# IEEE INFOCOM'97

## The Conference on Computer Communications

## Volume 2

Proceedings Volume 2

# IEEE INFOCOM'97

## The Conference on Computer Communications

## Sixteenth Annual Joint Conference of the IEEE Computer and Communications Societies

*Driving the Information Revolution*

---

April 7–12, 1997
Kobe, Japan

***Sponsored by***

IEEE Computer Society
Technical Committee on Computer Communications
IEEE Communications Society

***In cooperation with***

IEICE (the Institute of Electronics, Information and Communication Engineers) Japan
IPS (Information Processing Society) of Japan
ORS (The Operations Research Society) of Japan



IEEE Computer Society Press
Los Alamitos, California

Washington • Brussels • Tokyo

IEEE Computer Society Press
10662 Los Vaqueros Circle
P.O.Box 3014
Los Alamitos, CA 90720-1264



IEEE Computer Society Press Order Number PR07780 (Three-volume set)
IEEE Order Plan Catalog Number 97CB36034
ISBN 0-8186-7780-5
IEEE Order Plan ISBN 0-8186-7782-1
Microfiche ISBN 0-8186-7781-3
ISSN 0743-166X

*Additional copies may be ordered from:*

IEEE Computer Society Press
Customer Service Center
10662 Los Vaqueros Circle
P.O. Box 3014
Los Alamitos, CA 90720-1314
Tel: +1-714-821-8380
Fax: +1-714-821-4641
Email: cs.books@computer.org

IEEE Service Center
445 Hoes Lane
P.O. Box 1331
Piscataway, NJ 08855-1331
Tel: +1-908-981-1393
Fax: +1-908-981-9667
misc.custserv@computer.org

IEEE Computer Society
13, Avenue de l'Aquilon
B-1200 Brussels
BELGIUM
Tel: +32-2-770-2198
Fax: +32-2-770-8505
euro.ofc@computer.org

IEEE Computer Society
Ooshima Building
2-19-1 Minami-Aoyama
Minato-ku, Tokyo 107
JAPAN
Tel: +81-3-3408-3118
Fax: +81-3-3408-3553
tokyo.ofc@computer.org

Editorial production by Penny Storms
Printed in the United States of America by Braun-Brumfield, Inc.

The Institute of Electrical and Electronics Engineers, Inc.

# Table of Contents


Message from the General Co-Chairs .......... xvii
Message from the Technical Program Co-Chairs .......... xviii
Organizing Committee .......... xx
Technical Program Committee .......... xxi
Reviewers .......... xxiii

**Volume 1 Wednesday**

**Session 1A: ATM Switching I**

Design of a Gigabit ATM Switch .......... 2
*T. Chaney, J.A. Fingerhut, M. Flucke, and J.S. Turner*

Multi-Channel Deflection Crossbar (MCDC): A VLSI Optimized Architecture for Multi-Channel ATM Switching .......... 12
*P.Y. Yan, K.S. Kim, M.V. Hegde, and P.S. Min*

A High-Performance OC-12/OC-48 Queue Design Prototype for Input-buffered ATM Switches .......... 20
*H. Duan, J.W. Lockwood, S.M. Kang, and J.D. Will*

A General Purpose Cell Sequencer/Scheduler for ATM Switches .......... 29
*M.R. Hashemi and A. Leon-Garcia*

**Session1B: Multimedia I - Compressed Video over Networks**

Transporting Compressed Video over ATM Networks with Explicit Rate Feedback Control .......... 38
*T.V. Lakshman, P.P. Mishra, and K.K. Ramakrishnan*

VBR Video over ATM: Reducing Network Resource Requirements through Endsystem Traffic Shaping .......... 48
*M. Graf*

A Comparison of Bandwidth Smoothing Techniques for the Transmission of Prerecorded Compressed Video .......... 58
*W.-C. Feng and J. Rexford*

Exploiting the Temporal Structure of MPEG Video for the Reduction of Bandwidth Requirements .......... 67
*M. Krunz and S.K. Tripathi*

**Session 1C: Routing and Multicast I - QoS and Routing**

QoS-based Routing in Networks with Inaccurate Information: Theory and Algorithms .......... 75
*R. Guérin and A. Orda*

A Distributed Algorithm for Delay-Constrained Unicast Routing .......... 84
*H.F. Salama, D.S. Reeves, and Y. Viniotis*

Multi-Path Routing Combined with Resource Reservation .......... 92
*I. Cidon, R. Rom, and Y. Shavitt*

Loop-Free Internet Routing Using Hierarchical Routing Trees ........ 101
*S. Murthy and J.J. Garcia-Luna-Aceves*

**Session 1D: Wireless Networks I - Access Control Systems**
Broadcast Scheduling for Information Distribution ........ 109
*C.-J. Su and L. Tassiulas*
Asynchronous Multimedia Multihop Wireless Networks ........ 118
*C.R. Lin and M. Gerla*
Investigation of the IEEE 802.11 Medium Access Control (MAC) Sublayer Functions ........ 126
*B.P. Crow, I. Widjaja, J.G. Kim, and P. Sakai*
Collision Avoidance and Resolution Multiple Access with Transmission Groups ........ 134
*R. Garcés and J.J. Garcia-Luna-Aceves*

**Session 2A: ATM Traffic Control I - Optimization and Stability of Communication**
Connection Preemption: Issues, Algorithms, and a Simulation Study ........ 143
*M. Peyravian and A.D. Kshemkalyani*
A Performance Evaluation of Connectionless Overlay Networks for ATM ........ 152
*M. Schuba*
Stability in ATM Networks ........ 160
*C. Li, A. Raha, and W. Zhao*
VBR over VBR: The Homogeneous, Loss-Free Case ........ 168
*S. Giordano, J.-Y. Le Boudec, P. Oechslin, and S. Robert*

**Session 2B: Modeling and Analysis I - Traffic Modeling**
Fast Algorithms for Measurement-Based Traffic Modeling ........ 177
*H. Che and S.-Q. Li*
Multiplexing On-Off Sources with Subexponential On Periods: Part I ........ 187
*P.R. Jelenkovic and A.A. Lazar*
An Application of Superpositions of Two-State Markovian Sources to the Modelling of Self-Similar Behaviour ........ 196
*A.T. Andersen and B.F. Nielsen*
Time Scale Analysis of an ATM Queueing System with Long-Range Dependent Traffic ........ 205
*G. Mayor and J. Silvester*

**Session 2C: Distributed Systems and Protocols I - Protocol Design and Analysis**
Supporting DIS Applications Using ATM Multipoint Connection Caching ........ 213
*A. Kantawala, G. Parulkar, J. DeHart, and T. Marz*
Scalable Timers for Soft State Protocols ........ 222
*P. Sharma, D. Estrin, S. Floyd, and V. Jacobson*
Toward Formal TTCN-Based Test Execution ........ 230
*R. Hao and J. Wu*
Adaptive Control Strategy for the Multi-Layer Collision Resolution Protocol ........ 236
*D.-C. Twu and K.-C. Chen*

**Session 2D: Optical Networks I - Network Architecture and Design**
Design of a Survivable WDM Photonic Network ....................244
*J. Armitage, O. Crochat, and J.-Y. Le Boudec*
A Pipelined Single-Bit Controlled Sorting Network with $O(N \log^2 N)$ Bit Complexity ....................253
*R. Kannan*
Minimizing the Number of Optical Amplifiers Needed to Support a Multi-Wavelength Optical LAN/MAN ....................261
*B. Ramamurthy, J. Iness, and B. Mukherjee*
Wavelength-Routed Optical Networks: Linear Formulation, Resource Budgeting Tradeoffs, and a Reconfiguration Study ....................269
*D. Banerjee and B. Mukherjee*

**Session 3A: ATM ABR Services I - Control Theory Application and Flow Control**
A Linear Control Approach to Explicit Rate Feedback in ATM Networks ....................277
*C.E. Rohrs and R.A. Berry*
A Linear Dynamic Model for Design of Stable Explicit-Rate ABR Control Schemes ....................283
*Y. Zhao, S.Q. Li, and S. Sigarto*
A Control Theoretic Approach to the Design of Closed Loop Rate Based Flow Control for High Speed ATM Networks ....................293
*A. Kolarov and G. Ramamurthy*
Design of Robust Congestion Controllers for ATM Networks ....................302
*H. Zhang, O.W. Yang, and H. Mouftah*

**Session 3B: Traffic Control I - Scheduling 1**
Efficient Admission Control for EDF Schedulers ....................310
*V. Firoiu, J. Kurose, and D. Towsley*
Generalized Longest Queue First: An Adaptive Scheduling Discipline for ATM Networks ....................318
*D.-S. Lee*
A General Methodology for Designing Efficient Traffic Scheduling and Shaping Algorithms ....................326
*D. Stiliadis and A. Varma*
Characterizing Traffic Behavior and Providing End-to-End Service Guarantees within ATM Networks ....................336
*C.-S. Wu, J.-C. Jiau, and K.-J. Chen*

**Session 3C: Distributed Systems and Protocols II - Survivability and Restoration**
Comparative Study on Restoration Schemes of Survivable ATM Networks ....................345
*K. Murakami and H.S. Kim*
Restoration Strategies and Spare Capacity Requirements in Self-Healing ATM Networks ....................353
*Y. Xiong and L. Mason*
Design of a Fast Restoration Mechanism for Virtual Path-Based ATM Networks ....................361
*C.-J. Hou*

Addressing Network Survivability Issues by Finding the K-Best Paths through a Trellis Graph ..... 370
*S.D. Nikolopoulos, A. Pitsillides, and D. Tipper*

**Session 3D: Panel 1 - Broadband Services to the Home (ATM to the Home)** ..... 378
Moderator: Jeff Lynch, *IBM*
Panelists: Rhonda Hilton, *CableLabs*
Takao Kasahara, *Graphics Communication Laboratories*
Rob Norman, *IBM*
David Thorne, *British Telecom*

**Volume 2 Thursday**

**Session 4A: ATM ABR Services II**
Stability Analysis of Intelligent Marking EPRCA for ABR Congestion Control in ATM ..... 380
*W.K. Tsai, Y. Ge, and G. Huang*
Real-Time Block Transfer under a Link Sharing Hierarchy ..... 388
*G.G. Xie and S.S. Lam*
Constant-Time Dynamic ATM Bandwidth Scheduling for Guaranteed and Best Effort Services with Overbooking ..... 398
*D. Lin*
Virtual Queueing Techniques for ABR Service: Improving ABR/VBR Interaction ..... 406
*F.M. Chiussi, Y. Xia, and V.P. Kumar*

**Session 4B: Modeling and Analysis II - Traffic Characterization and Shaping**
$M/G/\infty$ Input Processes: A Versatile Class of Models for Network Traffic ..... 419
*M. Parulekar and A.M. Makowski*
Peakedness Measures for Traffic Characterization in High-Speed Networks ..... 427
*B.L. Mark, D.L. Jagerman, and G. Ramamurthy*
A Filtering Theory for Deterministic Traffic Regulation ..... 436
*C.-S. Chang*
Traffic Shaping at a Network Node: Theory, Optimum Design, Admission Control ..... 444
*A. Elwalid and D. Mitra*

**Session 4C: Routing and Multicast II - Reliable Multicast**
Bulk Multicast Transport Protocol ..... 455
*R. Morris*
Multicast Feedback Suppression Using Representatives ..... 463
*D. DeLucia and K. Obraczka*
Performance Modelling of Reliable Multicast Transmission ..... 471
*J. Nonnenmacher and E.W. Biersack*
A Delay Analysis of Sender-Initiated and Receiver-Initiated Reliable Multicast Protocols ..... 480
*M. Yamamoto, J.F. Kurose, D.F. Towsley, and H. Ikeda*

**Session 4D: Optical Networks II - Wavelength Conversion**

Multiwavelength Optical Networks with Limited Wavelength Conversion ........................... 489
*R. Ramaswami and G.H. Sasaki*

A Performance Model for Wavelength Conversion with Non-Poisson Traffic ........................ 499
*S. Subramaniam, A.K. Somani, M. Azizoglu, and R.A. Barry*

Fault Tolerant Multiwavelength Optical Rings with Limited Wavelength Conversion ........................ 507
*O. Gerstel, R. Ramaswami, and G.H. Sasaki*

Performance of Alternate Routing Methods in All-Optical Switching Networks .................. 516
*H. Harai, M. Murata, and H. Miyahara*

**Session 5A: ATM Switching II - Design and Performance Issues**

Performance of Multicasting Closed Interconnection Networks ........................ 525
*C.W. Chan and S.C. Liew*

The Single Queue Switch ........................ 533
*M.R. Hashemi and A. Leon-Garcia*

Analysis of Queueing Displacement Using Switch Port Speedup ........................ 541
*I. Cidon, A. Khamisy, and M. Sidi*

A New Method to Determine the Queue Length Distribution at an ATM Multiplexer ........................ 549
*J. Choe and N.B. Shroff*

**Session 5B: Traffic Control II - Scheduling 2**

Leap Forward Virtual Clock: A New Fair Queuing Scheme with Guaranteed Delays and Throughput Fairness ........................ 557
*S. Suri, G. Varghese, and G. Chandranmenon*

QLWFQ: A Queue Length Based Weighted Fair Queueing Algorithm in ATM Networks ........................ 566
*Y. Ohba*

A Near-Optimal Packet Scheduler for QoS Networks ........................ 576
*D.E. Wrege and J. Liebeherr*

Exact and Efficient Analysis of Schedulability in Fixed-Packet Networks: A Generic Approach ........................ 584
*S. Gorinsky, S. Baruah, T.J. Marlowe, and A.D. Stoyenko*

**Session 5C: Empirical Studies**

An Empirical Model of HTTP Network Traffic ........................ 592
*B.A. Mah*

Analyzing a Two-Stage Entry Monitor for High-Speed Networks ........................ 601
*G. Hjálmtýsson and A.G. Konheim*

Resource Reservation in Advance in Heterogeneous Networks with Partial ATM Infrastructures ........................ 611
*A. Schill, S. Kühn, and F. Breiter*

NFS Dynamics Over Flow-Controlled Wide Area Networks ........................ 619
*K. Chang, R. Morris, and H.T. Kung*

**Session 5D: Wireless Networks II - CDMA**

Uplink and Downlink Capacity Analysis for Two-Tier CDMA Cellular Systems....................626
*J.-S. Wu, M.-T. Sze, and J.-K. Chung*

Power Control and Time Division: The CDMA versus TDMA Question....................634
*J.M. Rulnick and N. Bambos*

On Algorithms Searching for Quasi-Optimal Subfamilies of GMW Sequences Suitable for CDMA Applications....................642
*X.H. Chen, T. Lang, and J. Oksman*

Call Admissibility for Multirate Traffic in Wireless ATM Networks....................649
*S.K. Biswas and B. Sengupta*

**Panel 2: Routing vs Switching**....................658

Moderator: Dimitrios Pendarakis, IBM

Panelists: Andrew Campbell, *Columbia University*
Dennis Ferguson, *Juniper Systems*
Srinivasan Keshav, *Cornell University*
Peter Newman, *Ipsilon Networks*
Martha Steenstrup, *BBN*

**Session 6A: ATM Traffic Control II - Pricing and Bandwidth Management**

Incentive Pricing in Multi-Class Communication Networks....................659
*A. Orda and N. Shimkin*

Charging Schemes for ATM Networks Based on Virtual Effective Bandwidths....................667
*J. Misic and S.T. Chanson*

Source Time Scale and Optimal Buffer/Bandwidth Trade-Off for Regulated Traffic in an ATM Node....................675
*F. Lo Presti, Z.-L. Zhang, J. Kurose, and D. Towsley*

**Session 6B: Multimedia II - Multimedia Multicast**

Adaptive Real-Time Group Multicast....................683
*M. Baldi, Y. Ofek, and B. Yener*

A Group Synchronization Mechanism for Stored Media in Multicast Communications....................692
*Y. Ishibashi, A. Tsuji, and S. Tasaka*

Gateway Based Approach for Conducting Multiparty Multimedia Sessions over Heterogeneous Signaling Domains....................701
*M. Sudan and N. Shacham*

Non Stationary Request Distribution in Video on Demand Networks....................711
*G. Bianchi and R. Melen*

**Session 6C: Distributed Systems and Protocols III - Network Security**

Secret Sharing in Graph-Based Prohibited Structures....................718
*H.-M. Sun and S.-P. Shieh*

Scalability and Flexibility in Authentication Services: The KryptoKnight Approach....................725
*P. Janson, G. Tsudik, and M. Yung*

An Adaptable and Reliable Authentication Protocol for Communication Networks ........ 737
*T. Kwon, M. Kang, and J. Song*
An Algorithm to Compute Collusion Paths ........ 745
*S.H. Low and N.F. Maxemchuk*

**Session 6D: Optical Networks II - WDM**
MetaRing Fairness Control Schemes in All-Optical WDM Rings ........ 752
*M. Ajmon Marsan, A. Bianco, E. Leonardi, F. Neri, and S. Toniolo*
SR$^3$: A Bandwidth-Reservation MAC Protocol for Multimedia Applications over All-Optical WDM Multi-Rings ........ 761
*M. Ajmone Marsan, A. Bianco, E. Leonardi, A. Morabito, and F. Neri*
Scalable WDM Network Architecture Based on Photonic Slot Routing and Switched Delay Lines ........ 769
*I. Chlamtac, V. Elek, A. Fumagalli, and C. Szabó*
STWnet: A High Bandwidth Space-Time-Wavelength Multiplexed Optical Switching Network ........ 777
*R. Kannan, R. Bartos, K.Y. Lee, and H.F. Jordan*

**Session 7A: ATM ABR Services III - Analysis of Flow Control Algorithms**
Performance and Correctness of the ATM ABR Rate Control Scheme ........ 785
*D. Lee, K.K. Ramakrishnan, W.M. Moh, and A.U. Shankar*
Performance Analysis of Rate Based Feedback Control for ATM Networks ........ 795
*L.A. Kulkarni and S.-Q. Li*
An ABR Feedback Control Scheme with Tracking ........ 805
*C. Fulton, S.-Q. Li, and C.S. Lim*
The Effect of Bottleneck Service Rate Variations on the Performance of the ABR Flow Control ........ 815
*M. Ritter*

**Session 7B: Advanced Topics I**
The APIC Approach to High Performance Network Interface Design: Protected DMA and Other Techniques ........ 823
*Z.D. Dittia, G.M. Parulkar, and J.R. Cox, Jr.*
Implementation and Analysis of PCC (Parallel Connection Control) ........ 832
*M. Veeraraghavan, G.L. Choudhury, and M. Kshirsagar*
Performance Analysis of Generalized Multihop Shuffle Networks ........ 842
*C.-L. Ng, S.-W. Seo, and H. Kobayashi*
An Analysis of Internet Inter-Domain Topology and Route Stability ........ 850
*R. Govindan and A. Reddy*

**Session 7C: Routing and Multicast III - Multicast Algorithms and Analysis**
Implementation and Analysis of IP Multicast over ATM ........ 858
*M.P. Maher and S.K. Bhogavilli*
SEAM: Scalable and Efficient ATM Multicast ........ 867
*M. Grossglauser and K.K. Ramakrishnan*

Restricted Dynamic Steiner Trees for Scalable Multicast in Datagram Networks ....876
*E. Aharoni and R. Cohen*
The Ordered Core Based Tree Protocol ....884
*C. Shields and J.J. Garcia-Luna-Aceves*

**Session 7D: Wireless Networks III - Channel Allocation and Call Blocking**
An Efficient Priority-Based Dynamic Channel Allocation Strategy for Mobile Cellular Networks ....892
*X. Dong and T.H. Lai*
A Unified Framework and Algorithm for (T/F/C)DMA Channel Assignment in Wireless Networks ....900
*R. Ramanathan*
Channel Carrying: A Novel Handoff Scheme for Mobile Cellular Networks ....908
*J. Li, N.B. Shroff, and E.K.P. Chong*
Effects of Erlang Call Holding Times on PCS Call Completion ....916
*Y.-B. Lin and I. Chlamtac*

**Volume 3 Friday**

**Session 8A: ATM Switching III - Multicast Switching**
Multicast ATM Switches Using Buffered MIN Structure: A Performance Study ....924
*Y. Xiong and L. Mason*
Design and Performance Analysis of a Growable Multicast ATM Switch ....932
*K. Wang and M.-H. Cheng*
Performance Analysis of a Multicast Switch Based on Multistage Interconnection Networks ....939
*J. Park, L. Jacob, and H. Yoon*
Performance and Complexity of Multicast Cross-Path ATM Switches ....947
*R.H. Lin, C.H. Lam, and T.T. Lee*

**Session 8B: Traffic Control III - Admission Control**
PSD-Based Neural-Net Connection Admission Control ....955
*C.-J. Chang, S.-Y. Lin, R.-G. Cheng, and Y.-R. Shiue*
Multi-Class Connection Admission Control Policy for High Speed ATM Switches ....963
*G. Ramamurthy and Q. Ren*
Comparison of Measurement-Based Admission Control Algorithms for Controlled-Load Service ....973
*S. Jamin, S.J. Shenker, and P.B. Danzig*
Measurement-Based Call Admission Control: Analysis and Simulation ....981
*D. Tse and M. Grossglauser*

**Session 8C: Distributed Systems and Protocols IV - Network Management and Resource Sharing**
Earthworm: A Network Memory Management Technique for Large-Scale Distributed Multimedia Applications ....990
*K.A. Hua, S. Sheu, and J.Z. Wang*

Checkpoint and Rollback in Asynchronous Distributed Systems ........ 998
*H. Higaki, K. Shima, T. Tachikawa, and M. Takizawa*
Atomic Resource Sharing in Noncooperative Networks ........ 1006
*L. Libman and A. Orda*
Server Selection Using Dynamic Path Characterization in Wide-Area Networks ........ 1014
*R.L. Carter and M.E. Crovella*

**Session 8D: Wireless Networks IV - Integrated Services**
Performance Evaluation of Packet Data Services over Cellular Voice Networks ........ 1022
*Y.Y. Kim and S.-Q. Li*
A Cellular Wireless Local Area Network with QoS Guarantees for Heterogeneous Traffic ........ 1030
*S. Choi and K.G. Shin*
Performance Analysis of Multicast Flow Control Algorithms over Combined Wired/Wireless Networks ........ 1038
*A.H. Wang and M. Schwartz*
On Accommodating Mobile Hosts in an Integrated Services Packet Network ........ 1046
*A.K. Talukdar, B.R. Badrinath, and A. Acharya*

**Session 9A: ATM Traffic Control III**
A Scalable Architecture for Fair Leaky-Bucket Shaping ........ 1054
*J. Rexford, F. Bonomi, A. Greenberg, and A. Wong*
Rate-Function Scheduling ........ 1063
*N.R. Figueira and J. Pasquale*
Real-Time Cell Loss Ratio Estimation and its Applications to ATM Traffic Controls ........ 1072
*S. Shioda and H. Saito*
Switch-Aided Flooding Operations in ATM Networks ........ 1080
*Y. Huang and P.K. McKinley*

**Session 9B: Modeling and Analysis III - Queueing Analysis**
Bounds for the Tail Distribution in a Queue with the Superposition of General Periodic Markov Sources ........ 1088
*F. Ishizaki and T. Takine*
Fitting Mixtures of Exponentials to Long-Tail Distributions to Analyze Network Performance Models ........ 1096
*A. Feldmann and W. Whitt*
Finite and Infinite QBD Chains: A Simple and Unifying Algorithmic Approach ........ 1105
*N. Akar and K. Sohraby*
Sensitivity Analysis of the Loss Probability in a Stationary Gradual Queue for High-Speed Networks ........ 1114
*Y. Yamada, N. Miyoshi, and T. Hasegawa*

**Session 9C: Advanced Topics II**
Copy Emulation in Checksummed, Multiple-Packet Communication ................................1122
*J.C. Brustoloni and P. Steenkiste*
SMART Retransmission: Performance with Overload and Random Losses ........................1131
*S. Keshav and S.P. Morgan*
Performance Characteristics of the D Channel Access Control Scheme ..............................1139
*S. Yagyu and H. Takagi*
Proactive Network Fault Detection ........................................................................................1147
*C.S. Hood and C. Ji*

**Session 9D: Panel 3 - Microcellular Personal Communication Systems - PHS, DECT and PACS** ........................................................................................1156
Moderator: Takeshi Hattori, *NTT Telecommunication Network Group*
Panelists: Giovanni Colombo, *CSELT*
Andy Gent, *PHS International Corporation*
Robert J. Hayes, *PCS Strategy, Motorola Corporation*
Nicolas Huery, *C.G.R.P.*
Y. Nakamura, *NTT Personal Communications Network Corporation*

**Session 10A: LANs and MANs**
Architecture for Two-Way Data Services over Residential Area CATV Networks ..........................................................................................................................1157
*C.-S. Wu, G.-K. Ma, and P.-N. Chen*
PCUP: Pipelined Cyclic Upstream Protocol over Hybrid Fiber Coax ..................................1165
*Y.-D. Lin, C.-J. Wu, and W.-M. Yin*
Multiple Priority CSMA-type Multichannel Local Area Network ........................................1174
*J.-W. Liao, J.-Y. Wang, W.-T. Lee, and L.-Y. Kung*
Group Allocation Multiple Access with Collision Detection ..................................................1182
*A. Muir and J.J. Garcia-Luna-Aceves*

**Session 10B: Traffic Control IV - Flow and Congestion Control**
Analysis of Packet Discarding Policies in High-Speed Networks .........................................1191
*Y. Lapid, R. Rom, and M. Sidi*
Window-Based Error Recovery and Flow Control with a Slow Acknowledgement Channel: A Study of TCP/IP Performance ............................................1199
*T.V. Lakshman, U. Madhow, and B. Suter*
TCP Boston: A Fragmentation-Tolerant TCP Protocol for ATM Networks ..........................1210
*A. Bestavros and G. Kim*
Client-Server Performance on Flow-Controlled ATM Networks: A Web Database of Simulation Results ..........................................................................................1218
*H.T. Kung and S.Y. Wang*

**Session 10C: Distributed Systems and Protocols V - Protocols and Software**
Two-Way TCP Traffic over ATM: Effects and Analysis ........................................................1227
*L. Kalampoukas, A. Varma, and K.K. Ramakrishnan*

Key to the Success of Asynchronous Transfer Mode: An Application Programming Interface ........ 1237
*M. Lin, A. Periyannan, and D. Singer*
Object-Oriented Network Protocols ........ 1245
*S. Böcking*
Analyzing Non-Determinism in Telecommunication Services Using P-Invariant of Petri-Net Model ........ 1253
*M. Nakamura, Y. Kakuda, and T. Kikuno*

**Session 10D: Optical Networks IV - Broadcast Star Networks**
On Dynamically Establishing and Terminating Isochronous Message Streams in WDMA-Based Local Area Lightwave Networks ........ 1261
*B. Wang, C.-J. Hou, and C.-C. Han*
HiPeR-ℓ: High Performance Reservation Protocol with ℓook-Ahead for Broadcast WDM Networks ........ 1270
*V. Sivaraman and G.N. Rouskas*
All-Optical LAN Interconnection with a Wavelength Selective Router ........ 1278
*A.K. Somani and M. Azizoglu*
On the All-to-All Broadcast Problem in Optical Networks ........ 1286
*H. Choi, H.-A. Choi, and M. Azizoglu*

**Session 11A: ATM ABR Services IV - Traffic Control Algorithms**
Integrated Rate and Credit Feedback Control for ABR Service in ATM Networks ........ 1295
*X. Zhang, K.G. Shin, and Q. Zheng*
The Rate Mismatch Problem in Heterogeneous ABR Flow Control ........ 1304
*N.T. Plotkin and J.J. Sydir*
Queueing Analysis of a Distributed Explicit Rate Allocation Algorithm for ABR Services ........ 1315
*N. Ghani and J.W. Mark*
Experimental Evaluation of ATM Congestion Control Mechanisms ........ 1324
*P. Chandra, A. Fisher, C. Kosak, and P. Steenkiste*

**Session 11B: Multimedia III - Video on Demand**
Long Term Resource Allocation in Video Delivery Systems ........ 1333
*K.C. Almeroth, A. Dan, D. Sitaram, and W.H. Tetzlaff*
A Shared Buffer Architecture for Interactive VOD Servers ........ 1341
*S. Sengodan and V.O.K. Li*
The Split and Merge (SAM) Protocol for Interactive Video-on-Demand Systems ........ 1349
*W. Liao and V.O.K. Li*
BiHOP: A Bidirectional Highly Optimized Pipelining Technique for Large-Scale Multimedia Servers ........ 1357
*K.A. Hua, J.Z. Wang, and S. Sheu*

**Session 11C: Routing and Multicast IV**
Performance of Congestion Control Mechanisms in Wormhole Routing Networks ........ 1365
*C. Roche, P. Palnati, M. Gerla, F. Neri, and E. Leonardi*

Re-Routing in Circuit Switched Networks ........ 1373
*E.W.M. Wong, A.K.M. Chan, and T.-S.P. Yum*
IP Multicasting for Point-to-Point Local Distribution ........ 1380
*G. Xylomenos and G.C. Polyzos*
Application-Layer Anycasting ........ 1388
*S. Bhattacharjee, M.H. Ammar, E.W. Zegura, V. Shah, and Z. Fei*

**Session 11D: Wireless Networks V - Routing and Internetworking**
Virtual LAN Internetworking over ATM Networks for Mobile Stations ........ 1397
*N.-F. Huang, Y.-T. Wang, B. Li, and T.-L. Liu*
A Highly Adaptive Distributed Routing Algorithm for Mobile Wireless Networks ........ 1405
*V.D. Park and M.S. Corson*
Dynamic Global Packet Routing in Wireless Networks ........ 1414
*N. Kahale and P.E. Wright*
A New Hierarchical Routing Protocol for Dynamic Multihop Wireless Networks ........ 1422
*I.F. Akyildiz, W. Yen, and B. Yener*

**Author Index** ........ A1

# Message from the General Co-Chairs

**Toshiharu Hasegawa**

**Raymond L. Pickholtz**

INFOCOM'97 comes at a critical juncture in networking. While the Internet's growth now threatens to exhaust address space and create congestion and extreme slowdowns, if not deadlock, new technologies, architectures and protocols are becoming available "just in time." Among these are high speed ATM networks at gigabit rates, a new IP protocol with enlarged address space and streamlined header processing, multi-gigabit optical links and more-versatile routers and switches. As a result of these developments, convergences of networking and services are occurring. We are beginning to see "cells in frames," gigabit Ethernet, gigabit ATM/SONET, gigabit switching, routing and protocols. The need for innovative design and the opportunities that this will open will engage researchers world-wide for decades. Most exciting are the potential applications that are difficult even to imagine at this time. The applications will likely go beyond our current framework of multimedia interactive communications, information access, and entertainment.

In the corporate world, new giants are forming such as BT/MCI and others to come. The brave new world of ultra high speed global networking will include untethered wireless communication and universal personal access with security.

The challenge is such that we envy our younger colleagues who will make the most-significant contributions to this enterprise. INFOCOM'97 starts the process with a program that clearly has the seeds of this revolution in networking. The conference committees have worked hard to insure this objective with a careful paper screening process, outstanding and up-to-date tutorials, a special Gigabit Workshop, keynote addresses by Vinton Cerf, VP of MCI and one of the visionaries of the Internet, and Toshiharu Aoki, Executive VP of NTT. We thank all of them. We also thank the host city of Kobe for making INFOCOM'97 a completely rewarding experience. As Kobe has seen a rebirth since the recent earthquake, so with similar ingenuity and vision, the participants of INFOCOM'97 in Kobe will initiate a rebirth in networking. We welcome you to INFOCOM'97, the networking conference in the beautiful new Kobe, where east, west, north and south will converge in April of 1997.

# Message from the Technical Program Co-Chairs

**Hideo Miyahara**

**Tatsuya Suda**

Greetings to everyone.

Welcome to the 16th annual IEEE INFOCOM'97 conference. This year, the INFOCOM'97 conference theme is "Driving the Information Revolution," and the technical program was created to advance our knowledge in computer communications and networking. It offers 42 technical sessions, 3 panels and 6 tutorials, all addressing the most recent advances in the field.

A number of people have contributed, creating a strong technical program. First of all, we received a large number of paper submissions — 524 to be exact. This is the second highest number of paper submissions in INFOCOM's history. Papers were submitted from all over the world: 250 from the North America, 171 from the Asia Pacific, 80 from the Europe, and 23 from other parts of the world. Second, a number of researchers served on the INFOCOM'97 Technical Program Committee; it has 127 members, 13 of whom served as area coordinators. They helped to evaluate paper submissions in a rigorous and fair, yet timely, manner and contributed significantly to the strength of the technical program. The excellent quality of this year's technical program is a reflection of the strong efforts of the researchers who submitted papers, the TPC members, and the area coordinators.

We employed a rigorous and fair review process with layers of check points, evaluating and re-evaluating the technical merits of the paper submissions. Paper submissions were first reviewed by at least 3 experts, including a TPC member, who were assigned the paper. In many cases, 4 to 6 experts reviewed a paper. Reviews and the TPC members' recommendations were then submitted to the corresponding area coordinators, who read all the paper submissions in their areas and integrated their evaluations into the review results. The recommendations of area coordinators were then discussed extensively at the TPC meeting in order to arrive at the 167 papers accepted to the conference.

The acceptance ratio for INFOCOM'97 this year was approximately 30% (167 papers accepted out of 524 submissions). Due to the competitive nature of this year's submission process, we were unable to accommodate a number of technically solid and qualified papers. We hope that the authors of these submissions will find other high quality conferences and journals in which to publish their fine results.

We would like to express our deep appreciation for the efforts of those who helped with the various administrative duties of the INFOCOM'97 TPC. They include Jaime Bae Kim, Duke Hong, Brett Vickers, Carlos Oliveira, Celio Albuquerque, George Lin, Larry Chen, Huy Phan, Sang Ahn, Leslee Xu, Hayato Ishibashi, Shinji Shimojo and Bernie Bender. Their aid was indispensable.

Finally we thank the conference attendees, whose engaging discussions with researchers will certainly make this year's conference a rousing success.

This year, INFOCOM'97 is held in Kobe, Japan, making this the second time in INFOCOM's history that the conference has been held abroad. April is considered one of the best times of the year to visit Japan. We are certain that the technical program will be thoroughly engaging and enjoyable, but we also hope that conference attendees allot some time to delight in Japan's springtime beauty.

# INFOCOM'97 Organizing Committee

**General Co-Chairs**
Toshiharu Hasegawa, *Kyoto University*
Raymond L. Pickholtz, *The George Washington University*

**Technical Program Committee Co-Chairs**
Hideo Miyahara, *Osaka University*
Tatsuya Suda, *University of California at Irvine*

**Local Aarrangements Co-Chairs**
Masayuki Murata, *Osaka University*
James Kurose, *University of Massachusetts at Amherst*

**Treasurer**
Tetsuya Takine, *Osaka University*
Jing-Fei Ren, *Texas Instruments*

**Publicity Co-Chairs**
Yuji Oie, *Nara Institute of Science and Technology*
Henning Schulzrinne, *Columbia University*

**Internet Arrangements Co-Chairs**
Shinji Shimojo, *Osaka University*
Kazuhiro Ohtsuki, *Kobe University*

**Publications Co-Chairs**
Miki Yamamoto, *Osaka University*
Joseph Bannister, *USC/Information Sciences Institute*

**Tutorials Co-Chairs**
Kiyoshi Nosu, *NTT Optical Network Systems Labs*
Tom LaPorta, *Bell Labs, Lucent Technologies*

**Panel Sessions Co-Chairs**
Shuji Tasaka, *Nagoya Institute of Technology*
Roch Guérin, *IBM T.J. Watson Research Center*

**Standing Committee Chair**
Harvey Freeman, *LANWORKS, Inc.*

## International Advisory Committee

**Chair**
Toshiharu Hasegawa, *Kyoto University, Japan*

**Members**
Hisashi Kobayashi, *Princeton University, USA*
Kojiro Watanabe, *NEC U.S.A., Inc., USA*
James Kurose, *University of Massachusetts at Amherst, USA*
Mark Karol, *Bell Labs, Lucent Technologies, USA*
Celia Desmond, *Stentor Resource Center Inc., Canada*
Hiromasa Ikeda, *Osaka University, Japan*
M. Naim Yunus, *VXL Holdings Sdn Bhd, Malaysia*
Tomonori Aoyama, *NTT, Japan*
Lye Kin Mun, *National Univ. of Singapore, Singapore*
Guy Pujole, *University of Versailles, France*
Seung-Taik Yang, *Electronics and Telecommunications Research Institute, Korea*
Tak-Shing Yum, *Chinese University, Hong Kong*
Lin-Shan Lee, *Academica Sinica, Taiwan*
Tetsuya Miki, *The University of Electro-Communications, Japan*
Koichi Matsuda, *NTT, Japan*

## Japan Local Committee

**Chair**
Hideo Miyahara, *Osaka University*

**Members**
Masayuki Murata, *Osaka University*
Tetsuya Takine, *Osaka University*
Yuji Oie, *Nara Institute of Science and Technology*
Kazuhiro Ohtsuki, *Kobe University*
Naoto Miyoshi, *Kyoto University*
Ken-ichi Aihara, *NTT*

# INFOCOM'97 Technical Program Committee

## Co-Chairs

Tatsuya Suda, *University of California at Irvine*
Hideo Miyahara, *Osaka University*

## Area Technical Program Coordinators

Joe Bannister, *USC/ISI*
Luigi Fratta, *Politecnico di Milano*
Roch Guérin, *IBM T.J. Watson Research Center*
Mark Karol, *Bell Labs, Lucent Technologies*
David Lee, *Bell Labs, Lucent Technologies*
Kin K. Leung, *AT&T Laboratories*
Biswanath Mukherjee, *University of California at Davis*
Shojiro Nishio, *Osaka University*
Giovanni Pacifici, *IBM T.J. Watson Research Center*
Guru Parulkar, *Washington University*
George Polyzos, *University of California at San Diego*
Hiroshi Saito, *NTT*
Lixia Zhang, *University of California at Los Angeles*

## Technical Program Committee Members

Ian F. Akyildiz, *Georgia Tech.*
Harmen R. van As, *Vienna University of Technology*
Abhaya Asthana, *Bell Labs*
Mohammed Atiquzzaman, *Monash University*
Ender Ayanoglu, *Bell Labs, Lucent Technologies*
Anindo Bagchi, *Bellcore*
Victor Bahl, *Digital Equipment Corporation*
Krishna Bala, *Bellcore*
Subrata Banerjee, *Stevens Institute of Technology*
Sujata Banerjee, *University of Pittsburgh*
Joe Betser, *The Aerospace Corp.*
Nicola Bléfari-Melazzi, *Univ. of Rome at Tor Vergata*
Michael S. Borella, *DePaul University*
Imrich Chlamtac, *Boston University*
Song Chong, *Sogang University*
Kee Chaing Chua, *National University of Singapore*
John N. Daigle, *University of Mississippi*
Rajiv Dighe, *NEC USA*
Christos Douligeris, *University of Miami*
Patrick W. Dowd, *University of Maryland*
Anwar Elwalid, *AT&T*
Anthony Ephremides, *University of Maryland*
Deborah Estrin, *University of Southern California*
Michael J. Ferguson, *Université du Québec*
Andrea Fumagalli, *Politecnico di Torino*
J.J. Garcia-Luna, *University of California at Santa Cruz*
Dipak Ghosal, *University of California at Davis*
Fengmin Gong, *MCNC*
Sanjay Gupta, *Illinois Institute of Technology*
Zygmunt J. Haas, *Cornell University*
Chao-Ju Jennifer Hou, *Ohio State University*
Tony Hsiao, *Sun Microsystems*
Pierre A. Humblet, *Eurecom Institute*
Toru Ishida, *Kyoto University*
Raj Jain, *Ohio State University*
Feiling Jia, *Optivision, Inc.*
Ahmed E. Kamal, *Kuwait University*
Dennis Karvelas, *New Jersey Institute of Technology*
Tohru Kikuno, *Osaka University*
Hyong S. Kim, *Carnegie Mellon University*
Jaime B. Kim, *California State University at Northridge*
Belka Kraimeche, *The Cooper Union*
Arvind Krishna, *IBM Research*
Jim Kurose, *University of Massachusetts at Amherst*

Jean-François Labourdette, *AT&T Laboratories*
T.V. Lakshman, *Bell Labs*
Simon S. Lam, *University of Texas at Austin*
Randall Landry, *DSP R&D Center, Texas Instruments*
Chin-Tau Lea, *Hong Kong Univ. of Science and Tech.*
Duan-Shin Lee, *NEC USA*
Bo Li, *Hong Kong Univ. of Science and Tech.*
Chung-Sheng Li, *IBM*
San-Qi Li, *University of Texas at Austin*
Jörg Liebeherr, *University of Virginia*
Kia Makki, *University of Nevada at Las Vegas*
Jon W. Mark, *University of Waterloo*
Ravi R. Mazumdar, *Université du Québec*
Deep Medhi, *University of Missouri-Kansas City*
Partho Pratim Mishra, *AT&T Research*
Melody Moh, *San Jose State University*
Sarit Mukherjee, *University of Nebraska at Lincoln*
Masayuki Murata, *Osaka University*
Klara Nahrstedt, *Univ. of Illinois at Urbana-Champaign*
K.S. Natarajan, *Motorola*
Yuji Oie, *Nara Institute of Science & Technology*
Guy Omidyar, *IITRI*
Ariel Orda, *Technion*
Teunis J. Ott, *Bellcore*
Sergio Palazzo, *University of Catania*
Pramod Pancha, *Bell Labs, Lucent Technologies*
Shivendra S. Panwar, *Polytechnic University*
Abhay Parekh, *Sun Microsystems*
Baiju V. Patel, *IBM T.J. Watson Research Center*
Krzysztof Pawlikowski, *University of Canterbury*
Andreas Pitsillides, *University of Cyprus*
K.K. Ramakrishnan, *AT&T Research*
G. Ramamurthy, *NEC USA*
Jing-Fei Ren, *Texas Instruments Inc.*
Raphael Rom, *Sun Microsystems Laboratories*
Catherine Rosenberg, *Ecole Polytechnique de Montreal*
Keith Ross, *University of Pennsylvania*
George Rouskas, *North Carolina State University*
Galen H. Sasaki, *University of Hawaii at Manoa*
Douglas C. Schmidt, *Washington University*
Bhaskar Sengupta, *NEC USA*
Adarshpal S. Sethi, *University of Delaware*
Syed Ijlal Shah, *Lahore Univ. of Management Science*
Ness B. Shroff, *Purdue University*
Moshe Sidi, *Technion*
Rahul Simha, *College of William and Mary*
Krishna Sivalingam, *Univ. of North Carolina at Greensboro*
Arun K. Somani, *University of Washington*
Rolf Stadler, *Columbia University*
Ioannis Stavrakakis, *Northeastern University*
James P.G. Sterbenz, *GTE Laboratories*
Hideaki Takagi, *University of Tsukuba*
Yutaka Takahashi, *Nara Institute of Science and Tech.*
Tetsuya Takine, *Osaka University*
Mallikarjun Tatipamula, *Northern Telecom*
David Tennenhouse, *MIT*
David Tipper, *University of Pittsburgh*
Terry Todd, *McMaster University*
Joe Touch, *USC/ISI*
Ljiljana Trajkovic, *University of California at Berkeley*
Srini Tridandapani, *Iowa State University*
Satish K. Tripathi, *University of Maryland*
Danny H.K. Tsang, *Hong Kong Univ. of Science and Tech.*
Anujan Varma, *University of California at Santa Cruz*
Indra Widjaja, *University of Arizona*
Johnny W. Wong, *University of Waterloo*
Bülent Yener, *New Jersey Institute of Technology*
Magda El Zarki, *University of Pennsylvania*
Ellen W. Zegura, *Georgia Institute of Technology*
Wei Zhao, *Texas A & M University*
Martina Zitterbart, *Technical Univ. of Braunschweig*

# Reviewers

Bob Aaron
Mohamed Abdelaziz
Tarek F. Abdelzaher
Arup Acharya
Abdelnaser Adas
Ron Addie
Yehuda Afek
Charu C. Aggarwal
Ehud Aharoni
Nima Ahmadvand
Masaki Aida
Nail Akar
Humayun Akhtar
Bora Aydin Akyol
Fouad Al-Hallel
Murat Alanyali
M. Mehmet Ali
Mohammad Ali Arad
Kevin Almeroth
Hussein M. Alnuweiri
Kemal Altinkemer
Onur Altintas
Eitan Altman
Mostafa Ammar
Nikos Aneroussis
P.N. Anirudhan
Nirwan Ansari
Rohan Aranha
Gerald R. Ash
Yukio Atsumi
Valery Augais
Cristina Aurrecoechea
Ra'ed Y. Awdeh
Daniel O. Awduche
Yossi Azar
Murat Azizoglu
B.R. Badrinath
Anantaram Balakrishnan
Mario Baldi
Ilia Baldine
Dhritiman Banerjee
Majid Barazande-Pour
B. Basch
Richard Barry
Jochen Behrens
George Benke
Lotfi Benmohamed
Jon Bennett
Brahim Bensaou
Arthur Berger
Randall A. Berry
Steven Berson
Maged Beshai
Riccardo Bettati
Pravin Bhagwat
Samrat Bhattacharjee
Partha P. Bhattacharya
Andrea Bianco
Subir K. Biswas
Gordon S. Blair
Chris Blondia
Raffaele Bolla
Christian Bonnet
Alberto Bononi
Maurizio A. Bonuccelli
Vanu Bose
Eric Bouillet
Raouf Boutaba
David Boyer
Lawrence S. Brakmo
Oliver Brand
Torsten Braun
Greg Brewster
Dale Buchholz
Jim Burns
Mehmet Ufuk Caglayan
Franco Callegati
Ken Calvert
Pietro Camarda
Jiannong Cao
Jeffrey Capone
Olga Casals
Christos G. Cassandras
Dirceu Cavendish
Mun Choon Chan
Shiu C. Chan
Y. Chandramouli
Cheng-Shang Chang
Chung-Ju Chang
Henry Chang
Jonathan H. Chao
Anna Charny
Hemant Chaskar
Hao Che
Biao Chen
Cheng C. Chen
Chien Chen
David Chen
Geping Chen
Hsiling Chen
Tom Chen
Wai Chen
Wen-Shyen E. Chen
Yao-Min Chen
Zhigang Chen
Chi-Chung Cheung
Kwan F. Cheung
Michael Cheung
Shun Yan Cheung
Marco Chiani
Franco Chiaraluce
Steve Chiu
Jinwoo Choe
Manhoi Choy
Hao-hua Chu
Hon-Wai Chu
John Chu
Anthony Chung
Israel Cidon
Reha Civanlar
Kimberly Claffy
John G. Cleary
Rosangela Coelho
Reuven Cohen
Blair Collier
Marco Conti
Adrian Conway
Giovanni E. Corazza
M. Scott Corson
R. Mitchell Cox
Brian P. Crow
Rene Cruz
Francesca Cuomo
Matteo D'Ambrosio
Walid Dabbous
Pankaj K. Das
Brian DeCleene
Amir Dembo
Sanjeev Deora
John Desmond
George Develekos
Michael Devetsikiotis
Jayanta Dey
Jason Ding
Tien V. Do
Matthew B. Doar
Wlodek Dobosiewicz
B.C. Domzy
Michael J. Donahoo
Lakshminath Dondeti
Pamela Drew
Oswald Drobnik
Alain Dupuis
Amitava Dutta
Deborah Dyson
Zbigniew Dziong
Viktoria Elek
Georgios Ellinas
Khaled Elsayed
Mike Erlinger
Cem Ersoy
Ted Faber
Sonia Fahmy
M. Faloutsos
Ruixue Fan
Romano Fantacci
Serge Fdida
Anja Feldmann
Kerry Fendick
Fang Feng
Wu-chi Feng
Wu-chun Feng
Gerhard P. Fettweis
J. Andrew Fingerhut
Stefan Fischer
Allan Fisher
Sally Floyd
Nelson L.S. Fonseca
Daniel Friedman
V.J. Friesen
Imed Frigui
Satoshi Fujita
Errin Fulp
Cathy Fulton
Toshitsugu Futagami
Maurice Gagnaire
Dominique Gaiti
Alexei A. Gaivoronski
Aura Ganz
Rodrigo Garces
Roberto Gaudino
Paul Gauthier
Constant Gbaguidi
Pawel Gburzynski
N. Georganas
Ori Gerstel
Nasir Ghani
J. Ghosh
Paolo Giacomazzi
Andre Girard
Aniruddha Gokhale
Andrea Goldsmith
Jamal Golestani
Jie Gong

Ramesh Govindan
Shri Goyal
Pawan Goyal
Rohit Goyal
Shri Goyal
Marcel Graf
J.-Ch. Grégoire
Albert G. Greenberg
Enrico Gregori
Wayne D. Grover
Fabrice Guillemin
Amit Gupta
Anil K. Gupta
Jun Han
Ibrahim Habib
Hisaya Hadama
Yaiche Haikel
Bruce Hajek
S. Louis Hakimi
Yukihiro Hamada
Babak Hamidzadeh
J. Han
Janelle J. Harms
Tim Harrison
Felix Hartanto
Kaname Harumoto
Hossam Hassanein
John Heidemann
Ahmed Helmy
Enrique J. Hernandez-Valencia
Meir Herzberg
Daniel P. Heyman
Manabu Higashida
Teruo Higashino
Atsushi Hiramatsu
Miwa Hiroyoshi
Gisli Hjalmtysson
Joseph Ho
Ricky Ho
David Hoffmeister
Markus Hofmann
Tad Hofmeister
Michael Honing
Steve Hotz
Chao-Ju Jennifer Hou
Yiwei Thomas Hou
Henry Houh
Fahad Hoymany
Scott Hrastar
Deh-Phone K. Hsing
Po-Chi Hu
Nian-Chi Huang
Jean-Francois Huard
Frank Huebner
Lucas Hui
Zbigniew Hulicki
Eoin Hyden
Chih-Lin I
Steve Iatrou
Noboru Iida
Chinatsu Ikeda
Jason Iness
Ichiro Inoue
Kenji Ishida
Fumio Ishizaki
Hiroyasu Itoh
Rauf Izmailov
X. Jia
Jonathan Jiang
Shengming Jiang
Shantigram Jagannath
Bjorn Jager
Prashant Jain
Andrzej Jajszczyk
Gabriel Jakobson
Ju-wook Jang
Anura Jayasumana
Predrag Jelenkovic
Seong-Ho Jeong
Hongbin Ji
Feiling Jia
Xiaohua Jia
Hong Jiang
S.M. Jiang
Song Jiang
David B. Johnson
Robert D. Johnston
H. Jonathan
Scott Jordan
Anupam Joshi
Y. Frank Jou
Jinoo Joung
Jason Jue
Youki Kadobayashi
Lampros Kalampoukas
C.R. Kalmanek
Shivkumar Kalyanaraman
Sanjay Kamat
Anshul Kantawala
Ezhan Karasan
Kamal Karlapalem
Shoji Kasahara
Irene Katzela
Fred Kaudel
Richard Kautz
Kenji Kawahara
Haruko Kawahigashi
Ryutaro Kawamura
Kai-wei Ke
S. Keshav
G. Kesidis
Asad Khamisy
Irfan Khan
Bhumip Khasnabish
Samir Khuller
Robert Kibler
Hyong S. Kim
Jeong Geun Kim
S.-C. Kim
Yonghwan Kim
Yasuhiko Kitamura
Hideo Kitazume
Masaru Kitsuregawa
John G. Klincewicz
Edward W. Knightly
Kazutomo Kobayashi
Ulf Koerner
Daniel Kofman
Aleksandar Kolarov
Takis Konstantopoulos
Willard Korfhage
Milan Kovacevic
W. Kreutzer
K.R. Krishnan
Ram Krishnan
Santosh Krishnan
Heiko Krumm
Marwan Krunz
Paul Krzyzanowski
Oguz Kucur
Seiya Kudoh
Vitaly M. Kuleshov
Lalita A. Kulkarni
Lakshmana N. Kumar
Srikantha Kumar
Joy Kuri
Seok-Kyu Kweon
Koenraad Laevens
Richard O. LaMaire
Yael Lapid
George Lapiotis
K.L. Eddie Law
Jean-Yves Le Boudec
Byoung-Joon Lee
Hung-Ju Lee
Kuo-Chun Lee
Ming-Jeng Lee
Tony T. Lee
Robert C. Lehr
William Lehr
Wolfram Lemppenau
Emilio Leonardi
Ian Leslie
Stefan Leue
Victor Leung
Charles Levert
Brian Neil Levine
Hanoch Levy
Yoni Levy
Bo Li
Chengzhi Li
Chih-Peng Li
Chung-Sheng Li
Junyi Li
Tony Li
Soung C. Liew
F. Joe Lin
Yow-Jian Lin
Ting-Li Ling
Marco Listanti
Kuo-Hui Liu
Te-Kai Liu
Wei Liu
Yao-Ching Liu
Zhao Liu
F.L. Lo
F. Lo Presti
Edwin Loecherbach
Alfio Lombardo
Steven Low
Steven Lowen
Chien-Chun Lu
Kevin W. Lu
Walter Lucchesi
Dante De Lucia
Qingshan Luo
Wenjun Luo
Bryan Lyles
Qingming Ma
Michelle MacRae
U. Madhow
Naoki Makimoto
Sam Makki
Nicholas Malcolm
Manu Malek
David A. Maltz
Dragos Manolescu
Weizhen Mao
Bill Marcus
Brian L. Mark
Doug Marquis
Saverio Mascolo
Lorne Mason
Rudolf Mathar
Ibrahim Matta
Jean McManus
D.C. McNickle
Aref Meddeb
Gopal Meempat

Marialuisa Merani
Zoran Miljanic
Frank Miller
Robert F. Miller
Jelena Misic
Sumita Mishra
Sanjay Mithal
Danny J. Mitzel
Naoto Miyoshi
Ahmed Mokhtar
José A.S. Monteiro
Robert Moose
Daniel Mossé
Hussain Mouftah
Andrew Muir
Sarit Mukherjee
Sumedh Mungee
Toru Murase
Shree Murthy
Nagi Naganathan
Shin'ichi Nagano
Ramesh Nagarajan
Erich Nahum
Philippe Nain
Hajime Nakamura
Masahide Nakamura
Sanjiv Nanda
Mahesan Nandikesan
Seffi Naor
Srinivas Narayan
B. Narendran
Tapas K. Nayak
Arnold L. Neidhardt
Tho Le Ngoc
BoFriis Nielsen
Ioanis Nikolaidis
Arne Nilsson
Joerg Nonnenmacher
Katia Obraczka
Toshikane Oda
Yoram Ofek
Richard Ogier
Nagao Ogino
Chang-Hwan Oh
Yoshihiro Ohba
Hiroyuki Ohsaki
Chikara Ohta
Masataka Ohta
Kazuhiro Ohtsuki
Yuji Oie
Sema Oktug
Lyndon Y. Ong
Luis Orozco-Barbosa
Timucin Ozugur
A.R. Pach
Leon Paley
Rajesh K. Pankaj
Daniela Panno
Christos Papadopoulos
M. Papamichail
Shyam Parekh
Jin-Soo Park
Gerard Parr
Sanjoy Paul
Rajesh S. Pazhyannur
Carlos M. D. Pazos
Jon M. Peha
Frank A. Pellegrino
Dimitrios E. Pendarakis
Wuxu Peng
Vinod Peris
Jim Perreault
Harry Perros
Hussain Pezeshki-Esfahani
Niki Pissinou
Gregory P. Pollini
Phil Porras
Greg Pottie
Balaji Prabakhar
Sharat C. Prasad
Robert L. Probert
Ramon Puigjaner
Hung Keng Pung
Irfan Pyarali
Kun Qian
Sonrong Qian
Yi Qian
Chunming Qiao
Lintian Qiao
R.Venkateswaran
Nabi Rafie
C. S. Raghavendra
Amitava Raha
Mahfuzur Rahman
Cynthia D. Rais
Gokul Rajaram
Byrav Ramamurthy
Rajiv Ramaswami
Ramachandran Ramjee
Nol Rananand
Sampath Rangarajan
Ramesh Rao
S. Rao
Anoop Reddy
Douglas S. Reeves
Kiran M. Rege
Amy R. Reibman
Peter Reiher
Martin Reisslein
Qiang Ren
Jennifer Rexford
Ronn Ritke
Charles E. Rohrs
Allyn Romanow
Zvi Rosberg
Oliver Rose
Jonathan Rosenberg
Kurt Rothermel
H. Rudin
John Rulnick
Chester Ruszczyk
Bong Ryu
Debanjan Saha
Anirudha Sahoo
Prescott Sakai
Charbel M. Sakr
Vijay K. Samalam
J.M. Didier Samfat
Pedro I. Sanchez
Huzur Saran
Chandramouli Sargor
Arvind Sathi
Stephen Schwab
Ahmet Sekercioglu
Abhijit Sengupta
Yetik Serbest
Srinivasan Seshan
Adarshpal Sethi
Sanjeev Setia
Faisal Shad
N. Shankar
Puneet Sharma
Jacob Sharony
Yuval Shavitt
Showi-Min Shen
Scott Shenker
Prashant Shenoy
Stephen Shew
Clay Shields
Cheul Shim
Nahum Shimkin
Shinsuke Shimogawa
Shinji Shimojo
N. Shivakumar
Adam Shwartz
Ikhlaq Sidhu
Rainer Siebenhaar
James Sienicki
Jim Sienicki
Sushil da Silva
Sundeep Singatwaria
Inderjeet Singh
Suresh Singh
Mukesh Singhal
Nishith Sinha
Rupam Sinha
H.R. Sirisena
Kumar N. Sivarajan
Vijay Sivaraman
Donald Smith
Kazem Sohraby
Cormac J. Sreenan
A. Srinivasan
Santhanam Srinivasan
K. Sriram
Mani Srivastava
Jerrold F. Stach
Mark Stahl
Pat Stakem
David Starobinski
James Stepanek
Donpaul C. Stephens
Dimitrios Stiliadis
Burkhard Stiller
Kris Struyve
Suresh Subramaniam
Dan Keun Sung
Hiroshi Suzuki
V. Swaminathan
Nina Taft-Plotkin
Masahiro Taka
G. Takahara
Yukio Takahashi
Yoshitaka Takahashi
Rajesh R. Talpade
Qiang Ming Tan
Ahmed N. Tantawy
Leandros Tassiulas
Daisuke Teratani
David Thaler
Chen-Khong Tham
Hideki Tode
Tom Tofigh
C-K Toh
Ozan K. Tonguz
Don Towsley
Ljiljana Trajkovic
John Trotter
Sophia Tsakiridou
Jason L. Tsay
David Tse
Kent H. Tseng
Thierry Turletti
Jonathan S. Turner
Hung-ying Tyan
Sathyadev V. Uppala
Huseyin Uzunalioglu
R. Vaidyanathan
Pravin Varaiya

Emmanouel Varvarigos
Gustavo de Veciana
Malathi Veeraraghavan
Paul A. Veitch
Nalini Venkatasubramanian
R. Venkateswaran
Dinesh Verma
Rajiv Vijayan
Yannis Viniotis
M. Vishnu
Krzysztof Wajda
Yasushi Wakahara
Bin Wang
Kuang-Yeh Wang
Kuochen Wang
Qiong Wang
Weiping Wang
Weyl K. Wang
Y.T. Wang
K. Watanabe
Kojiro Watanabe
Bernard M. Waxman
Gosse Wedzinga
Liming Wei
Martin Weiss
Ward Whitt
Jeffrey E. Wieselthier
Kenneth A. Williams
Sabine Wittevrongel
Ralph Wittmann
Joel Wolf
Kwok-Yee Michael Wong
P.C. Wong
Dallas E. Wrege
Fuxiang Wu
Gang Wu
Guo-Liang Wu
Tsong-Ho Wu
Geoffrey Xie
Shimpei Yagyu
Shalini Yajnik
S. Yalamanchili
Atsushi Yamada
Miki Yamamoto
Hideaki Yamanaka
O. Yang
Tao Yang
Keiichi Yasumoto
David Yates
Jennifer Yates
David K. Yau
Yi Ye
Uri Yechiali
Wei Yen
Liu Hui Yeo
Kwan L. Yeung
Makoto Yokoo
Kiroyuki Yokoyama
Jay Yoo
Masatoshi Yoshikawa
Chaoyu Yue
Jens Zander
Ali Zaringhalam
Pamela Zave
Ofer Zeitouni
Hui Zhang
Yongbing Zhang
Yaling Zhou
Moshe Zukerman

# Volume 2

# Technical Sessions
# 4A – 7D

# Stability Analysis of Intelligent Marking EPRCA for ABR Congestion Control in ATM

W.K. Tsai and Y.Ge

Department of Electrical
and Computer Engineering
University of California
Irvine, CA 92697

G. Huang

Department of Electrical
Engineering
Texas A. and M. University
College Station, TX 77843

## Abstract

*The EPRCA (Enhanced Proportional Rate Control Algorithm) is a leading congestion control protocol for Available Bit Rate (ABR) service in ATM networks. Even though the EPRCA has been adopted by the ATM forum as the standard for ABR congestion control, we show that this protocol is only marginally stable. The stability analysis presented in this paper does not consider interactions among network components and should be considered as a bottle-neck stability result. We show that, if a queue is the bottleneck of a congested path, then its queue size will eventually decrease. However, if a queue is not congested, its queue size can actually increase and a congestion can be self-induced.*

## 1 Introduction

With the advent of high speed networks such as ATM networks, congestion control has become a challenging research topic in recent years. Among the many proposed congestion control protocols for Available Bit Rate (ABR) service for ATM networks, the EPRCA (Enhanced Proportional Rate Control Algorithm) is a leading one which has been adopted by the ATM forum as the standard. The purpose of this paper is to provide perhaps the first theoretical stability analysis for EPRCA. As far as we know, all works on the stability of EPRCA has been basically simulation oriented and with some scattered theoretical analyses which do not provide conclusive theoretical foundation for the widely presumed stability of EPRCA. In this paper we show that this protocol is only marginally stable. The stability analysis presented in this paper does not consider interactions among network components and should be considered as a bottle-neck stability result. We show that, if a queue is the bottleneck of a congested path, then its queue size will eventually decrease. However, if a queue is not congested, its queue size can actually increase and a congestion can be self-induced.

The current standard uses modified forms of rate-based schemes based on several important ideas that were developed through the years [1, 2, 3, 4]. The current standard, EPRCA with Intelligent Marking(IM-EPRCA), comes from the original proportional rate control algorithm (PRCA) and the enhanced versions [5, 6, 7], which has many distinctive features and two of which are: positive feedback and counter-based approach. With this scheme, a congested switch (or queue) now has the responsibility to set the maximum cell rates of active connections via RM cells returning to the sources. This setting of rates is done by a scheme called intelligent marking [8]. Its important advantage over other schemes is that it does not require per-VC accounting at the switches so that complex hardware can be avoided.

Although IM-EPRCA has been shown to be stable from numerical simulations, no actual proof of stability has been known so far. This paper presents the first stability result of IM-EPRCA by assuming a deterministic queuing model and an average case synchronous discrete-time formulation. This formulation models both counter-based and interval-based EPRCA.

Because of the highly complex behaviors of the switches (queues) and the sources, most works on ABR congestion control assume a very simplistic modeling of the queues and the sources. This paper distinguishes from other works by modeling almost all the details of the IM-EPRCA protocol and the dynamics resulting from these details. For mathematical tractability we use a deterministic average case discrete-time formulation. The average case analysis is preferred to the worst case analysis in the sense that it describes the most probable operating conditions and provides insights into setting the parameters for the protocol. Our result does not consider explicitly the implications of the interactions among the queues in the network. This does not mean that our stability result is not realistic. On the contrary, our result is still realistic independent of the network interactions among the different queues. This will be self-evident after one reads our mathematical formulation. The approach we take in this paper is to analyze only the bottle-neck queue in a congested path. Using the identical formulation, studies and analyses for the IM-EPRCA in the face of interactions among the queues can be performed and will be treated in a forthcoming paper [12]. With the already complicated



0-8186-7780-5/97 $10.00 © 1997 IEEE

mathematical notations in this paper, consideration of the interactions among the queues will simply be beyond the scope of this concise paper.

The result of our analysis shows that once a queue becomes the bottleneck in a congested path, will have its queue size reduced so that the queue will eventually enter into an "uncontested" state. Such is what most numerical simulations have shown in the literature [8]. However, we also found that, if a queue is not congested, there exist possibilities that its queue size will also increase and it can enter into a "congested" state. There is no way to show that, once a queue enters into an "uncontested" state it will stay in that state forever. Thus each individual queue is "stable" in some sense. A new concept of marginal stability is defined to describe the unusual stability behavior of the algorithm. Both the stability and instability results in the paper are proved for the individual queues.

This paper is organized as follows. In section 2, an introduction of the IM-EPRCA is provided. This is done to provide the necessary background information in order to follow the modeling description in section 3 to section 5. The analysis is presented in section 5. The conclusions of the paper is given in section 6.

## 2 Background on Intelligent-marking EPRCA

Congestion occurs at a given transmission link whenever the total input rate is more than the available link capacity. Each transmission link is attached to an output port of an ATM switch. The purpose of congestion control is to prevent congestion from happening (if possible) and to stop congestion if it occurs.

Current ATM standards call for RM (Resource Management) cells to be sent from each source for every $N$ number of cells transmitted. The RM cells for a VC contain traffic control information such as ACR (Allowed Cell Rate) and the ER (Explicit or Expected Cell Rate) for the VC. If there is a congestion along the path of a VC, then a congested switch can set the ER to a lower value; while the RM cells originated from a source typically sets the ER to its PCR (Peak Cell Rate). The destination of each VC will return the RM cells backward in the path to the source. It is in the backward path that a congested switch will set the ER for the VC in congestion. This is done because one needs to find out the bottleneck link and the real bottleneck can only be found after an RM cell traverses the entire forward path.

The optimization objectives for the congestion control are to maximize the throughputs (maximally utilizing the transmission capacities) and to minimize congestions. Congestion can be defined in various ways, and one way is that a link is considered to be congested if the buffer occupancy exceeds a certain threshold. There is also a fairness issue in the congestion control. The most natural fairness criterion is the Max-Min fairness which states that each VC sharing the same most congested link should be awarded the same rate. In this paper, the Max-Min fairness doctrine is assumed.

The current standard for congestion control adopted by the ATM forum is the EPRCA with intelligent marking. Thus, in this paper, we will use terms IM-EPRCA and EPRCA interchangeably. The IM-EPRCA uses a variable to keep track of summary information of all the active VCs at each transmission link. This variable, which turns out to be the control reference value, is called the Modified ACR (MACR). The MACR associated with a link is designed to be an approximation of the fair share of the available capacity of the link; to be shared among the ABR users using the link. Because of the Max-Min fairness, the MACR associated with a link is understood to be an unweighted average of the rates of the active VCs in the respective link. When congestion occurs, the MACR will be reduced and each VC with an ACR greater than the MACR will be forced to reduce its rate by the switch setting a lower value on the ER field in the RM cell returning to the source. An outline of the EPRCA protocol is provided below.

1. A source transmits an RM(ACR,ER) for every $N$ data cells transmitted.

2. A source continually decreases its ACR.

3. Upon receiving each backward RM(ACR,ER), a source increases its ACR by no greater than ER.

4. A destination returns a backward RM(ACR,ER) cell upon reception of each forward RM cell.

5. Suppose a noncongested link receives a forward RM(ACR,ER) cell from a source. It replaces its MACR by MACR + $\beta\times$(ACR-MACR), where $\beta$ is an averaging factor which is a positive constant less than unity.

6. Suppose a congested link receives a forward RM(ACR,ER) cell from a source and if ACR $\leq$ MACR, it replaces its MACR by MACR + $\beta\times$(ACR-MACR); otherwise, its MACR is not replaced.

7. Suppose a congested link receives a backward RM(ACR,ER) cell from a destination and if the current queue size (buffer occupancy) is greater than DQT (fast Down Queue Threshold), it replaces the ER in the RM cell by min(ER, $\gamma$MACR); otherwise, if ACR $\geq$ MACR, it replaces the ER in the RM cell by min(ER,MACR), where $\gamma$ is a positive constant less than unity. $\gamma$ can be considered as a reduction factor to be used to reduce congestion.

## 3 Modeling

### 3.1 The Discrete-Time Average Case Assumption

The system can be described by a set of discrete time dynamic equations where the interval between two consecutive discrete time instants is given by $T_\alpha$ (measured in the continuous time scale). We assume that, during each $T_\alpha$ units of time, at all sources, there is exactly one reception of one backward (returning) RM cell and exactly one transmission of one forward

RM cell. Furthermore, during this same $T_\alpha$ time, there is exactly one reception of one forward RM cell from each VC and exactly one reception of one backward RM cell from each active VC at each switch. This peculiar parameter $T_\alpha$ is a device to bound the delay between the two consecutive repeated interesting events such as receptions of RM cells. This model will emulate both the cases of counter-based and interval-based EPRCA.

The implication of the above assumptions is that the delay for each RM cells traversing the network is *uniformly bounded.* Thus our model is effectively a *partially asynchronous* formulation and $T_\alpha$ is the *uniform* bound for the time between two interesting *consecutive repeated* events in our analysis. The interesting events are receptions and transmissions of the same type (either backward or forward) of RM cells for a particular VC, at a source, or at a switch. Because of the uniform bound assumption, we consider our analysis to be an *effective average case* analysis; even though we do allow *bounded variations* in the delays. For a truly asynchronous analysis, no uniform bound can be assumed and the analyze for the asynchronous case is reported in another paper of ours [13]. We use the peculiar notation of $T_\alpha$ in order to remind the reader that this number $T_\alpha$ is quite different from the period in an ordinary discrete time system. For ordinary discrete time systems, there are no interesting events occurring during the discrete time period $T$; all interesting events in an ordinary discrete time system occur at the boundaries of the time interval $T$. Our peculiar type of discrete time formulation enables us to write the dynamic equations in a concise form. This formulation is capable of exhibiting the essentials of our stability analysis while inhibiting the none-essentials in the overall system.

In our formulation, an event happening at a discrete time instant $n$ could happen at any time in the continuous time interval $[nT_\alpha, (n+1)T_\alpha]$.

### 3.2 The network:

i) The network consists of $S$ switches and $N$ transmission links. Let $\{1, 2, \ldots, S\}$ denote the set of nodes, and $\{1, 2, \ldots, N\}$ denote the set of transmission links.

ii) Each transmission link $i$ has an available capacity $c_i$ cells per $T_\alpha$ units time.

iii) The network load consists of traffic demand from all source-destination pairs denoted by $(ab)'s$, where $a$ and $b \in S$. The pair $(ab)$ will be referred to as the $(ab)$ virtual channel (VC). Let $C$ denote the set of all such connections. The number of active VCs is assumed to be constant during the congestion resolution time. This effectively assumes that no external disturbance exists except the initial disturbance (in terms of active VCs).

iv) For each $(ab)$ connection, the source at node $a$ sends cells to the destination at node $b$ through a sequence of links referred to as the path of the connection and denoted by $p(ab)$. According to the current ATM standard, $p(ab)$ is static. Let $C(i)$ be the set of all connections $(ab)$'s which traverse link $i$.

v) Each node (switch) has, for each of its outgoing links, a buffer for storing cells waiting to be transmitted. Let $Q_i$, $i \in N$, denote the number of cells buffered for transmission on link $i$ and referred to as link $i$'s buffer.

vi) Each switch has a congestion controller associated with each outgoing transmission link. For each link $i$, the controller computes its own modified allowed cell rate $MACR_i$ and determines the feedback explicit cell rate $ER$ for each VC whose backward RM cell is received. The controller compares the computed $MACR_i$ and the $ER$ in the backward RM cell received and compute a new ER for the VC involved. In the rest of this paper, we will use $R$ as a short form for $MACR$ and $E$ as a short form for $ER$. The short forms and the long forms will be used interchangeably.

vii) For each VC $(ab)$, we denote the delay of the RM cells from the source $a$ to switch $i$ (i.e., part of the forward trip) or from switch $i$ back to the source node $a$ (i.e., part of the backward trip) as $d_{ai}^{ab}$ and $d_{ia}^{ab}$ respectively. Furthermore, let $d^{ab}$ denote the average round trip delay for cells from the VC $(ab)$. Since we model the system in a discrete time formulation, all of these delays are integer. We will also assume that $d_{ai}^{ab} = d_{ia}^{ab}$. This assumption is used only to simplify our mathematical notations. This assumption is in no way reduce the generality of our analysis.

### 3.3 Buffer Equations

In what follows we will focus on a queue $i$ under consideration.

viii) The input traffics are viewed as deterministic flows.

ix) Let $f_i(n)$ denote the total input traffics to link $i$ at time $n$.

x) Let $A^{ab}(n)$ denote the average allowed cell rate of VC $(ab)$ during the time period $[nT_\alpha, (n+1)T_\alpha]$. Let $E_i^{ab}(n+1)$ denote the explicit cell rate which is determined by the switch (queue) $i$ and is to be carried in a backward RM cell of VC$(ab)$ to the source of $(ab)$, the RM is to be transmitted from the source during the time period $[nT_\alpha, (n+1)T_\alpha]$. Let $\rho^{ab}(n) \cdot E_i^{ab}(n+1-d^{ab})$ denote the explicit cell rate of VC $(ab)$ during the time $[nT_\alpha, (n+1)T_\alpha]$ carried in a backward RM cell arriving at link $i$. Therefore $\rho^{ab}(n)$ is the ratio of the ER seen by queue $i$ at time $n$ relative to the $ER_i^{ab}$ one round trip delay ago.

xi) Let $PCR^{ab}$ and $MCR^{ab}$ denote the peak cell rate and minimum cell rate of the source of VC $(ab)$.

Let $Q_i(n)$ denote the number of cells in link $i$'s buffer at time $n$ (the end of the time period $[nT_\alpha, (n+1)T_\alpha]$), then the buffer equation for link $i$ can be described by the following difference equation

$$Q_i(n+1) = max\{Q_i(n) + f_i(n) - c_i, 0\}; \quad (1)$$

¿From assumption ix), we have

$$f_i(n) = \sum_{(ab)\in C(i)} A^{ab}(n - d_{ai}^{ab}). \quad (2)$$

Note that in the above equation (2), $A^{ab}(n)$ should be taken to be the average ACR during the time period $[nT_\alpha, (n+1)T_\alpha]$. We assume that, for each VC, the average cell emission rate is the same as the average ACR rate in each discrete time period $T_\alpha$. In particular, for stability analysis, we will assume a worst case where $ACR^{ab}$ will be persistent, i.e. $ACR$ is not reduced continuously. For instability analysis, we will assume a best case analysis where $ACR$ will be reduced continuously.

### 3.4 The Source Cell Emission Rates

According to IM-EPRCA, each VC($ab$) source decreases its cell rate until receiving a feedback RM cell. After receiving the feedback RM cell, the $ACR$ is determined by the control protocol [8] as follows [?]:

$$A^{ab}(n) = \alpha_1^{ab}(n)\beta^{ab}(n)A^{ab}(n-1)+\alpha_2^{ab}(n)E^{ab}(n+1-d_{ia}^{ab}) \quad (3)$$

where

$$\alpha_1^{ab}(n) + \alpha_2^{ab}(n) = 1, \qquad \alpha_1^{ab}(n), \alpha_2^{ab}(n) \in \{0, 1\}$$

$$\alpha_1^{ab}(n) = \begin{cases} 0 & \text{if condition0} \\ 1 & \text{otherwise} \end{cases}$$

Condition0: $MCR^{ab} \leq E^{ab}(n+1-d_{ia}^{ab}) < \beta^{ab}(n)A^{ab}(n-1)$.

$$\begin{cases} \beta^{ab}(n) > 1 & \text{if } ACR^{ab}(n) > ACR^{ab}(n-1) \\ 0 < \beta^{ab}(n) \leq 1 & \text{if } ACR^{ab}(n) \leq ACR^{ab}(n-1) \end{cases} \quad (4)$$

### 3.5 The Switch/Link Update Equations:

If a noncongested switch/link receives a forward RM cell from the source, it will compute the modified allowed cell rate ($MACR$) as follows:

$$MACR \leftarrow k_1 \times MACR + k_2 \times A_{RM}^{ab},$$

where $A_{RM}^{ab}$ is the $ACR$ of VC ($ab$) contained in the forward RM cell, and $k_1$ and $k_2$ are two positive averaging factors: $k_1 + k_2 = 1$, $0 < k_2 < k_1 < 1$. In fact, $k_2 = \beta$ and $k_1 = 1 - \beta$ if using $\beta$ as in [8]. As noted earlier, in the rest of this paper, we will use $R$ as a short form for $MACR$.

If a congested switch receives a forward RM cell from a source, it will compute $R$ as follows only when $A_{RM}^{ab} > R$ [8]:

$$R \leftarrow k_1 \times R + k_2 \times A_{RM}^{ab}.$$

Therefore

$$\widehat{R}(n) = \begin{cases} k_1\bar{R}(n) + k_2 A_{RM}^{ab} & \text{if condition1} \\ \bar{R}(n) & \text{otherwise} \end{cases} \quad (5)$$

Condition1: $i$ is noncongested or $i$ is congested, $A_{RM}^{ab} < \bar{R}(n)$. Where $\bar{R}(n)$ is the latest Modified ACR which is stored at the switch before the forward RM cell of VC (ab) arrives at the switch, and $\widehat{R}(n)$ is the newly computed MACR right after the update, during the time period $[nT_\alpha, (n+1)T_\alpha]$.

During the time period $[nT_\alpha, (n+1)T_\alpha]$, we assume that a link $i$ will receive a forward RM cell from each of the active VCs on the link. The number of active VCs will be assumed to be $M$ and the VCs will be re-indexed to the set $\{1, 2, \ldots, M\}$. Let $R(n)$ denote the MACR at link $i$ at the end of the period $[nT_\alpha, (n+1)T_\alpha]$ after all the forward RM cells have been received and processed. We can solve a discrete difference equation to get:

$$R(n) = l^0(n) \cdot R(n-1) + \sum_{j=1}^{M} l^j(n) A_{RM}^j,$$

where

$$l^0(n) \in \{k_1, k_1^2, \cdots, k_1^M, 1\},$$

$$l^j(n) \in \{0, k_2, k_1k_2, k_1^2k_2, \cdots, k_1^{M-1}k_2\},$$

and

$$l^0(n) + \sum_{j=1}^{M} l^j(n) = 1. \quad (6)$$

Note that $A_{RM}^{ab}$ may or may not equal to $A^{ab}(n - d_{ai}^{ab})$, which is the average ACR for $(ab)$ at a delay $d_{ai}^{ab}$ ago. However, for the stability analysis, we assume the worst case where the sources are persistent and greedy, we have $A_{RM}^{ab} = A^{ab}(n - d_{ai}^{ab})$. For instability analysis, the calculation of MACR does not affect the dynamics of the queues involved (since noncongestion is assumed along the path, all links will not set ER in the backward RM cells for all the active VCs and ER is the only means for a congested link to enforce rate reduction at a source). Therefore, the equation for $R$ will be superfluous. For both cases, we can write:

$$R(n) = l^0(n) \cdot R(n-1) + \sum_{j=1}^{M} l^j(n) A^j(n - d_i^j), \quad (7)$$

where $d_i^j$ is the delay from the source of VC $j$ to link $i$.

Consider the case where a congested link $i$ receives a backward RM cell from a destination. If the current queue length $Q_i(n) > DQT$, the controller replaces $E$ in the RM cell by $\min(E, \gamma \times R)$. Otherwise, if $A > R$, the controller replaces $E$ in the RM cell by $\min(E, R)$; where $DQT$ is the fast-down queue threshold and $0 < \gamma < 1$ is the fast reduction ratio. Let $\widetilde{R}^{ab}(n)$ denote the latest $MACR$ stored in the switch for link $i$ at the time when the backward RM cell of VC(ab) arrives from the destination during the time period $[nT_\alpha, (n+1)T_\alpha]$. According to assumption $x$), the feedback explicit cell rate $E$ of VC($ab$) will be updated according to:

$$\begin{aligned} E^{ab}(n+1) &= g_1^{ab}(n)\gamma^{ab}(n)\widetilde{R}^{ab}(n) \\ &+ g_2^{ab}(n)\rho^{ab}(n)E^{ab}(n+1-d^{ab}) \quad (8) \end{aligned}$$

where

$$g_1^{ab}(n) + g_2^{ab}(n) = 1, \qquad g_1^{ab}(n), g_2^{ab}(n) \in \{0,1\}$$

$$g_1^{ab}(n) = \begin{cases} 1 & \text{if condition2} \\ 0 & \text{otherwise} \end{cases}$$

Condition2: $Q_i(n) > Q_i(n-1)$ and $\gamma^{ab}(n)\widetilde{R}^{ab}(n) < E^{ab}(n+1-d^{ab})$.

$$\gamma^{ab}(n) = \begin{cases} \gamma & \text{if } Q_i(n) > DQT \\ 1 & \text{otherwise.} \end{cases}$$

## 4 System Equations

Starting with this section, we will focus on a generic link $i$. Link $i$ will be the bottleneck link in the stability analysis where congestion is the problem. Link $i$ will be a generic link in the instability analysis where non-congestion is in the context. For link $i$, we assume that for all time, there are $M$ active VCs at link $i$, i.e. $C(i) = M$. Let all the VCs be re-indexed by $j = 1, 2, \ldots, M$. Let $d_i^j$ denote the delay of the cells of VC $j$ from its source to link $i$ in the forward path. From assumption vii), $d_i^j$ is also (assumed to be) the delay from link $i$ to source of VC $j$ in the backward path. Now equations (1) and (2) can be written as

$$Q_i(n+1) = max\{Q_i(n) + \sum_{j=1}^{M} A^j(n-d_i^j) - c_i, 0\}; \quad (9)$$

Equation (3) can be written as

$$A^j(n) = \alpha_1^j(n)\beta^j(n)A^j(n-1) + \alpha_2^j(n)E^j(n+1-d_i^j), \quad (10)$$

where

$$\alpha_1^j(n) + \alpha_2^j(n) = 1, \qquad \alpha_1^j(n), \alpha_2^j(n) \in \{0,1\},$$

$$\alpha_1^j(n) = \begin{cases} 0 & \text{if condition3} \\ 1 & \text{otherwise;} \end{cases}$$

Condition3: $MCR^j \leq E^j(n+1-d_i^j) < \beta^j(n)A^j(n-1)$.

$$\begin{cases} \beta^j(n) > 1 & \text{if } ACR^j(n) > ACR^j(n-1), \\ 0 < \beta^j(n) \leq 1 & \text{if } ACR^j(n) \leq ACR^j(n-1). \end{cases} \quad (11)$$

With the new indexing, the equation for $R$ can now be re-stated:

$$R(n) = l^0(n) \cdot R(n-1) + \sum_{j=1}^{M} l^j(n)A^j(n-d_i^j). \quad (12)$$

The equation for $E$ will be:

$$E^j(n+1) = g_1^j(n) \cdot \gamma^j(n)\widetilde{R}^j(n) + g_2^j(n) \cdot \rho^j(n) \cdot E^j(n+1-d^j), \quad (13)$$

where $d^j$ is the average round trip delay for VC $j$, $\widetilde{R}^j(n)$ is the value of MACR seen by the backward RM cell from VC $j$ at link $i$ at time $n$,

$$g_1^j(n) + g_2^j(n) = 1, \qquad g_1^j(n), g_2^j(n) \in \{0,1\},$$

$$g_1^j(n) = \begin{cases} 1 & \text{if condition4} \\ 0 & \text{otherwise;} \end{cases}$$

Condition4: $Q(n) > Q(n-1)$ and $\gamma^j(n)\widetilde{R}^j(n) < \rho^j(n) \cdot E^j(n-d^j)$.

$$\gamma^j(n) = \begin{cases} \gamma & \text{if } Q(n) > DQT, \\ 1 & \text{otherwise.} \end{cases}$$

Using a similar argument for equation (7), we can write:

$$\widetilde{R}^j(n) = m^0(n) \cdot R(n-1) + \sum_{k=1}^{M} m^k(n)A^k(n-1-d_i^k), \quad (14)$$

where

$$m^0(n) \in \{k_1, k_1^2, \cdots, k_1^M, 1\}$$

$$m^k(n) \in \{0, k_2, k_1k_2, k_1^2k_2, \cdots, k_1^{M-1}k_2\}, k = 1, 2, \cdots, M,$$

and

$$m^0(n) + \sum_{j=1}^{M} m^j(n) = 1. \quad (15)$$

In the above equations, we should have indexed the $A$, $m$ and $k$ variables by $j$, but we drop this indexing for the sake of simplicity.

The dynamics of all the sources and all the queues in the networks can be described by the above equations (9), (10), (12), (13). By writing all the equations together one will obtain a gigantic set of equations describing the overall dynamics of the entire network. However, in this paper, we will only consider the dynamics of a bottleneck congested link and the dynamics of a non-congested link. We will only be concerned with equations relevant to the queue under consideration; resulting in a greatly reduced number of equations, albeit this set of equations is still very large. These equations will be put into a state space formulation in the next section.

Using the above equations, the complete dynamics of the queue under consideration can be put into a state space form. The detailed description of the state space formulation can be found in [12].

## 5 Stability Analysis

### 5.1 Stability Results

First we formalize the definition of congestion.

**Definition 1** A link $i$ is said to be congested if $Q_i > Q_c$, where $Q_c$ is the congestion threshold; and link $i$ is said to be severely congested at time $n$ if $Q_i > DQT$. □

In order to analyze stability of the network, we will partition the state space into three regions: U, which is Noncongested region, C, which is Congested region and SC, which is Severely Congested region as follows:

Region U: $Q_i \leq Q_c$.
Region C: $Q_c < Q_i \leq DQT$.
Region SC: $Q_i > DQT$.

In the usual stability analysis, one considers the stability of the equilibrium points. However, the network is highly oscillatory and there exist no such points. We can only consider noncongestion regions such as region U. In the following theorem, we prove that the network is marginally stable in the sense that it can be controlled from congested regions to the noncongested region and it can also move from the noncongested region into congested regions. That is, there is no way to guarantee that the network will stay in the noncongested region even if the total number of active $VC$s is constant. The definition of stability needs to be modified for our problem if one wants to prove any stability result similar to the conventional definitions at all:

**Definition 2** The network is said to be *marginally stable* if every most congested link in any path will always become noncongested eventually, while there is no guarantee that other links will remain noncongested. □

**Assumptions for Stability Analysis:** For stability analysis, we assume that all sources are persistent and greedy: there are always cells waiting to be sent at all sources and all sources transmit data cells at the rate of their allowed cell rates.

To show marginal stability, it suffices to consider any congested link $i$. Now assume that link $i$ is congested or severely congested, i.e., in regions C or SC. Next, we will show that once queue $i$ enters into region C or SC, it will eventually enter into region U. To show this we need to observe that from item 6 and 7 of the EPRCA outline and (5) and (12), the value of $R$ is never increased when the queue $i$ is in region C or SC. $R$ is averaged with an $A$ ($ACR$) only if $A < R$. For any VC whose $A$ is less than $R$, the $A$ can be increased. However, for any VC whose $A$ is at least $R$, its $A$ will either remain the same or be decreased. Since $R$ may update upon every forward RM cells passing through link $i$, we let $R(n)$ denote the $R$ before any RM cell comes at link $i$ during $[nT_\alpha, (n+1)T_\alpha]$. We need to consider 2 cases: C and SC, in which, based on (5)

$$\widetilde{R}^{j+1}(n) \leq \widetilde{R}^j(n) < R(n) \leq R(n-1). \qquad (16)$$

Case 1: Queue $i$ is in region SC. In this case, for any VC $j$, in (13)

$$\gamma^j(n) = \gamma < 1.$$

Thus, for each VC $j$

$$E^j(n+1) \leq \gamma \widetilde{R}^j(n) \leq R(n), \qquad (17)$$

$$A^j(n+1-d_i^j) \leq E^j(n+1). \qquad (18)$$

If

$$R(n) \geq \frac{c_i}{M},$$

from (16) and (12), after a finite delay, $R$ will decrease until at some time $n_1$, $n_1 \geq n$,

$$R(n_1) < \frac{c_i}{M}.$$

Then from (17) and (18), at time $n_2 \geq n_1$, we obtain

$$A^j(n_2) \leq \gamma \widetilde{R}^j(n_2) < R(n_2). \qquad (19)$$

Then the total input rate is less than the output capacity $c_i$, queue $i$ decreases strictly until at a time $n_3 \leq n_2$,

$$Q_i(n_3) \leq DQT.$$

If $Q_c < Q_i(n_3) \leq DQT$, link $i$ enters case 2, otherwise, link $i$ enters region U directly.

Case 2: Queue $i$ is in region C. In this case, for any VC $j$,

$$\gamma^j(n) = 1.$$

From (13), the feedback explicit cell rate $E^j(n+1)$ of every VC $j$ is chosen as the minimum between $\widetilde{R}^j(n)$ and $\rho^j(n)E^j(n+1-d^j)$ only if $A^j(n-d_i^j) \geq \widetilde{R}^j(n)$. Then only those VCs with transmission rates higher than $\widetilde{R}^j(n)$ will set the backward $E^j$'s at a value no larger than $\widetilde{R}^j(n)$. Other VCs can still increase their $A^j$'s no larger than their feedback $E^j$'s, which are could be larger than $R^j(n)$. Thus VC $j$ may or may not increase its $A$.

If

$$R(n) \geq \frac{c_i}{M},$$

then those VCs with $A^j \geq \widetilde{R}^j(n)$ will have

$$E^j(n+1) \leq \widetilde{R}^j(n) \leq R(n).$$

If at time $n_1 \geq n$,

$$f_i(n_1) \geq c_i,$$

queue $i$ will increase its size, and even worse, it could enter region SC. However, once link $i$ is in region SC, link $i$ will eventually enter region U or C again. If at time $n_1 \geq n$,

$$f_i(n_1) < c_i,$$

then at time $n_2 \geq n_1$, from (16) and (12),

$$R(n_2) < \frac{c_i}{M},$$

the total input rate is less than the output capacity of link $i$. From (9), the queue size will decrease. If $Q(n) \leq Q_c$, link $i$ enters region U.

On the other hand, if queue $i$ is still in region C, those VCs whose previous $A$ is less than $R$ may increase their transmission rates no larger than their feedback explicit cell rate ($E^j$), which maybe as high as their peak cell rates. In this situation, link $i$ will see a set of VCs with $A^j > R$. For these VCs, the switch will set the backward $E^j$ at a value no larger than $R$. This will continue as long as queue $i$ is in region C until all the $A^j$'s, $j = 1, \ldots, M$ are no larger than $R$, which does not increase in this region. If there are at least one VC with an $A$ smaller than $R$, $R$ will continue to update as in (5). Thus $R$ continues to decrease until either all $A^j$s are no larger than $R$. Under this condition, $f_i(n) < c_i$, from (9). Consequently, queue $i$ will decrease to less than $Q_c$, forcing link $i$ into region U.

Unfortunately instability can also occur at this point. This will be described in the instability section which follows.

Therefore, though the buffer size may have overshoots, the queue length will eventually decrease to no larger than DQT or $Q_c$. This concludes the proof that the queue size will decrease once queue $i$ enters into region C or SC. Thus, a congested link $i$ is at least marginally stable.

## 5.2 Instability Result

**Spontaneous (Self-Induced) Congestion:** However, based on IM-EPRCA, the network can not be kept in the noncongested region even if the total number of active connections is constant. For this analysis, we assume that all sources are not persistent and greedy. Consider a link $i$ which is noncongested at time $n$, i.e., in region U. We will show that there is at least one intermediate link that can enter region C or SC. If the round trip delay is long that the queue length increases fast enough, then it is possible that the queue size will increase beyond $DQT$; forcing an intermediate link into region SC. The same result will happen if the control is not fast enough. A detailed proof can be found in [12]. We present a simple example to demonstrate the possibility of self-induced congestion as follows: Using the same parameters as those used in the simulation of [8], which are:

| | |
|---|---|
| $LinkSpeed = 155, Mbps$ | $PCR = 155Mbps,$ |
| $MCR = 0.155Mbps,$ | $ICR = 7.75Mbps,$ |
| $AIR = 0.053Mbps,$ | $N = 31,$ |
| $MD = 256,$ | $DQT = 50cells,$ |
| $k_1 = 1/16,$ | $\gamma = 0.25.$ |

Consider 10 active VCs of ABR traffics that are traversing link $i$ in which the available bandwidth for the ABR traffics is $77.5Mbps$ and the congestion threshold is $Q_c = 10$ cells. For simplicity, assume the 10 active VCs have the same round trip delay and the round trip delay is nearly equal to the time for each source to transmit $N$ data cells. Then each source receives a feedback RM cell every $N$ data cells transmitted. Initially, the queue length $Q_i = 0$. Let $t_k$ denote the $k$th RM cell each source receives, during the period $[0, t_1)$, the maximum cell rate of VC $j$ is the initial cell rate $7.75Mbps$, where $j = 1, \ldots, 10$. Since each source continuously decreases the cell rate until it receive an RM cell, the minimum cell rate is the 31th cell rate for VC$j$, $j = 1, \cdots, 10$:

$$ACR^j_{min} = 7.75 - (7.75/256) * 30 = 6.8418.$$

The average rate of VC$j$ in $[0, t_1)$ is:

$$ACR^j_{avg} = (ACR^j_{max} + ACR^j_{min})/2 = 7.2959$$

$$j = 1, \ldots, 10.$$

The average total input traffic in $[0, t_1)$ is:

$$f = \sum_j^{10} ACR^j_{avg} = 7.2959 * 10 = 72.959 < 77.5.$$

Link $i$ is noncongested. When the sources receive the feedback RM cells which show no congestion, each source will increase their cell rate as:

$$ACR^j = 6.8418 + 31 * (0.053 + 6.8418/256) = 9.3133$$

$$j = 1, \cdots, 10.$$

which is the maximum cell rate during $[t_1, t_2)$. Similarly, the minimum cell rate during $[t_1, t_2)$ is:

$$ACR^j_{min} = 9.3133 - (9.3133/256) * 30 = 8.2219$$

$$j = 1, \cdots, 10.$$

The average rate of VC$j$ in $[t_1, t_2)$ is:

$$ACR^j_{avg} = (9.3133 + 8.2219)/2 = 8.7676.$$

When these data cells arrive at link $i$,

$$f = \sum_j^{10} ACR^j = 8.7676 * 10 = 87.676 > 77.5.$$

and the queue length increases quickly,

$$\begin{aligned} Q = 87.676 - 77.5 &= 10.1760.Mbps \\ &= \frac{31}{8.7676} \times 10.1760 \\ &\approx 36cell > Q_c \end{aligned}$$

Link $i$ becomes very congested and enters region C.

Combining the stability and the instability properties of IM-EPRCA, we obtain that the network as described by equations (9), (10), (12), (13) is marginally stable.

**Theorem 1 1** *The closed loop system as described by (9), (10), (12) and (13), is marginally stable.*

## 6 Conclusion

In this paper, we prove the marginal stability of the counter-based *intelligent marking* of EPRCA in the rate-based control algorithms for ABR service developed in the ATM Forum. This result is significant in that current works on this adopted standard do not have any conclusive evidence of stability or instability of the protocol.

## References


[1] N. Yin, M.G. Hluchyi. On closed-loop rate control for ATM cell relay networks. *IEEE INFOCOM'94*, pp.99-109, June 1994.

[2] C. Ikeda, H. Suzuki. Adaptive congestion control schemes for ATM LANs. *IEEE INFOCOM'94*, pp.829-838, June 1994.

[3] P. Newman. Backward explicit congestion notification for ATM local area networks. *IEEE GLOBECOM'93*, pp.719-723, December 1993.

[4] A. Berger, F. Bonomi, K. Fendick, J. Swenson. Control of multiplexed connections using backward congestion control. *ATM Forum Contribution 94-064*, January 1994.

[5] L. Roberts et al. Closed-loop rate-based traffic management. *ATM Forum Contribution 94-0438R1*, June 1994.

[6] H. Hsiaw et al. Closed-loop rate-based traffic management. *ATM Forum Contribution 94-0438R2*, September 1994.

[7] L. Roberts et al. Enhanced PRCA (proportional rate-control algorithm). *ATM Forum Contribution 94-0735R1*, August 1994.

[8] K.Y. Siu, H.Y. Tzeng. Intelligent Congestion Control for ABR Service in ATM Networks. *Computer Communication Review*, April 1995.

[9] H. Ohsaki, M. Murata, H. Suzuki, and H. Miyahara. Rate-Based Congestion Control for ATM Networks. *Computer Communication Review*, April 1995.

[10] L. Benmohamed, S.M. Meerkov. Feedback Control of Congestion in Packet Switching Networks: The Case of a Single Congested Node. *IEEE/ACM Transactions on Networking*, vol.1, No.6, December 1993.

[11] L. Benmohamed, S.M. Meerkov. Feedback Control of Congestion in Store-and-forward Networks: The Case of Multiple Congested Nodes. *Control Group Report* No. CGR-93-3, The University of Michigan, February 1993.

[12] W.K. Tsai, G. Yan, and G. Huang Marginal Stability of the EPRCA with Intelligent Marking for ABR flow control in ATM networks. Submitted to *IEEE Communications Letters*, December, 1996.

[13] W.K. Tsai, G. Yan, and G. Huang Stability Analysis of Intelligent Marking EPRCA for ABR Congestion Control in ATM. Submitted to American Control Conference, 1997.

[14] M.S. Santina, A.R. Stubberud, G.H. Hostetter *Digital Control System Design*, 2nd. Edit., 1994

# Real-Time Block Transfer Under a Link Sharing Hierarchy*

Geoffrey G. Xie
Department of Computer Science
Naval Postgraduate School
Monterey, CA 93943
*xie@cs.nps.navy.mil*

Simon S. Lam
Department of Computer Sciences
The University of Texas at Austin
Austin, Texas 78712-1188
*lam@cs.utexas.edu*

## Abstract

*Most application-level data units are too large to be carried in a single packet (or cell) and must be segmented for network delivery. To an application, the end-to-end delays and loss rate of its data units are much more relevant performance measures than ones specified for individual packets (or cells). The concept of a burst (or block) was introduced to represent a sequence of packets (or cells) that carry an application data unit. In this paper, we describe how a real-time VBR service, with QoS parameters for block transfer delay and block loss rate, can be provided by integrating concepts and delay guarantee results from our previous work on burst scheduling, together with ideas from ATM block transfer. Two new contributions are presented herein. First, we design an admission control algorithm to provide the following classes of service: bounded-delay block transfer with no loss, and bounded-delay block transfer at a specified block loss rate. Second, we show how to extend existing end-to-end delay bounds to networks with hierarchical link sharing.*

## 1 Introduction

To an application, the end-to-end delays of its data units are much more relevant performance measures than ones specified for individual packets or cells. For example, a video picture (or file) being sent by an application over an IP network may be segmented into a sequence of IP datagrams. The delay incurred to deliver the entire video picture (or file) is much more important to the application than the delays of individual IP datagrams. As another example, an IP datagram carrying an email message may be segmented into a sequence of cells for delivery over an ATM network. The delay incurred to deliver the entire email message is more important than the delays of individual cells. From this observation, we introduced the concept of a burst to represent a sequence of packets that carry an application level data unit, and designed the class of burst scheduling networks to provide delay guarantees to bursts [8, 9].

The *ATM block transfer* (ABT) capability being standardized by ITU-T is based upon a similar observation [7]. The objective of ABT is to allow a data source to dynamically negotiate its bandwidth reservation on the basis of a block of cells. Note that a higher-layer protocol data unit, fragmented into a number of ATM cells, is lost if any one of its cells is lost. Therefore, even a low cell loss rate can cause a significant loss rate for the higher-layer protocol. As a result, the higher-layer protocol's throughput may be much less than the protocol session's throughput measured in delivered cells. The concept of a block was introduced to represent a sequence of cells, which may contain a single data unit or multiple data units for the higher-layer protocol. A block is bracketed by two RM cells. A leading RM cell requests a reserved bandwidth for the block, and a trailing RM cell releases the reserved bandwidth. Cells are handled in blocks by a switch. In particular, a block of cells is either discarded or accepted entirely.

For the ABT service, the concept of cell loss rate can be generalized to *block loss rate.* Such a generalization is backward-compatible with the existing ATM TM 4.0 service architecture [5] since a block is a sequence of cells, with a single cell being a special case. Similarly, the concept of cell transfer delay for real-time VBR services can be generalized to *block transfer delay* which, we believe, is a more relevant performance measure to many applications; for example, if every picture in a video sequence is carried by a block of cells, then the block transfer delays are the same as picture delays.

In this paper, we describe how a real-time VBR service called *real-time block transfer* with QoS parameters for block transfer delay and block loss rate can be provided by integrating concepts and delay guarantee results from our previous work on burst scheduling [8]

*Most of this work was done while G. Xie was a graduate student in the Department of Computer Sciences, the University of Texas at Austin. Research supported in part by National Science Foundation grant no. NCR-9506048, an Intel Graduate Fellowship, and the Texas Advanced Research Program grant no. 003658-220.



0-8186-7780-5/97 $10.00 © 1997 IEEE

and group priority [9], together with ideas from ATM block transfer. In particular, we have designed an admission control algorithm for real-time block transfer, which provides the following service classes: bounded-delay block transfer with no loss (deterministic delay guarantee), and bounded delay block transfer at a specified block loss rate.

It is envisioned that future integrated services networks will support not only link sharing by multiple service classes (real-time service, best-effort service, etc.) but also by multiple administrative classes (different agencies and organizations) [4]. Specifically, packets (or cells) from sessions belonging to different service classes and administrative classes interact with one another when they are statistically multiplexed at an output link of a switch. The switch's packet scheduling algorithm plays an important role in controlling such link sharing. Hierarchical link sharing has been proposed as a solution [1]. In this paper, we also describe a general approach for extending the end-to-end delay bounds for bursts[1] from networks in which links are shared by service classes only [8, 9] to networks in which links are hierarchically shared (e.g., by administrative classes first, and then by service classes within each administrative class). Specifically, we have proved two theorems that can be used to derive block delay guarantees by a *fluctuation constrained* server from block delay guarantees by a constant-rate server. The theorems are general. They are proved for a large class of well known servers.

The balance of this paper is organized as follows. In Section 2, we describe the basic idea of block-based admission control for ABT and the concept of burst scheduling. The end-to-end delay bounds of burst scheduling are shown. In Section 3, we design a flow level admission control algorithm for real-time block transfer services. We evaluated the algorithm using a simulator driven by MPEG video traces, and some experimental results are presented in this section. In Section 4, we introduce hierarchical link sharing. We model each logical server in a link sharing hierarchy as a fluctuation constrained (FC) server, and show how to extend end-to-end delay bounds such as the ones presented in Section 2 to networks with hierarchical link sharing.

# 2 Real-time Block Transfer

## 2.1 Block-based Admission Control

In ABT, dynamic bandwidth reservation and allocation for a block of cells can be carried out in two ways: (i) ABT with Delayed Transmission (ABT/DT), and (ii) ABT with Immediate Transmission (ABT/IT). For our discussion, we focus on the latter. In ABT/IT, the block is sent *immediately* after a preceding RM cell, which contains a request for a cell rate. The block proceeds on a switch by switch basis, with each switch either forwarding the block with guaranteed QoS for *every cell* in the block or discarding the *entire* block if a required resource such as bandwidth is not available. In other words, the switches perform admission control on a block by block basis.

With block-based admission control, cell losses are concentrated over a small number of blocks, and bandwidth is not wasted on delivery of partial blocks. (This is similar to the idea of early packet discard in recent studies on IP over ATM [13].) Therefore, ABT is able to avoid the situation in which cell losses spread over a large number of higher-layer data units causing throughput degradation of such data units.

With block-based admission control, ABT is also able to offer QoS measured in terms of blocks. In particular, the concept of cell loss rate can be generalized to *block loss rate*.

## 2.2 Burst Scheduling

For burst scheduling networks, we model a flow as a sequence of bursts [8]. A burst, a sequence of packets, corresponds to a block in ABT with some minor differences in detail. In particular, instead of two special packets being used, the first packet of each burst is marked and stored in it information on the size of the burst (in number of packets) and the average rate of the burst. Moreover for efficient packet scheduling and delay jitter control, packets of each burst satisfy a jitter timing constraint [8].

The following delay bound results are taken from [8] and [9].

*Consider a flow that traverses a sequence of nodes, indexed by $0, 1, 2, \ldots, K+1$, where node 0 denotes the source, node $K+1$ the destination, and the other nodes packet switches. If the capacity of every link on the network path is not exceeded, then the end-to-end delay[2] of every burst $m$ of the flow, denoted by $D_m$, $m = 1, 2, \ldots$, has the following upper and lower bounds:*

$$D_m \le \frac{b_m + g_m}{\lambda_m} + (K-1) \max_{1 \le n \le m} \{\frac{g_n}{\lambda_n}\} + \sum_{k=1}^{K} \alpha_k \quad (1)$$

$$D_m \ge (K-1)\frac{g_m}{\lambda_m} + \sum_{k=1}^{K} \alpha_k, \quad (2)$$

*where we use the following notation*

[1] End-to-end delay bounds for blocks are obtained by specifying a burst [8, 9] to represent a block of ATM cells.

[2] measured from the time when the first cell enters the network to the time when the last cell leaves the network.

| | |
|---|---|
| $b_m$ | *size of burst m (packets)* |
| $\lambda_m$ | *average rate of burst m (packets/second)* |
| $g_m$ | *group size (in packets) chosen for burst m by the switches for efficient scheduling;* $1 \le g_m \le b_m$ |
| $\alpha_k$ | *a small constant associated with the link from switch k to* $k+1$ |

Our design of burst scheduling networks consists of specialized components such as source and flow regulators. But the concept of burst scheduling, i.e. modeling a flow as a sequence of bursts and providing bounded delays to bursts (blocks) when link capacity is not exceeded, is quite general. It can be realized by many designs other than ours. In what follows, we refer to burst scheduling as a general concept independent of the design details.

### 2.3 Integration of ABT and Burst Scheduling

ABT is able to minimize block losses through the use of block-based admission control, and provide block loss rate as QoS. Burst scheduling networks provide bounded block transfer delays as QoS when link capacity is not exceeded. Integrating the concepts and results from ABT and burst scheduling, we define a real-time VBR service, called real-time block transfer, that provides the following two classes of services: (i) bounded-delay block transfer with zero block loss, and (ii) bounded-delay block transfer at a specified block loss rate.

Admission control at the flow level is the key for our integration. For class (i), peak rate reservation can be used for admission control to ensure that the link capacity allocated to this class is not exceeded without discarding blocks. For class (ii), overbooking of the class's allocated capacity is allowed at the time of connection setup while block-based admission control is used to ensure that link capacity is not exceeded at any time by discarding blocks if necessary. To limit the block loss rate to a specified value, the extent of overbooking is controlled by flow level admission control. In the next section, we describe in detail a flow level admission control algorithm for the real-time block transfer services.

## 3 Admission Control

In this section, we design an algorithm for flow level admission control at connection setup time for real-time block transfer.[3] Consider a flow whose source requests for a real-time block transfer service. We assume that at the time of connection setup, the source supplies the network two sets of flow parameters: (i) QoS parameters: block loss probability $BLP$ and block transfer delay bound $BTD$,[4] and (ii) traffic parameters: sustained cell rate $SCR$, peak cell rate $PCR$, and cell rate variation $CRV$. Whether or not to admit the flow is a decision made by each switch in the path of the flow. Specifically, each switch in the path accepts the flow only if doing so will not cause violation of QoS guarantees to accepted flows; the network admits the flow only if all switches in the path accept the flow.

### 3.1 System Model

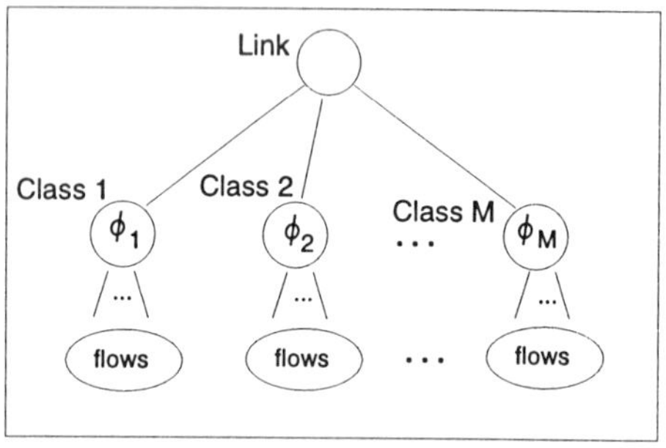


Figure 1: System model for admission control.

Our system model for admission control by a particular switch is shown in Figure 1. There are $M$ classes of real-time block transfer service. They share a link[5] with capacity $C$ bits/second. Each class is associated with a weight, $\phi_s$ for class $s$, which is a relative measure of its share of the bandwidth of the link. For ease of presentation and without loss of generality, we assume that $\sum_{s=1}^{M} \phi_s = 1$. Therefore, class $s$ has a share of the link equal to $r_s = \phi_s \cdot C$ (bits/second). Each class offers a block loss rate, $p_s$ for class $s$. Without loss of generality, we assume that

$$0 = p_1 < p_2 < \ldots < p_M < 1.$$

In other words, class 1 provides deterministic service, i.e., class (i) service defined in Section 2.3, and the other classes provide different levels of statistical service, i.e., class (ii) service defined in Section 2.3.

We also assume that an appropriate scheduling algorithm (such as WF$^2$Q+ [1]) is used by the link to provide a firewall between the service classes and guarantee each class its link share. (See Section 4.) As a result, admission control for each class can be performed independently.

### 3.2 Statistical Multiplexing

For flows requesting for the deterministic service, admission control should be based on peak rate reserva-

[3] We present the design in the context of ATM networks. Our design should be applicable to other types of networks.

[4] $BTD$ will not be considered further in our design of admission control, assuming that an appropriate scheduling algorithm is used by the network to ensure burst delay guarantees.

[5] The link could be a logical one; see Section 4.

tion, which is necessary to ensure that the class's link share cannot be exceeded without discarding blocks.[6]

We next consider a statistical class $s$. Flows that request for this class of service can tolerate some block losses. Therefore their admission control can be more aggressive to increase utilization of the class's bandwidth by taking advantage of statistical multiplexing. In what follows, we derive a set of conditions that are sufficient to limit the block loss probability of the class at approximately $p_s$.

Assume that the service of the class is currently shared by a set of $N$ flows (indexed by $1, 2, ..., N$). Let $BLP_i$, $SCR_i$, $PCR_i$ and $CRV_i$ be the QoS and traffic parameters[7] that are supplied to the switch by flow $i$. At any time, because of burst scheduling, at most one block from each flow is active [8]. Denote $\lambda_i(t)$ the reserved cell rate for the block of flow $i$ that is active at time $t$. ($\lambda_i(t) = 0$ if there is no active block for flow $i$ at $t$.) In our analysis below, $\lambda_i(t)$'s are considered independent random variables. Define

$$Y_s(t) = \sum_{i=1}^{N} \lambda_i(t) - r_s. \qquad (3)$$

Consider a block that becomes active at time $t$. The switch immediately performs admission control on the block, and will discard it if $(Y_s(t) > 0)$. Therefore $\Pr(Y_s(t) > 0)$ is a good approximation of the block loss probability of the class. The goal of our analysis is to find conditions sufficient for

$$\Pr(Y_s(t) > 0) \leq p_s. \qquad (4)$$

From a generalized version of the central limit theorem [11], we have

$$\frac{Y_s(t) - E[Y_s(t)]}{\sqrt{Var[Y_s(t)]}} \rightarrow \mathrm{N}(0,1), \qquad (5)$$

where N(0,1) is the standard normal distribution. Therefore, we can approximate $\Pr(Y_s(t) > 0) \leq p_s$ by

$$\Pr(X > \frac{-E[Y_s(t)]}{\sqrt{Var[Y_s(t)]}}) \leq p_s, \qquad (6)$$

where $X \sim \mathrm{N}(0,1)$.
The following condition is sufficient for (6):

$$\frac{-E[Y_s(t)]}{\sqrt{Var[Y_s(t)]}} \geq Z_s, \qquad (7)$$

where $Z_s$ is the constant that satisfies $(\Pr(X > Z_s) = p_s)$. We have

$$E[Y_s(t)] = \sum_{i=1}^{N} E[\lambda_i(t)] - r_s \qquad (8)$$

$$Var[Y_s(t)] = \sum_{i=1}^{N} Var[\lambda_i(t)]. \qquad (9)$$

Define

$$Z = \frac{r_s - \sum_{i=1}^{N} E[\lambda_i(t)]}{\sqrt{\sum_{i=1}^{N} Var[\lambda_i(t)]}}. \qquad (10)$$

Combining (7), (8), (9), and (10), we have the following approximate sufficient condition for (4):

$$\frac{Z_s}{Z} \leq 1. \qquad (11)$$

We refer to the value of $(Z_s/Z)$ as the Statistical Multiplexing Intensity (SMI) of class $s$. It should never exceed the threshold of 1 to limit the block loss rate at $p_s$. In practice, it is difficult to obtain the exact value of $Z$. However, $Z$ can be estimated as follows:

$$\hat{Z} = \frac{r_s - \sum_{i=1}^{N} SCR_i}{\sqrt{\sum_{i=1}^{N} CRV_i}}. \qquad (12)$$

Note that the source of flow $i$ may not have a good estimate of $CRV_i$ at the time of connection setup. In such a case, $CRV_i$ is upper bounded by $SCR_i \cdot (PCR_i - SCR_i)$, which can be used as a pessimistic estimate.

### 3.3 Algorithm Specification

The following admission control algorithm follows from the analysis in the previous section. The variables $B_s$ and $V_s$ are used to store respectively the available bandwidth and the total cell rate variance of class $s$. Initially $B_s = r_s$ and $V_s = 0$. We assume that if a source does not have a good estimate of $CRV$ at the time of connection setup, it will let the network know by setting $CRV = 0$.

```
Admission_Control (BLP, PCR, SCR, CRV)
s := find_class(BLP);
if (s = 1 )
  then if (B1 − PCR ≥ 0)
         then accept the flow;
              B1 := B1 − PCR;
         else reject the flow;
  else if (CRV = 0)
         then CRV := SCR * (PCR − SCR);
         SMI := Zs * (sqrt(Vs + CRV)/(Bs − SCR));
         if (SMI ≤ 1)
```

[6]If the switch has a priori knowledge of the traffic characteristics of flows in the class, peak rate reservation may not be necessary. But it is unrealistic with today's networks.

[7]Note that $BLP_i$ is the probability of block losses through one switch (i.e. a single hop) required for flow $i$. We will discuss how to distribute an end-to-end burst loss requirement to individual switches in a future report.

**then** accept the flow;
$B_s := B_s - SCR$;
$V_s := V_s + CRV$;
**else** reject the flow;

The algorithm is simple and straightforward. First, $BLP$ is used to find the service class desired by the source. Assume the class found is $s$. If $s$ is 1, the source requests for deterministic service. Therefore, the admission decision is based upon $PCR$ of the flow and the bandwidth currently available for class 1. Otherwise, the source requests for a statistical service. The admission decision is then based on $Z_s$ for class $s$, which has been calculated from $p_s$.

### 3.4 Experimental Results

We have performed a set of experiments to evaluate the performance of the admission control algorithm. We present the results in this section.

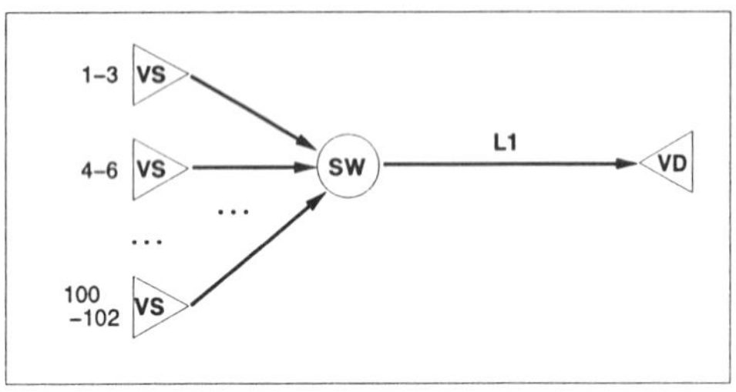


Figure 2: Simulated network.

The simulated network is shown in Figure 2. The nodes labeled by VS are video sources, and VD video destination. Each video source generates packets from a trace file obtained from one of the MPEG video sequences that we have downloaded from the Web.

Each video source makes reservation with the network before sending out data packets. The admission control algorithm is implemented for channel L1, and all video sources request for the same class of service with a targeted block loss rate, $p$. To evaluate the admission control algorithm, we varied the link bandwidth of L1 as well as the value of $p$. We ran each experiment for 10 seconds of simulated time.

In Figure 3, we show the channel utilization as a function of the targeted loss rate. Compared with deterministic guarantees, the network channel is used more efficiently for statistical guarantees; the price to pay is a small non-zero block loss probability. The utilization gain is more significant with a higher channel capacity, from below 30% to above 70% in the case where the capacity of L1 is 56 Mbps. This is because the improvement is due to statistical multiplexing gain, which is larger with a higher channel capacity.

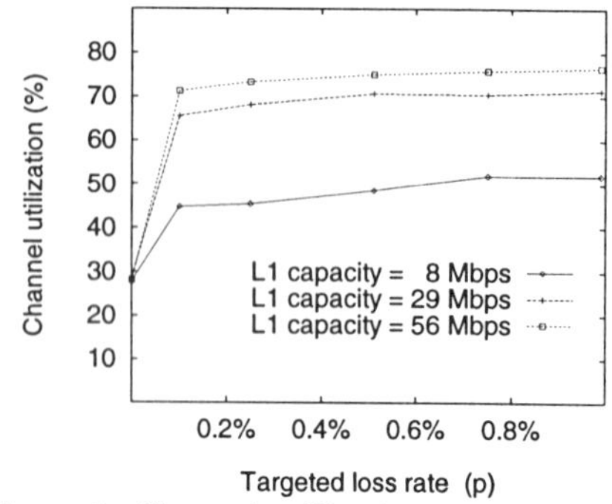


Figure 3: Channel utilization improvement

We also measured the actual block (picture) loss rate, averaged over five simulation runs using different random seeds. In Figure 4, a comparison of the actual and targeted loss rates is illustrated. The solid 45 degree line represents a perfect prediction by the central limit theorem. From the figure, we conclude that our admission control algorithm predicts the actual loss rate well when a large number of flows share the channel. (Around 30 flows were admitted when the channel capacity of L1 is 56 Mbps.) This agrees with our analysis; the larger the number of flows sharing the channel, the better the approximation based upon the central limit theorem.

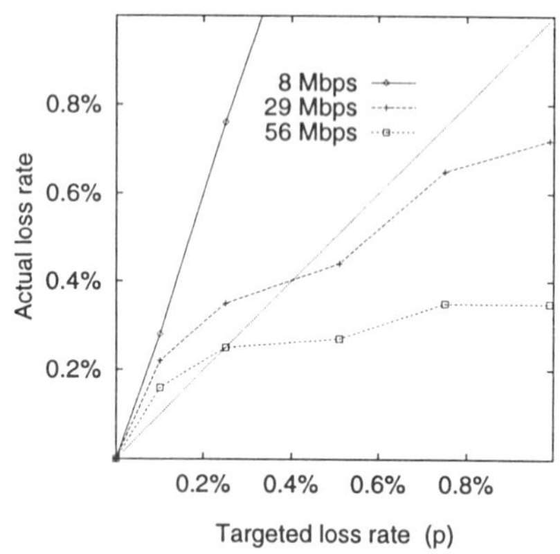


Figure 4: Actual vs. targeted loss rate

## 4 Hierarchical Link Sharing

Existing delay bounds for blocks (bursts), e.g. the ones presented in Section 2.2, were derived for networks with a flat one-level link sharing structure. In this section, we discuss how to generalize the delay bounds to networks in which links are hierarchically shared.

## 4.1 Directed Tree Model

First, we describe a directed tree model, largely borrowed from [1], for representation of a link sharing hierarchy. The root node, denoted by $R$, corresponds to the physical link, each leaf node corresponds to a flow with a queue of packets, and each non-leaf node (except for the root) corresponds to a link sharing entity, e.g., an administrative agency, a traffic type, or a service class. A non-leaf node $n$ is called backlogged if at least one flow in its leaf descendent node set, denoted by $leaf(n)$, is backlogged. Conceptually, node $n$ is a logical server for its descendents. The amount of work done by $n$ in the time interval $[t_1, t_2]$ is defined to be $W_n(t_1, t_2) = \sum_{f \in leaf(n)} W_f(t_1, t_2)$, where $W_f(t_1, t_2)$ is the amount of flow $f$ traffic served in the interval $[t_1, t_2]$. To achieve link sharing, each node $m$ is assigned a weight $\phi_m > 0$, which is a relative measure of the link share desired by entity $m$. For ease of presentation and without loss of generality, we assume that

$$\phi_R = 1 \quad (13)$$

$$\sum_{m \in children(n)} \phi_m \leq \phi_n, \ \forall \text{ non-leaf node } n. \quad (14)$$

**Notation.** Let $H(m)$ be the number of ancestors that node $m$ has. Let $p^h(m)$ be the ancestor node of $m$ that is $h$ levels higher than $m$ in the tree, $h = 1, 2, \ldots, H(m)$. Clearly $p^1(m) = parent(m)$ and $p^{H(m)}(m) = R$. For ease of presentation, we also set $p^0(m) = m$.

Hierarchical link sharing can have a big impact on the performance of flows that share the link. Specifically, packets of a flow under the link sharing hierarchy are scheduled jointly by *all* ancestor nodes of the flow before being served by the link [1]. For hierarchical link sharing to be useful, appropriate scheduling algorithms must be used at the logical servers to minimize any negative impact on flow performance. We next define ideal link sharing to set a performance target for designing such scheduling algorithms. Assume that the link bandwidth is $C$ (bits/second).

**Definition 1** *We say that ideal link sharing is achieved for logical server $n$ if for any time interval $[t_1, t_2]$ in which $n$ is continuously backlogged, the following holds*

$$W_n(t_1, t_2) \geq r_n \cdot (t_2 - t_1), \quad (15)$$

*where $r_n = \phi_n \cdot C$; that is, server $n$ is guaranteed its link share whenever it has work to do.*

It is straightforward to show that if every logical server is a Fluid model Fair Queueing (FFQ) server,[8] then ideal link sharing will be achieved for every logical server. Unfortunately, FFQ is not feasible. Therefore, scheduling algorithms that are good approximations of FFQ should be used at the logical servers.

[8] Also called General Processor Sharing (GPS) server in the literature [12].

## 4.2 Prior Work

In [1], Bennett and Zhang proposed a new approximation of FFQ, named Worst-case Fair Weighted Fair Queueing Plus (WF$^2$Q+), for providing tight delay bounds to flows under a link sharing hierarchy. They defined a metric for a logical server called Normalized Bit Worst-case Fair Index (NB-WFI).

**Definition 2** *A logical server node $n$ is said to guarantee a Normalized Bit Worst-case Fair Index (NB-WFI) of $\alpha_{m,n}$, for its child $m$, if during any time interval $[t_1, t_2]$ in which $m$ is continuously backlogged, the following holds*

$$W_m(t_1, t_2) \geq \frac{\phi_m}{\phi_n} W_n(t_1, t_2) - \alpha_{m,n}. \quad (16)$$

They then showed that delays of flow $f$ packets are bounded by

$$\frac{\sigma_f}{r_f} + \sum_{h=0}^{H(f)-1} \frac{\alpha_{p^h(f)}}{r_{p^h(f)}}, \quad (17)$$

where $\alpha_{p^h(f)}$ is the NB-WFI guaranteed to node $p^h(f)$ by node $p^{h+1}(f)$, if the flow is constrained by a leaky bucket $(\rho_f, \sigma_f)$ with $\rho_f \leq r_f$. Based on this result, Bennett and Zhang claimed that small NB-WFI values for the logical servers are necessary for providing tight delay bounds to the flows. They also showed that among all proposed packet fair queueing servers, a WF$^2$Q+ server offers the smallest NB-WFI, namely: the length of one packet when a fixed packet length is used by all flows.

The problem of scheduling packets for flows under a link sharing hierarchy was also studied by Goyal et al. in [6], where an algorithm called Start-time Fair Queueing (SFQ) was proposed. Goyal et al. observed that the intermediate logical servers no longer have constant service rates for their children. Therefore, they analyzed the performance of SFQ in the context of Fluctuation Constrained servers first defined by Lee [10].

**Definition 3** *A server is said to be Fluctuation Constrained (FC) with parameters[9] $(C, \delta)$, or simply a $FC(C, \delta)$ server, if for all intervals $[t_1, t_2]$ in a busy period of the server, the work done by the server, denoted by $W(t_1, t_2)$, satisfies:*

$$W(t_1, t_2) \geq C \cdot (t_2 - t_1) - \delta. \quad (18)$$

[9] A constant rate server is also FC with $\delta = 0$.

In addition, they showed that the service received by a flow from a FC SFQ server is also fluctuation constrained. Thus, if the logical servers (called virtual servers in [6]) are all SFQ servers, the packet delay bound for a flow under a link sharing hierarchy can be recursively computed. The exact bound is not given in [6].

### 4.3 A General Approach

While the authors cited above have made important contributions to the design of WF$^2$Q+ and SFQ, their approach is not the best. Specifically, too much emphasis was put on one good fair queueing algorithm for *both* link sharing and packet scheduling. For future networks, heterogeneous packet scheduling algorithms will likely be required at different parts of the link sharing hierarchy to achieve multiple design goals. For example, if implementation complexity is of primary concern, round robin scheduling may be more desirable than others. Also, there are a large number of performance results in the literature for one-level servers. It is not obvious from [1, 6] how these results, e.g. those for WFQ servers [2] or even FIFO servers, can be extended to networks with hierarchical link sharing.

Next we describe an approach in which link sharing and packet scheduling concerns are *separated.* In particular, a link sharing hierarchy is considered an extension of a one-level constant rate server.

Consider a particular flow $f$ under the link sharing hierarchy. Even with hierarchical link sharing, the flow is in essence scheduled by a one-level server, its parent node, but with a variable service rate. The impact of all non-parent ancestors of $f$ is indirectly accounted for by the service rate fluctuation of the parent node. Therefore, the analysis of flow $f$ performance can be carried out in two steps:

(1) characterization of the service rate fluctuation of the parent server.

(2) extension of the performance results for one-level servers to account for service rate fluctuations (characterized in the previous step).

For step 1, we characterize the parent server, $n = parent(f)$, as a FC server. That is, there exists a constant $\delta_n \geq 0$ such that for any time interval $[t_1, t_2]$ in which $n$ is backlogged (busy) throughout, the work (service) done by $n$ satisfies

$$W_n(t_1, t_2) \geq r_n \cdot (t_2 - t_1) - \delta_n. \qquad (19)$$

Note that the smaller $\delta_n$ is, the less service rate fluctuation for $n$. If all ancestors of $n$ are FFQ servers, $\delta_n = 0$. Therefore, good approximations of FFQ should be used for ancestors of $n$ to ensure a small value for $\delta_n$. Let us look at two examples.

**Example 1** *Assume that all ancestors of n are WF$^2$Q+ servers and all packets have a fixed length of L bits. From Definition 1 and the fact that WF$^2$Q+ guarantees a NB-WFI of L [1], it can be shown that $\delta_n$ is at most*

$$\left(\sum_{h=0}^{H(n)-1} \frac{r_n}{r_{p^h(n)}}\right)L. \qquad (20)$$

*Let us make the conservative assumption that $r_{p^h(n)}/r_{p^{h+1}(n)} = 0.5$, $h = 0, 1, \ldots, H(n) - 1$. (The ratio is usually much smaller in reality.) Then it is easy to show that $\delta_n \leq 2L$.*

**Example 2** *Assume that all ancestors of n are SFQ servers and all packets have a fixed length of L bits. Applying Theorem 2 of [6], it can be shown that $\delta_n$ is at most*

$$\left(1 + \left(\sum_{h=0}^{H(n)-1} \frac{r_n}{r_{p^{h+1}(n)}}(Q(h) + 1)\right)\right)L, \qquad (21)$$

*where $Q(h)$ is the number of branches that $p^{h+1}(n)$ has. Let us assume that $r_{p^h(n)}/r_{p^{h+1}(n)} = 0.5$ and $Q(h) = Q$, $h = 0, 1, \ldots, H(n) - 1$. Then $\delta_n$ could be as large as $(Q + 2)L$. Therefore in general, SFQ causes larger service rate fluctuations than WF$^2$Q+. On the other hand, SFQ appears to have a smaller implementation cost.*

For step 2, we next show how to extend delay guarantee results from constant rate servers to FC servers.

**Definition 4** *For a FC$(C, \delta)$ server, its* corresponding constant rate server *is defined to be identical to the FC server except that it has a constant service rate of C bits/second.*

Consider a class of *work conserving* servers, called the *priority class*, which can be described in general as follows. A priority value is computed and assigned to every packet upon its arrival, and queued packets are scheduled for service in the order of increasing priority values. Ties between packets are broken arbitrarily. Also, within a particular flow, the priority of each packet is non-decreasing in packet arrival time.

**Notation.** Consider an arbitrary sequence of packet arrivals to a priority server. (A packet arrival is represented by a tuple consisting of the packet arrival time and the packet size.) We use the following notation

| | |
|---|---|
| $A(p)$ | arrival time of packet $p$ in the arrival sequence |
| $s(p)$ | size of packet $p$ (in bits) |
| $P(p)$ | priority value assigned to packet $p$ |
| $L(p)$ | departure time of packet $p$ |

In what follows, we focus on a subclass called Service Independent Priority (SIP) servers, defined below.

**Definition 5** *An $FC(C, \delta)$ priority server belongs to the Service Independent Priority (SIP) subclass if for every packet p of an arrival sequence to the server, $P(p)$ depends exclusively upon the value of $C$ and packet arrivals up to and including p.*

Therefore for an $FC(C, \delta)$ SIP server, $P(p)$ is the same for different $\delta$ values.

It is easy to see that FC versions of Virtual Clock [15] and Delay-EDD [3] servers belong to the SIP class. FC versions of servers that approximate a hypothetical constant rate Fluid model Fair Queueing (FFQ) server (such as WFQ [2], PGPS [12] and $WF^2Q+$ [1]) can be defined so that their packet priority values depend upon virtual times in the constant rate FFQ server and are thus SIP servers as well. FC FIFO servers also belong to the SIP class since they in effect use the arrival time of a packet as the packet priority. (Lee obtained some delay bound results for FC FIFO servers with leaky bucket constrained sources [10].)

In particular, we consider two types of SIP servers: *preemptive-resume with no overhead*, and *nonpreemptive*. For a SIP server that is preemptive-resume with no overhead, it will immediately stop the service of a packet and serve a newly arrived packet if the new arrival has a smaller priority value. But no work will be lost because of the preemption, i.e., when resuming service for the preempted packet, the server will start from where it stopped. For a SIP server that is *nonpreemptive*, the service of a packet cannot be preempted once it is started.

Next we present two theorems on extension of delay guarantees for SIP servers.[10] (Their proofs are in the appendix.) They deal with preemptive and nonpreemptive SIP servers respectively. We say that a delay guarantee has the *firewall* property if the guarantees to packets of a flow are independent of how other flows behave.

**Theorem 1** *Consider an $FC(C, \delta)$ SIP server that is* preemptive-resume with no overhead. *If its corresponding constant rate server guarantees a departure deadline of $P(p) + \beta$ to every packet p of an arrival sequence, where $\beta$ is a constant, and the guarantee has the firewall property and is independent of the priority tie breaking method, then it guarantees to every packet p a departure deadline of $P(p) + \beta + \frac{\delta}{C}$*

**Corollary 1** *A $FC(C, \delta)$ FIFO server guarantees a delay bound of $\beta + \frac{\delta}{C}$ to every packet p of an arrival sequence if its corresponding constant rate server guarantees a delay bound of $\beta$ to every packet p.*

[10] Note that the servers need to perform some form of admission control to provide meaningful delay guarantees.

For nonpreemptive servers, the service may be out-of-order sometimes. It happens when a newly arrived packet has a priority value smaller than that of the packet being served, but preemption is not allowed.

**Definition 6** *Assume that a nonpreemptive server guarantees to packet p a deadline of $D(p)$. The guarantee is said to account for out-of-order service if with preemption the server can guarantee p a deadline of $D(p) - \frac{s_{max}}{C}$ where $s_{max}$ is the maximum packet size.*

**Theorem 2** *Consider a* nonpreemptive *$FC(C, \delta)$ SIP server. If its corresponding constant rate server guarantees a departure deadline of $P(p) + \beta$ to every packet p of an arrival sequence, and the guarantee has the firewall property, accounts for out-of-order service, and is independent of the priority tie breaking method, then it guarantees to every packet p a departure deadline of $P(p) + \beta + \frac{\delta}{C}$.*

Note that both theorems and Corollary 1 are quite general. They do not depend on specific admission control conditions or source control mechanisms. In contrast, most of Lee's analyses on FIFO FC servers [10] were done for leaky bucket constrained sources.

The burst (block) delay bounds presented in Section 2.2 were derived from a delay guarantee of Virtual Clock servers that has the firewall property and accounts for out-of-order service [14]. Using Theorem 2, it is straightforward to extend them to networks with hierarchical link sharing.

**Corollary 2** *Consider the end-to-end burst delay bounds presented in Section 2.2. If at each switch k, the packets of the flow are served by a $FC(C_k, \delta_k)$ logical server instead of a constant rate link with capacity $C_k$, then the end-to-end delay of burst m of the flow is bounded as follows:*

$$D_m \leq \frac{b_m + g_m}{\lambda_m} + (K-1) \max_{1 \leq n \leq m} \{\frac{g_n}{\lambda_n}\} + \sum_{k=1}^{K} (\alpha_k + \frac{\delta_k}{C_k}) \quad (22)$$

$$D_m \geq (K-1)\frac{g_m}{\lambda_m} + \sum_{k=1}^{K} \alpha_k. \quad (23)$$

## Appendix

### Proof of Theorem 1

Define

$N(p)$ — the set of packets in the arrival sequence whose priority values are less than or equal to that of packet $p$

$W_p(t_1, t_2)$ — total work (in bits) done by the FC server *for packets in* $N(p)$ in the time interval $[t_1, t_2]$

We will carry out a proof by contradiction. Specifically, we assume that there exists a packet $p$ in the arrival sequence such that

$$L(p) > P(p) + \beta + \frac{\delta}{C}. \tag{24}$$

Then we will show

$$W_p(0, P(p) + \beta + \frac{\delta}{C}) \geq \sum_{q \in N(p)} s(q), \tag{25}$$

which contradicts (24).

We use the superscript $c$ to label terms defined for the constant rate server. By definition of SIP servers, $p$ has the same priority value, $P(p)$, in both server systems, and

$$N^c(p) = N(p). \tag{26}$$

From (24), there exists a time period, of which $[A(p), P(p) + \beta + \frac{\delta}{C}]$ is a sub-interval and in which the FC server is continuously busy with $N(p)$ packets. Let $p^*$ be the packet that started this time period. (Note that $p^*$ may be $p$ itself.) In other words, there is no other $N(p)$ packet in the FC system when $p^*$ arrived. Consider the set of packets in $N(p)$ that arrived prior to $A(p^*)$ in the FC system (same as the packets in $N^c(p)$ that arrived prior to $A(p^*)$ in the constant rate system). Since all of them have been served in the FC system by $A(p^*)$ (but not necessarily in the constant rate system), we have

$$W_p(0, A(p^*)) \geq W_p^c(0, A(p^*)). \tag{27}$$

Since the FC server is busy exclusively with packets in $N(p)$ throughout the interval $[A(p^*), P(p) + \beta + \frac{\delta}{C}]$, we have

$$\begin{aligned} & W_p(A(p^*), P(p) + \beta + \frac{\delta}{C}) \\ \geq\ & C \cdot (P(p) + \beta + \frac{\delta}{C} - A(p^*)) - \delta \quad (28) \\ =\ & C \cdot (P(p) + \beta - A(p^*)) \quad (29) \\ =\ & W^c(A(p^*), P(p) + \beta). \quad (30) \end{aligned}$$

Combining (27) with (30), we have

$$\begin{aligned} & W_p(0, P(p) + \beta + \frac{\delta}{C}) \\ \geq\ & W_p^c(0, A(p^*)) + W^c(A(p^*), P(p) + \beta). \quad (31) \end{aligned}$$

Consider the constant rate server and a modification to the arrival sequence as follows. Those packets in $N^c(p)$ that arrive at or after $A(p) + \frac{s(p)}{C}$ in the original sequence will have their arrival times moved forward in the modified sequence such that they all arrive in the time interval $(A(p), A(p) + \frac{s(p)}{C})$ and the original order of arrivals for each flow is preserved. Note that the priority value of $p$ as well as the guaranteed deadline of $p$ are unaffected by the modification. Moreover, since the priority value of each packet within a flow is non-decreasing in packet arrival time (by definition of a priority class server), $N^c(p)$ is unaffected by the modification as well.

The deadline guarantee of $P(p) + \beta$ by the constant rate server still holds for the modified packet arrival sequence because of the firewall property. Moreover the guarantee is independent of the tie breaking method. Therefore it would hold even if $p$ were served last among all $N^c(p)$ packets. Also with the modified arrival sequence, the most amount of work that the constant rate server can do for $N^c(p)$ packets in the time interval $[0, P(p) + \beta)]$ is: $W_p^c(0, A(p^*)) + W^c(A(p^*), P(p) + \beta)$. Therefore, the following must hold

$$W_p^c(0, A(p^*)) + W^c(A(p^*), P(p) + \beta) \geq \sum_{q \in N^c(p)} s(q). \tag{32}$$

Combining (31) and (32), we have

$$W_p(0, P(p) + \beta + \frac{\delta}{C}) \geq \sum_{q \in N^c(p)} s(q). \tag{33}$$

Because of (26), $N^c(p)$ can be substituted by $N(p)$ in (33). Therefore (25) holds. □

### Proof of Corollary 1

For FIFO servers, $P(p) = A(p)$ for all $p$. Therefore a delay bound guarantee of $\beta$ is equivalent to a deadline guarantee of $P(p) + \beta$. The proof for the deadline guarantee generalization is identical to the one for Theorem 1 except for a simpler reasoning for (32): While a deadline guarantee by a FIFO server does not have the firewall property, there is no need for the condition because all packets in $N^c(p)$ arrive no later than $A(p)$; therefore we can reason for (32) with the original arrival sequence. □

### Proof of Theorem 2

Again we carry out a proof by contradiction. Specifically, we assume that for the nonpreemptive FC server, there exists a packet $p$ in the arrival sequence such that

$$L(p) > P(p) + \beta + \frac{\delta}{C}. \tag{34}$$

Then we will show

$$W_p(0, P(p) + \beta + \frac{\delta}{C}) \geq \sum_{q \in N(p)} s(q), \tag{35}$$

which contradicts (34).

In this proof, we also consider a third SIP server, which is identical to the constant rate server except that it is preemptive-resume with no overhead. We use the superscripts, $c$ and $pre$, to label terms for respectively the nonpreemptive and preemptive constant rate server systems. Note that by definition of SIP servers, $p$ has the same priority value, $P(p)$, for all three server systems, i.e.,

$$N^{pre}(p) = N^{c}(p) = N(p). \quad (36)$$

It is given that

$$L^{c}(p) \leq P(p) + \beta, \quad (37)$$

and the guarantee in (37) accounts for out-of-order service. Therefore we have

$$L^{pre}(p) \leq P(p) + \beta - \frac{s_{max}}{C}. \quad (38)$$

Note that the above guarantee also has the firewall property.

Similar to the proof for Theorem 1, we can show that there exists a packet $p^* \in N(p)$ such that

$$W_p(0, A(p^*)) \geq W_p^{pre}(0, A(p^*)), \quad (39)$$

$$W_p(A(p^*), P(p) + \beta + \frac{\delta}{C}) \geq C \cdot (P(p) + \beta - A(p^*)) - s_{max}. \quad (40)$$

The extra term $s_{max}$ in (40) is due to the fact that a part of the work done by the nonpreemptive FC server in $[A(p^*), P(p) + \beta + \frac{\delta}{C}]$ may be for out-of-order service of a packet that is not in $N(p)$.

Similar to the proof for Theorem 1, we have

$$W_p^{pre}(0, A(p^*)) + W^{pre}(A(p^*), P(p) + \beta - \frac{s_{max}}{C}) \geq \sum_{q \in N^{pre}(p)} s(q). \quad (41)$$

Moreover

$$\begin{aligned} W^{pre}(A(p^*), P(p) + \beta - \frac{s_{max}}{C}) &= C \cdot (P(p) + \beta - \frac{s_{max}}{C} - A(p^*)) \quad (42) \\ &= C \cdot (P(p) + \beta - A(p^*)) - s_{max}. \quad (43) \end{aligned}$$

Combining (41) and (43), we have

$$W_p^{pre}(0, A(p^*)) + C \cdot (P(p) + \beta - A(p^*)) - s_{max} \geq \sum_{q \in N^{pre}(p)} s(q). \quad (44)$$

From (39), (40) and (44), we have

$$\begin{aligned} W_p(0, P(p) + \beta + \frac{\delta}{C}) &= W_p(0, A(p^*)) + W_p(A(p^*), P(p) + \beta + \frac{\delta}{C}) \quad (45) \\ &\geq W_p^{pre}(0, A(p^*)) + C \cdot (P(p) + \beta - A(p^*)) - s_{max} \quad (46) \\ &\geq \sum_{q \in N^{pre}(p)} s(q). \quad (47) \end{aligned}$$

Because of (36), $N^{pre}(p)$ can be substituted by $N(p)$ in (47). Therefore (35) holds. □

## References


[1] Jon C.R. Bennett and Hui Zhang. Hierarchical packet fair queueing algorithms. In *Proceedings of ACM SIGCOMM '96*, pages 143–156, Stanford University, CA, August 1996.

[2] Alan Demers, Srinivasan Keshav, and Scott Shenker. Analysis and simulation of a fair queuing algorithm. In *Proceedings of ACM SIGCOMM '89*, pages 3–12, August 1989.

[3] D. Ferrari and D. Verma. A scheme for real-time channel establishment in wide-area networks. *IEEE JSAC*, pages 368–379, April 1990.

[4] Sally Floyd and Van Jacobson. Link-sharing and resource management models for packet networks. *IEEE/ACM Transactions on Networking*, 3(4):365–386, August 1995.

[5] The ATM Forum. *ATM Traffic Management Specification.* 1995. Version 4.0.

[6] P. Goyal, H. M. Vin, and H. Cheng. Start-time fair queueing: A scheduling algorithm for integrated services packet switching networks. In *Proceedings of ACM SIGCOMM '96*, pages 157–168, Stanford University, CA, August 1996.

[7] ITU-T Rec. I.371. *Traffic Control and Congestion Control in B-ISDN.* Perth, U.K., Nov. 6-14, 1995.

[8] Simon S. Lam and Geoffrey G. Xie. Burst Scheduling networks. Technical Report TR-94-20, University of Texas at Austin, Austin, Texas, July 1994. Revised, August 1996. An abbreviated version in *Proceedings of IEEE INFOCOM '95*, April 1995.

[9] Simon S. Lam and Geoffrey G. Xie. Group priority scheduling. Technical Report TR-95-28, University of Texas at Austin, Austin, Texas, July 1995. Revised, September 1996. An abbreviated version in *Proceedings of IEEE INFOCOM '96*, March 1995.

[10] Kam Lee. Performance bounds in communication networks with variable-rate links. In *Proceedings of ACM SIGCOMM '95*, pages 126–137, August 1995.

[11] Michel Loève. *Probability Theory I.* New York, 1977. 4th ed.

[12] Abhay K. Parekh and Robert G. Gallager. A generialized processor sharing approach to flow control in integrated services networks: The single node case. *IEEE/ACM Trans. on Networking*, 1(3):344–357, June 1993.

[13] A. Romanow and S. Floyd. The dynamics of TCP traffic over ATM networks. In *Proceedings of ACM SIGCOMM '94*, London, England, August 1994.

[14] Geoffrey G. Xie and Simon S. Lam. Delay guarantee of Virtual Clock server. *IEEE/ACM Trans. on Networking*, 3(6):683–689, December 1995.

[15] Lixia Zhang. VirtualClock: A new traffic control algorithm for packet switching networks. In *Proceedings of ACM SIGCOMM '90*, pages 19–29, August 1990.

# Constant-Time Dynamic ATM Bandwidth Scheduling for Guaranteed and Best Effort Services with Overbooking

Dong Lin
Harvard University
29 Oxford ST #110, Cambridge, MA 02138

## Abstract

*In this paper, we present an analysis of an existing rate-based ABR scheduling algorithm described in [1], and propose an enhanced rate-based round robin (RBR) scheduling algorithm for ATM switches and end systems. One of the novel aspects of RBR is that the scheduler supports available bit rate (ABR) traffic as well as guaranteed bandwidth reservations. In addition, bandwidth overbooking is allowed by the scheduler for ABR services to improve link efficiency as recommended by most flow control schemes. Under competition, the scheduler distributes the bandwidth in a max-min fair way. Any unused reservations for guaranteed services are reallocated to ABR services. Finally, the operations performed during each scheduling cycle are constant, independent of the number of connections. Simulation results are also presented and analyzed.*

## 1. Introduction

Many rate scheduling schemes have been proposed and investigated in the past, among which Fluid Fair Queueing (FFQ) [2], Virtual Clock [3], Generalized Processor Sharing (GPS) [5] and Self-Clocked Fair Queueing (SCFQ)[4] have received the most attention.

Three major problems are yet to be solved. First, a *practical* scheme is needed to do traffic shaping. Although VirtualClock, GPS and SCFQ provide guaranteed services, real time sorted insertions of large lists required in these schemes are expensive to implement. Second, a scheduler needs to handle overbooking. This can not be easily avoided in a flow controlled environment without losing efficiency. In addition to the requirement of statistical multiplexing, overbooking can still exist even if the downstream nodes do not overbook. Figure 1 shows this scenario. VC1 and VC2 are flow controlled by different downstream entities which grant 100% downstream output bandwidth to these two VCs. VC3 has 10% of its downstream bandwidth. The upstream scheduler is inevitably faced with the problem of making a distribution arbitration. It would be inappropriate to fairly and statically preassign the rates by (45%, 45%, 10%), because bandwidth will be wasted if any of the VCs' offered load is less than the preassigned rate. On the other hand, there will be no "firewall"[3] protection for VC 3 if VCs 1 and 2 are allowed to send at 100% of the link speed using Virtual Clock or GPS. Therefore, an alternative is needed to manipulate overbooking without losing firewall protections. Such firewall should be conditional in that, although each VC is entitled to reserve a fair share of the link bandwidth, no reservations should be kept exclusive unless they can be utilized, and any unused reservations should be reallocated to other VCs. Therefore, dynamic overbooking should be handled by the scheduler to work with the flow control mechanisms and to improve resource efficiency. Third, a

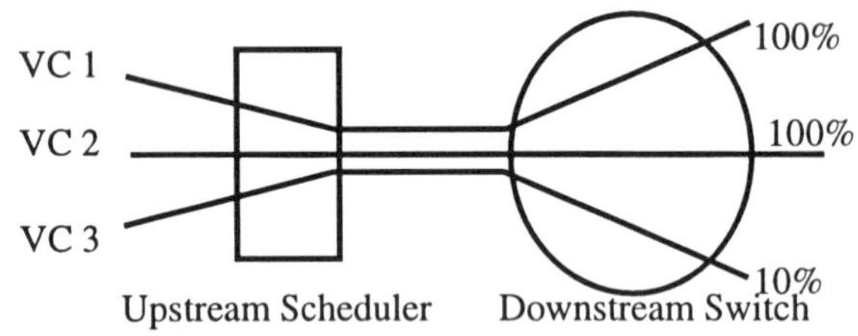


**Figure 1. Overbooking**

**The downstreams of VC1 and VC2 allow the upstreams to send at 100% link rate, whereas VC3's downstream constrains the transmission rate to be 10%. It is not efficient to map (100%, 100%, 10%) to (45%, 45%, 10%) if some of the VCs do not have enough offered load.**

scheduler should provide both guaranteed and best effort services in an efficient and unified way. For example, a video service may require 1.5 mbps minimum bandwidth to keep a movie running, but needs up to 6 mbps to deliver quality pictures. The scheduler should provide 1.5 mbps at any time and allocate more whenever possible to this video connection.

In this paper, we analyze an existing linear algorithm designed for scheduling ABR traffic for EPRCA[12] end systems. We show that this scheme enforces rate regulations and provides max-min fair allocation for competing VCs. Then we extend this baseline algorithm to provide both guaranteed and best-effort services in a unified way. In addition, the scheme supports bandwidth overbooking to improve output link utilization. The scheme also preserves the max-min fair allocation and linear operation time. In particular, we will prove that the algorithm achieves the following goals:

- No VCs can transmit faster than the assigned rates, and a VC can reach the assigned rate if there is no competition.
- The RBR scheduler guarantees each VC at least a fair share under overbooking while still maintaining high link efficiency. For example, for a 3-VC bandwidth request of (20%, 30%, 90%), the scheduler enforces a distribution of (20%, 30%, 50%) if all VCs have cells to send; or (10%, 10%, 80%) if the two low bandwidth VCs only have 10% offered load. Thus firewall protection and maximum utilization are both preserved. We will provide an extension to this property so that a VC can reserve an arbitrary fraction of the bandwidth, possibly more than the fair share 1/K where K is the total number of VCs sharing the link.
- The number of operations for each scheduling cycle is a constant and can be implemented by software and hardware at real time.

The rest of this paper is organized as follows: Section 2 defines the service models RBR supports and gives a definition of max-min fairness which determines the arbitration of



0-8186-7780-5/97 $10.00 © 1997 IEEE

bandwidth allocation for ABR traffic; Section 3 and Section 4 describe and analyze operations of the existing scheme described in [1] for the best effort traffic; Section 5 proposes an extension to the baseline scheduler for supporting both best effort and guaranteed services; Simulation results in Section 6 verify that our design goals are matched on various configurations; Section 7 outlines the differences between our scheduler and others; Section 8 concludes with a summary of our approach.

## 2. Services and Assumptions

### 2.1 Terminology and Environment

For simplicity, we choose the unit of rate to be the fraction of the link capacity. So the link rate is always 1, and all other rates are positive real numbers between 0 and 1. The time unit is cell cycles of the link rate. Under the flow controlled environment, a $VC_i$ has an allowed cell rate $acr_i$ assigned by the flow control mechanism. The RBR scheduler serves the VC with an allocated rate $a_i$ which satisfies the following constraints

$$a_i \le acr_i \quad (1)$$

$$\sum_{i=1}^{K} a_i \le 1 \quad (2)$$

where $K$ is the number of VCs served by the scheduler.

### 2.2 Service Models

In this section we define services the RBR scheduler provides. The goal is to provide guaranteed services to some VCs and at the same time use the leftover bandwidth for best effort traffic. In this paper, a guaranteed service for a VC is a portion of the link capacity allocated to the VC. A VC can request a guaranteed service and a best effort service at the same time. The scheduler would at least allocate the guaranteed bandwidth for the VC and let it share the leftover with other best effort VCs. In summary, we define the following two services:

**ABR**: a best effort service with no commitment from the scheduler. The VC is served with the available bandwidth. When serving more than one ABR VC, the scheduler allocates each VC a max-min fair share defined below.

**MCR+**: a guaranteed service with a minimum cell rate of $mcr$; the VC competes with ABR VCs for the available bandwidth if its allowed cell rate $acr$ is greater than its $mcr$.

Notice that an ABR service is just a special case of MCR+ with $mcr$ equal to 0. Assuming the scheduler provides the above two services to $K$ VCs in total, the following constraints must hold:

$$\sum_{i=1}^{K} mcr_i \le 1 \quad (3)$$

$$mcr_i \le acr_i, \text{ for all } i \quad (4)$$

Condition (3) requires no overbooking for guaranteed MCR+ service. Note that the aggregate allowed cell rate ($acr$) could be well over 1 which means overbooking is allowed for ABR service. Condition (4) requires that the flow control mechanism must allow a VC to send at least its minimum cell rate at any time.

We now define fairness for the ABR service. The concept of max-min fair share is not new [5,8,11].

**ABR max-min fair allocation**: given a vector of allocated cell rates $a = (a_1, a_2, \ldots, a_K)$ satisfies Condition (1) and Condition (2), let $\hat{a} = (\hat{a}_1, \hat{a}_2, \ldots, \hat{a}_K)$ be a permutation of $a$ such that $\hat{a}_i \le \hat{a}_j$ if $i < j$. then $a$ is max-min fair if $a$ is lexicographically greater than any other allocation $b$, i.e. either $\hat{a}_1 < \hat{b}_1$ or there exists an $1 < i \le K$ such that $\hat{a}_j = \hat{b}_j$ for $1 \le j < i$ and $\hat{a}_i < \hat{b}_i$.

### 2.3 Assumptions

We make the following minimum assumptions:

- At the scheduling node (switch or end system), per-VC queueing is used for buffering.
- Although potential extensions are possible, we assume that all rates are above a predefined minimum cell rate (call it $MCR$). See Section 3.3 for details on the value of $MCR$.

## 3. ABR Scheduling

We present the algorithm in two steps. This section describes scheduling for the ABR service as this is the fundamental baseline of the algorithm. In Section 5, we present extensions to the baseline for the guaranteed MCR+ service which allow VCs to have non-zero minimum cell rates.

We present the baseline algorithm described in [1] in a different but equivalent way so that extensions presented in Section 5 are straightforward.

### 3.1 VC Table

We begin with defining the VC table. Each table entry records the current state of a VC. Table 1 lists the contents of each VC table entry.

| Name | Unit | Description |
|---|---|---|
| vcid | none | VC identifier |
| rate | fraction of link | allowed cell rate. assigned by the flow control mechanism. |
| next cell time | cell cycles | departure time of the latest scheduled cell |
| queue length | cells | cells queued |

**Table 1. Contents of the VC table entry**

### 3.2 Operation Overview

The RBR scheduler performs four functions during each scheduling cycle. VCs with cell arrivals in the current cell cycle need to be activated if they have no cells queued previously. During each cycle, some VCs may be allowed to send cells after waiting long enough due to rate enforcement. The scheduler then picks a VC among those who are allowed to send cells. The choice must be max-min fair to all VCs. After a VC sends a cell, it needs to be rescheduled according to its assigned rate if more cells are queued. The following pseudo code describes the behavior of the top level scheduler.

```
VC_ID SCHED_CYCLE()
```

```
{ VC * vcp;
  for each arrived cell
    CellArrive(vc_tab[cell->vcid]);
  CycleUpdate();
  vcp = SchedOne();
  if( vcp ) {
    if( vcp->qlen )  // re-activate this vc
      ReschedVC(vcp)
    return vcp->id;
  }
  return NULL_VCID;
}
```

Notice that if each of the individual operations takes constant time, then the time complexity of the above procedure is proportional to the number of cell arrivals during each cell cycle.

### 3.3 Scheduler Operation Details

Similar to other rate schedulers[13,14], the RBR scheduler maintains a cycle slot table. Each slot has a list of events that need to happen at a particular cell cycle. The scheduler advances exactly one slot for each cell cycle. The number of slots is $1/MCR$, where $MCR$ is the predefined minimum cell rate mentioned in Section 2. This makes sure that the next cell departure time for a VC is within $1/MCR$ slots away from the current time.

Each VC with cells queued has a scheduled departure time for the next cell, represented by putting this VC in a particular slot. Because of overbooking or accidental overlapping, a slot could contain multiple VCs. The scheduler has a slot pointer which records the current cycle.

The scheduler also maintains a list of VCs which should have been scheduled in the past but have not been processed yet due to competition. We call it the backlog list. This term is used by [6] in a similar situation. Figure 2 depicts the data structure of the scheduler. During each cycle, the scheduler moves the list of VCs in the current slot to the end of the backlog list and advances the current slot pointer by one. We call this process cycle update. Figure 3 depicts the state after a cycle update from Figure 2. The following pseudo code describes the cycle update process:

```
CycleUpdate()
{
  VCS * vcsp = slots[cur_slot];
  slots[cur_slot++] = NULL;
  if( vcsp )
    bklog->AddVCS(vcsp);
}
```

After each cycle update, the scheduler removes and schedules a cell for the first VC in the backlog list if non-empty. Notice that all VCs in the list must have cells queued since idle VCs are never scheduled. If the backlog list is empty, the current cycle is wasted. Figure 4 depicts the state after scheduling a VC from Figure 3. The following code describes the action.

```
VC * SchedOne()
  { VC * vcp;
    if( bklog->Len() ) {
      vcp = bklog->DelVC();
      vcp->qlen--;
      return vcp;
    }
    return NULL;
}
```

After a VC is scheduled, its *next cell time* variable is incremented by $1/rate$. Because the increment is no greater than the size of the slots, this updated schedule time is either located at a different slot representing some future time or is still in the past meaning this VC is far behind schedule. In either case, the scheduler puts the VC in the slot representing the new *next cell time*, or at the end of the backlog list. This process is called re-scheduling and is presented below and in Figure 5.

```
ReschedVC(VC * vcp)
{
    vcp->next_celltime += 1/vcp->rate;
    slot_num=NextSlot(vcp);
    if( slot_num >= 0 )
      slots[slot_num]->AddVC(vcp);
    else
      bklog->AddVC(vcp);
}
```

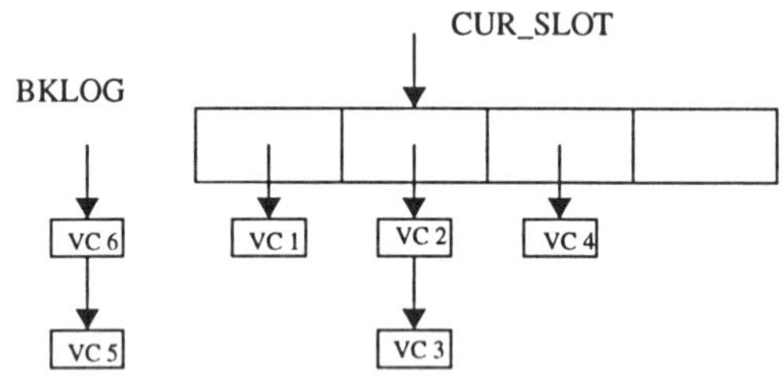


**Figure 2. Scheduler data structure**

**The scheduler has cell cycle slots and a backlog list. Each VC has a scheduled departure time for the next cell represented by putting this VC in a particular slot. The scheduler has a slot pointer which records the current cycle slot. The backlog list maintains a list of VCs which should have been scheduled in the past but have not been processed yet.**

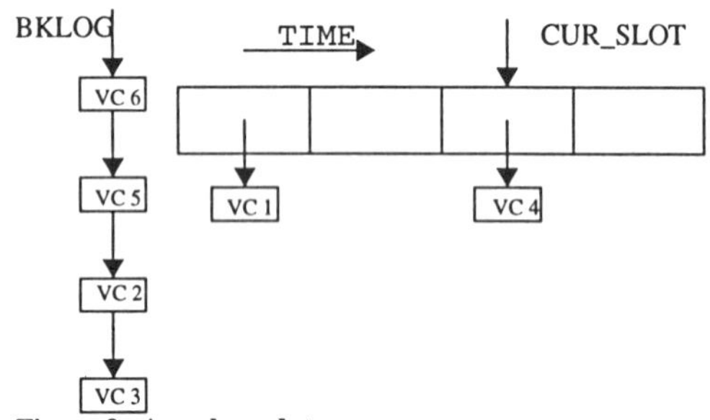


**Figure 3. A cycle update**

**During each cell cycle, the scheduler moves the list of VCs in the current slot to the end of the backlog list and advances the slot pointer by one.**

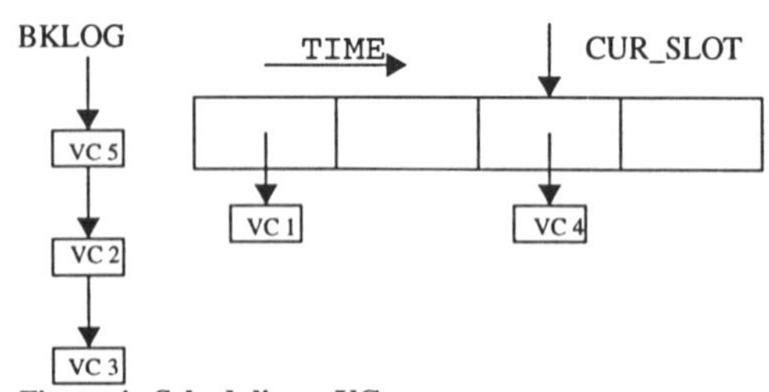


**Figure 4. Scheduling a VC**

**After a cycle update, the scheduler removes and returns the first VC in the backlog list to send a cell for this VC.**

Initially, a VC does not have any cells queued. Each cell arrival upon an empty queue triggers an activation procedure in which the VC gets rescheduled as if it had just sent a cell.

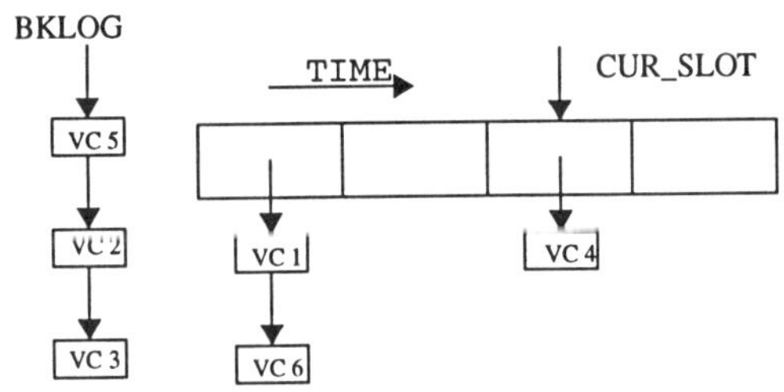


**Figure 5. VC re-scheduling**

**A VC is rescheduled by putting the VC in a new slot 1/rate slots away from its previous next_celltime.**

```
CellArrival(VC * vcp)
{ double t = vcp->next_celltime;
  double rate = vcp->rate;
  vcp->qlen++;
  if( vcp->qlen == 1) {
    if( t < now() - 1/rate )
      vcp->next_celltime = now()-1/rate;
    ReschedVC(vcp);
  }
}
```

Notice from the above pseudo code that when a VC is idle for too long, its next_celltime counter is reset to the current time when the next cell arrives. This is to prevent a VC from bursting back to back cells by being silent long enough. Without resetting the counter, the scheme will degrade to an "unrated" round robin scheduler when all VCs are infinitely behind schedule.

The following is a list of operations involved to perform the above procedures. Notice that all operations take constant time.

- Append an item or a list to a list (cycle update and rescheduling)
- Remove the first item from a list (VC scheduling)

## 4. Analysis

In this section, we provide some analysis and show that the baseline RBR scheme satisfies the goals presented in Section 1.

### 4.1 Rate Enforcement

If the output link is not overbooked, the backlog list is empty (except for some accidental overlapping). It is easy to see that the inter departure time is no less than $1/rate$ for all VCs.

Under overbooking, it is possible that a VC is delayed (inter-departure time is greater than $1/rate$), or made bursty (inter-departure time is less than $1/rate$). The overall average rate, however, is no greater than its assigned rate. More specifically, assume that the VC is not behind schedule at time $T_0$. We can show that during any period starting from $T_0$, the average rate is less than $rate$. To see this, notice that a cell can be scheduled only if its scheduled departure time is less than the current time, and that the next scheduled departure time is spaced by at least $1/rate$. That is, for any $T > T_0$,

$$CellsScheduled \le \frac{T - T_0}{1/rate} = (T - T_0)rate$$

Furthermore, we show that a VC is serviced at its assigned rate if its offered load can saturate the service and there is either no congestion at the server or the assigned rate is below the fair share. The first condition implies that the VC always has cells to send. The second condition has two possibilities:

- Each scheduled departure time is delayed by no more than a constant D or
- There is congestion, but the VC's assigned rate is less than its max-min fare share.

We defer the second bullet until Section 4.2. When the VC always has cells to send, the scheduled departure times are spaced by exactly $1/rate$. Therefore the Nth cell is served within the period $\left[\frac{N}{rate}, \frac{N}{rate} + D\right]$. This is equivalent to saying that the number of cells served for any period of $T$, denoted by C, satisfies the following condition

$$rate \cdot T - D \le C \le rate \cdot T \qquad (5)$$

Note the average rate, derivative of C, is exactly the assigned $rate$.

### 4.2 Fair Sharing

In this section, we show that fairness is guaranteed among competing VCs. Our goal is *no VC should get more than its fair share at the expense of others*. We first give a mathematical definition of a max-min fair share in our context. Let $a = (rate_1, rate_2, \ldots, rate_K)$ be the vector of the non-zero assigned cell rates. Without losing generality, assume it is in non-decreasing order. In other words, $rate_i \le rate_j$ if $i < j$. A $VC_n$'s assigned cell rate is below max-min fair share if the following condition holds:

$$rate_n \le \frac{1 - \sum_{i=1}^{n-1} rate_i}{K - (n-1)}, \; n \le K \qquad (6)$$

Notice that the above is an equivalent definition of max-min fairness from Section 2.2 [9]. We omit the simple proofs for the following two lemmas.

**Lemma 1** If $rate_n$ is a max-min fair share, $rate_i$ is also if $i < n$.

**Lemma 2** If $rate_n$ is a max-min fair share, then

$$\sum_{i=1}^{n} rate_i \le 1 \text{ and thus } \sum_{i=1}^{n-1} rate_i < 1$$

We now define an iterative algorithm to find the max-min fair allocation based on the above results,

- Among $K$ active VCs, any VC with $rate$ less than $1/K$ is 100% satisfied. If no such VC exists, give each VC a share of $1/K$ and stop.
- The remaining $K'$ VCs compete for the leftover bandwidth using these two steps recursively.

To see that the scheduler delivers max-min fair allocation, we first show, in the following statement, that a VC is guaranteed a service rate of $1/K$.

**Theorem 1** If a VC's allowed cell rate is $rate \le 1/K$, and its offered load can saturate $rate$, then the total number of cells C transmitted for this VC by the scheduler satisfies the following inequality for any period of length T

$$rate \cdot T - K \le C \le rate \cdot T \quad (7)$$

**Proof**: We claim that a VC can only appear in the slots or the backlog list exactly once. To see that, notice that CycleUpdate moves the VC from a slot to the backlog list and that a ReschedVC moves the VC from the backlog list to one slot or back to the backlog list. This implies the length of the backlog list is no more than K, the total number of VCs. So the worst case waiting time for a VC to transmit a cell after being removed from its slot is K. Since $1/rate \ge K$, this VC's next scheduled departure time is not overdue by the time this cell is actually transmitted. In other words, this VC will be moved from the backlog list to one slot representing a future cell cycle. From this we conclude that no departure time is delayed by more than K cell cycles.

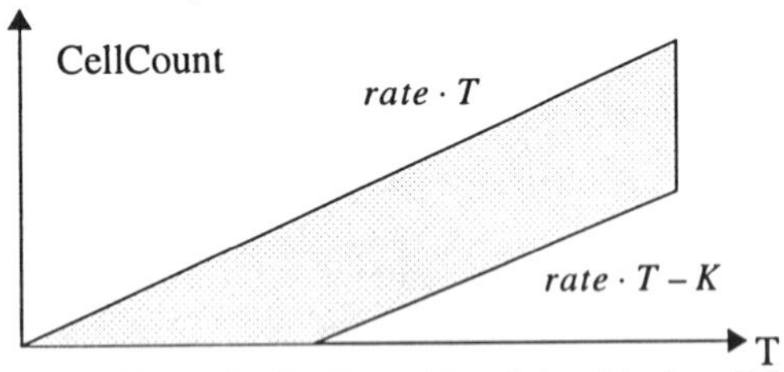


**Figure 6. Transmitted cell count for a below fair share VC**

**The output cell count curve for a below fair share VC must fall inside the shaded region. No departure time is delayed by more than K cell cycles.**

Figure 6 graphically shows that the transmitted cell count curve for a below fair share VC must fall inside the shaded area according to Theorem 1. The next theorem summarizes the general max-min case.

**Theorem 2** If a VC's allowed cell rate $rate_n$ is a max-min fair share defined by Equation (6), and its offered load can saturate $rate_n$, then the scheduler's average service rate for this VC is $rate_n$.

**Proof**: If $n = 1$, we know the theorem is true according to Theorem 1. Assume $n > 1$, let $S = \sum_{i=1}^{n-1} rate_i$, then Equation (6) becomes

$$rate_n \le \frac{1-S}{K-(n-1)} \quad (8)$$

therefore, $\frac{1}{rate_n} \ge \frac{K-n+1}{1-S}$. This implies the scheduled inter-departure time for each cell is at least $\frac{K-n+1}{1-S}$. We now estimate the average delay for each scheduled departure time. The delay is caused by the non-empty backlog list. The average length of the list is

$$L = \sum_{i=1}^{K} P_i \cdot 1 \quad (9)$$

where $P_i$ is the probability that $VC_i$ is on the list. By induction, VCs 1 through (n-1) are served at rates $rate_1, rate_2, \ldots, rate_{n-1}$ and thus they are not behind schedule. This implies $VC_i$ spends L cycles waiting in the list over the period of $1/rate_i$ and thus $P_i = \frac{L}{1/rate_i} = rate_i \cdot L$. Therefore the average length of the backlog list is $L = \sum_{i=1}^{n-1} rate_i \cdot L + \sum_{i=n}^{K} P_i \cdot 1 \le S \cdot L + (K-n+1)$ therefore $L \cdot (1-S) \le K-n+1$.

From Lemma 2, $S = \sum_{i=1}^{n-1} rate_i < 1$, therefore, $L \le \frac{K-n+1}{1-S} \le \frac{1}{rate_n}$.

The above result implies that the scheduled inter departure time is at least as long as the average delay. Therefore the scheduler is able to serve the VC at rate $rate_n$.

The crucial and unique feature of this scheme is that any VC can not introduce a delay of more than *1/K* cycles per cell cycle to other VCs because it can not appear in the backlog list more than once. In GPS and VirtualClock, a VC introduces a delay for each queued cell.

## 5. MCR+ Scheduling

This section describes extensions to provide bandwidth reservations as well as fair sharing. The goal is to let VCs run at specified minimum cell rate regardless of fairness concerns while using the leftover bandwidth to serve ABR VCs. An MCR+ VC can reserve a portion of the link bandwidth and share the unreserved portion with other VCs. However, no rates are reserved exclusively. Any unused reservations are allocated to other VCs. This feature is extremely desirable to most flow control schemes which use overbooking to statistically improve link efficiency

### 5.1 MCR+ Operation Details

The extended RBR scheduler consists of an MCR scheduler and an ABR scheduler. Each subscheduler is an instance of the baseline scheduler described in Section 3. For a VC of service $(acr, mcr)$, the MCR scheduler serves the VC at rate $mcr$ and the ABR scheduler serves the VC at rate $acr - mcr$. During each scheduling cycle, the MCR scheduler has higher priority for scheduling a cell. More specifically, the following rules define the exact scheduling behavior during each cell cycle:

- Each subscheduler does a cycle update.
- If the MCR scheduler's backlog list is not empty, send a cell for the first VC in the list.
- If the MCR scheduler's backlog list is empty, send a cell from the ABR scheduler, if possible.

When a cell arrives, each subscheduler executes the cell arrival procedure which makes the VC active in each scheduler even if there may only be one cell queued. To prevent either scheduler from scheduling a VC with no cells queued, the following modifications are needed after a cell is scheduled for a VC by either of the subschedulers:

- The subscheduler executes the reschedule procedure on a non-empty queue.
- If the VC has no more cells queued, the subscheduler triggers the other subscheduler to deactivate the VC.

During this deactivation, the scheduler removes the VC from its slot or the backlog list. The modified cell arrival and deactivation procedures preserve the fact that no empty queue VCs are dequeued from the backlog list. Therefore, no cell cycle is wasted as long as either backlog list is non-empty.

Notice that the above added operations require removing an item from the middle of a list which can be done in constant time with double-linked lists.[1]

## 5.2 Analysis

In this section we show that all reserved minimum cells rates are preserved while the leftover bandwidth are still fairly distributed in the max-min way. The following lemma provides the foundations of the extended scheduler.

**Lemma 3** If $a = (mcr_1, mcr_2, \ldots, mcr_K)$ is the vector of the assigned cell rates for the baseline scheduler and the minimum cell rates satisfy Condition (3), then $a$ is a max-min fair share.

**Proof**: Condition (3) implies that $mcr_K$ is a fair share for $VC_k$. This lemma becomes true by Lemma 1.

Based on this lemma and Theorem 2, we have proved the following.

**Theorem 3** The MCR subscheduler serves each VC at its minimum cell rate.

In order to show the ABR subscheduler delivers max-min fair service, we need to redefine max-min fair share to take the MCR+ service into account. Let $a = (rate_1, rate_2, \ldots, rate_K)$ be the vector of the assigned cell rates. Without losing generality, assume it is in non-decreasing order, in other words, $rate_i \le rate_j$ if $i < j$. A $VC_n$'s assigned cell rate is below max-min fair share if the following condition holds

$$rate_n \le \frac{1 - \sum_{i=1}^{n-1} rate_i - \sum_{i=1}^{K} mcr_i}{K - (n-1)}, n \le K \tag{10}$$

With the above redefinition of Equation (6), we now prove the following theorem

**Theorem 4** If a VC's allowed cell rate $rate_n$ is a max-min fair share defined by Equation (10), then the ABR subscheduler's average service rate for this VC is $rate_n$.

**Proof**: If $\sum_{i=1}^{K} mcr_i = 1$, then according to Equation (10), no none-zero assigned rate is a fair share. Therefore, assume $\sum_{i=1}^{K} mcr_i < 1$.

Let $S = \sum_{i=1}^{n-1} rate_i + \sum_{i=1}^{K} mcr_i$, then Equation (10) becomes

$$rate_n \le \frac{1 - S}{K - (n-1)} \tag{11}$$

therefore, $\frac{1}{rate_n} \ge \frac{K - n + 1}{1 - S}$. This implies the scheduled inter departure time for each cell is at least $\frac{K - n + 1}{1 - S}$.

We now estimate the average delay for each scheduled ABR departure time. Because the MCR subscheduler has higher priority over the ABR subscheduler, the delay for a scheduled ABR departure time is caused by both backlog lists in the two subschedulers. Using the method in the proof of Theorem 2, the average length of the MCR backlog list is $L_1 = 0$. Therefore, the average delay $W$ for a scheduled ABR departure time is the average number of cells scheduled from the MCR subscheduler during a period of $W$ plus the average length of the ABR backlog list, that is

$$W = \sum_{i=1}^{K} mcr_i \cdot W + \sum_{i=1}^{K} P_i \cdot 1 \tag{12}$$

where the first term represents the average number of scheduled MCR cells, and $P_i$ is the average probability that $VC_i$ is on the ABR backlog list.

If $n = 1$, by similar argument in the proof of Theorem 2, the average waiting time for $VC_1$ is $W = \sum_{i=1}^{K} mcr_i \cdot W + \sum_{i=1}^{K} P_i \le S \cdot W + K$, therefore, $W \le \frac{K}{1 - S} \le \frac{1}{rate_1}$. Thus the theorem is true for $VC_1$.

By induction, VCs 1 through (n-1) are served at rates $rate_1, rate_2, \ldots, rate_{n-1}$ and thus they appear in the ABR backlog list with probabilities $rate_1 \cdot W, rate_s \cdot W, \ldots, rate_{n-1} \cdot W$. Therefore the average waiting time for $VC_n$ is

$$W = \sum_{i=1}^{K} mcr_i \cdot W + \sum_{i=1}^{n-1} rate_i \cdot W + \sum_{i=n}^{K} P_i$$
$$\le S \cdot W + K - n + 1$$

therefore, $W \le \frac{K - n + 1}{1 - S} \le \frac{1}{rate_n}$. This implies that the scheduled inter-departure time is longer than the average delay. Therefore the ABR scheduler is able to serve the VC at rate $rate_n$.

## 6. Simulation Results

In this section we present simulation results of the RBR scheme. For each VC, we specify the minimum cell rate, the allowed cell rate, and the offered load. The scheduler steps through each cell cycle while cell arrivals are generated randomly with the specified offered load. The results are obtained by recording outgoing cells. We count the total number of outgoing cells for a fixed interval to measure bandwidth allocation. Throughout the simulations, most VCs' offered loads are far more than the assigned cell rates ($acr$). The results demonstrate that the scheduler output is independent of the aggressive offered load and therefore RBR is

1. We omitted the detail that the backlog list should now be a list of VC lists in order to remove an item from the middle of a list with constant time. We omitted this complication for simplicity.

perfect for input traffic shaping as well as providing quality of services.

### 6.1 Rate Scheduling

Table 2 shows the bandwidth distribution of 3 VCs with no overbooking. Three ABR VCs are assigned rates of 20%, 30% and 40% of the output link rate. When the offered load can saturate the output rate, the VCs are all running at the targeted rates. Figure 7 shows the measured cell counts for the three VCs at the scheduler output. Notice that the slopes representing the instant cell rate match the targeted rates for all VCs.

| | VC 1 | VC 2 | VC 3 |
|---|---|---|---|
| Service (mcr) | ABR | ABR | ABR |
| Rate(acr) | 20% | 30% | 40% |
| Offered Load | 100% | 100% | 100% |
| Allocated Bandwidth | 20% | 30% | 40% |

**Table 2. Bandwidth allocation without overbooking**

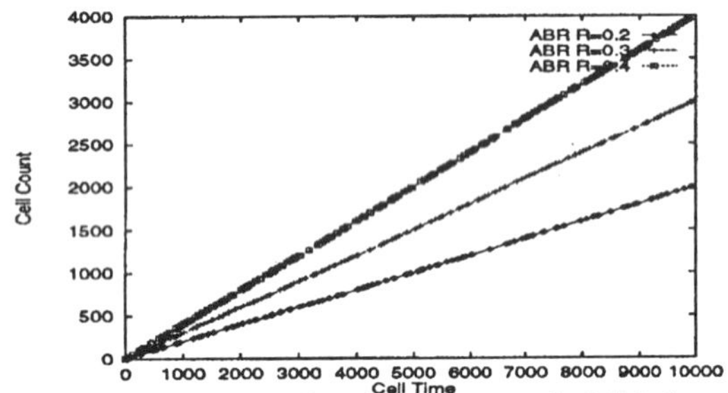


**Figure 7. Cell counts at the scheduler output for Table 2.**

**Three VCs, with assigned rates 20%, 30% and 40% of the link rate, are scheduled as targeted when the offered load can saturate the output rates.**

### 6.2 Fair Scheduling With Overbooking

Table 3 shows a greedy VC3 can only take leftover bandwidth under overbooking. Notice that VC1 is a 1st-level below fair share and VC2 is a 2nd-level below fair share. Figure 8 shows the slopes of the measured cell counts at the scheduler output.

| | VC 1 | VC 2 | VC3 |
|---|---|---|---|
| Service (mcr) | ABR | ABR | ABR |
| Rate(acr) | 10% | 40% | 90% |
| Offered Load | 100% | 100% | 100% |
| Allocated Bandwidth | 10% | 40% | 50% |

**Table 3. Bandwidth allocation with overbooking**

### 6.3 Guaranteed Service

In this simulation, we tested the scheduler on two ABR VCs competing with a guaranteed service VC3 which reserves 50% of the link bandwidth. Table 4 shows the bandwidth distribution when VC3 has enough offered load. Notice VC3 gets 50% of the link bandwidth for its reservation, plus 10% extra because 10% ( < 50%/3 ) is a fair share of the leftover 50% among the 3 VCs. Table 5 shows the distribution when VC3 has only 40% offered load. In this case, the unused

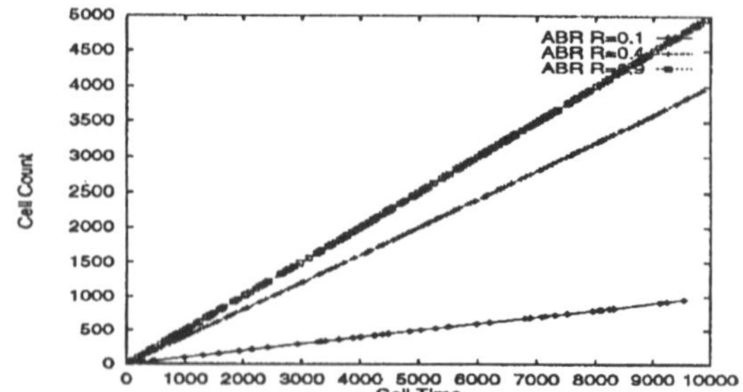


**Figure 8. Cell counts at the scheduler output for Table 3.**

**Three VCs, with assigned rates 10%, 40% and 90% of the link rate, are scheduled under max-min fair allocation when the offered load can saturate the output rates.**

bandwidth is given to VC2, even if this portion is reserved for VC3.

| | VC 1 | VC 2 | VC 3 |
|---|---|---|---|
| Service (mcr) | ABR | ABR | 50% |
| Rate(acr) | 10% | 60% | 60% |
| Offered Load | 100% | 100% | 100% |
| Allocated Bandwidth | 10% | 30% | 60% |

**Table 4. Bandwidth allocation for guaranteed services.**

| | VC 1 | VC 2 | VC 3 |
|---|---|---|---|
| Service (mcr) | ABR | ABR | 50% |
| Rate(acr) | 10% | 60% | 60% |
| Offered Load | 100% | 100% | 40% |
| Allocated Bandwidth | 10% | 50% | 40% |

**Table 5. Bandwidth allocation for unused reservations.**

## 7. Comparison with Other Approaches

There are two major categories for bandwidth scheduling [7]:

- Scheduler-based algorithms timestamp arriving packets with their departure times and make scheduling decisions based on the timestamp values. Such schemes include FFQ, VirtualClock, GPS and SCFQ. Scheduler-based schemes in general are "earliest deadline first" oriented. They seem to provide shorter delays than others, but they require intensive computation at real time.
- Frame-based algorithms poll packet queues sequentially and send a packet for each non-empty queue during each round. Round Robin, Weighted Round Robin and Deficit Round Robin belong to this type. These schemes emphasize "who gets how much" and operations take constant time.

Our RBR scheme differs from the scheduler-based schemes in many ways:

- RBR scheme enforces rate constraints for each connection. GPS and VirtualClock schemes are work-conserving. They can be fixed by holding packets until the virtual time and the real clock intersects, but that will prevent these schemes from handling greedy connections.
- RBR scheme does max-min fair allocation under contention due to overbooking. This prevents a greedy connection from taking more than its fair share at the expense of others. GPS and VirtualClock distributes the leftover bandwidth proportionally, i.e., the connection

with the largest guaranteed rate will get the most leftover bandwidth in addition to its reservation. This is illustrated by equation (2) of [9].

- RBR works perfectly for ABR traffic using overbooking. Since ABR connections do not have explicit rate requirements, there is no obvious way to augment GPS or VirtualClock to manage such uncommitted services.
- Scheduler-based schemes require at least LogN operations, where N is the number of connections. RBR operations take constant time.

RBR shares many properties with most frame-based schedulers, including max-min fairness[11] and constant operation time. However, the following properties are not shared by other round robin schedulers:

- RBR enforces explicit rates. Other round robin schedulers are work-conserving and have no knowledge of rates.
- RBR provides both guaranteed and best effort services. Although modified to provide some level of guarantees, weighted round robin schedulers cannot allow a connection to reserve an arbitrary portion of the link while fairly allocating the leftover bandwidth. The connection with the most weight not only gets its reserved bandwidth, but also most of the leftover.

## 8. Conclusions

In this paper, we have presented a constant time rate-based dynamic bandwidth allocation and scheduling algorithm. For traffic shaping, it is equivalent to a leaky bucket, but only requires constant number operations for each scheduling cycle. For dynamic bandwidth allocation, it applies overbooking to provide statistical multiplexing. Max-min fairness is guaranteed by preventing any greedy VC to cause a delay of more than $1/K$ to others, where $K$ is the number of competing VCs. For guaranteed services, the scheduler can serve a VC with a minimum cell rate while letting it share the leftover bandwidth with other ABR VCs. The link utilization is substantially improved by reallocating unused reserved bandwidth to ABR VCs dynamically.

## 9. References


[1] D. Kline "An event Driven EPRCA," ATM-Forum Contribution 94-0849

[2] A. Demers and S. Keshav "Analysis and Simulation of a Fair Queueing Algorithm," SIGCOMM'89

[3] L. Zhang "VirtualClock: A New Traffic Control Algorithm for Packet Switched Networks," ACM Trans. on Computer Systems Vol. 9, No 2, May 1991, pp101-124

[4] S. J. Golestani "A Self-Clocked Fair Queueing Scheme for Broadband Applications," Proc. IEEE INFOCOM'94

[5] A. K. Parekh and R. G. Gallager "A Generalized Processor Sharing Approach to Flow Control in Integrated Services Networks," Proc. IEEE INFOCOM'92

[6] M. Shreedhar and G. Varghese "Efficient Fair Queueing Using Deficit Round Robin," SIGCOMM'95

[7] D. Stiliadis, A. Varma "Latency-Rate Servers: A General Model for Analysis of Traffic Scheduling Algorithms," Proc. IEEE INFOCOM'96

[8] A. Charny "An Algorithm for Rate Allocation in Packet Switched Networks with Feedback," MIT/LCS/TR-601, April 1994

[9] D. Bertsekas and Robert Gallager, Data Networks, Prentice Hall, Englewood Cliffs, N.J.

[10] E. L. Hahne, "Round Robin Scheduling for Fair Flow Control in Data Communication Networks" Ph.D thesis, MIT, Dec 1986

[11] E. L. Hahne, "Round Robin Scheduling for Max-Min Fairness in Data Networks" IEEE Journal on Selected Areas in Communications, Vol. 9, No 7, Sept. 1991

[12] L. Roberts "Enhanced PRCA (Proportional Rate Control Algorithm." ATM Forum Contribution 94-0735R1

[13] Intel, IJET ATM PCI Host Adaptor

[14] Digital, OTTO ATM TurboChannel Host Adaptor

# Virtual Queueing Techniques for ABR Service: Improving ABR/VBR Interaction

Fabio M. Chiussi, Ye Xia, and Vijay P. Kumar
ATM Networks Research Department
Bell Laboratories, Lucent Technologies, Holmdel, NJ 07733, USA

**Abstract**

Several algorithms have been proposed for the switch behavior for congestion control of Available Bit Rate (ABR) services. Schemes such as the *Enhanced Proportional Rate Control Algorithm* (*EPRCA*) and the *Dynamic Max Rate Control Algorithm* (*DMRCA*), which use the queue length as congestion indicator to make a simple approximation of the fair share converge to the actual fair share, have become popular, because they offer good performance and are simple to implement. In particular, with no VBR traffic in the network, *DMRCA* has been shown to achieve fairness in all situations, good buffer control, and robust performance. In this paper, first we show that the performance of these schemes may degrade when ABR traffic interacts with highly-bursty VBR traffic. If VBR traffic induces congestion in the network, the length of the ABR queue cannot serve as a reliable indicator of congestion caused by ABR traffic, and the schemes perform poorly, introducing considerable unfairness. Then, we propose a simple technique to solve these problems. The switch constructs the length of a *virtual queue* which is not affected by the instantaneous behavior of VBR traffic, and does not depend on how the two types of traffic are served in order to share the common link capacity; thus, it can serve as a reliable indicator of congestion. We use this technique in *DMRCA with Virtual Queueing* (*DMRCA_VQ*), and show that the new scheme achieves fair rate allocation to the ABR connections also in presence of highly-bursty VBR traffic. *DMRCA_VQ* maintains the low hardware complexity of *DMRCA*. The virtual queueing technique is a solution for the more general problem of separating rate allocation based on the queue length from scheduling of multiple queues for sharing a common resource.

## 1. Introduction

The *Available Bit Rate* (ABR) service category has been recently introduced in Asynchronous Transfer Mode (ATM) networks to support highly-bursty data applications, where data packets are segmented into ATM cells. Most of these applications cannot predict their own traffic parameters, but have well-defined cell loss requirements, in order to avoid throughput collapse due to packet retransmission. Such applications cannot be addressed efficiently by the existing Constant Bit Rate (CBR) and Variable Bit Rate (VBR) services, where a traffic contract specifying the Quality of Service (QoS) guarantees (*e.g.*, delay, cell loss rate, bandwidth) is negotiated at the time a Virtual Connection (VC) is established, and maintained for the whole duration of the connection. In ABR, only lower and upper bounds on the bandwidth of a VC are specified at call set up, and the ABR service guarantees a cell loss rate only to those VC's whose source dynamically adapts its traffic in accordance with feedback received from the network.

The ATM Forum has adopted closed-loop *rate-based* congestion control schemes as the standard for ABR service [1]. Rate-based schemes, as the name implies, use feedback information from the network to control the rate at which each source can emit cells into the network [4,5,6,7,8,9,10]. The ATM Forum has specified source and destination behaviors, and has defined special control cells called *Resource Management* (RM) cells, which are used to convey control information to the endpoints. The ATM Forum requires each switch to control congestion by implementing at least one of three methods: i) *EFCI marking*, where the switch only marks a control bit in the data cells to indicate congestion, and relies on the destinations to convey information back to the sources by properly marking RM cells; ii) *Relative Rate (RR) marking*, where the switch uses RM cells to provide binary feedback on its state of congestion to each source; or iii) *Explicit Rate (ER) marking*, where the switch uses RM cells to explicitly provide the allowed rate to each source. The Forum has not standardized the specific algorithm implemented in the switches to perform the marking, leaving it to the switch manufacturers.

Several algorithms have been proposed for the switch behavior. In all these schemes, the central issue is the computation, at each node in the network, of the *fair share* of available bandwidth to which the rate of each connection is supposed to converge. As briefly reviewed in Section 2 below, an important class of these algorithms deliberately computes an *approximation* of the fair share, typically using a running average technique which is rather simple to implement, and uses congestion indication mechanisms to make the estimated fair share converge to the fair share [7,8,9,10]. These schemes achieve performance comparable with that of schemes based on a more accurate computation of the fair share, which have considerably higher implementation complexity. In certain circumstances, these scheme based on an approximation of the fair share may be even more resilient to errors than the schemes based on accurate computation, since they are designed to behave well even with relatively large transient discrepancies between the approximation and the actual fair share. Because of their simplicity and good performance, these schemes have become popular.

The *Enhanced Proportional Rate Control Algorithm* (*EPRCA*) [8,9] was the first example of such schemes to be proposed. This scheme uses the mean cell rate of all ABR VC's as the approximation of the fair share, and the length of the queue of cells waiting at the switch to be transmitted on the link as the congestion indicator mechanism. The scheme performs well when the mean cell rate converges to the fair share; however, as summarized in Section 2 below, it has been shown that there are situations where this does not hold, and *EPRCA* may introduce considerable unfairness [10]. Following a different approach, the *Dynamic Max Rate Control Algorithm* (*DMRCA*) [10], uses the maximum rate of all ABR VC's, filtered out

 0-8186-7780-5/97 $10.00 © 1997 IEEE

of short-term oscillations, and corrected by a function of the queue length as the approximation of the fair share. Because this approximation proves always to converge to the fair share, *DMRCA* solves the problems of *EPRCA*, and achieves fairness in all situations. *DMRCA* guarantees better control on the buffer size, and its performance is robust against imprecise tuning of the algorithm's parameters; the scheme maintains the low hardware complexity of *EPRCA*. Similarly to *EPRCA*, *DMRCA* uses the queue length as the congestion indicator mechanism to make the approximation converge to the fair share.

In this paper, we focus on the performance of these schemes which use the queue length as congestion indicator when ABR traffic interacts with VBR traffic. We first show that if VBR traffic is highly bursty, it may induce considerable congestion in the network, and negatively affect the performance of ABR traffic. The extent of the problem and the possible solutions depend on whether at the switches the two types of traffic are queued in a single queue or, as it is more common in current-generation switches, are assigned different delay priorities which are handled by separate queues. In the case where the two types of traffic share the same queue, highly-bursty VBR traffic can at times dominate the common queue and prevent ABR traffic queued behind it from being served. As a result, the queue length is not a reliable indicator of congestion caused by ABR traffic, and the ABR schemes perform poorly, causing unfairness in a network topology with multiple switches (this is true also in the case where the queue length is made equal to the number of ABR cells only, rather than to the total number of cells in the queue).

In the case where the two types of traffic are handled by separate queues and a work-conserving scheduling algorithm is used to share the link capacity between the two queues, the performance of ABR traffic depends on the rate at which VBR traffic is served when both queues are backlogged (since the scheduling algorithm is work conserving, when only a single queue is active, it is always served at full rate). If VBR traffic is only served at a rate equal to (or close to) the *average* rate of VBR traffic, and ABR traffic is given the remaining bandwidth, the two types of traffic are fully isolated, and the ABR schemes show the same good performance as in the case without VBR traffic. Obviously, with highly-bursty VBR traffic, the buffer size necessary to accommodate the VBR queue with such a scheduling policy becomes very large; other QoS parameters for VBR traffic, such as delay, are negatively affected as well. For this reason, in practice, VBR traffic is typically served at a rate higher than its average rate. A common choice is to use *strict priority* for VBR traffic, and serve ABR traffic only when there are no cells waiting in the VBR queue. In this case, the two types of traffic interact with each other, and the ABR performance degrades. The service rate of the ABR queue is modulated by the activity of the VBR queue, and the ABR queue length cannot serve anymore as a reliable indicator of congestion caused by the activity of the ABR sources. As a result, under these conditions, ABR schemes using the queue length as congestion indicator introduce considerable unfairness.

After having characterized the undesired effects of ABR/VBR interaction, we then propose a simple technique to solve these problems. The switch constructs the length of a *virtual queue*, which is the number of ABR cells that would be waiting at the switch if VBR traffic were not present, and the available bandwidth for ABR were made equal to the available bandwidth assuming VBR were allocated its *average* bandwidth. By construction, the virtual queue length is not affected by the short-term behavior of VBR traffic, and constitutes a reliable indicator of congestion induced by ABR traffic. We then modify *DMRCA* using the *virtual* queue length as congestion indicator, rather than the *real* queue length of cells waiting at the switch. The modified scheme, called *DMRCA with Virtual Queueing* (*DMRCA_VQ*) achieves fair rate allocation to the ABR connections also in presence of highly-bursty VBR traffic. The hardware complexity of *DMRCA_VQ* is only marginally higher than *DMRCA*, since the virtual queue is represented by a single counter that is easily maintained. We also present further refinements of *DMRCA_VQ* which use *both* the actual queue length and the virtual queue length as congestion indicators. These variations achieve performance similar to that of the basic *DMRCA_VQ* in terms of fairness, but substantially reduce the buffer requirements to accommodate ABR traffic. Similarly to the basic *DMRCA_VQ*, they are simple to implement.

The virtual queueing technique is a solution for the more general problem of separating rate allocation based on the queue length from scheduling of multiple queues to share a common link. Since the way the real queues are served directly impacts their length, scheduling influences rate allocation, if the latter is based on the real queue lengths. Using the virtual queue concept, this undesired interaction is eliminated, and scheduling and rate allocation can be treated separately. For this reason, the virtual queueing technique can be successfully applied also in other contexts. For example, an other application where scheduling and rate allocation potentially interact, and therefore the virtual queueing technique is useful, is ABR rate allocation when Per-VC queueing is implemented at the switches.

The rest of this paper is organized as follows. In Section 2, we briefly review the ABR standard, classify existing schemes for the switch behavior, and describe *DMRCA*. In Section 3, we describe the switch models, the traffic models, and the network configurations that we use in the paper. In Section 4, we characterize the problems of existing schemes using the queue length as congestion indicator when ABR traffic interacts with VBR traffic. In Section 5, we describe the basic version and the refinements of *DMRCA_VQ*, and show that these schemes perform very well also in presence of VBR traffic. Finally, Section 6 offers some concluding remarks.

## 2. Congestion Control for ABR

### *2.1. ABR Standard*

As mentioned in the Introduction, the ATM Forum has been defining a standard to support *EFCI* marking, *RR* marking, and *ER* marking [1]. The *EFCI* bit is provided in the header of every data cell, and can be used by the switches to indicate congestion to the destinations. The ATM Forum has defined special control cells, called *Resource Management* (RM) cells, to convey information to the sources about the state of congestion of the network. In particular, RM cells contain a bit, called *Congestion Indication (CI)* bit, which is used to have a source increase or decrease its rate by some predefined amount (a second bit, called *No Increase (NI)* bit, is also provided to have a source keep its rate unchanged), and a field, called the *ER field*, which carries a 15-bit floating point number representing the explicit rate. The RM cells also contain a field, called the *Current*

*Cell Rate (CCR)* field, which is set by the source to its current *Allowed Cell Rate (ACR)* when it generates a forward RM cell. The Forum has also defined the source and destination behavior. At connection set-up, a *Peak Cell Rate (PCR)* and a *Minimum Cell Rate (MCR)* for the ABR VC are negotiated. The source regularly sends to the destination a *forward* RM cell every *Nrm* data cells. When the destination receives a forward RM cell, it returns the RM cell to the source as a *backward* RM cell. Several mechanisms are provided to convey congestion information to the source via the RM cells: i) any intermediate switch can notify the source of congestion by marking the *CI* and *NI* bits, and/or by setting the *ER* field in the RM cells; ii) the destination can mark the *CI* bit in the RM cell if the EFCI bits in recently received data cells for that connection are marked; and iii) any intermediate switch (or the destination) can generate backward RM cells to directly communicate congestion to the sources.

When a source receives a backward RM cell with the *CI* bit set (indicating congestion), it decreases its *ACR* by a quantity *RDF*ACR*, where *RDF* is the *Rate Decrease Factor,* negotiated at call set up (however, the rate should not be reduced below *MCR*). When a source receives a backward RM cell with the *CI* bit not set, it increases its *ACR* by a quantity *RIF*PCR*, where *RIF* is the *Rate Increase Factor*, also negotiated at call set up (the rate should not be increased above *PCR*). The source sets its new *ACR* equal to the minimum of *ACR* adjusted according to the *CI* bit as described above, and *ER* (or to the minimum of the adjusted *ACR* and *MCR*, in case $ER < MCR$). The *ER* field in the forward RM cell is initially set by the source to a requested rate (such as *PCR*). Intermediate switches can only decrease the rate in the *ER* field in forward and/or backward RM cells.

### 2.2. Switch Behavior

As mentioned above, the ATM Forum has not defined the algorithm that should be used in the switches to control the rate of the connections. Several algorithms that use the RM cells and the end system behavior specified by the standard have been proposed for the switch behavior. In all these algorithms, the central issue is the computation of the *fair share* for every connection at each switching node in the network. According to the well-know *max-min fairness* criterion, the fair share for each connection competing for bandwidth at a given link is equal to:

$$Fair\_Share = (C - C_b)/(N - N_b) \qquad (1)$$

where $C$ is the total available bandwidth for ABR service on that link, $C_b$ is the total rate of *bottlenecked* connections, $N$ is the number of active connections, and $N_b$ is the number of bottlenecked connections. At a certain switch, *bottlenecked* connections are those connections which cannot achieve their fair share at that node because of constraints imposed either by their *PCR* or by limited bandwidth available at other switching nodes along their route [3]. In case of *RR* marking, the computed fair share is used as the threshold to perform *intelligent marking, i.e.,* to notify congestion only to VC's whose rate is above the fair share; in case of *ER* marking, the computed fair share is used as the explicit rate conveyed to the sources.

Existing schemes can be broadly divided in two classes.

i) Schemes based on *"exact" computation* of the fair share. These schemes use equation (1) directly to compute the fair share. In practice, due to a number of factors which introduce inaccuracies in the computation, the computed fair share may not be equal to the true fair share defined by equation (1) (hence, our use of quotes in referring to these schemes as using "exact" computation), and additional mechanisms may be provided to control congestion. Representative examples of such schemes are the MIT scheme [4], the UCSC scheme [5], and the *Fast Max-Min Rate Allocation* scheme [6].

ii) Schemes based on *approximation* of the fair share. These schemes do not use equation (1), and instead deliberately compute an approximation of the fair share, typically using a weighted averaging technique, and use congestion detection mechanisms to make the estimated fair share converge to the fair share. Representative schemes in this class are the *Explicit Rate Indication for Congestion Avoidance* (*ERICA*) scheme [7], *EPRCA* [8,9], and *DMRCA* [10]. These schemes can be further differentiated based on the congestion indicator mechanism used: *ERICA* uses the traffic load destined to the link; *EPRCA* and *DMRCA* use the queue length in the cell buffer. The focus of this paper is on algorithms which use the queue length as congestion indicator.

Schemes based on "exact" computation of the fair share, since they use equation (1) directly, need to perform floating-point division at each switch, and maintain state information for each connection, two operations that require considerable hardware complexity. Historically, schemes based on approximation of the fair share have been motivated by the desire of avoiding such complexity. As the field has evolved and more schemes have been proposed, the distinction between the two classes of schemes has become more philosophical, and translates more directly on the performance of these algorithms under different traffic scenarios. Schemes in the former class expect that the computed fair share be a relatively close estimation of the true fair share, and may use congestion detection mechanisms to achieve a desired incremental accuracy; such schemes may encounter difficulties in achieving good performance when, due to certain traffic conditions, the computed fair share deviates considerably from the true fair share. Schemes in the latter class are based on an estimation of the fair share that is by design not particularly accurate, and use additional mechanisms to correct for errors that are expected to be relatively large; such schemes may be better equipped to achieve robust performance under traffic scenarios that introduce significant inaccuracies in the fair share that can be computed at the switches. Because of their good performance and simple implementation, these schemes have gained considerable popularity.

*EPRCA* [8,9] was the first scheme to be proposed which avoided the floating-point division operation. In *EPRCA*, the switch uses the queue length in the cell buffer as congestion indicator, and maintains the *Mean ACR (MACR)* as an approximation of the fair share to perform intelligent marking. The *MACR* is computed every time the switch receives an RM cell using a *running exponential weighted average*, as

$$MACR = MACR(1 - AV) + CCR * AV \qquad (2)$$

where $AV$ is an averaging factor, typically equal to 1/16 [9]. As it is well known, *EPRCA* produces unfairness in situations when the *MACR* does not converge to the actual fair share. Examples of such circumstances are when some VC's are bottlenecked in other switches and cause the *MACR* to converge to an underestimation of the fair share, when rates oscillate due to transient behaviors and/or interactions among switches, and when the *CCR* of some VC's is incorrect [10].

### 2.3. DMRCA

We have recently introduced *DMRCA* [10] to solve the problems encountered with *EPRCA*, while maintaining the simplicity of *EPRCA*. Here we describe this scheme in detail, since the new schemes proposed in this paper are evolutions of *DMRCA*. *DMRCA* uses a function of the maximum rate of all ABR VC's and the queue length in the switch as the marking threshold. The motivation for using the maximum rate of all VC's is that the maximum rate jumps rapidly and remains *above* the fair share, and converges to the fair share in steady state. (This is markedly different from the *MACR* in *EPRCA*, which in general is not predictable if it is an overestimation or an underestimation of the fair share.) Since the maximum rate is always an overestimation of the fair share, a *reduction factor* can be used to improve convergence to the fair share. The correcting factor is a function of the degree of congestion in the switch.

More specifically, the pseudo code of *DMRCA* is shown in Fig. 1. The switch monitors the maximum rate *MAX* of all ABR VC's. Short-term oscillations of *MAX* are filtered out by computing an *adjusted maximum rate* *A_MAX* using a running exponential weighted average as:

$$A\_MAX = (1 - Alpha) * A\_MAX + Alpha * MAX \quad (3)$$

where *Alpha* is an averaging factor (*e.g.*, *Alpha* = 1/16). (In the pseudo code shown in Fig. 1, as a further refinement, we use the selection factor *Beta* which provides additional control on which *CCR's* are considered in updating *A_MAX*.) Then, the threshold to perform intelligent marking is computed as:

$$Marking\ threshold = A\_MAX * Fn(Queue\ Length) \quad (4)$$

where the correcting function *Fn(Queue Length)* is a discrete, non increasing function of the queue length, $0 \le Fn \le 1$. The algorithm works well using a simple linear function [10] (see Section 3). The same function can be used successfully for different network topologies and with different numbers of VC's. Although *A_MAX* depends on the value of *CCR* in the RM cells, we have shown that the algorithm is very resilient to incorrect *CCR*'s, due to the use of the correcting function which depends only on the level of congestion in the switch [10].

Similarly to *EPRCA*, *DMRCA* uses two thresholds *QT* and *DQT* on the queue length in the cell buffers for congestion detection. When the queue length exceeds the threshold *QT*, the switch is considered *congested* and intelligent marking is performed. In this region, we use *RR* marking only. In general, we have found that using *ER* marking in this region is not beneficial, and under some pathological situations may even give worse performance than *RR* marking (we observed this to be true also for *EPRCA*). If congestion persists and

```
Global Variables:
  MAX:               Current maximum rate of all connections (initialize to 0.0);
  A_MAX:             Current adjusted maximum rate of all connections
                     (initialize to 0.0);
  MAX_VC:            Current connection with maximum rate;
  Fn(Queue Length):  Discrete non-increasing function of the queue length,
                     0 ≤ Fn(Queue Length) ≤ 1;
  Alpha:             Averaging factor for A_MAX (e.g., Alpha = 1/16);
  Beta               Selection factor of CCR values for A_MAX averaging;
  MRF:               Major Reduction Factor for heavy congestion;
  MAX_Timeout:       Time interval used to timeout MAX (initialize to 0);
  QT                 Lower queue threshold;
  DQT                Higher queue threshold;

if (RM_cell->DIR == 0) {              /* forward RM cell for connection i      */
  /* update MAX, MAX_VC, MAX_Timeout, A_MAX */
  if (RM_cell->ID == MAX_VC) {        /* connection i is current MAX_VC        */
    MAX = RM_cell->CCR;               /* update MAX                            */
    if (MAX > 0.0)                    /* update MAX_Timeout                    */
      MAX_Timeout = 1.0/MAX * Nrm * 2;
    else
      MAX_Timeout = 0;
  } else {                            /* connection i is not MAX_VC            */
    if (RM_cell->CCR > MAX) {         /* CCR of connection i > MAX             */
      MAX = RM_cell->CCR;             /* update MAX                            */
      MAX_VC = RM_cell->ID;           /* update MAX_VC                         */
      if (MAX > 0.0)                  /* update MAX_Timeout                    */
        MAX_Timeout = 1.0/MAX * Nrm * 2;
      else
        MAX_Timeout = 0;
    }
  }

  if (RM_cell->CCR ≥ Beta*MAX){       /* CCR greater than Beta*MAX             */
                                      /* update A_MAX                          */
    A_MAX = (1 - Alpha) * A_MAX + Alpha * RM_cell->CCR;
  }

} else if (RM_cell->DIR == 1) {       /* backward RM cell for connection i     */
  /* set CI bit and ER field in RM cell, if necessary */
  if (Queue Length ≥ DQT) {           /* switch is heavily congested           */
                                      /* decrease rate of connection i         */
    RM_cell->CI = 1;                  /* mark CI bit                           */
                                      /* set ER field                          */
    RM_cell->ER = min(RM_cell->ER, MRF*A_MAX);
  } else if (Queue Length ≥ QT) {     /* switch is moderately congested        */
                                      /* intelligent marking                   */
    Marking_Threshold = A_MAX * Fn(Queue Length);
    if (RM_cell->CCR ≥ Marking_Threshold) {
                                      /* if CCR above marking threshold        */
                                      /* decrease rate of connection i         */
      RM_cell->CI = 1;                /* mark CI bit                           */
                                      /* (optional) set ER field               */
      RM_cell->ER = min(RM_cell->ER, Marking_Threshold);
    } else {                          /* if CCR below marking threshold        */
                                      /* rate increase allowed by this switch  */
    }
  } else {                            /* switch is not congested               */
                                      /* rate increase allowed by this switch  */
  }
}
```

Fig. 1. Pseudo code of *DMRCA*.

aggravates despite intelligent marking, and the queue length exceeds the threshold *DQT*, the switch is considered *highly congested*, and all the connections have their rate reduced. In this region, we use *ER* marking in conjunction with *RR* marking, since it is important to reduce the rate of the connections as rapidly as possible. The *ER* field of the RM cells is set equal to *A_MAX* * *MRF*, where *MRF* is the *Major Reduction Factor*, similar to the one used in *EPRCA* [2]. A typical value for *MRF* is 7/8.

## 3. Switch And Traffic Models

Before proceeding with our discussion, we describe the switch model, the traffic models, and the network configurations used throughout this paper. We consider output buffer switches with partitioned buffers and FIFO service discipline of their queue, and characterize the buffer requirements at the switches in order to achieve zero cell loss for ABR connections. All links are assumed to have the same rate. In our simulation, to make the results independent of the link rate, we use as the time unit the transmission time of one ATM cell (referred to as the *cell time*). For example, in the case of a link speed equal to 155 Mbps, the cell time unit for transmitting one ATM cell of 53 bytes is about 2.75 μs.

We consider the network topology shown in Fig. 2. This simple topology, known as the *parking-lot* configuration, is becoming popular in literature [9,10], because is very effective to illustrate fairness problems. The propagation time on each link between sources and switches, between switches, and between switches and destinations is 100 cell times. We assume both ABR and VBR traffic are present in the network, and study the scenario depicted in the figure. There are 6 ABR VC's in the network (VC1—VC6), all destined to the same port in switch 6; VC1 and VC2 start at the first switch in the chain, and traverse all 6 switches; one of the remaining ABR VC's starts at each one of the other switches in the chain. In addition, there are 4 VBR VC's entering each switch in the chain. For ABR VC's, we assume that the sources are greedy (*i.e.*, persistent), and can transmit cells at a certain *ACR*. We model *each* VBR VC with an on-off source which alternates between active and idle periods, and transmit cells at the link rate during active periods. For each VC, the bursts have geometrically-distributed length with average burst length *L*; the durations of the idle periods are also geometrically distributed, with average length *L'*; consequently, the load on each VC is *L*/(*L* + *L'*).

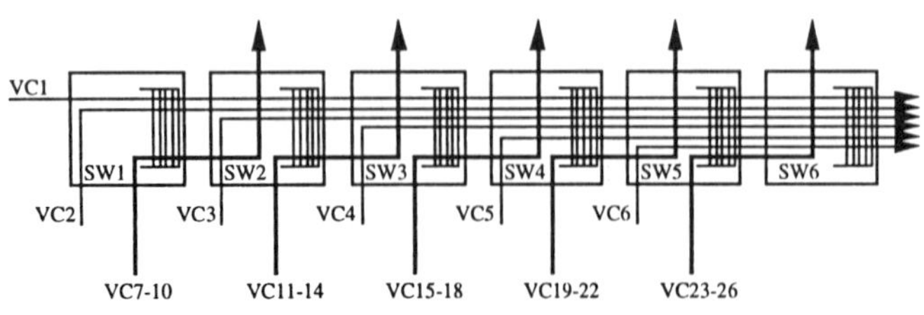


Fig. 2. Network model for the parking lot configuration used to study ABR/VBR interaction, with a total of 26 VC's. VC1—6 are greedy ABR VC's, VC7—26 are VBR VC's with on-off sources. Each VBR VC has an average rate equal to 10% of the link capacity (for a total average rate of VBR traffic on each link equal to 40% of the link capacity), and a peak rate equal to the link capacity.

The simulation parameters that are kept constant throughout this study are listed in the following table.

| | |
|---|---|
| *ICR* | 0.0% |
| *MCR* | 0.0% |
| *PCR* | 100.0% |
| *RIF* | 1/128 |
| *RDF* | 1/32 |
| *Nrm* | 32 |

(*ICR* is the *Initial Cell Rate*). All the rates are in percentage of the total available bandwidth. In *DMRCA*, we use a simple linear function for the *Fn*. The discrete values of *Fn* are listed in the following table.

| Queue Size | Function Value |
|---|---|
| *QT* + 50 | 1 |
| *QT* + 250 | 0.95 |
| *QT* + 450 | 0.9 |
| *QT* + 650 | 0.85 |
| *QT* + 850 | 0.8 |
| *QT* + 1050 | 0.75 |
| *QT* + 1250 | 0.7 |
| *QT* + 1450 | 0.65 |
| *QT* + 1650 | 0.6 |
| *QT* + 1850 | 0.55 |
| ≥ *QT* + 2050 | 0.5 |

## 4. ABR/VBR Interaction

As discussed in Section 2, ABR schemes based on an approximation of the fair share and using the queue length as congestion indicator are simple to implement and achieve good performance when highly-bursty VBR traffic is not present in the network. In this section, we study the performance of this class of ABR schemes when ABR interacts with VBR. The discussion is centered on the performance of *DMRCA*, since this is the scheme in this class that has been shown to offer the most robust performance without VBR traffic [10]. It should be clear, however, that the problems that we highlight in the following for *DMRCA* in presence of VBR traffic are common to *EPRCA* and to all other schemes in the class. To serve as a reference, in Fig. 3, we show the performance of *DMRCA*

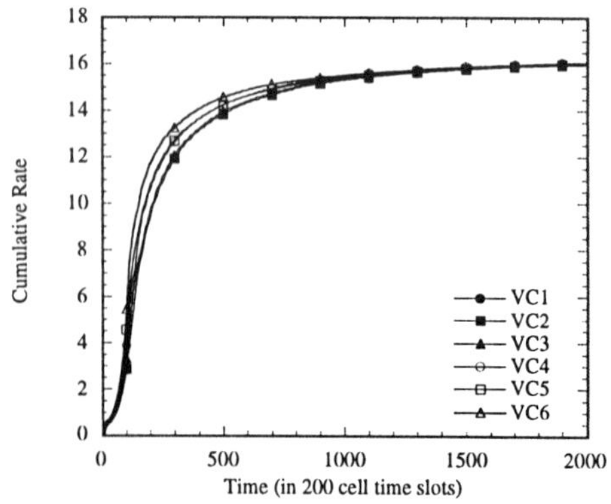


Fig. 3. Cumulative rate (in percentage of total available bandwidth) using *DMRCA* in the parking lot configuration, with no VBR traffic; *QT* = 50, *DQT* = 1000.

in the parking lot configuration of Fig. 2 when there are no VBR VC's; $QT = 50$, $DQT = 1000$. The scheme achieves excellent fairness; the same behavior is observed when bottlenecked VC's are present, and is maintained over other topologies [10]; in these conditions, we have shown that the behavior of the queue length at every switch is controlled, and except for rare transients the queue length oscillates well below *DQT* [10].

As it will become evident from the following discussion, for these ABR schemes to show performance degradation in presence of VBR traffic, VBR traffic must be highly-bursty and generate considerable congestion in the network. Here, we consider the parking lot configuration of Fig. 2 where each of the four VBR VC's entering each switch have an average rate equal to 10% of the link capacity, and a peak rate equal to the link capacity; the total average bandwidth of VBR on each link is therefore 40% of the link capacity, and the total peak bandwidth is 400% of the link capacity, *i.e.,* the available bandwidth is substantially overallocated, which can easily lead to congestion. Even with such heavy VBR traffic, we have observed that the *DMRCA* scheme does not show performance degradation if the average burst size for the VBR VC's is relatively small (*e.g.,* $L =$ 10 cells). The problems occur when the burst size become large, and increase with the burst size. As mentioned in the Introduction, the interaction between the two types of traffic depends on whether at the switches ABR and VBR share the same queue or are handled by separate queues.

We first consider the situation where a *single queue* is used to accommodate both traffic types. In this case, we can think of two variations of the ABR scheme. A first possibility is to use as congestion indicator the total queue length (*i.e.,* the number of *both* ABR and VBR cells in the queue); a second possibility, is to use the total number of ABR cells in the queue only.

In Fig. 4, we show the cumulative rate for the ABR VC's with *DMRCA* using the *total queue length* as congestion indicator, when the VBR sources emit bursts of average length $L = 100$ cells (Fig. 4(a)), and $L = 1000$ cells (Fig. 4(b)); $QT = 50$, $DQT = 1000$. Because of the highly bursty VBR traffic, the ABR VC's are treated unfairly, and the ABR VC's traveling through several switches receive a smaller share of available bandwidth than ABR VC's traveling for a shorter distance. (The fair share for each ABR VC should be 10% of the available bandwidth.) The reason for the poor performance is that in each switch cells belonging to VBR VC's account for a major portion of the cells in the queue. The queue length depends on the activity of *both* ABR and VBR traffic, and thus cannot be used to accurately control congestion caused by ABR. For example, a long queue may be due to congestion created by VBR, but would be misinterpreted by the switch, which would unnecessarily decrease the rate of ABR connections. A more simplistic way to see this phenomenon is that the queue length often increases above *DQT* due primarily to congestion caused by VBR, and intelligent marking is disabled unnecessarily, causing *beat-down* of the connections traveling through more switches. As the burst size increases, VBR dominates the queue more and more; controlling ABR rate allocation with the queue length becomes almost meaningless, and results in very

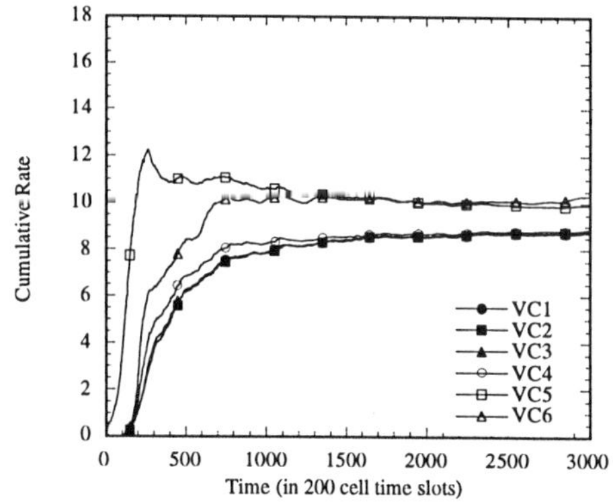


(a)

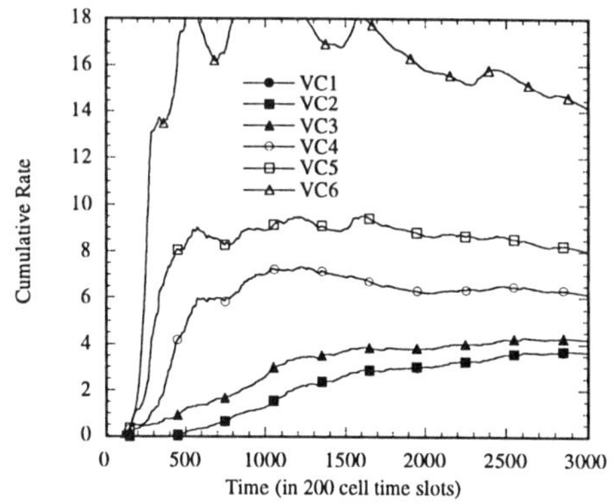


(b)

Fig. 4. Cumulative rate (in percentage of total available bandwidth) using *DMRCA* in the parking lot configuration of Fig. 2 in the case where ABR and VBR traffic share the same queue; the total number of both ABR and VBR cells in the queue is used as congestion indicator; $QT = 50$, $DQT = 1000$; a) $L = 100$, b) $L = 1000$.

substantial unfairness (see Fig. 4(b)). Some marginal improvement in fairness can be achieved by increasing the thresholds *QT* and *DQT*, so that more ABR cells are present in the queue. Unfortunately, the effect is negligible, since the number of VBR cells in the queue also increases, because the two types of traffic share the same queue. This is confirmed in Table I, where we report the average and maximum total queue length, number of ABR cells, and number of VBR cells, as well as the link utilization in switch 5 (by construction, switch 5 is the most congested switch in the parking-lot configuration considered here).

For relatively short average burst lengths in the VBR VC's, the situation can be partially improved by using as congestion indicator *only the number of ABR cells* in the queues, rather than the total queue

TABLE I

| *L* | *QT* | *DQT* | Utiliza-tion(%) | Total Queue Length | | Number of ABR Cells | | Number of VBR Cells | |
|---|---|---|---|---|---|---|---|---|---|
| | | | | Max | Mean | Max | Mean | Max | Mean |
| 100 | 50 | 1000 | 94.0 | 2457 | 580 | 1444 | 330 | 1481 | 246 |
| | 200 | 1000 | 96.5 | 2469 | 716 | 1637 | 416 | 1598 | 296 |
| | 200 | 2000 | 97.1 | 3606 | 1131 | 2504 | 666 | 2153 | 462 |
| | 1000 | 2000 | 97.6 | 6000 | 2201 | 3597 | 1304 | 3784 | 892 |
| 1000 | 50 | 1000 | 86.4 | 11533 | 1793 | 3249 | 578 | 9651 | 1206 |
| | 1000 | 10000 | 96.1 | 21672 | 7783 | 12185 | 3755 | 15631 | 4016 |

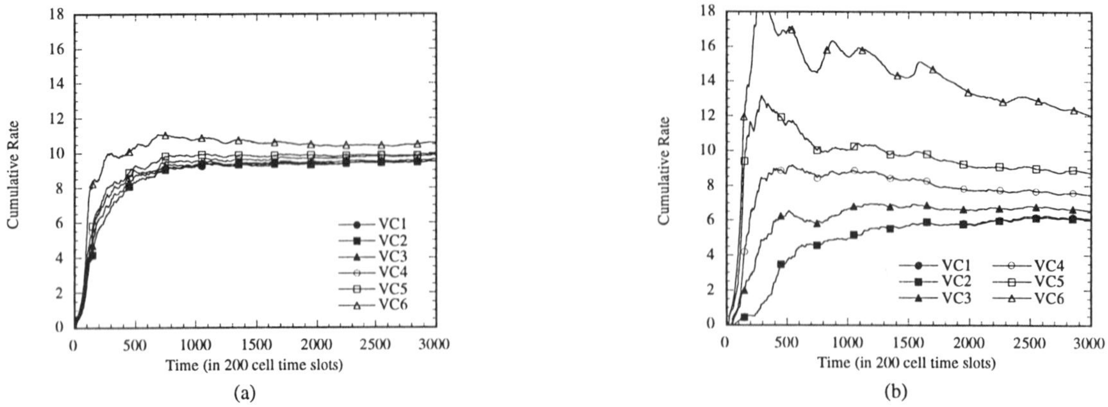


Fig. 5. Cumulative rate (in percentage of total available bandwidth) using *DMRCA* in the parking lot configuration of Fig. 2 in the case where ABR and VBR traffic share the same queue; only the number of ABR cells in the queue is used as congestion indicator; $QT = 50$, $DQT = 1000$; a) $L = 100$, b) $L = 1000$.

length. This is shown in Fig. 5(a), where we plot the cumulative rate for the ABR VC's using *DMRCA*, with average burst length $L = 100$ cells; $QT = 50$, $DQT = 1000$. For larger burst sizes, however, *DMRCA* still suffers heavy performance degradation, as shown in Fig. 5(b) for average burst length $L = 1000$ cells; $QT = 50$, $DQT = 1000$. The reason for the poor performance is that also in this case the queue length does not accurately reflect congestion caused by ABR. VBR traffic in the queue may prevent ABR traffic from being served for considerable periods of time, thus making the number of ABR cells in the queue depend on the activity of VBR. Again, marginal improvements in fairness can be obtained by increasing the threshold *QT* and *DQT*, at the expenses of very substantial increases in buffer requirements, as shown in Table II.

TABLE II

| *L* | *QT* | *DQT* | Utilization(%) | Total Queue Length | | Number of ABR Cells | | Number of VBR Cells | |
|---|---|---|---|---|---|---|---|---|---|
| | | | | Max | Mean | Max | Mean | Max | Mean |
| 100 | 50 | 1000 | 97.6 | 3555 | 1165 | 2627 | 685 | 1959 | 475 |
| 1000 | 50 | 1000 | 93.0 | 14206 | 2892 | 4429 | 1136 | 11440 | 1745 |
| | 1000 | 10000 | 99.0 | 28837 | 15032 | 16049 | 8007 | 20732 | 7011 |

We then consider the situation, typical in current-generation switches, where ABR and VBR traffic are given different delay priorities (since they belong to different service classes), and are handled by *separate queues*. In this case, the extent of the interaction between the two traffic types depends on the *scheduling algorithm* used to share the link capacity of the common link between the two queues. In this context, we are only interested in work-conserving scheduling algorithms; thus, if only a single queue has cells waiting to be served, it is always served at a rate equal to the link capacity. The performance of the ABR scheme depends therefore on the rate at which VBR traffic is served when both queues are backlogged. Specifically, we consider the two queues served according to a (work-conserving) weighted-round-robin discipline, and study the system as a function of the weights allocated to the two queues. Over the range of weights, one extreme is when VBR traffic is given a weight close to or equal to its *average* rate (in our specific case, the weight would be 40%), and ABR traffic is given a weight equal to the remaining bandwidth (in our case, the weight would be 60%); the other extreme is when VBR traffic is given a weight equal to 100% of the link capacity, *i.e.*, VBR traffic is given *strict priority* over ABR traffic, and ABR traffic is only served when there are no cells waiting in the VBR queue; the whole range of weights between these two extremes is possible.

In Fig. 6, we show the cumulative rate of the ABR VC's for different service rates (*i.e.,* weights) of the VBR queue, for average burst size in the VBR VC's $L = 100$ cells; $QT = 50$, $DQT = 1000$. The corresponding average and maximum size of the total queue length, ABR queue length, and VBR queue length in switch 5, as well as the link utilization at the output of switch 5 are summarized in Table III.

If the weight assigned to VBR is 40% (equal to the average rate of VBR traffic), ABR and VBR types of traffic are fully isolated, and *DMRCA* achieves the same good performance as in the case without VBR traffic, as shown in Fig 6(a). However, since VBR traffic is highly-bursty, the buffer size necessary to accommodate the VBR queue with such a minimum VBR weight is very large, as shown in the table above (and significantly larger than in the previous scenarios); other QoS parameters for VBR traffic, such as delay, are negatively affected as well. For this reason, in practice, VBR traffic is typically served at a rate higher than its average rate. A common choice is to use strict priority for VBR traffic (VBR weight = 100%), since this facilitates meeting the service guarantees for VBR.

If the VBR weight is larger than 40%, ABR and VBR traffic interact, and the ABR performance degrade. *DMRCA* introduces more

TABLE III

| VBR Weight (%) | Utilization(%) | Total Queue Length | | ABR Queue Length | | VBR Queue Length | |
|---|---|---|---|---|---|---|---|
| | | Max | Mean | Max | Mean | Max | Mean |
| 40 | 98.4 | > 5376 | > 2532 | 1890 | 666 | > 4391 | > 1862 |
| 50 | 97.3 | 3260 | 905 | 2637 | 681 | 1491 | 221 |
| 60 | 96.9 | 2764 | 789 | 2183 | 679 | 1147 | 107 |
| 80 | 95.3 | 3025 | 763 | 2962 | 720 | 827 | 41 |
| 100 | 94.1 | 3662 | 714 | 3662 | 696 | 706 | 17 |

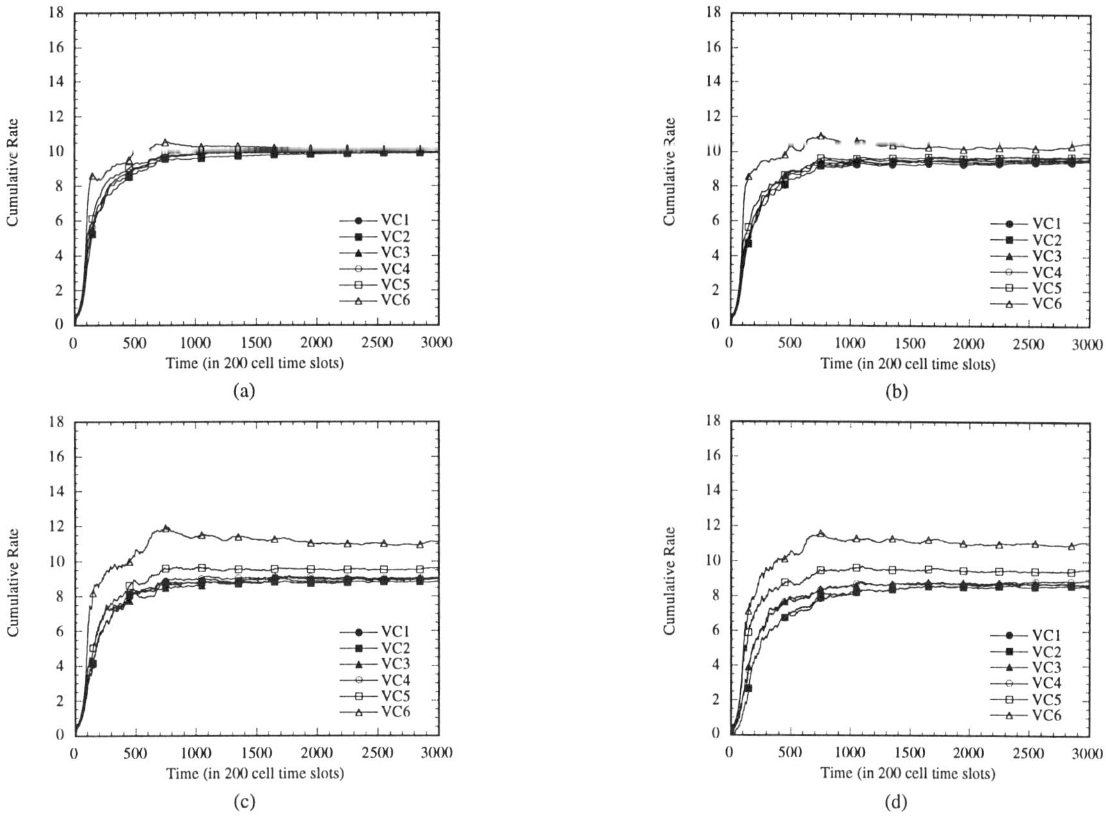


Fig. 6. Cumulative rate (in percentage of total available bandwidth) using *DMRCA* in the parking lot configuration of Fig. 2 in the case where ABR and VBR traffic are handled by separate queues, $L = 100$; $QT = 50$, $DQT = 1000$; a) 40% service rate of the VBR queue (*i.e.,* total average rate of VBR traffic); b) 50% service rate of the VBR queue; c) 80% service rate of the VBR queue; d) 100% service rate of the VBR queue (*i.e.,* strict priority of VBR traffic).

and more unfairness as the VBR weight increases (see Figures 6(b), 6(c), and 6(d)). The reason for the poor behavior is that the service rate of the ABR queue is now modulated by the activity of the VBR queue, and therefore the ABR queue length cannot serve anymore as a reliable indicator of congestion caused by the activity of the ABR sources, similarly to the previous cases. For example, at a certain time, the ABR queue may increase just because the VBR traffic is being served; the switch would erroneously interpret such an increase as due to congestion induced by ABR connections, and unnecessarily reallocate their rate. Similarly, a downstream switch may not receive ABR traffic for a certain time just because the ABR traffic is blocked upstream by VBR, and erroneously assume that the rate of ABR sources should be increased. As the ABR performance decrease, the link utilization also decreases. As far as the buffer requirements are concerned, the table above shows that both minimum and average VBR queue lengths decrease rapidly as the VBR weight increases. Of course, the minimum for the VBR queue length occurs when VBR has strict priority over ABR. We also observe that, as expected, the ABR queue is increases as the weight of VBR traffic increases. The minimum of the *total* buffer requirements occurs for a value of the VBR weight lower than 100% (in this specific case, the minimum occurs for a VBR weight equal to 70%).

Similar consideration can be made in the case where the average length for the VBR VC's is $L = 1000$. The only difference is that the effects are much more dramatic, as shown in Fig. 7, where we show the cumulative rate for the ABR VC's using *DMRCA*, $QT = 50$, $DQT = 1000$. The corresponding buffer sizes and link utilization in switch 5 are summarized in Table IV.

With such highly-bursty VBR traffic, as soon as the VBR weight is substantially larger than 40% (*i.e.,* average rate of VBR traffic), *DMRCA* practically allocates the ABR rates randomly, since the queue length has again very little relation with the activity of the ABR sources. To visually confirm this argument, in Fig. 8, we show the behavior of the VBR and ABR queue lengths for the case of strict priority given to VBR traffic (*i.e.,* corresponding to Fig. 7(d)). Both queues show a very "bursty" behavior, and the random, uncontrolled oscillations of the ABR queue length cannot be expected to give any reliable indication of ABR congestion.

TABLE IV

| VBR Weight (%) | Utiliza-tion(%) | Total Queue Length | | ABR Queue Length | | VBR Queue Length | |
|---|---|---|---|---|---|---|---|
| | | Max | Mean | Max | Mean | Max | Mean |
| 40 | 99.1 | > 30000 | > 12821 | 2139 | 729 | > 29551 | > 12617 |
| 50 | 97.7 | 15751 | 5417 | 3504 | 788 | 14869 | 4616 |
| 60 | 95.1 | 14659 | 2910 | 4955 | 1085 | 10042 | 1815 |
| 80 | 91.2 | 14472 | 2758 | 12178 | 2117 | 6577 | 633 |
| 100 | 86.4 | 21702 | 3673 | 21701 | 3443 | 3221 | 226 |

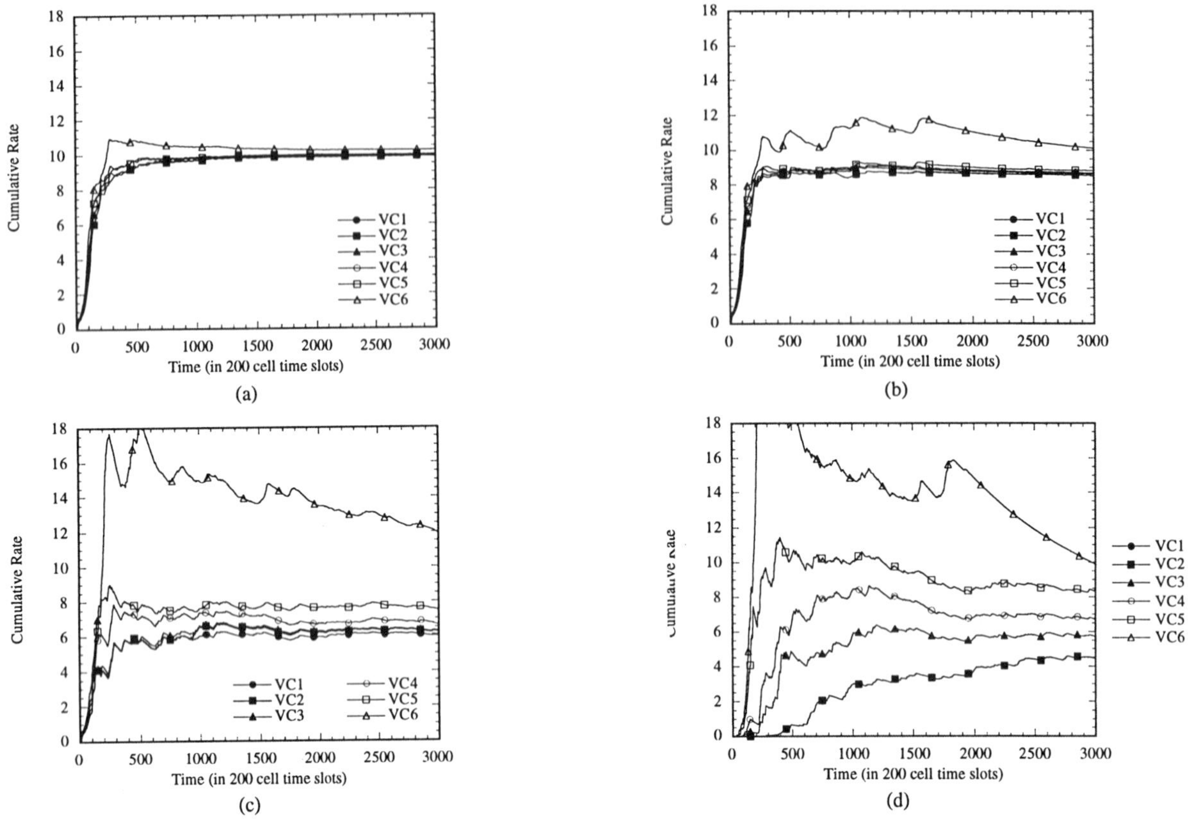


Fig. 7. Cumulative rate (in percentage of total available bandwidth) using *DMRCA* in the parking lot configuration of Fig. 2 in the case where ABR and VBR traffic are handled by separate queues, $L = 1000$. The number of cells in the ABR queue is used as congestion indicator; $QT = 50$, $DQT = 1000$; a) 40% service rate of the VBR queue (*i.e.,* total average rate of VBR traffic); b) 50% service rate of the VBR queue; c) 80% service rate of the VBR queue; d) 100% service rate of the VBR queue (*i.e.,* strict priority of VBR traffic).

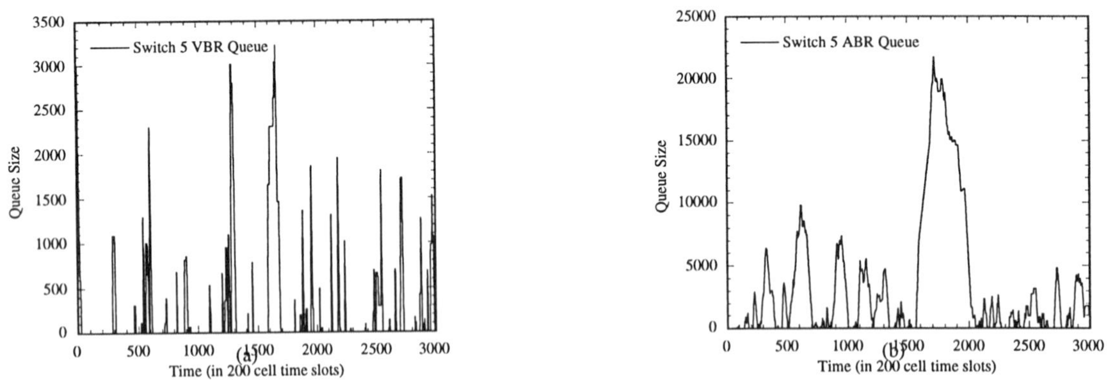


Fig. 8. Queue length in switch 5 using *DMRCA* in the case where ABR and VBR traffic are handled by separate queues, for 100% service rate of the VBR queue (*i.e.,* strict priority of VBR traffic). The number of cells in the ABR queue is used as congestion indicator; $QT = 50$, $DQT = 1000$; a) VBR queue; b) ABR queue.

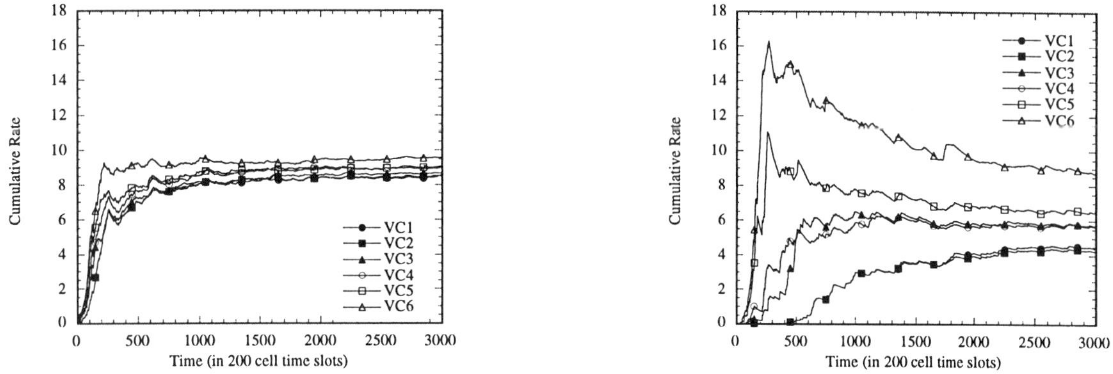


(a) (b)

Fig. 9. Cumulative rate (in percentage of total available bandwidth) using *DMRCA with Virtual Queueing* in the parking lot configuration of Fig. 2 in the case where an arrival at the virtual queue is posted every time a data cell arrives at the real ABR queue, for 100% service rate of the VBR queue (*i.e.,* strict priority of VBR traffic over ABR traffic). The number of cells in the virtual queue is used as congestion indicator; $QT = 50$, $DQT = 1000$; a) $L = 100$; b) $L = 1000$.

## 5. Dynamic Max Rate Control Algorithm with Virtual Queueing (*DMRCA_VQ*)

In this section, we introduce a simple technique to solve the problems identified above, and use it to modify *DMRCA* and achieve fairness also in presence of highly-bursty VBR traffic. In our technique, the switches construct the length of a *virtual queue*, which is the number of ABR cells that would be waiting at the switch if VBR traffic were not present, and the available bandwidth for ABR were made equal to the available bandwidth assuming VBR were allocated its *average* bandwidth. By construction, the virtual queue length is not affected by the instantaneous behavior of VBR traffic, and constitutes a reliable indicator of congestion induced by ABR traffic. We then apply the technique to *DMRCA*, and use the length of the virtual queue in place of the length of the real ABR queue as congestion indicator (*i.e., QT* and *DQT* are thresholds on the virtual queue length, and *Fn* is a function of the virtual queue length, rather than of the real queue length). We show that this scheme, referred to as *DMRCA with Virtual Queueing (DMRCA_VQ)*, can achieve performance comparable to that achieved with *DMRCA* in the case where no VBR traffic is present in the network. (Without VBR traffic, *DMRCA_VQ* reduces to *DMRCA*.) In the following, we concentrate on the case where VBR traffic is given strict priority over ABR traffic, which we have shown in the previous section is the case that causes the highest interaction between the two types of traffic, and leads to the highest unfairness.

The length of the virtual queue is constructed as follows. The service rate for the virtual queue is immediately computed once the average bandwidth of VBR is known, and only needs to be updated when a VBR connection is set up or terminated. Once the service rate is computed, the virtual queue length is decremented constantly at that rate (however, the virtual queue length is never decremented below zero). The arrival rate for the virtual queue requires some discussion. The simplest way to increment the length of the virtual queue is to post an arrival at the virtual queue every time an ABR data cell arrives at the switch. Unfortunately, this method does not produce a virtual queue which is independent of VBR traffic. Using such a virtual queue as congestion indicator gives better performance than using the real queue, but does not completely solve the fairness problems when the burst size of VBR traffic is very large. This is illustrated in Fig. 9, where we plot the cumulative rate in the parking-lot configuration with *DMRCA_VQ*, where the virtual queue length is updated when an ABR data cell arrives at the switch, for average burst length in the VBR VC's $L = 100$ and $L = 1000$; $QT = 50$, $DQT = 1000$. Although the performance has certainly improved with respect to *DMRCA* (compare with Fig. 6(d) for $L = 100$, and 7(d) for $L = 1000$), it is visibly worse than what can be achieved with *DMRCA* when VBR traffic is not present. In particular, in the case $L = 1000$, unfairness is still considerable. Table V summarizes buffer sizes and link utilization in switch 5.

The reason for the unsatisfactory performance is that, as noted in the previous section, VBR traffic affects the arrival process of ABR cells at downstream switches, because of strict-priority scheduling of VBR. A switch may not receive ABR cells for a certain period of time just because they are blocked upstream by VBR traffic being served. As a consequence, the virtual queue length is not updated in a way that is not affected by VBR.

In order for the virtual queue to become independent from VBR traffic, its arrival rate should also be equal to the rate in the case where ABR and VBR traffic were fully isolated. This can be simply achieved by giving *RM cells higher priority than VBR traffic* (VBR still maintains higher priority than ABR data cells). This is possible for the following reasons.

i) Current-generation switches typically support several delay-priority classes. For example, a rather common configuration provides support for four or five classes, with the highest priority class given to CBR traffic, and the remaining classes given to real-time and non-real-time VBR, ABR, and Unspecified Bit Rate (UBR) traffic.

TABLE V

| *L* | Utiliza-tion(%) | Total Queue Length | | ABR Queue Length | | VBR Queue Length | |
|---|---|---|---|---|---|---|---|
| | | Max | Mean | Max | Mean | Max | Mean |
| 100 | 92.0 | 4323 | 958 | 3816 | 940 | 706 | 15 |
| 1000 | 82.0 | 14089 | 2075 | 14089 | 1845 | 3221 | 226 |

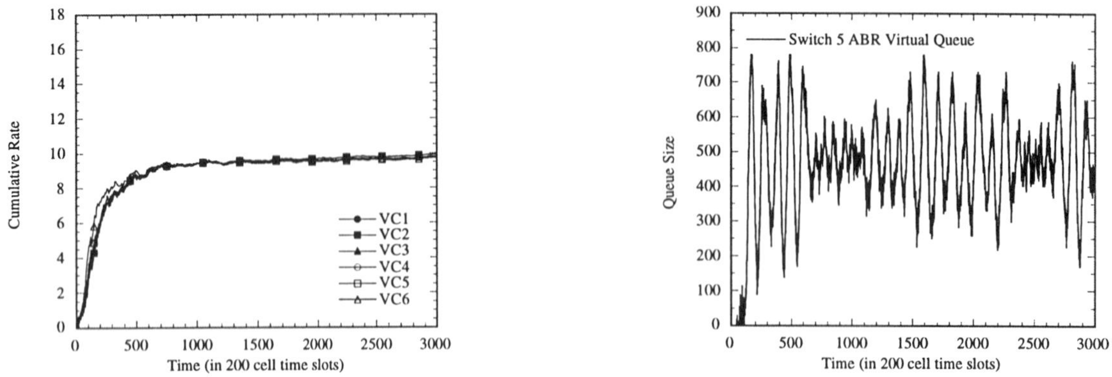


(a) (b)

Fig. 10. Performance of *DMRCA with Virtual Queueing* in the parking lot configuration of Fig. 2 in the case where RM cells are served with priority and *Nrm* arrivals at the virtual queue are posted every time an RM cell arrives at the real ABR queue, for 100% service rate of the VBR queue (*i.e.,* strict priority of VBR traffic over ABR traffic), $L = 100$. The number of cells in the virtual queue is used as congestion indicator; $QT = 50$, $DQT = 1000$; a) cumulative rate (in percentage of total available bandwidth); b) length of the virtual queue in switch 5.

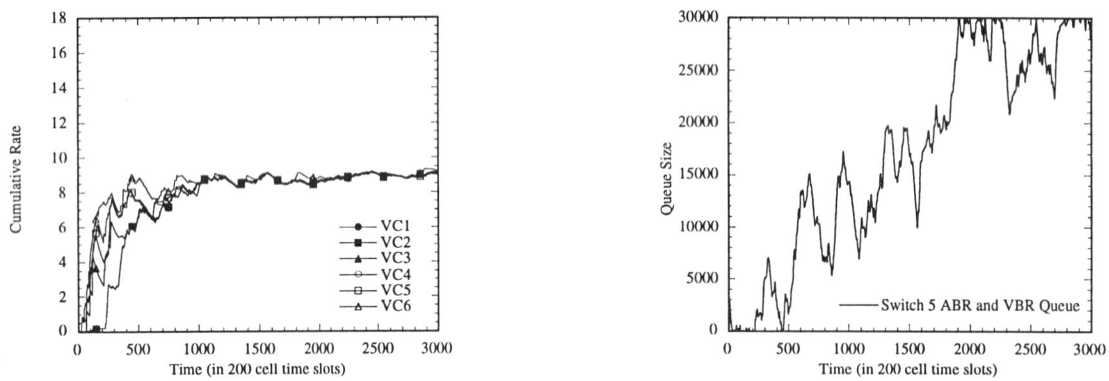


(a) (b)

Fig. 11. Performance of *DMRCA with Virtual Queueing* in the parking lot configuration of Fig. 2 in the case where RM cells are served with priority, and *Nrm* arrivals at the virtual queue are posted every time an RM cell arrives at the real ABR queue, for 100% service rate of the VBR queue (*i.e.,* strict priority of VBR traffic over ABR traffic), $L = 1000$. The number of cells in the virtual queue is used as congestion indicator; $QT = 50$, $DQT = 1000$; a) cumulative rate (in percentage of total available bandwidth); b) total length of both ABR and VBR queues in Switch 5.

ii) Modifying the priority of RM cells and placing them in the priority class immediately above VBR traffic does not affect the performance of the higher-priority service classes because of the small total bandwidth required by RM cells (less than 3% with 100% ABR traffic, and decreasing linearly with the volume of ABR traffic).

iii) Modifying the priority of the RM cells is compatible with current ATM Forum standard, which specifies that order be maintain within a VC among RM cells, but does not require to maintain the order between RM cells and data cells.

Once the RM cells are given priority over ABR, they travel in the network unaffected by VBR traffic, and can inform downstream switches of ABR data traffic under way, but temporarily blocked upstream because of VBR. This is achieved by posting *Nrm* arrivals in the virtual queue every time an RM cell arrives at the switch. (Further refinements, which we do not explicitly present in this paper, smooth the posting of the *Nrm* arrivals at the virtual queue over consecutive cell times, to take into account the fact that in reality ABR data cells would arrive at most one per cell time, rather than in bursts of *Nrm* cells at the time).

Indeed, the length of the virtual queue, when updated in this way, is not affected by the short-term behavior of VBR traffic and thus becomes a reliable indicator of congestion due to the activity of ABR sources. *DMRCA_VQ* with the virtual queue length incremented according to the RM cells arrivals achieves fairness with highly-bursty VBR traffic, as shown in Fig. 10(a), where we plot the cumulative rate for average burst size $L = 100$, $QT = 50$, $DQT = 1000$. In Fig. 10(b), we plot the behavior of the virtual queue length in switch 5. We observe the controlled oscillation of the virtual queue length, a behavior that is an indication that the queue length is used effectively to control congestion [10,11] (compare with the random oscillations of the ABR and VBR queue lengths in Fig. 8). *DMRCA_VQ* achieves fairness also with larger bursts, as plotted in Fig. 11(a), for $L = 1000$; $QT = 50$, $DQT = 1000$. The residual unfairness in the initial transient that shows in the cumulative rate can be further reduced by fine tuning the values of $QT$ and $DQT$. (The residual small oscillations in the rate can be eliminated by smoothing the arrivals at the virtual queue.) One problem that remains to be solved with *DMRCA_VQ* is that congestion control relies only on the virtual queue, and is totally detached from the state of the real ABR queue. As a result, the buffer requirements

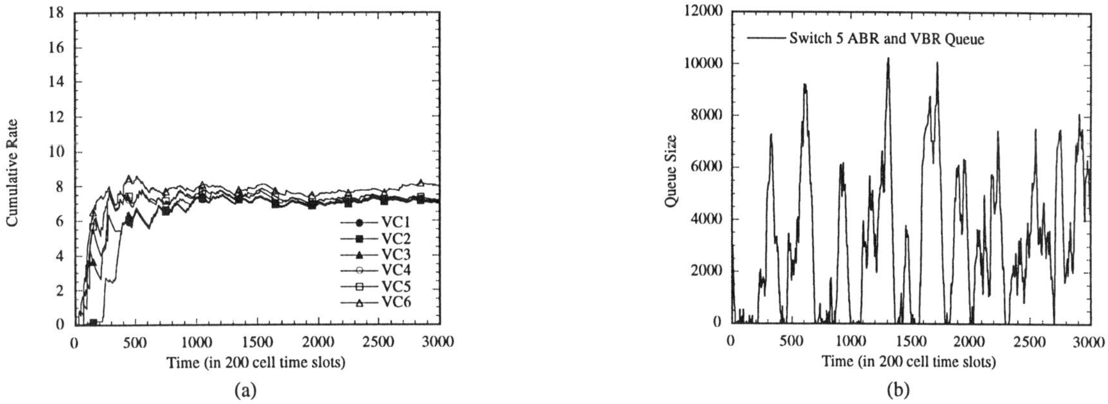


Fig. 12. Performance of *DMRCA with Virtual Queueing with Hard Limitation on the Real Queue* in the parking lot configuration of Fig. 2 in the case where RM cells are served with priority, and *Nrm* arrivals at the virtual queue are posted every time an RM cell arrives at the real ABR queue, for 100% service rate of the VBR queue (*i.e.,* strict priority of VBR traffic over ABR traffic), $L = 1000$. The number of cells in the virtual queue is used as congestion indicator; $QT = 50$, $DQT = 1000$, $RDQT = 5000$; a) cumulative rate (in percentage of total available bandwidth); b) total length of both ABR and VBR queues in Switch 5.

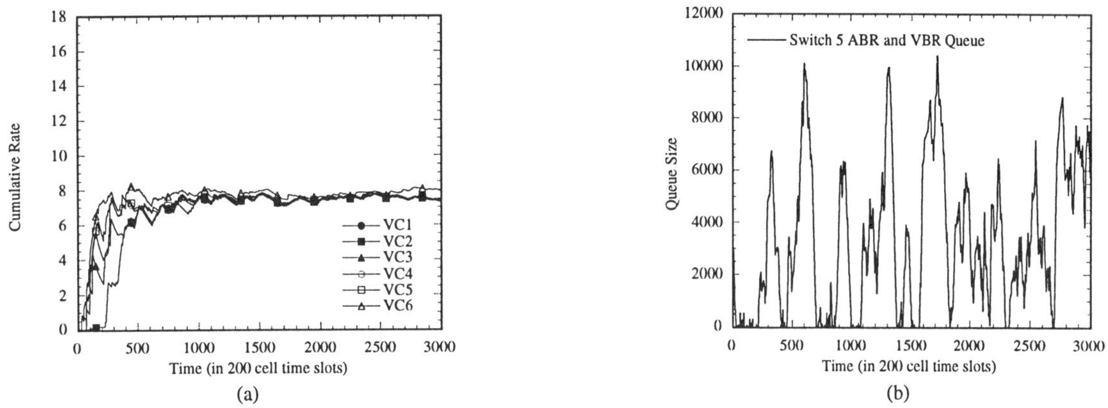


Fig. 13. Performance of *DMRCA with Virtual Queueing with Soft Limitation on the Real Queue* in the parking lot configuration of Fig. 2 in the case where RM cells are served with priority, and *Nrm* arrivals at the virtual queue are posted every time an RM cell arrives at the real ABR queue, for 100% service rate of the VBR queue (*i.e.,* strict priority of VBR traffic over ABR traffic), $L = 1000$. The number of cells in the virtual queue is used as congestion indicator; $QT = 50$, $DQT = 1000$; a) cumulative rate (in percentage of total available bandwidth); b) total length of both ABR and VBR queues in Switch 5.

to accommodate the real ABR queue and VBR queue may become very large; one of the desirable characteristics of schemes using the queue length for congestion control, *i.e.,* controlled buffer size, would be lost. As an example, in Fig. 11(b) we show the behavior of the total ABR and VBR queues in switch 5.

To reduce the buffer size, we introduce two variations of *DMRCA_VQ* which use *both* the virtual queue length and the real queue length as congestion indicators. In the first variation, called *DMRCA_VQ with Hard Limitation on the Real Queue*, a threshold *RDQT* is placed on the *real* queue length. If the real queue length is below the threshold *RDQT*, *DMRCA_VQ* is used, and congestion indication is based on the virtual queue, using the thresholds *QT* and *DQT*. If the real queue length is above the threshold *RDQT*, *DMRCA_VQ* is disabled, and all the sources have their rate decreased regardless of the length of the virtual queue. The cumulative rate using this variation of *DMRCA_VQ*, for average burst size $L = 1000$, is shown in Fig. 12(a); $QT = 50$, $DQT = 1000$, $RDQT = 5000$. With such a large burst size, we observe a marginal degradation in fairness with respect to *DMRCA_VQ* without the limitation on the real queue (with smaller burst sizes, no degradation would be observed). Because of the hard limitation, the behavior of the total ABR and VBR queue is much more controlled, as shown in Fig. 12(b).

The small degradation in fairness can be corrected using a second variation of *DMRCA_VQ*, called *DMRCA_VQ with Soft Limitation on the Real Queue*. In this scheme, rather than using a hard threshold *RDQT* on the real queue length, we use a function of the real queue length to adjust the drain rate of the virtual queue:

$$Drain\_Rate_{SoftLimitation} = Drain\_Rate_{NoLimitation} * Gn(Real\ Queue\ Length) \quad (5)$$

where the correcting function *Gn(Real Queue Length)* is a discrete, non increasing function of the real queue length, $0 \leq Gn \leq 1$. The idea is that if the real queue length increases, we reduce the drain rate of the virtual queue, which tends to increase the virtual queue length, and in turn possibly reduce the allocated rate to the ABR VC's. In Fig. 13(a), we show the cumulative rate using this variation, for average burst size $L = 1000$, $QT = 50$, $DQT = 1000$. In this case, we have used for *Gn* a discrete linear function between the values 1000 and 11000 of the real queue length, with step 1000. Further performance improvements can be obtained by fine tuning *Gn*. The behavior of the total ABR and VBR queue, shown in Fig. 13(b), is similar to what obtained with the hard limitation.

The average and maximum size of the total queue length, ABR queue length, and VBR queue length in switch 5, as well as the link utilization at the output of switch 5 for *DMRCA_VQ* without limitation on the real queue and for the variations with limitation on the real queue are compared in Table VI.

TABLE VI

| Limitation on Real Queue | Utiliza-tion(%) | Total Queue Length | | ABR Queue Length | | VBR Queue Length | |
|---|---|---|---|---|---|---|---|
| | | Max | Mean | Max | Mean | Max | Mean |
| No Limitation | 96.7 | > 30000 | > 16225 | > 30000 | > 16218 | 3527 | 216 |
| Hard Limitation | 90.3 | 10238 | 3042 | 10045 | 2794 | 3430 | 242 |
| Soft Limitation | 91.5 | 10700 | 3319 | 10679 | 3071 | 3421 | 243 |

The reduction in buffer requirements that can be achieved by using the variations of *DMRCA_VQ* with limitation on the real queue are very substantial. As a result of the more effective control of ABR connections, the total buffer requirements are also substantially smaller than what necessary when using *DMRCA* without virtual queueing (compare with tables in Section 4 above for VBR strict priority). The buffer requirements are dominated by ABR, as a consequence of the strict-priority scheduling of VBR, and of the highly-bursty characteristics of VBR traffic. Large buffers to accommodate ABR are intrinsically necessary to make ABR achieve high utilization of the available bandwidth with such traffic conditions and scheduling policy. Of course, the considerations made in Section 4 above on the impact of scheduling on the buffer size for ABR and VBR apply also here, and a minimum total buffer size can be achieved by using a VBR weight smaller than 100%.

Finally, *DMRCA_VQ* is simple to implement. Its hardware complexity is only marginally higher than that of *DMRCA*, since the virtual queue is represented by a single counter that is easily maintained (*i.e.*, it is decremented at a known constant rate, and is incremented when RM cells arrive). Modifying the priority of the RM cells as required to make the virtual queue most effective is a trivial operation in current-generation switches.

## 6. Conclusions

In this paper, we have shown that existing ABR schemes using the queue length experience heavy performance degradation when ABR traffic interacts with highly-bursty VBR traffic. We have studied both the case where ABR and VBR traffic share the same queue, and the case where the two types of traffic are handled by different queues. In the latter case, we have characterized the impact of scheduling of the two queues on the performance of the ABR scheme. In all these scenarios, we have shown that the length of the ABR queue is not a reliable indicator of congestion caused by the ABR sources, and leads to poor performance of the ABR schemes. To solve these problems, we have introduced the technique of *virtual queueing*. The switches construct a virtual queue, which represents the number of ABR cells that would be waiting at the switch if VBR were not present. By construction, the virtual queue is not affected by VBR traffic, and is a reliable indicator of congestion caused by ABR traffic. We have used the technique in *DMRCA with Virtual Queueing (DMRCA_VQ);* the new scheme achieves fair rate allocation also in presence of highly-bursty VBR traffic. We have also presented further refinements of *DMRCA_VQ* which use both virtual and real queue length as congestion indicators, and shown that these schemes not only achieve fairness, but also control congestion in the switch very effectively, thus requiring considerably smaller buffer sizes.

The virtual queueing technique can be viewed as a simple yet effective way to solve the more general problem of separating scheduling of multiple queues to share a common link from rate allocation based on the length of the queue(s). Scheduling directly impacts the length of the real queues, and thus influences rate allocation if the latter is based on the real queue length. Using the virtual queue concept, this undesired interaction is eliminated, and scheduling and rate allocation can be treated separately. In these terms, the virtual queueing technique has broader applications than what studied in this paper. For example, an other application where scheduling and rate allocation potentially interact, and therefore the virtual queueing technique is useful, is ABR rate allocation when Per-VC queueing is used.

## References


[1] ATM Forum Traffic Management Specification Version 4.0, ATM Forum Contribution 95-0013R10, Feb. 1996.

[2] H. Ohsaki et al., "Rate-Based Congestion Control for ATM Networks," *ACM SIGCOMM, Computer Communication Review*, Vol. 25 (2), April 1995.

[3] F. Bonomi and K. W. Fendick, "The Rate-Based Flow Control Framework for the Available Bit Rate ATM Service," *IEEE Network*, pp. 25-39, March/April 1995.

[4] A. Charny, "An Algorithm for Rate Allocation in a Packet-Switching Network with Feedback," *M.S. Thesis*, Dept. of Electrical Engineering and Computer Science, MIT, Cambridge, MA, May 1994.

[5] L. Kalampoukas, A. Varma, and K. K. Ramakrishnan, "Dynamics of An Explicit Rate Allocation Algorithm for Available-Bit-Rate (ABR) Service in ATM Networks," *Proc. 6th IFIP Int. Conf. High Performance Networking (HPN 95)*, pp. 143-154, Sept. 1995.

[6] A. Arulambalam, "A New Fair-Rate Allocation Algorithm for Available Bit Rate Services in ATM Networks," *Ph.D. Thesis*, Department of Electrical Engineering, New Jersey Institute of Technology, NJ, May 1996.

[7] R. Jain et al., "A Sample Switch Algorithm," ATM Forum Contribution 95-0178R1, 1995.

[8] H. Hsiaw *et al.*, "Closed-Loop Rate-based Traffic Management," *ATM Forum Contribution 94-0438R2*, Sept. 1994.

[9] K.-Y. Siu, and H.-Y. Tzeng, "Intelligent Congestion Control for ABR Service in ATM Networks," *ACM SIGCOMM, Computer Comm. Rev.*, 24, 5, pp. 81-106, Oct. 1995.

[10] F. M. Chiussi, Y. Xia, and V. P. Kumar, "Dynamic Max Rate Control Algorithm for Available Bit Rate Service in ATM Networks," *Proc. GLOBECOM '96*, pp. 2108-2117, London, UK, Nov. 1996.

[11] H. Osaki *et al.*, "Analysis of Rate-Based Congestion Control Algorithms for ATM Networks - Part 1: Steady State Analysis", *Proc. GLOBECOM '95*, pp. 296-303, Singapore, Nov. 1996.

# $M|G|\infty$ input processes: A versatile class of models for network traffic

Minothi Parulekar

Electrical Engineering Department
and Institute for Systems Research
University of Maryland
College Park, MD 20742

Armand M. Makowski

Electrical Engineering Department
and Institute for Systems Research
University of Maryland
College Park, MD 20742

## Abstract

We suggest the $M|G|\infty$ input process as a viable model for network traffic due to its versatility and tractability. We characterize the process as short or long–range dependent by means of a simple test. To gauge its performance, we study the large buffer asymptotics of a multiplexer driven by an $M|G|\infty$ input process. The decay rate of the tail probabilities for the buffer content (in steady–state) is investigated using large deviations techniques suggested by Duffield and O'Connell. We show that the selection of the appropriate large deviations scaling is related to the forward recurrence time of the service time distribution, and a closed–form expression is derived for the corresponding generalized limiting log–moment generating function associated with the input process. We apply our results to cases where the service time distribution in the $M|G|\infty$ input model is (i) Rayleigh (ii) Gamma (iii) Geometric (iv) Weibull (v) Log–normal and (vi) Pareto – cases (v) and (vi) have recently been found adequate for modeling packet traffic streams in certain networking applications. Finally, we comment on the insufficiency of the short– vs. long–range dependence characterization of an input process as a means to accurately describe the corresponding buffer dynamics.

## 1 Introduction

Several recent measurement studies have concluded that classical Poisson–like traffic models are ill-equipped to account for time dependencies observed at multiple time scales in a wide range of networking applications, including Ethernet LANs [8, 12, 22], VBR traffic [9], WAN traffic [21]. As the resulting temporal correlations are expected to have a significant impact on buffer engineering practices, this "failure of Poisson modeling" has generated an increased interest in a number of alternative traffic models which capture observed (long–range) dependencies. Proposed models include the fractional Brownian motion input model [15] and the fractional Gaussian noise input process [1]; already both have exposed clearly the limitations of traditional traffic models in predicting storage requirements and devising congestion controls.

In this paper we focus instead on the class of $M|G|\infty$ input processes as potential traffic models. An $M|G|\infty$ input process is understood as the busy server process of a discrete–time infinite server system fed by a discrete–time Poisson process of rate $\lambda$ (customers/slot) and with generic service time $\sigma$ distributed according to $G$. We argue that $M|G|\infty$ input processes constitute a viable alternative to existing traffic models; reasons which range from flexibility to tractability, are briefly presented below.

Firstly, the $M|G|\infty$ input model has been successfully investigated as a model for some wide area applications, e.g., Paxson and Floyd report a good fit to TELNET and FTP data using a log–normal service time [21]. However, the relevance of the $M|G|\infty$ input model to network traffic modelling is perhaps best explained through its connection to an attractive model for aggregate packet streams proposed by Likhanov, Tsybakov and Georganas [13]. They combine traffic generated by several on–off sources with a Pareto distributed activity period, and show that increasing the number of sources yields a limiting behaviour identical to the $M|G|\infty$ input stream with a Pareto distributed $\sigma$. As should be clear from their analysis, the limiting result holds for arbitrary activity period distributions,

*This work was supported through NSF Grant NSFD CDR-88-03012, NASA Grant NAGW277S and the Army Research Laboratory under Cooperative Agreement No. DAAL01-96-2-0002.

thereby providing a rationale for the view that $M|G|\infty$ input processes could provide a natural alternative to existing traffic models, at least for certain multiplexed applications. This limiting argument is similar to that of using the Palm–Khintchin Theorem to justify the Poisson model for interactive data traffic.

Secondly, the class of $M|G|\infty$ input processes has the desirable property of being stable under multiplexing, i.e., the superposition of several $M|G|\infty$ processes can be represented by an $M|G|\infty$ input process.

Thirdly, the $M|G|\infty$ model displays great flexibility in capturing positive dependencies over a wide range of time scales; this is achieved very simply through the tail behaviour of $\sigma$ [Prop. 3.1]. The degree of positive correlation can be further characterized by the sum of the autocovariances, or index of dispersion of counts (IDC), with the process being short-range dependent (i.e., IDC finite) if and only if $\mathbf{E}\left[\sigma^2\right]$ is finite [Prop. 3.2].

The temporal correlations of $M|G|\infty$ input processes are expected to affect queueing performance. Insights into this phenomenon can be gained by analyzing the behaviour of a multiplexer fed by an $M|G|\infty$ input process. For simplicity, we model the multiplexer as a discrete–time single server system consisting of an infinite size buffer and a server with a constant release rate $c$ (cells/slot). The number of customers in the input buffer at time $t$ is denoted by $q_t$. Our performance index is the steady–state buffer tail probability $\mathbf{P}[q_\infty > b]$, as this quantity is indicative of the buffer overflow probability in a corresponding finite buffer system with $b$ positions.

Computing these tail probabilities, either analytically or numerically, represents a challenging problem in the absence of any underlying Markov property for $M|G|\infty$ inputs. Instead, we focus on the simpler task of determining the tail behaviour of the queue–length distribution in some asymptotic sense. More precisely, we seek results of the form

$$\lim_{b\to\infty} \frac{1}{h(b)} \ln \mathbf{P}[q_\infty > b] = -\gamma \qquad (1.1)$$

for some positive constant $\gamma$ and mapping $h : \mathbb{R}_+ \to \mathbb{R}_+$; these quantities are characterized by $\lambda$, $G$ and $c$, and should be computable fairly easily. In Section 6 we present such asymptotics for several distributions, thin–tailed as well as heavy–tailed ones. Drastically different behaviors emerge depending on whether $v_t^\star = O(t)$ or $v_t^\star = o(t)$ [Thms. 5.1 and 5.2], where $v_t^\star = -\ln \mathbf{P}[\widehat{\sigma} > t]$ and $\widehat{\sigma}$ is the forward recurrence time (2.6) associated with $\sigma$.

Limits such as (1.1) provide a fair idea of the tail of the queue–length distribution, and suggest approximations of the form

$$\mathbf{P}[q_\infty > b] \sim e^{-h(b)\gamma} \quad (b \to \infty). \qquad (1.2)$$

Of course, the use of the right handside of (1.2) to estimate $\mathbf{P}[q_\infty > b]$ may be fraught with difficulties [4]. Nonetheless, (1.1) already provides some qualitative insights into the queueing behavior at the multiplexer, and could in principle be used to produce guidelines for sizing up its buffers.

Our focus here is primarily on large deviations techniques in order to obtain (1.1). This approach has already been adopted by a number of authors [7, 10, 11]. Applying results by Duffield and O'Connell [7] (and some recent extensions thereof [20]), we are able to compute $h(b)$ and $\gamma$ under reasonably general conditions. In fact, for a large class of distributions, we can select $h(b) = v_{[b]}^\star$, and the asymptotics (1.1)–(1.2) then take the compact form

$$\mathbf{P}[q_\infty > b] \sim \mathbf{P}[\widehat{\sigma} > b]^\gamma \quad (b \to \infty). \qquad (1.3)$$

Hence, in many cases, including Weibull, log–normal and Pareto service times, $q_\infty$ and $\widehat{\sigma}$ (thus $\sigma$) belong to the same distributional class as characterized by tail behavior.

Sometimes, in lieu of (1.1), these large deviations techniques yield only the weaker asymptotic bounds

$$-\gamma_\star \le \liminf_{b\to\infty} \frac{1}{h(b)} \ln \mathbf{P}[q_\infty > b] \qquad (1.4)$$

and

$$\limsup_{b\to\infty} \frac{1}{h(b)} \ln \mathbf{P}[q_\infty > b] \le -\gamma^\star. \qquad (1.5)$$

with $\gamma_\star \neq \gamma^\star$. This situation typically occurs when $\sigma$ is heavy–tailed with infinite $\mathbf{E}\left[\sigma^2\right]$, in which case large deviations excursions are only one of several causes for buffer exceedances [11]. Results such as (1.4) and (1.5) are still useful in providing *bounds* on decay rates.

Comparison of (1.3) with results from [15] and [17] points already to the complex and subtle impact of (long–range) dependencies on the tail probability $\mathbf{P}[q_\infty > b]$. Indeed, in [15] the input stream to the multiplexer was modeled as a fractional Gaussian noise process exhibiting long–range dependence (in fact, self–similarity), and the buffer asymptotics displayed Weibull–like characteristics. On the other hand, by the results described above, an $M|G|\infty$ input process with a Weibull service time also yields Weibull–like buffer asymptotics although the input process is now short–range dependent. Hence, the *same* asymptotic buffer behavior can be induced by two vastly different input streams, one long–range dependent and the other short–range dependent! To make matters worse, if the pmf $G$ were selected to be Pareto instead of Weibull, the input process would be long-range dependent, in fact asymptotically self-similar [17], but the buffer distribution would now exhibit Pareto-like asymptotics. To reiterate the main conclusion of [17], the value of the Hurst parameter as the sole indicator of long-range dependence (via asymptotic self-similarity) does not suffice for characterizing buffer asymptotics. Furthermore, buffer sizing cannot be determined adequately by appealing solely to the short versus long-range dependence characterization of the input model used, be it of the $M|G|\infty$ type or otherwise. Of course, long-range dependence (and its close cousin, self-similarity) are determined by second-order properties of the input process, while asymptotics of the form (1.1) invoke much finer probabilistic properties which are embedded in the sequence $\{v_t^\star,\ t=1,2,\ldots\}$. The finiteness of $\mathbf{E}\left[\sigma^2\right]$ (needed to ensure the finiteness of the IDC) is obviously a poor marker for predicting the behavior of this sequence. To close, the diverse queueing behavior, demonstrated here and tied to the tail behavior of $\sigma$, not only confirms the versatility of $M|G|\infty$ inputs as network traffic models, but also points to the need for a very careful and cautious approach in modeling network traffic when time dependencies are either observed or suspected.

The paper is organized as follows: We introduce both the class of $M|GI|\infty$ inputs as well as the multiplexer model in Section 2 along with various preliminaries. We discuss the correlation structure of the $M|GI|\infty$ input process in Section 3. Section 4 develops general results on buffer asymptotics which are applied to our specific model in Section 5. Finally, Section 6 illustrates the asymptotic results for various selections of distribution function $G$.

## 2 A multiplexer with $M|GI|\infty$ inputs

We model the multiplexer as a discrete-time single server queue with infinite buffer capacity which operates at a constant rate and in a first-come first-served manner: Let $q_t$ denote the number of cells remaining in the buffer by the end of slot $[t-1,t)$, and let $b_{t+1}$ denote the number of new cells which arrive at the start of time slot $[t,t+1)$. If the multiplexer output link can transmit $c$ cells/slot, then the buffer content sequence $\{q_t,\ t=0,1,\ldots\}$ evolves according to the Lindley recursion

$$q_0 = q; \quad q_{t+1} = [q_t + b_{t+1} - c]^+, \quad t=0,1,\ldots \tag{2.1}$$

for some initial condition $q$.

Here, we account for time dependencies in the cell input stream by modelling the arrival process $\{b_t,\ t= 0,1,\ldots\}$ as the busy server process of a discrete-time $M|G|\infty$ system. During time slot $[t,t+1)$, $\beta_{t+1}$ new customers arrive into the system. Customer $i$, $i=1,\ldots,\beta_{t+1}$, is presented to its own server and begins service by the start of slot $[t+1,t+2)$; its service time has duration $\sigma_{t+1,i}$. Let $b_t$ denote the number of busy servers, or equivalently of customers still present in the system, at the beginning of slot $[t,t+1)$, with $b$ denoting the number of busy servers initially present in the system at $t=0$.

The $I\!N$-valued rvs $b$, $\{\beta_{t+1},\ t=0,1,\ldots\}$ and $\{\sigma_{t,i},\ t=0,1,\ldots;\ i=1,2,\ldots\}$ satisfy the following assumptions: (i) The rvs are *mutually independent*; (ii) The rvs $\{\beta_{t+1},\ t=0,1,\ldots\}$ are *i.i.d.* Poisson rvs with parameter $\lambda>0$; (iii) The rvs $\{\sigma_{t,i},\ t=1,2,\ldots;\ i=1,2,\ldots\}$ are *i.i.d.* with common pmf $G$ on $\{1,2,\ldots\}$. We denote by $\sigma$ a generic $I\!N$-valued rv distributed according to the pmf $G$, and throughout we assume $\mathbf{E}[\sigma]<\infty$.

Many properties of $M|G|\infty$ input processes derive from the decomposition

$$b_t = b_t^{(0)} + b_t^{(a)}, \quad t=0,1,\ldots \tag{2.2}$$

where the rvs $b_t^{(0)}$ and $b_t^{(a)}$ describe the contributions to the number of customers in the system at the beginning of slot $[t,t+1)$ from those initially present (at $t=0$) and from the new arrivals, respectively. Under the enforced operational assumptions, we readily check for all $t=0,1,\ldots$ that

$$b_t^{(a)} = \sum_{s=1}^{t}\sum_{i=1}^{\beta_s} \mathbf{1}\left[\sigma_{s,i} > t-s\right] \tag{2.3}$$

and

$$b_t^{(0)} = \sum_{i=1}^{b} \mathbf{1}\left[\sigma_{0,i} > t\right]. \tag{2.4}$$

The rv $b_t^{(a)}$ can also be interpreted as the number of busy servers in the system at the beginning of slot $[t,t+1)$ given that the system was initially empty (i.e., $b=0$).

In the next proposition we state conditions for the queueing system (2.1) to admit a steady-state regime when driven by the busy server process $\{b_t,\ t= 0,1,\ldots\}$. Weak convergence is denoted by $\Longrightarrow$.

**Proposition 2.1** *If $\lambda\mathbf{E}[\sigma]<c$, then there exists an $\mathbb{R}_+$-valued rv $q_\infty$ such that $q_t \Longrightarrow_t q_\infty$ for any choice of the initial conditions $q$, $b$ and $\{\sigma_{0,i},\ i=1,2,\ldots\}$. The system is then said to be stable.*

In general, the busy server process $\{b_t,\ t=0,1,\ldots\}$ is *not* a (strictly) stationary process, and Proposition

2.1 will not follow directly from the well-known stability result of Loynes [14] for Lindley recursions driven by stationary and ergodic sequences. The characterization of stability flows instead from an extension of Loynes' result to driving sequences which *couple* with their stationary and ergodic versions [2]. Here, the busy server process $\{b_t,\ t = 0,1,\ldots\}$ indeed admits a stationary and ergodic version [16], thereafter denoted by $\{b_t^\star,\ t = 0,1,\ldots\}$, and with which it couples for any choice of the initial conditions $b$ and $\{\sigma_{0,i},\ i = 1,2,\ldots\}$. This stationary version $\{b_t^\star,\ t = 0,1,\ldots\}$ can represented through (2.2)–(2.4) with

$$b_t^{\star(0)} = \sum_{n=1}^{b} \mathbf{1}\left[\widehat{\sigma}_n > t\right], \quad t = 0,1,\ldots \tag{2.5}$$

where (i) the rvs $\{\widehat{\sigma}_n,\ n = 1,2,\ldots\}$ are independent of the rv $b$ which is Poisson distributed with parameter $\lambda\mathbf{E}[\sigma]$, and (ii) the rvs $\{\widehat{\sigma}_n,\ n = 1,2,\ldots\}$ are *i.i.d.* rvs distributed according to the *forward recurrence time* $\widehat{\sigma}$ associated with $\sigma$. This distribution is given by

$$\widehat{g}_r \equiv \mathbf{P}\left[\widehat{\sigma} = r\right] = \frac{\mathbf{P}\left[\sigma \geq r\right]}{\mathbf{E}\left[\sigma\right]}, \quad r = 1,2,\ldots \tag{2.6}$$

Throughout, we assume at a minimum the stability conditions $r_{in} < c$, where we have written $r_{in} \equiv \lambda\mathbf{E}[\sigma]$ to stress the fact that $\lambda\mathbf{E}[\sigma]$ indeed represents the average input rate into the multiplexer.

## 3 Correlation properties

We write

$$v_t^\star \equiv -\ln \mathbf{P}\left[\widehat{\sigma} > t\right], \quad t = 1,2,\ldots \tag{3.1}$$

The following properties are discussed in [5, 16].

**Proposition 3.1** *The stationary and ergodic version* $\{b_t^\star,\ t = 0,1,\ldots\}$ *of the busy server process has the following properties:*

**1.** *For each* $t = 0,1,\ldots$, *the rv* $b_t^\star$ *is a Poisson rv with parameter* $\lambda\mathbf{E}[\sigma]$;

**2.** *Its covariance structure is given by*

$$\begin{aligned} \Gamma(h) &\equiv \operatorname{cov}[b_t^\star, b_{t+h}^\star] \\ &= \lambda\mathbf{E}\left[(\sigma - h)^+\right] \\ &= \lambda\mathbf{E}[\sigma]\, e^{-v_h^\star}, \quad t,h = 0,1,2,\ldots \end{aligned} \tag{3.2}$$

*with the convention* $v_0 \equiv 0$.

The strength of the positive correlation exhibited by the sequence $\{b_t^\star,\ t = 0,1,\ldots\}$ can be formalized as follows: We say that the sequence $\{b_t^\star,\ t = 0,1,\ldots\}$ exhibits *short-range dependence* if

$$\sum_{h=0}^{\infty} \Gamma(h) < \infty. \tag{3.3}$$

Otherwise, the sequence $\{b_t^\star,\ t = 0,1,\ldots\}$ is said to be *long-range dependent* [3]. For $M|G|\infty$ processes this notion of dependence has a simple characterization.

**Proposition 3.2** *We have the relation*

$$\sum_{h=0}^{\infty} \Gamma(h) = \lambda\mathbf{E}[\sigma]\,\mathbf{E}[\widehat{\sigma}] = \frac{\lambda}{2}\mathbf{E}\left[\sigma(\sigma+1)\right], \tag{3.4}$$

*so that the stationary sequence* $\{b_t^\star,\ t = 0,1,\ldots\}$ *is short-range (resp. long-range) dependent if and only if* $\mathbf{E}\left[\sigma^2\right]$ *is finite (resp. infinite).*

## 4 General Buffer Asymptotics

Several authors [7, 10, 11] have derived asymptotics such as (1.1) by means of large deviations estimates associated with the sequence $\{t^{-1}(S_t - ct),\ t = 0,1,\ldots\}$, where

$$S_0 = 0; \quad S_t = b_1^\star + \ldots + b_t^\star, \quad t = 1,2,\ldots \tag{4.1}$$

These results have been obtained in varying degrees of generality, and are summarized below as they apply to the present context.

To fix the terminology, a scaling sequence is any monotone increasing $\mathbb{R}$-valued sequence $\{v_t,\ t = 0,1,\ldots\}$ such that $\lim_{t\to\infty} v_t = \infty$. A sequence of $\mathbb{R}$-valued rvs $\{x_t,\ t = 0,1,\ldots\}$ is said to satisfy the *Large Deviations Principle under scaling* $v_t$ if there exists a lower-semicontinuous function $I : \mathbb{R} \to [0,\infty]$ such that for every open set $G$,

$$-\inf_{x\in G} I(x) \leq \liminf_{t\to\infty} \frac{1}{v_t} \ln \mathbf{P}\left[x_t \in G\right] \tag{4.2}$$

and for every closed set $F$,

$$\limsup_{t\to\infty} \frac{1}{v_t} \ln \mathbf{P}\left[x_t \in F\right] \leq -\inf_{x\in F} I(x). \tag{4.3}$$

The *rate function* $I$ is said to be good if for each $r > 0$, the level set $\{x \in \mathbb{R} :\ I(x) \leq r\}$ is a compact subset of $\mathbb{R}$.

Consider a scaling sequence $\{v_t,\ t = 0,1,\ldots\}$ with the property that there exist functions $g, h : \mathbb{R}_+ \to \mathbb{R}_+$ such that $h$ is monotone increasing with $\lim_{b\to\infty} h(b) = \infty$, and the limit

$$\lim_{b\to\infty} \frac{v_{\lfloor b/y \rfloor}}{h(b)} = g(y), \quad y > 0 \tag{4.4}$$

holds. The following theorem is essentially due to Duffield and O'Connell [7].

**Proposition 4.1** *If the process* $\{t^{-1}(S_t - ct),\ t = 1, 2, \ldots\}$ *satisfies the Large Deviations lower bound (4.2) with good rate function* $I : \mathbb{R} \to [0, \infty]$ *(under scaling* $v_t$*), then we have (1.4) with*

$$\gamma_\star \equiv \inf_{y>0}\left(g(y) \inf_{x>y} I(x)\right). \qquad (4.5)$$

The existence of (4.2) (and for that matter, of (4.3)) is typically validated through the Gärtner–Ellis Theorem [6, Thm. 2.3.6, p. 45]: In that context, for each $t = 1, 2, \ldots$, we define

$$\Lambda_t(\theta) \equiv \frac{1}{v_t} \ln \mathbf{E}\left[\exp\left(\theta v_t \frac{S_t - ct}{t}\right)\right], \quad \theta \in \mathbb{R}, \ (4.6)$$

and it is required that for each $\theta$ in $\mathbb{R}$, the limit

$$\Lambda(\theta) \equiv \lim_{t\to\infty} \Lambda_t(\theta) \qquad (4.7)$$

exists (possibly as an extended real number). Under broad conditions, the process $\{t^{-1}(S_t - ct),\ t = 1, 2, \ldots\}$ then satisfies the Large Deviations Principle under scaling $v_t$ with good rate function $\Lambda^\star : \mathbb{R} \to [0, \infty]$, where $\Lambda^\star$ is the Legendre–Fenchel transform of the mapping $\Lambda : \mathbb{R} \to (-\infty, \infty]$ defined through (4.7), namely

$$\Lambda^\star(z) \equiv \sup_{\theta\in\mathbb{R}}\{\theta z - \Lambda(\theta)\}, \quad z \in \mathbb{R}. \qquad (4.8)$$

By the convexity of $\Lambda^\star : \mathbb{R} \to [0, \infty]$, and the fact that it is monotone non–decreasing on $[0, \infty)$, we easily check in cases of practical interest that

$$\gamma_\star \equiv \inf_{y>0} g(y)\Lambda^\star(y). \qquad (4.9)$$

In [7], the companion upper bound (1.5) was derived under a set of conditions which unfortunately do not cover some instances of the $M|G|\infty$ process considered here. Upon refining the arguments of [7], we have established the following asymptotic upper bound; details are available in [20].

**Proposition 4.2** *Assume the following conditions:*

**1.** *For each* $\theta$ *in* $\mathbb{R}$*, the limit (4.7) exists (possibly as an extended real number);*

**2.** *For some finite* $K \geq 0$*, we have*

$$\lim_{t\to\infty} \frac{\ln t}{v_t} = K. \qquad (4.10)$$

*Then, for each* $y > 0$ *we have*

$$\limsup_{b\to\infty} \frac{1}{h(b)} \ln \mathbf{P}[q_\infty > b] \leq -\min(\alpha(y), \beta(y))$$

*with the notation*

$$\alpha(y) = -Kg(y) + \sup_{\theta>0} \liminf_{n\to\infty}\left(\inf_{x>y}\left(\frac{v_n}{h(nx)}(\theta x - \Lambda(\theta))\right)\right) \qquad (4.11)$$

*and*

$$\beta(y) = (\Lambda^\star(0) - K)\, g(y). \qquad (4.12)$$

The case $K = 0$ is equivalent to Hypothesis 2.2(iv) in [7]. Moreover, the upper bound is trivial in cases where $\Lambda^\star(0) \leq K$. As the least upper bound is the sharpest, under the assumptions of Proposition 4.2 we immediately get (1.5) with

$$\gamma^\star = \sup_{y>0} \min(\alpha(y), \beta(y)). \qquad (4.13)$$

When the conditions of Propositions 4.1 and 4.2 are enforced, then the asymptotics (1.1) will follow *provided* $\gamma_\star = \gamma^\star$. As indicated in Section 6, such a result holds in the *linear* case ($v_t = t$) [7, 10, 11]; the calculations are detailed in [20]. However, it is certainly possible to have $\gamma_\star \neq \gamma^\star$, and we shall encounter such a situation in Section 6.

## 5 Evaluation of $\gamma_\star$, $\gamma^\star$ and $h(b)$

The key step in applying the results of the previous section consists in finding a scaling sequence $\{v_t,\ t = 0, 1, \ldots\}$ such that for each $\theta$ in $\mathbb{R}$, the limit (4.7) exists (possibly as an extended real number). In [18], we show that the selection of this scaling is governed by the behavior of (3.1). This is done under the assumption that the limit

$$\lim_{t\to\infty} \frac{v_t^\star}{t} = R \qquad (5.1)$$

exists (possibly infinite); this is a very mild assumption which holds in all known situations. The choice of the appropriate scaling $v_t$ turns out to depend on whether $R = \infty$ (Case I), $0 < R < \infty$ (Case II) and $R = 0$ (Case III).

To state the results more conveniently, we set

$$\Lambda_{b,t}(\theta) \equiv \frac{1}{v_t} \ln \mathbf{E}\left[\exp(\frac{v_t}{t}\theta S_t)\right], \quad \theta \in \mathbb{R} \qquad (5.2)$$

for each $t = 1, 2, \ldots$. Obviously, if the limit

$$\Lambda_b(\theta) \equiv \lim_{t\to\infty} \Lambda_{b,t}(\theta), \quad \theta \in \mathbb{R} \qquad (5.3)$$

exists (possibly infinite), so does (4.7) with

$$\Lambda(\theta) = \Lambda_b(\theta) - c\theta, \quad \theta \in \mathbb{R} \qquad (5.4)$$

and it suffices to concentrate on finding (5.3). The main facts along these lines are developed in the next two theorems; proofs are available in [16, 18]. Cases I and II are covered first:

**Theorem 5.1** *Assume $R > 0$, possibly infinite, and take the linear scaling*

$$v_t = t, \quad t = 1, 2, \ldots \tag{5.5}$$

*Then, for each $\theta$ in $\mathbb{R}$, the limit $\Lambda_b(\theta) \equiv \lim_{t\to\infty} \Lambda_{b,t}(\theta)$ exists and is given by*

$$\Lambda_b(\theta) = \lambda \mathbf{E}\left[e^{\theta\sigma} - 1\right], \tag{5.6}$$

*with $\mathbf{E}\left[e^{\theta\sigma}\right]$ finite (resp. infinite) if $\theta < R$ (resp. $R < \theta$).*

As we now turn to Case III, we find it convenient to say that the sequence $\{v_t^\star/t,\ t = 1, 2, \ldots\}$ is monotone decreasing in the limit if there exists a finite integer $T$ such that the tail $\{v_t^\star/t,\ t = T+1, T+2, \ldots\}$ is monotone decreasing.

**Theorem 5.2** *Assume $R = 0$ with $\{v_t^\star/t,\ t = 1, 2, \ldots\}$ monotone decreasing in the limit, and take the scaling*

$$v_t = v_t^\star, \quad t = 1, 2, \ldots \tag{5.7}$$

*Then, for each $\theta \neq 1$ in $\mathbb{R}$, the limit $\Lambda_b(\theta) \equiv \lim_{t\to\infty} \Lambda_{b,t}(\theta)$ exists and is given by*

$$\Lambda_b(\theta) = \begin{cases} \lambda \mathbf{E}[\sigma]\theta & \text{if } \theta < 1 \\ \infty & \text{if } \theta > 1, \end{cases} \tag{5.8}$$

*provided there exists a mapping $\Gamma : \mathbb{N} \to \mathbb{N}$ such that (i) $\Gamma(t) < t$ for all large $t = 1, 2, \ldots$, (ii) $\lim_{t\to\infty} v_t^\star \frac{\Gamma(t)}{t} = \infty$ and (iii) $\lim_{t\to\infty} \frac{v_t^\star}{t} \frac{\Gamma(t)}{v_{\Gamma(t)}^\star} = 0$.*

The assumptions of Theorem 5.2 are satisfied in all cases known to the authors, and are easy to check for broad classes of distributions. The boundary case $\theta = 1$ in (5.8) appears to depend crucially on the pmf $G$. However, it can be shown [16] that $\lim_{t\to\infty} \Lambda_{b,t}(1)$ does exist for the examples discussed here. In fact, a little thought indicates that the *existence* of this limit suffices for our purpose, in that its *specific* value is not of any consequence in evaluating $\gamma_\star$ given by (4.9). Indeed, in that case, under the assumptions of Theorem 5.2, we see from (4.8) and (5.4) that

$$\begin{aligned} \Lambda^\star(z) &= \sup_{\theta\in\mathbb{R}}\{\theta z - (\Lambda_b(\theta) - c\theta)\} \\ &= \sup_{\theta\le 1}\{(c+z)\theta - \Lambda_b(\theta)\} \\ &= \sup_{\theta< 1}\{(c+z)\theta - \lambda\mathbf{E}[\sigma]\theta\}, \quad z \in \mathbb{R} \end{aligned}$$

where in the last step we exploited the fact $\lim_{\theta\uparrow 1} \Lambda_b(\theta) \le \Lambda_b(1)$. From the stability condition $\lambda\mathbf{E}[\sigma] = r_{in} < c$, we get

$$\Lambda^\star(z) = z + c - r_{in}, \quad z > 0, \tag{5.9}$$

whence

$$\gamma_\star = \inf_{y>0} g(y)(y + c - r_{in}). \tag{5.10}$$

As became apparent when considering the examples presented in Section 6, the term $v_t$ often takes on a form which is computationally inconvenient to check the various technical conditions. Fortunately, only the *asymptotic* behavior of $v_t$ matters when applying the results of Sections 4 and 5: Indeed, with another scaling sequence $\{w_t,\ t = 1, 2, \ldots\}$, it is easy to see that the appropriate conditions can all be checked by replacing $v_t$ by $w_t$ provided these two scaling sequences are *asymptotically* equivalent in the sense that

$$\lim_{t\to\infty} \frac{w_t}{v_t} = 1. \tag{5.11}$$

Hopefully, the scaling sequence $\{w_t,\ t = 1, 2, \ldots\}$ is more tractable analytically.

For a number of distributions, as will be seen in Section 6, it is natural to select $h(b) = v_{[b]}^\star$, in which case the asymptotics (1.2) take the form

$$\mathbf{P}[q_\infty > b] \sim \mathbf{P}[\widehat{\sigma} > b]^{\gamma^*} \quad (b \to \infty). \tag{5.12}$$

Hence, for a number of distributions the tail behaviours of the service time $\sigma$ and of the queue length $q_\infty$ are of the same type.

## 6 Examples

We illustrate these asymptotic results for various choices of the pmf $G$; in each case we identify $h(b)$, and compute $\gamma_\star$ and $\gamma^\star$ in closed form (whenever possible). The results are presented in order of increasing weight on the tail of $G$, or equivalently, in order of increasing time dependence. Details of the calculations are available in [19].

We begin with a general result which covers Cases I and II. When $R > 0$, Theorem 5.1 suggests $v_t = t$, so that $h(b) = b$ and $g(y) = y^{-1}$, and we have

$$\Lambda(\theta) = \lambda\mathbf{E}\left[e^{\theta\sigma} - 1\right] - c\theta, \quad \theta \in \mathbb{R}. \tag{6.1}$$

The existence of the full Large Deviations Principle (hence of (4.2)) for $\{t^{-1}(S_t - ct),\ t = 1, 2, \ldots\}$ is readily obtained via the Gärtner–Ellis Theorem [6, Thm. 2.3.6, p. 45]. Next, from (4.9) we get

$$\gamma_\star = \inf_{y>0} \frac{\Lambda^\star(y)}{y} \tag{6.2}$$

while easy calculations, via (4.12)–(4.13), lead to

$$\gamma^\star = \sup\{\theta : \theta > 0, \Lambda(\theta) < 0\}. \tag{6.3}$$

Combining these facts with Propositions 4.1 and 4.2, we finally obtain the following asymptotics.

**Proposition 6.1** *Assume $R > 0$. Then, the asymptotics*

$$\lim_{b\to\infty} \frac{1}{b} \ln \mathbf{P}[q_\infty > b] = -\gamma \tag{6.4}$$

*holds, with $\gamma_\star = \gamma^\star \equiv \gamma$.*

Proposition 6.1 covers the situations where the tail of $G$ decays *at least* exponentially fast, e.g., the Rayleigh, Gamma and geometric cases. This result is of course not new; it has been obtained earlier by several authors [7, 10, 11] and paves the way to the notion of *effective bandwidth.* However, the arguments leading to it, which are detailed in [20], already show that the upper bound of Proposition 4.2 is good enough to recover this "classical" case.

The remaining examples fit Case III, so that by Theorem 5.2, we can take $v_t = v_t^\star$ (or any scaling sequence asymptotically equivalent to it) and we have

$$\Lambda(\theta) = \begin{cases} (\lambda\mathbf{E}[\sigma] - c)\theta & \text{if } \theta < 1 \\ \infty & \text{if } \theta > 1. \end{cases} \tag{6.5}$$

Unfortunately, the Gärtner–Ellis Theorem [6, Thm. 2.3.6, p. 45] will now yield a trivial lower bound (4.2) for $\{t^{-1}(S_t - ct),\ t = 1, 2, \ldots\}$. Nevertheless, for reasons argued below, we believe that such a lower bound holds in many cases of interest, with case–specific arguments needed to establish it.

The pmf $G$ of the rv $\sigma$ is an (integer–valued) Weibull distribution with parameters $(a, \beta)$ $(a > 0, 0 < \beta < 1)$ if $\sigma =_{st} \lceil X \rceil$ where the rv $X$ is a Weibull rv with parameters $(a, \beta)$, i.e.,

$$\mathbf{P}[X \le x] = 1 - e^{-ax^\beta}, \quad x \ge 0 \tag{6.6}$$

**Proposition 6.2** *If $G$ is a discrete Weibull distribution with parameters $(a, \beta)$ $(a > 0, 0 < \beta < 1)$, then*

$$\limsup_{b\to\infty} \frac{1}{b^\beta} \ln \mathbf{P}[q_\infty > b] \le -\gamma_{\mathrm{W}}^\star \tag{6.7}$$

*where*

$$\gamma_{\mathrm{W}}^\star = \frac{a}{\beta}\left(\frac{\beta(c - r_{in})}{1 - \beta}\right)^{1-\beta}. \tag{6.8}$$

The pmf $G$ of the rv $\sigma$ is an (integer–valued) log–normal distribution with parameters $(\mu, \delta)$ $(\delta > 0)$ if $\sigma =_{st} \lceil X \rceil$ for some log–normal rv $X$ of the form $X =_{st} \exp(Y)$ where $Y$ is a Gaussian rv with mean $\mu$ and variance $\delta^2$.

**Proposition 6.3** *If $G$ is a discrete log–normal distribution with parameters $(\mu, \delta)$ $(\delta > 0)$, then*

$$\limsup_{b\to\infty} \frac{1}{(\ln b)^2} \ln \mathbf{P}[q_\infty > b] \le -\gamma_{\mathrm{L}}^\star \tag{6.9}$$

*where*

$$\gamma_{\mathrm{L}}^\star = \frac{c - r_{in}}{2\delta^2}. \tag{6.10}$$

In all the cases considered thus far, $\mathbf{E}[\sigma^2]$ is finite, and the process $\{b_t^\star, t = 0, 1, \ldots\}$ is therefore short–range dependent by Proposition 3.2. Using the expression (4.9) for the constant entering the asymptotic lower bound (1.4), we readily confirm the equalities

$$\gamma_{\mathrm{W}}^\star = \gamma_{\star,\mathrm{W}} \quad \text{and} \quad \gamma_{\mathrm{L}}^\star == \gamma_{\star,\mathrm{L}}. \tag{6.11}$$

Hence, were we to apply Proposition 4.1 blindly (without further justification), we could then replace (6.7) and (6.9) by their appropriate version of the stronger limiting equality (1.1). Therefore, equality (6.11) raises one's hopes that the lower bound (4.2) indeed holds for $\{t^{-1}(S_t - ct),\ t = 1, 2, \ldots\}$ in the Weibull and log–normal cases. Work on this issue is in progress.

Finally, the pmf $G$ is said to be a Pareto distribution with parameter $\alpha$ $(1 < \alpha < 2)$ if

$$\lim_{r\to\infty} \frac{\mathbf{P}[\sigma > r]}{r^{-\alpha}} = 1. \tag{6.12}$$

**Proposition 6.4** *If $G$ is a discrete Pareto distribution with parameter $\alpha$ $(1 < \alpha < 2)$, then*

$$\limsup_{b\to\infty} \frac{1}{\ln b} \ln \mathbf{P}[q_\infty > b] \le -\gamma_{\mathrm{P}}^\star \tag{6.13}$$

*where*

$$\gamma_{\mathrm{P}}^\star = (\alpha - 1)(c - r_{in}) - 1. \tag{6.14}$$

Here, the condition $(\alpha - 1)(c - r_{in}) > 1$ is required for otherwise the bound (6.13) is trivial. It is easy to see that $\mathbf{E}[\sigma] < \infty$ while $\mathbf{E}[\sigma^2] = \infty$, and the process $\{b_t^\star, t = 0, 1, \ldots\}$ is long–range dependent. Moreover, we have $\gamma_{\mathrm{P}}^\star < \gamma_{\star,\mathrm{P}}$ with $\gamma_{\star,\mathrm{P}} = (\alpha - 1)(c - r_{in})$. Although this inequality is not sufficient by itself to reach any negative conclusion concerning the existence of the lower bound (4.2) for $\{t^{-1}(S_t - ct),\ t = 1, 2, \ldots\}$ in the Pareto case, it already implies at the very least that the asymptotic bounds (1.4) and (1.5) are certainly *not* tight in that case. This strongly suggests that in the long–range dependent case, the investigation of the buffer asymptotics will require that we look beyond large deviations techniques. Going back to the heuristics given in [11], we attribute this to the fact that now buffer exceedances cannot be explained entirely by large deviations excursions in the arrival stream, as there is a need to take into consideration the effect of a single customer with a large workload – the tail of the distribution has become too heavy to neglect such a customer! Hence, any argument based on large deviations techniques *alone* is bound to fall short. However, we conjecture that (1.1) still holds with scaling $h(b) = \ln b$ as specified through (4.4) but of course with a different value for $\gamma$. These issues are currently being investigated.

## References


[1] R.G. Addie, M. Zukerman and T. Neame, "Fractal traffic: Measurements, modeling and performance evaluation," in *Proceedings of Infocom '95*, Boston (MA), April 1995, pp. 985-992.

[2] F. Baccelli and P. Brémaud, *Elements of Queueing Theory: Palm–Martingale Calculus and Stochastic Recurrences*, Applications of Mathematics **26**, Springer–Verlag, Berlin Heidelberger, 1994.

[3] J. Beran, *Statistics for Long-Memory Processes*, Chapman and Hall, New York (NY), 1994.

[4] G.L. Choudhury, D.M. Lucantoni and W. Whitt, "Squeezing the most out of ATM," *IEEE Transactions on Communications* **COM–44** (1996), pp. 203–217.

[5] D. R. Cox, "Long–Range Dependence: A Review," *Statistics: An Appraisal*, H. A. David and H. T. David, Eds., The Iowa State University Press, Ames (IA), 1984, pp. 55–74.

[6] A. Dembo and O. Zeitouni, *Large Deviation Techniques and Applications*, Jones and Bartlett, Boston (MA), 1993.

[7] N. G. Duffield and N. O'Connell, "Large deviations and overflow probabilities for the general single server queue, with applications," *Mathematical Proceedings of the Cambridge Philosophical Society* **118** (1995), pp. 363–374.

[8] H. J. Fowler and W. E. Leland, "Local area network traffic characteristics, with implications for broadband network congestion management," *IEEE Journal on Selected Areas in Communications* **JSAC–9** (1991), pp. 1139–1149.

[9] M. Garrett and W. Willinger, "Analysis, modeling and generation of self-similar VBR video traffic," *Proceedings of SIGCOMM '94*, September 1994, pp. 269–280.

[10] P.W. Glynn and W. Whitt, "Logarithmic asymptotics for steady–state tail probabilities in a single–server queue," *Journal of Applied Probability* **31** (1994), pp. 131–159.

[11] G. Kesidis, J. Walrand and C.S. Chang, "Effective bandwidths for multiclass Markov fluids and other ATM sources," *IEEE/ACM Transactions on Networking* **1** (1993), pp. 424–428.

[12] W. Leland, M. Taqqu, W. Willinger, and D. Wilson, "On the self–similar nature of ethernet traffic (extended version)," *IEEE/ACM Transactions on Networking* **2** (1994), pp. 1–15.

[13] N. Likhanov, B. Tsybakov and N.D. Georganas, "Analysis of an ATM buffer with self–similar ("fractal") input traffic," in *Proceedings of Infocom '95*, Boston (MA), April 1995, pp. 985–992.

[14] R.M. Loynes, "The stability of a queue with non–independent inter–arrival and service times," *Proceedings of the Cambridge Philosophical Society* **58** (1962), pp. 497–520.

[15] I. Norros, "A storage model with self–similar input," *Queueing Systems – Theory & Applications* **16** (1994), pp. 387-396.

[16] M. Parulekar, *Buffer Engineering for Self–Similar Traffic*, Ph.D. Thesis, Electrical Engineering Department, University of Maryland, College Park (MD). Expected August 1996.

[17] M. Parulekar and A.M. Makowski, "Tail probabilities for a multiplexer with self–similar traffic," Infocom'96, April 1996, San Francisco (CA), April 1996, pp. 1452–1459.

[18] M. Parulekar and A.M. Makowski, "Tail probabilities for $M|G|\infty$ input processes (I): Preliminary asymptotics," *Queueing Systems – Theory & Applications*, submitted (1996).

[19] M. Parulekar and A.M. Makowski, "Tail probabilities for $M|G|\infty$ input processes (II): Buffer asymptotics" in preparation.

[20] M. Parulekar and A.M. Makowski, "Asymptotic tail probabilities for general single server queues: Another look," in preparation.

[21] V. Paxson and S. Floyd, "Wide area traffic: The failure of Poisson modeling," *IEEE/ACM Transactions on Networking* **3** (1993), pp. 226–244.

[22] W. Willinger, M. S. Taqqu, W. E. Leland and D. V. Wilson, "Self–similarity in high–speed packet traffic: Analysis and modeling of ethernet traffic measurements," *Statistical Science*, to appear.

# Peakedness Measures for Traffic Characterization in High-Speed Networks

Brian L. Mark, David L. Jagerman and G. Ramamurthy

C & C Research Laboratories
NEC USA, Inc.
4 Independence Way
Princeton, NJ 08540

## Abstract

*In high-speed networks based on Asynchronous Transfer Mode (ATM), variable bit rate (VBR) sources generate bursty cell streams which share link bandwidth wherever multiplexing occurs. In theory, the bandwidth requirement per stream to support a given quality-of-service at a multiplexer should generally decrease as the number of streams increases. In practice, high statistical multiplexing gain is difficult to achieve because good traffic characterizations are usually not available. This paper proposes the use of peakedness-based measures to capture the statistical information from traffic streams needed to determine bandwidth allocations. The standard definition of peakedness applies only to point process models of traffic. Yet fluid models of traffic have certain advantages in terms of tractability. Hence, we introduce a new measure called modified peakedness, which encompasses point process and fluid models under a common framework. We develop some of its properties and specialize it to several common traffic models. Finally, we study the effectiveness of the peakedness/modified peakedness as burstiness measures for real-time traffic.*

## 1 Introduction

High-speed networks will be able to support large numbers of connections with widely varying bandwidth requirements. Due to recent advances in switching and transmission technology, the potential bandwidth available to users has increased dramatically. However, with the emergence of new bandwidth intensive multimedia applications and increased network usage, bandwidth remains a precious commodity which must be allocated efficiently. An important first step in resource allocation is to obtain a simple, yet meaningful characterization of the traffic.

In networks based on the Asynchronous Transfer Mode (ATM), traffic streams consist of fixed sized cells which are transmitted and switched asynchronously over high-speed links. Traffic streams belonging to different connections share link bandwidth at switch output ports and access multiplexers. Typical variable bit rate (VBR) sources generate bursty cell streams. The burstiness of a cell stream is often defined as the ratio of the peak to mean cell arrival rate. For a given quality-of-service (measured in terms of cell loss or cell delay), the bandwidth required by a single bursty stream will be close to the peak rate. However, when a number of the these streams are multiplexed, the required bandwidth per stream may be much smaller than the peak rate (but larger than the mean rate), since the aggregate stream may be much less bursty than the individual stream. Accurate and efficient traffic characterization is essential to achieving statistical multiplexing gain in practice.

In this paper, we propose traffic characterization using measures based on the peakedness concept. Roughly speaking, peakedness is a statistical measure of the effect of an arrival stream on an infinite server system. As such, it is a measure of the amount of resource required by a stream in the context of a particular service system. The concept of peakedness was originally developed by teletraffic engineers to characterize call arrival arrival streams modeled as stationary point processes for approximating blocking probabilities at trunk groups. Our purpose here is somewhat different; we wish to characterize high-speed traffic streams in order to allocate bandwidth at multiplexing points within a network. We seek an empirical traffic characterization which captures the essential information needed for allocating resources. Moreover, the characterization should be capable of being mapped to a variety of traffic models which can then be used to perform resource allocation. While traffic streams are often modeled as point process arrivals, fluid models of traffic are often used in performance studies involving high-speed traffic because they are more computationally tractable. However, the definition of peakedness applies only to point processes.

We introduce a new statistical measure of traffic burstiness called *modified peakedness* which is applicable to both point process and fluid models. As such, it unifies the fluid and point process models under a common framework. Section 3 provides a definition for modified peakedness and develops several of its properties. From observations of a traffic stream, the modified peakedness can be obtained empirically and mapped to a simple traffic model which captures the



0-8186-7780-5/97 $10.00 © 1997 IEEE

main information about the traffic stream contained in the peakedness measure. Section 5 discusses how to obtain the peakedness measures empirically and provides an example for an MPEG video sequence. For brevity, we omit proofs of the results stated in the paper; they can be found in [1].

To set this work in its appropriate context, we mention some related work. Various authors have studied statistical multiplexing assuming that the streams are represented by certain traffic models. However, the crucial link between the actual observed traffic and the traffic model is usually not addressed. Some authors, have proposed a deterministic approach to network analysis (cf. [2]). By assuming worst-case traffic behavior conforming to leaky bucket parameters, deterministic end-to-end delay bounds can be derived for networks composed of basic network elements assumed to have infinite buffer capacities. An important feature of the leaky bucket-based descriptor is that it can be specified by the user and then enforced by the network (see [3] for a method of choosing appropriate leaky bucket parameters). Unfortunately, deterministic leaky bucket-based characterization can lead to overly conservative resource allocation. To improve network utilization, information from the observed traffic must play a role in resource allocation. Peakedness measures provide statistical information about traffic that can be obtained empirically and used to allocate resources efficiently in a real-time environment.

## 2 Peakedness

In this section, we give a brief overview of the peakedness theory for call arrival processes (cf. [4]). A call arrival process can be modeled as a *stationary point process* where each point event corresponds to an arrival of a call at a trunk group. The point process is specified by a *counting process* $\{N_t, t > 0\}$, where $N_t$ represents the number of arrivals in the interval $(0, t]$. With probability one, the sample paths of $N$ are positive integer-valued, increasing and right-continuous. The process experiences an integer-valued jump at each arrival epoch $T_i$. In addition, if each jump is of unit magnitude with probability one, then the point process is called *orderly*. However, in general, several arrival epochs may coincide, i.e., arrivals may occur in batches.

Peakedness of an arrival process is defined as follows. The arrivals are offered to an infinite group of servers with mutually independent service times (which are also independent of the process $N$) with common cumulative distribution function (cdf) $F$. Let $S_t$ be the number of *busy* servers at time $t \geq 0$. The mean service time, $\mu_F^{-1}$, is assumed to be positive and finite and is given by

$$\mu_F^{-1} = \int_0^\infty F^c(x)dx, \qquad (1)$$

where $F^c = 1 - F$ is the complementary service time distribution function.

The *peakedness functional* of the arrival process with respect to the service time distribution $F$ is defined by

$$z[F] = \lim_{t\to\infty} \frac{\mathrm{Var}[S_t]}{\mathrm{E}[S_t]}. \qquad (2)$$

Peakedness is more commonly expressed as a function of the service rate $\mu$. Let $F_1$ denote the cdf $F$ scaled so that the service rate is unity, i.e.,

$$F_1(x) \triangleq F(x/\mu_F), \quad x \geq 0. \qquad (3)$$

Define the scaled cdf $F_\mu$ with mean service rate $\mu$ by

$$F_\mu(x) = F_1(\mu x), \quad x \geq 0. \qquad (4)$$

The *peakedness function* with respect to the family of scaled service distributions represented by $F_1$ is defined by:

$$z_{F_1}(\mu) \triangleq z[F_\mu]. \qquad (5)$$

Peakedness can be expressed in terms of the second order statistics of the arrival process as follows [4]:

$$z[F] = 1 + \frac{\mu}{\lambda}\int_{-\infty}^{\infty} [k(x) - \lambda\delta(x)]F^*(x)dx, \qquad (6)$$

where $\delta(x)$ is the Dirac delta function, $F^*$ is the autocorrelation function of $F^c$ defined by

$$\begin{aligned} F^*(t) &= \int_0^\infty F^c(x)F^c(t+x)dx, \\ F^*(-t) &= F^*(t), \qquad \text{for } t \geq 0. \end{aligned} \qquad (7)$$

and $k(x)$ is the *covariance density* of the arrival process defined by

$$\frac{\partial^2}{\partial u \partial v}K_N(u,v) \triangleq k(u-v) = k(v-u), \quad u, v > 0, \qquad (8)$$

where $K_N(u,v) = \mathrm{Cov}[N_u, N_v]$ is the *covariance function*. The covariance density can be decomposed as $k(x) = k_1\delta(x) + k_0(x)$, where

$$k_0(x) = \frac{1}{2}\frac{d^2}{dt^2}K_N(x,x) \qquad (9)$$

is a (generalized) function containing no delta function at the origin and $k_1 = \lambda\beta_2/\beta_1$ , where $\beta_1$ and $\beta_2$ are, respectively, the first and second moments of the batch sizes [1]. From (6), we obtain a second representation for peakedness [4]:

$$z[F] = 1 + \frac{\mu}{\lambda}\left\{\frac{\lambda(\beta_2 - \beta_1)}{\beta_1}F^*(0) + \int_{0+}^{\infty}\frac{d^2}{dx^2}K_N(x,x)^*(x)dx\right\} \qquad (10)$$

[1] In the case of orderly arrivals, $\beta_1 = \beta_2 = 1$ and $k_1 = \lambda$.

Peakedness with respect to exponential service time distribution is of particular interest in teletraffic systems where the call holding times are usually well approximated by exponential random variables. The peakedness with respect to exponential service can be derived from (10) as:

$$z_{exp}(\mu) = \frac{k_1 + \lambda}{2\lambda} + \frac{1}{\lambda}\int_{0+}^{\infty} k_0(x)e^{-\mu x}dx. \qquad (11)$$

From (11), it can be deduced that knowledge of the peakedness function $z$ and the traffic intensity $\lambda$ is sufficient to reconstruct the covariance density $k$. Thus, the peakedness function together with the traffic intensity provides a complete second order characterization of the point process.

The pair $(\lambda, z(\cdot))$ provides a concise and meaningful characterization of a general call arrival stream. The peakedness function provides a quantitative measure of the concept of burstiness of a traffic stream. From (10), for fixed $\lambda$ and $k_0$, the peakedness function is increasing in the ratio of $\beta_2/\beta_1$, which is greater than one for non-orderly streams. Clearly, arrival streams with batch arrivals are very bursty. The ratio of peak-to-mean arrival rate fails as a measure of burstiness for such streams since the presence of batch arrivals implies that this ratio is infinite. Another measure of burstiness which has been used in teletraffic studies is the index of dispersion for counts (IDC) (cf. [5, 6]). The IDC is defined by

$$I = \lim_{t\to\infty} \frac{\mathrm{Var}[N_t]}{\mathrm{E}[N_t]}. \qquad (12)$$

Note the similarity between (2) and (12). In fact, peakedness may be viewed as a generalization of the IDC concept. It is easy to show that

$$I = 2z_{exp}(0^+) - 1. \qquad (13)$$

Thus, the peakedness function contains more statistical information about the arrival process than the IDC.

# 3 Modified Peakedness

A deficiency with the peakedness concept is that it is tied to the point process model of traffic. A point process may be characterized in terms of *counting properties*, which relate to the numbers of points lying in specified subsets of the state space $\mathbb{R}$ and *interval properties*, which relate to the relative spacings between the points. The process $\{N_t, t > 0\}$ specifies a point process in terms of a counting property, i.e., $N_t$ records the number of call arrivals occurring in the interval $(0, t]$. The peakedness concept essentially captures a counting property of the call arrival process. As far as the counting properties are concerned, the point nature of the process plays a subsidiary role.

Stochastic fluid models have become popular in recent years because of their conceptual simplicity and tractability relative to point process models. Moreover, for high-speed networks based on ATM with fixed size cells, the burst level behavior of cell streams can be modeled accurately with fluid models. In this section, we introduce a *modified peakedness* measure which is analogous to the standard peakedness, but has meaning for both point process and fluid models of traffic. We characterize a general arrival process in terms of a generalized random process which we call the *rate process*. The rate process provides a means for specifying a large class of traffic models and is the basis for our development of the modified peakedness measure.

## 3.1 Rate Process

We introduce a *rate process* $R = \{R_t : t \in \mathbb{R}\}$ to be understood as a generalized random process [7] with the interpretation that $R_t dt$ represents the *amount* of work arriving in the infinitesimal interval $[t, t+dt)$. The counting process, $\{N_t : t > 0\}$ for a general arrival process is then defined by

$$N_t \triangleq \int_0^t R_\tau d\tau = (R, 1_{(0,t]}), \quad t > 0. \qquad (14)$$

The rate process $\{R_t : t > 0\}$ can be viewed as the formal derivative of the process $\{N_t : t > 0\}$:

$$R_t = \frac{dN_t}{dt}. \qquad (15)$$

We view $\{R_t : t > 0\}$ as a stationary random process whose sample paths are generalized functions over $\mathbb{R}_+$. The mean of the rate process is a constant, i.e., $E[R_t] = \lambda$, where $\lambda$ is called the arrival rate or traffic intensity of the arrival process. Note that the covariance function of the rate process equals the covariance density of the counting process, i.e., $\mathrm{Cov}(R_u, R_v) = k(u - v)$.

### Point Processes

A point process can be represented by a rate process defined by

$$R_t = \sum_{i=-\infty}^{\infty} \delta(t - T_i), \qquad (16)$$

where $\delta(\cdot)$ denotes the Dirac delta function and $\{T_i\}_{i=-\infty}^{\infty}$ is the sequence of arrival times. The rate process (16) can be written in the form

$$R_t = \sum_{i=-\infty}^{\infty} b_i \delta(t - \tilde{T}_i), \qquad (17)$$

where $\tilde{T}_i$ is the $i$th distinct arrival epoch defined by

$$\tilde{T}_0 = T_0,\ \tilde{T}_{i+1} = \min_{j>0}\{T_j > \tilde{T}_i\},\ i \geq 0 \qquad (18)$$

$$\tilde{T}_{-1} = T_{-1},\ \tilde{T}_{i-1} = \max_{j<-1}\{T_j < \tilde{T}_i\},\ i < 0. \qquad (19)$$

and $b_i$ is the batch size at time $\tilde{T}_i$ defined by

$$b_i = \#\{j : T_j = \tilde{T}_i\}. \qquad (20)$$

With $b_i \in \mathbb{R}_+$, the form (17) is more general than (16). The counting process corresponding to the rate process (17) is given by

$$N_t = \int_0^t R_u du = \sum_{i=0}^{\infty} b_i u(t - \tilde{T}_i), \quad (21)$$

where $u(\cdot)$ denotes the unit step function. We call this type of process a *generalized batch process.* If $b_i \in \mathbb{Z}_+$, $\forall i$, the sample paths of $\{N_t\}$ are positive integer-valued and right-continuous; i.e., $N_t$ is the counting process which specifies a point process in the sense discussed in Section 2. Now if we impose the constraint

$$P\{\omega : b_i(\omega) = 1, \ \forall i \in \mathbb{Z}_+\} = 1, \quad (22)$$

then (17) represents an *orderly* point process. On the other hand, if we relax the requirement that $b_i \in \mathbb{Z}_+$ and require only that $b_i \in \mathbb{R}_+$, we obtain an arrival process that is not a point process, but shares many of the counting properties of a point process.

**Discrete-Level Fluid Process**

Let $\mathcal{X}$ be a finite set of fluid flow rates. At a given time $t$, the *discrete-level fluid process* produces fluid at one of the flow rates in the set $\mathcal{X}$ and then makes a transition to a new flow rate after a random time. We may represent such a process with a rate process defined by

$$R_t = \sum_{i=-\infty}^{\infty} f_i \ \text{rect}\left(\frac{t - T_i}{T_{i+1} - T_i}\right), \quad (23)$$

where $f_i \in \mathcal{X}$ is the fluid flow rate after the $i$th transition, $T_i$ is the epoch of the $i$th transition and $\text{rect}(t) \triangleq u(t) - u(t-1)$. The counting process corresponding to the rate process (23) is given by

$$N_t = \sum_{i=0}^{\infty} f_i[\ \text{ramp}(t - T_i) - \ \text{ramp}(t - T_{i+1})], \quad (24)$$

where $\text{ramp}(t) \triangleq tu(t)$.

## 3.2 Definition and Representations

The modified peakedness is defined in terms of a fictitious service system to which the arrival process is offered. The service system is represented by a random process $\{D_t, t > 0\}$ called the *service process.* In the infinitesimal interval $[t, t+dt)$, the arrival process offers $R_t dt$ units of work to a new server which is introduced at time $t$. The server removes this work from the system after a random duration $D_t$. The random variable $D_t$ represents the *lifetime* of the server introduced at time $t$. The random variables $D_t$, $t > 0$ are independent and identically distributed (i.i.d.) with common cumulative distribution function (cdf) $F$. The work which arrives in $[t, t+dt)$ remains in the system until the lifetime of the server expires. Let $\tilde{S}_t$ represent the amount of work present in the system at time $t$. We call $\{\tilde{S}_t, t > 0\}$ the *workload process* and define it by means of the following stochastic integral:

$$\tilde{S}_t \triangleq \int_0^t 1_{\{D_u > t-u\}}(u) R_u du, \quad (25)$$

where $1_A$ denotes the indicator function with respect to the set $A \subset \mathbb{R}$.

We now define the *modified peakedness functional* with respect to the service time distribution $F$ by

$$\tilde{z}[F] \triangleq \lim_{t\to\infty} \frac{\text{Var}[\tilde{S}_t]}{\text{E}[\tilde{S}_t]} = \lim_{t\to\infty} \frac{K_{\tilde{S}}(t,t)}{M_{\tilde{S}}(t)}, \quad (26)$$

where $M_{\tilde{S}}(t)$ and $K_{\tilde{S}}(u,v)$ denote the mean and covariance functions, respectively, of the workload process. As for the standard peakedness, we can define the modified peakedness as a function of the service rate $\mu$:

$$\tilde{z}_{F_1}(\mu) \triangleq \tilde{z}[F_\mu]. \quad (27)$$

Here $\{F_\mu : \mu > 0\}$ denotes the family of scaled service time distributions with shape determined by $F_1$ and mean given by $\mu^{-1}$ (cf. (3) and (4)).

The modified peakedness $\tilde{z}$ applies to a larger class of traffic models than the standard peakedness $z$, which is defined only for point process traffic models. A natural question to ask is for what point processes do the two measures coincide? In Theorem 3.3 below, we will establish necessary and sufficient conditions for the two peakedness measures to coincide. First we establish a representation of the modified peakedness functional with respect to a service time cdf $F$ with mean service rate $\mu$ for a rate process with covariance function $k(u)$.

**Lemma 3.1** *The mean of the workload process is given by*

$$M_{\tilde{S}}(t) = \lambda \int_0^t F^c(u) du. \quad (28)$$

*Hence,*

$$\lim_{t\to\infty} M_{\tilde{S}}(t) = \frac{\lambda}{\mu}. \quad (29)$$

**Lemma 3.2** *The covariance function of the workload process is given by*

$$K_{\tilde{S}}(t+\tau, t) = \int_{[0,t]^2 \cap \{x=y\}} F^c(x+\tau)F(y)k(x-y)dxdy$$
$$+ \int_{-t}^{t+\tau} dy\ k(\tau - y) \int_{\max(0,y)}^{t+\min(\tau,y)} F^c(x-y)F^c(x)dx \quad (30)$$

*for $t > 0$ and $\tau \geq 0$.*

In the double integral, $[0,t]^2$ denotes the square region $[0,t] \times [0,t]$. From the definition of modified peakedness and Lemmas 3.1 and 3.2 we have

**Theorem 3.1** *The modified peakedness functional can be expressed as:*

$$\tilde{z}[F] = \frac{\mu}{\lambda}\left[\int_{[0,t]^2 \cap \{x=y\}} F^c(x)F(y)k(x-y)dxdy + \int_{-\infty}^{\infty} k(y)F^*(y)dy\right]. \quad (31)$$

The result (31) is the analog of Eckberg's representation (6) for the standard peakedness functional. Note that the double integral in (31) is actually a line integral along the line $x = y$ which vanishes unless $k(x)$ contains a delta function at the origin. This observation motivates the following simpler representation.

**Corollary 3.1** *Suppose that $k(x)$ can be decomposed as*

$$k(x) = k_1\delta(x) + k_0(x),$$

*where $k_0(x)$ contains no delta function at the origin. Then*

$$\tilde{z}[F] = \frac{k_1}{\lambda} + \frac{\mu}{\lambda}\int_{-\infty}^{\infty} k_0(x)F^*(x)dx. \quad (32)$$

As discussed in Section 2, the covariance function of the rate process (i.e., covariance density) for a stationary point process can be decomposed as:

$$k(x) = k_1\delta(x) + k_0(x). \quad (33)$$

Recall that $k_0(t)$ is a generalized function with no delta function at the origin. Hence, using (31) we can specialize the modified peakedness functional to point processes.

**Theorem 3.2** *For stationary point processes, the modified peakedness has the following representation:*

$$\tilde{z}[F] = \frac{\beta_2}{\beta_1} + \frac{\mu}{\lambda}\int_0^{\infty} \frac{d^2}{dy^2}K_N(y,y)F^*(y)dy, \quad (34)$$

*where $\beta_1$ and $\beta_2$ are the first and second moments of the batch sizes and $K_N(\cdot,\cdot)$ is the covariance function of the counting process $\{N_t, t > 0\}$.*

Comparing (10) and (34), we have

**Corollary 3.2** *For stationary point processes, the modified peakedness and the standard peakedness functionals are related by*

$$\tilde{z}[F] - z[F] = \left(\frac{\beta_2}{\beta_1} - 1\right)(1 - \mu F^*(0)). \quad (35)$$

Corollary 3.2 leads to an important inequality relating the modified peakedness and standard peakedness measures and conditions under which they coincide. We state these results in the following

**Theorem 3.3** *For stationary point processes,*

$$\tilde{z}[F] \geq z[F]. \quad (36)$$

*with equality if and only if one of the following holds:*

*(i) The point process is orderly.*

*(ii) $F$ is the cdf for deterministic service times*

Consider modified peakedness with respect to exponential service. The cdf for exponential service times with mean $\mu^{-1}$ is given by

$$F_{exp}(x) = 1 - e^{-\mu x}, \quad x \geq 0, \quad (37)$$

with the normalized version obtained by setting $\mu = 1$. The autocorrelation function of $F^c_{exp}$ can be readily obtained:

$$F^*_{exp}(x) = \frac{1}{2\mu}e^{-\mu|x|}, \quad x \geq 0. \quad (38)$$

Let us assume that $k(x)$ can be decomposed as in (33). Then using (32), the modified peakedness function with respect to the exponential service can be expressed as follows:

$$\tilde{z}_{exp}(\mu) = \frac{k_1}{\lambda} + \hat{k}_0(\mu), \quad (39)$$

where $\hat{k}_0(s)$ denotes the unilateral Laplace transform of $k_0(x)$.

### 3.3 Superposition of Arrival Processes

In a broadband network environment, aggregate traffic streams are formed through statistical multiplexing. Therefore, it is of interest to characterize the superposition of a number of traffic streams in terms of the characteristics of the individual streams. Consider the superposition of $n$ arrival processes represented by the rate processes $R_1, R_2, \cdots, R_n$, respectively. The rate process of the superposition is given by $R = \sum_{i=1}^n R_i$ . The aggregate arrival rate is given by

$$\lambda = E[R] = \sum_{i=1}^{n} E[R_i] = \sum_{i=1}^{n} \lambda_i, \quad (40)$$

where $\lambda_i$ is the arrival rate of the $i$th stream. The covariance function of $R$ is given by

$$k(u-v) = \sum_{i=1}^{n}\sum_{j=1}^{n} k_{ij}(u-v),$$

where $k_{ij}(x)$ is the *cross-covariance* function of the $i$th and $j$th processes. We write $k_i(x) = k_{ii}(x)$ for the covariance function of process $i$. Let $\tilde{z}_i$ and $\tilde{z}$ denote the peakedness functional of the $i$th arrival process and the aggregate process, respectively.

**Theorem 3.4** *Let $F$ be an arbitrary service time cdf.*

$$\tilde{z}[F] = \sum_{i=1}^{n} \frac{\lambda_i}{\lambda} \tilde{z}_i[F] + \int_{-\infty}^{\infty} \sum_{i \neq j} k_{ij}(x-y) F^*(y) dy$$

$$+ \frac{\mu}{\lambda} \int_0^{\infty} \int_0^{\infty} F^c(x) F(y) \sum_{i \neq j} k_{ij}(x-y) 1_{\{x=y\}}(x,y) dx dy.$$

When the $n$ processes are statistically independent, we have

$$k_{ij}(x) \equiv 0, \tag{41}$$

whenever $i \neq j$. This observation immediately leads to the following important corollary.

**Corollary 3.3** *Suppose the $n$ processes are statistically independent. Then*

$$\tilde{z}[F] = \sum_{i=1}^{n} \frac{\lambda_i}{\lambda} \tilde{z}_i[F]. \tag{42}$$

# 4 Modified Peakedness for Some Traffic Models

In this section, we give closed-form expressions for the modified peakedness functionals for a number of traffic models. Like peakedness, the modified peakedness is equivalent to a second-order characterization of the stationary counting process $\{N_t,\ t > 0\}$ given in terms of $\lambda$ and $k(x)$. Given the pair $(\lambda, k(x))$, the peakedness functional can be obtained from the representation (6) while the modified peakedness can be obtained from the analogous representation (31). Eckberg [4] provides the peakedness functionals for several stationary point processes. For these models, the modified peakedness can be simply obtained from the peakedness via Corollary 3.2. We can also obtain the modified peakedness for several fluid-based traffic models. The modified peakedness serves as a common measure by which the fluid models can be compared with their point process counterparts.

## 4.1 Point Process Models

### Poisson Process

For a (homogeneous) Poisson process it is easy to show that $k(x) = \lambda\delta(x)$. Hence from (31) and (6), respectively, one has $\tilde{z}_P[F] = z_P[F] = 1$ for an arbitrary service time cdf $F$. Since the inter-arrival times are exponentially distributed, the Poisson process is necessarily orderly. Thus, the two peakedness measures coincide. The Poisson process has been used successfully to model call arrivals in teletraffic problems, but is not adequate for modeling bursty broadband network traffic at the cell level.

### Markov Modulated Poisson Process

*Markov Modulated Poisson Process* (MMPP) has been used extensively in the literature for modeling bursty traffic sources (see e.g., [8]). The MMPP is governed by an underlying Markov chain $X$, defined on a finite state-space $E$, which modulates the traffic intensity of a Poisson process. The MMPP can be specified in terms of a matrix $P$, the infinitesimal generator for the Markov chain $X$, and a diagonal matrix $H = [H_{ij}]$. When the Markov chain is in state $i$, the process generates arrivals according to a Poisson process of rate $H_{ii}$. Assume that $X$ is irreducible, with equilibrium probability vector $\pi$. For an MMPP so defined, the peakedness function with respect to exponential service can be obtained as [4]:

$$z_{MMPP,exp}(\mu) = 1 + \frac{\pi H(\mu I - P)^{-1} H\mathbf{1}}{\pi H\mathbf{1}} - \frac{\pi H\mathbf{1}}{\mu}, \tag{43}$$

where $\mathbf{1}$ represents the vector of all ones.

An important special case of an MMPP is the *Interrupted Poisson Process* (IPP). The IPP alternates between two states, an *on* state and an *off* state. During the on-state, the arrivals form a (homogeneous) Poisson process of rate $r$. During the off-state, there are no arrivals. The durations of the on and off periods are independent and exponentially distributed with means $\beta^{-1}$ and $\alpha^{-1}$. Identifying the on and off states as states 1 and 0, respectively, the IPP can be viewed as an MMPP with $E = \{0, 1\}$, $h(i) = i$, $i \in E$, and

$$P = \begin{bmatrix} -\alpha & \alpha \\ \beta & -\beta \end{bmatrix}. \tag{44}$$

From (43) one can easily obtain

$$z_{IPP,exp}(\mu) = 1 + \frac{r\beta}{(\alpha+\beta)(\mu+\alpha+\beta)}. \tag{45}$$

## 4.2 Stochastic Fluid Models

The initial motivation behind developing the modified peakedness measure was to extend the peakedness concept to encompass the popular stochastic fluid models used extensively in recent years to study the performance of high-speed networks. A fluid flow process is naturally represented in terms of its rate process $R_t$. At time $t$, $R_t$ represents the *rate* at which the fluid flow is produced. We define a fluid flow process as follows:

**Definition 4.1** *A fluid flow process is an arrival process for which the rate process is a stationary random process having piece-wise continuous sample paths.*

In fact, we will primarily be interested in fluid flow processes for which the rate process has piece-wise constant sample paths. By contrast, recall that for point process models the rate process is a stationary generalized random process whose sample paths are sequences of weighted Dirac delta functions. Furthermore, unlike a point process, it is not hard to see that the covariance density $k(x)$ for a fluid process will not contain a delta function at the origin (although it may be a generalized function). Therefore, from (31) the modified peakedness functional for a fluid process simplifies to

$$\tilde{z}_{fl}[F] = \frac{\mu}{\lambda}\int_{-\infty}^{\infty} k(x)F^{*}(x)dx. \qquad (46)$$

The peakedness function with respect to exponential service follows immediately from (46):

$$\tilde{z}_{fl,exp}(\mu) = \frac{1}{\lambda}\int_{0}^{\infty} k(x)e^{-\mu x}dx = \frac{\tilde{k}(\mu)}{\lambda}, \qquad (47)$$

where $\tilde{k}(s)$ is the Laplace transform of $k(x)$.

**Constant Flow**

The simplest fluid flow process is the constant fluid flow (CFF) process which outputs fluid at a constant rate $\lambda$. Clearly, this process is both deterministic and stationary. Its counting process and rate process are given, respectively, by

$$N_t = \lambda t \quad \text{and} \quad R_t = \lambda, \quad t > 0. \qquad (48)$$

Clearly,

$$E[N_t] = \lambda t, \quad t > 0 \quad \text{and} \quad k(x) = 0, \; x \in \mathbb{R}. \qquad (49)$$

Hence, from (31) we have $\tilde{z}_{CFF}[F] = 0$ for an arbitrary service time distribution $F$. Hence, one may regard the CFF process as the fluid process counter-part of the Poisson process. The smaller modified peakedness function of the CFF process indicates that it is less *bursty* than the Poisson process, a conclusion that is intuitively satisfying. Consider, for example, a buffer being emptied at a constant rate $c$ and fed by a CFF process with $\lambda < c$. Clearly the buffer will always be empty. However, a queue fed by a Poisson process and served at a constant rate $c > \lambda$ (i.e., an $M/D/1$ queue) will be non-empty with positive probability.

**Markov Modulated Fluid Process**

The Markov Modulated Fluid Process (MMFP) has been used extensively to model high-speed network traffic. It is the fluid process analog of the MMPP. The MMFP is governed by an underlying Markov chain $X = \{X, \; t > 0\}$, with infinitesimal generator $P$, on a finite state-space $E$ which modulates the rate at which the fluid flow is generated. The rate of fluid flow is a memoryless function $h : E \rightarrow \mathbb{R}_{+}$ of the state. Hence, the rate process is given by $R_t = h(X_t)$ . Let $H$ be a diagonal matrix with $H_{ii} = h(i), \quad i \in E$ and let $\pi = (\pi_i : i \in E)$ be the state probability vector for the Markov chain $X$. The traffic intensity is given by

$$\lambda \triangleq E[R_t] = \sum_{i \in E} \pi_i h(i) = \pi H \mathbf{1}, \qquad (50)$$

and the covariance density is given by

$$k(u-v) = \pi H e^{P(u-v)} H - (\pi H \mathbf{1})^2, \quad u, v > 0.$$

From (47), the modified peakedness function with respect to exponential service can be obtained as

$$\tilde{z}_{MMFP,exp}(\mu) = \frac{\pi H(\mu I - P)^{-1} H \mathbf{1}}{\pi H \mathbf{1}} - \frac{\pi H \mathbf{1}}{\mu}. \qquad (51)$$

analogy between the MMFP and the MMPP is obvious (cf. (43)). The rate process $R$ for the MMFP corresponds precisely to the process $\eta$, associated with the MMPP, which modulates the arrival rate of an inhomogeneous Poisson process. Note that the modified peakedness functions of an MMFP and its MMPP counterpart differ by the constant 1. Thus we have a generalization of the analogy between the CFF process and the Poisson process. An important special case of the MMFP is the on-off Markov fluid process (OOFP), which is the fluid process counterpart of the IPP. Its modified peakedness function with respect to exponential service time distribution is given by (cf. 45):

$$\tilde{z}_{OOFP,exp}(\mu) = \frac{r\beta}{(\alpha+\beta)(\mu+\alpha+\beta)}. \qquad (52)$$

## 5 Peakedness of Video Traffic

An important feature of the peakedness concept is that it has a meaningful interpretation in terms of a well-defined service system, i.e., an infinite-server group. The same is true of the related notion of modified peakedness introduced in Section 3. It is relatively straightforward, at least in principle, to obtain the peakedness function, $z_F(\mu)$, of an arbitrary point process traffic stream with respect to some service time distribution; for a given rate $\mu$ and service time distribution $F$, simply simulate a system in which the traffic stream is offered to a group of infinite servers with random service times distributed according to $F$. Since the peak rate of cell stream is usually well-defined, the peakedness and modified peakedness functions coincide in this case (cf. Theorem 3.3). This contrasts with call arrival streams in telephone trunk groups, where calls may arrive in batches simultaneously.

Variable bit-rate (VBR) video traffic streams will be major consumers of future broadband networks. Recently, much research effort has been devoted to the modeling of video traffic and video transmission over high-speed networks. In this section, we look at the peakedness function for an MPEG video stream. Our purpose is twofold: 1) to show that peakedness can be readily estimated for an actual high-speed traffic stream and 2) to demonstrate that peakedness is capable of capturing the burstiness of broadband traffic and hence is potentially useful in making resource allocation decisions.

### 5.1 Estimating Peakedness

As discussed above, one way of estimating the peakedness value $z_F(\mu)$ is to simulate an infinite server group system where the service times have mean $\mu^{-1}$ and are distributed according to $F$. When a cell arrives, a new server and service time are assigned to it. After the service time has elapsed, both the server and the cell leave the system. Denoting $S_t$ as the number of busy servers at time $t$, recall that the peakedness function is defined by

$$z_F(\mu) = \lim_{t\to\infty} \frac{\text{Var}[S_t]}{\text{E}[S_t]}. \quad (53)$$

Suppose we have an window of length $T_{obs}$ in which to observe the arrival process. Divide $T_{obs}$ into $M$ subwindows of length $T$. Let $S_{iT}$, $i = 1, \cdots, M$ be the number of busy servers in the system at time $iT$. Then unbiased estimates for $E[S_t]$ and $\text{Var}[S_t]$ are given, respectively, by (cf. [9]):

$$\hat{S}_1 = \frac{1}{M}\sum_{i=1}^{M} S_{iT}, \quad \hat{\sigma}_S^2 = \frac{1}{M-1}\sum_{i=1}^{M}(S_{iT} - \hat{S}_1)^2. \quad (54)$$

Hence, the peakedness can be estimated as $z_F(\mu) \approx \frac{\hat{\sigma}_S^2}{\hat{S}_1}$. The IDC can be estimated in a similar fashion. In this case there is no need to simulate a server system. Let $N_{iT}$ be the number of arrivals in the interval $((i-1)T, iT]$, $i = 1, \cdots, M$. Then an estimate of the IDC is $I \approx \frac{\hat{\sigma}_N^2}{\hat{N}_1}$, where $\hat{N}_1$ and $\hat{\sigma}_N$ are, respectively, the sample mean and sample variance of the sample sequence $\{N_{iT}; 1 \le i \le M\}$. The value of the peakedness function near $\mu = 0$ can be approximated using the relation $I = 2z_{exp}(0^+) - 1$.

When the service distribution is exponential, there is a simpler method to estimate the peakedness function discussed by Eckberg [10]. For an arrival process, let $U(t)$ be the number arrivals in $(0, t]$, given that an arrival occurred at time 0. The function $U(t)$ (sometimes called the *expectation function* [6]) is the analog of the renewal function in renewal theory for more general point processes. Eckberg [10] shows that peakedness can be expressed in terms of the expectation function as follows:

$$z_{exp}(\mu) = 1 + \tilde{U}(\mu) - \frac{\lambda}{\mu},$$

where $\tilde{U}(s)$ is the Laplace-Stieltjes transform of $U(t)$. Let $X$ be an exponentially distributed random variable with mean $\mu^{-1}$. One can show that

$$E[U(X)] = \tilde{U}(\mu). \quad (55)$$

The relation (55) is the basis for the following method for estimating peakedness (cf. [10]). Let $N_i$ be a random integer variable and let $X_i$ be an exponential random variable with mean $1/\mu$.

**for** $i = 1$ to $M$ **do**
1. Select next arrival after $N_i$ cells pass.
2. Generate random variate $X_i$.
3. Let $U_i$ be the number of cells which arrive within time $X_i$ from current cell

**end for**

Then an unbiased estimate for $\tilde{U}(\mu)$ is

$$\tilde{U}(\mu) \approx \frac{1}{M}\sum_{i=1}^{M} U_i.$$

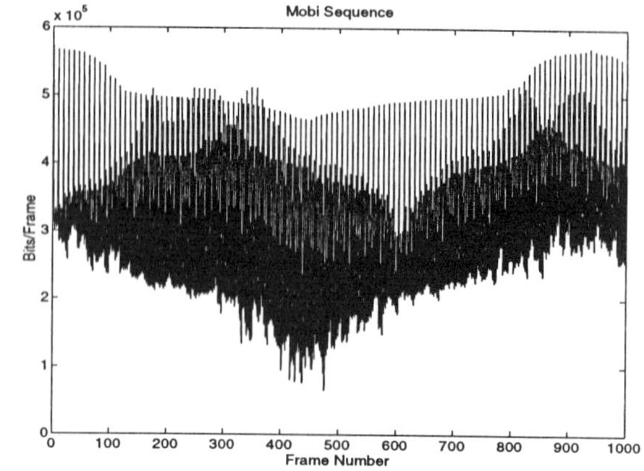


Figure 1: Bit-rate profile for 'mobi' MPEG sequence

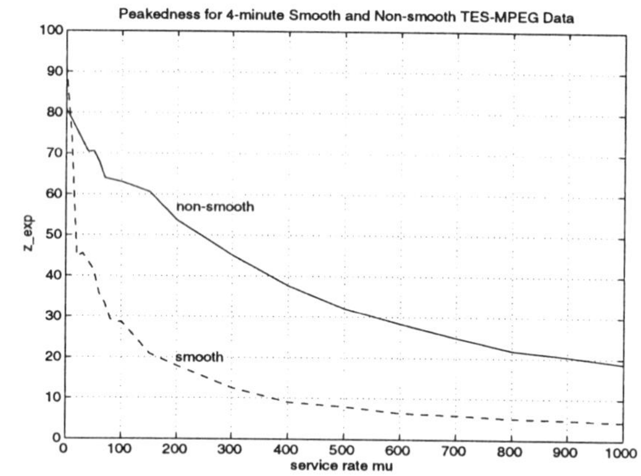


Figure 2: Peakedness Curves for 4 Minute MPEG Sequence

Here, $M$ is the maximum number of *trials* taken within the observation window $T_{obs}$. The mean of $N_i$ should be large enough to ensure that an "arbitrary" arrival is selected.

### 5.2 MPEG Video Stream

In the MPEG standard for video compression (cf. [11]), a video sequence is transmitted as a sequence of frames. The frames are of three types: intracoded (I), predicted (P), and bidirectional (B). A typical MPEG video sequence consists of a sequence of frames with a pattern, e.g., IBBPBBPBB, which repeats indefinitely. The frames are coded at a constant rate of 30 frames per second. The number of bits contained in a typical I frame is an order of magnitude larger than the number of bits in a B frame or P frame. Thus, the output of an MPEG encoder is a coded bit stream with a highly variable instantaneous bit rate. Figure 1 shows the bit-rate profile of 1000 frames (approximately 33.3 seconds) of an MPEG video sequence called 'mobi'.

For transmission over an ATM network, each MPEG frame must be divided into a group of ATM cells. We consider two modes of transmission of cells over a frame interval. In *non-smooth mode*, the cells are transmitted at a constant rate $\lambda_p$ starting at the beginning of the frame interval until the frame is fully transmitted. Then the source is silent until the beginning of the next frame interval. This results in an on-off type stream with highly correlated on and off periods. In *smooth mode*, the cells for the $i$th frame are transmitted at a constant rate $f(i)/\tau$ over the frame interval, where $f(i)$ is the total number of cells in the $i$th frame and $\tau$ is the inter-frame period. Thus, in *smooth mode*, buffering is done to smooth out the transmission of cells of each frame over the corresponding frame interval.

Figure 2 shows the peakedness curves with respect to exponential service distribution obtained empirically from a four-minute MPEG sequence. To make a fair comparison, the peak rate for the non-smooth mode was chosen to be the smallest rate needed to transmit the largest frame in the sequence over a frame interval. This example illustrates that the peakedness is able to capture the difference in burstiness between the smooth and non-smooth streams. Note that at the frame level, the two MPEG sequences are identical; the difference lies in how the frames are transmitted in the form of cells. If interframe smoothing were done (cf. [12]), the peakedness of the resulting cell stream would be further reduced.

## 6 Conclusion

In this paper, we have introduced a new measure of traffic burstiness called modified peakedness which shares many of the properties of standard peakedness. Modified peakedness is more general than standard peakedness in that it can be applied to both point process and fluid models of traffic. Peakedness-based measures can be an effective means for characterizing high-speed traffic because: (i) the measures can be readily obtained through real-time measurements; (ii) they capture the statistical burstiness of traffic streams; (iii) they can be used as the basis of traffic descriptors to be used in resource allocation. In [1], the application of peakedness measures to network resource allocation is investigated further.

## References


[1] B. L. Mark and G. Ramamurthy, "Peakedness measures for traffic characterization in high-speed networks," *NEC C&C Laboratories Technical Report*, 1996.

[2] R. L. Cruz, "A calculus for network delay, part i: Network elements in isolation," *IEEE Trans. on Information Theory*, vol. 37, no. 1, pp. 114–131, 1991.

[3] B. L. Mark and G. Ramamurthy, "Real-time estimation of UPC parameters for arbitrary traffic sources in ATM networks," in *Proc. INFOCOM '96*, (San Francisco, California), pp. 384–392, March 1996.

[4] A. E. Eckberg, "A generalization of peakedness to arbitrary arrival processes and service time distributions," in *Bell Laboratories Technical Memorandum*, 1976.

[5] D. R. Cox and P. A. Lewis, *Point Processes*. Methuen, 1966.

[6] D. L. Jagerman, B. Melamed, and W. Willinger, "Stochastic modeling of traffic processes," in *Frontiers in Queuing: Models, Methods and Problems* (J. Dshalalow, ed.), vol. 2, CRC Press, 1996 (to appear).

[7] I. M. Gelfand and N. Y. Vilenkin, *Generalized Functions*, vol. 4. New York: Academic Press, 1964.

[8] H. Heffes and D. M. Lucantoni, "A Markov modulated characterization of packetized voice and data and related statistical multiplexer performance," *IEEE Journal on Selected Areas in Commun.*, vol. 4, pp. 856–868, September 1986.

[9] H. Kobayashi, *Modeling and Analysis: An Introduction to System Performance Evaluation Methodology*. Addison-Wesley, 1978.

[10] A. E. Eckberg, "Approximations for bursty and smoothed arrival delays based on generalized peakedness," in *Proc. 11-th International Teletraffic Congress*, (Kyoto, Japan), 1985.

[11] D. Le Gall, "MPEG: A video compression standard for multimedia applications," *CACM*, vol. 34, pp. 46–58, April 1991.

[12] S. S. Lam, S. Chow, and D. K. Y. Yau, "An algorithm for lossless smoothing of MPEG video," in *Proc. of SIGCOMM'94*, pp. 281–293, 1994.

# A Filtering Theory for Deterministic Traffic Regulation

Cheng-Shang Chang[1]
Dept. of Electrical Engineering
National Tsing Hua University
Hsinchu 30043
Taiwan, R.O.C.
Email: cschang@ee.nthu.edu.tw

### Abstract

In this paper, we develop a filtering theory for deterministic traffic regulators that generate $f$-constrained outputs. We show that such regulators can be implemented by a linear time invariant filter with the impulse response $f$ under the $(\min,+)$-algebra if the function $f$ is increasing and subadditive. The filtering approach not only yields easier proofs for more general results than those in the literature, but also allows us to design traffic regulators via systematic methods such as concatenation, filter bank summation, linear system realization, and FIR-IIR realization. The theory has many applications, including leaky buckets, traffic regulation for periodic constraint functions, and service curves. In particular, we find a new linear system realization and a new FIR-IIR realization for a concatenation of leaky buckets. Moreover, we find a FIR-IIR realization for traffic regulators with periodic constraint functions. We also show that such regulators, in conjunction with maximum delay guarantee, guarantee shifted-subadditive service curves. Based on this, we provide a couple of rules for service curve allocation among a concatenation of servers.

Keywords: traffic regulation, leaky buckets, filtering, min-plus algebra, service curves

## 1 Introduction

Future high speed digital networks aim to serve integrated traffic, such as voice, video, fax, and so forth. To control interaction among traffic generated by different sources, traffic regulation seems inevitable. In the paper [4], Cruz proposed the following deterministic traffic characterization. For a nonnegative sequence $A \equiv \{a(t), t = 1, 2, \ldots\}$, it is $f$-upper constrained for some function $f$ if

$$A(t_2) - A(t_1) \leq f(t_2 - t_1), \quad \forall t_1 \leq t_2, \qquad (1)$$

where $A(t) = \sum_{s=1}^{t} a(s)$, $t \geq 1$ and $A(0) = 0$. Based on this characterization, he went on to develop a network calculus, including multiplexing and demultiplexing, so that deterministic performance, such as bounded delay and bounded queue length, can be guaranteed. To use the calculus, one needs to address the fundamental question of traffic regulation:

*How does one regulate traffic such that the constraint in (1) can be satisfied?*

In [4, 5], Cruz addressed the traffic regulation problem with the $(\sigma, \rho)$ regulator (leaky bucket) and the FIFO queue. Both only generate traffic that satisfies a linear constraint ($f$ is a linear function) in (1). For $f(t) = \sigma + \rho t$, Ananthram and Konstantopoulos [1, 8] recently showed that the leaky bucket is the best causal traffic regulator to generate such a constraint in terms of maximizing the total number of departures at any moment in time (an equivalent statement in terms of delay under FIFO is previously shown in Cruz [5]). Motivated by these important works, we propose in this paper a general filtering approach for the traffic regulation problem. Our approach is based on the following finding:

*Traffic regulation in (1) can be achieved by a linear time invariant filter with the impulse response $f$ under the* $(\min,+)$*-algebra if the function $f$ is increasing and subadditive.*

In such an algebra, one replaces the usual addition operator by the *min* operator and the usual multiplication operator by the addition operator. (Readers not familiar with the $(\min,+)$-algebra might consult [2].) We call such a filter the *maximal $f$-regulator* as it is also the best causal traffic regulator that one can implement in terms of maximizing the total number of departures from the regulator at any moment in time. The filtering approach not only yields easier proofs for more general results than those in the literature, but also allows us to design traffic regulators via systematic methods such as concatenation, filter bank summation, linear system realization, and FIR-IIR realization. In particular, we show that a concatenation of two maximal regulators yields another maximal regulator, independent of the order of the two maximal regulators. We also give a necessary and sufficient condition for "filter bank summation" of maximal regulators to yield another maximal regulator. Under such a condition, "filter bank summation" is equivalent to concatenation.

The theory has many applications, including leaky buckets, traffic regulation for periodic constraint functions, and service curves. When specialized to leaky buckets, our results for "filter bank summation" recover the known results in [5, 1]. Moreover, we find a new

[1]This research is supported in part by the National Science Council, Taiwan, R.O.C., under Contracts NSC-86-2221-E007-036 and NSC 86-2115-M007-025.

linear system realization and a new FIR-IIR realization for a concatenation of leaky buckets. These realizations are obviously suitable for VLSI implementation. The theory can also be applied to a traffic regulator with a periodic constraint function, where we derive a FIR-IIR realization for such a regulator. We also show that maximal regulators, in conjunction with maximum delay guarantee, guarantee shifted-subadditive service curves in [11]. Based on this, we provide a couple of rules for service curve allocation among a concatenation of servers.

The paper is organized as follows: in Section 2, we develop a general filtering theory for traffic regulation, including the maximal $f$-regulator, a concatenation of maximal regulators, and filter bank summation of maximal regulators. In Section 3, we apply the theory to leaky buckets, traffic regulation for periodic constraint functions, and service curves. We conclude the paper in Section 4 by discussing possible extensions of the theory.

## 2 Traffic regulation

Consider a nonnegative sequence $A \equiv \{a(t), t = 1, 2, \ldots\}$. Let $A(t) = \sum_{s=1}^{t} a(s)$, $t \geq 1$ and $A(0) = 0$. Cruz [4] introduced the following traffic characterization of the sequence $A$.

**Definition 2.1** *The sequence $A$ is $f$-upper constrained for some function $f$ if*

$$A(t_2) - A(t_1) \leq f(t_2 - t_1), \quad \forall t_1 \leq t_2. \tag{2}$$

Without loss of generality, we assume $f(0) = 0$ throughout the paper. It is shown in Chang [3] that if $A$ is $f$-upper constrained, then there exists a function $f^*$ such that (i) $A$ is still $f^*$-upper constrained, (ii) $f^*(t) \leq f(t)$ for all $t$, and (iii) $f^*(t)$ is increasing and subadditive. Recall that a function $f$ is increasing and subadditive (see e.g., [7]) if

$$f(s) \leq f(t+s) \leq f(s) + f(t), \quad \forall s, t \geq 0.$$

The function $f^*$ can be found by the following recursive construction:

$$\bar{f}(t) = \inf_{s \geq t} f(s)$$
$$f^*(t) = \min[\bar{f}(t), \min_{0<s<t} [f^*(s) + f^*(t-s)]], \tag{3}$$

where $f^*(0) = 0$. This leads to the following refined traffic characterization.

**Definition 2.2** *If $f$ is increasing and subadditive, and (2) holds, then the sequence $A$ is called $f$-upper enveloped.*

The importance of such a characterization lies in the fact that for a $f$-upper enveloped sequence $A$, there exists an upper envelope rate

$$\hat{a} = \lim_{t \to \infty} \frac{f(t)}{t}. \tag{4}$$

It is shown in [4, 3] that feeding such a sequence to a queue with capacity $c$ results in bounded queue length and bounded delay if the rate condition, $\hat{a} < c$, is satisfied. Moreover, there is an associated calculus for multiplexing and demultiplexing based on the envelope rate. The calculus allows us to decide whether a connection in a network meets its quality of service.

The question that remains to be answered is how one regulates a source such that it is $f$-upper enveloped. One of the main objectives in this paper is to develop a general traffic regulation theory based on filtering. The following theorem is the key to our theory. (As pointed out by one of the referees, Theorem 2.3(i) below has also been independently discovered by Sariowan [11].)

**Theorem 2.3** *For a nonnegative sequence $A \equiv \{a(t), t = 1, 2, \ldots\}$, construct a nonnegative sequence $B \equiv \{b(t), t = 1, 2, \ldots\}$ by*

$$B(t) = \min_{0 \leq s \leq t} [A(s) + f(t-s)], \tag{5}$$

*where $B(t) = \sum_{s=1}^{t} b(s)$.*

**(i)** *If $f$ is increasing and subadditive, then $B$ is $f$-upper enveloped.*

**(ii)** *For any $f$-upper constrained sequence $\tilde{B}$ that satisfies $\tilde{B}(t) \leq A(t)$ for all $t$, one has $\tilde{B}(t) \leq B(t)$ for all $t$.*

**(iii)** *If $A$ is $f$-upper constrained, then $B(t) = A(t)$ for all $t$.*

**Proof.** (i) Since both $A(t)$ and $f(t)$ are increasing, $B(t)$ is also increasing. This implies $B$ is a nonnegative sequence. To see that $B$ is $f$-upper enveloped, let $s^*$ be the the argument that achieves the minimum in $B(s)$, i.e., $B(s) = A(s^*) + f(s - s^*)$. Thus, for $0 \leq s \leq t$,

$$B(t) - B(s) \leq A(s^*) + f(t - s^*) - B(s)$$
$$= f(t - s^*) - f(s - s^*).$$

Applying the subadditivity of $f$ yields

$$B(t) - B(s) \leq f(t-s).$$

(ii) Note from (5) that $B(t) \leq A(t) + f(0) = A(t)$. Thus, it follows from (i) that $B$ is one of the sequences that satisfy the conditions in (ii). Since $\tilde{B}$ is $f$-upper constrained, $\tilde{B}(t) \leq \tilde{B}(s) + f(t-s)$ for all $0 \leq s \leq t$. In conjunction with the assumption that $\tilde{B}(t) \leq A(t)$ for all $t$,

$$\tilde{B}(t) \leq A(s) + f(t-s), \quad 0 \leq s \leq t.$$

Thus,

$$\tilde{B}(t) \leq \min_{0 \leq s \leq t} [A(s) + f(t-s)] = B(t).$$

(iii) As discussed in (ii), one has $A(t) \geq B(t)$. Since we assume that $A$ is $f$-upper constrained, the conditions in (ii) are satisfied and we have $A(t) \leq B(t)$. ■

Note that the condition $\tilde{B}(t) \leq A(t)$ is referred to one of the causal conditions in [1] as the number of departures cannot be larger than the number of arrivals. Theorem 2.3(i) shows that for any input sequence $A$, the construction in (5) generates a $f$-upper enveloped sequence $B$ if $f$ is increasing and subadditive. Theorem 2.3(ii) shows that it is the best construction that one can implement if one would like to maximize the number of departures by time $t$. Finally, Theorem 2.3(iii) shows that if $A$ is already $f$-upper constrained, then it will pass through the construction in (5) without any change.

To ease our presentation, we make the following definition.

**Definition 2.4** *If $f$ is increasing and subadditive, then the construction in (5) is called the* maximal $f$-regulator.

If one examines the maximal $f$-regulator carefully, one realizes that it is in fact in the form of convolution under the $(\min,+)$-algebra. In such an algebra, we replace the usual addition operator by the *min* operator and the usual multiplication operator by the addition operator. Analogous to the classical filtering theory, we may view the maximal $f$-regulator as a linear time invariant filter (under the $(\min,+)$-algebra) with the impulse response $f(t)$. The following theorem is a natural extension of its counterpart in the classical filtering theory.

**Theorem 2.5** *A concatenation of the maximal $f_1$-regulator and the maximal $f_2$-regulator, independent of the order, is the maximal $f$-regulator, where $f$ is the convolution of $f_1$ and $f_2$ under the $(\min,+)$-algebra, i.e.,*

$$f(t) = \min_{0 \leq s \leq t} [f_1(s) + f_2(t-s)]. \qquad (6)$$

**Proof.** We first prove that $f(t)$ in (6) is still increasing and subadditive. That $f(t)$ is increasing follows easily from the assumption that both $f_1(t)$ and $f_2(t)$ are increasing. To prove subadditivity, we need to show that for all $s, t \geq 0$,

$$f(s) + f(t) \geq f(t+s).$$

Let $s^*$ (resp. $t^*$) be the argument that achieves the minimum in $f(s)$ (resp. $f(t)$). Thus, $f(s) = f_1(s^*) + f_2(s-s^*)$ and $f(t) = f_1(t^*) + f_2(t-t^*)$. This implies

$$\begin{aligned} & f(s) + f(t) \\ &= f_1(s^*) + f_1(t^*) + f_2(s-s^*) + f_2(t-t^*) \\ &\geq f_1(s^*+t^*) + f_2(s+t-s^*-t^*) \\ &\geq \min_{0 \leq \tau \leq t+s} [f_1(\tau) + f_2(t+s-\tau)] = f(t+s), \end{aligned}$$

where we apply subadditivity for $f_1$ and $f_2$ in the first inequality.

Now consider an input sequence $A$ to the maximal $f_1$-regulator. Let $B_1$ be the output sequence of the maximal $f_1$-regulator, which is then fed into the maximal $f_2$-regulator. Let $B$ be the output of the maximal $f_2$-regulator. Thus, we have

$$B_1(t) = \min_{0 \leq s \leq t} [A(s) + f_1(t-s)]$$

and

$$\begin{aligned} B(t) &= \min_{0 \leq s \leq t} [B_1(s) + f_2(t-s)] \\ &= \min_{0 \leq s \leq t} \left[ \min_{0 \leq \tau \leq s} [A(\tau) + f_1(s-\tau)] + f_2(t-s) \right] \\ &= \min_{0 \leq \tau \leq t} \left[ A(\tau) + \min_{\tau \leq s \leq t} [f_1(s-\tau) + f_2(t-s)] \right] \\ &= \min_{0 \leq \tau \leq t} [A(\tau) + f(t-\tau)]. \end{aligned}$$

This shows putting the maximal $f_1$-regulator and the maximal $f_2$-regulator in tandem results in the maximal $f$-regulator. Since $f(t)$ is symmetric with respect to $f_1$ and $f_2$, the result is independent of the order of the concatenation. ∎

We note that the envelope rate of $f$ in (6) is $\hat{a} = \min[\hat{a}_1, \hat{a}_2]$, where $\hat{a}_1$ and $\hat{a}_2$ are the envelope rates of $f_1$ and $f_2$. This can be shown by the following argument. As discussed in [3], for every $\epsilon > 0$, there exists $\sigma_1 < \infty$ and $\sigma_2 < \infty$ such that

$$(\hat{a}_i - \epsilon)t - \sigma_i \leq f_i(t) \leq (\hat{a}_i + \epsilon)t + \sigma_i, \quad i = 1, 2.$$

From (6), it follows that

$$\begin{aligned} & (\min[\hat{a}_1, \hat{a}_2] - \epsilon)t - \sigma_1 - \sigma_2 \\ & \leq f(t) \leq (\min[\hat{a}_1, \hat{a}_2] + \epsilon)t + \sigma_1 + \sigma_2. \end{aligned}$$

Thus,

$$\begin{aligned} & \min[\hat{a}_1, \hat{a}_2] - \epsilon \leq \liminf_{t \to \infty} \frac{f(t)}{t} \leq \limsup_{t \to \infty} \frac{f(t)}{t} \\ & \leq \min[\hat{a}_1, \hat{a}_2] + \epsilon. \end{aligned}$$

Since $\epsilon$ is arbitrary, letting $\epsilon \to 0$ completes the argument.

Now we consider feeding a $f_1$-upper enveloped sequence to the maximal $f_2$-regulator.

**Theorem 2.6** *Let $A$ (resp. $B$) be the input (resp. output) of the maximal $f_2$-regulator. Let $q(t) = A(t) - B(t)$ be the queue length at the maximal $f_2$-regulator at time $t$, and $d(t) = \inf\{d \geq 0 : B(t+d) \geq A(t)\}$ be the virtual delay of the last customer that arrives at time $t$. Suppose that $A$ is $f_1$-upper enveloped. Then*

**(i)** *$B$ is $f$-upper enveloped, where $f$ is defined in (6).*

**(ii)** *$q(t) \leq \max_{0 \leq s \leq t}[f_1(s) - f_2(s)]$ for all $t$.*

**(iii)** *$d(t) \leq \inf\{d \geq 0 : f_1(s) \leq f_2(s+d), s = 1, \ldots, t\}$.*

**Proof.** (i) As shown in Theorem 2.3(iii), the output from the maximal $f_1$-regulator is the input itself if the input is $f_1$-upper enveloped. Thus, one can view $A$ as the output from the maximal $f_1$-regulator with $A$ as its input. In view of this, feeding $A$ into the maximal $f_2$

regulator is equivalent to feeding $A$ into the concatenation of the maximal $f_1$-regulator and the maximal $f_2$-regulator. From Theorem 2.5 and Theorem 2.3(i), $B$ is $f$-upper enveloped with $f$ specified in (6).

(ii) Note from (5) that

$$q(t) = \max_{0\le s\le t}[A(t) - A(s) - f_2(t-s)]. \tag{7}$$

Since we assume that $A$ is $f$-upper enveloped, $A(t) - A(s) \le f_1(t-s)$ and thus

$$\begin{aligned} q(t) &\le \max_{0\le s\le t}[f_1(t-s) - f_2(t-s)] \\ &= \max_{0\le s\le t}[f_1(s) - f_2(s)]. \end{aligned}$$

(iii) Observe that

$$\begin{aligned} &A(t) - B(t+d) \\ &= \max_{0\le s\le t+d}[A(t) - A(s) - f_2(t+d-s)] \\ &= \max_{0\le s\le t}[A(t) - A(s) - f_2(t+d-s)] \quad (8) \\ &\le \max_{0\le s\le t}[f_1(t-s) - f_2(t+d-s)] \quad (9) \\ &= \max_{0\le s\le t}[f_1(s) - f_2(s+d)], \quad (10) \end{aligned}$$

where we use $f_2(t) \ge 0$ in (8) and the assumption that $A$ is $f_1$-upper enveloped in (9). Thus, $d(t) \le \inf\{d \ge 0 : f_1(s) \le f_2(s+d), s = 1, \dots, t\}$. ■

Another important realization in filtering is the *filter bank summation*. Note that the summation in the (min, +)-algebra is the min operator. Consider feeding $A$ simultaneous to two maximal regulators. Let $B_1$ (resp. $B_2$) be the output from the maximal $f_1$-regulator (resp. maximal $f_2$-regulator). The output from the "filter bank summation", denoted by $B$, is

$$B(t) = \min[B_1(t), B_2(t)]. \tag{11}$$

**Theorem 2.7** *A "filter bank summation" of the maximal $f_1$-regulator and the maximal $f_2$-regulator is the maximal $f$-regulator with*

$$f(t) = \min[f_1(t), f_2(t)], \tag{12}$$

*if and only if*

$$\min_{0\le s\le t}[f_1(s) + f_2(t-s)] = \min[f_1(t), f_2(t)]. \tag{13}$$

Note that under (13), the realization using concatenation in Theorem 2.5 is equivalent to the realization using "filter bank summation" in Theorem 2.7.

**Proof.** Note from (12) and (5) that

$$\begin{aligned} B(t) &= \min[B_1(t), B_2(t)] \\ &= \min\Big[\min_{0\le s\le t}[A(s) + f_1(t-s)], \\ &\quad \min_{0\le s\le t}[A(s) + f_2(t-s)]\Big] \\ &= \min_{0\le s\le t}[A(s) + \min[f_1(t-s), f_2(t-s)]] \\ &= \min_{0\le s\le t}[A(s) + f(t-s)]. \quad (14) \end{aligned}$$

In view of this, it suffices to show that $f(t)$ defined in (12) is increasing and subadditive. Clearly, $f(t)$ is increasing as both $f_1(t)$ and $f_2(t)$ are increasing. It remains to show that $f(t)$ is subadditive if and only if (13) holds. Note that if (13) holds, then for all $0 \le s \le t$

$$\begin{aligned} &f(s) + f(t-s) \\ &= \min[f_1(s), f_2(s)] + \min[f_1(t-s), f_2(t-s)] \\ &= \min[f_1(s) + f_1(t-s), f_1(s) + f_2(t-s), \\ &\quad f_2(s) + f_1(t-s), f_2(s) + f_2(t-s)] \\ &\ge \min[f_1(t), f_1(s) + f_2(t-s), \\ &\quad f_2(s) + f_1(t-s), f_2(t)] \quad (15) \\ &\ge \min_{0\le s\le t}[f_1(s) + f_2(t-s)] \\ &= \min[f_1(t), f_2(t)] = f(t), \quad (16) \end{aligned}$$

where we apply subadditivity of $f_1$ and $f_2$ in (15). This show subadditivity of $f$ under (13). On the other hand, if $f(t)$ defined in (12) is subadditive, then for all $0 \le s \le t$

$$\begin{aligned} &\min[f_1(t), f_2(t)] = f(t) \le f(s) + f(t-s) \\ &= \min[f_1(s), f_2(s)] + \min[f_1(t-s), f_2(t-s)] \\ &\le f_1(s) + f_2(t-s). \quad (17) \end{aligned}$$

Since the inequality holds for all $0 \le s \le t$,

$$\min[f_1(t), f_2(t)] \le \min_{0\le s\le t}[f_1(s) + f_2(t-s)]. \tag{18}$$

Thus, (13) holds since one has clearly the other side of inequality, i.e.,

$$\min[f_1(t), f_2(t)] \ge \min_{0\le s\le t}[f_1(s) + f_2(t-s)]. \tag{19}$$

■

**Remark 2.8** The condition in (13) is satisfied for the family of functions

$$\mathcal{F} = \{f : f(0) = 0, f(s) \le f(t) \le \frac{t}{s} f(s), \forall s \le t\}. \tag{20}$$

Note that for all $f \in \mathcal{F}$, $-f$ is star-shaped, i.e., $-f(t)/t$ is increasing in $t$ and $f(0) = 0$ (see e.g., [9] pp. 453). Since a star-shaped function is superadditive, $f \in \mathcal{F}$ is subadditive. This can also be seen directly from

$$f(s) + f(t-s) \ge \frac{s}{t} f(t) + \frac{t-s}{t} f(t) = f(t), \quad \forall s \le t.$$

Moreover, the family of functions is min closed, i.e., for any $f_1(t) \in \mathcal{F}$ and $f_2(t) \in \mathcal{F}$, $f(t) = \min[f_1(t), f_2(t)] \in \mathcal{F}$. To see that (13) is satisfied, note that for $f_1$ and $f_2$ in $\mathcal{F}$ and for all $s \le t$,

$$\begin{aligned} f_1(s) + f_2(t-s) &\ge \frac{s}{t} f_1(t) + \frac{t-s}{t} f_2(t) \\ &\ge \min[f_1(t), f_2(t)]. \end{aligned}$$

A subclass of functions in $\mathcal{F}$ is the family of increasing concave functions, $\mathcal{F}_{icv}$ (with $f(0) = 0$). To see this, note from concavity and $f(0) = 0$ that for $s \le t$

$$f(s) \ge \frac{t-s}{t} f(0) + \frac{s}{t} f(t) = \frac{s}{t} f(t).$$

Moreover, $\mathcal{F}_{icv}$ is a strict subclass of $\mathcal{F}$.

## 3 Applications

In this section, we discuss some applications of the theory.

### 3.1 Leaky buckets

Consider a discrete-time leaky bucket with the token generation rate $\rho$ (the number of tokens generated per unit of time) and the size of the token buffer $\sigma$ (see e.g., [12]). Let $A = \{a(t), t = 1, 2, \ldots\}$ be the input sequence to the leaky bucket, where $a(t)$ is the number of cells that arrive at time $t$. The cell buffer size is assumed to be infinite. Denote by $q_1(t)$ (resp. $q_2(t)$) the number of cells in the cell buffer (the number of tokens in the token buffer) at time $t$. Assume $q_1(0) = 0$ and $q_2(0) = \sigma$. Let $z(t) = q_1(t) - q_2(t)$. Then $z(t)$ satisfies the following recursive equation:

$$z(t+1) = \max[z(t) + a(t+1) - \rho, -\sigma]. \tag{21}$$

This equation can be easily verified by considering the three cases: (i) $z(t) > 0$, (ii) $z(t) < 0$ and $z(t) = 0$. Due to page limitation, we omit the proof for (21) here.

The following theorem shows that leaky buckets are maximal $f$-regulators.

**Theorem 3.1** *The discrete-time $(\sigma, \rho)$-leaky bucket described in this section is the maximal $f$-regulator, where $f(t) = \rho t + \sigma$, $t \geq 1$ and $f(0) = 0$.*

**Proof.** Note that $q_1(t) = \max[z(t), 0]$ from the three cases. Let $B$ be the output from the $(\sigma, \rho)$-leaky bucket. Then

$$\begin{aligned} B(t) &= A(t) - q_1(t) = A(t) - \max[z(t), 0] \\ &= \min[A(t), A(t) - z(t)]. \end{aligned} \tag{22}$$

Let

$$y(t) = z(t) + \sigma. \tag{23}$$

It then follows from (21) that $y(t)$ satisfies Lindley's recursion

$$y(t+1) = \max[y(t) + a(t+1) - \rho, 0], \quad y(0) = 0.$$

Thus,

$$y(t) = \max_{0 \leq s \leq t} [A(t) - A(s) - \rho(t-s)].$$

In conjunction with (22) and (23), one has

$$\begin{aligned} B(t) &= \min\left[A(t), \min_{0 \leq s \leq t} [A(s) + \rho(t-s)] + \sigma\right] \\ &= \min\left[A(t), \min_{0 \leq s \leq t-1} [A(s) + \rho(t-s) + \sigma]\right], \end{aligned}$$

as $\sigma \geq 0$. Clearly, the function $f(t) = \rho t + \sigma$, $t \geq 1$ and $f(0) = 0$ is increasing and subadditive. This completes the argument. ∎

To gain more intuition on leaky buckets, we show that leaky buckets can be realized by the first order infinite duration impulse response (IIR) systems under the $(\min, +)$-algebra. To our best knowledge, such a realization appears to be new. Consider the following "linear system" under the $(\min, +)$-algebra.

$$\begin{aligned} x(t) &= \min[\rho + x(t-1), A(t)], \quad x(0) = 0, \\ B(t) &= \min[x(t) + \sigma, A(t)]. \end{aligned}$$

Recursive expansion yields

$$x(t) = \min_{0 \leq s \leq t} [A(s) + \rho(t-s)],$$

and thus

$$B(t) = \min\left[\min_{0 \leq s \leq t} [A(s) + \rho(t-s)] + \sigma, A(t)\right],$$

which is exactly the output from the $(\sigma, \rho)$-leaky bucket.

Note that the function $f(t)$ in Theorem 3.1 is not only subadditive, but also concave. Hence, the condition in Theorem 2.7 is satisfied and one can implement "filter bank summation" for a concatenation of $(\sigma_i, \rho_i)$-leaky buckets, $i = 1, \ldots, K$ (see Remark 2.8). This yields the maximal $f$-regulator with $f(t) = \min_{1 \leq i \leq K} [\rho_i t + \sigma_i]$, $t \geq 1$ and $f(0) = 0$. This result was previously shown in [5, 1]. In fact, such a system can be realized by the following "linear system" under the $(\min, +)$-algebra:

$$\begin{aligned} x(t) &= G \otimes x(t-1) \oplus O \otimes A(t), \quad x(0) = O, \\ B(t) &= H \otimes x(t) \oplus A(t), \end{aligned}$$

where $x(t)$ is the $K$ dimensional state vector, $G$ is the "diagonal" matrix with its $i^{th}$ diagonal element being $\rho_i$, $O$ is the $K$ dimensional column vector with all its elements being 0, and $H$ is the $K$ dimensional row vector with its $i^{th}$ element being $\sigma_i$. Here we use $\otimes$ and $\oplus$ to denote the matrix multiplication and addition under the $(\min, +)$-algebra. Once again, such a realization appears to be new. For example, if $K = 3$, then

$$G = \begin{bmatrix} \rho_1 & \infty & \infty \\ \infty & \rho_2 & \infty \\ \infty & \infty & \rho_3 \end{bmatrix}. \tag{24}$$

$$O = \begin{bmatrix} 0 \\ 0 \\ 0 \end{bmatrix}. \tag{25}$$

$$H = [\sigma_1, \sigma_2, \sigma_3]. \tag{26}$$

There is another systematic way to implement the maximal $f$-regulator with

$$f(t) = \min_{1 \leq i \leq K} [\rho_i t + \sigma_i], t \geq 1 \text{ and } f(0) = 0.$$

Note that for such a function, there exists a $t_0 < \infty$ such that $f(t) = \rho t + f(t_0)$ for all $t \geq t_0$ and $\rho = \min_{1 \leq i \leq K} [\rho_i]$. Define the following two functions

$$\begin{aligned} f_1(t) &= \rho t + f(t_0), \quad f_1(0) = 0, \\ f_2(t) &= \begin{cases} f(t) & \text{if } t \leq t_0, \\ \infty & \text{otherwise.} \end{cases} \end{aligned}$$

Since $f(t)$ is concave, $f_1(t)$ (as the tangent of $f(t)$ at $t_0$) provides a upper bound of $f(t)$. Thus, $f(t) =$

$\min[f_1(t), f_2(t)]$ and we may use the "filter bank summation" method to implement the maximal $f$-regulator. To be precise, we write

$$\begin{aligned}
&\min_{0\le s\le t}[A(s) + f(t-s)] \\
&= \min_{0\le s\le t}\Big[A(s) + \min[f_1(t-s), f_2(t-s)]\Big] \\
&= \min\Big[\min_{0\le s\le t}[A(s) + f_1(t-s)], \\
&\quad \min_{0\le s\le t}[A(s) + f_2(t-s)]\Big] \qquad (27)
\end{aligned}$$

Clearly, the first term in (27) is the maximal $f_1$-regulator and can be easily implemented by a $(f(t_0), \rho)$ leaky bucket. However, the second term in (27) is not the maximal $f_2$-regulator, as $f_2(t)$ is not subadditive. Since $f_2(t) = \infty$ for all $t \ge t_0$, the second term in (27) is in fact the output from a finite duration impulse response (FIR) systems under the $(\min, +)$-algebra, i.e.,

$$\begin{aligned}
&\min_{0\le s\le t}[A(s) + f_2(t-s)] \\
&= \min_{0\le s\le t}[A(t-s) + f_2(s)] \\
&= \min_{0\le s\le t_0}[A(t-s) + f_2(s)],
\end{aligned}$$

where we assume $A(t) = \infty$ for all $t \le 0$.

### 3.2 Traffic regulation for periodic constraint functions

Suppose that the input sequence $A = \{a(t), t = 1, 2, \ldots\}$ is claimed to be $f$-enveloped for a function $f$ that is periodic with period $p$, i.e., $f(t+p) - f(t)$ is a constant for all $t$. How does one find an efficient design for such a regulator? Note that such functions cannot be realized by leaky buckets due to periodicity.

Define the average rate $\rho = (f(t+p) - f(t))/p$. Thus, once $f(t)$, $t = 0, \ldots, p-1$, and $\rho$ are specified, the whole function $f$ is defined via the recursive equation

$$f(t+p) = f(t) + \rho p. \qquad (28)$$

It then follows that

$$\begin{aligned}
B(t) &= \min_{0\le s\le t}[A(s) + f(t-s)] \\
&= \min\Big[\min_{0\le s\le t-p}[A(s) + f(t-s)], \\
&\quad \min_{t-p<s\le t}[A(s) + f(t-s)]\Big] \\
&= \min\Big[\min_{0\le s\le t-p}[A(s) + f(t-p-s)] + \rho p, \\
&\quad \min_{t-p<s\le t}[A(s) + f(t-s)]\Big] \\
&= \min\Big[B(t-p) + \rho p, A(t-p+1) + f(p-1), \\
&\quad A(t-p+2) + f(p-2), \ldots, A(t) + f(0)\Big].
\end{aligned}$$

Such a regulator can be efficiently implemented by the FIR-IIR realization. One possible application for such a regulator is traffic policing for video sequence, e.g. MPEG, where a certain periodic structure exists.

### 3.3 Service curves

In the section we discuss the connections between the maximal $f$-regulator and the concept of service curves developed by Cruz [6] and Sariowan [11].

**Definition 3.2** *A server guarantees service curve $f(t)$ (with $f$ increasing and $f(0) = 0$) for an input sequence $A$ if its output sequence $B$ satisfies*

$$B(t) \ge \min_{0\le s\le t}[A(s) + f(t-s)] \qquad (29)$$

*for all $t$. If the inequality in (29) is satisfied for all input sequences, then we say the server guarantees service curve $f(t)$* universally.

Here the function $f$ is not necessarily subadditive. We note the service curve guarantee defined in [11, 6] is universal. Clearly, the maximal $f$-regulator defined in this paper guarantees service curve $f$ *universally* (with equality). Moreover, Theorems 2.5, 2.6 and 2.7 can be rephrased as follows:

**Theorem 3.3** *A concatenation of the first server that guarantees service curve $f_1$ for an input sequence $A$ and the second server that guarantees service curve $f_2$ for the output from the first server is a server that guarantees service curve $f$ for the sequence $A$, where $f$ is the convolution of $f_1$ and $f_2$ under the $(\min, +)$-algebra, i.e.,*

$$f(t) = \min_{0\le s\le t}[f_1(s) + f_2(t-s)]. \qquad (30)$$

*Moreover, if both servers are* universal, *then the result is independent of the order.*

**Theorem 3.4** *Consider a server that guarantees service curve $f_2$ for an input sequence $A$. Let $B$ be the output, $q(t) = A(t) - B(t)$ be the queue length at the server at time $t$, and $d(t) = \inf\{d \ge 0 : B(t+d) \ge A(t)\}$ be the virtual delay of the last customer that arrives at time $t$. Suppose that $A$ is $f_1$-upper enveloped. Then*

(i) *the server guarantees service curve $f$ for $f$ satisfying*

$$f_2(t) \ge \min_{0\le s\le t}[f_1(s) + f(t-s)] \quad \text{for all } t.$$

(ii) $q(t) \le \max_{0\le s\le t}[f_1(s) - f_2(s)]$ *for all $t$.*

(iii) $d(t) \le \inf\{d \ge 0 : f_1(s) \le f_2(s+d), s = 1, \ldots, t\}$.

**Theorem 3.5** *Consider an input sequence $A$. Let $B_1$ (resp. $B_2$) be the output from a server that guarantees service curve $f_1$ (resp. $f_2$) for the sequence $A$. The output from the "filter bank summation", denoted by $B$, is*

$$B(t) = \min[B_1(t), B_2(t)]. \qquad (31)$$

*Then the "filter bank summation" of a server that guarantees service curve $f_1$ for $A$ and a server that guarantees service curve $f_2$ for $A$ is a server that guarantees service curve $f$ for $A$ with*

$$f(t) = \min[f_1(t), f_2(t)]. \qquad (32)$$

All the proofs of these three theorems are identical to those in Theorems 2.5, 2.6 and 2.7, leaving out the arguments for subadditivity. We note that the result in Theorem 2.6(i) is in the form of "convolution" while the result in Theorem 3.4(i) is in the form of "deconvolution." Both of them are based on the fact that a $f_1$-upper enveloped sequence passes through the maximal $f_1$-regulator without any change. We also note that Theorem 3.3 and Theorem 3.4(ii) and (iii) were stated in [11]. The convolution result in Theorem 3.3 was previously derived in [6] under a stronger definition of service curve. Though the concept of service curves is originally developed for providing bounded end-to-end delay [6, 11], it is of the same importance to observe that a server that provides bounded delay also guarantees a service curve. In the following lemma, we show that maximum delay guarantee is equivalent to service curve guarantee.

**Lemma 3.6** *A server guarantees maximum delay d for an input sequence A if and only if the server guarantees service curve* $\mathbf{O}_d$ *for the sequence A with*

$$\mathbf{O}_d(t) = \begin{cases} 0 & \text{if } 0 \le t \le d \\ \infty & \text{otherwise} \end{cases}. \quad (33)$$

**Proof.** Let $B$ be the output from the server. Note that the server guarantees maximum delay $d$ for an input sequence $A$ if and only if

$$B(t) \ge A((t-d)^+) = \min_{0 \le s \le t}[A(s) + \mathbf{O}_d(t-s)]$$

with $\mathbf{O}_d$ defined in (33). ■

The following result strengthens the one-sided result for service curve specification in [11].

**Corollary 3.7** *Suppose that the input sequence A is* $f_1$*-upper enveloped. Then a server guarantees maximum delay d for the sequence A if and only if the server guarantees service curve f (for the sequence A) that is the convolution of* $f_1$ *and* $\mathbf{O}_d$ *(defined in (33)) under the* $(\min, +)$ *algebra, i.e.,*

$$f(t) = \min_{0 \le s \le t}[f_1(s) + \mathbf{O}_d(t-s)] = f_1((t-d)^+). \quad (34)$$

**Proof.** To see the *only if* part, one has from Lemma 3.6 that a server that guarantees maximum delay $d$ also guarantees service curve $\mathbf{O}_d$. Since $\mathbf{O}_d(t) \ge f_1((t-d)^+) = f(t)$ for all $t$, the server guarantees service curve $f(t)$.

For the *if* part, we have from Theorem 3.4(i) that the server also guarantees service curve $\mathbf{O}_d$ if the server guarantees service curve $f(t)$. From Lemma 3.6, the server then guarantees maximum delay $d$. We note that another way to prove this is to apply Theorem 3.4(iii). ■

Functions of the form in (34) are called shifted subadditive in [11] as $f_1$ (with $f_1(0) = 0$) is subadditive. From Corollary 3.7 and Theorem 3.3, one may view a server that guarantees a shifted subadditive service curve $f$ in (34) as a concatenation of a server that guarantees service curve $f_1$ and a server that guarantees service curve $\mathbf{O}_d$. This implies a server that guarantees a shifted subadditive service curve $f(t) = f_1((t-d)^+)$ can be achieved by a concatenation of the maximal $f_1$-regulator and a server that guarantees maximum delay $d$. Since the output from the maximal $f_1$-regulator is $f_1$-upper enveloped, bounded delay can be accomplished by proper admission control for simple scheduling policies such as the First Come First Served (FCFS) policy and the static priority policy, or more complicated deadline scheduling polices such as the Earliest Deadline First policy (EDF) (see [4, 3, 13]). We note that deadline scheduling policies usually provide a larger admission set, but they are at the cost of design complexity, e.g. time stamping and sorting.

Corollary 3.7 shows that the best service curve allocation for a server to yield bounded delay is shifted-subadditive. In a network environment, a server is often a concatenation of servers. The question is then how one allocates minimum service curves among a concatenation of servers so that the convolution of these service curves guarantees a shifted-subadditive service curve.

Without loss of generality, consider the case with a concatenation of two servers. In the following, we provide a couple of rules of thumbs for service curve allocation.

(i) Suppose we restrict ourselves to the problem that only shifted-subadditive service curves in these two servers are allocated. For instance, assume we allocate $h_1(t) = g_1((t-d_1)^+)$ for the first server and $h_2(t) = g_2((t-d_2)^+)$ for the second server, where $g_1$ and $g_2$ are increasing and subadditive. Then a better way is to allocate the first server $\tilde{h}_1(t) = g((t-d_1)^+)$ and the second server $\tilde{h}_2(t) = g((t-d_2)^+)$, where $g$ is the convolution of $g_1$ and $g_2$. To see this, note that the overall service curve for the original allocation is the convolution of $h_1$ and $h_2$, which is equivalent to the convolution of $g_1$, $\mathbf{O}_{d_1}$, $g_2$ and $\mathbf{O}_{d_2}$. Since $g$ is the convolution of $g_1$ and $g_2$, $g$ is also increasing and subadditive (Theorem 2.5) and the convolution of $g$ and $g$ is still $g$. Since the convolution is independent of the order, the overall service curve for the modified allocation is then the convolution of $g$, $\mathbf{O}_{d_1}$, $g$ and $\mathbf{O}_{d_2}$, which is the same as that of the original allocation. As $g$ is the convolution of $g_1$ and $g_2$, one has $g(t) \le g_i(t)$ for all $t$, and thus $\tilde{h}_i(t) \le h_i(t)$ for all $t$, $i = 1$ and 2.

(ii) Suppose we restrict ourselves to the problem that only shifted-concave service curves in these two servers are allocated. As the definition for shifted-subadditive functions, we call a function $h$ shifted-concave if it is of the form $h(t) = \tilde{h}((t-d)^+)$ for some increasing concave function $\tilde{h}$ (with $\tilde{h}(0) = 0$) and some $d \ge 0$. Thus, the class of shifted-concave functions is a subset of shifted-subadditive functions. Assume our goal is to guarantee the overall service curve $f(t) = g((t-d))^+$ for some increasing function $g$ and $d \ge 0$. (Without loss of generality, assume $g(1) > 0$. Otherwise, we may increase $d$.) Then the best allocation is in the following form:

$\tilde{h}_1(t) = \tilde{g}((t-d_1)^+)$ and $\tilde{h}_2(t) = \tilde{g}((t-d_2)^+)$, where $d_1 + d_2 \le d$ and

$$\tilde{g}(t) = \min_{z \ge 0} \Big[zt - \min_{\tau \ge 0}[z\tau - g((\tau - d + d_1 + d_2)^+)]\Big]. \quad (35)$$

Note that $\tilde{g}(t)$ is known as the concave envelope of $g((t-d+d_1+d_2)^+)$ and $\tilde{g}(t)$ is the smallest concave function that is not less than $g((t-d+d_1+d_2)^+)$ (see e.g. [10]). We first show such an allocation guarantees the overall service curve $g((t-d)^+)$. Note that the overall service curve is the convolution of $\tilde{g}$, $\mathbf{O}_{d_1}$, $\tilde{g}$ and $\mathbf{O}_{d_2}$. Thus, the overall service curve is guaranteed as $\tilde{g}(t) \ge g((t-d+d_1+d_2)^+)$. This inequality can also be seen directly from (35) by takes $\tau = t$. Now we argue such an allocation is optimal. From (i), it suffices to consider allocations of the following form: $h_1(t) = g_1((t-d_1)^+)$ and $h_2(t) = g_1((t-d_2)^+)$ for some increasing concave function $g_1$. Since the overall service curve $g((t-d)^+)$ is guaranteed, one has $g_1(t) \ge g((t-d+d_1+d_2)^+)$. As we assume $g(1) > 0$, one must have $d_1 + d_2 \le d$. Otherwise, the inequality cannot hold for $t = 0$. Recall that $\tilde{g}(t)$ is the smallest concave function that is not less than $g((t-d+d_1+d_2)^+)$. This implies $g_1(t) \ge \tilde{g}(t)$. Thus, $h_i(t) \ge \tilde{h}_i(t)$, $i = 1$ and 2.

## 4 Conclusions and future research

In this paper, we developed in Section 2 a general filtering theory for traffic regulation, including the maximal $f$-regulator, a concatenation of maximal regulators, and filter bank summation of maximal regulators. We also showed in Section 3 that the theory has many applications, including leaky buckets, traffic regulation for periodic constraint functions, and service curves.

Possible extensions of the filtering theory includes (i) transfer functions of the $f$-maximal regulators, (ii) traffic regulation with buffer and delay constraints, (iii) time varying filtering for traffic regulation, and (iv) traffic regulation with multiple inputs and outputs.

For (i), one may define the so called $z$-transform under the (min, +)-algebra by $F(z) = \min_t[f(t) + zt]$ (see [2]). This definition corresponds to the Legendre transform (the convex transform) [10] in the continuous time setting.

In [8], Ananthram and Konstantopoulos considered traffic regulation problems with buffer and delay constraints. Though they focused on the $(\sigma, \rho)$ regulators, the technique developed there might be applied to the general setting discussed in this paper.

Both topics in (iii) and (iv) are important. They also seem to be difficult problems. Obviously, time varying filtering is related to stochastic extension of the deterministic filtering theory developed here. Traffic regulation with multiple inputs and outputs corresponds to scheduling in a queue with multiple inputs.

**Acknowledgements:**

The author would like to thank the INFOCOM'97 referees for pointing out Sariowan's thesis [11]. This leads to the application of the filtering theory to service curves in Section 3.3. The author would also like to thank Rene Cruz for many helpful comments on Sections 3.2 and 3.3.

## References

[1] V. Anantharam and T. Konstantopoulos. "Optimality and interchangeability of leaky buckets in tandem," Univ. of Texas at Austin, Tech. Report SCC-95-01, 1995. Initial version also in: Proc. 32nd Allerton Conference, pp. 235-244, Monticello, IL, October 1994.

[2] F. Baccelli, G. Cohen, G. Oslder, and J. Quadrat, *Synchronization and Linearity: An Algebra for Discrete Event Systems*, Wiley, 1992.

[3] C.S. Chang, "Stability, queue length and delay of deterministic and stochastic queueing networks," *IEEE Transactions on Automatic Control*, Vol. 39, pp. 913-931, 1994.

[4] R.L. Cruz, "A calculus for network delay, Part I: Network elements in isolation," *IEEE Trans. Inform. Theory*, Vol. 37, pp. 114-131, 1991.

[5] R.L. Cruz, "A calculus for network delay, Part II: Network analysis," *IEEE Trans. Inform. Theory*, Vol. 37, pp. 132-141, 1991.

[6] R.L. Cruz, "Quality of service guarantees in virtual circuit switched networks," *IEEE J. Selected Areas in Communications*, Vol. 13, pp. 1048-1056, 1995.

[7] J.F.C. Kingman, *Subadditive processes* in Ecole d'ete de probabilities de Saint-Flour, edited by A. Dold and B. Eckmann, Lecture Notes in Mathematics, 539, Springer-Verlag, Berlin, pp. 165-223, 1976.

[8] T. Konstantopoulos and V. Anantharam. "Optimal flow control schemes that regulate the burstiness of traffic," IEEE/ACM Trans. Networking, Vol. 3, pp. 423-432, 1995.

[9] A.W. Marshall and I. Olkin, *Inequalities: Theory of Majorization and Its Applications.* New York: Academic Press, 1979.

[10] R.T. Rochafellar. *Convex Analysis.* Princeton: Princeton University Press, 1970.

[11] H. Sariowan, "A Service-Curve Approach to Performance Guarantees in Integrated-Service Networks," Ph.D. Dissertation, University of California, San Diego, 1996.

[12] J.S. Turner, "New Directions in Communications (or Which Way to the Information Age?)," *IEEE Communication Magazine*, Vol. 24, No. 10, Oct. 1986.

[13] H. Zhang, "Service displines for guaranteed performance service in packet-switching networks," *Proceedings of the IEEE*, Vol. 83, pp. 1374-1396, 1995.

# Traffic Shaping at a Network Node: Theory, Optimum Design, Admission Control

*Anwar Elwalid* *Debasis Mitra*

Bell Laboratories
Lucent Technologies
Murray Hill, New Jersey 07974

## Abstract

*This paper develops a framework of traffic shaping which has the goal of increasing the nodal connection-carrying capacity. The shaping filters are designed to interwork with statistical multiplexers which use FIFO buffers. Differences in delay tolerances between traffic classes are exploited to shape and smooth the less delay sensitive traffic. The source model used in the analysis is asynchronous, worst-case subject to Dual Leaky Bucket regulation, where the asynchrony is due to the assumption of independent sources. This, together with the allowance of small loss probabilities, makes statistical multiplexing feasible. We require the shapers to be lossless so that losses, if any, occur only at the multiplexer. We obtain the optimal design of the shaper such that a given delay tolerance for the connection is satisfied. For purposes of admission control we obtain the admissible region of combinations of sources of various types such that the QoS requirements in loss and delay are satisfied. By examining the regions obtained with and without shaping we quantify the capacity gain from shaping. Our numerical results show that the gain can be substantial.*

## 1. Introduction

Shaping of traffic at the points of ingress and egress to the network has been proposed for interworking between subnetworks and for increasing capacity, which is measured in terms of carried connections. Shaping at the ingress is the subject of this paper. We develop a theoretical basis for shaping a class of traffic source models, give guidelines for the optimum selection of the parameters of the shaper, show how admission control to the composite of the shaper and the multiplexer may be done and indicate how the capacity of the system may be calculated.

Shaping filters are envisaged to interwork with FIFO statistical multiplexers. The framework developed here is designed to exploit differences in delay tolerances between different traffic classes, such as real time and non-real time, to shape and smooth the less delay sensitive traffic and thus increase the capacity of the network node. Another motivating factor is that memory, which is required for shaping, may be cheaper at the ingress than at the multiplexer.

The basic network configuration is shown in Figure 1.1. It is assumed that regulated traffic is offered to the shaper. Specifically, the offered traffic is assumed to be conforming to a Dual Leaky Bucket Regulator $(r, B_T, P)$, where $r$ is the mean sustainable rate or token rate, $B_T$ is the burst tolerance or token buffer size, and $P$ is the peak rate. The shaper is in general a four-parameter device: the sustainable rate $r$ is carried over from the regulator and $B_{TS}$ is the token buffer size. The component which distinguishes the shaper from the regulator is the data buffer, with size denoted by $B_{DS}$, which, in contrast to the virtual buffering (in fact, a counter only) of tokens, actually stores traffic cells. The final parameter is $P_S$, the peak rate, which is considered a design variable in our formulation. However, we are able to accommodate designs in which $P_S$ is constrained to be $P$.

Two key features in our design of the shaper are that (i) the shaper is allowed to introduce a delay which cannot exceed $D_S$, a given positive parameter, and (ii) the shaping process is lossless.

A basic configuration which highlights the role of shaping is shown in Figure 1.2. There are $K_1$ regulated sources, possibly heterogeneous, with maximum delay tolerance $D$. In the configuration shown in the figure these sources feed directly into the multiplexer with buffer size $B$ and output port speed $C$, and consequently the delay requirement is satisfied if $B/C \leq D$. Now suppose that there are $K_2$ other regulated sources, possibly heterogeneous, with delay tolerance $D + D_S$ $(D_S > 0)$. The extra permissible delay of $D_S$ may be used to shape the traffic. The proce-



0-8186-7780-5/97 $10.00 © 1997 IEEE

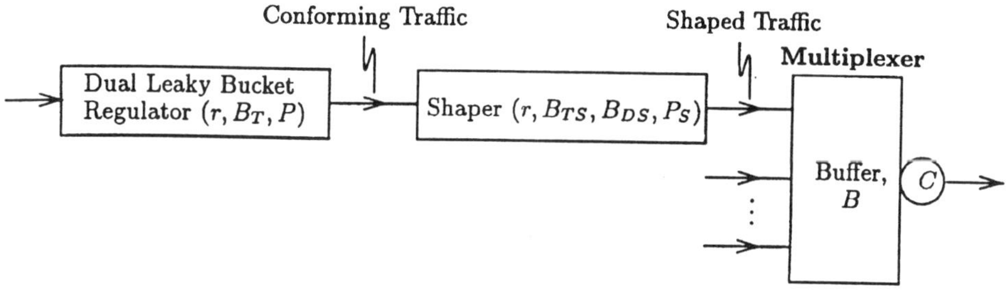


Figure 1.1: Network configuration with regulator, shaper and multiplexer.

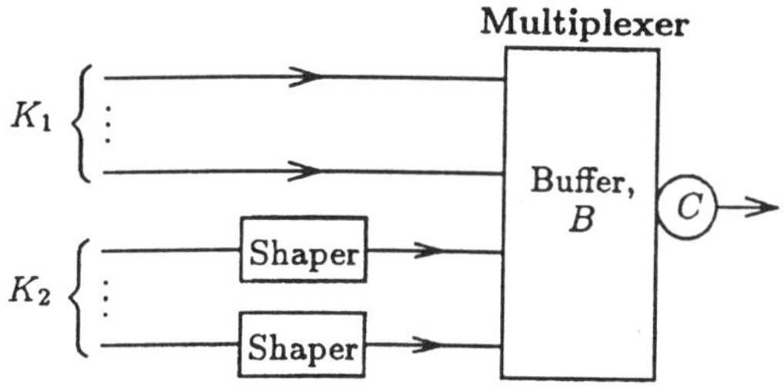


Figure 1.2: Role of shaping for heterogeneous traffic and delay tolerances.

dure given in this paper designs the shaper which will maximize the admissible number of connections. The scenario depicted above is fairly typical, since the essential elements are a mix of real and non-real-time traffic and a FIFO multiplexing buffer.

Our experience with numerical experiments has been that shaping, especially where the peak rate $P_S$ is allowed to be a design variable, gives significant increases in capacity in various typical scenarios.

A noteworthy feature of the work reported here is the traffic source model. Our starting point is the ubiquitous presence of the leaky bucket regulator [TUR86, CRU91, ROB92] in planned switches and service offerings. Works on traffic management based on the leaky bucket regulated source, such as [KBL92], [PGA93], [RBC93], [EMW95], [MMO95], [KNI96], [WKZ96] and this paper, are in contrast to works based on statistical source models, for instance [EMI91], [ROB92] and [HRO96]. The assumption here is that traffic sources are adversarial to the extent permitted by the regulators. Even so, there are interesting choices to be made. One option is to proceed with deterministic bounds to ensure that there are no losses in the network nodes. The growing literature on shaping and scheduling (see, for instance, [GGP96]) is largely devoted to this approach. Another option is to allow small losses, say $10^{-9}$, in the multiplexing and to extract capacity gains from the assumed statistical independence of traffic sources. This approach, based on *asynchronous, worst case sources* and quality of service guarantees in the form of a maximum delay and small loss probabilities, is taken here.

It should also be pointed out that current work on shaping and scheduling is largely non-statistical, as previously noted, and focussed on end-to-end network performance guarantees, while this paper focusses on a single network node. Also noteworthy is that we have relied on [EMW95], which does not consider shaping, for certain basic ideas and techniques, in particular, the optimal trading of bandwidth and buffers. On the other hand, here we work only with the constraints of regulation and shaping, while in [EMW95] adversarial sources transmit specific, extremal, on-off waveforms which satisfy the constraints. Thus, the ad hoc basis of the latter is removed.

In the next section we present certain preliminary, background facts, which are used later. Section 3 considers lossless shaping and the optimum selection of parameters of the lossless shaper. Section 4 considers lossless multiplexing, first by investigating systems with a single source. Statistical multiplexing is considered in Section 5. For ease of exposition, Sections 3–5 deal with a single homogeneous set of traffic sources. Heterogeneous sources are treated in Section 6. Numerical results are presented in Section 7. Concluding remarks are made in Section 8. This paper is necessarily brief; proofs and details are in [EMI96].

## 2. Preliminaries and Background Facts

**2.1. Flows, Rates, Dual Leaky Bucket Regulator.** Here we review some basic quantities and operations of the Dual Leaky Bucket Regulator $(r, B_T, P)$. Traffic streams are modelled as fluid flow here and throughout the paper. In Figure 2.1 $Q(t)$ and $R(t)$ are rate processes; $Q(t)$ is offered by the source and $R(t)$ is the conforming process which is passed by the regulator. We let $A_Q(t, t+\tau)$ and $A_R(t, t+\tau)$ de-

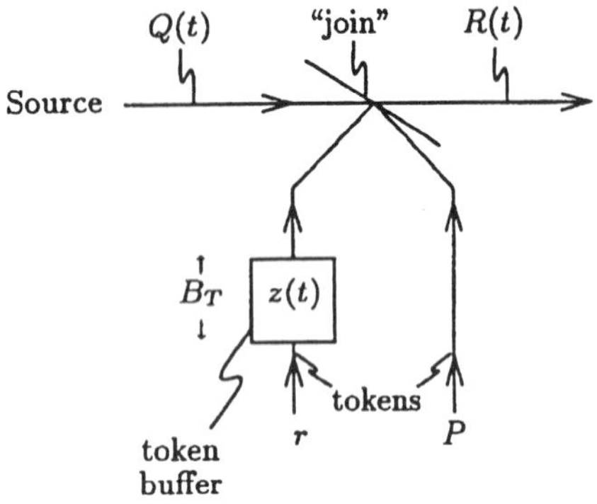


Figure 2.1: Schematic of the Dual Leaky Bucket Regulator

note the *total flows* during the interval $[t, t+\tau]$ for the $Q$ and $R$ rate processes, respectively, where rates and total flows are generally related thus:

$$A_R(t, t+\tau) = \int_t^{t+\tau} R(s)\,ds \ . \tag{2.1}$$

The basic relation describing the conforming process $R(t)$ is, for $\forall t$, $\forall \tau > 0$,

$$A_R(t, t+\tau) = \min(A_Q(t, t+\tau),\ P\tau,\ z(t)+r\tau) \ . \tag{2.2}$$

The "min" operation in (2.2) is performed by the "join" in the schematic of Figure 2.1. In (2.2) $z(t)$ is the token content of the token buffer at time $t$. The governing equations of $z(t)$ are

$$\left.\begin{aligned} \frac{d}{dt}z(t) &= r - R(t), && \text{if } 0 < z(t) < B_T \\ &= [r - R(t)]^+, && \text{if } z(t) = 0 \\ &= [r - R(t)]^-, && \text{if } z(t) = B_T \end{aligned}\right\} \ . \tag{2.3}$$

These equations are standard for fluid models with finite buffers. It may be verified from (2.1)–(2.3) that

$$\begin{aligned} R(t) &= \min(Q(t), P) && \text{if } z(t) > 0 \\ &= \min(Q(t), r) && \text{if } z(t) = 0 \ . \end{aligned} \tag{2.4}$$

**2.2. Chernoff Approximation.** The Chernoff large deviations approximation [PET65] is an effective technique for estimating loss in bufferless multiplexing systems. The procedure given here is due to Hui and Kelly [HUI90, KEL91]. Consider

$$P_{loss} = \Pr\,(U > C) \ , \tag{2.5}$$

where the total instantaneous load $U = \sum_{j=1}^{J} \sum_{k=1}^{K_j} u_{jk}$, and $\{u_{jk}\}$ are independent, nonnegative identically distributed random variables. Here there are $J$ source classes and $K_j$ sources of class $j$. When $C$ is the nodal bandwidth, $P_{loss}$ is the fraction of time that losses occur. Other performance measures related to $P_{loss}$ are discussed in [ROB92].

Assume that the instantaneous loads $u_{jk}$ have moment generating functions

$$M_j(s) = E[e^{su_{jk}}] \quad (j = 1, 2, \cdots, J) \ . \tag{2.6}$$

Also assume the stability condition $\sum_j K_j E(u_{jk}) < C$ and that $\lim_{s\to\infty} \sum_j K_j M_j'(s)/M_j(s) > C$, as otherwise there is no loss. Then

**FACT 1:** Chernoff's bound is

$$\log P_{loss} \le -F(s^*) \ , \tag{2.7}$$

where

$$F(s) = sC - \sum_j K_j \log M_j(s) \tag{2.8}$$

and $F(s^*) = \sup_{s \ge 0} F(s)$. $F(s)$ is strictly concave with an unique maximum at $s^*(s^* > 0)$, which is obtained by solving $F'(s) = 0$. Also, if $K_j = \gamma_j C$ with $\gamma_j = O(1)$ and $C \to \infty$, then

$$\log P_{loss} = -F(s^*)[1 + O(\log C/C)] \ . \tag{2.9}$$

□

Hence, the large deviations approximation is $P_{loss} \sim \exp(-F(s^*))$. Elementary techniques, such as bisections, are effective for calculating $s^*$.

For our numerical procedures we use a refinement [PET65] to (2.9). For the same asymptotic scaling,

**FACT 2:**

$$P_{loss} = \frac{\exp\{-F(s^*)\}}{s^*\sigma(s^*)\sqrt{2\pi}}[1 + o(1)] \tag{2.10}$$

where $\sigma^2(s) = \partial^2 \log E(e^{sU})/\partial s^2$. □

More specifically,

$$\sigma^2(s) = \sum_{j=1}^{J} K_j \left[\frac{M_j''(s)}{M_j(s)} - \left\{\frac{M_j'(s)}{M_j(s)}\right\}^2\right] \ . \tag{2.11}$$

**2.3. Distributions which Maximize the Chernoff Loss Estimate.** We briefly review a result due to Mitra and Morrison [MMO95], which is needed later. This result concerns the Chernoff approximation $P_{loss} \sim \exp(-F(s^*))$ and distributions of independent, nonnegative random variables $\{u_{jk}\}$, which possess moment generating functions and satisfy the following constraints: for $k = 1, 2, \cdots, K_j$ and $j = 1, 2, \cdots, J$

$$u_{jk} \le \bar{u}_j \,, \text{ and} \tag{2.12}$$

$$E(u_{jk}) \le \rho_j \,. \tag{2.13}$$

It is assumed that $\sum_{j=1}^{J} K_j \rho_j < C$, and that $\lim_{s\to\infty} \sum_{j=1}^{J} K_j M_j'(s)/M_j(s) > C$, as otherwise there is no loss. The result is

**Proposition 1:** For any independent random variables $u_{jk}$ with distributions $V_j(x)$, which satisfy the constraints (2.12) and (2.13), there exist on-off random variables $\hat{u}_{jk}$, with distributions $\hat{V}_j(x)$, which take values 0 and $\bar{u}_j$ only, and $E(\hat{u}_{jk}) = \rho_j$, i.e.,

$$\Pr(\hat{u}_{jk} = \bar{u}_j) = 1 - \Pr(\hat{u}_{jk} = 0) = \rho_j/\bar{u}_j \,, \tag{2.14}$$

for which the Chernoff approximation to the loss probability is at least as great, i.e.,

$$F(s^*) \ge \hat{F}(\hat{s}^*) \,,$$

with equality if and only if $V_j \equiv \hat{V}_j$ $(j = 1, 2, \cdots, J)$.
□

## 3. Lossless Shaping

**3.1. Coupled Regulator and Shaper.** Here we consider the composite system in order to prove an essential property. Figure 3.1 depicts the coupled system. As shown in the figure $z(t)$, $x(t)$ and $y(t)$ respectively denote the contents of the token buffer in the regulator, the data buffer in the shaper and the token buffer of the shaper. Define

$$w(t) \triangleq \{B_T - z(t)\} - [x(t) + \{B_{TS} - y(t)\}] \,. \tag{3.1}$$

In this subsection we also let the data buffer be sufficiently large so that no overflows occur there. Our goal is to establish the nonnegativity of $w(t)$. In [EMI96] we prove

**Proposition 2:** If at any time $t'$, $w(t') \ge 0$ then for all time $t > t'$, $w(t) \ge 0$. □

Since the shaper is under the control of the network management system, we are free to set its initial conditions, i.e., conditions at connection admission. To avoid trivialities we shall assume that at connection admission time, say $t = 0$, $w(0) \ge 0$. This is ensured, for instance, by having the data buffer empty, $x(0) = 0$, and the token buffer full, $y(0) = B_{TS}$. It then follows from Proposition 2 that

$$w(t) \ge 0 \qquad \text{for all } t \ge 0 \,. \tag{3.2}$$

As a consequence we have,

**Corollary 1:** For $t \ge 0$,

$$\text{if } x(t) = 0 \text{ then } \{B_{TS} - y(t)\} \le \{B_T - z(t)\} \,. \tag{3.3}$$

□

**3.2. Lossless Shaping.** We now estimate how large $x(t)$ can be in the framework of the system in Figure 1.1, where the Dual Leaky Bucket Regulator's parameters $(r, B_T, P)$ are given, as is $P_S$, where $r < P_S \le P$. The maximum of $x(t)$ will determine the size of the data buffer in the shaper, $B_{DS}$, necessary for lossless shaping.

Let $t_0$ be the start of a busy period of the shaper's data buffer, i.e., $x(t_0) = 0$ and $x(t_0+\ ) > 0$. Let $A(t, t+\tau)$ denote the total flow of the rate process $R$

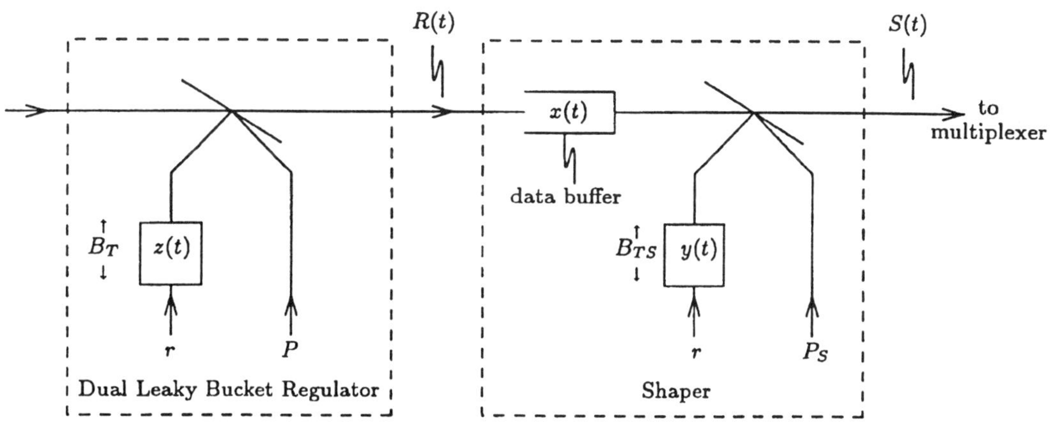


Figure 3.1: Coupled regulator and shaper.

in the interval $[t, t+\tau]$. A bound on $A(t, t+\tau)$ for all $t$ is $E(\tau)$:

$$A(t_0, t_0+\tau) \le E(\tau) \triangleq \min(P\tau, z(t_0)+r\tau) . \quad (3.4)$$

There are two cases to consider, depending upon whether the shaper's token buffer has the potential of emptying before or after the regulator's token buffer.

$$\text{Case (i):} \quad \frac{y(t_0)}{P_S - r} \le \frac{z(t_0)}{P-r} \quad (3.5)$$

$$\text{Case (ii):} \quad \frac{y(t_0)}{P_S - r} > \frac{z(t_0)}{P-r} . \quad (3.6)$$

Let $F(\tau)$ denote a lower bound on the total flow of the shaped rate process $S(t)$, which leaves the shaper's data buffer, during the interval $[t_0, t_0+\tau]$. It is assumed here that this interval is contained in the busy period of the data buffer. Clearly,

$$x(\tau) \le \bar{x}(\tau) \triangleq E(\tau) - F(\tau) . \quad (3.7)$$

Now, in Case (i),

$$\begin{aligned} F(\tau) &= P_S\tau \text{ for } 0 \le \tau \le y(t_0)/(P_S - r) \quad (3.8)\\ &= \frac{y(t_0)P_S}{P_S - r} + r\tau \quad y(t_0)/(P_S-r) < \tau . \end{aligned}$$

Since $x(t_0) = 0$, and noting that the peak buffer content is reached during the busy period,

$$x(\tau) \le z(t_0) - y(t_0) \quad \text{for all } \tau . \quad (3.9)$$

Now, by the final result of the analysis in the preceding subsection, which is stated in (3.3),

$$z(t_0) - y(t_0) \le B_T - B_{TS} . \quad (3.10)$$

Hence, for Case (i), the bound on the content of shaper's data buffer is,

$$x(\tau) \le B_T - B_{TS} . \quad (3.11)$$

Proceeding to Case (ii),

$$x(\tau) \le \frac{(P-P_S)z(t_0)}{(P-r)} \quad \text{for all } \tau, \quad (3.12)$$

again by virtue of $x(t_0) = 0$ and that the peak buffer content is attained during the busy period. We summarize the results below (see Fig. 3.2).

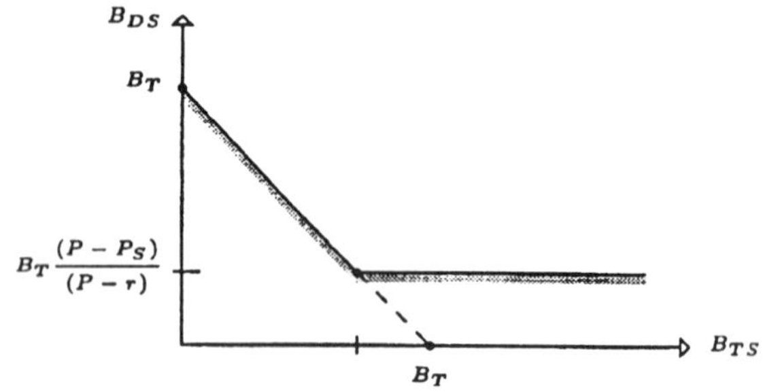


Figure 3.2: Sufficient conditions for lossless shaping.

**Proposition 3:** Sufficient conditions for lossless shaping are

$$B_{DS} \ge B_T - B_{TS}, \text{ and } B_{DS} \ge \frac{B_T(P-P_S)}{P-r}, \quad (3.13)$$

which respectively arise from Case (i) and Case (ii). □

The above result is tight in the following sense. The extremal on-off regulated process described in [EMW95], equation (2), is such that, if either inequality in (3.13) is violated, then the shaper is not lossless. Hence, the conditions in Proposition 3 are necessary for lossless shaping.

Let $D_S$ denote the prespecified bound on the delay introduced by the shaper. Now, the delay in the shaper can be as high as $B_{DS}/r$, clearly. Hence, the requirement on the maximum delay implies the constraint

$$B_{DS}/r \le D_S . \quad (3.14)$$

The system of inequalities (3.13)–(3.14) constitute the complete set of constraints for the selection of the parameters $B_{TS}$, $B_{DS}$ and $P_S$ of the shaper.

It is intuitively plausible, and also proven later, that, all else being equal, smaller values of $B_{TS}$ and $P_S$ lead to higher connection-carrying capacities at network nodes. This consideration is the motivation for the minimal solution to the above constraints, which is given in the following result.

**Proposition 4:** Given $(r, B_T, P)$ and the delay bound $D_S$, the selection of $(B_{DS}, B_{TS}, P_S)$, which satisfies the delay bound, the constraints due to lossless shaping and gives the smallest values of $B_{TS}$ and $P_S$, is obtained by replacing inequalities by equalities,

$$\begin{aligned} &B_{DS} = rD_S, \quad B_{TS} = B_T - rD_S, \\ &P_S = P - rD_S(P-r)/B_T . \end{aligned} \quad (3.15)$$

□

## 4. Lossless Multiplexing

**4.1. Single Source System.** As in [EMW95], it is helpful for the analytic development to consider a construct in which a *single* shaped traffic stream $S(t)$ feeds a buffer of infinite capacity, which is serviced by a trunk of capacity, i.e., bandwidth, $c$ ($c > r$). The physical multiplexing system is different, which is why the above construct is a "virtual" system. The schematic for the construct is shown in the following Figure 4.1.

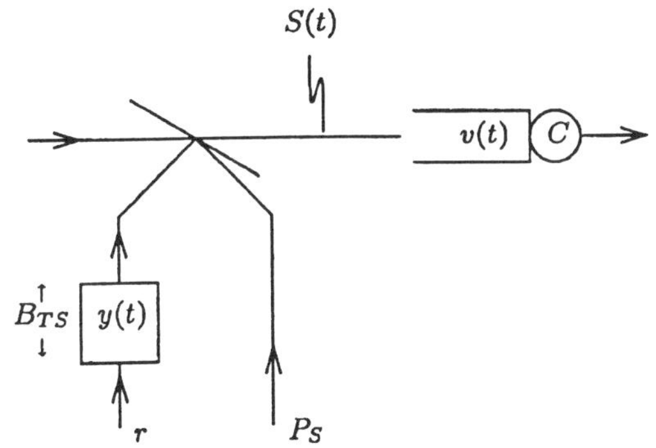


Figure 4.1: Coupling of the shaper and the single source system.

The content of the buffer is denoted by $v(t)$. The main goal of this subsection is to derive a simple expression for the supremum of the buffer content. For our purposes here the shaped stream $S(t)$ is such that the total flow in any interval $[t,\, t+\tau]$, $A_S(t,\, t+\tau)$, is bounded thus

$$A_S(t,\, t+\tau) \le \min(P_S\tau,\; y(t)+r\tau) \quad \forall t,\ \forall\tau > 0\,. \tag{4.1}$$

The presence of the token buffer content $y(t)$ on the right is on account of the coupling of the shaper with the single source system, which is necessary to get the following tight upper bound on the buffer content $v(t)$. The presence of other components, such as the shaper's data buffer, imply additional constraints on $v(t)$, which, it turns out, are not helpful and therefore not used.

**Proposition 5:** For all $t$

$$v(t) \le \frac{(P_S - c)B_{TS}}{(P_S - r)} \triangleq b\,. \tag{4.2}$$

**Proof:** Clearly the supremum of $v(t)$ occurs during a busy period of the buffer. Let $t_0$ correspond to the onset of a busy period, i.e., $v(t_0) = 0$ and $v(t_0+) > 0$. During the busy period the total flow into the buffer during the interval $[t_0,\, t_0+\tau]$ is, from (4.1), bounded by

$$\begin{cases} P_S\tau & 0 \le \tau \le y(t_0)/(P_S - r) \\ y(t_0) + r\tau & y(t_0)/(P_S - r) \le \tau\,. \end{cases} \tag{4.3}$$

On the other hand, since by assumption the interval $[t_0,\, t_0+\tau]$ is contained in the busy period, the total flow out of the buffer is at least $c\tau$. The difference, $\bar{v}(\tau)$, is a bound on the buffer content during the buffer's busy period. Hence, for $\tau \ge 0$,

$$\bar{v}(\tau) \le \frac{(P_S - c)\,y(t_0)}{(P_S - r)} \le \frac{(P_S - c)\,B_{TS}}{(P_S - r)}\,,$$

which completes the proof. □

It should be noted, once again, that the result is tight. The bound on $v(t)$ in (4.2) is realized by the extremal on-off process which turns on at rate $P_S$ when the token buffer is full and turns off when the token buffer first becomes empty.

As indicated in (4.2) the bound on the buffer content is given by $b$, which may conveniently be viewed as a function of the variable $c$, i.e., $b = b(c)$. This function is linear, decreasing.

**4.2. Lossless Multiplexing.** Here we consider the multiplexing of several, say $K$, shaped traffic streams by a FIFO buffer of capacity $B$, which is serviced by a trunk of capacity, i.e., bandwidth, $C$. The characteristics of the single source system of the preceding subsection are used to obtain the capacity of the lossless multiplexer, i.e., the maximum number of shaped streams, $K_{max}$, which may be admitted without any overflow of the multiplexer buffer occurring.

The total flow from the $k^{th}$ shaped stream $S_k(t)$ in any interval $[t,\, t+\tau]$, $A_{S_k}(t,\, t+\tau)$, is bounded as in (4.1). The aggregate flow in the interval from the superposition of $K$ shaped streams is bounded by $A_{agg}(t,\, t+\tau)$, where

$$A_{agg}(t,\, t+\tau) = \sum_{k=1}^{K} A_{S_k}(t,\, t+\tau)\,. \tag{4.4}$$

Hence,

$$\begin{aligned} A_{agg}(t,\, t+\tau) &\le K\min(P_S\tau, B_{TS} + r\tau) \\ &= \min(KP_S\tau, KB_{TS} + Kr\tau) \end{aligned} \tag{4.5}$$

Since the characterization of the aggregate flow is in terms of a single stream with parameters $(Kr, KB_{TS}, KP_S)$, we may now employ the same reasoning that was used in Proposition 5 to establish a tight bound on the content of the multiplexing buffer, $X(t)$. Assuming initially that the capacity of the multiplexing buffer is infinite, this reasoning gives

$$X(t) \le \frac{(KP_S - C)B_{TS}}{(P_S - r)}, \quad (4.6)$$

for all $t$. Hence, if

$$\frac{(KP_S - C)B_{TS}}{(P_S - r)} \le B, \quad (4.7)$$

then there is no loss in the multiplexer with a buffer of size $B$.

We will find it convenient to interpret the above result in the framework of the prior single source system.

**Proposition 6:** $K_{\max} = \lfloor C/e_0 \rfloor = \lfloor B/b_0 \rfloor$, where $(e_0, b_0)$ are solutions of the following pair of equations in $(c, b)$,

$$\frac{(P_S - c)B_{TS}}{(P_S - r)} = b \quad (4.8,\text{i})$$

$$B/b = C/c \quad (4.8,\text{ii})$$

□

The reader may verify the equivalence of (4.7) and (4.8). A graphical interpretation of (4.8) is in Figure 4.2. The line segment corresponding to (4.8,i) expresses the dependence of $b$ on $c$, as reflected in (4.2), from the analysis of the single source system. The line corresponding to (4.8,ii) states that each shaped stream is allocated each of the two resources, buffers and bandwidth, in equal proportion to their respective resource capacities. Thus, $e_0$ and $b_0$ may appropriately be called the effective bandwidth and effective buffer, respectively, for a single stream.

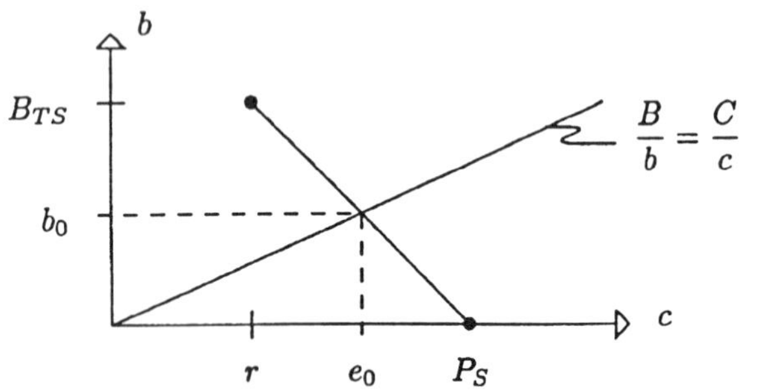


Figure 4.2: Effective bandwidth $e_0$ and effective buffer $b_0$ for lossless multiplexing.

The characterization of the capacity of the lossless multiplexing system, which is given by $K_{\max}$, is tight in the following sense: $K_{\max}$ is the maximum admissible number of shaped streams, which are extremal on-off and, furthermore, have coincident on periods. This fact follows from the analysis in [EMW95].

The reader may note that if $B_{TS}$ or $P_S$ are smaller, with all other parameters held fixed, then $e_0$ and $b_0$ are smaller and, consequently, the capacity $K_{\max}$ is greater. This claim was made earlier in Section 3.

## 5. Statistical Multiplexing

The preceding section arrived at an allocation of the two resources for each connection, which maximizes the capacity of the network node. A key requirement so far has been that no losses occur in either the shaper or the multiplexer. This requirement is relaxed in this section, where small losses upto a specified amount $L$ are allowed in the multiplexer. Furthermore, we make the assumption that the connections behave as independent statistical traffic sources, which disallows collusive behavior. The combination of the two features allows statistical multiplexing.

The key to statistical multiplexing is the observation that, (i) even though each connection is allocated resources, say bandwidth $e_0$, such allocations are not utilized all the time, and, hence, (ii) the probability that several connections will require their resource allocations simultaneously decays rapidly with the number of such connections. We rely on the Chernoff bound and asymptotic, large deviations approximation described in Section 2.2 to estimate the loss probability,

$$P_{\text{loss}} = \Pr\ (U > C), \quad (5.1)$$

where the total bandwidth load $U = \sum_{k=1}^{K} u_k$, and $u_k$ is the instantaneous random demand on bandwidth from connection $k$. The random variables $\{u_k\}$ are independent, identically distributed. Note that

$$0 \le u_k \le e_0 \text{ and } E(u_k) \le r \quad (1 \le k \le K)\ . \quad (5.2)$$

We may now use the result in Proposition 1, which gives the extremal distribution of independent, identically distributed random variables which satisfy (5.2) and maximize the Chernoff approximation to the loss probability. This gives

**Proposition 7:** The Chernoff approximation to the loss probability $P_{\text{loss}}$ in (5.1) is maximized by independent, on-off random variables $\hat{u}_k$ which only take values 0 and $e_0$, and $E(\hat{u}_k) = r$, i.e.,

$$\Pr\ (\hat{u}_k = e_0) = 1 - \Pr\ (\hat{u}_k = 0) = \omega\,, \quad (5.3)$$

where $\omega = r/e_0$. □

So far here we have only dealt with one of the resources, namely, bandwidth. We now observe that when we take into account in our capacity calculations the worst-case behavior of bandwidth demand as expressed in Proposition 7, then the constraints imposed by the other resource, namely, buffers, are also accounted for. To see this, note that buffers are utilized only when the bandwidth demand is positive. Specifically, when bandwidth demand in 0, then the buffer space demand is 0, and when the bandwidth demand is at its peak value of $e_0$, then the buffer demand, see Figure 4.2, may be conservatively bounded by $b_0$. With this bound, the bandwidth and buffer demand processes for each connection are mutually synchronized, on-off, and the loss probability expressed in (5.1) bounds the probability that either bandwidth demand exceeds $C$ or buffer space demand exceeds $B$.

Since the extremal distribution for the total bandwidth demand $U$ from $K$ connections is binomial, it is straightforward to obtain the extremal Chernoff asymptotic approximation for $P_{loss}$.

**Proposition 8:**

$$P_{loss} \sim \frac{e^{-F(s^*)}}{s^*\sigma(s^*)\sqrt{2\pi}}, \tag{5.4}$$

where

$$a = \frac{C}{K}\cdot\frac{1}{e_0}, \quad s^* = \frac{1}{e_0}\log\left[\frac{a}{1-a}\cdot\frac{1-\omega}{\omega}\right],$$

$$F(s^*) = K\left[a\log\left(\frac{a}{\omega}\right) + (1-a)\log\left(\frac{1-a}{1-\omega}\right)\right], \tag{5.5}$$

and

$$\sigma^2(s) = K\omega(1-\omega)e_0^2 \exp(se_0)/\{1-\omega+\omega\exp(se_0)\}^2 \tag{5.6}$$

□

The capacity $K_{max}$ is the value of $K$ for which

$$\frac{e^{-F(s^*)}}{s^*\sigma(s^*)\sqrt{2\pi}} = L. \tag{5.7}$$

It can be shown that the quality of service requirement $P_{loss} \le L$ is satisfied for all $K \le K_{max}$. The effective bandwidth in the context of statistical multiplexing is denoted by $e$, where $eK_{max} = C$. Clearly $e \le e_0$, the effective bandwidth for lossless multiplexing.

It requires simple calculus on (5.5) to establish the

**Corollary 2:** $F(s^*)$ is monotonic increasing with decreasing $e_0$, for fixed $r$. □

Together with the prior observation that $e_0$ is monotonic decreasing with decreasing $B_{TS}$ and decreasing $P_S$, this establishes the intuitively plausible result that the design of the shaper which maximizes capacity uses the smallest values of $B_{TS}$ and $P_S$ consistent with lossless behavior at the shaper, and these values are given in Proposition 4.

## 6. Heterogeneous Sources

Here we make some simple observations which allow the treatment in the prior sections to be extended to the case of multiple classes of connections. In fact, the observations and extensions apply only to the topics of lossless and statistical multiplexing, which are respectively treated in Sections 4 and 5. For class $j$ the regulators are specified by $(r^{(j)}, B_T^{(j)}, P^{(j)})$, the shaping filters by $(r^{(j)}, B_{TS}^{(j)}, B_{DS}^{(j)}, P_S^{(j)})$ and the number of connections by $K_j$.

The effective bandwidth and effective buffer of class $j$ sources for lossless multiplexing are obtained as described in Proposition 6, and denoted by $e_0^{(j)}$ and $b_0^{(j)}$, respectively. We now claim

**Proposition 9:** The sources $\mathbf{K} = (K_1, K_2, \cdots, K_J)$ allow lossless multiplexing if

$$\sum_{j=1}^{J} K_j e_0^{(j)} \le C. \tag{6.1}$$

**Proof:** As a first step note that it follows from (6.1) and (4.8,ii) that

$$\sum_{j=1}^{J} K_j b_0^{(j)} \le B. \tag{6.2}$$

Now consider a virtual partition of the bandwidth into components $\{C_j\}$ and the buffer into components $\{B_j\}$, such that $C_j \triangleq K_j e_0^{(j)}$ and $B_j \triangleq K_j b_0^{(j)}$, with $(C_j, B_j)$ dedicated to class $j$ sources. Note that

$$\frac{B_j}{B} = \frac{C_j}{C}, \tag{6.3}$$

so that the properties of lossless behavior described in Section 4 carry over here to each virtually partitioned system dedicated to all sources of a particular class. □

We let $\mathcal{A}_0$ denote the set obtained from the above proposition of admissible sources for lossless multiplexing, i.e., $\mathcal{A}_0 = \left\{\mathbf{K} \mid \sum_{j=1}^{J} K_j e_0^{(j)} \le C\right\}$.

Proceeding to statistical multiplexing, the loss probability, $P_{\text{loss}}$ is given by the expression in (5.1), where now $U = \sum_{j=1}^{J} \sum_{k=1}^{K_j} u_{jk}$ and $u_{jk}$ is the instantaneous demand on the bandwidth from connection $k$ of class $j$. The Chernoff asymptotic approximation is used to estimate $P_{\text{loss}}$. The result in Proposition 2 applies to the case of heterogeneous sources and hence the natural extension of Proposition 8 holds, i.e., the Chernoff asymptotic approximation to the loss probability $P_{\text{loss}}$ is maximized by independent on-off random variables $\hat{u}_{jk}$, which take values 0 and $e_0^{(j)}$ and $E(\hat{u}_{jk}) = r^{(j)}$, i.e.,

$$\Pr\,(\hat{u}_{jk} = e_0^{(j)}) = 1 - \Pr\,(\hat{u}_{jk} = 0) = \omega^{(j)}, \quad (6.4)$$

where $\omega^{(j)} = r^{(j)}/e_0^{(j)}$. Assume that $\sum K_j r^{(j)} < C$ and $\sum_j K_j e_0^{(j)} > C$.

**Proposition 10:** The worst-case Chernoff asymptotic approximation for $P_{\text{loss}}$ with statistical multiplexing and heterogeneous sources is

$$P_{\text{loss}} \sim \frac{e^{-F(s^*)}}{s^* \sigma(s^*) \sqrt{2\pi}}, \quad (6.5)$$

where $s^*$ is the unique positive real solution to the equation

$$\sum_j \frac{K_j \omega^{(j)} e_0^{(j)} \,\exp(s e_0^{(j)})}{1 - \omega^{(j)} + \omega^{(j)} \,\exp(s e_0^{(j)})} = C, \quad (6.6)$$

$$F(s) = sC - \sum_j K_j \log\left\{1 - \omega^{(j)} + \omega^{(j)} \,\exp(s e_0^{(j)})\right\}, \quad (6.7)$$

and

$$\sigma^2(s) = \sum_j \frac{K_j \omega^{(j)} (1 - \omega^{(j)}) (e_0^{(j)})^2 \,\exp(s e_0^{(j)})}{\left\{1 - \omega^{(j)} + \omega^{(j)} \,\exp(s e_0^{(j)})\right\}^2}. \quad (6.8)$$

□

Let $\mathcal{A}_L$ denote the set of connection $\mathbf{K} = (K_1, \cdots, K_J)$ such that $P_{\text{loss}}$ as estimated by the expression in (6.5) does not exceed $L$. For a wide variety of conditions the boundary $\partial \mathcal{A}_L$ is closely approximated by an appropriately chosen linear hyperplane, which, moreover, conservatively bounds $\mathcal{A}_L$. An optimistic upper bound on $\mathcal{A}_L$ is given by $\{\mathbf{K} : \sum K_j e_j \le C\}$, where $e_j$ is obtained by considering class $j$ in isolation and applying the explicit techniques in Section 5. When $\partial \mathcal{A}_L$ is close to being linear, which is typically the case, this approximation is close to the conservative estimate.

## 7. Numerical Investigation

The investigations reported in this section numerically illustrate the mathematical results of prior sections on the shaper design and the role of shaping in increasing the network capacity.

Figures 7.1 and 7.2 examine the effect of traffic shaping and the associated traffic delay on the effective bandwidth of the traffic sources, and demonstrate the advantage of optimizing the shaper's parameters. In Figure 7.1, we consider the system depicted in Figure 1.1, where a single class of sources is subject to dual leaky bucket regulation, then shaped and multiplexed on a link with transmission capacity of 45 Mbps and (FIFO) buffer size of 1000 cells. The parameters of the dual leaky bucket regulator are: mean rate $r = 0.15$ Mbps, peak rate $P = 1.5$ Mbps and maximum burst size $Q = 250$ cells, where $Q = B_T P/(P - r)$. The size of the data buffer, $B_{DS}$, of the lossless shaper (and hence its maximum delay) is varied from 0 to 225 cells, and the effective bandwidth of the shaped traffic when the cell loss probability at the link is not greater than $10^{-9}$ is plotted for the case when the peak rate of the shaper, $P_S$, is equal to the peak rate of the leaky bucket regulator, $P$, and for the case when $P_S$ is set to the optimum value which is stated in Proposition 4, Section 3, and referred to as $P_S^*$ in the figures. Observe first that increasing the data buffer, $B_{DS}$, from 0 to 225 cells (maximum delay from 0 to 636 msec) has the effect of reducing the effective bandwidth from 0.45 Mbps to the source mean rate value of 0.15 Mbps. Second, the optimization of the peak rate of the shaper results in an appreciable reduction in the effective bandwidth. Figure 7.2 is similar to Figure 7.1, except that the parameters of the regulator are $r = 0.15$ Mbps, $P = 6.0$ Mbps and $Q = 25$ cells. Notice that in this case varying the peak rate of the shaper $P_S$ does not reduce the effective bandwidth significantly.

In Figures 7.3 we consider the multiplexing of two classes of sources in the configuration shown in Figure 1.2; class 1 sources are real-time (delay-sensitive), while class 2 sources are non-real time (delay insensitive). The multiplexer parameters are $B = 18000$ cells and $C = 150$ Mbps, and hence it introduces a maximum delay of 51 msec, which may be considered to be the maximum delay tolerance of class 1. Since class 2 tolerates greater delay, its traffic is shaped to reduce its effective bandwidth. The boundary of the admissible region of class 1 and class 2 sources is plotted for different values of shaping delay, $D_S$, for class 2, ranging from zero to 200 msec. Observe that by shaping class 2 we are able to significantly increase

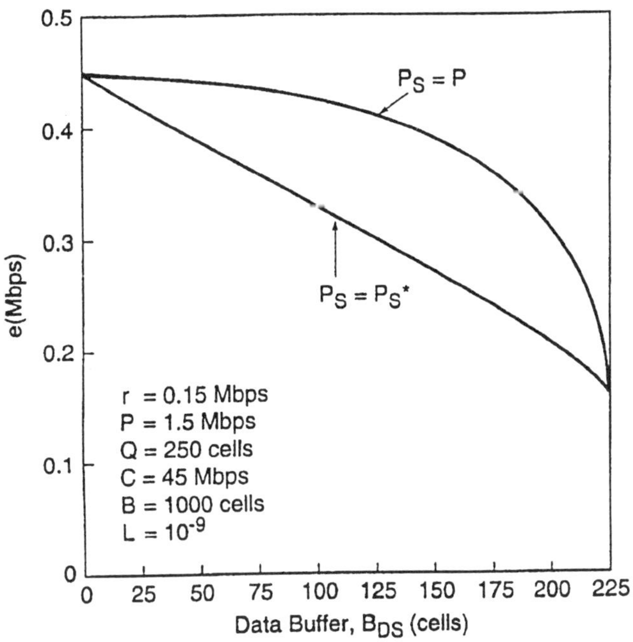


Figure 7.1: Effective bandwidth $e$ versus the size of shaper's data buffer, $B_{DS}$, showing the effect of optimizing the shaper's peak rate $P_S$.

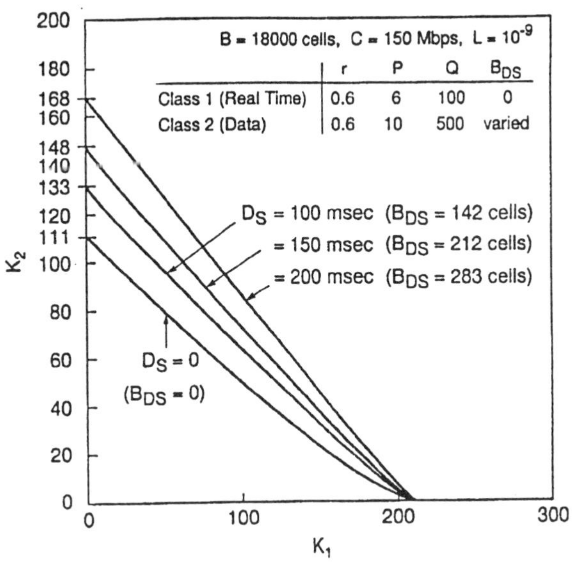


Figure 7.3: Admissible region for the multiplexing of a real-time source class and a non-real-time source class showing the effect of shaping the non-real-time sources.

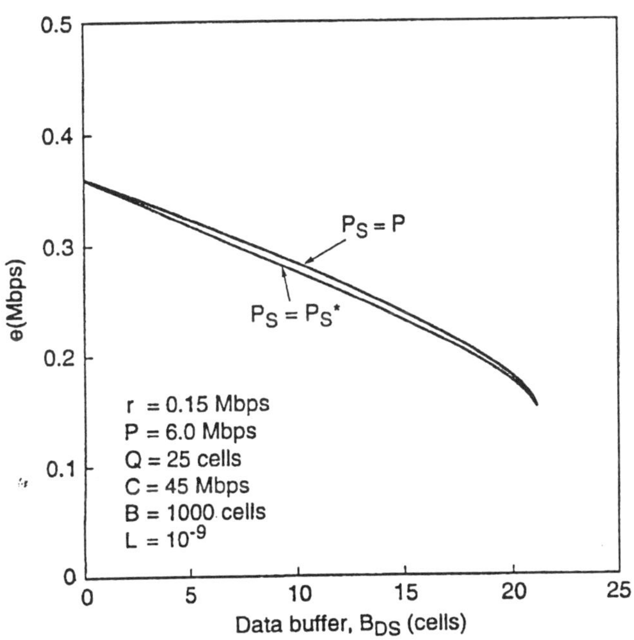


Figure 7.2: Effective bandwidth $e$ versus the size of shaper's data buffer, $B_{DS}$, showing the effect of optimizing the shaper's peak rate $P_S$.

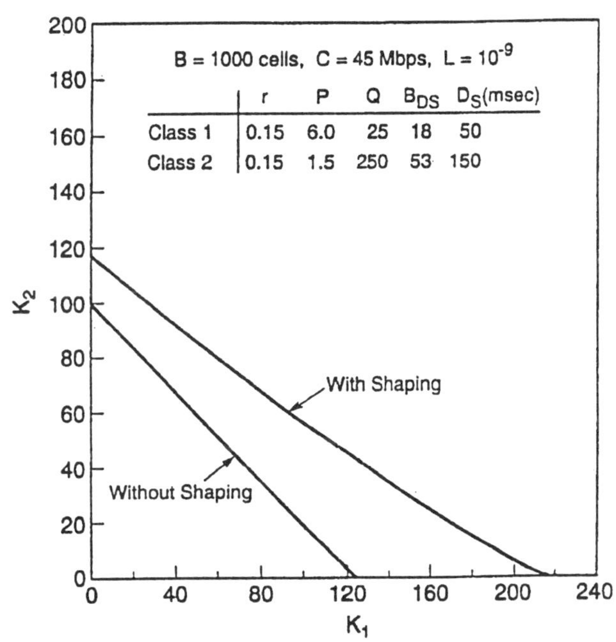


Figure 7.4: Admissible region for the multiplexing of two source classes showing the effect of shaping the two classes.

the capacity of the system while meeting the delay constraints of both classes. In Figure 7.4 the admissible region is plotted for the two class of sources considered separately in Figures 7.1 and 7.2. Each class is shaped according to a maximum delay constraint and the boundary of the admissible region with and without shaping are plotted, illustrating the significant gain in capacity due to shaping.

## 8. Concluding Remarks

The paper gives a framework for integrating shaping on a per-connection basis with FIFO statistical multiplexing. It is shown that differences in delay tolerances between different traffic classes may be exploited by shaping the less delay sensitive traffic. Shaping is shown to increase the nodal connection-carrying capacity, with the beneficial increase often quite substantial when the optimum shaper design is utilized. The framework of the paper is based on source models which are asynchronous, worst-case subject to Dual Leaky Bucket regulation. It is shown how admission control to the composite of the shaper and the multiplexer may be implemented efficiently by using effective bandwidth parameters for sources.

In future work we propose to enhance the framework in several respects. First, small cell losses are allowed in the shaper, so that the total loss has components arising from the shaper and the statistical multiplexer. Second, the data buffers from various shapers are designed to share a common memory pool. Both features will have the effect of increasing connection-carrying capacity for given total memory. Finally, we believe that the framework presented here extends readily to switches where the buffering is on a per-connection basis and the scheduling is weighted round-robin.

## Acknowledgement

The carryover of benefits from a prior collaboration with our colleague R. H. Wentworth is gratefully acknowledged.

## References

[CRU91] R. L. Cruz, "A calculus for network delay, Part I: Network elements in isolation", *IEEE Trans. Inform Theory* **37**, 1991, pp. 114–131.

[EMI91] A. I. Elwalid and D. Mitra, "Analysis and design of rate-based congestion control of high speed networks, I: stochastic fluid models, access regulation", *Queueing Systems* **9**, 1991, pp. 29–63.

[EMI96] A. I. Elwalid and D. Mitra, "Traffic shaping at a network node: theory, optimum design, admission control", *Bell Labs Tech. Report*, 1996.

[EMW95] A. I. Elwalid, D. Mitra and R. H. Wentworth, "A new approach for allocating buffers and bandwidth to heterogeneous, regulated traffic in an ATM node", *IEEE J. Select. Areas Commun.* **13**:(6), 1995, pp. 1115–1127.

[GGP96] L. Georgiadis, R. Guerin, V. Peris and K. N. Sivarajan, "Efficient network QoS provisioning based on per node traffic shaping", in *Proc. IEEE INFOCOM*, 1996, pp. 102–110.

[HRO96] M. Hamdi and J. W. Roberts, "Burstiness bounds based multiplexing schemes for VBR video connections in the B-ISDN", in *Broadband Communications*, Ed. B. Plattner, Springer, 1996, pp. 53–64.

[HUI90] J. Y. Hui, "Resource allocation for broadband networks", *IEEE J. Select. Areas Commun.* **6**, 1988, pp. 1598–1608.

[KBL92] K. Kvol and S. Blaabjerg, "Bounds and approximations for the periodic on/off queue with applications to ATM traffic control", in *Proc. IEEE INFOCOM*, 1992, pp. 487–494.

[KEL91] F. P. Kelly, "Effective bandwidths at multi-type queues", *Queueing Systems* **9**, 1991, pp. 5–15.

[KNI96] E. W. Knightly, "H-BIND: A new approach to providing statistical performance guarantees to VBR traffic", in *Proc. IEEE INFOCOM*, 1996, pp. 1091–1099.

[MMO95] D. Mitra and J. A. Morrison, "Multiple time scale regulation and worst case processes for ATM network control", in *Proc. 34th Conf. on Decision and Control*, 1995, pp. 353–358.

[PET65] V. V. Petrov, "On the probabilities of large deviations for sums of independent random variables", *Theory Probab. Applicat.* **10**, 1965, pp. 287–298.

[PGA93] A. K. Parekh and R. G. Gallager, "A generalized processor sharing approach to flow control in integrated services network – the single – node case", *IEEE/ACM Trans. Networking* **1**, 1993, pp. 344–357.

[RBC93] J. W. Roberts, B. Bensaou and Y. Canetti, "A traffic control framework for high speed data transmission", in *Proc. IFIP Workshop Modeling, Performance Eval. ATM Technol.*, 1993, pp. 243–262.

[ROB92] *Performance Evaluation and Design of Multiservice Networks*, Ed. J. W. Roberts, Commission of the European Communities, Final Rep. COST 224 project, 1992.

[TUR86] J. S. Turner, "New directions in communications (Or which way to the information age?)", *IEEE Commun. Mag.*, Oct. 1986.

[WKZ96] D. E. Wrege, E. W. Knightly, H. Zhang and J. Liebeherr, "Deterministic delay bounds for VBR video in packet-switching networks: fundamental limits and practical trade-offs", *IEEE/ACM Trans. Networking* **4**:(3), 1996, pp. 352–362.

# Bulk Multicast Transport Protocol

Robert Morris
Division of Engineering and Applied Sciences
Harvard University
Cambridge, MA 02138 USA

## Abstract

*BMTP offers rate controlled multicast with reliability, high throughput, and support for large numbers of receivers. A multicast sender needs feedback from receivers to recover from errors and to choose an appropriate send rate, but must avoid being overwhelmed as the number of receivers grows. BMTP does this by keeping the rate at which each receiver sends feedback inversely proportional to a running estimate of the number of receivers. BMTP bases its send rate on the minimum of the receive rates observed by the receivers, causing the sender to slow down in the face of packet loss or competing traffic, and to speed up when there is spare network capacity. BMTP's NAK-based retransmission rarely sends any data more than twice, a substantial improvement over iterated unicast. Rabin's Information Dispersal Algorithm can reduce this re-send rate as close as desired to the underlying loss rate of the network. Simulations with 1000 receivers substantiate these claims.*

## 1. Introduction

Lack of a suitable multicast transport protocol has prevented bulk data transfer applications from using the Internet multicast facilities. Netnews, mailing lists, and mass software updates, for instance, all distribute large amounts of identical information to many receivers. Currently, however, these applications use many one-to-one (or unicast) transfers over the Internet, sending the same data over the network many times. The idea of multicasting the data just once is old [11], but no existing multicast transport protocol provides the reliability and scalability required by these applications. BMTP addresses this need.

BMTP solves only the reliable high-throughput multicast problem; it does not cater to all multicast applications. These are its design goals:

- Allow a sender to transmit a long stream of data to many receivers over the Internet.
- Assure reliability by re-sending lost data.
- Send as fast as the network allows without overloading it.
- Limit the sender's complexity and the load placed on it, as it could be a bottleneck.
- Allow receivers to come and go at any time.
- Adapt to widely varying network capacities along the paths to different receivers.
- Do not require changes to the underlying Internet.
- Scale to thousands of receivers over a wide area.

BMTP's goals do not include low delay, coordination among multiple senders, and consistent message ordering. Interactive applications might work better with multicast transport protocols that provide low delay [2,5]. Protocols that guarantee consistency among multiple participants [1] are better suited than BMTP to distributed computations. Applications with a limited number of receivers or limited network complexity may be more efficient with protocols [3,10,12] that take advantage of such limits. BMTP's intended applications fall outside these classes, and BMTP takes advantage of the their tolerance of delay to provide scaling and adaptability to a wide range of network conditions.

The next section describes BMTP's relationship to existing work. Section 3 presents BMTP's design, and sections 4 and 5 describe further details. Section 6 uses simulation results to show how well BMTP works across a range of error rates and numbers of receivers. Section 7 presents the improvements in error recovery made possible by the Information Dispersal Algorithm.

## 2. Related Work

BMTP relies on IP Multicast [4] to deliver packets to receivers. An IP Multicast application can send packets to one of a number of special multicast IP addresses, or ask to receive all packets sent to such an address. IP Multicast routers keep track of all the receivers listening to each address; the receivers for each address are called a group. IP Multicast delivers packets along a tree rooted at the sender with a leaf at each group member. Figure 1 shows an example of a multicast delivery tree layered on top of an internet. This tree provides higher efficiency than separate unicasts to each receiver. No one entity, not even the sender, needs to keep track of the entire group membership; this allows IP Multicast groups to scale to thousands of members. Like the Internet, IP Multicast provides unreliable best-effort delivery. The distribution



0-8186-7780-5/97 $10.00 © 1997 IEEE 

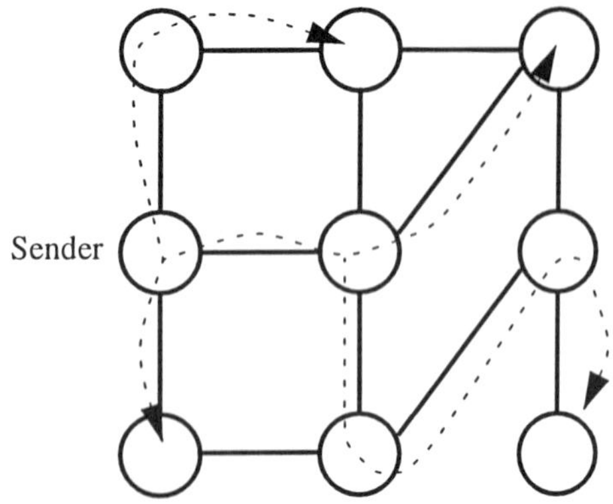


Figure 1: IP Multicast Distribution Tree Example

tree often causes a single packet loss near the sender to affect more receivers than a loss near a leaf.

A number of previous systems have addressed reliable multicast. One approach is to extend ideas in reliable unicast protocols such as TCP [8]. For instance, HPBFTP [3] and SCE [10] require that all receivers acknowledge the data as they are sent. The sender knows the identities of the receivers, so it can re-send any data not acknowledged by all receivers within one round-trip time of the initial transmission. Further, the acknowledgments (ACKs) allow the sender to use sliding window flow control to avoid overloading the network or receivers. While these are important properties, such a scheme cannot scale well: the sender cannot easily track a large and changing list of receivers, nor avoid being swamped by a large number of acknowledgments for each packet sent.

MTP [1] fixes some of these problems, though it focuses on ordering messages from many senders rather than bulk transfer. An MTP receiver does not acknowledge every data packet. Instead, it returns a negative acknowledgment (NAK) packet to the sender when it notices that it has failed to receive a data packet. Thus the sender receives NAK packets in proportion to the number of receivers times the loss rate, not times the send rate. However, if multiple receivers miss the same data packet, they may flood the sender with NAKs. This might happen constantly in a large network. In addition, because MTP does not use ACKs, it cannot use a sliding window for flow control. Instead the sender must pace itself with rate control. However, the protocol specification does not mention a general method for adapting this rate to changing conditions in a large network.

SRM [5] provides a solution to the problem of multiple NAKs for the same lost packet. A receiver delays transmission of a NAK packet in a manner designed to ensure that the receiver closest to the point where the packet was lost sends a NAK first. The receiver multicasts the NAK to all the other receivers as well as the sender, so that any participant with a copy of the lost data can re-send it. Again, participants that receive a NAK delay re-sending the data in a way that makes it likely that only the closest participant will re-send. Thus, in many situations, a lost data packet will result in only one NAK and re-sent data packet.

SRM is well suited to interactive traffic but has some drawbacks for bulk transfers. If retransmission is to be efficient, all the receivers must remember all recently transmitted data. This may not be reasonable for large amounts of data. SRM also includes no adaptive flow control mechanism to avoid overloading the network. Since the number of NAKs generated is only loosely related to the number of packet loss events, it might be hard for the sender to gather enough information to adjust its rate. For instance, suppose there are 1000 receivers, and the sender sees one NAK for every two data packets it sends. This could mean that all the receivers are seeing 50% packet loss, or that 999 of them are receiving perfectly and just one has a problem. The sender might wish to drastically reduce its rate in the first case, and keep it the same in the second, but has no way in SRM to distinguish the two.

The IVS video multicast system [2], while not reliable, does have adaptive rate control. Each receiver keeps track of the fraction of packets it failed to receive (presumably due to network overload). The sender decides what fraction of receivers are overloaded by probing a small subset of them, chosen randomly. The sender decreases its send rate by half if more than 1.4% of the receivers are losing packets. It increases its send rate slowly if none of the receivers report loss. BMTP, as well as providing reliability, allows more accurate flow control by giving the sender more specific information about receive rates.

The RMTP system [7] uses ACKs for reliability and a window for flow control. It avoids flooding the sender with ACKs by combining them as they flow back up the multicast tree. The combining nodes may re-send missing data if they have it stored locally. RMTP requires changes to multicast routers to allow such retransmissions to be sent only to the sub-tree below the combining node. RMTP lacks a mechanism to adapt the number and placement of combining nodes to changes in the number and location of receivers. Finally, RMTP's ACK combining scheme discards information that the sender needs to set its window size, and thus its transmission rate. An RMTP sender decreases its window when ACKs indicate that too many packets are being lost. Combining nodes that buffer and re-send lost data will not report losses to the sender unless they run out of buffer space.

Combining nodes that merely combine ACKs will tend to report every packet as lost if there are many receivers. In either case the information available to the sender may be misleading.

## 3. BMTP Architecture

BMTP bases its error and flow control on status packets sent from receivers to the sender. Each status packet contains the rate at which the receiver recently received data. This receive rate is the number of bytes per time successfully delivered to the receiver by the network; a receiver will report a rate lower than the send rate if the network is slow, if the network drops packets, or if the receiver cannot keep up with the sender. A status packet may optionally contain a NAK as well: the sequence number of a missing packet. Receivers unicast status packets to the sender at times described below.

The BMTP sender arranges to receive only one status packet per data packet it sends as follows. It maintains a number N, an estimate of the number of receivers. The sender includes N in each data packet it sends. Whenever a receiver gets a data packet, it sends back a status packets with probability 1/N. The sender measures the ratio of status packets it receives to data packets it has sent. If this ratio is higher than one, the estimate N is too low; and if lower, N is too high. The sender periodically divides N by the ratio to adapt to any changes in the number of receivers. Thus, no matter how many receivers miss a given data packet, the sender will not have to deal with a high rate of incoming status packets.

The sender maintains an estimate of a reasonable transmit rate, and the minimum receive rate recently reported in a status packet. When it receives a status packet which indicates a receive rate substantially less than the previous minimum, it immediately decreases the transmit rate to the indicated receive rate. The sender periodically increases the transmit rate to be slightly higher than the minimum receive rate recently reported. This algorithm will increase the send rate to just over the capacity of the slowest part of the system, whether that is a slow network link or a slow CPU. It knows when it has reached the bottleneck capacity because reported receive rates stop increasing. If network capacity decreases, or if packets are lost, one or more receivers will observe a decreased receive rate. These receivers will notify the sender of the lower rate, and the sender will send at that rate but no slower. The algorithm intentionally overloads the network slightly in order to detect spare capacity. As described below, BMTP can recover from the resulting packet losses with little loss in efficiency. This may seem a greedy policy, but it is analogous to TCP's congestion window increase algorithm [6].

Receivers detect missing data packets by looking for gaps in the packet sequence numbers. Each time the receiver sends a status packet, it can ask the sender to re-send one data packet. The receiver will only ask for a packet that has been missing for a while, in case the network re-orders packets and to allow the sender some flexibility in the order in which it sends data. The receiver will not ask for the same packet twice in quick succession, to give the sender time to respond to the earlier request.

The sender may need to make decisions about which packets to re-send; even though it will receive at most one NAK per data packet it sends, it may wish to limit the bandwidth used by re-transmissions. Note that the transmit rate described above applies to all packets the sender sends, including re-transmissions. The sender could record all NAK requests and service them in some order. However, this is not necessary. The sender is willing to use some fraction of its transmit rate for re-transmissions. As each NAK arrives, the sender responds to it if recent re-sends have used less than that fraction, and discards the NAK otherwise. If there are many NAKs, the sender will use up the allowed fraction with responses, and remembering NAKs won't cause it to re-send any faster. If there are only a few NAKs, the sender will be willing to respond to all of them. Receivers re-send NAKs periodically in case the sender ignores them or the network drops them.

As described, this scheme has trouble with very non-uniform packet loss. Suppose one receiver misses many packets, but 999 others have perfect reception. The one receiver can request only one re-transmission for every 1000 packets sent, which is only enough to recover from a tiny loss rate of 0.1 percent. Few of the status packets the sender gets will have a NAK in them; the others will be wasted from the point of view of error correction. BMTP handles non-uniform loss by weighting the receiver counting mechanism described above by the number of packets each receiver is missing. Call this number M for a particular receiver. Receivers cap M at a global constant K to avoid one receiver hogging all the NAK bandwidth. The receiver places MAX(MIN(M, K), 1) in status packets. The sender sends out its estimate N of the sum of these numbers in data packets. The receiver returns a status packet with probability MAX(MIN(M, K), 1) / N in response to each data packet. This scheme allows less reliable receivers to send more status packets and thus more NAKs. Note that this means the bandwidth samples in status packets are dominated by the receivers with high loss rates, which is appropriate since they will tend to have the lowest receive rates.

## 4. Timing Details

The discussion above omitted the details of timing

| Data Packet Field | Bytes |
|---|---|
| UDP/IP Header | 28 |
| # of Receivers | 4 |
| Measurement Interval | 4 |
| Packet Seq # | 8 |
| Data Seq # | 8 |
| Data Payload | 512 |

| Status Packet Field | Bytes |
|---|---|
| UDP/IP Header | 28 |
| Measurement Interval | 4 |
| Packets Received | 8 |
| Packets Lost | 8 |
| NAK Data Seq # | 8 |

Figure 2: Packet Formats

intervals. BMTP defines a constant control interval, which must be at least the maximum possible round trip time including queuing delay. The experimental implementation uses ten seconds. Control is exerted once per control interval. This includes the sender increasing the transmit rate and the sender changing the estimated number of receivers that it announces. Receivers wait for a control interval before sending a NAK for a missing packet, and between NAKs for the same packet. The idea is that any of these actions takes at least one round trip time before its effects will be noticed by the actor.

BMTP defines a measurement interval to be twice the control interval. All measurements are averaged over the measurement interval. For instance, the receivers measure the receive rate and the sender estimates the ratio of status packets to data packets over a measurement interval.

These intervals are conservative constants because it is difficult to estimate the round trip time adaptively. An accurate estimate would speed BMTP's response to lost data and increases in available network bandwidth (recall that BMTP immediately slows down in response to reports of decreased bandwidth). Low delay re-transmission is not critical for bulk transfers. The sender must retain data to re-send it, and the receiver must remember out of order arrivals, but they can do this on disk rather than in expensive main memory.

One danger of a short measurement interval is that the sender will not hear status packets from all receivers in each interval. The send rate in packets per second times the measurement interval yields the number of status packets the sender will hear. If reliability is critical, it may be necessary to increase the measurement interval to reflect the number of receivers. Another possibility is to allow more than one status packet per data packet. In practice it is enough that status packets give the sender a sample of the receive rates observed by the receivers, from which the sender need only select the minimum. As long as there are no tiny minorities among the receivers, such a sample will likely include a rate close to the minimum.

The experimental version of BMTP sends 5 percent faster than the minimum reported receive rate. The 5 percent figure is a trade-off between the speed at which BMTP can ramp up its rate to make use of spare bandwidth and the rate at which it forces the network to drop packets.

## 5. Practical Details

This description of BMTP assumes an infinite stream of bytes. Typical applications will want to transfer a stream of finite-size files. The intent is that an upper protocol layer place file identifiers and delimiters in the payload of BMTP data packets. The BMTP sender needs to be able to ask the file layer for a block of data, giving it a byte offset in the BMTP stream. The sender may ask for any given block of data more than once if it must re-send it. The BMTP receiver will deliver blocks to the file layer along with a byte offset. The receiver may deliver blocks out of order, expecting the file layer to store them until it accumulates a full file.

BMTP cannot guarantee complete reliability. A receiver may be powered down or disconnected from the net indefinitely. The sender may wish to place a limit on the age of data it re-sends, to avoid having to buffer it forever. The sender may also wish to enforce a minimum send rate, knowing that receivers on very slow links might not be able to keep up. These unlucky receivers will wish to generate many NAKs. For this reason, BMTP places the limit K on the weight allowed each receiver in the receiver count estimation algorithm. The sender could also ignore NAKs in status messages that report receive rates lower than the enforced minimum send rate.

If BMTP comes to the end of the data to be sent, it keeps sending empty data packets at a low rate, which allows receivers to continue to report lost packets.

Figure 2 shows the BMTP packet formats. The sender places the measurement interval in milliseconds in each data packet it multicasts so the receivers need not compile this number into their code; the measurement interval does not change over the life of a session. The sender includes two sequence numbers in each data packet. The packet sequence number uniquely identifies packets; a retransmission will have a different packet sequence number than the original transmission. Receivers use the packet sequence numbers to decide how many packets they have missed. The data sequence number indicates where the payload lies in the stream of bytes to transmit. Receivers use data sequence numbers to ask for specific data to be re-sent. Each status packet includes the total number of packets the receiver has recently received and missed. To allow receivers some flexibility, status packets include the interval over which those counts were taken. The status packet also includes one optional data sequence number which the receiver is missing and would like the sender to retransmit.

## 6. Experimental Results

A test version of BMTP exists, running as a user application on UNIX workstations. A single sender on a 10-megabit Ethernet can sustain about 5 megabits per second to half a dozen receivers. The system also works efficiently when one receiver is connected by way of a modem: the sender keeps the modem busy, losing only the expected 5% of packets.

Simulation with a wide variety of error rates and numbers of receivers illustrates BMTP's strengths and limitations. The simulator used for the following discussion models the network path from the sender to each receiver independently, as if the multicast tree consisted of a separate link from the sender to each receiver. For BMTP this topology is a worst case. Such a flat tree tends to produce different sets of lost packets at different receivers. Receivers in more tree-like topologies would tend to see similar sets of losses due to packets being dropped near the root of the tree. Thus the number of distinct lost packets over all receivers will tend to be higher in the simulated topology than in a tree-like topology. Since BMTP places a limit on the rate at which receivers can produce NAKs, it is at a disadvantage when many different packets are missing.

Each simulated path involves a queue which can hold at most 50 512-byte packets. Packets leave each queue at a rate specified in the description of each simulation below. If a packet arrives from the sender and the queue is full, the new arrival is dropped. Packets may also be dropped with a uniform probability on the way into each queue; this is meant to simulate transmission line errors. The receivers share a single channel on which to send status packets to the sender. This reverse channel runs at a rate of 500 packets per second, has a queue with maximum length 50, and suffers the same transmission line loss rate as the forward channels. The faster reverse bandwidth is reasonable because status packets are much shorter than data packets. Each link has a one-way propagation delay of 50 milliseconds.

Figure 3 depicts BMTP recovering from an initial

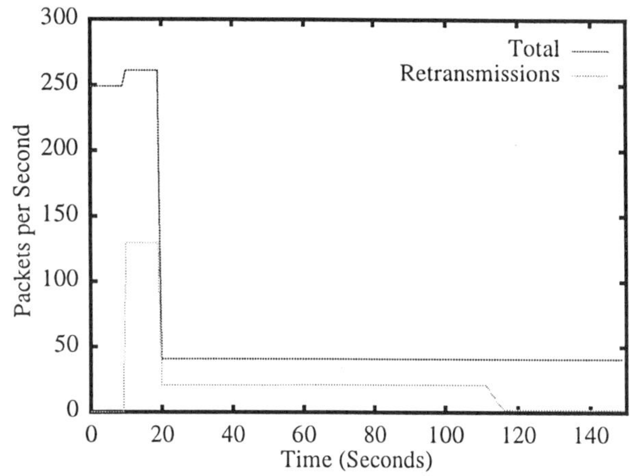


Figure 3: BMTP Start-up

overestimate of the network bandwidth. Ordinarily BMTP would start at a low rate; the high initial rate in this example is for illustration only. In this simulation there are 100 receivers. The slowest receiver can receive at 40 packets per second, and the rest receive at 100 packets per second. The graph's x axis is time in seconds, and the y axis indicates packets sent per second. The upper line indicates the total number of packets the sender sent in a second. The lower line indicates how many of these were retransmissions. The sender starts sending five times too fast, since it knows nothing about network conditions initially; it keeps up this rate for one measurement interval of twenty seconds. In ordinary operation, some receiver would tell the transmitter to slow down fairly quickly; however, the receivers do not report their receive rates until they have observed them for at least one measurement interval of 20 seconds. Thus BMTP's rate control mechanism begins to take effect at time 21, at which point the sender immediately decreases its rate. From then on the sender maintains a rate of about 42 packets per second, just over the capacity of the slowest receiver. Receivers start reporting losses at time 11; recall that they delay such reports for at least one control interval in case the packet is late. Until time 115 the sender uses half the bandwidth for re-transmissions, since over 3000 packets were lost when it was sending too fast. The server is willing to devote no more than half its bandwidth to re-transmissions. After time 120 the sender only needs to re-send the 5% of packets lost because it sends 5% too fast.

Figure 4 shows the effect of transmission line errors

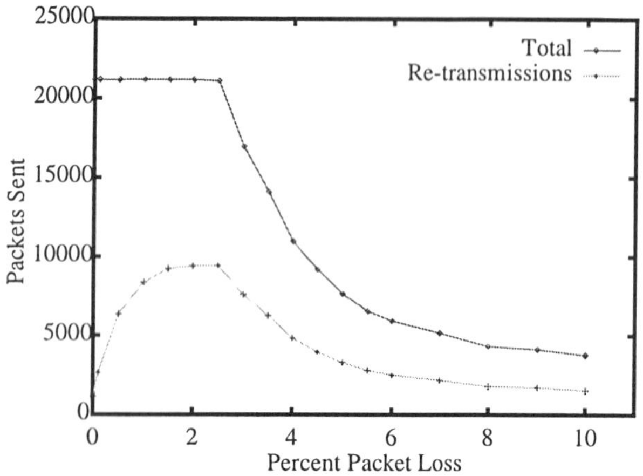


Figure 4: Effect of Transmission Errors

on BMTP performance. Such errors might include telephone line noise disrupting modem traffic. The x axis indicates the percent of packets the simulator throws away to simulate transmission line errors. Packets lost due to queue overruns are not included in the x value, so even at the origin of the graph, about five percent of packets are being lost due to overruns. The y axis shows total packets sent, and of those how many were re-transmissions. Each point represents one 500 second simulation run. The sender starts out at a send rate slightly higher than 40 packets per second; thus the expected number of packets sent in each simulated run is roughly 21000. The simulation configuration is otherwise as described in the previous paragraph.

The leftmost part of Figure 4 is not surprising. Even with no transmission errors, the sender must re-send the 5% of packets lost due to queue overruns. Thus 1113 of the 21000 packets were re-transmissions even when there were no transmission errors; that is just over 5%. As the error rate climbs towards 2%, the sender must re-send correspondingly more packets. The re-send rate flattens out briefly after 2% because the probability that two receivers lose the same packet increases. Such double losses are fixed by single re-transmissions. However, just before 3% loss the sender's overall transmission rate abruptly decreases. The receivers reflect losses not just with NAKs, but also in the receive rates they send back. Whenever the sender sees a reported receive rate more than 5% less than its current rate, it decreases the rate. So any transmission error rate approaching 5% will cause the sender to decrease its rate. If the losses were caused by congestion, they would soon go away, if only because BMTP decreases its offered load. However, transmission errors don't decrease when the load decreases. Thus a high enough error rate causes the sender to gradually decrease its send rate, even though it would be acceptable for it to send faster. In practice, few IP networks have transmission errors even as high as one percent. They may experience more congestion loss than that, but BMTP's rate reduction algorithm reacts correctly to congestion loss.

BMTP still works with 1000 users. Figure 5 shows

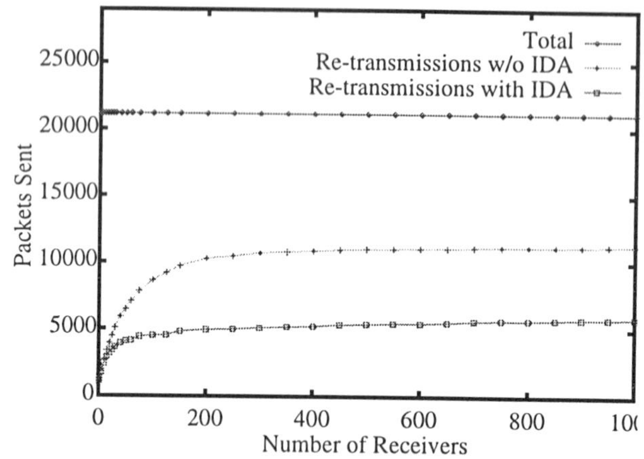


Figure 5: Effect of Many Receivers

the effect of increasing numbers of receivers. Each point in the top line represents the total number of packets sent, and each point in the middle line the number which were re-sends, during a 500 second simulation with the indicated number of receivers. In each simulation, the network bandwidth to one receiver was 40 packets per second, and to all the others 100 packets per second. Each receiver independently loses 1% of data packets because of transmission errors. Just for this simulation the sender always gives preference to retransmissions over sending new data, and places no limit on the fraction of bandwidth devoted to retransmission. From the fact that the total is always just over 20000 packets, or 40*500, we can conclude that the sender sustains the correct transmit rate. The danger, which BMTP avoids, is that status packets from the slowest receiver might not arrive at the sender often enough, allowing the sender to increase its bandwidth to the 100 packets/second available to all the other receivers.

Note also that the sender never needs to devote more than about half the bandwidth to re-transmissions. A typical packet is lost by 1% of the receivers. Thus, for 1000 receivers, there is a danger that up to 10 receivers might NAK each packet. Since the sender does not keep track of which packets it has recently re-sent, it risks using 90% of its bandwidth for re-transmissions. BMTP avoids this problem because the receivers return status packets one by one, not all at once. The expected interval between times when different receivers NAK the same lost packet is N/(40*N*1%), where N is the number of receivers, 40 is the rate in packets per second, and 1% is the packet loss rate. This comes out to 2.5 seconds. The round trip time, including the maximum queueing time and propagation delay of 50 milliseconds, is just over a second. Thus the re-send triggered by one receiver's NAK typically arrives back at all the receivers before a second receiver gets a chance to NAK the same packet.

All the simulations described above have asymmetric receiver bandwidths: there is some slowest receiver. BMTP would work poorly if all the receivers had identical bandwidths and queue lengths. In such a case all receivers would experience an independent 5% loss rate caused by the sender transmitting 5% too fast. At least one receiver would miss every packet, causing the sender to devote half its bandwidth to retransmission. On the other hand, if there is some slowest receiver, only that receiver misses 5% of packets. Note that the weighting mechanism allows that receiver to repair the misses. It's reasonable to expect that real networks (as opposed to simulators) will exhibit such asymmetry.

## 7. Effects of IDA

Rabin's Information Dispersal Algorithm (IDA) [9] can be added to BMTP in a straightforward manner. IDA allows correction of losses within a group of $m$ packets with a number of retransmissions equal to the maximum number of packets lost from the group by any one receiver. For instance, if each receiver loses a different two packets out of a particular group, the sender can repair all the losses with just two IDA retransmissions. This makes IDA particularly appropriate for multicast. The ideas in the ensuing discussion all spring from the original IDA paper.

BMTP with IDA treats successive groups of $m$ packets' worth of input data separately. Suppose a packet holds 512 bytes. Instead of sending each packet's worth of data in a packet, BMTP with IDA sends a packet-sized *piece* computed as follows:

$$\begin{bmatrix} p_1 & \cdots & p_{512} \end{bmatrix} = \begin{bmatrix} v_1 & \cdots & v_m \end{bmatrix} \cdot \begin{bmatrix} b_1 & \cdots & b_{511m+1} \\ \cdots & \cdots & \cdots \\ b_m & \cdots & b_{512m} \end{bmatrix}$$

$b_1$ through $b_{512m}$ are one group of input data. $v_1$ through $v_m$ are random numbers, chosen separately for each piece sent. The sender places $p_1$ through $p_{512}$ and $v_1$ through $v_m$ in a packet and multicasts it to all the receivers. Ordinarily the sender does this $m$ times for each group of data, sending $m$ packets. Call the $v$ and $p$ row-vectors the sender transmits $V_i$ and $P_i$ for i from 1 to $m$. The sender is essentially calculating the following, one $P$ and $V$ at a time:

$$\begin{bmatrix} P_1 \\ \cdots \\ P_m \end{bmatrix} = \begin{bmatrix} V_1 \\ \cdots \\ V_m \end{bmatrix} \cdot \begin{bmatrix} b_1 & \cdots & b_{511m+1} \\ \cdots & \cdots & \cdots \\ b_m & \cdots & b_{512m} \end{bmatrix}$$

When a receiver has received $m$ pieces for a group, it reconstructs the original data thus:

$$\begin{bmatrix} b_1 & \cdots & b_{511m+1} \\ \cdots & \cdots & \cdots \\ b_m & \cdots & b_{512m} \end{bmatrix} = \begin{bmatrix} V_1 \\ \cdots \\ V_m \end{bmatrix}^{-1} \cdot \begin{bmatrix} P_1 \\ \cdots \\ P_m \end{bmatrix}$$

If no packets are lost, this costs some extra cpu time and the extra bandwidth required to send the $V$ vectors.

Suppose a receiver fails to receive a packet from a group, and thus is missing a *V*/*P* pair. In BMTP with IDA, the receiver will ask the sender to send an additional piece from the group. The sender calculates the additional piece as described above. Since the new $V$ vector is randomly chosen, the new piece is unlikely to be the same as any previous piece from the same group. However, the equations above hold for any $m$ pieces, so the receiver will be able to reconstruct the group from any combination of $m$ pieces. A receiver will keep requesting new pieces for each group until it has $m$; it follows the rules previously described governing when it is allowed to send status messages.

Now suppose two receivers received only $m$-1 pieces from a group, but missed different pieces. An ordinary BMTP sender would have to re-send two packets to fix this. IDA allows both losses to be fixed with one re-send: the equations above allow the receivers to use any distinct $m$ pieces to reconstruct a group.

IDA does not help when fixing losses in different groups, so a group should contain as many bytes as possible. One could increase the piece size beyond 512 bytes to achieve this goal, but still send each piece in a packet. However, the Internet fragments large packets into small ones, and loss of any one fragment causes the remainder of the packet to be useless. Thus it seems most reasonable to avoid fragmentation by keeping pieces small. Another approach to making groups large is to make $m$ large. The matrix multiplies needed to create pieces and reconstruct the original data require O($m$) operations per byte. Thus large values of $m$ will consume large amounts of CPU time. For purposes of experimentation, BMTP with IDA uses groups of $m$=5 pieces of 512 bytes each.

There is a chance that the matrix of $V$ vectors will fail to invert. In this case, the receiver discards one randomly chosen piece and ask the sender for a new one. The sender could avoid this by choosing $V$ vectors that are linearly independent. The per-group state required in the sender does not seem worth the added efficiency.

All of the arithmetic described above is carried out in the field of integers mod 257. There are one too many field members to encode in a byte. BMTP with IDA uses an escaping mechanism to mark the extra value, which increases the packet size slightly.

An implementation of BMTP with IDA on 120 mHz Pentiums can send at four megabits bits per second, but receive at only one megabit per second. Essentially all of the time is in the matrix multiplies. The algorithms involved could certainly be improved.

The simulation of Figure 5, when run with IDA and $m$=5, results in about 28% re-sends with 1000 receivers, rather than the 50% without IDA. One would expect every group of five original packets to require roughly one extra piece to fix losses: a re-send rate of 16%. For a typical group, 50 receivers will need this extra piece. At a one percent loss rate, roughly 60% of these extra pieces will themselves be missed by one of the 50 receivers. This implies a total re-send rate of 26%, which agrees with the simulation result.

## 8. Further Work

Some of BMTP's mechanisms could be improved. It intentionally overloads the network by 5% in order to detect spare capacity. While this is arguably in the tradition of TCP, the impact could be decreased by a periodic probing algorithm. BMTP can recover from the 5% loss due to that overload, as well as a loss rate of a few percent due to transmission errors. Its tolerance to transmission errors could be increased if the sender noted any loss rate that persists despite substantial rate reduction. BMTP uses fixed measurement and control intervals, which slow its response to changing conditions; these could be based on dynamic measurements of round trip time. BMTP allows a fixed maximum weight for the probability with which a receiver sends a status packet; this maximum should be governed by the total number of receivers.

More experience is needed with the interaction between multiple BMTP sessions, and between BMTP and other protocols.

BMTP leaves some decisions up to the application, but lacks a well-defined interface with which an application can declare its policies. An application may wish to limit the maximum age of data BMTP should re-send, or to ignore very slow receivers, or to ensure complete reliability to a known set of receivers. BMTP could enforce these policies if the application could ask it to do so.

## 9. Conclusions

BMTP will allow applications like Netnews, mailing lists, and mass software distribution to take advantage of the Internet's multicast system. It multicasts bulk data with a reliability and capacity to scale not previously available. It avoids overloading the network with data or the sender with status packets. It sustains high throughput even with a large number of receivers or a modest transmission error rate. It usually avoids re-sending any one lost packet more than once even if multiple receivers missed it. BMTP achieves these effects by counting the receivers, using this count to limit the rate at which receivers can send status packets, and feeding rate information back to the sender from the receivers.

## References


[1] ARMSTRONG, S., FREIER, A., AND MARZULLO, K. Multicast Transport Protocol, RFC1301, 1992.

[2] BOLOT, J-C, TURLETTI, T., AND WAKEMAN, I. Scalable Feedback Control for Multicast Video Distribution in the Internet. *Proceedings of the Conference on Communications Architectures, Protocols and Applications (ACM SIGCOMM 1994).*

[3] DAKA, J., AND WATERS, A., A High Performance Broadcast File Transfer Protocol. *Proceedings of the Conference on Communications Architectures, Protocols and Applications (ACM SIGCOMM 1988).*

[4] DEERING, S., Multicast Routing in a Datagram Internetwork, Ph.D. thesis, Stanford University, December 1991.

[5] FLOYD, S., JACOBSON, V., MCCANNE, S., LIU, C., AND ZHANG, L. A Reliable Multicast Framework for Light-weight Sessions and Application Level Framing. *Proceedings of the Conference on Communications Architectures, Protocols and Applications (ACM SIGCOMM 1995).*

[6] JACOBSON, V., Congestion Avoidance and Control. *Proceedings of the Conference on Communications Architectures, Protocols and Applications (ACM SIGCOMM 1988).*

[7] LIN, J., AND PAUL, S. RMTP: A Reliable Multicast Transport Protocol. *IEEE INFOCOM 1996, March 1996.*

[8] POSTEL, J., Transmission Control Protocol, RFC793, 1981.

[9] RABIN, M., Efficient Dispersal of Information for Security, Load Balancing, and Fault Tolerance, *Journal of the ACM, Volume 36, Number 2, Pages 335 to 348. ACM Press, New York, 1989.*

[10] TALPADE, R., AND AMMAR, M. H., Single Connection Emulation: An Architecture for Providing a Reliable Multicast Transport Service, *Georgia Institute of Technology College of Computing Tech Report GIT-CC- 94-47, October 1994.*

[11] WEINSTEIN, L., Broadcasting of Netnews and Network Mail via Satellite, *USENIX Conference Proceedings, 1984.*

[12] XTP Protocol Definition, Revision 3.6. Protocol Engines Incorporated, Mountain View, CA, 1992.

# Multicast Feedback Suppression Using Representatives

Dante DeLucia
Hughes Research Laboratories
3011 Malibu Canyon Road
Malibu CA 90265
email: dante@usc.edu

Katia Obraczka
USC Information Sciences Institute
4676 Admiralty Way Suite 1001
Marina Del Rey, CA 90292
email: katia@isi.edu

## Abstract

*For a reliable, feedback dependent multicast transport protocol to scale, it must avoid the feedback implosion problem [3], particularly if the protocol targets arbitrarily large multicast groups communicating over lossy networks. Most existing suppression based feedback control mechanisms address the implosion problem using timers based on round-trip time (RTT) estimates between each receiver and the source.*

*The algorithm presented in this paper has three major benefits: it does not need to compute RTT from all receivers to the source, does not require knowledge of group membership, and provides prompt feedback. A small set of* representative *receivers and probabilistic suppression are used to limit feedback. We believe that this approach will perform well in real networks. Simulations show that for various multicast group sizes, a few representatives can keep the amount of feedback low while not degrading feedback timeliness.*

**Keywords: Multicast, feedback, suppression, representatives**

## 1 Introduction

While many existing multicast transport protocols such as SRM [5], and RTP [11], target delay sensitive, real-time applications, little has been done to address congestion issues that arise in multipoint bulk data transfer services.

The feedback suppression scheme presented addresses the problem of feedback implosion [3], while providing frequent and timely feedback required for congestion control, yet not requiring full knowledge of the multicast group membership nor special support from the network. Feedback implosion occurs when a multitude of receivers respond to a single event such as a packet loss. This flood of responses can rapidly congest the network.

Several existing reliable multicast transport protocols [5] use RTT-based probabilistic suppression to avoid feedback implosion. Each receiver measures RTT to the source and sets a timer based on its distance from the source. Receivers nearer the source will respond more quickly and will suppress feedback from receivers farther down the multicast tree. For conferencing applications in which many-to-many communication takes place, computation of RTTs to the source requires little additional overhead.

We present a solution to the feedback implosion problem that does not rely on RTT estimation to every member and hence has greater potential for scalability. Our mechanism targets applications with a single data source and multiple receivers. All communication is via multicast.

A small set of group members, or *representatives*, represents congested multicast subtrees. In addition to providing fast feedback to the source, representatives suppress feedback from the other group members.

For multicast groups of varying sizes communicating over randomly-generated network topologies subject to pessimistic loss rates, our simulation results show that representatives can greatly reduce the amount of feedback when compared to purely suppressive algorithms, yet still provide timely feedback to the source. Representatives also make the algorithm less sensitive to suppression timer settings, allowing the algorithm to perform well while avoiding RTT estimation between each receiver and the source. Simulations also show that representative set size scales well with multicast group size.

## 2 Related Work

Traditional reliable unicast transport protocols, such as TCP, use ACKs to recover from packet loss. This approach to achieving reliability is often referred to as *sender-initiated*, since it is the responsibility of the sender to detect packet losses. In a multicast environment, as group sizes increase, the sender-initiated scheme may cause ACK implosion since each delivered packet triggers an acknowledgment from every receiver in the group.

Alternatively, in the *receiver-initiated* approach to reliability, receivers detect packet losses and request retransmissions by generating NACKs. Placing the responsibility of recovering from packet losses on the receiver helps alleviate the ACK implosion problem. The performance comparison study presented in [10] confirms that receiver-initiated multicast transport protocols have better scalability propoerties than their sender-initiated counterparts. For this reason, most reliable multipoint transport protocols employ receiver-initiated or hybrid approaches to reliablity.

However, receiver-based protocols also suffer from the feedback implosion problem, especially when losses occur high in the multicast tree in large groups.

Grossglauser [6], classfies solutions to the feedback implosion problem as *structure-based* or *timer-based.* Structure-based approaches, such as the Log-Based Protocol [8], rely on a designated site (either a dedicated server in the case of the Log-Based Protocol [8] or a pre-assigned group member) to process and filter feedback information.

Timer-based solutions rely on probabilistic feedback suppression to avoid implosion at the source. Receivers in the SRM protocol [5] (designed to support the WB distributed whiteboard application) delay their retransmission requests for a random interval, uniformly distributed between the current time and the one-way trip time to the source. The goal is that group members closer to the source send their feedback sooner suppressing feedback from farther away members. A site uses periodic *session messages* to measure its distance (based on the resulting RTT) to the other group members.

The Deterministic Timeouts for Reliable Multicast (DTRM) [6] algorithm also uses RTT between receivers and the sender to compute the receivers' suppression timeouts such that only one receiver in a multicast subtree, the *representative receiver*, responds to losses.

The feedback control mechanism proposed in [9] does not fall into either the structure-based or the timer-based categories. In this approach to feedback control, which is used by the IVS videoconferencing tool [12] and is layered atop of RTP [11], video sources use probabilistic polling to select a set of receivers that should provide feedback.

## 3 The Model

Our feedback suppression mechanism focuses on the following application-level requirements and lower-layer services. Athough we target reliable data transfer applications, the model can also be applied to realtime applications like audio and video. In general, we believe that it can be applied to any multicast application requiring prompt feedback.

Our model has minimal assumptions:

- IP Multicast:

  Senders transmit data packets using internet multicast. There is no centralized group management. Hosts can join or leave the group at any time. Any host can transmit to the group.

- Single Data Source:

  All data is sent from a single source. The source is a member of the multicast group. Receivers send control messages, but no data.

- Unknown Group Membership: Like IP multicast, we assume the set of receivers is unknown to support scalability.

- Unknown Network Topology:

  No knowledge of the underlying physical network topology is assumed. Routers are not relied on to provide feedback about the network conditions, or filter feedback requests.

- Application Semantics

  Applications are responsible for the protocol semantics. When moving from a one-to-one reliability protocol such as TCP to a one-to-many protocol that would be used in multicast applications, it becomes much more difficult to build a single transmission protocol that can handle all the possible semantics that might be required. For instance, a higher level applications might require an explicit join protocol, or might guarantee atomic delivery. Others might only provide best effort delivery to receivers.

## 4 Feedback Suppression Algorithm

Our multicast feedback mechanism is based on the assumption that in a large multicast group, a small set of bottleneck links will cause the majority of the congestion problems. We exploit this by finding a small set of group members to represent the congested multicast subtrees. These group *representatives* provide immediate feedback that suppresses feedback from other group members, thus preventing feedback implosion.

The first challenge in selecting representatives is choosing them such that they represent the congested subtrees of the multicast tree. Ideally, each congested link would be represented by one representative in the affected subtree. The second challenge is to react to new congestion in a timely manner by choosing new representatives and discarding those that no longer contribute to the feedback efforts.

The congestion avoidance protocol we envision relies on both positive (ACK) and negative (NACK) acknowledgments. ACKs are required to prevent congestion collapse, while NACKs are required to provide feedback in the case of congestion. In the absence of feedback, the source assumes that either there are no other group members, or that there has been a catastrophic network failure.

Receivers selected as representatives provide immediate feedback to the source. Feedback from other receivers is scheduled over a random interval and is subject to suppression. We explain how suppression timers are set in Section 4.

At startup, the representative set is empty and suppression timers are set very loosely.[1] As feedback is received, the source builds the representative set. In the absence of NACKs, the receivers whose ACKs were received by the source will be selected as representatives. Since NACKs are an immediate indication of congestion, feedback suppression will give precedence to NACKs over ACKs. Receivers sending NACKs will take precedence over receivers sending ACKs for consideration as representatives. As network conditions change, new feedback is received by the source and the representative set is updated.

### The Source

The source maintains the representative set and computes the group's current maximum round-trip time (GRTT) defined in Section 4. The source is responsible for distributing the current representative set and GRTT to the group.

### Receivers

Upon receipt of a data packet, non-representative receivers schedule a NACK if a data packet N is received without having seen packet N-1[2], else an ACK is scheduled. A scheduled response is held for a random period. If another response is received before the scheduled send time and the received response is defined to be as "good or better" than the response scheduled, the scheduled response is suppressed. In our definition of "good or better", NACKs suppress NACKs and ACKs, while ACKs can only suppress other ACKs.

[1] In our simulation we initially set the suppression timers to 1500 milliseconds. Once the GRTT (see 4) is computed we use it as the basis to set timers.

[2] Since this is not a reliability mechanism, we only NACK the N-1 packet. We are not concerned with any other previous lost packets.

If a receiver never experiences any packet loss, or has its packet losses covered by a representative, it will never generate any messages.

### Representatives

Receivers designated as representatives send feedback to the source immediately, forgoing any suppression interval.

A receiver is designated a representative when it receives a representative set notification in which it is a member. A representative reverts to non-representative operation when it receives a representative set update in which it is not a member.

### Representative Selection

At startup, any receiver that provides feedback is eligible for selection as a representative. After a full representative set has been obtained, only NACKs qualify a receiver for selection as a representative. To prevent a sudden change of the representative set, only one new representative may be selected in response to any one packet. When the representative set is full and a new representative is selected, an existing representative must be ejected from the current set. The best candidate for ejection is obviously the "worst" representative, but the problem then lies in what constitutes the "worst". To keep things simple, the representative that has not sent a NACK in the longest time is selected. This criteria is based on the assumption that a representative that has not sent a NACK is having the fewest number of congestion problems.

### Timers

Avoiding computation of RTT between all receivers and the source means we cannot use "precise" suppression timers as done in SRM [5]. We compensate by using loose timers and representatives to provide fast feedback. Since representatives provide immediate feedback on behalf of the subtrees they cover, we need "backup" timers for those losses not covered by representatives.

We break our suppression timers into two components. The first is a simple *wait* period, and the second is a random *interval.* The wait period allows time for responses by representatives to traverse the group and suppress non-representative feedback. If the wait period is too long losses not covered by the current representative set cannot be detected in a timely fashion. The random interval spaces out feedback responses and allows probabilistic suppression to reduce non-representative feedback.

The wait and random intervals are set to a percentage of the estimated GRTT described below.

### GRTT Measurement

The maximum group round-trip (GRTT) time is computed by keeping a table of the worst RTTs received. Each table entry contains an RTT measurement and a time-to-live (TTL). Each time a packet is sent, the TTL is decremented. The current TTL values is set to 10. We chose this value to reduce rapid turnover in the RTT set in the case of lost packets. Since we are measuring RTT for every feedback packet received, the RTTs should be updated once for every data packet sent.

We keep track of the three worst RTTs received. When a new RTT is received it is assigned a TTL. Note that we do not generate any additional messages to estimate the GRTT.

### Timer Setting

Each receiver's wait period and suppression interval is defined as a percentage of the advertised GRTT. Since ACKs provide little control information, they can be suppressed to an arbitrary degree. Ideally we only need one ACK per packet. Currently we set the ACK wait interval to 1 GRTT.

In the case of NACKs, we are faced with the following tradeoff. On one hand we seek to minimize the number of NACKs. On the other, we wish to receive NACKs in a timely fashion since we need to react to them as quickly as possible. In the normal case, representatives should be selected in such a way as to maximize the probability of responding to packet loss. When representatives fail to cover the packet loss, the backup mechanism of non-representatives sending NACKs must react as quickly as possible.

### Overhead

Since our feedback control mechanism does not rely on RTT estimation, the only bandwidth overhead required by our scheme is the distribution of a new representative set and GRTT. GRTT measurements are sent as part of a packet header, and hence do require separate messages.

We minimize computation and space requirements at the source by bounding the size of the representative set and maximum RTT tables.

## 5 Results

We simulate our feedback suppression mechanism to evaluate the amount and timeliness of the feedback generated by the receivers in a multicast group connected using an arbitrary network topology with loss rates and delays specified per link.

### 5.1 Evaluation Methodology

#### 5.1.1 Network Topologies

Early tests of the feedback suppression mechanism utilized a simple binary tree network with the source transmitting at the root of the tree and all other nodes being receivers. While such networks were easy to generate and provided useful preliminary information on the feedback suppression mechanism, it was necessary to test the feedback suppression mechanism on more realistic networks.

To generate more realistic topologies we use Network Topology Generator [7]. The networks generated were three level networks with low delay links at the first and second levels and large delay links at the third level. The intent is to provide a loose approximation of a real internetwork topology with a high speed backbone, slower regional networks and finally slow edge links. The loss rates were randomly chosen over the interval 0-5%. Hotz describes more details on the generation of the networks in [7].

The receivers are all at the third level and hence will tend to be leaves, but still have different distances to the source. The source is at the top level.

#### 5.1.2 Simulator

The simulator generates a minimum delay spanning tree from a given network topology. Link delays and drop rates are specified per link. No capacity modeling is done, i.e. all links have infinite bandwidth. End-to-end delay is simply the sum of the link delays, and no delay jitter is introduced. The membership of the group is static.

The aggregrate network loss rate is very high. Our networks typically have a 9% loss rate since we wanted to test our feedback mechanism on the worst possible cases.

The source transmits data packets at a constant rate of 10 packets a second. We describe the simulation parameters below and Table 1 summarizes them.

- **Representatives** To measure the effect of representatives, we simulated groups with 0, 3, 5, and 10 representatives.

- **NACK Wait Interval** As explained in Section 4, the feedback timer delay has two components. The first is a simple wait interval, and the second is a random interval. The wait interval is a percentage of the estimated maximum group round-trip time (GRTT). Feedback time is scheduled by adding the wait and random intervals.

| | |
|---|---|
| Representatives | 0, 3, 5, 10 |
| NACK wait interval | 0, 0.25, 1 |
| Maximum link loss rate | 0.01, 0.02, 0.05, |

Table 1: Simulation Parameters

In our simulations we used wait times of 0, 25, and 100% of the maximum GRTT.

- **Maximum Link Loss Rate**

  Each link is randomly assigned a value between 0 and the maximum loss rate. The overall loss rate of the network is a function of the link loss rates, network size, and topology.

We ran our simulator using a randomly-generated, 650-node topology, with 50, 100, and 500 level-1, level-2, and level-3 nodes, respectively. In each simulation run, we vary one of the parameters in Table 1, while keeping all the other parameters constant.

## 5.2 Evaluation Metrics

In this evaluation we are concerned with two metrics. The first is the quantity of the feedback, and the second is timeliness. For feedback quantity, we look at the total amount of feedback received. The less the better. Ideally, we want a constant amount of feedback per packet. For timeliness, we normalize the feedback time to the maximum GRTT over the entire simulation.

## 5.3 Evaluation Results

In the graphs shown in this section, each point corresponds to the average of a sequence of 20 simulation runs where all parameters were kept constant. We evaluate the effects of the NACK wait timer, representatives, and group size in the quantity and quality of the feedback generated by the multicast group. The graphs that show amount of feedback generated by the group plot number of packets received at the source against data packet sequence number. The timeliness graphs plot the minimum time for the source to receive feedback normalized to GRTT against data packet sequence number.

Most of the simulations we ran used a maximum link loss rate of 1%, which resulted in an overall loss rate of approximately 9%, which is a considerably higher loss rate than what is observed in real networks. Therefore, in our simulations, we are driving our feedback control algorithms with pessimistic scenarios in terms of loss rates.

### 5.3.1 NACK Wait Timer Settings

We studied how the NACK wait interval influences the quantity and timeliness of the feedback received at the source. For these set of simulations, we used 650-member groups, 3 representatives, and a maximum link loss rate of 1%, but due to space limitations we omit the resulting graphs.

Our results show that representatives greatly reduce the impact of how the NACK wait timer is set. This is because when there are no representatives, feedback control relies on pure suppression and hence timer setting is crucial. Representatives provide immediate feedback and only rely on NACK timers for packet losses they still do not cover. If the current representative set covered all packet losses in their multicast group, longer NACK timers would be the way to go. However, since in real networks congestion occurs at different points at different times, NACK wait timers should be set so that non-representatives can still respond to losses not covered by the current representatives in a timely fashion.

Regarding timeliness, while shorter NACK timers allow feedback to be received sooner, longer NACK timers improve the chances of feedback being suppressed. As we discuss in the next section, representatives compensate for longer NACK timers by sending immediate feedback.

### 5.3.2 Representatives

Figures 1 and Figure 2 show the amount and timeliness of feedback for different representative set sizes. These simulations used 650-member groups, a maximum link loss rate of 1%, or approximately 9% overall loss rate, and NACK wait interval of 25% of GRTT. Graphs (a), (b), and (c) in each figure correspond to representative set sizes of 0, 3, and 10, respectively.

Figure 1 shows how representatives can reduce the amount of feedback received. We observe that using representatives result in a significant reduction in the amount of feedback generated. Overall, the 3-representative case (averaging 3 NACKs per packet sent) generates less feedback than the 0-representative case (7 NACKs per packet), but still perform effective suppression. The 10-representative case however seems to be more effective at limiting the variance in the amount of feedback. This is due to the fact that the 10-representative set provides a better coverage of packet losses, and therefore keeps the amount of feedback generated by the group more constrained.

For the non-empty representative set graphs, the amount of feedback is high during the first 10 packets

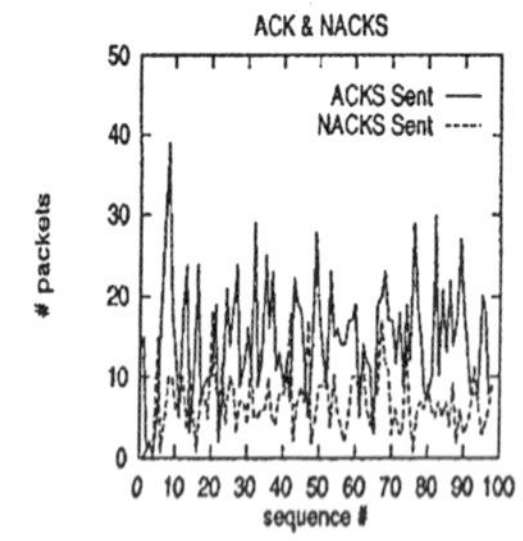


(a) No Representatives

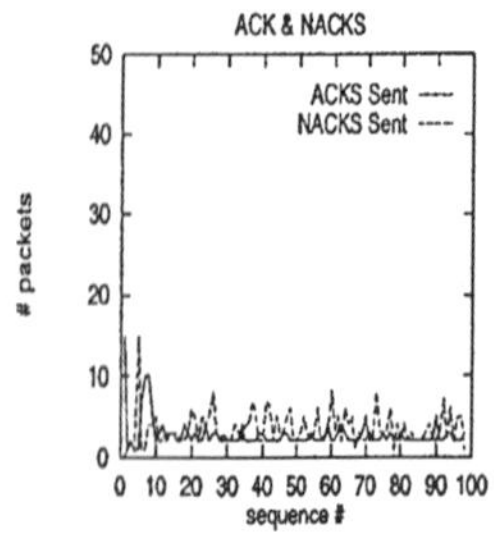


(b) 3 Representatives

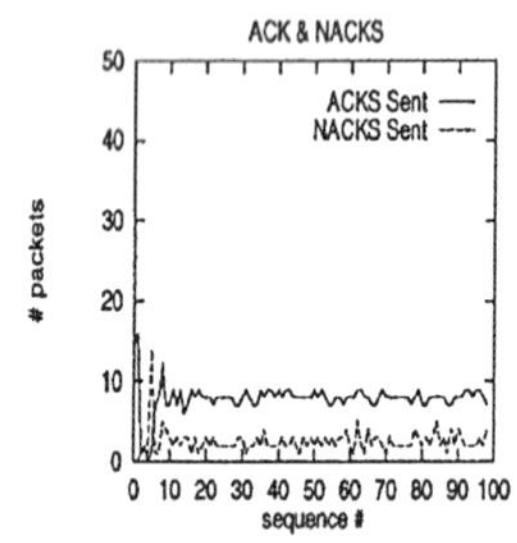


(c) 10 Representatives

Figure 1: Effects of representatives on feedback. We use 0, 3, and 10 representatives in a 650-member group. NACK wait time is 25% of GRTT, and maximum link loss rate is 1%. Network loss rate is approximately 9%.

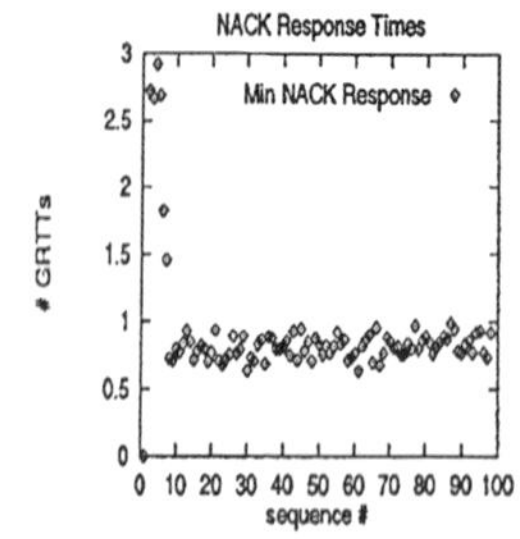


(a) No Representatives

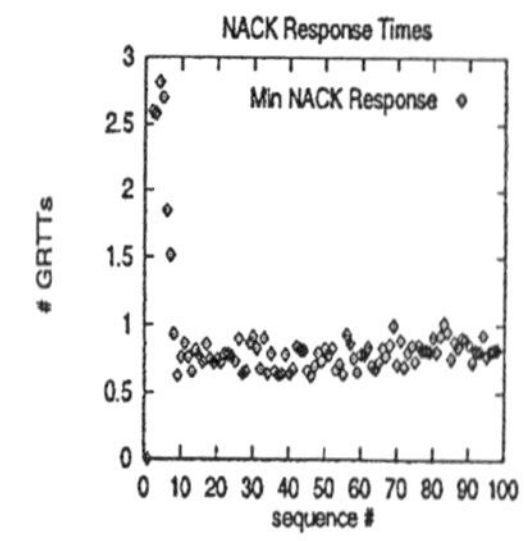


(b) 3 Representatives

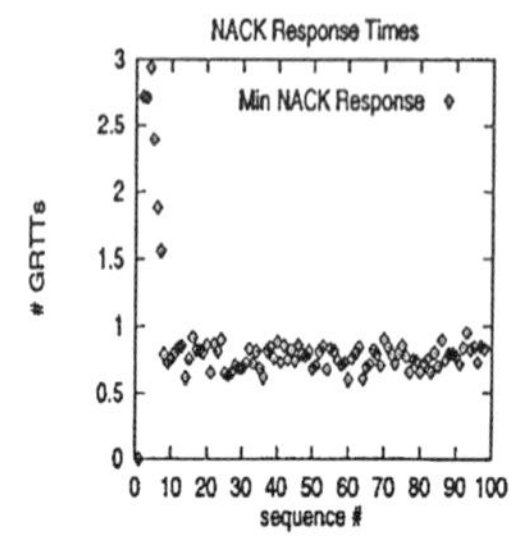


(c) 10 Representatives

Figure 2: Effects of representatives on timeliness. We use 0, 3, and 10 representatives in a 650-member group. NACK wait time is 25% of GRTT, and maximum link loss rate is 1%. Network loss rate is approximately 9%.

because representatives were still being elected.

In general there is a tradeoff between the amount of feedback generated and the timeliness of the protocol. In the case of representatives, the amount of feedback is reduced without incurring unreasonable latency in feedback to the source. Figure 2 illustrates this.

In our simple simulation model, representatives tend to be farther from the source. This is due to the fact that the farther down the tree a receiver is, the more likely it is to lose a packet. The more likely a receiver loses packets, the more likely it is that it be elected as a representative.

In this section we showed that for a given multicast group size, we can perform effective suppression with very few representatives. In the next section we show how our algorithm performs for different group sizes.

### 5.3.3 Group Size

Figures 3 and Figure 4 show the amount and timeliness of feedback generated by groups of different sizes. We use group sizes of 175, 300, and 650, and set the NACK timer at 25% of the GRTT, and the maximum link loss rate at 1%, or 9% approximate overall loss rate. We use a 3-representative set in all cases.

From Figure 3, we observe that the size of the group has relatively little impact on the overall feedback received. This confirms that a few representatives are quite effective in keeping feedback amount low. A larger representative set (5 representatives instead of 3) for the 650-member group (Figure 3(c)) results in less variation in the amount of feedback. As we pointed out in Section 5.3.2, this is due to the fact that more representatives provide a better coverage of packet loss.

Similarly to the amount of feedback generated, Figure 4 shows that feedback timeliness does not degrade as the group size increase. On average, the time for the source to receive feedback is kept under 1 GRTT for all groups sizes shown.

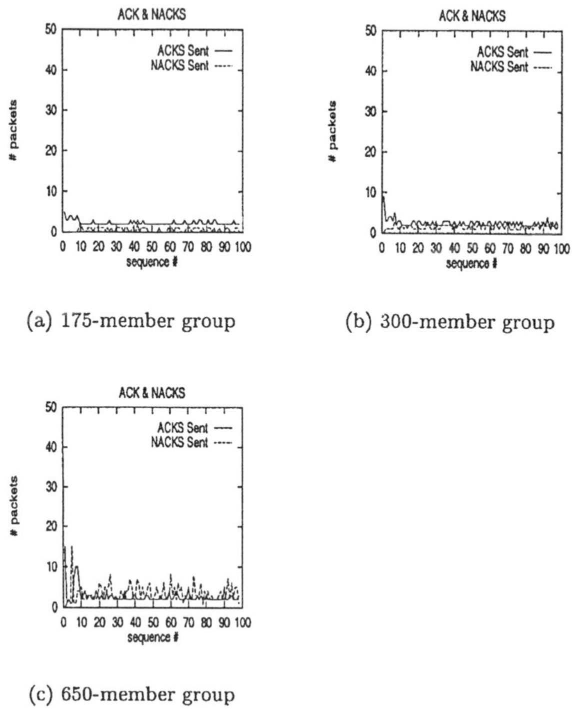


Figure 3: Effects of group size on amount of feedback. We use 175, 300, and 650-member groups. NACK wait time is 25% of GRTT, maximum link loss rate is 1%, and number of representatives is 3. The network loss rate is approximately 9%.

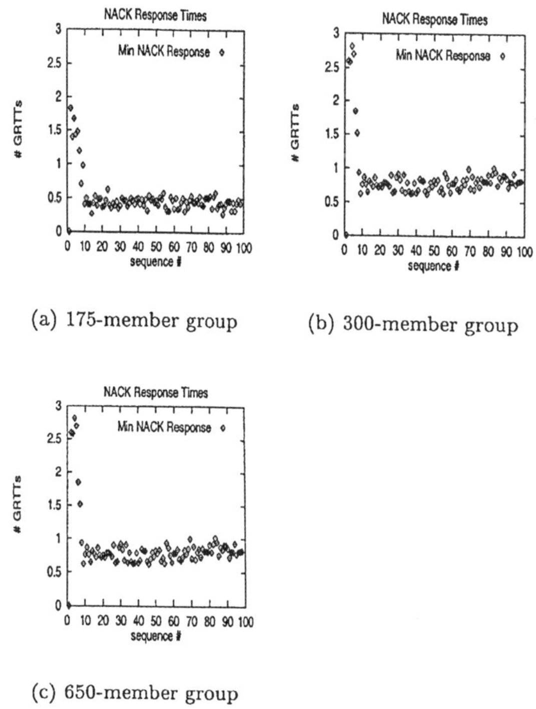


Figure 4: Effects of group size on timeliness of feedback. We use 175, 300, and 650-member groups. NACK wait time is 25% of GRTT, maximum link loss rate is 1%, and number of representatives is 3. The network loss rate is approximately 9%.

## 6 Future Work

We have evaluated the utility of representatives in purely lossy networks. We expect that performance will be even better in real networks in which losses result primarily from congestion. With this in mind, future simulations need to take into account network congestion and bottleneck links. In the short term, we can extend the current simple simulator to create especially lossy links to simulate congestion and vary these loss rates over time to simulate transient congestion in the network.

An obvious optimization to reduce feedback is to only allow representatives to send ACKs. This will greatly reduce ACKs while still providing protection in the case of congestion collapse. NACK feedback is not affected.

In addition to the random topologies we have examined, we will investigate other networks. We will also investigate the possibility of automatically determining a good representative set size.

Our goal is to build a full flow control mechanism suitable for bulk data distribution in a multicast environment. Since any flow control scheme must detect congestion in the network, we need to investigate congestion detection schemes. In addition to evaluating the use of packet loss as a congestion metric as is done in traditional TCP, we would also like to investigate delay-based metrics like that used in TCP-Vegas [2].

## 7 Conclusion

This paper described a multicast feedback control scheme that is part of our efforts to build a scalable reliable, flow-controlled, multicast transport protocol suitable for bulk data transfer applications.

The major benefit of our algorithm derives from the fact that we do not need to compute round trip time from receivers to the source, and we do not require knowledge of group membership or network topology.

We use a small set of representatives in combination with probabilistic suppression to limit feedback, yet not significantly degrading the timeliness of the feedback with respect to the worst round trip time for the group.

We investigated the performance of our feedback control mechanism in purely lossy networks with no capacity modeling. Representatives show a marked improvement over a purely suppression oriented algorithm.

## References


[1] A.J. Ballardi, P.F. Francis, and J. Crowcroft. Core based trees (cbt). *Proc. of the ACM SIGCOMM'93, San Francisco, CA*, August 1993.

[2] L.S. Brakmo, S.W. O'Malley, and L.L. Peterson. TCP Vegas: New techniques for congestion detection and avoidance. *1994 ACM SIGCOMM Conference*, pages 24–35, May 1994.

[3] P. B. Danzig. *Optimally Selecting the Parameters of Adaptive Backoff Algorithms for Computer Networks and Multiprocessors.* PhD thesis, University of California, Berkeley, December 1989.

[4] S. Deering, D. Estrin, D. Farinacci, V. Jacobson, C. Liu, and L. Wei. An architecture for wide-area multicast routing. 1994 ACM SIGCOMM Conference, February 1994.

[5] S. Floyd, V. Jacobson, S. McCanne, C.G. Liu, and L. Zhang. A reliable multicast framework for light-weight sessions and application-level framing. *1995 ACM Sigcomm Conference*, pages 342–356, October 1995.

[6] M. Grossglauser. Optimal deterministic timeouts for reliable scalable multicast. *Proc. of the IEEE Infocomm'96, San Francisco, CA*, pages 1425–1432, March 1996.

[7] S. Hotz and R. Nagamati. Network topology generator (NTG): A tool for generating network topology and policy for protocol simulation purposes. Technical Report, Computer Science Department, University of Southern California, Spring 1992.

[8] S.K. Singhal H.W. Holbrook and D.R. Cheriton. Log-based receiver-reliable multicast for interactive simulation". *1995 ACM SIGCOMM Conference*, pages 328–341, September 1995.

[9] T. Turletti J.C. Bolot and I. Wakeman. Scalable feedback control for multicast video distribution in the internet. *Proc. of the Conference on Communications Architectures, Protocols, and Applications, ACM SIGCOMM 1994*, August 1994.

[10] S. Pingali, D. Towsley, and J. F. Kurose. A comparison of sender-initiated and receiver-initiated reliable multicast protocols. *1994 ACM SIGMETRICS Conference*, May 1994.

[11] H. Schulzrinne. A transport protocol for real-time applications. Internet Draft, Internet Engineering Task Force, Audio-Video Transport WG, March 1993.

[12] T. Turletti. H.261 software codec for video conferencing over the internet. INRIA Research Report 1834, January 1993.

# Performance Modelling of Reliable Multicast Transmission

Jörg Nonnenmacher Ernst W. Biersack
Institut EURECOM
B.P. 193, 06904 Sophia Antipolis Cedex, FRANCE
{nonnen,erbi}@eurecom.fr

## Abstract

*Our aim is to investigate reliable transmission for multicast communication and explore its relationship to multicast routing. We derive two characterizations that enable the comparison of routing algorithms and error recovery mechanisms with respect to the multicast tree topology, namely the probability mass function of successful receptions and the expected number of retransmissions needed to deliver a packet from the source to all receivers. We also give a tight approximation of the computationally expensive expected number of retransmissions. These expressions allow to explore the relationship between routing and error recovery for multicast communication. We finally evaluate the impact of routing algorithms on the performance of reliable multicast transmission and give a realistic generic model for a multicast tree.*

Keywords: Reliable Multicast, MBONE, Multicast Routing, Performance Evaluation, ARQ

## 1 Introduction

The MBONE [1] has given raise to a number of conferencing applications such as vat, ivs, or vic where timely delivery is most important and packet loss can be tolerated. However, there is another class of dissemination-oriented applications where *reliable* multicast delivery from one source to many receivers is required such as

- Information delivery e.g., newspaper excerpts, software updates and software distribution.
- Distributed Simulation where state information must be exchanged.
- Web caching and replication for cache hierarchies such as Harvest.

In order to get a handle for designing and evaluating reliable multicast transport protocols one needs to be able to compute performance measures such as delay or the number of retransmissions. We will derive the formulas for computing

- the probability mass function ($pmf$) for the number of receivers that successfully receive a packet that is emitted once.
- the mean number of retransmissions until all receivers have successfully received a packet.

Since the exact expression is difficult to compute we also give a simple approximation for the mean number of retransmissions.

Our aim is to investigate reliable transmission for multicast communication and explore its relationship to multicast routing. Very little work [2] was done in this area and the effect of the topology on reliable multicast is not well understood.

Recent multicast routing algorithms have been evaluated in terms of cost and delay [3, 4, 5], blocking probability [6, 7] and overhead [8]. The impact of the routing algorithm on reliable multicast transmission has not yet been studied. Our results enable us to study the impact of multicast routing algorithms on reliable transmission. We will demonstrate the impact for two multicast routing algorithms that are known to perform best in terms of cost and delay.

Nearly all the research on the performance of reliable multicast communication [9, 10, 11, 12, 13] assumes multicast trees where the loss on any link affects only a single receiver.

We will take this special case of a multicast tree, referred to as $MFAN$ (see figure 3) into consideration and compare it both, with trees that are the outcome of routing algorithms and with two other generic multicast trees. We will show that the full binary tree (see figure 1) is a more realistic model for a multicast tree than $MFAN$.

## 2 Multicast Trees

The formulas we derive are valid for all types of multicast trees, i.e. they are independent of the topology of the multicast trees. In order to evaluate the formulas we define three generic multicast trees and additionally use two of the most popular multicast routing algorithms to compute multicast trees for artificially generated networks.

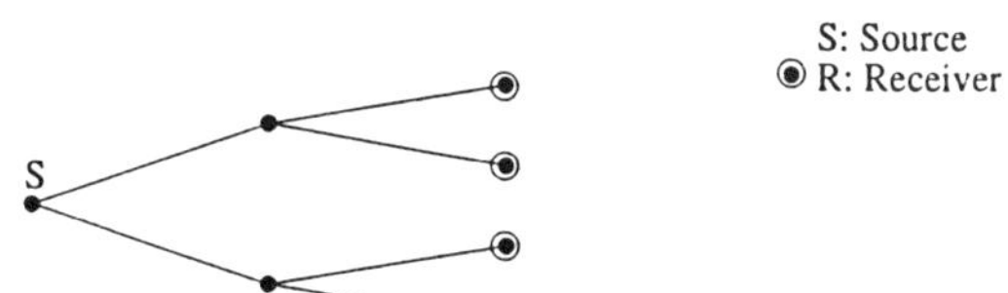


Figure 1: Full Binary Tree ($FBT$)

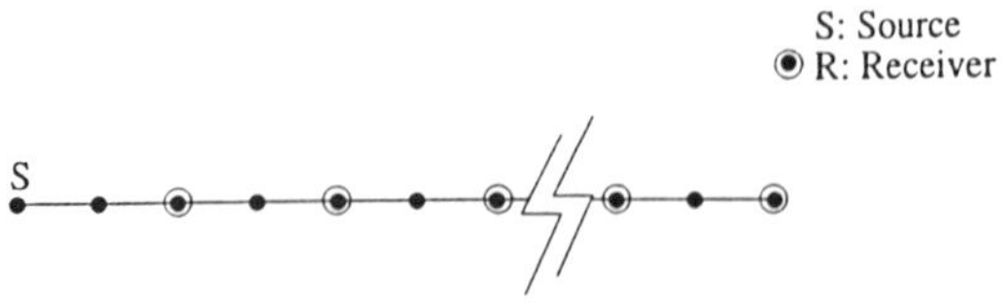


Figure 2: Linear Chain ($LC$)

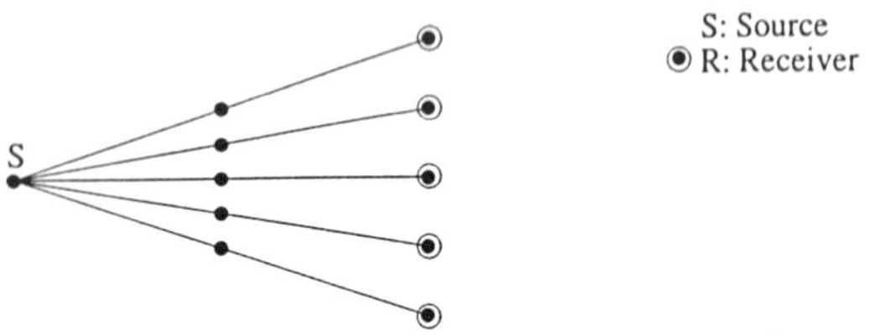


Figure 3: Multihop-Fanout ($MFAN$)

A 1:n – multicast connection forms a tree rooted at the source. The loss in a multicast tree is dependent on the topology. A tree topology has several parameters, each of them having a different influence on loss: (i) tree height, (ii) number of receivers (members in the multicast group), (iii) number of nodes in the tree[2], and (iv) the number of receivers affected by a loss over a single link.

We have chosen these particular three generic multicast trees because they behave very differently with respect to the impact of packet loss on a single link:

- For $MFAN$ (figure 3), always only a single receiver is affected.
- For the linear chain $LC$ (figure 2), depending on what link the loss occurs, the number of affected receivers can range from one to all receivers.
- For the full binary tree $FBT$ (figure 1), the impact of loss lies between the one for $MFAN$ and $LC$, affecting either a single receiver or a subgroup of all receivers.

By keeping the ratio of the number of receivers and the number of tree nodes for all three trees approximately at 0.5 (see Table 1) we collapse the two parameters (ii) and (iii) that influence loss into a single one.

However, as the tree grows, the tree height will vary if we keep the ratio of receivers and nodes in the tree fixed (see Table 1).

To generate "real" multicast trees we use two different multicast routing algorithms that base their routing decision on the optimization of cost or delay:

[2] The number of edges in a tree is not stated, since for a tree: $edges = nodes - 1$.

| | $MFAN$ | $FBT$ | $LC$ |
|---|---|---|---|
| the ratio $\frac{receivers}{nodes}$ | $\frac{1}{2+\frac{1}{r}}$ | $\frac{1}{2-\frac{1}{r}}$ | $\frac{1}{2+\frac{1}{r}}$ |
| tree height | 2 | $\log_2(r)$ | $2r$ |

Table 1: The characteristic of the three generic multicast trees with respect to the number $r$ of receivers

**Cost optimization** tries to minimize the sum of the edge costs in the multicast tree. The Kou Markovsky Berman algorithm [14], referred to as $KMB$, is presently the most famous heuristic to approach the optimal cost solution for a multicast tree. It constructs a **Heuristic Steiner Tree** ($HST$) [15] based on the minimum spanning tree algorithm.

**Delay optimization** minimizes the delay from the source to every receiver. The Shortest Path Algorithm, analyzed by Doar [4] optimizes delay and constructs a **shortest path tree** ($SPT$) that connects every receiver to the source via the shortest path.

10 random networks with 200 nodes and an average outdegree of 3.0 were constructed following Waxman [16], with the modification of Doar in [4] that avoids the influence of the number of nodes on the average outdegree. The method of Waxman is commonly used by the Multicast Routing community [3, 4, 16, 17] to compare the performance of different Multicast Routing Algorithms on random networks.

On each of the 10 random nets, 100 multicast groups with varying group sizes (5...140) and random receiver locations had been routed by the two algorithms for Cost and Delay optimization. A sample $SPT$ is shown in figure 4 and a sample $HST$ for the same network and the same group of 5 receivers is shown in figure 5.

The characteristics of the two multicast trees is shown in figure 6 and figure 7. In figure 6 it can be seen that the ratio between receivers and nodes in the multicast tree is not a constant. For $r = 40$, the trees have a ratio receiver to nodes that is about 0.5 and are therefore comparable with the generic trees.

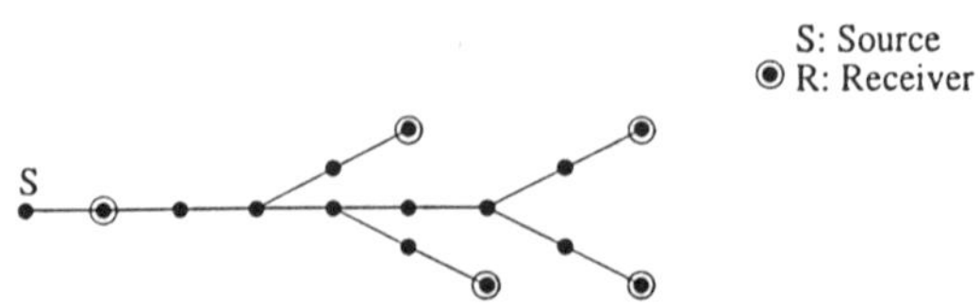


Figure 4: A $SPT$ with 5 receivers computed on a random network

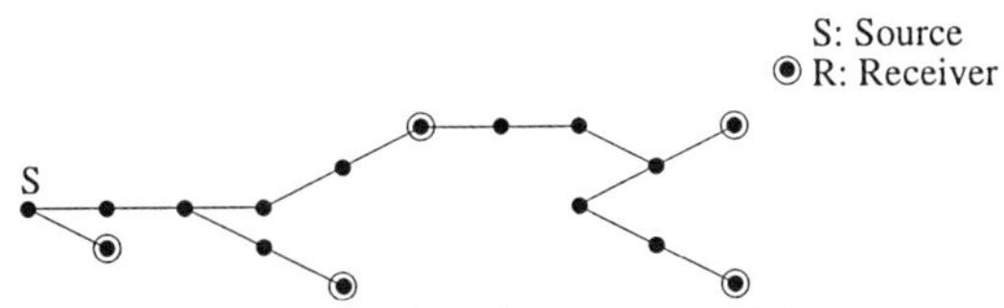


Figure 5: A $HST$ for the same multicast group in the same random network

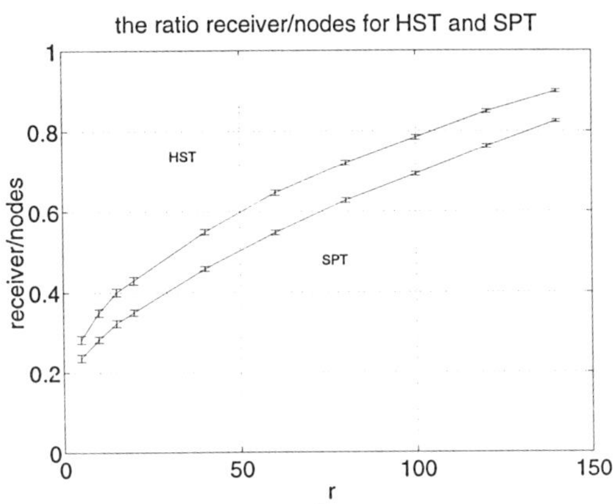


Figure 6: The ratio $\frac{receivers}{nodes}$ for $HST$ and $SPT$

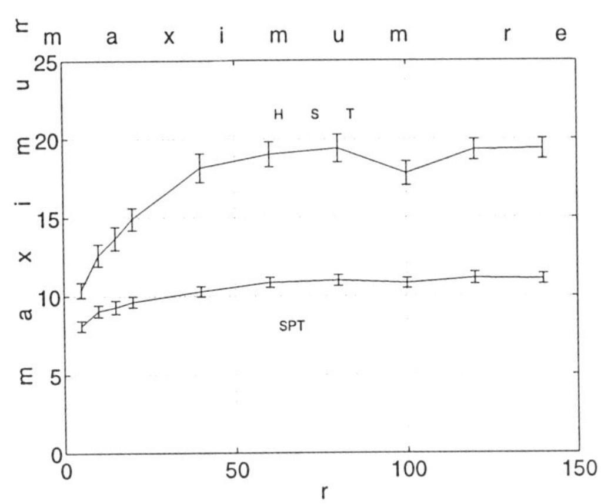


Figure 7: The tree height of $HST$ and $SPT$

## 3 Loss characteristics of a multicast tree

Loss in a multicast tree affects several receivers, if it happens on a link that leads to several receivers. We will call such a link **shared link**.

Reliable multicast transmission has to deal with two major problems:

- **Feedback implosion**: Receivers in a reliable multicast communication have to provide the source with the status of the reception. Loss on shared links causes loss at several receivers and increases the amount of feedback.

- **High number of retransmissions**: The higher the number of receivers the higher becomes the number of links in the multicast tree and the average number of retransmissions.

We derive a formula to analytically evaluate the **feedback implosion** at the source, by calculating the probability mass function ($pmf$) of successful and unsuccessful receptions for *a single packet emission*. We also give the expectation of the number of receptions and show its independence of shared links.

We give the expected number of **retransmissions** needed to deliver one packet to all receivers and propose a tight approximation that enables loss prediction for adaptive error control mechanisms.

### 3.1 The number of successful receptions in a multicast tree

Supposed that a packet is sent **once**, we are interested in the $pmf$ of the number of receivers that successfully receive this packet.

Given is a multicast tree $mct$:

- with source $S$ as the root

- $r$ receivers placed at arbitrary nodes and at all leaves. We allow at most one receiver at a node in the tree, and we assume not to have a receiver at the source

- homogeneous link loss probability $q$ of a packet.

Let $X_S$ be the number of receivers out of the $r$ receivers in the multicast tree rooted at $S$ that receive the packet successfully when transmitted once from $S$. We will give a method to calculate the corresponding probability mass function ($pmf$) $p(X_S = k)$, which enables us to capture the loss characteristic of different multicast trees. First of all, some definitions:

| | |
|---|---|
| $n$ | A node in the $mct$. |
| $child(n)$ | The set of children (successors) of $n$. |
| $c_n$ | The number of children of $n$, $c_n = card(child(n))$. |
| $r_n$ | The number of receivers in the subtree rooted at $n$. If $n$ is a receiver, it is **not** included. The number of receivers in the whole tree is therefore $r = r_S$. |
| $X_n$ | A random variable, describing the number of receivers out of the $r_n$ receivers in the subtree rooted at $n$ that successfully receive a packet, when transmitted from node $n$. |
| $p(X_n = k)$ | The $pmf$ of $X_n$, where $k = 0, \ldots, r_n$. |
| $s_n \in \{0,1\}^{c_n}$ | Link success vector, indicating the success or loss of a packet transported via the links leading to the children of $n$. |

| | |
|---|---|
| $s_n(i)$ | The $i$–th component of $s_n$. The success ($s_n(i) = 1$) indicator of the link leading from node $n$ to its child $i$. If the packet is lost on the link leading from $n$ to $i$, then $s_n(i) = 0$. |
| $x_n \in \{0,1\}^{c_n}$ | The children receiver vector. Indicates which child of $n$ is a receiver. |
| $x_n(i)$ | The $i$–th component of $x_n$. $x_n(i) = 1$ indicates that the child $i$ of node $n$ is a receiver, otherwise $x_n(i) = 0$. |
| $a_n \in \times_{i=1}^{c_n}\{0,\ldots,r_i\}$ | Behind child receptions vector. Gives the number of receivers behind the children of node $n$ that received the packet successfully. |
| $a_n(i) \in \{0,\ldots,r_i\}$ | The $i$–th component of $a_n$, gives the number of receivers in the subtree rooted at the child $i$ of $n$ that received the packet successfully. |

The *pmf* can now be calculated in a recursive way, starting at the leaves of the multicast tree. We need to distinguish two cases:

**Node $n$ is a leaf.** Then there are no receivers located behind node $n$ and the probability that no receiver is receiving a packet is 1 and the *pmf* evaluates trivially to:

$$p(X_n = 0) = 1 \qquad (1)$$

**Node $n$ is not a leaf.** The *pmf* $p(X_n = k)$ is given by the sum of the probabilities of all different combinations of $k$ successful receptions in the tree rooted at $n$. The recursive way of calculating the *pmf* allows the use of already known probabilities $p(X_i = a_n(i))$ at the children $i \in child(n)$ of $n$. For every node $n$ we have therefore just to look at the adjacent links leading to the children.

We must sum over all the combinations of link success that allow in total $k$ successful receiving receivers located at the children $i$ of $n$ and in the subtrees rooted at each of the children.

For one combination $s_n$ of link success the number of successful receptions at the direct children, being also receivers, is given by the inner product $s_n^T x_n$. The number of receptions in the subtrees rooted at the children is given by $s_n^T a_n$.

To obtain the number $k$ of successful receptions for a given $s_n$ the following condition must hold:

$$k = s_n^T(a_n + x_n) \qquad (2)$$

Since $x_n$ is constant and $s_n$ is given, equation (2) selects a subset of combinations of receptions in the subtrees rooted at the children of $n$: $A_n(s_n) = \{a_n | k = s_n^T(a_n + x_n)\} \subset \times_{i=1}^{c_n}\{0,\ldots,r_i\}$.

Different number of receptions in subtrees behind a failing link do not change the probability $p(X_n = k)$. $A_n(s_n)$ can therefore be reduced by masking the number of receptions in subtrees behind failing links.

$$A_n(s_n) = \{\, a_n \mid k = s_n^T(a_n + x_n) \wedge \forall i:\ s_n(i)a_n(i) = a_n(i)\} \qquad (3)$$

The probability for one combination $s_n$ of link success and one $a_n \in A_n(s_n)$ is then given by the product over the children:

$$p(a_n, s_n) = \prod_{i \in child(n)} \{\ s_n(i)(1-q)p(X_i = a_n(i)) + (1 - s_n(i))q\ \} \qquad (4)$$

Since the link to child $i$ is successful ($s_n(i) = 1$) with probability $(1-q)$ and the probability of $a_n(i)$ successful receptions in the subtree rooted at child $i$ is $p(X_i = a_n(i))$. The packet gets lost $((1 - s_n(i)) = 1)$ on the link to child $i$ with probability $q$ and $a_n(i)$ has no contribution.

The probability $p(X_n = k)$ is then given by summing over all link success combinations $s_n$ and all $a_n \in A_n(s_n)$:

$$p(X_n = k) = \sum_{s_n} \sum_{a_n \in A_n(s_n)} p(a_n, s_n) \qquad (5)$$

We show $p(X_S = k)$ for the generic multicast trees with a link loss probability of $q = 0.03$ in figure 8 for $r = 64$ receivers and, for $r = 128$ receivers in figure 9.

We can see that the *pmf*s vary significantly for the three generic multicast trees. This is due to the fact that the number of receivers affected by a loss on a single link also differs widely for the three generic multicast trees.

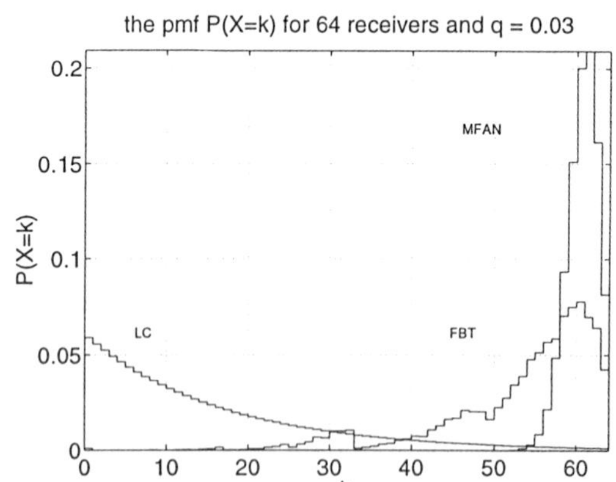


Figure 8: The probability mass function $P(X_S = k)$ for $FBT$, $MFAN$ and $LC$ for 64 receivers and a link loss probability of $q = 0.03$

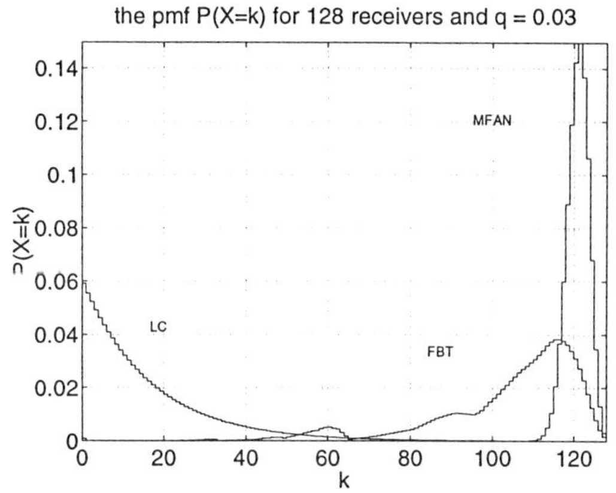


Figure 9: The probability mass function $P(X_S = k)$ for $FBT$, $MFAN$ and $LC$ for 128 receivers and a link loss probability of $q = 0.03$

The $pmf$ of the $MFAN$ is the binomial $pmf$, the $pmf$ of the $LC$ approximates the geometric $pmf$ for a large number of receivers. The curve of the $FBT$ is multimodal with peaks at $k = 2^{h-1}, 2^{h-1} + 2^{h-2}, \ldots$. These peaks are due to a high number of full binary subtrees with $2^{h-2}, 2^{h-3}, \ldots$ receivers and therefore a high number of possible combinations that lead to a sum of $k$ successful receptions, whereas for $k + 1$ successful receptions the number of possible combinations of full binary subtrees is much lower.

The $pmfs$ for the $HST$ and the $SPT$ for the same multicast group on the same network (figures 10 and 11) indicate that the variance of the number of successful receptions for the $HST$ is higher than for the $SPT$. The high probabilities for low numbers of successful receivers are due to shared paths near the source. We observe that the $pmfs$ for the $HST$ and the $SPT$ resemble most closely the $pmf$ for the $FBT$.

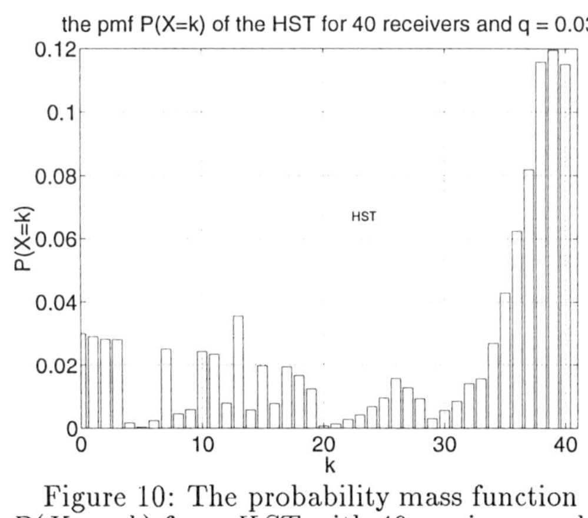


Figure 10: The probability mass function $P(X_S = k)$ for a $HST$ with 40 receivers and a link loss probability of $q = 0.03$

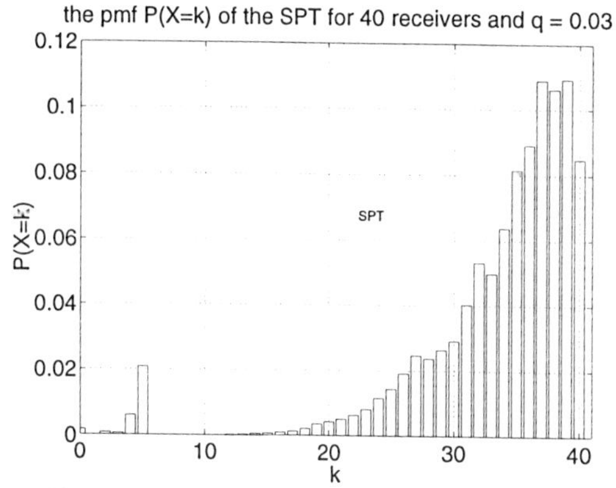


Figure 11: The probability mass function $P(X_S = k)$ for the $SPT$ with 40 receivers and a link loss probability of $q = 0.03$

### 3.2 The number of responses

We are interested in the number of responses, which can be either positive or negative ACKs, we can expect from the $r$ receivers in the multicast tree, when a packet is emitted once by the source. We make the assumption that the feedback reverse channel from the receivers to the source is loss–free, in which case the number of ACKs/NAKs is identical to the number of receivers that have received or have not received a packet.

$X_S$ is a random variable that describes the number of successful receptions in the whole multicast tree. $X_S$ is the sum of random variables $X_{S,i} \in \{0, 1\}$, each describing the reception of a single receivers $i$: $X_S = \sum_{i=1}^{r} X_{S,i}$. Since we assume uniform link loss $q$ on all links, the probability of a successful reception for receiver $i$, which lies $h_i$ hops away from the source, is $P(X_{S,i}) = (1-q)^{h_i}$. The expected number of ACKs for every single receiver is therefore $E(X_{S,i}) = P(X_{S,i})$. The expected number of successful receptions $E(X_S)$ in a tree with $r$ receivers is then:

$$E(X_S) = E(\sum_{i=1}^{r} X_{S,i}) = \sum_{i=1}^{r} E(X_{S,i}) = \sum_{i=1}^{r} (1-q)^{h_i} \tag{6}$$

We can also express $E(X_S)$ dependent on the receiver distribution over the tree levels $h$, by accumulating receivers that have the same distance from the source. Let $n_h$ be the number of receivers that lie in tree level $h$, e.g. $h$ hops from the source, then:

$$E(X_S) = \sum_{h=1}^{h_{max}} n_h (1-q)^h \tag{7}$$

gives the expected number of ACKs. Please note that $E(X_S)$ is **not** dependent on the number of shared links, since in (6) the path from the source to every receiver accounts by its full length.

The expected number $E(X_S)$ of ACK-packets at the source is shown in figure 12 as a function of the number of receivers in the multicast group for a link loss probability $q = 0.03$. For $HST$, the number of ACKs is slightly lower than for $SPT$, accounting for the fact that the number of links traversed between the source and a receiver is higher for $HST$ than for $SPT$.

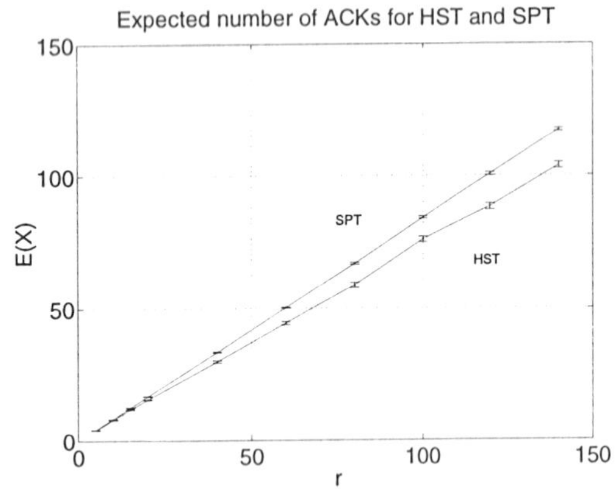


Figure 12: Expected number of ACK-packets at the source for a link loss probability of $q = 0.03$.

The error control scheme may use positive ACKs or negative ACKs (NAKs). Let $Y_S = r - X_S$ be the random variable that describes the number of unsuccessful receptions, then the $pmf$ of $Y_S$ is:

$$p(Y_S = k) = p(X_S = r - k)$$

and the expected number of NAKs for $r$ receivers is given as:

$$E(Y_S) = r - E(X_S)$$

.

### 3.3 The expected number of transmissions for reliable delivery

The expected number of multicast transmissions to deliver a packet to **all** receivers is an important measure in reliable multicast communication. The expected number of transmissions captures the global packet loss behaviour in the tree and the cost and the time of a reliable multicast delivery. The expected number of multicast transmissions depends on the link loss probability $q$ and the topology of the multicast tree.

In [2], the expected number of multicasted transmissions is given for the case of loss at **nodes** in the multicast tree. It is more appropriate to consider loss on a link due to two reasons: loss at the source node is unlikely and link loss can be associated with loss in output buffers in routers. In [18] the expected number of multicasted transmissions for link loss is given by a slight modification of the formula given in [2].

The Cumulative Distribution Function ($CDF$) $F_n(i)$ of the number of transmissions for the link leading to node $n$ and the tree rooted at $n$ is calculated in a recursive fashion starting at the leaves: It has to be distinguished, if node $n$ is a leaf $l$, an internal node, or the source $S$ (for details see [18]):

$$\begin{aligned} F_l(i) &= 1 - q^i \\ F_n(i) &= \sum_{u=0}^{i-1} \binom{i}{u} q^u (1-q)^{(i-u)} \prod_{c \in child(n)} F_c(i-u) \\ F_S(i) &= \prod_{c \in child(S)} F_c(i) \end{aligned} \tag{8}$$

Using $F_S(i)$, the expected number of multicasted transmissions $E(T(S))$ from the source $S$ is:

$$E(T(S)) = \sum_{i=0}^{\infty} (1 - F_S(i)) \tag{9}$$

The expected number of retransmissions $E(R(S))$ is:

$$\begin{aligned} E(R(S)) &= E(T(S) - 1) = E(T(S)) - 1 \\ &\overset{(9)}{=} \sum_{i=1}^{\infty} (1 - F_S(i)) \end{aligned} \tag{10}$$

### 3.4 A useful approximation for $E(R(S))$

Reliable multicast protocols need to know the expected number of retransmissions. However, the exact calculation as derived above is not practical:

- The expected number of retransmissions is hard to calculate, since the calculation of the recursive $CDF$ in (8) is computationally intensive for arbitrary topologies.
- Adaptive transport protocols need simple but effective mechanisms to decide.

We give a tight and very simple approximation. The expected number of retransmissions is approximately the product of the link loss probability $q$ and the number of links $L$ in the multicast tree:

$$E(R(S)) \approx qL \tag{11}$$

This approximation is tight for $qL \leq 1$.

For space reasons we limit ourselves to a sketch of the derivation of the approximation for $E(R(S))$ (for details see [19]). By induction over the children is shown that every $F_n(i)$ can be expressed in the form

$$F_n(i) = 1 - \sum_{j_n^-} (Q_{j_n^-})^i + \sum_{j_n^+} (Q_{j_n^+})^i$$

where $Q_{j_n^-}$ and $Q_{j_n^+}$ are polynoms in $q$: $Q = \sum_k \zeta_k q^k$, with a minimal exponent $k_{min} \geq 1$. The difference between the sum $\sum_{j_n^+} \zeta_{1_{j_n^+}}$ of the $\zeta_1$ of all the polynoms $Q_{j_n^+}$ with $k_{min} = 1$ and the sum $\sum_{j_n^-} \zeta_{1_{j_n^-}}$ of the $\zeta_1$ of all the polynoms $Q_{j_n^-}$ with $k_{min} = 1$ equals the number of links in the subtree rooted at $n$. If there is a link leading to node $n$ the difference is one greater than the number of links in the subtree rooted at $n$.

Afterwards, the expectation is calculated by:

$$E(R(S)) = \sum_{i=1}^{\infty}(1 - F_S(i))$$

Which results in:

$$E(R(S)) = \sum_{j_S^-} \frac{Q_{j_S^-}}{1 - Q_{j_S^-}} - \sum_{j_S^+} \frac{Q_{j_S^+}}{1 - Q_{j_S^+}}$$

Then, the ratios $\frac{Q}{1-Q}$ are approximated by $Q$, yielding

$$E(R(S)) \approx \sum_{j_S^-} Q_{j_S^-} - \sum_{j_n^+} Q_{j_n^+}$$

Finally, are we interested in the term $q$ of the polynom $Q$, due to its relevance compared with the terms $q^2, q^3, \ldots$. Every polynom $Q = \sum_k \zeta_k q^k$ is approximated by $\zeta_1 q$, resulting in an approximation of the expected number of retransmissions as:

$$E(R(S)) \approx q(\sum_{j_S^-} \zeta_{1_{j_S^-}} - \sum_{j_n^+} \zeta_{1_{j_S^+}}) = qL$$

The last approximation, where higher order terms are suppressed, also gives us the condition for which the whole approximation of the expected number of retransmissions (11) is valid:

$$qL \leq 1$$

since for $qL \geq 1$ a second order term $q^2$ has an impact of one or more links on the approximative expectation: $q^2 \cdot L = q(qL) \geq q \cdot 1$.

We compare the two most extreme cases of multicast topologies. The first one is called linear chain ($LC$) and is just a chain of $L$ links. The other extreme is called $MFAN$ and is the so beloved, frequently used, model for a multicast tree in performance evaluation of reliable multicast communication. The $MFAN$[3] has one separate link from the source to every of the $L$ receivers. In both cases, we have $L$ links. $LC$ is the deepest, $MFAN$ the broadest multicast tree that can be built with $L$ links. In figure 14 we compare the exact expected numbers of retransmissions for $MFAN$ and $LC$ with the approximation $qL$ as a function of the number of links. We previously saw that the loss characteristic and the $pmf$ for the number of successful receptions of the $FBT$ is similar to the one for real multicast trees. We therefore compare separately the expected number of retransmissions in the $FBT$ with the approximation $qL$ for $L = 30$ links in figure 13 and observe that the approximation is very tight.

[3] To get the most extreme multicast tree, we reduce the height of the $MFAN$ to $h = 1$, compared to the previous definition of MFAN, where we had chosen $h = 2$ (figure 3).

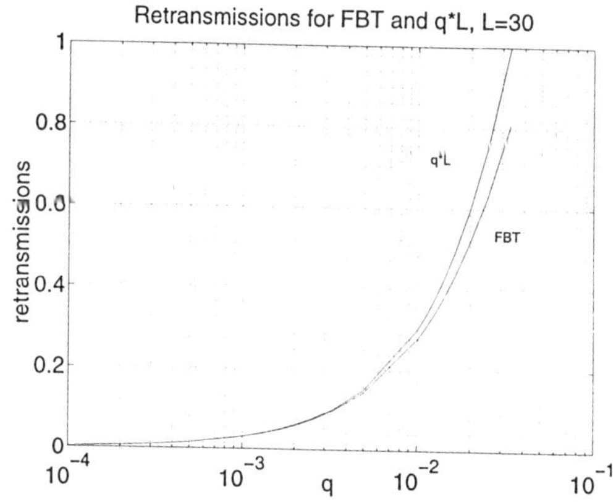


Figure 13: The expected number of retransmissions for the $FBT$ and the approximation $qL$ for different $q$.

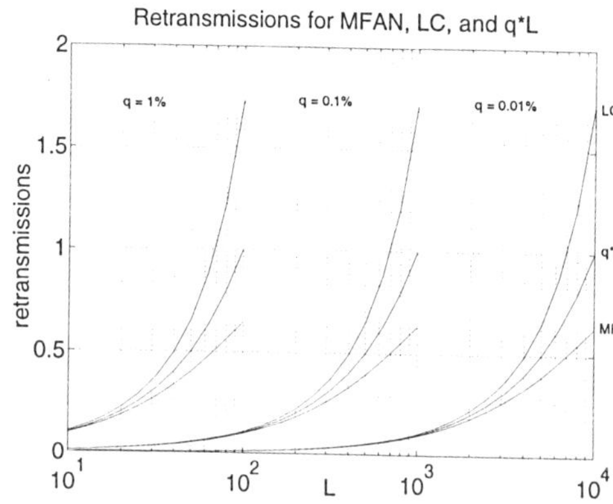


Figure 14: The expected number of retransmissions for the most extreme multicast trees and the approximation $qL$ with respect to the number of links $L$.

## 4 Implications of our work

We demonstrate the impact of our results in the following two domains:

- We show that multicast routing algorithms that optimize delay achieve better delay and throughput performance for reliable multicast communication, than algorithms that optimize cost.
- We show that the $FBT$ is a good generic model of a multicast connection and that more realistic results are obtained than with the usual used $MFAN$.

### 4.1 Impact of Routing on Error Recovery

Multicast routing algorithms have been designed that take into account several metrics. However, the performance of an algorithm is the most time evaluated for cost and delay – the performance for reliable transmission is left aside. We give a tight approximation for the number of retransmissions needed to deliver one packet from the source to all receivers: $E(R(S)) \approx qL$ that enables performance evaluation of routing algorithms with respect to loss.

In the case where a unique link cost is chosen, the cost of the multicast tree is proportional to the number of links $L$ in the multicast tree and therefore approximately proportional to the number of retransmissions.

For a given loss rate the performance of error recovery schemes for point to point connections is determined by the Round Trip Time ($RTT$) between the source and the receiver. We define the Round Trip Time as two times the sum of the propagation and transmission delays of the links on the path from the source to the receiver.

For a multicast connection, the receiver connected to the source via the longest path (in terms of delay) is the feedback bottleneck for the error recovery scheme. The $RTT$ of a multicast connection is therefore defined as two times the sum of the propagation and transmission time on the links on this longest path and depends on the routing algorithm. The $RTT$ for the $HST$ is about two times higher than the $RTT$ for the $SPT$ (see figure 7). On the other hand, the difference between $HST$ and $SPT$ in terms of the expected number of retransmissions, using $E(R(S)) \approx qL$, is minor (compare figure 15), with the values for $SPT$ being only slightly higher than for $HST$.

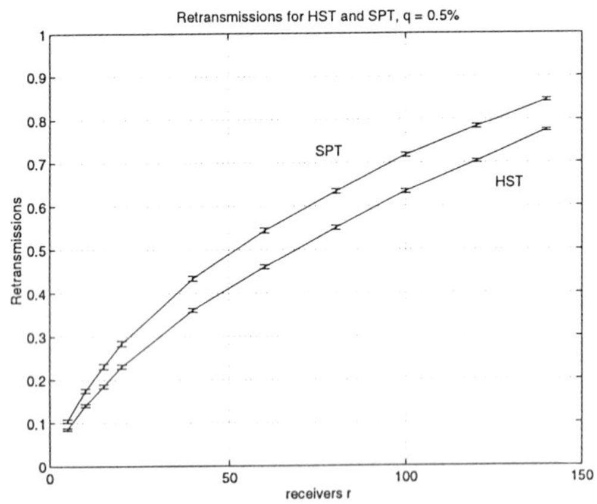


Figure 15: The expected number of retransmissions for $HST$ and $SPT$ for $q = 0.005$.

From these two observations, we can conclude that delay optimization ($SPT$) in multicast routing algorithms yields better delay and throughput performance for reliable transmission than does cost optimization ($HST$).

Applications with a stringent time-constraint profit also from routing algorithms that optimize delay. In recent years routing algorithms have been designed that optimize cost and try to meet a delay-constraint. However, most of the algorithms optimizing cost do not support dynamic multicast group membership changes – the $SPT$ does.

We believe that $SPT$ routing is the best solution for multicast routing. Due to its simplicity, it can use the routing of the underlying unicast algorithm, its support for dynamic membership changes and its good performance for reliable transmission as for applications that need timely delivery.

## 4.2 A better generic model for multicast trees: Full Binary Tree

We saw in previous sections that the loss characteristics of the $FBT$ is very close to the loss characteristics of $HST$ and $SPT$. To confirm that $FBT$ is a good generic model for a multicast tree, we compare the **link share** in different trees, i.e. to what degree do receivers in a tree share common paths.

Let $L$ be the number of links and $r$ be the number of receivers in the multicast tree, then the link share of one link $l_i$, $i = 1, \ldots, L$ can be defined as the number of receivers $rd(l_i)$ that share the cost on link $l_i$ divided by the total number of receivers: $ls(l_i) = \frac{rd(l_i)}{r}$. The link share $ls$ for the entire tree $mct$ is defined as the average link share of all links:

$$ls(mct) = \frac{1}{L}\sum_{i=1}^{L} \frac{rd(l_i)}{r} \tag{12}$$

For a tree, there are several methods to define a measure of link share. We compared measures of link share and found that the definition given in (12) reflects well the degree to which receivers share links in a tree. For a further discussion on definitions of link share see [20].

The link share of the $FBT$ is nearly identical with the link share of the $SPT$ (see figure 16). The choice of the $FBT$ as a model for a multicast tree is further confirmed by the degree to which receivers share the links in the multicast tree. The $HST$ has a higher link share than the $SPT$, since the routing algorithm tries to connect the receiver set with a minimal cost, resulting in a high number of receivers that share an average single link in the multicast tree.

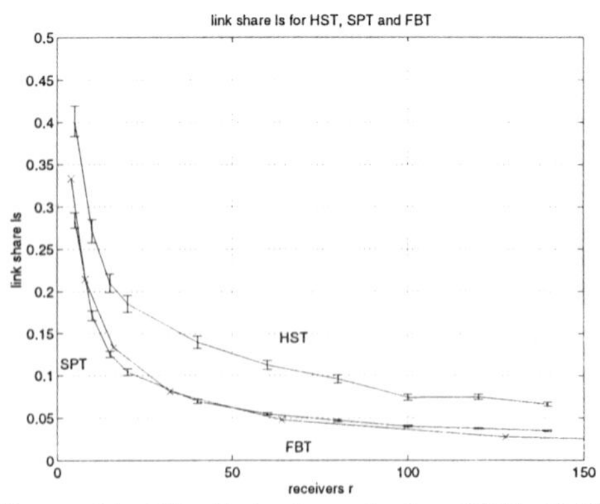


Figure 16: The link share $ls$ for $SPT$, $HST$ and $FBT$

## 5 Conclusion

We evaluated the impact of routing on reliable multicast and achieved two main results. First, multicast routing that optimizes delay achieves better throughput and delay performance for reliable multicast than cost optimal routing. Second, the full binary tree ($FBT$) is a good generic model for the loss characteristics of real multicast trees and provides more realistic results than the usual $MFAN$, in which a loss affects always only one receiver. We derived two characterizations that enable the comparison of routing algorithms and error recovery mechanisms with respect to the multicast tree topology, namely a $pmf$ for the number of successful receptions when a packet is emitted once from the source and the expected number of retransmissions needed to deliver a packet from the source to all receivers. We show that the product of the link loss probability $q$ and the number of links $L$ in an arbitrary multicast tree tightly approximates the expected number of retransmissions $E(R)$ under the condition that $qL < 1$:

$$E(R) \approx qL$$

## References


[1] H. Eriksson, "MBONE: The multicast backbone," *Communications of the ACM*, vol. 37, pp. 54–60, Aug. 1994.

[2] P. Bhagwat, P. P. Mishra, and S. K. Tripathi, "Effect of topology on performance of reliable multicast communication," in *Proceedings of INFOCOM'94*, vol. 2, (Toronto, Ontario, Canada), pp. 602–609, IEEE, June 1994.

[3] L. Wei and D. Estrin, "The trade-offs of multicast trees and algorithms," in *Proceedings of ICCN'94*, (San Francisco, CA, USA), Sept 1994.

[4] M. Doar and I. Leslie, "How bad is naïve multicast routing," in *Proceedings of INFOCOM'93*, vol. 1, pp. 82–89, IEEE, 1993.

[5] V. P. Kompella, J. C. Pasquale, and G. C. Polyzos, "Multicasting for multimedia applications," in *Proceedings of INFOCOM'92*, pp. 2078–2085, IEEE, 1992.

[6] C. A. Noronha and F. A. Tobagi, "Evaluation of multicast routing algorithms for multimedia streams," in *Proceedings of IEEE ITS'94*, (Rio de Janeiro, Brazil), IEEE, August 1994.

[7] R. Widyono, "The design and evaluation of routing algorithms for real-time channels," Tech. Rep. TR-94-024, University of California at Berkeley, International Computer Science Institute, June 1994.

[8] T. Billhartz, J. B. Cain, E. Farrey-Goudreau, and D. Fieg, "Performance and resource cost comparisons for the cbt and pim multicast routing protocols in dis environments," in *Proceedings of INFOCOM'96*, vol. 1, (San Francisco, CA, USA), pp. 85–93, IEEE, March 1996.

[9] D. Towsley and S. Mithal, "A selective repeat arq protocol for a point to multipoint channel," in *Proceedings of INFOCOM'87*, (San Francisco, CA, USA), pp. 521–526, IEEE, April 1987.

[10] D. Towsley, "An analysis of a point-to-multipoint channel using a go-back-n error control protocol," *IEEE Transactions on Communications*, vol. 33, pp. 282–285, March 1985.

[11] R. H. Deng, "Hybrid arq schemes for point-to-multipoint communication over nonstationary broadcast channels," *IEEE Transactions on Communications*, vol. 41, pp. 1379–1387, September 1993.

[12] N. Shacham and D. Towsley, "Resequencing delay and buffer occupancy in selective repeat arq with multiple receivers," in *Proceedings of INFOCOM'87*, pp. 512–520, IEEE, 1987.

[13] S. Pingali, D. Towsley, and J. F. Kurose, "A comparison of sender-initiated and receiver-initiated reliable multicast protocols," in *Proceedings of Sigmetrics, Conference on measurement and modeling of Computer Systems*, (Santa Clara, CA, USA), pp. 221–230, ACM, May 1994.

[14] L. Kou, G. Markowsky, and L. Berman, "A fast algorithm for steiner trees," *Acta Informatica*, vol. 15, pp. 141–145, 1981.

[15] P. Winter, "Steiner problem in networks: a survey," in *Networks*, vol. 17, pp. 129–167, 1987.

[16] B. M. Waxman, "Routing of multipoint connections," *IEEE JSAC*, vol. 6, pp. 1617–1622, December 1988.

[17] J. Kadirire, "Minimising packet copies in multicast routing by exploiting geographic spread," *ACM Computer Communication Review*, vol. 24, pp. 47–62, July 1994.

[18] J. Nonnenmacher and E. W. Biersack, "Reliable multicast: Where to use fec," in *Proceedings of IFIP 5th International Workshop on Protocols for High Speed Networks (PfHSN'96)*, (INRIA, Sophia Antipolis, FRANCE), IFIP, Chapman & Hall, October 1996.

[19] J. Nonnenmacher, "Reliable multicast: An approximation for the expected number of retransmissions," tech. rep., Institut EURECOM, 2229 route des Crêtes, B.P. 193, 06904 Sophia Antipolis Cedex, FRANCE, May 1996.

[20] J. Nonnenmacher, "Ressource sharing in multicast connections," tech. rep., Institut EURECOM, 2229 route des Crêtes, B.P. 193, 06904 Sophia Antipolis Cedex, FRANCE, February 1996.

# A Delay Analysis of Sender-Initiated and Receiver-Initiated Reliable Multicast Protocols

Miki Yamamoto† 1   James F. Kurose‡ 2   Donald F. Towsley‡ 2   Hiromasa Ikeda†

†Department of Communications Engineering
Faculty of Engineering, Osaka University
2-1 Yamadaoka, Suita, Osaka 565 JAPAN

‡Department of Computer Science
University of Massachusetts
Amherst, Massachusetts 01030 U.S.A.

**Abstract**

*A growing number of network applications require the use of a reliable multicast protocol to disseminate data from a source to a potentially large number of receivers. This paper presents an analytic performance analysis of the packet delay incurred under three generic sender- and receiver-initiated approaches towards reliable multicast. We focus on the host processing requirements of these protocols and derive expressions for average time between the initial arrival of a packet at a sender and its correct reception at a randomly chosen receiver. Our numerical results indicate that a NAK-based protocol that limits NAK generation by intentionally and randomly delaying NAK packets can achieve substantially higher throughput than the other two protocols examined, and can do so without suffering an appreciable higher delay over a range of system parameters.*

## 1 Introduction

A growing number of network applications require the use of a reliable multicast protocol to disseminate data from a source to a potentially large number of receivers. These applications include whiteboard teleconferencing [1], distribution of financial and billing data [4], and distributed interactive simulation . An earlier paper by Pingali *et al.*[6] identified two basic approaches towards reliable multicast – sender-initiated ACK-based protocols and receiver-initiated NAK-based protocols – and examined the maximum achievable sender and receiver throughputs for these approaches. It was shown that as the number of receivers grows large, receiver-initiated protocols provide substantially higher throughput than their sender-initiated counterparts when end system processing is the resource under consideration.

This present paper builds on the work in [6] by presenting a delay analysis of the three generic sender- and receiver-initiated protocols similar to identified in [6]: **A** (a sender-initiated ACK-based protocol), **N1** (a receiver-initiated NAK-based protocol in which NAKs are returned to the sender via a point-to-point channel), and **N2** (a receiver-initiated NAK-based protocol in which receivers multicast NAKs to the sender). Our results indicate that the **N2** protocol, which limits NAK generation by intentionally and randomly delaying NAK packets, can achieve substantially higher throughput than the other two protocols examined, and can do so without suffering an appreciable higher delay over a range of system parameters.

Our work differs from previous work in reliable multicast protocols in two important ways. First, our goal here is not to propose a specific reliable multicast protocol but rather to focus on the *fundamental differences* between sender- and receiver-initiated protocols and the sensitivity of their delay behavior to system parameters such as the number of receivers, network propagation delay, and timer values. Second, we focus on end-system protocol processing as the crucial resource. We expect the processing costs of end-system protocols to become increasingly important as network bandwidths continue to increase, particularly when there are many participants in a multicast group.

The remainder of this paper is structured as follows. Section 2 presents a description of the **A**, **N1,** and **N2** protocols. Section 3 describes our network model and presents an analysis of the reliable multicast packet delay – the time between the initial generation of a packet at the sender and its successful reception at a a randomly chosen receiver under the three generic protocols. Section 4 provides a numerical comparison of the protocols' performance under various scenarios. Section 5 concludes this paper.

---

1 This author was visiting the University of Massachusetts during the 1995-6 academic year, supported by a grant from the Ministry of Education, Science and Culture of Japanese Government.

2 This research was supported in part by the Defense Advanced Research Projects Agency under contract F19628-95-C-0146 and the National Science Foundation under grant NCR-95-08274.



0-8186-7780-5/97 $10.00 © 1997 IEEE

## 2 Three Generic Approaches Towards Reliable Multicast

In this section we present three generic approaches [6] towards reliable multicast. We emphasize that our intent here is not to present specific new reliable multicast protocols, but rather to identify generic protocols that capture important general characteristics of ACK- and NAK-based protocols. We describe these protocols assuming a single sender and $R$ receivers. However, the protocols below are equally applicable in the case where an end system can both send and receive data.

### 2.1 A Sender-Initiated Protocol: A

In the sender-initiated protocol, denoted **A**, each time a receiver correctly receives a packet, it sends a positive acknowledgment (ACK) to the sender. The sender maintains a list of the receivers from which it has received an ACK for each packet. A sender timeout mechanism is used to recover from lost packets. Specifically, the sender starts a timer when a packet is transmitted and, if the timer expires prior to it having received ACKs for this packet from every receiver, the sender retransmits the packet and restarts the timer.

Most traditional point-to-point reliable data transfer protocols (e.g., TCP, HDLC, TP4) and many early multicast/broadcast protocols [8, 7] follow this ACK-based approach. Rather than focus on a specific protocol, we will instead focus on a *generic* protocol which exhibits the following behavior:

- Whenever the sender transmits or retransmits a packet, it multicasts it to all receivers and starts a timer.
- Whenever a receiver receives a packet correctly, it transmits an ACK to the sender over a point-to-point connection.
- A timer is associated with each packet that has not been acknowledged by all receivers. Whenever a timer expires, the sender re-multicasts the corresponding packet (only) to the receivers.

This protocol can be optimized in numerous ways, such as grouping ACKs for different packets into a single ACK and hierarchically grouping receivers [8, 5]. We will not consider such optimizations here.

### 2.2 A Receiver-Initiated Protocol: N1

Receiver-initiated protocols place the responsibility for ensuring reliable packet delivery on the receivers. The sender transmits an initial copy of a packet and will only retransmit that packet if it receives a negative acknowledgment (NAK) from a receiver. When this occurs, the sender then re-multicasts the NAKed packet.

Under protocol **N1**, NAKs are generated by a receiver and sent point-to-point to the sender when it (the receiver) discovers that the sender has transmitted a packet that it (the receiver) has not yet received. This occurs when the receiver first receives a packet with sequence number $i + 1$ without having received packet $i$. As we will see, the time between the transmission of packet $i$ and packet $i + 1$ at the sender thus plays an important role in determining the delay until a receiver realizes that it has lost packet $i$. A number of researchers have proposed having the sender multicast another copy of packet $i$ (or its sequence number), even though no NAKs are receiver, whenever the delay between the arrival of packet $i$ and $i + 1$ exceeds some threshold. In the following, we will ignore these forced retransmissions in our analysis although they can be accommodated rather easily. In order to recover from the loss of a NAK or the subsequently retransmitted packet, a receiver uses a timer, as discussed below. The first generic receiver-initiated protocol, **N1**, operates as follows:

- The sender multicasts all packets.
- Whenever a receiver detects a lost packet, it transmits a NAK for that packet to the sender over a point-to-point channel and starts a timer.
- The expiration of a timer without prior reception of the corresponding packet causes the receiver to generate another NAK, which is sent point-to-point to the sender. The timer is also restarted.
- Whenever the sender receives a NAK, it re-multicasts the packet to all receivers.

### 2.3 A Second Receiver-Initiated Protocol: N2

The **N2** protocol presented below is a variation of the **N1** protocol discussed above. As suggested by Ramakrishnan and Jain [7] for a LAN and Jacobson and Floyd [1] for a WAN, it limits the number of NAKs generated using a NAK suppression mechanism. With NAK suppression, each receiver multicasts its NAK only after waiting a random amount of time after detecting packet loss. If a receiver receives a NAK from another receiver while waiting to transmit its own NAK for that packet, it cancels its pending NAK. **N2** thus has the following behavior:

- The sender multicasts all packets.
- Whenever a receiver detects a lost packet, it schedules a pending NAK transmission at a randomly chosen point of time in the future. In the meantime, if the receiver receives a NAK (generated by another receiver) for this packet, it cancels the transmission of its own pending NAK. This is called NAK suppression.

- If, at the scheduled time for a pending NAK transmission, a NAK for this packet has not been received since the pending NAK transmission was first scheduled, the receiver multicasts a NAK to the sender and all other receivers, and starts a timer.

- Upon receipt of a NAK for a packet that the receiver has not yet received, but for which it has initiated the random delay prior to sending a NAK, the receiver sets a timer and behaves as if it had sent that NAK.

- The expiration of a timer without prior reception of the corresponding packet causes the receiver infer that a packet has been lost, and operate as in item 2 above.

- Whenever the sender receives a NAK, it re-multicasts the packet to all receivers.

As with the sender-initiated protocols, there are numerous optimizations possible. For example, it is possible for a receiver that has correctly received a packet to itself retransmit a copy of the packet [1]. See [7, 1] for additional discussion of possible optimizations.

# 3 Delay Analysis of Reliable Multicast Protocols

The goal of the analysis outlined in this section is to determine the delay between the initial arrival of a packet at the sender and its correct reception at a randomly chosen receiver under the **A**, **N1**, and **N2** protocols. As we will see, this delay will be influenced by many factors, including the "processing" delays experienced by a packet at the sender and receiver, the end-to-end network propagation delay, the packet loss probability, and per-protocol parameters (e.g., the interval over which NAKs are delayed in **N2**). The delay analysis of each of the three protocols has two major steps:

1. In the first step, we first determine the packet arrival rates for the different types of requests (data packets plus ACK or NAK packets) at the sender and the receivers for a given protocol. Given this arrival rate, an M/G/1 queueing model of the sender and receiver gives the average delay of a request at that host: the time from the arrival/generation of a packet at a host to the completion of its "processing" at that host. Here, "processing" refers to the actions taken when a packet is sent and/or received. For example, the arrival of a NAK at the sender may result in the retransmission of a packet; NAK processing would thus include the host protocol processing needed to receive the incoming NAK and transmit the requested data packet. Packet arrival rates and sojourn times are derived in section 3.2 for the three protocols under study.
2. In the second step, we focus on a specific data packet when it first arrives at the sender for transmission to the senders, and analyze the sequence of message exchanges between the end systems that ultimately results in the data packet being successfully received at a randomly chosen receiver. The delays associated with these message exchanges together with the packet processing delays determined in step 1 together yield the overall delay between the initial arrival of the packet at the sender and its successful reception at the randomly chosen receiver. The delay analysis of the **A**, **N1** and **N2** protocols is detailed in sections 3.3, 3.4 and 3.5 respectively.

## 3.1 Network Model

Our network model is quite simple. As noted above, we assume a single sender and $R$ receivers. New packets to be sent to the receivers arrive at the sender according to a Poisson process with rate $\lambda$. We assume that a packet sent by the sender is lost by a receiver with probability $p$, which is the same for all receivers. In our ensuing analysis, this assumption can be relaxed without significant conceptual difficulties. We also assume that packet losses are independent in both space and time. That is, loss of a particular packet is independent among receivers and independent of the loss of any previously transmitted packet. [9] discusses the spatial and temporal loss correlation observed in the MBone, an operational multicast network overlayed on the Internet, and observes that a simple model of spatial loss correlation is often appropriate. We also assume that ACKs and NAKs are never lost. This assumption can be relaxed by following the analysis given in [8]. Finally, we assume that all participants in the multicast are separated from each other by a delay of $\tau$.

## 3.2 Processing Model

We assume that the time required to service a data packet (either receive or send) is a random variable $X$ and that the time to process an ACK or NAK packet (either receive or send) is a random variable $Y$ and that they have means and second moments $E[X]$, $E[X^2]$, $E[Y]$ and $E[Y^2]$. In section 4, we discuss our measured values for these random variables.

## 3.3 Mean Delays at Sender and Receivers

The flow of packets among the sender and receivers is shown in Figure 1 for the **A** and **N2** protocols and will be discussed shortly. The flows in **N1** are also similar to **N2**, except that **N1** receivers receive no NAKs via the network.

Important quantities that arise throughout the analyses are

- $M_i^{(r)}$ - the number of times a packet must be transmitted before receiver $i$ receives it correctly. When there is no confusion, we will drop the subscript $i$. $M^{(r)}$ has

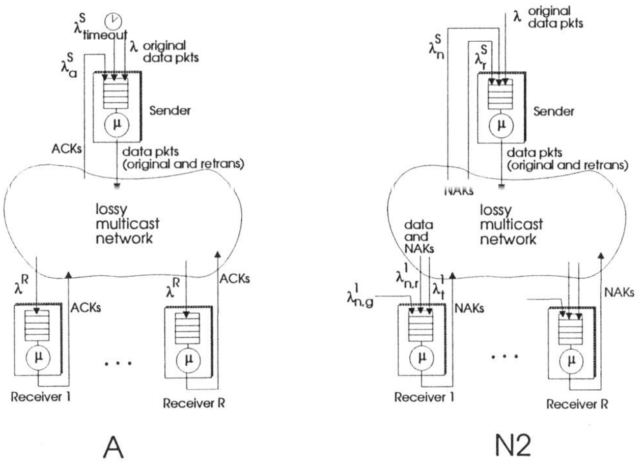


Figure 1: Packet flows under protocols A and N2

distribution $P[M^{(r)} = m] = (1-p)p^{m-1}$, $m \geq 1$, mean $E[M^{(r)}] = 1/(1-p)$.

- $M = \max_{1 \leq r \leq R} M_r^{(r)}$, the number of transmissions required until all receivers receive the packet, it has distribution $P(M \leq m) = P(M^{(r)} \leq m)^R = (1 - p^m)^R$ and mean $E[M] = \sum_{m=1}^{\infty}(1-(1-p^{m-1})^R)$.

### 3.3.1 Mean Waiting Times Under Protocol A

Consider first the sender under protocol **A.** Work performed by the sender comes from one of three sources. There are those packets that arrive for first time transmission at the sender. This flow, denoted $\lambda_t^S$, has rate $\lambda$. There are also those packets that are retransmitted due to a timeout. Since each packet is transmitted on average $E[M]-1$ times, the rate for this work flow, $\lambda_{timeout}^S$, is $\lambda(E[M]-1)$. Packets in both of these flows have a service requirement of $X$, as noted above. Finally, the arrival rate of ACK packets to the sender, $\lambda_a^S$, is $\lambda R E[M](1-p)$, with each request having a service requirement $Y$. Recall that a receiver always acknowledges a received packet, even it has already successfully received that packet.

Given these flows arriving at the sender, the total load on the sender then is

$$\rho_A^S = \lambda E[M]E[X] + \lambda R E[M](1-p)E[Y]$$

If we assume that the arrival processes are Poisson and that service times are independent random variables, independent of the arrival process, then the system can be modeled as an M/G/1 queue. The mean waiting time for a request (data (re)transmission or ACK) waiting to be processed at the sender under protocol **A**, $E[W_A^S]$, is given (using the Pollaczek-Khinchine formula, [3, p. 191]) by:

$$E[W_A^S] = \frac{(\lambda_t^S + \lambda_{timeout}^S)E[X^2] + \lambda_a^S E[Y^2]}{2(1-\rho_A^S)}.$$

Let us now focus on the receivers under **A**. At each receiver, there is only a single arriving flow, corresponding to the arrival of data packets, with rate

$$\lambda^R = \lambda E[M](1-p).$$

Servicing such a request corresponds to receiving the packet followed by the transmission of an ACK; hence the service time is $X + Y$. The load on the receiver is then $\rho_A^R = \lambda E[M](1-p)(E[X]+E[Y])$ and, under the assumption of Poisson arrivals, the mean waiting time, $E[W_A^R]$ is

$$E[W_A^R] = \frac{\lambda^R(E[X^2] + E[Y^2] + 2E[X]E[Y])}{2(1-\rho_A^R)}.$$

Note that $E[(X+Y)^2] = E[X^2] + E[Y^2] + 2E[X]E[Y]$ when $X$ and $Y$ are independent random variables.

Note that in deriving the equations for the flows at the sender, we have implicitly assumed that the timeout interval at the sender is always greater than the round trip propagation delay plus processing delay at the receivers, i.e., that there are no premature timeouts. We are currently investigating how to relax this assumption.

### 3.3.2 Waiting Times under Protocol N1

In [6], the assumption was made that the sender would never retransmit a packet more than once in response to NAKs due to the loss of the previous retransmission, i.e., it was assumed that the sender could determine whether or not a received NAK was a "duplicate" NAK. We assume this to be true in this paper as well but note that this is an *optimistic* assumption, since in practice it is difficult for the sender to determine whether or not a just-received NAK will be satisfied by its most recent retransmission or whether another retransmission should be made. Techniques such as having a receiver increment a count field in a NAK packet each time it generates a NAK for a given data packet, or having estimates of the delays between the source and the receivers [1] can help a source avoid retransmitting in response to duplicate NAK's. In [10] we also treat a pessimistic scenario where every NAK triggers a retransmission.

Under this scenario, the sender processes three flows. The first corresponds to the original transmissions. The second corresponds to the arrival of NAKs that trigger retransmissions and the third corresponds to the arrival of NAKs that are processed but do not generate a retransmission. The corresponding flow rates are

$$\lambda_t^S \;=\; \lambda,$$

$$\begin{aligned}\lambda_r^S &= \lambda(E[M]-1),\\ \lambda_n^S &= \lambda(RE[M^{(r)}]-E[M]-R+1).\end{aligned}$$

Here the subscripts $t$ and $r$ refer to the original transmissions and retransmissions respectively. The service times are $X$, $X+Y$ and $Y$ respectively. The load at the sender is then

$$\rho_{N1}^S = \lambda(E[X]E[M] + R(E[M^{(r)}]-1)E[Y]) \quad (1)$$

and the mean waiting time at the sender, $E[W_{N1}^S]$, is

$$\begin{aligned}&E[W_{N1}^S]\\ &= \{\lambda_t^S E[X^2] + \lambda_r^S(E[X^2]+E[Y^2]+2E[X]E[Y])\\ &\quad +\lambda_n^S E[Y^2]\}/2(1-\rho_{N1}^S) \quad (2)\end{aligned}$$

There are two work flows through the receiver under **N1.** One corresponds to the arrival of data packets from the sender and the other corresponds to the self-generation of NAK packets by the receiver. The respective arrival rates are

$$\begin{aligned}\lambda_t^R &= \lambda E[M](1-p),\\ \lambda_n^R &= \lambda(E[M^{(r)}]-1).\end{aligned}$$

The respective service times are $X$ and $Y$. The receiver load is thus

$$\rho_{N1}^R = \lambda(E[X]E[M](1-p) + (E[M^{(r)}]-1)E[Y])$$

and the mean wait time at a receiver, $E[W_{N1}^R]$ is

$$E[W_{N1}^R] = \frac{\lambda_t^R E[X^2] + \lambda_n^R E[Y^2]}{2(1-\rho_{N1}^R)}$$

### 3.3.3 Waiting Times Under N2

We next consider packet flows under protocol **N2**. Recall that **N2** has a more complicated NAK generation policy in which receivers needing to generate a NAK wait a random amount of time before doing so. The receipt of a NAK generated by another receiver causes the pending NAK transmission to be cancelled. As with our analysis of **N1**, we will again make an optimistic analysis of **N2**, assuming that a sender never retransmits a packet more than once in response to NAKs generated in response to the loss of the previous retransmission.

Define the random variable $N_{N2}$ to be the total number of NAKs received for packet $i$ by the sender under **N2.** Since NAKs are multicast, this is also the total number of NAKs of packet $i$ either transmitted or received by a receiver under **N2.** In [10], we derive the value of $E[N_{N2}]$.

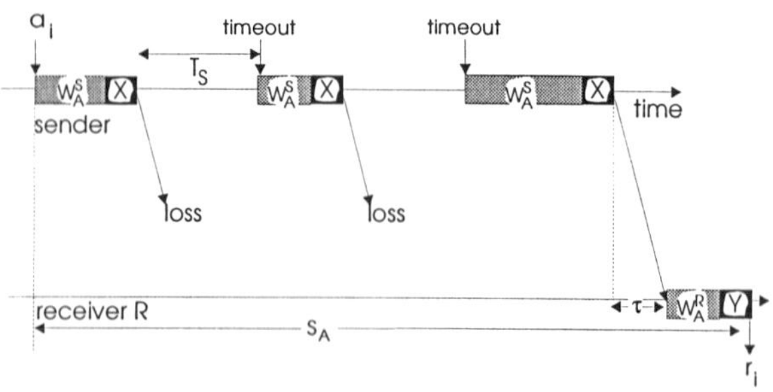


Figure 2: Delay components of the A protocol

Given this value and following similar reasoning as in the case of the optimistic **N1** protocol, we have the following expressions for the three flow rates into the sender,

$$\begin{aligned}\lambda_t^S &= \lambda,\\ \lambda_r^S &= \lambda(E[M]-1),\\ \lambda_n^S &= \lambda E[N_{N2}] - \lambda_r^S.\end{aligned}$$

The service times are $X$, $X+Y$ and $Y$ respectively. The load and mean waiting time at the sender under **N2**, $\rho_{N2}^S$ and $E[W_{N2}^S]$, are calculated using (1) and (2) (as in **N1**) using the values of $\lambda_t^S$, $\lambda_r^S$ and $\lambda_n^S$ immediately above.

There are three flows at the receiver with rates

$$\begin{aligned}\lambda_t^R &= \lambda E[M](1-p),\\ \lambda_{n,g}^R &= \frac{1}{R}\lambda E[N_{N2}]\\ \lambda_{n,r}^R &= \frac{R-1}{R}\lambda E[N_{N2}].\end{aligned}$$

$\lambda_{n,g}^R$ and $\lambda_{n,r}^R$ correspond to the rates at which the receiver generates NAKs and receives NAKs respectively. They each have service time $Y$. $\lambda_t^R$ is the flow of data packets, with service time $X$. Given these flows, the receiver load is

$$\rho_{N2}^R = \lambda(E[X]E[M](1-p) + E[N_{N2}]E[Y])$$

and the mean waiting time at the receiver under **N2**, under the assumption of Poisson flows, is

$$E[W_{N2}^R] = \frac{\lambda_t^R E[X^2] + (\lambda_{n,g}^R + \lambda_{n,r}^R)E[Y^2])}{2(1-\rho_{N2}^R)}.$$

## 3.4 Overall Delay Analysis of Protocol A

Having derived the rate of packet flows among the senders and receivers under the three protocols, we now consider the overall delay analysis of protocol **A**.

Figure 2 shows the operation of protocol **A.** Packet $i$ first arrives at the sender at time $a_i$. If there are other packets (data or ACK) waiting for processing at the sender, packet

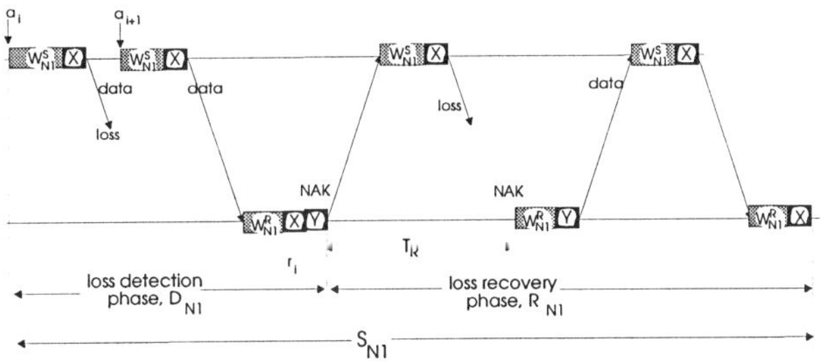


Figure 3: Delay components of the N1 protocol

$i$ waits for processing under FCFS scheduling and is eventually sent. After being lost twice in this example (and having to wait for retransmission processing after each timeout) the packet is received correctly at the receiver at time $r_i$.

Recall that the sender timeout delay and propagation delay have fixed values $T_s$ and $\tau$ respectively. The probability that a randomly chosen receiver requires exactly $j$ transmissions of the packets is $p^{j-1}(1-p)$. Given these considerations, the mean waiting times ($E[W_A^S]$ and $E[W_A^R]$) computed in section 3.3.1, and the service requirements $X$ and $Y$, the mean time between a packet's initial arrival to the sender and its successful receipt at a receiver under protocol **A** is given by

$$E[S_A]$$
$$= \left(\sum_{j=1}^{\infty} p^{j-1}(1-p)(j(E[W_A^S]+E[X])+(j-1)T_S)\right)$$
$$+\tau + E[W_A^R] + E[X]$$
$$= \frac{(E[W_A^S]+E[X]+pT_S)}{(1-p)} + \tau + E[W_A^R] + E[X]$$

## 3.5 Delay Analysis of Protocol N1

Figure 3 illustrates the operation of protocol **N1.** In this example, packet $i$ first arrives at the sender at time $a_i$, awaits processing at the sender, and is eventually sent. Let us focus on a randomly chosen receiver, which (along with $K$ other receivers) does not receive this initial copy of packet $i$. Upon the reception of the first packet, $j$, where $j > i$ at any of these $K+1$ receivers, a NAK is generated. We define the time from the initial arrival of packet $i$ at the sender to the generation of this initial NAK by *any* of the $K+1$ receivers as the *loss detection phase.* We present an approximate expression for the average length of this phase in section 3.5.1.

Once the loss is detected, those receivers that detect the loss will continue to generate NAKs periodically until they eventually receive packet $i$. We define the time between the end of the loss detection phase and the successful reception of the packet at the randomly chosen receiver as the *loss recovery phase.* We present an approximation for the length of the loss recovery phase in section 3.5.2. In section 3.5.3 we combine the results of sections 3.5.1 and 3.5.2 to derive the overall packet delay under protocol **N1.**

### 3.5.1 N1 Loss Detection Phase

Conditioning on the fact that our randomly chosen receiver has lost packet $i$, we further condition on the number of other receivers $K$ that have also lost packet $i$. As noted above, the loss detection phase ends when *any* of the $K+1$ receivers successfully receives a packet with a higher sequence number. Given that $K=k$, the conditional probability distribution for $L$, the number of subsequent packets (i.e., packets with higher sequence number) that are lost by the randomly chosen receiver and the other $K$ receivers is $P(L=l\,|\,K=k) = p^{l(k+1)}(1-p^{k+1}), l=0,\ldots; k=0,\ldots,R-1$, and $E(L|\,K=k) = p^{k+1}/(1-p^{k+1})$.

Once the $L+1$st packet (i.e., the first packet after $i$ that is successfully received by one of the $K+1$ receivers) arrives, it will experience a processing delay at the sender of $E[W_{N1}^S]+E[X]$, a propagation delay to the receiver of $\tau$ and a processing delay at the receiver of $E[W_{N1}^R]+E[X]$. We define the detection phase to end after the NAK is sent. Conditioning on the value of K, we have

$$E[D_{N1}]$$
$$= \sum_{k=0}^{R-1} \binom{R-1}{k} p^k(1-p)^{R-k-1}\frac{p^{k+1}/\lambda}{1-p^{k+1}}$$
$$+E[W_{N1}^S] + E[W_{N1}^R] + \tau + 2E[X] + E[Y].$$

We note that one simplifying assumption we have made in computing $E[D_{N1}]$ is that instead of using $E[W_{N1}^R]$, a more accurate expression would replace this quantity with the mean minimum processing time among the $j$ receivers out of the $k+1$ receivers that detect the loss of the $L+1$st packet.

### 3.5.2 N1 Loss Recovery Phase

The loss recovery phase of **N1** seen by our random receiver, denoted $R_{N1}$ and shown in Figure 3, is essentially a mirror image of protocol **A.** The receivers send one or more NAKs to the sender and the sender replies with a retransmitted packet, that is lost at the random receiver with probability $p$. From the random receiver's viewpoint, the loss recovery phase thus begins with a number of receiver timeout rounds, each of length $T_R + W_{N1}^R + E[Y]$ where $T_R$ is the length of the timeout period and $W_{N1}^R$ is the waiting time (see section 3.3.2). The loss recovery phase ends with a final propagation delay of the NAK to the sender, sender processing/retransmission of the data packet, and receiver processing of the received packet. Following our derivation of the delay of the **A** protocol, the mean recovery delay $E[R_{N1}]$:

$$
\begin{aligned}
&E[R_{N1}] \\
&= \left( \sum_{j=1}^{\infty} p^{j-1}(1-p)(j-1)(T_R + E[W_{N1}^R] + E[Y]) \right) \\
&\quad + 2\tau + E[W_{N1}^S] + E[X] + E[W_{N1}^R] + E[X] \\
&= \frac{p(T_R + E[W_{N1}^R] + E[Y])}{(1-p)} + E[W_{N1}^S] + E[W_{N1}^R] \\
&\quad +2(E[X] + \tau)
\end{aligned}
$$

### 3.5.3 Overall N1 Delay Analysis

Given the results from 3.5.1 and 3.5.2 for the lengths of the loss detection and recovery phases, respectively, for the N1 protocol, we may now easily derive the mean overall delay. With probability $(1-p)$ the randomly selected receiver receives the initial transmission of packet $i$ and experiences a delay equal to the sum of the sender processing delay, propagation delay, and receiver processing delay. With probability $p$ the receiver loses the initial transmission of packet $i$ and then experiences a delay equal to the sum of the loss detection and recovery phases, as discussed in sections 3.4.1. and 3.4.2. Given these considerations, the overall mean delay between the initial arrival of packet $i$ at the sender and its successful receptions at the randomly chosen receiver, $E[S_{N1}]$ is:

$$
\begin{aligned}
&E[S_{N1}] \\
&= (1-p)(E[W_{N1}^S] + E[W_{N1}^R] + 2E[X] + \tau) \\
&\quad +p(E[D_{N1}] + E[R_{N1}]) \\
&= E[W_{N1}^S] + E[W_{N1}^R] + 2E[X] + \tau \\
&\quad + \frac{p^2(T_R + E[W_{N1}^R] + E[Y])}{(1-p)} + p(E[D_{N1}] + \tau)
\end{aligned}
$$

Note that a simplifying assumption is that the $K+1$ receivers proceed in "rounds" after detecting the loss of packet $i$. Such synchronization is clearly idealized. It also overlooks the possibility that some of the $K+1$ receivers that lost the packets but were not among the subset of the $K+1$ receivers that initially detected the loss, might themselves detect the loss while the "rounds" are ongoing.

## 3.6 Delay Analysis of Protocol N2

Figure 4 illustrates the operation of protocol **N2,** using an example similar to that in Figure 3. The delay between the initial arrival of packet $i$ at the sender and its reception at a randomly chosen receiver under protocol **N2**, $S_{N2}$, divides into three segments:

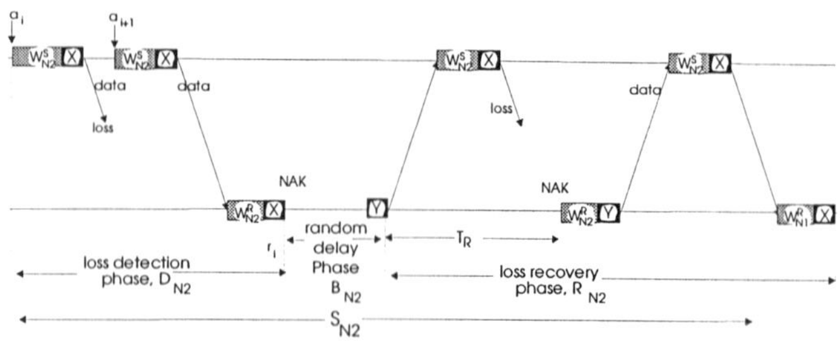


Figure 4: Delay components of the N2 protocol

- As in the **N1** protocol, the overall delay $S_{N2}$ begins with a loss detection phase of length $D_{N2}$. The derivation of the mean loss detection period length under **N2,** $E[D_{N2}]$ is identical to the derivation of $E[D_{N1}]$ in section 3.5. for the **N1** protocol, except that $E[W_{N2}^S]$ and $E[W_{N2}^R]$ are used instead of $E[W_{N1}^S]$ and $E[W_{N1}^R]$. Also, here we do not include the NAK transmission time in $E[D_{N2}]$.

- As in the **N1** protocol, $S_{N2}$ ends with a loss recovery phase of length $R_{N2}$. The derivation of the mean loss recovery period length is identical to the corresponding derivation in section 3.4.2 for the **N1** protocol, except that $E[W_{N2}^S]$ and $E[W_{N2}^R]$ are used instead of $E[W_{N1}^S]$ and $E[W_{N1}^R]$.

- Unlike the **N1** protocol, the receivers in **N2** wait a random amount of time until generating a NAK. This gives rise to the *random delay phase* shown in Figure 4. We denote the length of the random delay phase $B_{N2}$ and derive its mean, $E[B_{N2}]$ in [10].

Given the above considerations, the mean overall delay between the initial arrival of packet $i$ at the sender and its successful receptions at the randomly chosen receiver under protocol **N2** is:

$$
\begin{aligned}
&E[S_{N2}] \\
&= E[W_{N2}^S] + E[W_{N2}^R] + 2E[X] + \tau \\
&\quad +pE[B_{N2}] + \frac{p^2(T_R + E[W_{N2}^R] + E[Y])}{1-p} + \\
&\quad p\left( \sum_{k=0}^{R-1} \binom{R-1}{k} p^k(1-p)^{R-k-1} \frac{p^{k+1}/\lambda}{1-p^{k+1}} + \right. \\
&\quad \left. E[W_{N2}^S] + E[W_{N2}^R] + 2(E[X] + \tau) \right)
\end{aligned}
$$

# 4 Numerical Results

The analysis from sections 3.4, 3.5, and 3.6 give the expected delay between the initial arrival of a packet at the sender and its successful reception at the randomly chosen receiver under protocols **A**, **N1**, and **N2** respectively. We will refer to this measure simply as the *expected delay*.

In order to choose realistic values for the various processing times associated with sending and receiving a data or ACK/NAK packet, we use the measured values reported in [2]. Those measurements show that packet send and receive processing times for a Linux Ethernet/IP/UDP stack to be approximately 500 $\mu$secs on a 133Mhz Pentium. ACK/NAK send/receive times are approximately 100 $\mu$secs. In the following, we normalize the unit of time to be the data packet send and receive times, i.e., $E[X] = 1$, and $E[Y] = 0.2$. We assume these per-packet processing costs are constant (i.e., have no variability) and choose a normalized propagation delay of $\tau = 20.0$, corresponding to a 10 msec propagation delay.

Recall that an important parameter of the **N2** protocol is the backoff timer for NAK suppression. Figure 5 shows the expected number of NAKs generated by the receivers as a function of the backoff interval length (measured in units of propagation delay). As expected, the expected number of NAKs generated decreases with an increasing NAK suppression interval length since the receivers are randomizing their NAK transmissions over an increasingly longer period of time. Note that after an initial decrease, the expected number of generated NAKs does not decrease significantly as the backoff interval length is increased. In the case of a small loss probability ($p = 0.01$), the expected number of receivers that lose a packet is small and hence the number of generated NAKs is small, regardless of the receivers' timeout interval length. We note that a backoff interval of length 10 is a reasonable value for all of the loss probabilities shown, and so we use this value in subsequent computations for $R = 100$.

Figures 6, 7 and 8 plot the expected delay under each of the three protocols as a function of the arrival rate for $R = 100$ and various $p$. Figure 6, with an x-axis plotted logarithmically, shows the expected delay under the NAK-based protocols is high at very low arrival rates. This results from the fact that a receiver can only detect a packet loss when a packet with a larger sequence number arrives. At low arrival rates, this wait can be significant. For such low arrival rates, we see that **A** outperforms both **N1** and **N2**. As the arrival rate increases, **N1** and **N2** perform essentially identically (although **N2** achieves a slightly higher throughput). Figure 7 shows that for a larger loss probability of $p = 0.1$, **N1** and **N2** have comparable delays, up to the point where **N1** becomes saturated. Similar behavior is evidenced in Figure 8 for the case $p = 0.25$.

Figure 9 plots expected delay versus the arrival rate for the case of $R = 500$ receivers and $p = 0.1$. As in the case of Figure 7, **N1** and **N2** perform similarly up to the point where **N1** saturates. Also, the ACK overhead associated with **A** and the larger number of receivers again severely limits **A**'s throughput. Comparing Figures 7 and 9, we note that with the increased number of receivers, the relative size of the gap between the maximum throughput of **N1** and **N2** has increased noticeably. In summary, we conclude that **N2** can achieve substantially higher throughput than both **N1** and **A**, and can do so without suffering an appreciable higher delay due to delays associated with its NAK suppression mechanism.

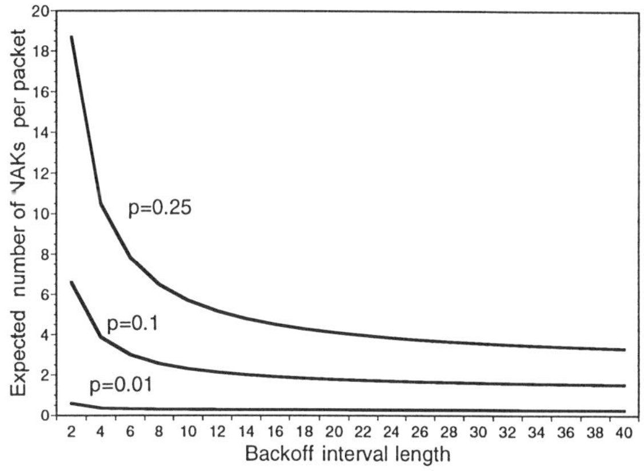


Figure 5: NAKs generated under **N2** versus receiver timeout interval

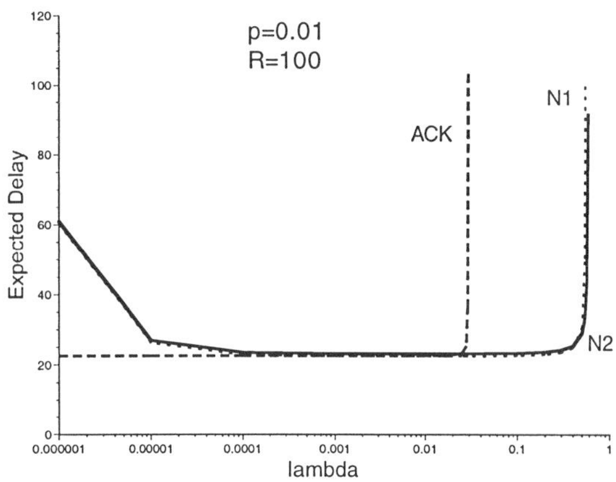


Figure 6: Average delay versus arrival rate, $p = 0.01$

## 5 Conclusion

In this paper we have derived analytic performance models of packet delay of three generic sender- and receiver-initiated protocols. For the range of parameter values studied, our results showed that **N2** can achieve substantially higher throughput than both **N1** and **A**, and do so

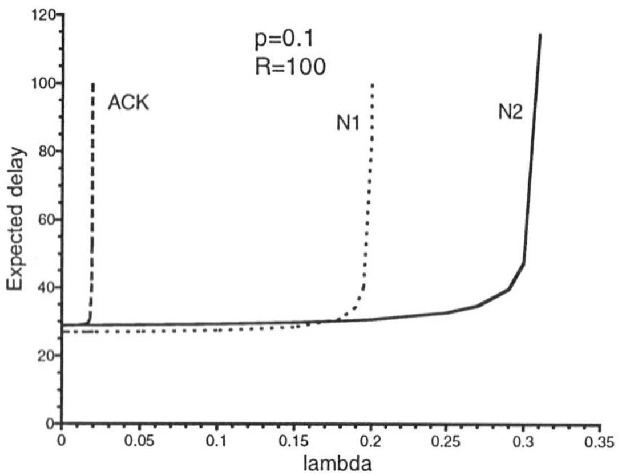


Figure 7: Average delay versus arrival rate, $p = 0.1$

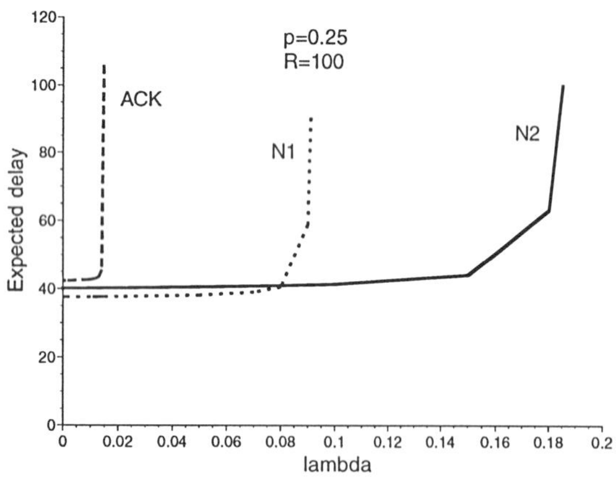


Figure 8: Average delay versus arrival rate, $p = 0.25$

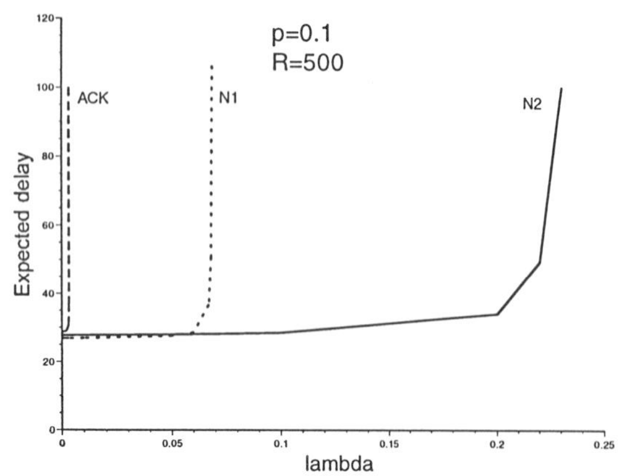


Figure 9: Delay versus arrival rate, $R = 500, p = 0.1$

without suffering an appreciable higher delay due to delays associated with its NAK suppression mechanism.

Our future work in this area is aimed at modeling packet loss correlation in the network (a problem we have examined experimentally in [9]), examining adaptive NAK generation policies under **N2**, and studying the distribution of the delay under the various protocols – an important consideration for real-time reliable multicast protocols.

## References


[1] S. Floyd, V. Jacobsen, S. McCanne, C.G. Liu, L. Zhang, "A Reliable Multicast Framework for Light-weight Sessions and Application-Level Framing," *Proc. ACM Sigcomm95,* (Aug. 1995, Boston MA), pp 342 - 356.

[2] S. Kasera, J. Kurose, D. Towsley, "Scalable Reliable Multicast Using Multiple Multicast Groups," to appear in *Proc. ACM SIgmetrics 97.*

[3] . L. Kleinrock, Queueing Systems: Part 1: Theory, Wiley-Interscience, 1974.

[4] J.C. Lin and S. Paul, "RMTP: A Reliable Multicast Transport Protocol," *Proc. IEEE Infocom96,* (San Francisco, March 1996), pp. 1414-1424.

[5] S. Paul, K. Sabnani, D. Kristol, Multicast Transport Protocols for High-Speed Networks," *Proc. IEEE Int. Conference on Network Protocols,* (Boston MA, 1994).

[6] S. Pingali, J.F. Kurose, D. Towsley, "A Comparison of Sender-initiated and Receiver-initiated Reliable Multicast Protocols," *Proc. 1994 ACM Sigmetrics Conf.,* May 1994, ftp://gaia.cs.umass.edu/pub/Ping94:Multicast.ps.Z.

[7] S. Ramakrishnan and B. N. Jain, "A Negative Acknowledgment with Periodic Polling Protocol for Multicast over LANs," *Proc. IEEE Infocom'87*, pp 502–511, Mar-Apr 1987.

[8] D. Towsley, "An Analysis of a Point-to-Multipoint Channel Using a Go-Back-N Error Control Protocol", *IEEE Trans. on Communications*, 33:282–285, March 1985.

[9] M. Yajnik, J. Kurose, D. Towsley, "Packet Loss Correlation in the MBone Multicast Network," submitted to *IEEE Global Internet Conference.* ftp://gaia.cs.umass.edu/pub/Yajn96:Loss.ps.

[10] M. Yamamoto, J. Kurose, D. Towsley, H. Ikeda, "A Delay Analysis of Sender- and Receiver-Initiated Reliable Multicast Protocols," Technical Report, Dept. of Computer Science, Univ. Massachusetts, June 1996. ftp://gaia.cs.umass.edu/pub/Yamamoto96:Delay.ps

# Multiwavelength Optical Networks with Limited Wavelength Conversion*

R. Ramaswami

IBM Research
30 Saw Mill River Road
Hawthorne, NY 10532 USA
*rajiv@watson.ibm.com*

G. H. Sasaki

Dept. Elec. Engg., U. Hawaii
2540 Dole Street
Honolulu, HI 96822 USA
*sasaki@spectra.eng.hawaii.edu*

## Abstract

*This paper proposes optical wavelength division multiplexed (WDM) networks with limited wavelength conversion that can efficiently support lightpaths (connections) between nodes. Each lightpath follows a route in the network and must be assigned a channel along each link in its route. The load $\lambda_{\max}$ of a set of lightpath requests is the maximum over all links of the number of lightpaths that use the link. At least $\lambda_{\max}$ wavelengths will be needed to assign channels to the lightpaths. If the network has full wavelength conversion capabilities then $\lambda_{\max}$ wavelengths are sufficient to perform the channel assignment.*

*We propose ring networks with fixed wavelength conversion capability within the nodes that can support all lightpath request sets with load $\lambda_{\max}$ at most $W-1$, where $W$ is the number of wavelengths in each link. We also propose ring networks with selective pairwise wavelength conversion capability within the nodes that can support all lightpath request sets with load $\lambda_{\max}$ at most $W$. We also propose a star network with fixed wavelength conversion capability at its hub node that can support all lightpath request sets with load $\lambda_{\max}$ at most $W$. We extend this result to tree networks and networks with arbitrary topologies. These results show that significant improvements in traffic-carrying capacity can be obtained in WDM networks by providing very limited wavelength conversion capability within the network.*

## 1 Introduction

Wavelength Division Multiplexing (WDM) is an important approach to utilize the large available bandwidth in a single mode optical fiber. WDM is basically frequency division multiplexing in the optical frequency domain, where on a single optical fiber there are multiple communication channels at different *wavelengths* (corresponding to carrier frequencies). There has been a great deal of interest in WDM networks that employ wavelength routing. These networks support *lightpaths*, which are end-to-end circuit-switched communication connections that traverse one or more links and use one WDM channel per link. These lightpaths could serve as the physical communication links for a variety of high-speed networks such as ATM (Asynchronous Transfer Mode) networks.

*This work was sponsored in part by grant MDA-972-95-C-0001 by ARPA and grant NCRI-93-96130 by NSF.

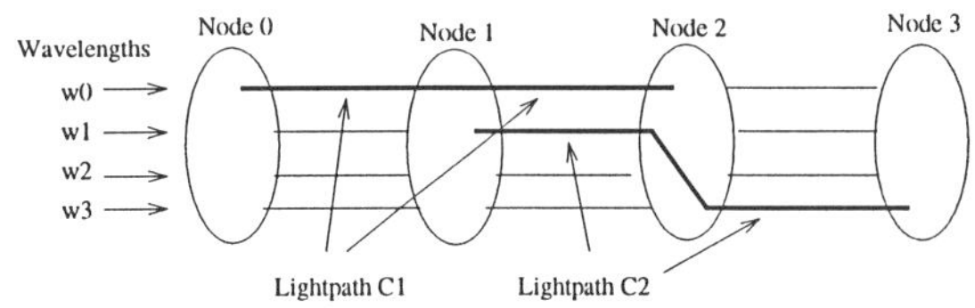


Figure 1: A network with wavelengths $\{\omega_0, \omega_1, \omega_2, \omega_3\}$. Channels are shown as lines between nodes.

An example of a WDM wavelength routing network is shown in Figure 1. It is composed of four nodes with three optical fiber links connecting nodes 0 and 1, nodes 1 and 2, and nodes 2 and 3. Each link has four WDM channels at wavelengths $\{\omega_0, \omega_1, \omega_2, \omega_3\}$. Switching is done at each node so that channels may be connected to form lightpaths. Note that if channels at different wavelengths are to be connected then *wavelength conversion* devices are needed that can shift the wavelength of an optical signal. For example, in Figure 1, lightpath $C1$ is composed of two WDM channels at wavelength $\omega_0$ on links 1 and 2. Hence, it does not need a wavelength converter. However, lightpath $C2$ needs a converter at node 2 because it is composed of two WDM channels at different wavelengths ($\omega_1$ and $\omega_3$). The advantage of wavelength conversion is that WDM channels will be used more efficiently, but the disadvantage is increased cost and complexity.

### 1.1 Limited Wavelength Conversion

In this paper we will explore circuit-switched wavelength routing WDM network architectures that employ *limited wavelength conversion*, i.e., WDM channels have restrictions on the channels they may be connected to on other links. For example, Figure 2 shows a ring network with seven WDM channels per link, where the channels are at wavelengths $\{\omega_0, \omega_1, ..., \omega_6\}$. The lines within nodes show which pairs of channels



0-8186-7780-5/97 $10.00 © 1997 IEEE

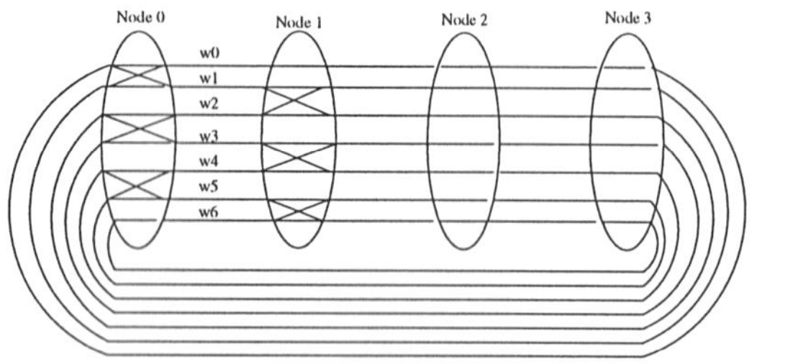


Figure 2: A ring network with wavelengths $\{\omega_0, \omega_1, ..., \omega_6\}$ to illustrate limited wavelength conversion. The lines between nodes represent channels, and lines within nodes indicate which channels may be connected.

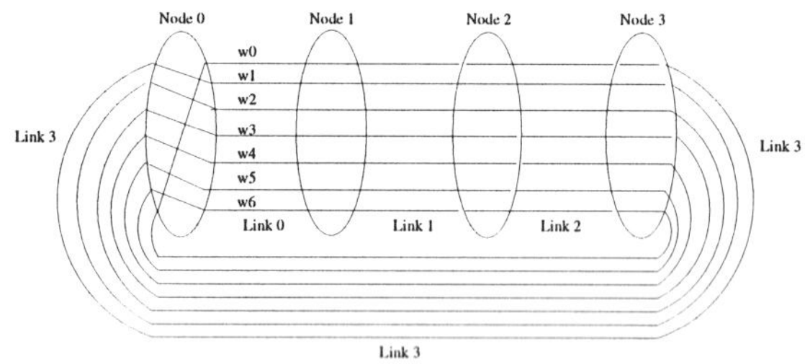


Figure 3: A ring network with wavelengths $\{\omega_0, \omega_1, ..., \omega_6\}$ to illustrate fixed wavelength conversion. The lines between nodes represent channels, and lines within nodes indicate which channels may be connected.

may be connected. Note that the network has some wavelength conversion, but with restrictions. For example, at node 0 channels at wavelengths $\{\omega_0, \omega_1\}$ may only be connected to other channels at wavelengths $\{\omega_0, \omega_1\}$. A special case of limited wavelength conversion is *fixed* wavelength conversion, where at each node, each channel may be connected to exactly one predetermined channel on every other link. Figure 3 shows an example ring network with fixed wavelength conversion. Here, the channel at $\omega_i$ in link 3 may be connected only to channel $\omega_{(i+1) \bmod W}$ in link 0 for $i = 0, 1, ..., W-1$. At all other nodes, only channels with the same wavelength are connected.

Networks with limited/fixed wavelength conversion will be less costly to implement than networks without restrictions on wavelength conversion (i.e., having full wavelength conversion capability), but may still provide enough conversion to use channels efficiently. The different types of conversion possible within the node are illustrated in Figure 4. Within each node the wavelength conversion can be done all-optically or by receiving the signal, switching it electronically and retransmitting it on another wavelength (O-E-O). The all-optical approach uses optical wavelength converter devices. In some of these devices, such as those based on four-wave mixing [27], the conversion efficiency is a strong function of the input and output wavelengths, naturally leading to limited conversion capability. Even otherwise we can save on the num-

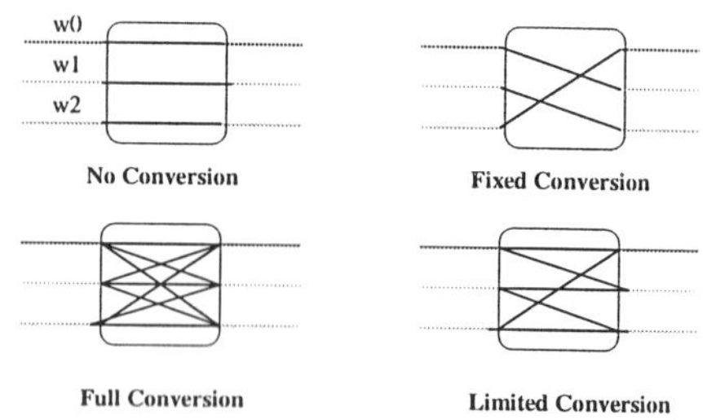


Figure 4: Different types of wavelength conversion.

ber of such devices required in the node. In the O-E-O approach we can implement limited conversion using much fewer electronic switches than would be needed for full conversion.

## 1.2 Network Model

We assume that the links and WDM channels are bidirectional (or full duplex). Network nodes are connected by fiber optic links, and for simplicity it is assumed that all pairs of nodes have at most one link between them. Each link has $W$ WDM bidirectional channels at wavelengths $\{\omega_0, \omega_1, ..., \omega_{W-1}\}$, where $\omega_0 < \omega_1 < ... < \omega_{W-1}$.

Each node has switching capability to connect WDM channels to form full duplex lightpaths. The switching capability will determine which pairs of channels may be connected to one another. We will refer to two channels that may be connected to one another as being *attached*. For example, at node 0 in Figure 2, channels at wavelengths $\{\omega_0, \omega_1\}$ are attached, channels at $\{\omega_2, \omega_3\}$ are attached, channels at $\{\omega_4, \omega_5\}$ are attached, and channels at $\omega_6$ are attached. A node has *wavelength degree* $k$ (for some integer $k > 0$) if for each pair of incident links, each channel in one link is connected to at most $k$ other channels in the other link. For example, node 0 in Figure 2 has wavelength degree two. A node has *full wavelength conversion* if its wavelength degree is $W$. A node is said to have *fixed wavelength conversion* if its wavelength degree is one (e.g., see Figure 3). Note that a node with no wavelength conversion has wavelength degree one. (Again these different types of conversion are illustrated in Figure 4.)

The network supports sets of lightpaths. A lightpath is specified by a path in the network that is referred to as a *route*. A lightpath is realized by a set of channels, one on each link along its route so that channels that are incident to a common node are attached at the node. Such a set of channels is referred to as a *channel assignment* for the route. This realization allows communication signals to be sent on a lightpath between the ends of the route by having them transported along attached channels.

A set of lightpaths is specified by a set of routes, one route per lightpath. A set of routes will be referred to as a *request*. A *channel assignment* for a request is a collection of channel assignments, one per route of the request, such that each channel is assigned to at most one route, i.e., no two routes share a channel. Note that a channel assignment for a request realizes the lightpaths corresponding to the request. An important parameter of a request is its *load*, which is the value $\lambda_{\max} = \max_{e \in E} \lambda_e$, where $\lambda_e$ denotes the number of routes using link $e$ and $E$ denotes the set of links in the network. Clearly at least $\lambda_{\max}$ wavelengths are needed for a channel assignment for a request with load $\lambda_{\max}$.

### 1.3 Organization

In this paper, we propose ring and star networks with limited wavelength conversion to support sets of lightpaths efficiently. In Section 2, we discuss our results for ring networks. We give a ring network with one node having fixed wavelength conversion and the rest of the nodes with no wavelength conversion such that all requests with load $\lambda_{\max} \leq W - 1$ have channel assignments. We also give a ring network with two nodes with wavelength degree two and the rest of the nodes with no wavelength conversion such that all requests with load $\lambda_{\max} \leq W$ have channel assignments. Note that the networks that have channel assignments for all requests with load at most $W$ utilize the channels as efficiently as networks with full wavelength conversion at all nodes. Also note that the first deployed WDM networks are likely to be rings, as seen from several recent testbeds (see for example [5, 23]).

In Section 3, we discuss our results for star networks as well as extensions to tree networks, and networks with arbitrary topologies where route lengths are at most two. We present a star network that has fixed wavelength conversion and has channel assignments for all requests with load $\lambda_{\max} \leq W$, when $W$ is an even number. In Section 4, we provide conclusions and discuss how our results can be extended when links and channels are *directed*.

Note that we consider the problem of finding channel assignments for sets of lightpaths all at one time. Thus, if a new lightpath is to be included to an existing set of lightpaths (while keeping the same routes for the lightpaths), the channel assignments for all lightpaths may have to be recomputed. In this sense, the channel assignment is done *offline*. There is also the more practical consideration of *online* channel assignment, i.e., setting up new lightpaths without changing the assignment for existing lightpaths. Although we only consider the offline case, we believe that its understanding can lead to fundamental insights to the online case, just as understanding *rearrangeable nonblocking networks* can help to understand efficient *wide-sense* and *strict-sense nonblocking networks* [13]. Also, offline channel assignment will be more efficient in utilizing channels than online channel assignment.

### 1.4 Related Work

Previous work focuses primarily on networks with either no wavelength conversion or networks with full wavelength conversion (i.e., any pair of WDM channels may be connected).

The joint lightpath routing and channel assignment problem in networks without wavelength conversion is known to be NP-complete [6] and remains NP-complete even for rings [8]. Given a routing already, an algorithm that finds a channel assignment in a ring network without wavelength conversion if $2\lambda_{\max} - 1 \leq W$ is given in [24] as well as [19]. An algorithm that finds channel assignments in a tree network without wavelength conversion if $\frac{3}{2}\lambda_{\max} \leq W$ is given in [19]. Sample requests can easily be constructed for these networks that require $W = 2\lambda_{\max} - 1$ wavelengths and $W = \frac{3}{2}\lambda_{\max}$ wavelengths for rings and stars respectively. [18] gives algorithms that find channel assignments for the case of a directed network without wavelength conversion and directed lightpath requests for trees, if $15\lambda_{\max}/8 \leq W$, and for rings, if $2\lambda_{\max} \leq W$. Several heuristic channel assignment schemes have also been proposed for networks without wavelength conversion [3, 21, 6, 15, 4, 25].

Variants of the limited conversion model are considered in [16, 17, 26, 22]. In [16, 17] it is assumed that each node has a limited number of wavelength converters and that each converter has no restrictions on the wavelengths of the channels it can connect. Here, the restriction is on the *number* of wavelength conversions at a node. In [26], a network with limited wavelength conversion is used to study the performance due to limited wavelength shifting capability of devices based on four wave mixing. The converters allow wavelengths to be shifted within a given range. Also, the work in [22] studies *sparse wavelength conversion*, where networks are comprised of a mix of nodes having full and no wavelength conversion. The channel assignment in these papers [16, 17, 26, 22] are simple heuristics, and their performance analyses are based upon probabilistic models and techniques (i.e., compute blocking probabilities of setting up lightpaths) which may not be as appropriate for networks that require channels to be highly utilized.

There are some recent results on the *online* channel assignment problem for ring and tree networks [9, 11], where lightpath requests arrive and leave the network dynamically. The problem of recovering from link and node faults in ring networks using limited wavelength conversion is addressed in [10].

## 2 Rings

In this section we will consider ring networks. Without loss of generality, it will be assumed that a ring network has a *clockwise direction* (and *counterclockwise direction*) as shown in Figure 5. Its nodes are numbered $0, 1, ..., N-1$ consecutively in the clockwise direction, where $N$ denotes the number of nodes. The links are also numbered $0, 1, ..., N-1$ in the clockwise direction such that for each $i = 0, 1, ..., N-1$, the link between node $i$ and node $(i+1) \bmod N$ is numbered $i$ (see Figure 5).

Most of the results of this section assume that there is a collection of lightpaths to be set up, and their set of routes (i.e., a *request*) is already given. However, we should note that for the ring network, there is an algorithm that can compute minimum load requests for sets of lightpaths, specified by their terminating nodes [7]. However, simple shortest path routing does not perform very poorly as shown below.

**Theorem 1** *Suppose we are given a request of source-destination pairs and the minimum possible load for*

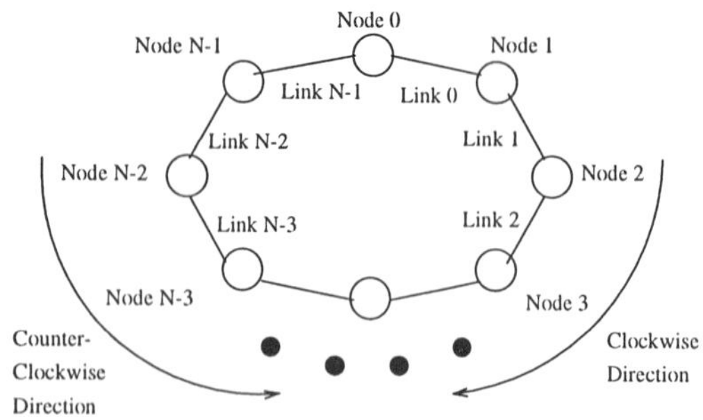


Figure 5: A ring network.

*satisfying this request is* $\lambda_{\max}$. *Then shortest-path routing yields a load of at most* $2\lambda_{\max}$.

**Proof.** Suppose shortest-path routing yields a load $\lambda_{sp}$. Consider a link $i$ with load $\lambda_{sp}$. Rerouting $k$ lightpaths using link $i$ using their longer routes on the ring can reduce the load on link $i$ to at most $\lambda_{sp} - k$. Note that since all these lightpaths are routed on paths of length $\leq \lfloor N/2 \rfloor$ initially, their longer routes on the ring will all use the link $(\lfloor N/2 \rfloor + i) \bmod N$, increasing its load by $k$. Therefore an optimal routing algorithm would have a load given by $\lambda_{\max} \geq \min_k(\lambda_{sp} - k, k)$, or $\lambda_{\max} \geq \lceil \lambda_{sp}/2 \rceil$. □

For the rest of the section, we describe ring networks that lead to efficient channel assignments for requests. To find channel assignments, we will use structures for the requests. In particular, for each request $R$, the structures are another request $R^c$ and a set of labels for the routes in $R^c$. The request $R^c$ will be referred to as the *cut request* for $R$ because it is generated from $R$ by "cutting" the routes of $R$ at node 0. The label for each route $p \in R^c$ will be denoted by $\gamma(p)$, which is an integer from the set $\{0, 1, ..., \lambda_{\max} - 1\}$, where $\lambda_{\max}$ is the load for $R$.

We will now define $R^c$ and then $\gamma(\cdot)$. For the sake of discussion, denote the routes of $R$ by $\{p_0, ..., p_{m-1}\}$, where $m$ is the number of routes. Also, refer to routes that pass through node 0 as *cut routes*, and ones that do not as *uncut routes*. $R^c$ is generated from $R$ as follows. For each uncut route $p_i \in R$, include $p_i$ in $R^c$. For each cut route $p_i \in R$, cut (or split) it at node 0 into a pair of routes $\{a_i, b_i\}$ such that each has node 0 as a terminating node. Include $a_i$ and $b_i$ into $R^c$. We will refer to $a_i$ and $b_i$ as the *residual routes* for $p_i$. Route $a_i$ is assumed to be the one that intersects link $N-1$ and is referred to as the *left* residual route, while $b_i$ is the one that intersects link 0 and is referred to as the *right* residual route. (Figure 6 shows a request $\{p_0, p_1, ..., p_6\}$. Note that $p_2$, $p_4$, and $p_6$ are cut routes since they pass through node 0. Figure 7 shows the routes of $R^c$.)

Next we define the labels $\gamma(\cdot)$ for $R^c$. The labels for the routes in $R^c$ are such that routes traversing a common link have distinct labels. This is like *coloring* paths in an *interval graph* [2, Sec.16.5] because no route of $R^c$ crosses through node 0. Hence, we can use a *greedy algorithm* assignment that requires $\lambda_{\max}$

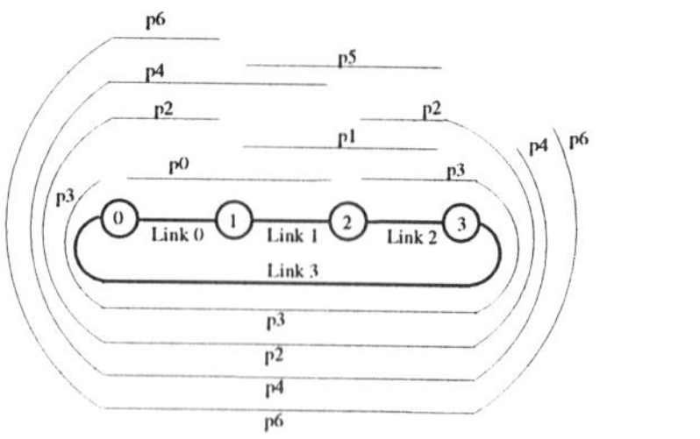


Figure 6: A request $R = \{p_0, p_1, ..., p_6\}$ for a four node ring network.

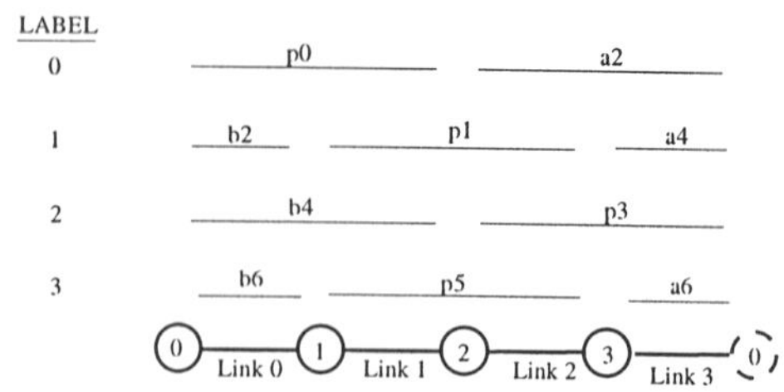


Figure 7: Cut request $R^c$ and label $\gamma(\cdot)$.

numbers [2, Sec.16.5]. Figure 7 shows the labels for $R^c$.

**Theorem 2** *Suppose the ring network has full wavelength conversion at one node and no wavelength conversion at the other nodes. Then any request with load at most $W$ has a channel assignment.*

**Proof.** Without loss of generality, assume that node 0 has the full wavelength conversion. Suppose we are given an arbitrary request $R$ with load $\lambda_{\max}$ at most $W$. Let $R^c$ be the cut request for $R$, and let $\gamma(\cdot)$ be the corresponding label. Consider the following channel assignment for $R$. For each uncut route $p_i \in R$, assign it the channels at wavelength $\omega_{\gamma(p_i)}$ on all its links. For each cut route $p_i \in R$, assign it the channels at wavelength $\omega_{\gamma(a_i)}$ on all links corresponding to its left residual route $a_i$, and assign it channels at wavelength $\omega_{\gamma(b_i)}$ on all links corresponding to its right residual route $b_i$.

The channel assignment is valid which can be checked as follows. Note that channels assigned to a route in $R$ are attached because they have the same wavelength, except at node 0, which has full wavelength conversion. Note that different routes of $R$ are assigned different channels because of the way $\gamma(\cdot)$ is defined. Finally, note that only $W$ wavelengths are used because $\gamma(\cdot)$ takes values from $\{0, ..., \lambda_{\max} - 1\}$ and $\lambda_{\max} \leq W$. □

The ring network of Theorem 2 has a channel assignment for every request with load at most $W$. However, one of its nodes has wavelength degree $W$. The next theorem states that there is a ring network with wavelength degree one (i.e., fixed wavelength conversion) that has channel assignments for every request with load at most $W - 1$.

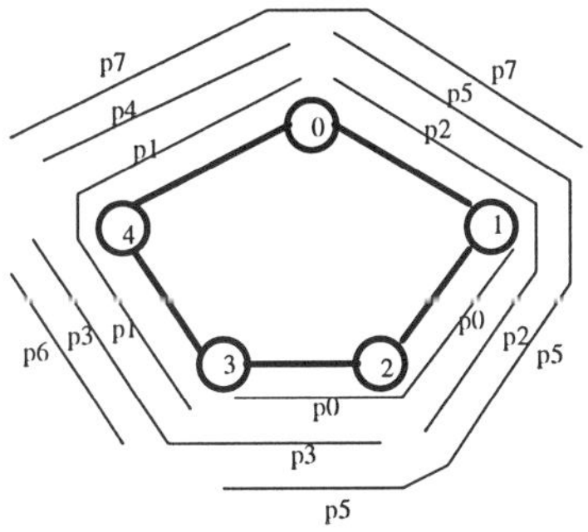


Figure 8: An MCR $(p_0, p_1, ..., p_7)$ that starts and ends at node 1.

First we will define additional structure for a request that will help determine a channel assignment. Consider a sequence of routes $(p_0, p_1, ..., p_{k-1})$, where $k$ is the number of routes. The sequence is referred to as a *multi-cycle of routes* (MCR) if for $i = 0, 1, ..., k-1$, the last node of $p_i$ is the first node of $p_{(i+1)\bmod k}$ when we consider the routes to be going in the clockwise direction. Hence, an MCR is just a sequence of routes that circumvents the ring in the clockwise direction one or more times. The number of times an MCR goes around the ring is called its *multiplicity*. Figure 8 shows an MCR with multiplicity three.

Now we will consider requests such that the number of routes traversing any link is the same. Such requests will be referred to as *uniform* requests. Given a uniform request $R$, we can define a collection of MCRs $\{M_0, M_1, ..., M_{k-1}\}$ (for some $k$) with the property that each route of $R$ is in exactly one MCR, and the MCRs are composed only of the routes of $R$. The collection is called an *MCR partition* for $R$.

We now describe how to construct an MCR partition from a uniform request $R = \{p_0, p_1, ..., p_{m-1}\}$, with load denoted by $\lambda_{\max}$. First, find the cut request $R^c$ for $R$ and its corresponding label $\gamma(\cdot)$. Note that $R^c$ is also a uniform request with load $\lambda_{\max}$. Second, construct an MCR partition for $R^c$. This MCR partition will be denoted by $\{M_0, M_1, ..., M_{\lambda_{\max}-1}\}$, where $M_j$ (for $0 \le j < \lambda_{\max}$) is the MCR with multiplicity one formed by the routes $p \in R^c$ that have label $\gamma(p) = j$. Notice that the MCRs each have at most one right residual route and at most one left residual route. Without loss of generality, assume that MCRs with residual routes start and end at node 0, and go clockwise around the ring. Thus, a right residual route would be the first route in an MCR, while a left residual route would be the last route.

Third, pair the MCRs that have exactly one residual route such that each pair has a left and a right residual route. (Note such a pairing is possible since the number of left residual routes is equal to the number of right residual routes.) Then merge each pair of MCRs to form new MCRs. To be more specific, consider a pair $(M_l, M_r)$, where $M_l$ and $M_r$ holds the left and right residual routes, respectively. Merge the pair by attaching $M_l$ after $M_r$.

Note that the MCRs are now of two types. The first type has no residual routes, and these are referred to as being *unmergeable*. The second type starts at node 0 with a right residual route, goes clockwise, and ends at node 0 with a left residual route. We refer to these MCRs as being *mergeable*. Now as long as there are mergeable MCRs do the following. Form a sequence of mergeable MCRs $(M'_0, M'_1, ...., M'_{j-1})$ (for some $j$) such that for $i = 0, 1, ..., j-1$, the last route of $M'_i$ and the first route of $M'_{(i+1)\bmod j}$ are the right and left residual routes, respectively, of some cut route in $R$. Merge the MCRs $M'_0, M'_1, ...., M'_{j-1}$ by attaching them in succession to form a new MCR. Then in the new MCR, for $i = 0, 1, ..., j-1$, replace the last route of $M'_i$ and the first route of $M'_{(i+1)\bmod j}$ with their corresponding cut route. The new MCR is now unmergeable, i.e., it has no residual routes.

After the merging, the set of MCRs only contain the routes of $R$. Thus, it is an MCR partition for $R$.

**Example 1:** The following is an example of constructing a MCR partition from a request, which is shown in Figure 6. Note that its cut request is shown in Figure 7. The MCR partition of the cut request is $M_0 = (p_0, a_2)$, $M_1 = (b_2, p_1, a_4)$, $M_2 = (b_4, p_3)$, and $M_3 = (b_6, p_5, a_6)$. Note that $M_0$ and $M_2$ are the MCRs with only one residual route. These are merged together to form a new MCR $M_{20} = (b_4, p_3, p_0, a_2)$. The remaining MCRs $\{M_1, M_{20}, M_3\}$ are all mergeable. Merge $M_1$ with $M_{20}$ to form the MCR $M' = (b_2, p_1, a_4, b_4, p_3, p_0, a_2)$. Replace $(a_4, b_4)$ with the cut route $p_4$, and replace $(a_2, b_2)$ with cut route $p_2$. This leaves the MCR $M' = (p_1, p_4, p_3, p_0, p_2)$, which is unmergeable. This leaves $M_3$ as the only mergeable MCR. Replace $(a_6, b_6)$ with $p_6$ which leaves $M_3 = (p_5, p_6)$. Then $M_3$ is unmergeable. Note that $\{M_3, M'\}$ is an MCR partition for the request in Figure 6. □

We will define ring networks that take advantage of the MCR partition structure. The channels of these ring networks can be organized into sequences of attached channels called *multi-cycles of channels* (MCC). An MCC is a sequence of distinct channels $(c_0, c_1, ..., c_{k-1})$, where $k$ is a multiple of $N$, that starts at some node $j$ goes around the ring in the clockwise direction one or more times and ends at node $j$. In addition, for $i = 0, 1, ..., k-1$, the channels $c_i$ and $c_{(i+1)\bmod k}$ must be attached. The *multiplicity* of an MCC is the number of times it goes around the ring, i.e., it is equal to $\frac{k}{N}$. Figure 9 shows an MCC with multiplicity 3 that starts and ends at node 1.

Note that an MCC with multiplicity $m$ (for $1 \le m \le W$) will lead to a channel assignment for the routes in an MCR with multiplicity $m$. In particular, the channel assignment can be computed as follows. First assume without loss of generality that the MCC and MCR start at the same node. Starting from the node, go clockwise around the ring $m$ times one link at a time. While going around the ring, keep track of the corresponding route of the MCR and the channel of the MCC, and assign the channel to the route.

Now consider ring networks with fixed conversion

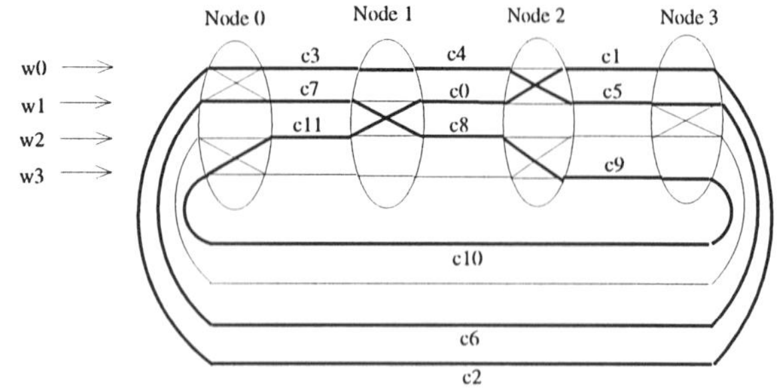


Figure 9: An example MCC with multiplicity 3 that starts and ends at node 1.

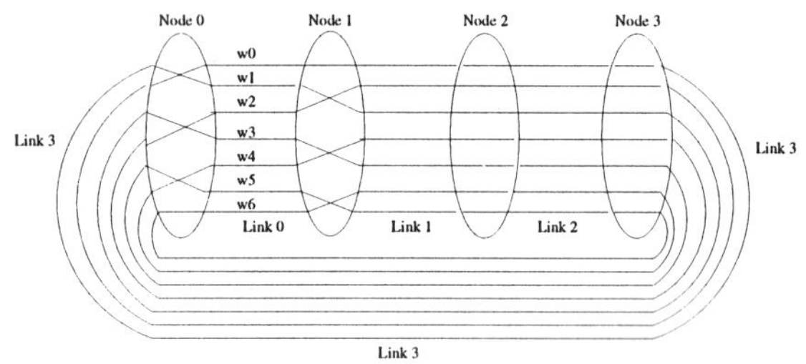


Figure 10: An example of a single-MCC ring network with wavelengths $\{\omega_0, \omega_1, ..., \omega_6\}$.

such that their channels form a single MCC, i.e., the MCC has multiplicity $W$. We will refer to such networks as *single-MCC* ring networks, and we give two examples.

**Example 2:** The network shown in Figure 3 is a single-MCC ring network. At node 0, the channel at $\omega_i$ in link 3 is attached to the channel at $\omega_{(i+1)\bmod W}$ in link 0 for $i = 0, 1, ..., W-1$. At the other nodes, for $i = 0, 1, ..., W-1$, channels at $\omega_i$ are attached to each other (no wavelength conversion). □

**Example 3:** The network shown in Figure 10 is a single-MCC ring network. At node 0, channels at $\omega_i$ are attached to channels at $\omega_{i+1}$ for even values of $i < W-1$. If $W$ is odd then channels at $\omega_{W-1}$ are attached to each other. At node 1, channel $\omega_i$ is attached to channel $\omega_{i+1}$ for odd values of $i < W-1$. Channels at $\omega_0$ are attached to each other, and if $W$ is even then channels at $\omega_{W-1}$ are attached to each other. At other nodes there is no wavelength conversion. □

**Theorem 3** *For a single-MCC ring network, any request $R$ with load at most $W-1$ has a channel assignment.*

**Proof.** Without loss of generality, assume that $R$ has uniform load (otherwise, we can add one-hop *dummy routes*). There is an MCR partition $\{M_0, M_1, ..., M_{k-1}\}$ for $R$, where $k$ is the number of MCRs in the partition. We will transform the MCR partition into a single MCR with multiplicity $W$ by adding dummy routes as follows.

For $i = 0, 1, ..., k-1$, let $x_i$ be the node where MCR $M_i$ starts and ends. Without loss of generality, let $x_0 \leq x_1 \leq ... \leq x_{k-1}$. Let $p' = \{p'_0, p'_1, ..., p'_{k-1}\}$ be a collection of dummy routes such that for $i = 0, 1, ..., k-1$, $p'_i$ starts at node $x_i$, ends at node $x_{(i+1)\bmod k}$, and goes clockwise around the ring. However, if $x_i = x_{(i+1)\bmod k}$ then the route $p'_i$ has zero length, i.e., it is a path that starts and ends at node $x_i = x_{(i+1)\bmod k}$ but does not traverse any links. Note that each link of the ring network has at most one route of $p'$ traversing it because $x_0 \leq x_1 \leq ... \leq x_{k-1}$, i.e., $p'$ has load at most one. Create a new MCR $M = (M_0, p'_0, M_1, p'_1, ...., M_{k-1}, p'_{k-1})$. Note that $M$ is an MCR because for $i = 0, 1, ..., k-1$, the dummy route $p'_i$ starts at the end of $M_i$ and ends at the beginning of $M_{(i+1)\bmod k}$.

The routes of $M$ have load that is either $W-1$ or $W$ because $R$ has load $W-1$ and the dummy routes have load at most one. If the routes of $M$ have load $W-1$ then another dummy route $p_k$ can be appended to $M$ that starts and ends at node $x_0$ (the starting and ending point for $M$) and circumvents the ring exactly once. Then $M$ will be an MCR with multiplicity $W$. Since $M$ is an MCR with multiplicity $W$ and the single-MCC ring network has an MCC with multiplicity $W$, there is a channel assignment for the routes of $M$. Thus, there is a channel assignment for $R$. □

The following theorem states that with fixed conversion, all requests with load at most $W$ are not guaranteed to have a channel assignment, proving that Theorem 3 provides the best possible construction and channel assignment for a fixed-conversion ring network. For brevity, the proof is omitted. Its outline can be found in [20].

**Theorem 4** *For any ring network with $W$ wavelengths, fixed wavelength conversion at every node, and a sufficiently large number of nodes, there is a request with load $W$ that does not have a channel assignment.*

Theorem 3 illustrates that providing fixed wavelength conversion is sufficient to obtain efficient channel assignments for the offline case, as long as the load of the request is at most $W-1$. By allowing a bit more wavelength conversion, a ring network may be designed to have channel assignments for all requests with load at most $W$. This is stated in the next theorem.

**Theorem 5** *There is a ring network that has wavelength degree two at two nodes and no wavelength conversion at the other nodes such that every request with load at most $W$ has a channel assignment.*

The proof of the theorem will be given after preliminary definitions and results. Consider a ring network with $W$ wavelengths. A vector $(m_0, m_1, ..., m_{k-1})$ is be referred to as a *multiplicity vector* if its elements are positive integers, $k \in \{1, 2, ..., W\}$, and $\sum_{i=0}^{k-1} m_i = W$. The ring network is referred to as a *multi-MCC ring network* if for each multiplicity vector $(m_0, ..., m_{k-1})$, it has a collection of MCCs $(H_0, H_1, ..., H_{k-1})$ that are channel disjoint and, for $i = 0, 1, ..., k-1$, $H_i$ has multiplicity $m_i$.

**Theorem 6** *For a multi-MCC ring network, any request with load at most $W$ has a channel assignment.*

**Proof.** Without loss of generality, we may assume that the request is uniform and has load $W$. (Otherwise, we can make it so by adding *dummy* one-hop routes.) Let $\{M_0, M_1, ..., M_{k-1}\}$ be an MCR partition for the request, where $k$ is the number of MCRs in the partition. For $i = 0, 1, ..., k-1$, let $m_i$ be the multiplicity of $M_i$. Note that $\sum_{i=0}^{k-1} m_i = W$. Therefore, from the definition of a multi-MCC ring network, there is a collection of channel disjoint MCCs $(H_0, H_1, ..., H_{k-1})$ such that for $i = 0, 1, ..., k-1$, $m_i$ is the multiplicity of $H_i$. It is now straight forward to construct a channel assignment for the request since for each $i = 0, 1, ..., k-1$, a channel assignment for the routes of $M_i$ can be constructed from the channels in $H_i$. □

We now describe a particular multi-MCC ring network which we refer to as a *paired wavelengths* (PW) ring network. The network has two nodes, called the *primary* and *secondary* nodes, that have wavelength conversion capability. All other nodes have no wavelength conversion.

To describe the wavelength conversion capability at the primary and secondary nodes we will use the following terminology. We say that a pair of wavelengths $(\omega, \omega')$ form a *switching pair* at a node if WDM channels at $\{\omega, \omega'\}$ are attached to channels at $\{\omega, \omega'\}$. At the primary node, the following pairs of wavelengths form switching pairs: $(\omega_0, \omega_1)$, $(\omega_2, \omega_3)$, and so forth. At the secondary node the following pairs of wavelengths form switching pairs: $(\omega_1, \omega_2)$, $(\omega_3, \omega_4)$, and so forth. Figure 2 shows how the channels are attached for the case $W = 7$, and where the primary and secondary nodes are nodes 0 and 1, respectively. Note that the network has channel degree two at the primary and secondary nodes.

**Proof of Theorem 5:** In light of Theorem 6 it is sufficient to prove that the PW ring network is a multi-MCC ring network. To do this consider an arbitrary multiplicity vector $(m_0, m_1, ..., m_{k-1})$. We now proceed to show that there is a collection $(H_0, H_1, ..., H_{k-1})$ of channel disjoint MCCs such that for $i = 0, ..., k-1$, $H_i$ has multiplicity $m_i$. We will do this by constructing the MCCs.

For each $i = 0, 1, ..., k-1$, assign $m_i$ wavelengths to construct $H_i$. In particular, assign wavelengths $\{\omega_0, \omega_1, ..., \omega_{m_0-1}\}$ to $H_0$, assign wavelengths $\{\omega_{m_0}, \omega_{m_0+1}, ..., \omega_{m_0+m_1-1}\}$ to $H_1$, and so forth. Since the MCCs use different wavelengths, they will be channel disjoint.

To complete the proof, we define the $H_i$ (for $0 \leq i < k$) from its $m_i$ assigned wavelengths $\{\omega_j, \omega_{j+1}, ..., \omega_{j+m_i-1}\}$, where $j = \sum_{s=0}^{i-1} m_s$. The definition is recursive. It starts by noting that there is an MCC with multiplicity one using channels only at wavelength $\omega_j$. Now for $s = 1, 2, ..., m_i - 1$, suppose there is an MCC $H'$ with multiplicity $s$ that only uses channels at wavelengths $\{\omega_j, \omega_{j+1}, ..., \omega_{j+s-1}\}$. Then we can form an MCC $H''$ with multiplicity $s+1$ that only uses channels at wavelengths $\{\omega_j, \omega_{j+1}, ..., \omega_{j+s}\}$ as follows. Note that there is an MCC $H^*$ with multiplicity one that uses channels only at wavelength $\omega_{j+s}$, and that there is a node $x$ (either the primary or secondary node) that has $(\omega_{j+s-1}, \omega_{j+s})$ as a switching pair. Let $H''$ be the MCC by joining $H'$ and $H^*$ at node 0 through the switching pair $(\omega_{j+s-1}, \omega_{j+s})$. In other words, $H''$ is the sequence of channels that starts at node $x$ at wavelength $\omega_{j+s}$, follows the channels of $H^*$ until returning to $x$ at wavelength $\omega_{j+s}$, then follows the channels of $H'$ starting at wavelength $\omega_{j+s-1}$ until it returns to $x$ at wavelength $\omega_{j+s-1}$. Finally, $H_i$ is defined to be $H''$ when $s = m_i - 1$. □

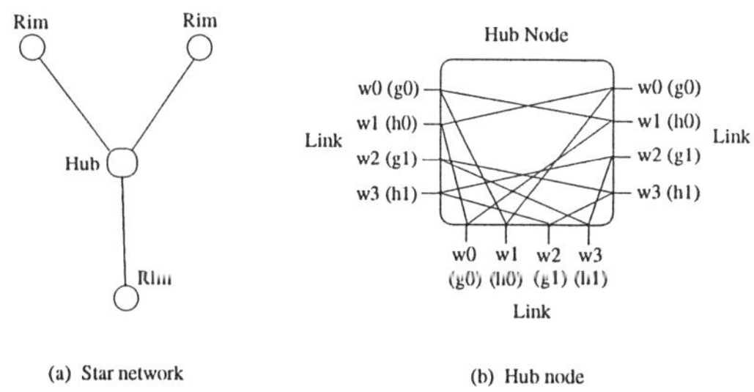


Figure 11: A star network with three rim nodes is shown in (a). A diagram showing how the channels in the hub are attached when $W = 4$ is shown in (b).

Another kind of multi-MCC ring network is described in [20]. It has its channels attached to form a *permutation interconnection network* such as the Benes network [1]. Although the ring network requires more switches/wavelength converters than the PW network, it is useful in handling failures in the network. This topic is explored in detail in [10].

## 3 Stars, Trees and Meshes

In this section, we will first consider star networks, and then consider more general networks. Throughout this section we will assume that $W$ is even, so that the wavelengths may be paired as follows: $(\omega_0, \omega_1), (\omega_2, \omega_3), ..., (\omega_{W-2}, \omega_{W-1})$. For $i = 0, 1, ..., \frac{W}{2} - 1$, let $(g_i, h_i)$ denote the pair $(\omega_{2i}, \omega_{2i+1})$.

A star network consists of a *hub* node and one or more *rim* nodes, as shown in Figure 11(a). There are links between the rim nodes and the hub only. The star network we consider has a hub node with fixed wavelength conversion such that for $i = 0, 1, ..., \frac{W}{2} - 1$, channels at $g_i$ are only attached to channels at $h_i$. We call such a node as one having *fixed conversion wavelength pairs* (FCWP). Figure 11(b) shows a hub node having FCWP. Notice that channels at the same wavelength are not attached.

As in the previous section, requests will be given structure that will lead to efficient channel assign-

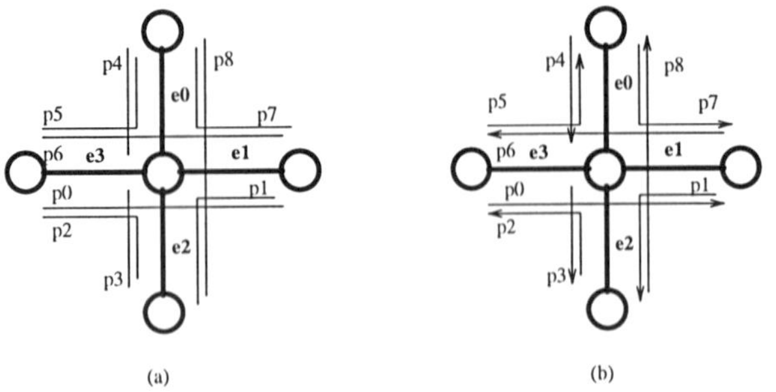


Figure 12: Shown in (a) is a request $\{p_0, p_1, ..., p_8\}$ for a star network of four links $\{e_0, e_1, e_2, e_3\}$. Shown in (b) is a balanced set of directions for the request.

ments. In particular, the routes of a request will be given *directions*, and these directions will be used to determine a channel assignment. To direct a route, one of its terminating nodes is designated as the *first* node, the other terminating node is designated as the *last* node, and the route is assumed to go from the first to the last node. Now consider a request, and suppose the routes of the request are directed. If the routes along each link are directed such that exactly half traverse the link in one direction and the other half traverse the link in the opposite direction then the request is said to have a *balanced set of directions.* Figure 12(a) shows a request for a star network, and Figure 12(b) shows a balanced set of directions for the request.

The following lemma considers tree networks, of which star networks are a special case. It also considers a uniform request with load $W$ (i.e., each link has $W$ routes traversing it).

**Lemma 1** *Consider a tree network $T$ with $W$ even. Every uniform request $R = \{p_0, p_1, ..., p_{m-1}\}$ with load $W$ may have its routes directed such that it has a balanced set of directions.*

**Proof.** First we will show that at each node in $T$, the number of routes of $R$ that terminate at the node is even. Consider an arbitrary node $u$ in $T$, and let $d$ denote the number of links that are incident to it. Note that each link has exactly $W$ routes traversing it. Thus, $\sum_{e \in E_u} \rho_e = d \cdot W$, where $\rho_e$ is the number of routes of $R$ that traverse link $e$, and $E_u$ is the set of links incident to $u$. Now let $n_1$ denote the number of routes that terminate at $u$, and let $n_2$ denote the number of routes that have $u$ as an intermediate node. Therefore, $n_1 + 2n_2 = \sum_{e \in E_u} \rho_e$. Thus, $n_1 + 2n_2 = d \cdot W$. Since both $W$ and $2n_2$ are even, $n_1$ must be even.

Second, consider the following *multigraph* $G$, i.e., a graph which can have multiple edges between vertices. The number of vertices in $G$ is equal to the numbers of nodes in $T$. Each vertex in $G$ represents a distinct node in $T$ and is labeled with the node it represents. $G$ has $m$ edges with labels $\{p_0, p_1, ..., p_{m-1}\}$. The edge labeled $p_i$ in $G$ is between vertices $u$ and $v$ if the route $p_i$ in $T$ has $u$ and $v$ as terminating nodes. Note that the vertices of $G$ have an even number of incident edges because the number of routes of $R$ that terminate at any node in $T$ is even. Thus, there is an Euler tour for $G$ [12, Chap. 7]. Traverse the edges of $G$ according to the tour, traversing each edge exactly once. Let $(\pi(0), \pi(1), ..., \pi(m-1))$ be the permutation of $(0, 1, ..., m-1)$ such that $(p_{\pi(0)}, p_{\pi(1)}, ..., p_{\pi(m-1)})$ is the sequence of edges traversed. Direct each edge according to how it was traversed. Direct each route $p_i$ in $R$ according to how its corresponding edge in $G$ is directed.

We will verify that the directions are balanced by checking an arbitrary link $e$ in $T$. Now note that for $i = 0, 1, ..., m-1$, the last node of $p_{\pi(i)}$ is the first node of $p_{\pi((i+1) \bmod m)}$. Then the traversal of $T$ that follows the sequence of directed routes $(p_{\pi(0)}, p_{\pi(1)}, ..., p_{\pi(m-1)})$ goes from node to neighboring node. Now notice that tree $T$ can be considered to be two subtrees connected by $e$. Thus, if the traversal crosses link $e$ in one direction, then the next time it crosses $e$ it will be in the opposite direction because the only way to get between the two subtrees is across $e$. Therefore, the traversal crosses link $e$ exactly $\frac{W}{2}$ times in both directions because link $e$ has $W$ routes going through it. Hence, there are $\frac{W}{2}$ routes crossing $e$ in either direction. This verifies that the directions for the request are balanced because $e$ is arbitrary. □

**Theorem 7** *Consider a star network with $N$ nodes, $W$ even, and where the hub node has FCWP. Then any request with load at most $W$ has a channel assignment.*

**Proof.** First let $\{e_0, e_1, ..., e_{N-2}\}$ denote the links of the star network. Next, consider a request $R$ and assume without loss of generality that it is uniform with load $W$ (otherwise, we can add dummy one-hop routes). Let $R_2 = \{p_0, p_1, ..., p_{m-1}\}$ denote the two-hop routes of $R$. The other routes of $R$ are one-hop routes, and denote these by $R_1$. From Lemma 1, we can direct the routes of $R$ so that they are balanced. Since the routes of $R_2$ are now directed, they have *first* and *second* links that they traverse.

The channel assignment for a route $p_i$ in $R_2$ will be specified by a number $n$, that satisfies $0 \leq n < \frac{W}{2}$ and which is referred to as the *wavelength pair index* (WPI) for $p_i$. In particular, the channels for $p_i$ is the channel at $g_n$ on the first link of $p_i$ and the channel at $h_n$ on the second link. Note that the channels are attached because the hub node has FCWP. Now refer to a collection of WPIs, one per route of $R_2$, as a *feasible* collection if, for each link $e$, the WPIs of routes that use $e$ as their first link are distinct and the WPIs of routes that use $e$ as their second link are distinct. Note that the resulting channel assignment will have each channel assigned to at most one route. Thus, a feasible collection of WPIs leads to a channel assignment for $R_2$.

To determine a feasible collection of WPIs, consider a bipartite graph $G$ (see Figure 13) which has two sets of vertices $\{f_0, f_1, ..., f_{N-2}\}$ and $\{s_0, s_1, ..., s_{N-2}\}$. (For $i = 0, 1, ..., N-2$, the vertices $f_i$ and $s_i$ both represent link $e_i$ in the star network, but $f_i$ corresponds to when $e_i$ is the first link of a route and $s_i$ corresponds

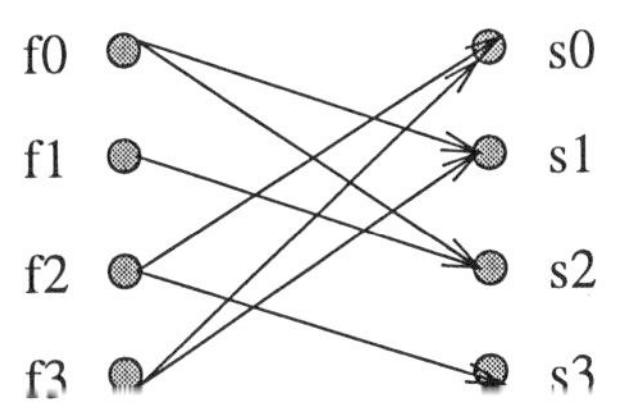


Figure 13: The bipartite graph $G$ corresponding to the star network and directed routes of Figure 12(b).

to when $e_i$ is the second link.) Bipartite graph $G$ has $m$ edges corresponding to the routes of $R_2$. In fact, they are labeled $p_0, ..., p_{m-1}$. For $i = 0, 1, ..., m-1$, if route $p_i$ has $e_j$ and $e_k$ as its first and second links, respectively, then the edge of $G$ labeled $p_i$ is between vertices $f_j$ and $s_k$.

Since the directions of the routes of $R$ are balanced, at any link in the star network, at most $\frac{W}{2}$ routes of $R_2$ are directed towards (resp., away from) the hub node. Therefore, for any link in the star network, at most $\frac{W}{2}$ routes of $R_2$ use the link as their first (resp., second) link. Hence, each vertex of $G$ has at most $\frac{W}{2}$ incident edges. Then numbers $\{0, 1, ..., \frac{W}{2} - 1\}$ can be assigned to the edges of $G$ such that, at each vertex, the numbers assigned to the edges incident to the vertex are distinct. In particular, the assignment can be accomplished using the scheduling algorithms used for Satellite Switched/Time Division Multiple Access (SS/TDMA) systems [14]. Let these numbers be the WPIs for the routes corresponding to their edges. Note that these WPIs for the routes in $R_2$ are feasible, and so there is a channel assignment for $R_2$.

To complete the channel assignment for $R$, we have to find channel assignments for the routes in $R_1$. This is trivial since the the routes in $R_1$ are one-hop. □

**Corollary 1** *Consider an arbitrary topology network $G$ with $W$ even and where all nodes with two or more incident links have FCWP. There is a channel assignment for each request that has load at most $W$ and routes traversing at most two links.*

**Proof.** A star network graph $G_{star}$ is used to represent the links of $G$. Each link $e$ in $G$ is represented by a distinct edge in $G_{star}$ which is also labeled $e$. A channel assignment for a request $R = \{p_0, p_1, ..., p_{m-1}\}$ in network $G$ can be determined as follows. Let $R' = \{p'_0, p'_1, ..., p'_{m-1}\}$ be a set of routes for $G_{star}$ such that for $i = 0, 1, ...., m-1$, $p'_i$ traverses the edges of $G_{star}$ with the same labels as the links traversed by $p_i$. Note that $R'$ has load at most $W$ on $G_{star}$ since it has the same load as $R$ on $G$. Thus, we can apply Theorem 7 to $R'$ on $G_{star}$ to get a channel assignment for $R'$. Note that this channel assignment can be translated into a channel assignment for $R$ on $G$ in a straightforward way because the channels assigned to the same route of $R$ are attached. The channels assigned to a route are attached because routes that traverse two links in $G$ have intermediate nodes with FCWP. □

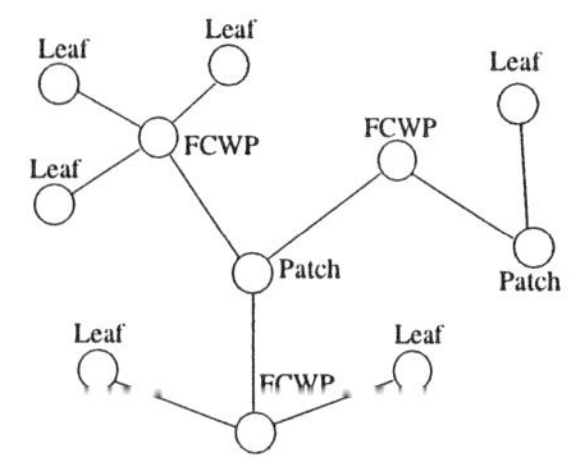


Figure 14: A tree network with leaf nodes, patch nodes, and nodes with FCWP.

In the next theorem, we consider a tree network. We will refer to nodes that have one incident link as a *leaf node*. We will refer to nodes that have channels at wavelengths $\{g_0, g_1, ..., g_{W/2-1}\}$ attached to channels at wavelengths $\{h_0, h_1, ..., h_{W/2-1}\}$ as *patch nodes*. Note that patch nodes have wavelength degree $\frac{W}{2}$.

**Theorem 8** *Consider a tree network with $W$ even and is composed of nodes that are patch nodes, leaf nodes, and nodes that have FCWP. Suppose that the network is such that all nodes with FCWP have neighboring nodes that are leaf or patch nodes. Then every request with load at most $W$ has a channel assignment.*

The proof of the theorem is omitted for brevity. Its outline can be found in [20].

## 4 Conclusion

The paper considered a network model with bidirectional links, WDM channels, and lightpaths for ring, star, and tree networks, as well as arbitrary topology networks with restrictions on lightpath route lengths. It was shown that there are ring and star networks with minimal wavelength conversion capabilities that can perform off-line channel assignment as well as networks with full wavelength conversion. In fact, the ring and star networks of Theorems 5 and 7 only required wavelengths to be shifted to their nearest wavelengths, i.e., the required range of wavelength shifting is minimal.

It should also be noted that the results of this paper can be extended to the case when links, WDM channels, and lightpaths are unidirectional. The results on ring networks in Section 2 can be extended in a straightforward way. Theorem 7 (the result on the bidirectional star network) can be extended to the unidirectional case and where the hub does not have any wavelength conversion (here, the bidirectional star has two unidirectional links that go in opposite directions between the hub and any rim node). Extending all these results to arbitrary topologies is an important open problem.

**Acknowledgement:** We thank Ori Gerstel for his comments on the paper.

## References


[1] V. Benes, *Mathematical Theory of Connecting Networks.* Academic Press, 1965.

[2] C. Berge, *Graphs and Hypergraphs.* North Holland 1976.

[3] A. Birman, "Computing approximate blocking probabilities for a class of optical networks," *IEEE JSAC/JLT Special Issue on Optical Networks*, vol. 14, no. 5, pp. 852-857, June 1996. An earlier version appeared in Proc. Infocom '95.

[4] A. Birman and A. Kershenbaum, "Routing and wavelength assignment methods in single-hop all-optical networks with blocking," *Proc. IEEE Infocom '95*, pp. 431-438, 1995.

[5] G. K. Chang, G. Ellinas, J. K. Gamelin, M. Z. Iqbal, and C. A. Brackett, "Multiwavelength reconfigurable WDM/ATM/SONET network testbed," *IEEE/OSA J. Lightwave Tech./IEEE JSAC*, vol. 14, no. 6, pp. 1320-1340, June 1996.

[6] I. Chlamtac, A. Ganz, and G. Karmi, "Lightpath communications: an approach to high-bandwidth optical WANs" *IEEE Trans. on Commun.*, vol. 40, pp. 1171-1182, July 1992.

[7] A. Frank, T. Nishizeki, N. Saito, H. Suzuki, and E. Tardos, "Algorithms for routing around a rectangle," *Discrete Applied Math*, vol. 40, pp. 363-378, 1992.

[8] M. Garey, D. Johnson, G. Miller, and C. Papadimitrou, "The complexity of coloring circular arcs and chords," *SIAM Journal on Discrete Math*, vol. 1, no. 2, pp. 216-227, 1980.

[9] O. Gerstel and S. Kutten, "Dynamic wavelength allocation in WDM ring networks," IBM Research Report RC 20462, May 1996.

[10] O. Gerstel, Rajiv Ramaswami, and G. Sasaki, "Fault-tolerant multiwavelength optical networks with limited wavelength conversion," to appear in *Proc. IEEE Infocom '97.*

[11] O. Gerstel, G. Sasaki, and R. Ramaswami, "Dynamic channel assignment for WDM optical networks with little or no wavelength conversion," to appear in *Proc. 1996 Allerton Conference*, Monticello, IL, 1996.

[12] F. Harary, *Graph Theory.* Addison-Wesley, 1969.

[13] J. Y. Hui, *Switching and Traffic Theory for Integrated Broadband Networks.* Kluwer Academic Publishers, 1990.

[14] T. Inukai, "An efficient SS/TDMA time slot assignment algorithm," *IEEE Trans. Commun.* vol. 27, pp. 1449-1445, Oct. 1979.

[15] M. Kovacevic and A. S. Acampora, "On the benefits of wavelength translation in all optical clear-channel networks," *IEEE JSAC/JLT Special Issue on Optical Networks*, vol. 14, no. 5, pp. 868-880, June 1996. An earlier version appeared in Proc. Infocom '95.

[16] K.-C. Lee and V. O. K. Li, "Routing and switching in a wavelength convertible lightwave network," *Proc. Infocom '93*, pp. 578-585, 1993.

[17] K.-C. Lee and V. O. K. Li, "A wavelength-convertible optical network," *IEEE/OSA J. Lightwave Tech.*, vol. 11, pp. 962-970, May/June 1993.

[18] M. Mihail, C. Kaklamanis, and S. Rao, "Efficient access to optical bandwidth," *Proc. of IEEE Symp. on Foundations of Computer Science*, pp. 548-557, 1995.

[19] P. Raghavan and E. Upfal, "Efficient routing in all-optical networks," *Proc. 26th ACM Symp. Theory of Computing*, pp. 134-143, May 1994.

[20] R. Ramaswami and G. Sasaki, "Multiwavelength optical networks with limited wavelength conversion," IBM Research Report RC 20503, July 1996.

[21] R. Ramaswami and K. N. Sivarajan, "Routing and wavelength assignment in all-optical networks," *IEEE/ACM Trans. on Networking*, pp. 489-500, Oct. 1995. An earlier version appeared in IEEE Infocom '94.

[22] S. Subramaniam, M Azizoglu, and A. K. Somani, "Connectivity and sparse wavelength conversion in wavelength-routing networks," *Proc. IEEE Infocom '96*, pp. 148-155, 1996.

[23] H. Toba, K. Oda, K. Inoue, K. Nosu, and T. Kitoh, "An optical FDM based self-healing ring network employing arrayed-waveguide-grating ADM filters and EDFAs with level equalizers," *IEEE JSAC/JLT Special Issue on Optical Networks,* vol. 14, no. 5, pp. 800-813, June 1996.

[24] A. Tucker, "Coloring a family of circular arcs," *SIAM Journal on Applied Math*, vol. 29, no. 3, pp. 493-502, 1975.

[25] N. Wauters and P. Demeester, "Design of the optical path layer in multiwavelength cross-connected networks," *IEEE JSAC/JLT Special Issue on Optical Networks*, vol. 14, no. 5, pp. 881-892, June 1996.

[26] J. Yates, J. Lacey, D. Everitt, and M. Summerfield, "limited-range wavelength translation in all-optical networks," *Proc. IEEE Infocom '96*, pp. 954-961, 1996.

[27] J. Zhou, N. Park, K. Vahala, M. Newkirk, and B. Miller, "Four-wave mixing wavelength conversion efficiency in semiconductor traveling-wave amplifiers measured to 65 nm of wavelength shift," *IEEE Photon. Tech. Lett.*, vol. 6, pp. 984-987, Aug. 1994.

# A Performance Model for Wavelength Conversion with Non-Poisson Traffic*

S. Subramaniam, A. K. Somani, M. Azizoğlu
Dept. of Electrical Engineering
Univ. of Washington
Seattle, WA 98195

R. A. Barry
MIT Lincoln Laboratory
Lexington, MA 02173

## Abstract

*This paper makes the first known attempt to study wavelength-routing networks and the effects of wavelength conversion under dynamic non-Poisson traffic. An approximation that characterizes any non-Poisson traffic by its first two moments is utilized. The arrival occupancy distribution of busy wavelengths for this approximate process is derived and is used to analyze the effects of wavelength conversion. The model predicts that traffic peakedness plays an important role in determining the blocking performance, and also that wavelength conversion gain is insensitive to traffic peakedness over a large range.*

## 1 Introduction

Wavelength-routing networks that employ wavelength division multiplexing (WDM) have emerged as the most attractive all-optical networks for information transfer in the wide area [1, 2]. Such networks are scalable in size and allow concurrent use of the same wavelength on different network links, in contrast to broadcast-and-select networks [1].

We consider networks operating in circuit-switched mode. Call requests arrive at a node according to a random point process and an optical circuit is established between the two communicating stations for the random duration of the call. The ability of a routing node to convert one wavelength to another plays an important role in the routing of arriving calls. When all nodes have wavelength converters, the situation is analogous to trunk switching in digital telephony [3] in that a call arriving on one circuit (wavelength) can be switched to any outgoing circuit, as long as one is available. On the other hand, in a network without any wavelength conversion, a call arriving on a certain wavelength on an input fiber has to be switched to an output fiber on the same wavelength. This requirement of wavelength continuity increases the probability of call blocking; in order to honor a call request, it is necessary that the *same* wavelength be free on all the links of the circuit.

*This work was supported by the University of Washington Royalty Research Fund, and the NSF under grants NCR-9502610, NCR-9309574, NCR-9628165, and NCR-9103485.

It is important to quantify the effect of wavelength conversion on network performance in order to assess whether it will be needed in future networks. A number of papers addressing this issue have appeared in the literature. A traffic model that considers the effects of path length, switch size, and interference length on the wavelength utilization in the presence and absence of conversion was presented in [4]. A model to iteratively evaluate the blocking probabilities for dense networks with and without wavelength conversion was presented in [5]. These models considered networks which have full wavelength conversion capability at every node and networks without any conversion capability. Because of the increased complexity and cost of a routing node with wavelength conversion [6, 7], a limited amount of wavelength conversion may be attractive in practice. Limited wavelength conversion can imply a limit on the number of wavelength conversions allowed per node, or on the number of nodes with full wavelength conversion capability (sparse wavelength conversion), or on the range of wavelengths to which a given wavelength can be converted. Recently, a model that extends the basic model in [4] to the case of limited range wavelength conversion was presented in [8]. In [9], we presented an analytical model to compute the blocking probabilities for an arbitrary wavelength conversion density. A more accurate, albeit more complex, version of this model as well as simulation results were presented in [10].

Previous work has established that wavelength conversion significantly improves the blocking performance in moderately dense networks such as the mesh-torus and does not have as significant an effect in sparse and very dense topologies such as the ring and the hypercube. Furthermore, the work in [9] showed that typically only a small fraction of routing nodes need to be equipped with conversion capability. Most of the dynamic traffic models in the literature have assumed a Poisson call arrival process. The Poisson process may not be representative of the input traffic in a wide area optical network [11].

The effect of wavelength conversion when the input traffic is non-Poisson needs to be investigated, in order to obtain the sensitivity of the conclusions on



0-8186-7780-5/97 $10.00 

the Poisson assumption. In this paper, we study the effect of dynamic non-Poisson traffic on wavelength conversion by employing the Bernoulli-Poisson-Pascal approximation [3] and extending the model in [9]. We evaluate the blocking probability and obtain the dependence of the blocking performance and the wavelength conversion gain on network parameters such as conversion density and peakedness of the link traffic.

In Section 2, we review the framework for modeling non-Poisson traffic by considering a single link. Section 3 presents a summary of our previous network model [9] and extends it to the case of non-Poisson traffic. Finally, we use this model to analyze the blocking performance of two networks, the mesh-torus and the hypercube, in Section 4 and present some results. Conclusions are presented in Section 5.

# 2 The Single Link Model

We first review the necessary background to characterize non-Poisson traffic offered to a single link.

Consider a single link with $F$ servers and assume that a superposition of several traffic streams is offered to this link. We assume that the holding times of the arriving calls are exponentially distributed and are independent of the arrival process.

Teletraffic models with arbitrary arrival processes are $G/M/F/F$ queues, i.e., the arrival process is arbitrary, the service times are exponentially distributed, the number of servers is $F$, and there is no waiting room. The nature of the traffic is thus completely determined by the nature of the arrival process. Two types of arrival processes have traditionally been studied in queueing theory literature. In the first approach, the arrival process is such that the queue can be analyzed as a birth-death process where the interarrival times are exponentially distributed, but dependent on the state of the system (the number of busy servers). In the second approach, the interarrival times are independent and identically distributed. These processes, called renewal processes, are completely characterized by the distribution of the interarrival times. Note that the Poisson process is a special case of both of the above types of processes.

Traffic is often characterized by the busy circuit distribution induced by it in an infinite trunk group [3, 12]. The busy circuit distribution for a general arrival process is difficult to obtain. More importantly, the exact statistical description of the interarrival process that will be realistic in future optical networks is very difficult to ascertain. Instead of attempting to study the effect of specific non-Poisson traffic types, we employ a moment-matching technique commonly used in teletraffic theory to study overflow streams in telephone networks.

Suppose that a few moments of the offered traffic are known. The moment-matching technique consists of choosing an *equivalent process* that yields the same moments and whose distribution is easily obtained, and using that equivalent process to obtain the busy circuit distribution [13, 14, 15, 16]. In practice, the number of moments that are matched vary from two to four. The two models mentioned above are candidates for the equivalent process.

The earliest and most widely accepted moment-matching method uses two moments [13, 14] and is the Bernoulli-Poisson-Pascal (BPP) approximation. This method provides fairly accurate results and is attractive because of its simplicity and the ease with which the model parameters can be obtained from the first two moments. For a more detailed discussion on moment-matching techniques, the reader is referred to [3].

## 2.1 Definitions and Notation

The following definitions about the input traffic will be used in this paper. Consider a single link with infinite servers with calls arriving at a Poisson rate $\lambda_k^*$ when the system is in state $k$ and exponentially distributed service times with mean $1/\mu$. Let $p_k^*$ denote the probability that the infinite-server system is in state $k$ in the steady state.

- The *offered load* is the average number of busy servers, $M$, when the traffic is offered to the link with infinite servers.
- Let $V$ denote the variance of the number of busy servers in the infinite-server system. The *peakedness* of the input traffic, $Z$, is defined as the ratio of the variance to the average number of busy servers in the infinite-server system, *i.e.*, $Z = V/M$. Peakedness has been used as a measure of a traffic's deviation from Poissonian nature [14].
- A traffic is called *smooth*, *regular*, or *peaked* depending on whether $Z$ is less than, equal to, or greater than 1, respectively. Note that a Poisson arrival process is regular.

Now, consider the link with the number of servers limited to $F$. Let $\lambda_k$ denote the Poisson rate of arrival of calls when the system is in state $k$.

- The *carried load* is the average number of busy servers, $m$, when the input traffic is offered to the $F$-server system.
- The *unconditional occupancy distribution* is the set of probabilities, $p_k$, that $k$ servers are busy in the $F$-server system at an arbitrary instant of time, in the steady state.
- The *arrival occupancy distribution* is the set of probabilities, $p'_k$, that an arriving call finds $k$ servers busy in the $F$-server system, in the steady state.
- The call congestion, $B = p'_F$, is the probability that an arriving call finds the $F$-server system full, and therefore gets blocked.

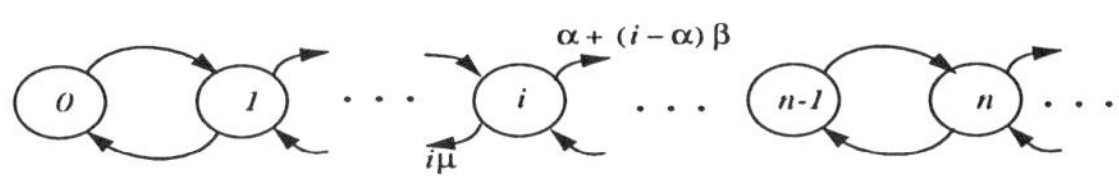


Figure 1. The Markov chain for the Pascal approximation

When the arrival process is a non-Poisson process, the arrival occupancy distribution is not the same as the unconditional occupancy distribution [3].

Peakedness is an indication of traffic burstiness. In a traffic with $Z > 1$, arrivals tend to happen in clusters and tend to find the system more congested than does an observer. Therefore, in order to carry the same amount of load with peaked traffic as with Poisson traffic, the number of servers must be increased, sometimes significantly [14]. The object of this paper is to explore the impact of traffic peakedness on the performance benefits due to wavelength conversion.

## 2.2 The BPP Approximation

In the following discussion, we present the BPP approximation of [13] and compute the arrival occupancy distribution using the approximation.

The BPP approximation consists of replacing an arbitrary arrival process by another process with the same first two moments (offered load and peakedness) for which the arrival occupancy can be obtained analytically. The Bernoulli, Poisson, or Pascal approximation is used when $Z$ is less than, equal to, or greater than 1, respectively, as described below.

### 2.2.1 The Pascal Approximation

Consider a single link with infinite servers where the interarrival times are exponentially distributed and state-dependent. Let the call arrival rate at state $i$, $\lambda_i^* = \alpha + (i - \alpha)\beta$ for some $\alpha > 0$ and $0 < \beta < 1$. The number of busy servers can be represented by the Markov chain shown in Figure 1.

The stationary probabilities of the infinite server system are given by

$$p_i^* = \left(1 - \frac{\beta}{\mu}\right)^a \left(\frac{\beta}{\mu}\right)^i \binom{a+i-1}{i}$$

where $a \equiv \frac{\alpha}{\beta}(1-\beta)$. This is the Pascal distribution with mean and variance

$$\begin{aligned} M &= \alpha \\ V &= \frac{\alpha}{1-\beta}, \end{aligned} \qquad (1)$$

where we have set $\mu = 1$. Hence, $Z = 1/(1-\beta) > 1$, and the Pascal approximation can be used to model a peaked arrival process with arbitrary offered load. Given $M$ and $Z$, the arrival process is approximated as the Markov process of Figure 1 with $\mu = 1$, $\alpha = M$, and $\beta = 1 - 1/Z$.

We will show later how the arrival occupancy distribution is obtained when the number of servers is restricted to $F$. We next proceed to the case with $Z < 1$ and discuss how the standard binomial distribution can be used as an approximation.

### 2.2.2 The Bernoulli Approximation

Let a single link with infinite servers be offered traffic from a finite number of sources $n$. Consider the Markov chain in Figure 2 for some $\lambda, \mu > 0$.

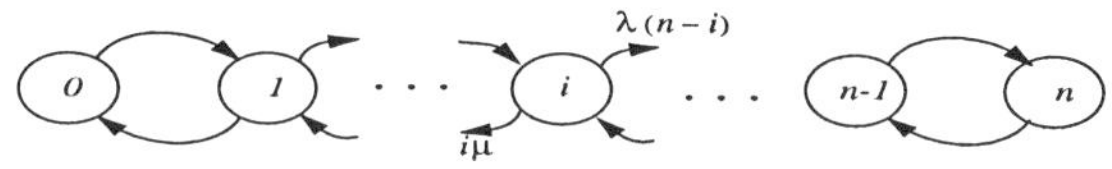


Figure 2: The Markov chain for the Bernoulli approximation

The stationary probabilities are given by

$$p_i^* = \binom{n}{i} \left(\frac{\lambda}{\lambda+\mu}\right)^i \left(\frac{\mu}{\lambda+\mu}\right)^{n-i}$$

which is the Bernoulli (the binomial) distribution.[1] The mean and peakedness of the offered traffic are given by

$$\begin{aligned} M &= n\frac{\lambda}{\lambda+\mu} \\ Z &= \frac{\mu}{\lambda+\mu}. \end{aligned} \qquad (2)$$

Hence, this can be used as an approximation for smooth traffic. Given an offered load $M$ and a peakedness $Z < 1$, the arrival process is assumed to be the process of Figure 2 with $\mu = 1$, and

$$\begin{aligned} \lambda &= \frac{1-Z}{Z} \\ n &= \frac{M}{1-Z} \end{aligned} \qquad (3)$$

Note that when $n$ above is not an integer, the physical interpretation of $n$ as the number of sources fails to hold; nevertheless, the approximation has been found to yield sufficiently accurate numerical results for congestion probabilities in telephony [13].

A limitation of the Bernoulli approximation when the number of servers is finite is that the number of

[1] Note that in [4], the arrival occupancy distribution in the finite-server system was modeled as a binomial. Here, we are using a binomial to model the unconditional distribution in an infinite-server system.

sources $n$ must be at least equal to the number of servers $F$. This places a restriction on the range of $Z$; in particular, $Z \geq 1 - M/F$.

Having presented models to approximate smooth, regular, and peaked traffic, we now proceed to derive the arrival occupancy distribution when these traffics are presented to a link where the number of servers is limited to $F$. This distribution will be used in analyzing the blocking performance in Section 3.

### 2.2.3 Arrival Occupancy Distribution

Suppose an arrival process is offered to a single link with $F$ servers. We derive below the arrival occupancy distribution for a general arrival process with state-dependent exponential interarrival times. Let $\lambda_i$ denote the arrival rate of calls when the system is in state $i$. Let the departure rate in state $i$ be $\mu_i$. The BPP model further assumes [13] that the unconditional occupancy distribution in the $F$-server system is a truncated Pascal, Poisson, or binomial distribution. In order to achieve this, we assume that $\lambda_i = \lambda_i^*$, $i = 0, 1, \cdots, F-1$.

Let $Q_{ij}$ denote the conditional probability that an arrival in steady state finds the system in state $i$ given that the previous arrival found the system in state $j$. The arrival occupancy distribution is the solution to the system of linear equations

$$p'_i = \sum_{j=0}^{F} p'_j Q_{ij}, \qquad i = 0, 1, \cdots, F. \tag{4}$$

We now determine $Q_{ij}$. Given that the system was in state $j$ when the previous call arrived, the system is in state $j+1$ immediately after this arrival (except when the system was in state $F$ in which case the state is unchanged). The probability that the next call finds the system in state $i$ is exactly the probability that $j+1-i$ calls depart the system before the arrival occurs.

Using the properties of the exponential distribution, we can write

$$Q_{ij} = \begin{cases} \frac{\mu_{j+1}}{\lambda_{j+1}+\mu_{j+1}} Q_{i,j-1}, & 0 \leq i \leq j \leq F-1 \\ \frac{\lambda_i}{\lambda_i+\mu_i}, & 1 \leq i \leq F-1,\ j = i-1 \\ \frac{\mu_{i+1}}{\lambda_{i+1}} \frac{\lambda_i}{\lambda_i+\mu_i} Q_{i+1,F}, & 0 \leq i \leq F-1,\ j = F \\ \frac{\lambda_F}{\lambda_F+\mu_F}, & i = F, j = F, F-1 \\ 0, & \text{otherwise} \end{cases} \tag{5}$$

with the understanding that $Q_{0,-1} = 1$.

After some manipulations involving (4) and (5), we obtain

$$p'_i = \frac{\lambda_i}{\mu_i} p'_{i-1}, \qquad i = 1, 2, \cdots F. \tag{6}$$

$p'_0$ can be determined from $\sum_{i=0}^{F} p'_i = 1$. Note the difference between the arrival occupancy distribution and the unconditional occupancy distribution which satisfies

$$p_i = \frac{\lambda_{i-1}}{\mu_i} p_{i-1}, \qquad i = 1, 2, \cdots F. \tag{7}$$

It is seen that for a Poisson arrival process the two distributions are the same.

It is important to observe that the unconditional occupancy probabilities are independent of $\lambda_F$ whereas the arrival occupancy probabilities are not. When the infinite-server system is truncated to an $F$-server system, the carried load $m$ can be computed using the unconditional occupancy distribution as $m = \sum_{i=0}^{F} i p_i$. Moreover, the carried load $m$ and offered load $M$ are related by

$$m = M(1 - B) \tag{8}$$

where $B$ is the probability that an arriving call finds all $F$ servers busy. Since $B = p'_F$, (6) and (8) define a relation between $\lambda_F$ and the unconditional occupancy distribution. It can be shown using $M = \sum_{i=0}^{\infty} i p_i^*$ that $\lambda_F = (\sum_{i=0}^{\infty} p_i^* \lambda_i^* - \sum_{i=0}^{F-1} p_i \lambda_i)/p_F$, where $\lambda_i^*$ is the arrival rate at state $i$ in the infinite-server system.

## 3 Network Blocking Analysis

In this section, we summarize the network model of [9] and extend it to the case of non-Poisson traffic using the approximation presented in Section 2.

### 3.1 Model assumptions

The following assumptions are used in our analytical model.

1. Calls arrive at each node according to a random process and the offered load is $\rho$. Each call is equally likely to be destined to any of the remaining nodes.
2. Call holding times are exponentially distributed with unit mean.
3. A shortest-path is chosen randomly to route a call.
4. Each call requires a full wavelength on each link it traverses.
5. The number of wavelengths, $F$, is the same on all links. Each node is capable of transmitting and receiving on any of the $F$ wavelengths.
6. A call is blocked if the chosen path is blocked.
7. Wavelengths are assigned to a session randomly from the set of free wavelengths on the associated path.
8. Link loads are statistically independent.[2]

[2]This assumption has been shown to yield accurate blocking probability estimates for Poisson traffic for the topologies we study in this paper [10].

### 3.2 Networks without Conversion

Throughout this section, all events regarding the status of wavelengths refer to events occurring when a call arrives. A wavelength is defined as "free" on a path if that wavelength is not used on any of the links constituting the path. A wavelength is "busy" on the path otherwise. First, consider the case of networks with no wavelength conversion. Given the load per station $\rho$, the load per link $M$ can be computed using the uniform traffic and shortest-path routing assumptions as

$$M = N\rho\overline{H}/L \qquad (9)$$

where $N$ is the number of nodes, $\overline{H}$ is the average path length and $L$ is the number of links in the network. The arrival occupancy distribution on a single link can be computed using this value of $M$ for various values of the link peakedness $Z$ using the analysis of Section 2. Note that the actual load carried by each link will be less than $M$ due to blocking (which in turn depends on $M$). We have observed that ignoring this feedback effect does not produce significantly different results when the blocking probabilities are low (on the order of $10^{-3}$) while considerably decreasing the computation time.

To compute the blocking probabilities in networks without conversion, the distribution of free wavelengths is required. In a two-hop path, the probability that $n$ wavelengths are free on the path is obtained as [9]

$$t_n^{(2)} = \sum_{i=0}^{F}\sum_{j=0}^{F} R(n|i,j)p'_{F-i}p'_{F-j}$$

where $R(n|i,j)$ is defined as

$$R(n|i,j) = \frac{\binom{i}{n}\binom{F-i}{j-n}}{\binom{F}{j}},$$

for $\max(0, i+j-F) \leq n \leq \min(i,j)$ and is 0 otherwise.

The free wavelength distribution on an $l$-hop path can be obtained recursively using the distribution for the two-hop path by considering the first $l-1$ hops as the first hop and hop $l$ as the second hop of a two-hop path. The probability of finding $n$ free wavelengths on an $l$-hop path is then written as

$$t_n^{(l)} = \sum_{i=0}^{F}\sum_{j=0}^{F} R(n|i,j)t_i^{(l-1)}p'_{F-j}.$$

where $p'_i$ is as obtained in Section 2. The probability of blocking on an $l$-hop path is simply given by $t_0^{(l)}$.

### 3.3 Networks with Conversion

Following the methodology of [9], we model networks with wavelength conversion by assuming that

Figure 3: An $l$-hop path with nodes numbered $s, 1, 2, \ldots, l-1, d$.

each node is capable of converting any wavelength to any other with probability $q$, independently of the other nodes. This leads to a binomial distribution with mean $Nq$ on the number of converter nodes in the network. The blocking performance we obtain is the ensemble average of the blocking probability over this distribution.

Consider an $l$-hop path and let the nodes on the path be numbered $s, 1, 2, \ldots, l-1, d$ as shown in Figure 3. Let $P_b^{(i)}$ denote the probability of blocking on an $i$-hop path. $P_b^{(1)}$ is clearly $p'_F$. $P_b^{(l)}$ can be computed recursively in terms of the blocking probabilities on paths of fewer hops and on paths with no converters as [9]

$$\begin{aligned} P_b^{(l)} &= t_0^{(l)}(1-q)^{l-1} + \\ & \sum_{i=1}^{l-1}[1-(1-P_b^{(i)})(1-t_0^{(l-i)})]q(1-q)^{l-i-1}. \end{aligned}$$

The first term is the probability that there are no converters in the intermediate nodes along the given $l$-hop path times the probability of blocking in this case (which is simply $t_0^{(l)}$). The $i^{th}$ term in the series is the probability that node $i$ is the last converter in the given $l$-hop path times the probability of blocking in this case. The probability that a call is not blocked in this case is the product of the probability that it is not blocked on the $i$-hop path (which is $1 - P_b^{(i)}$) and the probability that it is not blocked on the last $l-i$ hops given there are no wavelength converters on the last $l-i$ hops (which is $1 - t_0^{(l-i)}$). The network blocking probability is then computed as

$$P_b = \sum_{l=1}^{N-1} P_b^{(l)} r_l$$

where $r_l$ is the probability that an $l$-hop path is chosen to route an arriving call.

Given a network topology with an offered load per station of $\rho$, we first determine the hop-length distribution $r_l$ as described in [9]. The blocking performance for different values of link traffic peakedness can then be studied by using the analysis presented in Section 2 and this section. In the next section, we evaluate the effect of link peakedness on call blocking performance and wavelength conversion for two regular network topologies that have different degrees of connectivity – the mesh-torus and the hypercube.

## 4 Performance Results

We study the effects of traffic peakedness on networks with sparse wavelength conversion in two different ways. In the first approach, the blocking probability of a given network is evaluated as a function of the peakedness and conversion density. In the second approach, we define the *conversion gain* $G_q$ as the ratio of the offered load that can be supported with a given value of conversion density $q$ to the load that can be supported without conversion, for a given blocking probability. The evaluation is performed on two network topologies – an $11 \times 11$ mesh-torus and a 128-node binary hypercube, both with 10 wavelengths per fiber. The mesh-torus has four outgoing fibers per node and the hypercube has $7(= \log_2 128)$ outgoing fibers per node. The routing is shortest-path routing where each of the possible paths is chosen with equal probability.

First, for the mesh network, we plot the blocking probability against the offered load per station $\rho$ for link peakedness values of 1.0, 1.25, and 1.5 in Figure 4. Two observations can made from these figures. One is that for a given value of peakedness, the curves for no conversion and full conversion are essentially parallel indicating that the full conversion gain is not a sensitive function of the blocking probability. More importantly, as the peakedness increases, the supportable loads for a fixed blocking probability rapidly decrease.

Note that while the link load is simply given by the sum of the node traffic loads that are superposed on the link, the link peakedness depends on the exact proportions of the node traffic that are superposed on the link. This results in an interesting relationship between the peakedness of link traffic and that of node traffic. We omit the details here for lack of space. For instance, if the arrival process at a node of the mesh-torus is such that the peakedness values are $1, 4.11$, and $7.22$, then the aggregated link traffic has peakedness values of $1, 1.25$, and $1.5$, respectively.

Next, we show the blocking probability as a function of the conversion density for the mesh and the hypercube in Figures 5(a) and 5(b), respectively. As pointed out earlier by several researchers [4, 5, 9, 10], the blocking probability decreases sharply as conversion density increases for Poisson input traffic ($Z = 1$). From the figures, we observe that as the traffic becomes more peaked, the blocking probabilities do not diminish as rapidly as for Poisson traffic in either topology. This suggests that peaked traffic decreases the performance gain with wavelength conversion if it is measured as the decrease in blocking probability with wavelength conversion.

The graphs can also be used to determine the amount of conversion needed for a given traffic peakedness and blocking probability. For example, in the mesh with Poisson input traffic, a conversion density of approximately 40% is sufficient for realizing a blocking probability of $10^{-3}$ whereas when the link peaked-

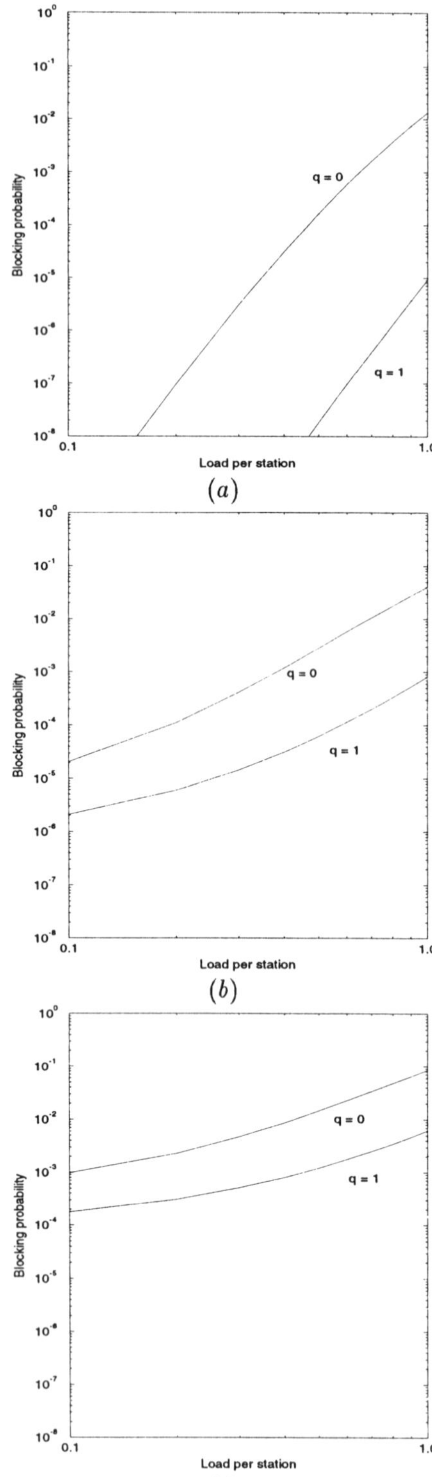


Figure 4: The blocking probability vs. the load per station for the mesh network with no conversion and full conversion. (a) $Z = 1.0$ (b) $Z = 1.25$ (c) $Z = 1.5$.

ness increases to 1.25, close to 100% conversion is required. The blocking probability is plotted as a func-

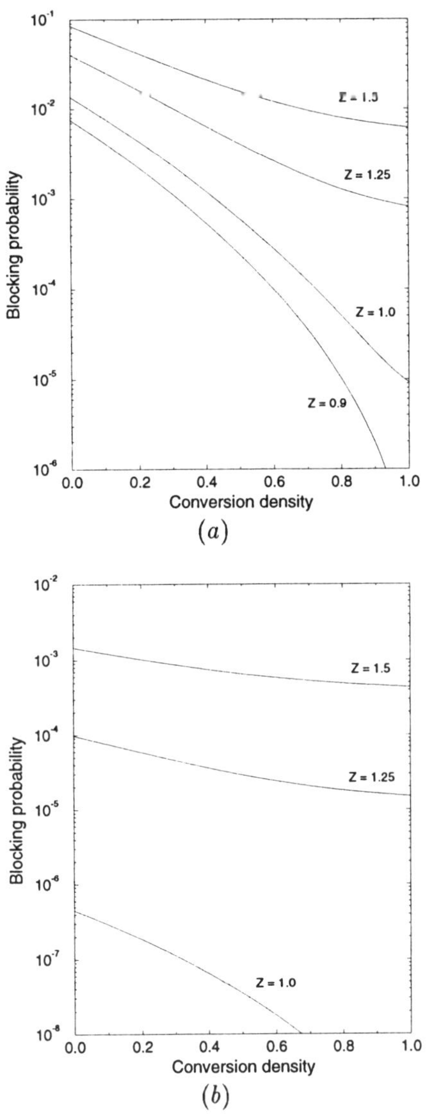


Figure 5: The blocking probability vs. the conversion density with a load of 1.0 per station for (a) the mesh, and (b) the hypercube.

tion of link peakedness for different values of conversion density in the hypercube with a load of $\rho = 1.0$ per station in Figure 6. It is observed that the probability of blocking increases dramatically as the link traffic becomes more peaked. The situation is similar in the mesh (not shown). This is due to the fact that an arrival sees a much more congested system with peaked traffic due to its "bursty" nature.

Finally, the conversion gain is plotted against link peakedness in Figure 7 for different values of conversion density in the mesh network. The blocking probability is maintained at $10^{-3}$. The graphs show that the gain is fairly insensitive to link peakedness up to a certain value (about 1.45 in this case) for any value of conversion density. Beyond this point, the gain dramatically increases. However in the region of large $Z$, the loads that can be supported with and without conversion are small (e.g., for $Z = 1.55$, the supportable loads with no conversion and full conversion are 0.015 and 0.297, respectively). Therefore even a modest increase in supportable load with conversion translates to a huge conversion gain (which is a ratio). For the hypercube (not shown in the paper) the breakaway point occurs at a higher peakedness.

## 5 Conclusions and Future Work

We have developed a methodology for studying the benefits of wavelength converters for non-Poisson dynamic traffic. We used the Pascal approximation which has been used by teletraffic engineers to characterize the non-Poisson nature of overflow traffic from a trunk. We derived the arrival occupancy distribution for this approximation and utilized it to analyze the effect of traffic peakedness on wavelength conversion benefits and call blocking performance.

For the two topologies considered, our models predict that for a fixed load, peakedness dramatically increases the blocking probability, and wavelength conversion can only mildly alleviate performance degradation. If the metric of interest is the reduction in blocking probability with wavelength conversion, then traffic peakedness reduces the benefits of wavelength conversion (Figure 5). However, if the performance metric is the increase in network throughput achievable with wavelength conversion at a fixed blocking probability, traffic peakedness does not affect the benefits of wavelength conversion for a large range of peakedness values (Figure 7). In this case, wavelength conversion assumes a more significant role at large peakedness values.

We are currently simulating smooth and peaked node traffic and comparing the observed network blocking performance with that obtained by using the matched BPP model. Our initial results indicate that the trends predicted by the model and those obtained via simulation are similar.

## References


[1] R. Ramaswami, "Multiwavelength lightwave networks for computer communication," *IEEE Communcations Magazine*, vol. 31, no. 2, pp. 78–88, Feb. 1993.

[2] B. Mukherjee, "WDM-based local lightwave networks – Part I: Single-hop systems," *IEEE Network*, vol. 6, no. 3, pp. 12–27, May 1992.

[3] A. Girard, *Routing and Dimensioning in Circuit-Switched Networks,* Addison-Wesley, 1990.

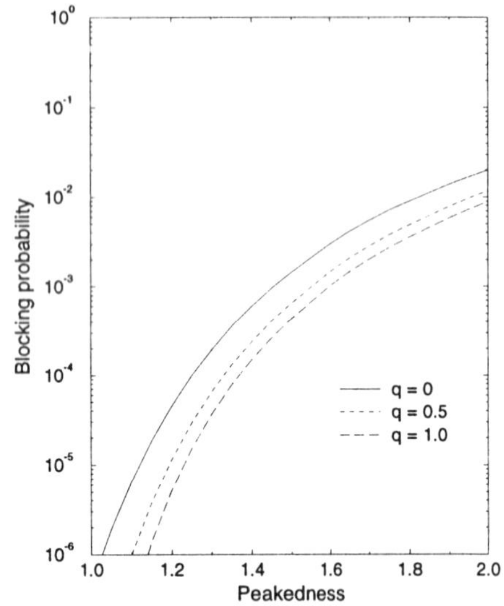


Figure 6: The blocking probability vs. the link peakedness for the hypercube. $\rho = 1$.

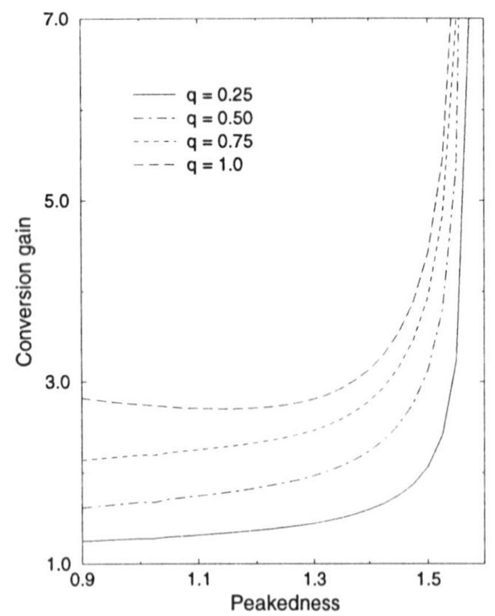


Figure 7: The conversion gain vs. the link peakedness for the mesh network. $P_b = 10^{-3}$.


[4] R. A. Barry and P. A. Humblet, "Models of blocking probability in all-optical networks with and without wavelength changers," *IEEE J. Sel. Areas in Commun.*, pp. 858–867, June 1996.

[5] M. Kovačević and A. S. Acampora, "Benefits of wavelength translation in all-optical clear-channel networks," *IEEE J. Sel. Areas in Commun.*, pp. 868–880, June 1996.

[6] K. C. Lee and V. O. K. Li, "A wavelength-convertible optical network," *J. Lightwave Technology*, vol. 11, no. 5/6, pp. 962–970, May/June 1993.

[7] B. S. Glance *et al.*, "New advances in optical components needed for FDM optical networks," *J. Lightwave Technology*, vol. 11, no. 5/6, pp. 882–890, May/June 1993.

[8] J. Yates *et al.*, "Limited-range wavelength translation in all-optical networks," *Proc. of IEEE INFOCOM'96*, pp. 954–961, Mar. 1996.

[9] S. Subramaniam, M. Azizoğlu, and A. K. Somani, "Connectivity and sparse wavelength conversion in wavelength-routing networks," *Proc. IEEE INFOCOM'96*, pp. 148–155, Mar. 1996.

[10] S. Subramaniam, M. Azizoğlu, and A. K. Somani, "All-optical networks with sparse wavelength conversion," *IEEE/ACM Trans. Networking*, pp. 544–557, Aug. 1996.

[11] I. P. Kaminow *et al.*, "A wideband all-optical WDM network," *IEEE J. Sel. Areas in Commun.*, vol. 14, no. 5, pp. 780–799, June 1996.

[12] E. A. van Doorn, "Some aspects of the peakedness concept in teletraffic theory," *Elektronische Informationsverarbeitung und Kybernetik*, vol. 22, no. 2–3, pp. 93–104. 1986.

[13] L. E. N. Delbrouck, "A unified approximate evaluation of congestion functions for smooth and peaky traffics," *IEEE Trans. Commun.*, vol. 29, no. 2, pp. 85–91, Feb. 1981.

[14] R. I. Wilkinson, "Theories for toll traffic engineering in the U.S.A.," *Bell Systems Technical Journal*, vol. 35, pp. 421–514, Mar. 1956.

[15] A. Kuczura and D. Bajaj, "A method of moments for the analysis of a switched communication network's performance," *IEEE Trans. Commun.*, vol. 25, no. 2, pp. 185–193, Feb. 1977.

[16] H. Heffes and D. Lucantoni, "A Markov-modulated characterization of packetized voice and data traffic and related statistical multiplexer performance," *IEEE J. Sel. Areas in Commun.*, vol. 4, no. 6, pp. 856–868, Sept. 1986.

# Fault Tolerant Multiwavelength Optical Rings with Limited Wavelength Conversion*

O. Gerstel
IBM Research Division
T.J. Watson Research Center
Hawthorne, NY 10532
ori@watson.ibm.com

R. Ramaswami
IBM Research Division
T.J. Watson Research Center
Hawthorne, NY 10532
rajiv@watson.ibm.com

G.H. Sasaki
Electrical Engineering Dept.
University of Hawaii
Honolulu, HI 96822
sasaki@spectra.eng.hawaii.edu

## Abstract

*This paper presents methods for recovering from channel failures, link failures, and node failures in wavelength-division multiplexed (WDM) point-to-point links and ring networks, with limited wavelength conversion/switching capabilities at the nodes. Different recovery schemes are presented to handle each type of failure. Each scheme is evaluated based on the network hardware configuration required to support it, and the performance and management overheads associated with fault-recovery.*

## 1 Introduction

Today's telecommunications infrastructure is based on SONET/SDH self-healing rings. To increase the bandwidth of their trunks, the carriers are actively deploying wavelength-division-multiplexed (WDM) point-to-point links. It is likely that WDM ring networks will come next, as a natural evolution of WDM links and SONET rings. A WDM network provides lightpaths. A *lightpath* is an end-to-end connection, comprising of channels interconnected by switches within the nodes with an appropriate configuration. A ring is a popular interconnection topology because it is simple and provides a fair degree of fault-tolerance.

All-optical ring nodes that perform add/drop functions are being actively researched today. It is likely however, that the first practical WDM ring networks will use electronics rather than optics to perform the switching functions within the nodes (O-E-O architecture). Whatever be the architecture of a node, providing limited wavelength conversion capabilities is more cost-effective than full wavelength conversion. This will be quantified later in the paper. Moreover, it has been shown in [7] that if the set of lightpath requests is given in advance, very limited conversion is as good as full conversion.

Failure restoration is particularly important in these networks where lightpaths carry data at very high bit-rates. A customer cannot have a lightpath fail due to a fiber cut, power outage or a component failure. It is also desirable that these failures be handled within the optical network, rather than have the higher layers deal with them, for the following reasons: If the optical network handles the recovery process, it can share the same set of failure-restoration resources among many higher-level networks. This point is further clarified in Section 2.1 where it is shown how many working channels can share a single protection channel. Also, the lightpaths provided by the optical network can support a variety of different protocols, and some of these protocols may not have their own fault-recovery mechanisms.

This work proposes various failure restoration schemes tailored for WDM ring networks with limited wavelength conversion. These schemes handle channel faults, wherein an individual channel fails, link faults, wherein an entire link fails, and node faults, wherein a network node fails. We also propose an integrated solution that can isolate and handle all these faults. These mechanisms are very different from those employed in SONET rings, mainly because WDM nodes are based on space switching while SONET is based on time switching. They are also very different from mechanisms for WDM rings with full or no conversion, since such networks allow for much simpler wavelength allocation schemes.

This paper is structured as follows. Section 1.1 describes related work. Section 1.2 describes the network and node models and identifies the different failure conditions. Section 2 proposes and analyzes different recovery schemes. In Section 3, we discuss fault-management aspects of these solutions, and conclude in Section 4.

### 1.1 Related Work

Extensive work has been performed on fault-tolerant network architectures in general and self-healing rings in particular (see [3] for a good overview). However, most networks that have such fault-tolerant mechanisms built into them use time division multiplexing on their fibers (SONET, ATM, FDDI are a few of the many examples), and thus can perform the recovery in the time domain. In contrast, WDM networks treat their channels as transparent, continuous streams, and can thus manipulate them only via space switching. This fact, combined with the careful design needed for limited wavelength conversion, substantially complicates the configurations for supporting fault-tolerance.

*This work was supported in part by grant MDA 972-95-C-0001 from DARPA.



0-8186-7780-5/97 $10.00 © 1997 IEEE

Some simple failure restoration techniques for WDM mesh networks have been proposed in [2, 5, 8]. In [2, 5], the idea is to set up an alternate link-disjoint route for each lightpath at the time it is set up. We will see in Section 2.2 that this method is inefficient in utilizing the available wavelengths. The work in [8] is useful for mesh networks, but is too resource and time consuming for rings, for which simpler schemes without any coordination between the nodes are possible, thereby enabling faster restoration.

Several recent papers have considered limited wavelength conversion [4, 10, 9, 7] from a routing and wavelength assignment perspective but none of these consider failure restoration. We believe that our work is the first one to explore different recovery procedures in detail for rings with limited conversion. The current architecture is further described in [7], however our solution can be coupled with any other wavelength allocation scheme to provide fault-tolerance in the network.

### 1.2 The Model

A WDM point-to-point link uses optical multiplexors (abbreviated herein to PTPMs) to combine multiple channels at different wavelengths into a single fiber and to separate the channels at the other end. It is conceptually simple to combine such devices into WDM add/drop multiplexors (WADMs) by taking a pair of such PTPMs, connecting their electronic interfaces back-to-back, and adding some switching and local ports. A WDM ring network is then obtained by interconnecting several such WADMs in a ring topology (and adding a control plane). This architecture is based on electronic switching at the nodes (O-E-O), however the fault-tolerance schemes presented herein are applicable with small change to many similar all-optical architectures.

Within each WADM, different types of wavelength conversion are possible, each requiring different amounts of switching and conversion capabilites, as shown in Figure 1. *Fixed* conversion does not require any switches, as shown in Figure 1(a). The case of *no* conversion is just a specific form of this interconnection pattern.

On the other hand, one could have a full blown non-blocking switch/conversion between the channels (as in Figure 1(b)). Such a solution enables any-to-any conversion in each and every node. It also allows for simple switch management and simple, yet optimal, wavelength allocation. However such a node is likely to be very expensive to realize. An intermediate solution is to install switches and converters of small-degree for each channel, and to connect them to the switches of other channels in some clever fashion (see Figure 1(c)). This solution is far less expensive than the full conversion case (depending on the degree $\Delta$ of the the switches), yet supports many of the scenarios that full conversion supports [7], provided that the interconnection pattern is carefully planned. However it does add some complexity to the failure restoration mechanisms required. It will be shown that careful planning enables the network to offer the same level of fault-tolerance that full conversion supports.

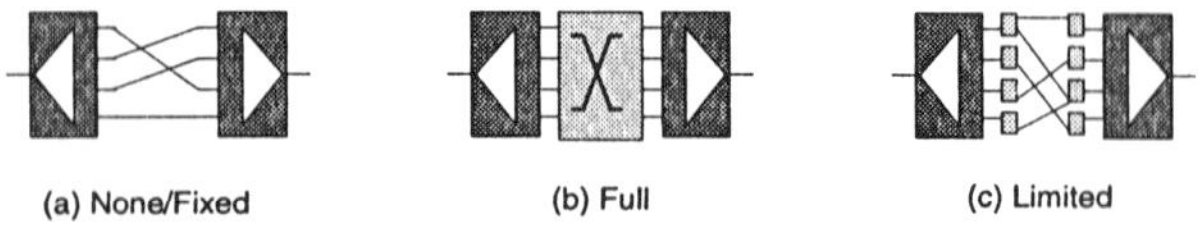


Figure 1: The spectrum of wavelength conversion capabilities in a WADM

We identify the following three main types of failure scenarios:

**Channel fault:** A single channel on a link between two nodes has failed. This failure can result from a failure of the designated laser or receiver for the channel, or wire disconnections.

**Link fault:** Typically caused by a fiber cut. Such failures can be dealt with by using a separate protection fiber, or by providing a "loopback" mechanism within each node on the same working fiber, without using a separate protection fiber. We describe these solutions in the next section.

**Node fault:** In this case, an entire WADM node has failed. This is the most severe fault of the three, and may result from power outages or catastrophic scenarios.

Throughout the paper we shall use $N$ to denote the number of nodes in the ring and $W$ to denote the number of wavelengths (channels) per fiber. We shall also use the term *link* to denote the transmission medium connecting adjacent nodes (typically a single fiber/fiber pair, with an additional fiber/fiber pair for protection if desired). The term *channel* is used to denote the logical link between nodes that uses a specific wavelength. Thus $W$ channels are multiplexed onto each of the $N$ links comprising the ring. We also assume full duplex links and lightpaths.

## 2 Fault Tolerant Configurations

In this section we present WADM node configurations that deal with the fault scenarios mentioned above. In all cases, cost considerations dictate that the fault-tolerance support require as few additional switches as possible, or even better, only a few additional ports in existing switches. This overhead will be referred to as the *switching overhead.* Another important design factor is to reduce the number of switching elements involved in the data path, since this reduces the deterioration in signal quality. The maximum number of switching stages in a node will be referred to as the *hop overhead.* A third crucial factor, which can dominate the reaction time from detection of a fault to restoration of service, is the need to coordinate between nodes in the ring (or between the nodes and the network management site). This will be referred to as the *coordination overhead.*

### 2.1 Channel Faults

The least cost solution for backing up channels for the case of single channel failures is to allocate one channel on each link between WADMs for backup

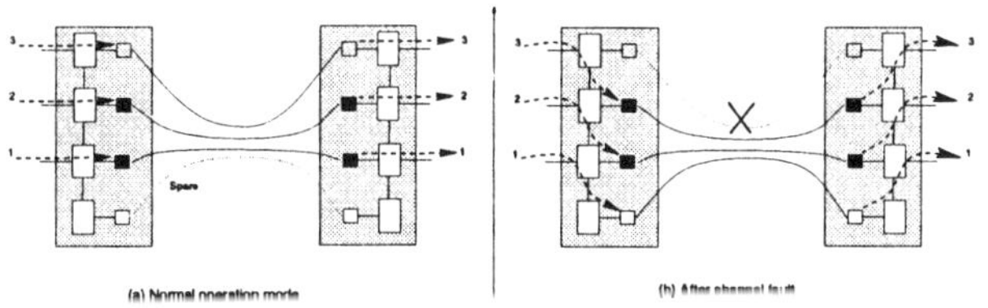


Figure 2: Protection against a single channel failure (solution 1)

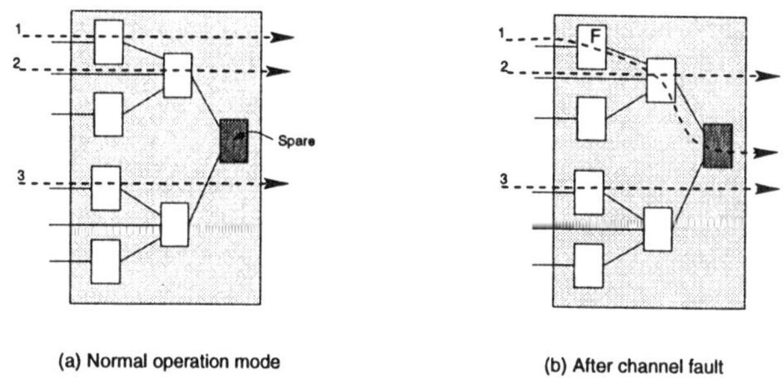


Figure 3: Protection against a single channel failure (solution 2)

purposes. Upon detection of a channel failure, the switches in the node switch the data from the failed channel to the backup channel. This solution can be extended to support multiple channel failures.

We propose three solutions, one having a very small switching overhead (two ports per channel are used for fault-tolerance) and a very low hop overhead (a maximum of two hops per channel), but with a big drawback: in order to move from the normal configuration to the backup configuration, the node needs to be fully reconfigured, resulting in short disruptions to all the lightpaths using the link. A second solution, which does not disrupt lightpaths that do not use the failed channel, has much larger switching overhead and hop overhead. Both solutions do not have a coordination overhead and allow $1:(W-1)$ and $2:(W-1)$ channel protection[1]. These solutions are primarily useful for point-to-point links (i.e., in each PTPM). A third solution that can be integrated with the mechanism to handle link failures is proposed in Section 2.2.

### 2.1.1 Solution 1: Allowing Full Reconfiguration

Logically arrange the channels in each PTPM in a chain. Use two ports of the switch of each channel $i$ to connect the switch to the switch of the previous and next channels, $i-1$ and $i+1$ in the chain respectively (see Figure 2(a)). Let channel 0 be the designated backup channel. Upon failure of some channel $i$, configure the switch of $i$ to transfer $i$'s data to channel $i-1$ on the link. Also configure the switch of channel $i-1$ to transfer its data to channel $i-2$. Repeat the process until channel 1's data is transmitted on channel 0 (see Figure 2(b)).

The same process is repeated in the PTPM on the other side of the link upon detection of a fault. As a result, after a short disconnection, many of the lightpaths use different channels than the original ones (the exact number being $i$).

This solution can be readily extended to support two channel failures: Designate channel $W-1$ as another backup channel. Now, upon the first failure (of, say, channel $i$), reroute connections $i, i-1, ..., 1$ to $i-1, i-2, ..., 0$, as before. Upon a second failure of channel $j$, reroute $j$ to $j+1$, $j+1$ to $j+2$ and so on, until channel $W-2$ is rerouted to the spare channel $W-1$.

[1] In $k:m$ protection, there are $k$ protection facilities shared by $m$ working facilities.

This configuration suffers from a large number of temporary disconnections for transforming from normal to fault configuration and vice versa. An improved configuration connects the switches in a ring rather than a chain. It is then possible to choose the shorter path from the failed channel to backup, resulting in a reduction of 50% in the number of channels that need to be rerouted (on the average).

In most cases, two backup channels should suffice. Larger numbers of channel faults can be dealt with more efficiently by the link fault solutions of Section 2.2.

**Overheads:**

Switching: A $2\times2$ switch per channel is required.

Hops: Each channel goes through at most two switches in a node: its own and that of the adjacent channel.

Coordination: Since both ends of the link perform identical operations, no coordination is needed.

### 2.1.2 Solution 2: No Unnecessary Disconnections

To support a single failure, arrange the channels within each PTPM in a tree structure as shown in Figure 3(a). The root of the tree is the switch of the backup channel $b$, and its degree, $\Delta > 2$, depends on the number of ports per switch that can be allocated for fault-tolerance purposes.

During normal operation, each switch transfers data from its I/O port to the link. When a channel $i$ fails, the switches on the path from $i$ to $b$ are configured to transfer $i$'s data to $b$. (See Figure 3(b) in which the switch of the faulty channel is marked "F". Note that it is assumed that the optics has failed but the switch itself has not failed.) This operation must be done without disrupting the transfer of data on the other channels from their I/O ports to the link. This requires the switch for each channel to be nonblocking. Clearly, the maximum length of the path from a node to the root is $\log_{\Delta-1} W$.

This case may again be generalized for two backup channels as follows. Arrange the switches in two trees, each tree rooted at a switch of a backup channel.

These trees are connected at the leaf level, to form a "dual tree". We defer the details to the full version.

**Overheads:**

Switching: Given $\Delta$ ports are allocated for protection purposes, $\Delta > 2$ is required for single channel protection and $\Delta > 3$ for supporting up to two failures.

Hops: Each channel goes through at most $\log_{\Delta-1} W$ switches in a node for single fault configurations and $2 + \log_{\Delta} \frac{W}{2}$ for dual faults configurations.

Coordination: Since both ends of a link perform identical operations, no coordination is needed.

## 2.2 Link Faults

There are four common techniques to protect against link faults:

**Span protection:** Add a protection fiber between each pair of adjacent nodes, which will be used by the nodes when the primary fiber has failed. Such a recovery scheme is deployed in SONET BLSR/4 rings[2].

**Line protection:** Mend the lightpaths affected by the fault locally, by replacing the faulty link by a loop around the ring on the working fibers but on separate backup wavelengths (see SONET BLSR/2 rings[3] and FDDI rings for similar schemes).

**Online path protection:** When a link fails, set new routes around the ring from the sources of affected lightpaths to their destinations, and reroute the lightpaths to the new routes.

**Proactive path protection:** For each lightpath, set two routes in advance, on the two alternatives around the ring. When one such route fails — switch to the other (e.g., UPSR rings[4] [2, 5]).

As mentioned earlier, despite the conceptual similarity of these schemes to TDM protection schemes, the implementation is quite different due to the fact that space switching is used.

Online path protection may not be a viable option for networks with limited conversion, because the complexity of coordinating the endpoints of a lightpath to find an available backup route around the ring may take hundreds of milliseconds, which is not likely to be tolerated by many higher level protocols. Proactive path protection, on the other hand, is very fast, however it is not a reasonable solution for densely deployed networks, as it is inefficient in utilizing the available wavelengths. With $W$ wavelengths available, one can only support a total of $W$ simultaneous lightpaths. Moreover if all $W$ happen to be single-hop lightpaths, then we end up using $(N-1)W$ channels for failure restoration and only $W$ channels for carrying the working traffic, a very poor channel utilization ratio. (Recall that a channel corresponds to a wavelength on a given link.) With line protection we can support many more than $W$ simultaneous lightpaths. In the best case, if all lightpaths are single-hop lightpaths, then our line protection scheme allows us to support $N\frac{W}{2}$ simultaneous lightpaths.

Span protection is an attractive solution as it is simple, fast, and can be done locally at the two ends of the failed link. All that is necessary is to add an optical switch in the node's output, just in front of the fiber, and to control which fiber is to be used based on detection of light on both fibers. This involves adding very little additional cost to the node hardware, unlike the other schemes. However, this solution is not viable if the cost of additional fiber is high (including a separate set of amplifiers). In order for it to be effective, the protection and working fibers must be routed over disjoint routes so that both do not get cut simultaneously. Moreover it cannot deal with node failures.

The advantage of line protection over proactive path protection is that the former requires only up to 50% of the channels in the network whereas the latter may consume many more of the channels. (This is clearly the minimum required in any scheme if all lightpaths must be protected.) Its advantage over span protection depends on the relative cost of the additional 50% hardware per node versus the cost of additional fiber.

In what follows we focus on the line protection mechanism. This mechanism is based on allocating up to half of the wavelengths for protection, with each data channel $i$ having its unique backup channel $B(i)$. When a failure occurs at a link, it is detected by the nodes adjacent to the failing link, which configure their switches to loop back all the lightpaths that use the link (see Figure 5(b)), through the rest of the ring all the way to its other end, where they are switched to the remaining part of their route. Since backup channels have a default configuration that enables a signal to travel around the ring ($B(i)$ of one link is configured by default to connect to $B(i)$ on the other link in each node), the operation can be completed locally at the nodes that discover the fault.

The intricate part of the design pertains to the actual loopback mechanism at the nodes. Take for example the lightpath in Figure 4(a). It uses wavelength 2 on link WX, wavelength 3 on XY and wavelength 1 on YZ. Suppose XY fails. After the failure, this lightpath must be looped around the ring via XW...ZY and converted from wavelength 2 (on link WX) to wavelength 1 (on YZ). We propose the configuration shown in Figure 5(a), which requires only a single additional port within each switch. Going back to the example in Figure 4(a), connect the switch of channel 3 on link

[2]Bidirectional SONET rings that use four fibers per link between adjacent nodes, two unidirectional working fibers in opposite directions and two protection fibers. Such rings are also called BSHRs.

[3]Bidirectional SONET rings that use two opposite unidirectional fibers per link between adjacent nodes, each of which is utilized up to half of its capacity for working traffic.

[4]Unidirectional SONET rings employing two opposite fibers, and transmitting the data on both of them simultaneously. Also termed USHR/Ps.

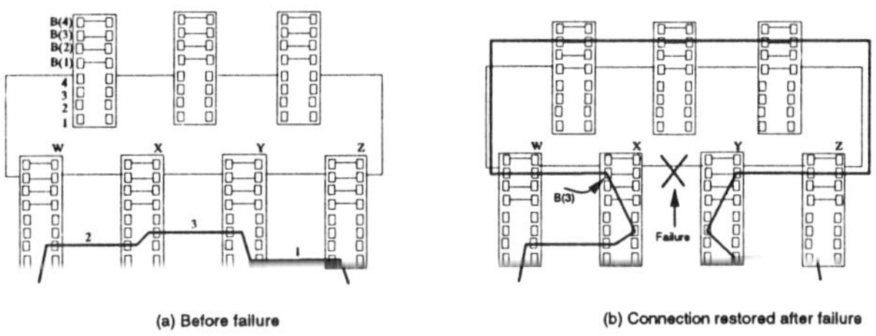


Figure 4: Line protection. All lightpaths are assumed to be bidirectional.

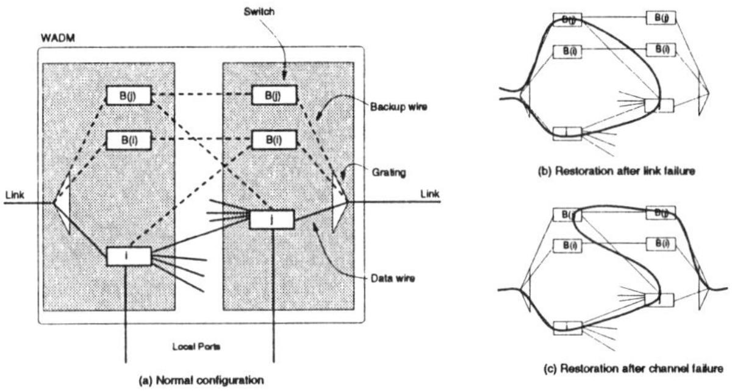


Figure 5: WADM node configuration supporting line protection

XY to the backup channel $B(3)$ on link WX, and activate this connection upon failure. The lightpath will now use channel 2 on link WX, get converted to 3 in node X, from which it will be converted again to $B(3)$, loop around the ring on channel $B(3)$ until it reaches node Y. At node Y it is converted to 3, and converted again to 1 on link YZ (see Figure 4(b)).

**Overheads:**

Switching: One additional port per working traffic switch is required. A $1 \times 2$ switch suffices for a backup channel.

Hops: Each channel goes through at most three switches in a node. However, a looped-back lightpath goes through $N$ additional nodes (2 switches per node).

Coordination: Since both ends of a link perform identical operations, no coordination is needed.

**Observation 1.** This scheme can handle individual channel failures as well. Consider the configuration in Figure 5(c). In it, if channel $j$ fails, its data can be switched to channel $B(j)$ on the same link. This type of restoration will require a management protocol to prevent a link failure event and a channel failure event from simultaneously triggering an attempt to use the same backup channel for recovery. This issue will be addressed in Section 3.

**Observation 2.** The channel failure restoration scheme described above does not allow channel $i$ on *both* links of a WADM to be restored in the event of both channels failing. This can be rectified by adding an additional connection between the $B(i)$ switches.

The amount of protection against channel failures in this case is maximized: it is possible to simultaneously recover all working channels in all the links around the ring.

## 2.3 Node faults

Node failures are complicated to handle in the context of limited conversion, because part of the conversion capability of the network as a whole is lost when a node fails. The rest of the network must compensate for this loss by incorporating more switching capability in the remaining nodes to support the failure. Note, as a corollary, that this problem becomes as simple as handling link faults in the context of no conversion or full conversion. In this section we present two solutions for supporting node failures.

### 2.3.1 Solution 1: More Hardware

In order to enable a solution along the lines of the link failure solution, one must overcome the following obstacle. Assume channel $i$ supporting lightpath $p$ has failed on the link between nodes X and Y. In the link failure case it is possible to convert to a backup wavelength, $B(i)$ at node X, and to use $B(i)$ to loop around the ring, arrive at node Y, and then convert back to $i$ in order to continue along the original course of the lightpath. In contrast, suppose that node X, converting $p$ from wavelength $i$ to wavelength $j$, fails. Then there is no suitable channel to convert $p$ to at both nodes adjacent to the failure (neither $B(i)$ nor $B(j)$ can be chosen without adding more conversion capabilities along the route).

Number the nodes from 0 to $N-1$ clockwise around the ring and call $(i+1) \bmod N$ the clockwise neighbor of $i$. Our scheme adds more conversion capability to the clockwise neighbor of a failing node, while the other neighbor performs the same operation as for the link fault case. Referring to Figure 6(a), the following additional wiring is necessary at node X: if node Y can convert wavelength $i$ on link XY to wavelengths $\{j_1, .., j_k\}$ on link YZ, then (at node X) we connect the switch of channel $i$ on link XY to an extra switch, $Next(i)$, which is connected back to channels $\{B(j_1), ..., B(j_k)\}$ on link WX. As in the link failure case, at node X we also connect channel $i$ on link WX to channel $B(i)$ on link XY and similarly channel $i$ on link XY to channel $B(i)$ on link WX.

Suppose now that node Y fails, as shown in Figure 7(b). Then its clockwise neighbor X converts the affected lightpath $p$ shown in the figure to $B(1)$, where 1 is the wavelength used by $p$ between the failed node Y and its other neighbor Z. At the same time, node Z converts from 1 to $B(1)$ as well, to re-establish the lightpath. Note that node Z performs the same function for the failure of node Y as for the failure of link YZ. However node X performs a different function depending on whether node Y has failed or whether link XY has failed. Distinguishing between these two cases is part of the management function to be discussed in Section 3.

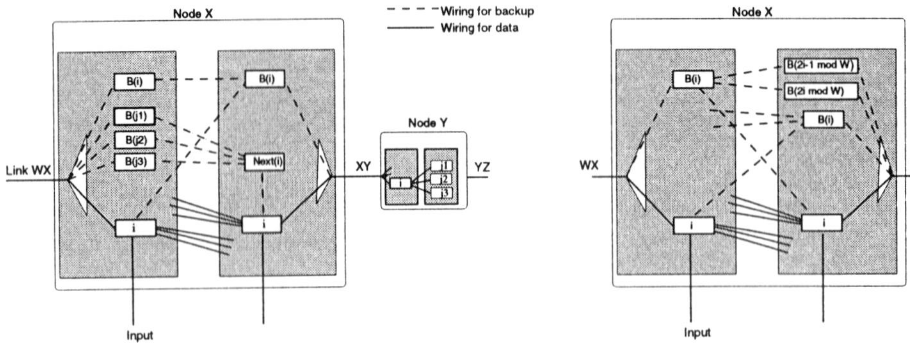


(a) Node configuration for solution 1

(b) Node configuration for solution 2

Figure 6: Node configurations to support recovery from node failures

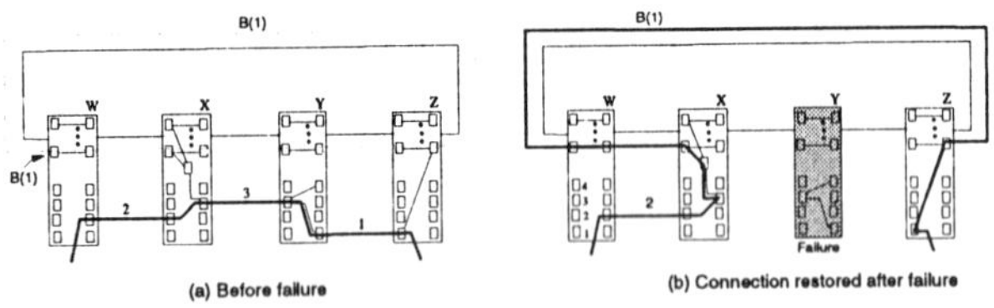


Figure 7: Protection against node failures (solution 1)

**Overheads:**

Switching: $\frac{W}{2}$ additional $Next(i)$ switches per node are required with a degree of $\Delta$ each (where $\Delta$ is the degree of a a switch without the protection mechanism). This represents an increase of 25% in the number of switches since there are $2W$ regular switches per WADM. As a result, the $\frac{W}{2}$ backup switches connected to the $Next(i)$ switches need $\Delta$ more ports each. All other switches need a single extra port (i.e., their degree in $\Delta + 1$).

Hops: Each channel goes through at most four switches in a node. However, a looped-back lightpath goes through $N$ additional nodes.

Coordination: Assuming that a node failure is diagnosed, this scheme can be performed with no additional coordination, as follows. Upon setup of a lightpath, each node records locally the conversion that the *next* clockwise neighbor performs on the lightpath. Returning to the example in Figure 7(a), node X records that the lightpath using wavelength 3 on link XY is converted to wavelength 1 at node Y. This can be elegantly done by setting the switch $Next(3)$ at node X to $B(1)$. Upon failure, node X sets the switch of channel 3 on link XY to $Next(3)$ (rather than to the multiplexer), and node Z sets its switch of channel 1 to $B(1)$ — both of which actions are based entirely on internal node information.

### 2.3.2 Solution 2: Global Coordination

The next solution requires no additional hardware (except for an additional port per switch), and the lost conversion capability due to a node failure is compensated for by having a richer conversion capability between the backup channels.

When a node Y fails, each lightpath $x_i$ that goes through Y uses some channel $Left_i$ to the left of Y and some channel $Right_i$ to the right of Y. For the sake of simplicity assume that all $\frac{W}{2}$ possible lightpaths go through Y (all of the wavelengths are used and none of them is dropped/added). Thus, the pairs $\{(Left_i, Right_i)\}_{i=1}^{W/2}$ represent a *permutation* of the values $\{1, ..., \frac{W}{2}\}$. If each neighboring node sends a failed channel $i$ to its backup $B(i)$ — as in the link failure case — and the set of backup channels is configured as a $\frac{W}{2} \times \frac{W}{2}$ permutation network (e.g., a Beneš network [1]), then the backup channels can route each $Left_i$ channel to the correct $Right_i$. Note that, as opposed to the classic use of permutation networks, we do not use it as a switch fabric configuration but distribute it over a whole ring, having a single stage of it in every node, as in [7].

For the current case it is important to choose the appropriate permutation network topology. For example, the Beneš network is not a good choice here, since we need a network that functions as a $\frac{W}{2} \times \frac{W}{2}$ switch, no matter where the node failure is. In other words, we need a cyclic configuration around the ring, that can be cut at any point, to yield a $\frac{W}{2} \times \frac{W}{2}$ rearrangeable permutation network. Clearly, if all the stages in a permutation network are identical, its input and output $\frac{W}{2}$ ports may be connected to arrive at the required configuration.

The basic building block for this configuration is the *Shuffle/Exchange* pattern from a set $S_1$ of switches to a set $S_2$ (where both sets contain $\frac{W}{2}$ switches). This pattern connects each switch $i \in \{1, ..., \frac{W}{2}\}$ in set $S_1$ to switches $(2i-1) \bmod \frac{W}{2}$ and $2i \bmod \frac{W}{2}$ in set $S_2$. The network resulting from concatenating $\log_2 \frac{W}{2}$ stages of Shuffle/Exchange in a row is called an *Omega network* for which the following result holds.

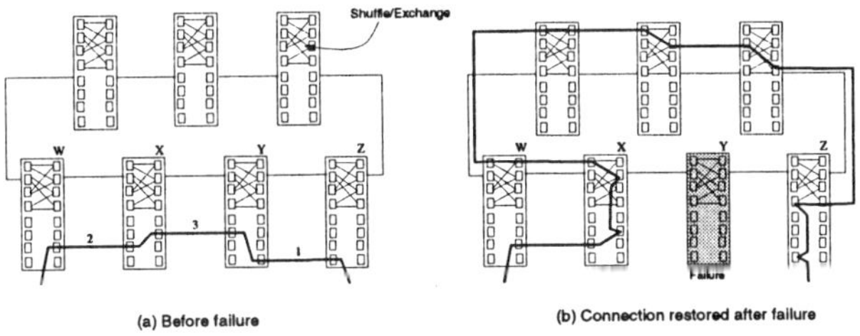


Figure 8: Protection against node failures (solution 2)

**Theorem 1 [6].** *Let a* Triple-Omega network *be the result of concatenating three Omega networks in a row. Then a Triple-Omega network is a full scale rearrangeable permutation network.*

*In addition, if $W \leq 16$, a Double-Omega network is also a full scale rearrangeable permutation network.*

Let $S_1$ be the set of switches of backup channels on the link connecting a given node to its clockwise neighbor, and $S_2$ the set of switches connecting the node to its other neighbor. We use the following configuration: Wire the switches of backup channels in each node according to a Shuffle/Exchange from set $S_1$ to $S_2$ (see Figure 8). If the size of the network is large enough, namely: $N \geq 3\log_2 \frac{W}{2} + 1$, then after a node failure, the backup switches in the remaining network form a Triple-Omega configuration and can route the broken lightpaths to realize the required permutation. If $W \leq 16$ it is enough to have $N \geq 2\log_2 \frac{W}{2} + 1$ nodes.

Note that the scheme effectively distributes the permutation network $P$ over the entire ring. Recovery from a node failure is done in a centralized manner by a network management entity by considering the permutation of $(Left_i, Right_i)$ pairs at the moment of failure and setting the switches along the ring to support it.

**Overheads:**

Switching: Switches of backup channels need only have four ports (two ports for the Shuffle/Exchange, one for connecting to the multiplexer and one for connecting to the corresponding non-backup channel). Data channel switches need only one extra port, as for the link failure case.

Hops: Each channel goes through up to three switches in a node. However, a looped-back lightpath goes through $N$ additional nodes.

Coordination: It is necessary to set up the entire configuration of backup switches to support the permutation. Thus all the network nodes have to be involved in the coordination.

## 3 Fault Management

So far we have described the mechanisms in the nodes to restore connections from a failure. Two additional higher level management aspects are still necessary to complete the picture. The first aspect addresses the need to manage individual channel failures versus link failures in the case of Section 2.2. The second aspect addresses the need to diagnose the fault type before action is taken. This enables us to integrate the schemes in this paper into one unified channel/link/node recovery scheme.

### 3.1 Managing channel and link faults

The scheme of Section 2.2 works correctly if a single link fails. The scheme can also handle multiple channel failures on different links. This is better than adding the costly hardware mechanism of Section 2.1 to deal specifically with channel faults. However, if no further steps are taken, channel faults and a link fault can cause collisions, since both of them use the same set of backup channels for protection. This will result in corrupting lightpaths that recovered from channel failures and lightpaths that recovered from a link failure and even more severe data security problems.

Network management must ensure that if $B(i)$ is already used for recovering from a channel fault, it will not be used to recover another lightpath at the same time. The challenge here is to devise a mechanism that does not require global processing at the time of a failure, in order to keep the restoration time as small as possible.

To manage the backup channels it is necessary to maintain local flags at each node which control the decision to use each backup channel for recovery purposes. The solution requires some global management entity (GME) to coordinate the flags. More specifically, each node $x$ maintains two boolean flags for each backup channel $B(i)$: $EnableChan[i, x]$ and $EnableLink[i]$. $EnableChan[i, x]$ controls channel recovery using $B(i)$ at $x$, while $EnableLink[i]$ controls the use of $B(i)$ for link recovery at $x$. Note, by the notation, that while an instance of $EnableLink[i]$ appears in every node, $EnableLink[i]$ is identical in all the nodes while $EnableChan[i, x]$ may be different. In addition to the nodes themselves, GME has an updated copy of all the flags (for every $i$ and $x$). All the flags are set only by GME. The algorithm to maintain these flags is given in Figure 9.

An important characteristic of this process is that *it does not slow down the actual recovery process*, since all real-time decisions are based on local flags only and executed by the nodes without any coordination between them. For example when a link failure occurs, the two nodes at the ends of the failed link sense the failure, check their local $EnableLink[i]$ flags and for each $i$ for which the flag is on, execute the line protection scheme. The two nodes then inform the GME about the event and the GME sets the local flags at all the nodes. This slower global coordination by the GME is adequate as long as two failures do not occur very close to each other (which is not expected to be the case).

### 3.2 Integrated recovery mechanism

This section attempts to merge the recovery scheme for channel and link faults presented in Section 2.2 and the *local* recovery scheme for node faults (Section 2.3, Solution 1). As all schemes are local, it is desirable to merge them into a unified scheme that handles all

1. Upon failure of an individual channel $i$ at node $x$:

(a) If $i$ is not used by any lightpath at node $x$, ignore the failure. Otherwise:

(b) Node $x$ checks *EnableChan*$[i, x]$. If it is on, $x$ proceeds with channel recovery as in Section 2.2 and informs GME of the event. Otherwise – no recovery is done.

(c) Upon receipt of a notification, GME turns the *EnableLink*$[i]$ flag off at all the nodes. It also turns *EnableChan*$[i, x]$ off.

2. Upon failure of channel $i$ as part of a link failure adjacent to node $x$:

(a) If $i$ is not used by any lightpath at node $x$, ignore the failure. Otherwise:

(b) Node $x$ checks its local instance of *EnableLink*$[i]$. If it is on, $x$ proceeds with link recovery as in Section 2.2 and informs GME of the event. Otherwise – no recovery is done.

(c) Upon receipt of a notification, GME turns *EnableLink*$[i]$ off at all the nodes. It also turns *EnableChan*$[i, y]$ off for every node $y$.

3. Upon restoration of service of channel $i$ at node $x$:

(a) If $i$ is using $B(i)$ as part of the channel recovery scheme, it resets the switches to normal mode and informs GME. Otherwise – it ignores the event.

(b) GME turns *EnableChan*$[i, x]$ on.

(c) If *EnableChan*$[i, y]$ is on for every node $y$, GME turns *EnableLink*$[i]$ on.

4. Upon restoration of service of a link adjacent to node $x$:

(a) For every channel $i$ that is using $B(i)$ as part of the link recovery scheme at node $x$, $x$ resets the switches to normal mode and informs GME.

(b) GME turns *EnableChan*$[i, y]$ on for every node $y$. It also turns *EnableLink*$[i]$ on.

Figure 9: Maintenance of protection resources for unified channel and link recovery

fault scenarios quickly, without coordination. Unfortunately, since these recovery schemes are not identical, it is necessary to diagnose the fault type in order to activate the appropriate scheme, a process that requires some coordination.

Diagnosing a channel failure from the other types is easy: upon failure of channel $i$, the node checks if channel $B(i)$ is operational. If so — this is a channel failure and the diagnosis is complete. Otherwise, it is either a link or a node failure. (This can also be detected by determining whether light is present on the other channels on the link or not.)

The following scheme integrates the diagnosis and recovery process and is demonstrated on the generic example in Figure 10.

**Node configuration.** We adopt the node configuration for node failures (Figure 6(a)) and add to it an additional connection between the switch of channel $i$ on link XY to that of $B(i)$ on link WX (thereby merging into it the wiring scheme for link faults).

**Phase 1.** The nodes adjacent to a fault *assume* it is a link fault and activate the link recovery procedure (nodes X and Y in Figure 10(a), nodes X and Z in Figure 10(b)).

**Phase 2.** The clockwise neighbor of a failed link XY (node X) sends a message to the second hop neighbor (node Z), announcing that link XY has failed. This is done via some out-of-band signaling network (e.g., IP) or via some in-band signal propagating anti-clockwise (e.g., on a dedicated supervisory wavelength).

**Phase 3.** Node Z receives the message and examines to see if link YZ has failed. If not, Z sends a reply to X diagnosing the fault as a link fault. If YZ has indeed failed, this is a failure of node Y, and Z notifies X of a node failure. Note that the switch setting of Z is already correct since the anti-clockwise neighbor of a fault activates the same reconfiguration regardless of the fault type.

**Phase 4.** If X receives a link failure diagnosis, nothing needs to be done (X is already configured for this case). If X receives a node failure diagnosis it reconfigures to support this case.

This integrated method yields fast restoration times: in case of a channel fault, the diagnosis is based on local data and the recovery can be completed very quickly. In case of a link fault, recovery is performed as fast as the original scheme of Section 2.2; in case of a node fault, there is an added delay of a round trip from node X to Z.

There is one potential problem with this approach. Suppose the failure is actually a node failure. In Phase 1, when the link recovery procedure is activated, it will result in some temporary misconnections for lightpaths that are affected by the failure. There are two ways to fix this problem: (1) rely on a higher layer protocol to discover the problem (e.g., rely on connection specific SONET bits), or (2) delay the actual switching

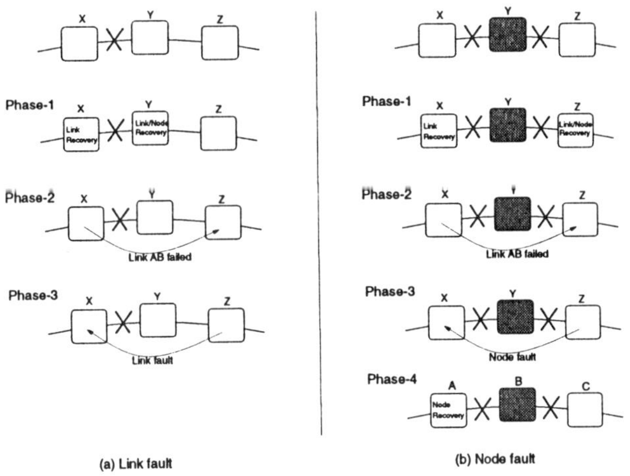


Figure 10: Integrated protocol for link and node faults

to the end of the diagnostics protocol, thereby choosing to degrade the performance of the protocol for the more prevalent link faults over having potential security threats in more rare cases of node faults.

## 4 Conclusions

In this paper we considered WDM ring networks with limited wavelength conversion capabilities in each node. While the paper mainly focuses on the O-E-O node architecture, most of it is applicable to many all-optical architectures as well. The main part which should be modified for these architectures are the channel protection mechanisms described in Section 2.1.

We considered three failure scenarios: individual channel failures, link failures, and node failures. For channel failures we presented three solutions. One has small overheads but requires a major reconfiguration of a node in case of a fault affecting all the other channels. The second requires more hardware (an additional port per switch), and has longer paths to a backup channel ($\log_2 \frac{W}{2}$ instead of two hops), but requires only the faulty channel to reconfigure. Both solutions provide $W:2$ protection. The third solution is integrated with link recovery and does not require additional hardware (over that of link protection) yet provides $1:1$ channel protection.

For link failures we proposed a solution requiring the faulty lightpaths to loop-back around the ring. This solution also supports multiple channel faults around the ring, provided that it is managed properly, and we presented a management scheme to ensure proper operation in case of multiple faults. The hardware overhead of the solution is low (one port per switch), but it requires 50% of the channels to be reserved for backup purposes (however, this is the minimum for any scheme), and long loop-back paths.

For node failures we presented two solutions. One is a simple extension of the configuration that handles link faults, requiring more hardware (25% more switches per node), and the other is based on sophisticated connection patterns between the nodes, requiring no additional hardware. We believe that the simpler solution is better suited to networks which require fast restoration, as it entails no coordination among the nodes.

Finally, we presented a scheme that combines all the recovery schemes, which we believe to be a practical integrated solution for such networks. This scheme requires limited coordination between nodes and we conjecture that this is an inherent property of such schemes.

**Acknowledgment.** We would like to thank W. Eric Hall for many useful discussions.

## References

[1] V.E. Beneš. *Mathematical Theory of Connecting Networks.* Academic Press, 1965.

[2] Y. Hamazumi, N. Nagatsu, and K-I. Sato. Number of wavelengths required for optical networks with failure restoration. In *OFC'94 Tech. Digest*, pages 67–68, 1994.

[3] I. Haque, W. Kremer, and K. Raychauduri. Self-healing rings in a synchronous environment. In C.A. Siller and M. Shafi, editors, *SONET/SDH: a sourcebook of synchronous networking*, pages 131–139. IEEE Press, New York, 1996.

[4] K-C. Lee and V.O.K. Li. A wavelength-convertible optical network. *IEEE/OSA Journal on Lightwave Technology*, 11:962–970, May/June 1993.

[5] N. Nagatsu, S. Okamoto, and K-I. Sato. Optical path cross-connect system scale evaluation using path accommodation design for restricted wavelength division multiplexing. *IEEE JSAC / IEEE/OSA JLT: Special Issue on Optical Networks*, 14(5):893–902, 1996.

[6] D.S. Parker. Notes on shuffle/exchange-type switching networks. *IEEE Transactions on Computers*, C-29(3):213–222, March 1980.

[7] R. Ramaswami and G.H. Sasaki. Multiwavelength optical networks with limited wavelength conversion. In *IEEE Infocom'97*, 1997.

[8] R. Ramaswami and A. Segall. Distributed network control for optical networks. *ACM/IEEE Transactions on Networking*, 1996. Submitted.

[9] S. Subramaniam, M. Azizoglu, and A. K. Somani. Connectivity and sparse wavelength conversion in wavelength-routing networks. In *IEEE Infocom'96*, pages 148–155, 1996.

[10] J. Yates, J. Lacey, D. Everitt, and M. Summerfield. Limited-range wavelength translation in all-optical networks. In *IEEE Infocom'96*, pages 954–961, 1996.

# Performance of Alternate Routing Methods in All–Optical Switching Networks

Hiroaki Harai, Masayuki Murata and Hideo Miyahara

Department of Informatics and Mathematical Science
Graduate School of Engineering Science, Osaka University
Toyonaka, Osaka 560, Japan

**Abstract**

*We study routing methods in all–optical switching networks. In all–optical switching networks, the connection with more hops encounters more call blocking, and it is especially true in optical networks with no wavelength conversions. We therefore consider an alternate routing method with limited trunk reservation in which connections with more hops are prepared more alternate routes. Through developing an approximate analytic approach, we show that our method keeps good performance when compared with the existing alternate routing methods, and also that the fairness among connections can be improved. Further performance improvement is investigated by introducing a wavelength assignment policy and a dynamic routing method. An effectiveness of the proposed method is investigated through simulation.*

## 1 Introduction

An amount of traffic that a network should handle is rapidly growing due to the recent advancement of multimedia computing and communication technologies. However, switching systems based on the current electronic technology cannot provide enough capacity to meet those requirements. An all–optical switching technology thus becomes important for future very high speed networks. In the optical switching network, switching nodes can be expected to have throughput of an order of gigabit per second. Moreover, no optical from/to electronic conversion is required. Recently, a lightpath architecture is proposed for optical switching based on a circuit–switching method in [1-4]. In the lightpath architecture, network nodes perform demultiplexing and linear operation such as power dividing and amplification on optical signals, which makes it possible to perform all operations in the optical domain and to simplify the network management (Fig. 1).

A main problem in optical networks is that the wavelength conversion at the optical node is difficult. Then, the same wavelength should be assigned to the connection on all the links along the route if a capability of wavelength conversion is not provided at the switching node. In [1,

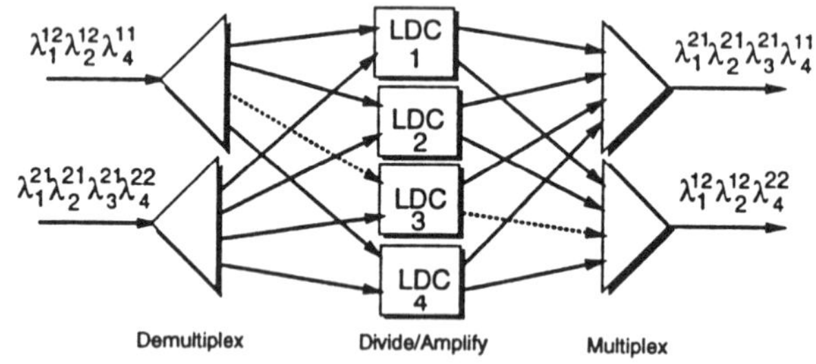


Figure 1: A switching process at a node

2], the performances of a fixed routing method with and without wavelength conversions are compared, and it is shown that the fixed routing method without wavelength conversions remarkably degrades performance in terms of call blocking probability through approximate analysis and simulation techniques. The alternate routing method and the dynamic routing method including LLR (least loaded routing) are then introduced in [2, 3, 5] to improve performance by providing more routes for each connection. In the alternate routing, if there is no available wavelength on the primary route, the secondary route is examined to seek the available wavelength. If it is found, the connection is established along the secondary route.

In this paper, we consider a new class of alternate routing to achieve high network performance as well as to improve a fairness among connections with different numbers of hop counts. In general, the connection with shorter hop counts is likely to be accepted while the one with more hops encounters more call blocking. It is because the latter requires to reserve more links at the connection setup time. It is especially true in optical networks with no wavelength conversions since the same wavelength must be available along the route. In fact, the authors in [1, 2] show that in optical networks without wavelength conversions, the performance is considerably degraded as the number of hop counts is increased. In order to sustain the performance degradation of connections with more hops, an *Rsv* (Wavelength Reservation) and a *Thr* (Protecting Threshold) methods are proposed in [2]. In the former method, a given



0-8186-7780-5/97 $10.00 © 1997 IEEE

number of wavelengths on each link is dedicated to connections with more hops while in the latter, the connections with shorter hops are assigned an idle wavelength only if the number of idle wavelengths on the link is at or above a given threshold. However, both methods degrade the overall network performance (i.e., call blocking probabilities averaged over all connections) due to the use of dedicated wavelengths for specific connections, which results in decrease of wavelength utilization. In this paper, we consider an *alternate routing method with limited trunk reservation* (a *limited alternate routing method* for short) in which connections with more hops are provided more alternate routes in proportion to the number of hop counts. By this method, we can expect the performance improvement of connections with more hops at the expense of larger blocking probabilities of ones with shorter hops, leading to improve a fairness among connections. Another notable feature obtained in our method is that overall network performance can also be improved as will be shown later.

A key issue in our method is how to determine the number of alternative routes dependent on the number of hop counts. In Section 2, we develop an approximate analytic approach for alternate routing methods including our proposed one. It is performed by extending an existing approach developed for the fixed routing [1, 2]. We then exhibit the effectiveness of our method by comparing with the conventional fixed routing and alternate routing, in which a fixed number of alternative routes is provided with every connection.

A wavelength assignment is a unique problem of optical networks. When the several wavelengths are available on the route, which one is better to be chosen for good performance? In our approximate analysis, we make an assumption that the wavelength is chosen randomly. However, in such a case, more call blocking tends to occur for later arriving connections with more hops. We can expect to decrease a call blocking probability by introducing the first–fit policy in which the available wavelength is always sought from the same wavelength on every route. By this policy, the connection with more hops can have more occasions to find the available wavelength on the route. In Section 3, through simulation experiments, we show that the routing method with first–fit wavelength assignment can slightly improve performance when compared to the one with random wavelength assignment.

Last, we investigate further performance improvement by introducing a dynamic routing. In this study, we focus on the combination of routing selection and wavelength assignment, which has not been paid much attention in the past literature. In the alternate routing, its route is determined by the predefined order. In the dynamic routing, on the other hand, its route and wavelength are determined by monitoring the global state of the network resources, more specifically the number of free wavelengths on all links. We will show the grade of performance improvement by our dynamic method in Section 4.

Finally, Section 5 presents our conclusions and future works.

## 2 Approximate Analysis and Performance of Alternate Routing Methods

### 2.1 Analytic Model

We introduce the following notations to describe our alternate routing method and its analysis.

(1) A network consists of $J$ links, each of which has $W$ wavelengths.

(2) By introducing $m_j$ for the number of idle wavelengths on link $j$, the network state can be represented as $\mathbf{m} = (m_1, m_2, \cdots, m_J)$. The state space is $\mathcal{M} = \{0, \cdots, W\} \times \cdots \times \{0, \cdots, W\}$.

(3) Any route $R$ is a subset of the link set $\{1, 2, \cdots, J\}$. The number of hop counts for route $R$ is denoted as $h(R)$.

(4) Denote $R_a^{(i)}$ for $i$ th route between source/destination pair $a$. In our model, it is assumed that every route for each source/destination pair does not share the same link in order to simplify description. The number $r(R_a^{(i)})$ of wavelengths is reserved for the route $R_a^{(i)}$. (See the next subsection for our routing method.)
Let $\mathcal{R}^{(1)}$ denote a set of primary routes. In alternate routing, let us denote $\mathcal{R}^{(i)}$ for the set of $i$ th routes. Further, we introduce $\mathcal{R}_j^{(i)}$ denoting the set of $i$ th routes that employ link $j$ . Moreover, $P_j^{(i-)}$ is introduced for representing the $i$ th route of route $P_j$ that employs link $j$ .

(5) In the analysis, we will assume that connection setup requests arrive at route $R_a^{(1)}$ following a Poisson distribution with rate $e_{R_a^{(1)}}$. The holding times of all connections are assumed to be exponentially distributed with unit mean.

### 2.2 Alternate Routing Method with Limited Reservation

An outline of our alternate routing method is performed when the connection setup request of the source/destination pair $a$ arrives.

(I) The following connection setup procedure is performed for routes $R_a^{(i)}, i = 1, \ldots, n_a$, where $n_a$ represents the number of routes provided for source/destination pair $a$.

(I-i) Determine the available number of wavelengths, $m$, for links on route $R_a^{(i)}$. If wavelength conversion is allowed, $m$ is the minimum number of idle wavelengths on the link on route $R_a^{(i)}$. If wavelength conversion is not permitted, on the other hand, $m$ is the number of idle wavelengths through all links on the route.

(I-ii) If the number of idle wavelengths is larger than the number of reserved wavelengths on $i$ th route, i.e., if $m > r(R_a^{(i)})$ for $m$ determined in Step (I-i), the connection is established using a wavelength selected randomly from idle wavelengths ($m$) on that route. If $m \leq r(R_a^{(i)})$, the connection is not accepted on route $R_a^{(i)}$ and next $(i+1)$ th route is examined.

(II) If the connection cannot be established on any route of $R_a^{(i)}, i = 1, \ldots, n_a$, the connection request is blocked.

### 2.3 Numerical Algorithm

Let $X_j$ be the random variable for the number of idle wavelengths on link $j$ in steady state. The corresponding density is denoted as

$$q_j(m_j) = \mathrm{P}(X_j = m_j), \qquad m_j = 0, \cdots, W$$

To make an analysis tractable, we assume that random variables $X_1, X_2, \cdots, X_J$ are independent;

$$q(\mathbf{m}) = \prod_{j=1}^{J} q_j(m_j), \qquad \mathbf{m} \in \mathcal{M}.$$

Furthermore, we assume that the interarrival time for the next connection setup request is exponentially distributed with parameter $\alpha_j(m_j)$ if there are $m_j$ idle wavelengths on link $j$ [5]. It follows that

$$q_j(m_j) = \frac{W(W-1)\cdots(W-m_j+1)}{\alpha_j(1)\alpha_j(2)\cdots\alpha_j(m_j)} q_j(0), \qquad m_j = 1, \cdots, W \tag{1}$$

where

$$q_j(0) = \left[1 + \sum_{m_j=1}^{W} \frac{W(W-1)\cdots(W-m_j+1)}{\alpha_j(1)\alpha_j(2)\cdots\alpha_j(m_j)}\right]^{-1} \tag{2}$$

We then determine the steady state probabilities $\{q(\mathbf{m}) : \mathbf{m} \in \mathcal{M}\}$ using the algorithm below.

(i) Choose $\alpha_j(\cdot), j = 1, \cdots, J$ arbitrarily for all links.

(ii) Determine $\{q(\mathbf{m}) : \mathbf{m} \in \mathcal{M}\}$ using Eqs.(1) and (2).

(iii) Calculate $\alpha_j(\cdot), j = 1, \cdots, J$ which will be described in the following subsection.

(iv) Calculate the blocking probability $L_a$ for all source–destination pair $a$ (see Eq. (3)). If new values of $L_a$ are converged to the older ones, the iteration is terminated. Otherwise go to Step (ii) for next iteration.

### 2.4 Determination of $\alpha_j(m_j)$ without Wavelength Conversions

We extend the analysis for fixed routing based on a reduced load approximation method in [1, 3, 5] to the alternate routing in all–optical switching networks. In this subsection, we show the case where wavelength conversions are not provided.

When the wavelength conversion is not allowed on the node, the same wavelength must be idle throughout the route for connection establishment. We introduce $u_i(m_j; P_j)$ which represents the probability that when the number $m_j$ of wavelengths is idle on link $j$, $i$ wavelengths are available on the route $P_j$ that includes link $j$. By letting the link set of $P_j$ be $\{j, j_1, j_2, \cdots, j_{h(P_j)-1}\}$, the probability $u_i(m_j; P_j)$ is given by the following equation [3].

$$u_i(m_j; P_j) = \sum_{m_{j_1}=0}^{W} \sum_{m_{j_2}=0}^{W} \cdots \sum_{m_{j_{h(P_j)-1}}=0}^{W} q_{j_1}(m_{j_1}) q_{j_2}(m_{j_2}) \cdots q_{j_{h(P_j)-1}}(m_{j_{h(P_j)-1}}) \times p_i^{h(P_j)}(m_j, m_{j_1}, m_{j_2}, \cdots, m_{j_{h(P_j)-1}})$$

where $p_i^n(\cdot)$ is determined by the following recursive relation [3].

$$p_i^n(m_{j_1}, m_{j_2}, m_{j_3}, \cdots, m_{j_n}) = \sum_{k=0}^{W} p_i^2(k, m_{j_n}) p_k^{n-1}(m_{j_1}, m_{j_2}, \cdots, m_{j_{n-1}})$$

$$p_i^2(x,y) = \begin{cases} \beta(x,y,i), & \text{if } x \geq i, \quad y \geq i, \\ & \quad x+y-i \leq W, \\ & \quad 0 \leq x, y \leq W \\ 0, & \text{otherwise} \end{cases}$$

The conditional probability $\beta(x, y, n)$ is the probability that there exist $n$ available wavelengths under the condition that $x$ and $y$ wavelengths are available on successive two links. From [1], $\beta(x, y, n)$ is given by

$$\beta(x,y,n) = \left(\prod_{i=1}^{n} \frac{y-i+1}{n-i+1}\right) \left(\prod_{i=1}^{x} \frac{x-i+1}{W-i+1}\right) \times \left(\prod_{i=1}^{x-n} \frac{W-y-i+1}{x-n-i+1}\right).$$

Now, we focus on some link $j$. By considering all primary routes traversing link $j$, the corresponding arrival rate of connection requests at link $j$ is given as

$$\sum_{P_j \in \mathcal{R}_j^{(1)}} e_{P_j} \left(1 - u_0(m_j; P_j)\right).$$

If link $j$ is included in some secondary routes, overflowing connection requests from the primary routes should also taken into account. Such a case takes place when $m_j > r(P_j)$ and contribution of such a rate becomes

$$\sum_{P_j \in \mathcal{R}_j^{(2)}} e_{P_j^{(1-)}} v_0\left(P_j^{(1-)}\right) \left[\sum_{k=r(P_j)+1}^{W} u_k(m_j; P_j)\right]$$

where

$$v_i(P_j) = \sum_{m_j=0}^{W} q_j(m_j)u_i(m_j;P_j).$$

If link $j$ is included in some tertiary routes, overflow rate from secondary routes becomes

$$\sum_{P_j \in \mathcal{R}_j^{(3)}} e_{P_j^{(1-)}} v_0\left(P_j^{(1-)}\right) \times \left[1 - \sum_{k=r(P_j^{(2-)})+1}^{W} v_k\left(P_j^{(2-)}\right)\right] \times \left[\sum_{k=r(P_j)+1}^{W} u_k(m_j;P_j)\right].$$

In a similar way, overflow rate can be also determined in the case where the route $P_j$ traversing link $j$ is $i$ th route. By introducing $r(P_j^{(1-)}) \equiv 0$, we have the following equation by collecting all the rates in the above.

$$\alpha_j(m_j) = \sum_{l=1}^{\max n_a} \left[\sum_{P_j \in \mathcal{R}_j^{(l)}} e_{P_j^{(1-)}} \times \left\{\prod_{n=1}^{l-1}\left[1 - \sum_{k=r(P_j^{(n-)})+1}^{W} v_k(P_j^{(n-)})\right]\right\} \times \left[\sum_{k=r(P_j)+1}^{W} u_k(m_j;P_j)\right]\right]$$

where $\max n_a$ is a maximum number of alternate routes provided for route $P_j$ traversing link $j$.

Finally, we derive the blocking probability. The probability that a connection cannot be established on the primary route $R_a^{(1)}$ is given by

$$\sum_{m_j=0}^{W} q_j(m_j)u_0(m_j;R_a^{(1)}).$$

By letting the above probability be $v_0(R_a^{(1)})$, the probability that the connection cannot be established on the secondary route is then determined as

$$v_0(R_a^{(1)}) \times \left\{1 - \sum_{k=r(R_a^{(2)})+1}^{W} v_k(R_a^{(2)})\right\}.$$

If $n_a$ routes are provided for some source/destination pair $a$, the blocking probability $L_a$ then becomes

$$L_a = v_0(R_a^{(1)}) \times \prod_{l=2}^{n_a}\left\{1 - \sum_{k=r(R_a^{(l)})+1}^{W} v_k(R_a^{(l)})\right\}$$

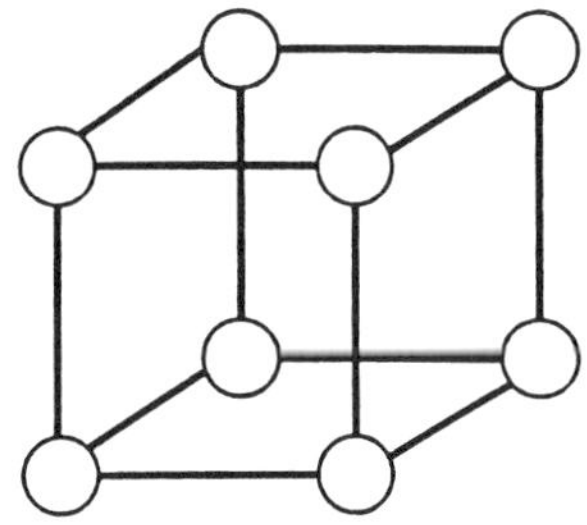

Figure 2: The network model (1)

$$= \prod_{l=1}^{n_a}\left\{1 - \sum_{k=r(R_a^{(l)})+1}^{W} v_k(R_a^{(l)})\right\}. \quad (3)$$

## 2.5 Numerical Examples and Discussions

In this subsection, we first assess the accuracy of our approximation approach. Then, numerical examples are provided to discuss the effect of the alternate routing method.

### 2.5.1 Assessment of Approximation

To assess the accuracy of the approximate analysis, we compare with simulation results by using the following model. The network model is depicted in Fig. 2 in which the bidirectional link connects two adjacent nodes. To clearly demonstrate the dependence of blocking probabilities on hop counts of routes, we limit generation of connection setup requests only at the source/destination pairs satisfying the following conditions.

(1) If there exists a 1-hop route between source/destination pair, it is used as the primary route. One of 3-hop routes is used as the secondary one (since we do not have 2-hop routes in this case). The tertiary route is not provided.
(2) If a smallest hop is two, it is used as the primary route. Another 2-hop route is used as the secondary route. The tertiary route is not provided.
(3) If the route with more than three hops is the shortest one, it is used as the primary route and the second and third shortest routes are used as the alternate routes. The forth route is not provided.

We note here that for brevity, the source/destination pair satisfying conditions (1) through (3) in the above are also referred to as 1-hop, 2-hop and 3-hop connections, respectively.

Alternative routes for each source/destination pair are set to have no common links. In simulation, the arrival rate, $e_R$, of connections setup request at all source/destination pairs are identical. Table 1 shows parameter sets we have used for comparison. In the table, the parameter, $r(R^{(i)})$, means that on $i$ th route of $h$-hop route, the connection is allowed to be established only if the number of idle wavelengths on the route is larger than $r(R^{(i)})$. The symbol "–" for $r(R^{(i)})$ shows that $i$ th route is not provided in the cases

Table 1: Parameter sets for comparison (1)

| | | $r(R^{(1)}), r(R^{(2)}), r(R^{(3)})$ | | |
|---|---|---|---|---|
| type | $W$ | for 1-hop | for 2-hop | for 3-hop |
| type 1 | 4 | $0, 4, -$ | $0, 0, -$ | $0, 0, 0$ |
| type 2 | 8 | $0, 2, -$ | $0, 0, -$ | $0, 0, 1$ |

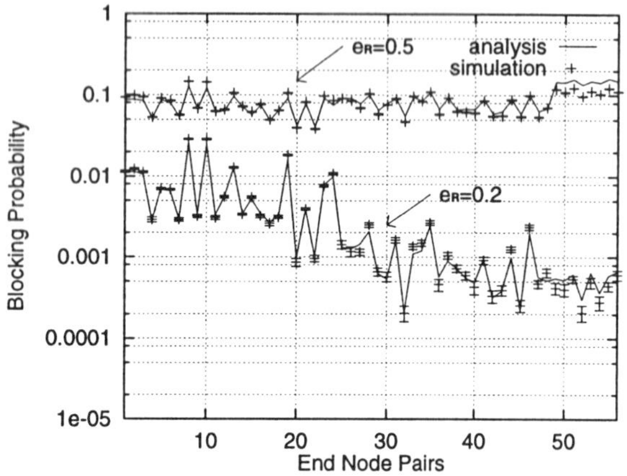


Figure 3: Comparison between analysis and simulation results (type 1)

of fixed and alternate routing methods.

Figures 3 and 4 present the results for different numbers of wavelengths, $W = 4$ and 8. The horizontal axis in the figures shows the index of the source/destination pair; indices from 1 to 24, from 25 to 48, and from 49 to 56, correspond to the source/destination pair satisfying the above conditions (1), (2), and (3), respectively. The vertical axis shows the blocking probability at each source/destination pair. In the approximate analysis, iteration is required and the convergence criteria was set to be $10^{-6}$ for the blocking probabilities. Simulation results are given with 95% confidence intervals. From two figures, we can observe that blocking probabilities of 3-hop connections obtained through the analysis are slightly overestimated than those by simulation. However, analytic results in other conditions are in good agreement with simulation results.

### 2.5.2 Numerical Results and Discussions

In what follows, we compare three routing methods based on our analytic approach. Connection setup requests only arrive at the source/destination pairs which satisfies one of conditions described in Subsection 2.5.1. Figure 5 depicts our network model, consisting of 16 nodes. Overall blocking probabilities (averaged over all source/destination pairs) and the blocking probabilities dependent on the hop count of the primary route are used as performance measures.

We employ the following routing methods for comparison purposes. Parameter sets for each routing method are shown in Table 2.

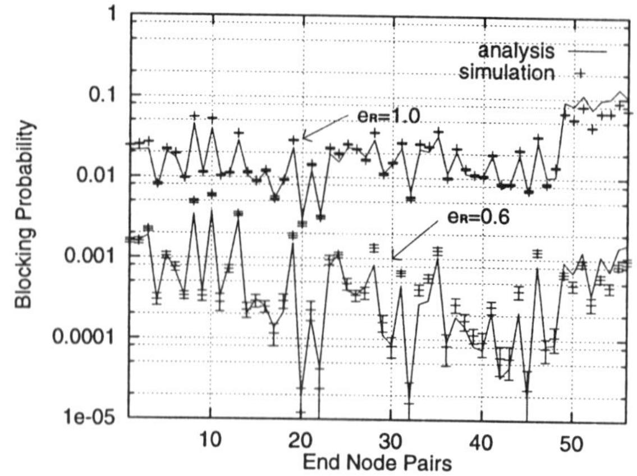


Figure 4: Comparison between analysis and simulation results (type 2)

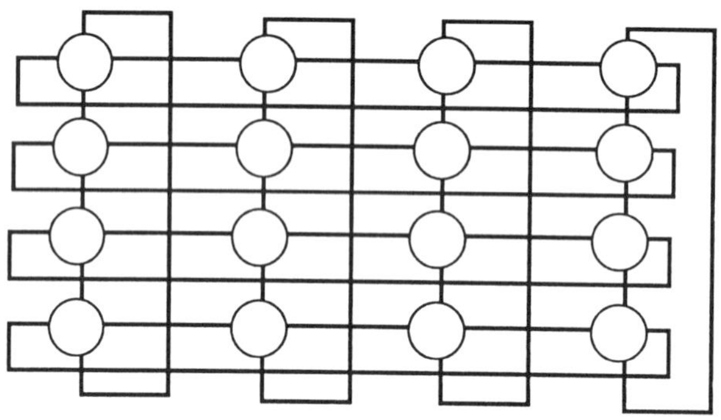

Figure 5: The network model (2)

(a) Fixed routing: no alternate route is provided.

(b) Alternate routing: two routes (one for the primary route and another for the secondary route) are always provided regardless of the number of hops of the route. When the primary (or secondary) route has at least one idle wavelength, the connection is established.

(c) Limited alternate routing: the number of alternate routes is controlled by parameter $r(R^{(i)})$. Its difference from ordinary alternate routing in the above is that 1-hop connections are less likely to be established on the secondary routes. Further, 3-hop connections are provided with the tertiary route while not in the alternate routing. We will use two sets of parameters (see (c-1) and (c-2) in the table).

Figures 6 through 9 correspond to the above four cases.

Table 2: parameter sets for comparison (2)

| | $r(R^{(1)}), r(R^{(2)}), r(R^{(3)})$ | | |
|---|---|---|---|
| Method | for 1-hop | for 2-hop | for 3-hop |
| (a)fixed | $0, -, -$ | $0, -, -$ | $0, -, -$ |
| (b)alternate | $0, 0, -$ | $0, 0, -$ | $0, 0, -$ |
| (c-1)limited | $0, 1, -$ | $0, 0, -$ | $0, 0, 1$ |
| (c-2)limited | $0, 2, -$ | $0, 1, -$ | $0, 0, 1$ |

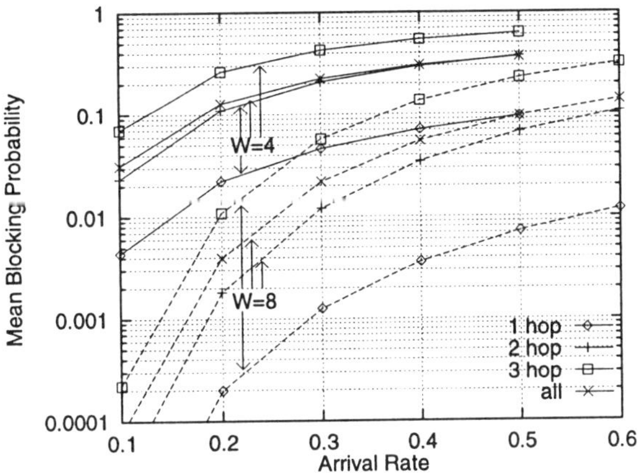


Figure 6: (a) fixed routing method

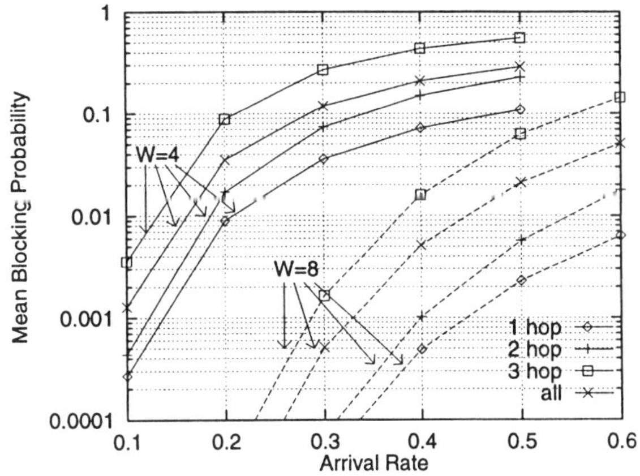


Figure 7: (b) alternate routing method

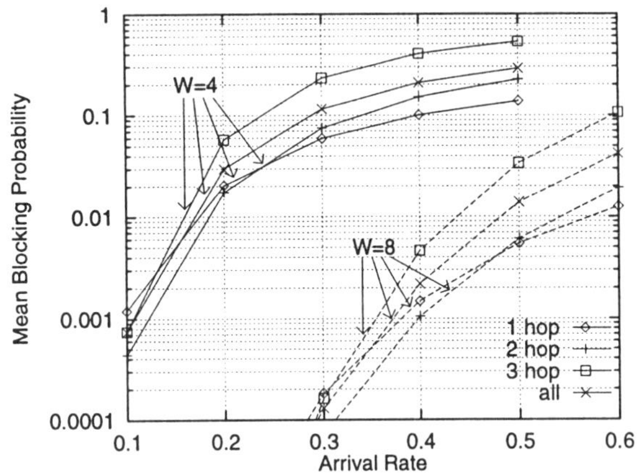


Figure 8: (c-1) limited alternate routing method

In the figures, we plot overall blocking probabilities as well as average blocking probabilities dependent on the number of hop counts to observe the fairness among connections. The arrival rates are identical among all source/destination pairs. In all figures, two cases for the number of wavelengths on each link are shown, i.e., $W = 4$ and 8.

Figures 6 and 7 show the analytic results of (a) fixed routing method and (b) alternate routing method, respectively. By comparing two figures, we can observe that blocking probability is improved by introducing alternate routes. However, in both routing methods, the differences in blocking probabilities between 1-hop and 3-hop connections are beyond an order of magnitude.

We next compare (b) alternate routing method (Fig. 7) and (c-1) limited alternate routing method (Fig. 8). As can be seen from the figures, our limited alternate routing method decreases an average blocking probability of 3-hop connections (labeled by "3-hop" in the figure) as expected. More notably, an overall blocking probability ("all") is also improved by limiting the call acceptance of 1-hop connections, which leads to more call establishments of 3-hop connections. As a consequence, our limited alternate routing method can improve the fairness among connections with different numbers of hop counts. This tendency is remarkable when the traffic load is low. The last figure (Fig. 9) shows that fairness can be further improved by adjusting parameters as shown in the row (c-2) in Table 2. This fairness property is established by less acceptance of 1-hop and 2-hop connections (i.e., $r(R^{(2)}) = 2$ for all 1-hop connections and $r(R^{(2)}) = 1$ for all 2-hop connections).

## 3 Effects of Wavelength Assignment Policies

In the previous section, we have assumed that the wavelength is randomly chosen if the multiple wavelengths are available on the route. However, a wavelength assignment is one of important issues in all–optical switching networks. In this section, we investigate the effect of following wavelength assignment policies by simulation.

(i) Random Assignment:
If a multiple number of wavelengths is available on the examined route between source/destination pair, the assigned wavelength is chosen randomly.

(ii) First–Fit Assignment:
The wavelength is assigned according to a predefined order [1]. In simulation, we assume that the wavelengths are indexed and the free wavelength with the smallest index is selected.

(iii) MaxWave Assignment [4]:
In the above two policies, the wavelength to be assigned is sought from the available wavelengths only on the predetermined (fixed or alternate) route. On the contrary, in the MaxWave policy, the wavelength is determined according to the usage status of wavelengths in the whole network. Namely, when a connection setup request arrives, the most used wavelength in the whole network is first selected. Then it is examined whether the selected wavelength is free on the route or not. If not, the secondly used wave-

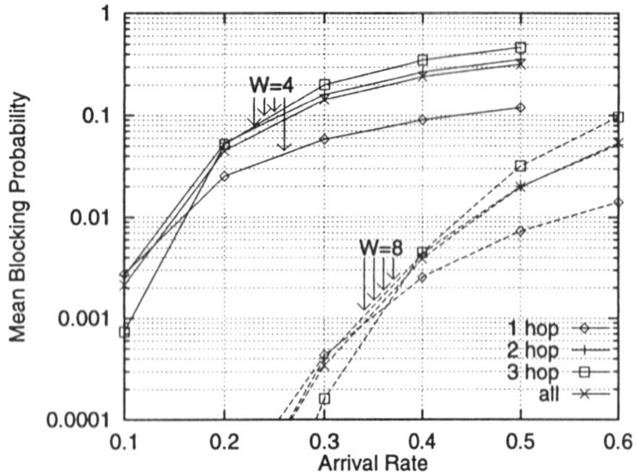


Figure 9: (c-2) limited alternate routing method

length is sought for a possible use to establish the connection, and so on. In this policy, the usage status of the wavelengths in the whole network should be maintained, which is different from the above two policies where the availability of the wavelength on the route is only examined. By the MaxWave policy, it is expected that some wavelengths with large indices are left unused in the network, which is likely to be used for the more hop connections.

In the current section, we treat this policy only for comparison purposes. A dynamic routing method which maintains the network global state will be further investigated in the next section.

Since the authors in [1] has compared random and first–fit assignment policies for fixed routing, our investigation in this section is devoted to the alternate routing method. We use the (c-1) limited alternate routing in Table 2 as the routing method, and it is applied to the network model depicted in Fig. 5.

Figures 10 and 11 show the simulation results for the random and the first–fit wavelength assignment policies. The result of the MaxWave policy is omitted due to space limitation. The number of connection setup requests at each source/destination pair during each simulation run is 100,000. By comparing the random and first–fit wavelength assignment policies, it is observed that the first–fit policy can improve the blocking probability of the connections with more hops (labeled by "3-hop" in Fig. 11) as one expects. However, it is very limited.

We also observe that performance of the MaxWave policy is very close to that of the first–fit policy. In the first–fit policy, the wavelength with the smaller index is likely to be used for the connection setup, and such a wavelength assignment policy is only applied to the selected route, not considering the usage of wavelengths in the whole network. However, we can observe from the figures that the wavelength assignment policy used in the first–fit policy is suffi-

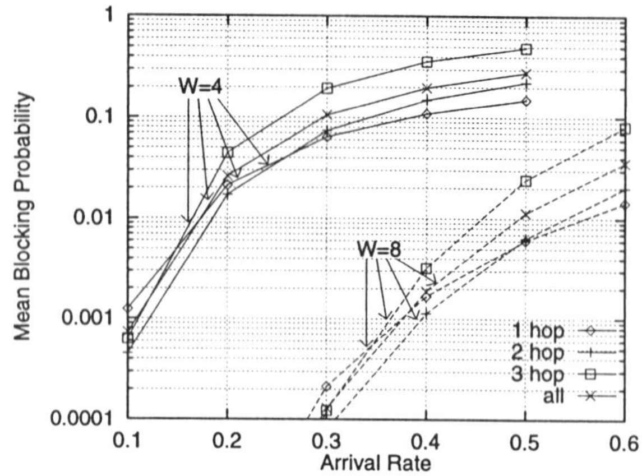


Figure 10: Blocking probability of (i) random policy

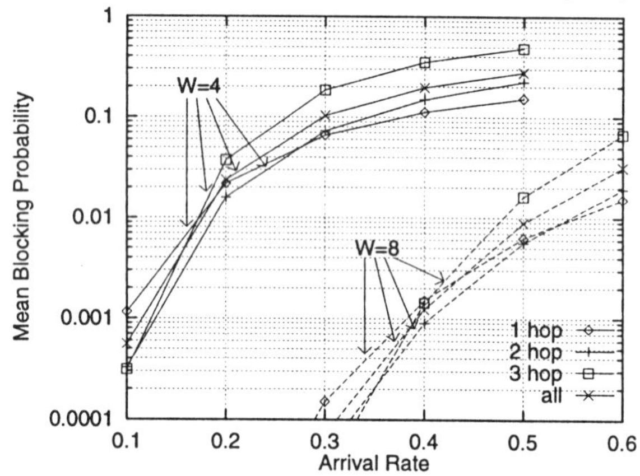


Figure 11: Blocking probability of (ii) first–fit policy

cient for the network model which we have tried. One point we should note here is that in the MaxWave policy, the order of routes examined for the wavelength assignment is preordered. In the next section, we will investigate the dynamic routing method in which the wavelength assignment and the routing determination are considered at the same time.

## 4 An Effect of Dynamic Routing

In the previous section, we have investigated the effects of wavelength assignments in the alternate routing method. In this section, we introduce the dynamic routing method in which the wavelength assignment as well as the route selection are determined according to the current global network status, i.e., the usage status of the wavelengths in the whole network. Since the dynamic routing requires the control overhead including the introduction of the center node which maintains the network global state, the main objective of the current section is limited to confirm how the performance can be improved by introducing such a dynamic routing method.

Basically, our dynamic routing method is an extension of the MaxWave policy mentioned in the previous section. The multiple routes are provided for each source/destination pair. Then, for each route, the number of free wavelengths is checked and selected in conjunction with the usage status of the wavelengths in the whole network. We introduce following notations to describe our dynamic routing method more specifically.

(i) For each wavelength $\lambda_i (1 \leq i \leq W)$, the number of links on which the wavelength is idle is counted, and it is denoted by $\beta_i$. A set of the wavelengths is represented by $\Lambda = \{\lambda_1, \lambda_2, \ldots, \lambda_W\}$ and a set of the corresponding number of links is denoted by $\mathcal{B} = \{\beta_1, \beta_2, \ldots, \beta_W\}$.

(ii) Let a set of routes provided for a source/destination pair $a$ be $\mathcal{S}_a = \{S_1, S_2, \ldots, S_{n_a}\}$ where $n_a$ is a number of routes on which a connection can be established for the pair $a$. A set of the corresponding number of hop counts is denoted by $\mathcal{H} = \{h_1, h_2, \ldots, h_{n_a}\}$. When the connection setup request arrives at the source/destination pair $a$, the number of free wavelengths on route $S_i$ is denoted as $\gamma_i$. Then, we have a set of $\Gamma = \{\gamma_1, \gamma_2, \ldots, \gamma_{n_a}\}$.

(iii) To determine the route and the wavelength, we have the number of idle links for each wavelength in the whole network ($\mathcal{B}$) and the information on each route. For the latter, we consider the available number of wavelengths ($\Gamma$) and the number of hop counts ($\mathcal{H}$). We then introduce a constant $\alpha_1$ $(0 \leq \alpha_1 \leq 1)$ and a function $\theta_j$ to represent the weighted sum of the above three variables;

$$\delta_{ij} = \alpha_1 \beta_i + (1 - \alpha_1)\theta_j(\gamma_j, h_j),$$

where the function $\theta_j$ is related to the local information regarding the possible routes for the source/destination pair $a$, i.e., $\theta_j$ is a function of the hop counts $h_j$ and the available number of wavelength $\gamma_j$. We then choose $\delta_{ij}$ with a smallest value to establish a connection using the wavelength $\lambda_i$ on the route $S_j$.

Note that when the hop count of each route is not taken into account, $\theta_j(\gamma_j, h_j)$ may be given as $W - \gamma_j$. Then, the smaller value of $\alpha_1$ gives a preference on the available number of the wavelength on the route. Or, we may set $\delta_{ij}$ as $\alpha_2 (0 \leq \alpha_2 \leq 1)$,

$$\delta_{ij} = \alpha_1 \beta_i + (1 - \alpha_1)\{\alpha_2(W - \gamma_j) + (1 - \alpha_2)h_j\}.$$

by introducing another constant $\alpha_2$ to incorporate the hop counts of the route. On the other hand, a larger value of $\alpha_1$ selects the wavelength which is more used in the network. As an example, we illustrate Fig. 12 where cases of $\alpha_1 = 0.25$ and 0.5 are shown. We further notice that $\alpha_1 = 0$ corresponds to the case where the usage status of wavelength in the whole network is not considered. In this case, the wavelength may be examined in the order of $\lambda_1, \ldots, \lambda_W$ which leads to the first-fit wavelength assignment policy presented in the previous section.

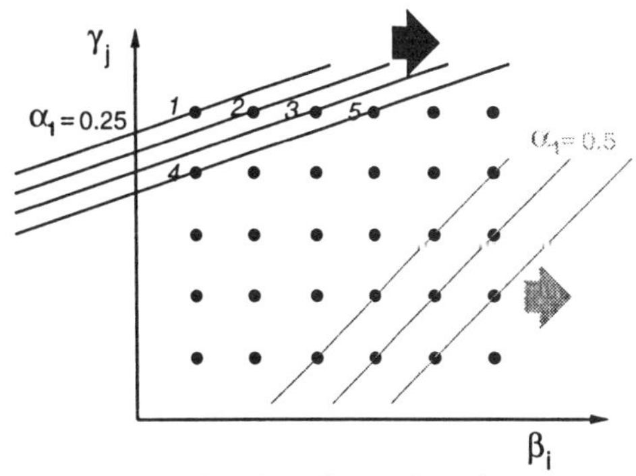

Figure 12: Selected order of wavelength and route in dynamic routing

The network performs the following steps at the connection setup request time for the source/destination pair $a$.

(I) Update the usage status of the wavelengths in the whole network $\mathcal{B} = \{\beta_1, \beta_2, \ldots, \beta_W\}$. However, if constant $\alpha_1 = 0$, this step is not performed.

(II) Evaluate the number of idle wavelengths $\Gamma = \{\gamma_1, \gamma_2, \ldots, \gamma_{n_a}\}$ on the route set $\mathcal{S}_a = \{S_1, S_2, \ldots, S_{n_a}\}$. If every route has no available wavelength, i.e., if $\gamma_1 = \gamma_2 = \ldots = \gamma_{n_a} = 0$, the request is blocked.

(III) Calculate $\delta_{ij}$ to order the set of routes and wavelengths. A smallest value of $\delta_{ij}$ is chosen to establish a connection using the wavelength $\lambda_i$ on the route $S_j$. If two or more sets of $\delta_{ij}$ are identical, then first choose the wavelength with the smallest $\beta_i$. If the order is not still determined, choose the route with the largest $\alpha_2(W - \gamma_j) + (1 - \alpha_2)h_j$ secondly. If it is impossible to establish the connection on the selected combination of the route and the wavelength, the next $\delta_{ij}$ is examined.

Now, we compare the dynamic and alternate routing methods. In simulation, the network model depicted in Fig. 5 is used to compare the alternate routing method using first-fit wavelength assignment and the above dynamic routing method. Simulation was run until 100,000 connection setup requests are generated for every source/destination pair. For the weighted function $\delta_{ij}$, we have used

$$\delta_{ij} = \alpha_1 \beta_i + (1 - \alpha_1)\theta_j(\gamma_j, h_j),$$

where

$$\theta_j(\gamma_j, h_j) = W - \gamma_j,$$

since the effect of consideration on hop counts was little in our model setting.

Figure 13 shows results dependent on the number of wavelengths on each link. In this case, $\alpha_1$ is set to be

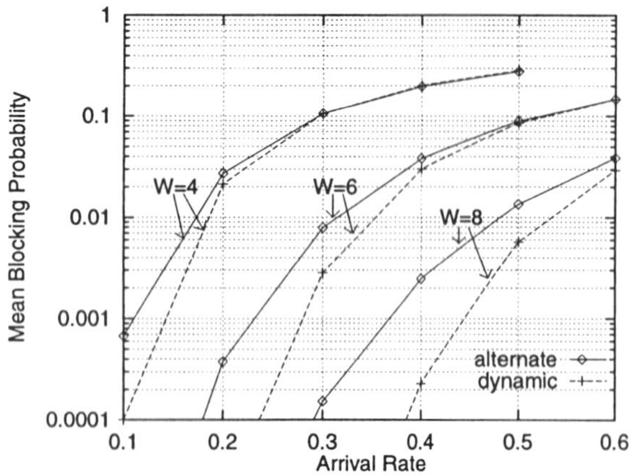


Figure 13: Comparison between alternate and dynamic routing

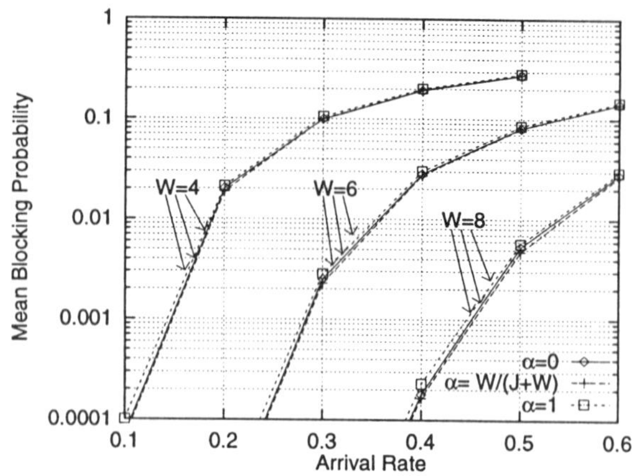


Figure 14: Performance of the dynamic routing dependent on $\alpha_1$

1. That is, $\mathcal{B}$ is considered to determine the wavelength, and the route is chosen according to the predetermined order. From the figure, we can observe that the dynamic routing outperforms the alternate routing as traffic load becomes low. The dynamic routing method also becomes efficient with the larger number of wavelengths. It is due to the fact that some specific wavelengths are likely to be idle by increasing wavelengths. It may conclude that if we have enough wavelengths on each link, the dynamic routing method can be useful. However, the effect becomes limited as the number of wavelengths is small, and in that case the alternate routing with the first-fit wavelength assignment is sufficient.

We next show results for three different values of constant $\alpha_1 = 0$, $W/(J+W)$, and 1 in Fig. 14. Recalling that $J$ represents the number of links in the whole network, the value $\alpha_1 = W/(J+W)$ corresponds to the case where both the number of idle links for each wavelength ($\mathcal{B}$) and the available number of wavelengths on each route ($\Gamma$) are equally weighted. Figure 14 shows that the equally weighted case ($\alpha_1 = W/(J+W)$) outperforms the other two cases, but the degree of performance improvement is very limited. That is, the dynamic routing is efficient, but a selection method of wavelengths and routes does not affect the performance with significant differences. Of course, such a conclusion cannot be drawn unless extensive evaluation is carried out using various network topologies, which should be a future research topic.

## 5 Concluding Remarks

In this paper, we have proposed a new class of alternate routing method in all–optical switching networks. We have developed a new approximate analytic approach for the alternate routing method including our proposed method. Numerical results have shown that our routing method can improve overall blocking probability as well as a fairness among connections with different numbers of hop counts. We have also investigated the effect of the wavelength assignment method. Performance improvement can be observed by introducing the first-fit method even for the alternate routing, but the network global information (i.e., the available number of wavelengths in the whole network required in the MaxWave method) is not necessary. The effect of introducing the dynamic routing method has also been investigated, showing that the dynamic routing method is efficient when traffic load is low or many wavelengths are prepared on the link.

In this paper, we have only shown results for one example network. More discussions are required for the various network configurations.

## References


[1] M. Kovačević and A. Acampora, "Benefits of Wavelength Tramslation in All–Optical Clear–Channel Networks," *IEEE J. Select. Areas in Commun.*, vol. 13, pp. 868–880, June 1996.

[2] A.Birman and A.Kershenbaum, "Routing and Wavelength Assignment Methods in Single–Hop All–Optical Networks with Blocking," *IEEE INFOCOM '95*, pp. 431–438, 1995.

[3] A. Birman, "Computing Approximate Blocking Probabilities for a Class of All–Optical Networks," *IEEE J. Select. Areas in Commun.*, vol. 13, pp. 852–857, June 1996.

[4] I. Chlamtac, A. Ganz, and G. Karmi, "Purely Optical Networks for Terabit Communication," *IEEE INFOCOM '89*, pp. 887–896, 1989.

[5] S.-P. Chung, A. Kashper, and K. W.Ross, "Computing Approximate Blocking Probabilities for Large Loss Networks with State-Dependent Routing," *IEEE/ACM Transactions on Networking*, vol. 1, pp. 105–115, February 1993.

# Performance of Multicasting Closed Interconnection Networks

Cathy W. Chan Soung C. Liew
Department of Information Engineering
The Chinese University of Hong Kong
Shatin, N.T., Hong Kong
*wcchan4@ie.cuhk.edu.hk, soung@ie.cuhk.edu.hk*

## Abstract

*This paper examines the application of a simple yet general packet replication scheme to achieve multicasting in closed interconnection networks. The performance of these networks is studied and a general throughput equation is obtained to express the overall network throughput in terms of the average routing delay of the corresponding point-to-point network. The multicast performance results are thus built on top of the previously-established, and often simpler, point-to-point results. Making use of this formula, we investigate the multicast closed shuffle-exchange network in detail. Analytical results are compared with simulation results to obtain further insights into the network operation and ways to improve the network performance.*

## I. Introduction

A simple way to perform multicasting in a closed interconnection network, such as the shuffle-exchange network and the Manhattan-street network, is to divide the process into replication and routing phases. The first phase generates the number of copies required by the multicast connection and the second phase routes the copies to the destinations. This two-phase approach has been widely used in constructing multicast packet switches by cascading a copy network and a point-to-point switch [1, 2, 3, 4]. In the closed network scenario, however, the same network is used to perform packet replication and routing simultaneously. Specifically, an input packet enters the network and duplicates itself in a "chain-reaction" manner until the required number of copies are generated. Each copy is then routed to one of the destinations of the multicast connection. Hence, the network appears to a packet as a copy network in the first part of its journey and a point-to-point routing network in the second. One can think of the multicast process as being divided into replication and routing phases in the time domain, rather than spatially as in the open network scenario.

In this paper, we consider closed multicast networks constructed by $2 \times 2$ switch nodes. In these networks, the network nodes are also the sources and destinations of the packets being transmitted. Each node consists of two components, a processor and a replication switch (Fig. 1). The processor is responsible for extracting arriving packets destined for the node and injecting new packets originating from it when unoccupied links are available. The replication switch performs packet duplication and routing depending on what packets arrive at it.

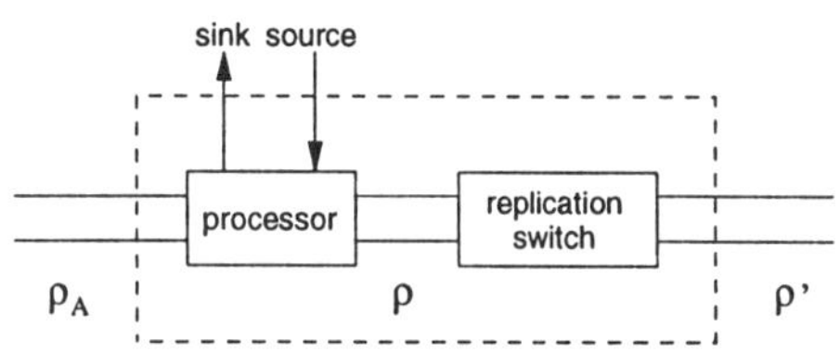


Figure 1: A $2 \times 2$ switch node.

Packet replication in the closed networks is performed by a simple replication scheme [4] applicable to arbitrary network topologies. Under this scheme, a replicating packet is duplicated at a network node if it is the only packet at the replication switch. Duplication is deferred to the next time slot otherwise. To implement this scheme, each packet has a copy-number ($CN$) field in its header. The $CN$ value is the number of copies that need to be further generated. When a packet first enters the network, its $CN$ value is initialized to its fanout request. Each time a replicating packet ($CN > 1$) is successfully duplicated, its



0-8186-7780-5/97 $10.00 © 1997 IEEE

$CN$ value is shared equally between the two resulting packets, one with $CN=\lceil K/2 \rceil$ and the other with $CN=\lfloor K/2 \rfloor$. When a packet's $CN$ value becomes 1, it enters the routing phase and is directed towards its final destination using the routing algorithm of the network. If two routing packets meet at the replication switch and desire the same output port, one of them is forwarded to the desired link and the other is deflected. If a routing packet meets a replicating one, the routing packet is forwarded to the link it desires and the replicating one to the other link. This is because replicating packets do not have specific destinations and can take arbitrary links. Finally, if two replicating packets meet each other, they are forwarded to the two outgoing links randomly. For both, duplication is deferred to the next node.

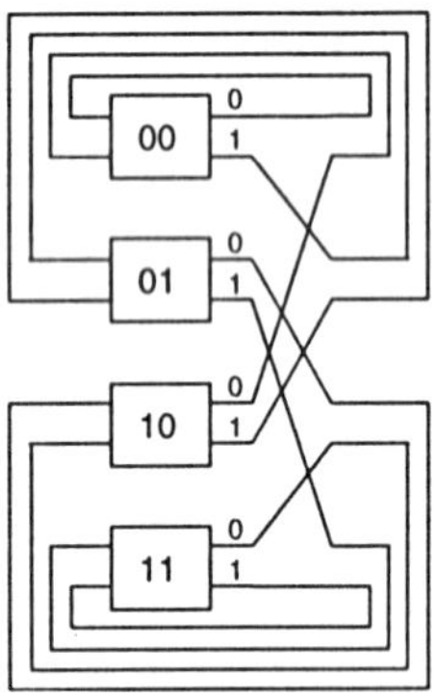


Figure 2: A 4-node closed shuffle-exchange network.

Figure 2 shows a four-node shuffle-exchange network that operates on a time-slotted basis. A spatial representation of the network operation over different times is given in Fig. 3 in which successive stages of the network represent the same network nodes but in successive time slots. Two multicast requests are shown as an example. Packet $A$ enters the network from node 10 at time slot 0 and three copies ($CN$=3) are to be delivered to nodes 00,01 and 11. It is immediately duplicated. The lower copy has $CN$=1 and starts routing at time slot 1, arriving at its destination at time slot 3. The remaining copy is further split into two copies which start routing at time slot 3 and arrive at their destinations at time slot 5. The other packet $B$ enters from node 11 at time slot 1 with $CN$=2. Its copies start routing at time slot 3 and reach their destinations at time slot 5.

This simple example shows that in closed networks,

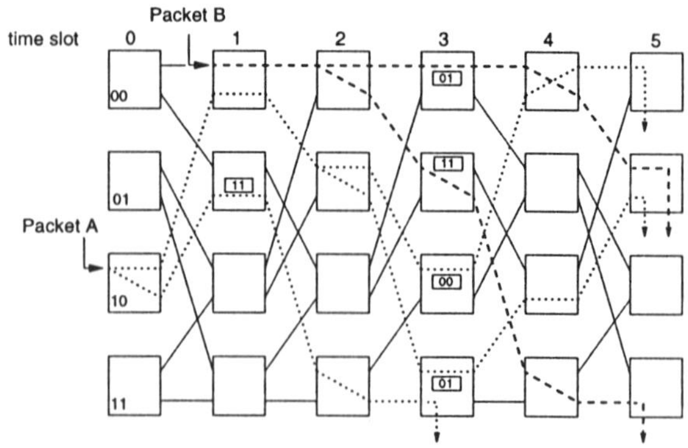


Figure 3: Applying the replication scheme to a closed shuffle-exchange network.

the replication phases of different packets and copies can be of different lengths. This is in contrast to the fixed replication time in the open copy networks [1, 2, 3, 4] in which every packet has to traverse all the stages of the entire copy network before they can be routed to their destinations. The flexibility in the replication time allows packets to start routing and exit the network as soon as possible, freeing more links for use by other packets.

Incorporating packet replication and routing in the same physical network results in more packet interactions and complicates the analysis of the multicast networks. We show in Section II that a general equation can be found to relate the overall network throughput with the average delay of the routing phase. The performance analysis of the multicast networks can then be built on top of the point-to-point routing analysis of the same network and it is much simplified. Based on these results, we study the multicast shuffle-exchange network in Section III and examine performance issues such as network stability and throughput penalty of the general multicast networks. Simulation results and their implications are shown in Section IV and the paper is concluded in Section V.

## II. General Throughput Equation

In this section, we derive a general equation describing the throughput of the closed multicast networks that are built on $2 \times 2$ switch nodes and operate on a time-slotted basis. The analysis can be extended to networks constructed by switch nodes of other degrees.

To simplify the analysis, we assume that the packets in the network are independent of each other and that the destinations of packets are distributed uniformly over all the nodes. These two assumptions are commonly used to simplify analysis of point-to-point routing in interconnection networks [7, 8] and their validity is generally accepted. We will adopt these assumptions in our analysis of the multicast network. Simulation results to be presented later show that these assumptions are justified.

Consider a network with $N$ nodes, each having the structure shown in Fig. 1. Let $\rho_A$, $\rho$ and $\rho'$ denote the link loading at each input of the processor, each output of the processor and each output of the replication switch, respectively. Furthermore, let $\overline{F}$ be the expected fanout of a packet and $\Lambda$ be the input load to the network, the average number of new packets entering the network per time slot. The average output load of the network is the expected number of routing packets reaching their destinations in a time slot and is equal to $\overline{F}\Lambda$. The relationship between these parameters can be obtained by inspecting the network operations in each time slot.

*Injection and removal of packets* : At equilibrium, in each time slot, there is on average a total of $2N\rho_A$ and $2N\rho$ packets entering and leaving the processors of the $N$ nodes, respectively. Since an average of $\overline{F}\Lambda$ packets arrive at their destinations and are removed, and an average of $\Lambda$ packets are introduced into the network at the processors, we have

$$2N\rho \quad = \quad 2N\rho_A - \overline{F}\Lambda + \Lambda \ . \qquad (1)$$

*Replication of packets* : At the output of the replication switch, there are either zero, one or two packets at the two links, depending on the number of packets at the inputs. If no packets enter the replication switch, no packets emerge at the outputs. If there is a single routing packet at the inputs, there is one packet at the outputs. There can be two packets at the outputs in two cases: either there are two packets at the inputs or there is one replicating packet only and it is duplicated in the switch. Let $P_r$ be the packet replication probability, the probability that a packet at the input link of the replication switch is a replicating packet. The expected number of packets at the two outputs of the switch is given by

$$\begin{aligned} 2\rho' \quad &= \quad 0 \cdot (1-\rho)^2 + 1 \cdot 2\rho(1-\rho)(1-P_r) \\ &\quad + 2 \cdot [\rho^2 + 2\rho(1-\rho)P_r] \ , \end{aligned}$$

which simplifies to

$$\rho' = \rho + \rho(1-\rho)P_r \ .$$

At equilibrium, all packets at the outputs of the replication switches are fed back to the inputs of the processors. Hence, $\rho_A = \rho'$ and (1) reduces to

$$P_r = \frac{(\overline{F}-1)\Lambda}{2N\rho(1-\rho)} \qquad (2)$$

which relates the packet replication probability at the input of the replication switch to the input load and the link loading of the network.

*Routing of packets* : At any replication switch, deflection occurs only if there are two packets present and they desire the same outgoing link. Since replicating packets are free to emerge at any node at the end of their replication process, they do not have any desired outgoing link at the replication switches. Thus, as far as routing and deflection is concerned, they can be ignored and only routing packets need to be considered. The routing phase, therefore, has link loading $\rho_s = \rho(1 - P_r)$, called the effective link loading, and throughput $\overline{F}\Lambda$. The routing delay is the delay incurred from the time a packet is generated from the replication process (and begins the routing phase) to the time it reaches its final destination. Denote the average routing delay by $D$. Applying Little's law on the routing process, we have

$$2N\rho(1-P_r) = \overline{F}\Lambda \cdot D \qquad (3)$$

Substituting (2) into (3) and rearranging gives the general throughput equation:

$$\boxed{\Lambda = \frac{2N\rho(1-\rho)}{\overline{F}-1+\overline{F}(1-\rho)D}} \qquad (4)$$

Equation (4) states that the input load $\Lambda$ (and hence, the throughput) of a multicast network at a given link loading is related to the network topology through the delay term $D$ only. For most networks, $D$ is a function of the network size $N$ and the effective link loading $\rho_s = \rho(1-P_r)$, which by (2), is in turn related to $\overline{F}$ and $\Lambda$. Thus, we can write

$$D = D(N, \rho, \Lambda, \overline{F}) \ . \qquad (5)$$

The exact expression of (5) can be obtained from the analysis of the point-to-point network. By solving it and (4) simultaneously, the network throughput at a particular link loading can be found. Although closed-form solutions may not always exist, the two equations can be solved numerically to obtain the performance of the multicast network.

## III. The Multicasting Closed Shuffle-Exchange Network

We have seen that the performance of the multicast network is related to its topology through the average routing delay of the network. This delay is determined by the routing algorithm, the specification of which includes how packets choose their outgoing links at a switch node and how output port conflicts between packets are resolved. We illustrate how the analysis is completed for the shuffle-exchange network in this section.

In a shuffle-exchange network with $N{=}2^n$ nodes, routing is performed by utilizing the destination address bits $d_n d_{n-1} \ldots d_1$ as the routing tag [5]. The routing tag specifies the preferred outgoing links of the packet as it traverses the network, starting from $d_n$ to $d_1$. When two packets at a node prefer the same link, one is chosen to be deflected to the unfavorable link and has to restart the routing process in the next time slot. Two strategies are commonly used in selecting the winning packet. The random contention resolution scheme chooses a packet randomly and the distance-priority scheme gives priority to the packet closer to its destination. It is known that the latter scheme improves the performance of the point-to-point shuffle-exchange network over the former in terms of achievable throughput and network stability [6, 7]. We will investigate whether this improvement carries through to the multicast scenario when these schemes are applied to the routing phase.

### A. Random Contention Resolution Scheme

In the $2^n$-node shuffle-exchange network, when contention is resolved by randomly deflecting a packet, the routing delay at link loading $\rho$ is given by [6]

$$D = \frac{1-(1-q)^n}{(1-q)^n q}$$

where $q{=}\frac{1}{4}\rho$ is the deflection probability of a routing packet. Recall that the link loading of the routing phase in the multicast shuffle-exchange network is equal to the effective link loading $\rho_s$. The average routing delay is therefore

$$D = \frac{1-(1-\frac{1}{4}\rho_s)^n}{(1-\frac{1}{4}\rho_s)^n \frac{1}{4}\rho_s} \tag{6}$$

The throughput of the multicast shuffle-exchange network at a particular link loading $\rho$ can be found by iterations. Initially, an arbitrary value is assigned to $\Lambda$. By (2), $P_r$ is found and $\rho_s$ $(=\rho(1-P_r))$ is substituted into (6) to obtain $D$. Finally, a new value of $\Lambda$ is computed using (4). This process is repeated until $\Lambda$ converges.

The results for such a multicast shuffle-exchange network with 256 nodes and an average fanout of 8 are shown in Fig. 4 and 5. Figure 4 plots the packet replication probability $P_r$ and the average routing delay $D$ against the link loading. In Fig. 5, the per-node throughput, or the average number of packets arriving at their destinations per node per time slot, is given by the average output load $\overline{F}\Lambda$ divided by $N$. The throughput of the same shuffle-exchange network used as a unicast routing network is shown in dashed line for comparison.

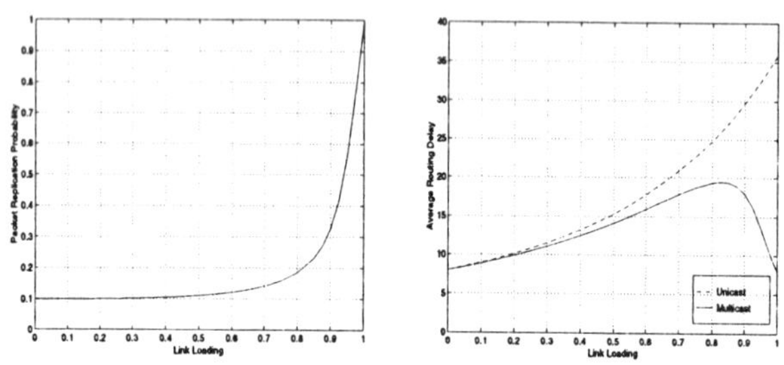


(a) (b)

Figure 4: (a) Packet replication probability and (b) routing delay of a multicast shuffle-exchange network using random contention resolution ($N$=256, $\overline{F}$=8).

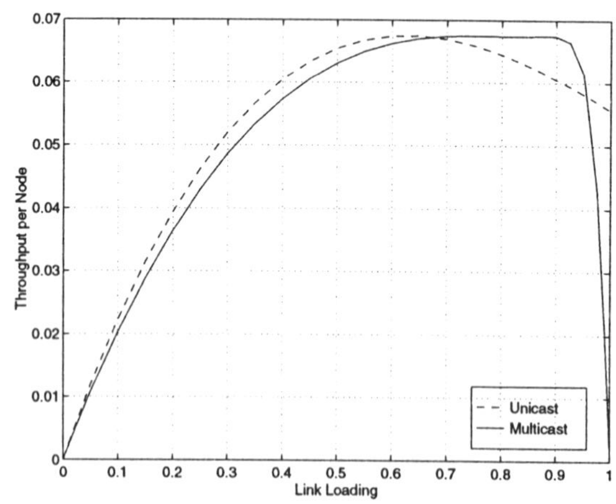


Figure 5: Unicast and multicast throughput of a 256-node shuffle-exchange network using random contention resolution.

At light load, the multicast throughput is very similar to the unicast throughput. In this region, there are very few packets in the network and replication processes are completed quickly. The fraction of replicating packets remains small (Fig. 4(a)). Hence, the multicast network behaves like a unicast network for $\rho \leq 0.6$.

As $\rho$ increases, the packet replication probability $P_r$ begins to increase with the link loading, giving rise to a smaller effective link loading $\rho_s$. For the same overall link loading $\rho$, there are actually fewer routing packets in the multicast network than in the unicast one. Contention between packets in the network is less severe in the multicast network and packets can be delivered with a smaller routing delay (Fig. 4(b)). Hence, the multicast throughput is higher than the unicast one.

When the link loading becomes very high, most of the packets in the network are replicating. Routing packets experience fewer conflicts and can reach their destinations in a shorter time. However, due to the large number of packets in the network, packet duplication is very difficult and the number of routing packets generated is small. On one hand, we expect the throughput to increase because of the smaller routing delay. On the other hand, we also expect the throughput to decrease because of the small number of routing packets in the network. The actual throughput is determined by the relative effects of the two opposing factors and, as indicated in Fig. 5, it is found to be decreasing with increasing $\rho$ in the high load region.

In the extreme case that the network is saturated, all packets in the network are replicating and none of them can have a chance to replicate or leave the network. These packets keep circulating in the network and no new packets can enter. This is a deadlock situation in that the overall status of the network remains unchanged over time. Since no routing packets can be obtained from replication, the saturation throughput of the network is zero.

The overall throughput of the multicast shuffle-exchange network is thus an increasing function of the link loading at light load and a decreasing function at high load. In general, for any networks, operation in regions in which the throughput decreases with link loading is unstable [6], meaning that any attempt to operate the network in such a region will evolve to a stable operating point either at the beginning or at the end of the unstable region. In our network, this stable operating point is the saturation point where the network is deadlocked: all links are occupied by replicating packets ($\rho$=1 and $P_r$=1) and the throughput is zero.

Note that this instability is not specific to the shuffle-exchange network but is a property common to all closed multicast networks that perform packet replication and routing in the same physical network. This is revealed by the throughput equation (4). The overall throughput of the multicast network is zero at $\rho$=0 and $\rho$=1. This requires the throughput to be an increasing function of the link loading in some regions and a decreasing function in others, in which the network would be unstable. This is independent of the value of the routing delay and hence, independent of the network topology and routing algorithm used. Consequently, the multicast networks can easily become deadlocked and useless when operating in the high load region. One possible solution for breaking deadlocks will be discussed in the next section.

Another performance issue we are interested in is whether adding multicast support to the closed networks results in any improvement or penalty in network performance in terms of the maximum achievable throughput. Intuitively, the introduction of the replication process uses up part of the network resources. It is impossible for the multicast network to have a better performance than the unicast network, which is purely responsible for routing packets to their destinations. This can be verified by observing that the overall throughput of the multicast network at a particular link loading $\rho$ is equal to the throughput of the embedded routing process with effective link loading $\rho_s=\rho(1-P_r)$. This routing throughput is in turn equal to the throughput of the same unicast network operating at $\rho_s$. Thus, the multicast throughput at any link loading must be achievable by the unicast network and the maximum multicast throughput must be smaller than (or equal to) the maximum unicast throughput.

Figure 5 shows that for the shuffle-exchange network, the maximum multicast throughput is approximately equal to the maximum unicast throughput. This indicates that the introduction of multicast connections does not result in any throughput penalty in the shuffle-exchange network that resolves conflicts by the random contention resolution scheme.

## B. Distance-Priority Contention Resolution Scheme

When output port conflicts in the shuffle-exchange network are resolved by the distance-priority contention resolution scheme, the network throughput and average routing delay are given by [6]

$$\Lambda = 2N\pi(1)\left(1 - \frac{\pi(1)}{4}\right),$$
$$D = \frac{2N\rho_s}{\Lambda} = \frac{\rho_s}{\pi(1)(1 - \frac{\pi(1)}{4})} \quad (7)$$

where $\pi(1)$ is obtained by iteratively solving the following recursive definition of $\pi(i)$ [6]

$$\pi(i) = \begin{cases} \pi(i+1) - \frac{\pi^2(i+1)}{4} & \\ \quad - \pi(1) + \frac{\pi^2(1)}{4}, & 1 \leq i \leq n-1 \\ \rho_s, & i = n. \end{cases} \quad (8)$$

When this routing delay is used in the iterations for computing the throughput of the multicast network, we obtain the results shown in Fig. 6. As before, the network has 256 nodes and the solid line shows the multicast throughput where the average fanout is 8 and the dashed line shows the unicast throughput. Compared with the random scheme, the distance-priority scheme can achieve a higher network throughput because of the reduction in routing time. This improvement is the same as in the unicast shuffle-exchange network. But unlike the point-to-point scenario, the multicast network remains to be unstable when the distance-priority scheme is adopted. This is in agreement with our previous observation that instability in multicast networks is independent of the routing algorithm and contention scheme used.

Figure 6 also shows that the maximum unicast throughput of the shuffle-exchange network using distance-priority contention resolution is achieved when the network links are all occupied by routing packets. Due to the presence of replicating packets, this can never be achieved in the multicast network. Hence, the maximum multicast throughput is smaller than the maximum unicast throughput. In general, throughput penalty results when the proportion of replicating and routing packets in the multicast network always gives rise to an effective link loading smaller than the link loading required to achieve the maximum throughput in the unicast network. For other networks, the introduction of multicast connections does not reduce the maximum achievable throughput of the network.

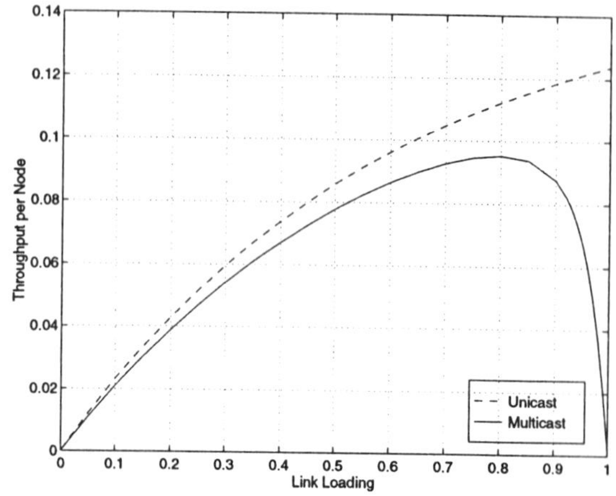


Figure 6: Unicast and multicast throughput of a 256-node shuffle-exchange network using distance-priority contention resolution.

# IV. Simulation Results

In this section, we show the simulation results for the multicast shuffle-exchange network. In our simulations, packets generated at each source node are stored at an input queue outside the processor. A packet is injected into the network if at least one of the output links of the processor is empty. At each time slot, a packet is generated at a node with probability $\Lambda_o/N$, where $\Lambda_o$, the total number of packets generated per time slot, is known as the offered load of the network. The offered load is varied to simulate the network under different link loadings. In each simulation run, statistics on the number of packets in and leaving the network is collected only after the network reaches equilibrium. These results are averaged to obtain the link loading and per-node throughput of the network on a per time slot basis. The throughput is plotted against the link loading and compared with the analytical results.

The fanout requests $F$ of the packets are truncated-geometrically distributed:

$$P\{F = k\} = \frac{(1-p)p^{k-1}}{1-p^{N-1}}, \quad 1 \leq k \leq N-1 \quad (9)$$

with average fanout

$$\overline{F} = \frac{1}{1-p} - \frac{(N-1)p^{N-1}}{1-p^{N-1}}$$

where the parameter $p$ is varied to generate the desired average fanout. We assume that no multicast connection requires copies to be sent to its source node so that the maximum fanout is $N$-1. The minimum fanout is one and corresponds to point-to-point routing packets.

The distribution of the destination addresses, on the other hand, is uniform. All nodes, except the source node, are equally likely to be chosen as one of the destinations of a multicast connection.

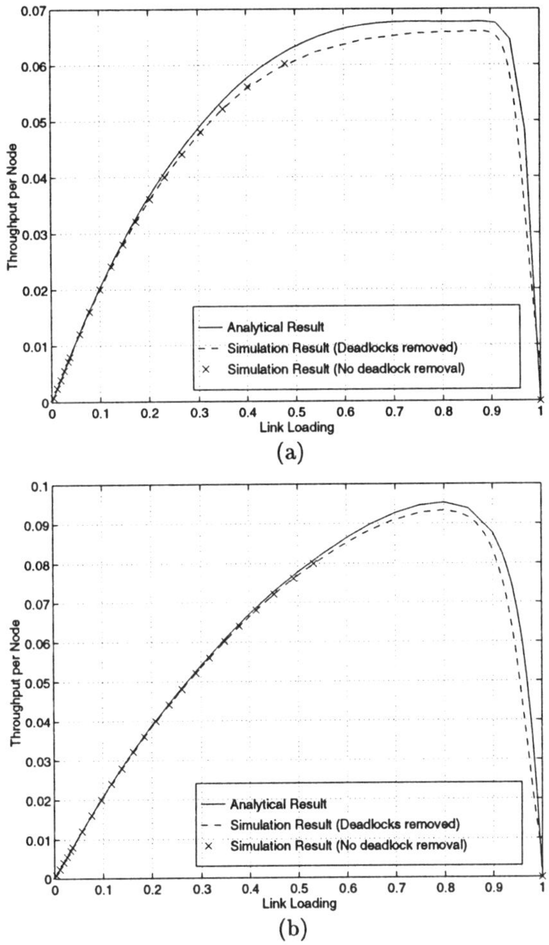


Figure 7: Simulation results of the multicast shuffle-exchange network using (a) random and (b) distance-priority contention resolution.

The simulation results for the multicast shuffle-exchange network are shown in Fig. 7. The crosses represent the results obtained from simulation and the solid lines are the analytical results. The throughputs achieved at small link loadings ($0 \leq \rho \leq 0.5$) agree with those predicted by numerical analysis except that the simulated values are slightly smaller than the analytical values. This discrepancy is due to the independence assumption used in the analysis. In simulations and actual implementations, packets may be correlated in such a way that there is a higher level of contention among them, causing the results to deviate slightly from the analytical ones.

As the multicast throughput approaches the maximum value (where $0.5 < \rho < 0.9$), no data points can be obtained. In this region, any slight variations in the offered load or throughput can easily shift the operating point to the negative-slope area ($0.9 < \rho < 1$), in which the network runs into saturation very quickly. Consequently, network operation cannot maintain equilibrium in either the "close-to-maximum" or the negative-slope regions and no data can be collected for $\rho > 0.5$.

To prevent the network from becoming useless due to deadlocks, we employ a deadlock-breaking mechanism in the network. An age counter is added to the header of each replicating packet. The age counter is incremented in each time slot, regardless of whether duplication is successful. When the age of a replicating packet reaches the lifetime limit $T_{max}$, the packet is discarded. In this way, old packets are removed and the links can be freed for duplication or injection of new packets. Hence, packet circulations are eliminated and deadlocks do not exist in the network.

The dashed lines in Fig. 7 show the results of applying this deadlock-breaking mechanism using $T_{max}$=40. At light loads, the results are similar to those obtained previously. When the network load increases, we are able to obtain results in the "unstable" regions. By removing some of the replicating packets and their embedded copies, the rate at which packets (and copies) leave the network is large enough to balance the rate at which they enter the network. Packet accumulation does not occur and the network can, therefore, operate at equilibrium in regions in which it was previously unstable. Thus, the network is now stable at all link loadings.

By varying $T_{max}$, it is found that the deadlock-breaking mechanism does not guarantee network stability. Figure 8 shows the results at different $T_{max}$. When the limit is small ($T_{max}$=10), the network throughput is much smaller than the analytical throughput. The replicating packets are removed so soon that many replication requests are not performed, leading to a smaller throughput than the network can achieve. On the other hand, when the limit is too large ($T_{max}$=200), the network becomes unsta-

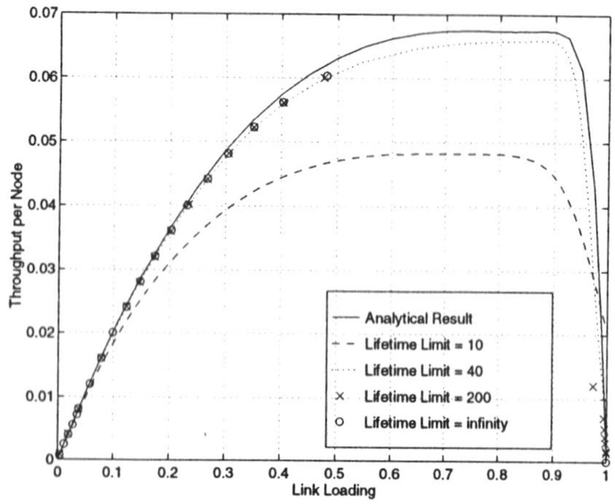


Figure 8: Simulation results of the multicast shuffle-exchange network using deadlock-breaking mechanism with different lifetime limits.

ble again. Because the replicating packets are allowed to stay in the network for too long, the network is easily saturated with replicating packets. Although the network is now deadlock-free (packets are removed from time to time), it cannot operate at equilibrium at the high load region. This is similar to when no lifetime limit is imposed ($T_{max}=\infty$). We conclude that the deadlock-breaking mechanism can stabilize network operation only when a suitable lifetime limit is chosen.

A final remark is that the deadlock-breaking mechanism is not a good solution to the instability problem due to inevitable packet loss. Discarding packets may lead to retransmission by the upper layers, thereby increasing the load of the network. Carefully designed access control schemes should be used to prevent instability while maintaining the performance of the closed multicast networks.

## V. Conclusions

In this paper, we have extended the general packet replication algorithm to closed interconnection networks. We showed that the performance of this kind of multicasting networks can be summarized by a general throughput equation. With this equation, any closed multicast networks can be analyzed based on the analysis of point-to-point routing in the network. We investigated the closed shuffle-exchange network using this method as well as by simulation. By comparing the results, we addressed some performance issues of the closed multicast networks. An important property common to these networks is network instability which cannot be overlooked in the design of these networks.

## References


[1] T.T. Lee, "Nonblocking Copy Networks for Multicast Packet Switching," *IEEE JSAC*, Vol. 6, No. 9, Dec. 1988, pp. 1455–1467.

[2] A. Huang and S. Knauer, "Starlite: A Wideband Digital Switch," *IEEE GLOBECOM '84*, 1984, pp. 121–125.

[3] J.S. Turner, "Design of a Broadcast Packet Switching Network," *IEEE INFOCOM '86*, 1986, pp. 667–675.

[4] S.C. Liew, "A General Packet Replication Scheme for Multicasting with Application to Shuffle-Exchange Networks," *IEEE Trans. on Commun.*, Vol. 44, No. 8, Aug, 1996, pp. 1021–1033.

[5] D.H. Lawrie, "Access and Alignment of Data in an Array Processor," *IEEE Trans. on Computers*, Vol. C-24, No. 12, Dec. 1975, pp. 99-109.

[6] S.C. Liew, "On the Stability of Shuffle-Exchange and Bidirectional Shuffle-Exchange Deflection Networks," to appear in *IEEE Trans. on Networking.*

[7] A. Krishna and B. Hajek, "Performance of Shuffle-Like Switching Networks with Deflection," *IEEE INFOCOM '90*, 1990, pp. 473–480.

[8] A.G. Greenberg and J. Goodman, "Sharp Approximate Models of Deflection Routing in Mesh Networks," *IEEE Trans. on Commun.*, Vol. 41, No. 1, Jan. 1993, pp. 210–223.

# The Single Queue Switch

Massoud R. Hashemi    Alberto Leon-Garcia
Department of Electrical and Computer Engineering
University of Toronto
Email: alg@comm.utoronto.ca, hashemi@comm.utoronto.ca

**Abstract**

*In this paper we introduce a new approach to ATM switching. We propose an ATM switch architecture which: uses only a single shift-register-type buffering element to store and queue the cells; and within the same physical queue switches the cells by organizing them in logical queues destined to different output lines. The buffer is also a sequencer which allows flexible ordering the cells in each logical queue to achieve any appropriate scheduling algorithm.*

*This switch is proposed for use as the building block of large-scale multi-stage ATM switches and as the scheduler/controller for the RAM-based switches.*

*The single queue switch implements output queueing and performs full buffer sharing. The hardware complexity is low. The number of input and output lines can vary independently without affecting the switch core. The size of the buffering space can be increased by simply cascading the buffering elements to each other.*

**Keywords:** ATM; ATM Switch Architecture; Scheduling; QoS; RAM-Based Switches, Shared-Buffer Switches.

## 1 Introduction

The design of an ATM switch architecture with minimum possible hardware complexity and maximum possible performance in throughput, buffer usage, and quality of service parameters such as delay and cell loss, has been a challenge for the past few years. Output queueing, complete buffer sharing, and scheduling capabilities for a guaranteed quality of service, are considered as major characteristics to be achieved by a successful ATM switch [1, 2].

Output buffering guarantees maximum throughput and buffer sharing reduces the amount of buffering space, which means less hardware complexity and lower cost [3]. While many of switches use output buffering, not all of them achieve a high degree of buffer sharing. Full buffer sharing can be achieved in RAM-based shared-buffer switches, but it comes with a large overhead in terms of hardware complexity, to control the buffering mechanism and to keep track of the cells and the queues and also the free spaces in the buffer [4].

When it comes to queue scheduling, there is always inflexibility in implementing an arbitrary algorithm. The scheduling mechanism has to fit within the constraints of the hardware. Scalability is also another major issue. It is not always possible to increase the number of input and output lines easily without reconstructing the whole switch. Increasing the buffering space also is not an easy task in the switches.

In this paper we describe a new ATM switch architecture which achieves the above goals. The switch is output buffered and offers full buffer sharing without extra overhead. The number of input and output lines can vary without affecting the switch core. The buffering space can be increased by simply cascading the buffering elements. The switch has the flexibility to implement a variety of scheduling algorithms.

This architecture is based on the cell sequencer architecture which we introduced in [13]. In the sequencer, cells are stored and queued in a shift-register-type buffering element. The structure of the buffer allows the cells to travel in the queue while finding their appropriate places in the queue, based on their priority level, age, or any other consideration. In this way it is possible to distinguish groups of cells with some common characteristics as logical queues within the same physical buffer. So, it is possible to have several logical queues and to schedule the service among them by adding appropriate tags to individual cells of each queue. As a result, a selected scheduling algorithm can be implemented simply by translating the algorithm into an appropriate tagging method.

In this paper we extend the same architecture to introduce a new and totally different approach to ATM switching. We propose an ATM switch architecture which uses a single sequencer-type queueing buffer for all of the output lines. Cells destined for different output lines are organized in different logical queues



0-8186-7780-5/97 $10.00 © 1997 IEEE

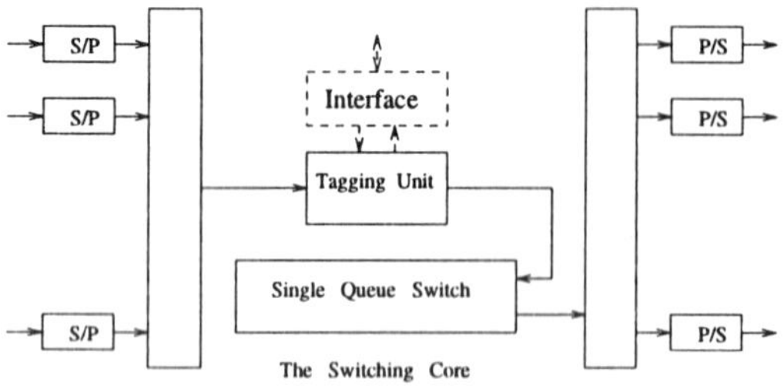


Figure 1: The single queue switch system

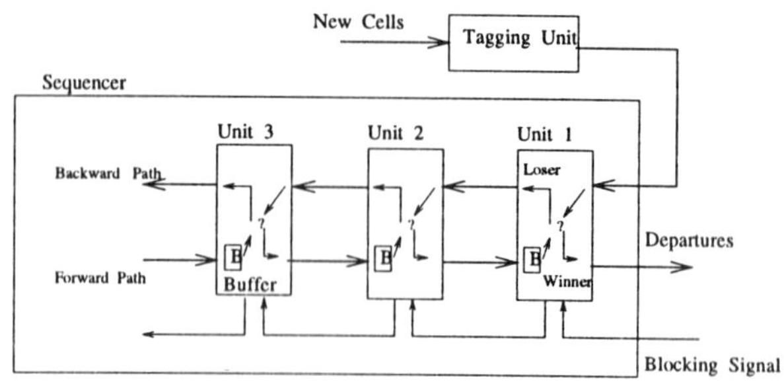


Figure 2: The sequencer architecture

within the same physical buffer. But, unlike the sequencer, these logical queues are interleaved into the single queue. Each of the logical queues can have other logical queues inside it as described in the sequencer.

Figure 1 shows the overall block diagram of the switching system. As mentioned above, the switch fabric is a single buffer only. Input lines are scanned and cells are transformed into parallel format, and sent to the tagging unit one after the other. The cells enter the single queue after being tagged. At the same time a departing cell leaves the queue and enters the output stage where it is directed to its output line in the serial format again.

Cells are inserted into the single queue one by one. This is similar to the RAM-based switch where the cells are written into the RAM one by one. This could become a bottleneck. In the RAM-based switch the speedup required to overcome this bottleneck is achieved by handling the cells in parallel format [5]. The same approach is used in the single queue switch to write the cells into the buffer.

A major characteristic of this new switch is its simplicity. The core hardware of the switch is just a shift-register-type buffering element. The buffering element has a modular structure and is composed of a collection of an arbitrary number of simple 1-cell-size buffering units which contain a very simple logic part.

There are two other sorting circuits presented in the literature, by Chao [6] and Roberts [7]. The first architecture cannot be transformed into a single queue switch because of the different approach used for sorting the cells which is based on bus structure. The second architecture logically provides the same function as our sequencer and can be modified to be used as a single queue switch using the algorithm introduced in this paper.

Full buffer sharing for output queues can be achieved using a searchable queue [8, 9, 10]. In these architectures all of the incoming cells are put in a shared buffer in a FIFO order, and a common search engine is used to find the first cell of each output line at each cell-time using a common bus. The mechanism is quite different from the single queue concept and achieves none of its goals except for the buffer sharing. Especially, scheduling is hardware dependent and is restricted to a limited number of static priority levels.

In the following we will first review the sequencer architecture. The single queue switch architecture and the switching mechanism will be introduced in detail in section 3. Both simple FIFO queueing and priority-based queueing will be presented. In section 4 we will discuss the buffer sharing, scalability, and finally the complexity of the switch. We will explain the application of the switch in large-scale multi-stage switches and also RAM-based switches in section 5.

## 2 The sequencer architecture

The single queue switch architecture is based on the sequencer architecture described in [13]. The following is a brief review of the sequencer architecture and its function. The sequencer consists of a chain of buffering units. Each buffering unit can accommodate one cell. Cells can travel from one unit to the adjacent units in forward and backward directions (Fig. 2). A logic section inside each unit decides about the replacement and direction of the cells. At each cell-time a new cell enters the queue from the head of the queue. The cell is compared to the cell at the head of the queue and based on the logic section's decision, one of them is sent out as the winner. The other cell, the loser, is sent one step back inside the queue where it is compared to the cell in that unit. The winner is sent forward to occupy the unit at the head of the queue, and the loser is sent backward to the next unit in the queue. This procedure is repeated spreading

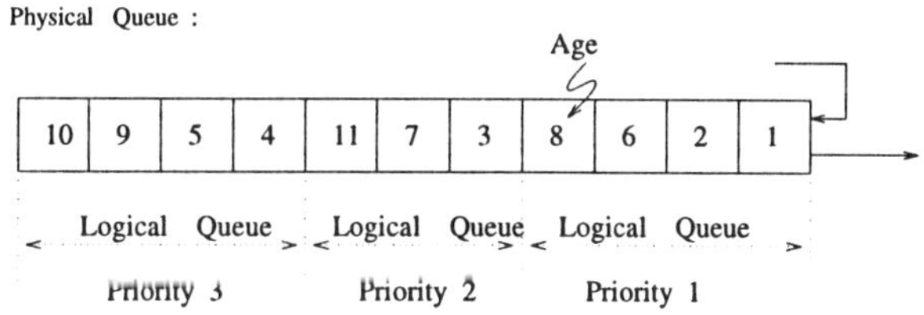


Figure 3: Priority based logical queues

into the buffer, like a wave, until it reaches the last unit. In this way, the winner of the unit $i$ is always forwarded to the unit $i-1$ ,( the forward path ), and the loser to the unit $i+1$, ( the backward path ).

Regardless of the situation of the travelling wave carrying the cell inside the queue, the next cell enters the buffer just after the previous one, generating a new wave. The events inside the sequencer are exactly synchronized. Therefore, whenever the new wave arrives at the unit $i$, the outcome of the previous wave is already in the unit and the comparison can start immediately. Each flying cell moves backward into the buffer until it finds its right place in the queue. The cell is inserted in that place, pushing the remaining cells one step back in the queue.

The logic section compares the cells based on the tag of each cell. Cells are tagged before entering the sequencer (Fig. 2). Tagging can be done in different ways to achieve different purposes. Scheduling can be achieved by means of tagging. The tagging criterion has to be derived from the desired scheduling algorithm which could satisfy the QoS requirements of the connections. For example, in a priority-based system cells can be tagged based on their priority levels. As another example, fair queueing can be achieved by using the virtual service time of each cell as its tag [11]. The tag can be composed of several distinct fields, each controlling a relative aspect in sequencing the cells. For example, age field can be used, in conjunction with the priority field, to arrange the cells with the same priority level, in the order of their ages (Fig. 3).

A blocking capability can be implemented in the sequencer, so that the cells can enter the queue even if there is no outgoing cell. To realize this capability,in case of blocking the winner in the comparison in each unit remains at the same unit instead of being forwarded to the adjacent unit. The loser is sent backward as before.

The basic achievement of the above architecture is

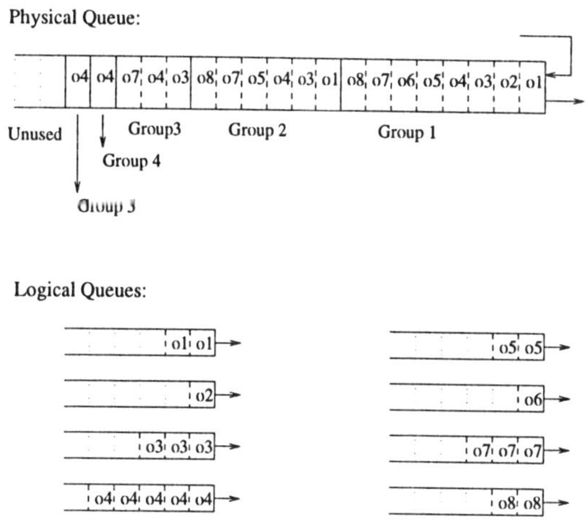


Figure 4: Grouping of cells for $N = 8$

the ability to have several logical queues within the same physical queue. In this paper we will explain how this capability can be extended to a new dimension, in which, we not only put the logical queues destined to the same output line in the same queue, but also merge the queues of different output lines into a single physical queue.

## 3 Single queue switch architecture Switching mechanism

As we saw before, the sequencer architecture has the capability of organizing the logical queues within the same physical queue. In our single queue switch architecture we use the same capability to interleave the queues of different output lines into the same physical queue. The interleaving mechanism is as following: The sequence of cells is divided into groups. Within each group, the cells of outputs 1 to N are placed in the first up to the Nth positions. The first group contains the first cell of each logical (output) queue. The second group contains the second cell of each logical (output) queue and so on.

The interleaved sequence of the cells seems very much like a TDM signal (Fig. 4). But unlike an ordinary TDM signal, in this sequence if the logical queue of one of the output lines has only $k$ cells, there will not be a reserved place for that output in groups $k+1$ and up. In this way, in each group only outputs which have cell for that group will occupy a place. But, this does not mean that new cells can not be inserted into the queue. For instance, in the above example, if a new cell comes in for the mentioned output, it will be inserted in the appropriate place in the group $k+1$,

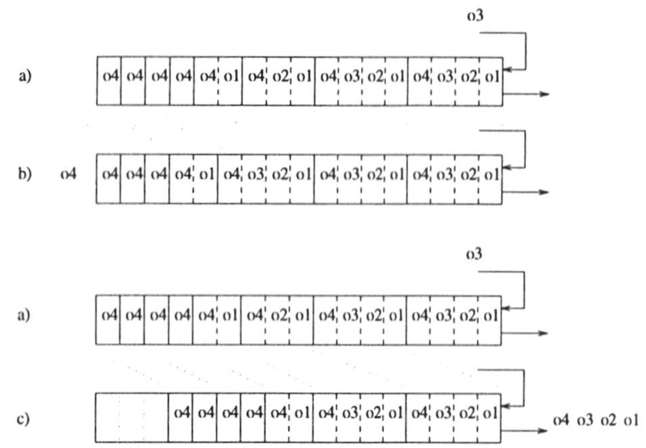


Figure 5: Cell insertion

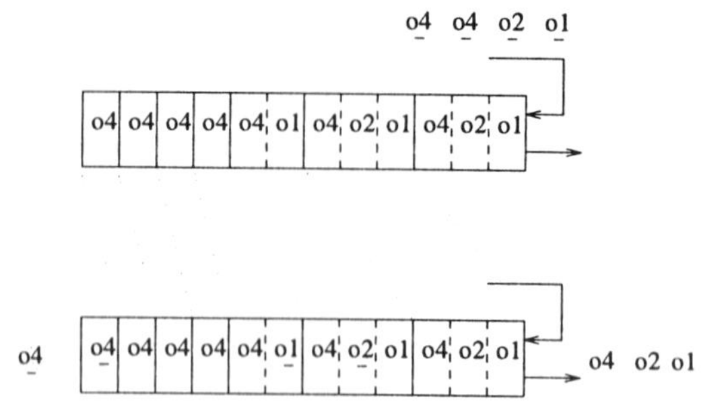


Figure 6: push out

pushing the rest of the cells one step back in the queue. Figure 5 illustrates this situation, assuming that the output is blocked for duration of one cell-time. If the queue has situation shown in (a), and a new cell for O3 (output number 3) comes in, the result will be as (b), while the last cell of O4 is pushed out because O4 has already occupied all the existing places in the buffer. Normally at each cell time each output with a non-empty queue will have a departure. As a result, one group will leave the queue at each cell-time. Therefore, the final situation in the above example will be as (c).

As a result, in this switch all of the buffering spaces are shared by all of the input and also output lines. Each unoccupied place in each group will be used by others. However, a newcomer cell destined for the output related to an unoccupied space will have priority to use the place. This cell will push the rest of the queue one step back in the queue. There will be a pushout only if: the physical queue is already full, the outgoing group is not full and the number of its cells is less than the number of newcomer cells at that time-slot, and the newly arriving cells do not include the missing cell in the outgoing group (Fig. 6). In case of priority-based queueing, the discarded cell will always be the one with the lowest priority.

## The function of the switch fabric

At this point we consider a switch with equal number of input and output lines (N), all of them with the same speed (Fig. 2). In the input side, the aggregate traffic of the input lines is given to the sequencer, where they are organized into the groups. With the above assumption, in the worst case there will be N newcomers in the queue in one cell-time. On the other side, the cells are sent to their related output lines using a synchronous round-robin scheme. The queue can have up to N departures at each cell time. This will happen only if the HoL group is full (a full group has one cell for each output line). If the group is not full, then one or some of the outputs will not be utilized during the time-slot. But still the group will be sent out during the same time. The output will be idle during the missing cells turns. Obviously, the queue will not move forward during the idle time but this will not harm the operation of the queue, because of the aforementioned blocking mechanism.

## Grouping mechanism

As was shown in the previous section, the grouping mechanism has the key role in extending the logical queueing mechanism from a single output queue to multiple output switch. In this section, we will explain how the cells entering the buffer are put in the groups. For simplicity, at this point we assume that the output queues are simple FIFO queues. In the next section we will extend the mechanism to priority-based queues.

Based on the operation of the sequencer which we explained earlier, each cell entering the sequencer carries a field in its tag which indicates the output line which is its destination. Each cell carries also two flag bits. Let's call these flags "X" and "Z".

The X flag of a cell in the queue indicates whether the cell is the last cell of a group or not. The groups are recognized and distinguished from each other by setting the X flag of the last cell of each group to "1". The X flag of a cell which occupies an empty unit is always set to "1". This in fact starts building the groups at the beginning or adding new groups later.

To explain the mechanism, we first consider a simpler case in which the order of the cells within the group is not fixed. We also assume that the queue is blocked. A newcomer cell always looks for the cells with the same address tag. Such a cell could be any-

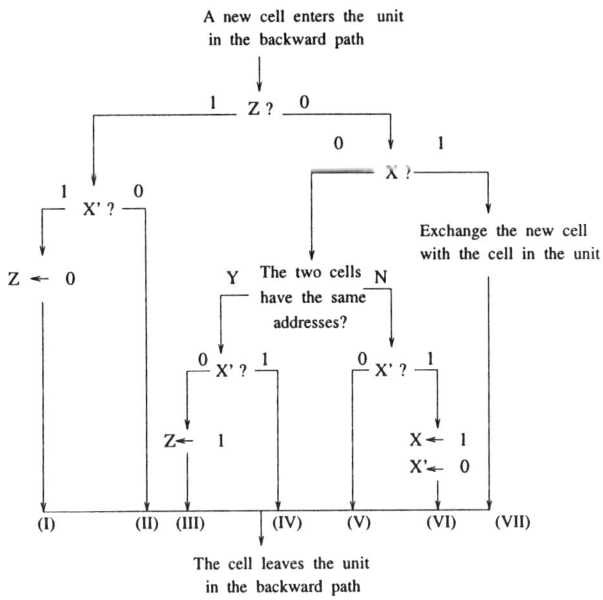


Figure 7: The comparison logic in the simplest case. The items with (') refer to the cell which is in the unit, the other items refer to the cell which enters the unit.

where in the group. Therefore, the cell examines all the cells in the group from the beginning of the group until it reaches a cell with the same address or the end of the group, whichever comes first. The cell always examines the X flag of the cells in the units to recognize the last cell of the group. If the cell meets a cell with the same address during its journey in the group, this means that it should continue its journey to the next group, to find the last cell of its related logical queue. The cell memorizes this, which is done by setting its Z flag to "1" (Figure 7, branch III), and continues its flight to the end of the group which is recognized by examining the X flag of the rest of the cells in the group (Figure 7, branch II). When the cell meets the cell with X flag set to "1" , it resets its Z flag to "0" and goes to the next unit which is the beginning of the next group (Figure 7, branch I). If the cell meets a cell with the same address which is the last cell of the group, it doesn't need to set its Z flag to "1" (Figure 7, branch IV).

If the cell meets a cell with a different address which is not the last cell of the group, it goes directly to the next unit (Figure 7, branch V). If the cell does not meet a cell with the same address in the group and reaches the end of the group, it means that the cell must stay at this group as the last cell of its related logical queue. In order to do this, the X flag of the last cell of the queue is reset to "0", and the X flag of the new cell is set to "1" instead (Figure 7, branch VI); Then the cell continues its flight to the next unit and stays at that unit as the last cell of the group, as well as the last cell of its related logical queue. To guarantee this operation, a cell with X=1 always occupies the unit (Figure 7, branch VII).

In this method, a new cell always enters the unit at the bottom of the first group without a cell for the same destination, and the cell in that unit , which is the first cell of the next group, is sent out and in a similar way eventually settles in the bottom of that group; and this procedure is repeated as a chain phenomenon until the end of the physical queue.

Now, we consider the case that the cells in the group are in increasing order from 1 to N, based on their destination addresses. This is necessary for the synchronous operation of the switch to prevent any extra latency at the output stage of the fabric. We still assume that the queue is blocked. In this case a flying cell not only looks for the cells with the same destination address, but also examines whether their address field is greater than its own address field or not. Since the addresses are in increasing order, if the cell with Z=0 meets a cell with a larger address first, it means that the cell must stay at that unit, as the last cell of its logical queue. The cell occupies the place sending out the cell in that place. This will start a chain phenomenon again which will push all the cells one step back.

In this method, if the cell meets a cell with the same address first , the procedure is as previous method; It sets the Z flag to "1", flies to the end of the group, and enters the next group while reseting the Z flag to "0".

Finally, we consider the case that the queue is not blocked (the normal case). In this case a new cell may enter the queue at the middle of a group (the HoL group). In order for the algorithm to be consistent, the "$Z$" flag of the cell entering the queue should be set to "0" or "1" respectively if the cell is entering the queue before or after the time-slot belonging to its related output line. This is done easily because the output stage of the switch operates synchronously and it has an assigned time-slot for each output line during which the cell destined for the output line departs or the queue remains idle ( blocked) if there is not such a cell in the group. The "$X$" flag must always be "0" when a cell enters the queue.

## Priority-based logical queues

The logical queues explained so far were simple FIFO queues. A newcomer cell in those queues was always put at the end of the logical queue. In this section we will show that priority based queueing can also be realized in this architecture.

In fact, despite the fact that all of the logical queues are interleaved in a single physical queue, according to the mechanism explained in the previous section, each logical queue can be virtually viewed as an independent queue built on an independent sequencer. And since the basic structure of the hardware backbone is the same as the sequencer structure [13] , briefly reviewed in section 2, we can easily implement the same functions as in the sequencer on top of the interleaving mechanism. So, let us assume that we have a single logical queue, with sequencing facilities (Fig. 2) . Now all we need is an appropriate tagging algorithm.

Obviously, the sequencing mechanism should take place after a flying cell finds the unit which belongs to its logical queue. We can summarize the whole procedure after a cells enters in a unit, as the following:

The address field of the cell is compared to the address field of the cell in the unit. If the two addresses are different the procedure continues as explained before. If the two addresses are the same, the priority fields of the two cells are compared to each other before any other action. If the flying cell is the loser, the procedure continues as before. If the flying cell is winner, it enters the unit and pushes its cell out, but at the same time their X, Y, and Z flags are exchanged. After this point, the situation is similar to the one in the previous section. So, the same procedures happen again.

The whole procedure is summarized in table 1. In the table, the items with (') refer to the cell which is in the unit. Rows number 8 and 9 are required only in the priority based queueing. Row number 10 is required only in the case that the cells in the group are in order.

| | Conditions | Action |
|---|---|---|
| 1 | Z=1 X'=0 | No change |
| 2 | Z=1 X'=1 | Z=0 |
| 3 | Z=0 X=0 A' < A X'=1 | X=1 X'=0 |
| 4 | Z=0 X=0 A' < A X'=0 | No change |
| 5 | Z=0 X=0 A' > A | Cell' ↔ Cell |
| 6 | Z=0 X=0 A'= A P' > P X'=1 | No change |
| 7 | Z=0 X=0 A'= A P' > P X'=0 | Z=1 |
| 8 | Z=0 X=0 A'= A P' < P X'=1 | Cell' ↔ Cell X,Z ↔ X',Z' |
| 9 | Z=0 X=0 A'= A P' < P X'=0 | Cell' ↔ Cell Z=1 |
| 10 | Z=0 X=1 | Cell' ↔ Cell |

Items with (') refer to the cell in the unit.
A: Address
P : Priority

Table 1: The complete logical function of the comparison unit

## 4 Specifications

### Buffer sharing

The single queue switch architecture allows full buffer sharing for the output queues. In this architecture, the buffering spaces are not dedicated or reserved for a specific queue. The buffer is filled from top to bottom. No space is left empty . When a new cell arrives, it is inserted in its right place and the rest of the queue is pushed one step back to use the next empty unit from the buffering space (Fig. 4 and 5).

Since the logical queues are filled independently, a shorter queue can grow independent of the situation in the other queues, as long as there are empty units in the buffer. If the buffer is full, a shorter queue still grows independently, but in this case other queues which occupy the rest of the physical queue, will lose their cells in the bottom of the queue. So we can conclude that the buffer sharing mechanism will show the push-out property if the buffer is full (Fig. 6).

In this way, there is a minimum guaranteed space available for each output, which its size is $B/N$ cells, where $B$ is the total buffer size and $N$ is the number of output lines. Each output queue can use free space on top of this number as long as the other outputs do not utilize their own shares of the buffer.

### The switch size (N)

The number of input and output lines in this architecture can vary independently. The core switch architecture is completely independent of the number of input and output lines, if the internal speed is high enough to carry excessive traffic. The only requirement is new modules at input and output stages.

The mechanism of grouping is independent of the number of input and output lines. Even though the length of the group will change if the number of output lines changes, the group size will be automatically adjusted to the number of the output lines.

### The buffer size (B)

The size of the buffer (max queue length) can easily grow by adding the number of buffering units in the switch. There is no impact on the operation of the switch. The maximum number of the units in each single chip switch would be limited by the technology used in manufacturing the chip. But still the buffer size can be increased by cascading the chips to each other. The structure is modular and the chips are cascadeable.

### Complexity

Fig 1 shows the overall block diagram of the single queue switch system. The input and output stages are required in all switching systems in various forms but with almost the same complexity. The tagging section is the only major difference in this switch. This section can be merged with the header translation section which usually uses a look up table RAM, by using a larger memory and extended header attachment. Additional processing is required to determine the tags dynamically for the cases that use complicated scheduling algorithms. As usual, the switching system relies on an attached computer, for required communication processes, as a controller. This controller, run by software, can program the tagging section based on the selected scheduling algorithm.

The core switching section of this switch, the sequencer, is very simple in structure in comparison to the other switches. The structure is modular and is composed of a chain of similar small units. Each unit is made up of a cell storage section and a logic circuit which controls the comparison operation. The logic section is not considered as a major factor, from the VLSI technology point of view. The storage section is a $W$-bit width shift-register-type memory whose length is $l/W$, in which $l$ represents the cell length and $W$ represents the width of the data path. The available memory technology can be customized to build the buffering section. Because of the simplicity of the hardware, including the buffering area which is the dominant part, single chip switch is feasible in this architecture. Later we will describe another version of the single queue in which the cell length and consequently the buffering area in each unit is much smaller, which further simplifies the hardware.

## 5 Applications

### Concentrator and expander

Since the core switch architecture is independent of the number of input and output lines, the switch can have different number of inputs and outputs . Therefore, it can be used as a concentrator or expander. As an example, assume that the number of input lines is $N_i$ and the number of output lines is $N_o$. The physical queue will have groups of $N_o$ cells. If $N_i = \alpha N_o$, and $\alpha = A/B$, where $A$ and $B$ are integer numbers, "$A$" groups will be built every "$B$" cell-times. If $N_i > N_o$, $A > B$ and the input traffic could exceed the output traffic if the line speed is the same.If the concentrator is used for statistical multiplexing, the speed of the output lines could be lower, based on the characteristics of the traffics. Otherwise, to be able to handle the worst case traffic, the speed of the output lines have to be $r_o = \alpha r_i$, $(\alpha > 1)$.

If $N_i < N_o$, then $A < B$ and the input traffic is always less than the output traffic if the speeds are the same. The output line speed can be as low as $r_o = \alpha r_i$, $(\alpha < 1)$, still being able to handle the worst case traffic.

### Multistage switching

Because of its simple structure and flexibility in handling different number of input and output lines, the single queue switch can be used as the building block of multi-stage switches. A wide range of configurations are possible and in each stage any group of lines can be selected to be handled by a single switch. Multi-stage switches can be used to handle larger number of input and output lines in cases that the number of lines is beyond the throughput limitations of the single queue switch.

If a priority-based scheduling scheme is used, the priority level of the cell is the same in all of the stages. Therefore, a single tagging section before the first stage of the switch is sufficient for the whole switch system. This further simplifies the structure of the multi-stage switch.

### RAM-based switches

The single queue switch architecture can be used as the centralized controller in RAM-based switches. In this case the original cells are saved in the RAM and the mini-cells are sent to the switch ( controller) instead. The mini-cells are composed of the tag of the cell and a pointer which addresses the original cell in the RAM ( Fig. 8).

The size of the buffer in each unit and the data path width are reduced to the length of the mini-cells. The advantage of the smaller size of the buffering section of the units is the feasibility of very large number of units in the buffer, since most of the area in each unit is covered by the storage section.

A major advantage of using the single queue switch as the queue controller in RAM-based switch is the capability to have any number of priority levels and the flexibility to use a wide range of scheduling algorithms while still benefiting from the RAM as the major storage resource in the switch. It is worth noting that in this new architecture illustrated in figure 8 , there is no need to have hardware which controls the virtual queues of chained cells for output lines or their priority levels. Usually a set of pointers and a linking mechanism is used for this purpose in RAM-based switches [12].

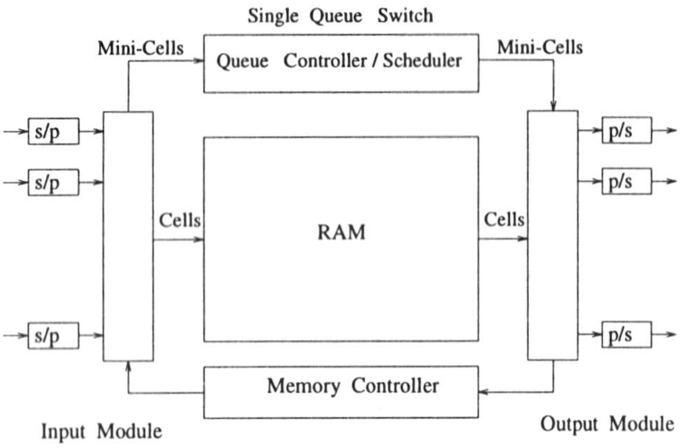


Figure 8: RAM-based ATM switch with the single queue switch as its controller

## 6 Conclusion

A new ATM switch architecture was described which is quite different from the architectures addressed in the literature. The core of the switch is a sequencer whose structure is similar to a shift-register. The sequencer can sequence the cells in the buffer based on a tag added to each cell prior to entering the buffer. In this paper we described a specific sequencing algorithm, called grouping, which changes the sequencer into a switch. This algorithm is controlled by two flag bits together with the destination output address bits which all are added to the tag of each cell. The queues of the cells destined for output lines ( output queues ) are interleaved to each other. Each output queue is independent of the others and all of the capabilities provided by a sequencer, such as priority based or other scheduling algorithms controlled by extra tag bits, are still applicable to them.

Besides the very simple and modular switching structure, the switch provides other unique characteristics: Full buffer sharing is experienced; The number of input and output lines can vary independently and without affecting the switching section; The buffering space can be extended by simply cascading the switching elements.

The architecture is proposed to be used as the building block of large-scale multi-stage switches and the controller/scheduler of RAM-based switches.

## References

[1] H. Ahmadi, *"A survey of modern high-performance switching techniques,"* IEEE Journal on Selected Areas in Communications, vol.7, no.7, pp.1091-1103, Sep. 1989.

[2] Y. Oie, T. Souda, M. Murata, D. kolson and H. Hiyahara, *"Survey of switching techniques in high-speed networks and their performance,"* Proc. INFOCOM'90, pp.1242-1251, 1990.

[3] M.G. Hluchyj and M.J. Karol, *"Queueing in high-performance packet switching,"* IEEE Journal on Selected Areas in Communications, vol.6, no.9, pp.1587-1597, Dec. 1988.

[4] A. Jajszczyk, M. Roszkiewicz, and J.Garcia-Haro, *" Comparison of ATM Shared-Memory Switches,"* Proc. ISS'95, PP. 409-413, 1995.

[5] K.J. Schultz and P.G. Gulak, *"Physical Performance Limits for Shared Buffer ATM Switches to the year 2005,"* Proc. ISS'95, PP.294-298, 1995.

[6] H.J.Chao, *"A Novel Architecture for Queue Management in the ATM Network,"* IEEE Journal on Selected Areas in Communications, vol.9, no.7, pp. 1110-1118, Sept.1991.

[7] J.W.Roberts, P.E.Boyer, and M.J.Servel, *"A Real Time Sorter with Application to ATM Traffic Control",* in Proc. ISS'95, pp. 258-262, 1995.

[8] H. Kondoh et al, *"A Scalable Nonblocking Shared Multibuffer ATM Switch with a New Concept of Searchable Queue",* in Proc. ISS'95, pp. 278-282, 1995.

[9] Y. Unekawa, et al, *"A 5 Gb/s* 8 × 8 *Switch Element CMOS LSI Supporting Five Quality-of-Service Classes with 200MHz LVDS Interface",* in Proc. IEEE ISSCC'96, pp. 118-119, 1996.

[10] K. Schultz and P. G. Gulak, *"CAM-Based Single-Chip Shared Buffer ATM Switch",* in Proc. ICC'94, pp. 1190-1195, 1994.

[11] A.K. Parekh and R.G. Gallager, *"A generalized processor sharing approach to flow control in integrated services networks,"* Proc. IEEE INFOCOM'93, pp.521-530, June 1993.

[12] H. Kuwahara, N. Endo, M. Ogino and T. Kozaki, *"A shared buffer memory switch for an ATM exchange,"* Proc ICC'89, pp.118-122, June 1989.

[13] M. R. Hashemi and A. Leon-Garcia, *"A General Purpose Cell Sequencer/Scheduler for ATM Switches,"* Proc. INFOCOM'97, Cobe, Japan, April 1997.

# Analysis of Queueing Displacement Using Switch Port Speedup*

**Israel Cidon**†
Department of Electrical Engineering
Technion - Israel Institute of Technology
Haifa 32000, Israel
cidon@ee.technion.ac.il

**Asad Khamisy**
SUN Microsystems Labs
2550 Garcia Avenue
Mountain View, CA 94043, U.S.A.
asad@eng.sun.com

**Moshe Sidi**‡
Department of Electrical Engineering
Technion - Israel Institute of Technology
Haifa 32000, Israel
moshe@ee.technion.ac.il

## Abstract

*Current high-speed packet switching systems, ATM in particular, have large port buffering requirements. The use of highly integrated ASIC technology for implementing high-degree and high-speed switch fabrics is facing a technology mismatch in the sense that today's chip technology does not allow to integrate on-chip the high-speed switching fabric with the large buffering requirements. Consequently, many designs are based on the principles of queueing displacement, i.e., they attempt to move the queueing point off-chip. This is usually done by considerably speeding-up the on-chip switch output ports and placing a second external stage of buffering between the switch fabric and the outgoing link circuitry. Such designs are very popular and are used by many current ATM switch vendors. While such schemes are widely used, no rigorous analysis has so far been offered to evaluate the design trade-offs and to quantify the design points.*

*The model we use to analyze the performance of the above system is a two-node tandem queueing system. The first node in the tandem corresponds to the internal buffer while the second node in the tandem corresponds to the external buffer. It is assumed that the internal buffer is capable to transfer $c_1$ cells per time unit to the external buffer, while the external buffer is served at a lower rate of $c_2$ cells per time unit.*

*The work of I. Cidon and M. Sidi was partially supported by Intel, Israel and by the Fund for the Promotion of Research at the Technion.

†also with SUN Microsystems Labs, 2550 Garcia Avenue, Mountain View, CA 94043, U.S.A.

‡Part of the work of this author was done while visiting SUN Microsystems Labs, Mountain View CA, U.S.A.

## 1 Introduction

This paper addresses basic design and performance issues in the architecture of hardware based fast packet switches. The ability to implement cost-effective high-speed switches in silicon is (along with the advance of fiber-optic technologies) the enabling technology behind the recent rise of broadband integrated networks, in particular the ATM architecture [1, 2, 3, 4, 5, 6]. Fast hardware based switches have also been at the core of the emerging switched LAN (also termed switching hubs) products as well as the new generation of Gigabit routers [www.bbn.com/magazine/techwatch/router.html].

Current switching system designs in high-speed packet-switching networks and in particular the emerging ATM market have large and consistently growing port buffering requirements. This trend follows the expected use of ATM networks for bursty data applications, the use of reactive flow control over ever increasing link speeds and the separation of different QoS classes and connection groups to dedicated buffers. While in the past ATM vendors have frequently offered switches with less than a hundred cell (5Kbytes) buffers, the numbers today have grown typically to more than 10K cell buffers. These numbers are expected to continue to grow with the speed of links, with the geographical distances, as well as with the use of more sophisticated buffer scheduling mechanisms. For example, Fore System [www.fore.com/html/products/datasheets/2famcamp.html] advertises buffer sizes of 53K cells (almost 3Mbytes) and 212K cells (11Mbytes) for its ASX-200 and ASX-1000 ATM switches, respectively.



0-8186-7780-5/97 $10.00 © 1997 IEEE

Cisco [www.cisco.com/warp/public/641/16.html] advertises 64K cells output buffers per link for its LightStream 2020 ATM switch. Stratacom provides 64K cells per port at its BPX switch [www.stratacom.com/products/bpxaxis.html]. The GTE [www.gte.com/Cando/Carrier/Docs/Wired/span4000.html] SPANet 4000 ATM switch is designed with a buffer size of 16K cells.

Most hardware based switch designs rely on the new generation of CMOS ASICs which are very popular within products which require fast turn-around and at the same time high integration and high performance. (Nevertheless, these following statements are also correct for today's fully custom VLSI designs.) The use of highly integrated ASIC technology for implementing high-degree and high-speed switch fabrics (8X8 to 32X32 with 155-622Mbps) is facing a technology mismatch in the sense that today's technology does not allow to integrate within the same ASIC the high-speed switching fabric logic of many ports with the large amount of fast memory required to buffer all switch output ports.

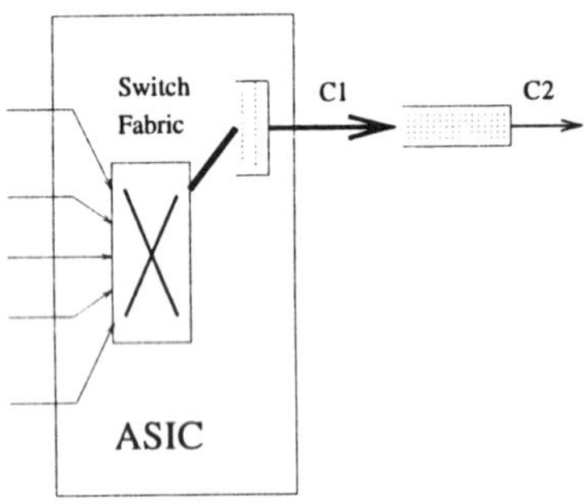


Figure 1: Speedup used to extend the memory in an ASIC based switch

Consequently, many designs are based on the principles of queueing displacement, i.e., the attempt to move the queueing point off-chip and implement the main buffer using standard RAM technology. This is usually done by considerably speeding-up the integrated switch output ports (compared to the actual link speed supported) and placing a second stage (external to the switch) of buffering between the switch fabric and the outgoing link. The much higher speed at which the internal buffer is off-loaded, considerably reduces its memory requirements for a given overflow probability design point. Such a design is very popular and is used by many current ATM switch vendors (usually termed as *speedup*). In particular, the ones which base their buffering design on output queueing techniques. (Other designs are also possible, for example, pure input queueing or a shared memory design based exclusively on off-the-shelf RAM.) Figure 1 depicts an ASIC with a limited on-chip buffer at the switching fabric being extended with an external memory using the speedup technique. For example, the IBM switch-on-a-chip Prizma chip is limited by the number of on-chip buffers and employs speedup technique [www.zurich.ibm.com/Technology/ATM/SWOCPWP] and [8]. Bay Networks, uses speedup in its Lattice Cell switch design to increase the effective amount of buffers in its multi-stage switching fabric.

While speedup schemes are widely used, no rigorous analysis has so far been offered to evaluate the design trade-offs and to quantify the design points. The designer would like to evaluate the size of the internal and external buffers required for a certain design point as well as the speed of the path connecting them together. In particular, it is attractive to map (or lower bound) such dual stage designs to the performance of an "ideal" output queueing design in order to be able to compare different switches of different design points. The following works have addressed the speedup problem or have used queueing models which are related to our problem. In [10], the speedup effect was explored using a tandem system model composed of an M/M/C queue feeding a dependent M/M/1 queue. This model was investigated by extensive simulation and no rigorous analysis was carried out for the speedup problem. In the relevant tandem queues models only limited results are available. In [9] a tandem of two single server discrete-time queues with independent and identically distributed external arrival processes, where the output of one queue is fed as an additional input for the other queue is solved. This is a special case of our solution when no speedup exists and the server can serve only a single cell at a time slot. In [11, 12] Boxma analyzes two exponential single server queues in series where the first queue has a Poisson arrival process and the second is fed by the output of the first. In both queues the same customers have the same service times. In this case, again, the system in question has no speedup. In [13] a tandem of multiple queues in which message sizes are preserved is considered. Several properties of the joint work load distribution (but no full solution) are presented and proved for such a system.

The model we use to analyze the performance of the system with speed-up is a two-node tandem discrete-time queueing system. The first node in the tandem corresponds to the internal (in-ASIC) buffer while the second node in the tandem corresponds to the external buffer. We begin the analysis of this system assuming that the external buffer can output at most one cell per slot and derive the generating function of the joint probability distribution of the lengths of the two buffers. Moments of the queue lengths are then derived. In addition, we introduce an explicit recursion to compute the joint probability distribution. From this we are able to compute tail probabilities that enable us to dimension the length of the buffers required to guarantee small loss probabilities when the buffers are finite. Speedup of two has special implementation importance as it is a very common and convenient speedup to design and use. It usually does not require tricky clock resynchronizations as either one clock is derived from the other or the path that connects the two buffer stages is of double width. Intuitively, with such speedup, the load on the first buffer stage is only half the load on the output port. In a well controlled network, no link should be overloaded (on the average) and hence the first port has a load limitation of 0.5. This rather low load should enable us to use very few buffers at the internal first stage. Our main numerical conclusion supports this intuition and shows that the internal buffer can be kept small without damaging the performance of the whole system. We extend the analysis to more general models in which the external buffer can output several cells per slot, and again obtain the generating function of the joint probability distribution of the lengths of the two buffers and the moments. The conclusions obtained are similar to the above.

## 2 The Model

The model we use to analyze the performance of the system with speed-up is a two-node tandem discrete-time queueing system. The first node in the tandem corresponds to the internal (in-ASIC) buffer while the second node in the tandem corresponds to the external buffer. Time is slotted into fixed size slots. It is assumed that during each slot the internal buffer is capable to transfer $c_1$ cells to the external buffer, while the external buffer is capable to output from the system $c_2$ cells. Since the internal buffer is faster than the external buffer, $c_1 > c_2$. Note that when $c_2 = 1$ we have integral speedups $(c_1 : 1)$, while for a general $c_2$ we can have any rational speedup $(c_1 : c_2)$.

Let $A_1^{(n)}$ and $A_2^{(n)}$ be the number of new cells arriving (from outside the system) during slot $n$ to the first node and the second node, respectively. The arrival process of these new cells at the system is assumed to be an independent and identically distributed (in each slot) process, namely, $\{A_1^{(n)}, A_2^{(n)}\}$ is independent of $\{A_1^{(k)}, A_2^{(k)}\}$ for any $n \neq k$, and $Prob(A_1^{(n)} = i, A_2^{(n)} = j) = a_{i,j}$ is independent of $n$. Let $A(z_1, z_2) = \sum_{i=0}^{\infty}\sum_{j=0}^{\infty} a_{i,j} z_1^i z_2^j$ be the joint generating function of the arrival processes to the two nodes. Note that arrivals to the two buffers in the same slot may be correlated. We let $r_l = \sum_{i_1=0}^{\infty}\sum_{i_2=0}^{\infty} i_l a_{i_1,i_2} = \partial A(z_1,z_2)/\partial z_l|_{z_1=z_2=1}$ be the arrival rate of cells to node $l$ $(l = 1, 2)$. For the sake of the analysis, we assume that both buffers are of infinite size. We will later discuss how this assumption can be dealt with to attain the performance of realistic switches. (Note that the speedup based output port system corresponds to the case with no external arrivals to the second node, i.e., $a_{i,j} = 0,\ j > 0$.)

## 3 Analysis

We begin our analysis with $c_2 = 1$, namely, a single cell can be transmitted by the second node and leave the system during a slot. Note that when $c_1 = 1$, our system is identical to the system analyzed in [9]. In our analysis we are interested in computing the steady-state probabilities of the lengths of the two nodes. Since at most one cell can leave the system during a slot, steady-state exists if $r_1 + r_2 < 1$.

Assume that departures take place at the end of slots and arrivals within slots. Let $Q_1^{(n)}$ and $Q_2^{(n)}$ denote the lengths of the first node and the second node at the end of slot $n$, respectively. Let $p_{i,j}^{(n)} = Prob(Q_1^{(n)} = i\ ,\ Q_2^{(n)} = j)$ and $G^{(n)}(z_1, z_2) = \sum_{i=0}^{\infty}\sum_{j=0}^{\infty} p_{i,j}^{(n)} z_1^i z_2^j$ be the generating function of the joint queue length distribution at both nodes. We let $p_{i,j} = \lim_{n\to\infty} p_{i,j}^{(n)}$ and $G(z_1, z_2) = \lim_{n\to\infty} G^{(n)}(z_1, z_2)$.

The evolution equation of the queue lengths for $n \geq 0$ is given by

$$\begin{aligned} Q_1^{(n+1)} &= (Q_1^{(n)} - c_1)^+ + A_1^{(n)} \\ Q_2^{(n+1)} &= (Q_2^{(n)} - 1)^+ \\ &\quad + \min(Q_1^{(n)}, c_1) + A_2^{(n)} \end{aligned} \quad (1)$$

From which we have in steady-state $(n \to \infty)$,

$$\begin{aligned} G(z_1, z_2) = A(z_1, z_2)\{p_{0,0} &+ \sum_{i=1}^{c_1-1} p_{i,0} z_1^i \cdot z_1^{-i} z_2^i \\ &+ \sum_{i=1}^{c_1-1}\sum_{j=1}^{\infty} p_{i,j} z_1^i z_2^j \cdot z_1^{-i} z_2^{i-1} \\ &+ \sum_{j=1}^{\infty} p_{0,j} z_2^j \cdot z_2^{-1} + \sum_{i=c_1}^{\infty} p_{i,0} z_1^i \cdot z_1^{-c_1} z_2^{c_1} \end{aligned}$$

$$+ \sum_{i=c_1}^{\infty}\sum_{j=1}^{\infty} p_{i,j} z_1^i z_2^j \cdot z_1^{-c_1} z_2^{c_1-1}\} \quad (2)$$

Simple algebraic manipulations yield the following,

$$G(z_1,z_2) = A(z_1,z_2)\frac{B(z_1,z_2)}{z_1^{c_1}z_2 - z_2^{c_1}A(z_1,z_2)} \quad (3)$$

where $B(z_1,z_2) = \sum_{i=0}^{c_1-1}[p_{i,0}(z_2-1)+g_i(z_2)](z_1^{c_1}z_2^i - z_1^i z_2^{c_1}) + G(z_1,0)z_2^{c_1}(z_2-1)$ and $g_i(z_2) = \frac{1}{i!}\frac{\partial G^i(z_1,z_2)}{\partial z_1^i}$ at $z_1 = 0$.

In (3), we encounter a common phenomenon in dependent queues, namely, that the generating functions $G(z_1,z_2)$ is expressed in terms of several boundary functions. In order to uniquely determine $G(z_1,z_2)$ we will have to determine the boundary functions, $G(z_1,0)$ and $g_i(z_2)$, $0 \le i \le c_1 - 1$. In what follows, we develop the method for obtaining these boundary functions. Along this process we mainly use the analytic properties of the generating functions $G(z_1,z_2)$ in the disk $|z_i| < 1$ , $i = 1,2$.

We begin by letting $z_2 \to 0$ in (2) to obtain $G(z_1,0) = A(z_1,0)[p_{0,0}+p_{0,1}]$. When $z_1 = 0$ we have that

$$p_{0,0} = a_{0,0}(p_{0,0}+p_{0,1}) \quad (4)$$

Therefore we can express $G(z_1,0)$ (and the corresponding probabilities $p_{i,0}$, $i \ge 1$) in terms of the constant $p_{0,0}$ as follows,

$$G(z_1,0) = A(z_1,0)\frac{p_{0,0}}{a_{0,0}} \;;\; p_{i,0} = a_{i,0}\frac{p_{0,0}}{a_{0,0}} \quad i \ge 1 (5)$$

To determine $g_i(z_2)$, $0 \le i \le c_1 - 1$, we use the fact that for any $|z_2| < 1$, the denominator $z_1^{c_1}z_2 - z_2^{c_1}A(z_1,z_2)$ of (3) has exactly $c_1$ roots within the unit disk $|z_1| < 1$ (the proof is based on Rouche's Theorem). Let these roots be denoted by $\sigma_l(z_2)$, $1 \le l \le c_1$. Since $G(z_1,z_2)$ is an analytic function in the disk $|z_i| < 1$ , $i = 1,2$, the nominator of (3) must vanish at each of these roots, i.e.,

$$B(\sigma_l(z_2),z_2) = 0 \quad , \quad 1 \le l \le c_1 \quad (6)$$

where in the above we use $p_{i,0}$ from (5) and $G(\sigma_l(z_2),0) = A(\sigma_l(z_2),0)p_{0,0}/a_{0,0}$. Expression (6) is a set of $c_1$ (linear) equations that determines the functions $g_i(z_2)$, $0 \le i \le c_1 - 1$ up to the constant $p_{0,0}$.

To complete the derivation of the generating function we need to compute that constant. To that end, let $z_1 = z_2 = z$ in (3) to obtain,

$$\begin{aligned} G(z,z) &= A(z,z)\frac{G(z,0)(z-1)}{z - A(z,z)} \\ &= A(z,z)\frac{A(z,0)p_{0,0}(z-1)}{a_{0,0}[z - A(z,z)]} \end{aligned} \quad (7)$$

Letting $z \to 1$ in the above and assuming that the steady-state condition $r_1 + r_2 < 1$ holds, we obtain by using L'Hôpital's law,

$$p_{0,0} = \frac{a_{0,0}(1 - r_1 - r_2)}{A(1,0)} \quad (8)$$

This completes the derivation of the joint generating function of the queue-length probability distribution.

Using the generating function we can obtain the average number of cells in node $i$ ($i = 1,2$), denoted by $L_i$. Letting $z_2 = 1$ in (3) we have

$$G(z_1,1) = A(z_1,1)\frac{\sum_{i=0}^{c_1-1} g_i(1)(z_1^{c_1} - z_1^i)}{z_1^{c_1} - A(z_1,1)}$$

Taking the derivative of the above expression with respect to $z_1$ and letting $z_1 \to 1$ we obatin,

$$L_1 = r_1 + \frac{\sum_{i=0}^{c_1-1} g_i(1)(c_1^2 - i^2) + r_1 - c_1^2 + \hat{A}}{2(c_1 - r_1)} \quad (9)$$

where $\hat{A} = d^2A(z,1)/dz^2|_{z=1}$.

Taking the derivative of (7) with respect to $z$ and letting $z \to 1$ we obatin (using (8)),

$$L_1+L_2 = r_1+r_2+\frac{dA(z,0)}{dz}|_{z=1}+\frac{\frac{d^2A(z,z)}{dz^2}|_{z=1}}{2(1-r_1-r_2)} \quad (10)$$

Subtracting (9) from (10) we obtain the average number of cells in the second node $L_2$.

## 4 The Probability Distribution

The joint generating function derived in the previous section allows us to compute $p_{0,0}$ and the average quantities easily. However, the computation of the probabilities themselves is difficult. In this section we develop a recursion for the computation of the steady-state probabilities $p_{n_1,n_2}$. From equation (4) we obtain $p_{0,1} = p_{0,0}(1 - a_{0,0})/a_{0,0}$. Together with equations (5) and (8) we have the initial conditions for the recursion, i.e., we know $p_{i,0}$, $i \ge 0$ and $p_{0,1}$.

Next, we compute the probabilities $p_{n_1,n_2}$ for $n_1 \ge 0$ and $1 \le n_2 \le c_1 - 1$ (except for $p_{0,1}$ that is known already). In order to have $n_2$, $1 \le n_2 \le c_1 - 1$, cells in the second queue, the number of cells in the first queue at the end of the previous slot have to be less or equal to $n_2$. Assume the number of cells in the first queue is $i$, $0 \le i \le c_1 - 1$, then in order to have $n_1$ cells in the first queue, all $n_1$ cells have to arrive from the external source. Further, assuming that $j$ cells arrive to the second queue from the external source, the total number of cells that arrive to the second queue is $i+j$. If the second queue is not empty at the end of the previous slot, then in order to have $n_2$ cells, the number of cells at the end of the previous slot have to be $n_2+1-i-j$, where the plus 1 accounts for the cell that must have departed the second queue. We have for $n_1 \geq 0,\ 1 \leq n_2 \leq c_1 - 1$ that

$$\begin{aligned} p_{n_1,n_2} &= \sum_{i=0}^{n_2} p_{i,0} a_{n_1,n_2-i} \\ &+ \sum_{i=0}^{n_2} \sum_{j=0}^{n_2-i} p_{i,n_2+1-i-j} a_{n_1,j} \end{aligned} \tag{11}$$

where the first sum corresponds to the case where the second queue is empty at the end of the previous slot. Note that $n_1$ appears in the right hand side of equation (11) only in $a_{n_1,l}$ for some $l$ (and does not appear in any of the $p$'s). In equation (11) we compute the probabilities $p_{n_1,n_2}$ in increasing order of $n_2$ as follows. We assume that $p_{i,j}$ for $i \geq 0,\ 0 \leq j \leq n_2 - 2$ as well as $p_{0,n_2-1}$ are known (initially, for $n_2 = 2$ this is true as explained at the beginning of this section). Next, we compute $p_{0,n_2}$, $p_{1,n_2-1}$ by solving two equations with two unknowns. These equations correspond to equation (11) with $p_{0,n_2-1}$ and $p_{1,n_2-1}$ in the left hand side. Note that the unknown $p_{0,n_2}$ appears only in the right hand side of (11), while the unknown $p_{1,n_2-1}$ appears also in the left hand side. After some simple algebra we obtain the solution for $p_{0,n_2}$, $p_{1,n_2-1}$ as,

$$\begin{aligned} p_{0,n_2} &= (\beta_{1,n_2}(1)a_{0,0} - \beta_{1,n_2}(0)(a_{1,0}-1))/a_{0,0} \\ p_{1,n_2-1} &= (\beta_{1,n_2}(0)a_{1,0} - \beta_{1,n_2}(1)a_{0,0})/a_{0,0} \end{aligned} \tag{12}$$

where we define

$$\begin{aligned} \beta_{1,n_2}(l) &\triangleq 1\{l=0\} p_{0,n_2-1} \\ &- \sum_{i=0}^{min(c_1,(n_2-1))} \sum_{j=1}^{n_2-i} p_{i,n_2-i-j} a_{l,j-1\{j=n_2-i\}} \\ &- \sum_{i=2}^{min(c_1,(n_2-1))} p_{i,n_2-i} a_{l,0} \qquad l = 0,1 \end{aligned} \tag{13}$$

Now the probabilities $p_{n_1,n_2-1}$ for $n_1 \geq 2$ are computed directly from equation (11). Recursing this procedure completes the computation of the probabilities $p_{n_1,n_2}$ for $n_1 \geq 0$ and $1 \leq n_2 \leq c_1 - 1$.

Next, we compute the probabilities $p_{n_1,n_2}$ for $n_1 \geq 0$ and $n_2 \geq c_1$. There are two cases to consider in the recursion, the first is when the number of cells in the first queue is less than $c_1$ in which case all cells move to the second queue, and the case where the number of cells in the first queue is greater or equal to $c_1$ in which case only $c_1$ cells move from the first queue to the second queue. Similar to the previous recursion, we have for $n_1 \geq 0, n_2 \geq c_1$,

$$\begin{aligned} p_{n_1,n_2} &= \sum_{i=0}^{c_1-1} p_{i,0} a_{n_1,n_2-i} \\ &+ \sum_{i=0}^{c_1-1} \sum_{j=0}^{n_2-i} p_{i,n_2+1-i-j} a_{n_1,j} \\ &+ \sum_{i=c_1}^{n_1+c_1} p_{i,0} a_{n_1+c_1-i,n_2-c_1} \\ &+ \sum_{i=c_1}^{n_1+c_1} \sum_{j=0}^{n_2-c_1} p_{i,n_2+1-c_1-j} a_{n_1+c_1-i,j} \end{aligned} \tag{14}$$

In the same way as before, we write two equations for $p_{0,n_2-1}$ and $p_{1,n_2-1}$, from which we obtain the probabilities $p_{0,n_2}$, $p_{1,n_2-1}$. Then we use equation (14) to compute the probabilities $p_{n_1,n_2-1}$ for $n_1 \geq 2$. The solution for $p_{0,n_2}$, $p_{1,n_2-1}$ in this case is given by:

$$\begin{aligned} p_{0,n_2} &= (\beta_{2,n_2}(1)a_{0,0} - \beta_{2,n_2}(0)(a_{1,0}-1))/a_{0,0} \\ p_{1,n_2-1} &= (\beta_{2,n_2}(0)a_{1,0} - \beta_{2,n_2}(1)a_{0,0})/a_{0,0} \end{aligned} \tag{15}$$

Where we define $\beta_{2,n_2}(0) \triangleq \beta_{1,n_2}(0)$ and $\beta_{2,n_2}(1) \triangleq \beta_{1,n_2}(1) + \sum_{j=0}^{n_2-c_1} p_{c_1+1,n_2-c_1-j} a_{0,j-1\{j=n_2-c_1\}}$. Now the probabilities $p_{n_1,n_2-1}$ for $n_1 \geq 2$ are computed directly from equation (14). This completes the computation of the probabilities $p_{n_1,n_2}$ for $n_1 \geq 0$ and $n_2 \geq c_1$.

The computation complexity of the probabilities $p_{n_1,n_2}$ for $0 \leq n_1 \leq N_1$ and $0 \leq n_2 \leq N_2$ is in the order of $O(N_1^2 N_2^2)$.

### 4.1 Overflow Probability

Since we use infinite buffers in our model, we approximate the cell loss probability by the buffer overflow probability. The first (second) node is in overflow state when the number of cells in the buffer exceeds $N_1$ ($N_2$).

If the state upon arrival is $(n_1, n_2)$, then the the number of cells in the second queue in front of this cell, when this cell arrives to the second queue, will be $n_1 + n_2 - \sum_{i=1}^{\lceil (n_1+1)/c_1 \rceil} A_2(i) - \lceil (n_1+1)/c_1 \rceil$, where $A_2(i)$ denotes the number of cells that arrive to the second queue in slot number $i$ (the slot of arrival of the cell is marked as slot number 1). This is true since 1. The cell will arrive at the second queue $\lceil (n_1+1)/c_1 \rceil$ slots after it arrived to the system, and 2. $c_1 > 1$ and hence the second queue will not empty in the next $\lceil (n_1+1)/c_1 \rceil$ slots after the arrival of this cell.

Correspondingly, we define the overflow probability in the system as the probability that the number of cells in the first and second nodes at slot boundaries fulfil the relation $(n_1, n_2) \in \{(n_1, n_2) \mid n_1 > N_1,\ n_1 + n_2 - \lceil (n_1+1)/c_1 \rceil > N_2\}$.

Next, we consider a system without external arrivals to the second queue, i.e., $a_{i,j} = 0,\ j > 0$. Then, the overflow probability in the system is equal to

$$P_{overflow} = 1 - \sum_{n_1=0}^{N_1} \sum_{n_2=0}^{N_2+\lceil (n_1+1)/c_1 \rceil - n_1} p_{n_1,n_2} \quad (16)$$

## 5 The case $c_2 > 1$

We now consider a system with $c_2 > 1$, namely, several cells ($c_2$) can be transmitted by the second node and leave the system during a slot. As before, we are interested in computing the steady-state probabilities of the lengths of the two nodes. Since $c_2 > 1$ cells can leave the system during a slot, steady-state exists if $r_1 + r_2 < c_2$.

With the same notations as in Section 3 the evolution equation of the queue lengths for $n \geq 0$ is given by

$$\begin{aligned} Q_1^{(n+1)} &= (Q_1^{(n)} - c_1)^+ + A_1^{(n)} \\ Q_2^{(n+1)} &= (Q_2^{(n)} - c_2)^+ \\ &\quad + \min(Q_1^{(n)}, c_1) + A_2^{(n)} \end{aligned} \quad (17)$$

Similar to the method for obtaining (2), we obtain in this case,

$$\begin{aligned} G(z_1, z_2) &= A(z_1, z_2)\{\sum_{i=0}^{c_1-1} \sum_{j=0}^{c_2-1} p_{i,j} z_1^i z_2^j \cdot z_1^{-i} z_2^{i-j} \\ &+ \sum_{i=0}^{c_1-1} \sum_{j=c_2}^{\infty} p_{i,j} z_1^i z_2^j \cdot z_1^{-i} z_2^{i-c_2} \\ &+ \sum_{i=c_1}^{\infty} \sum_{j=0}^{c_2-1} p_{i,j} z_1^i z_2^j \cdot z_1^{-c_1} z_2^{c_1-j} \\ &+ \sum_{i=c_1}^{\infty} \sum_{j=c_2}^{\infty} p_{i,j} z_1^i z_2^j \cdot z_1^{-c_1} z_2^{c_1-c_2}\} \end{aligned} \quad (18)$$

and after simple algebraic manipulations we get,

$$G(z_1, z_2) = A(z_1, z_2) \frac{B(z_1, z_2)}{z_1^{c_1} z_2^{c_2} - z_2^{c_1} A(z_1, z_2)} \quad (19)$$

where $B(z_1, z_2) = \sum_{i=0}^{c_1-1} [\sum_{j=0}^{c_2-1} p_{i,j}(z_2^{c_2} - z_2^j) + g_i(z_2)](z_1^{c_1} z_2^i - z_1^i z_2^{c_1}) + \sum_{j=0}^{c_2-1} f_j(z_1) z_2^{c_1}(z_2^{c_2} - z_2^j)$ and $g_i(z_2) = \frac{1}{i!}\frac{\partial G^i(z_1,z_2)}{\partial z_1^i}|_{z_1=0}$, $f_j(z_1) = \frac{1}{j!}\frac{\partial G^j(z_1,z_2)}{\partial z_2^j}|_{z_2=0}$. In order to uniquely determine $G(z_1, z_2)$ we will have to determine the boundary functions, $f_j(z_1)$, $0 \leq j \leq c_2 - 1$ and $g_i(z_2)$, $0 \leq i \leq c_1 - 1$. In what follows, we demonstrate the method for obtaining these boundary functions. Along this process we mainly use the analytic properties of the generating functions $G(z_1, z_2)$ in the disk $|z_i| < 1$, $i = 1, 2$.

We begin by taking the $l$-th derivative ($0 \leq l \leq c_2 - 1$) of both sides of (18) with respect to $z_2$ and let $z_2 \to 0$ to obtain,

$$f_l(z_1) = \sum_{k=0}^{l} \frac{\mathcal{A}_{l-k}(z_1)\, u_k}{(l-k)!} \quad (20)$$

where $\mathcal{A}_i(z_1) = \partial A^i(z_1, z_2)/\partial z_2^i|_{z_2=0}$, and $u_k = \sum_{j=0}^{c_2} p_{k,j} + \sum_{j=0}^{k-1} p_{j,c_2+k-j}$.

Consequently, $f_l(z_1)$ (and the corresponding probabilities $p_{i,l}$, $i \geq 0$) are expressed in terms of the constants $u_k$, $0 \leq k \leq l$. To determine these constants, we let $z_1 = z_2 = z$ in (19) to obtain,

$$G(z, z) = A(z, z) \frac{\hat{B}(z)}{z^{c_2} - A(z, z)} \quad (21)$$

where $\hat{B}(z) = \sum_{j=0}^{c_2-1}(z^{c_2} - z^j) \sum_{k=0}^{j} \mathcal{A}_{j-k}(z)\, u_k/(j-k)!$. Letting $z \to 1$ in the above and assuming that the steady-state condition $r_1 + r_2 < c_2$ holds, we obtain

$$c_2 - r_1 - r_2 = \sum_{j=0}^{c_2-1} (c_2 - j) \sum_{k=0}^{j} \frac{\mathcal{A}_{j-k}(1)\, u_k}{(j-k)!} \quad (22)$$

Furthermore, the denominator $z^{c_2} - A(z, z)$ of (21) has one root at $z = 1$ and exactly $c_2 - 1$ roots within the unit disk $|z| < 1$ (the proof is based on Rouche's Theorem). Let these roots be denoted by $\mu_l$, $1 \leq l \leq c_2 - 1$. Since $G(z, z)$ is an analytic function in the disk $|z| < 1$, the nominator of (21) must vanish at each of these roots, i.e., for $1 \leq l \leq c_2 - 1$,

$$\sum_{j=0}^{c_2-1} (\mu_l^{c_2} - \mu_l^j) \sum_{k=0}^{j} \frac{\mathcal{A}_{j-k}(\mu_l)\, u_k}{(j-k)!} = 0 \quad (23)$$

Equation (22) together with (23) is a set of $c_2$ (linear) equations that determines the constants $u_k$, $0 \leq k \leq c_2 - 1$, and hence the boundary functions $f_j(z_1)$, $0 \leq j \leq c_2 - 1$ are determined (using (20)). From $f_j(z_1)$ we can obtain $p_{i,j}$, $j \geq 0$ by taking the $i$-th derivative of $f_j(z_1)$ with respect to $z_1$ and letting $z_1 \to 0$.

To determine $g_i(z_2)$, $0 \leq i \leq c_1 - 1$, we use the same procedure described in Section 3. In particular, we note that for any $|z_2| < 1$, the denominator $z_1^{c_1} z_2^{c_2} - z_2^{c_1} A(z_1, z_2)$ of (19) has exactly $c_1$ roots within the unit disk $|z_1| < 1$ (the proof is based on Rouche's Theorem). Let these roots be denoted by $\sigma_l(z_2)$, $1 \leq l \leq c_1$. Since $G(z_1, z_2)$ is an analytic function in the disk $|z_i| < 1$, $i = 1, 2$, the nominator of (19) must vanish at each of these roots, i.e.,

$$B(\sigma_l(z_2), z_2) = 0 \qquad 1 \leq l \leq c_1 \tag{24}$$

Expression (24) is a set of $c_1$ (linear) equations that determines the functions $g_i(z_2)$, $0 \leq i \leq c_1 - 1$.

This completes the derivation of the joint generating function of the queue-length probability distribution. In [14] we provide the procedure for computing the joint probability distribution in this case.

Using the generating function we can obtain the average number of cells in node $i$ ($i = 1, 2$), denoted by $L_i$, as was done in Section 3. In fact, the average number of cells in the first node does not change with $c_2$, hence is identical to (9). Taking the derivative of (21) with respect to $z$ and letting $z \to 1$ we obatin,

$$\begin{aligned} L_1 + L_2 &= r_1 + r_2 + \frac{\frac{d^2 A(z,z)}{dz^2}|_{z=1}}{2(c_2 - r_1 - r_2)} \\ &+ \frac{\hat{\mathcal{A}} - c_2(c_2 - 1)}{2(c_2 - r_1 - r_2)} \end{aligned} \tag{25}$$

where $\hat{\mathcal{A}} = \sum_{j=0}^{c_2-1} \sum_{k=0}^{j} \frac{u_k}{(j-k)!} \{[c_2(c_2 - 1) - j(j - 1)]\mathcal{A}_{j-k}(1) + 2(c_2 - j) d\mathcal{A}_{j-k}(z)/dz|_{z=1}\}$. Subtracting (9) from (25) we obtain the average number of cells in the second node $L_2$.

## 6 Numerical Results

In the first example cells arrive to the system (through the first node only) according to a Poisson process with rate $\lambda$. We set $c_1 = 2$ and $c_2 = 1$. In Figure 2 we plot the overflow probability in the system versus the internal buffer size for external buffer size of 80 cells and load of $\lambda = 0.9$. We also plot the overflow probability in the internal buffer, external buffer and in an "ideal" output buffer switch with $c_1 = \infty$. From Figure 2 we notice that for internal buffer size greater or equal to 15, the overflow probability in the system is less than the overflow probability in the "ideal" system. Also, the main contribution to the total overflow probability for small (large) internal buffer sizes comes from the internal (external) overflow probability. Notice that the internal buffer reduces the burstiness of the input process to the external buffer by limiting the maximum number of cells that can arrive to the external buffer to $c_1 = 2$, and hence the overflow probability in the system and in the external buffer is smaller than the overflow probability in the "ideal" system.

We obtained numerical results for different external buffer sizes and loads where the overflow probability in the "ideal" system was kept at $10^{-7}$. In all examples, an internal buffer size between 12 and 14 cells was sufficient to bring the overflow probability in the system below $10^{-7}$. The same phenomena described in Figure 2 were observed in all examples.

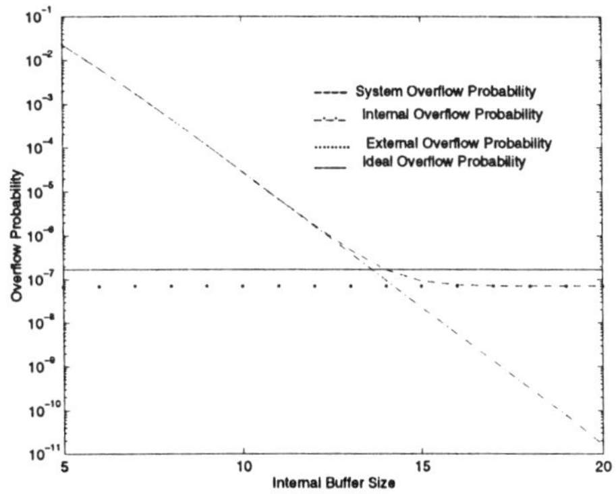


Figure 2: Overflow probability versus internal buffer size for load of 0.9 and external buffer size of 80 cells.

More numerical results are provided in Figure 3 where we plot the overflow probability versus the average load for internal buffer size of 15 and external buffer size of 40. We see again that internal buffer size of 15 is enough to achieve smaller overflow probability in the system compared to the "ideal" system, for average load of 0.75 or larger (for the range of $\geq 10^{-9}$ overflow probability this is the relevant load range). Numerical results for the case $c_2 > 1$ are provided in [14].

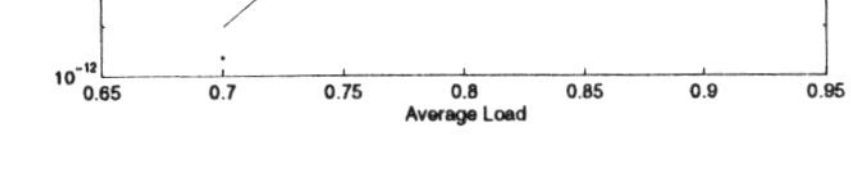


Figure 3: Overflow probability versus average load for internal buffer size of 15 and external buffer size of 40.

We also simulated a system with bursty traffic model that corresponds to VBR traffic class. Here we used three groups of sources. Each group consists of 10 identical sources. Each source corresponds to Interrupted Poisson Process (IPP) model, with sources in the first group having an average ON period of 100 slots and average OFF period of 100 slots. The second and third group sources have average (ON, OFF) periods of (100, 300) and (100, 900), respectively. The average load in the system is termed "VBR Load" and the total load of each group is "VBR Load"/3. Table 6 contains the overflow probability in the "ideal" system and in the system versus "VBR Load" for different internal buffer sizes. The conclusions are similar to the Poisson model.

| VBR Load | Ideal | IB = 8 | IB = 10 | IB = 15 | IB = 20 |
|---|---|---|---|---|---|
| 0.62 | $2.42\ 10^{-4}$ | $3.05\ 10^{-4}$ | $2.54\ 10^{-4}$ | $2.38\ 10^{-4}$ | $2.38\ 10^{-4}$ |
| 0.66 | $7.15\ 10^{-4}$ | $8.08\ 10^{-4}$ | $7.31\ 10^{-4}$ | $7.07\ 10^{-4}$ | $7.07\ 10^{-4}$ |
| 0.70 | $1.68\ 10^{-3}$ | $1.81\ 10^{-3}$ | $1.70\ 10^{-3}$ | $1.66\ 10^{-3}$ | $1.66\ 10^{-3}$ |
| 0.74 | $3.35\ 10^{-3}$ | $3.56\ 10^{-3}$ | $3.39\ 10^{-3}$ | $3.31\ 10^{-3}$ | $3.31\ 10^{-3}$ |
| 0.78 | $6.07\ 10^{-3}$ | $6.29\ 10^{-3}$ | $6.09\ 10^{-3}$ | $6.02\ 10^{-3}$ | $5.61\ 10^{-3}$ |
| 0.82 | $1.04\ 10^{-2}$ | $1.06\ 10^{-2}$ | $1.04\ 10^{-2}$ | $1.03\ 10^{-2}$ | $1.03\ 10^{-2}$ |

Table 1: Overflow probability versus VBR Load for external buffer size of 100.

## References


[1] J. S. Turner, "Design of an integrated services packet network," *IEEE Journal on Selected Areas in Comm.*, SAC-4:1373–1380, Nov. 1986.

[2] I. Cidon and I. S. Gopal, "PARIS: An approach to integrated high-speed private networks," *International Journal of Digital and Analog Cabled Systems*, 1(2):77–85, April 1988.

[3] J. N. Giacopelli and et al, "Sunshine: A high-performance self-routing broadband packet switch architecture," *IEEE Journal on Selected Areas in Comm.*, SAC-9:1289–1298, Oct. 1991.

[4] P. Newman, "A fast packet switch for the integrated services backbone network," *IEEE Journal on Selected Areas in Comm.*, SAC-6:1468–1479, 1988.

[5] Y. S. Yeh, M. G. Hluchyj, and A. S. Acampora, "The knockout switch: A simple, modular architecture for high performance packet switching," *IEEE Journal on Selected Areas in Comm.*, SAC-5:1274–1283, Oct. 1987.

[6] J. Hui, "A broadband packet switch for multirate services," *Proc. of International Conference on Comm. (ICC'87)*: 782–788, June 1987.

[7] AT&T Microelectronics, *Microelectronic Products Selection Guide*, AT&T Microelectronics, Jan. 1995.

[8] W. E. Denzel, A. P. J. Engbersen, I. Iliadis, and G. Karlsson, "A highly modular packet switch for GB/S rates," *Proc. of International Switching Symposium*, 2:A8.3, Oct. 1992.

[9] J. A. Morrison, "Two discrete-time queues in tandem," *IEEE Trans. on Comm.*, COM-27:563–573, 1979.

[10] J. S. C. Chen and T. E. Stern, "Throughput analysis, optimal buffer allocation, and traffic imbalance study of a generic nonblocking packet switch," *IEEE Journal on Selected Areas in Comm.*, SAC-9, 3:439–449, 1991.

[11] O. J. Boxma, "On a tandem queueing model with identical service times at both counters, I," *Adv. Appl. Prob.*, (11):616–643, November 1979.

[12] O. J. Boxma, "On a tandem queueing model with identical service times at both counters, II," *Adv. Appl. Prob.*, (11):644–659, November 1979.

[13] S. B. Calo, "Message delays in repeated-service tandem connections," *IEEE Trans. on Comm.*, COM-29:670–678, May 1981.

[14] I. Cidon, A. Khamisy and M. Sidi, "Analysis of Queueing Displacement Using Switch Port Speedup," CC PUB #170, October 1996.

# A New Method to Determine the Queue Length Distribution at an ATM Multiplexer *

Jinwoo Choe    Ness B. Shroff
School of Electrical and Computer Engineering
Purdue University
West Lafayette, IN 47907-1285
E-mail: {jinwoo, shroff}@ecn.purdue.edu

## Abstract

In this paper, we develop a simple analytical technique to determine $P(\{Q > q\})$, the tail of the queue length distribution, at an ATM multiplexer. The ATM multiplexer is modeled as a fluid queue serving a large number of independent sources. Our method is based on the central limit theorem and the *maximum variance approximation*, and enables us to avoid the state explosion problem. The approach is quite general and *not limited by a Markovian framework*. We apply our analytical method to study the buffer behavior for various traffic sources such as *multiplexed homogeneous and heterogeneous* Markov modulated sources, sources that are *correlated at multiple time scales*, sources whose *autocorrelation function exhibits heavy (sub-exponential) tail behavior*, and sources generated from real *MPEG-encoded video* sequences.

## 1 Introduction

High-Speed Asynchronous Transfer Mode (ATM) networks are envisioned to support various applications that will generate a variety of traffic types such as video, voice, still images, and data. Statististical multiplexing, which enables a large number of sources to share network resources, such as the buffer and link capacity, is crucial to the financial success of these networks. However, when these resources are shared, congestion can occur which may impact the quality of the underlying applications. A fundamental measure of congestion is $P(\{Q > q\})$, the steady state tail of the queue length distribution of an infinite buffer system. For example, $P(\{Q > B\})$ is often used to approximate the loss probability in the corresponding finite buffer system with buffer size $B$. Therefore, analyzing $P(\{Q > q\})$ is important for the control and design of these networks.

*This research was supported in part by NSF CAREER Grant NCR-9624525, NSF Grant CDA-9422250, and the Purdue Research Foundation Grant 690-1285-2479.

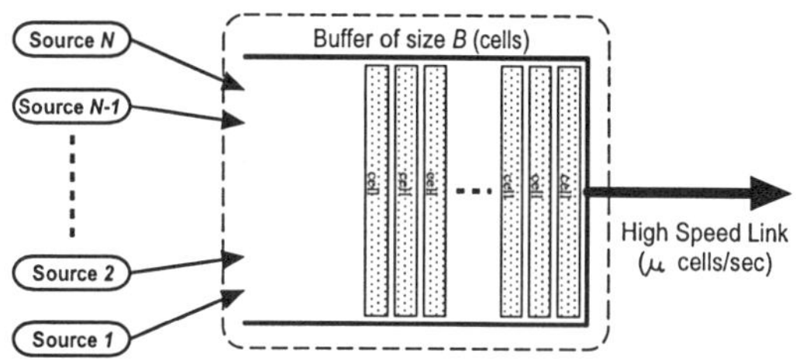


Figure 1: $N$ sources share an ATM Multiplexer with Buffer size $B$ and link rate $\mu$.

A typical ATM multiplexer serving $N$ sources, with buffer size $B$ and link capacity $\mu$, is shown in Figure 1. Since current ATM networks already support 155 Mbps link speeds and gigabit-per-second switches are well on their way, we expect that ATM multiplexers will serve a large number of heterogeneous sources. This causes computational difficulties in evaluating the tail probability $P(\{Q > q\})$. For example, we encounter the state explosion problem even for well behaved sources such as the Markov Modulated Poisson Process (MMPP) and the Markov Modulated Fluid (MMF). Thus, there is significant research interest in studying this problem.

We now briefly overview the research efforts undertaken to address this problem.

It has been shown under a variety of Cramer type assumptions (exponentially bounded marginals and autocorrelations of the arrival process) that $P(\{Q > q\})$, the queue length distribution of an infinite buffer queue, is asymptotically exponential, that is,

$$P(\{Q > q\}) \sim ce^{-\eta q} \qquad \text{as } q \to \infty. \qquad (1.1)$$

Here $\eta$ is a positive constant called the *asymptotic decay rate*, and $c$ is a positive constant called the *asymptotic constant.* We will call this approximation the *asymptotic approximation.* However, it is usually (computationally) infeasible to exactly determine $c$, the asymptotic constant in Equation (1.1). This has led some researchers to suggest a simpler approximation given by (setting $c = 1$) $P(\{Q > q\}) \approx e^{-\eta q}$ as $q \to \infty$. This approximation is the well known *effective bandwidth* approximation [3, 10]. However, there have been a number of recent papers that have shown that the effective bandwidth approximation is usually quite conservative and does not account for statistical multiplexing, which is so important in ATM networks [4, 13]. Therefore, there is renewed interest in the asymptotic approximation, and methods have been developed to approximate the asymptotic constant $c$ for special cases [5, 14]. However, even the asymptotic approximation may provide a poor lower bound for the tail probability (see [4] for examples using on-off sources). The error is expected to be especially significant (even for large buffers) when the aggregate traffic is correlated at multiple time scales. Multiple time-scale correlation will in general occur when heterogeneous sources are multiplexed. Also certain traffic sources (for example, MPEG and JPEG encoded video) themselves, are correlated at different time scales. For traffic exhibiting this type of correlation, the convergence to the asymptotic approximation is expected to be very slow. This implies that using the asymptotic approximation could result in significant errors over a large range of buffer sizes.

Further, empirical studies have shown that the marginal distribution and autocorrelation function of arrival processes that appear in communications networks may have a heavy (subexponential) tail [6]. For these sources, the Cramer type conditions are not satisfied and the asymptotic approximation given by Equation (1.1) may not even be asymptotically valid [8].

In this paper we address these problems by appealing to the *Central Limit Theorem* and model the aggregate arrival process by a normal stochastic process. Using this normal arrival process we are then able to accurately capture the tail probability $P(\{Q > q\})$ in all of the above described scenarios. We next define our problem in more detail.

## 2 Fluid Models

The ATM multiplexer is modeled by an infinite buffer fluid queue that serves $N$ independent arrival processes, as shown in Figure 2. We will derive the necessary equations to determine the tail of queue length distribution $P(\{Q > q\})$ for both discrete time and continuous time versions of this queueing system.

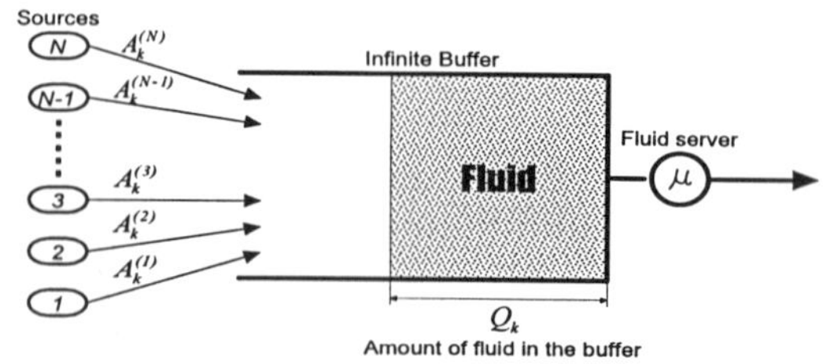


Figure 2: A fluid queue model of the ATM multiplexer shown in Figure 1. The information transmitted through the multiplexer is modeled as a fluid flow.

<u>Discrete Time Model:</u> In the discrete time queueing model the fluid is allowed to flow into and out of the buffer only at discrete times $k$. Let $X_k^{(n)}$, shown in Figure 2, represent the amount of fluid that arrives from source $n$ into the buffer at time $k$, let $N$ be the total number of sources served by the multiplexer, and let $Q_k \geq 0$ be the amount of fluid in the buffer at time $k$. Further, let $X_k^{(0)} \triangleq -\mu$, and $X_k \triangleq \sum_{n=0}^{N} X_k^{(n)}$. So $X_k$ is the aggregate fluid arriving at time $k$, less the capacity $\mu$. The behavior of $Q_k$ in the infinite buffer case is then completely described by the following (Lindley's) equation.

$$Q_k = (Q_{k-1} + X_k)^+ = \max\{Q_{k-1} + X_k, 0\}. \quad (2.2)$$

<u>Continuous Time Model:</u> In the continuous time queueing model, the fluid is allowed to flow in and out of the buffer at any time $t$. Now, let $X_t^{(n)}$, shown in Figure 2, represent the instantaneous rate of fluid arrival at time $t$ from source $n$, for $n = 1, \ldots, N$. As before, let $X_t^{(0)} \triangleq -\mu$, and $X_t \triangleq \sum_{n=0}^{N} X_t^{(n)}$. Then $Q_t$, the amount of fluid in the infinite buffer at time $t$, is given by

$$\frac{d}{dt}Q_t = \begin{cases} 0 & \text{if } Q_t = 0 \text{ and } X_t < 0, \\ X_t & \text{else.} \end{cases} \quad (2.3)$$

## 3 Extreme Value Problem

In this section we will relate the problem of determining the tail probability to that of determining the extreme value distribution of a stochastic process for both the discrete-time and the continuous-time fluid models.

### 3.1 Discrete Time Model

It is well known that solving Equation (2.2) uniquely determines $Q_k$ for $k \geq k_0$, given $\{X_k : k \geq k_0\}$ and $Q_{k_0}$. Therefore, given $Q_{k_0}$ and a stochastic process $\{X_k : k \geq k_0\}$, the stochastic process $Q_k$, that satisfies Equation (2.2) for all $k \geq k_0$, is uniquely determined.

Further, as long as $\bar{X} \triangleq E\{X_k\} < 0$ (the stability condition[1]), and some ergodicity and stationarity requirements on $X_k$ are satisfied, $P(\{Q_k > q\})$ converges to a steady state tail probability $P(\{Q > q\})$, regardless of the initial condition $Q_{k_0}$. Now let us view this problem a little differently. Instead of time starting at $k = 0$, let us assume that the fluid queue has always been operational (that is, since $k = -\infty$). Then, if $X_k$ (now $k \in \mathcal{Z} = \{\ldots, -1, 0, 1, \ldots\}$) is stationary and ergodic with $E\{X_k\} < 0$, it has been shown that Equation (2.2) uniquely determines a stationary process $\tilde{Q}_k$ $(k \in \mathcal{Z})$ that satisfies the equation for all $k \in \mathcal{Z}$, almost surely [11]. Not surprisingly, $P\left(\left\{\tilde{Q} > q\right\}\right)$ is equal to $P(\{Q > q\})$ for all $k \in \mathcal{Z}$ [11].[2] Also, the following relationship between an ergodic stationary process $X_k$ $(k \in \mathcal{Z})$ and the corresponding stochastic process $\tilde{Q}_k$ $(k \in \mathcal{Z})$

$$\tilde{Q}_k = \sup_{m \geq 0} \sum_{i=0}^{m-1} X_{k-i}, \qquad \text{almost surely,} \tag{3.4}$$

provides us a key to further investigating $P(\{Q > q\})$.

Since $P\left(\left\{\tilde{Q}_k > q\right\}\right) = P(\{Q > q\})$ for all $k$,

$$\begin{aligned} P(\{Q > q\}) &= P\left(\left\{\tilde{Q}_0 > q\right\}\right) \\ &= P\left(\left\{\sup_{m \geq 0} \sum_{i=0}^{m-1} X_{-i} > q\right\}\right). \end{aligned} \tag{3.5}$$

In other words, the limiting tail probability $P(\{Q > q\})$ is the same as the tail probability of the supremum of a stochastic process $\{W_m : m = 0, 1, 2, \ldots\}$ defined by $W_m \triangleq \sum_{i=0}^{m-1} X_{-i}$.

We call this stochastic process $\{W_m : m = 0, 1, 2, \ldots\}$, the *backward accumulation process.* The first two moments of $W_m$ are given by

$$E\{W_m\} = m\bar{X}, \tag{3.6}$$

$$Var\{W_m\} = lC_X(0) + 2\sum_{i=1}^{m-1}(m-i)C_X(i), \tag{3.7}$$

where $C_X(l) \triangleq E\{(X_k - \bar{X})(X_{k+l} - \bar{X})\}$ represents the autocovariance function of $X_k$. Note that $W_m$ is not stationary. We can now calculate $P(\{Q > q\})$ by determining the tail probability of the supremum of the backward accumulation process $W_m$.

[1] For an infinite buffer queueing system to be stable, the arrival rate must be less than the service rate.

[2] Since the limiting tail probability does not depend on the initial condition $Q_0$, it intuitively follows that the limiting tail probability of $\tilde{Q}_k$ should be the same as $P(\{Q > q\})$. Additionally, since the limiting tail probability of a stationary process is the tail probability $P(\{\tilde{Q}_k > q\})$ itself, $P(\{\tilde{Q}_k > q\}) = P(\{Q > q\})$.

### 3.2 Continuous Time Model

In the continuous time case, we consider $\{X_t : t \in \mathcal{R}\}$, to be a measurable mean ergodic continuous stochastic process with $\bar{X} = E\{X_t\} < 0$. Then, we have

$$\tilde{Q}_t = \sup_{s \geq 0} \int_{t-s}^{t} X_u du, \qquad \text{almost surely.} \tag{3.8}$$

As in the case of the discrete time model, we define a backward accumulation process $W_s$ as

$$W_s \triangleq \int_0^s X_{-u} du. \tag{3.9}$$

We then have

$$P(\{Q > q\}) = P\left(\left\{\sup_{s \geq 0} W_s > q\right\}\right). \tag{3.10}$$

So far the general problem of determining the tail probability $P(\{Q > q\})$ of a queueing system has been mapped to that of determining the tail probability of the supremum of the backward accumulation process for both discrete-time and continuous-time fluid models. The supremum of a stochastic process has been extensively studied in the *Extreme Value Theory* [1]. We next apply a result from this theory to obtain a simple approximation for $P(\{Q > q\})$.

## 4 Evaluating $P(\{Q > q\})$ at an ATM multiplexer

The results in this section are independent of whether we use the discrete time or continuous time queueing model to characterize our system. To avoid redundancies, however, we will focus on the discrete time case.

We let $X_k^{(0)} = -\mu$ be the link rate of the ATM multiplexer. $X_k^{(n)}$ is defined to be the fluid arrival process corresponding to source $n$, for $n = 1, \ldots, N$. We assume that $X_k^{(n)}$, $n = 1, \ldots, N$, are independent mean ergodic stationary arrival processes with finite mean $\bar{X}_n$, and autocovariance $C_n(l)$. Now, $A_k \triangleq \sum_{n=1}^{N} X_k^{(n)}$ corresponds to the *aggregate arrival process.* Then $A_k$ is a mean ergodic stationary arrival process with mean $\bar{A} = \sum_{n=1}^{N} \bar{X}_n$, and autocovariance $C_A(l) = \sum_{n=1}^{N} C_n(l)$. Also, $X_k = \sum_{n=0}^{N} X_k^{(n)} = A_k - \mu$ is a mean ergodic stationary process with mean $\bar{X} = \bar{A} - \mu$ and autocovariance $C_X(l) = C_A(l)$. As in Section 2, we assume that $\bar{X} = \bar{A} - \mu < 0$.

We now model the arrival process $A_k$ as a stationary *normal process*. We justify this characterization by appealing to the Central Limit Theorem [7] because, as mentioned in the introduction, we expect that ATM multiplexers will serve a large number of independent sources. It should be noted, however, that a normal process $A_t$ has both a negative and positive component. The negative component in our context implies that the buffer is being emptied due to the arrival process, which is not possible in reality. But because the mean $\bar{A}$ of the aggregate process (when many sources are multiplexed) is typically several times larger than its standard deviation $\sqrt{C_A(0)}$, the probability of this negative flow is negligible.

Since we model $A_k$ as a normal process, both $X_k$ and $W_m$ are normal processes. We now rewrite this problem so that determining the extreme value distribution of $W_m$ is equivalent to determining the extreme value distribution of a new stochastic process $\{Z_m : m = 0, 1, \ldots\}$, defined as

$$Z_m \triangleq \frac{W_m - \mu(1-\rho)m}{\mu((1-\rho)m + \kappa)}. \tag{4.11}$$

Here $\rho \triangleq \frac{\bar{A}}{\mu}$ is the utilization of the ATM multiplexer, and $\kappa \triangleq \frac{q}{\mu}$ is the time it takes for the fluid at buffer level $q$ to empty. It then follows that $Z_m$, defined by Equation (4.11), is a normal process with

$$\begin{aligned} E\{Z_m\} &= 0, \quad \text{and} \\ Var\{Z_m\} &= \frac{Var\{W_m\}}{\mu^2((1-\rho)m+\kappa)^2}. \end{aligned} \tag{4.12}$$

A few simple algebraic operations give us the following proposition.

**Proposition 1** *$W_m > q$ if and only if $Z_m > 1$.*

From Proposition 1 and Equation (3.5), we have the following relationship between the tail probability and extreme value distributions of $Z_m$ and $W_m$.

$$\begin{aligned} P(\{Q > q\}) &= P\left(\left\{\sup_{m\geq 0} W_m > q\right\}\right) \\ &= P\left(\left\{\sup_{m\geq 0} Z_m > 1\right\}\right). \end{aligned} \tag{4.13}$$

From the Dominated Convergence Theorem [2], it follows that if $\sum_{k=-\infty}^{\infty} |C_X(k)| < \infty$ (a sufficient condition for the ergodicity of a stationary normal process [15]), then

$$\lim_{m\to\infty} \frac{1}{m} Var\{W_m\} = \sum_{k=-\infty}^{\infty} C_X(k), \tag{4.14}$$

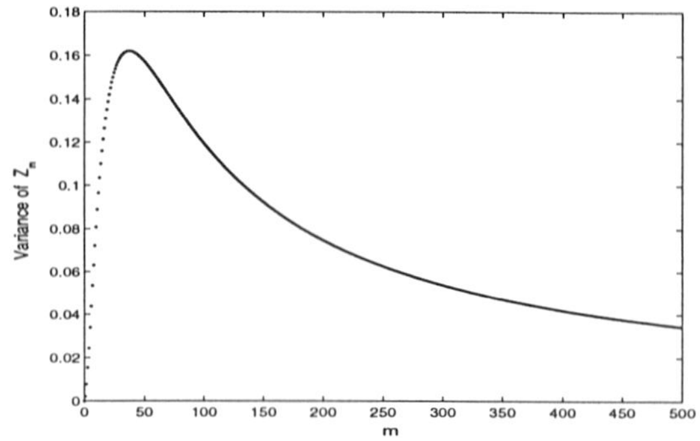


Figure 3: A typical plot of the variance of $Z_m$ versus $m$. Observe that the variance reaches a maximum value and then begins to converge to 0.

and

$$\lim_{l\to\infty} mVar\{Z_m\} = \frac{\sum_{k=-\infty}^{\infty} C_X(k)}{\mu^2(1-\rho)^2}. \tag{4.15}$$

Therefore, $Var\{Z_m\} \to 0$, as $m \to \infty$. This implies that $Var\{Z_m\}$ must reach its maximum value at some $m = m_{max} \geq 0$. In Figure 3 we illustrate this point by showing a typical plot of $Var\{Z_m\}$ versus $m$.

An important observation is that, since $W_m = \sum_{k=1-m}^{0} X_k$, it follows that both $W_m$ and $Z_m$ are "highly correlated" in time. We now state the following approximation used to solve the extreme value problem in our context.

**Maximum Variance Approximation:** *For a zero mean normal process $Z_m$ that is correlated in time and whose variance $Var\{Z_m\}$ achieves a maximum value for some finite $m_{max}$,*

$$P\left(\left\{\sup_{m\geq 0} Z_m > u\right\}\right) \approx P\left(\{Z_{m_{max}} > u\}\right), \tag{4.16}$$

*for sufficiently large $u$.*

The above approximation is taken from Adler [1]. Typically, $u > 1.5\sqrt{Var\{Z_{m_{max}}\}}$ is sufficiently large for the approximation to work well [1]. Therefore, if $Var\{Z_{m_{max}}\} \ll 1$, then we can use the above approximation to obtain

$$P(\{Q > q\}) \approx P\left(\{Z_{m_{max}} > 1\}\right). \tag{4.17}$$

Note that the right hand side of approximation (4.16) is a *lower bound* of the left hand side, that is, $P\left(\{\sup_{m\geq 0} Z_m > u\}\right) \geq P\left(\{Z_{m_{max}} > u\}\right)$. Since $P(\{Q > q\}) = P\left(\{\sup_{m\geq 0} Z_m > u\}\right) \geq P\left(\{Z_{m_{max}} > 1\}\right)$, and because we are interested in probabilities $P(\{Q > q\})$ much less than 1, the condition $Var\{Z_{m_{max}}\} \ll 1$ readily holds for our case.

Table 1: Source Specification Table.

| Type No. | Specification |
|---|---|
| 1 | Markov Modulated Fluid Process<br>Generating Matrix: -0.02 0.02 / [illegible] [illegible]<br>Arrival Rates (cells/sec): 0 / [illegible] |
| 2 | Markov Modulated Fluid Process<br>Generating Matrix: -2 2 / 2 -2<br>Arrival Rates (cells/sec): 0 / 83.33 |
| 3 | Markov Modulated Fluid Process<br>Generating Matrix: -10.02 10 0.02 0 / 30 -30.02 0 0.02 / 0.02 0 -10.02 10 / 0 0.02 30 -30.02<br>Arrival Rates (cells/sec): 2083 / 6250 / 3125 / 9375 |
| 4 | Superposition of three Markov Modulated Fluid (on-off) Processes with different time-scale autocovariance<br>Three Generating Matrices: -10 10 / 10 -10; -0.5 0.5 / 0.5 -0.5; -0.025 0.025 / 0.025 -0.025<br>Arrival Rates (cells/sec): 0 / 66.67 |
| 5 | Semi-Markov Modulated Fluid Process<br>Sojourn Time Distribution: $1-\left(1+\frac{x}{3}\right)^{-4}$<br>State Transition Matrix: 0.5 0.5 / 0.5 0.5<br>Arrival Rates (cells/sec): 0 / 600 |
| 6 | Real MPEG video sources simulated using MPEG (frame size) traces (760000 frames ≈ 8 hours 30 minute × 25 frames/sec) |

The above approximation, although simple, has been found to work quite well [1], as will also be illustrated in Section 5.

*We now summarize our procedure for obtaining the tail probability* $P(\{Q > q\})$.

1. Given the mean $\bar{X}_n$ and autocovariance $C_n(l)$ of the individual arrival processes, compute the mean $\bar{A} = \sum_{n=1}^{N} \bar{X}_n$ and autocovariance $C_A(l) = \sum_{n=1}^{N} C_n(l)$ of the aggregate arrival process.
2. Compute $Var\{Z_m\}$ using Equations (3.7) and (4.12) or explicitly compute
$$Var\{Z_m\} = \frac{mC_A(0) + 2\sum_{i=1}^{m-1}(m-i)C_A(i)}{\mu^2((1-\rho)m+\kappa)^2},$$
where $\mu > \bar{A}$ is the link rate, $\rho = \frac{\bar{A}}{\mu}$, and $\kappa = \frac{q}{\mu}$.
3. Determine $\sigma^2_{max}$, the maximum value of $Var\{Z_m\}$.
4. Compute the tail probability $P(\{Q > q\}) \approx P(\{Z_{m_{max}} > 1\}) = \int_{\frac{1}{\sigma_{max}}}^{\infty} \frac{1}{\sqrt{2\pi}} e^{-\frac{x^2}{2}} dx$, the tail distribution of the normal random variable $Z_{m_{max}}$.

To determine $P(\{Q > q\})$ for the continuous time queueing model, we can follow the above steps by replacing the discrete variable $m$ with the continuous variable $s$. Additionally, for the continuous time model, $Var\{Z_s\}$ (in step 2), is given by

$$Var\{Z_s\} = \frac{2\int_0^s (s-u)C_A(u)du}{\mu^2((1-\rho)s+\kappa)^2}.$$

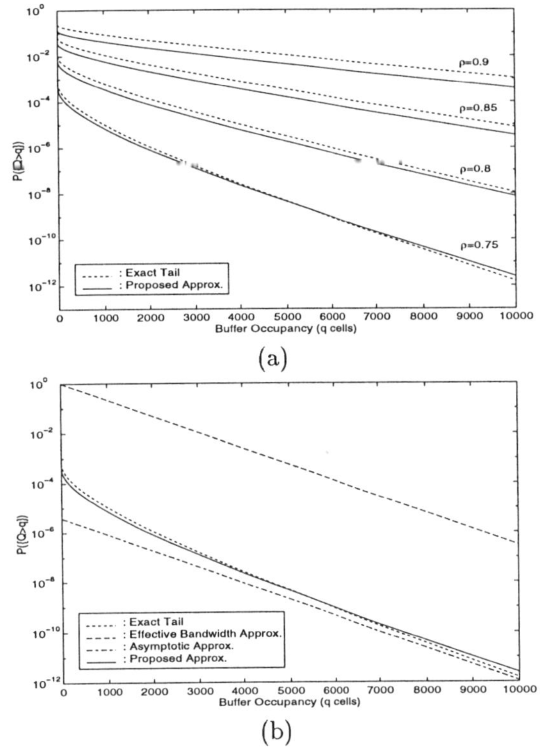


Figure 4: 100 type 1 sources are multiplexed: (a) Comparison with the exact tail probability for 4 different link capacities. (b) Comparison with the exact tail probability, the asymptotic approximation, and the effective bandwidth approximation for $\rho = 0.75$.

## 5 Results and Discussion

In the previous sections we have developed an analytical technique to determine the tail probability $P(\{Q > q\})$ for an infinite buffer fluid queue. Using numerical results, we will investigate the performance of our method.

We use six different types of sources in our experiments. They are summarized in Table 1. The continuous time version of the analytical model is used for all but the last experiment involving real MPEG video sources. *For our experiments, information transfer is measured in an abstract unit of "cells" per second.*

In the first experiment we consider the queue fed by 100 type 1 sources for which the exact tail probability can be computed. As is shown in Table 1, type 1 sources are symmetric on-off sources with exponentially distributed "on" and "off" periods. The mean sojourn time in both the on and off states is 50 sec and the arrival rate in the on period is 20 cells/sec. It then follows that the mean rate of each source is 10 cells/sec and the autocovariance $C(\tau) = 100e^{-0.04\tau}$. In Fig-

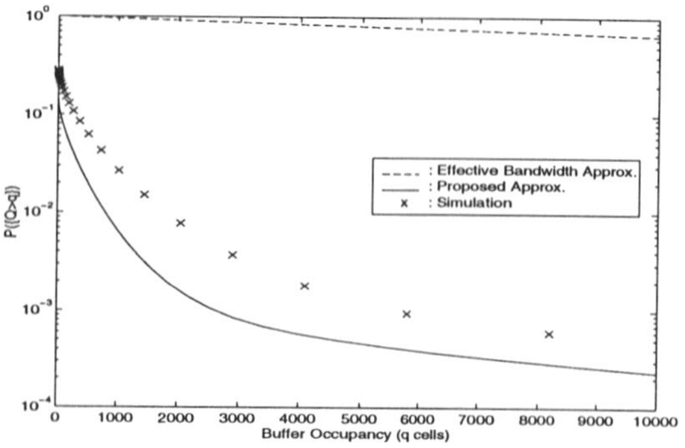


Figure 5: Comparing our proposed approximation with simulations and the effective bandwidth approximation for multiplexed heterogeneous (type 2 and type 3) sources.

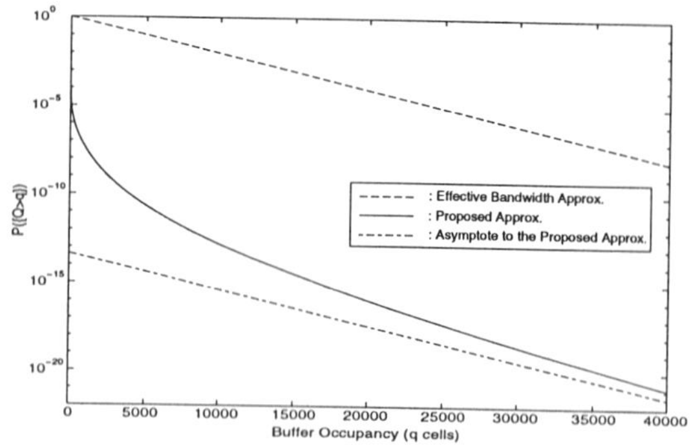


Figure 6: An emphatic illustration that using single exponential (asymptotic) approximations for the tail probability can lead to very poor results.

ure 4(a), four sets of curves are obtained for different utilization $\rho$ by varying the link capacity $\mu$. Our approximation is shown to closely match the exact tail over a large range of buffer sizes and tail probability. In Figure 4(b), we focus on the case when $\rho = 0.75$, and compare the tail probability with the effective bandwidth approximation (Equation (1.1) with $c = 1$), and the asymptotic approximation (Equation (1.1)). The effective bandwidth approximation is off by about four orders of magnitude. The asymptotic approximation performs well for large buffers but underestimates the tail probability considerably for small buffer sizes.

Since the exact solution to the tail probability can only be found for very special cases, we next concentrate on comparing our analytical technique with simulations.

In the next experiment, shown in Figure 5, we focus on the scenario in which two different types of sources, type 2 and type 3 sources, are multiplexed. A type 2 source is an on-off source with exponentially distributed on and off periods. The mean sojourn time in each state is 0.5 sec and the arrival rate during the on period is 83.33 cells/sec. This results in a mean rate of 41.67 cells/sec and autocovariance $C(\tau) = 1736.11e^{-4\tau}$. For an ATM cell size (48 byte payload), this results in a mean arrival rate of 16 Kbps, and an arrival rate, in the on state, of 32 Kbps. This corresponds to the traffic characteristics of a typical voice call [9]. The type 3 source is an MMF source having 4 states. Table 1 shows the arrival rate corresponding to each state and the generating matrix of the source. The mean rate and autocovariance function of the type 3 source are computed to be 3906.12 cells/sec and $203385e^{-40.08\tau} + 5086590e^{-40\tau} + 610547e^{-0.08\tau}$, respectively. Note that since the autocovariance function is the sum of weighted exponentials, type 3 sources have multiple time-scale correlations. In fact this source was generated so that it would have both short term and long term correlations often observed in video sources. Also, the mean data rate generated by the type 3 source based on the ATM cell format is 1.5 Mbps, which is approximately the rate generated by a typical MPEG encoded video source. Therefore, in this experiment, we are attempting to simulate a typical scenario of voice and video calls at an ATM multiplexer. In Figure 5, 2000 type 2 sources and 30 type 3 sources are being multiplexed resulting in a utilization of 0.94. Note that although many sources are multiplexed, the link capacity used is around 82 Mbps, which is almost half of an $OC-3$ line. The analysis and simulation results for Figure 5 match quite well over a large range of buffer sizes. In the figure one can observe that only at a very large buffer size does the tail probability curve predicted by our approximation parallel that of the effective bandwidth curve. This implies that the effective bandwidth approximation is quite conservative. Further (since the slope of the effective bandwidth approximation is the same as that of the asymptotic approximation), the asymptotic approximation given by Equation (1.1) provides a poor lower bound to the tail at small to moderate buffer sizes[3]. This effect is observed because the arrival process is correlated at multiple time scales.

A more pronounced demonstration of the above effect is shown in Figure 6. For this figure, 400 type 4 sources have been multiplexed resulting in a utilization of 0.91. Each type 4 source has mean 100 cells/sec,

[3] We do not show a curve for the asymptotic approximation, because the asymptotic constant in Equation (1.1) cannot be exactly determined.

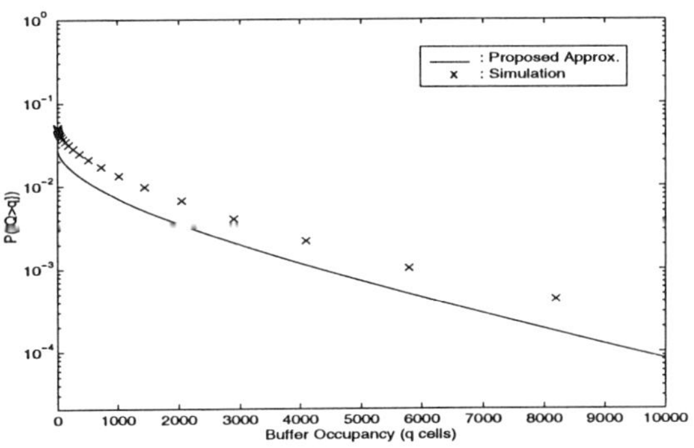


Figure 7: 200 subexponential or heavy tail (type 4) sources are multiplexed at $\rho = 0.88$.

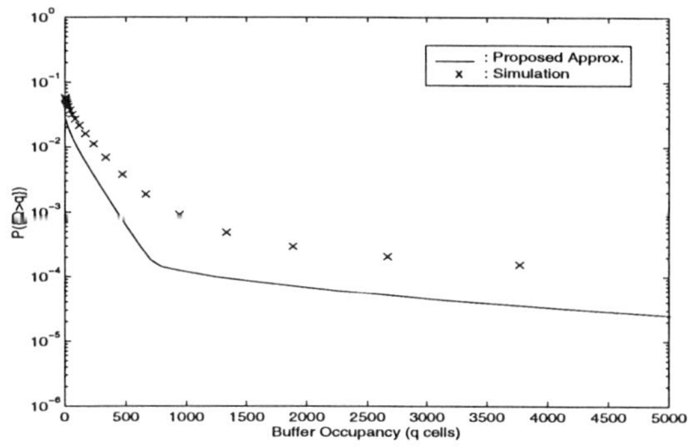


Figure 8: 100 MPEG video sources are multiplexed at $\rho = 0.84$. Note the shallow asymptotic slope predicted by both simulations and analysis.

and autocovariance function $1110.9(e^{-20\tau} + e^{-\tau} + e^{-0.05\tau})$. In Figure 6 one can observe that the tail predicted by our approximation parallels the effective bandwidth curve only at very small tail probabilities (less than $10^{-15}$). This means that the convergence of the tail probability to its asymptotic value is very slow. In Figure 6 we also include the asymptote to the tail probability curve predicted by our method, which can be used to approximate the asymptotic approximation given by Equation (1.1). At a tail probability of $10^{-9}$, this asymptote predicts a lower bound of over five orders of magnitude, while at a tail probability of $10^{-6}$, it is off by seven orders of magnitude! Therefore, the figure illustrates the difficulty in applying the asymptotic approximation to traffic that is correlated at multiple time scales.

In the next experiment we consider Semi Markov Modulated Fluid (SMMF) sources, in which the modulating process is semi-Markov (type 5 sources shown in Table 1). Unlike the Markov modulated sources, the sojourn time in each state is not exponential. The sojourn time distribution for each type 5 source is $1-(1+\frac{x}{3})^{-4}$. These types of sources are called "heavy tail" (or sub-exponential) types of sources. The arrival rate in the on state is 600 cells/sec, and the symmetric state transition matrix is shown in Table 1. This results in a mean arrival rate of 300 cells/s and autocovariance $C(\tau) = \frac{2340000}{(\tau+3)^3}$. In Figure 7, we multiplex 200 type 5 sources resulting in a utilization of $\rho = 0.88$. Since the Cramer types of assumptions fail for these sources, we cannot capture the tail behavior (even asymptotically) using the exponential type approximations (Eq. (1.1)). However, as one can see from Figure 7, our analytical technique predicts the tail probability quite accurately.

In our next experiment, we consider an ATM multiplexer fed by 100 MPEG video sources. These 100 video sources are obtained from a total of over 8 hours of MPEG video traces that were encoded at the Institute of Computer Science at the University of Wuerzburg [12]. For the experiment, we considered an ATM multiplexer with a link capacity of 56.5 Mbps, which corresponds to a utilization of $\rho = 0.84$. For the analysis we use our discrete time queueing model with a 10 msec time step. We obtain the autocovariance and mean directly from the various sequences. Figure 8 shows the tail probabilities computed by the proposed method and by simulation. Note that both the analysis and simulations predict a sharp decay in the tail probability followed by a shallow asymptotic slope. This phenomenon is due to the multiple time-scale correlation that we observed earlier in Figures 5 and 6. To explain this phenomenon in a little more detail let us first briefly review the MPEG encoding scheme. MPEG-encoded traffic, uses inter-frame coding as well as intra-frame coding. The whole MPEG sequence is separated into Groups of Pictures (GOPs). A GOP contains $N$ pictures (frames), of which the first is an Intra-frame coded ($I$ frame) picture. Within a GOP, there are predicted frames called $P$ and $B$ frames. An $I$ frame, since it represents only intra-frame coding, needs on average more coded bits than the $P$ or $B$ frames (typically twice as many bits as the $P$ frame and three times as many bits as the $B$ frame). So there is strong short term correlation within a GOP, between the $I$, $P$, and $B$ frames. In addition, there is long-term correlation across GOPs (between subsequent $I$ frames, for example). When the buffer size is initially increased, the short term correlations are quickly absorbed resulting in the sharp decay in the tail probability. However, it requires a significantly larger buffer size to absorb long-term correlations between GOPs. This results in the tail probability curve eventually flattening out.

**Discussion on our approximation**

Our analytical method involves two approximations: (1) Applying the Central Limit Theorem and characterizing the aggregate source by a normal stochastic process. (2) Applying the maximum variance approximation to calculate the extreme value distribution.

Our numerical results indicate that the maximum variance approximation provides a tight lower bound to the extreme value distribution. Therefore, to apply our analytical method, it seems sufficient to check whether the normal approximation is valid. The validity of the normal approximation depends on both the type and the number of sources multiplexed. However, for typical sources used in traffic modeling, we have found that a few hundred sources is usually enough to determine the tail probability accurately. This is not an unrealistically large number for ATM networks. For example, an $OC-3$ line (155.52 Mbps) can accommodate over 7700 voice calls (32 Kbps in the on state) at a link utilization of 0.8. Further, an $OC-12$ line (622.08 Mbps) can accommodate over 300 MPEG (1.5 Mbps) video calls at the same link utilization. FORE SYSTEMS has already built commercial ATM switches to support $OC-12$ lines, and ATM networks with $OC-24$ (1.2 Gbps) lines are already operational (at Cambridge University, for example). Also switches supporting link capacities of several gigabits-per-second (and higher) are on the horizon. All of the above discussion indicates that, for realistic ATM networks, the aggregate arrival process can be characterized by a normal stochastic process.

## 6 Conclusion

In this paper we developed a technique to capture the steady state queue length distribution at an ATM multiplexer serving a large number of sources. Our approach was based on the Central Limit Theorem which enabled us to characterize the aggregate fluid arrival process as a *normal* stochastic process, thus avoiding the classical state explosion problem that occurs when *heterogeneous sources* are multiplexed. We reformulated our problem as the *extreme value problem* of a normal stochastic process. We then applied an existing lower bound approximation to the extreme value problem to determine the tail probability. Our analytical technique is simple and does not require a detailed model for each source. It is also quite general, and not limited by a Markovian framework.

We have tested the validity of our model by numerical examples for a wide variety of traffic sources. Using numerical results, we also showed that, when traffic is correlated at multiple time scales, "large buffer" approximations (such as the *asymptotic approximation*) may yield poor results, even for large buffers.


### Acknowledgment

We wish to thank the anonymous reviewers for their detailed comments.


## References


[1] R. J. Adler, *An Introduction to Continuity, Extrema, and Related Topics for General Gaussian Processes.* Hayward, CA: Institute of Mathematical Statistics, 1990.

[2] P. Billingsley, *Probability and Measure.* New York: John Wiley & Sons, 1979.

[3] C.-S. Chang and J. Thomas, "Effective Bandwidth in High-Speed Digital Networks," *IEEE Journal On Selected Areas In Communications*, vol. 13, pp. 1091–1114, August 1995.

[4] G. Choudhary, D. Lucantoni, and W. Whitt, "Squeezing the most out of ATM," *IEEE Transactions on Communications*, vol. 44, pp. 203–217, February 1996.

[5] A. Elwalid, D. Mitra, and R. Wentworth, "A New Approach for Allocating Buffers and Bandwidth to Heterogeneous Regulated Traffic in an ATM Node," *IEEE Journal On Selected Areas In Communications*, vol. 13, pp. 1115–1127, August 1995.

[6] M. Garrett and W. Willinger, "Analysis, Modeling and generation of self-similar VBR video traffic," in *ACM SIGCOMM'94*, pp. 269–280, 1994.

[7] I. I. Gikhman and A. V. Skorokhod, *Introduction to the Thoery of Random Processes.* Philadelphia: W. B. Saunders, 1969.

[8] P. Jelenkovic and A. Lazar, "Subexponential Asymptotics of a Markov-Modulated G/G/1 Queue," Preprint: *Submitted to Journal of Applied Probability*, November, 1995.

[9] Y. Jenq, "Approximations for Packetized Voice Traffic in Statistical Multiplexer," in *Proceedings of IEEE INFOCOM'84*, pp. 256–259, 1984.

[10] F. Kelly, "Effective Bandwidth in Multiclass Queues," *Queueing Systems*, vol. 9, pp. 5–16, 1991.

[11] R. M. Loynes, "The Stability of a Queue with Non-independent Inter-arrival and Service Times," *Proc. Cambridge Philos Soc.*, vol. 58, pp. 497–520, 1962.

[12] O. Rose, "Statistical properties of MPEG video traffic and their impact on traffic modeling in ATM systems," in *Proceedings of the 20th Conference on Local Computer Networks*, pp. 397–406, Minneapolis,MN, Oct. 1995.

[13] N. Shroff and M. Schwartz, "Improved Loss Calculations at an ATM Multiplexer," in *Proceedings of IEEE INFOCOM*, vol. 2, pp. 561–568, March 1996.

[14] A. Simonian and J. Guibert, "Large Deviation Approximation for Fluid Queues Fed by a Large Number of On/Off Sources," *IEEE Journal On Selected Areas In Communications*, vol. 13, pp. 1017–1027, August 1995.

[15] E. Wong and B. Hajek, *Stochastic Processes in Engineering Systems.* New York: Springer-Verlag, 1985.

# Leap Forward Virtual Clock:
## A New Fair Queuing Scheme with Guaranteed Delays and Throughput Fairness

Subhash Suri  George Varghese  Girish Chandranmenon

Department of Computer Science
Washington University
One Brookings Drive
St. Louis, MO 63130-4899

### Abstract

*We describe an efficient fair queuing scheme, Leap Forward Virtual Clock, that provides end-to-end delay bounds similar to WFQ, along with throughput fairness. Our scheme can be implemented with a worst-case time $O(\log\log N)$ per packet (inclusive of sorting costs), which improves upon all previously known schemes that guarantee delay and throughput fairness similar to WFQ. Interestingly, both the classical virtual clock and the Self-Clocked Fair Queuing schemes can be thought of as special cases of our scheme, by setting the leap forward parameter appropriately.*

## 1 Introduction

The study of service disciplines in integrated services networks has gained significance with the emergence of multimedia applications and electronic commerce. Unlike traditional data applications, real-time applications such as video-on-demand and teleconferencing must meet stringent quality-of-service (QoS) standards to be successful. In an integrated services network, applications with widely different communication rates (ranging from few bits to several megabits per sec), traffic patterns, and QoS requirements share communication links. This makes it difficult to provide good bounds on end-to-end delay and bandwidth.

With many delay-sensitive traffic sources contending for bandwidth, a service discipline must provide a fast and effective mechanism for servicing packets so that real-time traffic is not affected by non-time-critical traffic such as file transfer. Also, both kinds of traffic must receive a (preset) fair share of bandwidth. A lack of "firewalls" can result in a rogue traffic source (either a misbehaving user or malfunctioning device) unjustly penalizing well-behaved sources. In today's Internet, for instance, a rogue user can send data at an uncontrolled rate, and seize a large fraction of the available bandwidth at the expense of "good" users. Weighted Fair Queuing(WFQ) [5] is a benchmark for comparing properties of packet schedulers. WFQ, however, requires $O(N)$ time to schedule a packet, where $N$ is the number of concurrent flows at a router. Other algorithms [14, 2] equivalent to WFQ require $O(\log N)$ time per packet. Our main result is a service discipline called *Leap Forward Virtual Clock (LFVC)* whose delay bound and throughput fairness is almost identical to WFQ, but whose computational overhead is only $O(\log\log N)$ per packet. Our $O(\log\log N)$ time bound is worst-case and includes all sorting overheads[1]. $O(\log\log N)$ is a small constant for all practical purposes—for instance, $\log\log N \leq 5$ for all $N \leq 4 * 10^9$; the underlying constants are also quite small.

Bennett and Zhang[1] introduced a more refined form of fairness called worst-case fairness (WFI). They showed that even WFQ could exhibit burstiness (i.e., high WFI), and described a scheme called WF$^2$Q that has optimal WFI. Our LFVC scheme has a WFI comparable to WF$^2$Q. Thus Leap Forward Virtual Clock appears to be the first service discipline that achieves near-ideal delay and throughput bounds, but has a computational overhead smaller than the $O(\log N)$ of prior schemes. We summarize the salient features of previous algorithms in Table 1, and compare them to our Leap Forward scheme. A detailed comparison can

[1] in contrast with some existing algorithms whose $O(1)$ time complexity bound accounts only for "tag computation" and not the additional $O(\log N)$ cost for sorting

| Scheme | Delay Bound | Fairness | Worst-case Fairness | Efficiency |
|---|---|---|---|---|
| GPS[10] | 0 | Fair | Excellent | Impractical |
| WFQ[5] | Small | Fair | Poor | $O(N)$ |
| SCFQ[9] | Large | Fair | Poor | $O(\log N)$ |
| Virtual Clock[17] | Small | Unfair | Poor | $O(\log N)$ |
| Deficit Round Robin[12] | Large | Fair | Poor | $O(1)$ |
| Frame Based FQ[14] | Small | Fair | Poor | $O(\log N)$ |
| $WF^2Q$[1] | Small | Fair | Good | $O(\log N)$ |
| Leap Forward VC | Small | Fair | Good | $O(\log\log N)$ |

Table 1: A comparison of several well-known scheduling algorithms. By a "small" delay, we mean a delay that is only a small additive constant larger than GPS delay, while "fair" throughput is fairness comparable to that of SCFQ or GPS. By poor worst-case fairness, we mean a worst-case index that grows with the number of flows.

be found in [15].

The paper is organized as follows. In Section 2, we formulate two conditions which are necessary and sufficient to guarantee WFQ-like delay and throughput bounds. In Section 3, we introduce our main algorithm, Leap Forward Virtual Clock (LFVC). We prove end-to-end delay bounds in Section 4, and throughput fairness in Section 5. In Section 6, we describe tag coarsening and how it leads to an $O(\log\log N)$ time implementation. In Section 7, we report on simulation experiments, and conclude in Section 8.

## 2 Virtual Clock Service Disciplines

Service disciplines based on a virtual clock work by assigning a tag (deadline) to each packet, representing the clock value by which the packet must be transmitted. Packets are serviced in non-decreasing order of tags. It is true but not obvious [7, 16] that such a scheme meets all tag deadlines. We have isolated two fundamental conditions that underlie delay and throughput guarantees. Our Leap Forward Virtual Clock scheme is an instance of a class of service disciplines that derive from these conditions. In particular, by setting parameters appropriately, both classical virtual clock [17] and Self-Clocked Fair Queuing [9] can be derived as special cases.

We begin with some useful notation. A *flow* is a logical connection between a source and a destination. Each packet in a flow carries the ID of the flow. Packets in a flow pass through a sequence of servers (or routers) along their path. We will later use the framework of *guaranteed rate clock* (GRC) algorithms introduced by Goyal et al. [8], to establish WFQ-like bounds on end-to-end delay. With this framework, it suffices to establish the delay bound at a single server. Hence, we concentrate on a server $S$, with output rate $B$ bits per second.

Let $f_1, f_2, \ldots, f_N$ denote the set of flows that are serviced at $S$, where flow $f_i$ has a guaranteed rate of $r_i$ bits/sec, and $\sum_{i=1}^{N} r_i \leq B$. The sequence of packets in a particular flow $f$ is denoted $p_f^1, p_f^2, \ldots, p_f^k$, and their sizes (in bits) are denoted $\ell_f^1, \ell_f^2, \ldots, \ell_f^k$. We also use the notation $\ell(p)$ to denote the length of $p$. We assume $S$ is work-conserving: $S$ does not idle when there is some packet to send. The virtual clock associated with the server is a counter that keeps track of the bits sent out by $S$. The output rate of $S$ is $B$ bits/sec, and thus servicing a packet $p$ of length $\ell$ increments the clock by $\ell/B$. Every packet to be serviced by $S$ receives a *tag*, indicating the server clock value by which it must be serviced. The tag of the $j$th packet in flow $f$ is denoted $T(p_f^j)$.

Let $t_s$ denote the *current* server time (clock value) at any instant. The arrival time of a packet $p_f^j$, denoted $A(p_f^j)$, is defined as the server time when $p_f^j$ reaches the head of its flow queue. Let $t_f^{prev}$ denote the tag of the last packet sent by $f$; it is zero if no packet of $f$ has been sent. We define the *tag* of $p_f^j$ as follows:

$$T(p_f^j) = \max\{A(p_f^j),\ T(p_f^{j-1})\} + \frac{\ell_f^j}{r_f} = \max\{t_f^{prev},\ t_s\} + \frac{\ell_f^j}{r_f}. \quad (1)$$

Next, we define the *current tag* of a flow $f$, denoted $t_f$. We say a flow $f$ is *active* if it currently has at least one packet in its queue. Otherwise, $f$ is called *idle*. If $f$ is active, let $p_f$ denote the packet at the head of $f$'s queue, and $l_f$ the length of $p_f$ in bits; this is the current packet for $f$. The current tag of $f$ is defined as follows:

$$t_f = \begin{cases} T(p_f) & \text{if } f \text{ is active} \\ \max\{t_f^{prev},\ t_s\} & \text{otherwise} \end{cases}$$

Finally, we define an important parameter $\Delta_f$ for each flow $f$:

$$\Delta_f = \frac{\ell_f^{max}}{r_f}, \qquad (2)$$

where $\ell_f^{max}$ is the size of the largest packet in flow $f$. Note that $\Delta_f$ is the time needed to send the largest packet by a flow at its guaranteed rate. Lastly, we use the notation $\tau$ to denote the time to transmit a largest packet at the server rate; thus, $\tau = \frac{M}{B}$, where $M$ is the size of the largest packet across all flows.

## 2.1 Delay Bound for Virtual Clock

Classical virtual clock[17] assigns a tag to each arriving packet using Eq. (1), and services packets in non-decreasing tag order. If one can show that each packet is transmitted no later than its tag value, then the GRC framework of Goyal et al. [8] provides a good end-to-end delay bound. We distill a fundamental invariant, called *Backlog Inequality*, that is essential to ensuring that a packet is serviced by its tag. Our analysis is new and simple; more importantly, it leads directly to our new scheme.

Let $t$ be an arbitrary server time such that $t \geq t_s$ and consider the time window $(t_s, t)$. The Backlog Inequality relates the backlog (both packets waiting and potential future arrivals) that must be serviced within the time window $(t_s, t)$ and the amount of bandwidth available: $B \times (t - t_s)$. A service discipline can meet all tag commitments only if the available bandwidth is no less than the backlog. Fig. 1 depicts the inequality.

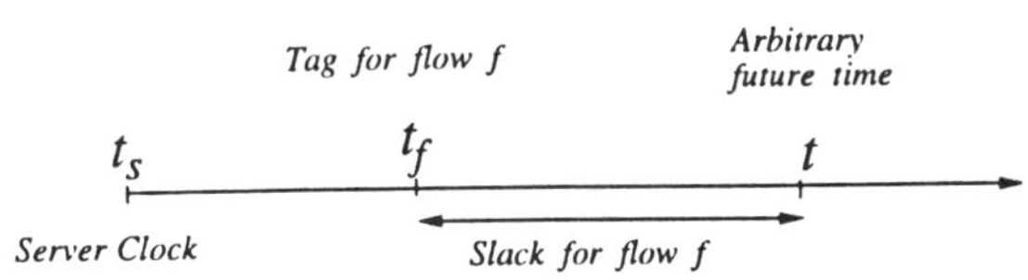


Figure 1: The Backlog Inequality.

More formally, let $\Phi_t$ denote the set of all flows whose current tags have value at most $t$:

$$\Phi_t = \{f \mid t_f \leq t\}.$$

Thus $\Phi_t$ is the set of flows whose most recent packet to receive service has tag less than $t$. These are the flows whose packets might need to be serviced before server clock reaches $t$.

**[Backlog Inequality:]** Given a server $S$ with output rate $B$, the current server time $t_s$ and a future server clock value $t$, we say that the Backlog Inequality holds if:

$$\sum_{f\in\Phi_t} \ell_f + \sum_{f\in\Phi_t} r_f(t - t_f) \leq (t - t_s) \times B \qquad (3)$$

On the left hand side, the first term is the current backlog, and the second term is the potential backlog or slack. The right hand side represents the available bandwidth in this time window. Later, we will show that *any service discipline that maintains the Backlog Inequality guarantees a WFQ-like delay bound.*

## 2.2 Delay and Throughput Conditions

The virtual clock discipline is known to suffer from throughput unfairness. The problem is caused by unbounded deviations between the server clock and a flow tag, which can happen when some flows send packets in bursts while others remain idle. (See [13] for examples.) Surprisingly, Bennett and Zhang [1] show that even WFQ exhibits a form of bursty behavior. Leap Forward Virtual Clock avoids both forms of unfairness. We show that a service discipline should satisfy the following delay and throughput conditions to deliver WFQ-like delay bounds and a good worst-case fairness index.

**[Delay Condition:]** A service discipline satisfies the delay condition if it satisfies the Backlog Inequality at all times.

**[Throughput Condition:]** Let $k$ be a constant independent of $N$. A service discipline satisfies the throughput condition if each flow $f$ satisfies the following condition at all times:

$$t_f \leq t_s + k \cdot \Delta_f.$$

These conditions are necessary for a virtual clock scheme to guarantee delay and throughput bounds similar to WFQ. Later, we establish the sufficiency of these conditions. These conditions motivate our Leap Forward algorithm, which modifies classical virtual clock by introducing two key ideas (quarantine and leap forward).

# 3 Leap Forward Virtual Clock

Our algorithm uses a strategy employed by parents for disciplining children: take them temporarily offline. For us, a flow in possible need of discipline is one that has recently received more than its allocated share of the bandwidth; the tag of such a flow might violate the Throughput Condition. We call such a flow *oversubscribed.* Any packets for an oversubscribed flow are placed in a holding area $L$

(see Figure 2). Other well-behaved flows are placed in a priority queue $H$. The server picks the packet with the lowest current tag in $H$ for servicing next. We note that the lowest tag in $H$ may very well be bigger than the lowest tag in $L$, yet the packet from $H$ is serviced first. The data structures $H$ and $L$ can be thought of as *High* and *Low* priority queues.

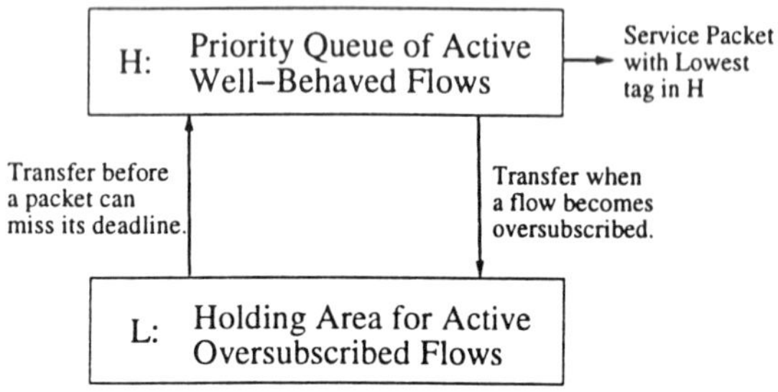


Figure 2: A conceptual picture of Leap Forward Scheme.

Just as children are forgiven after a "time off" period, we need to eventually transfer an active flow from $L$ to $H$. How long can we wait before doing so? We must transfer $f$ before we violate the delay condition. If $f$ is a flow in $L$ and $p$ is the packet at the head of its queue, a safe test for keeping $f$ in $L$ is:

$$T(p) - t_s \geq \Delta_f.$$

We must transfer $f$ to $H$ before this condition is violated. We show that this transfer policy maintains the delay condition, and every packet is serviced no later than its tag.

Thus, our scheme transfers a flow to $L$ when it is likely to cause a throughput problem, and restores it to $H$ before the delay guarantee of its packet can be violated. There remains, however, one problem: what happens if all flows are oversubscribed, and therefore $H$ is empty? To be work-conserving, we must transmit a packet; yet there is no eligible packet. This brings us to the second important feature of our algorithm. When $H$ is empty, we *advance the server clock as far forward as possible without violating the delay invariant of any flows in L.*

We can prove that the Delay Condition for a flow $f$ in $L$ is satisfied if the following holds: $t_f - t_s \geq \Delta_f$. We call our scheme Leap Forward Virtual Clock because the server clock can leap forward when all active flows are oversubscribed. After the leap forward step, at least one active flow in $L$ becomes eligible for transfer to $H$. Thus the server is work-conserving.

The leap forward step can be implemented by advancing the server clock to the smallest value of $(t_f - \Delta_f)$ among all active flows $f$ that are in $L$. This suggests organizing the flows in $L$ as a priority queue with key $t_f - \Delta_f$ (instead of $t_f$ as in $H$). The use of these offset flow tags allows us to check the Leap Forward and Transfer conditions only for the flow(s) at the head of $L$.

### 3.1 Transfer Thresholds

The description above can be used to generate a family of schemes. A particular implementation involves fixing certain parameters. For instance, maintaining the Delay Condition requires there be "sufficient time" left for the deadlines of all flows in $L$. In our implementation, we ensure that any flow $f$ in $L$ satisfies the following *No Rush* condition:

$$t_f - \Delta_f \geq t_s.$$

Any flow $f$ in violation of the "No Rush" condition must be transferred to $H$. Since $L$ is a priority queue with $t_f - \Delta_f$ as keys, it suffices to check this condition for the flow $g$ at the head of $L$. If $g$ violates the No Rush condition, we transfer it to $H$, and repeat the process on the new flow at the head of $L$, until we reach a flow that meets the condition. At this point, we can be sure that all flows remaining in $L$ satisfy the condition. While we may have to perform multiple transfers from $L$ to $H$, each packet is extracted from $L$ at most once. Thus, the amortized cost per packet is at most one Delete operation from $L$.

Finally, since server clock advances discretely, all tests use an additional slack parameter $\tau = \frac{M}{B}$, where $M$ is the largest packet in the system. To make the Throughput Condition concrete, we also fix $k = 2$.

### 3.2 Allowing Rounded Tags

The Internal Revenue Service allows tax filers to round numbers to the nearest dollar. The intent is reduced computation at the expense of a possible small loss. We investigate a similar tradeoff between accuracy of tags and computational overhead. Let $\rho$ be an arbitrary number. We will "round" up tag values to a whole multiple of $\rho$. Implementing the Leap Forward scheme with exact tags corresponds to setting $\rho = 0$.

Fix a value of $\rho$. The coarsened version of Leap Forward continues to compute fully accurate tags $t_f$ and $t_s$, but rounds them up to the nearest multiple of $\rho$ *before inserting them into the priority queues H or L.* Since rounding may introduce an error of $\rho$ in the relative values of two tags, all our tests, such as Throughput and Delay Conditions, can be off by $\rho$. We prove that this uncertainty increases the delay bound by at most $\rho$, and worsens the worst-case throughput fairness index by a small amount.

### 3.3 Leap Forward Code

**Leap Forward Virtual Clock**

```
ProcessHead (Q_f)
  if (Q_f is empty) return;
  p ← head(Q_f);
  t_f ← T(p) ← max(t_s, t_f) + ℓ(p)/r_f;
  if (t_f ≤ t_s + Δ_f + τ + ρ) then
    Insert(H, p, t_f));
  else Insert(L, p, t_f − Δ_f);
End.

Enqueue (* A new packet p_f arrives. *)

  AddToTail (Q_f);
  if (Q_f was empty) then
    ProcessHead (Q_f);

Dequeue (* The server is idle and there is a packet
in the system. *)

  k_min ← MinKey(L);
  Let f be the flow corresponding to
  the key k_min.
  if (H is empty) then
    t_s = max(t_s, k_min − ρ) (* Leap forward *)
  while (k_min < t_s + τ + ρ )
    p_f ← ExtractMin(L);
    Insert(H, p_f, T(p_f));     (* Transfer *)
    k_min ← MinKey(L);
  end
  p_f ← ExtractMin(H);
  t_s ← t_s + ℓ(p_f)/B.         (* Start Service *)
  RemovefromTail (Q_f)
  ProcessHead (Q_f);
  Transmit p_f;           (* Real time elapses *)
```

Figure 3: Leap Forward Virtual Clock: Algorithm

The Leap Forward algorithm asynchronously performs two operations repeatedly: Enqueue and Dequeue. The former handles the task of inserting a newly arrived packet in appropriate data structures, while the latter deals with prioritizing packets for service. The server always picks for transmission the packet $p$ with the current smallest tag in $H$. The server clock is advanced by $\ell(p)/B$, and $p$ is deleted from the flow queue. Only then does the server begin transmitting the packet $p$. Real time elapses only during packet transmission. All other events are assumed to be instantaneous. The server clock is incremented before the packet is actually transmitted!

The code for Leap Forward algorithm is described in Figure 3. The algorithm maintains two priority queues, $H$ and $L$, which allow *Insertion* and *Extract-Min* operations. Each flow $f$ has a FIFO queue $Q_f$ which contains flow $f$ packets that are waiting for service. $t_f$ maintains the flow tag of $f$, while $t_s$ is the server clock. Variables $t_s$ and $t_f$, for all $f$, are initialized to 0, and reset to zero whenever the server becomes idle.

The procedure $Insert(\mathcal{A}, p, x)$ inserts the *rounded* value of $x$ (assuming some fixed coarsening parameter $\rho$) into the priority queue $\mathcal{A}$. The value $x$ is the tag of $p$ if $\mathcal{A} = H$ and the offset tag if $\mathcal{A} = L$. In addition, the procedure *ProcessHead* is used to handle a packet $p$ when it reaches the head of its queue $Q_f$.

We show that:

**Theorem 3.1** *LFVC is a work-conserving service discipline.*

Due to lack of space, we omit the proof. Please refer to [15] for details.

## 4 Delay Bounds for LFVC

We establish the delay bound at a single server, and extend it to multiple hops.

### 4.1 Delay at a Single Server

We show that LFVC maintains the Backlog Inequality. Due to our use of rounded tags, we only require that this Inequality hold for times $t$ that are whole multiples of the parameter $\rho$. The following lemma collects some useful invariants on flow tags.

**Lemma 4.1 (Tag invariants)** *Consider a flow $f$, and its current tag $t_f$. LFVC maintains the following invariants with respect to the current server time $t_s$:*

**T1:** *If $t_f$ is in $H$, then $t_f \le t_s + \Delta_f + \tau + \rho$.*

**T2:** *If $t_f$ is in $L$ then $t_f \ge t_s + \Delta_f$.*

**T3:** *Let $\ell_f$ be the length of packet at the head of $f$'s queue (assume $\ell_f = 0$ if $f$ is idle). Then, $t_f \le t_s + \tau + \rho + \Delta_f + \ell_f/r_f$.*

Our next lemma proves a weaker version of the backlog inequality, which we use in establishing our final lemma. Let us recall the definition of the set $\Phi_t$ from earlier discussion: $\Phi_t = \{f \mid t_f \le t\}$ is the set of flows whose current tags are less than $t$, for a server time $t \ge t_s$. We call a flow *backlogged* if it currently has at least one packet in its queue.

**Lemma 4.2 (Sufficient Bandwidth)** *If, for all $t \geq t_s$, every backlogged flow $f \in \Phi_t$ satisfies $\ell_f \leq (t_f - t_s) r_f$, then the backlog inequality holds at $t_s$.*

Let us use the notation $R(n)$ to denote the value of $n$ *rounded up* to the nearest multiple of $\rho$. Abusing the notation slightly, we also use $R(p)$ to denote $R(T(p))$. We are now ready to state and prove the following key lemma.

**Lemma 4.3 (Backlog Lemma)** *In LFVC, the Backlog Inequality holds for all rounded values of $t$. That is, if $t$ is a whole multiple of $\rho$, then the following holds:*

$$\sum_{f \in \Phi_t} \ell_f + \sum_{f \in \Phi_t} (t - t_f)\, r_f \;\leq\; (t - t_s) \times B.$$

PROOF. Our proof is by induction on the number of *events*, where an event is either an Enqueue, or any of the following four steps of Dequeue: Leap Forward, Transfer, Start Service, and End Service. Due to lack of space, we only discuss the proof for the Enqueue; the remaining cases are similar and a complete proof can be found in the technical report [15].

[*Enqueue.*] Suppose a packet $p_f$ arrives at the head of queue for the flow $f$. Let $t_f$ be the current tag of $f$ before $p_f$ arrives. Then, the tag of $p_f$ is given by $T(p_f) = t_f + \frac{\ell_f}{r_f}$. We consider two cases, depending upon whether or not $T(p_f) < t$. If $T(p_f) \geq t$, then $f \notin \Phi_t$, and the lemma clearly holds. If $T(p_f) < t$, then the first term on the left hand side of the Backlog Inequality increases by $\ell_f$, but the second term *decreases* by $(t - t_f)\, r_f - (t - T(p_f))\, r_f = (T(p_f) - t_f)\, r_f = \ell_f$, and the right hand side remains unchanged, Hence the inequality is preserved.

□

The preceding lemma implies that at any time $t$ the server has sufficient bandwidth to service packets scheduled before $t$. This allows us to bound the service time of a packet:

**Lemma 4.4 (Service Time)** *A packet $p$ is completely transmitted by the time the server clock reaches $R(p) \leq T(p) + \rho$. Thus, no packet in $H$ or $L$ has a tag smaller than $t_s - \rho$.*

The preceding lemma bounds a packet's service time in terms of the virtual server clock. But we need a statement in terms of real time. Our next lemma establishes a connection between the server clock and real time. Let $I$ be a variable that maintains the value of the real time when the server was last idle. If the server is currently busy, then $I$ equals the real time when the last busy period began. If the server is idle, then $I$ equals the current value of real time. Similarly, let $L$ be a variable that maintains the amount of leap-forward done in the current busy period up to the current instant of time. At the start of a busy period, we set $L = 0$. The following lemma shows that real time equals server time plus $I - L$, except during packet transmission, when it can be behind by $\tau$.

**Lemma 4.5 (Server Clock Deviation)** *Let $t$ be real time and let $I$ and $L$ be defined as above. Then, the following holds:*

1. *During a packet transmission, $t \leq (t_s + I - L) \leq t + \tau$.*

2. *At all other times, $t = (t_s + I - L)$.*

The preceding two lemmas imply that a packet $p$ is serviced in the Leap Forward system no later than the real time value $R(p) + I - L$. We use this fact to prove end-to-end delay bounds.

We then show that our scheme is a Guaranteed Rate scheduling algorithm, as defined by Goyal et al. [8]. This provides an end-to-end delay bound from our single-server delay bound; we omit details, and state the result.

**Theorem 4.6 (End-to-end Delay Bound)** *Suppose that a flow $f$ conforms to a leaky bucket process with parameters $(\sigma_f, r_f)$, and the scheduling algorithm at each of the $K$ servers on its path is LFVC. Then, the end-to-end delay of a packet $p_f^n$, denoted by $d_f^n$, is given by the following:*

$$d_f^n \leq \frac{\sigma_f}{r_f} + (K - 1) \max_{j=1}^{n} \frac{\ell_f^j}{r_f} + \sum_{i=1}^{K} \alpha^i.$$

Leap Forward has $\beta = \rho + \tau$. If we eliminate tag coarsening (set $\rho = 0$), our result is identical to the standard delay bound of classical virtual clock and WFQ. Tag coarsening adds an additional delay of at most $\rho$ per server on the path. The parameter $\rho$ can be used to derive tradeoffs between additional delay and savings in computational overhead.

Goyal et al. [8] also show how to obtain probabilistic bounds on the end-to-end delay when the burstiness of a flow is bounded with a stochastic process, such as the exponentially bounded burstiness. The same results also apply to our scheduling algorithms. In next section, we address the throughput fairness of our algorithm.

# 5 Throughput Fairness of Leap Forward

Informally, a scheme is fair if each backlogged flow receives its fair share of the available server bandwidth. There are two commonly used fairness measures: the first, proposed by Golestani [9], is a gross measure, while the second, introduced recently by Bennett and Zhang [1], is a more refined measure. Bennett-Zhang call their measure *worst-case fairness index* (WFI), and show that while WFQ is fair by Golestani's measure, it falls short of the ideal GPS by the worst-case fairness index. WFI more closely measures short-term bursty behavior. We will show that our Leap Forward Scheme satisfies both Golestani's as well as Bennett-Zhang's definition of fairness.

## 5.1 Fairness Measure of Golestani

A flow is said to be *backlogged* during interval $(t_1, t_2)$ if the queue for flow $f$ is never empty during $(t_1, t_2)$. Let $sent_f(t_1, t_2)$ denote the total number of bits of $f$ transmitted during $(t_1, t_2)$ by the server. Throughput fairness of an algorithm is measured by the maximum (absolute) difference between rate-normalized values of $sent_f(t_1, t_2)$ and $sent_f(t_1, t_2)$ over all pairs of backlogged flows and over all intervals $(t_1, t_2)$. In other words, consider an execution of the Leap Forward algorithm, and define $F(t_1, t_2)$ as follows:

$$F(t_1, t_2) = \max_{f,g} \left| \frac{sent_f(t_1, t_2)}{r_f} - \frac{sent_g(t_1, t_2)}{r_g} \right|,$$

where max is over all pairs of flows that are backlogged during $(t_1, t_2)$. Then, throughput fairness is measured by the worst-case maximum value of $F(t_1, t_2)$ over all intervals and all executions of the algorithm:

$$F = \max_{(t_1, t_2)} F(t_1, t_2).$$

We call a service discipline *fair* if $F$ is a small constant. In particular, $F$ should be a constant, independent of the length of the time interval [9]. It is known that in the case of the classical virtual clock, $F \to \infty$. For LFVC, we prove:

**Theorem 5.1 (Throughput Fairness)**
*The fairness measure of LFVC Clock satisfies:* $F \leq \max_{f,g} 3(\Delta_f + \Delta_g) + 2\tau + 4\rho$, *where* $\tau = M/B$ *and* $\rho$ *is a tag coarsening parameter.*

## 5.2 Worst Case Fairness Index

The following measure of throughput fairness, due to Bennett and Zhang [2] provides a more refined measure of short term throughput unfairness than the Golestani measure. We start with some notation.

The delay $D(p)$ of a packet $p$ is the real time that elapses between the arrival time of $p$ and the time $p$ is completely transmitted. The arrival time of a packet $p$ is denoted by $A(p)$. Assume $p$ belongs to flow $f$. Let $Q(p)$ denote the size (in bits) of the queue in front of $p$ (including $p$) at the time of $p$'s arrival.

**Definition 5.2** *A service discipline is said to be worst-case for flow $f$ if, for any packet $p$ in $f$, the following holds:* $D(p) < \frac{Q(p)}{r_f} + C_f$, *where $C_f$ is a constant independent of other flows sharing this server. The normalized worst-case fair index (WFI) is defined as* $C = \max_f \frac{r_f C_f}{B}$.

Bennett and Zhang [1] have shown that Worst-case Weighted Fair Queuing has an optimal WFI equal to $\tau = M/B$. We show that the WFI of our scheme is nearly the same. Our proof depends critically on two facts: one, the current tag of a backlogged flow differs from the server clock by no more than $2\Delta_f + \tau + \rho$ (Lemma 4.1), and, two, during a backlogged period $(t_1, t_2)$, the difference of the initial and final tags of $f$ is (roughly) the number of bits of flow $f$ transmitted during $(t_1, t_2)$ divided by its rate $r_f$.

**Theorem 5.3** *The Worst-Case Fairness Index of Leap Forward Virtual Clock is bounded by* $\tau + \max_f 2(\tau + \rho) \frac{r_f}{B}$.

In practice, $r_f/B$ should be quite small, and if we set the coarsening parameter $\rho$ to roughly $\tau$, the WFI of Leap Forward approaches $\tau$, which is the optimal value of WFI [1].

# 6 Data Structures

The only nontrivial data structure needed for implementing LFVC is a priority queue. Using standard data structures for maintaining priority queues, we can implement LFVC in $O(\log N)$ time per packet. We can improve the processing cost to $O(\log \log N)$ per packet using two key ideas: *tag coarsening* and a *finite-universe priority queue.*

The basic idea of tag coarsening is that maintaining *exact* order among virtual clock tags is overkill if one is willing to tolerate a minor increase in latency. For instance, suppose the server rate is $B$ and the largest packet size in any flow is $M$. Then, rounding up all the tags to multiples of $M/B$ dramatically reduces the underlying key space of the priority queue, while increasing the delay by at most $M/B$. We further reduce the key space to a set of $O(N)$ integers, in the range $[1, cN]$ for a fixed constant $c$, by using a tag-separation property of our algorithm and *modular arithmetic* to recycle tags. With these ideas in place, we use "approximate sorting" and a finite-universe priority queue of van Emde Boas [6] to achieve $O(\log\log N)$ processing time per packet. Details can be found in [15].

The following theorem summarizes the main result of our paper.

**Theorem 6.1** *LFVC provides a guaranteed delay bound comparable to WFQ, throughput fairness comparable to worst-case WFQ, and can be implemented with the worst-case overhead of $O(\log\log N)$ per packet, where $N$ is the number of active flows.*

### 6.1 Preliminary Implementations

We have implemented the $O(\lg\lg N)$ priority queue. The constants are roughly 250 Sparc instructions per operation. We have found that a second scheme based on tries, outperforms the (unoptimized) Van Emde Boas structure for small values of $N$. The trie scheme views a $K$ bit tag $b$ bits at a time, and goes through a tree of arrays $b$ bits at a time. If $b$ is small we can avoid searching through empty array elements by keeping a bitmap and doing a table lookup to determine the lowest non-null array position. A trie-based implementation for values in the range $[0..2^{21}-1]$ requires worst-case 85 Sparc instructions for Insert and 183 instructions for ExtractMin. Note that for both the trie scheme and the Van Emde Boas scheme, reducing the size of the tag by coarsening is crucial for decreasing processing costs. We hope that further optimizations will reduce the cost to around 40 instructions for values of $N < 10000$.

## 7 Simulations

We used a stripped down version of the network simulator, freely available from Lawrence Berkeley Laboratories,[2] to carry out simulations. We implemented several fair-queuing algorithms and compared their performance to Leap Forward Virtual Clock scheme. The simulator allows us to examine packets that go through a link, and calculate delays of individual packets and overall bandwidth seen by each flow.

Due to space constraints, we show only one of the simulation results in Table 7 where we compare the delay experienced by different flows under four different fair queuing schemes. Average delay experienced by flows under LFVC are similar to those under VC and much smaller than those under DRR and SCFQ. Other results [15] illustrate the merits of LFVC over other fair queuing schemes.

[2] http://www-nrg.ee.lbl.gov/ns/

[3] The rate allocations in this experiment are borrowed from [13]; but the flows here send data at a constant bit rate as opposed to an on-off model used in their experiments.

Based on our experiments, we observe: **1)** LFVC rations the output link fairly among contending flows. The leap forward step prevents credit accumulation. **2)** Flows sending packets at or under their reserved rate experience very small delay in LFVC but the delay suffered by ill-behaved flows (on average) appears to be worse in Leap Forward. **3)** LFVC does not cause bursty behavior as can be exhibited by both SCFQ and WFQ.

## 8 Concluding Remarks

We believe there are several important contributions of this paper. The first contribution is the algorithm itself. Leap Forward Virtual Clock goes well beyond Virtual Clock by adding two non-trivial modifications: a quarantine mechanism and a leap forward mechanism. The resulting scheme provides throughput fairness, even in a worst-case sense, without compromising delay bounds. The algorithm is elegant and simple to implement, and should have practical appeal.

Second, our analytical techniques (i.e., separation of delay and throughput conditions) are new and simple. They may be useful for other schemes as well (WFQ, SCFQ etc.)

Third, the idea of trading off delay bounds for reduced computation, leads to an exponential speedup for our algorithm. The same ideas may well be applicable to other fair queuing schemes but requires careful proofs. We found a number of subtle bugs before we were able to make coarsening work for LFVC without compromising throughput fairness.

The *scalability* offered by $O(\log\log N)$ schemes holds promise as networks become larger and operate at increasingly higher speeds. Our preliminary implementation shows that the underlying constant is reasonably small (insert, delete, and successor/findmin operations cost between 200 and 300 Sparc instructions). We believe that with further optimization we can rival more conventional schemes (such as tries), for even small values of $N$.

Future work includes using LFVC in Hierarchical Fair Queuing systems and extending the scheme to provide jitter bounds. We also plan to implement LFVC in a real router testbed.

## References


[1] J. Bennett and H. Zhang Worst-case Fair Weighted Fair Queuing. *Proc. INFOCOM*, 1995.

[2] J. Bennett and H. Zhang Hierarchical Packet Fair Queuing Algorithms. in *Proc. SIGCOMM '96.*

[3] R. Brown Calendar Queues: a fast O(1) Priority Queue Implementation for the Simulation Event Set Prob-

| Flow | Reserved rate[3] | arrival rate | Delay (seconds) | | | |
|---|---|---|---|---|---|---|
| | | | DRR | SCFQ | VC | LFVC |
| 0 | 0.5 | 0.498 | 0.00143 | 0.00112 | 0.000213 | 0.000213 |
| 1 | 0.0625 | 0.1 | 0.368 | 0.365 | 0.382 | 0.382 |
| 2 | 0.0625 | 0.62 | 0.00242 | 0.00526 | 0.00186 | 0.00203 |
| 3 | 0.0625 | 0.61 | 0.00243 | 0.00535 | 0.002 | 0.00211 |
| 4 | 0.078125 | 0.076 | 0.00307 | 0.00404 | 0.000881 | 0.000861 |
| 5 | 0.078125 | 0.076 | 0.0035 | 0.00354 | 0.0025 | 0.00228 |
| 6 | 0.078125 | 0.076 | 0.00371 | 0.00335 | 0.00217 | 0.00229 |
| 7 | 0.078125 | 0.076 | 0.00392 | 0.00356 | 0.00114 | 0.00125 |

Table 2: Average delay experienced by flows under Deficit Round Robin (DRR), Virtual Clock, Self-Clocked, and Leap Forward. In this experiment we use constant bit rate flows with a packet size of 53 bytes. All flows except flow 1 are operating under their reserved rate. All these queuing algorithms provide fair sharing of the bandwidth. Since the columns representing throughput used by each flow under different schemes are identical to their allocated rate, they are not enumerated here. On the other hand, the delay experienced by flow 0 for example, varies widely across the different queuing disciplines. DRR and SCFQ do not provide good delay bounds, as can be seen from the table. Average delay experienced by flows under LFVC are similar to those under VC and much smaller than those under DRR and SCFQ.


lem. *Communications of the ACM, Vol 31,10, October 1988.*

[4] T. Cormen, C. Leiserson, and R. Rivest. Introduction to Algorithms. *MIT Press, 1990.*

[5] A. Demers, S. Keshav, and S. Shenker. Analysis and simulation of a fair queuing algorithm. *Proc. Sigcomm '89*, 19(4):1–12, September 1989.

[6] P. van Emde Boas, R. Kaas, and E. Zijlstra. Design and implementation of an efficient priority queue. *Math. Syst. Theory*, 10:99–127, 1977.

[7] N. Figuera and J. Pasquale. Leave-in-time: A new service discipline for real-time communication in a packet-switching data network. *Proc. Sigcomm '95*, September 1995.

[8] P. Goyal, S. S. Lam, and H. M. Vin. Determining End-to-End Delay Bounds in Heterogeneous Networks. In *Proceedings of Workshop on Network and OS Support for Audio-Video*, pages 287–298, April 1995.

[9] S. J. Golestani. A Self-Clocked Fair Queuing Scheme for High Speed Applications. In *Proceedings of IEEE INFOCOM '94*, pages 636–646, April 1994.

[10] A. K. Parekh and R. G. Gallager. A Generalized Processor Sharing Approach to Flow Control: The Single Node Case. In *Proc. of IEEE INFOCOM*, pp. 915–924, 1992.

[11] A. K. Parekh and R. G. Gallager. A Generalized Processor Sharing Approach to Flow Control in Integrated Services Networks: The Multiple Node Case. In *Proc. of IEEE INFOCOM*, pp. 521–530, 1993.

[12] M. Shreedhar and G. Varghese. Efficient Fair Queuing Using Deficit Round Robin. In *Proc. of SIGCOMM*, pp. 231–242, 1995.

[13] D. Stiliadis and A. Varma. Latency-Rate Servers: A General Model for Analysis of Traffic Scheduling Algorithms. *Technical Report UCSC-CRL-95-38, Dept. of Computer Engineering and Information Sciences, UC Santa Cruz*, July 1995.

[14] D. Stiliadis and A. Varma. Frame-based Fair Queueing: A New Traffic Scheduling Algorithm for Packet-Switched Networks. *Proc. of ACM SIGMETRICS '96, May 1996.*

[15] S. Suri, G. Varghese and G. Chandranmenon. Leap Forward Virtual Clock: A New Fair Queuing Scheme with Guaranteed Delays and Throughput Fairness. *Technical Report, Dept. of Computer Science, Washington University, Saint Louis*, 1996. Use the WWW link: `www.cs.wustl.edu/~suri/leapforward.ps` to access the report.

[16] G. G. Xie and S. S. Lam. Delay Guarantee of a Virtual Clock Server. *IEEE/ACM Transactions on Networking, December 1995*

[17] Lixia Zhang. Virtual Clock: A New Traffic Control Algorithm for Packet-Switched Networks. *ACM Transactions on Computer Systems*, 9(2), May 1991.

# QLWFQ: A Queue Length Based Weighted Fair Queueing Algorithm in ATM Networks

Yoshihiro Ohba

Research and Development Center, Toshiba Corporation
Komukai Toshiba-cho 1, Saiwai-ku, Kawasaki 210, Japan
ohba@csl.rdc.toshiba.co.jp

## Abstract

*A work conserving $O(1)$ per-VC queueing algorithm named QLWFQ (Queue Length based Weighted Fair Queueing) for high-speed ATM networks is proposed. The basic process in QLWFQ is the comparison of the current queue length with the weight when a cell arrival or departure occurs. QLWFQ has upward compatibility with Fair Queueing and FIFO, and can be considered to be a simplified version of Weighted Round Robin. A delay bound and a fairness index are derived analytically for the QLWFQ algorithm. The simulation results for heavily and lightly loaded conditions are also presented. The analytical and simulation results show that QLWFQ achieves a better balance between traffic isolation and traffic sharing than timestamp based algorithms.*

## 1 Introduction

In integrated services packet networks such as ATM (Asynchronous Transfer Mode), it is important to support different QoS (Quality of Service) for various types of realtime and non-realtime applications. For realtime applications, it is required that a maximum delay and delay variation be guaranteed for VCs (Virtual Channels) conforming to the traffic descriptors negotiated at the call setup time. On the other hand, there is no QoS requirement in terms of delay for non-realtime applications. Instead, fair use of the available bandwidth should be achieved even if a misbehaving user sends a large amount of cells at a higher rate. Per-VC queueing with different weights among VCs is considered to be a flexible method for satisfying these requirements, and many rate-based per-VC queueing algorithms have been proposed. These include WFQ (Weighted Fair Queueing) [1], VirtualClock [2, 3], SCFQ (Self-Clocked Fair Queueing) [4, 5], Delay-EDD (Delay Earliest Due Date), Jitter-EDD [6], and HOL-EDD (Head-Of-the-Line EDD) [7]. All these algorithms except for Jitter-EDD are work-conserving, which implies that the server never becomes idle when there is a packet to send.

WFQ is also referred to as PGPS (Packet-by-packet Generalized Processor Sharing), and has analytically attractive characteristics on delay and fairness [8, 9]. The computational cost, however, makes it impractical. VirtualClock and SCFQ can schedule packets in a relatively simple manner compared with WFQ. WFQ, SCFQ, and VirtualClock schedule packets by using the packet length, weight, and virtual time. Delay-EDD, Jitter-EDD, and HOL-EDD assign service deadlines to packets or packet queues and send packets in deadline based order. Delay bounds are guaranteed for all these algorithms. In other words, traffic isolation is achieved. Another similarity is that these algorithms are based on timestamps being assigned to packets or packet queues.

However, there are two problems in the timestamp based scheduling algorithms. One well-known problem is computational cost. If no approximation method is employed, the cost in timestamp based algorithms is $O(\log_2 N)$ where $N$ denotes the number of backlogged VCs. The $O(\log_2 N)$ complexity is large when several thousands of VCs are multiplexed into a high-speed link such as an ATM link. An $O(1)$ solution has been proposed by Rexford for the SCFQ algorithm [10].

Another problem is related to delay jitter. For example, a 99% delay for WFQ is known to be larger than that for FIFO (First-In-First-Out), which implies that the timestamp based scheduling algorithms are not the best choice from the viewpoint of traffic sharing [11].

In this paper we propose a work conserving $O(1)$ per-VC queueing algorithm named QLWFQ (Queue Length based Weighted Fair Queueing) for high-speed fixed-length packet switching networks such as ATM networks. The basic process in QLWFQ involves the comparison of the current queue length with the weight when a cell arrival or departure occurs. QLWFQ has upward compatibility with Fair Queueing [12] and FIFO, and can be considered to be a simplified version of WRR (Weighted Round Robin)[13]. We analytically derive a delay bound and a fairness index for the QLWFQ algorithm. We also present simulation results for heavily and lightly loaded conditions.

In Section 2, the basic QLWFQ algorithm is explained. The delay bound and fairness index for our algorithm is derived in Section 3. The enhanced QLWFQ algorithm which shows better multiplexing performance is described in Section 4, and the simulation results are presented in Section 5. Finally, we summarize this paper and describe the current status of the incorporation of the QLWFQ algorithm in our ATM switch products.


0-8186-7780-5/97 $10.00 © 1997 IEEE

## 2 Basic QLWFQ Algorithm

In this section, we describe the basic QLWFQ algorithm. A QLWFQ multiplexer is composed of VC queues, one scheduling queue, and a comparison section, as shown in Fig. 1.

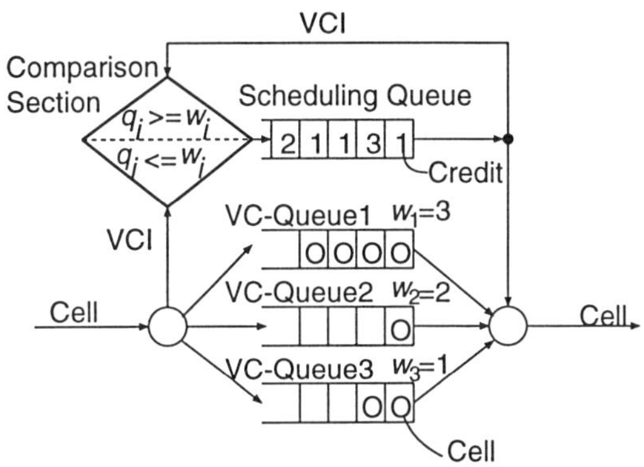


Figure 1: Example of QLWFQ

VC queues store cells on a FIFO basis and are provided for individual VCs. The scheduling queue is also based on the FIFO principle and stores VCIs (Virtual Channel Identifiers). The VCIs stored in the scheduling queue are referred to as *credits*. Let $w_i(\geq 1)$ be the weight in terms of service rate of VC queue $i$ and let $q_i$ be the current queue length (the current number of cells) of the same queue. For simplicity, we first assume that each $w_i$ takes an integral value. This assumption will be removed later.

When a cell of VC $i$ arrives, it is stored in VC queue $i$, and $q_i$ is incremented by one. A credit "$i$" is then entered in the scheduling queue if $q_i \leq w_i$ at the comparison section. For example, in Fig. 1, if a cell of VC 2 arrives, the credit "2" can enter the scheduling queue. However, if a cell of VC 1 arrives, the credit "1" cannot enter the scheduling queue anymore.

At the time of cell output, the credit, say "$i$", at the head of the scheduling queue, is removed and the corresponding VC queue $i$ gets service. Then $q_i$ is decremented by one and the credit "$i$" is re-entered in the scheduling queue if $q_i \geq w_i$. Again in Fig. 1, the credit "1" at the head of the scheduling queue is re-entered in the scheduling queue. The credit "2" is, however, not re-entered if no cell arrives from VC 2 until the credit "2" is dequeued from the scheduling queue. This re-entry process guarantees the work conservation property of the QLWFQ scheduler (this is shown later). Clearly, the complexity of QLWFQ is $O(1)$. The flowchart of this algorithm is shown in Fig 2. Note that there are several $O(1)$ non-timestamp-based algorithms such as DRR (Deficit Round Robin)[14] and CORR (Carry-Over Round Robin) [15], but these algorithms require a greater number of variables than QLWFQ.

QLWFQ behaves as a Fair Queueing algorithm if

**In the connection establishment phase**

```
qi := 0;
```

**At the cell arrival time**

```
i := VCI of the cell;
Enqueue the cell in VC-queue i;
qi := qi + 1;
if (qi ≤ wi) then begin
   Enqueue the credit "i" in the scheduling-queue;
end
```

**At the cell transmission time**
(if there is a cell to transmit)

```
Dequeue the credit "i" from the scheduling-queue;
Dequeue the cell from VC-queue i;
qi := qi − 1;
if (qi ≥ wi) then begin
   Enqueue the credit "i" in the scheduling-queue;
end
```

Figure 2: QLWFQ Algorithm

$w_i = 1$ for all $i$. FIFO queueing is also emulated by QLWFQ if $w_i = \infty$ for all $i$. So we can say that QLWFQ has upward compatibility with Fair Queueing and FIFO. QLWFQ can also be considered to be a simplified version of WRR[13] which originally has $O(\log_2 N)$ complexity [1]. The main difference between QLWFQ and WRR is that queue length information is used in QLWFQ, whereas WRR uses partial information on queue length, i.e., whether each per-VC queue is backlogged or not.

The fundamental characteristics of the QLWFQ algorithm are outlined in Theorem 1.

**Theorem 1** *Assume that $w_i$ is not changed during the connection holding time for all $i$. Let $n_i$ be the current number of credits for VC $i$ in the scheduling queue. Then, for all $i$,*

$$n_i = \min(q_i, w_i).$$

**Proof** A cell arrival or a cell departure is defined to be an event in the QLWFQ system. Let $e^{(m)}$ be the $m$-th event. Also let $q_i^{(m)}$ be the current number of cells in VC queue $i$ and let $n_i^{(m)}$ be the the current number of credits for $i$ in the scheduling queue. Note that $q_i^{(0)} = n_i^{(0)} = 0$ for all $i$.

(i) For $m = 1$, the event $e^{(1)}$ must be a cell arrival. Let the VCI of the cell be $i$. Since $w_i \geq 1$ and $q_i^{(1)} = 1$,

[1] It is stated in [16] that the complexity of WRR is $O(1)$. But we believe it should be $O(\log_2 N)$, since binary search is used for finding the next VC entry that is backlogged, still unvisited, and located at the nearest position from the current position in the scanning memory.

the credit "i" is entered in the scheduling queue and $n_i^{(1)} = q_i^{(1)} = 1 \leq w_i$. Hence, $n_i^{(m)} = \min(q_i^{(m)}, w_i)$ holds for $m = 1$.

**(ii)** For $m = k$, assume that $n_i^{(m)} = \min(q_i^{(m)}, w_i)$ for all $i$ and move to the case of $m = k + 1$. The event $e^{(m+1)}$ is either a cell arrival or a cell departure.

First consider the case that $e^{(m+1)}$ is the cell arrival of VC $i$. Then for all $j \neq i$, $n_j^{(m+1)} = n_j^{(m)} = \min(q_j^{(m)}, w_j) = \min(q_j^{(m+1)}, w_j)$. For $i$, if $q_i^{(m)} < w_i$ then $n_i^{(m+1)} = n_i^{(m)} + 1 = q_i^{(m)} + 1 = q_i^{(m+1)} \leq w_i$. On the other hand, if $q_i^{(m)} \geq w_i$ then $n_i^{(m+1)} = n_i^{(m)} = w_i < q_i^{(m+1)}$. Hence, $n_i^{(m+1)} = \min(q_i^{(m+1)}, w_i)$ is true in this case.

Next, consider the case that $e^{(m+1)}$ is the cell departure of VC $i$. Then $n_j^{(m+1)} = n_j^{(m)} = \min(q_j^{(m)}, w_j) = \min(q_j^{(m+1)}, w_j)$ holds for all $j \neq i$ as in the first case. For $i$, since the transmitted cell belongs to VC $i$, $n_i^{(m)}$ and $q_i^{(m)}$ must be positive. This implies that $q_i^{(m+1)} = q_i^{(m)} - 1$. Therefore if $q_i^{(m)} > w_i$, then $n_i^{(m+1)} = n_i^{(m)} - 1 + 1 = w_i \leq q_i^{(m+1)}$. If $q_i^{(m)} \leq w_i$, then $n_i^{(m+1)} = n_i^{(m)} - 1 = q_i^{(m)} - 1 = q_i^{(m+1)} < w_i$. Therefore, $n_i^{(m+1)} = \min(q_i^{(m+1)}, w_i)$ also holds in this case. □

The work conserving property of the QLWFQ scheduler is assured by Theorem 1.
Theorem 1 is also used to derive the delay upper bound as described in detail in the next section.

## 3 Analysis

In this section, we show several analytical results on the delay and fairness of the QLWFQ algorithm. First we define the notations used in this section. $A_i(t)$ and $S_i(t)$ denote the number of cells of VC $i$ that arrive at and depart from the QLWFQ scheduler during the time interval $(0, t]$, respectively. Initially, $A_i(0) = S_i(0) = 0$. The unit of time is expressed in cell slots. We assume that $A_i(t)$ and $S_i(t)$ are staircase integer functions. $Q_i(t) (= A_i(t) - S_i(t))$ denotes the number of cells of VC $i$ queued at the time $t$, and $w_i$ denotes the weight allocated to VC $i$. The current number of existing VCs are represented by $N$. For any function $f(t)$, we define $f(t_1, t_2) \triangleq f(t_2) - f(t_1)$, and for any real number $x$, $[x]^+ \triangleq \max(x, 0)$. In addition, $\lfloor x \rfloor$ denotes the maximum integer that is not greater than $x$ and $\lceil x \rceil$ the minimum integer that is greater than or equal to $x$. For simplicity, in the remainder of this paper, we assume that each input link and each VC-queue have infinite capacity.

### 3.1 Leaky Bucket Filter

In ATM networks, leaky bucket filters are widely used to monitor traffic entering the network. The leaky bucket filter for VC $i$ is characterized by two parameters $(\sigma_i, \rho_i)$. Tokens are generated at a fixed rate $\rho_i$ [cells/slot], and are stored in the token bucket unless the number of tokens in the bucket reaches $\sigma_i$. A cell can be released into the network only after removing a token from the token bucket. If there is no token in the token bucket, cells are buffered until a token becomes available.

If $A_i(t)$ satisfies the following inequality,

$$A_i(t_1, t_2) \leq \sigma_i + \rho_i(t_2 - t_1),$$

for the whole time interval $(t_1, t_2]$, then $A_i(t)$ is called leaky bucket conformant and is represented by the expression $A_i(t) \sim (\sigma_i, \rho_i)$. Cells are not buffered at the leaky bucket filter if $A_i(t) \sim (\sigma_i, \rho_i)$. When a dual leaky bucket is used for monitoring traffic, we set $\rho = m$ and $\sigma = b/(p - m)$ where $p$, $m$ and $b$ denote the peak rate, the mean rate and the maximum burst length, respectively. Next, let $l_i(t)$ be the available tokens in the token bucket for VC $i$ at time $t$. Then, $l_i(t)$ can be expressed as

$$l_i(t) = \min_{\tau \leq t}\{\sigma_i + \rho_i(t - \tau) - A_i(\tau, t)\}.$$

From reference [8], $l_i(t)$ is known to satisfy the following relations.

$$0 \leq l_i(t) \leq \sigma_i, \forall t \geq 0,$$

$$A_i(t_1, t_2) \leq \rho_i(t_2 - t_1) - l_i(t_1, t_2). \tag{1}$$

### 3.2 Delay Upper Bound

Next, we derive the delay upper bound of cells that are leaky bucket conformant and are multiplexed in a QLWFQ scheduler. Of course, we consider the case where the allocated weights are not dynamically changed.

VC $i$ is called *locally stable* when $\rho_i \leq \frac{w_i}{W}$, where $W = \sum_{j=1}^{N} w_j$. Here, $\frac{w_i}{W}$ [cells/slot] denotes the minimum service rate for VC $i$. Let $Q_i^*$ be the maximum number of cells queued in the VC queue $i$ and let $D_i^*$ be the maximum delay for VC $i$. Then the following upper bounds exist on $Q_i^*$ and $D_i^*$ for the QLWFQ scheduler.

**Theorem 2** *For any locally stable VC $i$ which satisfies $A_i(t) \sim (\sigma_i, \rho_i)$,*

$$\begin{cases} Q_i^* \leq \sigma_i + \rho_i(Z_i + W - w_i) \\ D_i^* \leq nW + (W - w_i) + m \end{cases},$$

*where*

$$Z_i = \min(W, \frac{\sigma_i + W - w_i}{1 - \rho_i})$$

*and*

$$n = \lfloor \frac{\sigma_i + \rho_i(Z_i + W - w_i)}{w_i} \rfloor,$$

$$m = \sigma_i + \rho_i(Z_i + W - w_i) - nw_i.$$

Before proving Theorem 2, we outline three lemmas.

**Lemma 1** *For a QLWFQ scheduler,*

$$S_i(t, t + \tau) \geq [w_i - W + \tau]^+,$$

*where*

$$0 \leq \tau \leq W - [w_i - Q_i(t)]^+.$$

**Proof** Theorem 1 shows that there are $\min(Q_i(t), w_i)$ credits for VC $i$ at any time $t$ in the scheduling queue. Also, there are in total a maximum of $W - w_i + \min(Q_i(t), w_i)$ credits at any time $t$ in the scheduling queue.
**(i)** If $0 \le \tau \le W - w_i$, at most $(W - w_i)$ credits in total for $j(\neq i)$s may exist in the scheduling queue. When all these $(W - w_i)$ credits precede any credit for $i$ in the scheduling queue, the credits for $i$ are not dequeued from the scheduling queue during the interval $[t, t+\tau]$. This is the worst queueing pattern for VC $i$. Therefore, $S_i \ge 0$, and the lemma holds.
**(ii)** If $W - w_i < \tau \le W - [w_i - Q_i(t)]^+$, at least $\tau - (W - w_i)$ cells of VC $i$ are served even in the worst queueing pattern for VC $i$. Therefore, $S_i(t, t+\tau) \ge w_i - W + \tau$, and the lemma holds. □

Next, as in reference [8], we define a *potential backlog* of VC $i$ by

$$\sigma_i^t \triangleq Q_i(t) + l_i(t),$$

which represents the maximum allowable queue length of VC queue $i$ at time $t$. For $t = 0$,

$$\sigma_i^0 = Q_i(0) + l_i(0) = Q_i(0) + \sigma_i - A_i(0) = \sigma_i.$$

On other hand, from Eq. (1),

$$\begin{aligned} Q_i(t_1, t_2) &= A_i(t_1, t_2) - S_i(t_1, t_2) \\ &\le \rho_i(t_2 - t_1) - l_i(t_1, t_2) - S_i(t_1, t_2). \end{aligned}$$

This yields

$$\sigma_i^{t_2} - \sigma_i^{t_1} \le \rho_i(t_2 - t_1) - S_i(t_1, t_2) \quad (2)$$

We have following lemmas related to the potential backlog.

**Lemma 2** *If $A_i(t) \sim (\sigma_i, \rho_i)$, then*

$$\sigma_i^t > \sigma_i \ \Rightarrow\ Q_i(t) \ge \sigma_i^t - \sigma_i.$$

**Proof** Since $l_i(t) \le \sigma_i$, $Q_i(t) = \sigma_i^t - l_i(t) \ge \sigma_i^t - \sigma_i$. □

**Lemma 3** *If VC $i$ is locally stable and satisfies $A_i(t) \sim (\sigma_i, \rho_i)$, then, for the discrete time series $\{t_j\}$ defined as*

$$\begin{cases} t_j = 0, & j = 0 \\ t_j = t_{j-1} + \tau_j, & j = 1, 2, \ldots \end{cases}$$

$$\tau_j = W - [w_i - Q_i(t_{j-1})]^+, \quad W - w_i \le \tau_j \le W,$$

*the potential backlog at each time $t_j$ is bounded by*

$$\sigma_i^{t_j} \le \sigma_i + \rho_i \min(W, \frac{\sigma_i + W - w_i}{1 - \rho_i}).$$

**Proof** We prove this lemma by induction.
**(i)** The lemma clearly holds for $j = 0$.
**(ii)** For $j = 1$, from Eq. (2),

$$\begin{aligned} \sigma_i^{t_1} - \sigma_i^0 &\le \rho_i\tau_1 - S_i(0, \tau_1) \\ &\le \rho_i\tau_1 - [w_i - W + \tau_1]^+ \\ &\le \rho_i\tau_1 - (w_i - W + \tau_1) \\ &\le -(1 - \rho_i)(W - w_i) + W - w_i \\ &\le \rho_i(W - w_i). \end{aligned}$$

Since $\sigma_i^0 = \sigma_i$,

$$\sigma_i^{t_1} \le \sigma_i + \rho_i(W - w_i) \le \sigma_i + \rho_i \min(W, \frac{\sigma_i + W - w_i}{1 - \rho_i}).$$

Therefore, the lemma also holds for $j = 1$.
**(iii)** For the case of $j = k$, we assume that the lemma is true. Then,

$$Q_i(t_k) \le \sigma_i^{t_k} \le \sigma_i + \rho_i \min(W, \frac{\sigma_i + W - w_i}{1 - \rho_i}).$$

Since $\rho_i W \le w_i$,

$$\sigma_i^{t_k} \le \sigma_i + w_i.$$

Next consider the case of $j = k + 1$. Then,

$$\begin{aligned} \sigma_i^{t_{k+1}} - \sigma_i^{t_k} &\le \rho_i\tau_{k+1} - S_i(t_k, t_{k+1}) \\ &\le \rho_i\tau_{k+1} - [w_i - W + \tau_{k+1}]^+ \\ &= \rho_i\tau_{k+1} - w_i + W - \tau_{k+1}. \end{aligned} \quad (3)$$

**(iii-a)** If $\sigma_i^{t_k} \le \sigma_i$, as in (ii),

$$\sigma_i^{t_{k+1}} \le \sigma_i + \rho_i(W - w_i) \le \sigma_i + \min(W, \frac{\sigma_i + W - w_i}{1 - \rho_i}).$$

**(iii-b)** If $\sigma_i^{t_k} > \sigma_i$, by Lemma 2, $Q_i(t_k) \ge \sigma_i^{t_k} - \sigma_i$. Then,

$$\tau_{k+1} = W - [w_i - Q_i(t_k)]^+ \ge W - [w_i - \sigma_i^{t_k} + \sigma_i]^+.$$

Thus,

$$\begin{aligned} W - \tau_{k+1} + \sigma_i^{t_k} &\le [\sigma_i + w_i - \sigma_i^{t_k}]^+ + \sigma_i^{t_k} \\ &= \sigma_i + w_i - \sigma_i^{t_k} + \sigma_i^{t_k} = \sigma_i + w_i. \end{aligned}$$

Hence, Eq. (3) can be rewritten as

$$\sigma_i^{t_{k+1}} \le \rho_i\tau_{k+1} - w_i + \sigma_i + w_i \le \sigma_i + \rho_i\tau_{k+1} \quad (4)$$

Now, consider the following two cases for $\sigma_i + \rho_i W$.
**(iii-b-1)** In the case of $\sigma_i + \rho_i W \le w_i$ (i.e., $W \ge \frac{\sigma_i + W - w_i}{1 - \rho_i}$), from the assumption that the lemma holds, $Q_i(t_k) \le \sigma_i^{t_k} \le \sigma_i + \rho_i \frac{\sigma_i + W - w_i}{1 - \rho_i} \le w_i$. This implies that

$$\begin{aligned} \tau_{k+1} = W - [w_i - Q(t_k)]^+ &= W - w_i + Q_i(t_k) \\ &\le W - w_i + \frac{\sigma_i + \rho_i(W - w_i)}{1 - \rho_i} \\ &= \frac{\sigma_i + W - w_i}{1 - \rho_i}. \end{aligned}$$

Therefore, Eq. (4) can be rewritten as

$$\sigma_i^{t_{k+1}} \le \sigma_i + \rho_i \frac{\sigma_i + W - w_i}{1 - \rho_i} = \sigma_i + \rho_i \min(W, \frac{\sigma_i + W - w_i}{1 - \rho_i}).$$

**(iii-b-2)** In the case of $\sigma_i + \rho_i W > w_i$, since $\tau_{k+1} \le W < \frac{\sigma_i + W - w_i}{1 - \rho_i}$, we obtain

$$\sigma_i^{t_{k+1}} \le \sigma_i + \rho_i W = \sigma_i + \rho_i \min(W, \frac{\sigma_i + W - w_i}{1 - \rho_i}).$$

Thus Lemma 3 is proven. □

Lemma 3 shows that the potential backlog and hence the queue length for any locally stable leaky bucket conformant VC is bounded at time $t_j$'s. Theorem 2 is finally obtained after deriving the bound of the potential backlog during intervals $(t_j, t_{j+1}]$ $(j = 0, 1, \ldots)$. Our approach to prove Theorem 2 is illustrated in Fig. 3.

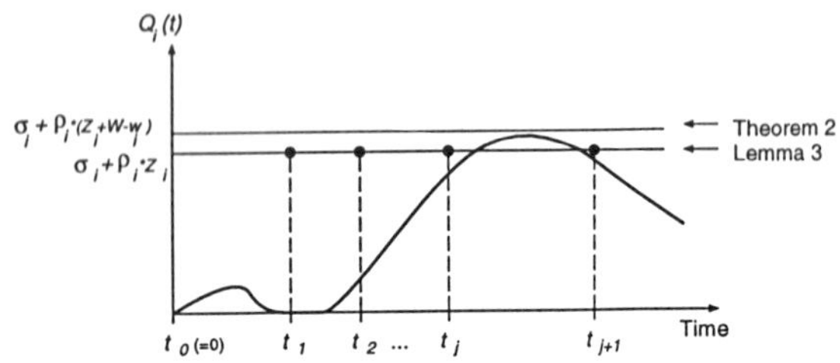


Figure 3: Approach to obtaining Theorem 2.

**Proof of Theorem 2** If $\frac{w_i}{W} = 1$, Theorem 2 is apparently true because there is only one VC in the QLWFQ system for this case. So we only consider the case of $\frac{w_i}{W} < 1$. Then, for any time $t(\geq 0)$, either of the following two cases is applied.

**(i)** In the case of $t = t_j, (j = 0, 1, \ldots)$, from Lemma 3 we obtain $Q_i(t) \leq \sigma_i + \rho_i \min(W, \frac{\sigma_i + W - w_i}{1-\rho_i})$.

**(ii)** In the case of $t \neq t_j, (j = 0, 1, \ldots)$, an integer $k(\geq 0)$ exists which satisfies $t_k < t < t_{k+1}$, $t - t_k < \tau_{k+1} \leq W$. If $\tau$ is defined as $\tau \triangleq t - t_k$, then $\tau$ satisfies the following relation.

$$\sigma_i^t - \sigma_i^{t_k} \leq \rho_i\tau - S_i(t_k, t_k + \tau) \leq \rho_i\tau - [w_i - W + \tau]^+.$$

**(ii-a)** If $\tau \leq W - w_i$, $\sigma_i^t - \sigma_i^{t_k} \leq \rho_i(W - w_i)$.
**(ii-b)** If $W - w_i < \tau < \tau_{k+1}$, then,

$$\begin{aligned} \sigma_i^t - \sigma_i^{t_k} &\leq \rho_i\tau - (w_i - W + \tau) \\ &\leq (\rho_i - 1)\tau - w_i + W \\ &< (\rho_i - 1)(W - w_i) - w_i + W \\ &= \rho_i(W - w_i). \end{aligned}$$

From (ii-a) and (ii-b), we obtain

$$\begin{aligned} Q_i(t) &\leq \sigma_i^t \leq \sigma_i^{t_k} + \rho_i(W - w_i) \\ &\leq \sigma_i + \rho_i\{\min(W, \frac{\sigma_i + W - w_i}{1 - \rho_i}) + W - w_i\}. \end{aligned}$$

Consequently, from (i) and (ii), the queue length is bounded according the following expression.

$$Q_i^* \leq \sigma_i + \rho_i(Z_i + W - w_i).$$

Consider the case where a cell of VC $i$, say $C$, arrives at time $t$ and the length of VC queue $i$ becomes $Q_i(t)$. The delay for cell $C$ is maximized when there are always $w_j$ credits in the scheduling queue for all VC $j(\neq i)$ and no more cells of VC $i$ arrive until cell $C$ is transmitted. In this case, Lemma 1 guarantees that at least $w_i$ cells of VC $i$ are served every $W$ cell slots as long as the length of VC queue $i$ is greater than or equal to $w_i$ at the beginning of each set of $W$ cell slots, and finally, when the queue length becomes $m(< w_i)$ at the beginning of a set of $W$ cell slots, then cell $C$ is transmitted within $W - w_i + m$ cell slots. Consequently, the following delay bound is obtained.

$$D_i^* \leq nW + (W - w_i) + m.$$

□

Note that one can easily find a delay bound without using the notion of potential backlog as follows. Consider a busy period $[t_1, t_2]$ during which $Q(t) \geq w_i$ holds. In such a period, at least $w_i$ cells are served within $W$ slots. In conjunction with the condition $A_i(t_1, t_2) \leq \sigma_i + \rho_i(t_2 - t_1)$, a delay bound is obtained. This method is often used for a flow control system such as TCP. However, the obtained bound is not tight since correlation between $l_i(t_1)$ and $Q_i(t_1)$ is not considered.

We can calculate the delay bound at the next node by substituting the bound on $Q^*$ at the current node for $\sigma_i$ at the next node. The end-to-end delay bound can also be obtained by repeating this calculation for all nodes along the path and summing up the delay bounds at all nodes.

We now present a comparative result on the delay bound for the single node case. Table 1 shows the delay bounds of VC $i$ for QLWFQ, SCFQ, and PGPS schedulers for various values of the total number of VCs $(N)$. The parameters are set as $(\sigma_i, \rho_i) = (30, 1/24)$ and $w_i = 1$. Here we assume that $W = 24$, which means that the minimum service rate $w_i/W$ is equal to $\rho_i$. VCs other than $i$ may create cells at any high rate. The results for VirtualClock and PGPS are the same and are considered to be the ideal result. The delay for QLWFQ is larger than that for SCFQ, but the difference becomes small as $N$ becomes large. It should be noted that the delay bound for QLWFQ depends not only on $w_i/W$ but also on the absolute values of $w_i$ and $W$. In the above example, if $w_i = 3$ and $W = 24 * 3$, the delay bound for QLWFQ becomes 863, whereas, if $w_i = 5$ and $W = 24*5$, the delay bound becomes 959. For SCFQ and PGPS, the delay bound is constant, however. Hence, it is important for QLWFQ to set the weights to values that are as low as possible, keeping the desired value for $w_i/W$. For this purpose, we present an enhanced QLWFQ algorithm in Section 4.

Table 1: Delay upper bounds (unit: cell slot)

| $N$ | QLWFQ | SCFQ | PGPS, VirtualClock |
|---|---|---|---|
| 2 | | 745 | |
| 5 | | 748 | |
| 10 | 767 | 753 | 721 |
| 20 | | 763 | |
| 24 | | 767 | |

### 3.3 Fairness

While it is crucial to guarantee the delay bound for realtime traffic, fair or weighted fair service is required for non-realtime traffic. In this section, we discuss the fairness of the QLWFQ scheduler.

We use the fairness index introduced in [16]. Consider a time $t_1$ at which VC $i$ and VC $j$ being compared have an infinite supply of cells. This forces them to be continuously backlogged in the servers. The fairness index $F$ is defined by the upper bound on $|\frac{S_i(t_1,t_2)}{r_i} - \frac{S_j(t_1,t_2)}{r_j}|$ for any set of VCs $(i, j)$ and for any time interval $(t_1, t_2]$, where $r_k = \frac{w_k}{W}r$ and $r$ [cells/sec.] denotes the link capacity. Then QLWFQ has the following characteristics in terms of fairness.

**Theorem 3** *For a QLWFQ scheduler,* $F = \frac{W}{r}$.

**Proof of Theorem 3** Let the discrete time series $\{\tau_m\}$ be defined as

$$\tau_m = \begin{cases} t_1, & m = 0 \\ \tau_{m-1} + w_i + w_j + \\ \sum_{k \neq i,j} \min(Q_k(\tau_{m-1}), w_k), & m > 0 \end{cases},$$

and let the index $M(\geq 0)$ be such that the following inequality is satisfied.

$$t_1 = \tau_0 < \tau_1 < \cdots < \cdots < \tau_{M-1} < \tau_M \leq t_2 < \tau_{M+1}.$$

Since VC queue $i$ has infinite number of cells in $[t_1, t_2]$,

$$Mw_i \leq S_i(t_1, t_2) < (M + 1)w_i,$$

then

$$M \leq \frac{S_i(t_1, t_2)}{w_i} < M + 1.$$

Therefore,

$$|\frac{S_i(t_1, t_2)}{w_i} - \frac{S_j(t_1, t_2)}{w_j}| < 1,$$

and Theorem 3 holds. □

The obtained fairness index is the same as that of Weighted Round Robin [16].

## 4 Enhanced QLWFQ Algorithm

If we allow only integer weights for the QLWFQ system, certain undesirable situations may arise. Consider the case where we allocate 20Mbps to VC 1 and 21Mbps to VC 2. In the original QLWFQ, the weights will be set to 20 and 21 for these VCs. This means that, when both VCs send cells at 21Mbps, their service rates will be indistinguishable until each queue length exceeds 20. In addition, the delay bound becomes large. In this section, we outline an enhanced QLWFQ algorithm in which the weights are not restricted to integer values.

The enhanced QLWFQ algorithm is shown in Fig. 4. Here, we allow each weight $w_i$ to take a real values that is greater than or equal to 1. Let $f_i$ be the fraction part of $w_i$, let $w'_i$ be the current weight for VC $i$, and let $n_i$ be the current number of credits in the scheduling queue for VC $i$. At the cell arrival time, $w'_i$ is used instead of $w_i$ for the comparison of the weight and the queue length. If $w'_i \leq q_i$, then the credit "i" is entered in the scheduling queue and $n_i$ is incremented by 1.

At cell transmission time, $w'_i$ is changed dynamically, i.e., $w'_i$ is decremented by one if $w'_i \geq \lfloor w_i \rfloor$ and then incremented by $f_i$, so that the expected value of $\lfloor w'_i \rfloor$ at the cell transmission time becomes $w_i$. In this case, however, Theorem 1 does not hold because of the dynamic changes in the weights. This is the reason for counting $n_i$ for each $i$. At the cell transmission time of VC $i$, the credit for $i$ is re-entered into the scheduling queue if $q_i \geq n_i$ and $w'_i \geq n_i$. Where the first condition checks whether there are enough cells to be scheduled, and the second checks that the weight is not decreased. The re-entry process is repeated in order to respond quickly to increases in the weight. The delay bound is also guaranteed by substituting $W$ for $W'$ and $w_i$ for $w'_i$ in Theorem 2, where $W' = \sum_i \lceil w_i \rceil$ and $w'_i = \lfloor w_i \rfloor$.

Note that treating real-number weights is not the only reason for dynamical weight changes. Some systems may change weights in accordance with requests from users, or by following a rate-based flow control protocol. We can also deal with these cases by repeating the re-entry process a maximum of $c + 1$ times, where $c$ is limited by hardware constraints.

**In the connection establishment phase**

> $f_i := w_i - \lfloor w_i \rfloor$;
> $w'_i := w_i$;
> $q_i := 0; n_i := 0$;

**At the cell arrival time**

> $i :=$ *VCI of the cell*;
> *Enqueue the cell in VC-queue* $i$;
> $q_i := q_i + 1$;
> `if` $(q_i \leq w'_i)$ `then begin`
>   *Enqueue the credit "i" in the scheduling-queue*;
>   $n_i := n_i + 1$;
> `end`

**At the cell transmission time**
(if there is a cell to transmit)

> *Dequeue the credit "i" from scheduling-queue*;
> *Dequeue the cell from VC-queue* $i$;
> $q_i := q_i - 1$;
> `if` $(w'_i \geq \lfloor w_i \rfloor + 1)$ `then` $w'_i := w'_i - 1$;
> `if` $(w'_i \geq n_i$ `and` $q_i \geq n_i)$ `then begin`
>   *Enqueue the credit "i" in the scheduling-queue*;
>   $c := 0$;
>   `while` $(w'_i \geq n_i + 1$ `and` $q_i \geq n_i + 1)$ `do begin`
>     *Enqueue the credit "i" in the scheduling-queue*
>     $n_i := n_i + 1$;
>     $c := c + 1$;
>     `if` $(c > c_{max})$ `then break`;
>   `end`;
> `end else` $n_i := n_i - 1$;

Figure 4: Enhanced QLWFQ Algorithm

## 5 Simulation Results

In this section, we show some of simulation results of QLWFQ related to traffic sharing. For comparison, we use SCFQ as a typical timestamp based scheduling algorithm.

### 5.1 Heavily Loaded Case

We use the simulation model used in reference [10] for the heavily loaded case. All VCs send one cell at every cell slot. There are three types of weights in this example and the parameters are shown in Table 2. For the SCFQ algorithm, the weight for all VCs of Class $i$ is set to $g_i$, whereas for the basic QLWFQ algorithm it is set to $g_i$ multipled by 120(=LCM(3,24,40)), which constitutes an integer weight. For the enhanced QLWFQ algorithm, it is set to a real value, $g_i$ multipled by $40(=\max(3, 24, 40))$, and the case of $c = 0$ is examined. The service curves of a selected VC of Class 1 are plotted for the three algorithm are in Fig. 5. Note that the dashed lines in these figures represent the ideal service curves based on the minimum service rates. Note also that there is no distinct difference among the service curves for VCs of Class 2 and 3, therefore the results are omitted.

Fig. 5 shows that all these algorithms guarantee the minimum bandwidth for each VC over an extended period of time. However, the short term fairness performance of the VC with higher weight is different in each of the three algorithms. From Fig. 5, Class 1 VCs in basic QLWFQ get less bandwidth than in SCFQ and enhanced QLWFQ in shorter periods. This is because in the basic QLWFQ algorithm a Class 1 VC has a weight of 40, and it takes longer time for the queue length to reach this weight relative to the VCs of other classes.

Table 2: Traffic parameters (heavily loaded case)
(MSR: Minimum Service Rate per VC)

| Class($i$) | Number of VCs | Weight($g_i$) | MSR |
|---|---|---|---|
| 1 | 10 | 1/3 | 1/20 |
| 2 | 20 | 1/24 | 1/160 |
| 3 | 100 | 1/40 | 3/800 |

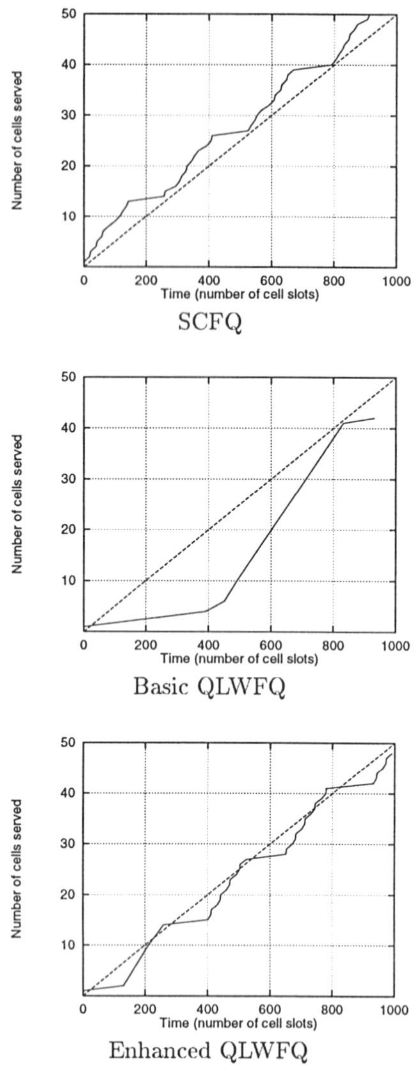


Figure 5: Cell departure process for class 1 traffic

### 5.2 Lightly Loaded Case

Next we show the results for lightly loaded conditions. In the simulation, two types of VCs with different weights were multiplexed into a single ATM link. Let $W_i$ be the weight of VCs of Class $i$ and let $N_i$ be the number of VCs of Class $i$. We set $W_2 = 1$ in all the remaining simulations. Each Class 1 VC is an ON-OFF source. Let $X$ (cells) be the minimum cell interarrival time during ON periods, let $L$ (cells) be the mean length of an ON period, and let $m_1$ be the mean arrival rate normalized against the link rate. Class 2 VCs are Poisson sources with the normalized mean arrival rate $m_2$. For example, FTP can be considered to be a Class 1 application, while TELNET can be considered to be a Class 2 application. The load of the system is denoted by $\rho(= N_1m_1 + N_2m_2)$. We examined three simulations, which are denoted as Simulation 1, 2, and 3. The simulation parameters are shown in Table 3. Two hundred thousand cell cycles were examined in Simulations 1 and 3, and a million cell cycles were studied in Simulation 2.

We examined various load conditions in Simulation 1. We set $m_2 = m_1/100$ and the load $\rho$ was changed with $m_1$. The mean delay and 99% delay for $W_1$=10,50,and 100 are shown in Fig. 6 and 7, respectively. In the case of $W_1 = 100$, the weight allocated for each class becomes proportional to the mean rate of the class. For all algorithms except for FIFO, different delay characteristics were obtained by changing the weight. As can be seen, there is a difference between the delay characteristics of QLWFQ and SCFQ, and this becomes pronounced as $W_1$ becomes large. The reason for the difference in behavior between the algorithms is that, in SCFQ, the arrival order among cells of different backlogged VCs is not considered in the scheduling decision. On the other hand, since the scheduling queue in QLWFQ is of the FIFO type, the length of this FIFO can be large for larger weights. This

Table 3: Traffic parameters (lightly loaded case)

| Class | | Simulation 1 | Simulation 2 | Simulation 3 |
|---|---|---|---|---|
| 1 | $X$ | 1 | 1 | $1,\ldots,4$ |
| | $L$ | 100 | $10\ldots1100$ | 100 |
| | $m_1$ | $0.01,\ldots,0.09$ | 0.01 | 0.01 |
| | $W_1$ | 10, 50, 100 | 50, 100, 1000 | 100 |
| | $N_1$ | 5 | | |
| 2 | $m_2$ | $m_1/100$ | 0.0001 | 0.0001 |
| | $W_2$ | 1 | | |
| | $N_2$ | 500 | | |
| $\rho$ | | $10m_1$ | 0.1 | 0.1 |

makes QLWFQ show FIFO-like behavior to some degree and leads to the difference in behavior between the two algorithms. A similar difference would also be seen between QLWFQ and other timestamp based algorithms such as WFQ.

Another reason for the difference between the algorithms is that the delay jitter of VCs with smaller weights tends to be large in the SCFQ algorithm even when the load is small. For example, in the case of $W_1 = 100$ in Fig. 7, Class 2 VCs suffer a 99% delay of 100 cell cycles when $\rho = 0.1$. This is because Class 1 cells are likely to be served consecutively prior to Class 2 cells, including those that arrived earlier than the Class 1 cells. Note that the mean delay of Class 1 cells in QLWFQ is larger than in SCFQ, but the difference is relatively small.

Of course we can give smaller weights, e.g., 10 rather than 100, to Class 1 VCs to diminish the 99% delay of Class 2 for SCFQ in the case of $\rho = 0.1$. In this case, however, the delay of Class 1 increases as the load becomes high. Hence, we can say that QLWFQ has preferable traffic sharing characteristics since balanced mix of different kinds of traffic with different weights can be achieved by using the queue length as part of the scheduling information.

The 99% delay characteristics were investigated in detail for $\rho = 0.1$. Various burst lengths $L$ were examined in Simulation 2. The results are shown in Fig. 8. The burst length of Class 1 affects the Class 2 performance in SCFQ. However, the increase of the 99% delay of Class 2 stops growing when $L$ is larger than $W_1$. This is due to the fact that, in the SCFQ algorithm, one cell of a Class 2 VC is always served every time $L$ cells of a Class 1 VC are served, if the two VC queues are always backlogged during the interval. In QLWFQ and FIFO on the other hand, the Class 2 delay is still not affected by Class 1 under a constant low load.

The last experiment, Simulation 3, shows the effect of the peak rate of Class 1. The results are plotted in Fig. 9 where $W_1$ was set to 100 and the minimum interarrival time $X$ of Class 1 VCs was changed. As can be seen in the figure, when $X$ is small the Class 1 delay in SCFQ decreases as in the cases of QLWFQ and FIFO. Therefore, some traffic shaping function may be required for SCFQ to be able to suppress the delay of VCs with smaller weights, whereas no special function is needed for QLWFQ even if bursty traffic enters the network.

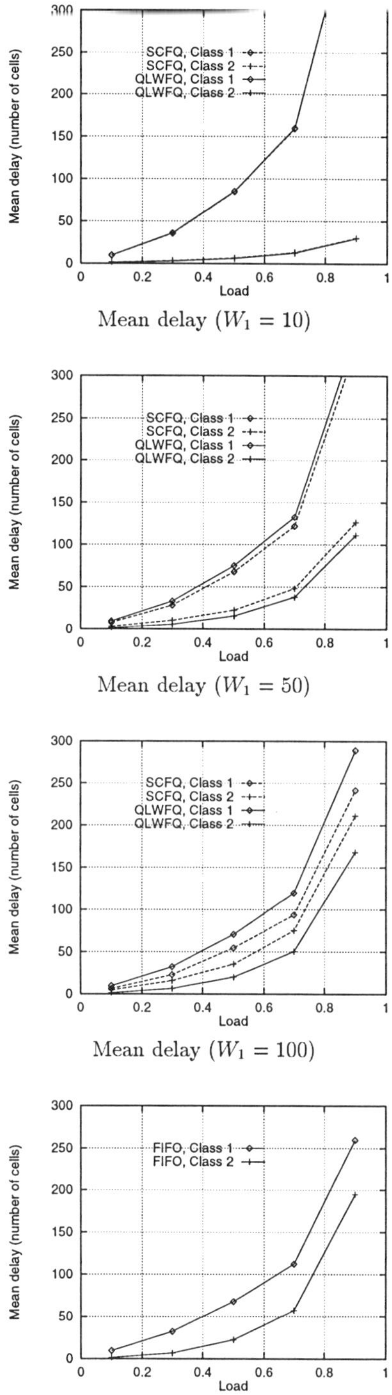


Mean delay ($W_1 = 10$)

Mean delay ($W_1 = 50$)

Mean delay ($W_1 = 100$)

Mean delay (FIFO)

Figure 6: Results of Simulation 1 (Mean delay)

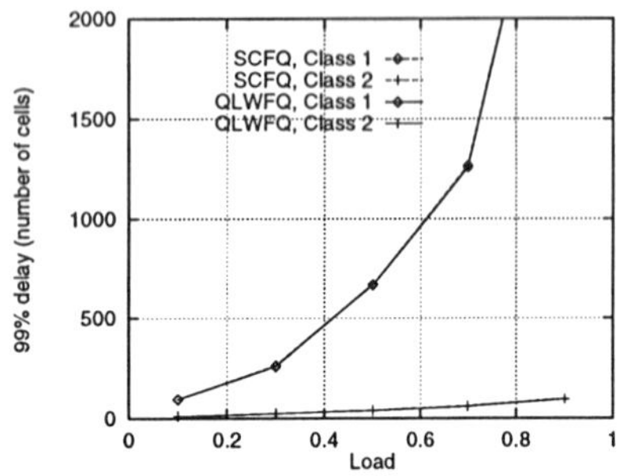


99% delay ($W_1 = 10$)

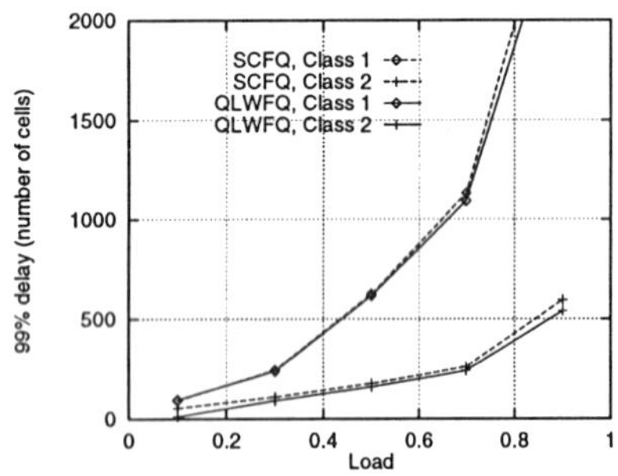


99% delay ($W_1 = 50$)

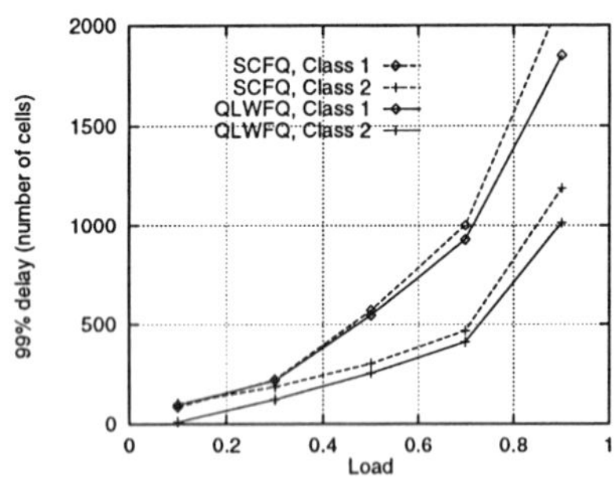


99% delay ($W_1 = 100$)

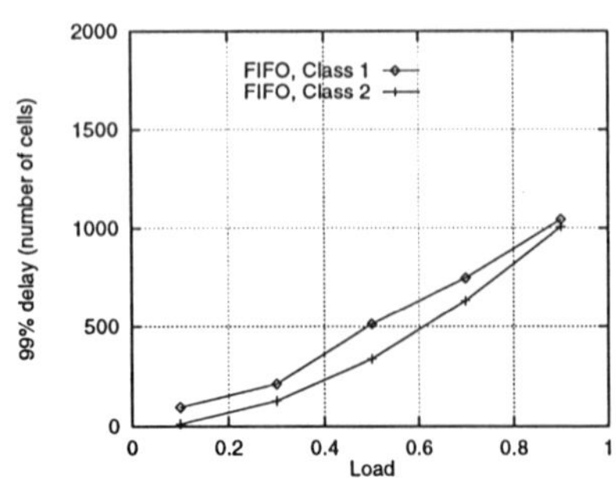


99% delay (FIFO)

Figure 7: Results of Simulation 1 (99% delay)

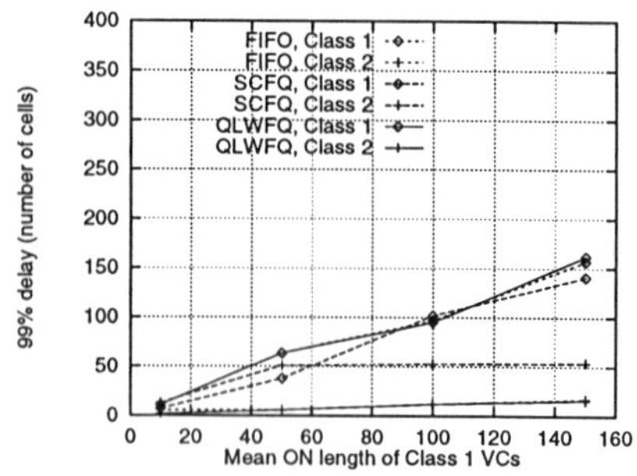


99% delay ($W_1 = 50$)

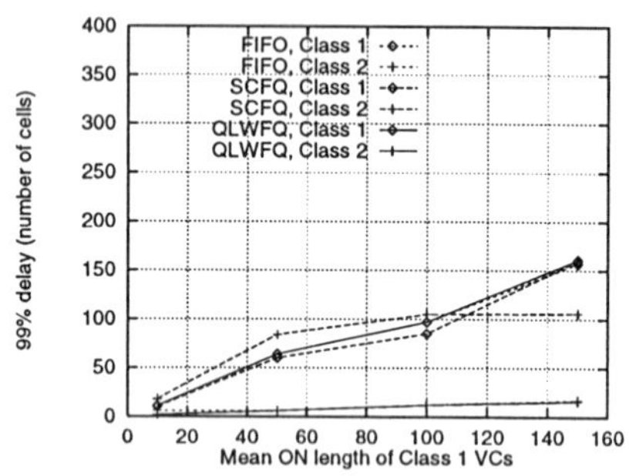


99% delay ($W_1 = 100$)

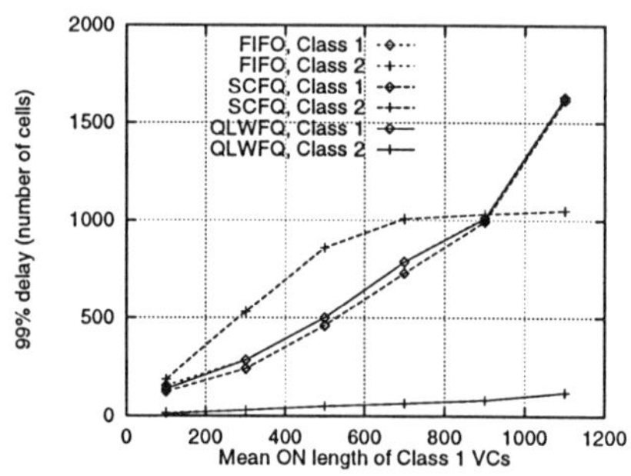


99% delay ($W_1 = 1000$)

Figure 8: Results of Simulation 2

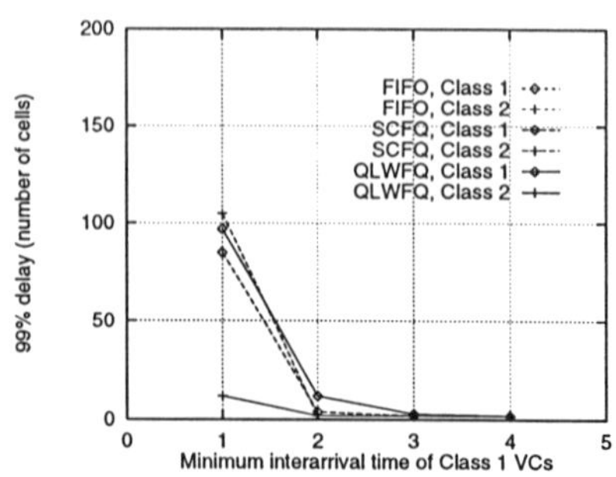


99% delay

Figure 9: Results of Simulation 3

## 6 Conclusion

We have proposed a work conserving, $O(1)$ per-VC queueing algorithm named QLWFQ for high-speed ATM networks.

We analytically derived the delay bound for cells that are leaky bucket conformant and are scheduled by QL-WFQ algorithm. We also performed several simulations for heavily and lightly loaded conditions. From the analytical and simulation results, it was concluded that QL-WFQ provides a better balance between traffic isolation and traffic sharing than timestamp based algorithms.

At present, we are incorporating the QLWFQ algorithm in interface modules of our ATM switch tip set [17, 18] together with an intelligent cell discarding algorithm and a scheduling algorithm for arbitration among different classes such as CBR (Constant Bit Rate), rt-VBR (Real-Time Variable Bit Rate), nrt-VBR (Non-Real-Time Variable Bit Rate), ABR (Available Bit Rate), and UBR (Unspecified Bit Rate). The total switch architecture will be reported in another publication. One of issues for the QLWFQ algorithm is the development of methods to obtain a tighter bound on the end-to-end delay. For this purpose, correlation among adjacent nodes should be considered.

## References


[1] A. Demars and S. Shenker, "Analysis and Simulation of a Fair Queueing Algorithm," in *Proc. ACM SIGCOMM 1989*, pp. 1–12.

[2] L. Zhang, "VirtualClock: A New Traffic Control Algorithm for Packet Switching Networks," in *Proc. ACM SIGCOMM 1990*, pp. 19–29.

[3] N. R. Figueira and J. Pasquale, "An Upper Bound on Delay for the VirtualClock Service Discipline," *IEEE/ACM Trans. Networking*, Vol. 3, No. 4, pp. 399-408, Aug. 1995.

[4] S. J. Golestani, "A Self-Clocked Fair Queueing Scheme for Broadband Applications," in *Proc. IEEE INFOCOM 1994*, pp. 636–646.

[5] ___, "Network Delay Analysis of a Class of Fair Queueing Algorithms," *IEEE J. Select. Areas Commun.*, Vol. 13, No. 6, pp. 1057–1070, Aug. 1994.

[6] H. Zhang and S. Keshav, "Comparison of Rate-Based Service Diciplines," in *Proc. ACM SIGCOMM 1991*, pp. 113–121.

[7] M. Vishnu and J. W. Mark, "HOL-EDD: A Flexible Service Scheduling Scheme for ATM Networks," in *Proc. IEEE INFOCOM 1996*, pp. 647–654.

[8] A. K. Parekh and R. G. Gallager, "A Generalized Processor Sharing Approach to Flow Control in Integrated Services Networks: The Single Node Case," *IEEE/ACM Trans. Networking*, Vol. 1, No. 3, pp. 344-357, June 1993.

[9] ___, "A Generalized Processor Sharing Approach to Flow Control in Integrated Services Networks: The Multiple Node Case," *IEEE/ACM Trans. Networking*, Vol. 2, No. 2, pp. 137-150, Apr. 1994.

[10] J. L. Lexford, A. G. Greenberg, and F. G. Bonomi, "Hardware-Efficient Fair Queueing Architectures for High-Speed Networks," in *Proc. IEEE INFOCOM 1996*, pp. 638–646.

[11] D. D. Clark, S. Shenker, and L. Zhang, "Supporting Real-Time Applications in an Integrated Services Packet Network: Architecture and Mechanism," in *Proc. ACM SIGCOMM 1992*, pp. 14–26.

[12] J. B. Nagle, "On Packet Switches with Infinite Storage," *IEEE Trans. Commun.*, Vol. COM-35, No. 4, pp. 435–438, Apr. 1987.

[13] M. Katavenis, S. Sidiropoulos, and C. Courcoubetis, "Weighted Round-Robin Cell Multiplexing in a General-Purpose ATM Switch Chip," *IEEE J. Select. Areas Commun.*, Vol. 9, No. 8, pp. 1265–1279, Oct. 1991.

[14] M. Shreedhar and G. Varghese, "Efficient Fair Queueing using Deficit Round Robin," in *Proc. ACM SIGCOMM 1995*, pp. 231–242.

[15] D. Saha and S. Mukherjee, "Carry-Over Round Robin: A Simple Cell Scheduling Mechanism for ATM Networks," in *Proc. IEEE INFOCOM 1996*, pp. 630–637.

[16] D. Stiliadis and A. Varma, "Latency-Rate Servers: A General Model for Analysis of Traffic Scheduling Algorithms," in *Proc. IEEE INFOCOM 1996*, pp. 111–119.

[17] Y. Unekawa, et al., "A 5GB/s 8 x 8 ATM Switch Element CMOS LSI Supporting Five Quality-of-Service Classes with 200MHz LVDS," *IEEE ISSCC Digest of Technical Papers*, pp. 118–119, 1996.

[18] Y. Kamatani, Y. Ohba, Y. Shimojo, K. Ise, M. Motoyama, and T. Saito, "VLSI-Oriented Input and Output Buffered Switch Architecture for High-Speed ATM Backbone Nodes, " *IEICE Trans. Commun.* , Vol. E79-B, No. 5, pp. 647–657, May 1996.

# A Near-Optimal Packet Scheduler for QoS Networks*

*Dallas E. Wrege*   *Jörg Liebeherr*
Department of Computer Science
University of Virginia
Charlottesville, VA 22903

## Abstract

*A packet scheduler in a quality-of-service (QoS) network should be sophisticated enough to support stringent QoS constraints at high loads, but it must also have a simple implementation so that packets can be processed at the speed of the transmission link. The Earliest-Deadline-First (EDF) scheduler is the optimal scheduler for bounded-delay services in the sense that it provides the tightest delay guarantees of any scheduler, but an implementation of EDF requires the sorting of packets, a complex operation that is not practical for high-speed networks. In this study we present the design, implementation, and analysis of the novel Rotating-Priority-Queues$^+$ (RPQ$^+$) scheduler that is near-optimal in the sense that it can approximate EDF with arbitrary precision. The RPQ$^+$ scheduler uses a set of prioritized FIFO queues whose priorities are rearranged (rotated) periodically to increase the priority of waiting packets. We derive admission control tests for RPQ$^+$ and show that it has the following desirable properties: its implementation requires operations independent of the number of queued packets, it can provide worst-case delay guarantees, and its efficiency is "between" that of EDF and Static-Priority (SP) schedulers. We use numerical examples, including examples based on MPEG video, to show that in realistic scenarios RPQ$^+$ can closely approximate EDF even for infrequent queue rotations.*

## 1 Introduction

Future integrated services networks based on Asynchronous Transfer Mode (ATM) technology are expected to support applications with a wide range of service requirements. Continuous media applications such as voice and video are particularly demanding since these applications require guarantees on their *quality-of-service* (QoS) in terms of bounded delay, loss, and jitter. To provide QoS, a network must reserve resources such as bandwidth and buffer space for individual connections; however, since resource availability is limited, the network must carefully manage its resources in order to ensure high achievable network utilization. One of the most important components in the design of such a network is the choice of *packet schedulers* at network switches that determine the transmission order of packets queued at output buffers. In this study, we consider the design of packet schedulers appropriate for use in networks with a *bounded-delay service*, that is, networks that provide deterministic (i.e., worst-case) delay guarantees to all packets on a connection.

Many packet schedulers have been considered for use in bounded-delay services (See [20] for a recent survey). The well-known *Earliest-Deadline-First* (EDF) scheduler has been studied in [6, 9, 12] and is distinguished in that it has optimal *efficiency*: for a given set of connections, EDF can support delay guarantees that are at least as tight as those provided by any other packet scheduler [9, 12]. Each packet arriving to an EDF scheduler is assigned a deadline equal to the sum of its arrival time and associated delay bound, and queued packets are transmitted in increasing order of deadline. Since an EDF scheduler selects packets for transmission according to their deadlines, its implementation requires sorting mechanisms. However, the high overhead costs of maintaining a sorted queue prohibit the use of EDF in high-speed networks. For this reason, we seek approximate scheduling disciplines with simpler implementations that can achieve an efficiency similar to EDF.

Recently, several packet schedulers have been designed to approximate the efficiency of EDF [11, 13, 15]. Unlike EDF, these approximation schedulers do not require a sorted transmission queue but rather insert packets into a set of prioritized FIFO queues. In each of these schedulers, a given FIFO contains only packets with *laxities* in a certain range, where the laxity of a packet is the time remaining until it violates its deadline. The *Head-of-Line with Priority Jumps* (HOL-PJ) scheduler moves individual packets between FIFOs according to their laxities [13]. HOL-PJ was shown to be an exact implementation of EDF, but its implementation requires a large number of timers and necessitates copying packets between FIFOs. Two schedulers that avoid manipulating individual packets are the priority relabeling architecture [15] and the Rotating-Priority-Queues (RPQ) scheduler [11]. These schedulers use so-called *calendar queues* [2, 10] that periodically relabel FIFOs to increase the priorities of queued packets.[1] Relabeling the FIFOs provides an efficient approximation to sorting, where the granularity of the approximation is determined by

*This work is supported in part by the National Science Foundation under Grant Nos. NCR-9309224 and NCR-9624106.

[1] Note that similar approaches have been used to approximate both fixed-rate and Virtual Clock schedulers [7, 10].



0-8186-7780-5/97 $10.00 © 1997 IEEE

the relabeling period. The RPQ scheduler is distinguished from the priority labeling architecture in that it can provide worst-case delay guarantees, but neither scheduler has an efficiency that always exceeds that of a *Static Priority* (SP) scheduler which does not change the priorities of queues.

In this paper we design, analyze, and evaluate a novel packet scheduling method that approximates EDF, the *Rotating-Priority-Queues*$^+$ (RPQ$^+$) scheduler. We will demonstrate that RPQ$^+$ can approximate the efficiency of the EDF scheduler with arbitrary precision. Similar to the priority relabeling architecture and RPQ, the RPQ$^+$ scheduler employs a set of prioritized FIFO queues whose priorities are periodically rotated. In switches with shared-memory output buffers, the RPQ$^+$ queue rotation can be implemented efficiently through pointer manipulation. The RPQ$^+$ scheduler has the following three key characteristics: (1) The operations of RPQ$^+$ are independent of the number of queued packets. (2) The RPQ$^+$ scheduler can provide worst-case delay guarantees. (3) RPQ$^+$ always yields a higher network utilization than a SP scheduler. So far no existing packet scheduler that tries to approximate EDF can satisfy all of the above characteristics. We derive necessary and sufficient conditions for schedulability in RPQ$^+$, that is, conditions for which all packets are guaranteed to be transmitted within their delay constraints. Using these conditions, we demonstrate that RPQ$^+$ is identical to SP if the FIFO queues are never rotated. We then show that increasing the frequency of queue rotations always yields a higher efficiency, converging to the efficiency of EDF in the limit. We note, however, that greater efficiency requires additional computational overhead in terms of added FIFO queues and more frequent rotations. We compare the efficiency of RPQ$^+$ against other packet schedulers using empirical examples, including an example based on MPEG-compressed video traces [8].

The remainder of this paper is structured as follows. We first discuss the framework of a bounded-delay service in Section 2. In Section 3 we present operations of the RPQ$^+$ scheduler and introduce an implementation approach for shared-memory switches. In Section 4 we derive necessary and sufficient conditions for schedulability in RPQ$^+$ and show that RPQ$^+$ is a hybrid between EDF and SP. We finally evaluate RPQ$^+$ in Section 5 using numerical examples as well as MPEG-compressed video traces.

# 2 Bounded-Delay Service Framework

We consider connection-oriented packet-switched networks where all packets on a single connection traverse the network on a fixed path of switches and links. A client desiring a new connection submits to the network (1) a *traffic characterization* that specifies the maximum traffic on the connection and (2) the desired delay bound [6]. The network uses these specifications in *admission control tests* to ensure the availability of network resources along the path of the connection. In this section we review traffic characterizations as well as packet schedulers and their admission control tests.

## 2.1 Traffic Characterization

Since a bounded-delay service provides worst-case guarantees, traffic characterizations that we consider must provide a worst-case bound for the maximum traffic arrivals on a connection. Let $\mathcal{C}$ denote the set of connections at a packet scheduler. For a given connection $i \in \mathcal{C}$, let $A_i[\tau, \tau+t]$ denote the total traffic on the connection in time interval $[\tau, \tau+t]$ measured in terms of transmission time of the link. A *traffic constraint function* $A_i^*$ provides a time-invariant bound on $A_i$ as follows [4]:

$$A_i^*(t) \geq A_i[\tau, \tau+t] \qquad \forall t \geq 0, \forall \tau \geq 0 \qquad (1)$$

In practice, traffic constraint functions for a connection are expressed with a small number of parameters using a *traffic model* [6, 12, 14, 18, 20]. As an example, we consider the traffic constraint function $A^*$ for the $(\sigma, \rho)$ traffic model [4] that corresponds with the traffic admitted by a leaky bucket mechanism [17]. The $(\sigma, \rho)$ model uses a burstiness parameter $\sigma$ and a rate parameter $\rho$, and its worst-case traffic is given as follows [4]:

$$A_i^*(t) = \sigma + \rho t \qquad \forall t \geq 0 \qquad (2)$$

## 2.2 Scheduling and Admission Control

Packets from different connections routed on a single outgoing link of a packet switch are stored in a transmission queue, and a packet scheduler determines the transmission order of these packets. Each connection $i$ has a local delay bound $d_i$ at a switch, and a packet on connection $i$ arriving to the switch at time $t$ is assigned a *deadline* of $t + d_i$. A *deadline violation* occurs if any packet is not fully transmitted before its deadline. Since propagation and processing delays are largely fixed due to physical constraints, we assume for clarity of presentation that these delays are zero, and so $d_i$ is a bound on the sum of the queueing delay and transmission time. In the remainder of the paper we restrict our attention to the delay at a single network switch. The case of multi-hop routes can be addressed by either quantifying the distortion of the worst-case traffic arrivals $A_i^*$ at different switches [5], or controlling the distortion of the arrivals by reshaping the traffic to conform to $A_i^*$ at each switch using so-called traffic shaping mechanisms [20].

For a given scheduler, we say that a set $\mathcal{C}$ of connections with traffic constraint functions and delay bounds $\{A_i^*, d_i\}_{i \in \mathcal{C}}$ is *schedulable* if a deadline violation cannot occur for any connection $i$ that conforms its traffic to $A_i^*$ as shown in equation (1). The conditions which determine if a set of connections is schedulable, called *schedulability conditions*, constitute the admission control test in bounded-delay services.

Table 1 shows necessary and sufficient schedulability conditions for the EDF, SP, and RPQ packet schedulers that are derived in [12]. In the EDF condition we use $s_j^{max}$ to denote the maximum transmission time of a packet from connection $j$. In the SP and RPQ conditions, the set of connections $\mathcal{C}$ is partitioned into $P$ connection sets $\{\mathcal{C}_p\}_{1 \leq p \leq P}$, and all connections in $\mathcal{C}_p$ have the same delay bound $d_p$, $d_p < d_q$ for $p < q$. The

| Packet Scheduler | Schedulability Conditions |
|---|---|
| EDF | For all $t \geq d_1$ : $t \geq \sum_{i \in \mathcal{C}} A_i^*(t - d_i) + \max_{d_j > t} s_j^{max}$ |
| SP | For all $p$ and all $t \geq 0$, there exists a $0 \leq \tau \leq d_p - s^{min}$ such that: $t + \tau \geq \sum_{q=1}^{p-1} \sum_{i \in \mathcal{C}_q} A_i^*(t + \tau) + \sum_{i \in \mathcal{C}_p} A_i^*(t) - s^{min} + \max_{q > p} s_q^{max}$ |
| RPQ | For all $t \geq d_1$ : $t \geq \sum_{i \in \mathcal{C}_1} A_i^*(t - d_1) + \sum_{p=2}^{P} \sum_{i \in \mathcal{C}_p} A_i^*(t - d_p + \Delta) + \max_{d_q > t - \Delta} s_q^{max}$ |

Table 1: Necessary and sufficient schedulability conditions.

RPQ scheduler also uses a so-called rotation parameter $\Delta$ that determines the frequency of FIFO relabeling; all supported delay bounds $d_p$ are multiples of $\Delta$, that is, $d_p = n_p\Delta$ for some integer $n_p$. We use $s_p^{max}$ to denote the maximum transmission time of any packet from a connection in set $\mathcal{C}_p$, while we use $s^{min}$ to denote the minimum packet transmission time of any packet.

## 3 The RPQ$^+$ Scheduler

In this section we introduce the *Rotating-Priority-Queues*$^+$ (RPQ$^+$) scheduler that approximates the optimal EDF scheduler. RPQ$^+$ can be implemented with a set of prioritized FIFO queues that are relabeled periodically. The efficiency of SP provides a lower bound on that of RPQ$^+$, and the efficiency of RPQ$^+$ increases with the frequency of relabeling, approaching that of EDF in the limit. Here we first describe the design principles and operations of the RPQ$^+$ scheduler. We then illustrate its operations using a simple example. Finally, we describe an efficient implementation strategy for shared-memory architectures where FIFO queues are implemented as linked lists.

### 3.1 Properties of RPQ$^+$

Connections submitting traffic to an RPQ$^+$ scheduler are partitioned into $P$ disjoint connection sets $\mathcal{C}_1, \mathcal{C}_2, \ldots, \mathcal{C}_P$, and all connections in $\mathcal{C}_p$ have identical delay bounds $d_p = p\Delta$, where $\Delta$ is the rotation interval.

The RPQ$^+$ scheduler employs $2P$ ordered FIFO queues, and these FIFOs are indexed as follows, from highest to lowest priority: $0^+, 1, 1^+, 2, 2^+, \ldots, (P-1), (P-1)^+, P$. We refer to the FIFO with index $p$ ($p^+$) as FIFO $p$ (FIFO $p^+$). The RPQ$^+$ scheduler always selects a packet from the highest-priority nonempty FIFO for transmission. All packets arriving on a connection in set $\mathcal{C}_p$ are placed in FIFO $p$. Arriving packets are never placed directly into FIFO $p^+$ for any $p$.

The FIFO queues for an RPQ$^+$ scheduler are relabeled every $\Delta$ time units. A RPQ$^+$ queue rotation can be viewed as a two-step process: a so-called "concatenation step" and a so-called "promotion step." In the concatenation step, the current FIFO $p$ and FIFO $p^+$ are merged to form FIFO $p$ for all $1 \leq p < P$. Packets from FIFO $p^+$ are concatenated to the end of those from FIFO $p$. In the promotion step, FIFO $p$ is relabeled as FIFO $(p-1)^+$ for all $1 \leq p \leq P$. Also, a new empty FIFO $p$ is created for all $p$ to hold packet arrivals during the next rotation interval. After the promotion step, all packets reside in some FIFO $p^+$. If a packet arrival occurs at the same time as a queue rotation, we assume that the queue rotation is performed before the packet arrives.

### 3.2 Illustration of RPQ$^+$ Scheduling

The operations of an RPQ$^+$ scheduler are best illustrated by means of a simple example. Figure 1 depicts the states of an RPQ$^+$ scheduler over the course of a queue rotation. We first consider Figure 1(a) which shows a snapshot of the scheduler. In this example, the scheduler is assumed to support three connection sets $\mathcal{C}_1$, $\mathcal{C}_2$, and $\mathcal{C}_3$ with delay bounds $d_p = p\Delta$ for $p = 1, 2, 3$. Packets from connection set $\mathcal{C}_p$ are labeled with index $p$ in the figure. An RPQ$^+$ scheduler that supports these connection sets requires 6 FIFO queues with indices $\{0^+, 1, 1^+, 2, 2^+, 3\}$. FIFO $p^+$ is indented for all $p$ to distinguish these queues from FIFO $p$. Packets are assumed to arrive from the left in Figure 1, and packets from connection set $\mathcal{C}_p$ are placed into FIFO $p$. When a packet is selected for transmission, it is assumed to leave the scheduler at right of the figure. If packets are in the scheduler as shown in Figure 1(a), the next packet selected will be the packet from connection set $\mathcal{C}_1$ since FIFO 1 is the highest-priority nonempty queue.

We next consider the queue rotation illustrated in the figure. Figure 1 shows, from left to right, (a) the state of the queues before a queue rotation, (b) the concatenation step of the queue rotation, and (c) the promotion step of the queue rotation. The concatenation step shown in Figure 1(b) involves merging FIFO $p$ and FIFO $p^+$ into a single FIFO $p$ for all $1 \leq p < P$. We indicate the queues to be merged with dashed lines at the left of the figure. When concatenating FIFO $p$ and FIFO $p^+$ for $1 \leq p < P$, all packets from FIFO $p^+$ are inserted at the tail of FIFO $p$. Figure 1(c) shows the promotion of packets from FIFO $p$ to FIFO $(p-1)^+$ for $p = 1, 2, 3$. Note that three new FIFO $p$ queues are included in Figure 1(c) for new arrivals during the next rotation interval.

Observe that we do not specify a location to which packets in FIFO $0^+$ are moved during a queue ro-

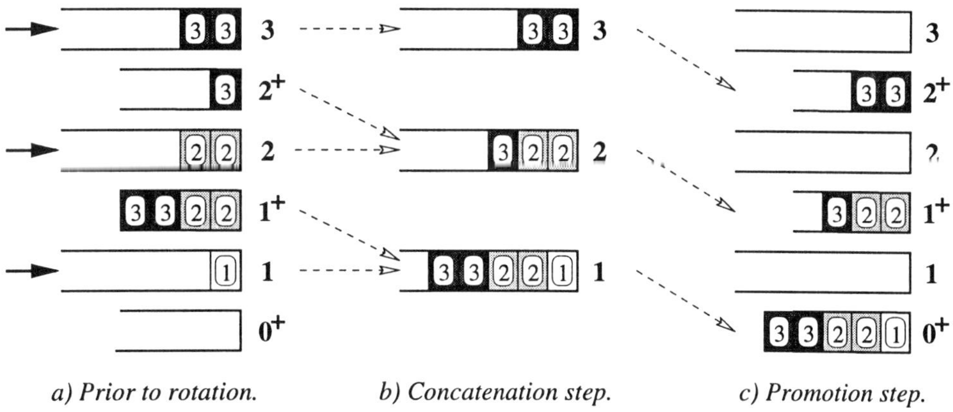


Figure 1: Example of RPQ$^+$ scheduling operations and queue rotations.

tation. This problem is not of concern if RPQ$^+$ is used in a bounded delay service where all packets are guaranteed to be transmitted before their deadlines. In this scenario, the delay bounds for the connection sets are selected such that FIFO $0^+$ will necessarily be empty at the end of all rotation intervals. However, for services other than a bounded-delay service, RPQ$^+$ can be designed to either (1) discard all packets in FIFO $0^+$ since they have necessarily violated their deadlines or (2) leave these packets in FIFO $0^+$ and concatenate new packets to the end of the FIFO.

### 3.3 An Efficient Implementation of RPQ$^+$

The overhead for implementing RPQ$^+$ is identical to that of an SP scheduler except for the queue rotations. Here we investigate the operations required for implementing the RPQ$^+$ queue rotation in switches with shared-memory output buffering.

In a switch with output buffering, arriving packets are passed through the switching fabric and then buffered until they are selected for transmission on an outgoing link. On a per-port or per-connection basis, the output buffer memory consists of either a single shared memory pool or physically separate memory. Most ATM switches use output buffers, and the majority of these are shared-memory buffers [1]. In switches with shared-memory output buffers, the FIFO queues of RPQ$^+$ can be implemented using linked lists, and queue rotations can be implemented with a small number of operations using simple pointer manipulations.

Figure 2 shows buffer management for an outgoing link of a shared-memory switch that employs the RPQ$^+$ scheduler. Figures 2(a) and 2(b) illustrate the state of the scheduler before and after a queue rotation, respectively. The figure illustrates FIFO queues that are each implemented as a linked list. For each FIFO queue, a "H" and a "T" pointer refer to the head and the tail of the queue, respectively. Packets arriving to FIFO $p$ are inserted at $T(p)$ its tail, and the scheduler selects packets for transmission from FIFO $p$ at its head.Comparing Figure 2(b) with Figure 2(a), we notice that only a small number of pointer manipulations are needed to implement the queue rotation.

## 4 RPQ$^+$ Schedulability Conditions

In this section we present schedulability conditions for the RPQ$^+$ scheduler and show that its efficiency is between EDF and SP. We first present in Theorem 1 the exact, that is, necessary and sufficient, schedulability conditions for a general class of traffic constraint functions. We then show explicitly that RPQ$^+$ is superior to SP and that its efficiency increases monotonically for a certain class of rotation intervals, converging to EDF in the limit.

### 4.1 Exact Schedulability Conditions

Here we present the necessary and sufficient conditions for schedulability in an RPQ$^+$ scheduler. These conditions assume that all connections have traffic constraint functions as described in Section 2.1.

**Theorem 1** *A set $\mathcal{C}$ of connections that is given by $\{A_i^*, d_i\}_{i\in\mathcal{C}}$ is RPQ$^+$-schedulable with rotation interval $\Delta$ if and only if for all priorities $p$ and for all $t \geq 0$, there exists a $\tau$ with $0 \leq \tau \leq d_p - s^{min}$ such that:*

$$t+\tau \geq \sum_{q=1}^{p-1}\sum_{i\in\mathcal{C}_q} A_i^*(\min\{t+\tau, t+d_p-d_q+\Delta\})+$$

$$+\sum_{q=p}^{P}\sum_{i\in\mathcal{C}_q} A_i^*(t+d_p-d_q) - s^{min} + \max_{r,d_r>t+d_p} s_r^{max} \quad (3)$$

A proof of the theorem is provided in [19].

### 4.2 RPQ$^+$ as a Hybrid between EDF and SP

Here we show that the RPQ$^+$ scheduler is a hybrid between EDF and SP in the sense that (i) RPQ$^+$ always achieves an efficiency at least as good as SP, (ii) the efficiency of RPQ$^+$ is nondecreasing as the rotation interval $\Delta$ is reduced,and (iii) the efficiency of RPQ$^+$ approaches that of EDF as $\Delta \to 0$. We consider each of these properties in turn.

To show Property (i), we argue that any set of connections schedulable with SP is also schedulable with

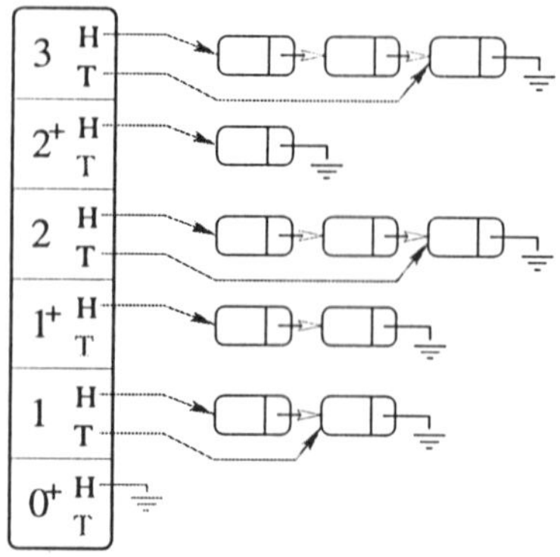


(a) Immediately before rotation.

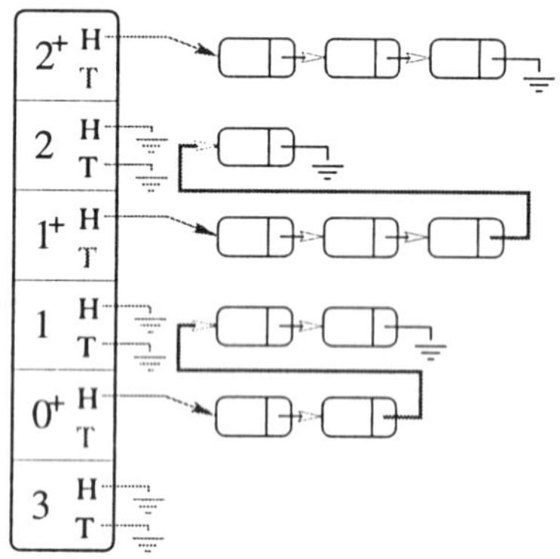


(b) After queue rotation.

Figure 2: Implementation of RPQ$^+$ queue rotation.

RPQ$^+$. Our argument relies on the following necessary condition for SP schedulability.

**Lemma 1** *If a set $\mathcal{C}$ of connections given by $\{A_i^*, d_i\}_{i\in\mathcal{C}}$ is SP-schedulable, then for all priorities p and for all $t \geq 0$, there exists a $\tau$ with $\tau \leq d_p - s^{min}$ such that:*

$$t+\tau \geq \sum_{q=1}^{p-1}\sum_{i\in\mathcal{C}_q} A_i^*(t+\tau) + \sum_{q=p}^{P}\sum_{i\in\mathcal{C}_q} A_i^*(t+d_p-d_q) -$$

$$-s^{min} + \max_{r,d_r>t+d_p} s_r^{max} \quad (4)$$

A complete proof of Lemma 1 is provided in [19]. With the lemma, note that the necessary condition for SP in equation (4) implies the sufficient condition for RPQ$^+$ in equation (3). This shows that RPQ$^+$ always achieves an efficiency at least as high as SP.

In order to show Property (ii), we observe that the right-hand-side of equation (3) increases with $\Delta$. As required, the efficiency of RPQ$^+$ is nondecreasing as the rotation interval $\Delta$ is reduced.

Finally, to show Property (iii), we compare RPQ$^+$ with EDF using a sufficient (but not necessary) schedulability condition for RPQ$^+$ that has a formulation similar to the exact EDF condition in Table 1. We obtain this condition directly from Theorem 1 by substituting $\tau = d_p - s^{min}$ in equation (3):

**Corollary 1** *A set $\mathcal{C}$ of connections given by $\{A_i^*, d_i\}_{i\in\mathcal{C}}$ is RPQ$^+$-schedulable with rotation interval $\Delta$ if for all priorities p and for all $t \geq d_1$ the following condition holds:*

$$t \geq \sum_{q=1}^{p-1}\sum_{i\in\mathcal{C}_q} A_i^*(t-d_q+\Delta) + \sum_{q=p}^{P}\sum_{i\in\mathcal{C}_q} A_i^*(t-d_q) + \max_{r,d_r>t} s_r^{max} \quad (5)$$

Comparing the condition in equation (5) with the EDF condition, we see that the only difference in the two conditions is the rotation interval $\Delta$. These two conditions become identical in the limit as $\Delta \to 0$, verifying that an RPQ$^+$ scheduler can approximate EDF with arbitrary precision.

## 5 Evaluation

In this section we compare the efficiency of the RPQ$^+$ scheduler against schedulers EDF and SP using empirical examples. Two sets of experiments are included. The first experiment uses traffic policed by leaky buckets, while the second experiment uses traces of MPEG-compressed video. In both experiments we use the most accurate, i.e., necessary and sufficient, admission control tests for each packet scheduler to obtain a precise comparison of the efficiency of the schedulers. We use the schedulability conditions from Theorem 1 for RPQ$^+$ and the conditions from Table 1 for EDF and SP.

### 5.1 Numerical Example

In the first experiment we compute the *schedulable region* of the packet schedulers for a set of three connection groups using an approach similar to one used in [12]. We vary the traffic rate of each connection group and use a surface plot to illustrate the rates for which all delay bounds are guaranteed. We can compare the efficiencies of different packet schedulers graphically by comparing the volumes of their schedulable regions.

We consider connections supported at a single packet scheduler that transmits packets at 155 Mbps, a rate that corresponds to OC-3. The three connection groups have traffic that conforms to the $(\sigma, \rho)$ traffic model, with traffic constraint functions $A^*$ of the form:

$$A^*(t) = \sigma + \rho t \quad (6)$$

Table 2 shows the traffic and QoS parameters for all connection groups. For a connection group with index $j$, the table shows the delay bound $d_j$ at the scheduler as well as the burst $\sigma_j$ and the range of rates $\rho_j$. The bursts $b_j$ in Table 2 are given in 53-byte ATM cells. In the example, we vary the rate parameter $\rho_j$ between 10 and 155 Mbps.

| Delay Group | Index $j$ | Delay Bound $d_j$ (ms) | Burst $\sigma_j$ (cells) | Rate $\rho_j$ (Mbps) |
|---|---|---|---|---|
| Low | 1 | 12 | 4000 | 10-155 |
| Medium | 2 | 24 | 2000 | 10-155 |
| High | 3 | 36 | 4000 | 10-155 |

Table 2: Parameter Set for Scheduler with 155 Mbps Transmission Rate.

We present our results with two sets of graphs in Figures 3 and 4. The schedulable region for different schedulers are shown using three-dimensional surface plots. We show the transmission rates for which all connection groups are admissible; the volume beneath a curve includes all operating points for which all packets are guaranteed to be transmitted before their deadlines. Note that the axes in these figures have a logarithmic scale.

Figure 3 depicts the schedulable regions for EDF and SP schedulers. Since EDF is the optimal packet scheduler with respect to number of admissible connections, the region shown in Figure 3(a) will contain the region corresponding to any other packet scheduler. For the parameter sets considered, observe that the schedulable region for EDF is much larger than that for SP shown in Figure 3(b).

In Figure 4, we show schedulable regions of the RPQ$^+$ packet scheduler for feasible rotation intervals in the range $\Delta = 2 - 12$ms. For this example, the number of queues that must be maintained for a particular choice of $\Delta$ is given by $72/\Delta$. Note that for all choices of rotation interval $\Delta$, the RPQ$^+$ schedulable region is superior to that of SP in Figure 3(b). Even for $\Delta = 12$ms, the largest possible choice of RPQ$^+$ rotation interval for this example, the RPQ$^+$ schedulable region completely contains the SP region. Notice in Figures 4(a)-(d) that the schedulable region increases as the rotation interval is decreased, approximating EDF closely when $\Delta = 2$ms.

## 5.2 MPEG Example

In this experiment all traffic characterizations are obtained from publicly-available traces of MPEG video [16]. We use two MPEG traces for the evaluation: a thirty-minute segment of the James Bond entertainment movie *Goldfinger* (*"Bond"*) and 200 seconds of a video conference recorded using a set top camera (*"Settop"*). Both traces were encoded in software at 24 frames/second with frame size 384x288 and frame pattern IBBPBBPBBPBB.

We again consider a packet scheduler that operates at 155 Mbps, and we assume that all traffic is packetized in 53-byte ATM cells with a payload of 48 bytes each. We use the so-called *empirical envelope* of a video sequence to characterize its traffic, where the empirical envelope $E^*$ of a sequence with traffic $A$ is given by [3, 18]:

$$E^*(t) = \sup_{\tau \geq 0} A[\tau, \tau + t] \qquad \forall t \geq 0 \qquad (7)$$

The empirical envelope is the tightest traffic characterization available for a video sequence and, when used with admission control, will result in the admission of a maximal number of connections. By using empirical envelopes for traffic characterization, we can determine the highest efficiency that can be achieved by a given packet scheduler.

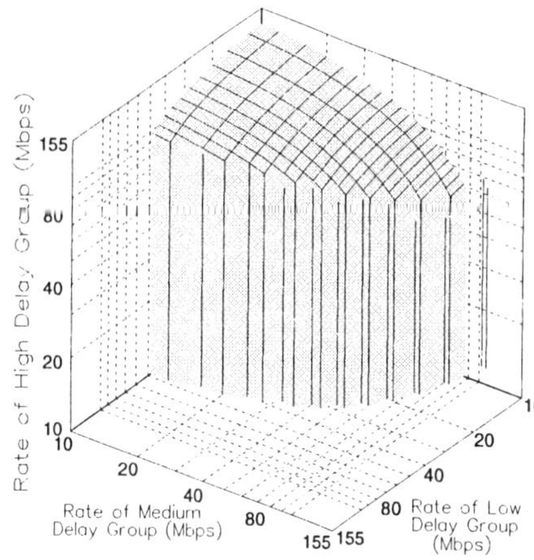


(a) EDF Scheduler.

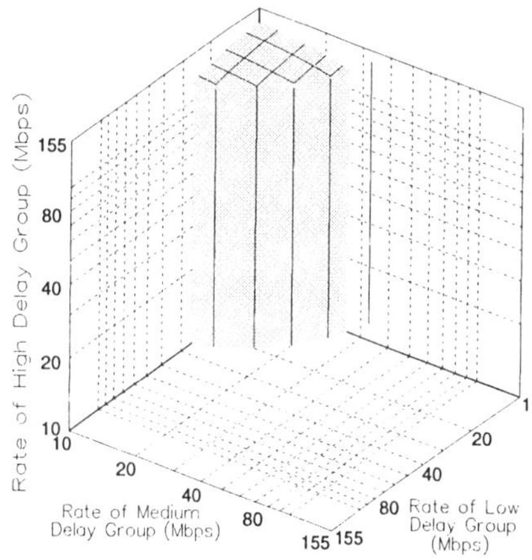


(b) SP Scheduler.

Figure 3: Benchmark schedulable regions.

Similar to the previous experiment, we consider two connection groups, one group consisting solely of *Bond* connections, and the second consisting solely of *Settop* connections. All connections in the same group have identical delay bounds: $d_{Settop} = 100$ms and $d_{Bond} = 200$ms.

Figure 5 illustrates the number of connections that can be supported at their delay constraints for the EDF, SP, and RPQ$^+$ schedulers as well as for a peak-rate allocation scheme.[2] We use a bold solid line for EDF, a bold dotted line for SP, a thin solid line for the peak-rate allocation scheme, and a series of dashed

[2]The peak rate of a connection is defined as the ratio of the largest-sized frame and the constant interframe time.

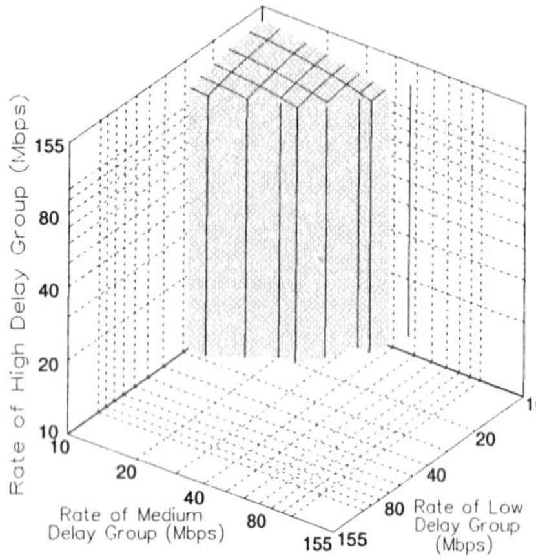


(a) RPQ$^+$ at $\Delta = 12$ms.

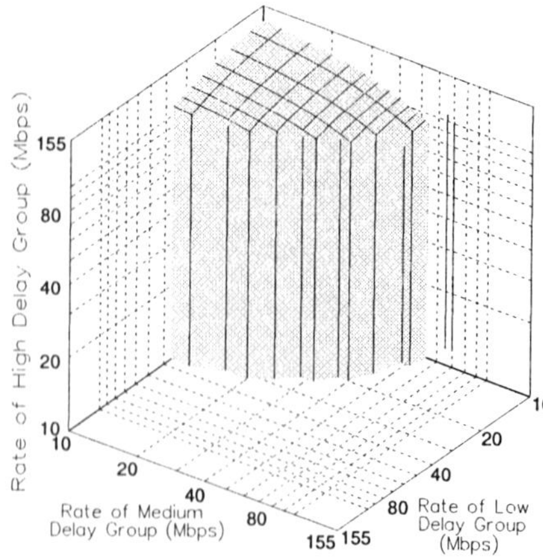


(b) RPQ$^+$ at $\Delta = 6$ms.

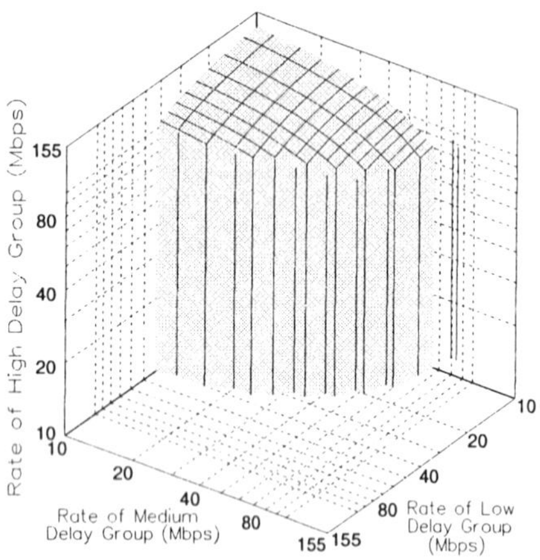


(c) RPQ$^+$ at $\Delta = 3$ms.

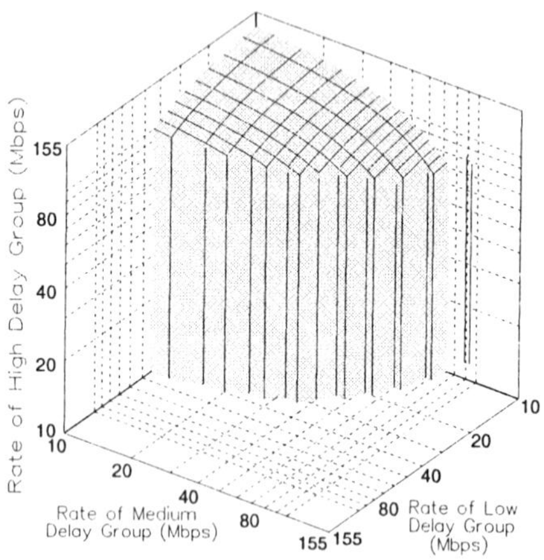


(d) RPQ$^+$ at $\Delta = 2$ms.

Figure 4: Schedulable regions for RPQ$^+$.

lines for RPQ$^+$ at different values of rotation interval $\Delta$. For the RPQ$^+$ curves we show the value of $\Delta$ as well as the number of required FIFOs. For each packet scheduler, we plot the maximum number of admissible *Bond* connections as a function of the number of *Settop* connections. For example, all packet schedulers (except the peak-rate scheme) can support 96 *Bond* connections if there are no *Settop* connections at the switch, and EDF can simultaneously support 60 *Bond* and 200 *Settop* connections.

We observe in the figure that all of the packet schedulers can admit many more connections than the peak-rate allocation. Additionally, EDF is superior to SP when the number of higher-priority *Settop* connections is large. Note in Figure 5 that RPQ$^+$ is identical to SP for $\Delta = 100$ms, and smaller values of $\Delta$ result in higher efficiency. For $\Delta = 10$ms, a point of operation requiring 40 FIFOs, RPQ$^+$ closely approximates EDF.

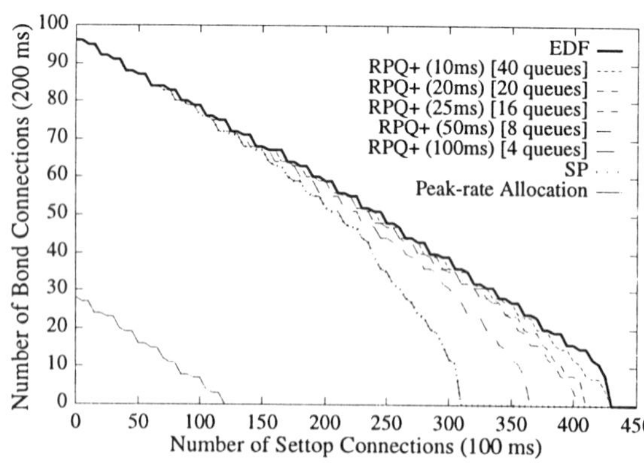


Figure 5: Example of RPQ$^+$ for MPEG video sequences.

## 6 Conclusions

In this paper we presented the novel Rotating-Priority-Queues$^+$ (RPQ$^+$) packet scheduler. We showed that in a bounded-delay service RPQ$^+$ can achieve a network utilization that approximates that of the optimal Earliest-Deadline-First (EDF) scheduler. We also showed that RPQ$^+$ can be implemented in shared-memory architectures with low overhead costs that make it practical for use in high-speed networks. The RPQ$^+$ scheduler places arriving packets into prioritized FIFO queues based on their delay constraints, and these queues are modified ("rotated") to increase the priority of waiting packets. RPQ$^+$ relies on a so-called rotation interval $\Delta$ that determines the frequency of these queue manipulations. When $\Delta$ is infinite, i.e., queues are never rotated, RPQ$^+$ behaves exactly the same as a SP scheduler and the two packet schedulers admit the same number of connections; as $\Delta$ is reduced, the number of admissible connections increases, approaching that of EDF in the limit. RPQ$^+$ can be implemented similar to SP except for the queue rotations which can be performed by manipulating pointers without moving any queued packets. We presented exact schedulability conditions for RPQ$^+$ that can be used for admission control tests in a bounded-delay service. We finally presented experiments that included MPEG traffic sources to illustrate that RPQ$^+$ can closely approximate EDF even for large values of $\Delta$.

## References


[1] N. Berry. Asynchronous Transfer Mode (ATM) Switch Technology and Vendor Survey. Technical Report NAS-95-001, National Aeronautics and Space Administration, January 1995.

[2] R. Brown. Calendar Queues: A Fast $O(1)$ Priority Queue Implementation for the Simulation Event Set Problem. *Communications of the ACM*, 21(10):1220–1227, October 1988.

[3] C.-S. Chang. Stability, Queue Length, and Delay of Deterministic and Stochastic Queueing Networks. *IEEE Transactions on Automatic Control*, 39(5):913–931, May 1994.

[4] R. L. Cruz. A Calculus for Network Delay, Part I: Network Elements in Isolation. *IEEE Transactions on Information Theory*, 37(1):114–131, January 1991.

[5] R. L. Cruz. A Calculus for Network Delay, Part II: Network Analysis. *IEEE Transactions on Information Theory*, 37(1):132–141, January 1991.

[6] D. Ferrari and D. C. Verma. A Scheme for Real-Time Channel Establishment in Wide-Area Networks. *IEEE Journal on Selected Areas in Communications*, 8(3):368–379, April 1990.

[7] N. R. Figueira. *A New Approach to the Control of Real-Time Traffic in Packet Switching Data Networks*. PhD thesis, University of California at San Diego, June 1995.

[8] D. Le Gall. MPEG: A Video Compression Standard for Multimedia Applications. *Communications of the ACM*, 34(4):305–313, April 1991.

[9] L. Georgiadis, R. Guerin, and A. Parekh. Optimal Multiplexing on a Single Link: Delay and Buffer Requirements. In *Proc. IEEE Infocom '94*, pages 524–532, June 1994.

[10] C. R. Kalmanek, H. Kanakia, and S. Keshav. Rate Controlled Servers for Very High-Speed Networks. In *Proc. Globecom '90*, pages 12–20, December 1990.

[11] J. Liebeherr and D. E. Wrege. A Versatile Packet Multiplexer for Quality-of-Service Networks. In *Proc. 4th International Symposium on High-Performance Distributed Computing (HPDC-4)*, pages 148–155, August 1995.

[12] J. Liebeherr, D. E. Wrege, and Domenico Ferrari. Exact Admission Control in Networks with Bounded Delay Services. To appear: *IEEE/ACM Transactions on Networking*, December 1996.

[13] Y. Lim and J. E. Kobza. Analysis of a Delay-Dependent Priority Discipline in an Integrated Multiclass Traffic Fast Packet Switch. *IEEE Transactions on Communications*, 38(5):659–665, May 1990.

[14] A. K. Parekh and R. G. Gallager. A Generalized Processor Sharing Approach to Flow Control in Integrated Services Networks: The Multiple Node Case. *IEEE/ACM Transactions on Networking*, 2(2):137–150, April 1994.

[15] J. M. Peha and F. A. Tobagi. Implementation Strategies for Scheduling Algorithms in Integrated-Services Packet-Switched Networks. In *Proc. IEEE Globecom '91*, pages 1733–1740, 1991.

[16] O. Rose. Statistical Properties of MPEG Video Traffic and Their Impact on Traffic Modeling in ATM systems. Technical Report 101, Institute of Computer Science, University of Wurzburg, February 1995.

[17] J. S. Turner. New Directions in Communications (or Which Way to the Information Age?). *IEEE Communications Magazine*, 25(8):8–15, October 1986.

[18] D. E. Wrege, E. W. Knightly, H. Zhang, and J. Liebeherr. Deterministic Delay Bounds for VBR Video in Packet-Switching Networks: Fundamental Limits and Practical Tradeoffs. *IEEE/ACM Transactions on Networking*, 4(3):352–362, June 1996.

[19] D. E. Wrege and J. Liebeherr. A Near-Optimal Packet Scheduler for QoS Networks. Technical Report CS-96-12, University of Virginia, June 1996.

[20] H. Zhang. Service Disciplines for Guaranteed Performance Service in Packet-Switching Networks. *Proceedings of the IEEE*, 83(10):1374–1399, October 1995.

# Exact and Efficient Analysis of Schedulability in Fixed-Packet Networks: A Generic Approach

Sergey Gorinsky* Sanjoy Baruah*† Thomas J. Marlowe*‡ Alexander D. Stoyenko*

Real-Time Computing Laboratory
Department of Computer and Information Science
New Jersey Institute of Technology
Newark, NJ 07102, USA

## Abstract

*A general model for traffic flows on packet-switched, virtual-circuit based, fixed-packet networks is introduced, and an exact schedulability test is obtained for systems of such flows. Rules are derived that make the evaluation of this schedulability test feasible and efficient under certain circumstances. The practical relevance of this approach is demonstrated by applying it to a number of standard traffic models.*

## 1 Introduction

*Rate-based scheduling* strategies are of particular interest in the design and implementation of virtual-circuit packet-switched computer networks that provide support for multimedia applications [9, 12, 14, 15, 16, 19, 21, 22]. It is assumed that the network traffic generated by each virtual-circuit connection satisfies certain pre-specified *rate constraints*, and that the scheduling strategy at the network nodes aims to provide each connection with certain *performance guarantees*, typically expressed in terms of (end-to-end) delay, delay jitter, throughput, et cetera.

Traditionally, the study of computer network performance has had a strong stochastic flavor, and sophisticated queueing-theoretic models have been developed to characterize network traffic, and measure performance under various traffic loads, service disciplines, etc. However, performance guarantees obtained through such modeling are necessarily probabilistic, and hence of limited usefulness when *deterministic* performance guarantees are required. There has therefore recently been considerable interest in deterministic modeling of network traffic, and design and implementation of network service disciplines that work well with such deterministic traffic.

A request for a new connection is admitted by the network if and only if the network possesses adequate resources to guarantee its desired level of performance — this process of determining whether to admit a request for a new connection is referred to as a *connection admission procedure.* A cornerstone of any connection admission procedure is *schedulability analysis:* given a set of connections that share a network link, can all packets be delivered before the requested delay bounds? The subject of this paper is the design of exact and computationally efficient schedulability tests for packet-switched virtual-circuit fixed-packet networks.

**Related work.** Schedulability analysis is greatly affected by two factors: the service discipline at network nodes and the traffic model employed to characterize data streams. First Come First Served (FCFS) has traditionally been a scheduling discipline of choice in ATM networks. Cruz [4, 5] has obtained delay bounds in FCFS networks using the leaky bucket model for traffic characterization. While simple to implement, FCFS lacks flexibility; the policy does not discriminate between traffic from different connections and therefore is not able to provide different levels of performance guarantees. Recently, new scheduling disciplines have been investigated: VirtualClock [22], Stop-and-Go [12], and Generalized Processor Sharing (GPS) and its packet-based version — Weighted Fair Queueing (WFQ) also known as Packet-by-packet

*Real-Time Computing Laboratory, Department of Computer and Information Science, New Jersey Institute of Technology, Newark, NJ 07102, USA. Research is supported in part by the U.S. ONR Grant N00014-93-1-1047 and by the NSF Grant CCR-9402827.

†Department of Computer Science and Electrical Engineering, The University of Vermont, Burlington, VT 05405, USA. Research is supported in part by the NSF Grant CCR-9596282. Dr. Baruah is on leave from the Real-Time Computing Laboratory at NJIT.

‡Department of Mathematics and Computer Science, Seton Hall University, South Orange, NJ 07079, USA.



0-8186-7780-5/97 $10.00 © 1997 IEEE

Generalized Processor Sharing (PGPS) [7, 19, 20]. The latter policy can take into account delay dependencies along the route of a connection and may provide smaller end-to-end delays than those obtained by summing up the worst case delays in each node.

Since deadline-based service disciplines, such as the Earliest Deadline First (EDF), have been proven optimal in the context of uniprocessor scheduling [8], they have captured the attention of networking researchers and are being used in various research studies as a traffic scheduling policy. Even though the derived performance guarantees are based on per-node analysis, it was shown by Georgiadis et al [11] that when accompanied with traffic reshaping inside the network, EDF outperforms GPS in terms of end-to-end delay bounds, buffer requirements, and implementation simplicity. This makes EDF an efficient service discipline to employ at network nodes. Ferrari and Verma [9] attempted to find schedulability conditions for the case when data streams abide by the Tenet model, when the minimum inter-arrival time for any connection is not less than the summation of packet transmission times over all connections. Zheng and Shin [23] derived necessary and sufficient feasibility conditions for the sporadic traffic model; Baruah, Mok, and Rosier [1] had earlier derived very similar results in the context of hard-real-time scheduling. Georgiadis, Guerin, and Parekh [10] provided necessary and sufficient schedulability conditions for the leaky bucket model. Liebeherr et al [16, 21] have provided similar analysis for more general constraints: the maximum traffic from a connection is characterized by a concave rate-controlling function.

Although the model of Liebeherr et al permits the representation of a large class of traffic specifications, traditional real-time streams of data, as well as traffic generated by many multimedia applications, cannot be accurately characterized by concave functions. Besides, the proposed testing bound is too pessimistic. For example, when the traffic is such that the link may be busy for an unbounded amount of time, the schedulability test may not terminate. Thus, the approach may fail even if the requested performance guarantees can in principle be provided.

**This research.** We study the problem of schedulability analysis within a very general framework, encompassing all of the work described above. Our approach is as follows:

- We define some very general constraints on traffic (Definition 1), which we refer to as the *Time-Independence Property* and the *Connection-Independence Property*. These properties are satisfied by the sporadic, Tenet, and leaky bucket models of traffic constraints and by all concave rate-controlling functions, as well as by significantly more general models of traffic constraints.
- For traffic constraints satisfying these properties (*well-formed constraints*), we define the notion of *extreme sets* (Section 4), and use this notion to derive necessary and sufficient conditions for schedulability in systems where all traffic satisfies such constraints.
- We identify guidelines (*TLTF*, *EQ*, *WIB*, and *Skip Rules* in Section 6) which assist in the efficient evaluation of these schedulability conditions. For particular kinds of traffic constraints, these rules can often be used to derive efficient schedulability tests.

This paper is organized as follows. Section 2 describes the network model and gives some definitions. Section 3 surveys existing traffic models and presents our generic traffic constraints. Section 4 introduces the notion of extreme sets. Section 5 discusses scheduling issues, and derives schedulability conditions. Section 6 provides general guidelines for identifying the smallest *testing set* and demonstrates these guidelines by examples of some specific traffic models. Finally, the results are summarized in Section 7.

## 2 The Network Model

In this study we consider packet-switched virtual-circuit fixed-packet networks of an arbitrary topology. Our model can be viewed as a generalization of ATM networks. Network nodes (switches) are interconnected by links. Point-to-point communication is supported by means of connections: data are transferred from a source node to a destination node along some fixed route in the network. Connection establishment takes place before transmission of user's data and succeeds only if requested performance guarantees can be provided. Traffic entering a network switch (from an input link or from an application process at the source node) is demultiplexed, and the packets are transferred to the buffers of appropriate output links (or application processes at the destination node). Every output link buffer is associated with a scheduler that decides in which order packets are sent over the link. As a general rule, the time to transfer a packet from an input link to an output link buffer (switching delay) is usually negligible in comparison with waiting time in the buffer (queueing delay) and transmission time of the packet (transmission delay) [3, 23]. In this study, we therefore assume that delay experienced by a packet in a switch comprises only queueing and transmission delays.

The basic unit of data transfer is the *packet*, and all packets are of the same size. A *message* is an ordered sequence of packets; different messages may contain different numbers of packets. Throughout this paper, we consider a model of time in which time is divided into discrete and indivisible fixed-size *time slots*. Each slot is equal to the time taken by one packet to be transmitted over a link[1]. For instance, if packets are 53 bytes long and the link bandwidth is 155 Mb/s, then the slot size equals to 2.7 $\mu$s. Messages are assumed to arrive instantaneously, and this arrival is aligned to the start of a time slot[2].

Let us define a *connection system* as the set $\{C_1, \ldots, C_n\}$ of all connections sending data over an output link of a network switch. Each connection $C_i$, $1 \le i \le n$, is characterized by an ordered pair $(Z_i, d_i)$ where $Z_i$ specifies a *traffic constraint* on the message arrival pattern, and $d_i$ denotes a *delay bound.* Every message having arrived from connection $C_i$ at time $t$ is called an *arrival* and has to be served before time $t+d_i$ which is called the *deadline* of the arrival. Throughout the paper, without loss of generality we assume that $d_1 \le d_2 \le \ldots \le d_{n-1} \le d_n$.

A set R of arrivals is said to be *schedulable* iff it is possible to service all the arrivals of R without missing any of their deadlines. R is *legal* iff all the constraints $Z_i$ are satisfied. The connection system is *schedulable* iff each legal set of arrivals is schedulable.

## 3 Traffic Constraints

In order to be able to provide useful performance guarantees, it is necessary that the traffic admitted along each connection be constrained in some manner. These constraints are formulated in terms of traffic models which can be categorized as *continuous* or *discrete*.

Traffic specification through continuous models simplifies network analysis but such models make the unrealistic assumptions that the traffic can be split into infinitesimally small packets and that multiple connections can simultaneously transmit data over the same link. As a result of these pessimistic assumptions, real traffic cannot be precisely described by continuous models; a connection admission request may be rejected even if its acceptance is safe for preserving performance guarantees in the actual (discrete-packet) network.

[1]Note that the slot size depends on the speed of data transmission and may vary for different links.

[2]In practice, this means that a message is considered to have arrived at the start of the slot following the instant that its last bit arrives. As a result, a packet can experience an additional (up to one slot) *alignment* delay in a node.

Discrete models take into account finite sizes of packets and can exactly describe network traffic. These models allow us to derive necessary and sufficient schedulability conditions for real traffic. On the other hand, performance analysis becomes more complicated.

Several kinds of constraints have been considered in the literature — we describe some of them briefly below.

**The sporadic model** of [1, 2, 17, 23] is a discrete traffic model. The description of a data stream is done by specifying pair of parameters $(p, s)$, where $p$ is the minimum message inter-arrival time and $s$ is the maximum message size. If traffic conforms to the sporadic model, the amount of data transferred during an interval of length $t$ is no larger than:

$$\mathsf{arrival}_s(t) = s\left\lceil \frac{t}{p} \right\rceil^+$$

where function $\lceil x \rceil^+ = n$ if $n-1 \le x < n$ for $n = 1, 2, \ldots$, and $\lceil x \rceil^+ = 0$ when $x < 0$.

A continuous version of the model limits maximum transmission rate over an arbitrary time interval by parameter $\rho$. As a result, the quantity of traffic having arrived during any interval of length $t \ge 0$ can not exceed:

$$\mathsf{arrival}_s^{cont}(t) = \rho t$$

**The Tenet model** [9] is a discrete traffic model defined by parameters $(x_{min}, x_{ave}, I, s)$. A data stream complies with the model if: (1) the maximum size of a message is not larger than $s$; (2) the message inter-arrival times are larger or equal to $x_{min}$; (3) over any interval of (fixed) length $I$, the average message inter-arrival time is not smaller than $x_{ave}$. Since $\frac{I}{x_{ave}}$ refers to the maximum number of messages having arrived during any interval $[t_1, t_2)$ where $t_2 - t_1 = I$, without loss of generality we may assume that $\frac{I}{x_{ave}}$ is an integer. The maximum amount of data having arrived during any period of length $t \ge 0$ is at most:

$$\begin{aligned}\mathsf{arrival}_T(t) &= s\Big(\left\lfloor \frac{t}{I} \right\rfloor \frac{I}{x_{ave}} \\ &\quad + \min\Big\{\left\lceil \Big(\frac{t}{I} - \left\lfloor \frac{t}{I} \right\rfloor\Big)\frac{I}{x_{min}} \right\rceil^+, \frac{I}{x_{ave}}\Big\}\Big),\end{aligned}$$

where the first term corresponds to the maximum number of messages in complete intervals of size $I$, and the second to the maximum number in the current fractional period.

A continuous version of the Tenet model can be defined through parameters $(\rho_{max}, \rho_{ave}, I)$. A traffic stream satisfying the model should have the following properties: (1) the maximum arrival rate is $\rho_{max}$; (2) over any interval of length $I$, the average arrival rate is not larger than $\rho_{ave}$. The worst-case amount of traffic during any interval of duration $t \geq 0$ equals:

$$\mathsf{arrival}_T^{cont}(t) = \rho_{ave}\left\lfloor\frac{t}{I}\right\rfloor I + \min\{\rho_{max}(\frac{t}{I} - \left\lfloor\frac{t}{I}\right\rfloor)I, \rho_{ave}I\}$$

Note that the sporadic model is a subcase of the Tenet model when $x_{min} = x_{ave} = p$ (or $\rho_{max} = \rho_{ave} = \rho$ for the continuous versions).

**The leaky bucket model** [4, 5, 6, 16] is a continuous traffic model and incorporates burstiness of data streams through parameter $\sigma$. This parameter denotes the amount of the maximum (possibly instantaneous) burst over the maximum average rate $\rho$. The quantity of traffic having arrived during any period of length $t \geq 0$ is not allowed to be larger than:

$$\mathsf{arrival}_l^{cont}(t) = \sigma + \rho t$$

A discrete version of the leaky bucket model is characterized by three parameters $(\sigma, p, s)$. $\sigma$ packets are allowed to arrive in addition to the maximum average rate represented by $s$ (the maximum size of a message) and $p$ (the minimum message inter-arrival time). The amount of data received during any time interval of length $t \geq 0$ is limited by:

$$\mathsf{arrival}_l(t) = \sigma + s\left\lceil\frac{t}{p}\right\rceil^+$$

When bursts are not allowed ($\sigma = 0$), the model reduces to the sporadic model.

While these constraints may all be a bit different from one another, they each attempt to do the same thing: restrict the rate at which traffic can arrive along any connection. In this work, we consider not only such rate-restricting traffic constraints, but also constraints that may specify to a certain degree the exact *pattern* of arrivals:

**Definition 1.** A traffic constraint $Z_i$ is defined to be *well-formed* if all legal sets of arrivals under constraint $Z_i$ possess the following two properties:

(1) *Time-Independence Property:* If R is a legal arrival set and set R′ can be derived from R by adding some integer $\delta$ to the arrival times of all messages, then R′ is also a legal set of arrivals.

(2) *Connection-Independence Property:* there is no correlation between arrivals from different connections.

According to the Time-Independence Property we only consider traffic constraints that restrict *relative* arrival times, and not absolute arrival times. For example, a constraint of the form "a message arrives at time-instant $3 + 10 \cdot k$ for all non-negative integers $k$" does not possess this property, while the constraint "successive arrivals are exactly 10 time units apart" does. The Time-Independence Property is not very restrictive since a priori knowledge of exact arrival times is usually unavailable. Besides, constraints based on absolute time values are necessarily location-specific and have to be different for all nodes traversed by a data stream.

The Connection-Independence Property says that our model *cannot* represent any cross-synchronization between different connections. Hence it is not possible to specify, for example: "messages from connections $C_i$ and $C_j$ do not ever arrive simultaneously."

The notion of well-formed traffic constraints is extremely general and encompasses a wide variety of the kinds of traffic constraints one may encounter in practice. The standard sporadic, Tenet, and leaky-bucket models are all included. So are more sophisticated ones, such as, for example: "for messages from the same connection, successive video-messages arrive at least $p_1$ time units apart, and each video-message is followed by an audio-message within $p_2$ time units ($p_2 < p_1$)".

It is important to be able to decide whether a considered connection system satisfies the imposed traffic constraints. Moreover, an algorithm for such a verification should be known. A constraint that conforms to these requirements is referred to as *constructively solvable.* Not every well-formed constraint is constructively solvable. For example, "for messages from the same connection, the inter-arrival time is equal to 420 if the Turing machine program P halts, and 666 otherwise" is not constructively solvable. In this paper we design schedulability tests for connection systems with *well-formed constructively-solvable* traffic constraints.

## 4 Worst-Case Traffic

For any well-formed traffic constraint $Z_i$, we can define an *arrival bound function* $\mathsf{arrival}_i(t)$, where $\mathsf{arrival}_i(t)$ equals the maximum amount of data that may be legally delivered from connection $C_i$ during any time interval of length $t$.

From $\mathsf{arrival}_i(t)$, we can construct an *extreme set* $\mathcal{R}_i$, such that the amount of data delivered by $\mathcal{R}_i$ over the interval $[0, t]$ is equal to $\mathsf{arrival}_i(t)$ for all $t \geq 0$. Observe that $\mathcal{R}_i$ is not necessary a *legal* set of arrivals:

**Example 1.** Let connection $C_1$ be characterized by the following traffic constraint $Z_1$ : "messages of size 4 arrive with period 13; each of them is followed by a message of size 3 in 3 time units and a message of size 5 in 7 time units." Figure 1 contains a legal set $R_1$ of arrivals, arrival bound function $\mathsf{arrival}_1(t) = 5\left\lceil\frac{t}{13}\right\rceil^+ + 2\left\lceil\frac{t-3}{13}\right\rceil^+ + \left\lceil\frac{t-4}{13}\right\rceil^+ + \left\lceil\frac{t-6}{13}\right\rceil^+ + 3\left\lceil\frac{t-7}{13}\right\rceil^+$, and

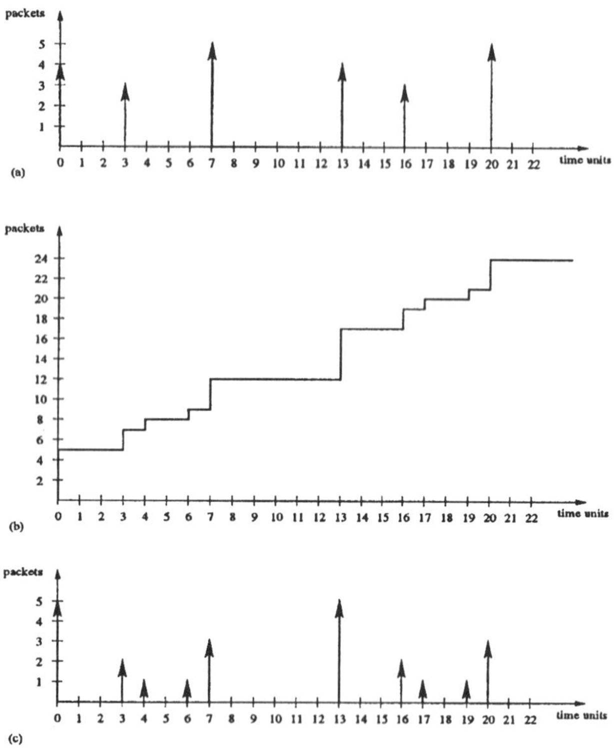


**Figure 1. (a) legal set $R_1$ of arrivals, (b) arrival bound function** $\mathsf{arrival}_1(t)$, **(c) extreme set $\mathcal{R}_1$ of connection $C_1$.**

extreme set $\mathcal{R}_1$ of connection $C_1$. Note that $\mathcal{R}_1$ is *not* legal since it does not satisfy constraint $Z_1$.

(A connection is called *greedy* if beginning from the first message it sends as much data as allowed by the corresponding traffic constraints. Constraints $Z_i$ are referred to as *zero-severe* if the greedy connection $C_i$ generates its extreme set. The class of zero-severe constraints includes, for example, the sporadic, Tenet, and leaky bucket models; however, observe that constraint $Z_1$ of Example 1 is *not* zero-severe. For constraints that are not zero-severe, the arrival bound function yields an extreme set that is not a legal set of arrivals)

Because of the Time-Independence and Connection-Independence Properties, connections may send their maximum traffic starting at the same time. Thus, the worst-case traffic from the connection system is a union of the connections' extreme sets, called a *system extreme set* $\mathcal{R}$ :

$$\mathcal{R} \stackrel{\text{def}}{=} \bigcup_{i=1}^{n} \mathcal{R}_i \tag{1}$$

The latter is represented by a *system arrival bound function:*

$$\mathsf{arrival}(t) = \sum_{i=1}^{n} \mathsf{arrival}_i(t)$$

The definition of the system extreme set $\mathcal{R}$ implies that for any $t_1, t_2 \geq 0$ we have[3]:

$$\mathsf{arrival}(t_1 + t_2 + 1) \leq \mathsf{arrival}(t_1) + \mathsf{arrival}(t_2) \tag{2}$$

## 5 Scheduling and Schedulability

**Result 1 (Dertouzos 74).** If set R of arrivals is schedulable, then it can be scheduled without missing any deadlines by the Earliest Deadline First (EDF) scheduling algorithm.

This optimality of EDF implies that EDF is a good scheduling discipline to employ at network nodes, at least from the view of satisfying delay bounds. Furthermore, remarkably efficient implementations of EDF have been devised, in both hardware and software [18]. However in this paper, we do not require that EDF be the scheduling discipline employed at the network nodes — *any* optimal discipline can be used.

If $\lim_{t\to\infty} \frac{\mathsf{arrival}(t)}{t} > 1$, then the amount of arrived traffic is asymptotically larger than a scheduler can serve, and bounded delay guarantees cannot be provided to all the connections. So, schedulability requires satisfaction of the *Utilization Condition:*

$$\lim_{t\to\infty} \frac{\mathsf{arrival}(t)}{t} \leq 1$$

Note that we do not exclude the cases when $\lim_{t\to\infty} \frac{\mathsf{arrival}(t)}{t} = 1$. Even if there are infinite busy periods (time intervals when the scheduler queue is not empty), it may be possible to schedule traffic from all the connections. For example, when the arrival bound function of the only connection of a connection system is $\mathsf{arrival}(t) = 2 + t$, any delay bound larger or equal to 2 can be guaranteed to this connection.

Let us define a *demand function* of an arrival set R as:

$$\mathsf{demand}_{\mathrm{R}}(t) \stackrel{\text{def}}{=} \sum_{i=1}^{n} A_i^{\mathrm{R}}(t - d_i)$$

where $t$ is time passed after the arrival of the first message, $d_i$ is the delay bound of connection $C_i$, $A_i^{\mathrm{R}}(t-d_i)$ is the amount of data delivered from connection $C_i$ by set R by time $t - d_i$.

**Theorem 1.** A set R of arrivals is schedulable if and only if $(\forall t \geq 0)[\mathsf{demand}_{\mathrm{R}}(t) \leq t]$.

**Proof:** Given in [13]. ■

Let us define a *system demand function* as the demand function of the system extreme set $\mathcal{R}$ (as defined in (1)): $\mathsf{demand}(t) \stackrel{\text{def}}{=} \mathsf{demand}_{\mathcal{R}}(t) = \sum_{i=1}^{n} \mathsf{arrival}_i(t - d_i)$.

[3] For continuous traffic models this condition becomes $\mathsf{arrival}(t_1 + t_2) \leq \mathsf{arrival}(t_1) + \mathsf{arrival}(t_2)$.

**Theorem 2.** A connection system is schedulable if and only if the system extreme set is schedulable.

**Proof:** Given in [13]. ■

**Corollary 1 (Schedulability Conditions).** A connection system is schedulable iff

$$(\forall t \geq 0)[\mathsf{demand}(t) \leq t] \qquad (3)$$

**Proof:** Follows from Theorems 1 and 2. ■

Checking condition (3) directly will take infinite time for any schedulable system. Fortunately, when the Utilization Condition is satisfied, it is usually possible to determine a finite *testing bound* $t_B$ and a finite *testing set* $S$ such that $\mathsf{demand}(t) \leq t$ for all $t \in S \subset \{d_1, d_1+1, \ldots, t_B\}$ implies condition (3) (Note that for $0 \leq t < d_1$ we always have $\mathsf{demand}(t) = 0 \leq t$). This fact allows us to derive the more practical schedulability test:

**Result 2.** A connection system is schedulable iff

$$(\forall t \in S)[\mathsf{demand}(t) \leq t] \text{ and}$$
the Utilization Condition is satisfied

## 6 Determination of the Testing Set

Even though the smallest testing set $S$ depends upon the specific traffic constraints being considered, there are several general guidelines for detecting $S$:

(1) The *Too-Late-To-Fail (TLTF) Rule:* if condition (3) is false, then there exists $t_f \geq 0$ such that $\mathsf{demand}(t_f) > t_f$. Sometimes, the latter inequality may be transformed to $t_f < B$ where $B$ does not depend on $t_f$. In such cases, the failure of $\mathsf{demand}(t) \leq t$ cannot occur for any $t \geq B$, and $t_{TLTF} = \lceil B \rceil - 1$ can be used as a testing bound.

(2) The *Empty-Queue (EQ) Rule:* if for some $t_{EQ}$ we have $\mathsf{arrival}(t_{EQ}) \leq t_{EQ} + 1$ and $\mathsf{demand}(t) \leq t$ for all $d_1 \leq t \leq t_{EQ}$, it means that all messages received during interval $[0, t_{EQ}]$ are served by time $t_{EQ} + 1$ without violation of their deadlines. Then the same is true for the messages arriving after $t_{EQ}$, since, according to (2), we have $\mathsf{arrival}(t_{EQ} + t + 1) - \mathsf{arrival}(t_{EQ}) \leq \mathsf{arrival}(t)$ for any $t \geq 0$. Thus, $t_{EQ}$ can be used as a testing bound.

(3) The *Worst-Is-Behind (WIB) Rule:* there may exist some $t_{WIB}$ such that $(\forall t > t_{WIB})$ $(\exists t' \leq t_{WIB})[\mathsf{demand}(t) \leq \mathsf{demand}(t') + (t - t')]$. If for all $d_1 \leq t \leq t_{WIB}$ the condition $\mathsf{demand}(t) \leq t$ is satisfied, then so is it for all $t \geq 0$. Thus, $t_{WIB}$ can be employed as a testing bound.

(4) The *Skip Rule:* if there exist some $t_1 \in S$ such that $(\forall t \in \{t_1 + 1, t_1 + 2, \ldots, t_2\})$ $[\mathsf{demand}(t) \leq \mathsf{demand}(t_1) + (t - t_1)]$, then numbers $t_1+1, t_1+2, \ldots, t_2$ may be excluded from the testing set S.

**Example 2.** Let us consider connection system $\{C_1, C_2\}$: $C_1$ is characterized by $Z_1$ (as introduced in Example 1) and $d_1 = 7$; $C_2$ conforms to the leaky bucket model with $\sigma = s = 1$, $p = 13$ and has delay bound $d_2 = 7$. The test presented in [16] runs forever and fails to assure schedulability of the system. However, applying the WIB and Skip Rules yields a testing bound $t_B = 19$ and testing set $S = \{7, 10, 14\}$. Therefore, checking condition $\mathsf{demand}(t) \leq t$ only for $t \in \{7, 10, 14\}$ suffices to verify schedulability of system $\{C_1, C_2\}$.

We have used the TLTF, EQ, WIB, and Skip Rules to derive necessary and sufficient schedulability conditions for the traffic models described in Section 3. The results are given in Figure 2. A detailed derivation of the obtained conditions for the leaky bucket model is provided in [13]; other may be derived similarly.

Comparative efficiency of the rules varies for different connection systems. In general, the TLTF Rule outperforms the EQ Rule; however, the latter may provide lower testing bounds when there exists a connection with a very large delay bound. Using the WIB Rule may yield smaller testing sets when the link utilization is high. A quantitative analysis given in [13] demonstrates the usefulness of each rule. [13] also offers recommendations for improving the efficiency of the connection admission in actual networks and provides efficient schedulability tests for the generic traffic model and the leaky bucket model.

## 7 Conclusions and Future Work

We have investigated the problem of schedulability at nodes of packet-switched virtual-circuit fixed-packet networks. We introduced very general constraints on traffic (*well-formed constraints*). For connection systems that satisfied those constraints, we defined the notion of *extreme sets*, and used this notion to derive necessary and sufficient schedulability conditions. We identified guidelines (*TLTF*, *EQ*, *WIB*, and *Skip Rules*) which could assist in the efficient evaluation of the obtained schedulability conditions.

In the near future, we plan on extending the research described here in several directions:

- We will explore the issue of designing additional rules, similar to the ones in Section 6, that help to improve the efficiency of the admission control.
- We will use the developed methodology for deriving efficient schedulability tests for different network and traffic models. For instance, this work can be extended in a straightforward manner to schedulability testing of systems where messages of the same connection are allowed to have different delay bounds.

| Traffic models | Schedulability conditions |
|---|---|
| The sporadic model | $\sum_{i=1}^{n} \frac{s_i}{p_i} \leq 1$ and $(\forall t \in S)[\mathsf{demand}(t) \leq t]$<br>where $S = \bigcup_{i=1}^{n} \{t:\ t \leq t_B,\ t = d_i + mp_i,\ m \in \mathbf{N}\}$,<br>$t_B = \min\left\{ \max\left\{ d_n, \left\lceil \frac{\sum_{i=1}^{n} s_i(1-\frac{d_i}{p_i})}{1-\sum_{i=1}^{n} \frac{s_i}{p_i}} \right\rceil -1 \right\}, \left\lceil \frac{\sum_{i=1}^{n} s_i - 1}{1-\sum_{i=1}^{n} \frac{s_i}{p_i}} \right\rceil -1,\ d_n + \underset{i=1,\ldots,n}{\mathsf{lcm}} \{p_i\} - 1 \right\}$, and<br>$\mathsf{demand}(t) = \sum_{i=1}^{n} s_i \left\lceil \frac{t-d_i}{p_i} \right\rceil^{+}$ |
| The continuous version of the sporadic model | $\sum_{i=1}^{n} \rho_i \leq 1$ |
| The Tenet model | $\sum_{i=1}^{n} \frac{s_i}{x_{ave,i}} \leq 1$ and $(\forall t \in S)[\mathsf{demand}(t) \leq t]$<br>where $S = \bigcup_{i=1}^{n} \{t:\ t \leq t_B,\ t = d_i + mI_i + kx_{min,i},\ m \in \mathbf{N},\ k = 0, 1, \ldots, \frac{I_i}{x_{ave,i}} - 1\}$,<br>$t_B = \min\left\{ \max\left\{ d_n, \left\lceil \frac{\sum_{i=1}^{n} \frac{s_i}{x_{ave,i}}(I_i-d_i)}{1-\sum_{i=1}^{n} \frac{s_i}{x_{ave,i}}} \right\rceil -1 \right\}, \left\lceil \frac{\sum_{i=1}^{n} \frac{s_i}{x_{ave,i}} I_i - 1}{1-\sum_{i=1}^{n} \frac{s_i}{x_{ave,i}}} \right\rceil -1,\ d_n + \underset{i=1,\ldots,n}{\mathsf{lcm}} \{I_i\} - 1 \right\}$, and<br>$\mathsf{demand}(t) = \sum_{i=1}^{n} \mathsf{threshold}(s_i \left( \left\lfloor \frac{t-d_i}{I_i} \right\rfloor \frac{I_i}{x_{ave,i}} + \min\left\{ \left\lceil (\frac{t-d_i}{I_i} - \left\lfloor \frac{t-d_i}{I_i} \right\rfloor) \frac{I_i}{x_{min,i}} \right\rceil^{+}, \frac{I_i}{x_{ave,i}} \right\} \right), t - d_i)$ |
| The continuous version of the Tenet model | $\sum_{i=1}^{n} \rho_{ave,i} \leq 1$ and $(\forall t \in S)[\mathsf{demand}(t) \leq t]$<br>where $S = \bigcup_{i=1}^{n} \{t:\ t \leq t_B,\ t = d_i + (m + \frac{\rho_{ave,i}}{\rho_{max,i}})I_i,\ m \in \mathbf{N}\}$,<br>$t_B = \min\left\{ \max\left\{ d_n, \frac{\sum_{i=1}^{n} \rho_{ave,i}(I_i-d_i)}{1-\sum_{i=1}^{n} \rho_{ave,i}} \right\}, \frac{\sum_{i=1}^{n} \rho_{ave,i} I_i}{1-\sum_{i=1}^{n} \rho_{ave,i}},\ d_n + \underset{i=1,\ldots,n}{\mathsf{lcm}} \{I_i\} - 1 \right\}$, and<br>$\mathsf{demand}(t) = \sum_{i=1}^{n} \mathsf{threshold}(\rho_{ave,i} \left\lfloor \frac{t-d_i}{I_i} \right\rfloor I_i + \min\left\{ \rho_{max,i}(\frac{t-d_i}{I_i} - \left\lfloor \frac{t-d_i}{I_i} \right\rfloor)I_i, \rho_{ave,i} I_i \right\}, t - d_i)$ |
| The leaky bucket model | $\sum_{i=1}^{n} \rho_i \leq 1$ and $(\forall j, 1 \leq j \leq n)[\sum_{d_i \leq d_j} (\sigma_i + \rho_i(d_j - d_i)) \leq d_j]$ |
| The discrete version of the leaky bucket model | $\sum_{i=1}^{n} \frac{s_i}{p_i} \leq 1$ and $(\forall t \in S)[\mathsf{demand}(t) \leq t]$<br>where $S = \bigcup_{i=1}^{n} \{t:\ t \leq t_B,\ t = d_i + mp_i,\ m \in \mathbf{N}\}$,<br>$t_B = \min\left\{ \max\left\{ d_n, \left\lceil \frac{\sum_{i=1}^{n} (\sigma_i + s_i(1-\frac{d_i}{p_i}))}{1-\sum_{i=1}^{n} \frac{s_i}{p_i}} \right\rceil -1 \right\}, \left\lceil \frac{\sum_{i=1}^{n} (\sigma_i + s_i) - 1}{1-\sum_{i=1}^{n} \frac{s_i}{p_i}} \right\rceil -1,\ d_n + \underset{i=1,\ldots,n}{\mathsf{lcm}} \{p_i\} - 1 \right\}$, and<br>$\mathsf{demand}(t) = \sum_{i=1}^{n} \mathsf{threshold}(\sigma_i + s_i \left\lceil \frac{t-d_i}{p_i} \right\rceil^{+}, t - d_i)$ |

**Notations:**
(1) threshold function: $\mathsf{threshold}(x, y) = x$ for $y \geq 0$, and $\mathsf{threshold}(x, y) = 0$ if $y < 0$;
(2) $\mathbf{N}$ is the set of natural numbers;
(3) $\underset{i=1,\ldots,n}{\mathsf{lcm}} \{x_i\}$ is the least common multiple of numbers $x_i$ where $i = 1, \ldots, n$.

**Figure 2. Necessary and sufficient schedulability conditions.**

- We plan to investigate providing performance guarantees to heterogeneous connection systems where different connections are described by different traffic models.
- The problem of verifying whether adding a new connection to a schedulable connection system is safe for system schedulability is important from a practical perspective. Often this problem can be solved more efficiently than by retesting the entire new system for schedulability. We plan to apply the techniques introduced in this paper to find exact and efficient solutions for this problem as well as for the problem of determination of the minimum delay bound that may be associated with the new connection.

## References


[1] S. Baruah, A. Mok, and L. Rosier. "The Preemptive Scheduling of Sporadic, Real-Time Tasks on One Processor," Proceedings of the 11th Real-Time Systems Symposium, pp. 182-190, 1990.

[2] S. Baruah. "The Uniprocessor Scheduling of Sporadic Real-Time Tasks," Ph.D. Thesis, The University of Texas at Austin, 1993.

[3] I. Cidon, I. Gopal, G. Grover, and M. Sidi, "Real-Time Packet Switching: A Performance Analysis," IEEE Journal on Selected Areas in Communications, 6(9):1576-1586, 1988.

[4] R.L. Cruz. "A Calculus for Network Delay, Part I: Network Elements in Isolation," IEEE Transactions on Information Theory, 37(1):114-131, January 1991.

[5] R.L. Cruz. "A Calculus for Network Delay, Part II: Network Analysis," IEEE Transactions on Information Theory, 37(1):132-141, January 1991.

[6] R.L. Cruz. "Quality of Service Guarantees in Virtual Circuit Switched Networks," IEEE Journal on Selected Areas in Communications, 13(6):1048 - 1056, August 1995.

[7] A. Demers, S. Keshav, and S. Shenker. "Analysis and Simulation of a Fair Queueing Algorithm," Proceedings of SIGCOMM '89, pp. 1-12, 1989.

[8] M. Dertouzos. "Control Robotics: the Procedural Control of Physical Processors," Proceedings of the IFIP Congress, pp. 807-813, 1974.

[9] D. Ferrari and D. C. Verma. "A Scheme for Real-Time Channel Establishment in Wide-Area Networks," IEEE Journal on Selected Areas in Communications, 8(3):368-379, April 1990.

[10] L. Georgiadis, R. Guerin, and A. Parekh. "Optimal multiplexing on a single link: delay and buffer requirements," Proceedings of INFOCOM '94, pp. 524-532, 1994.

[11] L. Georgiadis, R. Guerin, V. Peris, and K. N. Sivarajan. "Efficient Network QoS Provisioning Based on Per Node Traffic Shaping," IEEE/ACM Transactions on Networking, 4(4):482-501, August 1996.

[12] S. J. Golestani. "A Stop-and-Go Queueing Framework for Congestion Management," Proceedings of SIGCOMM '90, pp. 8-18, September 1990.

[13] S. Gorinsky, S. Baruah, T. J. Marlowe, and A. D. Stoyenko. "Exact and Efficient Analysis of Schedulability in Fixed-Packet Networks: A Generic Approach," Technical Report CIS-96-26, Department of Computer and Information Science, NJIT, 1996.

[14] P. Goyal, S. S. Lam, and H. M. Vin. "Determining End-to-End Delay Bounds In Heterogeneous Networks," Proceedings of NOSSDAV '95, pp. 287-298, April 1995.

[15] C.R. Kalmanek, H. Kanakia, and S. Keshav. "Rate-Controlled Servers for Very High-Speed Networks," Proceedings of GLOBECOM '90, pp. 300.3.1 - 300.3.9, December 1990.

[16] J. Liebeherr, D. E. Wrege, and D. Ferrari. "Exact Admission Control in Networks with Bounded Delay Sevices," to appear: IEEE/ACM Transactions on Networking, December 1996.

[17] A. Mok. "Fundamental Design Problems of Distributed Systems for the Hard Real-Time Environment," Ph.D. Thesis, MIT Laboratory for Computer Science, Technical Report MIT/LCS/TR-297, May 1983.

[18] A. Mok. "Task Management Techniques for Enforcing ED Scheduling on a Periodic Task Set," Proceedings of 5-th IEEE Workshop on Real-Time Software and Operating Systems, May 1988.

[19] A. K. Parekh and R. G. Gallager. "A Generalized Processor Sharing Approach to Flow Control in Integrated Services Networks: The Single-Node Case," IEEE/ACM Transactions on Networking, 1(3):344-357, June 1993.

[20] A. K. Parekh and R. G. Gallager. "A Generalized Processor Sharing Approach to Flow Control in Integrated Services Networks: The Multiple Node Case," IEEE/ACM Transactions on Networking, 2(2):137-150, April 1994.

[21] D. E. Wrege, E. W. Knightly, H. Zhang, and J. Liebeherr. "Deterministic Delay Bounds for VBR Video in Packet-Switching Networks: Fundamental Limits and Practical Tradeoffs," IEEE/ACM Transactions on Networking, 4(3):352-362, June 1996.

[22] Lixia Zhang. "Virtual Clock: A New Traffic Control Algorithm for Packet Switching Networks," ACM Transactions on Computer Systems, 9(2):101-124, May 1991.

[23] Q. Zheng and K. G. Shin. "On the Ability of Establishing Real-Time Channels in Point-to-Point Packet-Switched Networks," IEEE Transactions on Communications, 42(2/3/4):1096-1105, February/March/April 1994.

# An Empirical Model of HTTP Network Traffic

Bruce A. Mah
bmah@CS.Berkeley.EDU
The Tenet Group
Computer Science Division
University of California at Berkeley
Berkeley, CA 94720-1776

## Abstract

*The workload of the global Internet is dominated by the Hypertext Transfer Protocol (HTTP), an application protocol used by World Wide Web clients and servers. Simulation studies of IP networks will require a model of the traffic patterns of the World Wide Web, in order to investigate the effects of this increasingly popular application. We have developed an empirical model of network traffic produced by HTTP. Instead of relying on server or client logs, our approach is based on packet traces of HTTP conversations. Through traffic analysis, we have determined statistics and distributions for higher-level quantities such as the size of HTTP files, the number of files per "Web page", and user browsing behavior. These quantities form a model can then be used by simulations to mimic World Wide Web network applications.*

## 1 Introduction

Simulations are a popular tool for the evaluation of computer networks. To yield useful data, however, they require accurate models of the system under study and its expected workload. In particular, workloads need to capture various characteristics of network applications. While a number of synthetic workloads have been constructed for more traditional types of network traffic (such as remote logins and file transfers), new applications require the development of new traffic models.

One such example is the World Wide Web, a popular approach to retrieving information in the global Internet. The Web (along with its associated Hypertext Transfer Protocol) has come to strongly influence the nature of Internet network traffic.[1] To simulate networks under contemporary Internet traffic loads, we therefore require a model of this rapidly-growing application.

Section 2 of this paper provides background on the World Wide Web and HTTP. In Section 3, we describe some measurement methodologies used in prior studies of the Web and other Internet applications; we describe our actual approach to measurement-gathering in Section 4. Section 5 describes the various components of our model. We present our experimental results and apply them to our model in Section 6. In Section 7, we discuss the representation and use of our model's components.

## 2 Background

The *World Wide Web* (frequently shortened to *WWW* or *Web*) is a collection of documents and services available to the global Internet. Servers furnish these documents on request to clients (also known as *browsers*). Each document, or *page*, may consist of a number of files. For example, a multi-part document could consist of Hypertext Markup Language (HTML) text [3], plus some number of images, with each part in separate files.

The Hypertext Transfer Protocol (HTTP) [4] is a request-response protocol designed to transfer the files making up the parts of Web documents. Each transfer consists of the client requesting a file from the server, then the server replying with the requested file (or an error notification). Both the request and reply contain identification and control information in headers. HTTP uses the services of TCP [26]. In current versions of HTTP, each TCP connection can be used for at most one retrieval. Future versions of HTTP [12] will incorporate a proposal for the reuse of TCP connections for multiple retrievals between the same client and server [18, 23].

## 3 Prior work

In this section, we summarize three approaches to characterizing Internet applications. Two methods, server logs and client logs, are popular in Web measurements.

1. The last NSFNET traffic measurements in April 1995 showed that HTTP was the leading source of backbone network traffic, measured both by the number of bytes and number of packets transferred [22].



0-8186-7780-5/97 $10.00 © 1997 IEEE

The last approach, traffic traces, has been used for past studies of other Internet applications.

### 3.1 Server logs

Most Web servers keep logs of the files they have served; this information can be used to create a workload model. Such an approach is fairly easy, because the machinery for collecting model data already exists and, in fact, the data is very likely being collected anyway. Some studies, such as [2] and [18], require such a model of a stream of HTTP requests arriving at a Web server.

However, there are two principal drawbacks to this approach. One large disadvantage of using server logs is that they cannot easily capture user access patterns across multiple Web servers. In particular, it may be difficult to determine the locality of references during any given user session. Another shortcoming is that current server logs do not capture HTTP overheads such as protocol headers.

### 3.2 Client logs

[7], [8], and [9] relied on data gathered by instrumenting the NCSA Mosaic browser [19] to log all retrievals made during Web user sessions. These studies were concerned with investigating characteristics of Web accesses. Using this data, it would be possible to construct a corresponding model, suitable for generating a synthetic workload.

Unlike server logs, this approach captures user accesses between multiple Web servers. It can also characterize the effects of client document caching. However, this technique requires that browsers be able to log their requests, currently a rare capability.

### 3.3 Packet traces

A third method of gathering data consists of collecting packet traces taken from a subnet carrying HTTP traffic, typically an Ethernet or other shared-media LAN. From the packet traces and knowledge about the higher-layer protocols used, traffic analysis can yield a model of the behavior of the original application. This approach has been used in a number of other traffic studies, such as [6] and [24], that predate the Web. [27] analyzes the packets arriving at an HTTP server and presents some interesting statistics and observations. [10] describes a library of traffic models for common (circa 1991) Internet applications, which is designed for inclusion in network simulators. [25] describes analytic models derived from traffic traces, which have a more compact representation than purely empirical models and can be parameterized to more accurately reflect particular networks.

This approach eliminates the principal disadvantages of the two previous methods mentioned. However, it too introduces drawbacks. A packet trace misses higher-level information such as specific files requested and document types. In addition, the effects of client document caching are more difficult to ascertain, since only cache misses generate detectable network traffic.

## 4 Methodology

We chose to use a packet trace-based approach, principally because it allowed us to capture the behavior of individual users and we would be able to record the activity of any HTTP client. While this approach loses higher-level information such as filenames, we felt that such data is not essential to a network workload model.

We used the `tcpdump` packet capture utility [13], running on a DEC Alpha 3000/300, to record TCP/IP packet headers on a shared 10 Mbps Ethernet in the Computer Science Division at the University of California at Berkeley, during four periods in late 1995.

The subnet examined is a stub network (no transit traffic) with approximately one hundred hosts; almost all are UNIX workstations used principally by a single user. The user community consists primarily of Computer Science graduate students. While no statistics are available on the relative popularity of different Web clients in this environment, operational experience suggests that the most prevalent is Netscape Navigator [20]. There are also several Web servers on this subnet, associated with various research groups.

Most HTTP servers bind to TCP port 80.[2] By gathering all TCP packets to or from this well-known port, we captured what we believe is the vast majority of HTTP traffic. Table 1 summarizes our traffic traces. The first three traces were collected as a part of an effort to examine various types of LAN traffic (not just HTTP traffic); the packet counts from these traces include only those packets attributable to HTTP. The last traffic trace collected HTTP packets only. From these streams of packets, we extracted those for HTTP connections originating from clients on the local subnet. Our traces captured activity from between forty to sixty active client hosts.

Although we do not have complete packet loss figures for these traces, we recorded the loss of approximately 6000 out of 44,000,000 packets during the 1 November

2. In a recent study of the characteristics of HTML documents indexed by the Inktomi "web crawler", approximately 94% of the documents surveyed were accessed via the standard HTTP port [28].

| Starting Date | Duration (hr:min) | Packets |
|---|---|---|
| 19 Sep 1995 | 39:40 | 186,068 |
| 11 Oct 1995 | 29:31 | 458,264 |
| 1 Nov 1995 | 25:30 | 369,671 |
| 20 Nov 1995 | 138:14 | 676,256 |

**TABLE 1. Summary of Traffic Traces.**

1995 trace (before filtering to isolate HTTP packets). These figures yield a ratio of only 0.014%. Similar packet capture experiments using this hardware and network have produced figures consistent with this loss rate.

## 5 Model

Our model of HTTP traffic captures logically meaningful parameters of Web client behavior, such as file sizes and "think times". The traffic traces described in the preceding section provide us with empirical probability distributions describing various components of this behavior. We use these distributions to determine a synthetic workload. In this section, we present the components of our model, which are summarized in Table 2.

| Quantity | Description |
|---|---|
| request length | HTTP request length |
| reply length | HTTP reply length |
| document size | Number of files per document |
| think time | Time between retrieval of two successive documents |
| consecutive document retrievals | Number of consecutive documents retrieved from any given server |
| server selection | Used to select each succeeding server accessed |

**TABLE 2. Quantities Modeled.**

At the lowest level, our model deals with individual HTTP transfers, each of which consists of a request-reply pair of messages, sent over a single TCP connection. We model both the *request length* and *reply length* of HTTP transfers.[3]

At first glance, it may seem more appropriate for a model of network traffic to deal with the number, size, and interarrival times of TCP segments. However, we note that these quantities are governed by the TCP flow control and congestion control algorithms. These algorithms depend in part on the latency and effective bandwidth on the path between the client and server. Since this information cannot be known *a priori*, an accurate packet-level network simulation will depend on a simulation of the actual TCP algorithms. This is in fact the approach taken for other types of TCP bulk transfers in the traffic model described in [10]. In a similar fashion, our model generates transfers which need to be run through TCP's algorithms; it does not generate packet sizes and interarrivals by itself.

A Web document can consist of multiple files. A server and client may need to employ multiple HTTP transactions, each of which requires a separate TCP connection, to transfer a single document. For example, a document could consist of HTML text [3], which in turn could specify three images to be displayed "inline" in the body of the document. Such a document would require four TCP connections, each carrying one request and one reply. The next higher level above individual files is naturally the Web document, which we characterize in terms of the *number of files* needed to represent a document.

Between Web page retrievals, the user is generally considering her next action. We admit the difficulty of characterizing user behavior, due to its dependency on human factors beyond the scope of this study. However, we can model *user think time* based on our observations.

Assuming that users tend to access strings of documents from the same server, we characterize the locality of reference between different Web pages. We therefore define the *consecutive document retrievals* distribution as the number of consecutive pages that a user will retrieve from a single Web server before moving to a new one.[4]

Finally, the *server selection distribution* defines the relative popularity of each Web server, in terms of how likely it is that a particular server will be accessed for a set of consecutive document retrievals.

## 6 Experimental results

From our traffic traces and subsequent analysis, we derived the probability distributions for the different components of our model. They are consistent with existing Web measurement studies. We have summarized the more interesting facets of these measurements in Table 3.

3. In Section 6.5, we show it is appropriate to model the first HTTP transfer on a Web page separately from subsequent retrievals for that page. For simplicity, we have postponed discussion of this distinction.

4. We assume that all the components of a Web document come from the same server.

| |
|---|
| HTTP request sizes show a bimodal distribution. |
| HTTP reply sizes have a heavy-tailed distribution, and tend to be larger than request sizes. |
| A simple heuristic based on timing can be used to group individual files into documents |
| The number of files per document tends to be small; 80% of documents required less than four file transfers. |
| HTTP requests to retrieve the first file of a multi-file Web page tend to be longer than subsequent requests. |
| The first file of a Web page tends to be larger than subsequent files. |
| The number of consecutive documents retrieved from a given server tends to be small. 80% of visits to a server's document space resulted in fewer than six documents being retrieved. |

**TABLE 3. Selected Measurement Results.**

## 6.1 Anomalies

In some cases we noticed odd trends in our data, which indicated a large number of nearly-identical Web documents, transferred periodically. For example, the 11 October 1995 trace showed a number of retrievals with interarrival times of about five minutes. There were 291 instances of these transfers, accounting for approximately 20% of those transferred during the whole trace. Upon further investigation, we found that they contained real-time, still images of San Francisco. They used an extension to HTML which caused clients to automatically reload them every five minutes, thus updating the picture. As these (and other) periodic HTTP retrievals were skewing our data, we removed them from our traces.[5]

## 6.2 Request length

HTTP requests are sent from a client to a server. They typically specify a file to retrieve, although they may also provide information to a computation on the server.

The only data sent from client to server consists of the HTTP request, so we measured the request sizes by simply counting the number of bytes in the appropriate direction of each TCP connection, summed over all packets. We observed mean request lengths of about 320 bytes, with medians around 240 bytes.

5. While it may be argued that these retrievals should contribute to our traffic model since they actually occur in real life, this model cannot accurately capture the correlations between successive, periodic document retrievals. A model attempting to characterize such periodic Web traffic should explicitly account for this behavior.

The cumulative distribution functions (CDFs) for the request size distributions are shown in Figure 1. The request sizes in our traces all exhibited a bimodal distribution, with one large peak occurring around 250 bytes and another, smaller one around 1 KB. We believe that the former requests correspond to simple file retrievals, while the latter may contain more complex requests such as those generated by HTML forms. However, there is insufficient information in our existing traces to confirm this hypothesis. (Investigating further would require packet traces containing the payload bytes from each packet.)

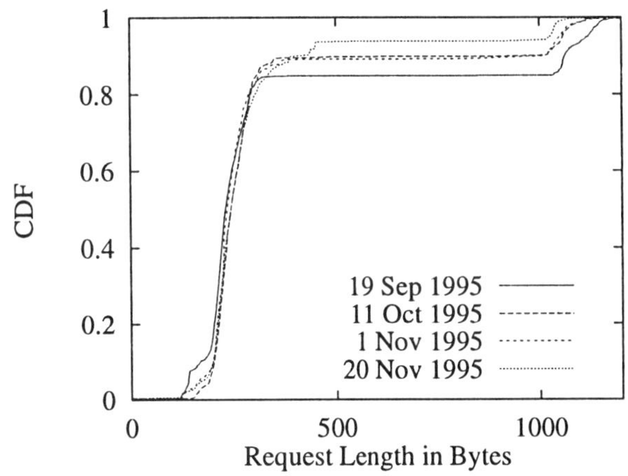


**FIGURE 1. HTTP Request Lengths.**

## 6.3 Reply length

Each HTTP reply consists of the bytes sent from server to client. Typically, the reply contains either HTML text or some multimedia data (e.g. an image or audio clip) to be displayed by the Web client. In the case of an error, the HTTP reply contains an error message.

The CDFs for the reply size distributions are shown in Figure 2. The mean file sizes ranged from 8–10 KB, with median files around 1.5–2.0 KB. We note that although many replies were short, we recorded some as long as 8 MB (upon further investigation we determined that they were binary file transfers).

In each of the traces, the minimum reply length was very short (tens of bytes). These replies probably represent either errors or "not modified" responses to conditional document retrieval requests. While some files may indeed be this short, the addition of HTTP headers lengthens the reply messages.

We note that the maximum reply sizes were rather large (over 1 MB in each of the traces). Further, the means (8–10 KB) were much larger than the median reply sizes (about 2 KB). These characteristics are consistent with distributions of reply sizes that are "heavy-tailed" (with a

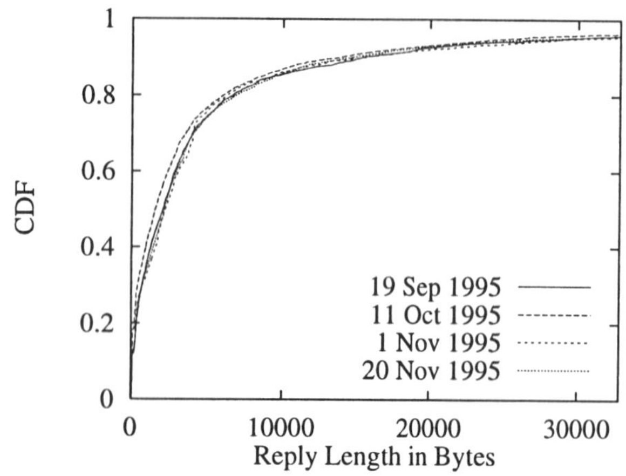


**FIGURE 2. HTTP Reply Lengths.**

large amount of the probability mass in the tail of the distribution), as shown for WWW file sizes in [8].

Assuming that HTTP retrievals generally result in the transfer of a WWW file (and in particular, the assumption that large HTTP replies contain WWW files), it seems natural to expect that HTTP replies would share this characteristic. We repeated the analysis of [8] on our data, and found that reply sizes above 1 KB are reasonably well-modeled by Pareto distributions with α estimates ranging from $\alpha = 1.04$ to $\alpha = 1.14$.[6] By comparison, [8] arrived at an estimate of $\alpha = 1.06$.

### 6.4 Page length

Determining the number of files per page is less straightforward, as we cannot exactly determine the set of TCP connections carrying parts of a single document. We therefore use two simple heuristics to determine whether two HTTP connections belong to the same document. First, they must originate from the same client machine. We note that it is possible for two connections from the same IP address to be associated with two unrelated documents, which can happen if two users fetch a document at the same time. Because our end hosts were workstations used by single users, we feel this occurrence is unlikely.

Second, the two connections cannot be separated by "too much time", an interval determined by a parameter we call $T_{thresh}$. More formally, let $c_1$ and $c_2$ be two HTTP connections. Let $S(c)$ be the arrival time of the starting packet of connection $c$ and let $E(c)$ be the arrival time of the ending packet of connection $c$. Assuming $S(c_1) < S(c_2)$, we judge $c_1$ and $c_2$ to belong to the same document only if $S(c_2) - E(c_1) \le T_{thresh}$. If $S(c_1) < S(c_2) < E(c_1)$, the two connections overlap and we judge their respective files to belong to the same document. This condition can occur with browsers that use multiple, overlapping TCP connections to improve interactive performance, such as Netscape Navigator [20].

Figure 3 illustrates the role of $T_{thresh}$ in determining the relation between two HTTP connections $c_1$ and $c_2$, between the same client and server. In the top timeline, $c_2$ starts within $T_{thresh}$ time after the end of $c_1$; we judge them to belong to the same document. In the center timeline, the inter-file gap is too long, so the files belong to different documents. In the bottom timeline, $c_2$ starts before $c_1$ finishes; they must be part of the same document.

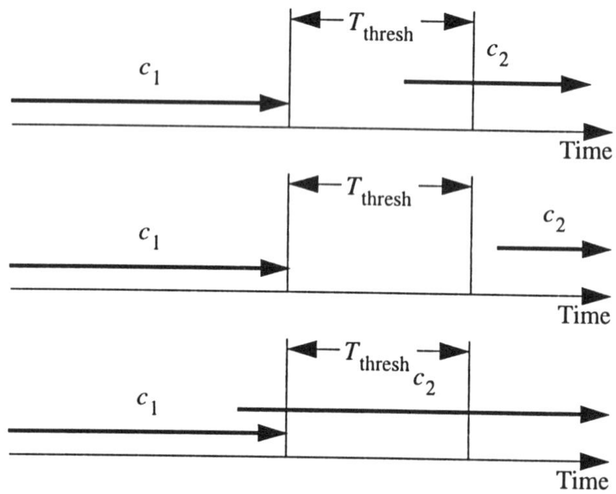


**FIGURE 3. Heuristic for Determining Relation Between Two HTTP Connections.**

This heuristic requires a suitable value of $T_{thresh}$. As $T_{thresh}$ becomes very short, it may become smaller than the time necessary for an HTTP client to initiate a file retrieval. In this case, related connections will be falsely classified as belonging to different documents. Conversely, as $T_{thresh}$ becomes long, it may become longer than the time for a user to react to the displayed document and request a new one. Files from different pages could then appear to be part of the same document.

The analysis in [8] classified files separated by less than one second of idle time as belonging to the same document, due to the limitations of the users' reaction time. Idle times greater than 30 seconds were assumed to delimit documents, as few items would take longer to be processed and displayed. Values in the intermediate range constituted a "transition" region. According to this reasoning, reasonable values for $T_{thresh}$ can be found in the range $1 \text{ sec} < T_{thresh} < 30 \text{ sec}$.

6. The "heavy-tailed" Pareto distribution has a CDF given by $F(x) = P[X \le x] = 1 - \left(\frac{k}{x}\right)^{\alpha}$, where $k$ is the minimum value of $X$ and $\alpha$ is a shape parameter.

We picked $T_{\text{thresh}} = 1$ sec for this study. The primary influence on our choice is that users will generally take longer than one second to react to the display of a new page and request the next document. For HTTP clients that perform overlapping file transfers, processing time does not affect the choice of $T_{\text{thresh}}$, as the various components of a multi-part document are downloaded, processed, and displayed in parallel.

Given our choice of an idle threshold, we can characterize the number of files per document. The mean number of files per document ranged from 2.8 to 3.2, with the median documents requiring only one file. We note that in the survey of HTML documents in [5], slightly more than half of all pages contained either zero or one inlined image (one or two connections). Considering that some of our "documents" were actually single-file downloads, which would tend to skew this distribution downward, we feel that our observations are consistent with this statistic.

[11] and [21] both analyzed a 5-minute trace from an Internet backbone for characteristics of flows (aggregations of TCP connections). The results in [21] implied average two-way flows of about 20 KB, considerably shorter than our averages of 26–32 KB. [11] found 90% of request flows to be shorter than 10 KB, with the 90th percentile of reply flows less than 100 KB. Our analogous measures (based on the sums of requests and replies for a page) were 7.4–9.0 KB and 168–249 KB respectively. We feel that the discrepancies are due both to the different metrics being examined and the short length of the trace these studies used.

We note that although the number of files per document varies as $T_{\text{thresh}}$ changes, the distributions were similar for values around $T_{\text{thresh}} = 1$ sec, as shown in Figure 4. Thus the exact choice of $T_{\text{thresh}}$ is not critical to our analysis.

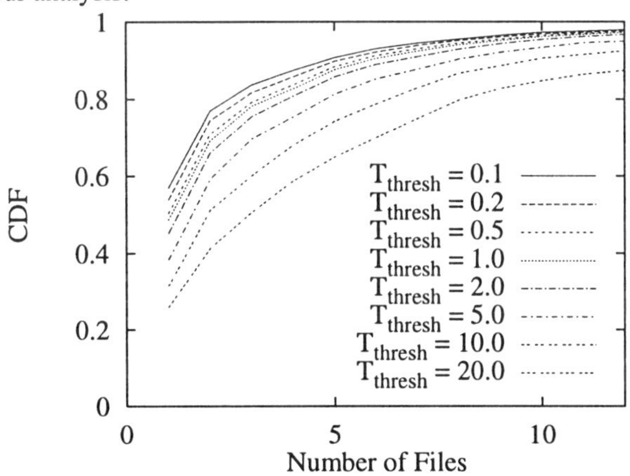


**FIGURE 4. Document Lengths, 19 September 1995. Curves correspond to varying values of $T_{\text{thresh}}$ in seconds.**

## 6.5 Primary and secondary retrievals

After classifying files into pages, we can partition their retrievals into two classes. The first, which we term *primary retrievals*, consists of the first file of each document. Typically the reply for a primary retrieval consists of HTML text, but the reply could also be an image, a data file, or an HTTP error message.

The other class of retrievals, called *secondary retrievals*, consists of any remaining files for a document, after its primary retrieval. Inlined images (referenced by a primary file consisting of HTML text) are the only known secondary retrievals.

We found that the sizes of requests and replies are slightly different for primary and secondary retrievals. Primary requests tend to be larger than secondary requests (for $T_{\text{thresh}} = 1$ sec, the median primary and secondary sizes were approximately 240 and 230 bytes respectively). This tendency is illustrated by the example of Figure 5.

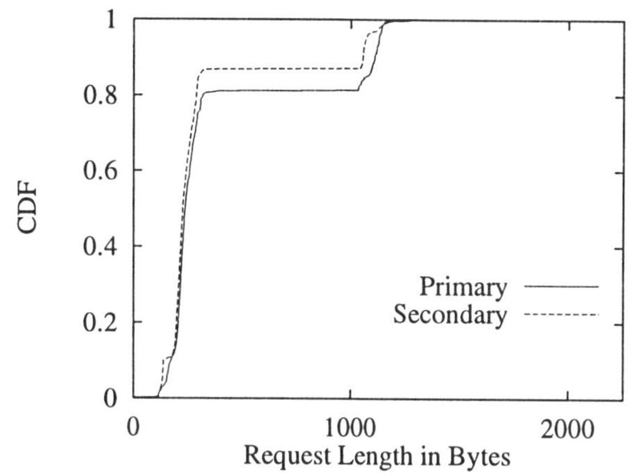


**FIGURE 5. Primary and Secondary Request Lengths, 19 September 1995.**

Primary reply sizes were also larger. The median primary replies ranged from 2.0–2.4 KB, while the median secondary replies were between 1.2–2.0 KB. When we fitted the reply sizes to Pareto distributions, the $\alpha$ parameter estimates were lower for primary replies than for secondary replies ($\alpha \in [0.85, 0.97]$ vs. $\alpha \in [1.12, 1.39]$).

To further distinguish the differences between primary and secondary request sizes, we computed confidence intervals for the estimates of $\alpha$, and determined that for all four datasets, the corresponding parameters for primary and secondary reply sizes are significantly different with 90% confidence. We believe that the differences between the sizes of primary and secondary retrievals are due to the dissimilar types of data being transferred. In particular, we note that arbitrary files downloaded from Web servers are transferred as primary transfers, as are HTML text files. Secondary transfers consist exclusively

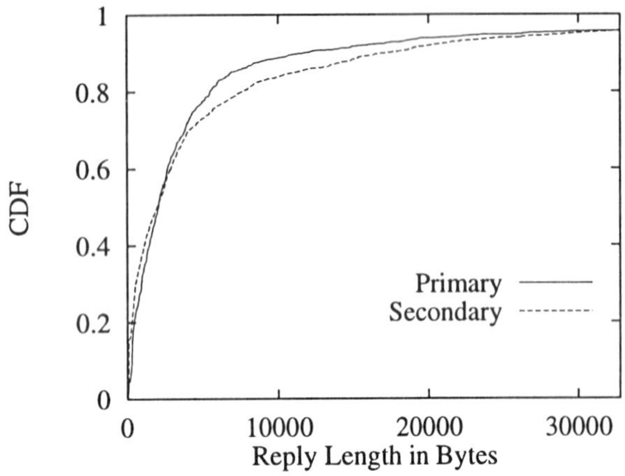


**FIGURE 6. Primary and Secondary Reply Lengths, 19 September 1995.**

of inlined images (many of which are small bitmaps). Based on this analysis, we conclude that it is appropriate to model these two types of retrievals differently.

### 6.6 User think time

Given a selection of $T_{thresh}$, the empirical distribution of user think times between pages is the set of interconnection idle times $T, T > T_{thresh}$. The median think times were short, only about 15 seconds. The 20 November 1995 trace had a much longer *mean* think time than the others (1900 vs. about 1000 seconds). We note that this trace spanned the American Thanksgiving holiday in late November, which could explain the long idle times. The CDFs for user think times are given by Figure 7.

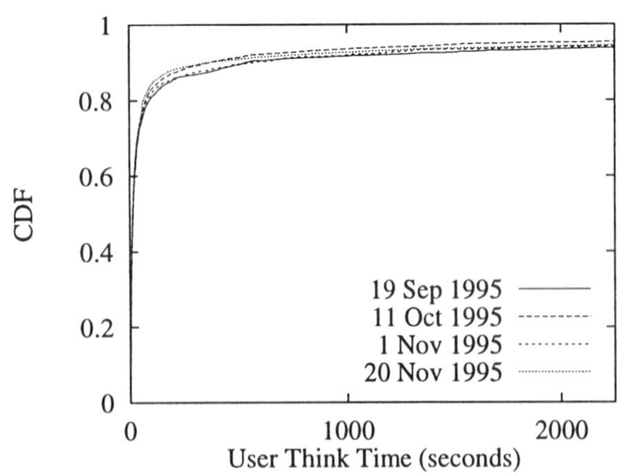


**FIGURE 7. Cumulative Distribution Functions of User Think Times.**

### 6.7 Consecutive document retrievals

The design of many Web sites is such that users will frequently access documents from the same server in succession. This fact may be important, for example, in networks that rely on locality of references in allocating virtual circuits or other network resources [17]. In our traces, users downloaded about four pages per server on average, with a median visit of two documents. By contrast, [7] noted that users accessed an average of ten consecutive pages per server. We believe that the difference is attributable to the interaction between user browsing strategies and client caching in Web browsers. Users tend to use a browsing strategy that has been described as "spoke and hub", which involves frequent backtracking to already-visited pages. In browsers that implement client side caching, revisited pages will not generate any network traffic (and thus would not appear in a network trace), but they would be counted in a client-side trace. Thus, we would expect our consecutive document retrieval count to be somewhat lower than that for a client access trace by about half, as we observed.

In Figure 8, we show the CDF for the consecutive document retrievals distribution. As can be seen, users tend to switch between servers fairly frequently. However, we noted cases in which visits to a server lasted for tens of consecutive documents.

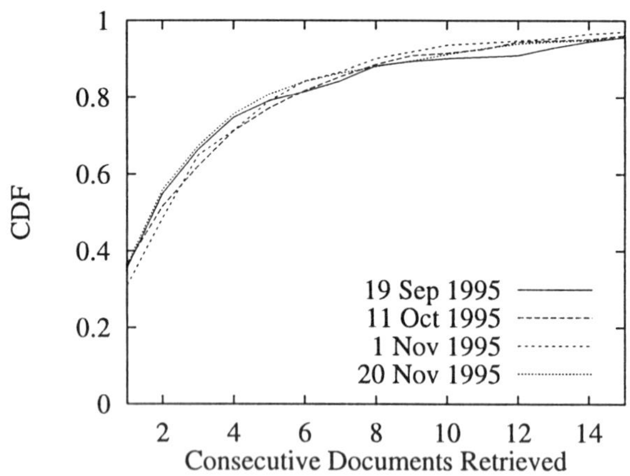


**FIGURE 8. Consecutive Document Retrievals.**

### 6.8 Server selection

The server selection distribution characterizes the relative frequency that each Web server was visited for some set of consecutive document retrievals. Using this metric, the most-visited server in this trace (indeed, for all four traces) was the local departmental Web server. It contains homepages for the vast majority of the users, as well as the initial document for many users. Four of the top ten servers, by this metric, were located on-site.

Given that so many of the servers accessed were local to the tracing site, we believe that we have insufficient information to properly characterize this aspect of our model. We have chosen instead to approximate the server selection distribution using a Zipf's Law distribution. Zipf's Law is a discrete, heavy-tailed distribution that states that the probability of selecting the $i$th most popular item in a set is proportional to $1/i$. Originally, it was used to describe the frequency of words in texts, as well as other human-related phenomena [29]. More recently, it has been applied to the access frequency of Web documents [2, 8]. It seems reasonable to apply Zipf's Law, or some other heavy-tailed distribution, to the access patterns of servers as well, but confirmation of this assertion requires a larger data sample than we had available.

In general, gauging the identity of Web servers from IP-layer packet traces is difficult. First, it is impossible to determine which of a machine's aliases were used to access it (given only its IP address). Second, if a hostname maps to multiple IP addresses (as is the case for the replicated Web server described in [15]), it may be difficult to associate these addresses with a single name.

## 7 Model representation

There were two possible representations for this traffic model. One approach was to fit the observed data to probability distributions that are easily described analytically. A simple analytic representation has the advantage of being compact and (perhaps) easy to manipulate. This approach was used in [25]; in fact, we performed some rudimentary curve-fitting in Sections 6.3 and 6.4. However, if a data set cannot be described by a well-known distribution (such as the bimodal request size distributions in Section 6.2), this technique cannot easily be used.

The alternative was to represent probability distributions by their CDFs, and to use the inverse transformation method (for example, as described in [14] and applied in [10]). While requiring more storage and perhaps being slower, this approach can represent arbitrary distributions.

Due to the flexibility of the latter method, we chose to maintain the CDF representation for all distributions except the Zipf's Law substitute for server selection, which is calculated analytically. We based our distributions on the traffic from the 19 September 1995 trace.

An earlier version of this model was incorporated into the INSANE network simulator, designed to help investigate the performance of IP-over-ATM designs [16]. It uses the distributions from this model to mimic the patterns of requests and replies sent by HTTP clients and servers.

We emphasize that for a meaningful Internet simulation, the actual request and reply data must be regulated by the TCP congestion control and flow control mechanisms, which are not included as a part of this model. It is not sufficient for network applications to simply transmit data into the network, as such an approach will not accurately model the timing and sizes of packets actually transmitted.

## 8 Conclusions

We have constructed an empirical model of network traffic produced by the Hypertext Transfer Protocol used by World Wide Web applications. This model consists of a number of probability distributions determined by analysis of actual HTTP conversations. From packet traces, we have built up higher-layer communication patterns, from individual HTTP retrievals to Web pages to groups of pages. This approach yields a sufficient level of detail to serve as a component of a workload generator for a packet-level simulation of an IP internetwork.

Our characterization of WWW-generated network traffic has shown that HTTP requests exhibit a bimodal distribution, and that (as revealed in prior studies) sizes of HTTP replies have a heavy-tailed distribution. We have shown that a simple heuristic can be used to separate HTTP transfers into Web pages, and that the differences between the first and subsequent transfers of a multi-file Web document are statistically significant. We have characterized some aspects of user Web page selection in terms of locality of consecutive documents referenced. Where possible, we have compared the results of our measurements and analysis to other Web measurement studies and found them consistent with those prior results.

## 9 Future work

We feel that the Zipf's Law substitute to the server selection distribution could be replaced with an empirical distribution, given an adequately-long trace of network data. It would also be desirable to investigate any correlations between the different components of our model (for example, between the popularity of a given server and the number of consecutive documents fetched from it). The constantly-changing nature of Web traffic calls for updates to this model to track trends over time. Persistent-connection HTTP will require new measurement and analysis methodologies.[7] Finally, the conversion of our empirical

7. We note that the advanced deployment of persistent-connection HTTP forces new analysis techniques even for late-1996 traffic. Examples can be found in recent versions of Netscape Navigator [20] and the Apache Web server [1].

distributions to closed-form analytic expressions would help make the models applicable to more environments.

## 10 Availability

A subset of the probability distributions gathered in this study, along with sample code, is available at:

`http://http.cs.berkeley.edu/~bmah/Software/HttpModel/`

## 11 Acknowledgments

The author gratefully acknowledges the comments of Kimberly Keeton and Venkata N. Padmanabhan, as well as the anonymous INFOCOM reviewers.

This work was funded by AT&T Bell Labs, the Corporation for National Research Initiatives, (DOE) DE-FG03-92ER-25135, Digital Equipment Corporation, Hitachi, the International Computer Science Institute, Mitsubishi Electric Research Laboratories, (NSF/ARPA) NCR-8919038, and Pacific Bell.

## 12 References

[1] The Apache Group. *Apache software*, 1996. This software is available at http://www.apache.org.

[2] Martin F. Arlitt and Carey L. Williamson. Web server workload characterization: The search for invariants. In *Proceedings of the ACM SIGMETRICS Conference on Measurement & Modeling of Computer Systems*, pages 126–137, Philadelphia, PA, May 1996.

[3] Tim Berners-Lee and Daniel W. Connolly. *Hypertext Markup Language – 2.0*. Internet Request for Comments 1886, November 1995.

[4] Tim Berners-Lee, Roy T. Fielding, and Henrik Frystyk Nielsen. *Hypertext Transfer Protocol – HTTP/1.0*. Internet Request for Comments 1945, May 1996.

[5] Tim Bray. Measuring the Web. In *Proceedings of the Fifth International World Wide Web Conference*, Paris, France, May 1996.

[6] Ramón Cáceres, Peter B. Danzig, Sugih Jamin, and Danny Mitzel. Characteristics of wide-area TCP/IP conversations. In *Proceedings of ACM SIGCOMM '91*, Zurich, Switzerland, September 1991.

[7] Lara D. Catledge and James E. Pitkow. Characterizing browsing strategies in the World-Wide Web. In *Proceedings of the Third International World Wide Web Conference*, Darmstadt, Germany, April 1995.

[8] Mark E. Crovella and Azer Bestavros. Self-similarity in World Wide Web traffic: Evidence and possible causes. In *Proceedings of the ACM SIGMETRICS Conference on Measurement & Modeling of Computer Systems*, pages 160–169, Philadelphia, PA, May 1996.

[9] Carlos R. Cunha, Azer Bestavros, and Mark E. Crovella. Characteristics of WWW client-based traces. Technical Report BU-CS-95-010, Computer Science Department, Boston University, July 1995.

[10] Peter B. Danzig and Sugih Jamin. tcplib: A library of TCP internetwork traffic characteristics. Technical Report USC-CS-91-495, Computer Science Department, University of Southern California, Los Angeles, CA, 1991.

[11] Rusty Eddy. HTTP analysis of IP level traces, February 1996. This document is available at http://catarina.usc.edu/eddy/http-traffic/http-traces.html.

[12] Roy T. Fielding, Jim Gettys, Jeffrey C. Mogul, Henrik Frystyk Nielsen, and Tim Berners-Lee. *Hypertext Transfer Protocol – HTTP/1.1*. Internet Draft draft-ietf-http-v1.1-spec-07, August 1996.

[13] Van Jacobson, Craig Leres, and Steven McCanne. *tcpdump software, Version 3.0.2*, 1995. This software is available at ftp://ftp.ee.lbl.gov/tcpdump.tar.Z.

[14] Raj Jain. *The Art of Computer Systems Performance Analysis*. John Wiley & Sons, Inc., New York, NY, 1991.

[15] Eric Dean Katz, Michelle Butler, and Robert McGrath. A scalable HTTP server: The NCSA prototype. In *Proceedings of the First International WWW Conference*, Geneva, Switzerland, May 1994.

[16] Bruce A. Mah. *INSANE Users Manual*. Computer Science Division, University of California at Berkeley, May 1996.

[17] Bruce A. Mah. *Quality of Service and Asynchronous Transfer Mode in IP Internetworks*. PhD dissertation, University of California at Berkeley, December 1996.

[18] Jeffrey C. Mogul. The case for persistent-connection HTTP. In *Proceedings of ACM SIGCOMM '95*, pages 299–313, Cambridge, MA, August 1995.

[19] National Center for Supercomputing Applications. *NCSA Mosaic software*, July 1995. This software is available at http://www.ncsa.uiuc.edu/SDG/Software/XMosaic/.

[20] Netscape Communications Corporation. *Netscape Navigator software*, 1996. This software is available at http://home.netscape.com/.

[21] Peter Newman, Tom Lyon, and Greg Minshall. Flow labelled IP: A connectionless approach to ATM. In *Proceedings of IEEE INFOCOM '96*, pages 1251–1260, San Francisco, CA, March 1996.

[22] NSFNET backbone traffic distribution by service, April 1995. This document is available at ftp://nic.merit.edu/nsfnet/statistics/1995/nsf-9504-ports.gz.

[23] Venkata N. Padmanabhan and Jeffrey C. Mogul. Improving HTTP latency. In *Proceedings of the Second International World Wide Web Conference*, Chicago, IL, October 1994.

[24] Vern Paxson. Measurements of wide area TCP conversations. Masters report, University of California at Berkeley, May 1991.

[25] Vern Paxson. Emprically derived analytic models of wide-area TCP connections. *IEEE/ACM Transactions on Networking*, 2(4):316–336, August 1994.

[26] Jon Postel. *Transmission Control Protocol*. Internet Request for Comments 793, September 1981.

[27] W. Richard Stevens. *TCP/IP Illustrated, Volume 3*. Addison-Wesley Publishing Company, Reading, MA, 1996.

[28] Allison Woodruff, Paul M. Aoki, Eric Brewer, Paul Gauthier, and Lawrence A. Rowe. An investigation of documents from the World Wide Web. In *Proceedings of the Fifth International World Wide Web Conference*, Paris, France, May 1996.

[29] George Kingsley Zipf. *Human Behavior and the Principle of Least Effort*. Hafner Publishing Company, New York, NY, 1949.

# Analyzing a Two-Stage Entry Monitor for High-Speed Networks

Gísli Hjálmtýsson*
Network Mathematics Research
AT&T Labs - Research
Murray Hill, New Jersey 07974

Alan G. Konheim†
Computer Science Department
University of California
Santa Barbara, California 93106

## Abstract

*Several researchers have suggested employing two-stage entry monitors for high-speed networks - the first stage enforcing a long term rate, the second stage enforcing a peak rate over a shorter time scale. In spite of this interest, little work on analyzing such systems has appeared. Not only is the analysis hard because of the the correlation between the stages, but for the most popular policing scheme, the leaky bucket, prior work is not easily generalized to two stages.*

*This paper presents a performance analysis of a two-stage entry monitor, by analyzing the combined queue length of a two-stage system. Our analysis is for a two-stage buffered moving window. Analyzing such a conservative scheme enables us to bound the penalty of more optimistic schemes, in particular a two stage leaky bucket based system. We obtain a closed form analytical result, and show how to evaluate it for a wide range of parameters of interest. Our results show that the performance penalty of having the second stage is minimal under reasonable rate assumptions.*

**Keywords:** Input Rate Control, Queuing Theory, ATM, Policing, Traffic Shaping, Integrated Services

## 1 Introduction

In high speed integrated services networks offering *quality of service* (QOS) guarantees, a connection is a contract between the user and the network. In addition to specifying quality of service parameters - e.g. delay and jitter bounds - a connection request specifies rate requirements, typically including peak rate, peak duration and sustainable rate. Connection admission control is responsible for establishing whether the requested connection can be accepted, based on the traffic description and the QOS requested by the user. *Input rate control* (IRC) enforces the users compliance with the contract by policing the actual rate at which the user delivers cells to the network.[1]

In the debate on flow control in ATM networks, several policing schemes have been proposed, the most celebrated being Turner's leaky bucket [3, 4, 5, 6, 7] and variations thereof. Others include the *credit manager* [11, 12], the *jumping window* [6], the *triggered jumping window* [6], the *moving window* [6], the *sticky buffer* [7], and the *exponentially weighted average* [6]. In addition *spacers* [13, 14, 15] have been proposed and studied as input rate schemes [14, 15].

In spite of the considerable body of work on IRC and traffic shaping, none of the proposed schemes attempt to monitor multiple parameters. It is suggested in several papers [2, 4, 8, 16, 20] that the policer might be complemented by a spacer for enhanced traffic shaping at the *User-Network Interface* (UNI), but only [8] presents a queuing analysis of such a system. There are several reasons for multiple parameter policing, the most obvious to enforce a peak rate as well as a sustainable rate. Even if the traffic contract only calls for single rate policing, statistical multiplexing performance may be improved by shaping at the UNI based on feedback from the network. However, strictly spacing out cells limits the granularity of bandwidth assignments, and may be too conservative.

Whereas the ITU [1] and the ATM Forum [2] have adopted the leaky bucket as a standard for determining connection compliance to a traffic contract the same documents specify that if two rates are negotiated then both must be policed. Still, to our knowledge, there has been no mathematical analysis of a two stage leaky bucket based scheme. Existing analysis for the leaky bucket is largely based on a token deficit model [4, 5, 7, 10]. While elegant and significantly reducing the complexity of the analysis for a

*This research was supported by NSF Grant NCR-9103998, by Minningarsjódur Helgu Jónsdóttur og Sigurlida Kristinssonar, and by Vísindarád through a Nato Fellowship. The bulk of this work was conducted as part of Ph.D. research at University of California, Santa Barbara.

†This research was supported by NSF Grant NCR-9103998.

[1] Although the results in this paper may have wider applicability than only ATM/B-ISDN, we assume a deterministic unit service time per packet, and thus adhere to ATM terminology using the term cell for a fixed length packet.

single stage leaky bucket system, it does not generalize to two stages. The token deficit state reduction factors out the very information of importance to the two stage analysis, namely the behavior of the token-pool.

In this paper, we provide a discrete-time queuing analysis of a two-stage entry monitor. Each stage is a buffered moving window input rate enforcer. We do a discrete-time analysis, since continuous or fluid flow models abstract out the combinatorial interplay of the two stages and thus do not provide insight into buffering and delay caused by the second stage. Indeed, contrary to the system herein, a tandem fluid system is only of interest if the downstream servers are progressively slower [18]. While our analytical results constitute a significant contribution, for practical purposes it is of equal importance that we are able to evaluate our formulas for wide range of parameters. Therefore, the fact that our analytical approach leads to a numerically tractable solution is of substantial importance. In addition the numerical techniques are a contribution by themselves.

There are two parts to solving the two stage system; deriving an analytical expression that is useful for evaluation, and overcoming numerical difficulties in evaluating the analytical expressions. While analytical results have appeared for various single stage input rate controllers, and hold for rather general Markovian sources, the difficulty of evaluating the analytical results typically reduces numerical examples to some trivial special cases, and/or very small parameter values. In particular, whereas multi-phase arrival sources lead to comparable analytical results, evaluating those results is rather tricky. (Indeed, numerical examples for such models are almost universally given solely for two stages, most typically for the special case of an on/off source.) For this reason we choose to model arrivals as independent identically distributed (iid) random variables. Whereas perhaps a less "realistic" arrival model, the processes we choose encompass enough parameters to model sources of various burstiness (see [7]). Our reward is an analytical result, which we are able solve numerically for a wide range of parameters for the input monitor, as well as for a wide range of source characteristics.

The two-stage system analyzed in this paper consists of a tandem connection of buffered moving window policers, where the rate of the second stage *exceeds* that of the former. Since the moving window is the most conservative of the above mentioned schemes [6, 7] its performance at the UNI bounds that of two stage systems based on more optimistic mechanisms[7]. This work builds on [7] and [8], the former analyzing a buffered moving window - the sticky buffer - and comparing it to the leaky bucket, the latter reporting preliminary results for a buffered moving window policer in tandem with a spacer. Here, we emphasize the results and their implications, and omit most proofs. Additional details can be found in [9].

While there are several ways to assess the performance cost of second rate enforcement, we achieve it by comparing the (overall) performance of the two-stage system to that of a single stage. We therefore start from the relations for the random variables for the queue length of the first stage, and for the *combined* queue length of the first and the second stage, both conditioned on the two-stage history. From this we obtain a two dimensional generating function in the respective probabilities. However, since from [7] we know the single stage result, we only seek to solve for the combined variable, and thus are able to eliminate the first variable, reducing the problem to a one dimensional analysis. Although still complex, this reduction is key to the analytical solution. Once the analytical part is solved, we give an algorithm to evaluate our results. Although elementary, each step of the algorithm requires some ingenuity for numerical stability.

The paper is organized as follows: Section 2 formulates the problem and gives our first result, a rate condition on the second stage with respect to the rate of the first, ensuring that the intermediate queue is bounded. We then give the backward equations for the discrete-time queuing analysis of the two-stage entry monitor. Section 3 contains analytical results; we give a closed-form formula for the probability generating function (pgf) of the combined queue length distribution. In Section 4 we show a pgf for the leaky bucket system, use it to compare to that of the buffered moving window and argue how our results carry over to more optimistic systems. Section 5 explains a numerical algorithm to evaluate the formulas of Section 4. In Section 6, we then give numerical examples to illustrate and quantify the performance penalty caused by the second stage, showing that it is indeed small. The paper ends with conclusions in Section 7.

## 2 Formulation

The entry monitor is modeled as a discrete-time queuing system. Transmission is over a slotted and synchronous system; the slot length $\Delta$ is sufficient to transmit a single cell. We adhere to the ITU-T convention that slot arrivals occur at the end of a slot, whereas transmission begins just after the start of a slot. This implies that before a cell can enter the network it *must first be buffered.*

The arrival of cells is modeled by a sequence of independent and identically distributed (iid) random variables $\{ X(n) : n \geq 1 \}$; $X(n)$ is the number of cells entering in the $n^{th}$-slot $\Delta(n)$. We use the notation

$$P(z) = \sum_{k=0}^{\infty} p_k z^k, \quad p_k = Pr\{X(n) = k\}$$

$$\mu = E\{X(n)\} \qquad \sigma^2 = Var\{X(n)\}$$

for the probability generating function, mean and variance of $X(n)$.

### 2.1 Specification of a Buffered Moving Window

The output process of the (single stage) buffered moving window is determined by two negotiated parameters $(R, T)$; in every window of size $T$, no more than $R$ cells are permitted to enter the network. The window moves (slides) in time with each slot so that it always covers the $T$ most recent slots. Cells are buffered to prevent the output rate from exceeding $R/T$. The buffered moving window strictly ensures that the rate at which cells enter the network (as measured over any window of size $T, 2T, \cdots$) never exceeds the allocated rate. Furthermore the maximum burst length permitted to enter the network is at most $R$.

### 2.2 The $(\mathbf{R},\mathbf{T})/(\mathbf{R_2},\mathbf{T_2})$ Entry Monitor

We form a two-stage entry monitor by connecting a pair of buffered-moving-windows in tandem. The parameters of the stages are denoted by $(R, T)$ and an $(R_2, T_2)$ respectively.

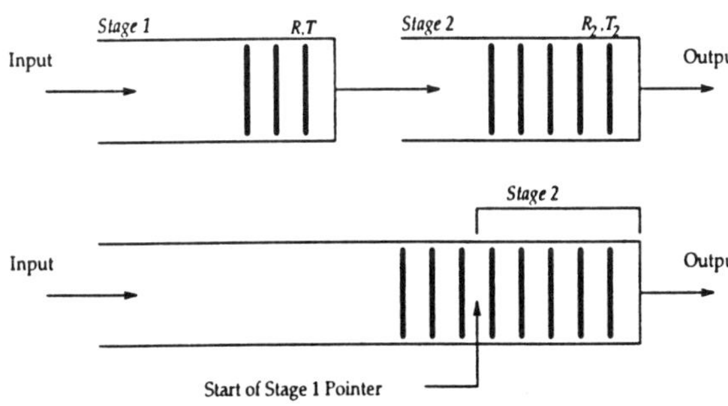


Figure 1: A Single Shared Queue for Both Stages

We assume $\mu < R/T < R_2/T_2$; namely *(i)* the average number of cells entering the buffer in a window of size $T$ is smaller than the maximum number $R$ that can leave the buffer; *(ii)* that the rate of the second stage exceeds the rate of the first. The first condition is necessary for the stochastic process of the system to have a non-degenerate equilibrium distribution. Since we desire the second stage to monitor rate on smaller time scale, we take $T > T_2$, and $R > R_2$.

A Markovian state description of the entry monitor is determined by the queue lengths at each stage, plus the output *history* of each stage over their respective window sizes. The state is denoted by $\left(\vec{L}(n), \vec{W}(n)\right)$ where

- $L_i(n)$ is the number of cells buffered at stage $i$ at start of the $n^{th}$-slot.
- $\vec{L}(n) = (L_1(n), L_2(n))$.
- $W_i(n) = 1$ if a cell is output from stage $i$ in the $n^{th}$-slot, and 0 otherwise.
- $\vec{W}_i(n) = (W_i(n-1), W_i(n-2), \ldots, W_i(n-T_i))$.
- $\vec{W}(n) = (\vec{W}_1(n), \vec{W}_2(n))$.

The state process evolves according to the rules:

1. A cell is output from *stage 1* of the entry monitor in $\Delta(n)$ if at the start of this slot *(i)* there is at least one cell buffered, and *(ii)* fewer than $R$ cells have been output from *stage 1* in the last $T-1$ slots. Formally

$$\begin{aligned} W_1(n) &= 1 \text{ iff } L_1(n) > 0 \text{ and } \\ &\quad \textstyle\sum_{j=n-(T-1)}^{n-1} W_1(j) < R \\ L_1(n+1) &= L_1(n) - W_1(n) + X(n) \end{aligned}$$

2. A cell is output from *stage 2* of the entry monitor in $\Delta(n)$ if at the start of this slot *(i)* there is at least one cell, either buffered in the second buffer or being output from the first stage, and *(ii)* fewer than $R_2$ cells have been output from *stage 2* in the last window of $T_2 - 1$ slots. Formally

$$\begin{aligned} W_2(n) &= 1 \text{ iff } W_1(n) + L_2(n) > 0 \text{ and } \\ &\quad \textstyle\sum_{j=n-(T_2-1)}^{n-1} W_2(j) < R_2 \\ L_2(n+1) &= L_2(n) - W_2(n) + W_1(n) \end{aligned}$$

Observe that a cell may pass through both stages in one time unit provided neither rate constraint is violated.

Unless the rate of the second stage "sufficiently" exceeds the rate of the first stage, the second stage queue may build up arbitrarily. Suitable rate restrictions exist so that the second stage queue flushes out in *every cycle* of the first stage - i.e. a busy period of the second stage never exceeds $T-1$ cells. These conditions are contained in (for proof see [9])

**Proposition 1** *If for some integer $q$, the parameters of the entry monitor $(R,T)/(R_2,T_2)$ satisfy*

$$(q-1)R_2 < R \leq qR_2 \qquad qT_2 \leq T \tag{1}$$

*then the stage 1 history $\vec{W}_1(n)$ determines the stage 2 history $\vec{W}_2(n)$ and queue length $L_2(n)$. Moreover, $\vec{W}_2(n)$ and $L_2(n)$ are the same as would evolve with the initial state $\vec{W}_i(0)=\vec{0}, L_i=0$.*

Condition (1) guarantees that the first stage history *uniquely determines* the second stage. The reduction in complexity is dramatic; instead of the state space growing exponentially in both $T$ and $T_2$, Proposition 1 dictates that it "only" grows exponentially in $T$. Moreover, condition (1) is reasonable given the purpose of the second stage and is not limiting in practice. In particular, if the second stage is a spacer (i.e., $R_2=1$), condition (1) simply restates the requirement that the rate of the second stage exceeds that of the first. We henceforth assume condition (1) to hold.

## 2.3 The Backward Equation

We define the equilibrium state probabilities by

$$\begin{aligned}\pi_{\vec{\omega}}(j,k) &= \lim_{n\to\infty} Pr\{L_1(n)=j, L_1(n)+L_2(n)=k,\\ &\quad \vec{\omega}_i(n)=\vec{\omega}_i \ \ (i=1,2)\}.\end{aligned}$$

Let the generating function (gf) with respect to the two variables $j$ and $k$ be

$$G_{\vec{\omega}}(z_1,z_2)=\sum_{j=0}^{\infty}\sum_{k=0}^{\infty}\pi_{\vec{\omega}}(j,k)z_1^j z_2^k$$

Since we are only seeking the combined queue length distribution, we define

$$H_{\vec{\omega}}(z)\equiv G_{\vec{\omega}}(1,z).$$

Write $\vec{\omega}=(i,j:\vec{\tau})$ and $\vec{\sigma}=(\vec{\tau}:i,j)$ for the histories that 'begin'[2] and 'end' with $i$ and $j$. Using Proposition 1, and observing that $H_{\vec{\omega}}(z)$ satisfies the backward equations of $G_{\vec{\omega}}(z_1,z_2)$, we obtain the backward equations for $H_{\vec{\omega}}(z)$

$$\begin{aligned}z^i H_{(0,i:\vec{\tau})}(z)+z^j H_{(1,j:\vec{\tau})}(z) &\\ = P(z)\left[H_{(\vec{\tau}:0,k)}(z)+H_{(\vec{\tau}:1,\ell)}(z)\right] & \quad (2)\\ z^i H_{(0,i:\vec{\tau})}(z) = P(z)\ H_{(\vec{\tau}:0,k)}(z) & \quad (3)\end{aligned}$$

where the Equation (2) applies when $\vec{\tau}_1$ contains fewer than $R$ ones, and (3) applies when $\vec{\tau}_1$ contains exactly $R$ ones. Observe that $k$ and $\ell$ are uniquely determined by $i$ and $j$.

The backward equations are deceiving in this compact form, partly because the powers of the $z$ terms, $i$ and $j$, hide different variations of each equation. Because of that, standard queuing theory techniques fail to solve this system. Specifically, this system does not yield a product form solution, and we are not able to solve for $H_{\vec{\omega}}(z)$. However, using a graph theoretic analysis of the state transition graph, we are able to exploit product forms over selected paths in the graph, to give a relatively simple expression for the *sum* of the generating functions of the combined queue length distribution *over all histories* $H(z)\equiv\sum_{\vec{\omega}}H_{\vec{\omega}}(z)$.

# 3 Analytical Results

**Theorem 1** *For some $R$ uniquely determined constants $\{\alpha_i\}$,*

$$H(z)=P(z)(z-1)\frac{\sum_{i=0}^{R-1}\alpha_i z^{R-i}P^{\phi(i)}(z)}{z^R-P^T(z)} \tag{4}$$

*where $\phi(i)=\lfloor i/R_2\rfloor T_2+i \bmod R_2$.*

Two special cases of this formula are important enough to state separately; *(i)* the second stage is a spacer, i.e. when $R_2=1$; *(ii)* the second stage does not interfere with the traffic.

**Corollary 1 (A Buffered Moving Window in tandem with a Spacer)** *If $R_2=1$, then (4) holds with $\phi(i)=iT_2$.*

**Corollary 2 (A Buffered Moving Window)** *If $R_2=T_2=1$, then (4) holds with $\phi(i)=i$.*

Interestingly, the denominator of $H(z)$ does not depend on the second stage parameters. This is a rather strong statement, since the decay of the queue length tail probabilities is determined by the smallest real root outside the unit circle of the denominator $z^R-P^T(z)$ in (4). The theorem and the corollaries

---

[2] If

$$\vec{\tau}=(\vec{\tau}_1,\vec{\tau}_2) = \begin{pmatrix}\tau_1(1)\cdots\tau_1(T_2)\cdots\tau_1(T-1)\\ \tau_2(1)\cdots\tau_2(T_2)\end{pmatrix}$$

$$\text{then}\quad (i,j:\vec{\tau}) = \begin{pmatrix}i & \tau_1(1)\cdots\tau_1(T_2)\cdots\tau_1(T-1)\\ j & \tau_2(1)\cdots\tau_2(T_2)\end{pmatrix}$$

is a history which begins with $\begin{pmatrix}i\\ j\end{pmatrix}$; similarly for $(\vec{\tau}:i,j)$, a history which ends with $\begin{pmatrix}i\\ j\end{pmatrix}$.

therefore show that this decay rate is independent of the second stage. For network engineering this implies that buffer requirements tend to be insensitive to second rate policing.

Differentiating the formula for $H(z)$ and evaluating at $z = 1$, we obtain the expected queue length

$$
\begin{aligned}
E\{L\} &= \mu + [1 - (R + \mu T)] + \frac{T\sigma^2}{R - \mu T} \\
&\quad + \frac{\sum_{i=0}^{R-1} \alpha_i (R - i + \mu\phi(i))}{R - \mu T} \qquad (5)
\end{aligned}
$$

## 4 Comparison to the Leaky Bucket

To compare the two-stage entry monitor to a leaky bucket based system we build on the approach by M. Sidi *et al* [4] and used in [4, 5, 10] encoding the state of the leaky bucket at token regeneration intervals by the *token deficit*,[3] the number of regeneration intervals needed to bring the token pool to its limit.[4] Let $\psi_i(0)$ be the probability that the token deficit equals $i$ at token regeneration and let $a_j$ denote the probability that $j$ cells arrive occur during a regeneration interval of length $D$. Then the backward equations for the $\{\psi_i(0)\}$ and its generating function $\Psi_0(z)$ are

$$
\begin{aligned}
\psi_i(0) &= \psi_0(0)a_0 + \sum_{j=0}^{i} \psi_{j+1}(0)a_{i-j} \qquad i \geq 0 \\
\Psi_0(z) &= (1 - \mu D)\frac{(z-1)P^D(z)}{z - P^D(z)}
\end{aligned}
$$

To extend these formulas to an arbitrary slot, observe that within a regeneration interval the token deficit will only increase, as determined by the arrival process. Thus $j < D$ slots after token regeneration,

$$\Psi_j(z) = P^j(z)\Psi_0(z)$$

Averaging over the $D$ slots of the regeneration interval we obtain

$$\Psi(z) = \frac{1}{D}\sum_{j=0}^{D-1} \Psi_j(z) = \frac{1 - P^D(z)}{D(1 - P(z))}\Psi_0(z) \qquad (6)$$

[3] A Markovian state description of the leaky bucket at token regeneration intervals is specified by $(m, L)$ where $m$ is the number of tokens in the pool and $L$, the number of cells in queue. The analyses given in [4, 5, 10] assume that cells are queued in the buffer only if the token pool is empty. This allows the state $(m, L)$ to have a more compact description, namely, the *token deficit* $F = M - m + L$, where $M$ is the size of the token pool.

[4] The token deficit is an equivalent description of the state only if *(i)* zero or one cell arrives in a slot or, if this is not the case *(ii)* multiple departures in a slot are allowed.

Differentiating (6) and evaluating at $z = 1$ gives the expected token deficit

$$
\begin{aligned}
\left.\frac{d}{dz}\Psi(z)\right|_{z=1} &= \Psi_0'(1) + \frac{1}{2}\mu(D-1) \\
&= D\mu - \frac{1}{2}\mu + \frac{D\sigma^2}{2(1 - D\mu)} \qquad (7)
\end{aligned}
$$

We use these to compare the leaky bucket with the buffered moving window. For comparison we choose the parameters $(R, T)$ and $D$ so that $R/T = 1/D$ in order for the long-term policed rates of the leaky bucket and the buffered moving window to be the same. Using the fact that the cell loss probability is primarily determined by the root $\zeta_{LB} > 1$ of $z - P^D(z)$ closest to the unit circle, we find that with these parameters $\zeta_{BMW} = \zeta_{LB}$, implying that the cell loss probabilities are asymptotically identical. Since the dominating root for the buffered moving window, $\zeta_{BMW}$, is independent of the second stage parameters, the same equality holds for the two stage buffered moving window versus the leaky bucket. Therefore, the performance curves of a two stage buffered moving window (in particular a buffered moving window followed by a spacer) will dominate a two stage leaky bucket system in buffer requirements at the UNI. The same holds true for other two stage systems based on more optimistic disciplines than the buffered moving window.

## 5 Algorithm to Numerically Solve for the Terms of $H(z)$

To obtain engineering values, we need to evaluate the terms of $H(z)$. Since $H(z)$ is analytic in the unit disk and $H(1) = 1$, the $\alpha$'s in (4) are uniquely determined so as to ensure that the roots of the numerator cancel the roots of the denominator. This however, causes difficulties in the numerical inversion. To obtain the terms we use the following algorithm

1. Find the roots of $z^R - P^T(z)$, using standard numerical techniques.
2. Determine the $\alpha$'s
3. Numerically invert by:
   - *i)* Expanding the numerator of (4) as a power series
   - *ii)* Expanding the power series of $z^R - P^T(z)$, the denominator of (4)
   - *iii)* Computing the series for $H(z)$ as their ratio.

### 5.1 How the $\alpha$'s are Determined

Using Rouché's Theorem we conclude that, $z^R - \zeta P^T(z)$ has $R$ zeros $\{\vartheta_j(\zeta)\}$ in the (closed) unit disk in the $z$-plane for every $\zeta$ of modulus at most 1 when $\mu T < R$. An argument in [19] can be modified to prove $\vartheta_j = lim_{\zeta \to 1} \vartheta_j(\zeta)$ exist and the limiting values are distinct. Unless $P(z)$ is a function of $z^R$, all but one of the limiting roots lie within the unit $z$-disk. Since $H(z)$ is analytic in the unit disk, the zeros $\{\vartheta_j\}$ in the denominator of equation (4) must be canceled by corresponding zeros in the numerator. This with the normalization condition $H(1) = 1$ gives $R$ conditions

$$R - \mu T = \sum_{i=0}^{R-1} \alpha_i, \qquad 0 = \sum_{i=0}^{R-1} \alpha_i \vartheta_j^{R-i-1} P^i(\vartheta_j), \quad (8)$$

$1 \leq j < R$, which uniquely determine the $\{\alpha_i\}$. In the two special cases when $\phi(i) = Ki$, the summation in the numerator of (4) can be written as a polynomial in $w = P^{\phi(i)}(z)/z$, transforming the linear system into an interpolation problem. However, for the general case the linear system system determined by (8) must be solved.

### 5.2 The Numerical Inversion

Even after determining the $R$ roots, and the $\alpha$-coefficients, the computation of the queue length distribution still requires some care. The defining relation

$$H(z) = (z-1)\frac{\sum_{i=0}^{R-1} \alpha_i z^{R-i} P^{\phi(i)}(z)}{z^R - P^T(z)} = \sum_{i=0}^{\infty} h_i z^i$$

may be written as

$$\left\{\sum_{i=0}^{\infty} h_i z^i\right\}[z^R - P^T(z)] = (z-1)\sum_{i=0}^{R-1} \alpha_i z^{R-i} P^{\phi(i)}(z) \quad (9)$$

Given the coefficients for $[z^R - P^T(z)]$ and $(z-1)\sum_{i=0}^{R-1} \alpha_i z^{R-i} P^{\phi(i)}(z)$ the $\{h_i\}$ are obtained recursively by matching coefficients.

Unfortunately, we cannot use equation (9) in this manner directly as the roots $\{\vartheta_j\}$ of the denominator of $H(z)$ have been computed with error. Therefore, while both the numerator and the denominator are "small" at the numerical roots they are not equal. Numerically, the numerator has a zero at $\tilde{\vartheta}_j = \vartheta_j + \epsilon_j$ while the denominator has a (numerical) zero at $\hat{\vartheta}_j = \tilde{\vartheta}_j + \delta_j$. Because of that

$$\frac{z - \hat{\vartheta}_j}{z - \tilde{\vartheta}_j} = \frac{z - \tilde{\vartheta}_j - \delta_j}{z - \tilde{\vartheta}_j} = 1 + \frac{\delta_j}{\tilde{\vartheta}_j}\sum_{i=0}^{\infty} z^i \tilde{\vartheta}_j^{-i}.$$

Since $|\tilde{\vartheta}_j| < 1$, this series *diverges* for $z$ close to 1.

Therefore, since the roots of the numerator do not *exactly* cancel the zeros in the denominator, the terms $h(n)$ are determined with an error that grows exponentially with $n$. The problem is not merely of technical interest; to determine the buffer size for a loss probability of $10^{-9}$, it is necessary to find $h(n)$ for $n \approx 500$ so that even what otherwise would be regarded as harmless error in the value of $\vartheta_j$ may cause havoc in the recursion.

For the arrival processes that we use for our examples, some effort allows us to *factor* the $z - \vartheta_j$ from both sides of equation (9) *without* knowing the *exact* value of $\vartheta_j$. For the special cases when $\phi(i) = Ki$, we can *formally factor* both sides, whereas for the most general case we factor the numerator numerically. The reward for our efforts is that after the factorizations, the queue length probabilities $\{h(n)\}$ may be computed without numerical difficulties. The details are described in [9].

## 6 Numerical results

Numerical results are derived modeling the arrival of cells by a discrete time compound Poisson process, given by $P(z) = e^{\lambda(Q(z)-1)}$, in which multiple cells are permitted to arrive at the same 'time'[5]. The compounded process, describing the "magnitude" of arrival, is described by a pgf $Q(z)$ which in our examples takes the form $Q(z) = qz + (1-q)z^M$. By varying $M$ we vary the burstiness of the source. For more discussion on this arrival process see [7]. The probability generating functions, means and variances for the compound Poisson process are summarized in the Table 1.

| | |
|---|---|
| **PGF** | $P(z) = e^{\lambda(Q(z)-1)}$<br>$Q(z) = \sum_{k=1}^{K} q_k z^k$ |
| **Mean** $\mu$ | $\lambda Q'(1)$ |
| **Variance** $\sigma^2$ | $\lambda[Q''(1) + Q'(1)]$ |
| **CV²** | $\frac{1}{\lambda Q'(1)} \left[1 + \frac{Q''(1)}{Q'(1)}\right]$ |

Table 1: Parameters of the Compound Poisson Process

[5] Multiple cells may arrive when traffic is described by a compound Poisson process. This is also the case in multi-phase models, e.g. [4, 5], where the arrivals in *state k* are according to a general renewal process. We interpret simultaneous arrivals as occurring in consecutive slots.

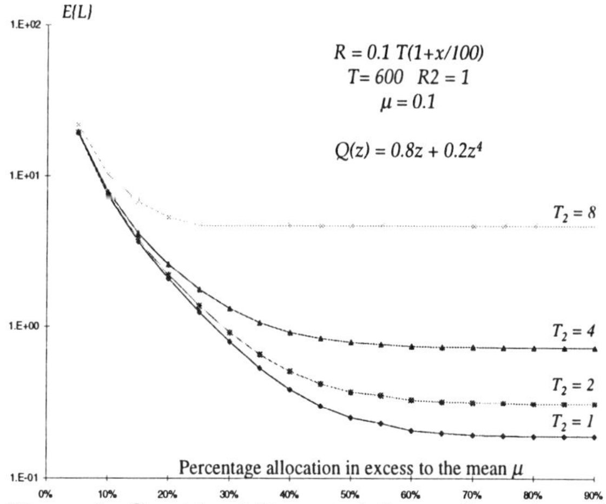


Figure 2: Combined Expected Queue Length vs. Excess Allocation

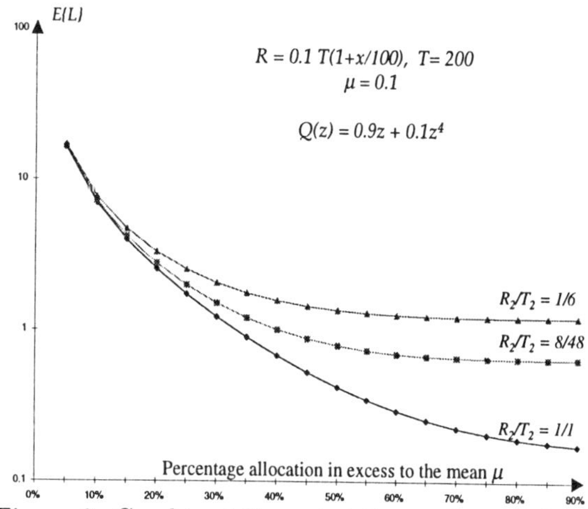


Figure 3: Combined Expected Queue Length for Second Stage Scaling

## 6.1 Expected Queue Length

Figure 2 compares the expected queue length $E\{L\}$ as the allocated rate (of the first stage) is increased; we use a Compound Poisson arrival process with bursty traffic, mean rate $\mu = 0.1$, $Q(z) = 0.8z + 0.2z^4$ ($CV^2 = 25$). The window size of the first stage is $T = 600$. The horizontal scale is the percentage of *excess allocation*, allocation in excess of the mean $\mu$, and varies from 10% to 90%. As can be seen from Figure 2, the expected queue length decreases rapidly as allocation is increased. In spite of a very bursty source, even with only 10% allocation over the mean, less than 10 cells are being buffered.

For allocation close to the mean, all four curves agree. Except for the top curve,[6] the agreement is good at least up to about 30%. We conclude that in this range, $\leq 30\%$, the expected queue length of the monitor is insensitive to the second stage.

As the first stage allocation increases, however, the second stage increasingly restricts the departure of cells; the combined expected queue length decreases to that of the second stage itself. For $R/T \geq R_2/T_2$, the expected queue length is constant. For example, when $T_2 = 8, R_2 = 1$ (Figure 2, the top curve) and allocation is 25% in excess of $\mu$, the rate limitation of the first stage is equal to that of the second $R/T = R_2/T_2$. The two components of the monitor limit the flow to the same long term rate, although the second stage restricts the departure of cells more than the first. The expected queue length is that of the second stage alone.

A similar effect is seen in Figure 3, which shows the effect of scaling the second stage parameters. The rate of the first stage is kept at $R/T = 22/200$ or 11%, whereas the second stage rate is $R_2/T_2 = 1/6 = 8/48$ or 16.7%. For reference we show the curve corresponding to no second stage shaping ($R_2 = T_2 = 1$). Although the second stage slows the drop in $E\{L\}$, the larger window (middle curve - $R/T = 8/48$) is less restrictive than strictly spacing out cells at the same rate $R_2/T_2 = 1/6$ (top curve). The asymptotic value is that of the second stage alone. For small excess allocation (say $\leq 30\%$) the penalty in expected queue length is still negligible.

[6]The spacer rate of the top curve corresponds to a rate 1/8 which is very restrictive.

## 6.2 The Queue Length Distribution

To assess the penalty in throughput, or equivalently, the buffer requirements to obtain a prescribed cell loss ratio, we investigate the tail of the queue length distribution. We consider the changes in these tail probabilities in three scenarios: *(i)* when the second stage peak rate control is enhanced (becomes more stringent), *(ii)* when the second stage parameter values are changed while the peak rate is fixed (scaling), and *(iii)* when the burstiness of the source is changed. Figure 4 shows the effect of varying the peak rates enforced by the second stage on the tail of the queue length distribution $Pr\{L \geq n\}$. In the figure $R_2 = 1$, whereas $T_2$ takes values in $\{1, 2, 4, 8\}$. Apart from the curve corresponding to $T_2 = 8$ (top curve), the tails agree to the level of being almost indistinguishable. However, a careful look revels that as peak rate control becomes stricter, the tail shifts up, implying increased buffer occupancy, increased delay and increased buffer requirements to achieve a prescribed cell-loss ratio. This penalty is, however, small; indeed so small that even very strict smoothing $T_2 = 8$ requires no more than 3 buffers to achieve the same

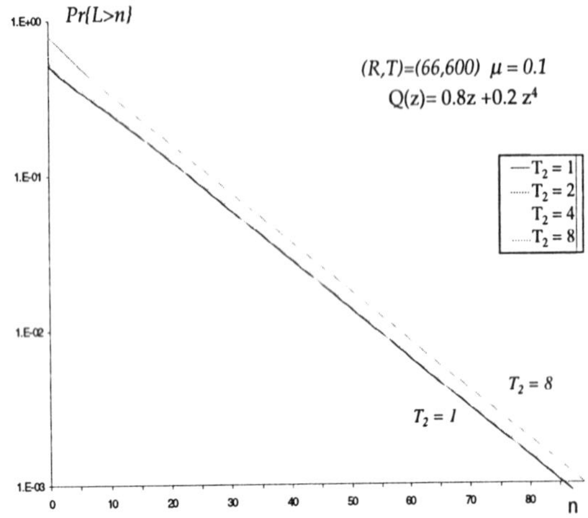


Figure 4: Effect of Stricter Peak Rate Control on the Tail of the Queue Length Distribution

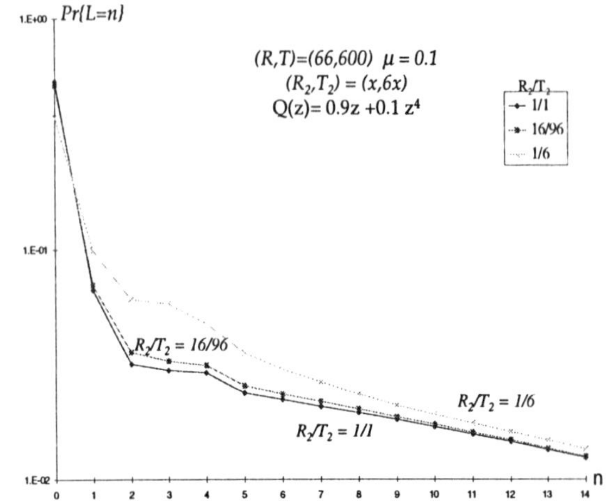


Figure 6: Effects of Second Stage Window Size on the Buffer Probabilities

throughput as without second stage shaping. We conclude that the second stage peak rate shaping is obtained with practically no penalty in buffer requirements.

Effects of changing the second stage parameters for a fixed peak rate is demonstrated in Figures 5 and 6. Three tails appear, one without the second stage interfering ($R_2 = T_2 = 1$), the other two enforcing peak rate using $T_2 = 6R_2$, $R_2 \in \{1, 16\}$. In Figure 5

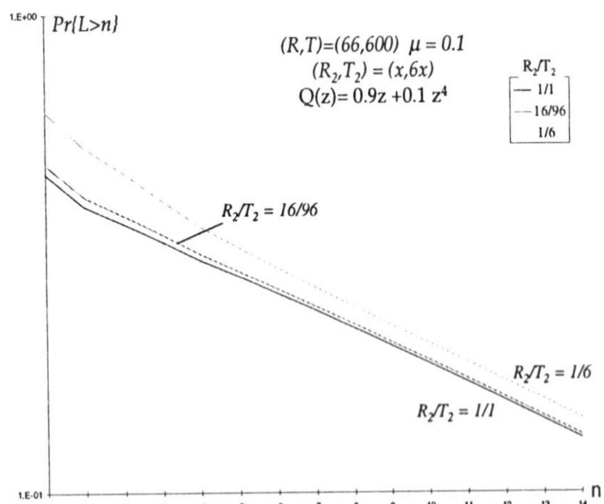


Figure 5: Effects of Scaling on Asymptotic Tail Probabilities

we see that the smaller the window (smaller $T_2$), the more the tail shifts up. Since a smaller window means stricter peak rate control, this is consistent with Figure 4. As before the shift represents a performance penalty in terms of higher buffer requirements, queuing probabilities and delay. To articulate the increased buffer occupancy as a result of stricter peak rate control, Figure 6 shows the first terms of $H(z)$. From it we see that the probabilities of queuing and therefore delay increase as control is enhanced. We conclude that while buffer requirements are insensitive to the second stage parameters, some additional queuing delay is incurred. Again, however, this penalty appears small.

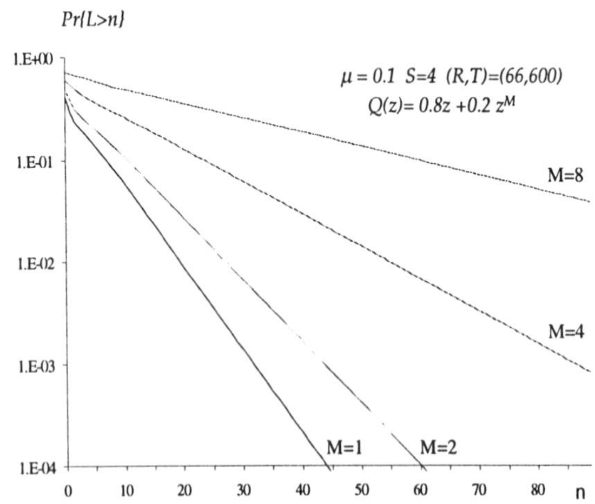


Figure 7: Effect of Burstiness on the Tail of the Queue Length Distribution

Figure 7 illustrates the effect of bursty traffic on the performance of the monitor, using as input the compound Poisson process with generating function

|  | $Q(z) = .8z + .2z^M$ | | | |
|---|---|---|---|---|
| $M$ | 1 | 2 | 4 | 8 |
| $Var\{X\}$ | 0.1 | 0.133 | 0.25 | 0.567 |
| $CV^2$ | 10.0 | 13.333 | 25.0 | 56.667 |
| $Pr\{L = 0\}$ | 0.589 | 0.519 | 0.405 | 0.292 |
| $E\{L\}$ | 2.107 | 3.260 | 7.785 | 21.450 |
| $Var\{L\}$ | 18.493 | 36.661 | 152.335 | 862.514 |
| $N(10^{-9})$ | 106.0 | 127 | 275 | 633 |
| $\vartheta^*$ | 1.206 | 1.150 | 1.076 | 1.033 |

Table 2: Performance Values For Varying Burstiness

$P(z) = e^{\lambda(Q(z)-1)}, Q(z) = 0.9z + 0.1z^M$. Burstiness is varied by letting $M$ range from 1 (simple Poisson process) through 2,4, and 8. By increasing $M$ the burstiness of the source is increased, flattening the tail of the queue length distribution. Except for the values of $Pr\{L \geq n\}$ with $n$ near 0, the curves with different $M$-values are linear on a logarithm scale with slopes determined by $M$.

However, since by equation (4) the second stage parameters do not affect the "dominant root" of $H(z)$, and therefore do not affect the slope (the asymptotic decay rate) of the tail probabilities this sensitivity to variability of the arrival traffic is not caused by second stage policing. Comparison to other work [4, 5, 7] further supports that assertion. Table 2 lists $Var\{X\}$ and $CV^2$ for the arrival process and some performance values.

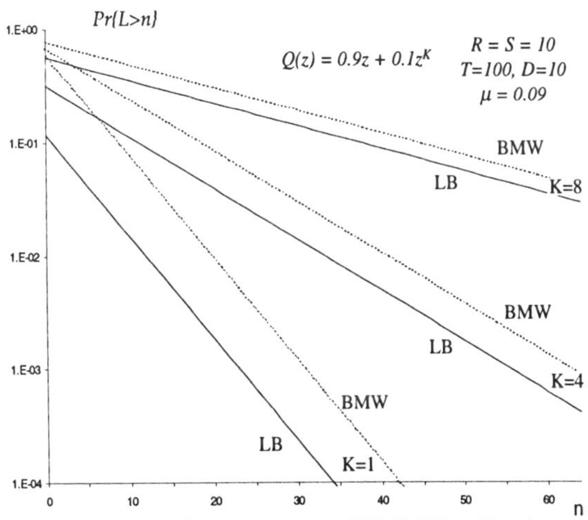


Figure 8: Comparison of Tail Distribution

Figure 8 compares the queue length tail probabilities of a buffered moving window (BMW) to that of the leaky bucket (LB). Three tail-pairs appear, for variously bursty arrival sources. For comparison, we make the long term rates of the systems the same, taking $R/T = 1/D$. Furthermore, we make the size of the leaky buckets token pool, $S$, equal to $R$.[7] We use the same arrival process as for Figure 7. We see that each pair rapidly approaches their common asymptote. Whereas the difference in buffer requirements is not large, and apparently does not depend on the burstiness (horizontal distance between each pair appears approximately the same), the key observation is that the curves for the buffered moving window dominate those of the leaky bucket in all cases.

In summary, we conclude that the tail probabilities of the queue length distribution is insensitive to second stage peak rate enforcing. Therefore, buffer requirements, or equivalently throughput, is indifferent of the second stage. However, some delay penalty is incurred by second stage shaping. This penalty is aggravated the stricter the peak rate control. We furthermore conclude that the same holds for a leaky bucket based two stage system.

## 7 Conclusion and Discussion

We have analyzed a two-stage entry monitor, each stage consisting of a buffered moving (sliding) window. Rate enforcement at each stage is achieved by buffering cells, delaying their entry into the network to strictly satisfy the rate enforced. If the traffic contract only specifies a single rate, the second stage is used to smooth traffic at the networks discretion. This smoothing may be done adaptively based on feedback.

We conclude that the cost of second rate policing is insignificant. The performance penalty appears minimal; in our numerical examples the penalty is hardly visible, and since the denominator of $H(z)$ does not depend on the second stage parameter, the difference in tail probabilities is asymptotically negligible. This means that buffer requirements to achieve prescribed cell loss ratio are insensitive to second rate policing. However, buffer occupancy is increased, showing that some additional delay penalty is suffered for enhanced control. Stricter peak rate control - scaling or lower peak rate - aggravates this difference. However, for reasonable allocation this penalty is still minimal.

Whereas not reported here, a generalization to systems of three or even more stages is of potential interest. In theory, an arbitrary level of control can be achieved by connecting $n$ buffered moving windows in tandem (or another basic scheme). Assuming that

[7] The buffered moving window may be viewed as having a token pool of size $R$ replenished $T$ slots after a token is used. Still, putting $R = S$ favors the leaky bucket, because tokens arrive during bursts and therefore the leaky bucket allows larger bursts than the token pool size to enter the network.

each stage exceeds the rate of the previous one, in a manner consistent with (1), we conjecture that the performance would remain acceptable. Some preliminary analysis of a three stage system seems to indicate how Theorem 1 and its implications would extend to three and more stages. We conjecture, however, that the numerical inversion will become progressively more difficult with additional stages.


## Acknowledgments

Thanks to Albert Greenberg and Ward Whitt, at AT&T Research, for their help on the presentation of this work.


## References


[1] Recommendation I.371, "Traffic and Congestion Control in B-ISDN", June 1992.

[2] ATM : User-Network Interface Specification (Version 3.0), Prentice-Hall, 1993.

[3] J. S. Turner, "New Directions in Communications (or Which Way to the Information Age?)", *IEEE Communication Magazine*, Vol. 24, pp. 8-15, number 10, October 1986.

[4] M. Sidi., Wen-Zu, Israel Cidon and Inder Gopal, "Congestion Control Through Input Rate Regulation", *IEEE Transactions on Communication*, vol. 41, number 3, pp. 471-477, 1993.

[5] K. Sohraby and M. Sidi., "On the Performance of Bursty Correlated Sources Subject to Leaky Bucket Rate-based Access Control Schemes", in *Proc. INFOCOM 1991*, 1991, pp. 426-434.

[6] E.P.Rathgeb, "Modeling and Performance Comparisons of Policing Mechanisms for ATM Networks", *IEEE Journal on Selected Areas in Communications*, volume 9, number 3, April 1991.

[7] G. Hjálmtýsson,A.G. Konheim, "The Sticky Buffer, A flow control mechanism for ATM," *Performance Evaluation*, 26, pp. 289-320, 1996.

[8] G. Hjálmtýsson, A.G. Konheim, "A Two-Stage Entry Monitor - The Sticky Buffer in Tandem with a Spacer," in *Proc. ICCCN*, San Francisco, CA, September 1994, pp. 52-58. To appear in *Telecommunication Systems.*

[9] G. Hjálmtýsson, "Input Rate Control and Traffic Shaping in ATM/B-ISDN", *Ph.D. Dissertation*, University of California, Santa Barbara, June 1995.

[10] M. Butto, E. Cavllero and A. Tonietti, "Effective of the "Leaky Bucket" Policing Mechanism in ATM Networks," *IEEE Journal on Selected Areas in Communications*, vol. 9, no. 3, April 1991, pp. 335-341.

[11] Bellcore, "Generic System Requirements in Support of Switched Multimegabit Data Service," Tech. Adv. TA-TSY-000772, iss. 3, October 1989.

[12] I. Rubin and K. D. Lin, "Queueing Behavior under Flow Control at the Subscriber-to-Network Interface for High Speed Metropolitan Area Networks," in *Proc. INFOCOM'91*, Bar Harbour, FL, April 1991, pp. 382-390.

[13] P. Boyer, F. M. Guillemin, M. J. Servel, J-P. Coudreuse, "Spacing Cells Protects and Enhances Utilization of ATM Network Links," *IEEE Network Magazine*, Vol 6, No 5, September 1992.

[14] E. Wallmeier, T. Worster, "The Spacer Policer, an Algorithm for Efficient Peak Bit Rate Control in ATM networks", in *Proc. ISS*, October 1992.

[15] Frank M. Brochin, "A Cell Spacing Device for Congestion Control in ATM Networks", *Performance Evaluation*, 16, 1992, pp. 107-127

[16] A. I. ElWalid and D. Mitra. "Analysis and Design of Rate-based Congestion Control of High Speed Networks, I: Stochastic Fluid Models, Access Regulation," *Queueing Systems*, No. 9, pp. 29-64, 1991.

[17] Pierre Humblet, A. Bhargava. M. G. Hluchyi, "Ballot Theorems Applied to the Transient Analysis of nD/D/1 Queues", *IEEE/ACM Transactions on Networking*, No. 1, February 1993.

[18] Offer Kella and Ward Whitt, "A tandem fluid network with Lévy input", *Queueing and Related Models*, Oxford Science Publications, Clarendon Press, Oxford 1992, pp. 112-128.

[19] Paul E. Boudreau, J. S. Griffin Jr. and Mark Kac, "An Elementary Queueing Problem", *American Mathematical Monthly*, October 1962, pp. 713-724.

[20] R. O. Onvural, "Asynchronous Transfer Mode : Networks," Artech House, 1994.

# RESOURCE RESERVATION in ADVANCE in HETEROGENEOUS NETWORKS with PARTIAL ATM INFRASTRUCTURES

Alexander Schill, Sabine Kühn, Frank Breiter
Dresden University of Technology

## Abstract

*Resource reservation in advance (ReRA) enables scheduling and allocation of resources at an early stage in time. This way, the availability of resources can actually be guaranteed for the point in time when the resources are needed. As opposed to that, current reservation protocols such as RSVP perform an "immediate" reservation without advance scheduling. They can therefore suffer shortage of resources with subsequent rejection of applications.*

*This paper describes our new approach for providing resource reservation in advance in ATM networks. As a foundation, we first present experiences of IPng and RSVP over ATM. Based on this work, we then discuss major design issues of an appropriate ReRA solution. Important aspects are the signalling model for ReRA, the admission control strategy, the duration of connections, and various other time-related parameters. We also discuss our ongoing implementation of ReRA as an extension of RSVP and outline directions for future research in this area.*

## 1: Introduction

ATM networks have recently gathered great interest in research and practice. According to the current UNI 3.1 (User Network Interface) specification and the UNI 4.0 specification of the ATM forum [3,4], important quality of service (QoS) characteristics are supported. However, there are two major problems with this approach:

*(1) Heterogeneous networks:* Most current and future networks are not purely based on ATM but consist of a mix of various technologies (ATM, FDDI, Ethernet etc. with switches, hubs, routers etc. for network interconnection). Therefore, higher-level protocols on top of ATM such as IP are necessary to enable heterogeneous interoperability. Moreover, reservation protocols at this level such as RSVP (resource reservation protocol; e.g. for reserving resources within routers) are also necessary to achieve QoS guarantees.

*(2) Drawbacks of immediate reservation:* Current resource reservation facilities, both within ATM and on top of it, perform a so-called "immediate" reservation: They reserve resources just at the point in time when they are actually needed. If resources cannot be granted at this time, QoS cannot be guaranteed as desired or important applications such as broadband videoconferences even have to be rejected. An advance scheduling of reservations could help to solve this problem.

The major contributions of this paper to address these problems are as follows:

*(1) Experiences with IP/IPng and RSVP over ATM:* In order to address the first problem, we present an implementation of the IP/IPng (IP next generation) and RSVP (resource reservation) protocols at OSI layer 3 on top of ATM. This enables extended addressing capabilities in Internet environments, enhanced QoS specifications, and associated resource reservation in heterogeneous networks.

*(2) Resource reservation in advance (ReRA):* In order to address the second problem, we present a new approach for implementing advance scheduling of reservations. This way, the availability of resources can actually be guaranteed for the point in time when the resources are needed. Important design decisions discussed are the signalling model for ReRA, the admission control strategy, the duration of connections, and various other time-related parameters. We also discuss our ongoing implementation of ReRA as an extension of RSVP.

The paper is organized as follows. In section 2, we discuss the current situation in terms of standards and common protocols in the context of ATM. In particular, IP/IPng over ATM is discussed. Moreover, related work concerning resource reservation in advance is outlined. Section 3 presents our implementation and experiences with RSVP over ATM. Section 4, the main part of the paper, discusses concepts and design decisions of our resource reservation in advance approach. In section 5, implementation aspects of ReRA as an RSVP extension are presented as a synergy of the former considerations.

## 2: Background and Related Work

As of today, ATM networks mainly offer adaptation layer AAL5 supporting available bit rate (ABR) traffic, and, in some cases, AAL1 offering a constant bit rate (CBR). Although applications could in principle directly



0-8186-7780-5/97 $10.00 © 1997 IEEE

use the AAL interface, the dominance of heterogeneous networks and the required migration of existing applications onto ATM makes higher-level protocols necessary.

A typical approach standardized is IP over ATM [14]: Applications just use conventional TCP/IP or UDP/IP, and IP communication is mapped onto virtual ATM connections. IP addresses are mapped onto ATM addresses by an ATMARP server (address resolution protocol), and IP packets are segmented into ATM cells and reassembled at the receiver's site transparently. The ATMARP approach requires that communication between different IP subnetworks is performed via routers, even if two communicating nodes are attached to the same physical ATM network. The emerging NHRP (next hop resolution protocol) will solve this problem by enabling direct ATM shortcuts whenever possible. The use of a MARS (multicast address resolution server) [20] also enables the implementation of IP multicast over ATM. As opposed to the current overlay model (overlay of IP routing on top of an ATM network), the peer model [1] is a direct algorithmic mapping of all network layer addresses onto ATM addresses, and there is only one kind of signalling, i.e. ATM signalling as defined by the PNNI specification (private network node interface) [19]. This leads to an environment with combined ATM switches and routers. An alternative solution for mapping existing applications onto ATM is LANE (LAN Emulation) [12, 13], which only enables the interconnection of homogeneous LANs via ATM. Therefore, we do not consider LANE in this paper. Currently, MPOA (multiprotocol over ATM) [1] is also discussed as a kind of integration approach; it supports LAN protocols, IP, IPX and other protocols over ATM.

With these solutions, however, ATM is merely a "large pipe" with significant throughput, but without any quality of service guarantees. Only best-effort traffic based on ABR can be supported as the given protocols do not provide QoS specification and resource reservation facilities. Therefore, problems with realtime applications such as videoconferences with shared applications, remote video monitoring, time-constrained bulk transactions etc. arise. An early, sender-oriented reservation protocol addressing these issues was ST-II [8]. More recently, RSVP (resource reservation protocol) [5] has observed growing interest. Basically, RSVP enables the reservation of bandwidth and other resources at the time when a resource-intensive communication scenario is initiated. This way, actual QoS guarantees can be given. RSVP coexists with IP or IPng (also known as IPv6 [11], as a successor of IPv4); it operates only during call setup and maps reservation requirements directly onto underlying networks (such as ATM) and network components (such as routers). Due to its importance in the upcoming Integrated Services Internet [7], RSVP has been selected as a basis of our implementation work, too.

Even with RSVP, however, reservations can of course fail if resources are not sufficiently available at the time when they are needed. Therefore, some first approaches towards providing resource reservation in advance facilities have been developed.

In summary, it can be stated that most of the known papers briefly describe more general problems to be solved: [10] concentrates on resource partitioning; [15] describes a possible exchange of advance reservation information using the ST-II [8] reservation protocol. Dealing with the Integrated Services Internet, [9] presents an explicit admission control algorithm for predictive service. Moreover, [17] already introduces a possible ReRA architecture and [16] compares the suitability of the Internet-based reservation protocols ST-II and RSVP to support ReRA. However, implementations have obviously not reached a mature stage yet.

Our approach differs from these solutions with respect to two major aspects: First, we consider quite a large number of design parameters in terms of signalling, admission control, and timing aspects and aim at achieving a large degree of flexibility. Secondly, our solution is directly based on RSVP and ATM as emerging standards.

## 3: RSVP over ATM

As originally conceived, the Internet, and also solutions based on IP over ATM offer only a very simple kind of QoS: best effort. Hence, before realtime applications like video conferencing can be used, the Internet has to be modified to support real time service. This is only possible by resource reservation. A protocol like RSVP is crucial for the negotiation of the corresponding reservation parameters and for guaranteeing quality of service (QoS) characteristics based on explicitly reserved network, memory and processing resources [6]. It is of particular importance in heterogeneous networks with partial ATM infrastructures. With the assistance of RSVP, the specification of QoS (Quality of Service) and traffic parameters for dedicated flows can be performed by the applications on top of the IP/IPng protocol stack. The usage of the new Internet protocol in conjunction with RSVP allows a more efficient handling and classification of packets as belonging to an already reserved flow.

### 3.1: RSVP - An IP Signalling Protocol

With the usage of RSVP [18], recently proposed as a Request for Comments, the Integrated Services Internet [7] especially supports realtime applications with guaranteed, predictable and controlled end-to-end performance across networks. The main task performed by RSVP is signalling of resource requirements at connection setup time. To be precise, RSVP does not actually reserve or allocate resources but rather indicates reservation requests to the underlying systems.

Moreover, the protocol offers a flexible handling of heterogeneous receivers as well as an adaptation to dynamically changing multicast groups. The transmission of RSVP control information is implemented by encapsulating RSVP packets into IP or IPng packets. The basis of a reservation is a detailed description of flow traffic and QoS characteristics. In accordance with this fact, RSVP defines the so-called flow (describing the traffic and the required QoS parameters) and filter specification (identifying the flow for which reservations have been performed). All reservation and state information are managed in soft states in all nodes which facilitates the renegotiation of resource reservations within RSVP.

Even though the reservation is receiver-oriented, the initiator of a reservation is the sender, which informs appropriate receivers about the characteristics of the flow to be sent. Figure 1 shows the main protocol elements.

In contrast to the RSVP model, the QoS setup time in

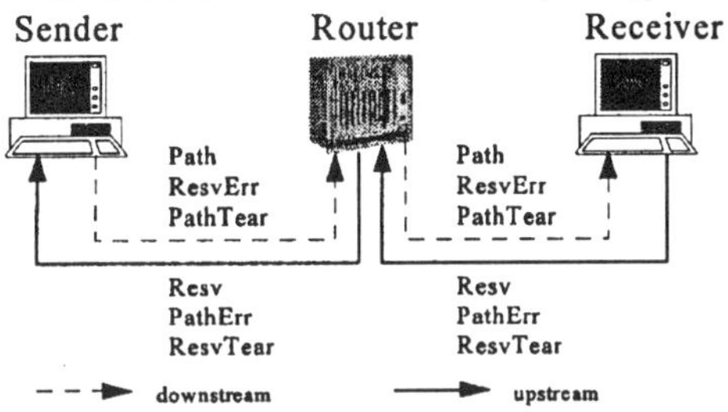


**Figure 1: Exchange of RSVP messages**

ATM is directly combined with the connection setup. Considering both the ATM and the RSVP service classes (of IETF), the latter are characterized by delay, whereas, in ATM, classes of bit rates (ABR, CBR etc.) are specified. Moreover, ATM allows both variable bit rate (burst, peak) and constant bit rate for transmission of non bursty traffic as opposed to RSVP. The traffic parameters of ATM accordingly comprise Maximum Burst Size, Sustainable Cell Rate and Peak Cell Rate. The mapping of the particular RSVP traffic parameters is discussed in conjunction with an assignment of the service classes in [2].

## 3.2: RSVP-IP/IPng-ATM Protocol Stack

Within our development work, an RSVP implementation on top of ATM has been completed under the Digital Unix operating system. As part of the IP/IPng convergence modules (CM), and hence part of the ATM subsystem, the RSVP specific API supports real time handling and transport of IP/IPng flows (figure 2).

The API is able to receive reservation information from a local RSVP daemon. Based on information contained in a given flow specification, a new ATM VC reservation is performed after completing the mapping of service classes and parameters. The classification of the IP/IPng flows belonging to a dedicated reserved reservation (virtual channel) is done in the IP/IPng CM, too.

As a basis for the implementation of ReRA, we use the full RSVP/IP(IPng)/ATM protocol stack which we have completed in cooperation with Digital Equipment.

The following section describes the general approach

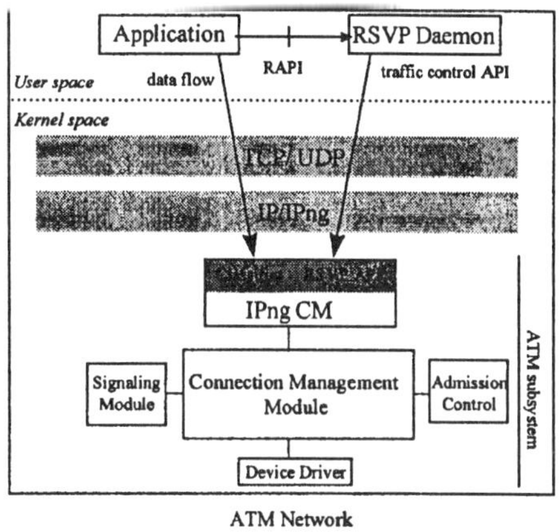


**Figure 2: ATM subsystem and RSVP**

to realize an extension of the "immediate" reservation mechanisms of RSVP and ATM with advance scheduling and planning techniques.

# 4: Resource Reservation in Advance

## 4.1: An Introduction

Considering, for instance, the „real world“, activities such as a meeting in a conferencing room are scheduled for a specific time. With this example, reservation means that limited resources are reserved a certain time in advance to get an assurance that the resources are available at the requested time. The definition of reservation in current QoS based networks like ATM covers another kind of semantics: reservations are being performed in conjunction with a connection establishment; this means that reservations are done at the time when the network resources are actually needed. This is an element of uncertainty, because in the worst case the required resources are used by other applications and therefore the application request must be rejected. However, using ReRA, a future lack of resources during actual reservations can be avoided.

From our point of view, it shall be possible to schedule applications, e.g. an important videoconference with several partners, for a given time in the future. The system shall then calculate and virtually reserve the required resources for that time, however without immediately blocking them. In order to grant the required QoS, it is necessary to provide mechanisms of resource reservation in advance.

The advantage of introducing a ReRA concept is also reasonable in QoS based high performance networks, in which a lot of users have to share the same resources.

## 4.2: ReRA Connection Parameters

Comparing the negotiation of immediate and advance reservation, one of the differences is the specification of additional parameters for setting up a reservation in advance. As the resources for advance reservations will be reserved for a given time in the future, one of the necessary parameters is the time at which the resources will be needed.

Furthermore, it seems to be meaningful to specify a duration for ReRA-connections which describes how long the reservation will be alive. Based on this information the admission control is able to recognize whether the reservation is overlapping with others or not. On one hand, specifying a reservation duration results in a more effective utilization of bandwidth (discussed in more detail in 4.4.2). On the other hand, many applications are not always able to specify a concrete duration for their reservations.

## 4.3: Signalling Model Description

The differences between the ImRe and ReRA communication model is shown in figure 3. For describing the extended communication to set up a resource reservation in advance, we have introduced time marks at which messages are sent or actions are performed.

To specify how much of the resource capacities have to be reserved, the client issues a REQUEST at the time $t_{request}$. It also specifies the points in time that define beginning ($t_{start}$) and duration ($d_{res}$) of the reservation. After successfully completed negotiation and admission control, the service provider CONFIRMs the reservation (at the time $t_{confirm}$). Moreover, each reservation is assigned an identifier for later access. The service provider RELEASEs the request in the case of rejection.

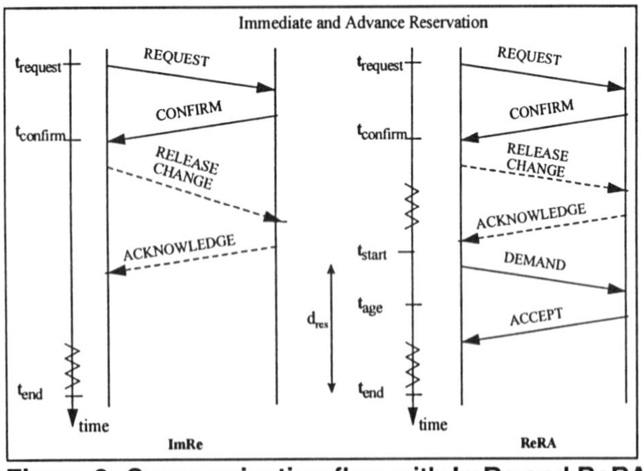


**Figure 3: Communication flow with ImRe and ReRA**

After a successful negotiation, the users might want to re-negotiate the communication resources. This covers the cancellation (RELEASE) or an increase or decrease (CHANGE) of the requested resources. If the changes are acceptable or the reservation was successfully released the service provider ACKNOWLEDGEs it. Re-negotiation concerns not only the traffic and QoS parameters of the reserved connection but also the starting point and duration. A re-negotiation can be performed until $t_{end}$ is reached. To realize a more flexible handling of changes, policy data within a CHANGE request have been introduced to indicate that the reservation should either be deleted or kept in the intermediate nodes if the modification fails. Another possible policy is that any rejection carries suggestions for alternative reservations: (1) If a reservation cannot be granted for the whole duration requested, the admission control has to determine the possible (shorter) duration. (2) It is also possible that the system suggests a new start time at which the requested resources will be available or (3) it just provides the currently available resources (i.e. less than requested) for the given time.

The decision, which of the policies should be used for ReRA or ImRe is a responsibility of the network administrator or provider. In our solution such information is exchanged with the user whenever a request fails.

As the interval between $t_{confirm}$ and $t_{start}$ could cover a long time, it is possible that intermediate nodes may be unplugged from the network for a short time, may crash or the topology may change. The occurrence of such kinds of failures is not different from failures within traditional QoS-based systems during the data transmission phase [17]. However, the handling of these failures differs dependent on the applied reservation system. The handling of failures before the data transmission starts via a ReRA connection requires special attention. In chapter 5 an example of such a special handling is given for RSVP.

In particular, the transition to the data transmission phase can be considered as a special case. When the start time is reached, the DEMAND for using the reservation has to be performed within $t_{start}$ - $t_{age}$. If the sender is not sending a DEMAND by then, the reservation will be aged and all state information corresponding to it is removed. In contrast to immediate reservation, ReRA therefore requires additional communication at $t_{start}$. We prefer this solution because last changes should be possible and resources are only reserved if they are really needed. If an application exceeds its requested duration without a recently requested prolongation, the system handles it as an immediate reservation.

## 4.4: Call Admission Control

### 4.4.1: Desired Features

The design of a suitable ATM traffic control is considered as a fundamental challenge for the success of the ReRA mechanism. The primary role of traffic control is to protect the network and the user in order to achieve predefined network performance objectives. Dealing with advance reservation, an additional role of traffic control is to optimize the use of network resources for the purpose of achieving: (1) sufficient network efficiency, that means the effectiveness in utilizing bandwidth, (2) a minimal blocking probability and (3) a fair handling of the advance and the immediate reservations. Obviously, it seems to be difficult to combine these features in such a way that the Call Admission Control (CAC) will achieve all these goals in an optimal way. Therefore, we are investigating influence parameters (e.g. bandwidth awarding, connection parameters) and their effects on the characteristics of the CAC.

#### 4.4.2: Impacts on the Admission Control Features

These and other influences concern the awarding of the resources between the two types of reservations. That means precisely the kind of policing of resource awarding and management that should be used between ImRe and ReRA. Another interesting point which shall be investigated is the sending of immediate versus deferred acknowledgements after receiving a setup request. Corresponding to this fact, the introduction of a granularity of time intervals is investigated, influencing the determination of starting time of a future reservation and of its duration.

Moreover, the knowledge of the connection duration has an important impact on the effectiveness of CAC and also on the acceptance of applying reservations. Finally, a minimum and maximum advance notice time for submitting reservations should be specified.

#### 4.4.3: Awarding of Bandwidth

Basically, there are the following policies to handle the two different kinds of reservations: sharing and partitioning. Sharing the resources allows the awarding of the whole bandwidth e.g. in the case of an aggressive access to ReRA connections. A partitioning of the bandwidth for instance for ImRe and ReRA is heading towards an equitable handling of the single reservations as the bandwidth is dedicated to each reservation type. But, assuming an adverse allocation of resources between ImRe and ReRA, it can result in an inefficient utilization of bandwidth caused by the two boundaries.

#### 4.4.4: Immediate and Deferred Acknowledgements

To optimize the bandwidth utilization and to reduce blocking probability, an investigation of immediate versus deferred acknowledgement of reservations is interesting. Generally considered, there are two models based on the time when scheduling decisions are made. In the case of immediate acknowledgement, scheduling decisions are made as soon as a request arrives. The other model is based on delayed acknowledgements, only applicable to reservations in advance. Every request has an associated decision point which is given by the system. Focusing on a reduced blocking probability, for example, the following simple heuristics can be used. We assume, that the bandwidth requests of all reservations with a synchronous starting point are sorted in an ascending way. Accepting all reservations beginning with the smallest resource request until the whole bandwidth is awarded, results in an reduced blocking probability. Obviously, assuming synchronous starting points of an amount of reservations is an abstract model and only conceivable with relatively coarse-grained time intervals. In the future, we also have to investigate and develop reasonable heuristics to achieve a better utilization of resources by a special handling of requests according to their attributes (e.g. bandwidth requirements).

#### 4.4.5: Duration of Connections

The specification of the connection duration will influence the effectiveness in utilizing bandwidth dependent on the selected resource awarding strategy. If the bandwidth between ImRe and ReRA is shared, then the bandwidth utilization is optimized by specifying the duration for all ImRe and ReRA connections.

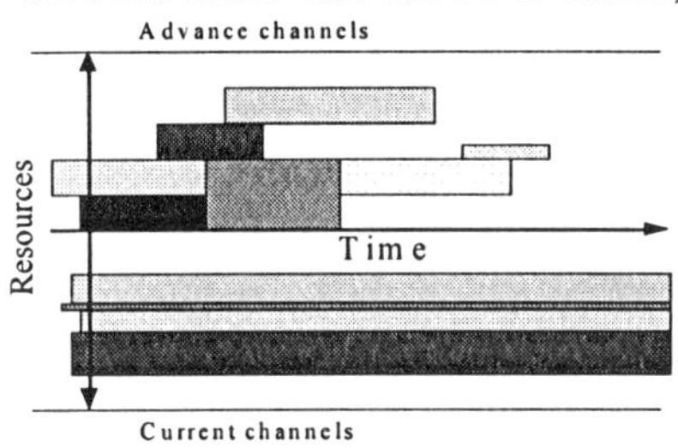

**Figure 4: Resource partitioning**

While this allows the system to make more efficient use of resources by explicitly limiting the duration of connections, it may be unacceptable to some applications. Using partitioning between ImRe and ReRA (figure 4), a definition of the duration is necessary only for ReRA connections to make decisions about future resource allocation. To be precise, in the case of static partitioning, the immediate partition treats any new requests exactly as usual. The advance partition must instead use a different mechanism to test new requests for admission.

#### 4.4.6: Granularity of Starting Points and Duration

Basically, an introduction of a granularity of time intervals has an effect on the administration of the reservations on the various intermediate nodes. Using a granularity results in a more effective mutual coincidence of reservation start and end points, that means connections could only be allowed to be pre-reserved at certain times. From this point of view, a rough granularity is more convenient. Considering typical applications, reservations are generally made in steps of five or up to 15 minutes [15].

For example (figure 5), a mapping of the event C onto the next starting time of the next granularity unit results in an inaccuracy of up to 1 time slot G; with a reasonable choice of C, this should usually be acceptable for most applications.

In spite of these facts, the approach has the side-effect that a clock synchronisation throughout the network must be assumed, as different times on different nodes may result in askew starting times due to different roundings.

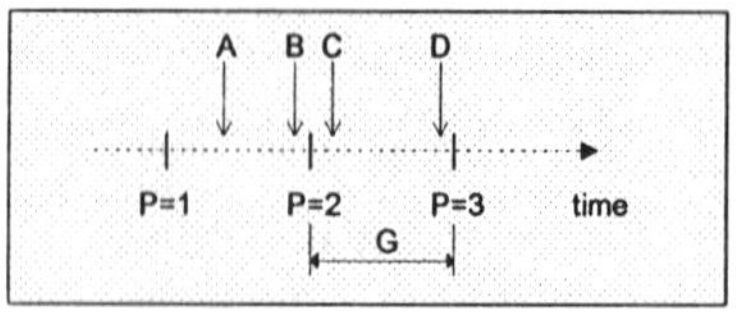


**Figure 5: Usage of time granularity**

### 4.4.7: Minimum and Maximum Advance Notice

The maximum notice as well as the minimum advance notice should be reasonable values with which a reservation can be submitted (e.g. for less than three hours and not more than 3 months) if such limits were imposed by the provider. As the value of the maximum advance notice has an impact on the management overhead of the admission control, it should not exceed a reasonable value. Moreover the minimum advance notice is also used to differ between ImRe and ReRA requests.

## 4.5: An Approach of ReRA in ATM

For implementing ReRA in an ATM environment, the following aspects have to be considered: (1) how to realize the necessary communication for advance reservation in ATM; (2) which components have to be changed and (3) how to realize the call admission control.

Although, there is more than one communication mechanism in ATM possible for exchanging ReRA information, the extension of the signalling protocol seems to be the most general approach. Considering ReRA in a private ATM network, an extension and modification of the signalling concerns both the User-Network-Interface and the Network-Network-Interface signalling protocol.

Recognizing ReRA in ATM means not only the transmission of ReRA information (4.5.1) and the decision on the acceptance or rejection of a new call (4.5.2). Because ReRA differs from immediate reservations, a possible QoS (load sensitive) routing and reactions to switch failures should also be considered. In the case of ImRe, the state and load information are exchanged between the switches by conveying appropriate cells as a part of the routing protocol of the PNNI [19]. A ReRA-QoS routing algorithm would allow the network capacity to be engineered efficiently, by virtue of its ability to take into account the future network state in making routing decisions. This may enable more effective operation and can reduce blocking probability.

### 4.5.1: ReRA Signalling

Introducing an extended signalling to negotiate ReRA parameters is realized in modifying existing and defining new message types. Modifying messages comprises the addition of newly defined and extended information elements (IE). These IE are necessary to convey the following parameters: starting time, duration and policy information for the requested ReRA. As the IEs will be handled as optional, the message types can be further used for immediate reservations in their original meaning.

The negotiation of immediate and advanced reservation are nearly the same, so that the **SETUP**[1] message is always used to *REQUEST* the needed resources. Concerning ImRe, sending a **SETUP** message results in a connection establishment. As opposed to that, it requests the setup of an advance reservation with ReRA. Based on the information of the included ReRA IE, the system then calculates and virtually reserves the required resources for that time, however without immediately blocking them. Furthermore, the **CONNECT, RELEASE_COMPLETE, CALL_PROCEEDING** and the **RELEASE** message are used without any modifications. Except the former message, all other messages can be used within the time $t_{request}$ - $t_{end}$.

After a successful negotiation of a reservation, it is possible to modify the starting time and duration of the ReRA connection, whereas the renegotiation of traffic and QoS parameters is allowed in the intermediate phase, too. Analogous to the recent ATM signalling, it is not possible to change any other parameter than traffic and QoS parameters in the usage phase without releasing the old and establishing the new connection. New message types were necessary due to an additional communication making modifications and demands of the already requested resources (ReRA) possible:

Hence, the *CHANGE* message is comparable to the **SETUP** message; in relation to the conveyed parameters, however, it has a different meaning. To be more precise, a *CHANGE* message is used to modify an existing request whereas a **SETUP** message should be used to initiate a new request. In the *CHANGE* message policy data can be used to indicate that the request should be either deleted or kept in the intermediate nodes if the modification fails. Concerning the specification of the policy data for *CHANGE*, it is sufficient to provide one IE in which each policy is represented by setting the corresponding bit.

The transition from the intermediate phase to the usage phase will be done by sending a *DEMAND* message. In analogy to the *CHANGE* message, the *DEMAND* message looks like the **SETUP** message.

---

[1] Words in bold face indicate ATM signalling messages and italic ones indicate ReRA messages.

Most of the IEs in the *DEMAND* message are optional as well as in the *CHANGE* message. Hence, it is possible to create a „very short" *DEMAND* message, which results in a decreased processing time in the end systems and the switch. We call this behaviour a "fast setup". Moreover, by setting up the appropriate IEs, it is allowed to make last minute changes by the user, sending a *DEMAND*. The messages which are sent to indicate an *ACCEPTion* are similar to the acknowledgement of the **SETUP** message.

### 4.5.2: CAC Decisions

As we consider ReRA only as an additional service, the impacts or influences on ImRe shall be small. So we decided that the underlying policy of admission control should be awarding bandwidth fairly between both kinds of reservations based on an optimized bandwidth utilization: a partitioning with a moveable boundary [10]. This means, each reservation has its own partition, but with the option of using available resources of the other partition if the own partition is completely allocated. To avoid a sharing across the whole bandwidth, we have introduced watermarks to protect e.g. the advance partition. Moreover, the immediate reservation can be handled as a special case of ReRA with starting time 0. In the case of a fully utilized ImRe bandwidth, the ReRA part can be used by reservations with start time "now" only with the maximum duration of minimum advanced notice. A part of the immediate reservation partition should be protected by a watermark, too. Considering the immediate partition, the following characteristics are notable: (1) it can be used for infinite immediate reservations, and (2) only for advance reservations if the advance partition is saturated.

The advance partition can be used: (1) for advance reservations and (2) limited immediate reservations.

Figure 6 shows an example that immediate reservations could be limited by the system. Obviously,

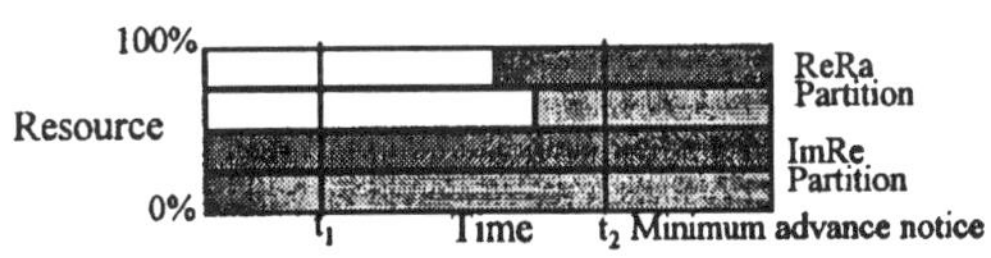


**Figure 6: Filling gaps caused by ReRA with limited ImRe**

this was also introduced to realize a more efficient utilization by filling gaps caused by the reservations in advance. This refers to bandwidth which is available in the time interval $t_1$ to $t_2$ and cannot be used by advance reservations in the advance partition. It can therefore be allocated to ImRe with limited duration.

If an infinite ImRe was requested and only resources within a limited duration are available, the user could be informed by the system as part of a rejection of the request according to the policies described in chapter 4.3.

## 5: ReRA in RSVP

In this chapter essential changes and extensions of RSVP to support ReRA will be described. In particular, this includes the negotiation of ReRA information, and the behaviour of RSVP in case of a temporary router failures before the starting time of the advance reservation is reached.

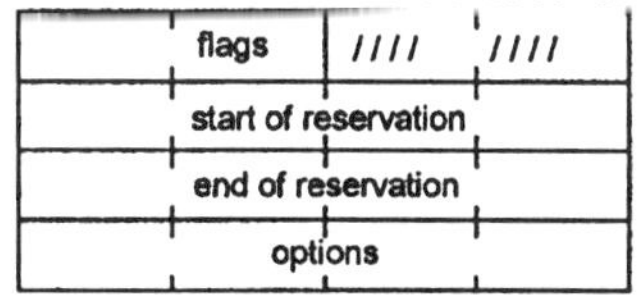


**Figure 7: RSVP ReRA class**

The ***negotiation*** of ReRA information is done by sending Path and Resv messages carrying an additional instance: a new RSVP class which is shown in figure 7.

As the ReRA object is an additional and optional object in an RSVP message, a result of this solution is that the semantics of the messages will be preserved for ImRe. This implies, that no new messages have to be defined in RSVP; instead the new RSVP class has been introduced which includes the points in time when the reservation starts and finishes. The flags can be used, for example, to distinguish between a normal Resv message and a Resv message (the latter complies with a DEMAND message, chapter 4.3), which is send at the starting point to indicate that the user wishes to use the reserved resources. Moreover, to change the end of an already requested reservation, in the ReRA object carried by a Resv message a special flag is set and the options field carries the new end time.

Moreover, to realize a ***complete extension of the RSVP specification*** to support ReRA we have performed the following steps:

- the extension of the messages (described above) and the corresponding extension of the message processing rules,
- the extension of the state control blocks (Path-, Reservation- and Traffic Control blocks) to support the pseudo hard state concept (see below) and to hold the new reservation parameters,
- the extension of the specific RSVP interfaces (e.g. RAPI, traffic control API, chapter 4.3) and the introduction of new functions, for example, as part of the RAPI, to allow: (1) a LEAVE of a session without releasing the soft states. This is used to inform the RSVP daemon that the application is not actual available for the whole time until the starting point is reached (for instance 3 months). The application should save session information to be able to re-register by calling the session function. (2) As we allow more than one reservation in one session (which can be distinguished by the start and end time of the reservation) the TEARDOWN function can be called to remove a specific reservation.

To avoid that soft states which hold the ReRA information will be deleted caused by temporary router failure or a longer termed unplugged endsystem we use a modified refreshing mechanism and the concept of pseudo hard states and proxy routers. Considering the soft state approach of RSVP (chapter 3), the periodic sending of Path and Resv messages (default: every 30 seconds) produces a considerable overhead. The refreshing of the states is controlled by the refresh time R and the lifetime L. The relationship between R and L is expressed by the following equation: $L \geq (K + 0.5) * 1.5 * R$ (K-1 successive messages may be lost without state information being deleted). From our point of view, L should increased in such a way that reservations are insensitive to temporary router failures. This can be achieved by an adequate increase of R at the time the ReRA connection was requested and a reduction of R step by step until the starting time is reached. At this time, R is set to the default value. It should be emphasized that concrete values of R and K have to be determined based on future measurements in our experimental environment.

As the advance notice of an advance reservation request can take a long time (e.g. 3 months), the actual availability of endsystems have to be considered. If an endsystem is not actually available (for instance a PC which was turned off), this results in missed Path and Reserve refresh messages and in a loss of the corresponding soft states of the neighboured router. In order to avoid this, the routers which are situated immediately behind the sender and the receiver, respectively, should react if no new refresh message arrives. Because these routers take over the function of the endsystems in sending Path and Resv refresh messages, they will be called proxy routers.

Moreover, each router has to determine if the next host is the receiver downstream or the sender upstream, itself. Is one of cases fulfilled, this results in holding the soft states the router. More precisely, these soft states are kept and only removed if the user sends a teardown message or if the starting time of the reservation is already exceeded. Therefore, the states are called pseudo hard states and so we are able to deal with unplugged endsystems.

## 6: Conclusions

This paper has presented the current situation in terms of standards and common protocols in the context of ATM. In particular, IP and IPng over ATM were discussed. Due to its importance in the upcoming Integrated Services Internet, RSVP has been selected as the basis of our implementation work. As a main contribution of this paper, a general model of advance reservation was described and an enhancement of RSVP and ATM was presented to support reservation in advance. Special emphasis was put on the problem of signalling the appropriate ReRA information within the integrated services Internet and the ATM network. For mapping the general model onto RSVP and ATM, differences in handling failure situations must be considered; they closely depend on the current handling of routing changes and neighbour losses concerning traditional reservations.

The presented concepts for resource reservation in advance are also under refinement and we expect to have further implementation experiences soon.

## 7: References


[1] Alles, A., „ATM Internetworking“, 1995

[2] Schill, A., Kühn, S., Breiter, F., Internetworking over ATM: Experiences with IP/IPng and RSVP, 7th Joint European Networking Conference, Budapest, Hungary, 1996

[3] ATM-Forum, „UNI Signaling 4.0“, ATM Forum 94-1019R6, Work in Progress, 1995

[4] ATM-Forum, „Traffic Managment Specification Version 4.0“, ATM Forum 95-0013R6, Work in Progress, 1995

[5] Braden, R., Zhang, L., „Resource ReSerVation Protocol (RSVP) -- Version 1 Functional Specification“, Work in Progress, 1996

[6] Campbell, A., Coulson, G., Hutchison, D., „A Quality of Service Architecture“, Computer Communication Review, Vol. 1, No. 2, April 1994, pp. 6-27

[7] Integrated Services Model, RCF 1633, 1995

[8] Delgrossi, L., Herrtwich, R.G., Hoffmann, F., „An Implementation of ST-II for the Heidelberg Transport System“, Internet-working: Research and Experience, Vol. 5, 1994, pp. 43-69

[9] Degermark, M., Köhler, T., Pink, S., Schelén, O., „Advance Reservation for Predictive Service“, 5th International Workshop on Network and Operating System Support for Digital Audio and Video, Durham, April 1995

[10] Ferrari, D., Gupta A., Ventre, G., „Distributed advance Reservation of real-time connections“, 5th International Workshop on NOSSDAV, Durham, April 1995

[11] Hinden, R., Deering, S., „IP Version 6 Addressing Architecture“ ,Work in Progress, 1995

[12] Jeffries, R., „ATM LAN Emulation“, Data Communications, No. 9, 1994, pp. 95-100

[13] ATM-Forum, „LAN Emulation over ATM Version 1“, 1995

[14] Laubach, M., „Classical IP and ARP over ATM“, RFC 1577, January 1994

[15] Reinhardt, W., „Advance Reservation of Network Resources for Multimedia Applications“, Proceedings of the 2nd IWACA94, Heidelberg, 1994

[16] Reinhardt, W., „Advance Resource Reservation and its Impact on Reservation Protocols“, Technical Report, 1995

[17] Wolf, L.C., Delgrossi, L., Steinmetz, R., Schaller, S., Wittig, H., „Issues of Reserving Resources in Advance“, IBM European Network Center Heidelberg, TR 43.9503, 1995

[18] Zhang, L., Deering, S., Estrin, D., Shenker, S., Zappala, D., „RSVP: A New Resource Reservation Protocol“, IEEE Network, Sept. 1993, pp. 8-18

[19] ATM-Forum, „PNNI Spezification Version 1.0“, 1996

[20] Armitage, G., „Support for Multicast over UNI 3.0/3.1 based ATM Networks“, RFC 2022, 1996

# NFS Dynamics Over Flow-Controlled Wide Area Networks

Koling Chang, Robert Morris and H.T. Kung
Division of Engineering and Applied Sciences, Harvard University
29 Oxford Street, Cambridge, MA 02138, USA
{chang, rtm, htk}@eecs.harvard.edu

## Abstract

*The Network File System protocol (NFS) has been the leading distributed file system for workstations since it was first introduced by Sun Microsystems in 1986. The geographical scale of NFS has been limited to the local area due to its relatively low performance on the wide area Internet. However, with the advent of high bandwidth wide area networks such as ATM, NFS over WANs may become more promising. In this paper, the performance of NFS over various sizes of WAN is studied. The effects of ATM flow-control and queuing strategies on NFS are discussed, as are the performance of TCP and UDP as NFS transport protocols. The primary conclusion is that standard NFS over UDP works well over ATM WANs as long as ATM-level flow control keeps the cell loss rate under one percent. In some cases, NFS over TCP works badly with small packets due to unfortunate interactions with TCP's congestion window.*

## 1. Introduction

In this paper we study the performance of NFS [1, 3] over flow-controlled ATM networks with various geographical scales and drop rates. NFS has poor performance over wide area networks such as the Internet mainly because of three factors: high drop rate, long propagation delay, and low available bandwidth. The latter is most significant for NFS operations such as read and write that involve large amounts of data. However, large transfers are substantially less common than small ones in most NFS workloads [4]. In such cases, NFS performance is affected more by packet drop rate and propagation delay.

Our research explores four issues relating to NFS and WANs. ATM WANs may use flow control to reduce losses; NFS is affected by both the flow control and the remaining losses. NFS can be used over TCP on WANs, and we wish to compare this with NFS over UDP on a flow-controlled ATM. Even the best WAN cannot reduce propagation delay, and we identify the situations in which propagation is the limiting factor in performance. Finally, sophisticated ATM switches may provide per-VC queuing and round-robin scheduling, and we show the degree to which this improves NFS performance.

### 1.1 NFS Overview

Sun Microsystems' Network File System (NFS) [1, 3] allows programs to access remote files in the same way as local files. It has seen wide use on a variety of computers since its introduction in 1986. This is mainly due to its simplicity and independence of machine and operating system. NFS is a client-server system. The protocol is defined in terms of a set of procedures, and their arguments, results, and effects. These procedures are implemented using Sun's RPC (Remote Procedure Call) protocol [2] to simplify programs.

All NFS procedures involve a client sending a request to the server and waiting for the reply. RPC automates this by making the client block until the server has completed the call and returned the result. If the server does not respond because of a crash or packet loss, the client periodically resends the request.

The most common operations are client requests to look up file names or to fetch file attributes such as read/write permissions or file length; these involve small transfers of a few hundred bytes over the network, and their performance is dominated by propagation latency rather than bandwidth. In contrast, NFS read and write operations usually transfer file blocks of 8192 bytes and more than one outstanding request is allowed. In this case, network bandwidth can potentially limit their performance.

NFS can be implemented on top of different transport protocols because Sun's RPC is designed to be transport independent. However, the implementation on top of UDP is mostly used since UDP has historically incurred less CPU overhead than TCP [9], and because NFS is almost always used on local networks where TCP's sophisticated error recovery and congestion control are not required [5].



0-8186-7780-5/97 $10.00 © 1997 IEEE

However, implementations of NFS on TCP have recently demonstrated performance better than UDP over congested networks [4]. The reason is that TCP has better congestion control and faster error recovery than UDP-based NFS. Whenever a packet is lost, NFS/UDP waits a timeout period on the order of one second and retransmits the entire request, which might involve multiple packets. TCP, in contrast, can often respond to a single dropped packet in one round trip time, and under many circumstances it re-sends only the lost packet rather than a whole request. Thus NFS over TCP should tolerate higher loss rates than NFS over UDP.

### 1.2 Flow-Controlled ATM

The high drop rate and low bandwidth on current wide area networks may eventually be improved when Broadband ISDN using ATM becomes available. ATM [7], which aims at high bandwidth and low data loss rate, has been adopted by telecommunication providers as the standard for future wide area digital networks. Several flow-control protocols have been proposed for use at the ATM level to provide "available bit-rate" (ABR) services and reduce data loss; these include rate-based flow-control [8,10] and credit-based flow-control protocols [15]. Both of these approaches will allow heavily loaded networks to achieve high utilization and low data loss.

The rate-based flow control method recommended by ATM Forum, Enhanced Proportional Rate Control Algorithm (EPRCA) [11], is an end-to-end protocol in which the source of a connection adjusts its sending rate depending on the network congestion status along its path. EPRCA does not eliminate cell loss due to congestion. The cell drop rate varies depending on the available buffer space in the network switches and protocol parameters. In general EPRCA allows a trade-off between drop rate and bandwidth utilization when the switch bandwidth and buffer resources are limited.

Credit protocols such as QFC [15] and FCVC [12,13,14] use hop-by-hop buffer based flow-control. FCVC eliminates cell loss by reserving buffer space, but requires per-VC queueing inside the network switches. While per-VC queuing may increase a switch's cost, it provides performance benefits beyond those provided by other flow controls. A number of switch vendors provide it independently of flow-control algorithm. For instance, the Fore Runner ASX-200BX ATM Switch from FORE SYSTEMS is a per-VC queueing switch even though it does not support credit-based flow-control.

### 1.3 Paper Outline

This paper is arranged as follows: In Section 2, we describe our trace-gathering setup, simulator test-bed, and benchmarks. In Section 3, we use trace-driven simulations to explore NFS performance on a lossless network with various propagation delays. The TCP overhead due to slow-start is also shown. In Section 4, we simulate NFS over a loaded network with various cell drop rates, and with the EPRCA rate-based flow-control protocol. In Section 5, we show the performance advantages of per-VC queueing and credit-based flow-control for NFS performance. We conclude this paper in Section 6.

## 2. Experimental Test-Bed

In order to evaluate the performance of NFS without a wide-area ATM net dedicated to our experiments, we used a network simulator. This simulator is an event-driven ATM network simulator featuring rate-based EPRCA flow-control, credit-based FCVC flow-control, TCP, and AAL5 tail dropping mechanism with partial packet discard. The EPRCA implementation follows the latest ATM Forum Traffic Management specification of March 1996 [8]. The TCP stack in this simulator is taken from the source code of NetBSD 1.1.

Our NFS simulations are trace-driven; we do not model the applications that use NFS. We collected traces of real NFS traffic on a network which directly connects an NFS client and server. The traces contain the following data:

- Type
- Time of Request
- Time of Response
- Request Packet Size
- Response Packet Size

The simulator calculates the amount of time the client computes between requests and the amount of time the server takes to serve each request by assuming a propagation time of zero. The simulator preserves the computation times when it uses the trace, and varies only the amount of time it takes the network to forward requests and responses. The details of this procedure are:

- If a request is not a READ or a WRITE, only one outstanding request is allowed. When the reply arrives, the interval until the next request is sent will be the same as in the trace.

- The time between when a client issues a request and when it receives the response is composed of three parts. The first part is the time it takes the network to forward the request; the simulator calculates this based on propagation and queuing delay. The second part is the amount of time the server spends serving; this is taken from the trace. The third is the simulated time taken by the network to forward the response.
- Some READ transactions are actually read-ahead, for which the client does not wait. Similarly, some WRITE requests are actually write-behind, for which the client also does not wait. The simulator decides whether the client must wait for READs and WRITEs by analyzing their original Request and Response Times in the trace. If the difference between Request Times of consecutive READs or WRITEs is smaller than a threshold, or the Request Time of the next transaction is smaller than the Response Time of current transaction, the interpreter treats these transactions as read-ahead or write-behind. In this case, more than one outstanding request is allowed.

The client machine in these traces was a 133 mHz Pentium PC running NetBSD 1.0. The server was a 133 mHz DEC Alpha 3000/400 running OSF/1 3.0. Each traced benchmark was run after a reboot to prevent data being cached between runs. They are connected by a 10 Mbps Ethernet with no other competing traffic.

The main performance metric in these experiments is the task completion time (TCT) of a particular benchmark listed in Table 1. These tasks involve the Berkeley MPEG encoder "mpeg_encode-1.3" source code distribution. As detailed in Table 1, these traces include "ls -l" on the source directories, "cp -r" of the source directory before compiling, "make" inside the source directory which compiles an mpeg_encode executable file, and finally running the executable with 200 frames of non-compressed 360x240 video as input to produce a 1.2 MByte compressed mpeg file. All of these commands are run on the NetBSD client, with all files accessed using NFS to the server. For comparison, we also execute the encoder with the input raw frame data stored locally and output mpeg file remotely.

## 3. Effects of Propagation and TCP Overhead

Most NFS transactions are small independent requests, each of which must complete before the next can start. Thus as propagation time increases it will eventually dominate the task completion time. Before this point, the TCT is mainly affected by the underlying flow-control protocols, network congestion status, and processing time on the client and server.

**Table 1: Command Task List**

| Command | Description |
|---|---|
| | S:bytes sent by client, R:bytes sent by server, TC=transaction count, TCT=Task Completion Time of original trace in seconds |
| ls | ls -l * */* of 37 files in the mpeg_encode source directory |
| | S:54KB, R:62KB, TC=453, TCT=2.11 sec. |
| cp | cp -r of the mpeg encoder source tree, 0.95 MegaBytes |
| | S:1034K, R:1032K, TC=771, TCT=9.58 |
| cp-1 | copy single 1 megabyte file |
| | S:1122K R 1126K, TC=268, TCT=5.23sec |
| make | compile mpeg_encoder which reads 0.95 mb source and generate 0.3 mb output. |
| | S: 672K, R: 1196K, TC=2023, TCT=60sec. |
| encode-remote | read 23 mb frame data and generate 1.2mb mpeg file; input and output are remote. |
| | S:1680K, R:23M, TC=3519, TCT=66.59 sec |
| encode-local | same as encode remote except the 23 mb input is stored on client local disk |
| | S:1247K, R: 157K, TC=173, TCT=50.094sec |

In this section, we show simulation results for a lossless network with varying client-server distances. The network has link rates of 155 Mbps and carries no competing traffic. Figure 1 shows the TCT of several benchmarks that use NFS/UDP. Both X and Y axes are in log scale. When the network delay is small, the TCT is dominated by disk latency and processing time. However, once the network delay exceeds roughly 10 milliseconds, it is the major factor in TCT, and the TCT increases linearly with delay. We can see that the propagation delay dominates the TCT of ls earlier than the other benchmarks. This is because ls has only short requests and is not CPU bound. An RTT of less than 100ms appears to be the most tolerable, since beyond that even simple tasks such as ls take a minute or more.

One interesting detail of these results is that the TCT of encode-local increases relatively modestly with propagation delay. Encode-local only uses NFS to write output to a file, and produces data slowly enough that NFS write-behind can avoid blocking the process. NFS can keep up to five write requests outstanding at a time; since each completes in roughly one network round trip time, NFS write throughput is limited to five blocks per round trip time. encode-local starts to slow down when the round trip time is so high that this throughput drops below the rate at which encode-local produces output.

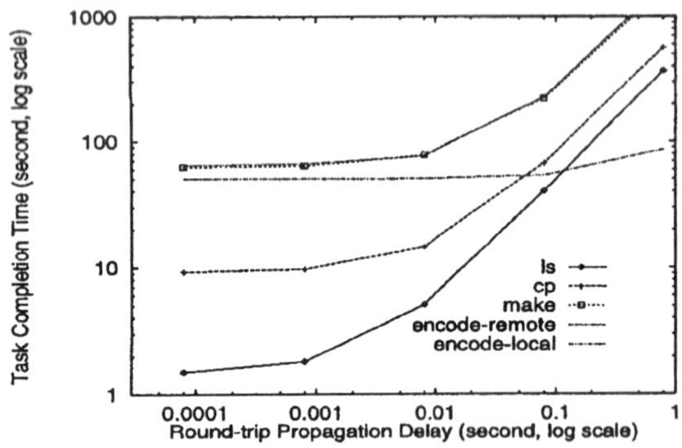


**Figure 1: Task Complete Time vs. Round-trip Propagation Delay for NFS/ UDP over Perfect Net**

NFS over TCP performs as well as NFS over UDP as long as the packet size (called MSS) is large, or 9192 bytes for these simulations. This packet size is typical for ATM networks. With packets of only 512 bytes, as are typically used over WANs, the TCTs of make and encode-local are around 15% and 30% larger with TCP than UDP respectively (see Figure 2). This degradation is due to TCP's slow-start ramp up time. If TCP is about to send something, but the connection has been idle for at least one round trip time, TCP first shrinks its congestion window. This decreases NFS write performance, since an 8192-byte NFS write will require many round trip times to send if the congestion window is only a few 512-byte packets. There is no similar effect for read requests because TCP does not consider the connection idle when the server sends the response: the client's request made the connection not idle. The congestion window does not affect requests other than read or write because all other requests can fit in the minimum size window. TCP with large packets always works well because even an 8192-byte write fits in a single packet.

A close reading of Figure 2 reveals that the TCT for encode-local over TCP actually decreases when the network delay increases. When the delay is small, the idle time between client requests is large relative to the round trip time; thus TCP often shrinks the client's congestion window. When the network delay is large, the client's relatively short inter-requests delays do not

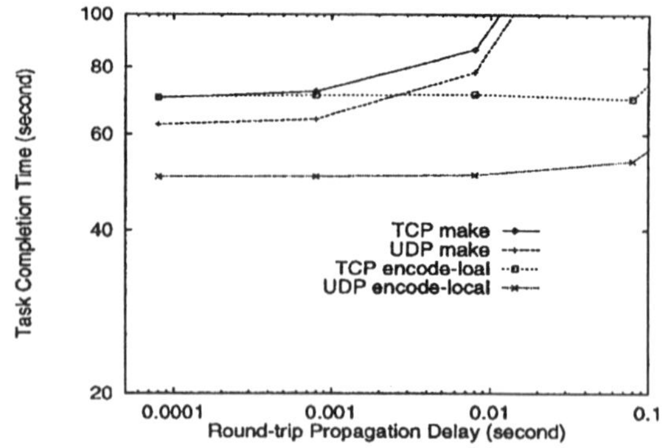


**Figure 2: Comparing of TCP and UDP on "make" and "encode-local"**

trigger TCP's idle behavior. Figure 3 compares the congestion windows of these two cases over time, for round-trip delays of 8 and 80 milliseconds. This phenomenon does not happen with encode-remote, which issues NFS requests much more often than encode-local because it reads input over NFS. These read requests prevent TCP from considering the connection idle.

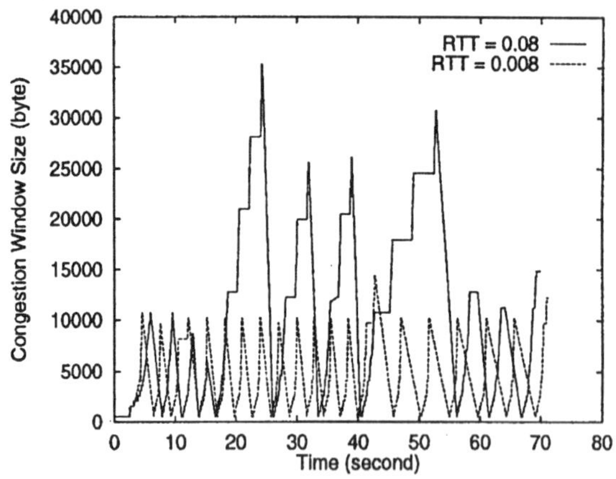


**Figure 3: Congestion Window Size for Two "encode-local" Cases with Different RTT**

## 4. Performance with Loaded Networks

Other work [4] has demonstrated that NFS/UDP performs badly over heavily loaded networks, and that NFS/TCP offers performance advantages. TCP recovers from packet loss faster than NFS/UDP, and can re-send just the lost packet rather than an entire request. TCP's adaptive congestion control window also allows it to use less switch or router buffer space than NFS/UDP, which decreases packet loss. These advantages hold primarily when all competing traffic uses TCP. If other traffic relies on ATM flow control, as is expected in future networks, TCP's advantages for NFS are less significant. This section reports simulation results for NFS with both ATM flow control and either TCP or UDP, as detailed in Table 2.

**Table 2: NFS Transport Protocols**

| Name | Description (MSS:Packet Size) |
|---|---|
| TCP-9192 | TCP with MSS = 9192 |
| TCP-512 | TCP with MSS = 512 |
| UDP | Raw AAL5 packet |

The simulations involve a heavily loaded network depicted in Figure 4. Each VC is flow-controlled by the rate-based EPRCA protocol. The parameters for EPRCA are adjusted to vary the network's cell drop rate. The bottleneck switch has 2500 to 3500 cells of buffering depending on the drop rate. The 50 competing connections, 25 in each direction, send data as fast as EPRCA will allow. The NFS connection uses either TCP with no NFS retransmission timers or UDP with standard 0.875 second based retransmission timer.

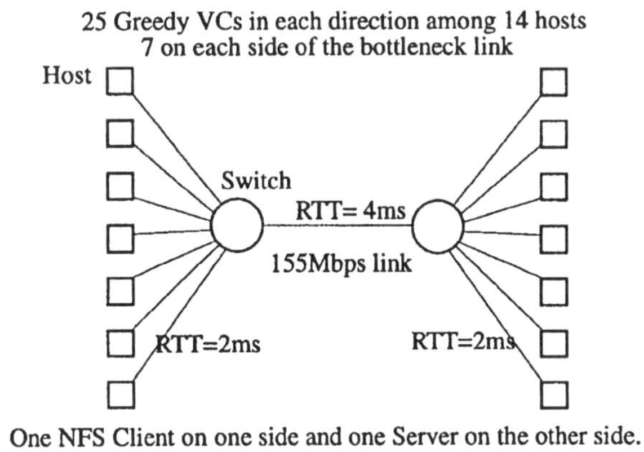


**Figure 4: Loaded ATM Network Configuration**

NFS over UDP and NFS over TCP with 9192-byte packets perform similarly in most cases. TCP-512 does not perform well when the drop rate is high and the amount of data to transfer is large. As seen in Figure 5 and Figure 6, TCP-512 performs slightly worse for "ls" and "make" than TCP-9192 and UDP. However, TCP-512 performs much worse than TCP-9192 and UDP in encode-remote and "cp-1" as seen in Figure 7 and Figure 8. This is because encode-remote transfers much more data than make. The cell loss causes the server's TCP congestion window to shrink often, which causes TCP-512 in particular to spend many round-trip times increasing the window again.

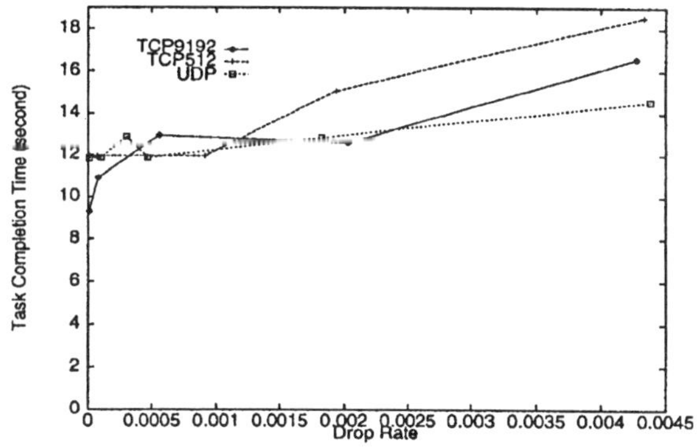


**Figure 5: Task Completion Time of "ls"**

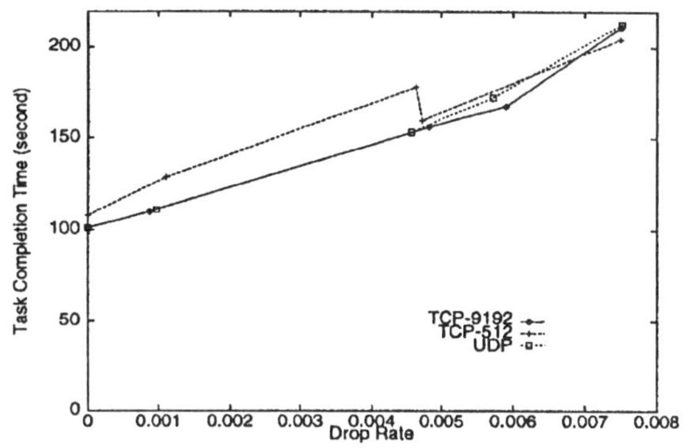


**Figure 6: Task Completion Time of "make"**

In these simulations, cell drop rate itself is not a configurable parameter. Instead, it is the measured result of a specific buffer size and EPRCA parameter set. That is why the drop rate index distance between each of the sample points in these graphs vary.

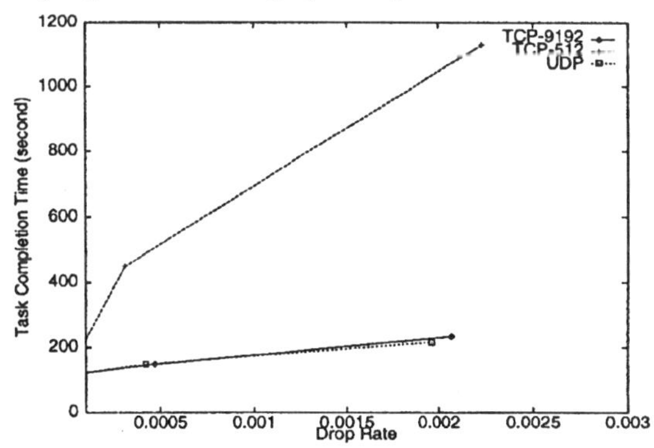


**Figure 7: Task Completion Time of "encode-remote"**

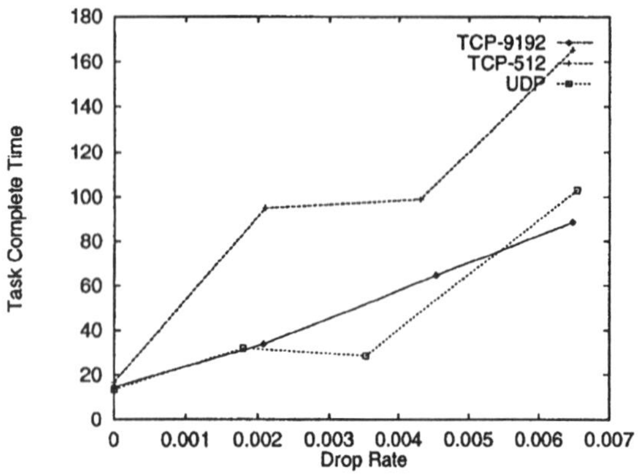


**Figure 8: Task Completion Time of "cp-1"**

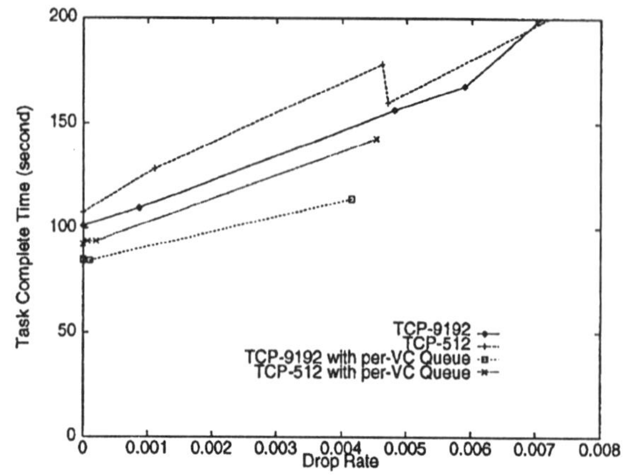


**Figure 9: Per-VC Queueing vs. Shared Queueing in "make"**

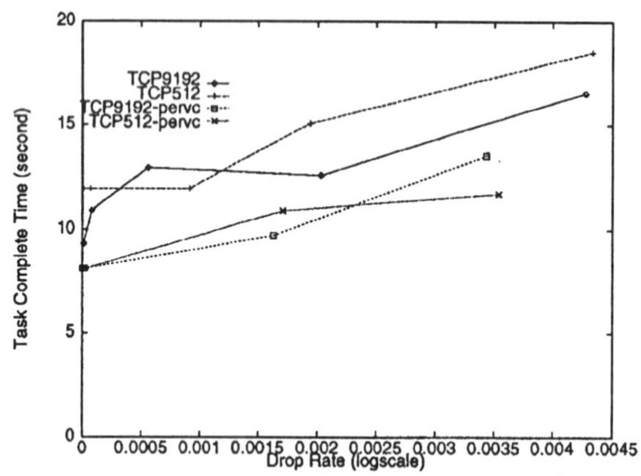


**Figure 10: Per-VC Queueing vs. Shared Queueing in "ls"**

## 5. Per-VC Queueing and Credit-Based Flow-Control

NFS, as a request-response protocol, is at a disadvantage when competing with "greedy" sources that always have data ready to send. Flow control mechanisms, while limiting the rate at which such sources send, typically allow them to keep fairly large amounts of data buffered in network switches. This leads to extra queuing delay. Senders that are limited only by flow control can maintain a high rate regardless of delay. Most NFS transactions, however, must slow down as queuing delay increases, since the client waits for each response before sending the next request. Even for READ and WRITE transactions, only 2 outstanding READ and 5 outstanding WRITE requests are allowed.

Switches that maintain separate queues for each connection (called per-VC queuing) and serve the queues fairly will decrease this effect. When an NFS request arrives at a switch, the NFS VC queue will be empty; thus the request will be sent relatively soon.

In the simulations discussed in the previous section, switch queue lengths varied from 0 to 3500 cells. At 155 megabits/second, this would impose a queuing delay of up to 10 milliseconds per NFS request. Figures 9 and 10 show the advantages of per-VC queuing for the "make" and "ls" benchmarks with EPRCA flow control.

Credit-based flow control performs better than rate-based for these traces for two reasons. First, credit flow control does not spend time ramping up its rate. Second, credit systems have round-robin scheduling among VCs. The simulation results of NFS over static FCVC with round trip propagation delay equal to 8 millisecond are listed in Table 3.

**Table 3: Performance Improvement in FCVC with RTT = 8 millisecond**

| Task | ls | cp | cp1 | make | encode -r |
|---|---|---|---|---|---|
| Perfect Net | 5.1437 | 14.701 | 11.681 | 78.21 | 76.73 |
| Static FCVC | 5.3016 | 17.239 | 12.144 | 80.392 | 96.729 |
| EPRCA Single FIFO with TCP-9192 and No Drop | 9.1898 | 23.97 | 13.612 | 101.07 | 114.80 |

## 6. Conclusions

The performance of typical NFS tasks starts to suffer significantly when client and server are separated by more than about 500 miles ($RTT \cong 10ms$). At that time a single "ls" command might take more than a minute to finish.

If ATM flow control is used to decrease packet loss, NFS over UDP performs as well as NFS over TCP when TCP uses large packets. With small packets, TCP spends an excessive amount of time with a congestion window smaller than an NFS request; this causes single requests to take many round trip times to transmit.

If ATM switches also implement per-VC queuing and round-robin scheduling, NFS can compete fairly with other traffic, further increasing performance. The combination of ATM flow control and per-VC queuing promise high performance for NFS over wide-area networks of reasonable size.

## References


[1] R. Sandberg, D. Goldberg, S. Kleiman, D. Walsh, and B. Lyon, "Design and Implementation of the Sun Network Filesystem", Proceedings Summer 1985 USENIX Conference, Portland OR, June 1985.

[2] "RPC: Remote Procedure Call Protocol Specification", RFC 1057, Internic, http://www.internic.net/rfc/rfc1057.txt, June 1988.

[3] "NFS: Network File System Protocol Specification", RFC 1094, SRI Network Information Center, Menlo Park, CA March 1989.

[4] Rick Macklem, "Lessons Learned Tuning the 4.3 BSD Reno Implementation of the NFS Protocol", Winter USENIX Conference, Dallas, TX, 1991.

[5] Bill Nowicki, "Transport Issues in the Network File System", Computer Communication Review, pg 16-20, March 1989.

[6] Rick Macklem, "The 4.4BSD NFS Implementation", Sun Microsystems Inc.

[7] ATM Forum ATM User-Network Interface Specification, Version 3.0, 1993.

[8] "Traffic Management Specification Version 4.0", ATM Forum Technical Committee, af-95-0013R11, March 1996.

[9] Van Jacobson, "Congestion Avoidance and Control", in Proceedings of SIGCOMM 1988.

[10] Charny, A., Clark, D.D., Jain R., "Congestion Control With Explicit Rate Indication", Proc. ICC95, June 1995.

[11] L. Roberts, "Enhanced PRCA (Proportional Rate Control Algorithm)", AF-TM 94-0735R1, August 1994.[

[12] Kung, H.T., R. Morris, "Credit -Based Flow Control for ATM Networks", IEEE Network Magazine, Vol. 9 No.2 March/April 1995.

[13] Kung, H.T. and K. Chang, "Receiver-Oriented Adaptive Buffer Allocation in Credit-Based Flow control for ATM Networks", Proceedings of INFOCOM 1995, April 2-6, 1995.

[14] Kung, H.T., T. Blackwell, A. Chapman, "Credit-Based Flow Control for ATM Networks: Credit Update Protocol, Adaptive Credit Allocation, and Statistical Multiplexing", Proceedings of ACM SIGCOMM '94.

[15] "Quantum Flow Control", Version 2.0, FCC-SPEC-95-1.

# Uplink and Downlink Capacity Analysis for Two-Tier CDMA Cellular Systems

**Jung-Shyr Wu , Ming-Tzong Sze and Jen-Kung Chung,**
**Department of Electrical Engineering**
**National Central University, 32054 Chung-Li, Taiwan, R.O.C.**
**Fax:+886-3-4255830**
**E-mail: jswu@wireless.ee.ncu.edu.tw**

**Abstract**

The combination of macrocell and microcell in a two-tier cellular system is attractive because it provides a balance between maximizing the number of users per unit area and minimizing the network control associated with handoff. In this paper, we study system capacity of a two-tier cellular architecture employing 3 TDMA/CDMA strategies. Both the uplink and downlink are evaluated via mathematical analysis. It shows that system performance degrades for larger macrocell or microcell and the capacities are poor for users near the macrocells' boundary. It also shows that huge discrepancy between the results obtained for the center cell versus those obtained for the boundary cell.

## 1. Introduction

The DS-CDMA cellular system is a good approach to provide more capacity than AMPS system that meets the increasing demand for mobile communication service[1-5].

On the other hand, microcells can provide more capacity than macrocells per unit area[6]. The combination of macrocell and microcell with a two-tier overlayed and underlayed cellular system will be popular in the near future, because this provides a balance between maximizing the number of users per unit area (which favors microcells) and minimizing the network control associated with handoff (which favors macrocells). However, the cochannel interference from microcell to macrocell and vice versa in a two-tier system is different from that in the homogeneous structure (i.e. consisting of only macrocells or only microcells). Moreover, system performance also depends on the access methods such as TDMA or CDMA. Thus, it is interesting to study the system performance for various TDMA/CDMA sharing strategies in a two-tier system.

I et al[7] studied the capacity issue for a two-tier cellular architecture with respect to 4 different accessing approaches (via CDMA and TDMA). However, they only consider the performance for the center microcell in a dedicated macrocell and only for the uplink performance. In this article, we extend I's results in two ways. First, we also analyze the system performance for any microcells and macrocells in terms of interference and capacity. Secondly, downlink capacity for users located at the boundary among microcells and macrocells is also discussed. It shows that the capacities are poor especially for users near the macrocell boundary because of the large amounts of cross-tier interference.

The paper is structured as follows. In Section 2, we describe the network model and assumptions. In Section 3, we analyze the capacities for uplink. In Section 4, we perform capacity analysis in downlink and in Section 5, we present the comparison data and draw our conclusion.

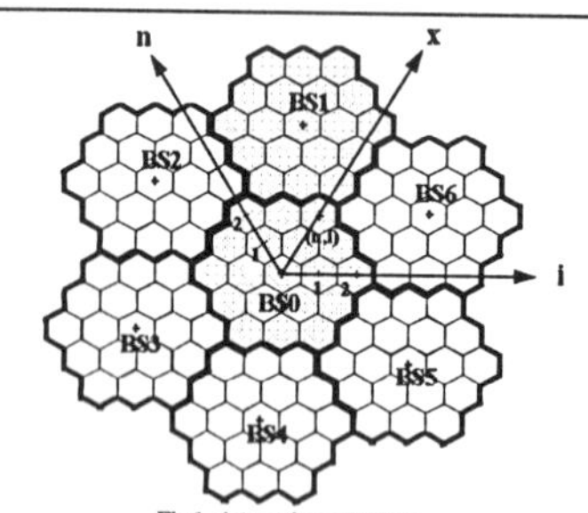


Fig.1 A two-tier structure

## 2. Network model and assumptions

A narrowband TDMA system has been accepted as a standard for the second-generation cellular system, such as GSM and DECT. As an alternative to the digital system based on TDMA method, a CDMA cellular system proposed by QUALCOMM has also become a standard as IS-95[8] recently. In a two-tiered system, performance study concerning with various CDMA/TDMA sharing strategy in macrocells and microcells is very interesting. In this article, we study the following three systems.

(1) System I : CDMA is used in macrocells and TDMA is used in microcells.
(2) System II : TDMA is used in macrocells and CDMA is used in microcells.
(3) System III : CDMA is used in both the macrocells and microcells.

In each system, the same spectrum is used for both CDMA and TDMA. Hence, user capacities are limited by cross-tier interferences. In Section 3, we shall study cochannel interference and capacity issues only for System I while similar analytic technique can be applied for studying System II and System III. Additional assumptions and conditions are described as follows.

A two-tier cellular configuration is illustrated in Fig.1, where a macrocell is the union of many equal microcells. The size of macrocell is also the same. Given a cell (macrocell or microcell), we refer to the cells immediately contiguous to it as ring-1 cells, those contiguous to the ring-1 cells as ring-2 cells, etc. Thus a $(n,i)_{th}$ microcell relative to a macrocell base station is referred to the *i-th* microcell belonging to the $n^{th}$ ring, where $i=1,2,\ldots,n$. The *(0,0)* microcell denotes the center microcell in a macrocell.

We assume that a TDMA radio channel bandwidth of *30*KHz with three time slots can have an equivalent channel bandwidth of 10KHz (i.e. $B_{ch}$=30KHz). The required carrier to interference power ratio, $(C/I)_{TDMA}$ in both the uplink and downlink is 18db. The frequency reusing factors in



0-8186-7780-5/97 $10.00 © 1997 IEEE

the macrocellular and microcellular tiers are 7.

For a CDMA system, the bit rate per user is 9.6 kbits/s. The spread-spectrum bandwidth is $W_{ss} = 1.25$ MHz and the chip rate is 1.288 MHz. The required $E_b/N_0$ for uplink and downlink are about 7db and 5db respectively for bit error rate less than 0.001. Since the processing gain is 21db, the threshold values of $(C/I)_{CDMA}$ is -14db for uplink and -16db for downlink, respectively.

The propagation model is similar to [7], where shadow fading is assumed to be negligible and propagation law exponents are 2 and 4 for shorter distances and longer distances, respectively. Thus,

$$P_r = \begin{cases} \left(\dfrac{\lambda}{4\pi}\right)^2 \dfrac{P_t}{d^2} & ; \quad d \le r = \dfrac{4\pi h_b h_m}{\lambda} \\ (h_b h_m)^2 \dfrac{P_t}{d^4} & ; \quad d > r \end{cases} \tag{1}$$

where $P_r$ and $P_t$ are received power and transmitted power, respectively; $\lambda$ is the wavelength, $h_b$ and $h_m$ are antenna heights of basestation and mobiles respectively, $d$ is the distance between base antenna and mobile antenna. Typical values being used are $\lambda = 0.33$ m (frequency = 900 MHz), $h_m = 1.5$ m, macrocell $h_b^M = 60$ m, and microcell $h_b^u = 9$ m. Thus, break points for macrocell and microcell are $r_o^M = 3426$ m and $r_o^u = 514$ m, respectively.

In the uplink, we assume ideal power control for CDMA and TDMA tiers. That is, CDMA basestation receives the same power from CDMA users (denoted as $P_C$). Similarly, TDMA basestation receives the same power from TDMA users (denoted as $P_T$).

## 3. Capacity analysis for uplink

In the following, we shall derive the uplink capacity for System I where macrocells use CDMA and microcells use TDMA. First, we evaluate the interference to a TDMA microcell.

### 3.1 TDMA microcells

In this subsection, we consider an arbitrary $(n,i)_{th}$ TDMA microcell in a CDMA macrocell, and calculate the interference to this microcell which mainly consisting of (1) the interference due to six adjacent CDMA macrocells, $I_{ct1}$. (2) interference due to CDMA users in the same macrocell, $I_{ct2}$, and (3) cochannel interference due to TDMA users, $I_{tt}$ from other microcells.

**Part I :** ***Calculation of $I_{ct1}$***

To calculate the interference due to CDMA users from six adjacent CDMA macrocells, we denote the macrocell base station $BS_j$, $j$=1~6, in the following analysis. Besides, we divide the users in two parts: inside break point $r = r_o^M$ and outside the break point for discussion.

**(A) For users located in $0 \le r \le r_o^M$**

Assume a perfect power control, the received power at the macrocell basestation would be the same for each mobile station (denoted as $P_C$). According to Fig.2, mobile emission power is

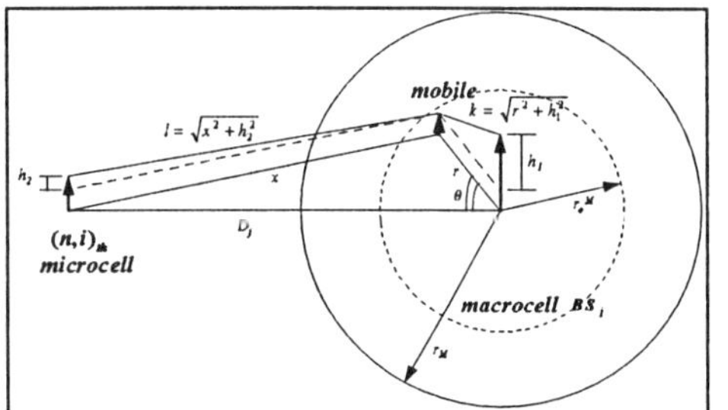


Fig.2 Calculation of $I_{ct1}$ (interference from adjacent macrocells to a microcell)

$$P_t = P_C \left(\frac{4\pi}{\lambda}\right)^2 k^2 \tag{2}$$

where $k = \sqrt{r^2 + h_1^2}$ and $h_1 = h_b^M - h_m$.

In eq(2), $k$ and $r$ denote the path length and mobile-to-macrocell base ground distance, respectively.

Thus, the power received by the $(n,i)_{th}$ microcell base station is

$$P_r = (h_b^u \cdot h_m)^2 \cdot \frac{P_t}{l^4} \tag{3}$$

where $l = \sqrt{x^2 + h_2^2}$, $x^2 = D_j^2 + r^2 - 2D_j r\cos\theta$, and $h_2 = h_b^u - h_m$.

In eq (3), $x$ is mobile-to-microcell base ground distance and $D_j$ is the distance between the $(n,i)_{th}$ microcell base and the macrocell base $BS_j$ which is derived in the Appendix.

We assume that $N_C$ mobiles are uniformly distributed in a circular macrocell of radius $r_M$ so the density of mobiles is $\rho = N_C/\pi r_M^2$.

If the microcell is rather distant from the macrocell, then the distance between macrocell base antenna and mobile's antenna is almost the same as the ground distance, i.e. $l \cong x$ shown in Fig.2. Thus, we can obtain a close-form solution for $I_{ct1}$ due to users located in $0 \le r \le r_o^M$. We denote this quantity as $P_{1j}$ where

$$P_{1j} = 2P_C \cdot N_C \left(\frac{4\pi h_b^u h_m}{\lambda r_M}\right)^2 \left[1 + \frac{D_j^4}{2\cdot(r_o^{M2} - D_j^2)^2} + \frac{3D_j^2}{2\cdot(r_o^{M2} - D_j^2)} + \tfrac{1}{2}\ln\left(\frac{D_j^2}{D_j^2 - r_o^{M2}}\right)\right] \tag{4}$$

Otherwise, $P_{1j}$ in eq (4) still can be calculated by performing numerical integration.

**(B) For users located in $r_o^M < r \le r_M$**

Similarly, the mobile emission power is

$$P_t = \frac{P_C \cdot k^4}{(h_b^M \cdot h_m)^2}$$

The interference due to CDMA macrocell users located in $r_o^M < r \le r_M$ is denoted as $P_{2j}$ and

$$P_{2j} = 2 \cdot \int_0^{\pi} \cdot \int_{r_o^M}^{r_M} P_r \cdot \rho \cdot r \cdot dr \cdot d\theta$$

$$= 2P_C \cdot N_C \cdot \left(\frac{h_b^u}{h_b^M \cdot r_u}\right)^2 \cdot \left[\frac{r_o^{M\,2}}{2} - \frac{r_M^{\;2}}{2} - \frac{D_j^6}{2\cdot(r_o^{M\,2} - D_j^2)^2}\right.$$

$$- \frac{5D_j^4}{2\cdot(r_o^{M\,2} - D_j^2)} + \frac{D_j^6}{2\cdot(r_M^{\;2} - D_j^2)^2} + \frac{5D_j^4}{2\cdot(r_M^{\;2} - D_j^2)}$$

$$\left. + 2D_j^2 \cdot \ln\left(\frac{D_j^2 - r_o^{M\,2}}{D_j^2 - r_M^{\;2}}\right)\right] \tag{5}$$

where $P_r$ is the same as in eq (3).

Thus, the total interference from six adjacent CDMA macrocells is

$$I_{ct1} = \sum_{j=1}^{6}(P_{1j} + P_{2j}) \times \frac{B_{ch}}{W_{SS}} \tag{6}$$

where $B_{ch}$ is equivalent bandwidth of each channel in the TDMA system and $W_{SS}$ is the spread-spectrum bandwidth in the CDMA system.

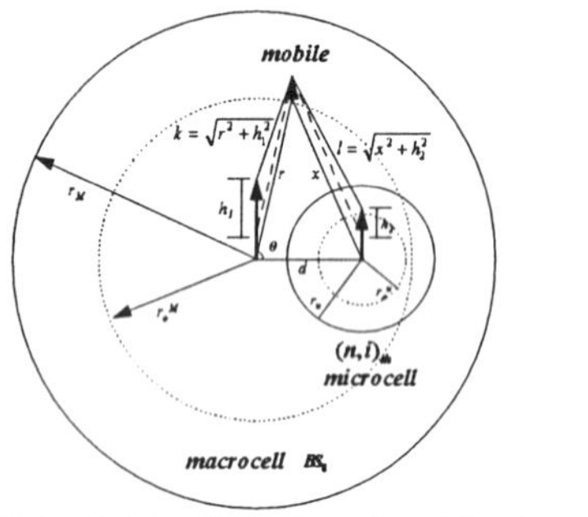


Fig.3 Calculation of $I_{ct2}$ (interference from a dedicated macrocell users to a microcell)

**Part II** : ***Calculation of*** $I_{ct2}$

The interference $I_{ct2}$ is due to CDMA users belonging to the dedicated macrocell where the microcell is embedded in, say $BS_0$. The calculation of $I_{ct2}$ depends on the location of a CDMA user (it may be located in the microcell or macrocell) and mobile's power.

**(A)** ***If a CDMA mobile is located in*** $0 \le r \le r_o^M$, its emission power is

$$P_t = P_C\left(\frac{4\pi}{\lambda}\right)^2 k^2$$

where $k = \sqrt{r^2 + h_1^2}$ is shown in Fig.3.

Then the power received by the $(n,i)_{th}$ microcell is

$$P_r = \begin{cases} \dfrac{(h_b^u \cdot h_m)^2 P_t}{l^4}, & if \quad r_o^u < l \le r_u \\[2ex] \dfrac{\left(\dfrac{\lambda}{4\pi}\right)^2 \cdot P_t}{l^2}, & if \quad 0 \le l \le r_o^u \end{cases} \tag{7}$$

where $l = \sqrt{x^2 + h_2^2}$, $x^2 = D_j^2 + r^2 - 2D_j \cdot r\cos\theta$, and $D_j$ can be obtained from eq (A-5) in the Appendix.

**(B)** ***If a CDMA mobile is located in*** $r_o^M < r \le r_M$ shown in Fig.3, its emission power is

$$P_t = \frac{P_C \cdot k^4}{(h_b^M \cdot h_m)^2}$$

and the power received by the $(n,i)_{th}$ microcell is

$$P_r = \begin{cases} \dfrac{(h_b^u \cdot h_m)^2 P_t}{l^4}, & if \quad r_o^u < l \le r_u \\[2ex] \dfrac{\left(\dfrac{\lambda}{4\pi}\right)^2 \cdot P_t}{l^2}, & if \quad 0 \le l \le r_o^u \end{cases} \tag{8}$$

where $l$ is the same as in eq (7).

Thus,

$$I_{ct2} = \left[2\int_0^{\pi}\int_0^{r_M} P_r \cdot \rho \cdot r \cdot dr \cdot d\theta\right] \times \frac{B_{ch}}{W_{SS}} \tag{9}$$

where $P_r$ is denoted in eq (7) and eq (8) for $0 \le r \le r_o^M$ and $r_o^M < r \le r_M$, respectively. There is no close-form expression for eq (9) so $I_{ct2}$ must be calculated by numerical integration.

**Part III :** ***Calculation of*** $I_{tt}$

Assume a perfect power control and the received power at the TDMA microcell basestation is $P_T$. In order to obtain the interference caused by other TDMA microcells, we follow a similar analysis as Lee[2] and get

$$I_{tt} = 6P_T\left(\frac{r_u}{D}\right)^4$$

and

$$\left(\frac{r_u}{D}\right)^4 = \frac{N_t^2}{9\left(\dfrac{W_{SS}}{B_{ch}}\right)^2}$$

where $N_t$ is the number of TDMA users in each microcell and $D$ is the cochannel distance. Thus,

$$I_{tt} = \frac{6P_T \cdot N_t^2}{9\left(\dfrac{W_{SS}}{B_{ch}}\right)^2} \tag{10}$$

In order to maintain the quality of communication, the uplink carrier-to-interference ratio must be greater than a threshold $(C/I)_{TDMA}$ (e.g. 18db for a TDMA system), so

$$\frac{P_T}{(I_{ct1} + I_{ct2}) + I_{tt}} \ge \left(\frac{C}{I}\right)_{TDMA} = 18db \tag{11}$$

For the sake of convenience, we let $I_{ct} \cdot P_C \cdot N_C \cdot (B_{ch}/W_{SS}) = I_{ct1} + I_{ct2}$, then eq (11) becomes

$$P_T \ge \frac{\left(\dfrac{C}{I}\right)_{TDMA} \times \dfrac{B_{ch}}{W_{SS}} \times I_{ct} \times P_C \times N_C}{1 - \left(\dfrac{C}{I}\right)_{TDMA} \times \dfrac{6N_t^2}{9\left(\dfrac{W_{SS}}{B_{ch}}\right)^2}} \tag{12}$$

### 3.2 CDMA macrocells

In this subsection, we consider the interference to a CDMA macrocell which consists of (1) the interference due to CDMA users in macrocells, $I_{cc}$, and (2) the interference from microcells, $I_{tc}$.

For the first part, according to [7], the interference caused by CDMA macrocell users is given by

$$I_{cc} = (1.5N_C - 1)P_C$$

To calculate $I_{tc}$, we consider 20 rings of microcells and the $n^{th}$ ring consists of $6n$

microcells. Based on the location of microcells, we can form three categories: (1) the microcell is located inside a radial distance of macrocell's break point. (2) the coverage of microcell intersects macrocell's break point and (3) the microcell is located outside macrocell's break point.

**Part I** : ***The microcell is located inside macrocell's break point, i.e.*** $\boldsymbol{d + r_u \le r_o^M}$.

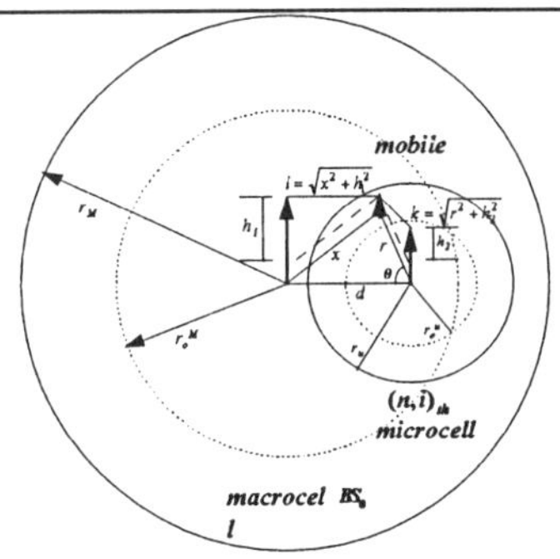


Fig.4 Calculation of $I_{tc}$

In this case, the emission power of a mobile in a microcell also depends on the microcell's breakpoint. Thus,

$$P_t = \begin{cases} \left(\dfrac{4\pi}{\lambda}\right)^2 P_T \cdot k^2; & if \quad 0 \le k \le r_o^u \\ \dfrac{P_T \cdot k^4}{(h_b^u \cdot h_m)^2} & ; \; if \quad r_o^u < k \le r_u \end{cases} \tag{13}$$

Because mobiles are located inside macrocell's breakpoint shown in Fig.4, the power received by macrocell basestation is

$$P_r = \left(\frac{\lambda}{4\pi}\right)^2 \frac{P_t}{l^2}$$

Hence, $P_r$ consists of two parts, i.e.

$$P_{r1} = P_T \frac{k^2}{l^2} \quad ; \; if \quad 0 \le l \le r_o^u$$

and

$$P_{r2} = P_T \left(\frac{\lambda}{4\pi \cdot h_b^u \cdot h_m}\right)^2 \frac{k^4}{l^2} \quad ; \; if \quad r_o^u < l \le r_u$$

Thus, the interference caused by the $(n,i)_{th}$ TDMA microcell is

$$I_{(n,i)} = 2\int_0^{\pi}\int_0^{r_o^u} P_{r1} \cdot \rho \cdot r \cdot dr \cdot d\theta + 2\int_0^{\pi}\int_{r_o^u}^{r_u} P_{r2} \cdot \rho \cdot r \cdot dr \cdot d\theta \tag{14}$$

where $\rho = N_t / \pi r_u^2$ is mobiles' density in a TDMA microcell.

**Part II** : ***The microcell's coverage intersects the macrocell's break point, i.e.*** $\boldsymbol{d + r_u > r_o^M}$ ***and*** $\boldsymbol{d - r_u < r_o^M}$.

The transmission power of a microcell's mobile is the same as in eq (13). However, the power received by the macrocell basestation depends on the location of microcell's mobiles.

*(i) If* $0 \le k \le r_o^u$, then mobile's emission power becomes

$$P_t = P_T \cdot \left(\frac{4\pi}{\lambda}\right)^2 \cdot k^2$$

and the power received by macrocell base station is

$$P_r = \begin{cases} P_T \cdot \dfrac{k^2}{l^2} & ; \; if \quad 0 \le l \le r_o^M \\ P_T \cdot \left(\dfrac{4\pi \cdot h_b^M \cdot h_m}{\lambda}\right)^2 \cdot \dfrac{k^2}{l^4}; & if \quad r_o^M < l \le r_M \end{cases} \tag{15}$$

*(ii) If* $r_o^u \le k \le r_u$, then mobile's emission power becomes

$$P_t = \frac{P_T \cdot k^4}{(h_b^u \cdot h_m)^2}$$

and the power received by macrocell basestation is

$$P_r = \begin{cases} P_T \cdot \left(\dfrac{\lambda}{4\pi \cdot h_b^u \cdot h_m}\right)^2 \cdot \dfrac{k^2}{l^2}; & if \quad 0 \le l \le r_o^M \\ P_T \cdot \left(\dfrac{h_b^M}{h_b^u}\right)^2 \cdot \dfrac{k^4}{l^4} & ; \; if \quad r_o^M < l \le r_M \end{cases} \tag{16}$$

Thus, the interference from the $(n,i)_{th}$ TDMA microcell is

$$I_{(n,i)} = 2 \cdot \int_0^{\pi}\int_0^{r_u} P_r \cdot \rho \cdot r \cdot dr \cdot d\theta$$

depending on $P_r$ in eq (15) or eq (16)

**Part III** : ***The microcell is located outside macrocell's break point, i.e.,*** $\boldsymbol{d - r_u \ge r_o^M}$.

The mobiles' emission power still follow eq (13). Because the microcell is located outside macrocell's break point, the power received by the CDMA macrocell base station is

$$P_r = (h_b^M \cdot h_m)^2 \frac{P_t}{l^4}$$

Hence, $P_r$ consists of two components, i.e.

$$P_{r1} = P_T \cdot \left(\frac{4\pi \cdot h_b^M \cdot h_m}{\lambda}\right)^2 \cdot \frac{k^2}{l^4} \quad ; \; if \quad 0 \le k \le r_o^u$$

and

$$P_{r2} = P_T \cdot \left(\frac{h_b^M}{h_b^u}\right)^2 \cdot \frac{k^4}{l^4} \quad ; \; if \quad r_o^u < k \le r_u$$

Again, the interference to the macrocell (due to the $(n,i)_{th}$ microcell) becomes

$$I_{(n,i)} = 2\int_0^{\pi}\int_0^{r_o^u} P_{r1} \cdot \rho \cdot r \cdot dr \cdot d\theta + 2\int_0^{\pi}\int_{r_o^u}^{r_u} P_{r2} \cdot \rho \cdot r \cdot dr \cdot d\theta$$

From the above discussions, the interference caused by the closest 20 rings of microcells is

$$I_{tc} = 6 \cdot \sum_{n,i} I_{(n,i)} + I_{(0,0)}, \quad n = 1,\cdots,20 \quad i = 1,\cdots,n$$

In order to maintain the quality of communication, the required average bit energy-to-noise density ratio must be greater than a threshold, $(E_b/N)_{CDMA}$. Thus,

$$\frac{\dfrac{P_C}{R}}{\dfrac{I_{cc}}{W_{SS}} + \dfrac{I_{tc}}{\left(W_{SS}/7\right)}} \ge \left(\frac{E_b}{N}\right)_{CDMA} \tag{17}$$

where $R$ is the data rate for a CDMA user and we assume frequency reusing factor in a TDMA system is 7.

We let $I_{tc'} = I_{tc}/(P_T \cdot N_t)$. Combining eq (12) and eq (17) and eliminating $P_T$, we can get the relation of uplink capacity in terms of macrocell users and microcell users as follows.

$$N_C\left\{\left(\frac{E_b}{N}\right)_{CDMA}\cdot\frac{1.5R}{W_{SS}}+\left(\frac{E_b}{N}\right)_{CDMA}\cdot\frac{7R}{W_{SS}}\cdot\left(\frac{C}{I}\right)_{TDMA}\cdot\frac{B_{ch}}{W_{SS}}\cdot I_{ct}\right.$$

$$\left.\cdot I_{tc'}\cdot\frac{N_t}{1-\left(\frac{C}{I}\right)_{TDMA}\cdot\frac{6N_t^2}{9(W_{SS}/B_{ch})^2}}\right\}\leq 1+\left(\frac{E_b}{N}\right)_{CDMA}\cdot\frac{R}{W_{SS}} \quad (18)$$

## 4. Capacity analysis for downlink

The downlink capacity for a microcell or a macrocell will get worse if multiple microcells or macrocells are neighbouring. The downlink power received by mobiles near a cell boundary is usually the weakest. The mobiles located at the cell boundary suffer the interference from adjacent microcells and macrocells and the dedicated microcell or macrocell. In the following analysis, we shall consider the downlink capacity for mobiles near the boundary for microcells and macrocells.

### 4.1 For TDMA microcells

For a microcell's mobile at the cell boundary, it suffers the interference mainly from (1) adjacent first ring 6 TDMA microcell base stations, $I_{tt}$ and (2) neighbouring 12 macrocell basestations, $I_{ct}$. Thus we obtain

$$I_{tt}=6(h_b^u\cdot h_m)^2\cdot\frac{P_T}{D^4}$$

and

$$I_{ct}=P_C\cdot N_C\cdot(h_b^M\cdot h_m)^2\cdot[3r_u^{-4}+3(2r_u)^{-4}+6(2.63r_u)^{-4}]\times\frac{B_{ch}}{W_{SS}}$$

$$=3.312\cdot P_C\cdot N_C\cdot(h_b^M\cdot h_m)^2\cdot\frac{B_{ch}}{W_{SS}}\cdot r_u^{-4}$$

For a microcell, the downlink $(C/I)$ must be greater than a threshold of $(C/I)_{TDMA}$ to satisfy the quality of service. Thus,

$$\frac{P_T\cdot r_u^{-4}\cdot(h_b^u\cdot h_m)^2}{I_{ct}+I_{tt}}\geq\left(\frac{C}{I}\right)_{TDMA}=18db \quad (19)$$

Substituting $I_{ct}$ and $I_{tt}$ into eq (19), we obtain

$$P_T\geq\frac{3.312\cdot N_C\cdot P_C\cdot\left(\frac{r_u}{r_M}\right)^4\cdot\frac{B_{ch}}{W_{SS}}\cdot h_b^{M2}\cdot\left(\frac{C}{I}\right)_{TDMA}}{h_b^{u2}\cdot\left[1-\frac{6\cdot N_t^2}{9\cdot\left(\frac{W_{SS}}{B_{ch}}\right)^2}\cdot\left(\frac{C}{I}\right)_{TDMA}\right]} \quad (20)$$

### 4.2 For CDMA macrocells

If a macrocell user is located at the cell boundary, it suffers the interference mainly from (1) 12 closest macrocell base stations (including its dedicated macrocell BS), $I_{cc}$, and (2) 12 closest microcell base stations, $I_{tc}$. Thus we obtain

$$I_{cc}=P_C\cdot(h_b^M\cdot h_m)^2\cdot[(N_C-1)\cdot r_M^{-4}+2N_C\cdot r_M^{-4}+3\cdot N_C(2r_M)^{-4}+6\cdot N_C(2.63r_u)^{-4}]$$

$$=(3.312N_C-1)\cdot P_C\cdot(h_b^M\cdot h_m)^2\cdot r_M^{-4}$$

and

$$I_{tc}=3.312N_t\cdot P_T\cdot(h_b^u\cdot h_m)^2\cdot r_u^{-4}$$

For a macrocell, the downlink $(C/I)$ has to be greater than a threshold of $(C/I)_{CDMA}$ in order to satisfy the quality of service, i.e. ,

$$P_C\cdot r_u^{-4}\cdot(h_b^u\cdot h_m)^2/[(h_b^M\cdot h_m)^2\cdot(3.312N_C-1)\cdot P_C\cdot r_M^{-4}+3.312\cdot 7\cdot N_t\cdot P_T\cdot(h_b^u\cdot h_m)^2\cdot r_u^{-4}]\geq\left(\frac{C}{I}\right)_{CDMA}=-16db \quad (21)$$

Combining eq (20) and eq (21), we can get the relation of downlink capacity in terms of macrocell users and microcell users as follows.

$$N_C\cdot\left\{3.312\cdot\left(\frac{C}{I}\right)_{CDMA}+(3.312)^2\cdot 7\cdot\left(\frac{B_{ch}}{W_{SS}}\right)\cdot\left(\frac{C}{I}\right)_{TDMA}\cdot\left(\frac{C}{I}\right)_{CDMA}\cdot N_t/\left[1-6\cdot\left(\frac{C}{I}\right)_{TDMA}\cdot\frac{N_t^2}{9\left(\frac{W_{SS}}{B_{ch}}\right)^2}\right]\right\}\leq 1+\left(C/I\right)_{CDMA} \quad (22)$$

## 5. Numerical results

In this subsection, we will discuss the relation between microcell capacity and macrocell capacity with respect to microcell's location and size. In addition to uplink performance, we also consider downlink performance for macrocell or microcell users at the boundary. Assume macrocell's radius is *6000m*, then microcell's radius is $r_u=6000m/(2n+1)$ if *n* rings of microcells are fully deployed in a macrocell.

In Table 1, we show the interference to $(n,i)_{th}$ microcell for System I (microcells use TDMA and macrocells use CDMA) where $I_{ct1}$ and $I_{ct2}$ denote the interference caused by ring-1 macrocells users and its dedicated macrocell users, respectively, and $I_{tc}$ denotes the interference to a dedicated macrocell caused by 20 rings of nearby TDMA microcells users. We observe that (1) $I_{ct2}$ is greater than $I_{ct1}$ for any microcell. (2) a microcell located far from the base station of its dedicated macrocell suffers more interference from its dedicated macrocell users and from adjacent macrocell users, and (3) if a microcell's radius is increased (i.e. the number of microcells in a ring is decreased), then a dedicated CDMA macrocell base station suffers more interference from TDMA microcell users because their emission power become stronger.

Fig 5 shows the permissible capacity region in terms of macrocell users and microcell users that System I can accommodate. Due to the effect of cochannel interference, microcell capacity is decreased if the number of macrocell users increases and vice versa. Besides, microcell's capacity gets worse if it is close to macrocell's boundary. Fig.6 and Fig.7 show similar results for 4 rings and 5 rings of microcells in a dedicated macrocell, respectively.

Fig.8 shows that the permissible capacity region of central microcell with respect to its size.

The smaller the microcell is, the more users it can accommodate. Alternatively, macrocell capacity is increased with the decreasing of microcell's radius if the number of microcell users is fixed. The reason is that macrocell base station suffers less interference from microcells if the latter's radius and emission power get smaller.

Fig.9 shows similar characteristics for the $(n,n)_{th}$ microcell. Because the microcell is near macrocell's boundary, its capacity will degrade especially if a microcell's area is getting bigger due to cross-tier interference.

Fig.10 shows the capacity region for System I, System II (macrocells use TDMA and microcells use CDMA method), and System III (macrocells and microcells use CDMA method). Although eq (18) shows the capacity relation for system I, the analysis can be easily extended for system II and System III. From Fig.10, System I and System II exhibit similar characteristics while system III performs the best because the required $(C/I)$ threshold for CDMA is -14db while that for TDMA is 18db. The system capacity degrades for microcells near the macrocell boundary shown in Fig.11. Also System III performs the best among the three systems.

Fig.12 shows the downlink capacity region for users located at macrocell's boundary. It demonstrates that system capacity degrades due to stronger cochannel interference caused by adjacent macrocells or microcells. In Fig.13, we compare the downlink capacities for three systems. Again it shows that system III performs the best due to smaller $(C/I)$ threshold for the CDMA system.

From the above discussions, we see that the uplink capacity for $(0,0)_{th}$ microcell (i.e. center microcell) is better than that of $(5,5)_{th}$ microcell by about 300 times due to smaller interference from macrocells if the microcell size is the same. This also means that I's results[7] overestimated the capacity per cell too much if only considering the center microcell's performance.

## 6. Conclusion

The capacity of a two-tier overlayed /underlayed cellular system were discussed in this paper. We extend the previous result not only for off-center microcells but also for downlink via mathematical analysis.

It showed that the capacities are poor especially for users near the macrocell's boundary because of large amounts of cross-tier interference. Besides, we compare the performance results for three systems. It showed that the system that both macrocells and microcells use CDMA accessing method exhibits the best performance in the uplink and in the downlink.

The results points out that cochannel interference between microcells and macrocells is much stronger and is difficult to perform power control. We thus conjecture that a better way is to assign different RF channels to different tier in order to avoid power control problem and excessive interference.

## Appendix. Calculation of the distance between $(n,i)_{th}$ microcell basestation and a adjacent macrocell base station, $D_j$

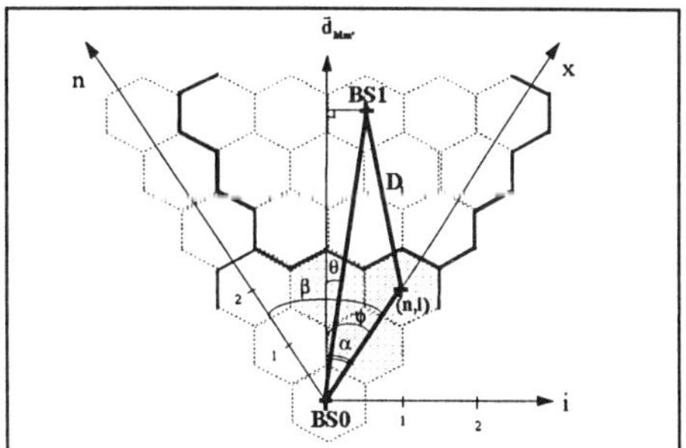


**Fig.A Calculation of the distance between a microcell base and a macrocell base**

In Fig. A, we consider a $(n,i)_{th}$ microcell in a dedicated macrocell with base station $BS_0$ and wish to find out the distance between the center of $(n,i)_{th}$ microcell and a adjacent macrocell base station $BS_1$. First, the distance between the $(n,i)_{th}$ microcell and $BS_0$, $d_{r_u,n,i}$, is given by [4]

$$d_{r_u,n,i} = 2 \cdot r_u \cdot \sqrt{n^2 + i^2} \qquad ; \quad i = 1,2,\cdots,n \qquad \text{(A-1)}$$

where $r_u$ is the radius of a microcell, and the distance between two adjacent macrocell base station is $2 \cdot R_M$. Hence, if we can determine the angle $\alpha$, then $D_1$ can be obtained.

From Fig.A, the angle $\theta$ is obtained by

$$\theta = \sin^{-1} \frac{r_u}{2R_M} \qquad ; \quad 0 < \theta \leq 30^\circ \qquad \text{(A-2)}$$

and the angle $\beta$ is determined by the following expression

$$\cos\beta = \frac{(2nr_u)^2 + d_{r_u,n,i}^{\;2} - (2ir_u)^2}{2(2nr_u) \cdot d_{r_u,n,i}} ; 0 < \beta \leq 60^\circ \qquad \text{(A-3)}$$

The relation between angle $\phi$ and angle $\beta$ is

$\phi = \beta - 30^\circ$

Thus, we obtain

$\alpha = \phi - \theta = \beta - 30^\circ - \theta$

Since the angle between the vectors $\overrightarrow{BS_0, BS_j}$ and $\overrightarrow{BS_0, BS_{j+1}}$, $j=1,\ldots,5$ , is $60^\circ$, we can determine the angle, $\gamma_j$, between the vectors $\overrightarrow{BS_0, BS_j}$ and $\overrightarrow{BS_0,(n,i)}$ as follows.

$$\gamma_j = \alpha + (j-1) \times 60^\circ \qquad ; \quad j = 1,2,\cdots,6 \qquad \text{(A-4)}$$

Finally, we obtain the distance between $(n,i)_{th}$ microcell base station and the base station of an adjacent macrocell,

$$D_j = \sqrt{(2r_M^2)^2 + d_{r_u,n,i}^{\;2} - 2(2r_M^2) \cdot d_{r_u,n,i} \cdot \cos r_j}$$
$$for \quad j = 1,2,\ldots,6 \qquad \text{(A-5)}$$

**Table. 1**

**Uplink Cochannel Interference for System I**

| 5 rings of microcells | | | | | | |
|---|---|---|---|---|---|---|
| | (0,0) | (1,1) | (2,2) | (3,3) | (4,4) | (5,5) |
| $I_{ct1}$ | 6.393E-3 | 6.987E-3 | 8.957E-3 | 1.385E-2 | 2.627E-2 | 6.310E-2 |
| $I_{ct2}$ | 4.312E-2 | 7.685E-2 | 1.809E-1 | 6.735E-1 | 8.720 | 20.644 |
| $I_u = 2.854$ | | | | | | |
| **4 rings of microcells** | | | | | | |
| | (0,0) | (1,1) | (2,2) | (3,3) | (4,4) | |
| $I_{ct1}$ | 6.393E-3 | 7.272E-3 | 1.061E-2 | 2.077E-2 | 5.739E-2 | |
| $I_{ct2}$ | 4.312E-2 | 9.361E-2 | 2.552E-1 | 6.180 | 19.053 | |
| $I_u = 3.328$ | | | | | | |
| **3 rings of microcells** | | | | | | |
| | (0,0) | (1,1) | (2,2) | (3,3) | | |
| $I_{ct1}$ | 6.393E-3 | 7.881E-3 | 1.505E-2 | 4.985E-2 | | |
| $I_{ct2}$ | 4.312E-2 | 1.272E-1 | 2.135 | 16.669 | | |
| $I_u = 4.377$ | | | | | | |

## References


[1] K.S. Gilhousen, I.M. Jacobs, R. Padovani, A.J. Viterbi, L.A. Weaver, and C.E. Wheatley, "On the Capacity of a Cellular CDMA Systems," IEEE Trans. Veh. Technol., vol. VT-40, pp. 303-312, May 1991.

[2] W.C.Y. Lee, "Overview of Cellular CDMA," IEEE Trans. Veh. Technol., vol. VT-40, pp. 291-302, May 1991.

[3] P. Jung, P.W. Baier and A. Steil, "Advantages of CDMA and Spread Spectrum Techniques over FDMA and TDMA in Cellular Mobile Radio Application," IEEE Trans. Veh. Technol., vol. VT-42, pp. 357-364, Aug. 1993.

[4] K. Kim, "CDMA cellular engineering issues," IEEE Trans. Veh. Technol., vol. 42, no. 3, pp. 345-350, Aug. 1993.

[5] Alfred Baier, Uwe-Carsten Fiebig, "Design Study for a CDMA-Based Third-Generation Mobile Radio system," IEEE Journal on Selected Area in Communications, Vol. 12, pp. 733-743, May 1994.

[6] J. Shapira, "Microcell Engineering in CDMA Cellular Networks," IEEE Trans. Veh. Technol., vol. 43, pp. 817-825, Nov. 1994.

[7] C-L. I *et al.* , "A Microcell/Macrocell Cellular Architecture for Low- and High-Mobility Wireless Users," IEEE Journal on Selected Area in Communications, vol. 11, no. 6, pp. 885-891, Aug. 1993.

[8] THE CDMA NETWORK ENGINEERING HANDBOOK, March 1991, Qualcomm.


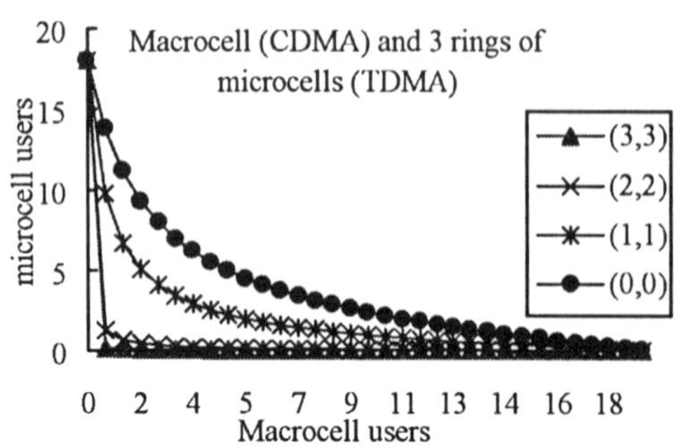


**Fig.5 Capacity region with 3 rings of microcells**

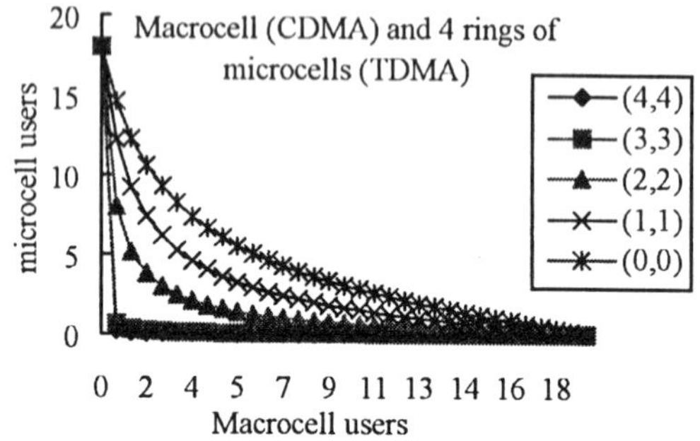


**Fig.6 Capacities with 4 rings of microcells**

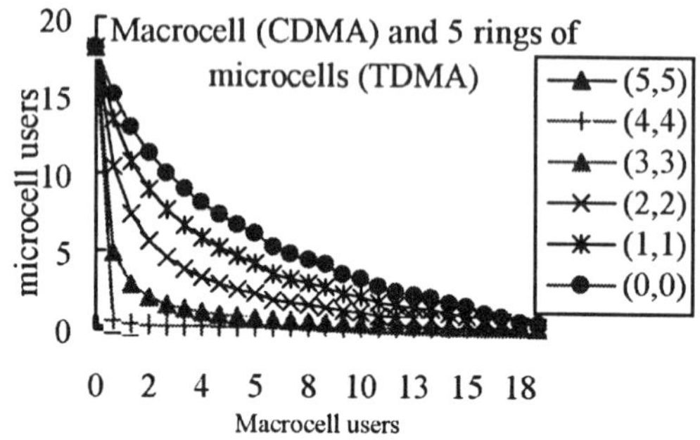


**Fig.7 Capacities with 5 rings of microcells**

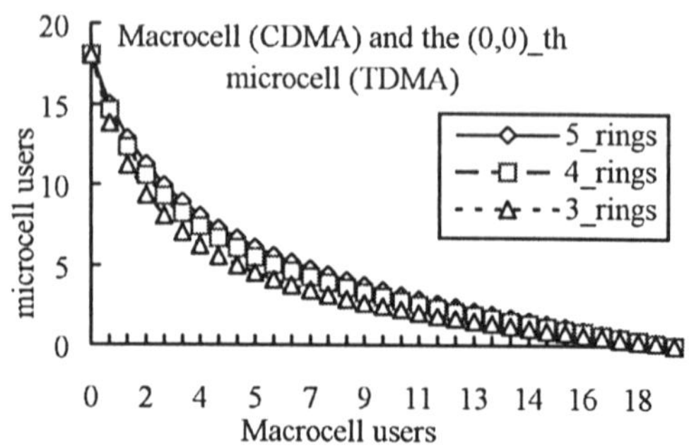


**Fig.8 Capacities in the $(0,0)_{th}$ microcells**

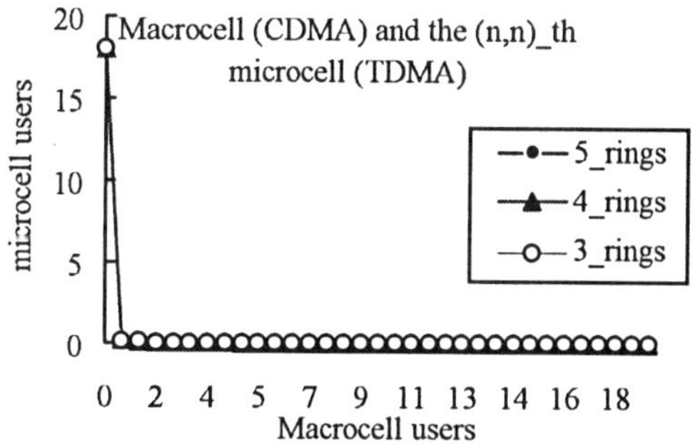


**Fig.9 Capacities in the (n,n)$_{th}$ microcells (n=3,4,5)**

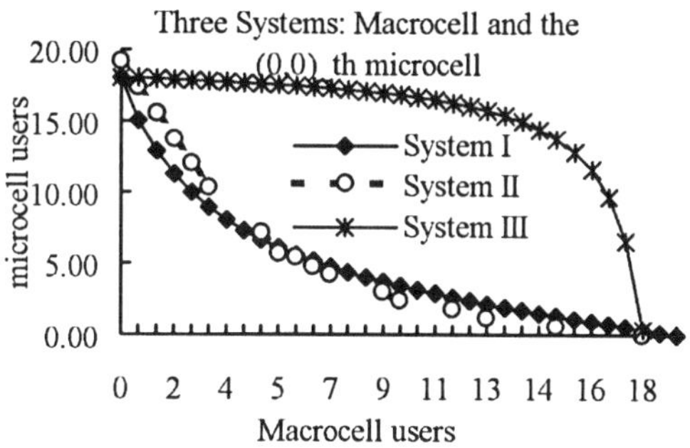


**Fig.10 Performance Comparision of three Systems (for the (0,0)$_{th}$ microcell)**

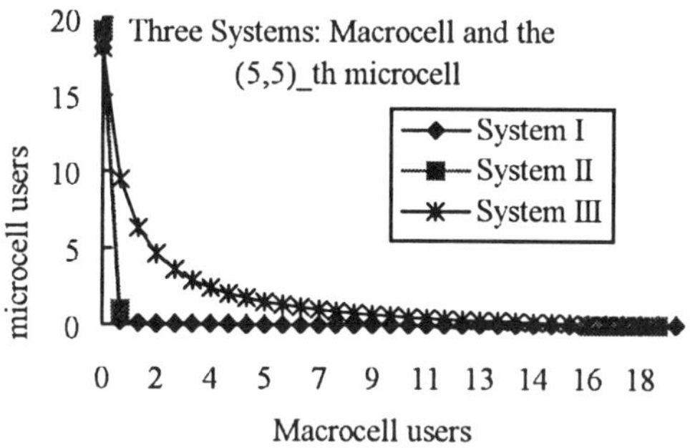


**Fig.11 Performance Comparision of three Systems (for the (5,5)$_{th}$ microcell)**

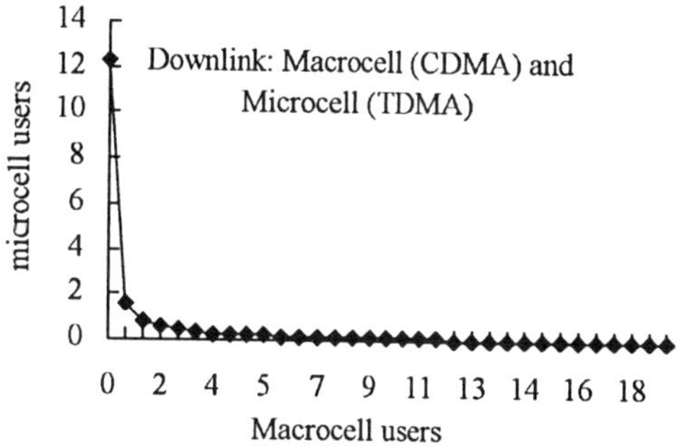


**Fig.12 Downlink capacity**

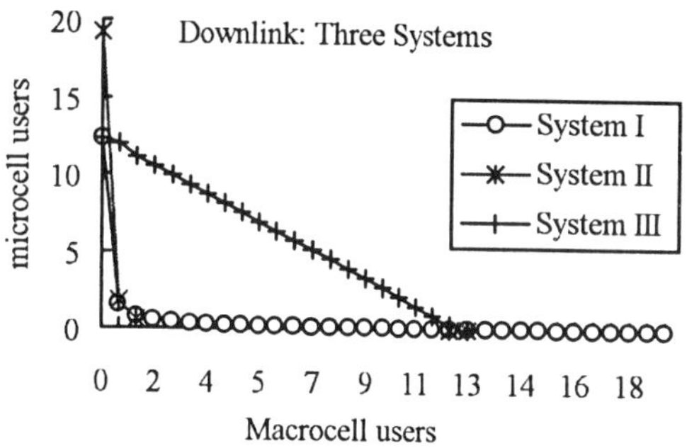


**Fig.13 Downlink capacities of three Systems**

# Power Control and Time Division: The CDMA versus TDMA Question

John M. Rulnick
Dept. of Electrical and Computer Eng.
WPI, Worcester, MA 01609
rulnick@ece.wpi.edu

Nicholas Bambos
Dept. of Eng. Econ. Syst. and Oper. Res.
Stanford U., Stanford, CA 94305
bambos@leland.stanford.edu

**Abstract**

*For wireless networks, time division multiple access (TDMA) offers certain well-known advantages over methods such as spread spectrum code division (CDMA). Foremost among them is the guarantee that other users will not interfere during a node's dedicated time slots. For this desirable isolation, the cost is synchronization. Viewing arbitrary time intervals as potential TDMA time slots, we ask whether it is possible to obtain some of the benefit of time division without incurring the synchronization cost. In particular, we address the question of whether a TDMA-like state can be induced on asynchronous channels in such a way as to reduce interference and energy consumption. Through analysis and simulation we find conditions under which it is desirable to use time division. We then show how autonomous power management may be used as a mechanism to induce a form of time division. In this context a backlog-sensitive power management system is presented.*

Keywords: CDMA, cellular network, code division, mobile, multiple access, power control, power management, TDMA, time division, wireless network.

## 1 Introduction

Considerable recent research attention and standards activity have focused on the question of whether code or time division is best for wireless networks [2, 4, 14]. In fact, the lack of standardization on either code or time division has been identified as "the biggest hurdle for the wireless revolution" [10]. Two operational factors in the competition are interference management and energy consumption. Examples included below show that for some parameters code division yields preferred operating modes, while for others time division is better. While this may not be particularly surprising, it is interesting for the question it raises: Can a single network effectively switch itself between modes in some way so as to take advantage of the preferred multiple access method? Better still, can this switching be achieved without the intervention (and added complexity and cost) of a central controller?

Our goal is to begin addressing these questions, and our main tool will be transmitter power control [1, 3, 5–8, 11–13, 18–21]. In section 2 we briefly explain the conventional, constant-SIR method of power control (CSPC), and show by a simple example how an alternative method can lead to substantial reduction in total transmitter power. Then in section 3 we examine a fundamental stability criterion (achievability) in the context of CSPC and our alternative, which we associate with time division multiple access (TDMA), and discuss how to detect which mode is preferred when target throughputs are achievable either way. Next, in sections 4 and 5, we review interference-based power *management*, introduce a form of backlog-sensitive power management, and show how the two can be integrated. The aim is to show that it is possible to achieve some of the benefits of TDMA in a code division multiple access (CDMA) or other non-TDMA system, through the use of power management. In section 6 we discuss simulation results which show the progress and shortcomings of the proposed system. Some concluding remarks are included in section 7.

## 2 Power-Controlled Wireless Networks

Consider a network with $N$ mobile transmitters, each communicating with another node or nodes over wireless channels, with the channels separated by codes, space, and/or frequency. For $i$ and $j$ in $\{1, \dots, N\}$ let $g_{i,j}$ represent the interfering-link gain from transmitter $j$ to $i$'s receiver when $j \neq i$, and the intended-link gain (including path loss and signal processing gain) between $i$ and $i$'s receiver when $j = i$, so a signal transmitted by $j$ with power $p_j$ is received by $i$'s receiver with power $g_{i,j}p_j$. Define the $N \times N$ gain matrix $G = [g_{i,j}]$. In addition, denote by $\xi_i$ the noise power at $i$'s receiver, and by $\mathcal{P}_i$ the set of admissible power functions for transmitter $i$.

Given such a network and some power control objective, we call the objective *achievable* iff it is satisfied for a set of power functions $\{p_i \in \mathcal{P}_i : i = 1, \dots, N\}$. For instance, the objective may be to attain a set of $N$ specified signal to interference ratios (SIRs) $\gamma_i$, one for each transmitter/receiver pair. If also each $\mathcal{P}_i$ is the set of nonnega-



0-8186-7780-5/97 $10.00 © 1997 IEEE

tive real-valued constant functions, we have a constant-SIR power-controlled (CSPC) system. Then in vector/matrix notation (abbreviating subscripts "$i$, $j$" to "$ij$") we desire a solution to the equation

$$p = \hat{Z}p + \hat{\xi}, \tag{1}$$

where

$$\hat{Z} = \hat{G} - \text{diag}(\gamma), \quad \hat{G}_{ij} = \frac{\gamma_i g_{ij}}{g_{ii}}, \quad \hat{\xi}_i = \frac{\gamma_i \xi_i}{g_{ii}}.$$

The objective SIR vector $(\gamma_1, \ldots, \gamma_N)$ is achievable iff the determinant $|I - \hat{Z}|$ is positive, in which case the solution is given by [5]

$$p = (I - \hat{Z})^{-1}\hat{\xi}. \tag{2}$$

For instance, the solution exists for $N = 2$ iff

$$\gamma_1\gamma_2 \frac{g_{12}g_{21}}{g_{11}g_{22}} < 1. \tag{3}$$

When we can confirm that a network objective is achievable, our attention turns to whether there exists an algorithm to realize the desired state, over time, starting from a given initial condition. In particular, we are interested in algorithms for selecting transmitter powers $p_i^{n+1}$ at times $n = 0, 1, \ldots,$ and starting from $p_i^0$. Let us say that a network, together with an algorithm (or collection of algorithms), is *power-stable* iff the algorithm generates a sequence of admissible power vectors $\{p^n : p_i^n \in \mathcal{P}_i^n, n = 1, 2, \ldots\}$ such that for all $i$,

$$p_i^n \to p_i \in \mathcal{P}_i, \quad n \to \infty,$$

and such that the objective is satisfied for the limiting powers $\{p_i\}$. For example, let us write $\gamma_i^n$ for the SIR at time $n$ on channel $i$; then Foschini and Miljanic [5] have shown that whenever a CSPC system (as described above) with constant noise power vector $\xi$ has an achievable vector $\gamma$, the network/algorithm

$$p_i^{n+1} = \frac{\gamma_i}{\gamma_i^n} p_i^n$$

is power-stable; that is, the power vector converges to a value which yields the target SIR vector $\gamma$.

For the remainder of this section let us focus on the case $N = 2$. If the $i$th channel's receiver noise is $\xi_i^n$ at time $n$ then the SIR on channel $i$ is

$$\gamma_i^n = \frac{g_{ii} p_i^n}{g_{ij} p_j^n + \xi_i^n}.$$

Given the error rate as a function of SIR, we can calculate the successful data transmission rate as a function of these parameters. Assume, for instance, that the error rate at SIR $\gamma$ is

$$e = \frac{1}{1+\gamma}. \tag{4}$$

While power control performance may be sensitive to the form of $e$, equation (4) represents a reasonable upper bound on the bit error rate (BER) relative to BERs obtained with many conventional modulation schemes (see [15]). In order to transmit at respective rates (or throughputs) $r_1$, $r_2$, the transmitter powers would have to be sufficient to attain receiver SIRs of $\gamma_1 = r_1/(1 - r_1)$ and $\gamma_2 = r_2/(1 - r_2)$, respectively. Solving for $p_1$ and $p_2$ simultaneously in terms of rates and gains we obtain

$$p_1 = \frac{r_1(g_{12}r_2\xi_2 + g_{22}(1 - r_2)\xi_1)}{(g_{11}g_{22} - g_{12}g_{21})r_1r_2 + g_{11}g_{22}(1 - r_1 - r_2)} \tag{5}$$

and

$$p_2 = \frac{r_2(g_{21}r_1\xi_1 + g_{11}(1 - r_1)\xi_2)}{(g_{11}g_{22} - g_{12}g_{21})r_1r_2 + g_{11}g_{22}(1 - r_1 - r_2)}, \tag{6}$$

as long as the rates $r_i$ are achievable, i.e.,

$$\frac{r_1}{1 - r_1}\frac{r_2}{1 - r_2}\frac{g_{12}g_{21}}{g_{11}g_{22}} < 1.$$

Using this constant-SIR transmission scheme, the total energy used to obtain rates $r_1$ and $r_2$ over a unit time interval is therefore

$$\mathcal{E} = \frac{r_1\xi_1(g_{21}r_2 + g_{22}(1 - r_2)) + r_2\xi_2(g_{11}(1 - r_1) + g_{12}r_1)}{(g_{11}g_{22} - g_{12}g_{21})r_1r_2 + g_{11}g_{22}(1 - r_1 - r_2)}.$$

The immediate question is: Can the same rates be obtained using less energy?

Certainly the answer is "no" under CSPC; the solution to (1) is unique for non-zero receiver noise powers. However, it is possible, given certain values of the gain matrix $G$ and rates $r_i$, to save energy by switching to a time-division-like access protocol.

**Example 1.** Consider the following parameters, which might represent reasonable values in a cellular code division multiple access (CDMA) system: $r_1 = r_2 = 1/3$, $g_{11} = g_{21} = 1$, $g_{22} = g_{12} = 1/16$, $\xi_1 = \xi_2 = 1$. The values obtained using (5) and (6) are

$$p_1 = 1 \quad \text{and} \quad p_2 = 16.$$

If the time period of interest is the unit interval, then the transmitters will use 1 and 16 units of energy, respectively, for a total of $\mathcal{E} = 17$, the total area under the constant-power curves of figure 1

On the other hand, if the two transmitters were permitted *piecewise* constant power control functions, and used

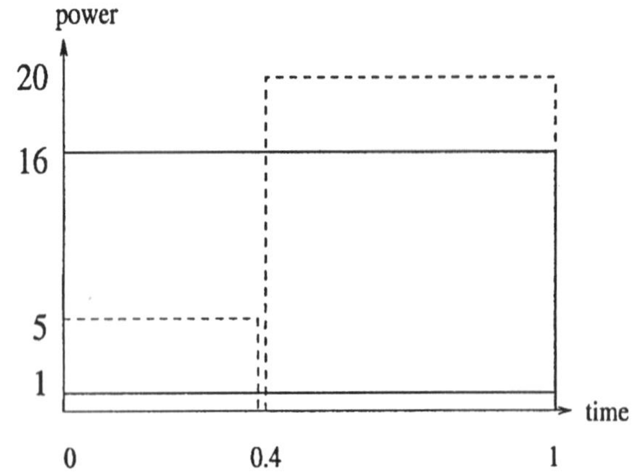


**Figure 1: Power levels for two transmitters under the CSPC (solid) and time division (dashed) systems.**

distinct time segments—only transmitter one during $(0, \tau]$, only transmitter two during $(\tau, 1]$—then it would be possible to lower the total energy used. For instance, if $\tau = 2/5$ then

$$p_1(t) = \begin{cases} 5, & t \in (0, 2/5], \\ 0, & t \in (2/5, 1], \end{cases}$$

and

$$p_2(t) = \begin{cases} 0, & t \in (0, 2/5], \\ 20, & t \in (2/5, 1], \end{cases}$$

would also yield rates $r_1 = r_2 = 1/3$ but would consume only $\mathcal{E} = 14$ units of energy, versus 17 under CSPC. The above situation might be called *ad hoc* TDMA. We use the term "induced TDMA" (iTDMA) for power control algorithms which bring on the this effect.

In the preceding example there is a nearly twenty percent reduction in energy usage under the induced TDMA. Moreover, the lower total transmitter power means lower interference to other users, and hence potential benefits like improved network throughput and stability. What are the drawbacks? First, one of the transmitters is called on to *increase* its energy consumption from 1 to 2 in switching to the more globally efficient time division scheme; this is likely to be unsatisfactory if the user is not eventually compensated. Second, the asynchronous static scheme is replaced by a synchronized system wherein each transmitter must know when to turn on and off, meaning increased system complexity.

While the first drawback is inherent to the protocol, the second can be at least partially avoided. In fact, it may be possible to reap much of the benefit usually associated with TDMA without using central control or synchronization to force users into time slots. The idea is to have sufficient incentive for the users to automatically detect conditions favorable to a TDMA structure and implement them *without* the intervention of a base station or other mediator. One such incentive may be provided by power management, to which we will turn shortly.

Example 1 illustrates the potential benefits of inducing time division. The next question is: When is it the right thing to do?

## 3 When Is TDMA Better Than CDMA?

In example 1 we used transmission rates rather than SIRs as our performance objective. While the two are usually related in a one-to-one manner (rates are usually increasing functions of SIR), focusing on the rate and letting the SIR vary over the interval of interest allowed us to consider non-static solutions. This, in turn, makes iTDMA power control systems possible. Hence the question of interest becomes: When, in general, is it better to use iTDMA than CSPC? In terms of access protocols, this is essentially the same as asking: When is TDMA better than CDMA?[1]

For an iTDMA system, one easily finds that the rates $\{r_i\}$ are achievable iff

$$\sum_{i=1}^{N} \frac{r_i}{1 - e_i(p_i)} < 1,$$

where $e_i$ is the error rate for channel $i$ during $i$'s slot, i.e., the portion of time that transmitter $i$ is alone using non-zero power. If we assume (as we have so far) that the admissible power functions are unbounded above then $e_i$ can be made arbitrarily close to 0 and the achievability condition becomes the intuitively satisfying expression

$$\sum_{i=1}^{N} r_i < 1.$$

Before we turn to the general CSPC achievability condition, let us look at a special case which will set the stage.

**Example 2.** Let us again restrict our scope to the case $N = 2$. From the above we know the rates $r_1$ and $r_2$ are achievable under iTDMA iff

$$r_1 + r_2 < 1. \tag{7}$$

Now consider the CSPC system. If we let $e_i = e$ as given in (4) then the achievability condition is (3); writing it to facilitate comparison with iTDMA,

$$\frac{r_1 r_2}{1 - (r_1 + r_2) + r_1 r_2} < \frac{g_{11} g_{22}}{g_{12} g_{21}}. \tag{8}$$

[1]More generally, when is a time division system better than a non-time-division system? We mean "better" in the sense of power and interference control, not other important factors such as complexity, resistance to multipath fading, etc. Also, real systems almost always include some implicit use of frequency division (FDMA), so CDMA is really CDMA/FDMA, etc. To be precise we might say we are comparing CDMA/FDMA with CDMA/FDMA/TDMA.

Now it is a consequence of physical conditions existing in typical systems that, for all $i = 1, \ldots, N$, either

$$g_{ii} \geq g_{ji} \text{ for all } j \neq i \quad \text{or} \quad g_{ii} \geq g_{ij} \text{ for all } j \neq i. \quad (9)$$

Indeed, in a code-separated system (such as under CDMA) one would expect the first condition to hold, while in a frequency- and/or space-separated system one would expect the second. Hence we take the liberty of assuming

$$\frac{g_{11}g_{22}}{g_{12}g_{21}} \geq 1. \quad (10)$$

It follows easily from (10) and conditions (7) and (8) that if the rates $(r_1, r_2)$ are achievable under iTDMA, then they are achievable under the CSPC. The converse is not true (consider $r_1 + r_2 \geq 1$ with $g_{12}$ and $g_{21}$ sufficiently small).

We can follow reasoning from example 2 to the proposition below. Let $\gamma_i(r)$ be the SIR necessary to achieve rate $r$ on channel $i$.

**Proposition 1.** *The rate vector $(r_1, \ldots, r_N)$ is achievable under iTDMA iff*

$$\sum_{i=1}^{N} r_i < 1.$$

*Under the assumption (9), the same rate vector is achievable under CSPC if $|\Gamma| > 0$, where $\Gamma$ equals*

$$\begin{bmatrix} 1 & -\gamma_1(r_1) & -\gamma_1(r_1) & \cdots & -\gamma_1(r_1) \\ -\gamma_2(r_2) & 1 & -\gamma_2(r_2) & \cdots & -\gamma_2(r_2) \\ \cdots & \cdots & \cdots & \cdots & \cdots \\ -\gamma_N(r_N) & \cdots & -\gamma_N(r_N) & -\gamma_N(r_N) & 1 \end{bmatrix}.$$

*Proof.* The first (iTDMA) statement is immediate. Now for the CSPC system, recall from section 2 that $|I - \hat{Z}| > 0$ is necessary and sufficient for achievability of the SIR vector $\gamma$. One can easily verify that under assumption (9), $|I - \hat{Z}| \geq |\Gamma|$. It follows that $|\Gamma| > 0$ is sufficient for the vector of SIRs $(\gamma_1(r_1), \ldots, \gamma_N(r_N))$ to be achievable. □

In situations where the objective is achievable under both iTDMA and CSPC, it is worth exploring which system will operate at lower total power. The first step is to find out how to optimally divide the interval among the users. If the optimal solution yields a total energy greater than that used under CSPC, there is no reason to continue with the iTDMA approach.

Assuming the rates $(r_1, \ldots, r_N)$ are achievable for iTDMA, we wish to find the values $t_i$, $i = 1, \ldots, N$, which solve

$$\min \sum_{i=1}^{N} p_i t_i \quad (11)$$

subject to

$$t_i(1 - e_i(p_i)) \geq r_i, \quad i = 1, \ldots, N, \quad (12)$$

and

$$\sum_{i=1}^{N} t_i = 1.$$

Again assuming $e_i$ is known and is strictly decreasing for each $i$, we can use Lagrange's method to find the $t_i$; or in simpler cases, if we can take equality in the equations (12) and solve each for $p_i$ in terms of $t_i$, then we can plug the results into the objective (11) and use ordinary calculus to find the optimal $t_i$.

Let us return to the tractable case $N = 2$ and find the optimal values for $t_1$ and $t_2$.

**Example 3.** For $N = 2$ let $t_1 = \tau$ and $t_2 = 1 - \tau$. The constraints become

$$\tau(1 - e_1(p_1)) \geq r_1, \quad (13)$$

and

$$(1 - \tau)(1 - e_2(p_2)) \geq r_2. \quad (14)$$

Solving and plugging into the objective function gives the expression

$$\tau = \frac{r_1 r_2^2 \tilde{\xi}_2 - r_1^2(1 - r_2)\tilde{\xi}_1 \pm r_1 r_2 (1 - r_1 - r_2)\sqrt{\tilde{\xi}_1 \tilde{\xi}_2}}{r_1^2 \tilde{\xi}_1 r_2^2 \tilde{\xi}_2},$$

where $\tilde{\xi}_i = \xi_i / g_{ii}$. We may also obtain

$$\frac{p_1}{p_2} = \sqrt{\frac{g_{22}\xi_1}{g_{11}\xi_2}}.$$

These equations may be used to show that the iTDMA scheme of example 1 is optimal, with $\tau = 2/5$.

Once the $t_i$ are known the minimum energy can be calculated. This value can then be compared to the minimum CSPC energy calculated from (2), and in cases where optimal time division uses less energy than CSPC, there will be interest in using iTDMA, and hence finding an efficient way to induce the TDMA effect. We turn now to power management for some clues on how this might be done without a central controller.

## 4 Interference-Based Power Management

Conventional power control schemes such as CSPC call for constant or increased power when increased interference is encountered. By contrast, power management, i.e., power control for battery life maximization [15, 16], typically dictates that power be *decreased* if interference exceeds certain thresholds. Given this, one can envision two or more power-managed, mutually interfering transmitters effectively taking turns accessing a channel. Before we elaborate, let us summarize some earlier work on power management.

Generally speaking, the power management problem is to select transmitter power as a function of receiver interference and possibly other information in order to minimize the rate of energy consumption, subject to various quality-of-service (QOS) constraints. For example, let us consider a discrete-time system such that the receiver interference in successive time instants forms an independent, identically distributed (i.i.d.) positive-integer-valued stochastic sequence independent of the transmitter power. One may then write $P_I(i)$ for the probability that interference is $i$, and express the power management problem in the form

$$\min \sum_{i=1}^{\infty} p(i) P_I(i)$$

subject to

$$\sum_{i=1}^{\infty} e(i, p(i)) P_I(i) \leq 1 - r,$$

where $r$ is a specified data transmission rate, and $e$ is the data error rate as a function of interference and transmitter power. (This formulation generously assumes the receiver interference at each time instant is known to the transmitter.)

In [15, 16] it was shown for the analogous continuous-time problem that if the error rate $e$ is known then the optimal power management function can be found, independent of the interference distribution, by solving for $p$ in the equation

$$\frac{\partial e}{\partial p} = \text{constant}, \tag{15}$$

with the right-hand side determined by the QOS constraint. This is a useful expression which lends itself well to a dynamic algorithm; the form of the solution $p$ can often be found analytically, and then the algorithm need only calculate and update the constant as it learns more about its operating (interference) environment (see [15, 16]). Basic simulations showed that the use of power management may lead to increased network capacity and stability in addition to reduced energy consumption at the mobile nodes.

Of course the target transmission rate $r$ is not the only measure which might form a quality constraint, and it is probably not the most useful one when the data being generated for transmission arrive randomly. In such cases it is more meaningful to consider QOS measures such as average delay (as in [17]) or, in the case of finite (i.e., real) data buffers, blocking or buffer overflow probabilities (also known as loss probabilities or loss rates). For brevity we have covered only rate constraints above; suffice it to say that in systems which are severely delay-constrained, our form of power management is not a viable option.

When a constant-SIR scheme is used, power levels tend to track one another; in response to higher power from transmitter two, and hence higher interference, transmitter one will increase its power. This causes transmitter two's power to increase, and so on; likewise with power decreases. This behavior is well known and the stability consequences well understood (see, e.g., [5,6,8,19,20] and references therein). However, a non-constant-SIR, power-managed system can behave quite differently. Depending on the particular parameters, simulations of power-managed systems similar to those in [15,16] show that transmitters using power management sometimes track one another, sometimes alternate, and often do a little of both. As opposed to CSPC, the dynamics are highly nonlinear.

Given this, it is certainly of interest to know if there is a way that one might design a power management scheme to specifically encourage alternating power levels. To do this it seems necessary to add at least one dimension to the space over which power levels are determined. Below we specifically consider selecting transmitter power as a function of interference *and backlog*, i.e., the number of data elements queued and waiting for transmission. Then the natural QOS constraint is an upper bound on the buffer overflow probability (data loss rate), rather than the data transmission rate.

## 5 Backlog-Sensitive Power Management

Assume that data arrive to the transmitter according to an i.i.d. Bernoulli process, with the probability of an arrival at any instant being $a \in (0, 1]$. Consider the problem of selecting transmitter power as a function of queue length in order to minimize energy consumption, subject to ensuring a buffer overflow probability less than or equal to some constant $\beta \in (0, 1]$. More precisely, if we assume interference is fixed then we may write

$$\min \sum_{q=1}^{b} p_q \pi_q$$

subject to

$$\pi_b(1 - r_b) \leq \beta,$$

$$\sum_{q=0}^{b} \pi_q = 1.$$

Here $b$ is buffer size, $p_q$ is the transmitter power to be used when the queue length is $q$, $\{\pi_q : q = 0, \ldots, b\}$ is the steady state distribution of the queue, and $r_q$ is the transmission rate (or departure rate) when the queue length is $q$. We find by standard computations for the discrete-time birth-death Markov chain associated with the queue (see, e.g., [9]) that

$$\pi_q = \pi_b \left(\frac{a}{1-a}\right)^{q-b} \frac{r_{q+1} \cdots r_b}{(1-r_q)\cdots(1-r_{b-1})},$$
$$q = 0, \dots, b-1. \quad (16)$$

Of course to solve we need a relation between $r_q$ and $p_q$; let us use

$$r_0 = 0 \quad \text{and} \quad r_q = \frac{p_q}{p_q+1}, \quad q = 1, \dots, b,$$

which is consistent with (4). It follows that $p_q = r_q/(1-r_q)$. Omitting details, the objective becomes

$$\min \frac{a^b}{(1-a)^b} \frac{r_b}{(1-r_b)^2} + \sum_{q=1}^{b-1} \frac{r_{q+1}\cdots r_b}{(1-r_q)\cdots(1-r_b)} \frac{a^q}{(1-a)^q} \frac{r_q}{1-r_q} \quad (17)$$

and the constraints become

$$\frac{1}{1-r_b} \frac{a^b}{(1-a)^b} + \sum_{q=0}^{b-1} \frac{r_{q+1}\cdots r_b}{(1-r_q)\cdots(1-r_b)} \frac{a^q}{(1-a)^q} = \beta^{-1}\left(\frac{a}{1-a}\right)^b. \quad (18)$$

Defining $\lambda = a/(1-a)$, $\mu_q = r_q/(1-r_q)$, and

$$\Phi_q = \begin{cases} \frac{r_{q+1}\cdots r_b}{(1-r_q)\cdots(1-r_b)}, & q = 0, \dots, b-1, \\ \frac{1}{1-r_b}, & q = b \end{cases}$$

this can be written more concisely as

$$\min \sum_{q=1}^{b} \Phi_q \lambda^q \mu_q \quad (19)$$

subject to

$$\sum_{q=0}^{b} \Phi_q \lambda^q = \frac{\lambda^b}{\beta}. \quad (20)$$

The system (19) and (20) can be partially solved using Lagrange's method. Then numerical methods can be used to find values for the $r_q$s, to desired precision.

**Example 4.** In the case $b = 2$ we obtain

$$r_1 = \frac{(\lambda+1)\alpha - 1}{(\lambda+1)\alpha + 1}$$

and

$$r_2 = \frac{\lambda^2(1-\beta)(1-r_1)}{\beta(\lambda + r_1)},$$

with a rather more complicated expression (omitted) for the Lagrange constant $\alpha$ in terms of $r_1, r_2$, and $\lambda$.

Next we will explain how these can be used to integrate backlog-sensitivity into the interference-based power management system discussed in the preceding section. However, a cautionary note is in order: The assumption that the queue is Markovian is certain to be invalid in all but the most contrived of implementations. Hence the rates $r_q$ should be expected to be less than ideal, and future research may be well-directed to alternate schemes for selecting these rates.

The interference-based dynamic power management algorithm (DPMA) found in [15, 16] works roughly as follows:

1. Interference power is measured at the receiver and communicated to the transmitter, or estimated at the transmitter based on other information.
2. The transmitter updates a quantized distribution $F$ of measured or estimated interference values.
3. The transmitter calculates a new power level based on the updated interference distribution, effectively by finding the constant on the right-hand side of (15) as a function of $F$ and the target data transmission rate, $r$.
4. Transmission is attempted at the new power level.

These steps are executed at each time instant, and if the network is stable and stationary (loosely, if transmitters' target rates are achievable and constant over the time interval of interest) then $F$ will gradually reflect the interference distribution encountered on the channel, and the rate of energy consumption will approach a minimum (approximately so except under the ideal conditions of the model, of course). For our purposes, however, the key point is the calculation of the constant—let us call it $\delta$—in step 3.

Because of the way the new transmitter powers are calculated, it is fairly straightforward to integrate backlog-sensitivity into the DPMA. Instead of using a single constant $\delta$ to be updated at each time instant, a vector of $b$ constants $\delta^q$, $q = 1, \dots, b$, is used. Likewise, a $b$-vector of rates $r^q$ replaces the single target rate $r$. These $r^q$s are precisely the values $r_q$ whose calculation was discussed above. The $r^q$s do not need to be updated regularly; rather, they are simply calculated once at the start of operation.

## 6 Network Simulation Results

We used computer simulation to examine the effectiveness of CSPC, interference-based power management (DPMA), and interference-and-backlog-based power management (modified DPMA), and to see the extent to which TDMA-like behavior is induced. We will provide just a

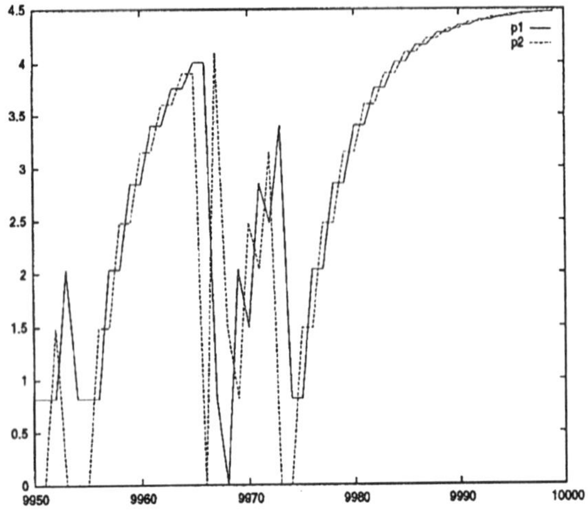


Figure 2: Transmitter powers under CSPC.

summary here. Some operational details concerning the simulator are included in the appendix.

In figure 2 is shown a randomly selected portion of a transmitter powers sample path under CSPC. Two transmitters are operating with achievable rates $r_1 = r_2 = 0.45$, so the network is power-stable. The arrival probabilities are $a = 0.4$, and each transmitter has a data buffer of size 10. Receiver noise powers are constant ($\xi_1 = \xi_2 = 1$), and the gain matrix is highly interfering:

$$G = \begin{bmatrix} 1 & 1 \\ 1 & 1 \end{bmatrix}.$$

As expected, the two transmitters' powers track one another, occasionally going to zero when an input buffer empties.

Now consider figure 3, which shows a modified DPMA system under identical circumstances. (Figure 3 also shows the queue backlogs, labeled "q1" and "q2.") Notice the dramatically different behavior of the power sample paths. It is evident that the transmitter powers are alternating, showing at least a partial iTDMA effect. The alternating is quite typical, and rather understated relative to some simulations, which show dramatic on-off behavior. Notice also that transmitter powers "voluntarily" drop to zero even with a non-zero backlog.

It is worth noting again that a power-managed system will in general require larger buffers to achieve the same blocking probabilities as a constant-SIR system, since queue lengths and delays tend to fluctuate more when energy conservation is made a high priority. This is the case in our simulation example above, as the average queue length and blocking probabilities are lower for the CSPC system.

The original DPMA system (not shown) yields transmitter power paths that lie somewhere between the modified DPMA and CSPC, in terms of the degree of iTDMA effect. Notably, though, the DPMA tends to outperform its two rivals by operating at lower power for similar rates and loss probabilities.

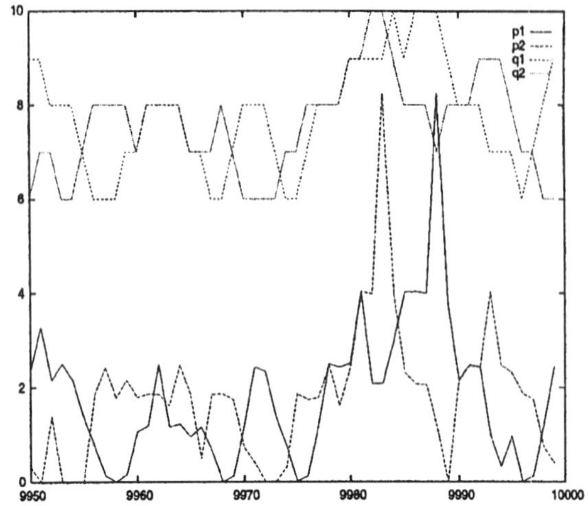


Figure 3: Transmitter powers (and queue lengths) under modified DPMA.

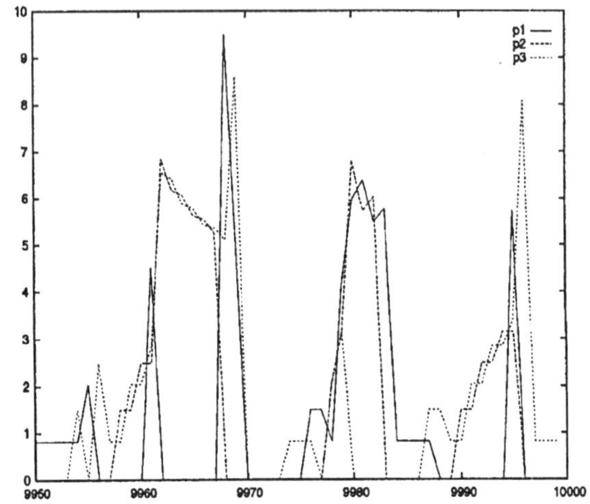


Figure 4: Transmitter powers under CSPC, N=3.

Shown in figures 4 and 5 are roughly comparable samples for $N = 3$ transmitters. Again, the alternating behavior of the modified DPMA scheme is evident relative to the power level tracking which occurs under CSPC for transmitters whose queues are non-empty.

## 7 Conclusion

On the one hand, the modified, backlog-sensitive DPMA shows great promise as an iTDMA mechanism. On the other, it is typically outperformed by the unmodified version. Both do well compared with CSPC, however, so what remains is to examine the shortcomings of the particular approach taken here in modifying the DPMA. In particular, as noted above, there is probably a great deal of room for

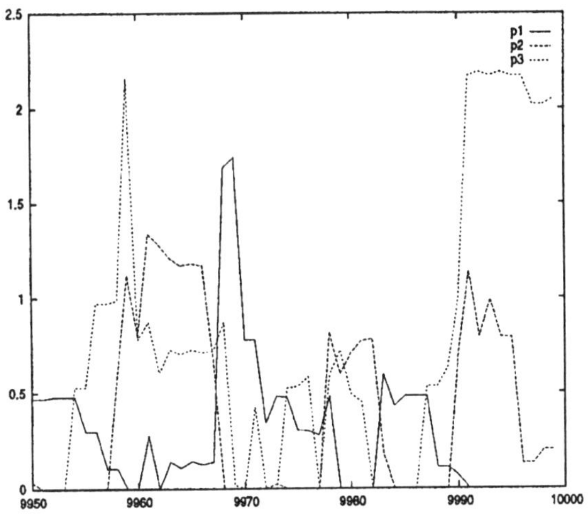


**Figure 5: Transmitter powers under modified DPMA, N=3.**

improvement in selecting the buffer-dependent transmission rates—perhaps they should be adjusted dynamically, rather than calculated a priori. In any event, the analysis of sections 2 and 3 suggests that the reward for developing a decentralized, genuine iTDMA algorithm would be substantial.

## Appendix: Some Computer Simulation Details

First, we assumed the error rate on each channel followed equation (4). Second, in contrast to the simulator used in [15, 16], the one used here incorporated the following two important features:

1. Non-Zero communication delay: Information gathered at the receiver arrives one time step later to the transmitter.

2. Simultaneous updates: All users update their power levels at each time instant, as opposed to round-robin updating.

Of course both changes lead to more realistic (and less optimistic) results. The performance of the highly nonlinear power management systems was far more susceptible to degradation from these changes than the linear CSPC system. Nonetheless, results are encouraging; for a wide range of parameters, the DPMA system outperforms CSPC.

## Acknowledgments

The authors thank the referees for their helpful comments.

## References

[1] AEIN, J. Power balancing in systems employing frequency reuse. *Comsat Technical Review 3*, 2 (1973).

[2] BAIER, P. W., JUNG, P., AND KLEIN, A. Taking the challenge of multiple access for third-generation cellular mobile radio systems—a European view. *IEEE Communications Magazine 34*, 2 (February 1996), 82–89.

[3] BOCK, F., AND EBSTEIN, B. Assignment of transmitter powers by linear programming. *IEEE Transactions on Electromagnetic Compatibility 6* (July 1964), 36–44.

[4] DA SILVA, J. S., BARANI, B., AND ARROYO-FERNANDEZ, B. European mobile communications on the move. *IEEE Communications Magazine 34*, 2 (February 1996), 60–69.

[5] FOSCHINI, G. J., AND MILJANIC, Z. A simple distributed autonomous power control algorithm and its convergence. *IEEE Transactions on Vehicular Technology 42*, 4 (November 1993), 641–646.

[6] GRANDHI, S., VIJAYAN, R., AND GOODMAN, D. A distributed algorithm for power control in cellular radio systems. In *Proceedings of the Thirtieth Annual Allerton Conference on Communications, Control, and Computing* (1992).

[7] GRANDHI, S. A., VIJAYAN, R., AND GOODMAN, D. J. Distributed power control in cellular radio systems. *IEEE Transactions on Communications 42*, 2–4 (February–April 1994), 226–228.

[8] GRANDHI, S. A., AND ZANDER, J. Constrained power control in cellular radio systems. In *Proceedings of the IEEE Vehicular Technology Conference* (1994), pp. 824–828.

[9] HOEL, P. G., PORT, S. C., AND STONE, C. J. *Introduction to Stochastic Processes.* Waveland Press, Inc., Prospect Heights, Illinois, 1972.

[10] KANESHIGE, T. Developments fuel wireless revolution. *IEEE Computer 29*, 8 (August 1996), 16–17.

[11] MEYERHOFF, H. J. Method for computing the optimum power balance in multi-beam satellites. *COMSAT Technical Review 4*, 1 (Spring 1974), 139–146.

[12] MITRA, D. An asynchronous distributed algorithm for power control in cellular radio systems. In *Proceedings of the 4th WINLAB Workshop on 3rd Generation Wireless Information Networks* (1993).

[13] NETTLETON, R. W., AND ALAVI, H. Power control for a spread spectrum cellular mobile radio system. In *Proceedings of the IEEE Vehicular Technology Conference* (1983), pp. 242–246.

[14] POLLINI, G. P. Trends in handover design. *IEEE Communications Magazine 34*, 3 (March 1996), 82–90.

[15] RULNICK, J. M., AND BAMBOS, N. Mobile power management for maximum battery life in wireless communication networks. In *Proceedings of IEEE Infocom* (1996).

[16] RULNICK, J. M., AND BAMBOS, N. Mobile power management for wireless communication networks. *Wireless Networks* (1996). To appear.

[17] RULNICK, J. M., AND BAMBOS, N. Performance evaluation of power-managed mobile communication devices. In *Proceedings of IEEE International Communications Conference (ICC)* (1996).

[18] YATES, R. D. A framework for uplink power control in cellular radio systems. *IEEE Journal on Selected Areas in Communications 13*, 7 (September 1995), 1341–1347.

[19] ZANDER, J. Distributed cochannel interference control in cellular radio systems. *IEEE Transactions on Vehicular Technology 41*, 3 (August 1992), 305–311.

[20] ZANDER, J. Performance of optimum transmitter power control in cellular radio systems. *IEEE Transactions on Vehicular Technology 41*, 1 (February 1992), 57–62.

[21] ZANDER, J. Transmitter power control for co-channel interference management in cellular radio systems. In *Proceedings of the 4th WINLAB Workshop on 3rd Generation Wireless Information Networks* (1993).

# On Algorithms Searching For Quasi-Optimal Subfamilies Of GMW Sequences Suitable For CDMA Applications

X. H. CHEN[1], T. LANG[1] and J. OKSMAN[2]

[1] Department of Electrical Engineering, National University of Singapore, Singapore 119260

[2] Telecommunication Laboratory, University of Oulu, 90570 Finland

*Abstract* - This paper studies several algorithms for constructing quasi-optimal GMW sub-families in terms of minimized bit error rate under co-channel interference. The results show that performance of resultant sub-families is very sensitive to the algorithms applied and sub-family sizes. A new criterion based on combinational (even plus odd) maximum cross-correlation is introduced for code selection and the resultant highest-peak-deleting and most-peak-deleting algorithms are effective to construct the GMW quasi-optimal sub-families.

## I. INTRODUCTION

The GMW sequences have relatively large code family. In this paper, we shall propose some promising algorithms to construct the sub-families from the original GMW sequence family by deliberately eliminating those sequences which could not meet certain criteria. Take the degree-12 GMW sequence as an example. There are in total 864 different members in its original family. For the applications in a finite CDMA system, a sub-family with, say, 50 members might be sufficient. Thus, it is natural to envisage that, by deliberately choosing 50 codes from the original family, the sub-family with the 50 codes could offer much better performance than that by using the 50 codes chosen randomly from the original family. Three different optimization algorithms, reciprocal code deleting, highest-peak-deleting and most-peak-deleting, will be introduced and the performance of their resultant sub-families will be compared in terms of bit error rate (BER) under the CDMA co-channel interference.

The outline of this paper is given as follows. In Section II, the correlation features of GMW sequences are introduced. Section III discusses the criteria of code performance with the help of the cross-correlation metric. Three algorithms to construct quasi-optimal sub-families of GMW sequences are proposed in Section IV. Section V is dedicated to performance comparison among those algorithms under various sub-family sizes. Finally, the concluding remarks are given in Section VI.

## II. GMW SEQUENCES

The definition for the GMW sequences should also be addressed. Assuming $M$ is a composite integer, or $M = JK$, by using the trace function $tr_J^M(\alpha)$, the GMW sequence $\{b_n\}$ can be specified as

$$b_n = tr_1^J\left\{\left[tr_J^M(\alpha)\right]^r\right\}, \tag{1}$$

where $\alpha$ is a primitive element of GF($2^M$), and $r$ is any integer relatively prime to $2^J$-1 and in the range $1 \le r < 2^J$-1. Note that for $r$=1, this reduces to an m-sequence. Also interesting is that if primitive elements $\alpha$ and $\beta$ are reciprocal, two sequences $\{b_n\}$ and $\{b'_n\}$ given in (2) will also be reciprocal, which is exactly the same as m-sequences.

$$b_n = tr_1^J\left\{\left[tr_J^M(\alpha)\right]^r\right\},\; b'_n = tr_1^J\left\{\left[tr_J^M(\beta)\right]^r\right\} \tag{2}$$

For a fixed $M$ and $J$, the number of cyclically distinct GMW sequences, or the maximum family size available, is given by

$$N_{GMW} = N_p(M)\, N_p(J), \tag{3}$$

where $N_p(D)$ denotes the number of primitive polynomials of degree $D$ over GF(2), or equivalently, the number of integers $j$ in the range $1 \le j < 2^D$ -1, which are relatively prime to $2^D$ -1 and have cyclically nonequivalent base-2 representations. This is clearly a significant increase over the available number of m-sequences of the same degree. For each degree



0-8186-7780-5/97 $10.00 © 1997 IEEE

$M$, the selected $J$ must maximize $N_{GMW}$ in order to get as many sequences as possible. The generator of GMW sequence can be mechanized by a Galois-configured shift-register in addition to a ROM. However, it is also convenient to deal with it directly from (3), as we did when generating the all GMW sequences concerned in this paper.

## III. The Criteria of Code Performance

In order to evaluate a spreading code family, it is very important to setup appropriate criteria. In many early studies on the topic, maximum value of even periodic CCLs $\theta_{max}$ was adopted as the criterion, based on which both Welch and Sidelnikov lower bounds were established in order to judge the code performance. In fact, most CDMA systems operate in an asynchronous mode, where both even and odd CCLs appear equally likely and they both are responsible for the system BER. Therefore, only even periodic CCL is not a sufficiently good parameter measuring the spreading code performance.

Pursley [5] derived an expression of signal to noise ratio (SNR) and introduced a new parameter $\gamma(x,y)$, named as the average interference parameter (AIP), which is directly associated with the SNR and hence the BER performance of an asynchronous DS/CDMA system (the equation for the AIP is given in (6)). Therefore, the AIP can also be taken as a parameter for measuring the average-case performance, whereas the parameter $\theta_{max}$ (the maximum even periodic CCL) reflects the worse-case performance. It should be pointed out at the same time that the mean-square aperiodic cross-correlation is sometimes considered as an alternative to the AIP since they are in fact very close with each other in values [6].

In order to link the parameters of the spreading codes to the BER performance under the co-channel interference due to the non-perfect correlation functions, we presented in our previous work [7] a new method, the convolution/multiple-variable-Bernoulli method, to evaluate BER performance directly from the auto-correlation and cross-correlation functions for different CDMA spreading codes. The procedure can be briefly illustrated as follows (assuming that a CDMA system employs a spreading code family of $N$ members with length $L$).

1. Calculate both the even (periodic) cross-correlation functions $\theta_{x,y}(l)$ and the odd (periodic) cross-correlation functions $\hat{\theta}_{x,y}(l)$ as defined in [1] respectively, where $l$ ranges from 0 to $L$-1 when $x \neq y$ and $l$ ranges from 1 to $L$-1 otherwise. Count the probability of appearance for each emerged correlation level $m$. Then the statistical distribution $D_{x,y}(m)$, which denotes the probability of CCL taking the value $m$, can be obtained.
2. For all possible pairs of spreading codes $x$ and $y$ selected from $N$ sequences, repeat the step 1 and let $\overline{D}(m)$ be the statistical average of CCL distribution for the whole family given by
$$\overline{D}(m)=\frac{1}{N^2}\sum_{x=1}^{N}\sum_{y=1}^{N}D_{x,y}(m). \qquad (4)$$
3. $\overline{D}(m)$ in (4) can be viewed as the average distribution of the CDMA co-channel interfering noise caused by a single interfering user. To take into account of multiple user situation, the convolution is used to obtain the statistical distribution of the co-channel interference with $n$ simultaneously active users, each of which is assumed to contribute the same CCL distribution $\overline{D}(m)$ and is independent of each other. It gives
$$\overline{D}^{(n)}(m)=\underbrace{\overline{D}(m)\otimes\cdots\otimes\overline{D}(m)}_{n-\text{fold convolution}}. \qquad (5)$$
Alternatively, (5) is also obtainable by using the multi-variable-Bernoulli distribution method from $\overline{D}(m)$, as shown in [7].
4. by summing up the probabilities of $\overline{D}^{(n)}(m)$ at which $m$ exceeds the pre-set decision threshold, the BER caused by $n$ simultaneously active users is obtained.

## IV. Three Algorithms for Constructing Sub-Families

Based on the two criteria parameters mentioned in Section III, namely maximum (both even and odd) periodic CCLs $\theta_{max}(x,y)$, $\hat{\theta}_{max}(x,y)$ and AIP $\gamma(x,y)$, three algorithms for construction of quasi-optimal sub-families are presented in this section.

(1) *Algorithm 1: Reciprocal-deleting*

The basic idea of this algorithm is to eliminate the pairs of sequences which contribute high AIP values. It has been known that the AIP for a real-valued sequence $x$ and its reciprocal $y$ is identical to the AIP for the sequence and itself, that is, $\gamma(x,y) = \gamma(x,x) = \gamma(y,y)$ [1,5], due to the fact that the two aperiodic auto-correlation functions $C_x(l)$ and $C_y(l)$, based on which the AIP is calculated, are the same [1]. Thus, the AIPs for them should also be the same, which is given as follows

$$\gamma(x,y)=2\sum_{l=1-N}^{N-1}C_x(l)C_y(l)+\sum_{l=1-N}^{N-1}C_x(l)C_y(l+1) \qquad (6)$$

However, if $x$ and $y$ are neither identical nor reciprocal with each other, the corresponding AIP function $\gamma(x,y)$ should always be smaller than $\gamma(x,x)$ or $\gamma(y,y)$, which is the result obtainable by simply using "*Cauchy inequality*". Therefore, an immediate conclusion is that, in order to construct a quasi-optimal sub-family based on the AIP criteria, a direct way is to delete all reciprocal codes from the original family. It can be seen from the obtained results that the GMW sequence benefit quite much from the reciprocal-deleting algorithm. Although only degree-12 of GMW sequences are discussed here, the algorithm is also valid for any other sequences of different degrees, however with different effectiveness.

(2) *Algorithm 2: Highest-peak-deleting*

Now we shall first define the combined maximum CCL as follows. Let $\theta_{max}(x,y)$ and $\hat{\theta}_{max}(x,y)$ be the maximum values of the even and odd (periodic) CCLs between sequences $x$ and $y$ respectively. Then the combined maximum CCL, $\xi(x,y)$, is defined as

$$\xi(x,y)=\max\{|\theta_{max}(x,y)|,|\hat{\theta}_{max}(x,y)|\}. \qquad (7)$$

The reasons why introducing the combined maximum CCL function as a new parameter for the code selection algorithm is that even and odd cross-correlation levels appear at a receiver equally likely in a practical (asynchronous) CDMA system, given that +1 and -1 bits are sent also equally likely, and they both should be responsible for the BER.

To optimize the performance of a sub-family, a natural idea is to remove those pairs from the original family which contribute high $\xi(x,y)$ values. One way to do so is to use so called "*Highest-peak-deleting*" algorithm which is implemented in the following steps:

1. Start with the original complete family and eliminate the sequences $x$ and $y$ whose $\xi(x,y)$ is the largest among the all codes.
2. Get the next largest combinational CCL value $\xi(x,y)$ and locate the sequences $x$ and $y$ which generate the value and remove them.
3. Repeat the step 2 until the remaining code group size satisfies the pre-set value, say 30.

It can be shown that the highest $\xi(x,y)$ value after the algorithm is only about the half of that before the algorithm. The fluctuation of resultant $\xi(x,y)$ can also be greatly reduced.

(3) *Algorithm 3: Most-peak-deleting*

In Algorithm 2 introduced just now, each deleted sequence-pair has the highest value of $\xi(x,y)$ in the entire residual family, hence generating a sub-family with $max[\xi(x,y)]=\xi_{max}$ lower than the value in the previous step. However, in some cases, keeping $\xi_{max}$ lower may not necessarily be as effective as keeping the average value of $\xi(x,y)$ lower in order to improve the BER under the co-channel interference. Thus, Algorithm 3 is introduced, whose rule is to remove the sequences which contributes too many high $\xi(x,y)$ values and its algorithm is given as follows:

1. Let $\xi_{max}$ and $\xi_{average}$ be the maximum and average values of all $\xi(x,y)$ in the entire code

(sub-)family respectively. Set the threshold $T$ to be the median of the two, or

$$T=(\xi_{max}+\xi_{average})/2. \quad (8)$$

2. For each sequence $x$, count the times ($N_x$) that $\xi(x,z)>T$, where $z$ takes all available sequence index numbers. Let $N_{max}$ be the maximum value of all $N_x$.
3. If there is only one $N_x$ equal to $N_{max}$, the sequence $x$ will then be deleted straight away. Otherwise, the one with maximum $S_x$ is deleted, where $S_x$ is defined as

$$S_x = \sum_{\xi(x,z)>T} \xi(x,z). \text{ (for all available sequence } z) \quad (9)$$

4. Return to step 1 and repeat the algorithm until the number of sequences left satisfies the pre-set value.

The strategy of this algorithm is to first delete those codes which contribute most high-valued $\xi(x,y)$, so that the algorithm ensures to obtain an optimal sub-family.

By summarizing the three algorithms for constructing a quasi-optimal sub-family from the original large families, we have the following conclusions. The reciprocal-deleting algorithm based on AIP parameter fails to work as effectively as the highest-peak-deleting and most-peak-deleting algorithms. As a matter of fact, the AIP parameter is never a good criterion for constructing optimal sub-families.

## V. BER PERFORMANCE

So far, the three algorithms have been introduced to construct quasi-optimal sub-families, one of which is based on AIP criterion and the other two are based on the combined maximum CCLs. The BER analysis based on statistical distribution of CCLs, as mentioned in Section II, is necessary to evaluate both original family and the three different sub-families generated by different algorithms introduced in the previous section. We will not deliberate the BER analytical method again here. Rather, we only give the results for various family sizes and algorithms.

Figs. 1(a) and 1(b) show the results for the GMW sequences of degree 9 and 10 respectively, whereas Fig. 2 shows the BERs for the GMW sequences of degree 12. Generally speaking, with the increase of sub-family sizes, the achievable BER gain through the algorithms reduces. In order to construct a satisfactory sub-family for CDMA applications, the original family should be relatively large. For instance, for degree-9 GMW sequences, only 96 sequences exist. Therefore, the improvement in BER of its sub-family of a size 30 by using any algorithm is marginal, as shown in Fig. 1(a). On the other hand, for degree-12 GMW sequences, there are in total 864 members in its original family. Thus, a well-constructed sub-family of 30 codes offer a significant BER improvement over that obtainable by using any 30-code sub-families randomly selected from its original family, as shown in Fig. 2.

Not surprisingly, the BER performance of all different-sized sub-families constructed by the reciprocal-deleting algorithm is close to that of their original families. Therefore, it verifies again that the AIP is not a suitable parameter for constructing an optimal sub-family, even though it was widely taken as the figure of merit for the spreading codes in the literature [1,5,9]. In fact, the AIPs for different spreading codes are very similar, so that it hardly tells the difference among the spreading codes if only using AIP as the criterion. On the contrary, the other two algorithms based on the combined maximum CCL (both the highest-peak-deleting and most-peak-deleting algorithms) are fairly effective in improving the BER performance of a constructed sub-family, although their effectiveness is also dependent of the types and the degrees of the spreading codes of concern.

To understand better about the highest-peak-deleting and most-peak-deleting algorithms, different-sized sub-families for the GMW sequences are constructed and studied. Let us take degree 12 as an example. The original entire family of GMW sequences of degree 12 contains 240 (due to the computational complexity, only 240 out of totally 864 available GMW sequences are randomly selected to form the original family) cyclically distinct sequences, five different-sized sub-families according to

Algorithm 2 and 3 are constructed and their BER curves are plotted in Fig. 2, from which the following observations can be made. Firstly, the Algorithm 2 and 3 are efficient in order to obtain an optimal sub-family in terms of BER in a finite CDMA system. For example, employing a GMW sequence sub-family constructed by Algorithm 2 or 3 can achieve an BER gain at least 20 dB over the original family under the same number of simultaneously active users. Secondly, the BER gain achieved by the Algorithm 2 or 3 is very sensitive to the sub-family sizes. The remarkable improvement exists only when the sub-family size is about one-third of the size of its original family. Moreover, the increase in the BER gain is not evenly distributed over different family sizes. Fig. 2 shows that the 60-sequence sub-family has a great gain over the 70-sequence sub-family, whereas a further reduction to 50-sequence sub-family could obtain only very limited improvement. Hence, it is necessary to find a proper sub-family size at which both capacity and BER can be optimized. Such optimized sub-family sizes are 30 and 60 for GMW sequences.

In general, the highest-peak-deleting algorithm outperforms the most-peak-deleting algorithm, although the difference between the two is small.

## VI. Conclusions

In this paper, the method of constructing quasi-optimal sub-families of the GMW sequences is studied. Three Algorithms, based on either AIP or combined maximum CCLs are introduced. Using the BER analysis based on statistical CCL distribution, it is concluded that both highest-peak-deleting and most-peak-deleting algorithms based on the combined maximum CCLs produce satisfactory sub-families with a significant BER gain over that of their original families. The reciprocal-deleting algorithm based on AIP parameter fails to work well if compared with the other two.

## References


[1] D. V. Sarwate and M. B. Pursley, "Cross-correlation Properties of Pseudo-Random and Related Sequences," *Proc. IEEE*, vol. 68, pp. 593-619, 1980.

[2] R. A. Scholtz and L. R. Welch, "GMW Sequences," *IEEE Trans. Inform. Theory*, vol. IT-30, pp. 548-553, 1984.

[3] S. W. Golomb, *Shift Register Sequences*. Laguna Hills, CA: Aegean Park Press, 1982.

[4] L. B. Milstein et al., "On the feasibility of a CDMA overlay for personal communications networks," *IEEE JSAC*, vol. 10, pp. 655-668, May 1992.

[5] M. B. Pursley, "Performance Evaluation for Phase-Coded Spread-Spectrum Multiple-Access Communications-Part I: System Analysis," *IEEE Trans. Commun.*, vol. COM-25, pp. 795-799, 1977.

[6] K. H. A. Kärkkäinen, "Mean-Square Cross-Correlation as a Performance Measure for Spreading Code Families," in *Proc. 1992 IEEE ISSSTA*, pp. 147-150, YoKohama, Japan, 1992.

[7] T. Lang and X. H. Chen, "Spreading Code Dependent Capacity in a Finite CDMA System-a Multiple Variable Bernoulli Co-Channel Interference Model," submitted to MINDEF'95 Seminar, Singapore, 1995.

[8] W. W. Peterson and E. J. Weldon, Jr., *Error-Correcting Codes*. 2nd ed. Cambridge, MA: M.I.T Press, 1972.

[9] M. B. Pursley and H. F. A. Roefs, "Numerical Evaluation of Correlation Parameters for Optimal Phases of Binary Shift-Register Sequences," *IEEE Trans. Commun.*, vol. COM-27, pp. 1597-1604, 1979.

[10] R. Skaug, "Numerical Evaluation of the Nonperiodic Autocorrelation Parameter for Optimal Phases of Maximal Length Sequences," *IEE Proc. -F*, vol. 127, pp. 230-237, 1980.

[11] T. Lang and X. H. Chen, "Comparison of Correlation Parameters of Binary Codes for DS/CDMA Systems," *Proc. IEEE Singapore ICCS'94*, pp. 1059-1063, Singapore, 1994.

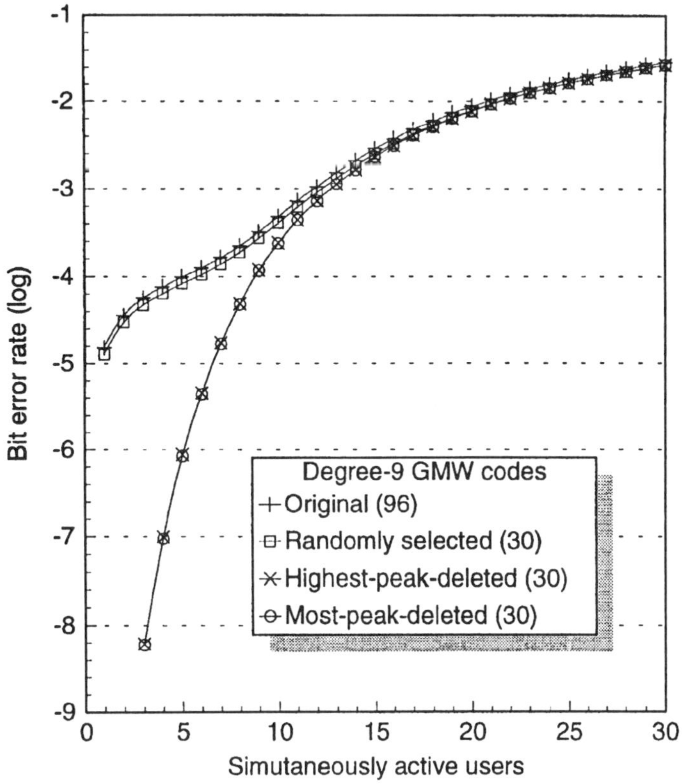


Fig. 1(a). BER of GMW sub-families of degree 9

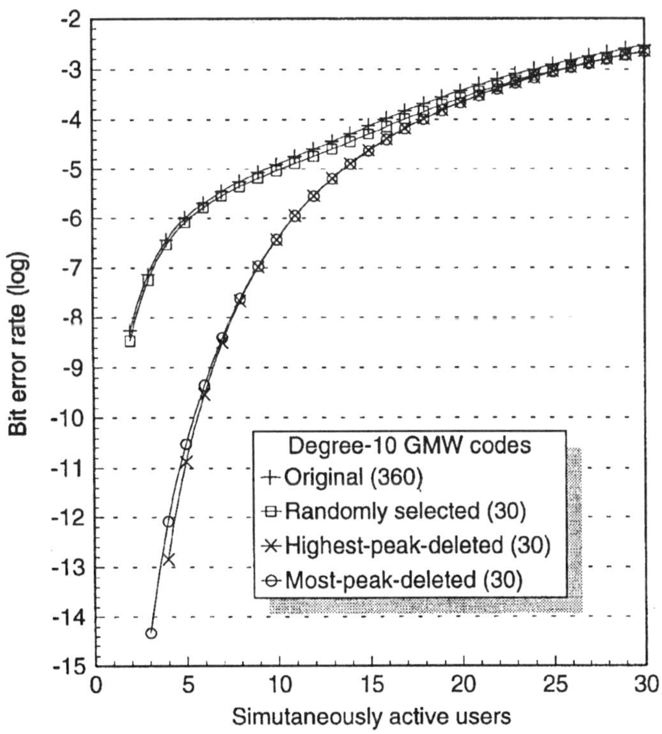


Fig. 1(b). BER of GMW sub-families of degree 10

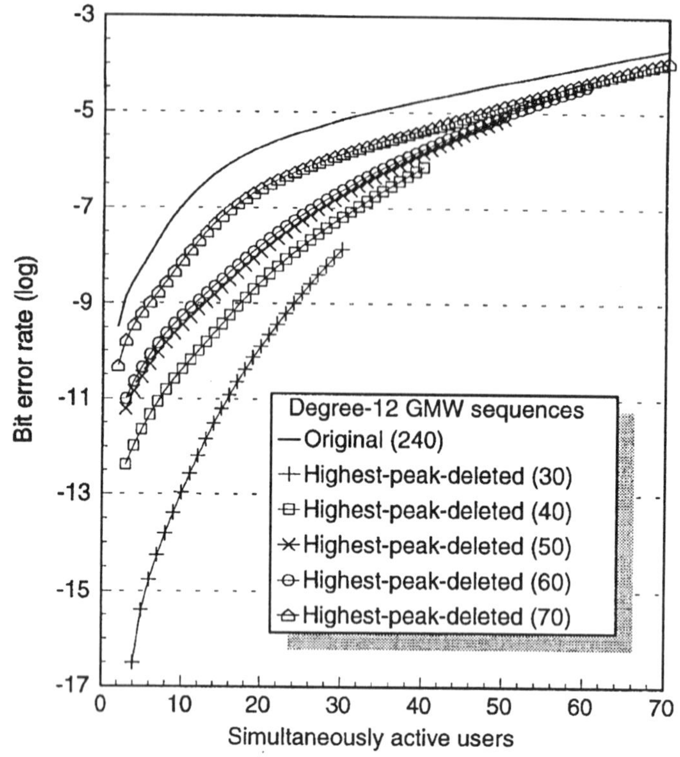


Fig. 2 (a). BER of different sized GMW sub-families with Highest-peak-deleting algorithm

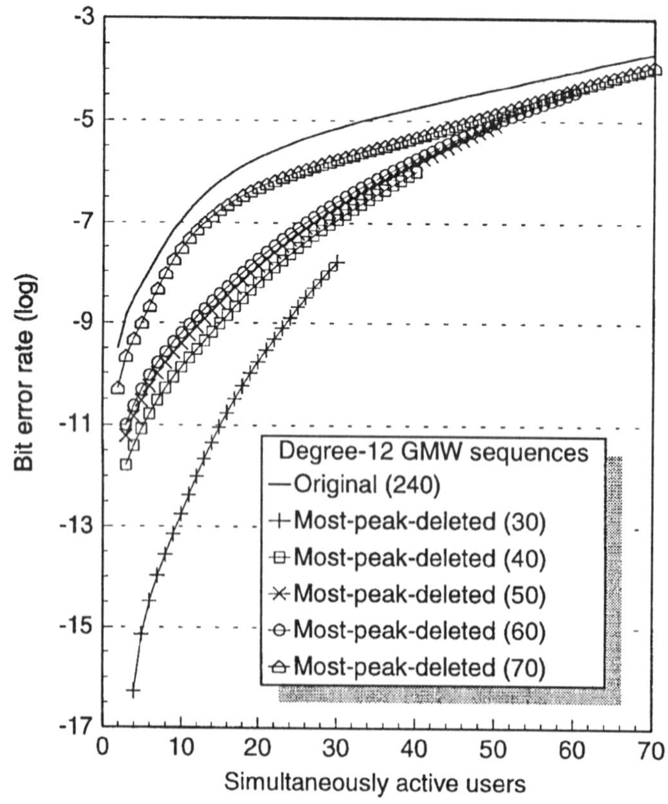


Fig. 2 (b). BER of different sized GMW sub-families with Most-peak-deleting algorithm

# Call Admissibility for Multirate Traffic in Wireless ATM Networks

Subir K. Biswas and Bhaskar Sengupta
NEC USA Inc., C&C Research Laboratories
4 Independence Way, Princeton NJ 08540.

## Abstract

*For multirate wireless ATM traffic, the first part of the call admission process is to determine whether to admit calls as long as bandwidth is available or to deny admission to a call of a particular class even if there is enough bandwidth available, in the hope of admitting calls of some other class later. A second part of the process is to determine if the quality of service requested by the call can be met. A scenario in which the first part is particularly important is when the blocking probability requirements for different classes is different. In this paper, we consider four policies to determine the circumstances under which calls of different types are admissible. For each of these policies, we show how to compute the blocking probabilities. For three of these policies, the blocking probabilities can be found by using results from product form networks. For the fourth, we provide an approximation which works extremely well in practice. We also formulate a non-linear programming problem which attempts to determine the parameters of the admissibility policies in such a way to maximize the call arrival rates while keeping the blocking probabilities under specified bounds. We provide an algorithm for solving the non-linear programming problem and use this as a basis for comparing the policies. We show that under some circumstances, it is possible to improve the system throughput by as much as 35% by a suitable use of the admissibility policies. This improvement in throughput is particularly important in wireless ATM networks, supporting high rate multimedia traffic because of the inherent limitations in bandwidth availability.*

## 1 Introduction

Wireless ATM (WATM) can be viewed as a general solution for next-generation personal communication networks (PCN) which will be required to support multimedia traffic. One of the goals of WATM is to provide a seamless extension of the services provided to applications connected to the wired ATM network. WATM protocols and algorithms are already being discussed for early standardization at the ATM forum. An architecture for a wireless ATM system is proposed in [9] where mechanisms for unified wired and wireless services are provided. The proposed system is intended to be an integral part of a high-speed ATM network with signaling and control layers, augmented for supporting mobility [14]. In order to maintain uniformity of service classes and quality-of-service (QoS) parameters, the network is designed to support standard ATM service interfaces, including constant bit rate (CBR), available bit rate (ABR) and variable bit rate (VBR) traffic. Supporting multi-class traffic over a multi-access medium, like radio, requires a specialized medium access control (MAC) protocol for providing QoS support to the upper layers. Such a QoS based MAC architecture and the related allocation algorithms for CBR, ABR and VBR traffic were reported in [2] and [13].

While such allocation and scheduling is performed at ATM cell-level, a call-level admission control strategy is also necessary for successful QoS provisioning to the multi-class virtual circuits. The problem of Call Admission Control (CAC) is a well known one in the context of emerging multi-class communication networks. The first part of the admission control problem could be viewed as the determination of call *admissibility*. The second part of the problem is to determine if the network can guarantee the QoS requested by the call. In the first part, we only try to figure out whether or not the admission controller should even attempt to admit the call. If the call is classified as admissible, then the admission controller performs additional checks to figure out if the call should be admitted. One possible reason for taking this approach is to give preferential treatment to a particular class of service because that class offers better revenue prospects for the operating company. In this paper, we are concerned with the first of the two steps only and we assume that each class of service has its own blocking probability requirement and the admissibility policy must be designed to satisfy these requirements. A naive policy for determining admissibility is one which admits all calls for which sufficient bandwidth is available. Our principal focus is to find good methods of determining admissi-



0-8186-7780-5/97 $10.00 © 1997 IEEE

bility in wireless ATM networks which are better than the naive method. Note that a good method of determining admissibility is of paramount importance to operating companies whose revenues are tied directly to the throughput that they can sustain. This is particularly important in the context of wireless networks since the physical medium has inherent bandwidth limitation compared to the terrestrial network. Given these constraints, even a small throughput gain can be very significant to the operating companies.

The main performance criterion that we are interested in is the blocking probability of various classes. We assume that the designer of the network would like to determine an admissibility policy which gives the maximum throughput subject to satisfying some requirements on the blocking probabilities. Simultaneously, he or she would like to determine the optimum values of the parameters of these policies. In this paper, we examine four admissibility policies and show how to compute the call blocking probabilities for these policies. For three of the four policies, it is known that the blocking probabilities can be found from the theory of product form networks. For one of the policies, we develop a method of computing the blocking probabilities which is significantly better than the existing known methods. Indeed, our goal is to be able to predict the blocking probabilities within about 10% of their true values found from simulation experiments. Having found the blocking probabilities, we formulate and solve a non-linear programming problem which maximizes the throughput while keeping the blocking probabilities within some specified bounds. The solution of this non-linear programming problem serves two functions. First, it enables us to determine the optimum values of the parameters of the admissibility policies and second, it enables us to objectively compare the performance of the four policies. We provide a method of solving this non-linear programming problem and through our numerical experiments, we are able to identify the scenarios in which one policy clearly outperforms the naive admissibility policy (which is to classify any call as admissible if sufficient bandwidth is available). We also identify scenarios in which all of the policies perform about equally well. This insight should enable the designers of future wireless networks to decide which admissibility policy to use and how to tune the parameters of the best policy.

This paper is divided into four more sections. In section 2, we describe the medium access control architecture that we consider in this paper. In sections 3 and 4 we provide the details of the models and algorithms used and the numerical results. Finally, in section 5, we draw some conclusions.

## 2 Medium Access Control (MAC)

In this section, we provide a brief description of the MAC architecture and the the multiclass slot allocation that we consider in this paper. Readers who are only interested in the analytical aspects of this paper may skip this section on first reading without any loss of continuity. A dynamic Time Division Multiple Access (TDMA) approach is adopted for medium access control within a transmission cell (the area controlled by a base station) where several virtual circuits are multiplexed in a single radio channel. Bandwidth allocation within a transmission cell works in a centralized manner where a base station is responsible for TDMA slot allocation and ATM cell scheduling for all the upstream and downstream virtual circuits within that cell. The allocation schedule for a TDMA frame is computed at the beginning of the frame and the allocation information is sent by the base station during an early part of the frame. After receiving the schedule, all the mobile terminals within that transmission cell transmit ATM cells according to the received allocation instruction.

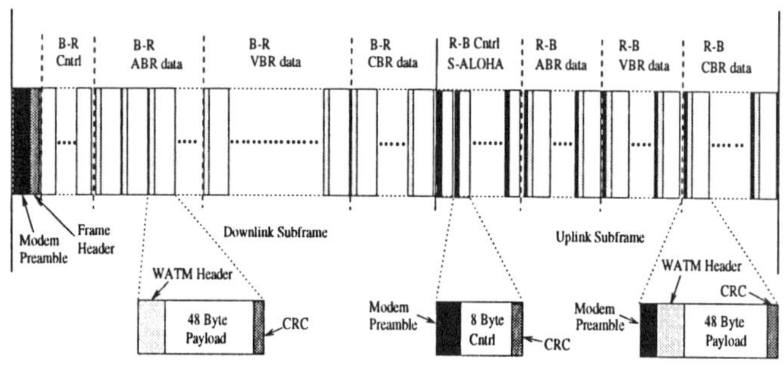


Figure 1: Wireless ATM MAC frame structure

Figure 1 illustrates the TDMA frame structure for supporting CBR, VBR and ABR traffic classes within a base station transmission cell. While the downlink transmissions are done as a single burst from the base to the remote terminals, the uplink transmission is allocated to multiple upstream virtual circuits using a dynamic TDMA scheme. The MAC frame is divided into an uplink and a downlink part and each of those are further partitioned into several subframes, carrying different classes of traffic. The boundaries between these subframes are varied gradually with time in order to respond to the changing traffic needs.

A brief description of the different frame parts and their functions [13] is given below. The downlink preamble provides frame synchronization as well as a training sequence for the purposes of equalization. The base station uses frame header to transmit its identifier and information about the positions and sizes of different subframes in the current frame. The downlink control messages, transmitted in the Base-to-Remote (B-R) control region, include slot allocation information, B-R acknowledgements and other wireless network control messages. The B-R data region consists of ABR, VBR and CBR data as shown in Figure 1. The R-B control region is used by the remote stations to transmit control messages to the base station in a slotted ALOHA mode. Both the uplink data and R-B acknowledgement messages are transmitted in the R-B data region.

Channel access scheduling, both uplink and downlink, for all the virtual circuits (CBR, ABR or VBR) is done by a supervisory MAC (S-MAC) process within the base station. The S-MAC receives all slot allocation requests for the VCs present in the transmission cell. Based on the User Parameter Control (UPC) specification and QoS requirement of each VC, the S-MAC arrives at a transmission schedule for data and acknowledgements (to enable error recovery by the data-link control layer [13]) to be sent in the next frame. At the remote terminals, this schedule information is received in each frame within the B-R control region and once received, a terminal first transmits the WATM cells and then the acknowledgement packets based on that received schedule.

CBR circuits are assigned slots periodically according to their bit-rate. The amount of this periodic allocation is decided at connection setup time and the allocation rate for a CBR stream does not change during the lifetime of the connection. ABR virtual circuits are handled in a burst-by-burst basis where an explicit allocation request is sent (through R-B ALOHA control slots) to the base station when an upstream ABR VC requires to transmit a new burst. Based on the available slots, a dynamic ABR allocation is done by the base station. Although an ABR like scheme (burst-by-burst) can be used for VBR allocation, the randomized nature of R-B allocation-request transmission makes it difficult to bound the delay and jitter within an acceptable range. Instead, an adaptive allocation scheme that tracks the short and long term variation of the source can be used for VBR. A set of such tracking based algorithms are used [2] for VBR allocation where the User Parameter Control (UPC) and required QoS information for each VBR VC is used for computing the slot requirements in each frame. For each VBR stream, a minimum rate allocation is provided like a CBR circuit and additional ABR type dynamic allocation is done based on an instantaneous bit-rate estimation at the base station.

It should be noted that cell retransmission requires instantaneous slot allocation which cannot be done a-priori, and that is why it is necessary to have a pool of slots for retransmission of the corrupted cells. In the present MAC framework, bandwidth from the ABR partition is utilized for cell retransmission of all the traffic classes. Since there is no QoS restrictions for ABR traffic, only the slots available after CBR/VBR transmission and retransmission, are actually allocated to the ABR streams. The performance of CBR and ABR joint allocation was reported in [13].

## 3 Models for Call Admissibility

In this section, we first describe the admissibility policies and the models used to determine the blocking probabilities for each policy. Then we describe a method which we use to compare the policies.

### 3.1 The Call Admission Policies

We consider four admissibility policies in this paper. They are *complete sharing* (CS), *upper limit* (UL), *guaranteed minimum* (GM) and *trunk reservation* (TR). Each of these policies allows the bandwidth to be shared differently by multiple classes of service. The key performance metric of interest to us is the blocking probability experienced by different classes of traffic. For each of these policies, we first show how to compute the blocking probabilities. Later, we formulate and solve an optimization problem which will allow us to compare the performance of each of these policies.

For all of the admissibility policies, we assume that there are $c$ traffic classes and the arrival rate for class $i$ calls is $\lambda_i$ and the call holding times are exponentially distributed with a rate of $\mu_i$ (note that the results for all policies except the TR policy will hold even if the exponential assumptions are relaxed and there is empirical evidence to suggest that the results are quite accurate for the TR policy also (see Tran-Gia and Hübner [12])). We assume that bandwidth is available to each call as a multiple number of some basic unit, where the basic bandwidth unit is equivalent to an allotment of exactly one slot per frame described in the previous section. We assume that there are $n$ slots available per frame. Let $\alpha_i$ be the number of units of bandwidth needed by a class $i$ call. If it is a CBR call, then $\alpha_i$ times the basic bandwidth unit is exactly the bandwidth needed by the call. If it is a VBR call, then $\alpha_i$ times the basic bandwidth unit is exactly the effective bandwidth [7] of the call. From here on, we do not distinguish between VBR and CBR calls except to say that unlike CBR calls, the VBR calls may not receive exactly $\alpha_i$ slots in every single frame. At the discretion of scheduler, the slots allocated to all the VBR calls can be pooled and redistributed among the ongoing VBR calls in an attempt to give larger chunks of bandwidth to those calls that need it most. This is actually a scheduling issue and we do not consider it any more in this paper, since the method of scheduling the slots does not affect the blocking probability of the calls. More about VBR scheduling can be found in [2].

The CS policy (which is also the naive policy described in section 1) allows the full use of the available number of slots to all incoming calls. Thus if a call of type $i$ arrives to find more than $n - \alpha_i$ slots already in use, then it will be blocked, otherwise it will be admitted. In the UL policy, there cannot be more than $u_i$ calls of type $i$ ongoing at any time; otherwise the policy is the same as CS. In the GM policy, calls are admitted in such a way that there is always enough room left for having at least $g_i$ ongoing calls of type $i$ (for this policy to work, the inequality $\sum_{i=1}^{c} g_i\alpha_i \leq n$ must hold). Finally, in the TR policy, we associate a trunk reservation parameter $\gamma_i$ with class $i$ and admit a class $i$ call if and only if the number of occupied slots is strictly less than $\gamma_i$ (clearly, for this policy to work, the inequality $\gamma_i \leq n - \alpha_i + 1$ must hold and we assume this to be true in the rest of the paper). We note that the CS policy is a special case of the UL, GM and TR policies and is therefore, certain to performs no better than the others.

In what follows, we describe methods of obtaining the blocking probabilities for each class of call under each policy. In order to do that, we first need to find the joint distribution of the number of calls in progress for the different classes of traffic. For the CS, UL and the GM policies, this joint distribution is known to have the the product form (see Choudhury, Leung and Whitt [3]). There are many ways of calculating this joint distribution and we now describe one method which is simple to implement. First, we define $p_{ij} = (\lambda_i/\mu_i)^j/j!$. Then the joint probability that there there are $j_i$ calls of type $i$ in progress is given by

$$q_\pi(j_1, \ldots, j_c) = C_\pi \prod_{i=1}^{c} p_{ij_i}, \qquad (1)$$

when using policy $\pi$ (which could be CS, UL or GM) provided that policy $\pi$ allows $j_i$ calls of type $i$ to be in progress simultaneously. The constant $C_\pi$ is a normalization constant and must be chosen so that the joint probabilities add to one over the appropriate allowable state space. Let the allowable state space be denoted by $S_{CS}, S_{UL}$ and $S_{GM}$ for the three policies. Let an element of this state space be denoted by the vector $j = \{j_1, \ldots, j_c\}$, which is a $1 \times c$ vector of the number of calls in progress of each class. Let $\alpha$ denote a $c \times 1$ vector, whose $i$th element is $\alpha_i$. The definition of the allowable state spaces for the three policies now follow:

$$j \in S_{CS} \iff j\alpha \leq n, \qquad (2)$$

$$j \in S_{UL} \iff j\alpha \leq n \text{ and } j_i \leq u_i \text{ for } i = 1, \ldots, c \qquad (3)$$

$$j \in S_{GM} \iff \sum_{i \neq k} j_i\alpha_i + \alpha_k \max\{g_k, j_k\} \leq n \text{ for } k = 1, \ldots, c. \qquad (4)$$

Let $r_\pi(k)$ denote the probability that $k$ slots are in use under policy $\pi$. Then, for $\pi$ = CS, UL and GM,

$$r_\pi(k) = \sum_{\substack{j \in S_\pi \\ j\alpha = k}} q_\pi(j) \, . \qquad (5)$$

Let $B_\pi(i)$ denote the blocking probability for class $i$ calls when using policy $\pi$. Then

$$B_\pi(i) = \sum_{\substack{j \in S_\pi \\ j + e_i \notin S_\pi}} q_\pi(j) \qquad (6)$$

where $e_i$ is a $1 \times c$ vector whose $i$th element is 1 and all other elements are zero. Note that it is possible to obtain the blocking probabilities by inverting the generating function associated with the normalization constant (see Choudhury, Leung and Whitt [3, 4, 5]). Indeed, the inversion method, when implemented carefully, produces answers for the blocking probability very efficiently. However, we have chosen not to use the inversion method because of its complexity of implementation and for the size of the problems that we are concerned with, the direct method works very well.

### 3.2 The Blocking Probability for the TR Policy

We now turn our attention to the TR policy. The distribution of customers present in the system is no longer of product form. However, a very nice heavy traffic theorem is available from the work of Bean, Gibbens and Zachary ([1]). Using this heavy traffic theorem, they have proposed an approximation for the TR policy. While this approximation works very well in the heavy traffic regime, its performance under light to moderate traffic conditions can be quite poor. Further, the BGZ approximation does not produce the right results for the special case of CS. Since wireless networks are likely to be designed for moderate traffic conditions (because of the presence of VBR calls and also because of fairly stringent QoS requirements), there is much to be gained in refining the BGZ approximation. We note that we consider an approximation to be good if it is within 10% of the actual blocking probabilities. With this in mind, we now propose a refinement to the BGZ approximation. Our goal is to produce an approximation which is exact for the special case of CS and also which works very well under light to moderate traffic. Let

$$B_{TR}^A(i) = \sum_{k=\gamma_i}^{n} r_{CS}(k) \tag{7}$$

and $B_{TR}^B(i)$ denote the BGZ approximation for the blocking probability for class $i$ traffic. The BGZ approximation is quite difficult to understand from the original source. For this reason, we provide a simple description of it now (see also Greenberg and Srikant [6]).

**Step 1:** Set $B_{TR}^B(i,0) = 0$ for $i = 1,\dots,c$ and set $\nu = 1$.

**Step 2:** Let $\beta_i^\nu = (1 - B_{TR}^B(i,\nu-1))\lambda_i/\mu_i$ for $i = 1,\dots,c$. Define a continuous time Markov chain whose state space is given by $\{0,\dots,n\}$ and the transitions are

- $k \to k + \alpha_i$ with rate $\lambda_i \delta(\gamma_i - k)$ for $i = 1,\dots,c$ and $k = 0,\dots,n$
- $k \to k - \alpha_i$ with rate $\mu_i k \frac{\beta_i^\nu}{\sum_{i=1}^{c} \alpha_i \beta_i^\nu} \delta(k - \alpha_i + 1)$ for $i = 1,\dots,c$ and $k = 0,\dots,n$.

In the above, $\delta(x) = 1$ if $x > 0$, otherwise it is 0. Solve for the steady state probabilities of this Markov chain and let the solution be $P_k^\nu$ for $k = 0,\dots,n$. Let $B_{TR}^B(i,\nu) = \sum_{k=\gamma_i}^{n} P_k^\nu$.

**Step 3:** If $\max_i |B_{TR}^B(i,\nu) - B_{TR}^B(i,\nu-1)| < \epsilon$, then stop and set $B_{TR}^B(i) = B_{TR}^B(i,\nu)$. This is the BGZ approximation. If the inequality is not true, then increase $\nu$ by 1 and go back to step 2. In our implementation, we took $\epsilon = 10^{-7}$.

Our proposed approximation for the blocking probability for class $i$ calls when using the TR policy is now given by

$$B_{TR}(i) \approx \omega B_{TR}^A(i) + (1-\omega) B_{TR}^B(i) \tag{8}$$

where

$$\omega = (1 - \delta(\theta)\sqrt{\sigma})e^{-\xi} \tag{9}$$

$$\sigma = \frac{1}{n}\sum_{i=1}^{c} \alpha_i \lambda_i / \mu_i \tag{10}$$

$$\theta = \frac{1}{(c-1)n}\sum_{i=1}^{c} n + 1 - \gamma_i - \alpha_i \tag{11}$$

$$\xi = \frac{\theta}{c}\sum_{i=1}^{c} \alpha_i. \tag{12}$$

As can be seen easily, our approximation is a linear combination of the BGZ approximation and $B_{TR}^A(i)$. First, the quantity $B_{TR}^A(i)$ is the exact blocking probability for the special case of CS and second, it provides a very good answer under light traffic conditions. Note that under light traffic conditions, the occupancy is low and that it is reasonable to say that each class determines its slot occupancy as if other classes were not present. Then, one can simply take a convolution of these distributions to determine the total slot occupancy since the total slot occupancy is quite likely to be far below the capacity $n$. It is readily verified that the quantity $B_{TR}^A(i)$ has this feature built into it. Now it is easy to see that the linear combination of $B_{TR}^A(i)$ and the BGZ approximation has been taken in such a way that the overall approximation preserves the good characteristics of each. For instance, as the traffic becomes heavy (high value of $\sigma$), it favors the BGZ approximation. As the parameters of the system get close to the CS policy ($n + 1 - \alpha_i - \gamma_i = 0$ for all $i$), most of the weight is on $B_{TR}^A(i)$. It is also easy to verify that the weighting function $\omega$ has been specifically designed to produce the exact answer for the special case of CS. This results in a very accurate approximation, which works extremely well over a wide range of parameter values of interest in wireless ATM.

### 3.3 Comparison of the Policies

In this section we turn our attention to the task of determining optimum values of the parameters of these policies and also finding a method of comparing these policies. Since most operators of wireless ATM systems are likely to be interested in maximizing their revenues while keeping the blocking probabilities within some prespecified bounds, we propose a non-linear programming problem along the following lines. Assume that a traffic profile curve is given. This traffic profile curve specifies the relative arrival rates of the various classes and is denoted by $f(i)$. Thus the actual arrival rate $\lambda_i = \zeta f(i)$ for $i = 1,\dots,c$. Assume further that the prespecified bound on the blocking probabilities for class $i$ is denoted by $b(i)$ for $i = 1,\dots,c$. Then our problem is to find the parameters for policy $\pi$ (*i.e.*, find $u_i, g_i$ and $\gamma_i$ for the policies UL, GM and TR respectively) so as to

$$\text{maximize} \quad \zeta_\pi \tag{13}$$

$$\text{subject to} \quad \lambda_i = \zeta_\pi f(i) \tag{14}$$

$$\text{and} \quad B_\pi(i) \le b(i) \ \text{ for } i = 1,\dots,c, \tag{15}$$

where the formulas for $B_\pi(i)$ for various values of $\pi$ have been derived earlier. Note that we have indexed the value of $\zeta$ by $\pi$ to denote explicitly its dependence on the specific policy chosen. Note that for the CS policy, there are no parameters to be chosen; nevertheless, the problem is still quite valid for the CS policy also. Indeed, the CS policy (being fairly obvious) provides a baseline for us to make comparisons and state the amount of improvement that one can achieve over a naive approach. Note that Choudhury, Leung and Whitt [3] have also considered a similar optimization problem, although it is not in the context of wireless ATM networks.

For the CS policy, the solution of the non-linear programming problem is quite easy. We first choose a high enough value of $\zeta_{CS}$ so that at least one of the constraints on the blocking probabilities is not satisfied. Then we perform a binary search on the value of $\zeta_{CS}$ until we find a value that just satisfies the constraints.

For the UL, GM and TR policies, the difficulty of solving the non-linear programming problem is that in the absence of known structural properties of the functions involved (like convexity, monotonicity etc.), it is not possible to use one of the known methods with confidence. For this reason, we have devised a search technique which attempts to solve this problem. The technique is quite similar for all three policies, so we now describe it fully for the TR policy only.

The technique works at all times with an upper and a lower bound for $\zeta_{TR}$, called $\zeta_{TR}^U$ and $\zeta_{TR}^L$. The property of $\zeta_{TR}^U$ is such that for this value, it is not possible to satisfy the constraint on blocking probabilities for any choice of the parameters $\gamma_i$. The property of $\zeta_{TR}^L$ is such that one can find suitable values of the parameters $\gamma_i$ for which the constraints are satisfied (obviously, a possible initial value of $\zeta_{TR}^L$ is 0). A high level description of the algorithm for finding $\zeta_{TR}$ is presented as the following pseudo code.

```
set ε = 0.02;
set ζ^L_TR = 0;
/* ζ^U_TR selection procedure */
set ζ_TR = 1;
while (it is possible to find suitable
        values of TR policy parameters
        which satisfy constraints){
        ζ_TR = 2ζ_TR;
}
ζ^U_TR = ζ_TR;
/* ζ^U_TR selection is done; now search for ζ_TR */
do{
    ζ_TR = (ζ^L_TR + ζ^U_TR)/2;
    if (it is possible to find suitable
        values of TR policy parameters
        which satisfy constraints)
        ζ^L_TR = ζ_TR;
    else
        ζ^U_TR = ζ_TR;
}while ((ζ^U_TR − ζ^L_TR)/ζ_TR ≥ ε);
use the current value of ζ_TR;
```

We now turn our attention to the problem of determining whether it is possible to satisfy the constraints for a particular value of $\zeta_{TR}$.

```
/* begin forward pass */
set γ_i = n − α_i + 1 for i = 1,...,c;
do{
    compute B_TR(i) for all i;
    if (B_TR(i) ≤ b(i) for all i){
        can satisfy the constraints;
        STOP and return;
    }
    set γ_k = γ_k + 1, where k = the index i for which
                        B_TR(i) − b(i) is maximum;
}while (all γ_i are feasible);
/* forward pass ends; initiate backward pass */
do{
    set γ_k = γ_k − 1, where k = the index i for which
                        B_TR(i) − b(i) is minimum;
    if (all γ_i are not feasible){
        cannot satisfy the constraints;
        STOP and return;
    }
    compute B_TR(i) for all i;
    if (B_TR(i) > b(i) for all i){
        cannot satisfy the constraints;
        STOP and return;
    }
}while (!(B_TR(i) ≤ b(i) for all i));
can satisfy the constraints;
STOP and return;
```

The search procedure for the UL and GM policies is similar. We vary the parameters $u_i$ or $g_i$ (as the case may be) in much the same way (with suitable and fairly obvious modifications).

We now turn our attention to a special case in which the blocking probability requirements are all the same. For this problem, Tran-Gia and Hübner [12] have already given a heuristic which says that by setting the parameters ($\gamma_i$) of the TR policy to be all equal, one obtains equal blocking probabilities for all classes. We now give a simple proof of this statement. Associated with the equal values of $\gamma_i$ is the distribution of slot occupancy $r_{TR}(k)$ as derived in equation (5). Since the arrivals are Poisson, the different classes see the same slot occupancy distribution on arrival. It is easy to see that the blocking probability for class $i$ is $B_{TR}(i) = \sum_{k=\gamma_i}^{n} r_{TR}(k)$. These blocking probabilities are obviously equal if the values of $\gamma_i$ are equal.

## 4 Results

There are two parts in this section. First, we compare the results found from the approximation for the

TR policy to simulations and show that the approximation is extremely good. Second, we compare the four policies by solving the non-linear programming problem described earlier and comment on their performance.

In the results to follow, we assume that a frame has 125 slots and that there are 5 classes of service. The overall bandwidth of the medium is assumed to be 8 Mbps (this corresponds to the WATMnet prototype system [10]), so the allocation of one slot per frame to a particular call corresponds to 64 kbps (equivalent to a voice call today). We assume that calls belonging to classes 1, 2, 3, 4 and 5 require 1, 4, 7, 10 and 13 slots per frame respectively. This corresponds to 64, 256, 448, 640 and 832 kbps for the five classes. While the first one corresponds to a voice call, the remaining may correspond to data or high-quality audio or video or multi-media calls (either CBR with suitable bandwidth allocation or VBR with effective bandwidth allocation). We further assume that the average call duration is 5 minutes for all classes, which gives $\mu = 0.2$. For the traffic profile curve, we assume that $f(i) = \phi^{i-1}$, where $\phi$ is a parameter and was chosen to be 0.5, 1.0 and 1.5. Further, we assume that $\lambda_i = \zeta f(i)$ and $\zeta$ is chosen appropriately to yield a value of $\sigma = 0.5, 0.55, 0.6, 0.65$ (note that $\sigma$ was defined in eq. (10)). Finally, for the TR policy, we chose six different sets of values for $\gamma_i$. the vectors of $\gamma_i$ were (125,122,119,116,113), (121,119,117,115,113), (117,116,115,114,113), (113,113,113,113,113), (109,110,111,112,113) and (105,107,109,111,113). Thus, with three choices of $\phi$, four choices of $\sigma$ and six choices of $\gamma_i$, there are a total of 72 scenarios that we tested. Since each scenario involves the computation of five blocking probabilities for the five classes, there are 360 numbers that we compared against simulations. We set our goal of acceptable blocking probability as one which is within 10% of the value reported by the simulation. Further, we carried out the simulation for a long enough period so that in all cases tried, the half-width of the 95% confidence interval was less than 1% of the value reported. Note that these percentages have been chosen in such a way that we are very sure that the analytical results are off by at least 10% when the results actually indicate it. The BGZ approximation had 55 numbers (out of 360) that were off more than 10% from the simulation. This is to be contrasted with only 5 numbers for our approximation which were off by more than 10%. Based on this evidence (and many others which we do not cite here), we conclude that our method significantly improves the BGZ approximation while maintaining its good qualities. We also note that we have tested the same data set against another approximation proposed by Tran-Gia and Hübner ([12]). The results for this method (referred to as T-H approximation) are also very good. Their method had 11 numbers which were off by more than 10%. We present an example in table 1 for $\phi = 0.5$, $\sigma = 0.50$ and the vector of $\gamma_i$s given in the table. As can be seen in this example, the BGZ approximation can be off by quite a bit, whereas our approximation is very accurate.

We present another example in table 2, in which $\phi = 1.0$ and $\sigma = 0.5$. Again one can see that our approximation is significantly more accurate than the BGZ approximation.

We now turn our attention to the second problem at hand and that is to set optimum values of the parameters of the admissibility policies and also to compare the policies. Throughout this discussion, we assume that $n = 125, c = 5, \mu_i = 0.2$ for all $i$ and that the values of $\alpha_i$ are 1, 4, 7, 10 and 13 as before. As a first experiment, we solved the non-linear programming problem for 14 problems which are separated into two groups of 7 problems each. In both the groups, the value of $\phi$ was chosen to be 0.1, 0.2, 0.5, 0.75, 1.0, 1.25 and 1.5. In the first group (identified as Group I in table 3), the requirement on the blocking probabilities ($b_i$) were (0.05, 0.04, 0.03, 0.02, 0.01) and for the second group (identified as Group II), these were chosen to be (0.01, 0.02, 0.03, 0.04, 0.05). The results are shown in table 3 in which we show the ratio of the optimum value of $\zeta$ of a particular policy to that of the CS policy. This ratio represents the throughput gain that the policy (UL, GM or TR) can give over the CS policy. We observe from these results that there is not too much to be gained from the use of these policies under Group II whereas in Group I, there are instances in which the gain is substantial. In particular, the gains are largest in the TR policy when the arrival rate ($\lambda_i$) falls off sharply as the bandwidth required by a call ($\alpha_i$) is increased *and* the blocking probability requirement ($b_i$) falls off moderately as the bandwidth required by a call is increased. When the arrival rates do not fall sharply or when the blocking probability requirement increases moderately as the bandwidth required by a call is increased, the gains are quite modest. These observations lead us to believe that the specialized admissibility policies (UL, GM and TR) are useful only when the parameters are skewed in a special way, otherwise, the gains are small. A second observation is that the TR policy seems to outperform the UL and GM policies whenever there is a substantial gain over the CS policy.

To test this hypothesis further and to see if further gains in throughput are possible, we considered another group of more skewed problems for which the results are shown in table 4. In these problems, the value of $\phi$ was chosen to be 0.5, 0.1 and 0.05 and the blocking probability requirement was divided into three groups, A, B and C. The blocking probability requirement vec-

| | Class 1 | Class 2 | Class 3 | Class 4 | Class 5 |
|---|---|---|---|---|---|
| $\gamma_i$ | 109 | 110 | 111 | 112 | 113 |
| Simulation | 0.011782 | 0.009663 | 0.007976 | 0.006413 | 0.004848 |
| BGZ approx. | 0.010564 | 0.008540 | 0.006970 | 0.005472 | 0.004126 |
| Our approx. | 0.011506 | 0.009523 | 0.007943 | 0.006445 | 0.005095 |
| T-H approx. | 0.011342 | 0.009557 | 0.008066 | 0.006697 | 0.005442 |
| % error, BGZ | -10.335618 | -11.619339 | -12.608237 | -14.679589 | -14.890621 |
| % error, ours | -2.341978 | -1.444413 | -0.410921 | 0.495418 | 5.092761 |
| % error, T-H | -3.732860 | -1.098886 | 1.128185 | 4.432359 | 12.253221 |

Table 1: Blocking probabilities and errors, $\phi = 0.5$ and $\sigma = 0.5$

| | Class 1 | Class 2 | Class 3 | Class 4 | Class 5 |
|---|---|---|---|---|---|
| $\gamma_i$ | 121 | 119 | 117 | 115 | 113 |
| Simulation | 0.004282 | 0.007290 | 0.010663 | 0.014429 | 0.018502 |
| BGZ approx. | 0.003888 | 0.006852 | 0.010244 | 0.014025 | 0.018257 |
| Our approx. | 0.004320 | 0.007253 | 0.010614 | 0.014388 | 0.018625 |
| T-H approx. | 0.004676 | 0.007521 | 0.010795 | 0.014553 | 0.018808 |
| % error, BGZ | -9.196003 | -6.006027 | -3.931573 | -2.797823 | -1.322810 |
| % error, ours | 0.885589 | -0.509239 | -0.461237 | -0.281267 | 0.666181 |
| % error, T-H | 9.203446 | 3.168411 | 1.239140 | 0.858521 | 1.653360 |

Table 2: Blocking Probabilities and errors, $\phi = 1.0$ and $\sigma = 0.5$

| | Group I | | | Group II | | |
|---|---|---|---|---|---|---|
| $\phi$ | UL | GM | TR | UL | GM | TR |
| 0.10 | 1.093 | 1.000 | 1.173 | 1.015 | 1.000 | 1.021 |
| 0.20 | 1.086 | 1.000 | 1.201 | 1.016 | 1.000 | 1.026 |
| 0.50 | 1.047 | 1.017 | 1.154 | 1.006 | 1.000 | 1.016 |
| 0.75 | 1.019 | 1.011 | 1.120 | 1.011 | 1.011 | 1.017 |
| 1.00 | 1.012 | 1.019 | 1.094 | 1.000 | 1.000 | 1.010 |
| 1.25 | 1.009 | 1.007 | 1.074 | 1.005 | 1.000 | 1.005 |
| 1.50 | 1.011 | 1.011 | 1.062 | 1.000 | 1.004 | 1.004 |

Table 3: Optimum Throughput Relative to the CS Policy

tors for these groups were taken as (0.16, 0.08, 0.04, 0.02, 0.01), (0.0625, 0.0125, 0.0025, 0.0005, 0.0001) and (0.1, 0.01, 0.001, 0.0001, 0.00001) respectively. What characterizes these blocking probability requirements is that they do not change moderately with class; rather, in all cases, they fall quite sharply when the bandwidth requirement of the call increases. In these cases, it is readily seen that the throughput gains are consistently higher. In fact, it is possible to achieve a throughput gain of as much as 35% in some instances and that the TR policy consistently performs the best. For an operating company, this kind of gain is almost a windfall as it directly translates to 35% extra revenue with hardly any extra cost of implementation (note that an admissibility criterion based on the TR policy is practically as easy to implement as one based on the CS policy). We point out that the skewness of traffic and blocking probabilities is something to be expected in multirate wireless networks of the future. It is easy to foresee that with voice and video calls of highly different bandwidths, the dollar rate charged per minute would be quite different and this in turn would make the arrival patterns quite skewed. Further, the operating companies may choose to block one type of call much less than another because the former offers more revenue per unit of bandwidth than the latter. We further note that the actual implementation of the TR policy can be refined so that its parameters are chosen based on historical information of traffic patterns. This would enable the operating company to take advantage of multiple peaks during a day, when the arrival rates of different call types dominate. Implementation of the dynamic version of a TR policy is rather simple, when it is based on hourly histories of traffic data and so we shall not discuss this anymore.

| $\phi$ | Group | UL | GM | TR |
|---|---|---|---|---|
| 0.50 | A | 1.081 | 1.017 | 1.249 |
| 0.10 | A | 1.237 | 1.000 | 1.335 |
| 0.01 | A | 1.256 | 1.034 | 1.351 |
| 0.50 | B | 1.018 | 1.014 | 1.228 |
| 0.10 | B | 1.120 | 1.008 | 1.165 |
| 0.01 | B | 1.171 | 1.000 | 1.146 |
| 0.50 | C | 1.022 | 1.022 | 1.297 |
| 0.10 | C | 1.185 | 1.013 | 1.168 |
| 0.01 | C | 1.228 | 1.032 | 1.160 |

Table 4: Relative Optimum Throughput for Skewed Problems

## 5 Conclusions

We have examined four call admissibility policies in the framework of wireless ATM. For the TR policy, we have proposed an approximation for calculating the blocking probabilities which performs better than the earlier known methods. For all practical considerations, the errors in blocking probabilities are less than 10%. We have formulated a non-linear programming problem which has two functions. First, for a given policy, the non-linear programming problem can be used to tune the parameters of the policy. Second, the solution to the problem forms the basis of comparison of these policies. In the comparisons, we found that the policies work about equally well when the blocking probability requirements of the different classes do not differ by too much. However, there are interesting situations in which there is very significant differences between the policies. These differences occur when the class with low arrival rate requires high bandwidth and low blocking probability. When these conditions are met, the TR policy seems to work the best and it can outperform the CS policy by as much as 35% in throughput. This is a very significant potential gain since the additional throughput will directly translate to extra revenue.

## References


[1] N. Bean, R. J. . Gibbens and S. Zachary, "Analysis of large single resource loss systems under heavy traffic, with applications to integrated networks", *Adv. App. Prob.*, Vol. 27, 273-292, 1995.

[2] S. K. Biswas and D. Reininger, "Bandwidth Allocation for VBR Video in Wireless ATM Links", *Proc. 3rd International Workshop on Mobile Multimedia Communications, Princeton, NJ.*, 1996.

[3] G. L. Choudhury, K. K. Leung and W. Whitt, "Efficiently Providing Multiple Grades of Service with Protection Against Overloads in Shared Resources", *AT&T Technical Journal*, 50-63, July-August 1995.

[4] G. L. Choudhury, K. K. Leung and W. Whitt, "An Algorithm to Compute Blocking Probabilities in Multirate Multi-class Multi-resource Loss Models", *Adv. in App. Prob.*, Vol. 27, no. 4, 1104-1143, 1995.

[5] G. L. Choudhury, K. K. Leung and W. Whitt, "An Inversion Algorithm to Compute Blocking Probabilities in Loss Networks with State-Dependent Rates", *IEEE/ACM Tran. in Networking*, Vol. 3, No. 5, 585-601, October 1995.

[6] A. Greenberg and R. Srikant, "Computational Techniques for Accurate Performance Evaluation of Multirate, Multihop Communication Networks", *Sigmetrics 1995*, Ottawa, Canada.

[7] R. Guerin, H. Ahmadi and M. Naghshineh, "Equivalent Capacity and Its Application to Bandwidth Allocation in High-Speed Networks", *IEEE JSAC*, Vol. 9, No. 7, 968-981, 1991.

[8] J. S. Kaufman, "Blocking in a Shared Resource Environment", *IEEE Tran. in Comm.*, Vol. 29, No. 10, 1474-1481, 1981.

[9] D. Raychaudhuri, "ATM-based transport architecture for multiservices wireless personal communication networks", *Proc. ICC*, 317.1.1-317.1.7, 1994.

[10] D. Raychaudhuri, L. J. French, R. J. Siracusa, S. K. Biswas, R. Yuan, P. Narasimhan and C. Johnston, "WATMnet: A Prototype Wireless ATM System for Multimedia Personal Communication", *to appear in IEEE JSAC.*

[11] J. W. Roberts, "A Service System with Heterogeneous User Requirements - Application to Multi-Service Telecommunications Systems", *Performance of Data Communication Systems and Their Applications*, G. Pujolle (ed.), North-Holland, 423-431, 1981.

[12] P. Tran-Gia and F. Hübner, "An Analysis of Trunk Reservation and Grade of Service Balancing Mechanisms in Multiservice Broadband Networks", *Modelling and Performance Evaluation of ATM Technology*, H. Perros, G. Pujolle and Y. Takahashi (eds.), Elsevier Science Publishers, 83-97, 1993.

[13] H. Xie, P. Narasimhan, R. Yuan, and D. Raychaudhuri, "Data Link Protocols for Wireless ATM Access Channels", *Proc. ICUPC, Tokyo, Japan*, 753-757, 1995.

[14] R. Yuan, S. K. Biswas and D. Raychaudhuri, "A Signalling and Control Architecture for Mobility Support in Wireless ATM Networks", *Proc. ICC, Dallas*, 478-484, 1996.

# Panel 2

## Routing vs. Switching

**Moderator**

Dimitrios Pendarakis, *IBM*

**Panelists**

Andrew Campbell, *Columbia University*
Dennis Ferguson, *Juniper Systems*
Srinivasan Keshav, *Cornell University*
Peter Newman, *Ipsilon Networks*
Martha Steenstrup, *BBN*

# Incentive Pricing in Multi-Class Communication Networks

Ariel Orda and Nahum Shimkin
Department of Electrical Engineering and the S. Neaman Institute
Technion, Israel Institute of Technology
Haifa 32000, Israel
{ariel,shimkin}@ee.technion.ac.il

## Abstract

*We consider a communication network that offers multi-class services to multiple types of traffic. Users choose service classes so as to optimize their own performance. The network associates with each traffic type a* nominal *service class.* Optimal prices *should provide incentives for the users to assign each traffic type to its nominal service class.*

*We establish necessary and sufficient conditions for the existence of optimal prices and provide an algorithm for their computation. We indicate that optimal prices can tolerate fluctuations in the various parameters. We then devise a distributed algorithm, with which the network can compute optimal prices even when it does not have sufficient knowledge on the traffic characteristics. Next, we consider an extended model which explicitly includes congestion effects. A key factor which emerges here is the amount of traffic at the disposal of each user. We consider the typical cases of individual, social and type optimization, for which we generalize our results.*

## 1 Introduction

Emerging broadband networks will offer multi-class services and support multiple types of traffic. Users of these networks will be able to choose the service class for their traffic, thus playing an active role in the supervision of network flows. The above scenario could lead to a deficient usage of the network resources. Users are concerned with the performance of their own traffic, rather than with the overall system performance. Thus, a user could be tempted to choose the best class of service for its traffic, even if a lower class of service would suffice. The network, on the other hand, needs its resources to be used in the most efficient way, meaning that, from a system point of view, premium service should be consumed only by those who really need it.

Our study is motivated by the fundamental distinction between *traffic types* and *service classes*: the traffic type is a property that characterizes the traffic requirements as perceived by user, and is typically known only to the user; the service class is a parameter assigned to the traffic stream (e.g., to each connection), which identifies the grade of service to be granted by the network. Consequently, the network relies on the user to specify the required service class for its traffic. The basic idea of incentive pricing is to assign different prices to available service classes, which would provide the required incentive for the users to choose the service class which the *network* deems appropriate for their requirements. Obviously, service classes which require more resources should be assigned relatively higher prices, which will prevent their usage by those who can settle for less, but not deter those who actually need them. A key point in the pricing scheme is that prices must depend only on the service class, and not on the traffic type, as follows from the network inability to identify traffic types. We aim at providing the required user incentives through a simple, fixed pricing scheme.

The incorporation of pricing in modern networking has been gaining increasing interest in the past few years [1, 2, 3, 4, 5, 6, 7, 8, 9]. Some of these studies, e.g. [1, 6], concentrated on best-effort networks such as the Internet, while others, e.g. [2, 3], concentrated on ATM-based networks. Several studies proposed pricing mechanisms that are load-sensitive, often based on some bidding scheme such as the "smart market" approach [6]. Such schemes typically focus on the access to a *single-class* network, which offers the same type of service to all accepted packets. Multi-class services have been typically tackled by pricing schemes that maximize some prescribed social function (e.g., [2, 8]).

Our study focuses on traffic allocation in networks that provide multi-class services. The fundamental standpoint is that the network associates with each traffic type a nominal service class, which it considers as the proper one for that type. The objective of pricing is to provide incentives for the users to assign each traffic type to its nominal service class. The determination of the nominal classes should take into account both the user satisfaction as well as the availability and cost of network resources. Often, the proper choice presents itself naturally, and it is inherent in the design of the network service classes.

Our basic model assumes that the quality of each service class does not depend on the traffic volume. This is expected to hold in a properly designed network, which operates near nominal conditions. Moreover, it fits well a "rigid" interpretation of an advertized grade of service, as is the case, for example, with guaranteed QoS connections in ATM networks. We also consider a different model, where the effects of congestion are explicitly included. In [10] we extend



0-8186-7780-5/97 $10.00 

both models to handle uncertainties in the user parameters and preferences.

For the basic model, we establish necessary and sufficient conditions for the existence of *optimal* prices, which lead each user to allocate its traffic according to the nominal choice. We specify these prices, provide an algorithm for their computation, and indicate that they can tolerate fluctuations in the traffic and service parameters. We also establish a relation to a class of network design problems. We then turn our attention to the practical problem of establishing the required price assignment when the network does not have sufficient knowledge on the traffic characteristics, or needs to adapt to changes. For such scenarios, we devise a distributed, iterative algorithm, whereby each service class updates its price by solely measuring its current traffic. We show that the algorithm converges to optimal prices, thereby inducing the nominal traffic allocation. Next, we consider the congestion model. Here, a distinction must be made among different kinds of users, based on the amount of flow that they control. First, we consider the typical case of *individual optimization*, where each user controls only a small part of the total traffic, and extend our results to this case. Next, we specialize our model, and consider in detail the effect of different user kinds. These include the other extreme, namely *social optimization*, in which a single user is responsible for the whole traffic. In [10] we also consider a typical intermediate case, termed *type optimization*, where each traffic type constitutes a different user.

The paper is structured as follows. In section 2 we formally define the basic model. The existence and structure of the corresponding optimal price assignments is presented in Section 3, while the dynamic distributed algorithm is formulated and analyzed in Section 4. Section 5 deals with the congestion model. Finally, in Section 6 we discuss these results and suggest several directions for further research. Due to space limits, proofs are omitted from this version, and can be found in [10].

## 2 Model Formulation

We formulate in this section the model that will be considered in this paper. We first present the model in its most basic form, and then consider some important extensions that will also be treated in the sequel.

### 2.1 The Basic Model

Consider a communication network which offers several classes of service, denoted by the set $\mathcal{K} = \{1, 2, \ldots, K\}$. We assume that the traffic in this system is divided into a finite number of distinct traffic types, denoted $\mathcal{I} = \{1, 2, \ldots, I\}$. The traffic types differ in their service requirements, as specified below.

Traffic is composed of data units, or flow units, which may be packets, sessions, etc., depending on the application. The flow units of all traffic types are assumed to be similar, and, in particular, they cannot be distinguished from each other by the network. The arrival process is assumed to be ergodic, with rate $\Lambda^i$ for type $i \in \mathcal{I}$. The users of the system are free to allocate any part of their traffic to any service class.

A basic premise of our formulation is that the "proper" traffic distribution is specified by a unique allocation of each traffic type to one of the service classes. We refer to this allocation as the *nominal class allocation*, and denote by $k(i)$ the nominal service class for traffic type $i$. The nominal allocation reflects the intent, or design, of the network service provider. While we do not specify at this stage a specific mechanism through which this allocation is chosen, it is obvious that a proper allocation should take into account the suitability of the service class for the traffic type, and a balanced utilization of network resources. Moreover, such an allocation is expected to underly the design of a multi-class network.

To be more precise, we introduce some additional notation. Denote by $\lambda_k^i$ the rate of type $i$ traffic which is directed to service class $k$, and let $\lambda_k = \sum_{i \in \mathcal{I}} \lambda_k^i$ denote the total rate of traffic allocated to service class $k$. The vector $\boldsymbol{\lambda}^i = \{\lambda_k^i, k \in \mathcal{K}\}$ denotes the *traffic flow of type* $i$, and $\boldsymbol{\lambda} = \{\boldsymbol{\lambda}^i, i \in \mathcal{I}\}$ is the *(global) traffic flow*. The set of *feasible flows* for traffic type $i$ is the set of allocation as $\boldsymbol{\lambda}^i$ which are non-negative and flow conserving, namely $\mathcal{L}^i = \{\boldsymbol{\lambda}^i : \lambda_k^i \geq 0, \sum_k \lambda_k^i = \Lambda^i\}$. Similarly, $\mathcal{L} = \{\boldsymbol{\lambda} : \boldsymbol{\lambda}^i \in \mathcal{L}^i\}$ is the set of *feasible traffic flows*. The *nominal flow allocation* $\boldsymbol{\lambda}^*$ may now be defined as

$$\lambda_k^{i*} = \begin{cases} \Lambda^i & k = k(i) \\ 0 & k \neq k(i) \end{cases} . \qquad (1)$$

Here $k(i) \in \mathcal{K}$ is the nominal service class for traffic class $i$, as specified by the nominal class allocation $\{k(i), i \in \mathcal{I}\}$.

We now introduce performance measures and the proposed pricing mechanism for this system. Each flow unit may be charged a certain price, which may depend on its service class (but not on its traffic type attribute, which, as mentioned above, is indistinguishable by the network). The price per unit flow in service class $k$ is denoted by $p_k$, and $p = (p_1, \ldots, p_K)$ is the *price vector*. In this paper we explore the use of this differential pricing mechanism as a means to regulate the traffic distribution between the different service classes, so that it will coincide with the nominal flow allocation.

To model the service requirements and preferences of the different traffic types, we associate with each traffic type $i$ and service class $k$ a number $c_k^i$. This number measures the subjective cost (or dissatisfaction) per unit flow of traffic type $i$ with respect to the performance offered by service class $k$. We assume that these costs are normalized to the same units as the prices $p_k$, so that the total cost per unit flow of traffic type $i$ using service class $k$ equals $c_k^i + p_k$. Obviously, the interest of each network user is to choose for its type-$i$ traffic the service class $k$ for which this cost is minimal. A traffic flow which obeys this rule is called a *user-optimal flow* for the price vector $p$ (a more precise definition will be given in the next section). In the following sections, we seek to characterize those price vectors $p$ for which the user-optimal allocation coincides with the nominal traffic allocation.

## 2.2 Extensions to the Basic Model

We now outline some important extensions to the basic model. While the first may be incorporated into the model by suitable definitions, the last two will require separate consideration.

1. *Elastic demand:* Our model assumes that all available traffic enters the system. However, the important case of elastic demand (where total service demand may depend on service costs) may be incorporated into this model, simply by appending a "null" service class (say, $k = 0$) to the actual ones. The costs $c_0^i$ associated with this class should reflect the cost incurred by type-$i$ traffic for not getting service, and the service price $p_0$ must naturally be set to 0. The latter does not interfere with the results in the following sections, since all price vectors are specified in relative terms (i.e., up to a common bias, which may be chosen to obtain $p_0{=}0$).

2. *Uncertain costs:* An important consideration in any pricing scheme should be its robustness to the cost coefficients $c_k^i$. Indeed, these costs may represent a subjective estimate which may be imprecisely known. Furthermore, some variation in these costs may be present *within* a given traffic class. In [10] we consider a model where the cost coefficients $c_k^i$ are only known to reside in an interval $[\underline{c}_k^i, \bar{c}_k^i]$, with arbitrary distribution within this interval. The main results described in this paper are extended to this important case.

3. *Congestion:* In highly congested networks, service quality may depend on the traffic volume and distribution. Thus, the cost coefficients $c_i^j$ become functions of the traffic flows. The effects of this extension on our model will be analyzed in some detail in Section 5.

# 3 Optimal Pricing

This section is devoted to the characterization of optimal prices. In accordance with the objectives set forth in the previous section, a price vector is optimal if it induces the nominal flows of all traffic types. We start by stating the precise definitions. We then consider the existence of optimal prices, and state explicit conditions for existence in terms of the system data. Computation of optimal prices is considered next, followed by an indication of some connections which exist between optimal prices and network design.

## 3.1 Definitions

**Definition 3.1** *Given a price vector $p$, the flow allocation $\boldsymbol{\lambda} \in \mathcal{L}$ is* user-optimal *if, for every traffic type $i$,*

$$\lambda_k^i > 0 \text{ implies } c_k^i + p_k \le c_l^i + p_l \quad \text{for all } l \neq k. \quad (2)$$

The last condition means simply that each traffic type is allocated to the service class (or classes) with minimal cost. Obviously, such user-optimal flow allocation always exists; however, it will be unique if and only if it satisfies the inequalities in (2) strictly.

It is easily verified that an allocation $\boldsymbol{\lambda}$ is (uniquely) user-optimal if and only if it is a (unique) solution of the following "social" minimization problem:

$$\min\{\sum_{i,k}(c_k^i + p_k)\lambda_k^i \ : \ \boldsymbol{\lambda} \in \mathcal{L}\}, \quad (3)$$

or, by collecting terms,

$$\min\{\sum_{i,k} c_k^i \lambda_k^i + \sum_k p_k \lambda_k \ : \ \boldsymbol{\lambda} \in \mathcal{L}\}. \quad (4)$$

These equivalent characterizations will be useful in the sequel. We note that this equivalence of individual and social optimization is a consequence of the assumed congestion-independent cost structure. We may now define the class of price vectors we are interested in:

**Definition 3.2** *A price vector $p$ is said to be* optimal *if the user-optimal flow allocation induced by $p$ is unique, and coincides with the nominal flow allocation.*

A flow allocation which is the unique user-optimal allocation for *some* price vector will be termed *price-inducible.*

## 3.2 Existence of Optimal Prices

Existence of an optimal price vector is not guaranteed. Intuitively, some consistency should be maintained between user service preferences (expressed by the cost coefficients $c_i^k$) and the nominal flow allocation, specified by the set $\{k(i),\ i \in \mathcal{I}\}$. To give a concrete example, consider the case of two traffic types and two service classes. Assume that $c_1^1 < c_2^1$ and $c_2^2 < c_1^2$, namely, with no external pricing, traffic type 1 prefers service class 1, and traffic type 2 prefers service class 2. Assume further that the nominal class allocation was chosen as $k(1) = 2$ and $k(2) = 1$ (traffic type 1 to service class 2, and type 2 to class 1). It is easily seen that no pricing vector $p = (p_1, p_2)$ can induce this allocation. Fixing $p_2$, if $p_1$ is chosen high enough so that type 1 traffic prefers service class 2, then so will type 2 traffic. The class allocations which may be enforced in this system are: $\{k(1) = 1, k(2) = 2\}$ (with null pricing), $k(1) = k(2) = 1$ (set $p_1$ low enough), and $k(1) = k(2) = 2$ (set $p_1$ high enough).

Existence of an optimal price vector is resolved in the following theorem. To present this result, define the constants

$$\alpha(k,l) = \min_{i:k(i)=k}(c_l^i - c_k^i). \quad (5)$$

If the minimization domain is empty, i.e., no $i$ exists with $k(i) = k$, define $\alpha(k,l) = \infty$. The minimized term may be interpreted as the difference in cost for traffic type $i$ between service classes

$k$ and $l$; the minimum is taken over all traffic types which are allocated to class $k$ as their nominal service class. Furthermore, define a *cycle* $C$ as a cyclic sequence of service class pairs: $C = \{(k_1, k_2), (k_2, k_3), \ldots, (k_{m-1}, k_m), (k_m, k_1)\}$, $m \geq 2$. A cycle is simple if it does not contain any sub-cycle, namely, all participating classes $\{k_n\,, n = 1, \ldots, m\}$ are distinct. Obviously, the number of simple cycles is finite.

**Theorem 3.1** *An optimal price vector exists if and only if*

$$\sum_{(k,l)\in C} \alpha(k,l) > 0 \tag{6}$$

*for every simple cycle $C$. Service classes which are empty under the nominal allocation need not be included in these cycles.*

The proof of the above theorem is based on the following basic observation:

**Lemma 3.1** *A price vector $p$ is optimal if and only if*

$$p(k,l) := p_k - p_l < \alpha(k,l) \text{ for all } k,\ l \neq k. \tag{7}$$

An alternative form for the condition of the last theorem is provided by the following corollary.

**Corollary 3.1** *Let $\lambda_k^*$ denote the total flow allocated to service class $k$ under the nominal allocation $\boldsymbol{\lambda}^*$. Consider the following constrained minimization problem:*

$$\min_{\boldsymbol{\lambda}}\{\sum_{i,k} c_k^i \lambda_k^i \ :\ \boldsymbol{\lambda} \in \mathcal{L},\ \sum_i \lambda_k^i = \lambda_k^*\}. \tag{8}$$

*An optimal price vector exists if and only if this problem has a unique solution, which coincides with the nominal flow allocation.*

This corollary is most naturally interpreted in terms of the optimization problem (3). The cost function of that problem may be written as

$$\sum_{i,k} c_k^i \lambda_k^i + \sum_k p_k \lambda_k\,.$$

This reflects the fact that pricing at each service class is insensitive to the traffic type. The minimization in (3) may now be divided into the following two steps:

$$\min_{\{\lambda_k\}}\{\min_{\{\lambda_k^i\}}\{\sum_{i,k} c_k^i \lambda_k^i : \sum_i \lambda_k^i = \lambda_k\} + \sum_k p_k \lambda_k\}. \tag{9}$$

The outer minimization is over the set of feasible *total* allocations to each service class, and the inner one over the feasible flow allocations given these total allocations. The necessity of (8) is now an immediate consequence. The sufficiency part may be interpreted as follows. For a required allocation $\boldsymbol{\lambda}^*$ to be realizable as a user-optimal one, it is only required to comply with the internal (price-independent) minimization. If it does, then pricing may be used to make the required total class-allocations optimal (in the outer minimization, hence for the overall problem).

### 3.3 Computation of Optimal Prices

The set of optimal price vectors is defined by condition (7), which is a set of linear constraints. Hence, if non-empty, this set is an open polyhedron (in particular, it is convex). An optimal price vector may be obtained by one of the standard methods for obtaining a feasible point with respect to a set of linear inequalities. A particular (finite) algorithm, implied by the proof of theorem 3.1, is presented in [10].

Since in general there is a whole set of optimal price vectors, one may want to choose the particular price vector from this set by exercising additional considerations. If these may be expressed through a cost function, this leads to a minimization problem subject to the linear constraints (7), for which efficient algorithms exist. A possible criterion for choosing the price vector may be to choose a "centrally located" element of this set (in some appropriate sense), in order to guarantee some robustness with respect to model variations. This approach to robust design is discussed in a more explicit way through the uncertain-cost model treated in [10].

### 3.4 Pricing and Network Design

Up till now we have not considered a specific way through which the nominal allocation is chosen. Here we consider briefly the case where the nominal allocation is chosen as an outcome of a network design problem. In particular, consider the following problem:

$$\min_{\boldsymbol{\lambda}}\{\sum_{i,k} c_k^i \lambda_k^i + \sum_k g_k \lambda_k\}.$$

In the minimized cost, the first term stands for the user negative utility (with $c_k^i$ the same cost coefficients as considered in our model so far). The second term, with $g_k > 0$, measures the cost, for the service provider, of setting up and maintaining the service class $k$ to support a traffic volume $\lambda_k$.

Generically, this design problem has a unique solution, which may be specified as the nominal flow allocation. The following simple result, which is a direct consequence of the formulation (9) of user-optimality, shows how the optimal price vector may be chosen in this case.

**Proposition 3.1** *Let the nominal allocation be chosen as the solution of the above network design problem (assumed to be unique). Then an optimal price vector, which makes this allocation user-optimal, is given by $p_k = g_k$.*

An alternative network design criterion, which directly takes into account the revenues obtained by the service provider through pricing, is the following one:

$$\min_{\boldsymbol{\lambda}}\{\sum_{i,k} c_k^i \lambda_k^i + \sum_k g_k \lambda_k - \sum_k p_k \lambda_k\}.$$

This cost function is appropriate when prices have an absolute meaning, which prevents addition of an arbitrary bias to all elements of the price vector. This is the situation in the elastic demand case, discussed at the end of the previous section. With this cost function, an identical result to the last corollary is obtained, except that now the price vector should be chosen as $p_k = g_k/2$.

## 4 Iterative Pricing

In the previous section we addressed the issue of price determination from an "open loop" design viewpoint - the prices are computed using a model of the system. Here we look at this problem from an operational viewpoint. Assuming that the system is in operation, using a fixed price vector, it is expected that some deviation from the expected performance will be observed, or perhaps develop over time. One option, then, is to update our model of the system based on the new information, and compute a new price vector according to this model. The second possibility is to update the price vector as a direct function of the observed performance parameters. This second option is explored in this section.

Consistent with our basic assumption, whereby different traffic types may not be discernable by the system, we assume that the observed quantities are the total flow at each service class (but not the distribution according to traffic types). Thus, we observe the vector $\{\lambda_k, k \in \mathcal{K}\}$, to which we refer as the *total flow.*

As a preliminary result, we show first that, under user-optimality, the total flow uniquely determines the flow allocation vector (i.e., the distribution of user types among the service classes may be determined even if we observe only the total flow at each service class). This implies, in particular, that just by looking at the total flow we can determine whether a given (user-optimal) flow allocation is the nominal one. Thus motivated, we propose an iterative algorithm for updating the price vector according to the observed total flow, and analyze its convergence to the optimal prices.

We note that the results in this section can be obtained are valid for the extended model with cost coefficient uncertainties, as described in [10].

**Proposition 4.1** *Let $\boldsymbol{\lambda}$ be a unique user-optimal allocation induced by some price-vector p, and let $\hat{\boldsymbol{\lambda}}$ be a unique user-optimal allocation corresponding to $\hat{p}$. If the total flow is the same in both cases ($\lambda_k = \hat{\lambda}_k$, $k \in \mathcal{K}$), then $\boldsymbol{\lambda}$ and $\hat{\boldsymbol{\lambda}}$ coincide.*

Let $\lambda^o = \{\lambda_k^o\}$ denote a nominal total-flow vector, which we seek to enforce through an appropriate price vector $p^o$. The following iterative update law is suggested for determining a price $p^o$ vector that will lead to the nominal total flow allocation $\lambda^o$.

**Iterative Procedure:** For every $t = 0, 1, 2, \ldots$:

$$p_k(t+1) = p_k(t) + d_k(\lambda_k(t) - \lambda_k^o), \quad k \in \mathcal{K}, \quad (10)$$

where each $d_k$ is a positive constant.

The interpretation is as follows: at each step $t$ we employ the price vector $p(t)$, and observe the resulting flow $\lambda(t) = \{\lambda_k(t)\}$. If it deviates from the required (nominal) one, we update the price in proportion to that deviation, and with the proper sign – if the flow is too high the price for that class is increased, and vice-versa.

Note that the proposed procedure is distributed, in the sense that only local flow information is used at each service class to update the price for that class.

Let us formulate the assumptions that will be used in the convergence analysis of this scheme. First, we shall assume that the observed response $\lambda(t)$ to the price vector $p(t)$ is *user-optimal.* Another crucial assumption is that the user-optimal response is unique, and depends *continuously* on the price. In terms of our cost model, this implies that the distribution of the cost coefficients $c_k^i$ *within* each traffic type must be continuous (as opposed to the basic model, for example, where all traffic of a given type ideally share precisely the same coefficients). This assumption seems reasonable in practical scenarios. The required assumptions are stated more precisely as follows.

**Assumptions I:**

(I1) For each price vector $p$, the user-optimal flow allocation is unique.
The total flow vector $\{\lambda_k\}$ corresponding to that user-optimal flow will be denoted by $\lambda^*(p)$.

(I2) $\lambda(t) = \lambda^*(p(t))$ for evert $t \geq 1$.

(I3) If the price $p_k$ changes by $\Delta p_k$, the corresponding change $\Delta\lambda_k^*$ in $\lambda_k^*(p)$ is bounded by

$$|\Delta\lambda_k^*| \leq \alpha_k |\Delta p_k|,$$

where $\alpha_k$ is a finite constant. Note that this may be written as $|\frac{\partial\lambda_k^*(p)}{\partial p_k}| \leq \alpha_k$ if $\lambda_k^*(\cdot)$ is differentiable.

(I4) The nominal total flow vector $\lambda^o$ is user-optimal for some price vector $p^o$, i.e., $\lambda^o = \lambda^*(p^o)$. (Note that $p^o$ need not be unique.)

**Theorem 4.1** *Consider the algorithm (10), with the coefficients $d_k$ chosen so that $d_k\alpha_k < 1$. Then, for any initial condition $\lambda(0)$,*

$$\lim_{t\to\infty} \lambda(t) = \lambda^o,$$

*and $p(t)$ converges to a constant price vector.*

## 5 Congestion Model

Till now we have not included in our model an explicit representation of the effects of possible congestion. If the impact of congestion is limited and reasonably small, then it may be handled within the uncertainty model, discussed previously: the lower bound would correspond to the ideal, uncongested state, whereas the upper bound would correspond to the worst (congested) state. However, if the impact of congestion is major, it may be required to model it explicitly and analyze its effect. This is the subject of the current section.

We thus consider a modification of our former model. In the new model, the subjective cost $c_k^i$ is a *function* of the load (total flow) at the service classes, $c_k^i(\lambda)$, which grows as congestion builds up. Here $\lambda = \{\lambda_k\}$ is the total flow vector, where $\lambda_k$ is the total flow at service class $k$.

A major difference between this and the previous (uncongested) model is that now each part of the traffic may affect the performance of the other parts. Therefore, the concept of "user optimality" now depends on the amount of flow that each user controls. We shall focus on the two extreme cases. The first is the typical case of *individual optimization*, where each user controls an infinitesimally small part of the total traffic. This is the case, for example, when each individual call is optimized independently. We then explore the other extreme case, termed *social optimization*, where a single user is responsible for the whole traffic.[1] In [10] we also consider a typical intermediate case, namely *type optimization*, where each traffic type constitutes a user that optimizes performance of the *overall* traffic of *that* type, but is indifferent to the performance of other types.

The case of individual optimization is analyzed in subsection 5.1 for the general model. The impact of the different user optimality concepts will be explored within a specialized model, as defined in subsection 5.2.

### 5.1 General Congestion Costs

As mentioned above, $c_k^i = c_k^i(\lambda)$ is a function of the total traffic flow vector $\lambda$. We assume that, for all $i \in \mathcal{I}$ and $k \in \mathcal{K}$, $c_k^i$ is continuous, strictly increasing in $\lambda_k$ and nondecreasing in $\lambda_l$ for all $l \in \mathcal{K}$. When no further assumptions are made, we shall term such functions as *general congestion costs.* In the following we discuss these costs in the context of individual optimization.

The inherent complication of general congestion costs is that, in absence of an appropriate form of convexity, there may exist multiple equilibrium points, which may be unconnected and result in different performance for the users. As we shall see, it is fairly easy to identify price vectors under which the nominal allocation is an equilibrium. However, the co-existence of other equilibria cannot be prevented in general.

We proceed with a formal definition of individual optimality, and indicate the relevant local results. We then formulate appropriate convexity-type conditions which guarantee the uniqueness of the equilibrium solution.

**Definition 5.1** *Given a price vector p, the flow allocation* $\boldsymbol{\lambda} \in \mathcal{L}$ *is* individually optimal *if, for every traffic type i,*

$$\lambda_k^i > 0 \textit{ implies } c_k^i(\lambda) + p_k \le c_l^i(\lambda) + p_l \quad \textit{for all } l \ne k. \tag{11}$$

*It is* strictly *individually optimal if the above inequalities are strict.*

[1] It might be argued that there is no reason to give incentives to the user in the case of social optimization. However, we should distinguish between optimality as perceived by the users (even if they are "social") and that perceived by the network.

A price vector is *locally optimal* if the nominal traffic allocation is individually optimal with respect to it. Observe that the total flow vector $\lambda$ corresponding to the nominal allocation is known, hence so are the values of the associated costs $c_k^i(\lambda)$. It is then trivial to show that a complete characterization of locally optimal prices may be obtained exactly as in the uncongested case, i.e. when $c_k^i$ are constants, simply be replacing these constants by their nominal values. This result, while local in nature, has independent significance. Indeed, frequently, the user is not likely to consider drastic alterations of the nominal allocation. Rather, starting from this assignment, it would consider (or try) small deviations. In this case, the local result is sufficient to maintain the nominal allocation.

In order to obtain a global result, paralleling the one obtained for the uncongested case, further assumptions are required. For example, the following *diagonal monotonicity* condition is sufficient for guaranteeing a unique individually optimal flow allocation for each given price vector (a similar result was stated in [11], in the context of transportation networks).

**Proposition 5.1** *Suppose that, for every pair of feasible traffic flows* $\boldsymbol{\lambda}, \hat{\boldsymbol{\lambda}} \in \mathcal{L}$, *with* $\lambda \ne \hat{\lambda}$ *(unequal total flows), there exist positive numbers* $\{r^1, r^2, \dots, r^I\}$ *for which the following relation holds:*

$$\sum_{i \in \mathcal{I}} \sum_{k \in \mathcal{K}} r^i (\hat{\lambda}_k^i - \lambda_k^i)(c_k^i(\hat{\lambda}) - c_k^i(\lambda)) > 0. \tag{12}$$

*(i) If* $\boldsymbol{\lambda}$ *and* $\hat{\boldsymbol{\lambda}}$ *are individually optimal allocations, their corresponding total flow vectors* $\lambda = \{\lambda_k\}$ *and* $\hat{\lambda} = \{\hat{\lambda}_k\}$ *are identical.*

*(ii) If an individually optimal allocation is strict, then it is unique, i.e., no other individually optimal allocation exists.*

A particular case, with no coupling between the service classes, for which this condition is satisfied is studied in the next subsection. As another example, in [10] we show that (12) holds in a network with a two-priority server.

### 5.2 Proportional Congestion Costs

Suppose that, for each service class $k$, there is a function $T_k$ and constants $c^1, c^2, \dots, c^I$, such that $c_k^i(\lambda) = c^i \cdot T_k$. We assume that $T_k$ depends on the flow at only service class $k$, i.e., $T_k = T_k(\lambda_k)$, and that the number of service classes matches the number of traffic types, i.e., $K = I = N$. Within this framework, we shall consider the three user behavior models mentioned above, namely individual, social and type optimization. To any user behavior model, and for each price vector, there corresponds a user-optimal (equilibrium) point. Whenever possible, we shall aim at establishing the uniqueness of that point for any given price vector. This will enable to obtain price vectors which are optimal is a global sense.

The classes of service are ordered by descending quality, i.e., service class 1 offers the best service quality and service class $N$ offers the worst quality, in a sense defined below (Assumption (T2)). Similarly, traffic types are ordered by descending quality of service requirements, meaning that $c^i > c^{i+1}$ for all $1 \leq i < N$. Service classes are matched to the traffic types accordingly, so that the $i$-th service class is the nominal one for the $i$-th traffic type.

We make the following technical assumption on the functions $T_k$:

(T1) $T_k(\lambda_k)$ is positive, strictly increasing, convex and continuously differentiable.

In addition, we make the following assumption, that differentiates among service classes:

(T2) $T_k(\Lambda^k) < T_{k+1}(\Lambda^{k+1})$ for all $1 \leq k < N$,

i.e., at nominal flow allocation, the quality of service is indeed descending in the class number.

As before, a flow unit pays a price $p_k$ for getting service from the $k$-th server. Thus, a flow unit belonging to the $i$-th traffic type, sent by the user to the $k$-th server, incurs a total cost of $c^i \cdot T_k(\lambda_k) + p_k$, when the total traffic sent to that server is $\lambda_k$.

### 5.2.1 Individual Optimality

We consider first the case where flow allocations are determined according to an individually optimal decision structure, as defined in Definition 5.1 of the previous subsection.

We first note that the diagonal monotonicity condition (12) in Proposition 5.1, hence the uniqueness results of that proposition, hold for the present cost structure. Indeed, choosing $r^i = \frac{1}{c^i}$, on the LHS (left-hand side) of 12 becomes $\sum_k(\hat{\lambda}_k - \lambda_k)(T_k(\hat{\lambda}_k) - T_k(\lambda_k))$ which is positive for any $\lambda \neq \hat{\lambda}$, by Assumption (T1).

**Definition 5.2** *A price vector p is* globally optimal *with respect to individually optimal allocations if, given this price vector, the nominal flow allocation is a unique and strict individually optimal flow allocation.*

We are now ready to present a complete characterization of optimal price vectors.

**Theorem 5.1** *Assume strict individually optimal allocations.*

(*i*) *A price vector p is optimal if and only if it satisfies*

$$c^{k+1}(\tau_{k+1} - \tau_k) < p_k - p_{k+1} < c^k(\tau_{k+1} - \tau_k), \tag{13}$$

*where* $k = 1, \ldots, N-1$ *and* $\tau_k = T_k(\Lambda^k)$.

(*ii*) *An optimal price vector always exists.*

(*iii*) *Any optimal price vector is class-monotonic, namely* $p_k > p_{k+1}$ *for* $k \in \mathcal{K}$.

Note that condition (13) only deals explicitly with the benefit of shifting flow to an *adjacent* service class. The point of the above theorem is that, under our class and type ordering assumptions, this is enough to ensure that no flow unit will find it advantageous to shift to *any* other service class rather than its nominal one. We also note that condition (13) guarantees a range of optimal price vectors, i.e., it provides a robust solution.

### 5.2.2 Social Optimality

Social optimality applies when all modeled traffic is controlled by a single user. As used here, the term refers only to the user point of view. The network's interests may be quite different, induced perhaps by looking at a "larger picture" of network performance. Pricing is used in our model as a tool which allows the network to enforce these interests.

Given a price vector $p$, a flow allocation $\boldsymbol{\lambda}$ is *socially optimal* if it minimizes the following cost function, which represents the social (i.e., averaged) cost:

$$J(\boldsymbol{\lambda}) = \sum_{k,i}(c^i \lambda_k^i T_k(\lambda_k) + \lambda_k^i p_k). \tag{14}$$

This cost function is not convex in general, and may exhibit multiple local minima. (A notable exception is when all the cost coefficients $c^i$ are equal, in which case the problem reduces to the standard single-class routing problem. This case is obviously of no interest here.) For this reason, price optimality results for the socially optimal formulation will be of local nature. The main results for the general problem are contained in the following theorem.

**Theorem 5.2** *Assume socially optimal allocations.*

(*i*) *Assume that the price vector p satisfies*

$$c^{k+1}(\tau_{k+1}-\tau_k)+(Z_{k+1}-Z_k) < p_k - p_{k+1} < \tag{15}$$
$$c^k(\tau_{k+1} - \tau_k) + (Z_{k+1} - Z_k)$$

*for* $k = 1, \ldots, N-1$, *where* $\tau_k = T_k(\Lambda^k)$, *and* $Z_k = c^k \Lambda^k T_k'(\Lambda^k)$. *Then the nominal flow allocation* $\boldsymbol{\lambda}^*$ *is locally socially optimal, i.e., it is a (strict) local minimizer of (14).*

(*ii*) *Such a price vector always exists.*

The condition of the last theorem may be interpreted similarly to the condition (13) of the individual case, in the sense that it concerns directly only infinitesimal flow shifts from the nominal service classes to adjacent ones. The additional "Z" terms result out of the so-called cost externalities, namely, the influence of shifted traffic on the performance of the rest.

The pricing policy (15) guarantees that the nominal flow allocation is a local minimum point. Whether this allocation is the global minimum needs to be checked for the specific problem at hand. However, as already mentioned, the local result has independent significance. In case that a global result must be ensured, the network may be forced to employ additional measures, such as allowing only a ('reasonable') subset of all possible flow allocations. One such reasonable restriction would be that the performance of a higher service class would always be kept better than that of the lower ones – this may be ensured simply by reassigning part of the traffic (independently of its type) to a lower service class if necessary. In [10] it is shown that, for the case of only two service classes, this mild restriction suffices to ensure the global result.

## 6 Conclusions

This paper proposes a general methodology for incentive pricing in multi-class networks. This methodology consists of two phases: in the first phase, which is typically interconnected with the network design, distinct traffic types are identified, and a nominal service class is assigned to each traffic type. In the second phase, an appropriate pricing vector is specified, which induces the nominal traffic allocation by providing the required incentives to the users.

The basic premise which underlies incentive pricing is that the choice of service class, among several available options, is (and should) be left to the user. Differential pricing is a key tool through which the network can induce efficient use of network resources, while keeping high performance service available for those who require it. The pricing scheme proposed in this paper is simple, based on per-unit pricing at each service class.

User performance preferences are captured by cost coefficients, allowed to vary in given intervals, which depend on the traffic type and service class. Prices are levied on a per-unit basis at each service class. For this fundamental model, a complete characterization of pricing vectors and their computation is presented, as well as an iterative algorithm for on-line price adjustment.

In a congestion-prone system, an explicit consideration of congestion and its effect on user preferences may be required. In this case the identity of the user, in terms of the amount of traffic at its disposal, is a key factor. We have considered the two extreme cases, namely many small users on one hand and a single user on the other hand, as well as an intermediate case where each user controls a single traffic type. The results highlight the differences between these cases, as well as the difficulties that emerge in the congestion-prone model, which are closely related to the inherent non-uniqueness of the equilibrium conditions in these systems. Results here are far from being complete, and additional research into these issues is called for.

The pricing mechanism studied in this paper is the simplest, fixed, per-unit pricing. More involved pricing schemes have been suggested in the literature, including schemes which are meant to mitigate congestion by using congestion-adaptable prices [6]. (Flow dependent pricing has been touched upon very briefly in [10].) The incorporation of such pricing mechanisms in our framework for *multi-class* networks seems worthy of further investigation.

## References


[1] R. Cocchi, S. Shenker, D. Estrin, and L. Zhang, "Pricing in Computer Networks: Motivation, Formulation and Example," *IEEE/ACM Transactions on Networking*, vol. 1, pp. 614–627, December 1993.

[2] S. H. Low and P. P. Varaiya, "A New Approach to Service Provisioning in ATM Networks," *IEEE/ACM Transactions on Networking*, vol. 1, no. 3, pp. 547–553, 1993.

[3] F. P. Kelly, "Tarrifs and Effecitve Bandwidths in Multiservice Networks," in *Proccedings of ITC'94*, pp. 401–410, Elsevier Science, 1994.

[4] R. P. McLean and W. W. Sharkey, "An Approach to the Pricing of Broadband Telecommunication Services," *Telecommunication Systems*, vol. 2, pp. 159–184, 1994.

[5] S. Jordan and H. Jiang, "Connection Establishment in High Speed Networks," *IEEE Journal on Selected Areas in Communications*, vol. 13, pp. 1150–1161, Sept. 1995.

[6] J. K. MacKie-Mason and H. R. Varian, "Pricing Congestable Network Resources," *IEEE Journal on Selected Areas in Communications*, vol. 13, pp. 1141–1149, September 1995.

[7] R. J. Edell, N. McKeown, and P. P. Varaiya, "Billing Users and Pricing for TCP," *IEEE Journal on Selected Areas in Communications*, vol. 13, pp. 1162–1175, September 1995.

[8] J. Sairamesh, D. F. Ferguson, and Y. Yemini, "An Approach to Pricing, Optimal Allocation and Quality of Service Provisioning in High-Speed Packet Networks," in *Proceedings of the IEEE INFOCOM*, (Boston, MA), April 1995.

[9] F. Toutain and O. Huber, "A General Preemption-based Admission Policy Using a Smart Market Approach," in *Proceedings of the IEEE INFOCOM*, (San Francisco, CA), March 1996.

[10] A. Orda and N. Shimkin, "Incentive Pricing in Multi-Class Communication Networks," EE Pub. No. 1031, Department of Electrical Engineering, Technion, Haifa, Israel, June 1996. "ftp://ftp.technion.ac.il/pub/supported/ee/Network/orda.shimkin.price96.ps".

[11] S. C. Dafermos, "Traffic equilibrium and variational inequalities," *Transportation Science*, vol. 14, pp. 42–54, 1980.

# Charging Schemes for ATM Networks Based on Virtual Effective Bandwidths

Jelena Mišić Samuel T. Chanson
Department of Computer Science
The Hong Kong University Of Science and Technology
Clear Water Bay, Kowloon, Hong Kong

## Abstract

*In this paper, we propose charging schemes for ATM networks based on the concept of virtual effective bandwidths (VEB). VEBs were initially developed by the authors to support real-time Connection Admission Control (CAC) in a framework where traffic sources with different quality of service (QoS) requirements are multiplexed into the same finite length queue [6]. VEBs allow different QoS requirements to be related which is important for charging purposes. We propose three charging schemes which can be included in real-time CAC: the first one depends solely on the resource requirements of the call; the second is dependent on resource as well as QoS requirements of the call; the third is dependent on the current traffic intensity of the other connections also.*

*Keywords:* ATM networks, QoS, charging, Connection admission control.

## 1 Introduction

Among the various issues related to ATM research, the problem of appropriate charging for different types of traffic has not received much attention, although it must be solved if ATM is to be offered as a public service. Charging schemes can generally be classified into two categories: usage-sensitive charging and time-sensitive charging. In a usage-sensitive charging scheme, the user pays according to the required QoS and to the number of packets sent. The general framework for usage-sensitive pricing (see [1] and its references) is based on the elements of microeconomic theory [7]. In this approach, network services with different QoS are priced dynamically according to user demand. However, algorithms which implement this kind of pricing are complex and therefore not suitable for ATM networks, where charging must be implemented in real-time together with CAC. On the other hand, the telephone network often uses time-sensitive charging, i.e., charges are based on connection time. Time-sensitive charging requires less overhead in monitoring and computation than usage sensitive charging and is therefore more appropriate for ATM networks.

Parameters that are related to charging in ATM networks are the distance between the source and destination, holding time (i.e., length of call), traffic characteristics, type and value of QoS bound(s), and traffic intensity of the network at the moment of call arrival.

Network traffic can be grouped into two broad classes – real-time and non-real-time, based on their properties and requirements. Real-time traffic is sensitive to average delay, delay variations, and cell loss, while non-real-time traffic is only loss sensitive. A traffic source is commonly characterized by traffic descriptors such as the peak rate, average rate, and average burst length. Also specified is the quality of service descriptors, which are usually either cell loss probability, delay, or delay jitter.

Charging in ATM networks has been addressed in [10, 11]. In [10], both usage-sensitive and time-sensitive charging are considered in the framework where cell loss probability is the only QoS criterion. One value of cell loss probability is associated with a buffer, and multiple buffers are needed for various types of traffic. In [11], time-sensitive charging is considered using only delay as the QoS criterion. This approach charges for the combination of buffer and bandwidth allocation. However, since no cell loss is allowed, statistical multiplexing is prevented, and therefore network resources can not be used efficiently.

In the connection admission phase of an ATM network, the amount of resources allocated to the connection is based on the specified traffic pattern and the QoS bound. If the traffic characteristics do not change throughout the duration of a connection, time-sensitive charging can be effectively used. The problem is in determining the appropriate traffic descriptor and its value to accurately estimate network usage and provide enough information for charging traffic with different QoS bounds.

One possible traffic descriptor which can be used for charging (as well as in CAC) is the effective bandwidth, defined as the minimum bandwidth required by a source to satisfy its QoS requirements. Effective bandwidths have been investigated mostly using two approaches: spectral expansions for Markov fluid models [2, 5], and theory of large deviations (for calculating large buffer asymptotics) [4, 12]. Both approaches assume an infinite buffer, and equal QoS requirement for all the connections. Under these assumptions the criterion for admission of a connection is simple: If the sum of effective bandwidths of the arriving call and the existing connections is less than the capacity of the output channel, the new connection can be admitted. However, when QoS bounds are different, a set of parallel FIFO queues is needed which share the output link's bandwidth using some scheduling policy, such as the packetized general processor sharing policy (PGPS) [9]. Connection requests with the same QoS requirement are placed in the same queue. The drawbacks of this approach include complex implementation (in particular, the need for a scheduler) and low buffer utilization. The charging problems related to this approach are:

– Various QoS descriptors are not related, e.g., it is not known what the cell loss probability bound means in terms



0-8186-7780-5/97 $10.00 © 1997 IEEE

of delay and delay jitter and vice versa.
– Charging is dependent on the scheduling policy also, e.g., the amount of time given to each queue.

In this paper we consider charging in the situation when $N$ traffic classes with (possibly) different QoS requirements are multiplexed into a single ATM queue (with cell loss control implemented using the Partial Buffer Sharing Mechanism (PBS) [3]), sharing the same buffer and the total bandwidth of the link. We define a capacity domain as the union of all connections with the same QoS criterion. We will characterize a target QoS traffic class (capacity domain) $t$ with the following descriptors: (a) sum of effective average arrival rates of the connections within $t$, and (b) QoS requirement of $t$.

In order to model the charging descriptor which reflects the value of the target capacity domain QoS descriptor as well as the occupancy of the other capacity domains, the effective bandwidth of a connection is determined within a capacity domain. This parameter represents the fraction of the capacity domain allocated to the source. Hence we will refer to it as virtual effective bandwidth (VEB). The VEB of a source depends on the traffic descriptors of the source, the QoS bound for the associated capacity domain, and the sum of the effective average arrival rates of connections in the other capacity domains.

In this way, we can consider capacity domains as linear combinations of VEB's, and represent them as $\sum_i A_i\alpha_i'(Qd) \leq 1$, where $A_i$ corresponds to the number of class $i$ connections (all connections within a traffic class have the same traffic descriptors), and $\alpha_i'(Qd)$ denotes the VEB of class $i$ connections with regard to the value of QoS descriptor $Qd$.

All traffic sources are assumed to be ON-OFF. However, when we analyse the behavior of a target connection, the background traffic is approximated as Poisson (see section 2).

We estimate how the average queue length, queue length jitter (defined as the ratio of standard deviation of queue length and the mean queue length), and aggregate traffic losses change under different Poisson traffic intensities. The changes in QoS descriptors depend on the buffer size, threshold position and the ratio of low and high priority cells. We then use these results to determine values of QoS descriptors for combinations of various classes of ON-OFF sources, which we model as an ON-OFF Poisson sources with exponentially distributed ON and OFF times. These expressions relate value of the QoS descriptor with the number and type of ON-OFF connections within capacity domain, and therefore expressions for effective bandwidth within a domain, with respect to the given value of QoS descriptors, can be derived.

The expressions for VEBs show that the QoS bounds are related. For example, if delay and delay jitter bounds are given, we can calculate the equivalent QoS limit on target connection loss. Because a simple relationship exists between the VEB's in a domain and the sum of effective average rates in the other domains, the capacity domains can be simply managed. Therefore, both time-sensitive charging and real-time connection admission control can be implemented efficiently.

The rest of the paper is organized as follows. Section 2 gives basic assumptions and definitions. In Section 3 QoS descriptors are determined for PBS queue for various intensities of Poisson input traffic. Section 4 analyses the PBS queue using a combination of Poisson traffic and various classes of ON-OFF sources. In Section 5 we discuss the virtual effective bandwidths (VEBs) for three classes of performance criteria: average queue length, queue length jitter, and loss probabilities. In Section 6 we discuss the properties of capacity domains and VEBs related to charging. In Section 7 we propose three simple charging policies based on VEB which can be used for time-sensitive charging. They also allow charging to be integrated with CAC. Finally, Section 8 concludes the paper.

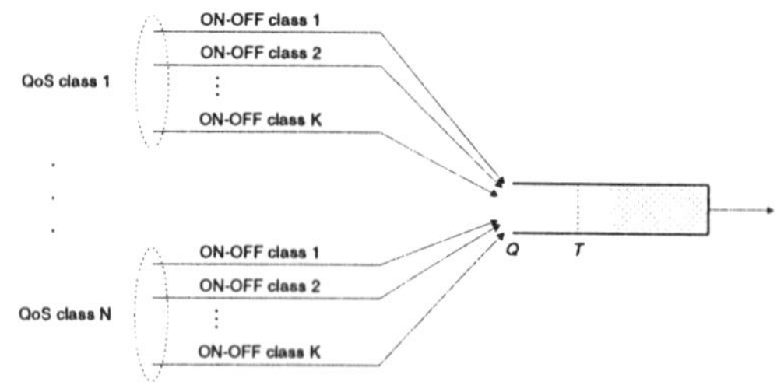


Figure 1: PBS queue with a combination of Poisson traffic and $N$ classes of ON-OFF traffic sources.

## 2 Background

In this section we consider a PBS queue fed by $N$ traffic classes with different QoS requirements (Fig. 1). Each QoS traffic class $j$ consists of $K$ classes of ON-OFF sources ('ON-OFF classes') and comprises one capacity domain. Each ON-OFF class ($i$) within the QoS class (i.e., the capacity domain) $j$ consists of $A_{i_j}$ independent and identical ON-OFF Poisson sources. Each ON-OFF class $i$ source has exponentially distributed ON and OFF periods, and is represented with a triplet $(\beta_i, \alpha_i, \lambda_{it})$, where $\beta_i$ is the transition rate from the OFF state to the ON state, $\alpha_i$ is the transition rate from an ON state to an OFF state, and $\lambda_{it}$ is the average cell generation rate while the source is in the ON state. The probability generating function (PGF) of the cell generation process with the source in the ON state is $f(x) = e^{\lambda_t(x-1)}$. The activity factor of the source is $p_{ion} = \frac{\beta_i}{\alpha_i+\beta_i}$, and the average arrival rate of the connection is $p_{ion}\lambda_{it}$. Let the traffic intensities for low and high priority traffic be $\lambda_{itl}$ and $\lambda_{ith}$, respectively. Then the probability of cell arrival from a connection at a slot boundary (given that there is an arrival from this connection) is $p_{ih} = \frac{\lambda_{ith}}{\lambda_{ith}+\lambda_{itl}}$, for a high-priority cell, and $p_{il} = \frac{\lambda_{itl}}{\lambda_{ith}+\lambda_{itl}}$, for a low-priority cell. In subsequent analysis we shall assume that for all types of sources, $p_{ih} = p_h = 1/3$, and $p_{il} = p_l = 2/3$.

In order to obtain specific values of QoS descriptors (average queue length, queue length jitter, low- and high-priority cell loss probabilities) for the target capacity domain $t \in [1..N]$, we shall concentrate on the ON-OFF sources in that domain, and model other the $N-1$ capacity domains as 'background' traffic. We model the PGF of the background traffic from capacity domains $j$, ($j \in [1..N], j \neq t$), by the following expression:

$$\Phi(x) = \sum_{\substack{j=1\\ j\neq t}}^{N} \sum_{p_{1,j}=0}^{A_{1,j}} \cdots \sum_{p_{K,j}=0}^{A_{K,j}} e^{\sum_{i=1}^{K} p_i \lambda_{it}(x-1)} .$$

$$\prod_{i=1}^{K} \binom{A_{i,j}}{p_{i,j}} p_{ion}^{p_{i,j}} (1-p_{ion})^{A_{i,j}-p_{i,j}} \quad (1)$$

For large $A_{i,j}$ and small $p_{ion}$, $\Phi(x)$ becomes $\Phi(x) = \exp(\sum_{j\neq t}\sum_i A_{i,j}p_{ion}(e^{\lambda_{it}(x-1)}-1))$, with an error less than 1% when $A_{i,j} \geq 10$ and $P_{ion} \leq 0.5$, and less than 5% when $A_{i,j} \geq 3$ and $P_{ion} \leq 0.5$. The first and second moments of the background traffic PGF are $\sum_{j\neq t}^{N}\sum_i A_{i,j}p_{ion}\lambda_{it}$ and $\sum_{j\neq t}^{N}\sum_i A_{i,j}p_{ion}\lambda_{it}(1+\lambda_{it})$, respectively. In practice, however, $\lambda_{it}$ is small (0.065 for 10Mbps connection rate and outgoing line capacity of 155Mbps, or 0.016 for the same connection rate and outgoing line capacity of 622Mbps), hence we can approximate $e^{\lambda_{it}(x-1)}$ with $1+\lambda_{it}(x-1)$, and the PGF of the background traffic becomes the PGF of a Poisson process, $\Phi_a(x) = \exp(\sum_{j\neq t}\sum_i A_i p_{ion}\lambda_{it}(x-1))$.

This approximation has the same average as the original input process, but with smaller variance. For large number of connections with diversity of peak rates and high capacity of the output channel, the difference in variance should not differ by more than a few percents. The average arrival rate of the background traffic Poisson process is $\lambda_{sl} = \sum_{j\neq t}\sum_i A_{i,j}p_{ion}\lambda_{it}$. We shall refer to the average arrival rate of the background traffic as $\lambda_s$, and the number of sources within the target QoS class as $A_i$. The total average arrival rate is $\lambda_{tot} = \sum_j\sum_i A_{i,j}p_{ion}\lambda_{it}$. The average arrival rate within the capacity domain $t$ is $\lambda_{ct} = \sum_{i=1}^{K} A_{i,t}p_{ion}\lambda_{it}$ (in the text that follows we shall refer to the average arrival rate within the target capacity domain as $\lambda_c$).

However, as will be shown in Section 5, the impact of the connections with high peak rates on QoS descriptors varies exponentially with the connection peak rate. Therefore, the Poisson approximation of the input process has to be modified such that connections contribute to the total average arrival rate with their 'effective' average arrival rates instead of their real average arrival rates.

## 2.1 Relationship between effective average arrival rate, effective bandwidth and virtual effective bandwidth

Consider the situation depicted in Fig. 1. Assume that all QoS traffic classes are characterized with the same QoS descriptor $Qd$ which may be cell loss probability, average queue length or queue length jitter. Each QoS class $j$ will have a different value of $Qd$, $Qd_j = C_j$ (without loss of generality, we assume $C_1 < C_2 \ldots < C_t \ldots < C_N$). We concentrate on the target QoS traffic class (capacity domain) with the required value of QoS descriptor $C_t$, the background traffic arrival rate $\lambda_s$, and the average domain arrival rate $\lambda_c$.

Let's assume that the transfer characteristics $\log Qd = f(\lambda)$, which relates the input traffic (Poisson) arrival rate with the consumed value of the QoS descriptor, may be approximated by a linear function $\log(Qd) = \log K_1 + K_2\lambda$ in the vicinity of $\lambda = \lambda_s + \lambda_c$, as shown in Fig. 2. (In fact, both $K_1$ and $K_2$ are functions of $\lambda$, but for the sake of clarity, we shall consider them as constants for the time being). We shall use this transfer characteristics to model a target ON-OFF connection from the aspect of the amount of QoS descriptior ($Qd$) it consumes.

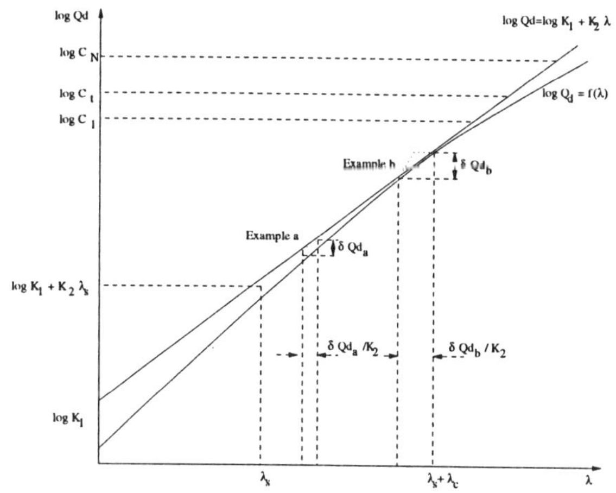


Figure 2: Representation of effective average arrival rate, effective bandwidth and virtual effective bandwidth

According to Fig. 2, the amount of $Qd$ spent on the background traffic is $\log K_1 + K_2\lambda_s$. The available amount of $Qd$ for the target capacity domain is $\Delta Qd = \log Qd_1 - \log K_1 - K_2\lambda_s$.

The target connection within the target capacity domain consumes some amount of $Qd$, denoted as $\delta Qd$. As will be shown in Section 5, $\delta Qd = p_{ion}(e^{K_2\lambda_{it}} - 1)$, where $p_{ion}$ represents the connection activity factor, and $\lambda_{it}$ is the average arrival rate when the connection is active (for ON-OFF source this is equivalent to the peak rate). For small peak rates, $\delta Qd = p_{ion}\lambda_{it}K_2$, which means that a connection with an average arrival rate $p_{ion}\lambda_{it}$ consumes an amount of $Qd$ which is linearly proportional to its average arrival rate (this is shown as example $a$ in Fig. 2). However, for high peak rates, $\delta Qd$ grows exponentially with the connection peak rate, and has higher slope than $K_2$. In that case, $\frac{\delta Qd}{K_2} > p_{ion}\lambda_{it}$ (this is shown as example $b$ in Fig. 2). The value $\frac{\delta Qd}{K_2} = \lambda_{it}^{eff}$ corresponds to the effective average arrival rate of the connection with respect to the consumed amount of traffic descriptor and to the transfer characteristics for the aggregate traffic, $\log Qd = \log K_1 + K_2\lambda$. The total amount of effective average arrival rates for connections from all capacity domains is determined by the most stringent value of $Qd$ (in the example shown in Fig. 2 this value is $C_1$). The total amount of QoS descriptor is equal to $\log C_1 - \log K_1$, and the total amount of effective arrival rates is equal to $\lambda_{tot}^{eff} = \frac{\log C_1 - \log K_1}{K_2}$.

Then, effective bandwidth $\alpha(Qd)$ of the connection with respect to the tightest value of QoS descriptor $Qd = C_1$ is defined as:

$$\alpha(Qd) = \frac{\delta Qd}{\Delta Qd_1} = \frac{\delta Qd}{\log C_1 - \log K_1} = \frac{\lambda_{it}^{eff}}{\lambda_{tot}^{eff}}. \quad (2)$$

Effective arrival rates and effective bandwidths have additive property across all capacity domains.

Since the amount of traffic from the various QoS classes varies in time, and the tightest value of the QoS descriptor may change, it is useful to define the effective bandwidth of the connection with respect to its QoS class, as well as the amount of traffic in the other capacity domains. We define the virtual effective bandwidth $\alpha'(Qd)$ of an ON-OFF connection within a given target capacity domain as the ratio of the amount of $Qd$ consumed by the target connection and the available amount of $Qd$ for the target capacity domain $t, t \in [1..N]$:

$$\begin{aligned}\alpha'(Qd) &= \frac{\delta Qd}{\Delta Qd_t} = \frac{\delta Qd}{\log C_t - \log K_1 - K_2\lambda_s^{eff}} \quad (3)\\ &= \frac{\lambda_{it}^{eff}}{(\log C_t - \log K_1 - K_2\lambda_s^{eff})/K_2}\end{aligned}$$

where $C_t$ is the value of $Qd$ for capacity domain $t$, and $\lambda_s^{eff}$ is the sum of effective average arrival rates in all the non-target capacity domains.

## 3 PBS queue QoS descriptors for the Poisson input process

In [6], probability generating function $G(x) = \sum_{j=0}^{Q-1} \pi(j)x^j$ for queue length distribution was derived (buffer size is denoted by Q and queue threshold is T). After obtaining stationary distribution of the queue length, the relevant moments of the distribution as well as cell loss probabilities for aggregate traffic can be calculated. The average queue length is $Q_{av} = G'(1)$, and the variance of the queue length is: $Var_Q = G''(1) + Q_{av} - Q_{av}^2$.

Knowing the average queue length and its variance, we can compute the jitter as: $J = \sqrt{Var_Q}/Q_{av}$.

Figs. 3 and 4 show the average queue length and jitter as functions of the average arrival rate of the input traffic. Since the analytical results for the queue length distribution are very complex, these functions are approximated using standard regression method in the range of average arrival rates of input traffic from 0.6 to 0.95. As a measure of the adequacy of approximation, the determination coefficient ($R^2$) [8] was computed. Values calculated from the PGF are shown by dots, and exponential approximation is given by the full line. In all examples the following values are used: Q=50, T=40, $p_l = 2/3$.

Fig. 5 shows low priority cell loss probabilities as functions of the average arrival rate of the input traffic. For the range of average arrival rate of input traffic from 0.6 to 0.95, this function is also approximated by exponential function using linear regression method. A similar graph was constructed for high priority cell loss and approximated by the function $e^{D_0^{Bh}+D_1^{Bh}\lambda+D_2^{Bh}\lambda^2}$, where $D_0^{Bh} = -172.144$, $D_1^{Bh} = 228.234$, and $D_2^{Bh} = -78.510$ (determination coefficient $R^2 = 0.99997$).

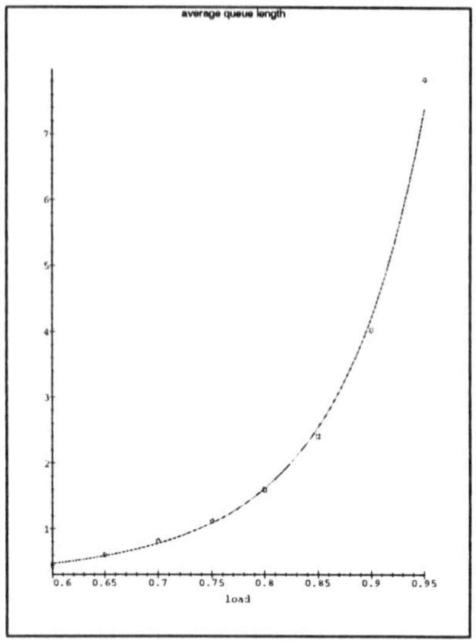


Figure 3: Average queue length and its approximation $e^{D_0^Q+D_1^Q\lambda+D_2^Q\lambda^2}$ with $D_0^Q = 0.946$, $D_1^Q = -9.599$ and $D_2^Q = 11.2744$ ($R^2 = 0.9970$).

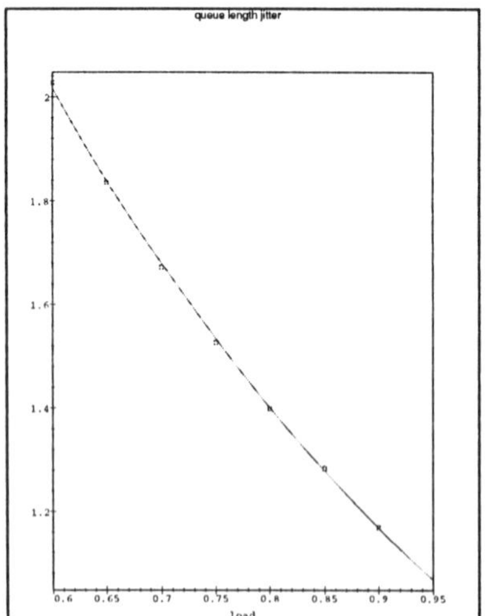


Figure 4: Queue length jitter and its approximation $e^{D_0^J+D_1^J\lambda}$ with $D_0^J = 1.791$, $D_1^J = -1.817$ ($R^2 = 0.99948$).

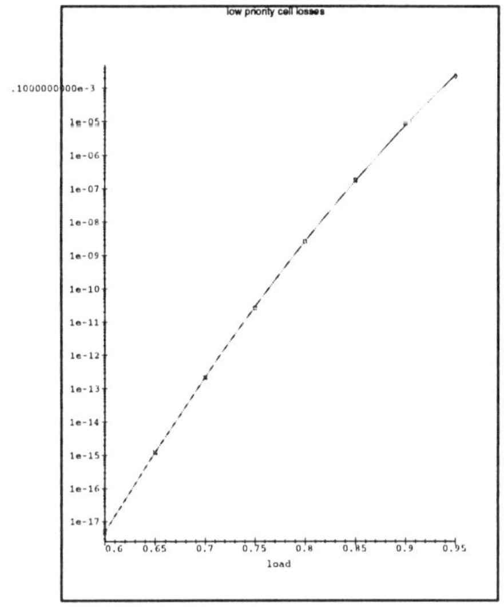


Figure 5: Low priority cell loss probability and its approximation $e^{D_0^{Bl}+D_1^{Bl}\lambda+D_2^{Bl}\lambda^2}$, with $D_0^{Bl} = -133.438$, $D_1^{Bl} = 197.296$, and $D_2^{Bl} = -69.001$ ($R^2 = 0.99995$).

## 4 Derivation of QoS descriptors in the presence of ON-OFF sources

In this section, the QoS descriptors are derived for a PBS queue fed by $N$ QoS traffic classes (Fig. 1). Each QoS traffic class $j$ consists of $K$ classes of ON-OFF sources and comprises one capacity domain. Each ON-OFF class $i$ of sources within the QoS class $j$ consists of $A_{i,j}$ independent and identical ON-OFF Poisson sources (as presented in Sec. 2).

Under the assumption that the offered load is less than 1, and that the queue can reach steady state, the steady state PGF of queue length and the state of ON-OFF sources are defined below (detailed derivation is presented in [6]) :

$$W(x, u_1, \ldots, u_K) = \sum_{p_1=0}^{A_1} \cdots \sum_{p_K=0}^{A_K} G(x)_{p_1 \ldots p_K, \lambda_s^{eff}} \cdot \quad (4)$$
$$\prod_{i=1}^{K} \begin{pmatrix} A_i \\ p_i \end{pmatrix} p_{ion}^{p_i} (1 - p_{ion})^{A_i - p_i} \cdot \left(\sum_{a_i=0}^{A_i} Ki_{p_i, a_i}^{A_i} u_i^{a_i}\right)$$

where $G(x)_{p_1 \ldots p_K, \lambda_s^{eff}}$ is the steady state generating function obtained for $p_1, p_2, \ldots, p_i, \ldots, p_K$ sources from classes $1, 2, \ldots, i, \ldots, K$ respectively, being constantly turned ON in the presence of Poisson traffic with effective average arrival rate $\lambda_s^{eff}$.

The coefficient $Ki_{p_i, a_i}^{A_i}$ is associated with the $i$-th class of ON-OFF sources and denotes the probability of switching from $p_i$ active sources to $a_i$ active sources in the next time slot ($\sum_{a_i=0}^{A_i} Ki_{p_i, a_i}^{A_i} = 1$ [6]).

Expression 4 gives the joint distribution of queue length, losses and the number of active ON-OFF sources. The average queue length in this case is:

$$Q_{av} = W_x'(1, 1, \ldots, 1) = \sum_{p_1=0}^{A_1} \cdots \sum_{p_K=0}^{A_K} G_x'(1)_{p_1 \ldots p_K, \lambda_s^{eff}} \cdot$$
$$\prod_{i=1}^{K} \begin{pmatrix} A_i \\ p_i \end{pmatrix} p_{ion}^{p_i} (1 - p_{ion})^{A_i - p_i} \quad (5)$$

The variance of the queue length is:

$$Var_Q = \sum_{p_1=0}^{A_1} \cdots \sum_{p_K=0}^{A_K} G''(1)_{p_1 \ldots p_K, \lambda_s^{eff}} \cdot \quad (6)$$
$$\prod_{i=1}^{K} \begin{pmatrix} A_i \\ p_i \end{pmatrix} p_{ion}^{p} (1 - p_{ion})^{A_i - p_i} + Q_{av} - Q_{av}^2$$

The jitter is equal to $J = \frac{\sqrt{Var_Q}}{Q_{av}}$.
The low priority cell loss probability is :

$$B_l = \sum_{p_1=0}^{A_1} \cdots \sum_{p_K=0}^{A_K} B_{l, p_1 \ldots p_K, \lambda_s^{eff}}$$
$$\prod_{i=1}^{K} \begin{pmatrix} A_i \\ p_i \end{pmatrix} p_{ion}^{p_i} (1 - p_{ion})^{A_i - p_i} \quad (7)$$

where $B_{l, p_1 \ldots p_K, \lambda_s^{eff}}$ denotes the low priority cell loss probability for $p_1, p_2, \ldots, p_i, \ldots, p_K$ sources from classes $1, 2, \ldots, i, \ldots, K$ respectively, being constantly turned ON in the presence of background traffic with effective average arrival rate $\lambda_s^{eff}$. The high priority cell loss probability is determined in a similar manner.

## 5 Virtual effective bandwidths

Results (5), (6), and (7) must be further simplified in order to model the capacity domain satisfying the condition $\sum_{i=1}^{K} A_i \alpha_i'(Qd) = 1$, where $\alpha_i'(Qd)$ denotes the VEB of the target ON-OFF class $i$ connection with respect to the QoS descriptor Qd.

**VEB based on low priority cell loss probability.** We will simplify expression (7) using the exponential approximation shown in Fig. 5, $\log(B_l) = D_0^{Bl} + D_1^{Bl}\lambda + D_2^{Bl}\lambda^2$. Furthermore, at the point $\lambda = \lambda_{tot}$, the transfer characteristics can be approximated with a linear function with the same slope, i.e., $\log(B_l) \approx [2D_2^{Bl}\lambda_{tot} + D_1^{Bl}]\lambda + [D_0^{Bl} - D_2^{Bl}\lambda_{tot}^2]$.

Expression (7) can then be rewritten as:

$$B_l = \sum_{p_1=0}^{A_1} \cdots \sum_{p_K=0}^{A_K} \left[\prod_{i=1}^{K} \frac{(A_i p_{ion})^{p_i}}{p_i!} e^{-A_i p_{ion}}\right]. \quad (8)$$

$$
\begin{aligned}
& e^{D_0^{Bl} - D_2^{Bl}\lambda_{tot}^2} \cdot e^{[2D_2^{Bl}\lambda_{tot} + D_1^{Bl}](p_1\lambda_{1t} + \ldots p_K\lambda_{Kt} + \lambda_s^{eff})} \\
= \;& e^{[D_0^{Bl} - D_2^{Bl}\lambda_{tot}^2]} e^{[2D_2^{Bl}\lambda_{tot} + D_1^{Bl}]\lambda_s^{eff}} e^{-\sum_i A_i p_{ion}} \cdot \\
& \sum_{p_1=0}^{A_1} \cdots \sum_{p_K=0}^{A_K} \frac{(e^{[2D_2^{Bl}\lambda_{tot} + D_1^{Bl}]\lambda_{1t}} A_1 p_{1on})^{p_1}}{p_1!} \cdot \\
& \cdots \frac{(e^{[2D_2^{Bl}\lambda_{tot} + D_1^{Bl}]\lambda_{Kt}} A_K p_{Kon})^{p_K}}{p_K!}
\end{aligned}
$$

If the values $e^{[2D_2^{Bl}\lambda_{tot} + D_1^{Bl}]\lambda_{it}} p_{ion} \leq 0.5$ and $A_i \geq 10$, the previous summation can be expressed as:

$$
\begin{aligned}
B_l \; = \; & e^{[D_0^{Bl} - D_2^{Bl}\lambda_{tot}^2]} e^{[2D_2^{Bl}\lambda_{tot} + D_1^{Bl}]\lambda_s^{eff}} \\
& e^{-\sum_i A_i p_{ion}} \prod_{i=1}^{i=K} e^{A_i p_{ion} e^{[2D_2^{Bl}\lambda_{tot} + D_1^{Bl}]\lambda_{it}}}
\end{aligned} \tag{9}
$$

Previous limitation means that for connections with high peak rates (e.g., 0.016, which corresponds to 10Mbps peak rate and 622 Mbps outgoing line capacity), the activity factor must be less than 0.3. Taking logarithm of both sides, we obtain $\sum_{i=1}^{K} A_i \alpha_i'(B_l) = 1$, where $\alpha_i'(B_l)$ (the VEB of the target ON-OFF class $i$ connection with respect to the low priority cell loss limit) is given by

$$
\frac{p_{ion}(e^{[2D_2^{Bl}\lambda_{tot} + D_1^{Bl}]\lambda_{it}} - 1)}{\log B_l - [D_0^{Bl} - D_2^{Bl}\lambda_{tot}^2] - [2D_2^{Bl}\lambda_{tot} + D_1^{Bl}]\lambda_s^{eff}} \tag{10}
$$

Similar expressions can be derived with high priority cell loss probability as the QoS descriptor.

Graphical representation of the VEB with low priority cell loss probability as QoS descriptor in the case of a single capacity domain is shown in Fig. 6. Exponential approximation is determined for $\lambda_{tot} = 0.85$.

**Effective average arrival rate of ON-OFF connection.** By combining the results from Section 2.1 with Eqn. 10, we can extract the expressions for the consumed amount of QoS descriptor and effective average arrival rate as $\delta Bl = p_{ion}(e^{[2D_2^{Bl}\lambda_{tot} + D_1^{Bl}]\lambda_{it}} - 1)$ and $\lambda_{it}^{eff} = \frac{\delta Bl}{[2D_2^{Bl}\lambda_{tot} + D_1^{Bl}]}$, respectively.

**VEB based on average delay and delay jitter.** Effective bandwidths based on average queue length and queue length jitter can be obtained using exponential approximations (shown in Figs. 3 and 4), in the same manner as those for losses; $\sum_{i=1}^{K} A_i \alpha_i'(Q_{av}) = 1$, where $\alpha_i'(Q_{av})$ (the VEB of the target class $i$ ON-OFF connection with respect to the average queue length) is given by:

$$
\frac{p_{ion}(e^{[2D_2^{Q}\lambda_{tot} + D_1^{Q}]\lambda_{it}} - 1)}{\log Q_{av} - [D_0^{Q} - D_2^{Q}\lambda_{tot}^2] - [2D_2^{Q}\lambda_{tot} + D_1^{Q}]\lambda_s^{eff}} \tag{11}
$$

Also, $\alpha_i'(J)$ which denotes the VEB of the target class $i$ ON-OFF connection with respect to queue length jitter is given by

$$
\alpha_i'(J) = \frac{p_{ion}(e^{D_1^{J}\lambda_{it}} - 1)}{\log J - D_0^{J} - D_1^{J}\lambda_s^{eff}} \tag{12}
$$

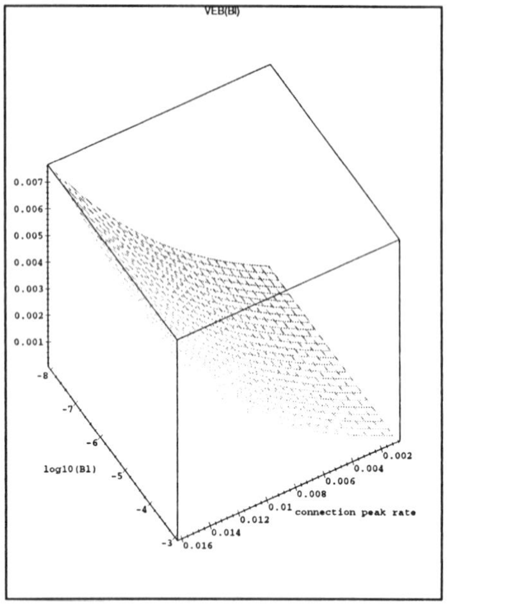


Figure 6: VEB for one capacity domain as a function of the source peak rate ($p_{on} = 0.2$) and low priority cell loss probability as QoS criterion.

Graphical representation of the VEB with average queue length and queue length jitter as QoS criteria in the case of a single capacity domain are shown in Figs. 7 and 8 respectively ($\lambda_{tot} = 0.85$).

## 6 Properties of capacity domains

VEBs provide a basis for obtaining the relationships between different QoS bounds. This is important for charging schemes based on specified QoS requirements. The following example shows how a real-time connection with given delay and delay jitter requirements can obtain information about the limit on its cell loss behavior. In the example, we will consider a PBS queue with Q=50, T=40 and $p_l = 2/3$. For simplicity, we will assume that there is only one capacity domain, i.e., $\lambda_s = 0$. Suppose that the imposed limit on average queue length is $Q_{av} = 1$. According to the transfer characteristic $Q_{av} = f(\lambda)$ for Poisson input traffic shown in Fig. 3, this limit corresponds to the total effective arrival rate $\lambda_{tot} = 0.75$, and to the jitter limit $J = 1.53$ (Fig. 4), and low priority cell loss limit $Bl = 0.5 \cdot 10^{-9}$ (Fig. 5). The effective bandwidths of the connection with peak rate 0.004 and activity factor $pon = 0.2$ are $\alpha'(Q_{av}) = \alpha'(J) = \alpha'(Bl) = 0.0011$.

Consider a source belonging to QoS traffic class $t$, with burstiness $1/p_{on}$, and peak rate $\lambda_t$. Assume that the QoS descriptor $Qd_t$ for the traffic class $t$ is given by $Qd_t = K_{1,Qd_t} e^{K_{2,Qd_t}\lambda}$ and that the QoS descriptor bound is $Qd_t = C_t$. Then the virtual effective bandwidth of the source is given by the following expression:

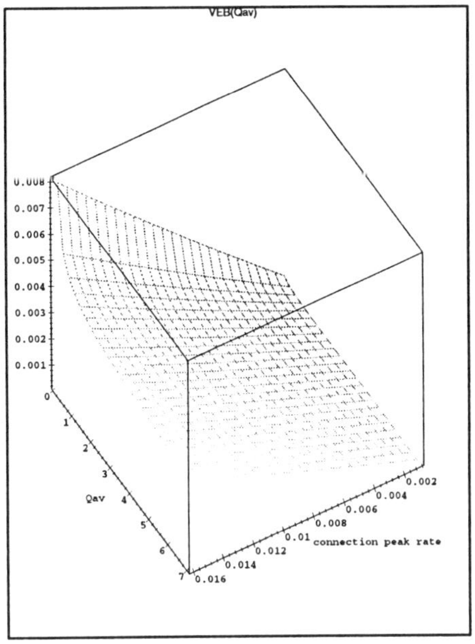


Figure 7: VEB for one capacity domain as a function of source peak rate ($p_{on} = 0.2$) and average queue length as QoS criterion.

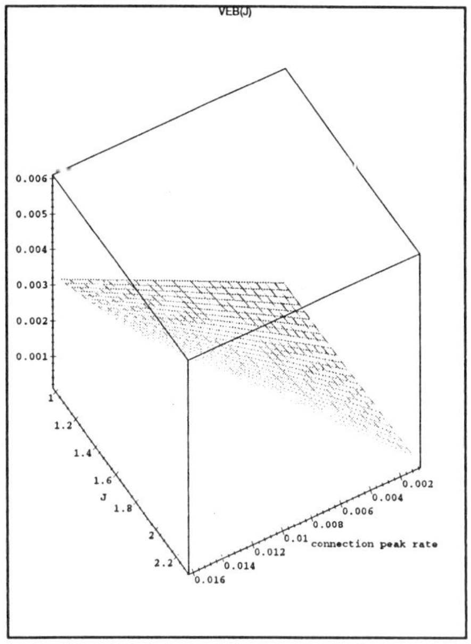


Figure 8: VEB for one capacity domain as a function of source peak rate ($p_{on} = 0.2$) and queue length jitter as QoS criterion.

$$\alpha_l'(Qd_t) = \frac{p_{on}(e^{K_{2,Qd_t}\lambda_t} - 1)}{\log\frac{C_t}{K_{1,Qd_t}} - K_{2,Qd_t}\lambda_{st}^{eff}}, \qquad (13)$$

where

$$\lambda_{st}^{eff} = \sum_{\substack{j=1 \\ j \neq l}}^{N} \sum_{i=1}^{K} A_{i,j}\lambda_{it}^{eff}.$$

Therefore, the VEB depends on the traffic parameters of the source, the value of QoS descriptor for the given capacity domain, and the sum of the effective average arrival rates of all connections in the other traffic classes. In the presence of multiple capacity domains, the total effective average traffic rate is: $\lambda_{tot}^{eff} = \sum_{j=1}^{N}\sum_i A_{i,j}\lambda_{it}^{eff}$.

## 7 Charging Policies

In this section we will present charging policies based on:
- traffic descriptors of the connection only,
- traffic descriptors and QoS requirements of the connection, and
- traffic descriptors, QoS requirement of the connection, and intensity of traffic in all capacity domains.

### 7.1 Charging policy based on the traffic descriptors of the call only

From the fairness point of view, traffic intensity in the other capacity domains should not be taken into consideration for charging. In this case, a connection should be charged only on the consumed amount of QoS descriptor $\delta Qd$, or equivalently on its effective average arrival rate $\lambda_{it}^{eff} = \frac{\delta Qd}{K_{2_{Qd}}}$. However, the transfer characteristics for a particular QoS descriptor is approximated by a linear approximation (in the log scale) $Qd = K_1 e^{K_2\lambda}$, around the point $\lambda_{tot}^{eff}$. Therefore, $K_1$ and $K_2$ depend on the value and slope of the transfer characteristic at the point determined by total effective arrival rate. They also include information about the buffer length, PBS threshold position, and outgoing line capacity. Since the slope of the transfer characteristics for all QoS descriptors except queue length jitter decreases with total load, $\delta Qd$ and $\lambda_{it}^{eff}$ will decrease slightly when the total load increases. This means that the values of these charging descriptors decrease as the utilization of the outgoing link increases. The charging unit can be determined according to one of two policies:

- based on the normalized server rate which is equal to 1 (or total amount of QoS descriptor $K_2 \log K_1 - \log K_1$), or
- based on the current maximum admissible traffic rate which is imposed by the tightest QoS bound $\lambda_{lmax}^{eff} = \frac{1}{K_{2_{Qd}}}\log\frac{C_t}{K_{1_{Qd}}}$ (or the amount of QoS descriptor $\log Qd_t - \log K_1$).

The second approach tends to discourage data-transfer users from establishing connections when real-time connections are present (see Fig. 2).

## 7.2 Charging policy sensitive to the traffic descriptors and QoS requirement of the connection

In this case, the appropriate charging descriptor is the VEB of the connection. To exclude the information about connections in other capacity domains, $\lambda_s^{eff}$ should be set to 0. Therefore, connections with same traffic descriptors will be charged differently if they have different QoS requirements.

## 7.3 Charging policy sensitive to the traffic descriptors, QoS requirement and current traffic intensity

This type of charging is harder to implement than the previous ones since the traffic intensity changes when a call arrives or terminates and must be recalculated.

The appropriate charging descriptor is the ratio of the amount of the QoS descriptor consumed by the connection and the available amount of QoS descriptor across all capacity domains. For a particular connection within target domain $t$ with QoS descriptor bound $C_t$, let us assume that the occupancy of capacity domain changes at time instances $t_0, t_1, \dots t_k, \dots t_Q$, where $t_0$ denotes the time of target call arrival, $t_Q$ denotes the time of target call termination, and $t_k$, $0 < k < Q$ denotes instances of other call arrivals or terminations. Then, the 'scaled' charging descriptor for the connection at time $t_k$, $0 \geq k \geq Q$ can be defined as:

$$\gamma(Qd_t, t_k) = \frac{p_{on}(e^{K_{2P_{cl}}\lambda_t} - 1)}{\log \frac{C_t}{K_{1Q_{d_t}}} - \sum_j \sum_i A_{i,j}(t_k) p_{ion}(e^{K_{2Q_{d_t}}\lambda_t} - 1)}$$

where $\sum_{j=1}^{N} \sum_{i=1}^{K} A_{i,j}(t_k) p_{ion}(e^{K_{2Q_{d_t}}\lambda_t} - 1)$ denotes the occupancy of all capacity domains at $t_k$. We will refer to this descriptor as a 'scaled VEB' or SVEB. The total price of the connection is then proportional to the value $\sum_{k=0}^{Q-1} \gamma(Qd_t, t_k)(t_{k+1} - t_k)$. This policy tends to discourage users from making connections when the network is heavily loaded.

# 8 Conclusions

In this paper we have investigated the possibility of charging ATM connections using traffic descriptors that are similar to those used in connection admission control. We have derived expressions for virtual effective bandwidths which allow different QoS requirements to be related. This is important for charging purposes. The two other features of VEB which are important to pricing are that VEB has an exponential relationship with connection peak rate which imposes penalty for underutilization of link capacity, and VEB increases with the traffic intensity outside the capacity domain. We have proposed three charging schemes. The first one is insensitive to the network traffic intensity and is based only on the characteristics of the connection being charged. The second scheme is dependent on the traffic descriptors as well as the QoS requirement of the connection.

The third scheme provides charging which is dependent on the current network traffic intensity. For this type of charging, a 'scaled VEB' (SVEB) descriptor is proposed. All charging descriptors can be computed during the call negotiation phase and returned to the user. The relations among different QoS bounds for VEB provide a sound basis for simple, real-time charging schemes for ATM connections.

# References


[1] R. Cocchi, S. Shenker, D. Estrin, L. Zhang. "Pricing in Computer Networks: Motivation, Formulation and Example". *IEEE/ACM Trans. Networking*, 1(6):614–627, 1993.

[2] R. J. Gibbens, P. J. Hunt. "Effective Bandwidths for the Multi-Type UAS Channel". *Queuing Systems*, 9:17–28, 1991.

[3] H. Kroner, G. Hebuterne, P. Boyer, A. Gravey. "Priority Management in ATM Switching Nodes". *IEEE Journal on Selected Areas in Communications*, 9(3):418–427, 1991.

[4] G. Kesidis, J. Walrand, C. S. Chang. "Effective Bandwidths for Multiclass Markov Fluids and Other ATM Sources". *IEEE/ACM Trans. Networking*, 1(4):424–428, 1993.

[5] A. Elwalid, D. Mitra "Effective Bandwidth of General Markovian Traffic Sources and Admission Control of High Speed Networks". *IEEE/ACM Trans. Networking*, 1(3):329–343, 1993.

[6] J. Mišić, S. Chanson. "Multiparameter QoS Admission Control for ATM Queues with Partial Buffer Sharing Mechanism". technical report *HKUST-SC96-07*, Dept. Of Computer Science, The Hong Kong University of Science and Technology, March 1996.

[7] W. Nicholson. *Microeconomic Theory Basic Principles and Extensions*. Dryden Press, 1989.

[8] W. W. Hines and D. C. Montgomery. *Probability and Statistics in Engineering and Management Science*, third edn, New York: John Wiley and Sons, 1990.

[9] A. K. Parekh, R. G. Gallager. "A Generalized Processor Sharing Approach to Flow Control in Integrated Services Networks: A Single Node Case". *IEEE/ACM Trans. Networking*, 1(3):344–357, 1993.

[10] H. Saito. "Resource Management and Charging in ATM Networks". *Computer Networks and ISDN Systems*, 28:641–644, 1996.

[11] S. H. Low, P. P. Varaiya. "A New Approach to Service Provisioning in ATM Networks". *IEEE/ACM Trans. Networking*, 1(5):547–553, 1993.

[12] G. de Veciana, J. Walrand. "Effective Bandwidths: Call Admission, Traffic Policing, and Filtering for ATM Networks". *Queuing Systems*, 20:37–59, 1995.

# Source Time Scale and Optimal Buffer/Bandwidth Trade-off for Regulated Traffic in an ATM Node*

Francesco Lo Presti Zhi-Li Zhang Jim Kurose Don Towsley

## Abstract

*In this paper, we study the problem of resource allocation and control for an ATM node with regulated traffic. Both guaranteed lossless service and statistical service with small loss probability are considered. We investigate the relationship between source characteristics and the buffer/bandwidth trade-off under both services.*

*Our contributions are the following. For guaranteed lossless service, we find that the optimal resource allocation scheme suggests a time scale separation of sources sharing an ATM node with finite bandwidth and buffer space, with the optimal buffer/bandwidth trade-off is determined by the sources' time scale. For statistical service with a small loss probability, we present a new approach for estimating the loss probability in a shared buffer multiplexor with the so called "extremal" on-off, periodic sources. Under this approach, the optimal resource allocation for statistical service is achieved by maximizing both the benefits of buffering sharing and bandwidth sharing. The optimal buffer/bandwidth trade-off is again determined by time scale separation.*

## 1 Introduction

Resource allocation is an extremely challenging and important problem in the design and control of high-speed networks such as ATM networks. The problem is particularly complicated by the need to support *Quality-of-Service* (QoS) guarantees for a variety of applications with very diverse traffic characteristics.

In [5], a new approach to resource allocation in an ATM node with fixed bandwidth and a finite, shared buffer is presented. In this approach, an ATM node is modeled by a shared buffer multiplexor with the so-called "extremal" on-off, periodic arrival processes, which account for the worst-case stochastic behavior (as proved for the bufferless multiplexor in [8, 14]). The ingenuity of the approach is the reduction of the two-resource (*i.e.*, buffer and bandwidth) allocation problem to a single-resource allocation problem, *i.e.*, the known problem of estimating loss probability of a bufferless multiplexor. This reduction is made possible by introducing the concept of a virtual buffer/trunk system and establishing the "exchangeability" of buffer and bandwidth. Based on the analytical results, a qualitative theory is then described which provides many insights in call admission control.

Motivated and inspired by the work in [5], we study source characteristics and their impact on buffer/bandwidth trade-off in the design and control of an ATM node. The starting point of our approach is the examination of optimal resource allocation schemes for guaranteed lossless service. We find that under such service, the optimal resource allocation scheme for an ATM node where each virtual circuit has its own allocated bandwidth and buffer space with no resource sharing (referred to as a lossless segregated system) is no different from that for an ATM node with all virtual circuits sharing the resources (*i.e.*, a lossless multiplexing system). Hence, in this case, there are no benefits in resource sharing, and the two systems are effectively equivalent. We also find that the optimal resource allocation scheme suggests an interesting separation of time scales among sources sharing an ATM node with finite bandwidth and buffer space, with the optimal buffer/bandwidth trade-off being determined by this time scale separation. Sources are classified as having either "fast" or "slow" time scales, reflecting the efficacy of either buffer sharing or bandwidth sharing among the sources.

For statistical service where a small loss probability is allowed, we derive a new approach to estimate the loss probability using our results for the optimal buffer/bandwidth trade-off obtained for lossless service. By giving a new interpretation to the virtual trunk/buffer systems introduced in [5], we are able to transform the two-resource allocation problem into two independent single-resource allocation problems. The best buffer/bandwidth separation is explored by optimizing resource allocation along the optimal buffer/bandwidth trade-off curve. Through numerical examples, we demonstrate that source time scales also have a major impact on the optimal resource allocation under statistical service, and the optimal buffer/bandwidth trade-off is again reflected by the source time scale separation.

Our work differs from [5] in several aspects. First, our perspectives on resource allocation and control problems are somewhat different. The authors in [5] are primarily interested in call admission control. This is reflected in their fixing the system bandwidth $C$ and buffer space $B$. Resource allocation to each source is independent of the sources' characteristics. In our approach, we fix one resource (bandwidth $C$) and find the optimal allocation of the other resource (buffer space $B$). Furthermore, resource

*This work was supported in part by the National Science Foundation under grant CCR-9119922. Any opinions, findings, and conclusions or recommendations expressed in this paper are those of the author and do not necessarily reflect the views of the National Science Foundation. Francesco Lo Presti is with Dip. di Informatica, Sistemi e Produzione, Università di Roma "Tor Vergata", Roma, Italy. Zhi-Li Zhang is with Department of Computer Science, University of Minnesota, EE/CS Building, 200 Union Street S.E., Minneapolis, MN 55455-0159. Jim Kurose and Don Towsley are with Computer Science Department, University of Massachusetts, Amherst, MA 01003. The authors' email addresses are: lopresti@russell.ce.utovrm.it, zhzhang@cs.umn.edu, {kurose,towsley}@cs.umass.edu.



0-8186-7780-5/97 $10.00 © 1997 IEEE

allocation is made according to the time scale separation of the system and the source's own time scale. Due to this difference in perspectives, we are able to study the role of source time scale and investigate optimal buffer/bandwidth trade-off for both lossless service and statistical service with a given loss probability. We are also able to explore the maximal benefits of both buffer sharing and bandwidth sharing. This is important, as the efficacy of buffer sharing and that of bandwidth sharing for sources with different time scales are quite different. Numerical examples indicate that our approach provides a better estimate of the system loss probability than [5].

The remainder of this paper is organized as follows. We start with the optimal resource allocation problem for guaranteed lossless service in Section 2.In Section 3, we study the optimal resource allocation problem for statistical service with small loss probability. In Section 4, numerical examples are presented to illustrate the relationship between source time scale and buffer/bandwidth trade-off. The paper is concluded in Section 5.

## 2 Guaranteed Lossless Service

The starting point of our study is the analysis of the optimal resource allocation scheme for guaranteed lossless service. Consider an ATM node with a total amount of bandwidth $C$ and buffer space $B$. Suppose there are $N$ virtual circuits sharing the node. Each virtual circuit is associated with a traffic source that is leaky bucket regulated [12]. We consider the following two scenarios. In the first scenario, each virtual circuit is allocated a fixed portion of the total bandwidth and buffer space with no resource sharing among the virtual circuits. We call this system *lossless segregated system*. In the second scenario, the resources are shared among the virtual circuits. We call such a system *lossless multiplexing system*. We are interested in optimal resource allocation schemes that, for given bandwidth $C$, minimize the buffer requirement while ensuring that no virtual circuits ever incur losses in the above scenarios. We show that for guaranteed lossless service, the optimal resource allocation schemes for both systems are the same. Hence in terms of resource requirements, the lossless multiplexing system is effectively equivalent to the lossless segregated system. First, we describe the regulated traffic sources.

A leaky bucket regulator is characterized by three parameters: the token rate $\rho$, the token bucket size $\sigma$ and the peak rate $P$, where $P \geq \rho$. Let $A[\tau, \tau+t]$ denote the amount of traffic passing through the regulator in the time interval $[\tau, \tau+t]$. Then

$$A[\tau,\tau+t] \leq \mathcal{E}(t) := \min\{Pt, \sigma+\rho t\}, \ \tau \geq 0, \ t \geq 0 \quad (1)$$

where $\mathcal{E}(t)$ is called the minimum envelope process for the regulated source [3]. It bounds the amount of traffic departing from the regulator during any time interval of length $t$.

Let $T_{on}$ denote the maximum length of a peak rate burst, *i.e.*, $T_{on} = \frac{\sigma}{P-\rho}$. A traffic source which generates traffic at peak rate $P$ for $T_{on}$ time and switches to rate $\rho$ for the rest of the time has a regulated traffic such that $A[0,t] = \mathcal{E}(t)$. We call such a traffic source *greedy*.

For the purpose of exposition, we assume that the $N$ traffic sources are classified into $J$ classes according to their regulator characterization, where all regulated sources in class $j$ have the same leaky bucket parameters $(\rho_j, \sigma_j, P_j)$, $1 \leq j \leq J$. There are $K_j$ Class $j$ sources, and $\sum_{j=1}^{J} K_j = N$. We assume that all classes have different peak rate burst length $T_{on}$. Without loss of generality, let $T_{on_1} > T_{on_2} > \cdots > T_{on_J}$. In order to have a stable system, we require that $\sum_{j=1}^{J} K_j\rho_j \leq C$. Also in order to avoid triviality, we assume that $C \leq \sum_{j=1}^{J} K_j P_j$.

### 2.1 Lossless Segregated System

We first consider the optimal resource allocation problem for the lossless segregated system. We fix the total bandwidth $C$ for the system, and consider allocation schemes that minimize the total buffer space required to ensure that no virtual circuits incur any losses.

For $j = 1, \ldots J$, suppose each source in class $j$ is allocated bandwidth $c_j$ and buffer space $b_j$. Let $C_j = K_j c_j$ denote the total amount of bandwidth allocated to class $j$ sources. The stability condition requires that $c_j \geq \rho_j$ for each $j$. In order to ensure that no losses occur for any virtual circuit, the amount of buffer space $b_j$ allocated to a class $j$ source is determined by the maximum queue length for each segregated virtual circuit $j$, *i.e.*,

$$b_j \geq \sup_{t\geq 0}\{\mathcal{E}_j[t] - c_j t\} = \sigma_j - T_{on_j}(c_j - \rho_j). \quad (2)$$

The overall buffer space required to ensure that no virtual circuits encounter losses is thus $B_{seg} = \sum_{j=1}^{J} K_j b_j$. This determines the buffer requirement under the segregated allocation scheme.

Given the linearity of (2), the optimal buffer allocation problem can be formulated as the following Linear Programming (LP) problem:

**Problem** Minimize
$B_{seg} = \sum_{j=1}^{J} K_j\sigma_j - \sum_{j=1}^{J} T_{on_j}(C_j - K_j\rho_j)$
subject to:
$$\sum_{j=1}^{J} C_j = \sum_{j=1}^{J} K_j c_j \leq C,$$
$$\rho_j \leq c_j \leq P_j, \quad j = 1, \ldots, J.$$

It is clear that the objective function decreases whenever bandwidth is taken from classes with smaller $T_{on}$ and is allocated to classes with larger $T_{on}$. As a consequence, the optimal allocation scheme consists of allocating peak rate to as many classes with large $T_{on}$ as possible without violating the constraint $\sum_{j=1}^{J} C_j \leq C$, while allocating only average rate to classes with small $T_{on}$. Formally, let $k$ be the smallest index such that

$$\sum_{j=1}^{k-1} K_j P_j + \sum_{j=k}^{J} K_j\rho_j \leq C < \sum_{j=1}^{k} k_j P_j + \sum_{j=k+1}^{J} K_j\rho_j. \quad (3)$$

Then the optimal resource allocation scheme that results in the minimum buffer requirement for the given bandwidth $C$ is as follows:

$$c_j = \begin{cases} P_j, & j = 1, \ldots, k-1, \\ \frac{C - \sum_{l\neq k} K_l c_l}{K_j}, & j = k, \\ \rho_j, & j = k+1, \ldots, J \end{cases} \quad (4)$$

and

$$b_j = \begin{cases} 0, & j = 1, \dots, k-1, \\ \sigma_j - T_{on_j}(c_j - \rho_j), & j = k, \\ \sigma_j, & j = k+1, \dots, J. \end{cases} \quad (5)$$

Note that $\sum_{j=1}^{J} C_j - \sum_{j=1}^{J} K_j c_j = C$, and the buffer requirement $B_{seg}$ has the following closed-form expression in terms of the regulated source parameters

$$B_{seg} = \sum_{j=k+1}^{J} K_j\sigma_j + [K_k\sigma_k - K_k T_{on_k}(c_k - \rho_k)]. \quad (6)$$

## 2.2 Lossless Multiplexing System

We now consider the optimal resource allocation problem for the lossless multiplexing system. Again we fix the total bandwidth of the system which is shared by all virtual circuits, and determine the minimal buffer space required to guarantee no losses. This shared buffer multiplexing system is equivalent to a shared single queue serviced by a server of capacity $C$. Given the regulated traffic sources defined earlier, the maximum queue length of the system is given by the following expression

$$Q_{max} \leq \sup_{t\geq 0}\{\sum_{j=1}^{J} K_j \mathcal{E}_j(t) - Ct\} \quad (7)$$

where the equality is attained when all sources are greedy and start at the same time. Hence in order to ensure that no losses occur in the system, a minimum buffer size $B_{mux} = Q_{max}$ is required.

We proceed to derive a closed-form expression for $B_{mux}$ in terms of the parameters of the regulated sources. By substituting the expression for $\mathcal{E}_j(t)$ in (7), we readily obtain that the supremum is attained at the point $t_{max} = T_{on_k}$, where $k$ is exactly as defined in (3). Hence, $T_{on_k}$ has the following physical meaning: $T_{on_k}$ is the time the system reaches its maximum queue length when all sources are greedy.

From (7), we derive that the minimum buffer requirement is

$$B_{mux} = \sum_{j=k+1}^{J} K_j\sigma_j + [K_k\sigma_k - T_{on_k}(C - \sum_{j=1}^{k-1} K_j P_j - \sum_{j=k}^{J} K_j\rho_j)]$$

Comparing this with (6), we observe that $B_{seg} = B_{mux}$. Hence the minimum buffer requirement for the lossless multiplexing system is exactly the same as for the lossless segregated system. Thus we can define $B_{min} = B_{seg} = B_{mux}$ as the buffer requirement for lossless service.

From (3), we observe that if, for $1 \leq j \leq J$, we define $c_j$ and $b_j$ as in (4) and (5), then $\sum_{j=1}^{J} K_j c_j = C$ and $\sum_{j=1}^{J} K_j b_j = B_{min}$. This observation provides the following interesting interpretation as to how the system resources are optimally shared among the regulated sources in the lossless multiplexing system. Specifically, when resources are optimally allocated in the lossless multiplexing system, the virtual circuits behave *as if each of them was allocated fixed bandwidth $c_j$ and fixed buffer space* $b_j$, just as in the lossless segregated system. Hence the lossless multiplexing system can be effectively treated as if it were the lossless segregated system. This observation provides a motivation for the approach we take in Section 3 for studying resource allocation schemes under statistical multiplexing with small loss probability.

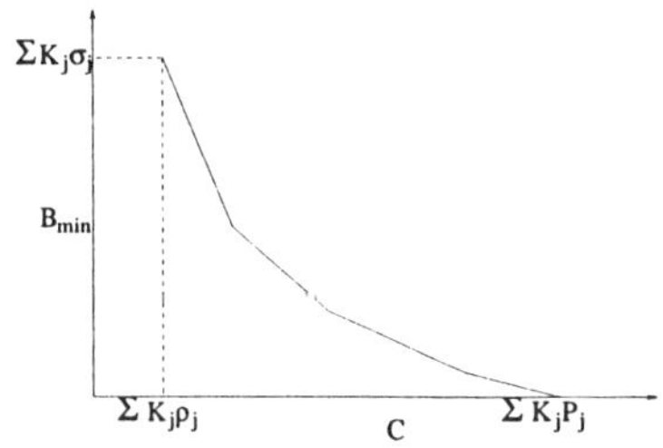


Figure 1: Optimal buffer/bandwidth trade-off curve.

## 2.3 Source Time Scale and Optimal Buffer/ Bandwidth Trade-off Curve

This far we have studied the resource allocation problem by fixing the bandwidth $C$. Now we consider the buffer/bandwidth trade-off for lossless service with a given set of regulated sources.

For any bandwidth $C$ such that $\sum_{j=1}^{J} K_j\rho_j \leq C \leq \sum_{j=1}^{J} K_j P_j$, the index $k$ defined in (3) is determined solely by the regulated source parameters and plays a key role in determining the minimal buffer requirement $B_{min}$ (see (6)). Hence in order to study the buffer/bandwidth trade-off, it suffices to study $k$ as a function of $C$. From (3), we see that $k$ is non-decreasing in $C$: $k = 1$ when $C = \sum_{j=1}^{J} K_j\rho_j$, and $k = J$ when $C = \sum_{j=1}^{J} K_j P_j$. As a consequence, from (4) and (5), we have that the allocated bandwidth $c_j$ to class $j$ sources is a non-decreasing function of $C$, whereas the buffer space $b_j$ allocated to these sources is a non-increasing function of $C$. Therefore, the buffer requirement $B_{min}$ is a decreasing function of $C$. Moreover, from (4) and (5), we have $\frac{dB_{min}}{dC} = -T_{on_k}$. Thus, the buffer requirement $B_{min}$ is a piece-wise linear, decreasing convex function of $C$(see Figure 1). We call the curve $(C, B_{min})$ in Figure 1 the buffer/bandwidth trade-off curve for lossless service.

The optimal resource allocation scheme also suggests a taxonomy of the regulated sources according to their maximum peak rate burst length $T_{on_j}$, which we shall also refer to as the time scale of the regulated sources. Subsequently, we call the index $k$ the source *time scale index* with respect to $(C, B_{min})$. Sources in class $j$ are said to have either have "fast" time scale or "slow" time scale with respect to $(C, B_{min})$ according to whether $T_{on_j} < T_{on_k}$ or $T_{on_j} > T_{on_k}$. Under the optimal resource allocation scheme, we see that the most efficient way to accommodate "fast" time scale sources under lossless service is to allocate minimum amount of bandwidth (equal to their mean rates) and maximum buffer space (equal to their token bucket sizes), while the most efficient way to accommodate "slow" time scale sources is to allocate maximum bandwidth (equal to their peak rate) and zero buffer space.

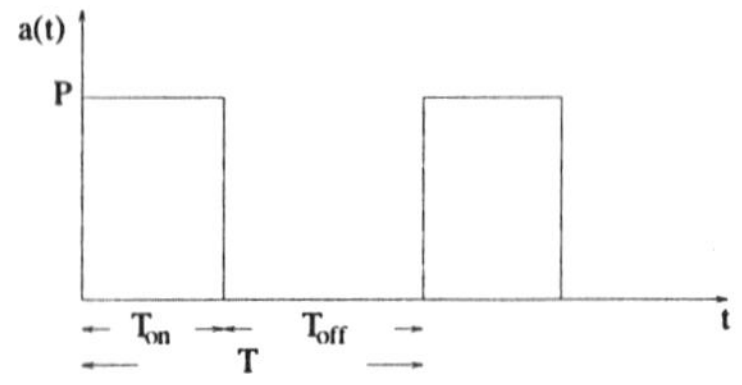


Figure 2: Extremal on-off, periodic curve.

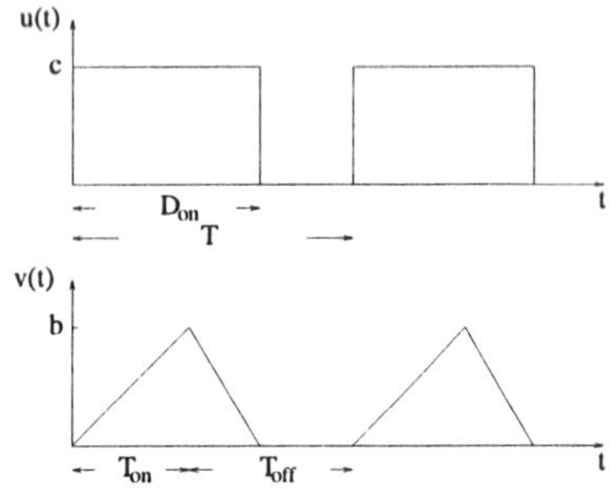


Figure 3: Buffer/bandwidth separation.

## 3 Statistical Service with Small Loss Probabilities

In the preceding section we established that under guaranteed lossless service, the optimal resource allocation is the same, regardless of whether resources are shared among sources. In this section, we study the benefits of resource sharing under statistical service where a small probability of loss, say, $10^{-9} \sim 10^{-7}$, is allowed, and investigate the buffer/bandwidth trade-off under such statistical service.

Once again, consider an ATM node with $N$ virtual circuits. Each virtual circuits is associated with a leaky bucket regulated traffic source. Suppose the node has a total amount of bandwidth $C$ and buffer space $B$, shared by all the sources. We assume that the system resources are not sufficient to provide guaranteed lossless service. In other words, the lossless service buffer requirement $B_{min}$ for the given value of bandwidth $C$ exceeds $B$. This implies that $(C, B)$ lies below the buffer/bandwidth trade-off curve in Figure 1. In this section, we explore the possibility of exploiting statistical multiplexing gains by considering statistical service with small loss probabilities.

Statistical multiplexing gains can be extracted by exploiting the bursty nature and statistical independence of traffic sources [5]. To exploit the bursty nature of traffic sources regulated by leaky buckets with parameters $(\sigma, \rho, P)$, we follow [5] and assume that the regulated sources after passing through leaky bucket regulators are extremal on-off, periodic processes (see Figure 2), where, when a source is active, it generates data at the peak rate $P$ until the depletion of its token bucket; it then stays inactive until the token bucket is completely filled again. Use of such processes are justified to a large extent by the work of [4, 8, 13, 14]. In particular, such processes account for the *worst-case* statistical behavior in a bufferless multiplexor in the sense that they maximize the average loss rate [14] and the loss probability estimated by the Chernoff bound [8, 14].

Let $a(t)$ denote an extremal on-off, periodic departure process from a leaky bucket regulator with parameters $(\rho, \sigma, P)$ as shown in Figure 2. Then the lengths of the on and off periods are $T_{on} = \frac{\sigma}{P-\rho}$ and $T_{off} = \frac{\sigma}{\rho}$. The source period is $T = T_{on} + T_{off} = P/\rho T_{on}$. Let $S$ denote the total amount of data generated during the on period. Then $S = PT_{on} = \sigma\frac{P}{P-\rho}$. $S$ is known as the source *burst-size*.

In order to model the statistical independence of traffic sources, we introduce indeterminate "phases" to the sources as in [5]. Assume that traffic sources are grouped into $J$ classes, and for $1 \le j \le J$, there are $K_j$ sources in class $j$, $\sum_{j=1}^{J} K_j = N$. Each source $i$ of class $j$, $a_{ji}(t)$, is an extremal on-off, periodic process with leaky bucket parameters $(\rho_j, \sigma_j, P_j)$, but having an associated phase $\theta_{ji}$, *i.e.*, $a_{ji}(t) = a_j(t + \theta_{ji})$. For $1 \le j \le J$ and $1 \le i \le K_j$, the phases $\theta_{ji}$ are independent random variables uniformly distributed in the interval $[0, T_j]$.

In order to provide robust service, it is imperative to estimate the loss probability $P_{loss}$ at the ATM node due to buffer overflow. However, the loss probability of such a two-resource system with the given on-off sources is very difficult to compute directly. Several bounding and approximate approaches has been developed [6, 10, 11], based on the so-called Benes approach [1]. A new approach is presented in [5] by trading one resource for the other, using the notion of the virtual buffer/trunk.

Based on the work of [5], in this section, we present a new approach to the problem of estimating system loss probability by transforming the two-resource problem into two independent single-resource problems which allows us to explore the optimal trade-off between buffer and bandwidth. This reduction is achieved via a virtual lossless segregate system functioning as a "resource separator", a new interpretation of the notion of the virtual buffer/trunk system introduced in [5].

The rest of this section is organized as follows. In Section 3.1, we introduce the concept of virtual buffer/trunk system. In Section 3.2, we describe our approach for determining the optimal buffer/bandwidth separation and trade-off. The effectiveness of our approach is evaluated via numerical examples in section 4.

### 3.1 Virtual Buffer/Trunk System

Consider a virtual circuit with a single extremal on-off, periodic traffic source $a(t)$ characterized by parameters $(\rho, \sigma, P)$. Suppose it is allocated a trunk of bandwidth of $c$ where $\rho \le c \le P$. Then the maximum backlog at the virtual circuit is $b = \sigma - T_{on}(c - \rho) = T_{on}(P - c)$. Hence if the virtual circuit is allocated buffer space $b$, no losses will occur. Following [5], we call such a virtual circuit a *virtual* buffer/trunk system.

Let $u(t)$ and $v(t)$ denote, respectively, the utilized bandwidth and the buffer content of the virtual circuit at time $t$. As shown in Figure 3, the two processes $u(t)$ and $v(t)$ are periodic with period $T$, the source period. Let $D_{on}$ denote the time in each cycle that the system is busy, *i.e.*, the buffer is not empty; $D_{on}$ exceeds the length of the source on period by the time required to deplete the buffer.

We can view the virtual buffer/trunk system as a "resource separator" as it splits the traffic process $a(t)$ into two separate processes $u(t)$ and $v(t)$, representing, respectively, the bandwidth requirement and buffer requirement of the source at time $t$. Under this interpretation, by varying the trunk bandwidth $c$, the virtual buffer/trunk system can "regulate" the source's buffer and bandwidth requirements, thus providing an interesting buffer/bandwidth trade-off when allocating resources. When $c$ is increased, the source's bandwidth requirement during the system busy period is also increased. However, the system busy period is shortened and the source' buffer requirement is decreased. On the other hand, when $c$ is decreased, the reverse is true.

The effect of varying $c$ on $u(t)$ and $v(t)$ can be concisely stated using the theory of stochastic orderings. The details can be found in [7].

### 3.2 Estimating Loss Probability for Statistical Service

Recall that we are assuming that the system resources are not sufficient to support lossless service, i.e., $(C, B)$ lies below the buffer/bandwidth trade-off curve in Figure 4. In this section, we present a new approach for estimating the system loss probability in such cases. This approach exploits the buffer/bandwidth separation determined by a virtual buffer/trunk system and exploits the optimal buffer/bandwidth trade-off curve for lossless service.

Consider a lossless segregated system with a total amount of bandwidth $C_v$ and buffer space $B_v$ where $(C_v, B_v)$ lies on the buffer/bandwidth trade-off curve. Because the system resource pair $(B, C)$ lies below the buffer/bandwidth trade-off curve, we must have either $C_v > C$ or $B_v > B$ or both. We call such a system a *virtual* lossless segregated system. In the virtual lossless segregated system, each source $i$ of class $j$, $a_{ji}(t)$, $1 \le j \le J, 1 \le i \le K_j$, has a trunk of fixed bandwidth $c_j^v$ and a buffer of fixed size $b_j^v$ such that $\sum_{j=1}^{J} K_j c_j^v = C_v$, $\sum_{j=1}^{J} K_j b_j^v = B_v$, and the resources $c_j^v$ and $b_j^v$ are allocated to each virtual buffer/trunk system according to the optimal resource allocation scheme described in Section 2.1. Hence no sources suffer any losses in the virtual buffer/trunk systems.

Let $u_{ji}(t)$ and $v_{ji}(t)$ denote the utilized bandwidth and the buffer contents of source $a_{ji}(t)$ in the virtual buffer/trunk system, where $u_{ji}(t)$ and $v_{ji}(t)$ are two periodic processes synchronized with source $a_{ji}(t)$ (*i.e.*, they all have the same phase $\theta_{ji}$). Interpreting the virtual buffer/trunk system as a "resource separator", then $u_{ji}(t)$ and $v_{ji}(t)$ represent, respectively, the bandwidth and buffer consumed by source $a_{ji}(t)$ at time $t$. Thus at any time $t$, the total bandwidth requirement of all sources is $U(t) = \sum_{j=1}^{J} \sum_{i=1}^{K_j} u_{ji}(t)$, while the total buffer requirement of all sources is $V(t) = \sum_{j=1}^{J} \sum_{i=1}^{K_j} v_{ji}(t)$. The virtual lossless segregated system separates the bandwidth and buffer requirements of the sources, thus enabling us to treat them separately.

By imagining that the traffic sources go through a virtual lossless segregated system that separates their bandwidth and buffer requirements, we reduce the difficult task of estimating the system loss probability in a buffered multiplexor with finite resources into that for two simpler systems: a trunk with bandwidth $C$ (but no buffer) and a storage system with buffer space $B$ (but no server). *At any time $t$, the sources demand a total amount of bandwidth $U(t)$ from the trunk and a total amount of buffer space $V(t)$ from the storage system. The sources will incur losses if either $U(t) > C$ or $V(t) > B$.* Therefore, we can use the probability that either event occurs as an upper bound on the loss probability $P_{loss}$ of the real system. (This buffer/bandwidth separation approach for estimating the system loss probability is justified and made rigorous in [7].) By choosing different resource pairs $(C_v, B_v)$ along the buffer/bandwidth trade-off curve, the virtual lossless segregate system "regulates" the sources' bandwidth and buffer requirements, thus providing a trade-off between them. The rest of this section is devoted to the determination of the resource pair $(C_v, B_v)$ that optimizes the system loss probability estimate.

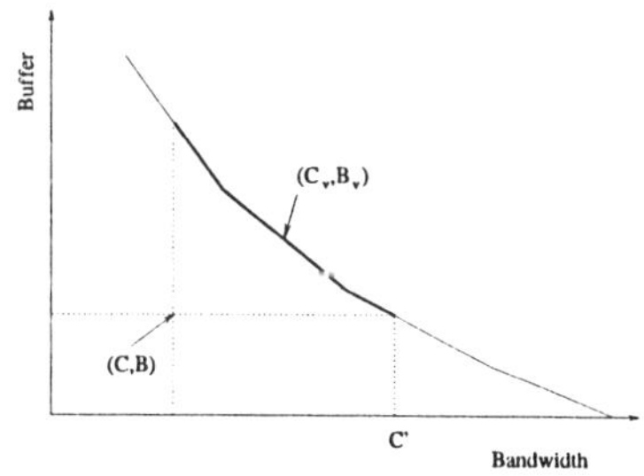


Figure 4: Relationship between $(C, B)$ and the buffer/bandwidth trade-off curve $(C_v, B_v)$.

Let $u_{ji}$ and $v_{ji}$ be two random variables that represent respectively the instantaneous bandwidth requirement and buffer requirement of source $a_{ji}$ at a random time. Then $u_{ji}$ is a Bernoulli random variable taking value $c_j^v$ with probability $w_j = \frac{\rho_j}{c_j^v}$ and 0 with probability $1 - w_j$, and $v_{ji}$ has the distribution $Pr\{v_{ji} \le x\} = 1 - w_j + w_j \frac{x}{b_j^v}$, $0 \le x \le b_j^v$. Moreover, $u_{ji}$, $1 \le j \le J, 1 \le i \le K_j$, are all independent, as are $v_{ji}$, $1 \le j \le J, 1 \le i \le K_j$.

Define $U = \sum_{j=1}^{J} \sum_{i=1}^{K_j} u_{ji}$ and $V = \sum_{j=1}^{J} \sum_{i=1}^{K_j} v_{ji}$. From the above discussion it follows that

$$P_{loss} \le \Pr\{V > B \text{ or } U > C\} \le \Pr\{V > B\} + \Pr\{U > C\} \quad (8)$$

Since (8) is valid for any choice of a resource pair $(C_v, B_v)$ on the buffer/bandwidth trade-off curve, we have

$$P_{loss} \le \inf_{(C_v, B_v)} \{\Pr\{U > C\} + \Pr\{V > B\}\}. \quad (9)$$

The minimization problem on the right hand side of (9) reveals an interesting trade-off between buffer and bandwidth in the virtual buffer/trunk systems. Intuitively, the resource pair $(C_v^*, B_v^*)$ that minimizes the probability on the right hand side of (9) represents the "best" separation of bandwidth and buffer requirements of the resources. This separation is obtained by optimizing the resource allocation along the optimal buffer/bandwidth trade-off curve.

For any $C_v$, $\Pr\{U > C\}$ and $\Pr\{V > B\}$ can be estimated using the Chernoff bound. For $1 \le j \le J$, let $M_{u_j}(\theta) = E[e^{\theta u_{ji}}]$ and $M_{v_j}(\theta) = E[e^{\theta v_{ji}}]$ denote the moment generating functions of $u_{ji}$ and $v_{ji}$.

Define $\Lambda_{C_v}(\theta) = \sum_{j=1}^{J} \kappa_j \log M_{u_j}(\theta)$ and $\Lambda_{B_v}(\theta) = \sum_{j=1}^{J} \kappa_j \log M_{v_j}(\theta)$ where $\kappa_j = \frac{K_j}{N}$, $1 \le j \le J$, and $\sum_{j=1}^{J} \kappa_j = 1$. Then Chernoff bound yields $\Pr\{U > C\} \le e^{-N\Lambda^*_{C_v}(C/N)}$ and $\Pr\{V > B\} \le e^{-N\Lambda^*_{B_v}(B/N)}$ where $\Lambda^*_{C_v}(\alpha) = \sup_{\theta\ge0}\{\theta\alpha - \Lambda_{C_v}(\theta)\}$, and $\Lambda^*_{B_v}(\alpha) = \sup_{\theta\ge0}\{\theta\alpha - \Lambda_{B_v}(\theta)\}$. Hence,

$$P_{loss} \le \inf_{(C_v,B_v)} \left\{ e^{-N\Lambda^*_{C_v}(C/N)} + e^{-N\Lambda^*_{B_v}(B/N)} \right\}. \quad (10)$$

The optimization problem can be greatly simplified by considering the asymptotic scaling $N \to \infty$ with $C/N = \bar{c}$, $B/N = \bar{b}$ and $K_j/N = \kappa_j$, $1 \le j \le J$, held constant. In this case, we have that

$$\lim_{N\to\infty} \frac{1}{N} \log P_{loss} \le - \sup_{(C_v,B_v)} \left\{ \min\{\Lambda^*_{C_v}(\bar{c}), \Lambda^*_{B_v}(\bar{b})\} \right\}. \quad (11)$$

Since $\Lambda^*_{C_v}(\bar{c})$ is a decreasing function in $C_v$ while $\Lambda^*_{B_v}(\bar{b})$ is an increasing in $C_v$, the above optimization can be solved in a straightforward manner [7]. Let $C_v^*$ denote the solution to the optimization problem, then the loss probability $P_{loss}$ can be estimated by $e^{-N\Lambda^*_{C_v^*}(\bar{c})} + e^{-N\Lambda^*_{B_v^*}(\bar{b})}$. This estimate can be further refined by adding a prefactor that represents an asymptotic correction term for the Chernoff bound [2].

## 4 Numerical Examples

In this section, we present numerical examples to illustrate the results of the previous sections. Our focus is on the relationship between source time scale and the optimal buffer/bandwidth trade-off, and on the effect of this buffer/bandwidth trade-off on admissible regions under both deterministic lossless service and statistical service with small loss probabilities. In comparison to previous works that consider multiplexing of periodic on-off sources [5, 6, 9, 10, 11], an important contribution of our present work lies in exploiting the different sources times scales existing in heterogeneous traffic sources. In particular, we show how the buffer/bandwidth trade-off is determined by the source time scale separation and that the boundary of the admissible region for heterogeneous sources can be severely non linear if the sources have very different time scales.

In the following examples, we describe regulated sources using the token rate $\rho$, the peak rate $P$, and the burst-size $S$ in place of the usual token bucket size $\sigma$. $\sigma$ can be obtained from $S$ from the identity $S = \sigma\frac{P}{P-\rho}$. The burst-size $S$ is preferred because it is related to the source time scale $T_{on}$ via $T_{on} = S/P$.

We begin by illustrating the relationship between source time scale and the optimal buffer/bandwidth trade-off. We first consider the case where there is a single class of sources. Under lossless multiplexing, for a multiplexor of bandwidth $C$ with $K$ homogeneous sources, from (2.2), we have that the minimal buffer requirement is given by $B_{min} = T_{on}(KP - C)$. With $K$ fixed, the buffer requirement decreases linearly with the bandwidth and is proportional to the source time scale. At $C = KP$, it becomes zero. The source time scale also determines the rate of

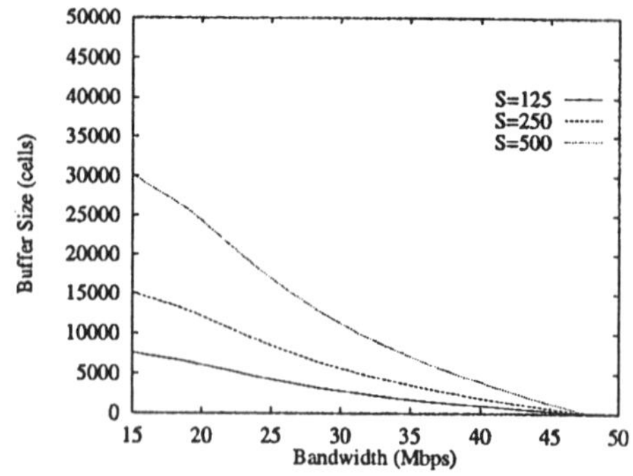


Figure 5: Buffer/bandwidth trade-off for a single class.

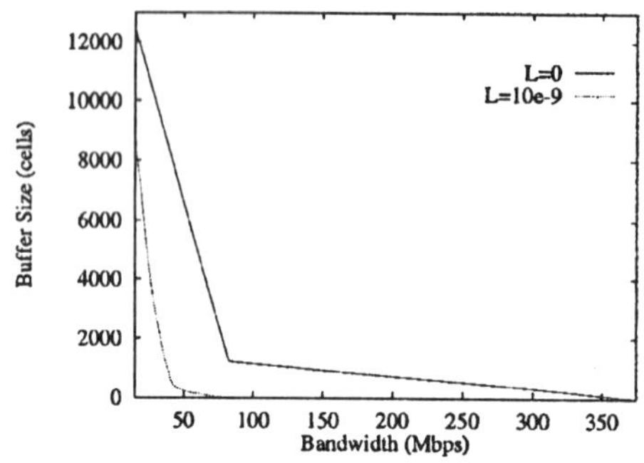


Figure 6: Buffer/bandwidth trade-off for two classes.

change in the buffer requirement, as $dB_{min}/dC = -T_{on}$. In Figure 5, we plot the bandwidth/buffer trade-off for statistical service with a loss probability of $L = 10^{-9}$, where for each given bandwidth value, the buffer requirement is computed as the minimum buffer size such that $P_{loss} \le L$. The curve is plotted with $K = 100$ for three types of single-class sources with the same mean rate $\rho = 0.15$ Mbps and peak rate $P = 1.5$ Mbps, but three different burst-sizes $S = 125, 250, 500$, measured in cells (*i.e.*, 53 Bytes), yielding $T_{on} = 35, 70, 140$ ms, respectively. With $K = 100$, the aggregate average rate is 15 Mbps and the aggregate peak rate 150 Mbps. In this case, the buffer requirement also decreases with the bandwidth, and is proportional to the source time scale. Note that the buffer requirement under statistical service is much less than under lossless service. For example, in this case, the buffer requirement drops to 0 as bandwidth approach 50 Mbps, as opposed to 150 Mbps in the case of lossless service. The presence of statistical multiplexing gains is clearly evident.

We now consider multiplexing two classes of sources. The parameters for the two classes are listed in Table 1. The parameters are chosen so that the two classes have drastically different $T_{on}$ ($T_{on_1} \gg T_{on_2}$), so as to highlight the effect of source time scale on the buffer/bandwidth trade-off curve when heterogeneous classes are multiplexed. We assume that $K_1 = K_2 = 50$. The aggregate average and peak rate of the two classes are 15 Mbps and 375 Mbps, respectively.

The optimal buffer/bandwidth trade-off curve for loss-

| class | $\rho$ | $P$ | $S$ | $T_{on}$ |
|---|---|---|---|---|
| 1 | 0.15 | 1.5 | 250 | 70 |
| 2 | 0.15 | 6 | 25 | 1.7 |

Table 1: Sources leaky bucket parameters.

less service ($L = 0$) is plotted in Figure 6(a). We can distinguish two distinct components in the curve: the first one with a very steep slope, and the second one with a much lower slope. The knee point is at $C = 82.5$. This phenomenon can be explained by considering the structure of the optimal resource allocation scheme. With small values of bandwidth $C$, class 2 sources have a "fast" time scale (the time scale index $k$ defined in (3) is 1), and are thus allocated an amount of bandwidth equal to their mean rate $\rho_2$ and buffer space equal to their maximum token bucket size $\sigma_2$, while the remaining bandwidth and buffer space are allocated among class 1 sources, which have much larger time scale, $T_{on_1}$. As $C$ increases, the bandwidth allocated to class 1 sources increases, hence their buffer requirement decreases as a rate of $dB_{min}/dC = -T_{on_1}$. When $C$ reaches 82.5 Mbps, class 1 sources are allocated peak rate (the time scale index, $k$, is 2), thus turning into "slow" time scale sources with no buffer requirements. As a consequence, as $C$ further increases, additional bandwidth is allocated only among class 2 sources, reducing their buffer requirements at a rate of $dB_{min}/dC = -T_{on_2}$.

In Figure 6, we also plot the buffer/bandwidth trade-off for statistical service with a loss probability of $10^{-9}$. As expected, both bandwidth and buffer requirements are reduced under statistical service, again providing evidence of statistical multiplexing gains. At $C = 85$ Mbps, the buffer requirement drops to 0. For statistical service, the time scale separation of the two classes is easier to discern by examining the trade-off curve in log-scale (Figure 6). Observe that as the bandwidth $C$ approaches 50Mbps, the curve bends. As in the deterministic case, this phenomenon can be explained in terms of the structure of the optimal resource allocation for the virtual segregated system, which is determined by the optimization in (11). Due to statistical multiplexing gains, the time scale separation evident in the bandwidth/buffer trade-off curve occurs at a lower value of bandwidth.

Next, we study the impact of source characteristics on the system admissible region, defined as the number of sources that can be admitted without violating a given QoS requirement. We consider the same two classes of traffic discussed above. We fix the value of the system bandwidth $C$ at 45 Mbps and study the admissible region as a function of the system buffer size $B$. Because the two classes have the same average rate, the system utilization is maximized when the number of sources of both classes, $K_1 + K_2$ is maximized. Because $\rho/C = 1/300$, the utilization is $\frac{K_1+K_2}{3}\%$.

The admissible regions for lossless service with various values of buffer size are plotted in Figure 7. The key observation here is the non-linearity of the boundary of the admissible region for all values of the buffer size $B$ except for $B = 0$. As we will see, this non-linearity is caused

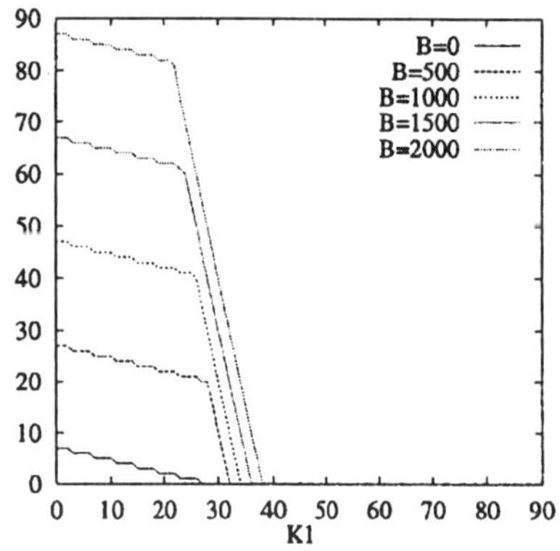


Figure 7: Admissible region for two heterogeneous classes: $T_{on_1} \gg T_{on_2}$.

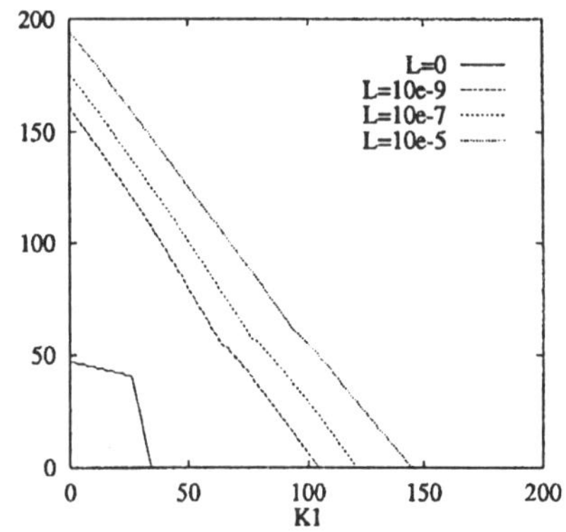


Figure 8: Admissible region: $B = 1000$.

by the different source time scales, $T_{on}$, of the sources. For $B = 0$, the boundary is linear with a slope given by the ratio of the source peak rates $dK_2/dK_1 = -P_1/P_2$. This is because in the bufferless case, sources are allocated peak rate. For a nonzero buffer size, we can identify two distinct segments of different slopes on the boundary of the admissible region. For relatively small numbers of class 1 sources, the boundary has the same slope as in the bufferless case, as shown in the figure. On the other hand, for relatively small numbers of class 2 sources, it is not difficult to show that the slope of the boundary is

$$\frac{dK_2}{dK_1} = -\frac{P_1}{\sigma_2/T_{on_1} + \rho_2} \leq -\frac{P_1}{\sigma_2/T_{on_2} + \rho_2} = -\frac{P_1}{P_2} \quad (12)$$

as $T_{on_1} \geq T_{on_2}$. As a result, the admissible region is convex.

In Figures 8 and 9, we plot the admissible regions for statistical service with various loss probabilities. The system bandwidth is again fixed at $C = 45$ Mbps, and two values of the system buffer size are considered: $B \in \{1000, 10000\}$ cells. Note that statistical service provides considerable improvement in system utilization. It is also interesting to observe that for large buffer, a form of system saturation takes effect that limits statistical multiplexing gains. For example, for $B = 10000$ (Figure 9), because the most

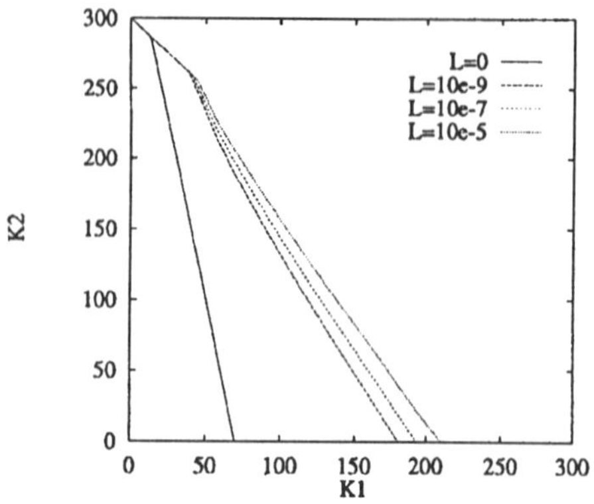


Figure 9: Admissible region: $B = 10000$.

resource-efficient way to accommodate "fast" time scale is to allocate minimum bandwidth and maximum buffer space, when the input traffic is dominated by the "fast" time scale class 2 sources, it is possible to admit up to 300 sources, corresponding to 100% utilization under lossless service. The same buffer size is less effective when input traffic is dominated by the "slow" time scale class 1 sources. In this case, because the most resource-efficient way to accommodate "slow" time scale is to allocate maximum bandwidth and no buffer space, no more than 70 sources can be admitted under lossless service (resulting in an utilization below 25%) and no more than approximately 210 sources can be admitted under statistical service with a loss probability of $10^{-5}$ (resulting in an utilization of approximately 70%). For statistical service, the resulting admissible region is also clearly non-linear. We can distinguish two distinct components in the boundary: a linear region for $K_1 \leq 45$ and a concave region otherwise.

## 5 Conclusions

In this paper, we studied the problem of resource allocation and control for an ATM node with regulated traffic. Both guaranteed lossless service and statistical service with small loss probability were considered. We investigated the relationship between source characteristics and buffer/bandwidth trade-off under both services.

For guaranteed lossless service, we identified the optimal resource allocation scheme for an ATM node with finite bandwidth and buffer space, and found that the optimal resource allocation scheme suggests an interesting time scale separation of sources sharing the ATM node. With respect to this time scale separation, the time scale of a source can be defined and the optimal buffer/bandwidth trade-off determined by the sources' time scale. For statistical service with small loss probability, we presented a new approach for estimating loss probability in a shared buffer multiplexor with extremal on-off, periodic sources. Under this approach, the optimal resource allocation for statistical service is achieved by maximizing both the benefits of buffering sharing and bandwidth sharing. The optimal buffer/bandwidth trade-off is again determined by the time scale separation and reflects the efficacy of buffer sharing and bandwidth sharing among sources with different time scales. Through numerical investigations, we illustrated the relationship of source time scale and the optimal buffer/bandwidth tradeoff and discussed the implications of our results in resource allocation and call admission control.

Our results have many other implications in network design and control such as network dimensioning and traffic shaping, in addition to resource allocation and call admission control in an ATM node. This will be the subject of future research.

## References


[1] V. Benes. *General Stochastic Processes in the Theory of Queues*. Reading, MA: Addison Wesley, 1963.

[2] R. Bahadur and R. Rao. On deviations of the sample mean. *Ann. Math. Statis.*, Vol. 31, pp. 1015-1027, 1960.

[3] C. S. Chang. Stability, Queue Length and Delay of Deterministic and Stochastic Queueing Networks, *IEEE Transaction on Automatic Control*, Vol. 39, No. 5, pp. 913-931, May 1994.

[4] B. Doshi. Deterministic Rule Based Traffic Descriptors for Broadband ISDN: Worst Case Behavior and Connection Acceptance Control, *Proceedings of IEEE INFOCOM 93*, pp. 1759-1764, San Francisco, March 1993.

[5] A. Elwalid, D. Mitra and R.Wentworth. A New Approach for Allocating Buffer and Bandwidth to Heterogeneous, Regulated Traffic in an ATM Node, *IEEE Journal on Selected Area in Communications*, Vol. 13, No. 6, pp. 1115-1127, August 1995.

[6] K. Kvols and S. Blaabjerg. Bounds and Approximations for the Periodic on/off Queue with Applications to ATM Traffic control, *Proceedings of IEEE INFOCOM 92*, pp. 487-494, Florence, May 1992.

[7] F. Lo Presti, Z.-L. Zhang, J. Kurose and D. Towsley. Source Time Scale and Optimal Buffer/Bandwidth Trade-off for Regulated Traffic in an ATM Node, *Technical Report* UM-CS-96-38, Computer Science Department, University of Massachusetts, June 1996.

[8] D. Mitra and J. Morrison. Multiple Time Scale Regulation and Worst Case Processes for ATM Network Control, *Proceedings of the 34th Conference on Decision and Control*, pp. 353-358, New Orleans, December 1995.

[9] I. Norros, J. Roberts, A. Simonian and J. Virtamo. The Superposition of Variable Bit Rate Sources in an ATM Multiplexer, *IEEE Journal on Selected Area in Communications*, Vol. 9, No. 3, pp. 378-387, April 1991.

[10] J. Roberts and J. Virtamo. Evaluating Buffer Requirements in an ATM Multiplexer, *Proceedings of GLOBECOM 89*, pp. 1473-1477, 1989.

[11] J. Roberts and J. Virtamo. The Superposition of Periodic Cell Arrival Streams in an ATM Multiplexer, *IEEE Trans. on Communications*, Vol. 39, No. 2, pp. 298-303, February 1991.

[12] J. Turner. New Directions in Communications (or Which Way to the Information Age?), *IEEE Comm. Mag.*, October 1986.

[13] T. Worster. Modeling Deterministic Queues: the Leaky Bucket as an Arrival Process, *Proc. ITC-14*, J. Labetoulle and J. Roberts, Eds. New York: Elsevier, 1994, pp. 581-590.

[14] Z.-L. Zhang, J. Kurose, J. Salehi and D. Towsley. Smoothing, Statistical Multiplexing and Call Admission Control for Stored Video, To appear in *IEEE Journal of Seleced Areas in Communications*, Special Issue on "Real-Time Video Services in Multimedia Networks", 1996.

# Adaptive Real-Time Group Multicast

Mario Baldi * Yoram Ofek † Bülent Yener ‡

## Abstract

This paper shows how to provide an *adaptive real-time group multicast* (many-to-many) communication service. Such a service can be used by applications, like audio/video tele-conferencing, that require low loss, and bounded delay and jitter. In order to meet deterministic quality of service (QoS) requirements of a real-time group multicast, some communication resources are reserved. In this work we show (i) how bandwidth is reserved for each group, and (ii) how an active user in a multicast group can *dynamically* share, in an efficient and fair manner, the bandwidth allocated to its group.

Quality of service support for a real-time multicast group is based on *time driven priority* [3]. In this scheme the time is divided into *time frames* of fixed duration and all the time frames are aligned by using a global time reference which can be obtained from GPS (global positioning system). Bandwidth is allocated to a multicast group as a whole, rather than individually to each user. The allocation is done by reserving time intervals within time frames in some periodic fashion.

This sort of allocation raises two problems that are studied in this paper: (1) *Scheduling:* how time intervals are reserved to each multicast group, and (2) *Adaptive sharing:* how the participants dynamically share the time intervals that have been reserved for their multicast group. The proposed approach is based on embedding multiple *virtual rings*, one for each multicast group. By using the virtual rings it is simple to route messages to all the participants, while minimizing the bound on the buffer sizes and queuing delays.

**Key words:** multicast, real-time.

## 1 Introduction

Group or many-to-many real-time multicast is a demanding service. It is usually exploited by applications which require guaranteed (sometimes large) bandwidth with small loss, and bounded end-to-end delay and jitter**. Given the finite network resources, applications should be performed in an *efficient* and *adaptive* manner. Efficient means that the communication links can operate near full utilization.

The number and the identity of transmitting nodes in a real-time multicast group changes over time. This has two implications: (i) the resources should be allocated to the group and not individually to each participants, and (ii) the active nodes (i.e., the source nodes) should *adapt* their transmission rate for dynamic sharing of the bandwidth allocated to their multicast group.

The solution presented in this paper exploits a combination of *space* (virtual ring embedding) and *time* (packet forwarding driven by time). Using virtual rings for many-to-many communications is simple and "natural", since a message sent from one member of the group travels around the ring until it comes back to the sender. We simply exploit this property by embedding multiple virtual rings, one for each multicast group. In a previous work it has been shown that the virtual ring can be instrumental in designing a *reliable multicast protocol* from *bursty sources* [4]. The ring circular property is used to adapt, in real-time, the share of capacity each *active node* obtains. It is done in a fair manner according to the number of nodes that are trying to transmit to the group at any given time.

An external timing information which comes, for example, from the global positioning system (GPS) [1], is used to control the forwarding of packets inside the network. This real-time forwarding is used for:
(i) Minimizing the *queuing delay* bound in the virtual ring, as we discuss in Section 2.
(ii) Sharing the capacity of a link among multiple virtual rings traversing the link in the same direction, as described in Section 3.
(iii) Adaptive sharing of bandwidth to ensure that each active node in a virtual ring gets a fair share of the capacity, as discussed in Section 4.

## 2 Principles of Operation

### 2.1 Network Model

In this work we consider a general topology network with bidirectional links. A virtual ring (VR) is associated with each group multicast by constructing cycles that includes each participant at least once [4]. For example, Figure 1 shows two VRs (continuous and dashed lines) embedded onto a arbitrary topology network (bold lines). In this example, the two VRs share link (i,j) that will carry packets for both the VRs.

A virtual ring has three types of nodes: (i) active participants (ii) passive participants (e.g., listeners in a video conferencing), and (iii) the transit nodes that are not the members of the multicast group but they needed to construct the VR (shaded circles in Figure 1).

Although, some nodes are traversed more than once by the packets pertain to the same multicast group (e.g., f and j in Figure 1), these packets will be received only the first time

*Dip. di Automatica e Informatica, Politecnico di Torino, Torino, Italy 10129, baldi@leonardo.polito.it. This work was done in part while the author was visiting IBM T. J. Watson Research Center.

†IBM T.J.Watson Research Center, P.O.Box 218, Yorktown Heights, NY 10598, (914) 945-3171, ofek@watson.ibm.com.

‡Networking and Communication Lab. Department of Computer and Information Sciences, New Jersey Institute of Technology, Newark, NJ 07102-1982, (201) 596-2666, yener@cis.njit.edu. This work was supported in part by the Office of Naval Research under Grant N00014-96-1-0825.

**The jitter is defined as the difference between maximum and minimum delay.



0-8186-7780-5/97 $10.00 © 1997 IEEE

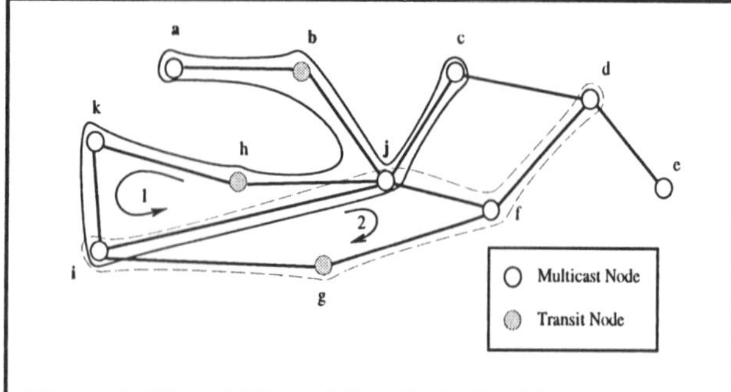


Figure 1: Virtual Rings (VRs) Embedded in the Network.

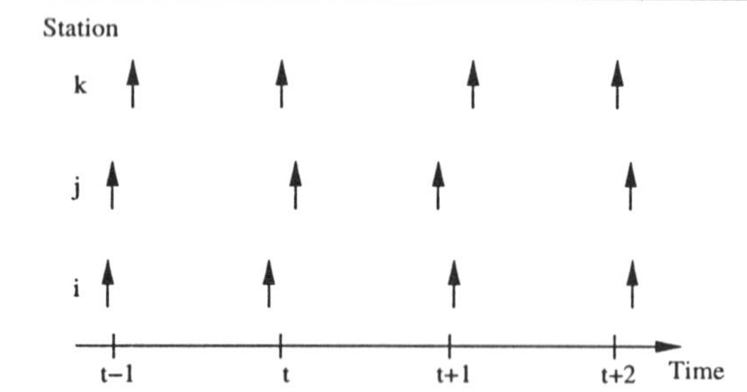


Figure 2: Clock Ticks.

they reach to these nodes.

## 2.2 Network Timing

All the nodes are provided with a global timing structure. If, for example, GPS is used for this purpose, each node in the network receives clock ticks from a GPS receiver and uses them to keep its internal clock synchronized. As shown in Figure 2, there is a period of time in which the clocks of all the nodes have the same time value.

The time between two successive ticks is called a *Time Frame* (TF) and has a typical duration of 125 $\mu$s or 8KHz. Thanks to this global timing structure all nodes have the same knowledge of the *temporal value* of the current TF.

## 2.3 Packet Forwarding

Nodes forward packets according to the *pseudo-isochronous* or *RISC-like* forwarding principle proposed in [2, 3]. The basic idea is that packet hopping in the network is a function of TFs. Precisely, a packet received by a node in TF t, is forwarded by the node so that it reaches the next node along the path in TF t+i (for $i \geq 1$). Note that in wide area internetworking environments $i$ may be large due to the processing and propagation delays. Furthermore, this scheme assumes that the delay between the output port of a node and the output port of the next node along the path is a constant integer number of TFs. If this does not fit actual delays, receiving nodes can introduce extra delay by buffering packets and moving them to the output port at the predefined

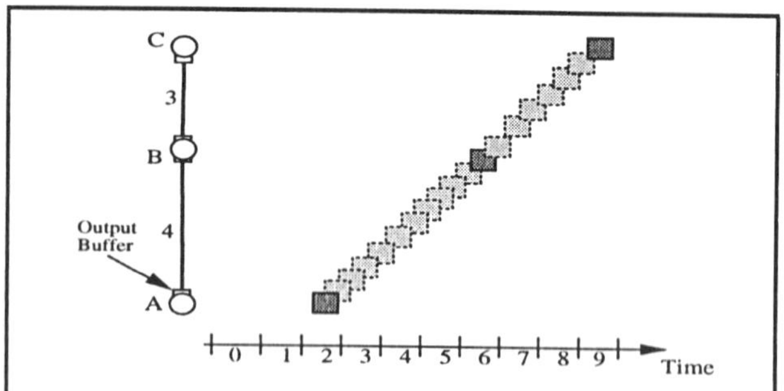


Figure 3: Packet Forwarding.

instant.

Consider as an example the simple topology depicted in Figure 3; links are labeled with the delay (in TF units) between the output port of the node transmitting on the link, and the output port of the receiving node. Node A has a packet to send on its output port (buffer) at TF 2. This packet will arrive to node B and will be ready to be sent from B's output port at TF 6; the destination node C receives the packet at TF 9. The propagation delay from the source A to the destination C is fixed; the jitter is bound by two TFs and is due to the uncertainty on when node A's transmission begins, during TF 2, and when node C's reception ends, during TF 9.

The packet forwarding on a VR follows the same principle such that a packet is forwarded along the VR and after a fixed number of TFs (say $n_r$) it is received back by its source node. Note that the integer $n_r$ gives the *length* of the VR in terms of time frames.

## 2.4 Bandwidth Allocation

Some bandwidth is allocated to each multicast group and is shared by the members of the group that are ready to transmit. Section 3 shows how bandwidth allocation is performed while Section 4 shows how bandwidth is dynamically shared among the active nodes of the group.

We assume that a node in the network can forward from its output port up to $125\mu s \cdot BMb/s$ bits during each TF. For example, if the data rate of a link is 100 Mb/s then 12.5 Kb can be transmitted in every TF. The source of the bits can be from this node, from its multicast group, or any other multicast group sharing this link. Note that $125\mu s \cdot BMb/s$ is also the output buffer requirement on every port. This establish a *small bound* on the queueing delay of every node along the virtual ring. If the many-to-many group multicast would be done over a tree, the propagation delay would be shorter but the queuing delay bound would be much larger. This is significant, since the delay bound is a critical parameter for real time applications.

The bandwidth is allocated on a link for a VR (i.e., multicast group) by reserving time intervals in some TFs in a periodic manner. (Unused reserved bandwidth can be used for "best effort" traffic). For example, allocating a 64 Kb/s

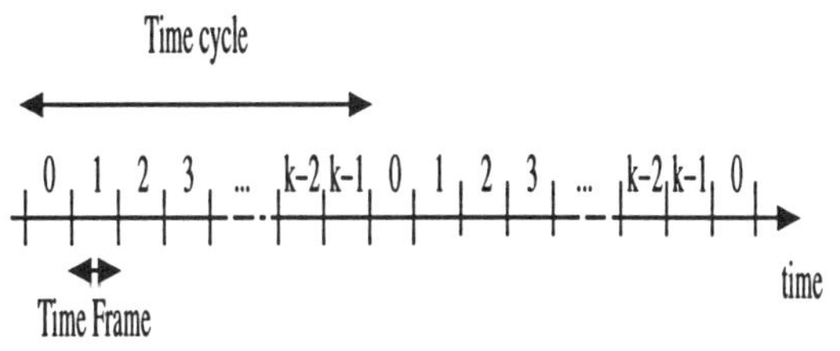


Figure 4: Timing Structure and Time Cycle.

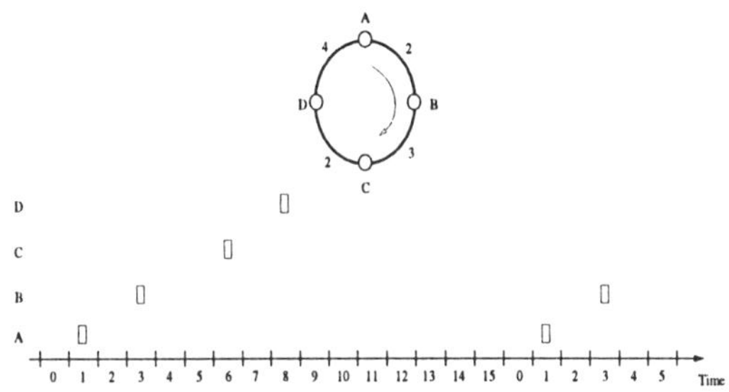


Figure 5: Sample Bandwidth Allocation for a Multicast Group.

for a multicast group means the transmission of 1 byte†† (i.e., $0.064 \cdot 125 = 8$ bits) during each TF (in each virtual node). A packet size of one byte is obviously not practical. Thus, we have to use a packet size that keeps low the percentage overhead of the packet headers. For example for video-conferencing over IP networks, a 500 bytes payload is a reasonable size in order to keep the overhead due to IP, UDP, and RTP headers under 10%. Therefore, in our example, the 64 Kb/s can be allocated to a multicast group by reserving 500 bytes every 500 TFs.

TFs are grouped into *Time Cycles* (TCs) of fixed length $k$ and are enumerated from 0 to $k-1$, as shown in Figure 4. Allocation of bandwidth to a multicast group is done by reserving a fraction of the bits that a node in the VR can send during some of the $k$ TFs in the TC.

Figure 5 shows a sample reservation of one packet per TC for a VR. In the figure a rectangle represents the bits reserved during the TF on the virtual ring nodes (i.e., A, B, C and D). Each node on the ring sends or forwards packets of its multicast group during the TFs in which transmission time for packets have been reserved, i.e., it uses always the same TFs in each TC for transmitting packets pertaining to its multicast group.

Assume for simplicity that packets are fixed size of $s$ bytes. If we reserve a packet worth of bytes in $p_r$ TFs for a multicast group $r$, then the bandwidth allocated to the multicast group

†† In the following examples when dealing with bandwidth we consider the gross bandwidth allocated to a multicast group, not the net bandwidth offered to applications. I.e., the overheads due to protocol encapsulation are not taken into account. This is not a limitation because these overheads can be taken into account by simply having the gross allocated bandwidth larger.

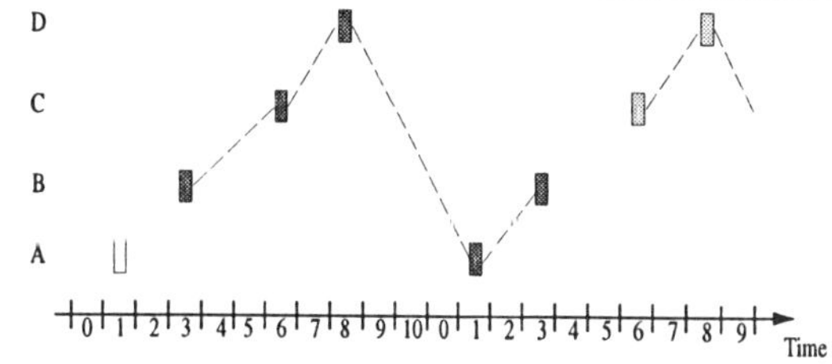


Figure 6: Forwarding of a Packet on a Virtual Ring.

is given by

$$MB_r = \frac{p_r \cdot s \cdot 8}{k \cdot 125} \text{ Mb/s}. \qquad (1)$$

Bandwidth is allocated in multiples of a base quantity which is given by the reservation of 1 packet per TC. In this work we assume $s = 500$ bytes and, as we want the base bandwidth allocation unit to be 64 Kb/s, we fix the number of TFs per TC (length of the TC) to

$$k = \frac{500 \cdot 8}{64 \cdot 10^3 \cdot 125 \cdot 10^{-6}} = 500.$$

Without loss of generality, we assume that only one packet is sent in each TF. As a consequence, bandwidth is allocated by giving to each virtual node on the ring exclusive usage of outgoing links during the whole reserved TFs. Such TFs are said to have been reserved on the node for a specific multicast group or VR.

## 2.5 Forwarding on a Virtual Ring

As an example, consider now the packet forwarding in the sample VR topology with the bandwidth allocation shown in Figure 5. If node B has a packet to transmit to the multicast group, it waits until TF 3 and then sends the packet which reaches the output port of C in TF 6, as shown in Figure 6. The packet travels on the VR and gets back to node B by TF 3 of the following TC. If node B at this point does not transmit any packet, C will be able to transmit a packet in TF 6 if it is not used for forwarding a packet from some other node.

Figure 7 shows the forwarding of packets on the same VR when $k = 16$. Virtual node A receives B's packet by TF 12, but it has no TF reserved until TF 1 of the following TC. Thus, node A buffers B's packet until the next TF reserved for its VR. Node A is named the *buffering node* of this VR. Each VR must have a buffering node in order to *adapt the length of the VR (virtual ring) to the length of the TC (time cycle)*. (Note that due to the presence of a buffering node a node does not necessarily receive its own packet at the same TF, in the next TC, in which it has transmitted it.)

## 2.6 Relative Time

When the timing structure is applied to a ring, the concept of *Relative IDentifier* (RID) of TFs is useful for two purposes:

1. To handle the reservation of TFs in the nodes (Section 3) and

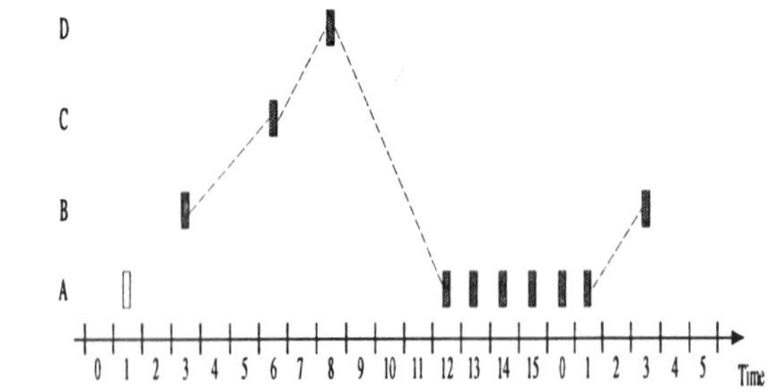


Figure 7: Forwarding of a Packet Originated from B on a Virtual Ring with Buffering Node A.

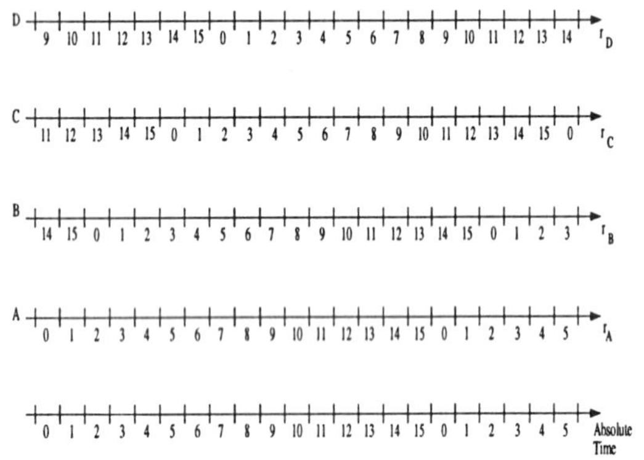


Figure 8: Relative Time.

2. To dynamically share the allocated TFs among the participants to the multicast group (Section 4).

Each node $j$ keeps its *relative time* by assigning a RID to TF $i$ through the expression:

$$r_i(j) = (i - d_{b,j} + k) \bmod k \quad (2)$$

where $r_i(j)$ is the RID given to TF $i$ by node $j$ and $d_{b,j}$ is the delay, expressed in number of TFs, experienced by a packet traveling from node $b$ chosen as the *base* for the relative time, to node $j$. The base node has the property that

$$r_i(b) = i, \; \forall i \; 0 \leq i \leq k-1$$

, i.e., the relative time in the base node equals the absolute time.

Figure 8 shows the relative time for the nodes of the VR shown in Figure 5 when node A is the base node. By comparing the two figures, it is easy to note that the TF reserved to the VR has RID 1 in each node. In general, the relative time has the useful property that each node of a VR identifies the TFs reserved to the multicast group through the same RID.

# 3 Scheduling

In this Section we consider how to allocate resources to a new multicast group $M_r$ with bandwidth request $MB_r$. As explained in section 2.4, the bandwidth request is mapped to a number ($p_r$) of TFs needed for the new multicast group.

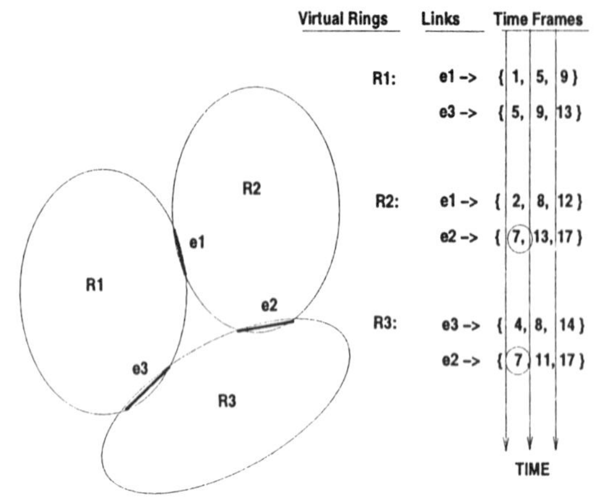


Figure 9: Inability to reserve bandwidth to virtual ring due to scheduling conflicts of time frames

Let $VR_r$ be the VR associated with this multicast group and let $E$ be the set of links included in this VR. Since the links of a synchronized network are shared by various types of traffic, some of the TFs (say $f$) on a link $e$ in $E$ may already be reserved.

It is necessary (*not sufficient*) to reserve $p_r$ unused (available) TFs on each link in $E$, in order to guarantee $MB_r$ bandwidth for this multicast group. Having $p_r$ available TFs on each link is not sufficient because a TF (on the same link) may need to be allocated to two or more different VRs.

In other words, it is possible that there is available bandwidth (i.e., time frames) for a new multicast group (or to increase the allocation of an existing group), but there is no available *schedule* to assign time frames (of fraction of time frames) such that a time interval in a time frame is *not* allocated to more than one virtual ring, see an example in Figure 9. This problem is like the Pigeon Hole Problem where there are enough available TFs on each link, but there is no schedule that can fit them in the right linear (sequential) order, on each of the VRs. The impact of such scheduling conflict is that some of the link bandwidth cannot be allocated to the multicast groups (however, note that this bandwidth can still be used by non-reserved traffic).

The scheduling problem is examined in a hierarchical way. First, we consider a single link used by the multicast group and define the necessary condition for *feasibility* of a link. Next, we consider the whole VR and define *feasible ring scheduling*.

A link of a VR is *feasible* if it has at least $p_r$ available TFs such that $p_r$ satisfies the equation (1). Note that if there is even one link in $E$ with less available TFs than $p_r$ (i.e., the link is highly loaded), then this multicast group cannot be allocated the required bandwidth. Next, we introduce the following definitions to be used in this section:

**Definition 1 –Feasible Schedule:** *Given a virtual ring*

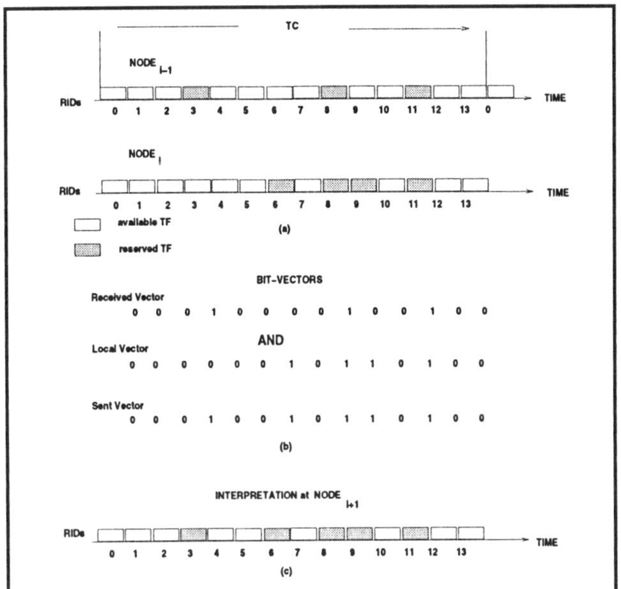


Figure 10: Example: Processing and Interpretation of Bit-Vectors to Determine a Feasible Schedule.

*$VR_r$, a schedule $\sigma$ is called feasible schedule for $VR_r$ if $\sigma$ chooses exactly $p_r$ (available) TFs on each link such that each TF has the same RID at each node.*

**Definition 2 –Feasible Ring:** *A virtual ring $VR_r$ is called feasible if there exists a* feasible schedule *$\sigma$ for $VR_r$.*

**Definition 3 –Feasible Network:** *Given a network and a set of multicast groups on it, the network is called feasible, if there exists a feasible scheduling for each one of the VRs.*

**Proposition 1** *In a feasible network, no TF on a link is used by two different rings.*

## 3.1 Feasible Ring-Scheduling Algorithm

In this section we present a distributed algorithm to find a feasible assignment of TFs to a VR. The algorithm is initiated by a predetermined origin node (e.g., the base node) and executed by each node in a VR. In Figure 10 the steps of the algorithm are shown.

In the algorithm a node first assigns a RID to each TF by using equation (2). Next, a bit-vector $BV_i$ of size $k$ is constructed at node $i$. In $BV_i$ a bit is set to 1 (see Figure 10.a), if the corresponding relative TF is not available (i.e., it has been previously reserved for another VR or a point-to-point connection).

The origin node on the VR *sends* its bit-vector to its downstream neighbor. Upon receiving a bit-vector, a node performs a logical AND operation between the received and local vector (see Figure 10.b). The result is stored as the updated local bit-vector, and sent to the downstream node (see Figure 10.c).

When the origin receives a bit-vector from its neighbor (step 1), the first phase of the algorithm is completed. Note

**Algorithm:** *Feasible_Ring_Schedule* performed at node $i$
**Input:** $VR_r$; origin node $o_r$; $p_r$
**Preprocessing:** for each TF on this link
compute its RID (for example, $o_r$ can be used as base)
construct $BV_i$ to indicate the status of TFs
**Begin**
RECEIVE a bit-vector $BV_{i-1}$
1 **if** node $i = o_r$ then
1.1 **if** $BV_{i-1} == RBV$ then STOP
1.2 **else**
1.2.1 **if** number of 0's in RBV $< p_r$ then
print INFEASIBLE
1.2.2 **else**
RBV = $MinMax\_Link\_Schedule(VR, RBV, p_r)$
SEND $RBV$ to downstream node $i+1$
2 **else**
2.1 **if** $BV_{i-1} == RBV$ then $BV_i = RBV$
2.2 **else** $BV_i = BV_{i-1}$ AND $BV_i$
2.3 SEND $BV_i$ to downstream node $i+1$
**End**

Figure 11: Ring Scheduling Algorithm to Ensure Ring Feasibility.

that at this point each node knows what all the upstream nodes (from the origin to its upstream neighbor) know about available TFs. Thus, when the origin receives the bit-vector from its neighbor, it learns the ringwise availability of TFs (global information).

If the number of zeros in the received bit vector $BV$ is less than $p_r$, the origin concludes (step 1.2.1) that the VR is *not feasible*. If $BV$ contains at least $p_r$ zeroes, then any choice of $p_r$ TFs will result in a *feasible scheduling*. The origin calls the procedure $MinMax\_Link\_Schedule(VR, BV, p_r)$ (see algorithm in Figure 13), to choose $p_r$ TFs for optimal scheduling (step 1.2.2). The bit-vector returned by this procedure indicates the TFs reserved for this multicast group. This bit-vector becomes the bit-vector of the reservation for this ring ($RBV$). The origin sends $RBV$ to its downstream node and it is propagated on the ring to inform all the nodes. When the origin receives $RBV$ (step 1.1), the algorithm terminates and each node on the ring has the same RID for the newly reserved TFs.

## 3.2 Optimal Selection of TFs

In this section we consider the problem of optimally choosing $p_r$ TFs for a VR. First we introduce an objective function then an algorithm to construct a solution.

### 3.2.1 Objective Function to Minimize Jitter

Delay jitter determines buffer size at nodes and performance of real-time protocols. The larger the jitter the larger the buffers needed to compensate for it. A uniform distribution of TFs in the TC is beneficial in reducing the end-to-end delay, its variation (jitter), and the size of buffers in the buffering node. Ideally, if reserved TFs are uniformly distributed, the buffering node receives the packets at a (almost) regular

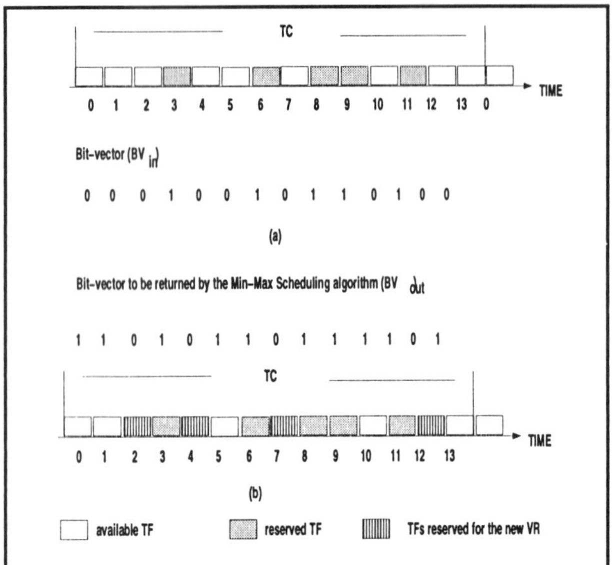


Figure 12: Example: Time Cycle with 9 Available TFs.

pace and forwards them at almost the same regular pace. As a consequence

1. packets are buffered shortly in the buffering node. Thus, the buffer must not be very large and the delay experienced by packets is small;
2. subsequent packets experience similar delays thus yielding small jitter.

Thus, one objective function for optimal schedule is to ensure equal *time distance* among TFs allocated in a TC. Let $FS$ denote the set of all feasible schedules; we consider as optimal schedule $\sigma$ the one which satisfies

$$\min_{\sigma \in FS} \left\{ \max_{1 \le i \le p_r} \left| [(t(\sigma)_{i \bmod p_r + 1} - t(\sigma)_i + k) \bmod k] - \frac{k}{f} \right| \right\} \quad (3)$$

where $t(\sigma)_i$ denotes the $i^{\text{th}}$ TF reserved for the multicast group according to the schedule $\sigma$.

Note that if all the TFs were available, the best spacing (timewise) between the $p_r$ TFs would be: $\lfloor \frac{k}{f} \rfloor$. Thus, equation (3) compares the maximum difference between the spacing imposed by each feasible schedule to the best possible spacing and chooses the schedule which minimizes this difference.

### Complexity of Link Scheduling

The size of the feasible scheduling set $FS$ is determined by two parameters: $p_r$ and $k - f$: enumeration can be obtained by $C(k - f, p_r)$ (i.e., number of ways to pick a subset of $p_r$ out of $k - f$ distinct objects). Since the enumeration involves factorial operation, if $p_r$ and $k - f$ are close to each other, it is possible to choose the best allocation by enumeration. However, for large factorial computations $FS$ can be too large to enumerate; we propose a min-max algorithm to solve this problem with acceptable complexity.

```
Algorithm: MinMax_Link_Schedule
Input: VR_r; BV_in; p_r
Output: BV_out with exactly p_r zeros to indicate
    which TFs will be used by VR_r
Preprocessing: construct a weighted line-graph such that
    nodes represent available TFs
    a link connects two consequent TFs
    the weight (cost) on a link is the difference between
      RIDs of the end point TFs
    mark the line-graph as "active" segment
Begin
1 Set all the bits to 1 in BV_out
  Begin FOR i <= p_r DO
2 Choose the median of the active segment and reset the bit
    in BV_out identified
  by the median's index
3 Compute the total cost of each "active" segment
4 Store the costs and end points of the segments in list
5 Choose the segment with maximum total cost from this
    list and make this segment "active"
  End
6 Return(BV_out)
End
```

Figure 13: A TF Choice Algorithm to Minimize Jitter in a VR

### 3.2.2 Min-Max Algorithm

The input of the algorithm is a bit vector $BV_{in}$ (Figure 12.a) which represents at least $k - f \geq p_r$ available TFs for a VR. The algorithm returns a bit vector $BV_{out}$ (Figure 12.b) that indicates which TFs should be reserved for the multicast group.

The algorithm shown in Figure 13 builds a Line-Graph (LG) from the information carried by $BV_{in}$. Define a *median* of a LG as a node to which maximum *distance* from any other node in the graph is minimum. The *distance* between two nodes is defined as the sum of the link *costs* on the path between them as explained in Figure 13.

The algorithm takes $p_r$ steps and at each step finds a median of an updated (reduced) graph as shown in Figure 14. Each median node corresponds to a TF selected by the algorithm for optimal scheduling. The location of median nodes in $BV_{out}$ is identified by zero while all the other bits are set to 1. Each time a median node is chosen the LG is divided into two connected components (called segments). A new median is chosen from the segment with maximum total cost computed during the selection of the previous median node (see Figure 14). The selected segment is called the *active segment*; initially the entire LG is considered a single active segment.

### 3.2.3 Objective Function for Load Balancing

In this Section we relax the assumption that a TF is used to transmit a single packet. In this case different amounts of bits can be reserved during TFs. Balancing the load over the TFs allows a larger number of VRs to be allocated on the network since it decreases the blocking probability. Thus, we

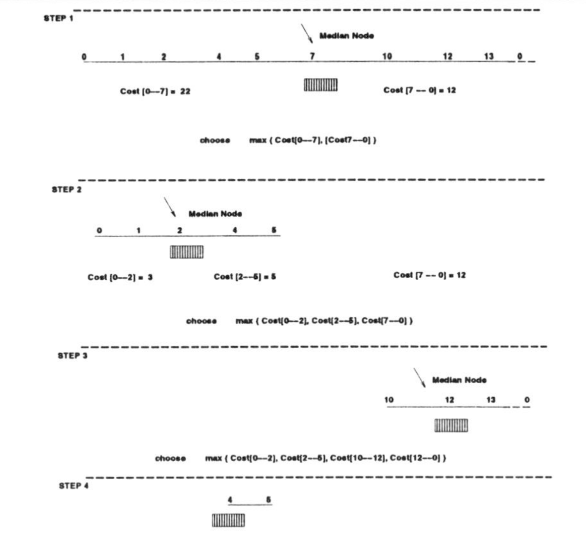


Figure 14: Example: Execution of the Algorithm to Choose 4 TFs.

introduce a new objective function which aims at balancing load when scheduling TFs for a VR. This objective function minimizes the differences among the amounts of non reserved bits in each of the $k$ TFs of a TC. The optimal schedule is the one which satisfies

$$\min_{\sigma \in FS} \left\{ \sum_{i=1}^{p(\sigma)_r} \left( \beta(\sigma)_i - \overline{\beta(\sigma)} \right)^2 \right\} \qquad (4)$$

where $\beta(\sigma)_i$ is the number of non reserved bits during the $i^{\text{th}}$ TF, *after* the schedule $\sigma$ has been applied. The variable $\overline{\beta(\sigma)}$ is the average amount of non reserved bits over the whole TC. The two objective functions (3) and (4) can be in conflict and thus a tradeoff between them must be found.

# 4 Adaptive Bandwidth Sharing

The adaptive bandwidth sharing concerns a single VR and does not affect any other VR embedded in the network. Active stations actually share the allocated bandwidth by sending their own packets during some of these TFs. Both passive stations and transit nodes just forward packets during the reserved TFs. The set of active stations changes dynamically as, for example, in a video-conference call the set of active speakers changes. The stations participating in a multicast group run a signaling protocol that allows each of them to know the actual set of active stations‡‡.

As the number $a_r$ of active stations changes, the share of bandwidth available to each station changes and they have to (1) adapt their transmission rate to it (Section 4.1) and (2) agree on which TF each station is using (Section 4.2).

‡‡This signaling protocol is out of the scope of this paper; some possible candidate protocols are available for the purpose.

## 4.1 Rate Adaptation

Through one of the algorithms described in Section 4.2, each active station knows the amount of bandwidth it can use for transmission. When the bandwidth available to an active station changes, the application is notified in order to change the rate at which data is produced.

Some applications require some time in order to make this change. For example, in a video-conferencing with compression data is produced through a process starting with capturing video frames, going through a number of processing steps, and ending with quantization and run-length encoding of the video information. The compressed data is buffered and retrieved from the buffer at a constant bit rate. Changing the amount of data produced by this process implies tuning the parameters that regulate some of these processing steps. The earlier the involved processing step, the longer the time for having the change take effect at the network interface.

When a station becomes passive, it notifies other stations and immediately stops transmitting. Each active station realizes that its share of the bandwidth is larger and notifies the application to increase the data generation rate. Even though the increment of the bandwidth share is immediately available to the active nodes, it takes some time before the change in the application generation rate has effect and is propagated to the network interface; i.e., the transmission rate of active nodes does not increase instantly.

When a station becomes active, it notifies other stations. However, it does not start transmitting immediately. All the previously active stations immediately notify their application to lower the data generation rate. Since it takes some time before the actual transmission rate of all the active stations decreases, the new active station waits for its bandwidth share to be available before starting transmitting. We assume that newly active stations wait a fixed time (in the order of a second) before transmitting. This is needed in order to assure that no packet is dropped in either the network interface of active stations or inside the network, due to unavailability of communications resources.

This waiting time is acceptable as the time scale in which stations change their activity status is usually long. For example, in a video-conferencing application a station becoming active implies that somebody is asking the right to speak. Thus, waiting should not be of concern since the new speaker will usually have to wait before getting the permission to speak.

## 4.2 Bandwidth Sharing

Given the set of the $p_r$ TFs reserved to a multicast group $r$, the bandwidth sharing problem consists in having each active station using a subset of them to send its own packets***. The subset used by each active station should be built satisfying the following criteria:

***Whenever dealing with TFs in this Section, we mean TFs reserved to the VR.

1. each node gets a fair share of the bandwidth $MB_r$ allocated to the multicast group;
2. the end-to-end jitter experienced by packets is minimum;
3. the unused bandwidth (i.e., the TFs during which no multicast data is transmitted) is minimized*.

### 4.2.1 Round Robin Allocation

The allocated bandwidth can be shared fairly among the active stations by having each active station using each TF in a round robin fashion. Active stations transmit their packets in any *free* or unused TF. When a station receives a packet originated by itself, it must not use the next TF to send another packet of its own. This allows downstream stations to use the TF, in a round robin manner, for their own transmissions. The fraction of unused bandwidth due to this phenomenon is:

$$\frac{1}{a_r + 1}$$

This unused bandwidth is analogous to the unused bandwidth due to the token walk time in token ring.

### 4.2.2 Fixed Allocation

A fixed allocation scheme can be used to reduce the amount of bandwidth unused due to the bandwidth sharing procedure. According to the fixed allocation scheme, active stations come to an agreement on which TFs each of them is using†. When a station receives back a packet sent by itself, it can use the next TF for sending its data. Figure 15 shows an example in which 4 TFs (RID 1, 4, 8, 12) have been reserved for the VR depicted in Figure 5 and nodes B and C are active. Each active node is using two TFs to transmit its data.

Note that the RIDs of the two TFs each node is using change over time because the buffering node A buffers and forwards packets in a different TF. Moreover, some bandwidth is still unused because in each moment only 3 TFs out of the 4 reserved are used. This is due to the behavior of the buffering node, the distribution of the TFs in the TC, and the relationship between the lengths of VR and TC. This situation can be accepted because with this behavior the buffering node delays packets for a short time as shown in the example of Figure 15.

In the example shown in Figure 15 the phenomenon is particularly harmful as the unused TF is always one of the 2 assigned to station C which is getting only half of the fair bandwidth share.

This unfairness is much smaller as larger is the number of TFs assigned to each station. This unfairness can be avoided by applying more complex bandwidth sharing schemes or buffering policies in the buffering node. When dealing with

*Even though unused bandwidth can be used to transmit best effort traffic, the VR should try and use as much as possible of the bandwidth allocated to it.

†This can be done through some signaling mechanism that is out of the scope of this paper.

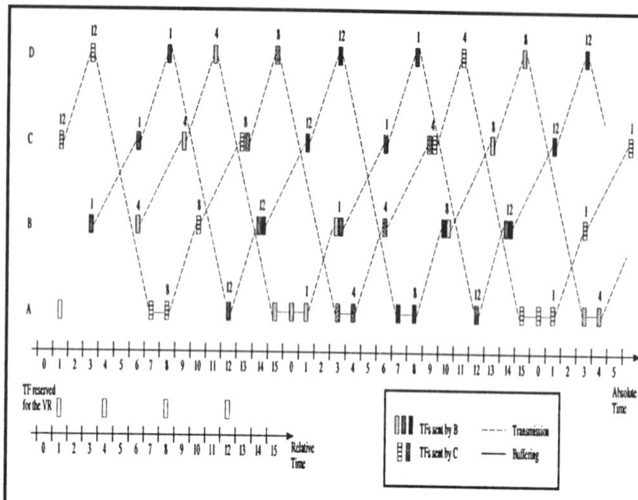


Figure 15: Fixed Allocation of TFs

unused bandwidth in the following, the contribution given by the foregoing phenomenon is not taken into account.

The fixed allocation of TFs to active stations is possible only if $a_r \leq p_r$, otherwise a different scheme (e.g., round robin allocation) must be applied.

Nevertheless, one of the main fields of application for real-time group multicasting is large scale video-conferencing, where it is possible to have a large number of listeners (i.e., large $p_r$) and a small number of active speakers (i.e., small $a_r$). Only the active speakers can transmit to the group.

When $p_r \bmod a_r = 0$, fixed allocation of TFs lets each active station use $\frac{p_r}{a_r}$ TFs per TC, i.e., active stations share the bandwidth fairly and do not leave unused any fraction of it. The jitter introduced depends on the distribution of TFs in the TC and the allocation of TFs to active stations.

When $p_r \bmod a_r \neq 0$, $p_r$ can be written as

$$p_r = I \cdot a_r + N, \text{ where } I = \lfloor \frac{p_r}{a_r} \rfloor \text{ and } N = p_r \bmod a_r$$

Each active node uses the fixed allocation criteria on $I$ TFs; for the remaining $N$ TFs several approaches can be followed.

1. The $N$ TFs are allocated to the active nodes in a round robin fashion. As a result, with this approach some bandwidth is not used and a large jitter is introduced because usually a node sends $I$ packets per TC and seldom it sends $I + 1$ packets. This exceptional packet received between two regular packets can sharply reduces the packet inter-arrival time, thus yielding a large variation of the end-to-end delay (increase of the delay jitter).
2. $N$ of the $a_r$ active nodes fixedly use $I + 1$ TFs for sending their packets. The bandwidth is not shared fairly, but all the allocated bandwidth is used and the bandwidth sharing scheme does not contribute to the jitter.
3. The $N$ TFs are left unused; the multicast group does not use some of the bandwidth allocated to it, but the

bandwidth allocation scheme does not contribute to jitter and it is very simple.

## 5 Conclusions

The combination of virtual rings and timing information is interesting and intriguing. In this work we have shown how useful this combination can be for *adaptive real-time multicast*, while in a previous work we have shown that it is also useful for *reliable multicast* for data processing applications [4].

The proposed approach to adaptive real-time multicast is characterized by having a *deterministic behavior*. This is important for real-time applications in two ways: (1) it minimizes the *bound* on the delay and delay variation across each virtual ring, and (2) it ensures no loss due to congestion. The no loss property is important for real-time video applications using compression. In compression a loss of a single packet can result in the inability to properly display multiple consecutive video frames, which can annoy the viewer.

Multicast communication over embedded virtual rings has a drawback that the delay is increased with the ring physical size and number of participants. Approaches based on trees do not suffer from this problem. However, tree based multicast suffers from two basic problems: (i) loss due to congestion, and (ii) queuing delay bound that can be very large. It is interesting to investigate ways to exploit some of the tree properties while maintaining the virtual rings virtues: (i) fair sharing of the bandwidth among the active nodes in the multicast group, (ii) high and stable utilization of the bandwidth, and (iii) deterministic performance with (very) small packet loss and (very) small queueing delay bound.

There are several open issues which require more research. The scheduling and allocation of time frames to the various multicast groups (virtual rings) can be improved by further investigating how to reduce the blocking probability. Blocking is defined as the impossibility of allocating enough bandwidth for a new multicast group while some capacity is still available, but not in the proper time frames. Another issue concerns the unused capacity assigned to a virtual ring due to the bandwidth adaptation schemes proposed in this work.

## References


[1] P. H. Dana. Global positioning system overview. http://www.utexas.edu/depts/grg/gcraft/notes/gps/gps.html.

[2] C-S. Li, Y. Ofek, A. Segall, and K. Sohraby. Pseudo-isochronous cell switching in atm networks. *Proc. IEEE INFOCOM'94*, pages 428–437, 1994.

[3] C-S Li, Y. Ofek, and M. Yung. "Time-driven priority" flow control for real-time heterogeneous internetworking. *IEEE INFOCOM'96*, 1996.

[4] Y. Ofek and B. Yener. Reliable concurrent multicast from bursty sources. *To Appear in IEEE JSAC (preliminary version is in Proc. IEEE INFOCOM'96)*, 1996.

# A Group Synchronization Mechanism for Stored Media in Multicast Communications

Yutaka Ishibashi, Akihiro Tsuji and Shuji Tasaka
Department of Electrical and Computer Engineering,
Nagoya Institute of Technology, Nagoya 466, Japan

***Abstract*** – This paper proposes a group synchronization mechanism, which synchronizes slave destinations with the master destination, for stored media in multicast communications. At the master and slave destinations, intra-stream and inter-stream synchronization mechanisms which were proposed by the authors are employed to output the master media stream and slave media streams synchronously. We achieve group synchronization by adjusting the output timing of the master media stream at each slave destination to that at the master destination. We also deal with traffic control by media scaling and control of joining an in-progress multicast group. Furthermore, the paper presents experimental results using an ATM network. It shows the validity of the mechanism and illustrates the influence of parameters on the system performance.

## 1 Introduction

Multimedia applications such as multimedia conferencing and distance learning bring challenging work to us. For example, delay jitters of a digital network have to be compensated to keep the temporal relationships among media streams. This compensation technique is referred to as media synchronization. In addition, multicasting is an important technique for the efficient use of network resources.

Media synchronization control is required for the preservation of the timing relation in a single media stream as well as among plural media streams [1]. The former is called ***intra-stream*** synchronization control, and the latter is ***inter-stream*** synchronization control. Furthermore, another kind of synchronization algorithm is necessary in multicast communications. In distance learning, for instance, we suppose that a tutor distributes a movie (i.e., a *stored* stream) to students, and he/she sometimes makes some comments (i.e., a *live* stream) on the movie. In this case, it is necessary to output the stored and live streams simultaneously for all the students. Even if only the stored stream is outputted, each *media unit* (*MU*; e.g., a video frame) of the stream should be outputted simultaneously at different destinations since the tutor may make some comments on the stream and the students may discuss the content of the stream. We refer to this type of synchronization as the *group* (or *inter-destination*) synchronization.

Very few papers have dealt with group synchronization [2]–[4]. Escobar *et al.* propose a flow synchronization protocol in [2]. They assume that there is an initiator which manages the dissemination of control information among destinations, and that *globally synchronized clocks* are employed; that is, clock ticks at the sources and destinations have the same advancement, and the current local times are also the same. They have not sufficiently demonstrated the validity of the protocol. In [3], Ohno *et al.* handle synchronization among stored and live media streams with interactive control. The synchronization mechanism tries to output MUs with an identical generation time simultaneously at each destination. However, destinations are not necessarily synchronized to each other. The mechanism also requires the globally synchronized clocks. Akyildiz and Yen present a group synchronization mechanism in [4], where clocks run at different rates. By simulation, they evaluate the maximum, minimum, and average asynchrony in seconds. The network delay bounds are assumed to be known. However, the bounds are not always known (especially, in the Internet, where a variety of multimedia services are becoming available at a reasonable cost).

One of important problems in multicast communications is traffic control. If sources distribute MUs at the speed of the slowest among the destinations to prevent the MUs from overflowing, the quality of media seriously deteriorates. Delgrossi *et al.* proposed a function of media scaling to avoid this deterioration [5]. On the other hand, destinations should be able to join or leave an in-progress multicast group freely. We have to offer such a function, which enables destinations to attain high quality synchronization as soon as the destinations join an in-progress group. However, most of the references including the above three papers do not address these problems.

Previously, the authors proposed a media synchronization mechanism for *nonperiodical* stored and live media in the case of *unknown network delay bounds* [6], [7]. The proposed method consists of intra-stream and inter-stream synchronization mechanisms. They further confirmed the validity of the mechanism using an FDDI LAN [8] or an ATM network [7]. However, the mechanism does not support multicast communications.

This paper proposes a stored media synchronization mechanism for multicast communications. The method consists of a group synchronization mechanism as well as the intra-stream and inter-stream synchronization mechanisms in [6] and [7]. The group synchronization mechanism is employed to output each MU simultaneously at all the destinations. This paper also deals with traffic control by media scaling and control of joining an in-progress multicast group. We have implemented the mechanism for stored media using an ATM network provided for *the Joint Utilization Tests of Multimedia Communications* by NTT. In the experimental system, stored video of a speaker and her voice are transferred from a source workstation to plural destination workstations by means of multicast.



0-8186-7780-5/97 $10.00 

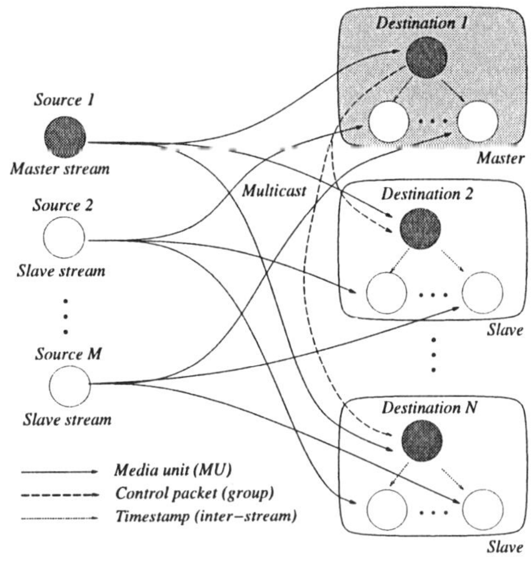


Figure 1: A media synchronization model.

Then, the streams are synchronized and outputted at the destinations (i.e., *lip-synch*). Using the system, we have confirmed the validity of the mechanism and have measured the performance.

The rest of this paper is organized as follows. Section 2 describes a synchronization model. Section 3 specifies the media synchronization mechanism. The experimental system is explained in Section 4, and measurement results are presented in Section 5. Section 6 concludes the paper.

## 2 Synchronization model

We assume in this paper that $M$ sources and $N$ destinations are connected through a digital network as shown in Fig. 1. MUs of stream $i$ $(i = 1, 2, \cdots, M)$ have been stored with timestamps in source $i$, and they are distributed to all the destinations by multicasting. The timestamp contained in an MU indicates its generation time. The streams fall into a master stream and slave streams. At each destination, the slave streams are synchronized with the master stream by using timestamps. It is also assumed that MUs in a single stream arrive at the destinations in order of sequence number.

On the other hand, the destinations are grouped into a master destination and slave destinations. The master destination may be supposed to be a chairperson's terminal in multimedia conferencing or a tutor's one in distance learning. The slave destinations should output MUs at the same timing as the master destination.

Let $\Delta_{\max}^{(i,j)}$ and $\Delta_{\min}^{(i,j)}$ denote the estimates of the maximum and minimum values, respectively, of the network delay in seconds between source $i$ and destination $j$ $(i = 1, 2, \cdots, M,\ j = 1, 2, \cdots, N)$. Also, let the estimates of the maximum and minimum values of the network delay between the master destination (say, destination 1) and slave destination $j$ be denoted by $\Delta_{\mathrm{MSmax}}^{(j)}$ and $\Delta_{\mathrm{MSmin}}^{(j)}$, respectively. Without loss of generality, we set $\Delta_{\min}^{(i,j)} = 0$ and $\Delta_{\mathrm{MSmin}}^{(j)} = 0$.

We assume that clock ticks at the sources and destinations have the same advancement, and that the current local times are also the same (i.e., globally synchronized clocks). Using the Network Time Protocol (NTP) [9], we can adjust the clock ticks to each other within a few milliseconds.

## 3 Synchronization mechanism

### 3.1 Principles

Since we deal with stored media streams and the master destination is not influenced by the other destinations, the master destination can employ the stored media synchronization mechanism in [6]. However, the slave destinations cannot use the same mechanism as that of the master destination. This is because the slave destinations have to be synchronized with the master destination. When large network delays happen to occur, the stored media synchronization mechanism may delay the output of MUs to reduce the frequency of occurrence of asynchrony by modifying *the target output time* [6], which is defined as follows: $t_1^{(i)} = D_1$, $t_{m+1}^{(i)} = t_m^{(i)} + \sigma_{m,m+1}^{(i)}$ $(m = 1, 2, \cdots)$, where $\sigma_{m,m+1}^{(i)}$ is the difference between timestamps of the $m$-th and $(m+1)$-st MUs in stream $i$, and $D_1$ denotes the output time of the first MUs. Since we use the target output time of an MU in determining its output time (see Subsection 3.3 or [6]), we can delay the output timing by increasing the target output time. However, the mechanism does not quicken the output timing of MUs since it has been designed just for stored media. The media synchronization mechanism for the slave destinations have to quicken the MU output timing as well as delaying it according to the status of the master destination. In order to synchronize the slave destinations with the master destination, the master destination distributes control packets to the slave destinations at adequate instants (see Fig. 1). The control packets include the status information of the master destination. Using the information, each slave destination adjusts the output timing of MUs. On the other hand, the live media synchronization mechanism in [7] has a function of reducing the target output time which has been increased by the modification. We can employ this function of the mechanism to decrease the target output time which have been increased independently of the master destination; note that the target output time may be modified if pausing owing to large delays happens to occur. When the target output time of the master destination is changed, the slave destinations also need to delay the output timing by the same time interval. However, neither stored nor live media synchronization mechanisms have this function. Therefore, we propose a method to perform the function in this paper.

Furthermore, the master destination multicasts control packets at the output time $D_1$ of the first MUs as well as each time the target output time is modified. Each destination outputs the first MUs of the streams under the simultaneous output control of the first MUs in [6]. Note that all the first MUs are assumed to have the same output time for simplicity. Since the destinations cannot output the first MUs at exactly the same instant, we have to adjust the output timing among the destinations later. The above mechanism can also be used for this adjustment.

In the following, we show a group synchronization mechanism and a media synchronization mechanism for the slave destinations.

### 3.2 Group synchronization mechanism

We achieve group synchronization by adjusting the output timing of the master MUs at the slave destinations to that at the master destination. We can adjust the timing by modifying the target output times at the slave destinations. This is because we determine the output time of an MU by referring to the target output time of the MU.

In order to synchronize the slave destinations with the master destination, the master destination sends control packets to the slave destinations. At first, the master destination multicasts a control packet including the output time of its first MUs to the slave destinations. In addition, when the target output time of the master destination is modified, the master notifies all the slaves of the modification by distributing a control packet which has the amount of time which is modified and the sequence number of the MU at which the target output time have been changed.

Let $\delta$ denote the difference between the target output time of the master and that of a slave. If $\delta > 0$, then the master has larger target output time than the slave (i.e., the master is late); otherwise, the target output time of the master is smaller than or equal to that of the slave. When the slave receives a control packet, it calculates the difference $\delta$. A small difference is allowed. Therefore, we assume that the slave need not adjust the output timing if $|\delta|$ is less than a threshold value $T_{h7}$[1]. Otherwise, the slave continues to adjust the output timing till $|\delta|$ becomes smaller than $T_{h7}$. A method for this adjustment will be presented in the next subsection.

When $|\delta|$ exceeds a threshold value $T_{h8}$ ($T_{h8} > T_{h7}$), the slave sends a control packet to the master to notify the master of large delay differences between the two. When $|\delta|$ becomes smaller than a threshold value $T_{h9}$ ($T_{h9} \leq T_{h8}$), the slave notifies the master of its recovery. If the number of slaves which are largely delayed exceeds a pre-defined percentage, the master delays the target output time in the same way as in the next subsection. We call this function *"the probabilistic synchronization."*[2]

Furthermore, to enable a new slave to join an in-progress multicast group, the master should distribute control packets at fixed intervals. When a slave joins an in-progress multicast group, the slave starts to output MUs by carrying out the intra-stream and inter-stream synchronization control. It adjusts the output timing by the group synchronization mechanism when it first receives a control packet.

[1]Note that $T_{h1}^{(j)}$ through $T_{h6}^{(i,j)}$ have already been defined in [7] and [8] (see Table 2).

[2]When the master is too late, it is also possible to quicken the output timing at the master.

### 3.3 Synchronization mechanism for slave destinations

For the intra-stream synchronization control, on receiving the $m$-th MU in stream $j$ ($j = 1, 2, \cdots, M$), each slave destination compares the arrival time $A_m^{(j)}$, the target output time $t_m^{(j)}$ and *the accumulated output time* $D_{m-1}^{(j)} + \sigma_{m-1,m}^{(j)}$, where $D_{m-1}^{(j)}$ is the output time of the ($m-1$)-st MU in stream $j$ [6]. Then, the destination determines *the scheduled output time* $d_m^{(j)}$, which will be used in determining the output time $D_m^{(j)}$ in the inter-stream synchronization control. In [7], we classify the relationship among the three time measures (i.e., $A_m^{(j)}$, $t_m^{(j)}$, and $D_{m-1}^{(j)} + \sigma_{m-1,m}^{(j)}$) into twelve patterns. These patterns are also used in our mechanism and are shown in Table 1[3], where $Timestamp_m^{(j)}$ is defined as follows: $Timestamp_m^{(j)} = D_1 + \sum_{k=2}^{m} \sigma_{k-1,k}^{(j)}$. Note that $Timestamp_m^{(j)}$ differs from $t_m^{(j)}$ in that the value of the former is not changed by our mechanism. The other thresholds and parameters defined here and in [6] are listed in Table 2. In this paper, we adopt *the graceful recovery policy* [6] to recover from asynchrony. In Table 1, patterns *(a')*, *(b')* and *(g')* is for the function of reducing the target output time.

If $|\delta| \leq T_{h7}$, we do not need to modify the MU output timing. Patterns *(a)*, *(b)* and *(g)* include the condition of $|\delta| \leq T_{h7}$ in Table 1, but patterns *(c)*, *(d)*, *(e)*, *(f)*, *(h)* and *(i)* do not have any condition of $\delta$. This means the latter patterns are also applicable to the case where $|\delta| > T_{h7}$ because of the reason explained later.

If $\delta < -T_{h7}$, we use pattern *(a')*, *(b')* and *(g')* to quicken the output timing instead of patterns *(a)*, *(b)* and *(g)*, respectively. In order to quicken the timing, the slave destination tries to set $d_m^{(j)}$ at the value which is smaller than that determined as pattern *(a)*, *(b)* or *(g)* by $r_D$ ($\geq 0$) [7]; then, the destination reduces the target output time and $|\delta|$ by the same amount. This modification of the target output time quickens the output timing of the following MUs. It is also possible to quicken the output timing in patterns *(c)*, *(d)*, *(h)* and *(i)*, where intra-stream asynchrony is recovered gradually; that is, we could define new patterns *(c')*, *(d')*, *(h')* and *(i')* instead of patterns *(c)*, *(d)*, *(h)* and *(i)* like patterns *(a')*, *(b')* and *(g')*. For simplicity, however, we here do not use these new patterns to quicken the output timing. We confirmed that the use of the patterns hardly improves the performance. It should be noted that since patterns *(e)* and *(f)* indicate late arrivals of MUs, it is impossible to quicken

[3]The relationships among the variables in patterns *(a)* through *(i)* excluding *(a')*, *(b')* and *(g')* correspond to those in Figs. 3 (a) through (i) in [6]. The timing diagrams of patterns *(a')*, *(b')* and *(g')* are shown in Figs. 1 (a) through (c) in [7].

Table 1: Patterns of intra-stream and inter-stream synchronization control at destinations.

| pattern | outline |
|---|---|
| | **intra-stream synchronization control** |
| | $A_m^{(j)} \le \min(t_m^{(j)}, D_{m-1}^{(j)} + \sigma_{m-1,m}^{(j)})$ |
| *(a)* | if $0 < (D_{m-1}^{(j)} + \sigma_{m-1,m}^{(j)}) - t_m^{(j)} \le T_{h1}^{(j)}$ & $\lvert\delta\rvert \le T_{h7}$, then $d_m^{(j)} = D_{m-1}^{(j)} + \sigma_{m-1,m}^{(j)}$ |
| *(a')* | if $0 < (D_{m-1}^{(j)} + \sigma_{m-1,m}^{(j)}) - t_m^{(j)} \le T_{h1}^{(j)}$ & $\delta < -T_{h7}$, then $d_m^{(j)} = \max(D_{m-1}^{(j)} + \sigma_{m-1,m}^{(j)} - r_D, Timestamp_m^{(j)}, A_m^{(j)})$ |
| *(a")* | if $0 < (D_{m-1}^{(j)} + \sigma_{m-1,m}^{(j)}) - t_m^{(j)} \le T_{h1}^{(j)}$ & $\delta > T_{h7}$, then $d_m^{(j)} = D_{m-1}^{(j)} + \sigma_{m-1,m}^{(j)} + \max(r_I, \delta)$ |
| *(b)* | if $0 \le t_m^{(j)} - (D_{m-1}^{(j)} + \sigma_{m-1,m}^{(j)}) \le T_{h1}^{(j)}$ & $\lvert\delta\rvert \le T_{h7}$, then $d_m^{(j)} = D_{m-1}^{(j)} + \sigma_{m-1,m}^{(j)}$ |
| *(b')* | if $0 \le t_m^{(j)} - (D_{m-1}^{(j)} + \sigma_{m-1,m}^{(j)}) \le T_{h1}^{(j)}$ & $\delta < -T_{h7}$, then $d_m^{(j)} = \max(D_{m-1}^{(j)} + \sigma_{m-1,m}^{(j)} - r_D, Timestamp_m^{(j)}, A_m^{(j)})$ |
| *(b")* | if $0 \le t_m^{(j)} - (D_{m-1}^{(j)} + \sigma_{m-1,m}^{(j)}) \le T_{h1}^{(j)}$ & $\delta > T_{h7}$, then $d_m^{(j)} = D_{m-1}^{(j)} + \sigma_{m-1,m}^{(j)} + \max(r_I, \delta)$ |
| *(c)* | if $(D_{m-1}^{(j)} + \sigma_{m-1,m}^{(j)}) - t_m^{(j)} > T_{h1}^{(j)}$, then $d_m^{(j)} = D_{m-1}^{(j)} + \sigma_{m-1,m}^{(j)} - c^{(j)}$ (graceful recovery) |
| *(d)* | if $t_m^{(j)} - (D_{m-1}^{(j)} + \sigma_{m-1,m}^{(j)}) > T_{h1}^{(j)}$, then $d_m^{(j)} = D_{m-1}^{(j)} + \sigma_{m-1,m}^{(j)} + c^{(j)}$ (graceful recovery) |
| | $A_m^{(j)} \ge \max(t_m^{(j)}, D_{m-1}^{(j)} + \sigma_{m-1,m}^{(j)})$ |
| *(e)* | $d_m^{(j)} = A_m^{(j)}$ (pausing occurs) |
| | $\min(t_m^{(j)}, D_{m-1}^{(j)} + \sigma_{m-1,m}^{(j)}) < A_m^{(j)} < \max(t_m^{(j)}, D_{m-1}^{(j)} + \sigma_{m-1,m}^{(j)})$ |
| *(f)* | if $0 < t_m^{(j)} - (D_{m-1}^{(j)} + \sigma_{m-1,m}^{(j)}) \le T_{h1}^{(j)}$, then $d_m^{(j)} = A_m^{(j)}$ |
| *(g)* | if $0 \le (D_{m-1}^{(j)} + \sigma_{m-1,m}^{(j)}) - t_m^{(j)} \le T_{h1}^{(j)}$ & $\lvert\delta\rvert \le T_{h7}$, then $d_m^{(j)} = D_{m-1}^{(j)} + \sigma_{m-1,m}^{(j)}$ |
| *(g')* | if $0 \le (D_{m-1}^{(j)} + \sigma_{m-1,m}^{(j)}) - t_m^{(j)} \le T_{h1}^{(j)}$ & $\delta < -T_{h7}$, then $d_m^{(j)} = \max(D_{m-1}^{(j)} + \sigma_{m-1,m}^{(j)} - r_D, Timestamp_m^{(j)}, A_m^{(j)})$ |
| *(g")* | if $0 \le (D_{m-1}^{(j)} + \sigma_{m-1,m}^{(j)}) - t_m^{(j)} \le T_{h1}^{(j)}$ & $\delta > T_{h7}$, then $d_m^{(j)} = D_{m-1}^{(j)} + \sigma_{m-1,m}^{(j)} + \max(r_I, \delta)$ |
| *(h)* | if $t_m^{(j)} - (D_{m-1}^{(j)} + \sigma_{m-1,m}^{(j)}) > T_{h1}^{(j)}$, then $d_m^{(j)} = \max(A_m^{(j)}, D_{m-1}^{(j)} + \sigma_{m-1,m}^{(j)} + c^{(j)})$ (graceful recovery) |
| *(i)* | if $(D_{m-1}^{(j)} + \sigma_{m-1,m}^{(j)}) - t_m^{(j)} > T_{h1}^{(j)}$, then $d_m^{(j)} = \max(A_m^{(j)}, D_{m-1}^{(j)} + \sigma_{m-1,m}^{(j)} - c^{(j)})$ (graceful recovery) |
| | **inter-stream synchronization control** |
| | the $n$-th MU in stream $i$ has been outputted by $d_m^{(j)}$ |
| *(a)* | if $0 < d_m^{(j)} - (D_n^{(i)} + \Delta) \le T_{h3}^{(i,j)}$, then $D_m^{(j)} = d_m^{(j)}$ |
| *(b)* | if $0 \le (D_n^{(i)} + \Delta) - d_m^{(j)} \le T_{h3}^{(i,j)}$, then $D_m^{(j)} = d_m^{(j)}$ |
| *(c)* | if $(D_n^{(i)} + \Delta) - d_m^{(j)} > T_{h3}^{(i,j)}$, then $D_m^{(j)} = d_m^{(j)} + c^{(i,j)}$ (graceful recovery) |
| *(d)* | if $d_m^{(j)} - (D_n^{(i)} + \Delta) > T_{h3}^{(i,j)}$, then $D_m^{(j)} = \max(d_m^{(j)} - c^{(i,j)}, A_m^{(j)})$ (graceful recovery) |
| | the $n$-th MU in stream $i$ has not been outputted by $d_m^{(j)}$ |
| *(e)* | if the $n$-th MU in stream $i$ is outputted within $T_{h4}^{(i,j)}$, $D_m^{(j)} = \max(d_m^{(j)} + c^{(i,j)}, D_n^{(i)})$ (graceful recovery) |
| *(f)* | otherwise, $D_m^{(j)} = d_m^{(j)} + T_{h4}^{(i,j)}$ |

For thresholds and parameters used in this table, the reader is referred to Table 2.

the output timing in these patterns.

If $\delta > T_{h7}$, the slave destination has to delay the MU output timing. For this purpose, we require new patterns; that is, patterns *(a")*, *(b")* and *(g")* (see Fig. 2). In each of the three patterns instead of patterns *(a)*, *(a')*, *(b)*, *(b')*, *(g)* and *(g')*, the slave destination tries to set $d_m^{(j)}$ at the value which is larger than that determined in the corresponding pattern *(a)*, *(b)* or *(g)* by $r_I$ ($> 0$). However, the amount which is increased should not be larger than $\delta$ (see patterns *(a")*, (b") and (g") in Table 1). Fig. 2 illustrates the relationship among $d_m^{(j)}$ and the above three time measures; the values of $d_m^{(j)}$ in patterns *(a")*, *(b")* and *(g")* are denoted by solid arrows, and those in patterns *(a)*, *(b)* and *(g)* by dotted arrows[4]. The destination also increases the target output time and decreases $\delta$ by the same value. The output timing of the following MUs as well as the current MU is delayed by this increase of the target output time. In this case, we also have a chance to delay $d_m^{(j)}$ in the other patterns. For simplicity, however, we do not use the other patterns as in the case of $\delta < -T_{h7}$

As for the inter-stream synchronization control, we use the same algorithm as in [6]. Table 1 shows the fifteen patterns in the above for the intra-stream synchronization and six patterns[5] for the inter-stream synchronization.

### 3.4 Traffic control

We use a media scaling technique [5] to control network traffic in multimedia communications. A single media stream is divided into several substreams. For example, we can suppose that an MPEG video stream consists of three substreams: sequences of I frames, P frames and B frames; each substream is assumed to be distributed to a single multicast group. When the traffic is heavy, destinations select only substream I (that is, they join only a single group). Otherwise, they

[4] In patterns *(a)*, *(b)* and *(g)*, we select the accumulated output time rather than the target output time as $d_m^{(j)}$ because of smooth change [6].

[5] The relationships between the variables in patterns *(a)* through *(f)* correspond to those in Figs. 5 (a) through (f) in [6].

Table 2: Thresholds and parameters.

| threshold/ parameter (stream $j$) | meaning | value: master (voice) ($j=1$) | value: slave (video) ($j=2$) |
|---|---|---|---|
| $r_I$ | the constant used to increase the target output time | 20 ms | |
| $r_D$ | the constant used to reduce the target output time | 20 ms | |
| $c^{(j)}$ | the constant used for graceful recovery (intra-stream) | 80 ms | |
| $c^{(i,j)}$ | the constant used for graceful recovery (inter-stream) | — | 80 ms |
| $T^{(j)}_{h1}$ | the threshold value of allowable output jitter (intra-stream) | 80 ms | |
| $T^{(j)}_{h2}$ | the threshold value for modification of the target output time (intra-stream) | 320 ms | $\infty$ |
| $T^{(i,j)}_{h3}$ | the threshold value of allowable output jitter (inter-stream) | — | 80 ms |
| $T^{(i,j)}_{h4}$ | the maximum waiting time of a slave MU for the corresponding master MU (inter-stream) | — | 160 ms |
| $T^{(j)}_{h5}$ | the threshold value used to judge asynchrony (intra-stream) | $\infty$ | 160 ms |
| $T^{(i,j)}_{h6}$ | the threshold value used to judge asynchrony (inter-stream) | — | 160 ms |
| $T_{h7}$ | the threshold value of allowable output jitter (group) | 0 ms | |
| $T_{h8}$ | the threshold value used to judge asynchrony (group) | $\infty$ | |
| $T_{h9}$ | the threshold value used to judge recovery from asynchrony (group) | $\infty$ | |

Stream $i$ is a master stream of stream $j$.

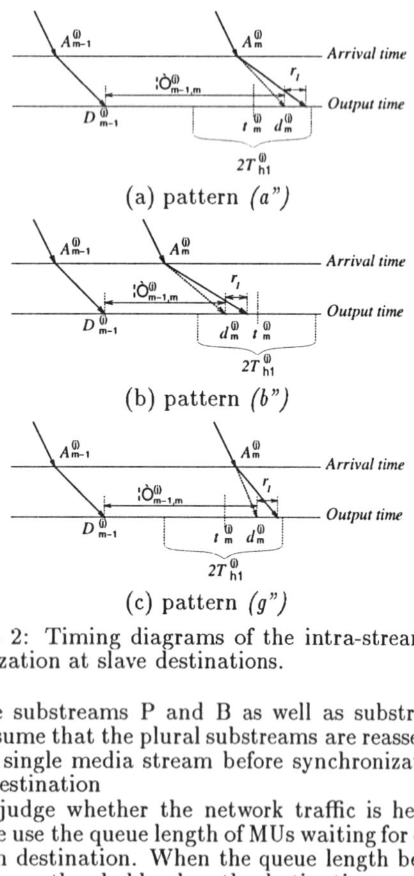


(a) pattern *(a")*

(b) pattern *(b")*

(c) pattern *(g")*

Figure 2: Timing diagrams of the intra-stream synchronization at slave destinations.

receive substreams P and B as well as substream I. We assume that the plural substreams are reassembled into a single media stream before synchronization at each destination

To judge whether the network traffic is heavy or not, we use the queue length of MUs waiting for output at each destination. When the queue length becomes less than a threshold value, the destination recognizes network congestion and leaves some multicast groups, to which ancillary information to improve the quality of media is carried. This is because if the network load becomes heavier, MUs arrive late at the destination. In the IP multicast, for instance, routers stop relaying multicast packets if the routers have no destinations; this alleviates the network load. When the queue length exceeds the threshold value, the destination recognizes congestion-clear and joins some multicast groups[6]. Instead of joining/leaving a multicast group, the destination may return control packets to the sources to notify of the network state; the sources change the number of substreams transmitted according to the state.

## 4 Experimental system

We carried out a lip-synch experiment, in which video images of a lady's head view and her voice were multicast from a source workstation to plural destination workstations using an ATM network. The media scaling function has not been included in our experimental system.

As shown in Fig. 3, the experimental system consists of an ATM LAN at Nagoya Institute of Technology and one at Shinshu University, which are connected through a 156 Mbps VP of NTT's ATM WAN. The ATM LAN at Nagoya Institute of Technology includes an ATM switch (Fujitsu E-7550AS) and two workstations; a source and a master destination. The other LAN has the same ATM switch and a workstation, which is a slave destination. The ATM WAN includes an ATM SLT located in Nagoya and one in Nagano, which are connected by a 622 Mbps transmission link through an ATM XC in Maebashi. The distance along the path between Nagoya Institute of Technology and Shinshu University is 1,089 km. Each workstation is SPARCstation 2 with 32 Mbyte RAM (SunOS 4.1.3+OpenWindow 2.1), and it has a 156 Mbps ATM board (FORE's SBA-200/OC3C), in which we employ AAL type 5. It also has a video board (PowerVideo from Parallax Graphics, Inc.)

[6]As the CPU load of the destination becomes larger, the queue length increases. Thus, we have to differentiate this situation from congestion-clear.

Table 3: Specifications of voice and video.

| item | voice | video |
|---|---|---|
| coding scheme | ITU-T G.711 $\mu$-law | JPEG |
| image size [pixels] | — | 320x240 |
| average MU size [bytes] | 600 | 4650 |
| total number of MUs | 1523 | 1771 |
| original total output time [sec.] | 124.4 | |
| average MU rate [MU/s] | 12.2 | 14.2 |
| average inter-MU time [ms] | 64.1 | 70.2 |
| average bit rate [kbps] | 64 | 528 |

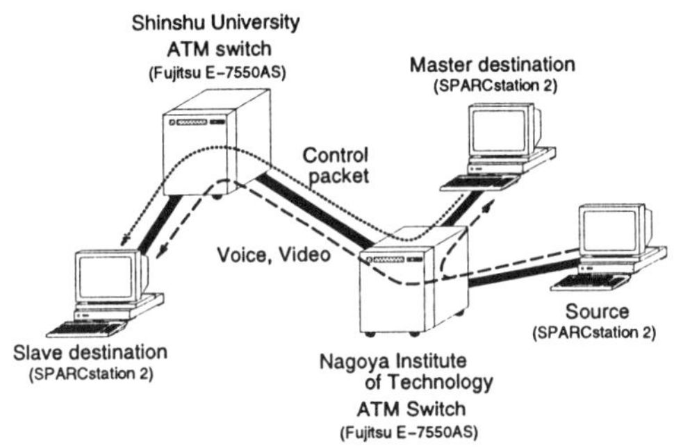


Figure 3: The experimental system.

handling a continuous bit stream of NTSC-standard video coded by the JPEG compression scheme. For lip-synch experiment, video images of a lady's head view and her voice have been inputted to the source workstation from a CCD camera and a microphone of the workstation, respectively. The specifications of video and voice are shown in Table 3. Each MU of video corresponds to a video frame whose size changes from frame to frame, and that of voice has a constant size of 600 bytes. The video and voice were stored with timestamps as two different files. Timestamps are necessary since the generation of video MUs by PowerVideo is not perfectly periodical.

In the experiment, the voice was selected as the master stream (stream 1) because of its more stringent delay constraints than those of the video (stream 2). The stored video images and voice were multicast independently by UDP, where the buffer capacity at each workstation is 51,200 bytes. Multicast is realized by broadcasting on a point-to-multipoint PVC connection of the ATM switch. Control packets were transferred from the master to the slave by UDP on an ATM point-to-point PVC connection. To reduce the frequency of MU overflow at the master destination, we performed window flow control only between the source and the master destination. After synchronization, the video images and voice were outputted at the destination workstations with PowerVideo and the speaker of the workstations.

Since the ATM network was lightly-loaded as in [7], we also independently generated a pseudo-delay which was exponentially distributed with a mean of $\Delta_{\rm av}$ seconds at the transmission of each MU as in [7].

Instead of the slave destination at Shinshu University, we also experimented using another slave destination in the ATM LAN at Nagoya Institute of Technology. We obtained almost the same results as those in this paper and confirmed high quality of group synchronization subjectively.

## 5 Experimental results

Here we examine the system behavior to see the validity of the mechanism, and we demonstrate the influence of the parameters on the performance.

We employ the same values of the thresholds and parameters for the intra-stream and inter-stream synchronization as those in [8], where we determined the value by referring to the results of subjective assessment in [10] (see Table 2). In [10], Steinmetz investigates the influence of the time difference between video and voice MUs in a lip-synch experiment. He concludes that a time difference within ±80 ms leads to synchronization of high quality; however, a time difference beyond ±160 ms corresponds to asynchrony. As for group synchronization, how large time difference between the master and slave destinations is allowable is not clear. In order to answer this question, we need to carry out subjective assessment for a wider range of the threshold values. This is for further study. In this paper, we set $T_{h7} = 0$ ms so that we can assess the quality of group synchronization subjectively[7].

In what follows, we set $\Delta_{\rm max} = \Delta^{(i,j)}_{\rm max} = \Delta^{(j)}_{\rm MSmax}$ for simplicity. We also set $T_{h8} = T_{h9} = \infty$; this means the probabilistic synchronization is disabled. It is assumed that only the master stream triggers the modification of the target output time. Furthermore, no voice MUs are assumed to be skipped so as not to degrade the voice quality largely.

### 5.1 System behavior

Figures 4 (a) and (b) show timing diagrams of the voice at the master and slave destinations, respectively, under the condition that $\Delta_{\rm av} = 200$ ms, $\Delta_{\rm max} = 1$ second, and $r_I = r_D = 20$ ms[8]. The figures exhibit the system behavior for a period within which the target output time is modified. Since we obtained the timing diagrams for video similar to those in [7], we do not show the diagrams here.

Figure 4 (a) plots $D_n^{(1)}$, $t_n^{(1)}$, $A_n^{(1)}$, and $Timestamp_n^{(1)}$ for the $n$-th MU ($n$ =1, 2, $\cdots$, and 100) in the voice

[7] In our experiment, we perceived high quality synchronization between the master stream of the master destination and the slave stream of the slave destination.

[8] We examined the influence of $r_I$ and $r_D$ on the performance. As a result, we noticed that the mean square error decrease gradually as $r_I$ ($r_D$) becomes larger if $r_I(r_D) \geq 5$ ms; otherwise, the mean square error is large. It is also found that the average MU rate is hardly dependent on $r_I$ ($r_D$). Too large $r_I$ ($r_D$) increases (decreases) output intervals between MUs largely; this leads to serious degradation of media quality, especially for voice. Considering the tradeoff between the mean square error and the degradation of media quality, we have adopted $r_I$ ($r_D$) of 20 ms in this experiment.

stream at the master destination. The figure also includes comments on the patterns (see Table 1) appeared in the intra-stream synchronization control. In the figure, the second through 59-th MUs are outputted on time (i.e., within the threshold value $T_{h1}^{(1)}$) as pattern *(b)*[9]. The next MU arrives 510 ms late. This case corresponds to pattern *(e)* with a value of $d_n^{(1)} - t_n^{(1)}$ beyond $T_{h2}^{(1)}$. As a result, $t_n^{(1)}$ is changed (the curve of $t_n^{(1)}$ coincides with that of $D_n^{(1)}$). The following 29 MUs are outputted on time as pattern *(b)*. Then, the 90-th MU arrives 126 ms late. In this case, the value of $d_n^{(1)} - t_n^{(1)}$ is within $T_{h2}^{(1)}$, and the MU is outputted as pattern *(e)*. After the graceful recovery (i.e., pattern *(i)*), the following MUs in the figure are outputted as pattern *(a)*.

Figure 4 (b) illustrates a timing diagram for the voice stream at the slave destination. Comments on the patterns appeared for voice in the intra-stream synchronization control are also written in the figure. We notice that pattern *(b")* appears at the second through fifth MUs since the master destination has outputted the first MUs 72 ms later than the slave destination. As a result, the target output time $t_n^{(1)}$ at the slave destination is delayed by 72 ms; to synchronize the slave with the master perfectly, it takes 4 MUs ($= \lceil 72/r_I \rceil$, which denotes the smallest integer not less than $72/r_I$). In the figure, the 17-th MU arrives 414 ms late (i.e., pattern *(e)*); therefore, $t_n^{(1)}$ is delayed by $|\delta| = 342$ ($= 414 - 72$). After the modification, $t_n^{(1)}$ is reduced gradually as pattern *(b')* as in [7]; since the amount of time which is decreased per MU is smaller than or equal to $r_D$ ms, it takes 18 MUs ($= \lceil |\delta|/r_D \rceil = \lceil 342/20 \rceil$). However, 34 MUs after $t_n^{(1)}$ catches up with $Timestamp_n^{(1)} + 72$ ms, the slave destination knows that the target output time of the master destination have been modified; note that the 60-th MU of the master destination is outputted at 5.41 second; owing to network delay, the slave destination knows the modification at the 70-th MU. Thus, in this case we have $|\delta| = 510$ ms. Then, $t_n^{(1)}$ is increased gradually as pattern *(a")* or *(b")* excluding pattern *(e)* at the 86-th MU. Since the 86-th MU arrives 6 ms late, the arrival increases $t_n^{(1)}$ by 6 ms (note that the destination could increase $t_n^{(1)}$ by 20 ms, but it does not). Finally, the slave destination catches up with the master destination at the 97-th MU; it takes 27 MUs (including the 86-th MU) to recover from asynchrony since $\lceil (|\delta| - 6)/r_I \rceil = 26$.

To illustrate the modification of the target output time in more detail, we show the behavior of *the accumulated maximum network delay* $\hat{\Delta}_{max}$[11] in Fig. 5, where $\hat{\Delta}_{max}$ is defined as the sum of $\Delta_{max}$ and the accumulation of the increment or decrement of the modified target output time; we can regard the sum at

[9]Note that the first MU is irrelevant to the patterns since the MU is outputted under the simultaneous output control of the first MUs.

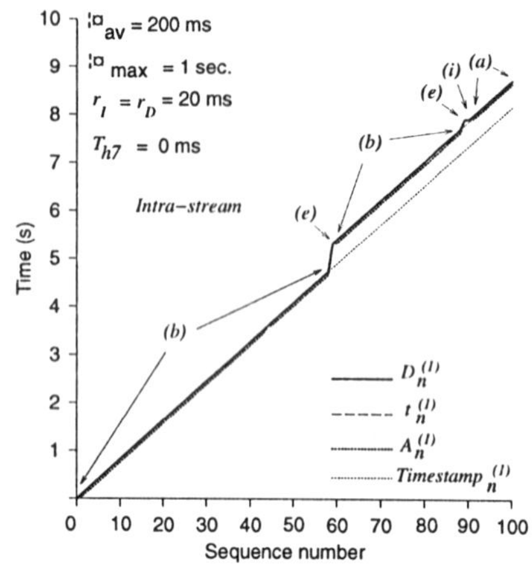


(a) Master destination

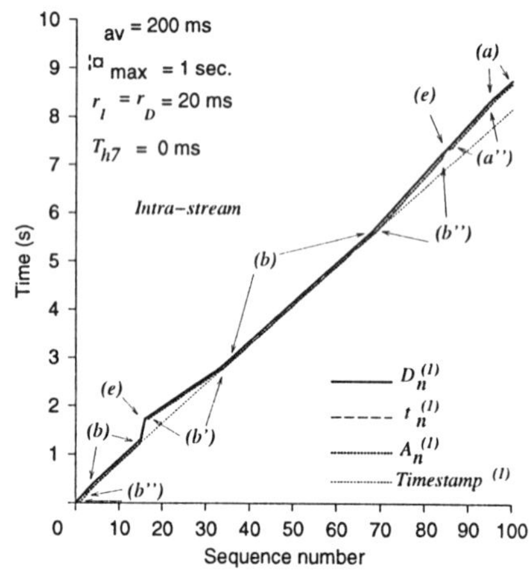


(b) Slave destination

Figure 4: Timing diagrams of media synchronization control for voice in the case where the target output time is modified.

the master destination as an estimate of the maximum network delay. The figure displays examples of $\hat{\Delta}_{max}$ as a function of the video MU sequence number in the same experimental result as that for Fig. 4. Note that the initial value of $\hat{\Delta}_{max}$ is $\Delta_{max}$. We can confirm that $\hat{\Delta}_{max}$ of the master destination is a monotonically nondecreasing function of time, but that of the slave destination is not. The values of $\hat{\Delta}_{max}$ of the master and slave destinations are changed discontinuously at the same MUs as those at which the target output times are modified in Figs. 4 (a) and (b), respectively. We also see that the values of $\hat{\Delta}_{max}$ of the master and slave destinations increase to 1.510 and 1.582 seconds, respectively, at the sequence number of 100; this difference (72 ms) is owing to the initial delay of the master destination. This property of $\hat{\Delta}_{max}$ enables us to apply our mechanism to environments of

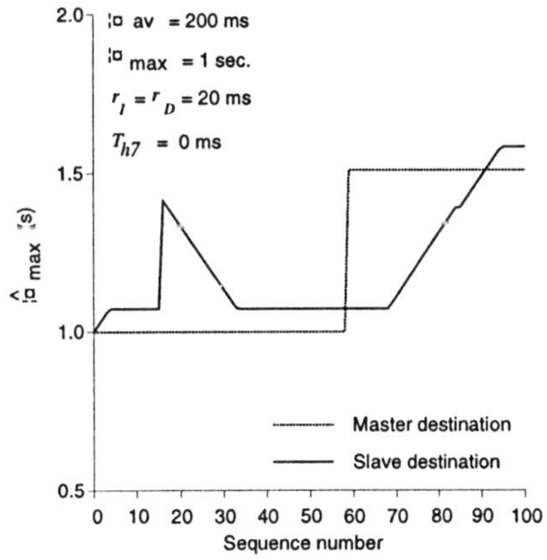


Figure 5: Behavior of $\hat{\Delta}_{\max}$.

unknown bounds on network delay.

## 5.2 Influence of $\Delta_{\mathrm{av}}$

We depict mean square error, average MU rate of video, and total output time as a function of $\Delta_{\mathrm{av}}$ in Figs. 6 (a)–(c), respectively, where $\Delta_{\max} = 1$ second and $r_I = r_D = 20$ ms. The mean square error is used to evaluate the quality of inter-stream synchronization and that of group synchronization. The mean square error for inter-stream synchronization (denoted by "inter-stream") is defined as the average square of the difference between the output time of each MU and that of the corresponding master MU. The error for group synchronization (by "group") denotes the mean square of the difference between the output time of each MU at the master destination and that of the MU at the slave destination. The average MU rate of video is the average number of video MUs outputted per second at each destination. It should be noted that voice MUs are not skipped in this paper. The total output time represents the time interval in seconds it takes for video and voice streams to be outputted at each destination.

In Fig. 6 (a), we notice that the mean square errors of "inter-stream" are smaller than 6,400 ms$^2$ ($= 80^2$; this value means the square of $T_{h3}^{(1,2)}$) at the master and slave destination when $\Delta_{\mathrm{av}}$ is less than or equal to 250 ms and 225 ms, respectively. Thus, high quality of inter-stream synchronization is achieved in this area. Moreover, we see that the mean square errors of "group" tend to increase as $\Delta_{\mathrm{av}}$ becomes larger. We also observe that when $\Delta_{\mathrm{av}} \geq 150$ ms, the mean square error of voice is almost the same as that of video. To judge whether the quality of group synchronization is high or not, we need to carry out subjective assessment for a wider range of the threshold and parameter values. Since the group synchronization mechanism does not usually require smaller mean square error than the inter-stream synchronization mechanism, we can say that high quality of group synchronization is achieved if the mean square error is smaller than at least 6400 ms$^2$. In the figure, when

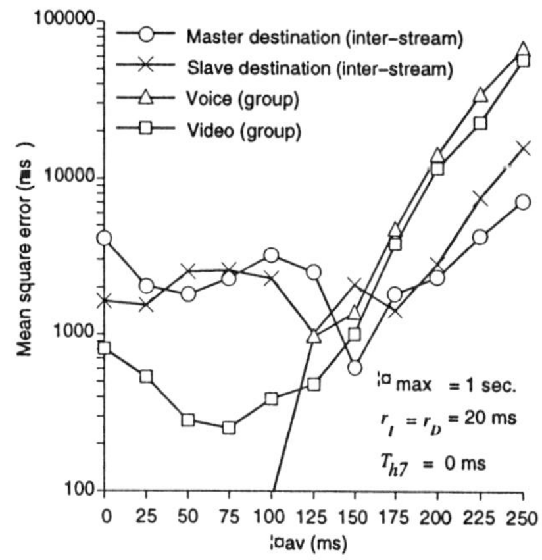


(a) Mean square error

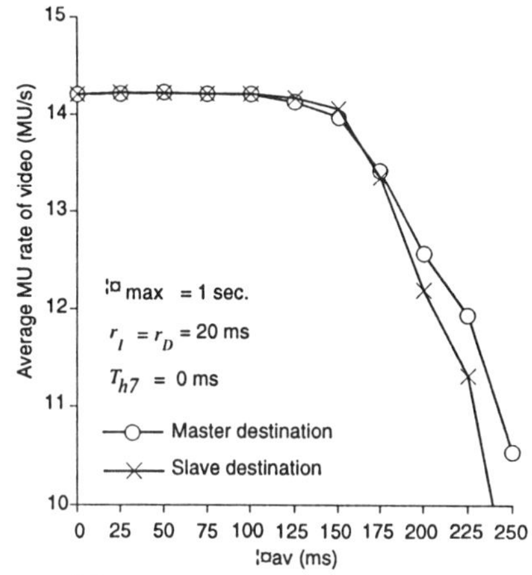


(b) Average MU rate of video

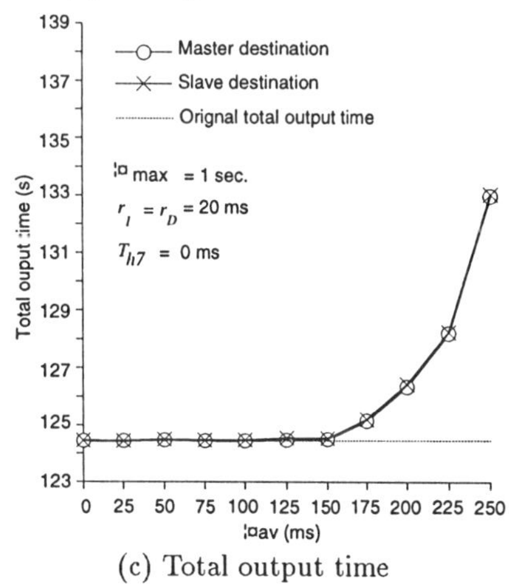


(c) Total output time

Figure 6: Mean square error, average MU rate, and total output time versus $\Delta_{\mathrm{av}}$.

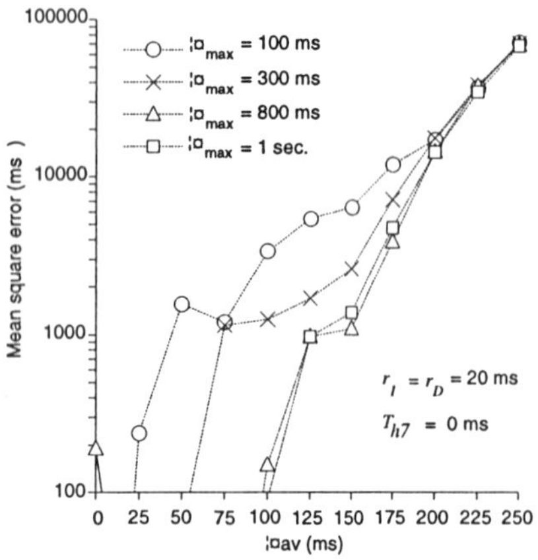


Figure 7: Influence of $\Delta_{max}$.

$\Delta_{av} \leq 175$ ms, we have mean square errors less than 6400 $ms^2$.

Figures 6 (b) and (c) reveal that the average MU rate and total output time of the master destination are almost the same as those of the slave destination in the whole range of $\Delta_{av}$ considered here. We also notice that the rate and time start to decrease and increase, respectively, at 125 ms.

### 5.3 Influence of $\Delta_{max}$

Figure 7 shows the influence of $\Delta_{max}$ on the performance. We plot the mean square error for group synchronization versus $\Delta_{av}$ for various values of $\Delta_{max}$; namely, $\Delta_{max}$ =100, 300, 800, and 1000 ms. In the figure, we set $r_I = r_D = 20$ ms.

We can confirm from Fig. 7 that when $\Delta_{max} \leq$ 800 ms, the mean square error has a tendency to decrease as $\Delta_{max}$ becomes larger. Hence, for stored media, we can improve the quality of synchronization by choosing large $\Delta_{max}$ at the expense of the response time. However, when $\Delta_{max} \geq 800$ ms, the mean square error is not improved. This is because the buffer capacity is 51,200 bytes; that is, the destination can buffer around 11 video MUs; the output period of these MUs is about 772 ms (see Table 3).

## 6 Conclusions

This paper proposed a group synchronization mechanism for stored media. The mechanism, together with the intra-stream and inter-stream synchronization mechanisms, can be used for multicast communications. In the lip-synch experiment, stored video and voice were multicast by UDP through an ATM network, and they were synchronized and outputted at destinations. Using the experimental system, we confirmed the validity of the mechanism and measured the performance. Further experimental studies under more heavily-loaded conditions of the ATM network are required. We are now adding a function of media scaling to the mechanism for traffic control. An extension of our mechanism to MPEG-coded video systems is also in progress. In addition, we plan to enhance the mechanism to support live media streams. In this case, the master destination can employ the live media synchronization mechanism in [7].


### Acknowledgment

The authors would like to acknowledge NTT for giving them the opportunity to join the "Joint Utilization Tests of Multimedia Communications." This work was also supported by Network Systems Laboratory, Hypermedia Research Center of SANYO Electric Co., Ltd., which they wish to thank. In addition, they are grateful to Prof. Yatsuka Nakamura and Prof. Yasushi Fuwa of Shinshu University for their cooperation in the experiment. Furthermore, this work was supported in part by the Toyota Physical & Chemical Research Institute.


## References


[1] G. Blakowski and R. Steinmetz, "A media synchronization survey: reference model, specification, and case studies," *IEEE J. Sel. Areas in Commun.*, vol. 14, no. 1, pp. 5–35, Jan. 1996.

[2] J. Escobar, C. Partridge, and D. Deutsch, "Flow synchronization protocol," *IEEE/ACM Trans. Networking*, vol. 2, no. 2, pp. 111–121, Apr. 1994.

[3] R. Ohno, H. Aida, and T. Saito, "A media synchronization mechanism for a distributed multimedia system with interactive control," *IEICE Trans. Commun.*, vol. E78-B, no. 7, pp. 980–986, July 1995.

[4] I. F. Akyildiz and W. Yen, "Multimedia group synchronization protocols for integrated services networks," *IEEE J. Sel. Areas in Commun.*, vol. 14, no. 1, pp. 162–173, Jan. 1996.

[5] L. Delgrossi, C. Halstrick, D. Hehmann, R. G. Herrtwich, O. Krone, J. Sandvoss, and C. Vogt, "Media scaling in a multimedia communication system," *ACM/Springer-Verlag Multimedia Syst.*, vol. 2, no. 4, pp. 172–180, Oct. 1994.

[6] Y. Ishibashi and S. Tasaka, "A synchronization mechanism for continuous media in multimedia communications," in *Proc. IEEE INFOCOM'95*, pp. 1010–1019, Apr. 1995.

[7] Y. Ishibashi, S. Tasaka, and A. Tsuji, "Measured performance of a live media synchronization mechanism in an ATM network," in *Conf. Rec. IEEE ICC'96*, pp. 1348–1354, June 1996.

[8] Y. Ishibashi, S. Tasaka, and E. Minami, "Performance measurement of a stored media synchronization mechanism: quick recovery scheme," in *Conf. Rec. IEEE GLOBECOM'95*, pp. 811–817, Nov. 1995.

[9] D. L. Mills, "Internet time synchronization: the network protocol," *IEEE Trans. Commun.*, vol. 39, no. 10, pp. 1482–1493, Oct. 1991.

[10] R. Steinmetz, "Human perception of jitter and media synchronization," *IEEE J. Sel. Areas in Commun.*, vol. 14, no. 1, pp. 61–72, Jan. 1996.

[11] S. Tasaka, Y. Ishibashi, and H. Imura, "Stored media synchronization in wireless LANs," to appear in *Conf. Rec. IEEE GLOBECOM'96*, Nov. 1996.

# Gateway Based Approach for Conducting Multiparty Multimedia Sessions over Heterogeneous Signaling Domains *

Madhu Sudan
Computer Science Laboratory
SRI International
Menlo Park, CA 94025, USA

Nachum Shacham
Computer Science Laboratory
SRI International
Menlo Park, CA 94025, USA

## Abstract

*Emerging networking technologies are being introduced with their own management protocols for routing, resource reservation and signaling. This diversity restricts the interoperability among QOS-aware multimedia applications written for different networks. We present an approach for managing multiparty, multimedia sessions in a heterogeneous internetwork spanning multiple signaling domains. Participants utilize the native signaling on their respective domains and interact with participants on other domains through signaling gateways that bridge the domains and provide translation of signaling procedures and QOS semantics. Data streams are transmitted using a hierarchical representation, which allows participants to independently adjust the reception quality of each stream according to their resources and interests. We present a particular design and implementation details for connecting ATM and IP signaling domains and conclude with its extension to an arbitrary number of interconnected domains.*

## 1 Introduction

The proliferation of multimedia applications has led to the deployment of various networking technologies (e.g., IP, ATM, Wireless) providing applications with interface for specifying quality-of-service (QOS). Applications use network specific *signaling* to demand predictive service. For instance, the Reservation Protocol (RSVP) [16] and the User Network Interface (UNI) [5] are the signaling protocols for the IP protocol suite and the Asynchronous Transfer Mode (ATM) networks, respectively.

This diversity restricts the interoperability among QOS-aware multimedia applications that run over a heterogeneous infrastructure spanning multiple signaling domains (a domain refers to a network where all the entities communicate using the *same* signaling protocol). The conventional approach for achieving interoperability is to impose *a uniform signaling* protocol throughout the internetwork. For example, the existing approach in the current Internet is to use the IP protocol suite as the universal protocol. Applications use IP signaling interface (e.g., RSVP) but are unaware of the interface between IP and the underlying network such as ATM [2, 7, 6, 8, 1].

This universal interface approach prevents applications from taking advantage of the more powerful native signaling and requires translation of addresses, QOS parameters and signaling messages between IP and the underlying domains. Such translation is necessary even when all the communicating entities are connected to a single domain (e.g., ATM).

We propose an alternative approach based on performing *signaling translation* at the domain boundaries. For intra-domain communication, the applications utilize the native signaling in their respective domains, and for inter-domain communication the interaction is through signaling *gateways* that bridge the domains and provide translation of signaling procedures and QOS semantics. This approach allows applications in different domains to communicate with each other *without* any changes to the existing signaling or resource reservation protocols. If communication involves end-points in the same domain, unnecessary translations are avoided.

Teleconferencing and broadcasting applications provide a good example for the utility of the proposed approach. At the user level most desktop teleconferencing programs provide similar services namely, session management and control, and the delivery of participants' video images. These applications, however, differ in the methods whereby their services are rendered. For example, RSVP and ATM-UNI 3.x sessions are based on leaf- and source-initiated join, respectively. The two also differ in their connection type,

*This work was supported partly by the U.S Naval Surface Warfare Center under contract number N00174-92-C-0129 and partly by the U.S Army Communications-Electronics Command under contract number DAAB07-90-D-A037.



0-8186-7780-5/97 $10.00 © 1997 IEEE

namely, dynamic routing with soft state (RSVP) versus virtual circuit (ATM). The objective is to let such multiparty applications interoperate by bridging their differences in session setup, resource reservation, and data representation.

*Heterogeneous MultiCast* (HMC) [11], is a communication paradigm for operating multiparty, multimedia sessions (MMS) in environments where the participants differ in the constraints they impose on the session and receive different levels of service. HMC originally addressed the issues of different transmission and reception capacities available to the session participants. Enhanced signaling and *hierarchical encoding* of the real-time streams enable participants to customize the fidelity of their reception to their individual needs and constraints.

This paper describes the gateway based approach for realizing HMC paradigm in a heterogeneous signaling internetwork. HMC and its implementation in the IP and ATM domains, are discussed in Section 2 alongwith the enhancements required in the signaling procedures for supporting HMC sessions. Section 3 outlines the functionalities of the signaling gateway. Sections 4 and 5 specify the methods whereby heterogeneous HMC sessions spanning IP and ATM domains are established and maintained. The implemented prototype is described in Section 7. In Section 8 we mention some research issues and present a methodology for extending the architecture to a large number of signaling domains interconnected in an arbitrary mesh. Section 9 contains concluding remarks.

## 2 Heterogeneous Multicast

An HMC session comprises of a set of end-systems, consisting of sources offering real-time streams to the destinations. A source can offer multiple streams, and all the streams are assumed to be encoded hierarchically to facilitate viewing at multiple fidelity levels. The lowest layer is considered to be the core layer and higher layers (enhancement layers) are considered to be dependent on the lower layers. Each destination independently signals to the network the streams it prefers to receive, and the desired fidelity level (layers) for each of the streams. Destinations can change their requests for streams during the session, and the stream delivery to them changes accordingly.

MMS applications (e.g., teleconferencing) are feasible over ATM and IP domains, and in each domain they use different schemes for transmission and switching, namely, virtual connections (VCs) and datagrams, respectively. Both domains provide signaling protocols and API for multicast support, but in both cases that support is not adequate for HMC. Table 1 summarizes the current capabilities of ATM and IP pertinent to HMC.

| Characteristic | ATM (UNI 3.0) | IP/RSVP |
|---|---|---|
| Orientation | Sender-driven | Receiver-driven |
| QOS modifications | Not allowed. Static QOS | Dynamic QOS |
| Heterogeneous receivers | Not supported | Supported |
| Group Reservations | Not supported | Not supported |

Table 1: Comparison between ATM (UNI 3.0) and IP signaling (RSVP)

In the rest of this section we briefly describe implementations of HMC over ATM and IP and discuss the enhancements in both domains' signaling procedures to support HMC.

### 2.1 HMC over ATM Network

As shown in Table 1, currently, ATM lacks support in two areas that are crucial for HMC sessions. First, ATM signaling (UNI 3.x [5]) does not allow heterogeneity among receivers in a multicast VC (all the receivers in a point-to-multipoint VC get the same QOS). Second, ATM receivers cannot renegotiate VC QOS in mid-session. Given these constraints, we have chosen to implement HMC over ATM by transporting each layer of each stream over a separate multipoint VC. Thus, the fidelity at which a stream is received is determined by the number of layers delivered to that receiver. A receiver renegotiates its QOS by adding or deleting layers, that is, by connecting to or disconnecting from multipoint VCs representing the corresponding layers.

This approach was accomplished by the following enhancements to the ATM signaling[1] to support the transport of layered streams.

- Ability to open multiple VCs in a single round-trip of a signaling message - It reduces the time to establish a multi-layer connection (a "connection" refers to a set of point-to-multipoint VC's), and causes all those VCs to follow the same route, thereby facilitating admission and resource allocation decisions.

[1]The new UNI 4.0 signaling standard includes provisions that accomplish some of these goals (e.g.,leaf initiated join).

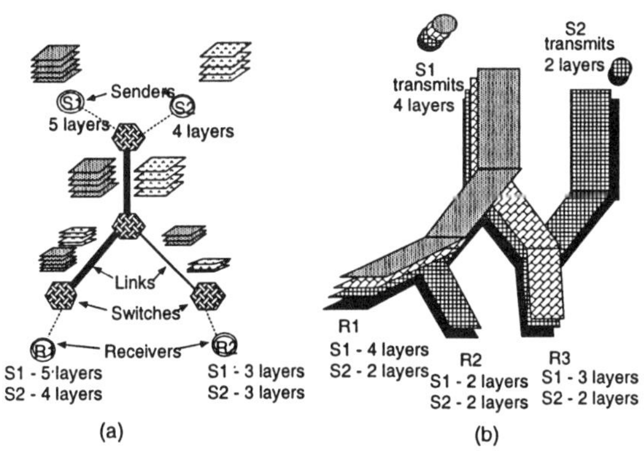


Figure 1: HMC Distribution trees in (a) ATM domain (b) IP domain - each shade represents a different multicast address (and hence a different layer).

- All the VCs for a particular stream are related by a connection identifier, which remains unchanged throughout the network and during the session. This *ConnectionID* enables a destination to initiate a join to the session, and is used by switches for admitting VCs according to their ranking in the stream hierarchy.

The main features of the HMC enhancements to the ATM signaling are summarized in Table 2.

Data from the source to the receivers is carried over a distribution tree consisting of as many point-to-multipoint VCs as the number of layers, as shown in Figure 1(a). A participant wishing to receive a stream sends a signaling message that causes the participant to be added to the corresponding tree. A more detailed description of HMC implementation over ATM can be found in [13].

### 2.2 HMC over IP/RSVP Network

The simplest way to implement HMC over IP multicast [3] is to assign different layers to different multicast addresses. According to this scheme, first proposed by Deering, destinations change their reception fidelity by joining or leaving multicast groups using IGMP messages. This approach is illustrated in Figure 1(b). In this scheme destinations are responsible for managing their connections and receiving layers according to their ranking in the hierarchy. Note that under IP multicast all sources transmit a particular layer on the same address, so a destination listening on an address, receives all the corresponding streams. Consequently, to receive the second layer from a given source, a destination must receive the base layer from all sources. This, of course, adversely affects the bandwidth management aspects of HMC.

RSVP, as the Internet's signaling protocol, is used by destinations to select the sources from which they want to receive, and specify the reservations needed for the corresponding streams [16]. However, IP/RSVP currently lacks two aspects of support for layered streams, namely, (1) the ability to make *group reservations* and (2) the performing of *ordered* admission control. We suggest the following enhancements to IP signaling.

- A *group identifier* to relate all the multicast addresses carrying data for a layered stream.
- Group related processing of reservation message at every router.

A detailed discussion of mechanisms to support transmission of layered streams in RSVP can be found in [15]. Table 2 summarizes the properties of the signaling in the IP domain to support layered streams.

The signaling modifications in both the domains must be accompanied by proper network support, in the form of admission control and QOS based routing, to efficiently conduct sessions in the internetwork. In Section 6 we suggest the criterion for admission control in both the domains that takes into consideration layer ordering.

As a final note, we summarize the means for identifying source, streams and layers. In ATM the VC carries all that information, i.e., each layer from each source and stream has a distinct VC. In IP, the source, stream, and layer are identified by source IP address, UDP port, and IP multicast address respectively.

## 3 The Gateway: Functionalities

The *session*-level *gateway* has an interface to both the domains. Participants on ATM and IP domains are aware of the respective interfaces. The gateway has the following functionalities.

**Signaling translation:** The gateway translates the signaling messages (and QOS semantics) from one domain to the other (for instance, the `PATH` and `RESV` messages to the corresponding messages in the ATM domain and vice versa) and thus provides *transparent* interconnection of the participants in two domains.

**Data forwarding:** Any inter-domain session, in turn, is composed of two intra-domain sessions (one on ATM and one on the IP network). The gateway maintains appropriate mapping information between the sessions in the two domains and uses this to forward the inter-domain data from a sender in one domain to the correct set of receivers in the other domain.

**Multiplexing/demultiplexing of data:** The gateway plays the unique role of a *proxy source*, representing the actual sources to receivers in a different domain (see Figure 2). Hence, streams from different

| Characteristic | ATM (for HMC) | IP/RSVP (for HMC) |
|---|---|---|
| Transport of layered stream | Each layer carried on different point-to-multipoint VC | Each layer carried on a separate multicast address |
| Receiver QOS | Aggregate QOS of all the received layers | Aggregate QOS of all the received layers |
| Orientation | Could be receiver or sender-driven | receiver-driven |
| QOS modifications | Dynamic QOS. Receivers can add or drop layers. | Dynamic QOS. Receivers can add or drop layers as well as change the QOS of individual layers. |
| Heterogeneous receivers | Yes. Different receivers can subscribe to different numbers of layers. | Yes |

Table 2: Comparison between enhanced ATM and IP signaling

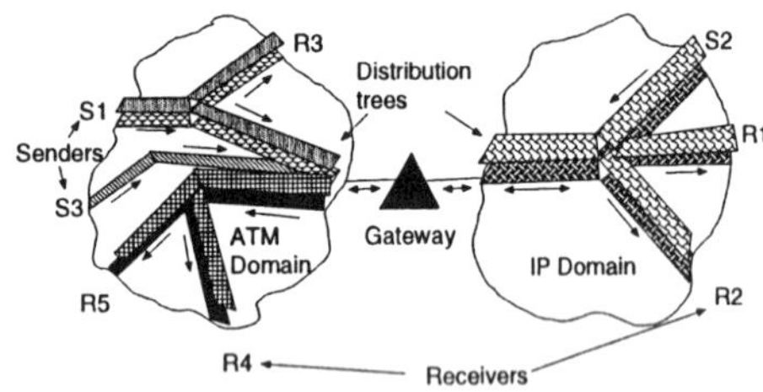


Figure 2: Gateway as a proxy source. Different shades in the ATM domain represent different VCs, and shades in the IP domain represent different multicast addresses.

senders in one domain are multiplexed at the gateway. Figure 2 shows layers from sender S1 and S3 being multiplexed by the gateway (which is a part of both the distribution trees from S1 and S3) to the same set of multicast addresses in the IP domain.

**Data encapsulation and de-encapsulation:** ATM data is transmitted in AAL PDUs and IP data is transmitted in the form of IP packets. In addition, the audio and video packets have encapsulation headers to enable the receivers to assemble and play them correctly. The gateway receives data from respective domains and performs encapsulation or de-encapsulation such that it is suitable for transmission in the other domain.

**Efficient distribution:** If sender and receivers in an HMC session are separated by domain boundary, the gateway tries to maintain a balance between the number of layers desired by the receivers and the number of layers actually delivered by the sender. For instance, in Figure 2, if no one in the IP domain is interested in receiving layer 2, the corresponding distribution tree is pruned from the actual source in the ATM domain.

# 4 Participating in an Inter-Domain Session

In Section 2 we described the enhancements to ATM and IP signaling to enable HMC sessions in the individual domains. With such a signaling at our disposal, we now consider a joint session with participants scattered in ATM and IP domains.

## 4.1 Addressing

Communication between two end points can be established only if their addresses are known. In an HMC session, two end-points can belong to two different domains. Since addressing schemes in IP and ATM domains are completely different, it does not make sense to provide receivers on the IP domains with the address of the source in the ATM domain and vice versa. Designing a common addressing scheme and mapping ATM (IP) addresses to IP (ATM) is a significant problem in itself, and a detailed discussion of a common addressing scheme is beyond the scope of this paper. Our approach to resolve this incompatibility among addresses is based on the following.

All the participants are assigned *names* (or IDs), which are independent of the domain-specific addresses. Each domain maintains a mapping between the names and the domain-specific addresses of participants in that domain. The participants on either domain identify each other by their names instead of the addresses, when trying to initiate communication with each other. Inter-domain requests for connection establishment, teardown and modification are received by the gateway (it can access mappings in *both* the domains), which translates the names (mentioned in the requests) into actual IP (or ATM) address and helps in establishing communication between the participants.

## 4.2 Participating in a Session

All the participants in a session receive the following information in advance by an out-of-band mechanism: (1) start time of the session, (2) source IDs, (3) maximum number of layers in the transmission (layers are ranked in the order 1...$k$, where rank 1 is the lowest and $k$ is the highest). (4) QOS for each layer, and (5) multicast addresses on which each layer is transmitted (for participants on IP only).

Tables 3(a) and 3(b) show different signaling messages used in the ATM and IP domains. This section describes the procedures followed by the participants to join, modify and leave a session and how the aforementioned messages are used.

#### 4.2.1 Joining a Session

**Actions taken by the source:** A source in the ATM domain waits for connection request (`hmc_connect`) to arrive from receivers. The request specifies the number of layers desired by the receiver. On receipt of such a request, the source tells the ATM network to create a multilayer (one for each layer), point-to-multipoint (so that other destinations can be added later) VC to the destination and sends an acknowledgment to the receiver. The source can also send a request to initiate a connection to the receivers.

A source in the IP domain sends a `PATH` message (indicating the source traffic specifications) for each layer that it is transmitting on the corresponding multicast address (known in advance). If the source generates multiple streams, it uses a different port number (UDP) to transmit each stream. **Actions taken by the destinations:** A receiver in ATM domain sends a connection request to the source specifying the number of layers desired and waits for an acknowledgment for the request. If resources are available, the ATM network adds this receiver to the distribution tree from the source to the destination(s); otherwise it reports the number of layers for which resources could not be allocated. The receiver can then choose to leave the session (described later) or continue with the available number of layers.

In the IP domain, any participant interested in receiving $k$ layers joins the multicast groups for layers 1...$k$, in that order. After receiving `PATH` messages from the sender, it sends `RESV` messages, one for each layer, in the order of lowest- to highest-ranked layer (this restriction is observed by the destination and is not currently imposed by RSVP). It assumes that the `RESV` requests succeeded, unless a `RESV_ERROR` message is received; in which case it leaves all the multicast groups corresponding to the current as well as the higher ranked layers (since a higher ranked layer is of no use without the lower ranked layers). This is done to maintain consistent reservations for the lowest $n$ layers, where $1 \leq n \leq k$. Note that this assumes no changes in the admission control procedures in the IP domain. Destinations do not expect the network to know about the ordering amongst the layers.

#### 4.2.2 Changing QOS in a Session

Each layer has a certain QOS associated with it. Consequently, the QOS perceived by a receiver is the sum[2] of the QOS of the individual layers received. A receiver can change its QOS in two ways - either by changing the QOS of a received layer or by changing the number of layers received.

As mentioned in Section 2.1 receivers in ATM domain change their QOS by changing the number of layers. The `hmc_modify` message specifies the layer to be added or dropped. If a layer is to be added to the set of received layers, this request results in the creation of a new point-to-multipoint VC from the source (if one does not exist) or causes the receiver to be added to an existing point-to-multipoint VC in the network. If a layer is to be dropped from the set of received layers, the corresponding branch of the point-to-multipoint VC (leading to this receiver) is deleted.

In the IP domain, the receivers can change either the QOS of an individual layer or change the number of layers received. To increase (decrease) the number of layers received, a receiver joins(leaves) the corresponding multicast group. To change the QOS of an individual layer, the receiver starts sending refresh `RESV` messages with the new QOS desired. Since RSVP maintains "soft state", the new `RESV` messages update the reservation state in the network.

#### 4.2.3 Leaving a Session

In the ATM domain, a receiver or sender sends an `hmc_close` message which closes all the associated point-to-multipoint VCs in the distribution tree. In the IP domain, a receiver first tears down the existing reservations (`RESV_TEAR`) and then leaves the corresponding multicast groups.

## 5 Gateway Procedures

As mentioned in Section 3, the gateway acts as a *proxy source* to either domain, whenever the actual sender is separated from the receiver(s) by a domain boundary.

In the following, we describe information maintained by the gateway and the actions taken in order

[2] We consider only bandwidth to be the measure of QOS for the purpose of this document. If there are other parameters to specify QOS, the receiver QOS may not be the sum but some *aggregate* of the individual QOS.

| ATM | | IP | |
|---|---|---|---|
| Message | Purpose | Messages | Purpose |
| hmc_connect | Connect to a destination/source with a certain number of layers (specified by caller). Returns a *ConnectionID* to be used later to refer to this connection. | IGMP_JOIN | Join a particular multicast group. The message specifies the group address. |
| | | IGMP_LEAVE | Leave a particular multicast group. The message specifies the group address. |
| hmc_modify | Change the number of layers being received. The message specifies the layers to be added/deleted and the connection identifier. | PATH | Inform the receivers about the source traffic specifications. |
| | | RESV | Reserve resources for a particular traffic flow. |
| hmc_close | Teardown reservation for a connection (close all the relevant VC's). The message specifies the corresponding *ConnectionID*. | RESV_TEAR | Tear down the existing reservations for a particular traffic flow. |
| | | RESV_ERROR | Notify a reservation error. |

(a) (b)

Figure 3: Messages used in (a) ATM domain (Enhanced Signaling) (b) IP domain

to carry out the functions required to achieve interoperability.

### 5.1 Signaling Translation

**Source on IP and receivers on ATM domain:** The gateway acts as a receiver in the IP domain and a sender in the ATM domain. For each stream in the IP domain, a multipoint VC is created in the ATM domain. Figure 4(a) is the state diagram of the gateway which shows the connection establishment and data flow process for a single layer.
• To receive all the layers from any IP source, the gateway joins all the multicast addresses corresponding to the different layers. Then it waits for the PATH messages to arrive (WAIT_IP_PATH).
• On receipt of the PATH messages, the receivers in the ATM domain are informed about the *traffic specifications* of the IP source by some out-of-band mechanism.
• It then waits for a hmc_connect message from any receiver (WAIT_ATM_CONNECT). Note that the hmc_connect message from the first receiver helps in creating the distribution tree in the ATM domain. All successive receivers in the ATM domain are added to this distribution tree by the network. The gateway does not necessarily have to know about all the receivers.
• On receiving a hmc_connect message, it sends out a *separate* RESV message for *each* of the layers that the receivers wish to receive (and for which a PATH message has been received), in order, from lowest- to the highest-ranked layer (PENDING_IP_RESV). If the gateway receives a RESV_ERROR message, it sends a hmc_modify request to the ATM network to tear down the VCs corresponding to the layers for which reservations failed in the IP domain.
• No errors imply that the reservation was successful (READY_IP_DATA_RECV). Subsequently, the gateway records the mapping between the sender (<Source_IP_Address, Source_UDP_Port>, received as a part of the PATH message) and the receivers (ConnectionID) in the *IP-to-ATM translation table*. This table is used in data forwarding.
• Once the session is established, the gateway tries to maintain a balance between the layers received from the IP domain and the layers being delivered to the receivers in the ATM domain. If there are no receivers in the ATM domain receiving layer $i$, then it sends a RESV_TEAR for this layer on the IP domain to release the reservations.

**Source on ATM and receivers on IP domain:** Figure 4(b) shows the corresponding state diagram of the gateway which illustrates the connection establishment and data flow process for a single layer.
• The gateway receives information about the *traffic specifications* of the source in the ATM domain by an out-of-band mechanism and sends out separate PATH messages (one for each layer) to the receivers on the IP domain (SEND_IP_PATH). The messages are sent in increasing order of the ranking of the layers. This step is repeated for all the streams sent from the ATM domain to IP domain. To the IP domain, the gateway acts as the source of these streams. So that the receivers can distinguish the various streams, the PATH messages for different streams are sent from a different UDP port.
• It waits for an IP receiver to send a RESV message indicating its interest in a particular layer (WAIT_IP_RESV).
• Depending on the number of RESV requests

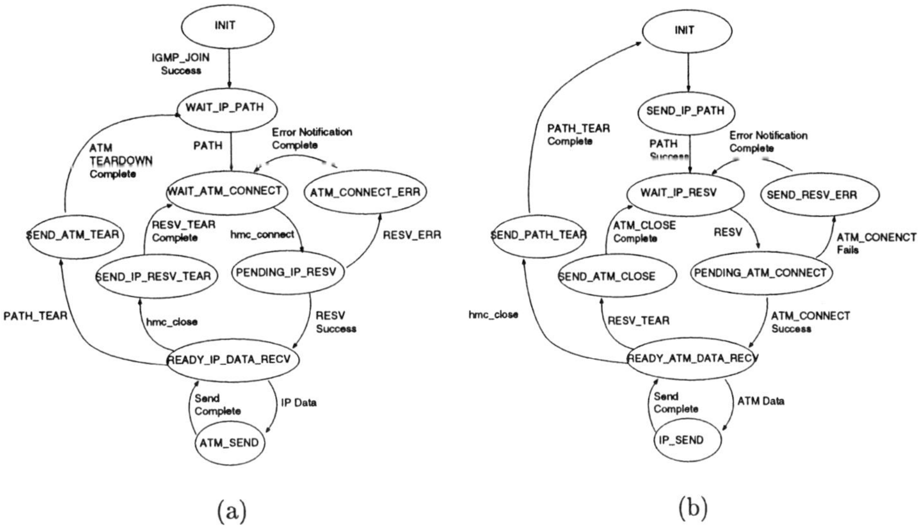


Figure 4: State diagram of the gateway showing connection establishment and data flow (for one layer) (a) Source in IP and receivers in ATM domain. (b) Source in ATM and receivers in IP domain.

received for a stream, it sends a hmc_connect (indicating the requested number of layers) message to all the identified sources in the ATM domain (PENDING_ATM_CONNECT).
• If a reservation request for a given layer is rejected by ATM, a RESV_ERR is sent for that as well as all the higher ranked layers for that stream.
• If there are no errors (READY_ATM_DATA_RECV), the gateway records the mapping between the ATM source (ConnectionID) and the IP receivers (UDP port and the multicast address of the layers) in the *ATM-to-IP translation table* (described later). This is used for data forwarding.
• It tries to maintain a balance between the layers received from the ATM domain and the layers delivered in the IP domain. If there are no receivers in the IP domain receiving layer $i$, then it sends a hmc_modify in the ATM domain to tear down the corresponding VCs.

The gateway must also translate the QOS parameters in addition to translating the signaling messages. Currently, bandwidth is assumed to be the only measure of QOS and hence the translation is relatively simple.

## 5.2 Data Forwarding

To forward the data streams from the senders to the correct set of receivers, the gateway first demultiplexes the data, i.e., identify the sender and the stream (if a sender is sending multiple streams). Then the data is sent to the corresponding set of receivers (associated with that stream) in the other domain. To achieve this functionality, the gateway uses the following tables, which are set up as part of the signaling process ( as described in Section 5.1).

**Layer-to-multicast address mapping:** This table is used by the gateway to determine the correspondence between the layer number and the IP multicast address. It is set up at the configuration time. The number of entries correspond to the maximum number of layers transmitted by any source. Each entry contains (1) a layer number, and (2) the multicast address of the layer.

**IP-to-ATM translation table:** This table is used in forwarding data from the IP domain to the ATM domain. Since the gateway is the root of the distribution tree in the ATM domain, it suffices to know the identity of the distribution tree (ConnectionID) rather than knowing all the individual recipients of the stream in the ATM domain. The number of entries in this table corresponds to the number of active streams in the IP domain. Each entry contains (1) IP stream identification (source IP address, source UDP port number) and, (2) ATM destination identification (ConnectionID of the ATM distribution tree).

When the gateway receives data from an IP source, it demultiplexes the data by looking at the source IP address and the UDP port, searches the corresponding entry in the translation table, and sends data over the appropriate distribution tree.

**ATM-to-IP translation table:** This table is

used to forward data from the ATM domain to the IP domain. Receivers on the IP domain are (collectively) identified by the IP multicast address corresponding to each layer. The number of entries in the table correspond to the number of active streams in the ATM domain. Each entry contains (1) ATM stream identification (ConnectionID of the ATM distribution tree) and, (2) sending UDP port (one port per ATM stream). Note that different UDP ports are needed for transmission because the single gateway represents (proxy) multiple ATM sources to the IP domain.

When the gateway receives data from an ATM source, it identifies the stream (the VC number determines the source, stream, and layer), looks up the corresponding entry in the table to determine the sending port (UDP), and sends data on the multicast address (determined from the layer-to-multicast address map) and the port number.

## 6 Network support for HMC

In addition to the enhanced signaling, the **admission control** procedures in both domains should take into account the ordering of the layers in a hierarchical stream being transmitted. A layer ranked $i$ should not be admitted before admitting layer $i-1$. This constraint can easily be observed in the ATM domain, since the enhanced ATM signaling (section 2.1) uses a *single* signaling message to request resources for *all* the layers desired by the receivers. Hence the switches can allocate resources for layers in ranking order. References [12, 14] provide different algorithms for admission control of layered streams. Things are more complicated in the IP domain since the `RESV` messages for each layer are sent asynchronously and might arrive out of order at the routers. We suggest the following rules to be observed by the routers:

1. A router *admits* a reservation request (indicated by the tuple <Source_IP_Address, IP_Multicast_Address, Source_UDP_Port> ) if: (A) resources for all the layers of lower rank from the same source have been reserved and (B) resources are sufficient to admit the current reservation requests.

   Failure in condition (A) implies that either the requests for admission of lower layers were denied because of unavailable resources, or the `RESV` messages for the lower layers were lost in the network. Hence, the RSVP router waits for a *refresh period*[3], at the end of which:
   • All the requests for which condition (A) is satisfied are processed (resources are reserved for the lowest $m$ layers that can be admitted).
   • If condition (A) is still false, the current reservation request is ignored (it might be a duplicate request floating around in the network).

   If (A) is true, but (B) is false, the router sends back an `RSVP_ERROR` message downstream, which indicates that *only* the current request was denied.

2. A reservation for layer $i$ is *forwarded* only if all the layers ($\leq i$) have been admitted by the router.

[3]The `RESV` messages are sent once every refresh period.

## 7 Implementation

We have implemented a research prototype of the gateway and the HMC systems running on ATM and IP domains in our laboratory. The focus was on using the gateway to interoperate between the tools written for individual domains.

The ATM network consists of a number of Sun SPARCstation-20's (running Solaris 2.5) directly connected to FORE systems ASX-200 switches. Enhanced ATM signaling (as explained in Section 2) is implemented as a separate module and incorporated in the ASX daemon running on the switches. The IP network consists of similar machines connected to a multicast capable network. The gateway is a SPARCstation-20 (running Solaris 2.5) having an interface to the ATM as well as the IP network.

Hierarchical encoding is emulated by varying the JPEG quantization factor for each captured frame and through temporal resolution by layer. Each layer is actually a JPEG encoded image at a different quantization factor. The base layer (layer 1) has the highest quantization factor, producing the blockiest looking image. The quantization factors decrease with each subsequent layer and the resolution of the image is improved. Figure 5(a) shows the variation in aggregate bit rates for a sample set of quantization factors for different layers. The rates pertain to a 320 x 240 size image, using parallax boards for video capture and display, with quantization factors of 500,300,100 and 30 applied to the first, second, third and fourth layer of video, respectively. Although our technique is not truly hierarchical, it utilizes the existing hardware in such a manner that hierarchical emulation is noticeable and thus it provides a temporary solution to test the concept.

We developed our own audio/video conferencing tool to run on native ATM using the HMC signaling we have described. The tool provides the participants the capabilities to join or leave the session or modify the number of layers received, during mid-session.

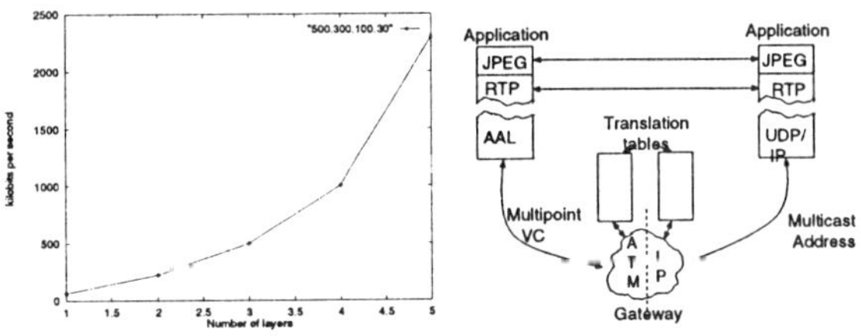


(a) (b)

Figure 5: (a) Variation in bit rates for 320 x 240 size video images (b) Translation using the gateway

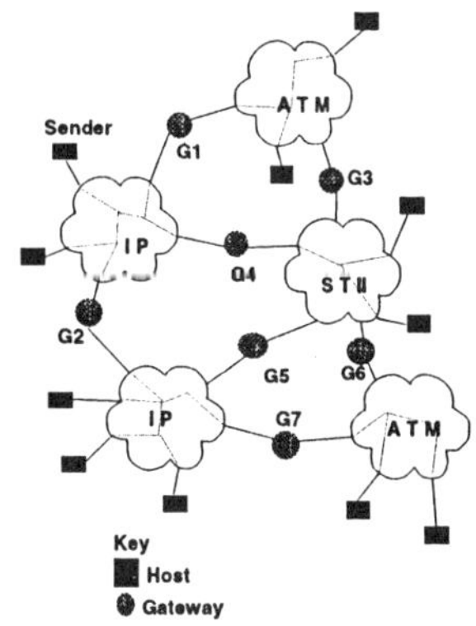


Figure 6: An Internetwork consisting of an arbitrary number of domains connected by gateways.

In the IP domain, we used the publicly available audio (VAT) and video (VIC) tools which were modified to receive data on multiple multicast addresses (and hence receive multiple layers). All the audio and video data is encapsulated end-to-end in RTP [9] format. The video packets are in the format as described in [4], and the audio packets use the format as suggested in [10]. The audio and video tools in both the domains communicated using the gateway (see Figure 5(b)), which implements the state diagrams mentioned in Section 5.1.

## 8 Issues for Further Research

The design that has been described takes into account a single IP domain connected to a single ATM domain. If several domains are connected by gateways (see Figure 6 ) then the gateway architecture becomes more complex. We discuss how to extend the current architecture to several domains and some other issues that need to be explored further.

**Extending the architecture to multiple domains:** In a situation shown in Figure 6, the gateways must be organized into a tree before data transmission can begin. The tree must be dynamically reconfigurable depending on the changing participant population.

Since the tree spans multiple domains, all the gateways communicate using a *Meta Signaling Protocol* (MSP). We call it "Meta" signaling protocol, since it tells the gateways *when* and *how* to use the the native signaling in their respective domains. Because of the heterogeneity of domains, it is possible that two gateways (for instance, gateways G1 and G6 in Figure 6) in the internetwork do not understand each other (since they use two different signaling protocols). However, G1 and G6 can communicate via G3, since G3 can understand the signaling protocol in both domains. The details of MSP are a subject of further research.

The following issues are also related to conducting a session and are under further study.

**Session control:** To advertise a session in the internetwork, a session directory service is needed, which can be used by the participants in different domains to find information about a session such as the offered traffic by the sources and the participant population. The current implementation uses an out-of-band mechanism to deliver this information.

**Route computation:** To construct a *tree of gateways* in the internetwork, an appropriate *route* (based on available resources) must be selected from the source to the destinations. The current architecture has a single gateway and hence does not need this functionality.

**QOS mapping between the different domains:** In order to preserve the semantics of actual QOS desired by the receiver and sender, we need appropriate mappings between the QOS parameters across domains. This paper assumes that received bandwidth is the only parameter for determining the QOS of a receiver. If other parameters (delay variation, loss) are considered, then efficient QOS translation becomes more complex.

**Scalability:** In order to improve scalability of the gateway based approach, it is preferable to have multiple gateways between two domains such that each gateway handles only a fraction of the total inter-domain traffic. We are investigating into various ways of load sharing between the gateways.

## 9 Conclusion

This paper outlined a design for conducting multimedia sessions in a heterogeneous internetwork with multiple signaling domains using hierarchically encoded data. Although we have discussed in detail only two domains, the idea is extendible to more than two domains (as described in Section 8). The concepts that are the key to such a design are:

- Use of the *native signaling* capabilities of the individual domains for intra-domain interaction and use of the gateway for inter-domain interaction.
- Use of the gateway to achieve interoperability. It performs *signaling translation* and acts as a *proxy source* to represent the actual source in a different domain. It also maintains *efficient distribution of data* by maintaining a *balance* between the flows in different domains.

Use of hierarchical data causes the communication in either domain to be unaffected by the resource constraints of the other domain. ATM signaling and IP signaling (RSVP) are still evolving, and we suggested the enhancements to be made to both the signaling domains to transport a layered stream. The requirements of the gateway and the procedures to achieve desired translation between both domains were described. The current implementation proves the feasibility of a gateway based approach for realizing the HMC communication paradigm in a heterogeneous internetwork. Certain aspects (as mentioned in Section 8) need further attention and are a part of ongoing research.

## Acknowledgments

We would like to acknowledge Raj Yavatkar, Don Hoffman and Michael Speer for their fruitful discussions about translation procedures. We would also like to thank Michael Brown and Danny Lee of SRI International, who were heavily involved in the development and testing of the HMC software.

## References

[1] Grenville Armitage. Suport for Multicast over UNI 3.0/3.1 based ATM Networks. *Internet Draft, Work in Progress*, February 1996.

[2] R.G Cole, D. H. Shur, and C. Villamizar. IP over ATM: A Framework document. *Internet Draft, Work in Progress*, February 1996.

[3] Stephen E. Deering and David R. Cheriton. Multicast Routing in Datagram Internetworks and Extended LANs. *ACM Transactions on Computer Systems*, 8(2):85–110, May 1990.

[4] W. Fenner, L. Berc, R. Fredrick, and S. McCane. RTP Encapsulation of JPEG-compressed video. *Internet draft, Work in progress*, November 1995.

[5] ATM Forum. *ATM User Network Interface Specification, Version 3.0.* Prentice Hall, 1993.

[6] M. Laubach. Classical IP and ARP over ATM. *RFC 1577*, Jan 1994.

[7] Walter Milliken. IP Multicasting over ATM: System Artitecture Issues. *Internet Draft, Work in Progress*, July 1995.

[8] M. Perez, F. Liaw, A Mankin, E. Hoffman, D. Gossman, and A. Malis. ATM Signaling Support for IP over ATM . *RFC 1755*, February 1995.

[9] H. Schulzrinne, S. Casner, R. Fredrick, and V. Jacobson. RTP: A Transport Protocol for Real-Time Applications. *RFC 1889*, January 1996.

[10] Henning Schulzrinne. RTP Profiles for Audio and Video with Minimal Control. *RFC 1890*, January 1996.

[11] Nachum Shacham. Multipoint Communication by Hierarchically Encoded Data. In *Proceedings of IEEE INFOCOM*, pages 2107–2114, 1992.

[12] Nachum Shacham. Preemption Based Admission Control in Multimedia Multiparty Communications. In *Proceedings of IEEE INFOCOM*, pages 827–834, 1995.

[13] Nachum Shacham, Madhu Sudan, and Michael Brown. A Flexible Multimedia teleconferencing System over ATM using Hierarchically encoded Data. *Unpublished Report*, May 1996.

[14] Nachum Shacham and Hidetoshi Yokota. Admission Control Algorithms for Multicast Sessions with Multiple Streams. In *Network and Operating Systems Support for Digital Audio and Video*, 1996.

[15] Madhu Sudan, Don Hoffman, Nachum Shacham, and Michael Speer. Supporting Session Groups in RSVP. *Internet draft, Work in Progress*, June 1996.

[16] L. Zhang, S. Deering, D. Estrin, S. Shenker, and D. Zappala. RSVP: A New Resource Reservation Protocol. *IEEE Network Magazine*, 7(5), September 1993.

# Non stationary request distribution in Video on Demand Networks*

Giuseppe Bianchi, Riccardo Melen
Politecnico di Milano, Dipartimento di Elettronica e Informazione
Piazza L. da Vinci 32, 20133 Milano - ITALY
Fax: +39-2-2399-3413; E-mail: bianchi@elet.polimi.it

## Abstract

*Several works have recently appeared in the literature on the design, performance and dimensioning of networks supporting Video on Demand and Multimedia services. It has been shown that performance is strongly dependent on the model adopted to describe the user's behaviour in terms of requests for programs. In this paper we provide a detailed investigation of a non stationary model for the user's request distribution. Numerical results are provided for a network scenario proposed in the literature to investigate the error achieved when the non stationary distribution is approximated with a stationary exponential one.*

## 1 Introduction

The convergence of technological, regulatory and market-related factors has recently generated a strong interest in Interactive Video and Multimedia services provisioning for residential users [1, 2, 3]. Various proposals have been put forward regarding the architecture necessary to support such services [4, 5, 6, 7, 8], and some key points seem to be present in most of the proposed designs: the use of ATM transport, and the presence of two points of control in the network, a Level 1 Gateway acting as a unique, trusted interface for the subscriber, offering various flavors of directory and navigation services, and a Level 2 Gateway controlling the service delivery functions of each provider. Most of the envisioned architectures are based on hierarchical storage systems, and employ the caching effect to reduce the bandwidth requirements of both video servers and transport network.

Performance evaluation and dimensioning issues for these architectures have been widely considered in the literature [9, 10, 11, 12, 13, 7, 14, 15]. In general, the attention is focussed on a class of information retrieval services where the information format consists in real time video segments (programs), lasting from few minutes (as in the case of some advertisement applications) up to two-hours movies. Note that such class of services is not limited to Video on Demand, but it contemplates a much wider set of applications. For instance, the navigation of a user through a video database organized as a hypermedia space can viewed as the delivery of a succession of video segments, intertwined by control informations.

*This work has been partially supported by CNR and MURST, Italy.

A major problem in the performance evaluation and dimensioning of these systems is that results are heavily dependent [14] on the model adopted to characterize the behaviour of the users in terms of probability of selecting a particular program. In general, *stationary* models have been adopted, by associating a constant *Viewing Probability* $p_i$ to each program $i$ stored in the server. However, results are strongly affected by the shape of this probability distribution (exponential and piecewise constant distributions have been generally adopted as *realistic*).

These models are biased because none of them accounts for the fundamental fact that each program reduces its popularity at every request (generally a user requires a program at most once, in VOD-like services). Moreover, new programs are periodically introduced, and contribute to reduce the popularity of those already present, by attracting the attention of the customers.

To account for such a non stationarity of the viewing probabilities associated to programs, we have developed a non stationary *token model*, where a number of permissions is associated to each program, and represents an estimate of the number of subscribers that will require it during its life time. In this paper, we show that such a model leads to a viewing probability distribution with exponential shape. The time-varying nature of the viewing probabililities is enclosed in the model by considering that programs are re-indexed according to their insertion time in the video server.

Since a stationary distribution is much easier to use in the developement of analytical models for the performance evaluation of these networks, a further aim of this paper is to quantify the error occurring when the non stationary distribution is approximated with a stationary one. For this purpose, numerical results are presented on a reference network architecture with hierarchical storage previously studied in the literature [9, 14].

The rest of the paper is organized as follows. In Section 2, the stationary models used in the literature are reviewed, and the non stationary model is introduced. In Section 3, the shape of the resulting viewing probability distribution is analytically derived. In Section 4, the reference network architecture is briefly reviewed. Section 5 is dedicated to the numerical results, and in Section 6 conclusions are drawn.



0-8186-7780-5/97 $10.00 © 1997 IEEE

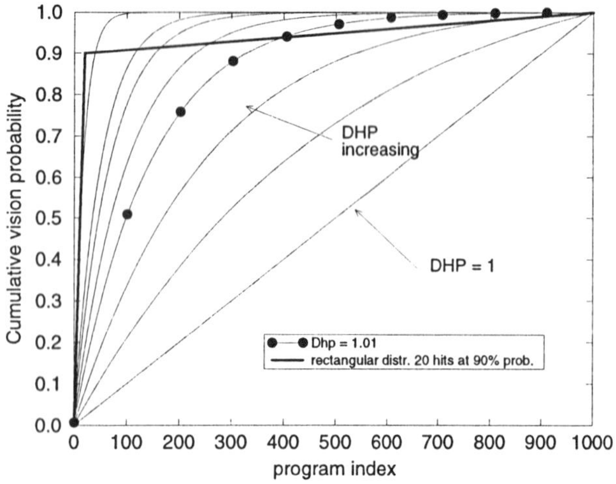


Figure 1: *Cumulative viewing probability for exponential and rectangular user request distributions.*

## 2 User Request Distribution Models

Consider a set of $N$ programs stored in a Video Server, and suppose, for convenience, to index them from 0 to $N-1$. In order to characterize the behaviour of the users accessing to the video server, we need to suitably model the *viewing probability* $p_i$ that a request is addressed to program $i$ ($0 \leq i < N$).

As discussed in the introduction, a common approach is to adopt stationary viewing probability distributions, i.e. to consider the values $p_i$ constant in time. Numerical results have been obtained in the literature (see for example [9, 10, 14, 15]) for two particular distribution cases, which we shall refer to as *Exponential distribution* and *Rectangular distribution*.

In the Exponential distribution case, programs are sorted on the basis of their popularity, and the probability $p_i$ associated to program $i$ ($i \geq 1$) is defined as:

$$p_i = \frac{p_{i-1}}{D_{HP}} \tag{1}$$

Where $D_{HP}$ is a constant greater or equal than 1. In case $D_{HP} = 1$, all the programs have the same viewing probability $1/N$, while, if $D_{HP} > 1$, the viewing probabilities $p_i$ are readily obtained as:

$$p_i = \frac{1 - \left(\frac{1}{D_{HP}}\right)}{1 - \left(\frac{1}{D_{HP}}\right)^N} \left(\frac{1}{D_{HP}}\right)^i \tag{2}$$

The higher the value of $D_{HP}$, the less probable the viewing for the highly ranked programs. Figure 1 shows the cumulative probability distribution with $N = 1000$ programs and several values of the parameter $D_{HP}$.

The Rectangular distribution consists in dividing all the programs in a small number of groups, and assigning to each group a certain overall value of viewing probability. Inside a group, all programs have the same viewing probability. The simplest case is to divide the programs in two sets, a very small set containing the *hit* programs, whose overall value of viewing probability is high, and the remaining low probability set containing all the other programs. An example of rectangular distribution is shown in figure 1, with 20 hit programs, over a total number of 1000, sharing a viewing probability of 90%.

These models are not able to account for two fundamental facts. First, each program reduces its viewing popularity at every request, as a user generally requires a program at most once. Second, the information providers periodically make available new programs, which contribute to reduce the popularity of the already present programs by attracting the attention of the customers. According to the authors' knowledge, the first attempt to define a non stationary model for the viewing probability has been done in [14]. However, the model therein defined was incomplete, and it is substantially improved by the following approach.

Let us define a *token model*, by associating to each program a number of permissions $T_i$, which represent an estimate of the number of subscribers that will view program $i$ during its lifetime. Being $T = \sum_{k=0}^{N-1} T_k$ the total number of tokens in the system, the viewing probability of program $i$ is clearly defined as the ratio $p_i = T_i/T$. Every time program $i$ is requested, $T_i$ (and thus $T$) are decremented.

The model can capture the effect of the insertion of a new program in the set of programs available to the users. In particular, new programs are periodically inserted in the video server with an initial amount $I$ of tokens. The value $I$ can be related to the number $n$ of users in the system by assuming that the new program will be likely viewed by a fraction $\gamma$ of users ($\gamma \leq 1$), i.e. $I = \gamma \cdot n$. The insertion of new programs has also the effect of avoiding that the total number of tokens in the system, $T$, drops to zero. In order to keep constant the total balance $T$ of tokens, a solution is to assume the rate of insertion of new tokens equal to the rate of extraction, i.e. to assume a frequency of insertion of new programs given by $\lambda_{ins} = \lambda/I$, being $\lambda$ the arrival rate of requests. However, in order to leave $\lambda_{ins}$ independent of $\lambda$, in our simulations we have kept the number of tokens $T$ approximately constant by proportionally restoring the number of tokens $T_i$ associated to each program, when the value $T$ was departing from the initial value for more than 5%. Finally, to keep constant the number $N$ of available programs, a newly inserted program replaces the program with the lowest number of remaining tokens.

According to the model outlined above, the viewing probabilities $T_i/T$ associated to each program $i$ are clearly non constant in time. However, if we assume a Poisson insertion of new programs, and we suppose to re-index the programs after each new insertion, assigning index 0 to the newcomer, we will show in the next section that the following approximate expression for $p_i$ holds:

$$p_i = \frac{I}{I+T} e^{-\frac{I}{I+T} i} \tag{3}$$

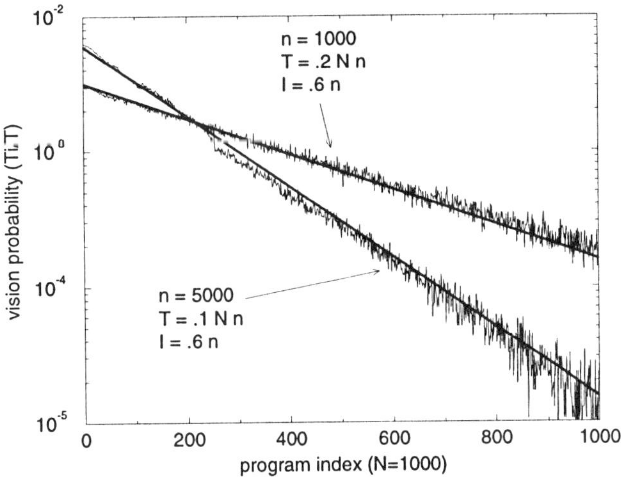


Figure 2: *Non stationary distribution: analysis versus simulation*

to be interpreted as the stationary viewing probability of the i-th most popular program. This is an exponential stationary distribution, where the non stationarity is accounted by the fact that each program has a variable index $i$ during its lifetime.

In conclusion, the non stationary token model is fully defined by the following four parameters:

- the number of users $n$;
- the fraction of users interested in a new program, $\gamma$; in this first study, $\gamma$ has been for simplicity supposed equal for all programs;
- the initial number of tokens in the system, $T$, or, alternatively, the desired shape $D_{HP}$ of the resulting exponential distribution;
- the average insertion rate of a new program, $\lambda_{ins}$.

## 3 An exponential approximation for the non stationary model

Let us concentrate on a *tagged program*, introduced at time $t = 0$ with an initial number of tokens $n(0) = I$. Let $T(t)$ and $n(t)$ be the overall number of tokens in the system and the number of tokens of the tagged program at time $t$, respectively. The time-varying viewing probability of the tagged program, $p(t)$, is defined as $p(t) = n(t)/T(t)$. Let now $\lambda$ be the (Poisson) rate of arrival of requests, and $\lambda_{ins}$ the (Poisson) rate of insertion of new programs. At time $t + dt$, the viewing probability of the tagged program modifies according to one of the following occurrences:

1. with probability $\lambda\ dt\ p(t) + o(dt)$, a request addressed to the tagged program arrives into the system. The new viewing probability of the tagged program becomes $(n(t) - 1)/(T(t) - 1)$, with a decrement equal to:

$$\Delta p_1 = \frac{n(t)}{T(t)} - \frac{n(t)-1}{T(t)-1} = \frac{T(t)-n(t)}{T(t)[T(t)-1]} = \frac{1-p(t)}{T(t)-1}$$

2. with probability $\lambda\ dt\ (1 - p(t)) + o(dt)$, a request arrives for a program different than the tagged one. The viewing probability of the tagged program becomes $n(t)/(T(t) - 1)$, with an increment given by:

$$\Delta p_2 = \frac{n(t)}{T(t)-1} - \frac{n(t)}{T(t)} = \frac{n(t)}{T(t)[T(t)-1]} = \frac{p(t)}{T(t)-1}$$

3. a new program is inserted with probability $\lambda_{ins}\ dt + o(dt)$. Assuming $I$ tokens associated to the new program, the probability of the tagged program decreases of an amount equal to:

$$\Delta p_3 = \frac{n(t)}{T(t)} - \frac{n(t)}{T(t)+I} = \frac{In(t)}{T(t)[T(t)+I]} = \frac{Ip(t)}{T(t)+I}$$

Combining the described events with their probabilities, and neglecting the $o(dt)$ terms, the following equality holds:

$$p(t+dt) = p(t) - \lambda p(t) dt \Delta p_1 + \lambda(1-p(t)) dt \Delta p_2 - \lambda_{ins} dt \Delta p_3 =$$

$$= p(t) - \lambda p(t) dt \frac{1-p(t)}{T(t)-1} + \lambda(1-p(t)) dt \frac{p(t)}{T(t)-1} - \lambda_{ins} dt \frac{Ip(t)}{T(t)+I} =$$

$$= p(t) - \lambda_{ins} \frac{I}{T(t)+I} p(t) dt$$

which leads to the following differential equation:

$$\frac{dp(t)}{dt} = -\lambda_{ins} \frac{I}{T(t)+I} p(t) \qquad (4)$$

that can be easily solved if we suppose that $T = T(t)$ is constant in time, a reasonable approximation if T is large compared to I, and either the condition $\lambda = I\lambda_{ins}$ occurs, or the renormalization of $T$ previously described takes place. Solving equation (4) with the boundary condition $p(0) = I/(I + T)$, we obtain:

$$p(t) = \frac{I}{I+T} e^{-\lambda_{ins} \frac{I}{T+I} t} \qquad (5)$$

From this result we can find the viewing probability of the $i$-th program available. To this purpose, we suppose that programs are indexed on the basis of their introduction order. Therefore, a program indexed with $i$ ($i = 0, \cdots, N-1$) has been introduced in the server in the average at time $t - i/\lambda_{ins}$, where $t$ is the present time instant. Combining this fact with equation (5), the viewing probability of the $i$th indexed program is readily obtained as:

$$p_i = \frac{I}{I+T} e^{-\frac{I}{I+T} i} \qquad (6)$$

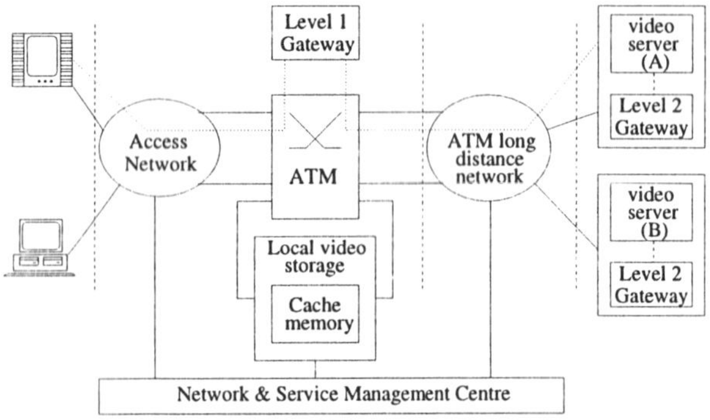


Figure 3: *Architectural model for Interactive Video Services provisioning*

Letting now $\alpha = I/(I+T)$, and imposing that the number of available programs is finite (i.e. $p_i = 0$ for $i \geq N$), we can renormalize expression (6) obtaining

$$p_i = \frac{1-e^{-\alpha}}{1-e^{-\alpha N}} \cdot e^{-\alpha i} \qquad (7)$$

Note that expression (7) is equivalent to the expression given in equation (2) for the exponential stationary user request distribution, with $D_{HP} = e^{\alpha}$.

The result reported in equation (7) has been tested by simulation. In particular, starting from uniform distribution of tokens among the programs, we have computed the "steady state" distribution of programs obtained by re-indexing programs after a new insertion, and running the simulation until convergence to a fixed distribution. Figure 2 reports a comparison between the simulation results and the analytic exponential distribution for two cases. Here, the overall number of programs considered is $N = 1000$, and the total number of tokens, $T$, as well as the number of new tokens per program, $I$, are expressed in terms of the number of programs $N$ and the number of users $n$. Simulations have been stopped after the insertion of $10 \cdot N$ new programs. We see that the error of the exponential approximation is negligible in both considered cases.

## 4 Reference Network Model

Figure 3 depicts a possible architecture capable of supporting Interactive Video Service provisioning. All the video material is stored in a small number of centralized databases, namely the *Video Servers* or *Video Libraries*. To control the video servers and to process the users requests, a *Level 2 Gateway* is associated to each video server, and is in charge of several service operation functionalities (billing, introduction of new video programs, privacy and security).

The video servers are connected to local switching nodes by means of a *Backbone Transport Network*, capable to carry traffic streams up to several Mbit/s, typical of video connections. The Broadband Integrated Services Digital Network (B-ISDN), based on the Asynchronous Transfer Mode (ATM) technique, is the most promising candidate for this role. On the other side, an *Access Network* connects the end-user to the local switching node. Different non mutually exclusive solutions, based on radio, twisted pair, coaxial cable or fiber optic technology have been envisioned (for a detailed overview, refer to [1, 8]).

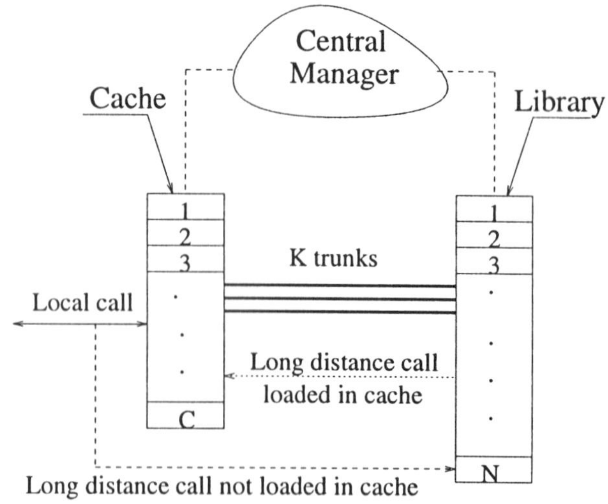


Figure 4: *simplified support model*

Local switching nodes are in charge to connect users with the requested programs. Those nodes implement several functionalities, among which a a primary role is assumed by the *Level 1 Gateway*, in charge to process each user request, and to localize and provide a connection with the video server containing the selected program. The local switching nodes can be equipped with a small video database (hereafter referred to with the name *Cache Memory*), containing a certain number of highly requested programs.

The performance evaluation and dimensioning of the capacity of the local storage has been first studied in [9], by assuming that the set of programs with higher viewing probability was stored in the cache memory. When the viewing probability of programs is not known a priori, or in the case of non stationary viewing probabilities, in which these values are varying in time, it is necessary to provide a suitable *cache management policy* in charge to decide whether a new program must be stored in the cache.

Different policies have been studied in [14]. In order to obtain numerical results, the simplified network model given in figure 4 has been considered, and it will be considered also in this paper. Here, one cache memory is connected to a single library. Each memory is composed of $C$ ($C << N$) locations, each containing one program. When a user selects a program, the service manager is in charge of determining whether the program is present in the cache or it is only stored in the library. In the former case, a local connection between the user and the local switching node is set up, while in the latter the network sets up a long distance connection between the library and the user.

In this process, there is the possibility that a program being downloaded from the library is recognized as a "popular" program, i.e. the service manager recognizes that there is a high probability of another user overlapping the former user view of the program. In this case, it allocates space in the cache, at the expense of programs previously loaded and presently unused, and it signals the library to download the program into the cache. A local independent connection between the cache and the user is also set up, so that the user is able to see the program, unaware that it is simultaneously downloaded in the cache.

It has been shown in [14] that a well performing policy, in terms of probability that a request is found in the cache (*cache hit probability*), is the one referred to as Conditional Overwrite (CO) Policy. This policy is based on an estimation of the viewing probability of the program to load. When a user requests a program not stored in the cache, the service manager compares the estimation of the viewing probability of the current program with the ones of the programs already stored in the cache, and currently inactive. If the viewing probability estimate of the new program is greater that the program with the worst estimate among those inactive in the cache, a replacement occurs.

A simple, but effective method to provide these estimates is to count the number of requests for the considered programs in a given sliding window time. Of course, the window size strongly affects these estimates: the wider is the window, the better is the estimate of the viewing probability of the program, assuming it is stationary, but the reaction time to the variations of this probability (in the non stationary case) will increase. On the contrary, if the sliding window is too narrow, the estimate of the viewing probability will follow time variations due to non stationarity, but only rough estimates will be obtained. More complex techniques to provide these estimates, for example autoregressive models, are out of the scopes of the present paper.

## 5 Numerical Results

The result reported in equation (7) is particularly important since it shows that the process of insertion of new programs leads to an exponential shape of the user request distribution. However, this does not mean that the system performance results are equivalent to those obtained with a stationary exponential request distribution, because the stationary model cannot account for the side effects on the performance of some systems (such as the reference network model outlined in the previous section) caused by the insertion of new programs and the variation in the programs popularity.

To provide the comparison between stationary and non stationary viewing probability distribution models, we have used the reference network model described above. The main performance index is the cache hit probability, i.e. the probability that a program is found in the cache. In the simulations, we have assumed $N = 1000$ programs stored in the video server, and each program has been modeled as a 9 Gbit movie, transmitted at a speed equal to 1.5 Mbit/s, which results in a fixed program length of 100 minutes. We have assumed that requests for programs arrive according to a stationary Poisson process of rate $\lambda$ arrivals/min. For convenience, time has been also measured in consecutive "days" of 8 hours each.

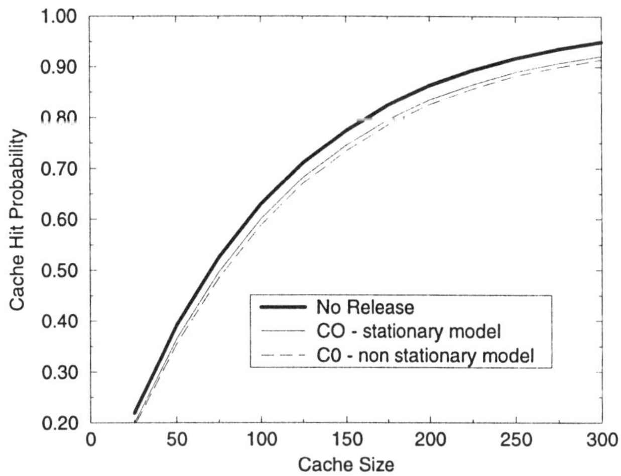


Figure 5: *Cache hit probability versus cache size*

Figure 5 shows the cache hit probability versus the cache size, considering an offered load of 50 Erlangs, and a (stationary and non stationary) user request distribution with $D_{HP} = 1.01$. For the CO policy, a sliding window size of 7 days has been assumed. For the non stationary case, we have considered 5000 users, with $\gamma = 1$ (i.e. I=5000), and a 3 days average insertion time for new programs. The process of insertion of new programs has been modeled as a Poisson process. With the label *No Release*, we have reported the results obtained storing in the cache the programs with higher viewing probability, supposed to be stationary and known a priori. These results can be considered as the upper bound for any management policy.

As the figure shows, the performance of the CO policy in the stationary case is not far from the optimal

| cache | stat. 50 erl | non stat. 50 erl | stat. 100 erl | non stat. 100 erl |
|---|---|---|---|---|
| 25 | 0.1997 | 0.1941 | 0.2075 | 0.2018 |
| 50 | 0.3647 | 0.3548 | 0.3770 | 0.3671 |
| 75 | 0.4967 | 0.4848 | 0.5105 | 0.4993 |
| 100 | 0.6012 | 0.5885 | 0.6151 | 0.6036 |
| 125 | 0.6820 | 0.6705 | 0.6966 | 0.6865 |
| 150 | 0.7460 | 0.7350 | 0.7600 | 0.7511 |
| 175 | 0.7957 | 0.7857 | 0.8096 | 0.8015 |
| 200 | 0.8345 | 0.8255 | 0.8483 | 0.8413 |
| 225 | 0.8644 | 0.8561 | 0.8788 | 0.8722 |
| 250 | 0.8896 | 0.8819 | 0.9024 | 0.8967 |
| 275 | 0.9072 | 0.8993 | 0.9208 | 0.9160 |
| 300 | 0.9215 | 0.9140 | 0.9351 | 0.9307 |

Table 1: *CO policy: comparison of the cache hit probability between stationary and not stationary models*

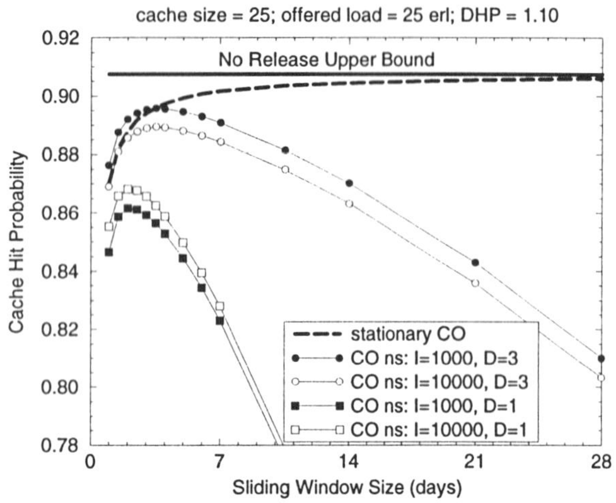


Figure 6: *Cache Hit probability versus sliding window size, for stationary and non stationary User Request Distribution*

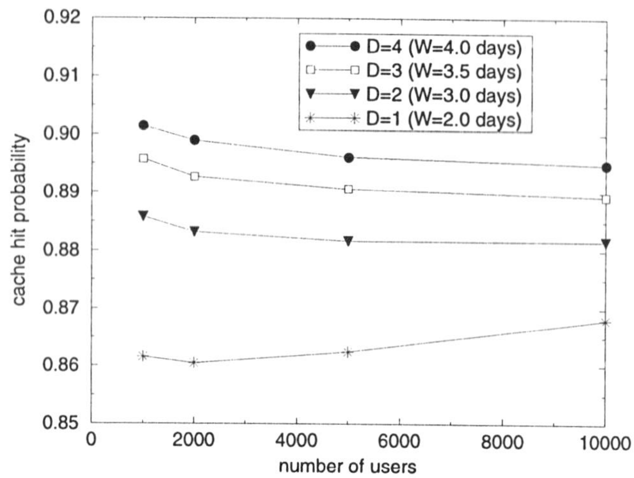


Figure 7: *Cache Hit probability versus population, for non stationary User Request Distribution*

one provided by the No Release policy. The offered load slightly affects the performance: in particular, simulations performed with a 100 Erlangs offered load (one case is reported in table 1) show that in this case the performance is slightly better, since the viewing probability estimate (the number of requests in the sliding window) is about double that of the 50 Erlangs case. However, the most interesting conclusion we can draw from figure 5 and table 1 is that the non stationary model affects the system performance in a negligible manner. A closer look to the numerical results (see table 1) shows that the difference in terms of cache hit probability between the stationary and non stationary cases is never greater than 2%. This unexpected similarity of results can be justified considering that the insertion of a new program has little effect on the viewing probability of the other programs, because either the $D_{HP}$ value of the exponential shape is very low (1.01 in the considered case), and the frequency of insertion of new programs is low. As shown below, we will find greater differences when the $D_{HP}$ coefficient is greater, which means that a new program captures the attention of more users on itself, and the frequency of insertion of new programs is higher.

Figure 6, obtained with a $D_{HP} = 1.1$ value and an offered load of 25 Erlangs, shows the effect of the sliding window size on the cache hit probability, for a cache size equal to 25. The two upper curves report the cache hit probability for the stationary case, in the case of No Release and Conditional Overwrite policies. The other curves report the results obtained with a non stationary user request distribution and the CO policy. Two different average insertion times of new programs have been simulated, namely, $D = 1$ and $D = 3$ days, as well as two different populations (1000 and 10000 users). $\gamma$ has been chosen equal to 1.

As expected, figure 6 shows that, in the stationary case, the cache hit probability for the CO policy increases as the window size increases, since the effectiveness of the estimation increases with the sliding window size. Clearly, this is no more true for the non stationary case, as with a long sliding window the effect of the non stationarity of the viewing probability of programs prevails. On the countrary, a short sliding window captures the slow variations of the programs popularity, but at the expense of a rough estimate. Note that a reasonable value for the sliding window size is in the range from 1 to 3 times the average interarrival time ($D$) of new inserted programs.

The same figure shows that a major difference between stationary and non stationary models occurs when the rate of insertion of new programs is high. In the case of $D = 1$ day, regardless of the sliding window size, the maximum performance achieved in the non stationary case is well below the corresponding performance for the stationary case. This difference significantly reduces as the value of $D$ increases.

An interesting comparison takes place between results reported in table 2 and the ones reported in table 1. As in the latter case, table 2 has been obtained with a sliding window of 7 days, and an interarrival time between new programs of 3 days. However, here the value of $D_{HP}$ has been assumed equal to 1.1, with a fixed cache size (25). Unfortunately, a direct comparison between the two tables is meaningless, since the cache sizes to provide the same value of hit probability are completely different. However, we note that,

| offered load [Erl] | population | | | | |
|---|---|---|---|---|---|
| | 1000 | 2000 | 5000 | 10000 | stat. |
| 25 | 0.8907 | 0.8880 | 0.8856 | 0.8842 | 0.9017 |
| 50 | 0.8973 | 0.8954 | 0.8926 | 0.8911 | 0.9044 |
| 100 | 0.8984 | 0.8996 | 0.8976 | 0.8964 | 0.9059 |

Table 2: *Cache hit probability for different population and offered load*

in table 2, the differences between stationary and non stationary cases are slightly greater than the differences noted in table 1. This fact is mainly due to the increase of the $D_{HP}$ value. In any case, results obtained for the stationary case may be still considered a very good approximation of the non stationary ones.

Finally, the effect of the population slightly affects the system performance. Figure 7 reports the maximum value of the cache hit probability for different values $D$ of the interarrival time between programs. The window size $W$, used to maximize these values is reported in the figure. Results have been obtained with a $D_{HP} = 1.1$ value, an offered load of 25 Erlangs, $\gamma = 1$, and a cache size equal to 25. Strangely, in the case of short interarrival time of new programs, performance are better as the population increases, while the converse is true in the more realistic case of large $D$. However, in all cases, the difference due to the population is practically negligible.

## 6 Conclusions

In this paper we have detailed a non stationary token model for the viewing probability of programs in a Video on Demand Network. The necessity of such a model has been pointed out by noting that, in a wide class of interactive video services, the assumption that the user requires a program with a probability constant in time definitely does not match reality.

Moreover, we have demonstrated that the proposed token models leads to an exponential shape of the viewing probability of programs. The parameters of the resulting exponential distribution are directly related with practical system parameters, such as the number of users in the system and the probability that a user is interested to a program freshly inserted in the system.

Finally, a further scope of this paper was to quantify the error occurring when the non stationary model is approximated with the stationary one. Our results clearly show that the differences between the two models in terms of performance on the considered reference network scenario are generally negligible, even in the case of very popular new inserted programs (i.e. high value of the coefficient $D_{HP}$). Significant differences have been found only in the (unrealistic) case of very high frequency of insertion of new programs.

## References


[1] P. D. Lattner, R. L. Fike, G. A. Nelson: "Business and Residential Services for the evolving Subscriber Loop". *IEEE Communications Magazine*, March 1991, pp. 109-114.

[2] J. Sutherland, L. Litteral: "Residential Video Services". *IEEE Communications Magazine*, July 1992, pp. 36-41.

[3] H. J. Kafka, L. K. Steffes, "Interactive Video and Multimedia Servers in Public Networks", *Proceedings of ISS'95*, Berlin, Germany, April 1995, Vol. 2, pp. 271-275.

[4] W. D. Sincoskie, "System Architecture for a Large Scale Video On Demand Service", *Computer Networks and ISDN Systems*, 1991, vol. 22, pp. 155-162.

[5] A. Gelman, L. S. Smoot, "An Architecture for Interactive Application", *Proceedings of IEEE ICC'93*, Geneva, Switzerland, May 1993, pp. 848-852.

[6] D. Deloddere, W. Verbiest, H. Verhille, "Interactive Video On Demand", *IEEE Communications Magazine*, May 1994, pp. 82-88.

[7] G. H. Petit, D. Deloddere, "A Video-On-Demand Network Architecture Optimizing Bandwidth and Buffer Storage Resources", *Proceedings of ISS'95*, Berlin, Germany, April 1995, Vol. 1, pp. 319-323.

[8] Yee-Hsiang, D. Coggins, D. Pitt, D. Skellern, M. Thapar, C. Venkatraman: "An Open-System Approach to Video On Demand", *IEEE Communication Magazine*, May 1994, pp. 68-80.

[9] L. De Giovanni, A. M. Langellotti, L. M. Patitucci, L. Petrini: "Dimensioning of Hierarchical Storage for Video On Demand Services", *Proceedings of IEEE ICC'94*, New Orleans, June 1994, pp. 1739-1743.

[10] H. Ghafir, H. Chadwick: "Multimedia Servers: Design and Performance", *Proceedings of IEEE ICC'94*, New Orleans, June 1994, pp. 886-890.

[11] P. N. Mouchtaris, "Traffic Analysis for a Custom Video Architecture", *IEEE J. Sel. Areas in Communications*, Vol. 10, No. 9, December 1992.

[12] R. Ramarao, V. Ramamoorthy: "An Architectural Design of On-Demand Video Delivery Systems: the Spatio-Temporal Storage Allocation Problem", *Proceedings of IEEE ICC'91*, pp. 506-510.

[13] A. Gelman, S. Halfin: "Analysis of Resource Sharing in Information Providing Services", *Proceedings of IEEE GLOBECOM '90*, pp. 312-316.

[14] G. Bianchi, R. Melen, "Performance and Dimensioning of a Hierarchical Video Storage Network for Interactive Video Services", *European Transactions on Telecommunications*, Vol. 7, No. 4, July-August 1996, pp. 349-358.

[15] G. Bianchi, R. Melen, "Traffic Management for Interactive Video Services on ATM Networks", *Proceedings of ITC '96*, Istambul, April 1996, pp. 237-244.

# Secret Sharing in Graph-Based Prohibited Structures

Hung-Min Sun
Department of Information Management
Chaoyang Institute of Technology
Wufeng, Taichung County, Taiwan 413
Email: hmsun@dscs2.csie.nctu.edu.tw

Shiuh-Pyng Shieh
Department of Computer Science
and Information Engineering
National Chiao Tung University
Hsinchu, Taiwan 30050
Email: ssp@csie.nctu.edu.tw

**Abstract**

*A secret sharing scheme for the prohibited structure is a method of sharing a master key among a finite set of participants in such a way that only certain pre-specified subsets of participants cannot recover the master key. A secret sharing scheme is called perfect if any subset of participants who cannot recover the master key obtains no information regarding the master key. In this paper, we propose an efficient construction of perfect secret sharing schemes for graph-based prohibited structures where a vertex denotes a participant and an edge does a pair of participants who cannot recover the master key. The information rate of our scheme is 2/n, where n is the number of participants.*

## 1: Introduction

In 1987, Ito et al. [1] described a general method of secret sharing called *secret sharing scheme* (SSS) which allows a master key to be shared among a finite set of participants in such a way that only certain pre-specified subsets of participants can recover the master key. Let $\boldsymbol{P}$ be the set of participants. The collection of subsets of participants that can reconstruct the master key in this way is called *access structure* (denoted by $\Gamma$). The collection of subsets of participants that cannot reconstruct the master key is called *prohibited structure* (denoted by $\Delta$) [2]. The natural restriction is that $\Gamma$ is monotone increasing and $\Delta$ is monotone decreasing, that is,

if $\boldsymbol{A} \in \Gamma$ and $\boldsymbol{A} \subseteq \boldsymbol{B} \subseteq \boldsymbol{P}$, then $\boldsymbol{B} \in \Gamma$, and

if $\boldsymbol{A} \in \Delta$ and $\boldsymbol{B} \subseteq \boldsymbol{A} \subseteq \boldsymbol{P}$, then $\boldsymbol{B} \in \Delta$.

If $\Delta = 2^P \setminus \Gamma$, then we say the structure $(\Gamma, \Delta)$ is *complete* [2]. In the special case where $\Gamma = \{ A \mid A \subseteq P \text{ and } |A| \geq m \}$ and $\Delta = \{ A \mid A \subseteq P \text{ and } |A| \leq m\text{-}1 \}$, the secret sharing scheme is called an $(m, n)$-threshold scheme [3,4], where $|P| = n$. Let $\mathbf{K}$ be the master key space and $\mathbf{S}$ be the share space. The information rate of the secret sharing scheme is defined as $\log_2 |\mathbf{K}| / \log_2 |\mathbf{S}|$ [5]. A secret sharing scheme is *perfect* if any set of participants in the prohibited structure $\Delta$ obtains no information regarding the master key [6-9]. Secret sharing schemes are classified into the following types:

**Type I**: A secret sharing scheme for the *access structure* $\Gamma$ is a method of sharing a master key among a finite set of participants in such a way that only subsets of participants in $\Gamma$ can recover the master key while other subsets cannot. That is, $\Delta$ $(= 2^P \setminus \Gamma)$ is implied.

**Type II**: A secret sharing scheme for the *prohibited structure* $\Delta$ is a method of sharing a master key among a finite set of participants in such a way that only subsets of participants in $\Delta$ cannot recover the master key while other subsets can. That is, $\Gamma$ $(= 2^P \setminus \Delta)$ is implied.

**Type III**: A secret sharing scheme for the *mixed structure* $(\Gamma, \Delta)$ is a method of sharing a master key among a finite set of participants in such a way that subsets of participants in $\Gamma$ can recover the master key but subsets of participants in $\Delta$ cannot recover the master key. That is, the privileges of subsets in $2^P \setminus (\Gamma \cup \Delta)$ are not cared. Any subset of participants in $2^P \setminus (\Gamma \cup \Delta)$ may either recover the master key or not. Note that here $\Gamma \cap \Delta = \emptyset$, and $\Gamma \cup \Delta \subseteq 2^P$.

This research was supported by the National Science Council, Taiwan under grant number NSC-85-2213-E-009-032 and NSC-86-2213-E-324-002.



0-8186-7780-5/97 $10.00 © 1997 IEEE

Given any access structure $\Gamma$, Ito et al. [1,8] showed that there exists a perfect secret sharing scheme to realize the structure. Benaloh and Leichter [10] proposed a different algorithm to realize secret sharing schemes for any given monotone access structure. In both constructions, the information rate decreases exponentially as a function of $n$, the number of participants.

There are several performance and efficiency measures proposed for analyzing secret sharing schemes [5,11-14]. Their goal is to maximize the information rate of a secret sharing scheme. Brickell and Stinson [5] studied a perfect secret sharing scheme for graph-based *access structure* $\Gamma$ where the monotone-increasing access structure $\Gamma$ contains the pairs of participants corresponding to edges (the prohibited structure is implied to be the collection of subsets of participants corresponding to any independent set of the graph). They proved that, for any graph $G$ with $n$ vertices having maximum degree $d$, there exists a perfect secret sharing scheme for the access structure based on $G$ in which the information rate is at least $2/(d+3)$. Stinson [14] improved the general result that there exists a perfect secret sharing scheme realizing access structure based on $G$ in which the information rate is at least $2/(d+1)$. After that, van Dijk [12] showed that Stinson's lower bound is tight because he proved that there exists graphs having maximum degree $d$ such that the optimal information rate is at most $2/(d+1-\varepsilon)$ for all $d \geq 3$ and $\varepsilon > 0$. Secret sharing schemes for *mixed structures* $(\Gamma, \Delta)$ proposed by Shieh and Sun in 1994 [15] were based on the graph where $\Gamma$ contains the pairs of participants corresponding to edges and $\Delta$ contains the pairs of participants corresponding to non-edges. The information rate of their scheme is $1/(2n)$, where $n$ is the number of participants. In 1996, Sun and Shieh [16] improved the information rate of the secret sharing scheme to be $1/(n-1)$. They also presented an application of the secret sharing scheme for a graph-based structure to reduce storage and computation load on the key distribution server in a secure network [16].

In this paper, we study the perfect secret sharing scheme for a *prohibited structure* based on the graph where the monotone-decreasing prohibited structure $\Delta$ contains all participants and the pairs of participants corresponding to edges (the access structure is implied to be the union of $\{A \mid A \subseteq P$ and $|A| \geq 3\}$ and the pairs of participants corresponding to non-edges of the graph). We propose an efficient perfect secret sharing scheme for the graph-based prohibited structure. The information rate of our scheme is $2/n$, where $n$ is the number of participants. Our scheme can be also applied to the reduction of storage and computation loads on the key distribution server in a secure network and can obtain better efficiency than the scheme proposed in [16].

This paper is organized as follows. In section 2, we give some preliminaries which will be used later on to construct the perfect secret sharing schemes for graph-based prohibited structures. In section 3, we propose a construction of perfect secret sharing schemes for graph-based prohibited structures. An example of perfect secret sharing scheme for the graph-based prohibited structure is demonstrated in section 4. Finally, we conclude the paper in section 5.

## 2: Preliminaries

### 2.1: Perfect $(m, n)$ Threshold Schemes

The $(m, n)$ threshold schemes were introduced by Blakley and Shamir in 1979 [3,4]. The main idea underlying an $(m, n)$ threshold scheme is to divide the master key $K$ into $n$ shares $S_i$'s corresponding to $n$ participants ($1 \leq i \leq n$) in such a way that the master key $K$ cannot be reclaimed unless $m$ shares are collected. Apparently, the $(m, n)$ threshold scheme is the special case of secret sharing schemes when the qualified subsets of participants are all subsets whose order are larger than or equal to $m$ and the non-qualified subsets of participants are all subsets whose order are less than or equal to $m$-1.

A secret sharing scheme is *perfect* if any unqualified subset of participants provide no information about the shared secret $K$ [6,8]. It means that the prior probability $p(K = K_0)$ equals the conditional probability $p(K = K_0 \mid$ given any or less secret shares of an unqualified set). By using the entropy function $H$ from [6,7,9], we can state the requirements for an $(m, n)$ threshold scheme as follows:

(1) $H(K \mid S_{i_1}, \ldots, S_{i_m}) = 0$

(2) $H(K \mid S_{i_1}, \ldots, S_{i_{m-1}}) = H(K)$

for an arbitrary set of $m$ indices $\{i_1, \ldots, i_m\}$ from $\{1, \ldots, n\}$.

As an example, we review the $(m, n)$ threshold scheme proposed by Shamir [4] as follows.

We assume that the master key $K$ is taken randomly from GF($q$). Therefore, $H(K) = \log q$.

Let $f(x) = a_{m-1} x^{m-1} + \ldots + a_1 x + K \pmod q$ be a polynomial of degree $m$-1 over the finite field GF($q$). The $n$ shares $S_i$'s are computed from $f(x)$ as follows, $S_i = f(i) \pmod q$, $i = 1, \ldots, n$.

Obviously, given any $m$ secret shares $S_{i_1},\ldots,S_{i_m}$, $\{i_1,\ldots,i_m\} \subset \{1, \ldots, n\}$, $f(x)$ can be reconstructed from the Lagrange interpolating polynomial as follows [6],

$$f(x)=\sum_{k=1}^{m}(S_{i_k}\cdot\prod_{j=1,j\neq k}^{m}\frac{(x-i_j)}{(i_k-i_j)}) \quad (\text{mod } q).$$

Thus, the master key $K$ can be obtained by $f(0)$. On the other hand, given any $m$-1 secret shares $S_{i_1},\ldots,S_{i_{m-1}}$, $\{i_1,\ldots,i_{m-1}\} \subset \{1, \ldots, n\}$, $f(0)$ can be written as follows.

$$f(0)=a+S_{i_m}\cdot b \quad (\text{mod } q), \text{ where}$$

$$a=\sum_{k=1}^{m-1}(S_{i_k}\cdot\prod_{j=1,j\neq k}^{m}\frac{(0-i_j)}{(i_k-i_j)}) \text{ and } b=\prod_{j=1}^{m-1}\frac{(0-i_j)}{(i_m-i_j)}.$$

Because $S_{i_m}$ is uniformly distributed over GF($q$), $H(K|\ S_{i_1},\ \ldots,\ S_{i_{m-1}}) = H(f(0)|\ S_{i_1},\ \ldots,\ S_{i_{m-1}}) = H(a+S_{i_m}\cdot b) = H(S_{i_m}) = \log q = H(K)$. Therefore, the ($m$, $n$) threshold scheme is perfect.

## 2.2: Perfect Secret Sharing Schemes for Mixed Structures ($\Gamma$, $\Delta$)

In the section, we give a construction of perfect secret sharing schemes for mixed structures ($\Gamma$, $\Delta$), where $\Gamma = \{P\}$ and $\Delta = \{A \mid A \subseteq P \text{ and } |A| \leq |P|-2\}$. The secret sharing scheme will be used later on to construct the perfect secret sharing schemes for graph-based prohibited structures.

We assume that the master key $K = (K_1, K_2)$ is taken randomly from GF($q$)×GF($q$). It is clear that $H(K)= 2\log q$.

Let $f(x)=a_{n-1}x^{n-1}+\cdots+a_2x^2+K_1x+K_2 \pmod q$ be a polynomial of degree $n$-1 over the finite field GF($q$). The $n$ shares $S_i$'s are computed from $f(x)$ as follows, $S_i = f(i) \pmod q$, $i$ = 1, ..., $n$.

Obviously, given $n$ secret shares $S_i$, $i$ = 1, ..., $n$, $f(x)$ can be reconstructed from the Lagrange interpolating polynomial as follows [6],

$$f(x)=\sum_{k=1}^{n}(S_k\cdot\prod_{j=1,j\neq k}^{n}\frac{(x-j)}{(k-j)}) \quad (\text{mod } q).$$

Thus, the master key $K$ can be obtained from $f(x)$. On the other hand, given any $n$-2 secret shares $S_{i_1},\ldots,S_{i_{n-2}}$, $\{i_1,\ldots,i_{n-2}\} \subset \{1, \ldots, n\}$, we can get the following relations:

$$\begin{bmatrix} i_1^{n-1} & \cdot & \cdot & i_1 & 1 \\ \cdot & \cdot & \cdot & \cdot & \cdot \\ \cdot & \cdot & \cdot & \cdot & \cdot \\ i_{n-4}^{n-1} & \cdot & \cdot & i_{n-4} & 1 \\ i_{n-3}^{n-1} & \cdot & \cdot & i_{n-3} & 1 \\ i_{n-2}^{n-1} & \cdot & \cdot & i_{n-2} & 1 \end{bmatrix} \begin{bmatrix} a_{n-1} \\ \cdot \\ \cdot \\ a_2 \\ K_1 \\ K_2 \end{bmatrix} = \begin{bmatrix} S_{i_1} \\ \cdot \\ \cdot \\ S_{i_{n-4}} \\ S_{i_{n-3}} \\ S_{i_{n-2}} \end{bmatrix} \quad (\text{mod } q).$$

Because there are $n$ unknown variables, $a_{n-1}, \cdots, a_2, K_1, K_2$, among these $n$-2 equations, it is clear that the total number of possible solutions for $K = (K_1, K_2)$ is $q^2$. Note that once the secret $(K_1, K_2)$ is chosen, the system has a unique solution over the field GF($q$). Hence, $H(K|S_{i_1},\ldots,S_{i_{n-2}}) = H(K_1, K_2|S_{i_1},\ldots,S_{i_{n-2}}) = 2\log q = H(K)$. Therefore, the secret sharing scheme for the mixed structure ($\Gamma$, $\Delta$) is perfect.

## 3: Construction of Perfect SSS for Prohibited Structures Based on Graphs

Let $\boldsymbol{P}$ be the set of participants, and $G$ be a graph where a vertex denotes a participant in $\boldsymbol{P}$ and an edge does a pair of participants. In a *perfect* secret sharing scheme for the prohibited structure based on $G$, a pair of participants corresponding to an edge of $G$ cannot obtain any information regarding the master key. In addition, we also assume that each participant corresponding to a vertex of $G$ cannot obtain any information regarding the master key. This is because that if one participant is allowed to recover the master key by himself, we can assign the master key as his share and remove him from the graph $G$. The graph we consider here may include disconnected graphs and isolated vertices. A participant corresponding to an isolated vertex can be interpreted as that he can recover the master key in cooperation with any participant in the graph except himself. We use $E(G)$ to denote the set of edges of $G$; $E(\overline{G})$ to denote the set of edges of $\overline{G}$, where $\overline{G}$ is the complement of $G$; $\boldsymbol{S}$ to denote the set of pairs of participants corresponding to edges in $E(G)$; $\boldsymbol{R}$ to denote the set of pairs of participants corresponding to edges in $E(\overline{G})$. It is reasonable to restrict that the prohibited structure and the access structure are monotone. Thus, given a graph $G$, the prohibited structure is denoted by $\Delta = \{A \mid A \subseteq \boldsymbol{P} \text{ and } |A| = 1\} \cup \{A \mid A \in \boldsymbol{S}\}$, and then the access structure is decided by $2^{P} \setminus \Delta = \{A \mid A \subseteq \boldsymbol{P} \text{ and } |A| \geq 3\} \cup \{A \mid A \in \boldsymbol{R}\}$.

In the following, we will use the conventional threshold schemes [3,4] to construct the perfect secret sharing schemes for graph-based prohibited structures.

We assume that all computations are over GF($q$) where $q$ is a prime.

Given a graph $G$ for the prohibited structure, a perfect secret sharing scheme is constructed as follows. Assume that $P = \{ p_1, p_2, \cdots, p_n \}$ is the set of participants corresponding to the vertices of the graph $G$. We first construct $n$+1 conventional (2, $n$)-threshold schemes [3,4], named $TS_1$, $TS_2$, ⋯, and $TS_{n+1}$. To avoid ambiguity, we call the master key and the shares of each $TS_i$ sub-master key and sub-shares, respectively. For each (2, $n$)-$TS_i$, let $Sk_i$ be its sub-master key and $s_{i,1}, s_{i,2}, \cdots, s_{i,n}$ be its $n$ sub-shares. Thus, given any two sub-shares, $s_{i,j}$ and $s_{i,k}$ ($1 \le j < k \le n$), the sub-master key $Sk_i$ can be recovered, but less than two sub-shares provide no information about $Sk_i$.

The master key of the secret sharing scheme for the prohibited structure based on the graph $G$ is given by $K = (K_1, K_2)$, which is protected by these sub-master keys $Sk_1$, $Sk_2$, ⋯, $Sk_n$, $Sk_{n+1}$ in such a way that all $n$+1 sub-master keys $Sk_1$, $Sk_2$, ⋯, $Sk_n$, $Sk_{n+1}$ collected together, the master key $K$ can be recovered, but any $n$-1 or less sub-master keys provide no information regarding the master key. It is easy to construct such protection mechanism following the method proposed in section 2.2.

The share of participant $p_i$ is given by

$S_i = < a_{i,1}, \cdots, a_{i,t}, \cdots, a_{i,n}, a_{i,n+1} >$,

where $1 \le t \le n+1$,

$a_{i,t}$ is empty if $t = i$,

$a_{i,t} = s_{t,i}$ if $t = n+1$ and $p_t$ is an isolated vertex,

$a_{i,t} = Sk_t$ if $t = n+1$ and $p_t$ is not an isolated vertex,

$a_{i,t} = s_{t,i}$ if $t \ne i$, $t \ne n+1$, and $\overline{p_i p_t}$ is an edge of $G$,

$a_{i,t} = Sk_t$ if $t \ne i$, $t \ne n+1$, and $\overline{p_i p_t}$ is not an edge of $G$.

Thus, the constructed secret sharing scheme satisfies:

(1) if $A \in S$, $A$ obtains no information regarding the master key,

(2) if $A \subseteq P$ and $|A| = 1$, $A$ obtains no information regarding the master key,

(3) if $A \in R$, $A$ can recover the master key,

(4) if $A \subseteq P$ and $|A| \ge 3$, $A$ can recover the master key.

THEOREM 1. If $A \in S$, $A$ obtains no information regarding the master key of the constructed secret sharing scheme for the prohibited structure based on the graph $G$.

PROOF. We assume that $A = \{ p_i, p_j \}$, where $i \ne j$. The share of $p_i$ is $S_i = < a_{i,1}, a_{i,2}, \cdots, a_{i,n+1} >$ and the share of $p_j$ is $S_j = < a_{j,1}, a_{j,2}, \cdots, a_{j,n+1} >$. Because $A \in S$, $\overline{p_i p_j}$ is an edge of $G$. We conclude that for any $t$, $1 \le t \le n+1$, one of the following four cases holds.

(1) $a_{i,t} = Sk_t$ and $a_{j,t} = Sk_t$ if $t = n+1$,

(2) $a_{i,t}$ = empty and $a_{j,t} = s_{t,j}$ if $t = i$,

(3) $a_{i,t} = s_{t,i}$ and $a_{j,t}$ = empty if $t = j$,

(4) $a_{i,t} = s_{t,i}$ or $Sk_t$, and $a_{j,t} = s_{t,j}$ or $Sk_t$ if $t \ne n+1$, $t \ne i$, and $t \ne j$.

In case (1) and (4), the sub-master key $Sk_t$ can be recovered. In case (2), $a_{i,i}$ and $a_{j,i}$ can obtain only one sub-share $s_{i,j}$ of the (2, $n$)-$TS_i$. Therefore, $p_i$ and $p_j$ get no information about the sub-master key $Sk_i$. In case (3), $a_{i,j}$ and $a_{j,j}$ can obtain only one sub-share $s_{j,i}$ of the (2, $n$)-$TS_j$. Therefore, $p_i$ and $p_j$ get no information about the sub-master key $Sk_j$. Hence, $p_i$ and $p_j$ can obtain only $n$-1 sub-master keys which provide no information regarding the master key $K$.

**(Q.E.D.)**

THEOREM 2. If $A \subseteq P$ and $|A| = 1$, $A$ obtains no information regarding the master key of the constructed secret sharing scheme for the prohibited structure based on the graph $G$.

PROOF. This means the case that each participant obtains no information regarding the master key. We assume that $A = \{ p_i \}$ and the share of $p_i$ is $S_i = < a_{i,1}, a_{i,2}, \cdots, a_{i,n+1} >$. If $p_i$ is not an isolated vertex, then there exists a vertex $p_j$ such that $\overline{p_i p_j}$ is an edge of $G$. From Theorem 1, we know that $\{ p_i, p_j \}$ obtains no information regarding the master key. Therefore, $A = \{ p_i \}$ obtains no information regarding the master key. If $p_i$ is not an isolated vertex, we conclude that for any $t$, $1 \le t \le n+1$, one of the following three cases holds.

(1) $a_{i,t} = s_{t,i}$ if $t = n+1$,

(2) $a_{i,t}$ = empty if $t = i$,

(3) $a_{i,t} = Sk_t$ if $t \ne n+1$, $t \ne i$.

In case (1) and case (2), $p_i$ gets no information about the sub-master key $Sk_{n+1}$ and $Sk_i$. Hence, $p_i$ can obtain only $n$-1 sub-master keys which provide no information regarding the master key $K$. **(Q.E.D.)**

THEOREM 3. If $A \in \boldsymbol{R}$, $A$ can recover the master key of the constructed secret sharing scheme for the prohibited structure based on the graph $G$.

PROOF. We assume that $A = \{ p_i , p_j \}$, where $i \neq j$. The share of $p_i$ is $S_i = < a_{i,1}, a_{i,2}, \cdots, a_{i,n+1} >$ and the share of $p_j$ is $S_j = < a_{j,1}, a_{j,2}, \cdots, a_{j,n+1} >$. Because $A \in \boldsymbol{R}$, $\overline{p_i p_j}$ is a non-edge of $G$. We conclude that for any $t$, $1 \leq t \leq n+1$, one of the following three cases holds.

(1) $a_{i,t}$ = empty and $a_{j,t} = Sk_t$ if $t = i$,

(2) $a_{i,t} = Sk_t$ and $a_{j,t}$ = empty if $t = j$,

(3) $a_{i,t} = s_{t,i}$ or $Sk_t$, and $a_{j,t} = s_{t,j}$ or $Sk_t$ if $t \neq i$, and $t \neq j$.

In all these cases (1),(2), and (3), the sub-master key $k_t$ can be recovered. Thus, participant $p_i$ and participant $p_j$ can recover all $n$+1 sub-master keys $Sk_1, Sk_2, \cdots, Sk_{n+1}$ and hence the master key $K$. **(Q.E.D.)**

THEOREM 4. If $A \subseteq \boldsymbol{P}$ and $|A| \geq 3$, $A$ can recover the master key of the constructed secret sharing scheme for the prohibited structure based on the graph $G$.

PROOF. Without loss of generality, we assume that $A = \{ p_i , p_j , p_k \}$, where $i$, $j$, and $k$ are distinct. If there exists a pair of participants of $A$ belongs to $\boldsymbol{R}$, then the master key can be recovered from Theorem 3. All we need to consider is the case that all $\overline{p_i p_j}$, $\overline{p_i p_k}$, and $\overline{p_j p_k}$ are edges of $G$. From Theorem 1, we know that $p_i$ and $p_j$ can recover all sub-master keys except $Sk_i$ and $Sk_j$. Similarly, $p_i$ and $p_k$ can recover all sub-master keys except $Sk_i$ and $Sk_k$. Also, $p_j$ and $p_k$ can recover all sub-master keys except $Sk_j$ and $Sk_k$. Therefore, $p_i$, $p_j$, and $p_k$ can recover all sub-master keys $Sk_1, Sk_2, \cdots, Sk_{n+1}$ and hence the master key $K$.

**(Q.E.D.)**

The share of participant $p_i$ (= $<a_{i,1}, \cdots, a_{i,t}, \cdots, \cdots, a_{i,n}, a_{i,n+1}>$) is an ($n$+1)-dimensional vector. Except that $a_{i,i}$ is empty, every $a_{i,j}$ is over GF($q$). Therefore, the size of the share space is $q^n$. Because the master key $K$ is equal to ($K_1$, $K_2$), the size of the master key space is $q^2$. It is clear that the information rate of our secret sharing scheme for the graph-based prohibited structure is $\log q^2 / \log q^n = 2/n$, where $n$ is the number of participants.

## 4: An Example of Perfect SSS for a Prohibited Structure

We demonstrate the use of our method in the following example. In Figure 1, the graph $G$ denotes the prohibited structure with six participants. Therefore, $E(G) = \{ \overline{p_1p_3}, \overline{p_1p_5}, \overline{p_2p_5}, \overline{p_2p_6}, \overline{p_3p_5}, \overline{p_3p_6} \}$ and $E(\overline{G}) = \{ \overline{p_1p_2}, \overline{p_1p_4}, \overline{p_1p_6}, \overline{p_2p_3}, \overline{p_2p_4}, \overline{p_3p_4}, \overline{p_4p_5}, \overline{p_4p_6}, \overline{p_5p_6} \}$. The secret sharing scheme for the prohibited structure based on the graph $G$ is constructed as follows.

Let $\boldsymbol{P} = \{ p_1, p_2, p_3, p_4, p_5, p_6 \}$. Thus,

$\boldsymbol{S}$ = $\{\{ p_1, p_3 \},\{ p_1, p_5 \},\{ p_2, p_5 \},\{ p_2, p_6 \},\{ p_3, p_5 \},\{ p_3, p_6 \}\}$ and

$\boldsymbol{R}$ = $\{\{ p_1, p_2 \},\{ p_1, p_4 \},\{ p_1, p_6 \},\{ p_2, p_3 \},\{ p_2, p_4 \},\{ p_3, p_4 \},\{ p_4, p_5 \},\{ p_4, p_6 \},\{ p_5, p_6 \}\}$.

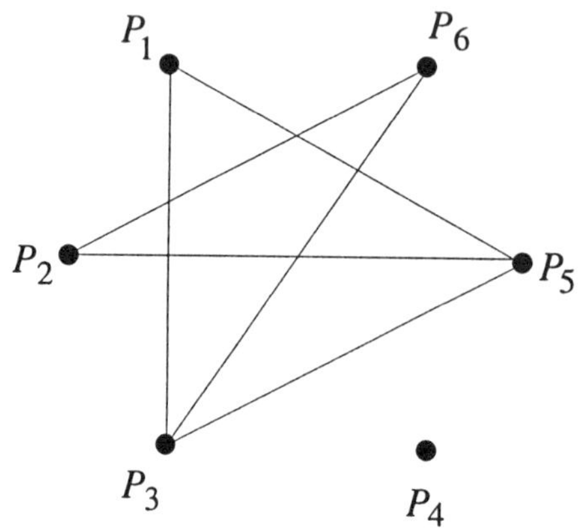


**Figure 1: Graph $G$ with six participants**

The prohibited structure

$\Delta$ =

$\{\phi,\{ p_1 \},\{ p_2 \},\{ p_3 \},\{ p_4 \},\{ p_5 \},\{ p_6 \},\{ p_1, p_3 \},$
$\{ p_1, p_5 \},\{ p_2, p_5 \},\{ p_2, p_6 \},\{ p_3, p_5 \}, \{ p_3, p_6 \}\}$.

The access structure

$\Gamma$ =

$\{\{ p_1, p_2 \},\{ p_1, p_4 \},\{ p_1, p_6 \},\{ p_2, p_3 \},\{ p_2, p_4 \},$
$\{ p_3, p_4 \},\{ p_4, p_5 \},\{ p_4, p_6 \},\{ p_5, p_6 \},$
$\{ p_1, p_2, p_3 \},\{ p_1, p_2, p_4 \},\{ p_1, p_2, p_5 \},$
$\{ p_1, p_2, p_6 \},\{ p_1, p_3, p_4 \},\{ p_1, p_3, p_6 \},$
$\{ p_1, p_4, p_5 \},\{ p_1, p_4, p_6 \},\{ p_1, p_5, p_6 \},$
$\{ p_2, p_3, p_4 \},\{ p_2, p_3, p_5 \},\{ p_2, p_3, p_6 \},$

$\{ p_2, p_4, p_5 \}, \{ p_2, p_4, p_6 \}, \{ p_2, p_5, p_6 \}$,
$\{ p_3, p_4, p_5 \}, \{ p_3, p_4, p_6 \}, \{ p_3, p_5, p_6 \}$,
$\{ p_4, p_5, p_6 \}, \{ p_1, p_2, p_3, p_4 \}, \{ p_1, p_2, p_3, p_5 \}$,
$\{ p_1, p_2, p_3, p_6 \}, \{ p_1, p_2, p_4, p_5 \}, \{ p_1, p_2, p_4, p_6 \}$,
$\{ p_1, p_2, p_5, p_6 \}, \{ p_1, p_3, p_4, p_5 \}, \{ p_1, p_3, p_4, p_6 \}$,
$\{ p_1, p_3, p_5, p_6 \}, \{ p_1, p_4, p_5, p_6 \}, \{ p_2, p_3, p_4, p_5 \}$,
$\{ p_2, p_3, p_4, p_6 \}, \{ p_2, p_3, p_5, p_6 \}, \{ p_2, p_4, p_5, p_6 \}$,
$\{ p_3, p_4, p_5, p_6 \}, \{ p_1, p_2, p_3, p_4, p_5 \}$,
$\{ p_1, p_2, p_3, p_4, p_6 \}, \{ p_1, p_2, p_3, p_5, p_6 \}$,
$\{ p_1, p_2, p_4, p_5, p_6 \}, \{ p_1, p_3, p_4, p_5, p_6 \}$,
$\{ p_2, p_3, p_4, p_5, p_6 \}, \{ p_1, p_2, p_3, p_4, p_5, p_6 \} \}$.

Let $TS_1$, $TS_2, \cdots$, and $TS_7$ be seven (2, 6)-threshold schemes. We assume that $Sk_i$ is the sub-master key of $TS_i$ and $s_{i,1}, s_{i,2}, \cdots$, and $s_{i,6}$ are the sub-shares of $TS_i$, for $1 \le i \le 7$. Here we use Shamir's method [4] to construct these threshold schemes. For each (2,6)-$TS_i$, let

$$f_i(x) = r_i \cdot x + Sk_i \qquad (\text{mod } q)$$

be a secret polynomial of degree 1 over the finite field GF($q$), where $q$ is a prime. Let $ID_j$ denote the identity of the participant $p_j$. The 6 sub-shares $s_{i,1}, \cdots, s_{i,6}$ are computed from $f_i(x)$ as follows:

$$s_{i,j} = f_i(ID_j) \quad (\text{mod } q), j = 1, \ldots, 6.$$

Obviously, given any two sub-shares, $s_{i,j}$ and $s_{i,k}$, $f_i(x)$ can be reconstructed from the Lagrange interpolating polynomial as follows [6]:

$$f_i(x) = s_{i,j} \cdot \frac{(x - ID_k)}{(ID_j - ID_k)} + s_{i,k} \cdot \frac{(x - ID_j)}{(ID_k - ID_j)} \qquad (\text{mod } q).$$

Thus, the sub-master key $Sk_i$ ( $= f_i(0)$ ) can be obtained, but less than two sub-shares provide no information about the sub-master key.

The master key of the secret sharing scheme is given by $K = (K_1, K_2)$ which is protected by these sub-master keys $Sk_1, Sk_2, \cdots, Sk_7$ in such a way that all seven sub-master keys collected together, the master key $K$ can be recovered, but any five or less sub-master keys provide no information regarding the master key (See section 2.2). The shares of participants are given by:

$$S_1 = < -, Sk_2, s_{3,1}, Sk_4, s_{5,1}, Sk_6, Sk_7 >,$$
$$S_2 = < Sk_1, -, Sk_3, Sk_4, s_{5,2}, s_{6,2}, Sk_7 >,$$
$$S_3 = < s_{1,3}, Sk_2, -, Sk_4, s_{5,3}, s_{6,3}, Sk_7 >,$$
$$S_4 = < Sk_1, Sk_2, Sk_3, -, Sk_5, Sk_6, s_{7,4} >,$$
$$S_5 = < s_{1,5}, s_{2,5}, s_{3,5}, Sk_4, -, Sk_6, Sk_7 >,$$
$$S_6 = < Sk_1, s_{2,6}, s_{3,6}, Sk_4, Sk_5, -, Sk_7 >,$$ where '–' denotes empty entry.

In the following, we demonstrate the constructed secret sharing scheme satisfies:

(1) if $A \in \boldsymbol{S}$, $A$ obtains no information regarding the master key,
(2) if $A \subseteq \boldsymbol{P}$ and $|A| = 1$, $A$ obtains no information regarding the master key,
(3) if $A \in \boldsymbol{R}$, $A$ can recover the master key,
(4) if $A \subseteq \boldsymbol{P}$ and $|A| \ge 3$, $A$ can recover the master key.

If $A = \{ p_1, p_3 \} \in \boldsymbol{\Delta}$, $A$ can not recover $Sk_1$ and $Sk_3$. Therefore, $A$ obtains no information about the master key $K$.

If $A = \{ p_4 \} \in \boldsymbol{\Delta}$, $A$ can not recover $Sk_4$ and $Sk_7$. Therefore, $A$ obtains no information about the master key $K$.

If $A = \{ p_1, p_2 \} \in \boldsymbol{\Gamma}$, $A$ can recover the master key $K$ as follows.

(1) Participant $p_1$ can obtain $Sk_2$, $Sk_4$, $Sk_6$, and $Sk_7$ because he owns his share $S_1$.
(2) Participant $p_2$ can obtain $Sk_1$, $Sk_3$, $Sk_4$, and $Sk_7$ because he owns his share $S_2$.
(3) Participants $p_1$ and $p_2$ can recover $Sk_5$ from $s_{5,1}$ of $S_1$ and $s_{5,2}$ of $S_2$.

Therefore, participants $p_1$ and $p_2$ can recover all seven sub-master keys and hence the master key $K$.

If $A = \{ p_1, p_3, p_5 \} \in \boldsymbol{\Gamma}$, $A$ can recover the master key $K$ as follows.

(1) Participant $p_1$ can obtain $Sk_2$, $Sk_4$, $Sk_6$, and $Sk_7$ because he owns his share $S_1$.
(2) Participants $p_3$ and $p_5$ can recover $Sk_1$ from $s_{1,3}$ of $S_3$ and $s_{1,5}$ of $S_5$.
(3) Participants $p_1$ and $p_5$ can recover $Sk_3$ from $s_{3,1}$ of $S_1$ and $s_{3,5}$ of $S_5$.
(4) Participants $p_1$ and $p_3$ can recover $Sk_5$ from $s_{5,1}$ of $S_1$ and $s_{5,3}$ of $S_3$.

Therefore, participants $p_1$, $p_3$, and $p_5$ can recover all seven sub-master keys and hence the master key $K$.

## 5: Conclusions

In this paper, we give a construction of perfect secret sharing schemes for mixed structures ($\Gamma$, $\Delta$), where $\Gamma = \{\boldsymbol{P}\}$ and $\Delta = \{A \mid A \subseteq \boldsymbol{P}$ and $|A| \le |\boldsymbol{P}| - 2\}$. Based on the proposed perfect secret sharing schemes, we propose an efficient construction of perfect secret sharing schemes for graph-based prohibited structures where a vertex denotes a participant and an edge does a pair of participants who cannot recover the master key. The information rate of our scheme is $2/n$, where $n$ is the number of participants.

## References


[1] M. Ito, A. Saito and T. Nishizeki, "Secret sharing scheme realizing general access structure," in *Proc. IEEE Globecom'87*, Tokyo, pp. 99-102 (1987).

[2] W.A. Jackson, K.M. Martin and C. M. O'Keefe, "Multisecret threshold schemes," in *Advances in Cryptology-Crypto'93 Proceedings*, Lecture Notes in Computer Science, Vol. 773, Springer-Verlag, Berlin, pp. 126-135 (1994).

[3] G.R. Blakley, "Safeguarding cryptographic keys," in *Proc. AFIPs 1979 National Computer Conference*, New York, Vol. 48, pp. 313-317 (1979).

[4] A. Shamir, "How to share a secret," *Commun. of the ACM* **22** (11) 612-613 (1979).

[5] E.F. Brickell and D.R. Stinson, "Some improved bounds on the information rate of perfect secret sharing schemes," *Journal of Cryptology* **5** 153-166 (1992).

[6] D.E.R. Denning, *Cryptography and Data Security*, Addison-Wesley, Reading, MA (1983).

[7] R.W. Hamming, *Coding and Information Theory*, Englewood Cliffs, Reading, NJ:Prentice-Hall (1986).

[8] M. Ito, A. Saito and T. Nishizeki, "Multiple assignment scheme for sharing secret," *Journal of Cryptology* **6** 15-20 (1993).

[9] C.E. Shannon, "Communication theory of secrecy systems," *Computer Security Journal*, **VI**(2) 7-66 (1990).

[10] J. Benaloh and J. Leichter, "Generalized secret sharing and monotone functions," in *Advances in Cryptology-Crypto'88 Proceedings*, Lecture Notes in Computer Science, Vol. 403, Springer-Verlag, Berlin, pp. 27-35 (1990).

[11] R.M. Capocelli, A. De Santis, L. Gargano and U. Vaccaro, "On the size of shares for secret sharing schemes," in *Advances in Cryptology-Crypto'91 Proceedings*, Lecture Notes in Computer Science, Springer-Verlag, Berlin, pp. 101-113 (1992).

[12] M. van Dijk, "On the information rate of perfect secret sharing schemes," *Designs, Codes and Cryptography* **6** 143-169 (1995).

[13] D.R. Stinson, "New general lower bounds on the information rate of secret sharing schemes," in *Advance in Cryptology-CRYPTO'92, Lecture Notes in Comput. Sci.*, Vol. 740, pp. 168-182 (1993).

[14] D.R. Stinson, "Decomposition constructions for secret sharing schemes," *IEEE Trans. Inform. Theory* **40**(1) 118-125 (1994).

[15] S.P. Shieh and H.M. Sun, "On constructing secret sharing schemes," in *Proceedings of the 1994 IEEE International Conference on Computer Communications, Networking for Global Communications (INFOCOM'94)*, pp. 1288-1292 (1994).

[16] H.M. Sun and S.P. Shieh, "An efficient construction of perfect secret sharing schemes for graph-based structures," *Journal of Computers and Mathematics with Applications* **31**(7) 129-135 (1996).

# Scalability and Flexibility in Authentication Services: The *KryptoKnight* Approach

Philippe Janson* Gene Tsudik† Moti Yung‡

**Abstract**

This paper studies the issues of *flexibility* and *scalability* in the context of network security. In particular, it concentrates on authentication and key distribution services suited for a variety of communication paradigms, network environments, and end-devices. We present the design criteria, specification, and step-by-step construction of authentication and key distribution services based on experience in the *KryptoKnight* project.

The central goal of the *KryptoKnight* project was the construction of basic network security functions in a *minimal, flexible* (thus, versatile) and *scalable* manner. Protocol minimality (in terms of resource usage) and flexibility are not merely theoretical goals; they have clear advantages in environments where computational resources are limited and connectivity is restricted. *KryptoKnight* was aimed at such environments: small and *anemic* wireless devices, simple network and data-link entities, embedded micro-devices and other special-purpose communication equipment and configurations. Furthermore, *scalability* of protocols makes their deployment possible in the presence of rapid network growth and inter-domain communication.

## 1 Introduction

The objective of the *KryptoKnight* project was the design of minimal, flexible and scalable authentication and key distribution protocols for various network settings such as low-level networking environments (e.g., link and network adapters) and small devices with limited computing power (e.g., PDAs and mobile telephones). Such components increasingly find their way into various areas, e,g., office, field, home, entertainment and education. Moreover, resarch on "ubiquitous computing" is advancing rapidly [10]. Unlike a workstation in a client-server setting, these limited-ability devices still require security features: device authentication to prevent wireless fraud, calling and called address identification to keep intruders out, low-level authentication to secure booting from a LAN adapter and so on. Security functions, in turn, typically require cryptographic support and, thus, key distribution protocols. However, integration of security features into primitive components must take into account restrictions such as: small packet sizes, low bandwidth, high transmission costs, limited processing and storage resources, real-time constraints and export regulations.

Under these conditions, designing simple, secure and versatile mechanisms is not obvious. Solutions must be flexible, i.e., suitable for various network configurations and connectivity patterns. Solutions must *fit* into devices with a wide range of computational capabilities, including: palm-top, lap-top, desk-top, set-top, or floor-top devices. Moreover, the most primitive devices must be able to inter-operate securely with the most powerful ones, which implies the need to provide common security functions to meet the minimal needs. Furthermore, solutions must be scalable so as to accommodate growth both within and across interconnected administrative domains.

In general, achieving minimal and flexible design is desirable because of the prevailing view that security mechanisms are expensive, performance-impairing, and cumbersome. (Since security mechanisms typically require complex administration and their deployment is subject to limitations such as export control or licensing.) This often results in users and organizations avoiding, disabling, or downgrading security mechanisms.

Finally, minimality of mechanism really pays off whenever security features must be *retrofitted* into existing, established protocols or applications. If, as is often the case, security features are introduced as an afterthought, security parameters have to be squeezed into the meager space available in memory or packet headers.[1]

In this paper we review the *KryptoKnight* protocol family which was designed with the explicit goals of flexibility, minimality and scalability. Early aspects of this work have been already reported on and have had their impact. The basic 2-party protocol [5] influenced the ISO basic authentication standard [17], and [7]–the ISO key management standard. The early work also initiated a research topic of proof correctness in cryptographic protocols based on matching of protocol histories and defending against replay and interleaving attacks [5, 11, 3, 4].

This paper, on the other hand, discusses other issues experienced and learned in the course of the *KryptoKnight* project. In particular, we consider the issues of flexibility and scalability in both intra- and inter-domain protocol design. More specifically, we present the rationale for the design concepts and develop the initial design of the protocol family geared towards various communication scenarios. Then, we concentrate on the inter-domain protocols that provide scalability of the overall architecture and show how the basic protocols' properties enable modular design of their inter-domain counterparts.

**Organization:** Section 2 addresses some background issues and the basic protocol building blocks. In Section 3, the optimized key distribution protocols are derived and a set of 3-party protocol scenarios and protocols is presented. Section 4 discusses the requirements for, and design of, the inter-domain protocols. Section 5 concludes with the summary of this work.

## 2 Basic Concepts and Preliminaries

A number of schemes have been designed for authentication and key distribution services in distributed systems and networks, e.g., [25, 8, 1, 26, 29, 21, 27]. Some of these have lead to implementations or standards, e.g. the Kerberos [32, 28] and ANSI X9.17 [18] schemes, which use DES technology, or the ISO-CCITT X.509 Directory Authentication scheme

*IBM Research, Rüschlikon, Switzerland; *pj@zurich.ibm.com*.
†USC/ISI, Marina del Rey, CA; *gts@isi.edu*.
‡CertCo, New York, NY; *moti@certco.com*.

[1] This point is best illustrated by considering what it takes to "secure" IP, Telnet or ATM networks.



0-8186-7780-5/97 $10.00 

[19], which relies on public key technology. Kerberos is the basis for the security component provided by the Open Software Foundation (OSF) as part of its Distributed Computing Environment (DCE) offering. The *KryptoKnight* concept and resulting architecture differ from the above mainly owing to the specific computing restrictions and the general flexibility/scalability requirements we next discuss. As a private-key based system, a scalable design must be based on trusted servers [25], which assure that various parties are able to undergo mutual authentication without initially sharing cryptographic keys and based solely on the established trust with the server(s).

## 2.1 Basic Concepts and Design Issues

Before delving into the actual protocols, we begin (in the next subsection) with the review of the key design issues.

### 2.1.1 Minimal Resource Utilization

Keeping in mind resource-poor, restricted network environments, our main requirement is to minimize bandwidth usage and computational overhead. This translates into small messages, small cryptographic tokens, few cryptographic operations and minimal storage at the device. This economy of mechanism rules out using public key designs (ISO-CCITT X.509 Directory). Even Kerberos with its relatively verbose tokens and liberal use of encryption may be too costly. Of course, our approach implies a certain trade-off with the semantic richness of cryptographic tokens in designs like X.509 or Kerberos. However, such richness is typically unnecessary at the basic level of communication protocols and devices that we have in mind.

We note that constructing cryptographic primitives on top of basic functions is an on-going research effort in theoretical cryptography (e.g., digital signature schemes have been shown to require only one-way functions [24, 31]). We concentrated on building key distribution and authentication primitives in the trusted server model without the full capacity of encryption/decryption functions but, with only pseudo-random one-way functions.[2] In addition, we minimize the use of cryptographic operations and the number of message flows in order to minimize the software that the resulting protocols require. Related minimization ideas have been independently developed by Gong [14, 15].

### 2.1.2 Freedom from Export Restrictions

The usability of global networks connecting numerous users across many businesses *requires* that authentication services be unrestricted between countries. In a mobile environment where users move from country to country, the situation can easily become intractable if authentication protocols were restricted. For example, how can one deal with a situation where a user from country A visits country B and communicates with a user in country C, using equipment produced in country D? Such problematic issues can only be resolved with the availability of a universally-accepted technology which is free of any governmental limitations. Lastly, experience with the design of cryptographic systems shows that maintaining different system versions - exportable and non-exportable - can be quite costly. There are a number of ways to assure exportability, by employing weakened cryptography (e.g., a 40-bit DES keys), or tight encapsulation of the crypto module. In our design we employ a well defined cryptographic module that employs only a one-way function rather than a block-cipher; this limits the applicability of our cryptography for bulk data encryption (which is the major concern for governments). In addition, modularity may help in careful design for exportability. For example, using different kinds of cryptographic tools at different levels.

### 2.1.3 Flexible Operational Scenarios

Most existing key distribution methods have been tailored to the relatively narrow operational scenarios of specific distributed applications. For instance, any scheme relying on time-stamps favors Local Area Network (LAN) environments, where all network users have easy access to a common trusted time server. While requiring tightly-synchronized reliable clocks in a Wide Area Network (WAN) is conceivable, it is certainly harder.

More importantly, existing schemes make specific assumptions about network configuration and connectivity models. For instance they may dictate a specific communication paradigm for contacting a trusted server or key distribution center (KDC): when a client A needs a key to communicate with a server B, Kerberos specifies that A must obtain the desired key from the KDC prior to communicating with B, which is sometimes called the *push model.* By contrast, in the same situation, X9.17 specifies that A must contact B first, and let B get the necessary key from the KDC, which is sometimes referred to as the *pull model.* Both models are justified in their respective environments. In a LAN environment - for which Kerberos was initially designed - requiring clients (rather than servers) to obtain the keys makes sense because it distributes the burden over many clients, thus alleviating the task of the few shared servers. In a WAN environment - for which X9.17 was designed - the opposite approach is justified because there are typically many more clients than servers and KDCs are typically located closer to servers than to clients. Under such circumstances, the amount of system definition (configuration) and the cost of client-KDC connections required by the Kerberos approach could become prohibitively high in a WAN context. In conclusion, dictating a fixed connectivity pattern is possible in well-defined application environments with clear operating assumptions. However, it becomes unrealistic in general network environments. In the setting of a wireless-network, clients contact communication servers (base stations) at their entry point to the network, the pull model is mandatory in such a case.

### 2.1.4 Scalable Design

Closely related to flexible operation is the notion of scalable design. Networks are often interconnected and portions thereof are administrated by different authorities. A general authentication and key distribution solution must be extensible to large internetworks comprised of many interconnected domains. Flexibility in connectivity and in access pattern to the security servers eases and enhances scalability, since it allows different clients and servers (under various mobility scenarios) to establish authenticated sessions. For this reason, the *KryptoKnight* design attempts to cover a number of different inter-domain environments. This is in contrast with the Kerberos inter-domain model which puts the burden on the client by making it responsible for searching and accessing the appropriate security server outside its own domain.

[2] In practice, typically a keyed cryptographic hash suffices.

## 2.2 Basic Building Block: 2-Party Authentication

A family of simple 2-party authentication protocols was presented in [5, 6]. The protocols are efficient in message size and computation overhead and minimal in use of cryptography (e.g., can use a block cipher or even a one-way hash function employing a common key as a private portion of the message). They were shown resistant to a wide set of attacks known as interleaving attacks. In addition, essential ideas for formal model and proofs of correctness for these and similar protocols were suggested initially in [5] and further developed in [11, 3]. Simple design eases these complexity-theoretic proofs. Conceptually, we attempted to have a uniform design basing our protocols on similar basic operation; this eases the design's conceptual complexity and its validation, while making it widely (and incrementally) applicable to numerous scenarios.

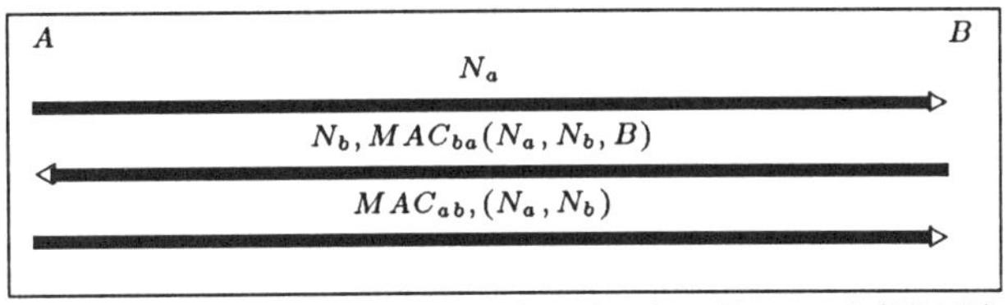


Figure 1: 2-Party Mutual Authentication Protocol (2PAP)

One of the protocols derived from the work of [5] is called 2PAP and is represented in figure 1. In this figure, the letters A and B stand for the identifiers of two network entities performing mutual authentication. The variables $N_a$ and $N_b$ are one-time random numbers (called nonces) used by each party to challenge the other to prove its identity. The notations $MAC_{ba}$ and $MAC_{ab}$ denote cryptographic one-way hash functions, called *Message Authentication Codes*, computed with keys $K_{ba}$ and $K_{ab}$ respectively, and used to guarantee the authenticity of their parameter string. (The commas between the MAC parameters indicate different blocks to which the MAC function is subsequently applied, e.g. as in CBC mode of block ciphers. Namely the key is applied to the first block the result is ex-ored with the next block and the key is applied, and so on.. ). Implementing MAC functions with a symmetric cryptographic system such as DES [9] (CBC mode), $K_{ab}$ and $K_{ba}$ are (typically equal) secret keys shared by A and B. Instead of using an encryption function to implement the MACs, one can also use a plain one-way hash function (e.g. the MD5 algorithm employed on fixed size blocks [30] is believed to be such a function, another function is SHA1) applied a number of times in some way to the authenticated string concatenated with the secret key (see, e.g., [33]). Using a plain one-way hash function (under the assumption that it is pseudo-random [13]) instead of an encryption function has the added advantage that even the source code or the detailed design of the resulting implementation are not subject to the export controls applicable to cryptographic technology in many countries (i.e., one can argue that using this function for *bulk data encryption* is either highly inefficient or requires additional cryptographic support). (As a matter of practicality, our designs, in fact, have gotten export license).

In addition, the protocol uses MAC operation twice (or three times if we count block encryptions in CBC mode.) The number of message flows (three) is *minimal* for a nonce-based protocol. Furthermore, the combined size of all cryptographic messages in terms of data blocks (four) is also *minimal*. The use of nonces is robust since nonces are typically generated with cryptographic means and require no *state* maintenance as opposed to alternative methods that rely on synchronized clocks or counters. This basic protocol serves as the foundation for the design of the entire *KryptoKnight* protocol family discussed in this paper.

## 3 Server Based Key Distribution

Key distribution by a server to users is central in our architecture. We now proceed to discuss key distribution issues and their various shapes, forms and flavors. After introducing the notation and discussing some preliminaries, we go into 2-party and (server-based) 3-party protocol scenarios.

### 3.1 Notation

| | |
|---|---|
| A,B,C,X,Y | principals |
| $K_x$ | KEK of X (known only to KDC and X) |
| $K_{xy}$ | Secret key shared by X and Y |
| $E_x(M)$ | Encryption of M under key $K_x$ |
| $E_{xy}(M)$ | Encryption of M under key $K_{xy}$ |
| $MAC_x(M)$ | MAC of message M under key $K_x$ |
| $MAC_{xy}(M)$ | MAC of message M under key $K_{xy}$ |

### 3.2 Tickets

Distribution of secret keys from the KDC to its constituent principals (clients and servers) requires the use of secret channels. In the realm of symmetric cryptography this requires that each principal in the network share at least one secret key with the KDC. This key is often referred to as the principal's *key-encryption key* (KEK).

The nature of the messages exchanged between a KDC and its clients is reminiscent of public key certificates: a key distribution expression issued by the KDC (also referred to as a *ticket*) must, by definition, include the new key. It must also include a *freshness indicator* (such as a unique key version number, time-stamp, or nonce) indicating to the recipient that the key is fresh and valid. In addition, a ticket must include the identifier(s) of the principal(s) for whom the key is intended. It may also include such information as key expiration time and other usage parameters.

### 3.3 Basic Key Distribution

Drawing on our discussion above, a simple and secure 2-party key distribution protocol can be easily constructed from 2PAP (as depicted in Figure 2.)

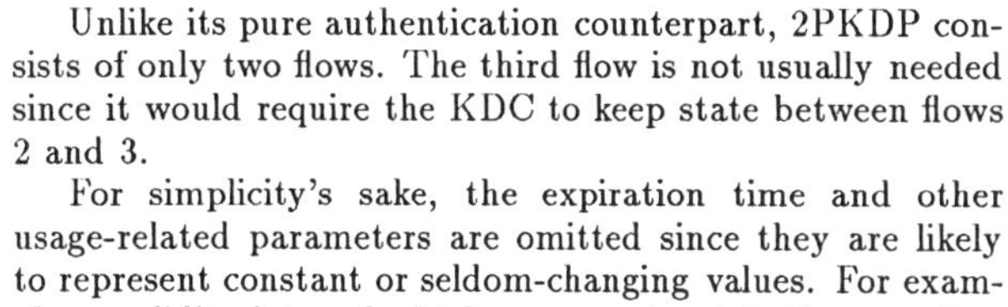


Figure 2: Basic 2-Party Key Distribution Protocol (2PKDP)

Unlike its pure authentication counterpart, 2PKDP consists of only two flows. The third flow is not usually needed since it would require the KDC to keep state between flows 2 and 3.

For simplicity's sake, the expiration time and other usage-related parameters are omitted since they are likely to represent constant or seldom-changing values. For example, a validity interval of 8 hours may be globally agreed on by default, or it may be included in ticket construction (i.e. its value may be added to the arguments being MAC-ed).

The resulting ticket syntax is minimal and exportable. It yields simple and short messages, and exhibits minimal redundancy in message parameters. Such economy of mechanism is certainly not present in any of the existing, application-layer designs for key distribution (Kerberos, X9.17, X.509). This may be due to several reasons:

- Keys requiring many more attributes (semantics) in such higher-layer environments,
- The designs make unnecessary use of encryption, encrypting many parameters that have nothing secret about them (in many cases, the notion of authentication is mistakenly associated with encryption),
- Key attributes are encrypted with the key rather than folded into it through notarization (except in X9.17),
- Economy of mechanism was clearly not an objective in these designs.

### 3.4 Authenticated Key Distribution

It can be easily seen that the 2PKDP provides key distribution and nothing else. The protocol is secure in the sense of key confidentiality, i.e., no one other than A and the KDC is able to obtain $K_a^{new}$. (The security of this protocol is discussion in detail in [34].) However, it is clearly not secure with respect to key integrity. This means that any intruder can modify the key distribution and cause A to extract a key *not issued* by the KDC. In fact, the KDC may be unavailable and the entire second flow can be concocted by the intruder. We note that the original design of the protocol family relied on such non-authenticated exchange and further verified the distributed key via subsequent 2-party mutual authentication handshake [7]; here we base the entire system on more novel authenticated key exchanges while not compromising the minimality achieved earlier.

In summary, 2PKDP lacks two features: i) integrity of the new key and ii) timeliness of the KDC's response. In order to address this issue, we construct a protocol which provides both features and, at the same time, retains the advantages of the basic protocol, most importantly, its compactness.

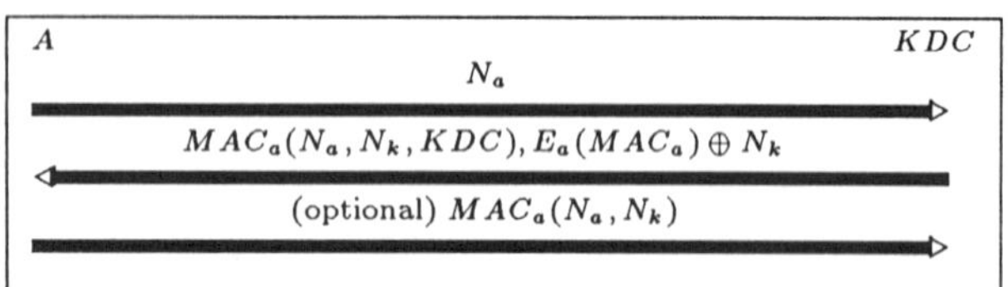


$MAC_a = MAC_a(N_a, N_k, KDC)$ $\quad N_k = K_a^{new}$

Figure 3: 2-Party Authenticated Key Distribution Protocol (2PAKDP)

The resulting protocol (2PAKDP) is illustrated in Figure 3. Its format is very similar to 2PAP in Figure 1. In fact, the only difference is that the KDC's nonce $N_k$ in flow 2 (which also happens to be the new key $K_a^{new}$) is hidden. The technique used to construct message flow 2 is called *braiding* [20]. Upon receiving the message, A first performs block encryption on the MAC value and factors out the new key $N_k$. Then, it computes the MAC – as in the basic 2PAP – over $(N_a, N_k, KDC)$ and checks that it matches the KDC's MAC in the message. The third protocol flow is identical to 2PAP and is, once again, optional.

The security of 2PAKDP is based directly on the security of the more basic 2PAP. Moreover, it is not difficult to see that 2PAKDP is, essentially, a superset of 2PAP. The arguments for supporting these assertions as well as the detailed derivation of 2PAKDP can be found in [20].

A remark on 2PAKDP is that, like its ancestors 2PKDP and 2PAP, it is a minimal protocol. In terms of composite message length, it is not possible for a principal to supply a challenge to the KDC and get back a new, unpredictable key and its integrity check in less than two messages and three data fields. Also, 2PAKDP requires only *one* additional (on top of 2PAP) block encryption operation in order to hide the key.

Finally, we remark that the protocol can be combined with a hard-to-compute function like Diffie-Hellman key exchange [12], to achieve better security (i.e., breaking the shared key does not give away the distributed key as in [2]). For example $N_a$ and $N_k$ may be the (authenticated) exchange messages of the key-exchange protocol (assuming the MAC is large enough, as for this technology, a larger key size is required).

### 3.5 Protocol Scenarios

We now proceed with the design of 3-party protocols. As mentioned before, two of our main guiding principles are i) protocol minimality, and ii) flexibility with respect to network configurations and connectivity patterns. We present optimized design that achieves authenticated key distribution in a minimal fashion (improving on the previous unauthenticated design in [7] where it was implicitly assumed that authentication is followed by key distribution).

The common setting for all protocol scenarios discussed below is exemplified by two entities A and B that want to authenticate with each other and, perhaps, subsequently engage in secure communication. Since initially A and B have no shared secret, they (or, rather, one of them) must contact the mutually-trusted KDC with whom they each share a secret.

#### 3.5.1 A-B-K Pull Scenario

The first scenario is called A-B-K or *pull model*. The A-B-K scenario assumes that A is either unable, unauthorized, or unwilling to contact the KDC or it is simply willing to let B choose if it wants to contact the KDC.

Our realization of A-B-K is shown in figure 4. It is constructed by simply combining and interleaving two 2PAKDP protocols ($A \leftrightarrow KDC$ and $B \leftrightarrow KDC$) and one 2PAP protocol ($A \leftrightarrow B$).

In more detail, the protocol is executed as follows:

1. As in the basic 2PAP, A contacts B in flow 1 challenging it to authenticate based on a nonce $N_a$.

2. B contacts the KDC in flow 2 passing along A's identifier, A's nonce $N_a$ and its own nonce $N_b$. (We assume that B's name can be inferred from the underlying communication context.)

3. KDC replies in flow 3 by sending two tickets which contain the same freshly-generated key Kab. The tickets (or key-distribution expressions) follow the same syntax as in 2PAKDP.

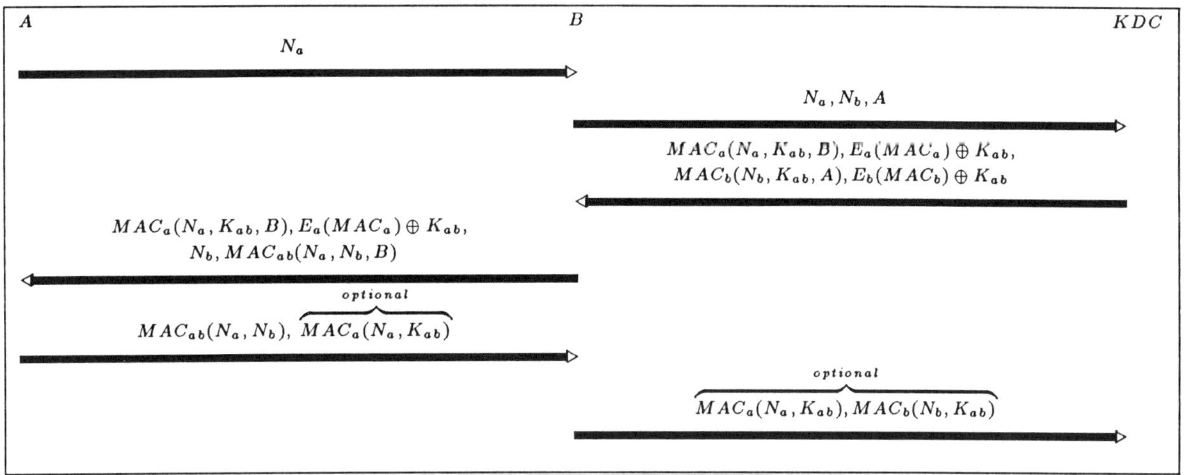


$MAC_a = MAC_a(N_a, K_{ab}, B) \qquad MAC_b = MAC_b(N_b, K_{ab}, A)$

Figure 4: A-B-K 3-Party Key Distribution Protocol

4. Having received the tickets, B may or may not cache them for reuse in later communication with A. (The issue of caching tickets is discussed in a later section.) B extracts $K_{ab}$ and checks its integrity and freshness by re-computing the MAC expression.

5. In flow 4, B forwards to A the appropriate ticket and adds its own nonce along with the expected authentication expression $MAC_{ab}(N_a, N_b, B)$.

6. In a similar fashion, A extracts and verifies $K_{ab}$, verifies the authentication expression from B, and replies with its own $MAC_{ab}(N_a, N_b)$. Optionally, A can add a confirmation token $MAC_a(N_a, K_{ab})$ that completes mutual authentication between A and the KDC.

7. Upon receipt of flow 5, B authenticates A's token thus completing the $A \leftrightarrow B$ 2PAP. Next, B can optionally compute its own confirmation, $MAC_b(N_b, K_{ab})$, and forward it along with A's confirmation to the KDC in the last flow.

The purpose of the optional confirmation flows is to acknowledge to the KDC that both A and B received the intended key $K_{ab}$ and successfully authenticated one another. Such information may be useful for logging and subsequent auditing. Of course, if auditing is desired, the KDC needs to either maintain or archive state information associated with each protocol run.

This completes the description of the basic 3-party protocol. Whether A and/or B should cache its own and/or each other's tickets depends on the operational assumptions of the scenario at hand. If we assume that keys like $K_{ab}$ are valid for one single interaction (message exchange or session duration) between A and B, then tickets need not be cached and keys should be stored and later erased at session termination time. This would force A and B to get a new key for each interaction. On the other hand, if the ticket usage conditions (e.g., validity interval) allows spanning more than one interaction, A and/or B may want to cache tickets for the span of their lifetime. Each can cache its own tickets knowing the other does the same or one of them can cache both tickets knowing the other does not cache any. In either case, at least one copy of each ticket must be cached between the two partners, so that both can retrieve $K_{ab}$ if and when they resume interaction after a period of inactivity and within the lifetime $K_{ab}$.

### 3.5.2 K-A-B Push Scenario

The second scenario is called K-A-B or *push model*. In it, the KDC is contacted by A instead of B, as shown in figure 5. The KDC is contacted by A because, for some reason, B is unable, unwilling or unauthorized to do it.

One distinguishing feature of this protocol is that it provides authentication on the forward flows to the KDC. By issuing the tickets in flow 4, the KDC confirms to both A and B that their respective authentication tokens – $MAC_b(N_a, N_b, B)$ and $MAC_a(N_a, \eta_b, A)$ – are valid. However, if either of the tokens is corrupted (B's in flow 2 or A's in flow 3), the KDC is unable to tell which one is at fault. In other words, the KDC can confirm that both tokens are valid or none are. In case it is desirable to pinpoint the corrupt token, flow 3 can be extended to include $MAC_b(N_a, N_b, B)$.

The most important consequence of forward-flow authentication is that the direct *handshake* (2PAP) between A and B is no longer needed (since it already takes place indirectly, through the KDC.) We note that the KDC only checks the authenticity of A's and B's tokens, but it does not and **cannot** assert the freshness of either token. The latter is inferred by A and B individually in flows 4 and 5, respectively.

We also note that $MAC_{ab}(N_a, N_b)$ in the last protocol flow is not always required. If we can guarantee no *crosstalk* between different 3-party protocols (as described in Section 3.6 below) then the $MAC_{ab}$ expression can be safely omitted.[3]

Another distinguishing feature of K-A-B is that it does not provide the same assurances as A-B-K. In K-A-B, both principals are satisfied at the end that their peer is authentic and is currently on-line. In K-A-B, on the other hand, both principals gain an additional assurance that their peer is currently in possession of the new key $K_{ab}$. This difference becomes moot when the two principals engage in subsequent communication secured with $K_{ab}$. However, since this is not always the case, we present a slight variation of K-A-B where $A \leftrightarrow B$ authentication is direct (see Figure 6.) The present protocol includes an extra flow that is required to complete

[3] We leave it as an exercise to the interested reader to see why $MAC_{ab}(N_a, N_b)$ is needed otherwise.

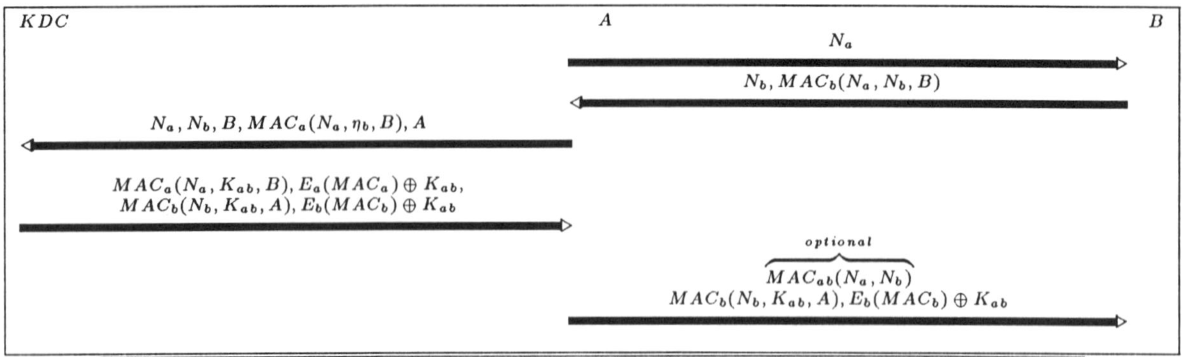


$\eta_b = MAC_b(N_a, N_b, B) \quad MAC_a = MAC_a(N_a, K_{ab}, B) \quad MAC_b = MAC_b(N_b, K_{ab}, A)$

Figure 5: K-A-B 3-Party Key Distribution Protocol

the handshake. It is easy to see the resemblance to the A-B-K protocol discussed in the previous section. In fact, K-A-B* can be obtained by simply re-arranging the flows and message contents of A-B-K.

### 3.5.3 Time-Based Push Scenario

Under certain conditions, it may be desirable to use another flavor of the *push protocol*, referred to as K-A-B(t) and represented in figure 7. This protocol forces A to get the tickets from the KDC before communicating with B. There can be several reason for choosing K-A-B(t):

1. The main reason may be that A (or A's KDC) has to adhere to a policy whereby all requests have to be processed/approved by the KDC before any contact can be made. This is an issue which often depends on whether Mandatory Access Control is being enforced (connection between parties is strictly controlled by servers), in highly sensitive communication systems (e.g., military systems) such a policy is typically enforced.
2. B is not available (i.e., is not on-line) at the time when A contacts the KDC. Also, B may be a busy/popular service which cannot be burdened with maintaining state. (We note that both K-A-B and A-B-K require B to maintain state – $N_b$, A's name, etc. – from the time of initial contact by A until the ticket from the KDC is received.) In contrast, K-A-B(t) requires B to start keeping state starting only from flow 3.
3. B has no connection to, or is otherwise unable to contact the KDC. For example, B is a mobile entity that can only connect to the rest of the world through A. Of course, in this case K-A-B can be used as well but K-A-B(t) requires one message less than K-A-B.

Although the message structure of K-A-B(t) is quite different, it is not hard to see its resemblance to the Kerberos model. As the Kerberos protocol, K-A-B(t) assumes loose clock synchronization between B and the KDC. (however, no clock synchronization between A and KDC or A and B is assumed.[4])

The main distinguishing factor of K-A-B(t) is the lack of a challenge from B to the KDC. Instead, the timeliness/freshness of the KDC's ticket for B is established on the basis of the KDC-supplied time-stamp, $TS_k$. The protocol, as depicted, is a **hybrid** in a sense that $KDC \rightarrow A$ authentication is challenge-based as is $A \leftrightarrow B$ authentication while $KDC \rightarrow B$ is time-based. If tight clock synchronization between A and B is available, the protocol can be simplified to resemble even more the Kerberos model. In particular, instead of waiting for B's challenge, A can authenticate to B in flow 3 by including $MAC_{ab}(N_a, TS, A)$. Flow 4 can then be reduced to just $MAC_{ab}(N_a, TS)$ and the last flow can be omitted altogether. (See Figure 8.)

### 3.6 Protocol Coexistence

In order to provide seamless and flexible service, all protocol types described above have to coexist under a common *umbrella*, i.e., within the same body of code. This raises some concerns regarding an intruder being able to take advantage of any cross-talk or interplay between different 3-party protocols.

One intuitive argument against this type of attack is that only *quality ingredients* were used in the construction of the 3-party protocols. In other words, every 3-party protocol combines – in one way or another – two parallel runs of 2PAKDP and one run of 2PAP (and these components have been shown to withstand attacks of this kind). Thus, we argue that the security of 3-party protocols is based on the security of the underlying 2-party protocols. A rigorous proof of this assertion is outside the scope of this paper. It is based on (formally) having each flow of each protocol instance being independent of other cryptographic expressions to avoid reusing them either on- or off-line. One very effective measure for avoiding many types of attacks is the assignment of a unique identifier and include sender and receiver names in every cryptographic expression ($MAC$ or $E$ operation) in supported protocols, and the inclusion of this identifier in the computation of all such cryptographic expressions. This creates independence between cryptographic tokens of different protocols, and then we have also to pay attention to independence between instances of the same protocol. (In practice, this can be realized by appending or pre-pending the expression identifier to the cleartext before computing the $MAC$ or $E$ function over it. Alternatively, the key itself can be varied for every distinct cryptographic operation.) The formal argument can then be based on complexity theory (reducing breaking to breaking assumptions about the strength of the underlying tools) and/or be formalized in a logic that argues about properties of such protocols. Elegant formal complexity arguments have recently been developed based on the above intuition experienced in the project, see

[4] In practice, clocks of all principals involved must anyway be loosely synchronized in order to interpret the key expiration times that may be included as part of KDC-issued tickets.

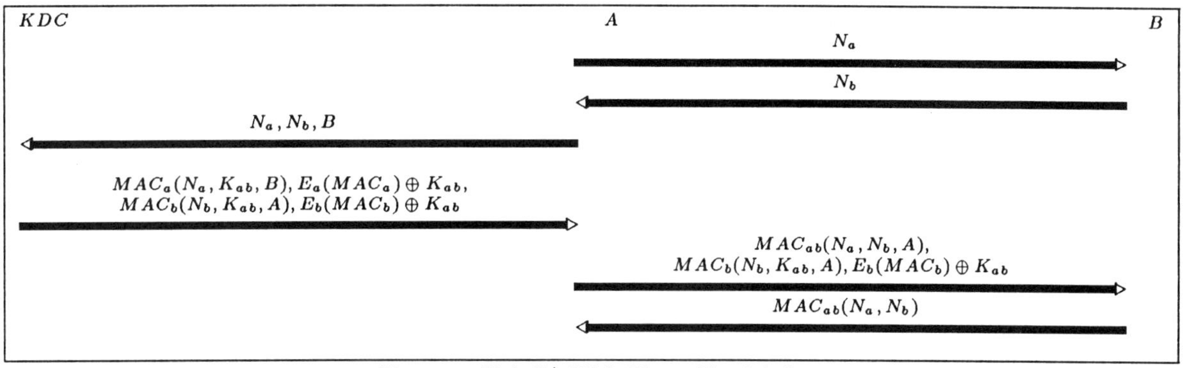


Figure 6: K-A-B* With Direct Handshake

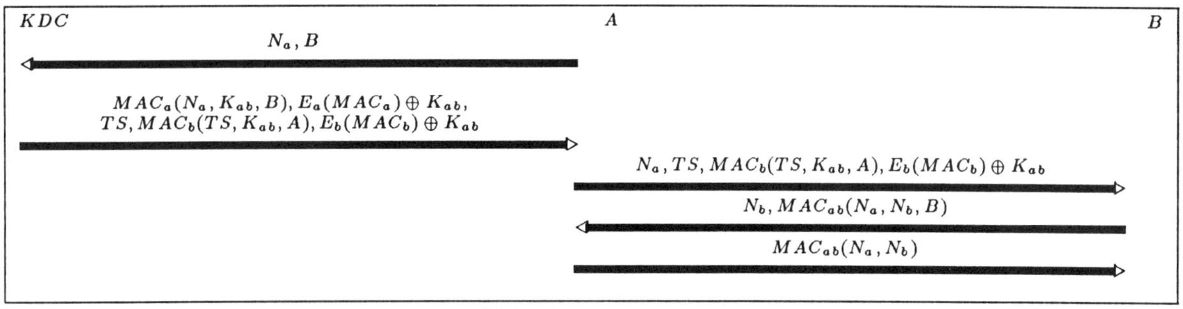


Figure 7: K-A-B(t) With Partial Clock Synchronization

[3, 4].

Other aspects of protocol coexistence are the criteria for selecting a particular protocol (which depends on the environment definition, such as whether Mandatory Access Control is required).

## 4 Inter-Domain Protocols

There are many well-known reasons for partitioning electronic space into so-called realms or domains: scale, geographical distance and administrative heterogeneity, as well as security considerations are the most common of them. The growth of the Internet and its potential to be the universal host of many domains is one typical example. Whether it takes place across a private, relatively secure network or across the uncharted wilderness of the global Internet, communication increasingly crosses such *domain boundaries*. This prompts the need for security services to take into account the "inter-domain-ness" of communication. More specifically, authentication and key distribution protocols must be extended to operate across domains.

This requirement is certainly not new; for example, both MIT and DCE Kerberos breeds include an inter-domain key distribution protocol. (See Figure 9.) The Kerberos model puts most of the load on the initiating client A which is reasonable in the context of a traditional, LAN communication environment. However, the Kerberos model is not applicable to many other environments:

- Client A may be a mobile unit in which case it has no connection to its own KDC, least of all to a "foreign" KDC.
- Client A might have a means to reach its own KDC but not a foreign one. In fact, KDCs can migrate from one host to another, crash and come up again. Ideally, this should not be of any concern to anyone outside their own domain.
- Client A may have a policy prohibiting it from communicating with the outside without establishing a secure "context". This would be the case if packet filtering is being applied at domain boundaries. We note that recently there is a growing popularity to employ such filtering by means of "firewall" bridges.
- Client B may have a policy requiring it to consult its own KDC first before contacting A's KDC. (One example is a mandatory access control environment where external connections must be strictly monitored by KDCs.)

Keeping in mind the above conditions and the goal to design flexible protocols, we now extend our 3-party protocols to support inter-domain communication. Like Kerberos designers, we assume the existence of inter-domain keys – keys that secure communication among KDCs in different domains. An inter-domain key, $K_{12}$ shared by $KDC_1$ and $KDC_2$ is assumed to be a strong, long-term key. In the descriptions below we assume symmetric, shared-key encryption, however, there is no reason why public key encryption could not be used for inter-KDC authentication and key distribution. The use of public key encryption can be made *visible* only to the KDCs and transparent to the regular principals. It would, however, imply longer messages and packet headers; thus, it is better suited to the versions with direct KDC-to-KDC communication.

Implicit in the above is the assumption that KDCs in different domains know one another *by name*. In other words, a KDC in every domain has a well-known (perhaps, reserved) name. Thus it should be easy to construct a name of a KDC given the name of its domain. However, we do not address any mechanisms for establishing relationships and distributing/refreshing keys between KDCs in different domains.

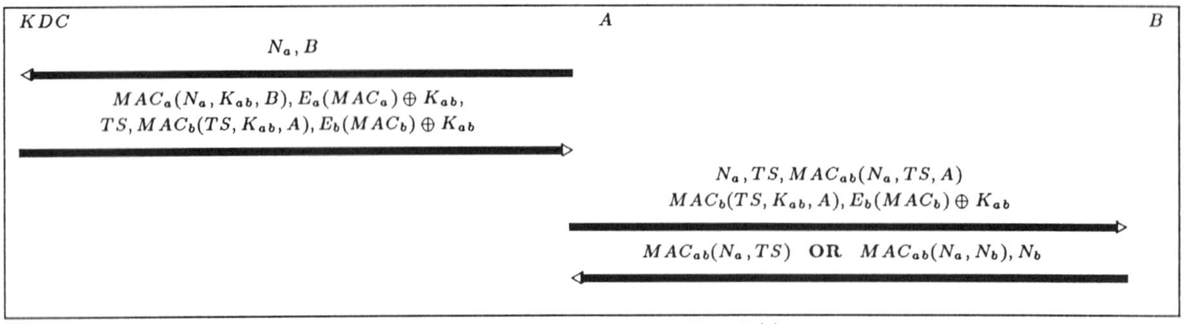


Figure 8: Fully Time-Based K-A-B(t)

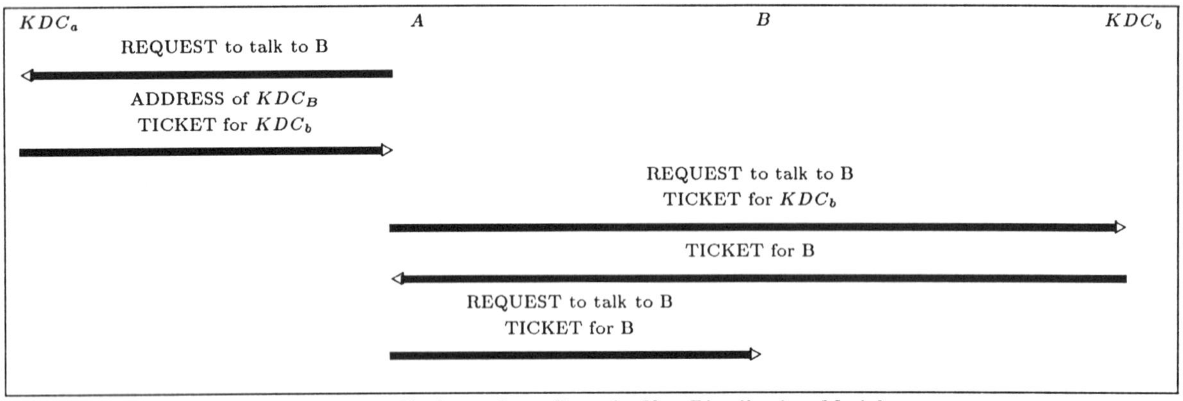


Figure 9: Kerberos Inter-Domain Key Distribution Model

### 4.1 Without Inter-KDC Communication

In the simplest inter-domain model we assume that KDCs do not engage in inter-domain communication. This restriction is realistic since the KDC is a special, perhaps protected entity and communication with the outside may result in its undue exposure. Furthermore, inter-domain communication is often less predictable and less reliable than intra-domain communication. Thus, the burden on the KDC can be reduced by disallowing outside communication. Finally, as mentioned before, KDCs can crash and migrate from host to host. Keeping track of the availability and the whereabouts of the KDCs is certainly more viable within a domain (where the KDCs are located) rather than outside.

Since direct communication between KDCs is unavailable, the obvious solution is for one of the KDCs to issue both tickets and for the other KDC to translate the appropriate ticket for its constituent principal. The protocol in Figure 10 depicts an example of this technique. It is essentially a straight-forward extension of the A-B-K protocol discussed in Section 3.5.1.

The protocol is executed as follows:

1. The first two flows are the same as in the intra-domain A-B-K protocol.
2. After receiving the request in flow 2, $KDC_2$ in B's domain discovers that one of the principals (A) is not local, i.e., not registered in the local database.
   (a) $KDC_2$ extracts A's domain name from A's name.[5]
   (b) From the domain name, $KDC_2$ determines the name of the peer KDC in that domain ($KDC_1$) and obtains the key ($K_{12}$) that it shares with that KDC. (The key can be stored, for example, in a normal principal entry in the local database of $KDC_2$.)
   (c) As in normal A-B-K, $KDC_2$ generates a new key $K_{ab}$ and issues a ticket for B. However, since it does not know A's KEK $K_a$ it cannot issue a ticket for A directly. Thus it issues a ticket for $KDC_1$ instead and forwards the reply to B.
3. B reads its own ticket and, behaving as usual, forwards A's ticket along with its own authentication token to A. We note that, throughout the protocol, B remains **oblivious** to the fact that A is in a different domain.
4. When A receives a ticket from B, it may do one of two things: i) try to read it (i.e., try to extract the key with $K_a$) or ii) simply determine from B's name that B is in a different domain and, therefore, the ticket coming from $B$ is not readable. In any case, $A$ forwards the ticket to $KDC_1$ for translation.
5. $KDC_1$ verifies the ticket and extracts $K_{ab}$. In doing so, it confirms that the ticket has been issued by $KDC_2$ and it authorizes A to "talk" to B. (The latter is confirmed by including both names in the computation of $MAC_{12}$.) However, $KDC_1$ can not draw any conclusions about the timeliness/freshness of the ticket it is translating. We do not consider this problematic since expiration time is expected to be factored into the ticket computation (although the protocol figures omit it.) In this sense, as long as the ticket is not expired, the KDC is willing to translate it.

[5] We assume that a principal name is always fully qualified, i.e., it includes as one of its components the domain name, e.g., *userX@domainY*.

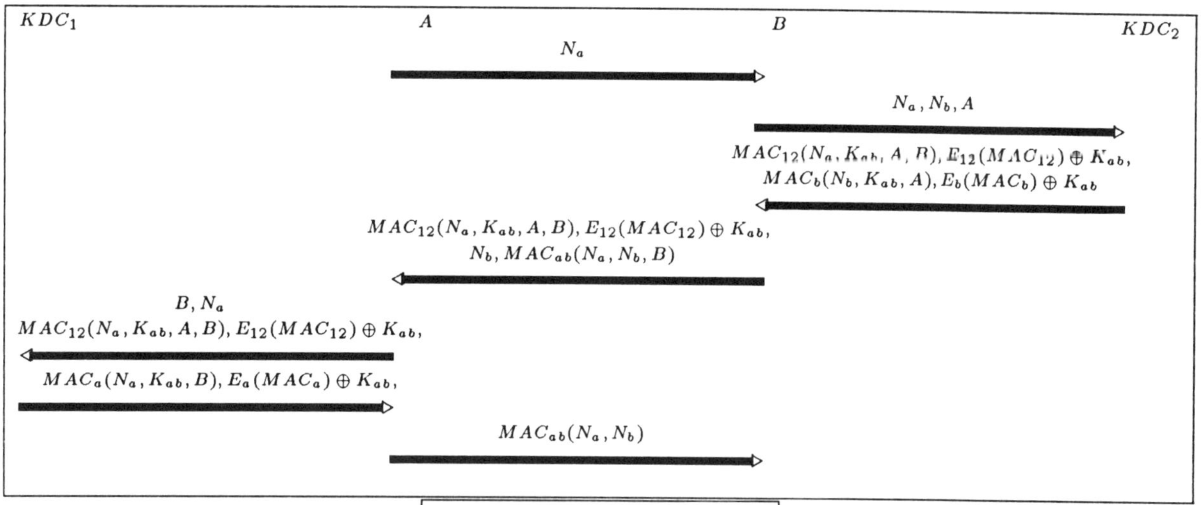


$MAC_{12} = MAC_{12}(N_a, K_{ab}, A, B)$

Figure 10: A-B-K Inter-Domain Protocol

This yields an unexpected benefit. Suppose that B caches A's ticket (as issued by $KDC_2$) and A does not cache its own ticket. At some later time B can supply A's ticket and $A$ can get the ticket translated by simply asking $KDC_1$. Consequently, the two-message ticket translation sub-protocol (flows 5 and 6) can be thought of as an independent protocol in its own right.

6. The final flow from A to B is the same as in intra-domain A-B-K.

Other 3-party protocols can be extended in a similar fashion. The inter-domain version of the time-based K-A-B(t) protocol is shown in Figure 11. The main difference with A-B-K is that now $KDC_1$ issues the tickets and $KDC_2$ acts as a translator for B.

An inter-domain version of K-A-B is also possible but its construction is somewhat less straight-forward. (See Figure 12.) As discussed in Section 3.5.2, the distinguishing feature of K-A-B is the so-called *pre-authentication* on forward flows whereby the KDC authenticates both principals before issuing the tickets. This is no longer possible because, while $KDC_1$ can still authenticate $A$, it is unable to check B's $MAC_b(N_a, N_b, B)$ expression. The solution is to let $KDC_1$ issue the tickets *provisionally* by including B's MAC expression in B's ticket (which is, of course, not readable by B.) This is a slight compromise since in the original K-A-B both parties obtain their respective tickets only after both are authenticated.

We can avoid the compromise by constructing a rather *ugly* protocol where $KDC_1$ super-encrypts A's ticket with $K_{12}$. Then, A would have to forward its own ticket along with B's to $KDC_2$ (via B.) $KDC_2$ would, in turn, check B's MAC expression and only then "unscramble" A's and translate B's ticket. In addition to having an extra flow (from B to A to deliver the ticket), this protocol would require longer messages (in flows 5, 6 and 7.)

## 4.2 With Inter-KDC Communication

Although inter-KDC communication should be avoided at times, under certain circumstances it becomes a necessity:

1. One of the principals (A or B) has no connection to its own KDC. More generally, a principal may have no means of contacting a KDC be it its own or a foreign one.
2. Software (code) size at one or both principals is critical. In this case, it is necessary to hide the *inter-domain-ness* of the protocols from both principals. In other words, principals can pretend that their "world" consists of a single domain while the burden and the complexity due to inter-domain issues can be isolated in KDCs.
3. KDCs have separate (perhaps faster and/or more secure) communication facilities, i.e., KDCs can communicate among themselves more efficiently than principals. (This is precisely the case with many wireless/cellular networks.)

As can be expected, allowing inter-KDC communication is commensurate with additional protocol complexity. In particular, a KDC not only has to "know" its peer KDC(s) in a foreign domain (and the corresponding key), but it also has to be aware of their whereabouts and operational status.

## 4.3 Inter-KDC Communication

The actual protocol modifications needed to support inter-KDC communication are fairly trivial. Three resultant protocols: A-B-K-K, K-K-A-B and K-K-A-B(t) are shown in Figures 13-15 below. It is easy to see that each of the three protocols differs from its *intra*-domain counterpart only insofar as two additional flows between KDCs. As mentioned above, the protocols are transparent to the principals, e.g., A and B do not need to differentiate between, say, A-B-K and A-B-K-K.

The main consequence of this convenience is the sacrifice of the KDC's *stateless* nature. Recall that all 2-party, 3-party and inter-domain protocols discussed so far allow KDCs to operate without having to keep state.[6] In other words, a KDC receives a request and replies to it; it does not wait for any external event or keep any state with respect to a request. A KDC never initiates communication; it only responds. All this keeps the design and operation of a KDC relatively simple. Inter-KDC communication changes the

[6] Excepting the password change protocol.

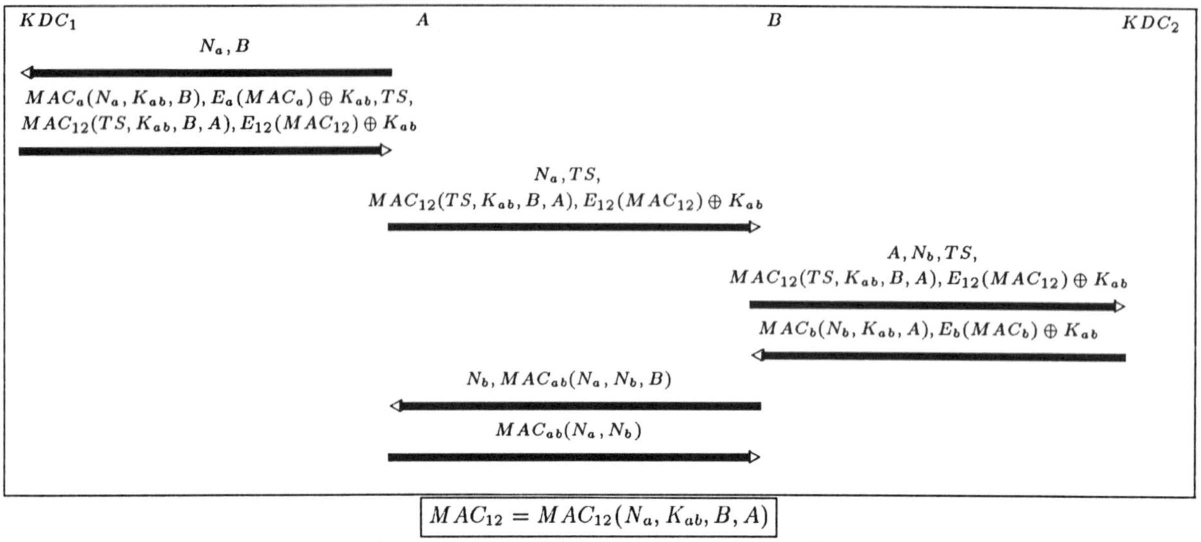


Figure 11: K-A-B(t) Inter-Domain Protocol

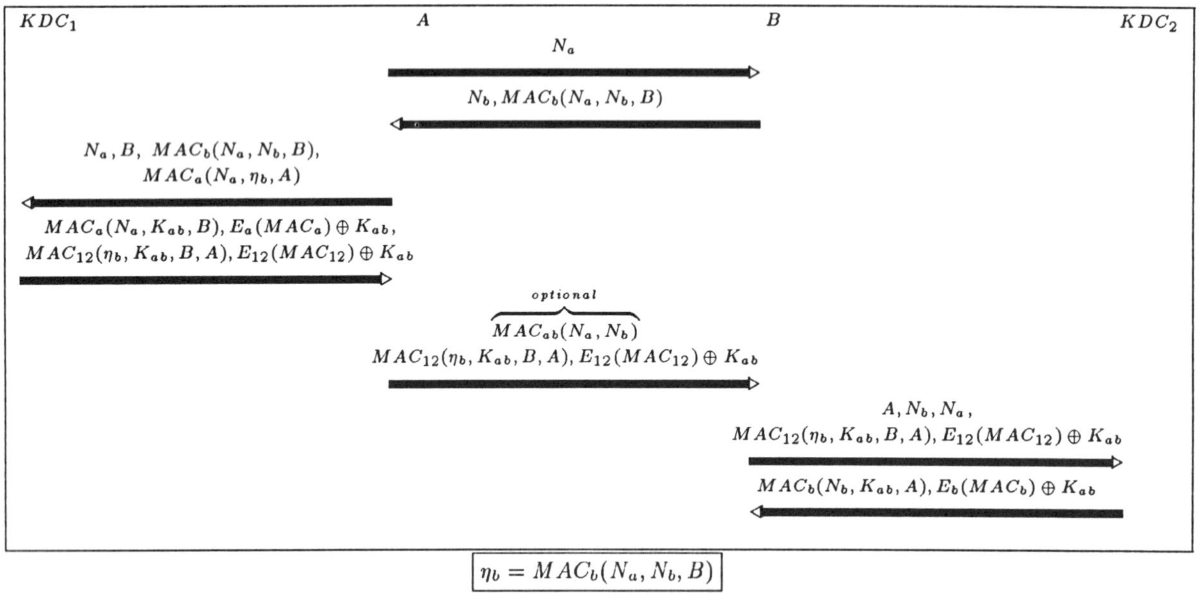


Figure 12: K-A-B Inter-Domain Protocol

simple nature of a KDC since it is now required to initiate communication with peer KDCs, wait for the response and deliver the results to the requesting principal. The ensuing complexity and ways of dealing with it pose a number of interesting systems questions which, due to space limitations, we discuss only briefly in this paper.

#### 4.3.1 A-B-K-K Protocol

As the contents of inter-KDC flows in Figure 13 indicate, $KDC_1$ issues the tickets (containing the new key) while $KDC_2$ only translates the ticket for B. Alternatively, the roles of the two KDCs can be switched as follows:

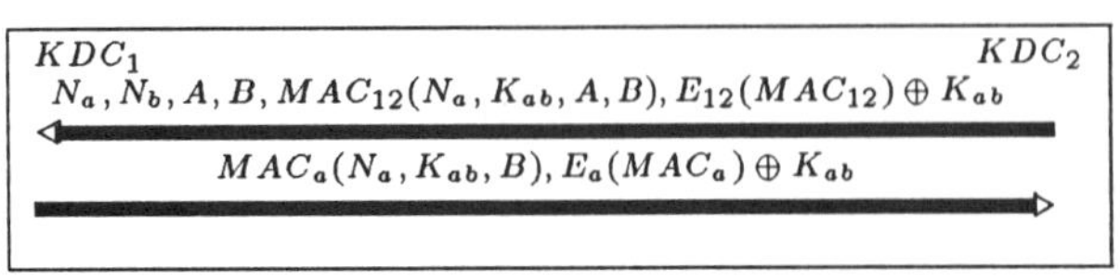


This variation would result in smaller messages but would also complicate things for $KDC_2$. This is because $KDC_2$ now has a choice: either it pre-issues a ticket for $B$ before contacting $KDC_1$ (in which case it has to store the ticket in the meantime) or it has to issue the ticket for $B$ when $KDC_1$ replies. In the latter case, $KDC_2$ still has to keep state between flows (at least $A$, $B$, $K_{ab}$ and $N_a$ must be kept.) Alternatively, $KDC_2$ can "export" the state information that it otherwise has to keep. This can be done by including the state variables in the flow to $KDC_1$; $KDC_1$ then simply echoes them back in its reply. (Of course, state variables can not be exported unprotected; $K_{ab}$ must be encrypted and the rest must be at least integrity-protected.) This would, once again, involve longer and more complicated messages. It becomes clear that the basic trade-off is between state retention (as well as implementation complexity) and message sizes.

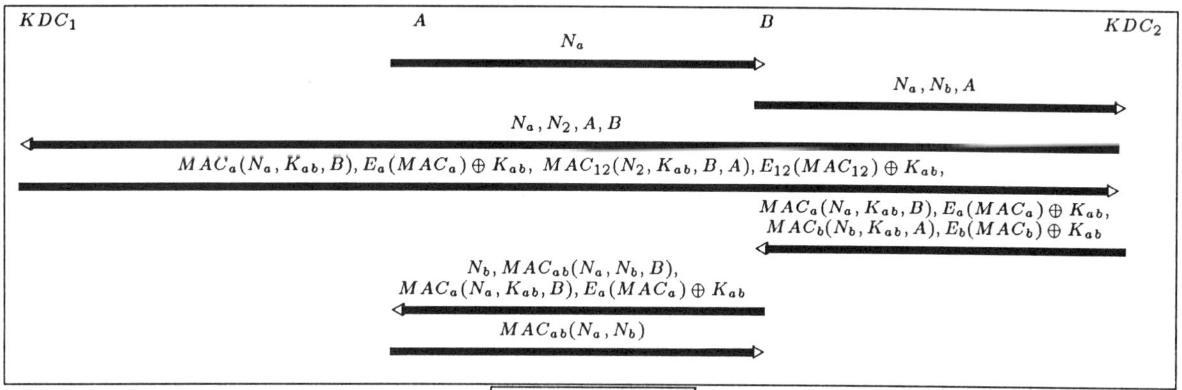


$N_2$ – nonce of $KDC_2$

Figure 13: A-B-K-K Inter-Domain Protocol

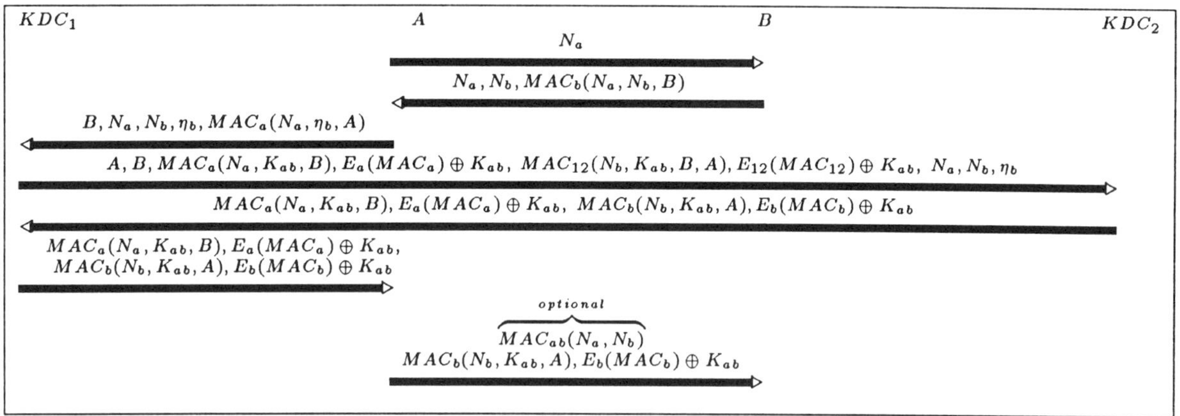


$\eta_b = MAC_b(N_a, N_b, B)$

Figure 14: K-K-A-B Inter-Domain Protocol

Similar issues and trade-offs arise in the other two protocols: K-K-A-B and K-K-A-B(t).[7]

### 4.4 Other Protocols

In addition to the protocols described above, a complete protocol family must contain auxiliary protocols targeted at actual human users.

- *Login or Single Sign-On (SSO)*: protocol that authenticates the human user and distributes a session key. In its minimal form (user only has a weak password) it is susceptible to so-called dictionary attacks unless stronger techniques (e.g., encrypted-key-exchange [2], public-key encryption, or smartcards/tokencards) are used in conjunction. The *KryptoKnight* SSO protocol is discussed in [22].

- *Single Sign-On for Mobile Users*: protocol that handles the case of a mobile user attempting to log in from a foreign domain. In spite of the operational scenario being similar to the A-B-K protocol, mobile SSO has some rather esoteric requirements (see [23] for a complete discussion of this topic and *KryptoKnight* mobile SSO protocol.)

- *Password Change*: protocol for changing users' long-term passwords and keys. Like mobile SSO, this protocol has some special requirements (mainly in terms of fault-tolerance) that influence protocol construction. An in-depth treatment of the subject and the description of the *KryptoKnight* password change protocol can be found in [16].

[7] One interesting aspect of K-K-A-B(t) protocol is that, unlike its immediate ancestor K-A-B(t), it does not require clock synchronization between the ticket-issuing KDC ($KDC_1$) and B. Instead, B's clock only needs to be synchronized with its own $KDC_2$. This is because $KDC_2$ has the option of updating the time-stamp (from $TS_1$ to $TS_2$) when translating B's ticket.

## 5 Summary

The protocols presented in this paper form a comprehensive family that addresses most authentication and key distribution requirements for any network environment. We circumvent some limitations of existing designs by supporting a flexible range of network configurations, avoiding reliance on tightly-synchronized clocks or counters, minimizing message sizes and cryptographic operations, assuring scalability, and staying clear of export restrictions. Overall, the protocols are light-weight in terms of resource usage and suitable for low-end devices with limited memory and processing capability.

## References


[1] R. K. Bauer, T. A. Berson, R. J. Feiertag, "A key distribution protocol using event markers," ACM TOCS 1 3 (1983) 249-255.

[2] S. Bellovin and M. Merritt, *Augmented Encrypted Key Exchange: a password-based protocol secure against dictionary attacks and password file compromise*, ACM Symp. on Comp. and Comm. Sec., 1993, 244–250.

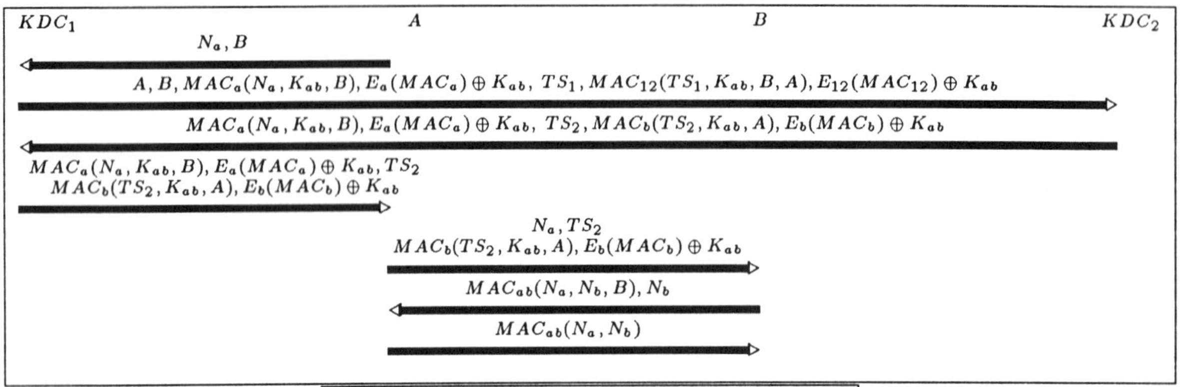


$TS_1, TS_2$ – time-stamps of $KDC_1$ and $KDC_2$, respectively

Figure 15: K-K-A-B(t) Inter-Domain Protocol

[3] M. Bellare, P. Rogaway, "Entity authentication and key distribution", Proc. Crypto'93, Advances in Cryptology, Springer Verlag.

[4] M. Bellare, P. Rogaway, Provably Secure Session Key Distribution- The Three Party Case, STOC'95.

[5] R. Bird, I. Gopal, A. Herzberg, P. Janson, S. Kutten, R. Molva, M. Yung, "Systematic design of 2-party authentication protocols," Proc. Crypto 91, Santa Barbara, CA (Aug.91) 44-61. Lecture Notes in Comp. Sc. 576, Springer Verlag (1991).

[6] R. Bird, I. Gopal, A. Herzberg, P. Janson, S. Kutten, R. Molva, M. Yung, "Systematic design of a family of attack-resistant authentication protocols," IEEE JSAC special issue on secure communications (1992).

[7] R. Bird, I. Gopal, A. Herzberg, P. Janson, S. Kutten, R. Molva, M. Yung, "The *KryptoKnight* Family of authentication and key distribution protocols", IEEE/ACM Trans. on Netw. (March 95).

[8] D. E. Denning, G. M. Sacco, "Time-stamps in key distribution systems", CACM 24 8 (Aug.81) 533-536.

[9] "Data Encryption Standard", FIPS 46, NBS (Jan.77).

[10] Research Issues in Ubiquitous Computing, The 13-th ACM Symp. on Principles of Distributed Computing (PODC), 1994, 2–8.

[11] W. Diffie, P. Van Oorschot, M. Weiner, *Authentication and Authenticated Key Exchange* Designs, Codes and Cryptography,2, 1992, 107-125.

[12] W. Diffie and M. Hellman, *New Directions in Cryptography*, IEEE Transactions on Information Theory, November 1976.

[13] O. Goldreich, S. Goldwasser, S. Micali, *How to Construct Random Functions*, J. of the ACM, V. 33, 1986, 210-217.

[14] L.Gong, *Using One-Way Functions for Authentication*, ACM Com. Comm. Review 19 5 (Oct.89) 8-11.

[15] L.Gong, Lower Bounds on Messages and Rounds for Network Authentication Protocols, The 1-st ACM Conf. on Compu. and Comm. Security, 1993, 26-37.

[16] R. Hauser, P. Janson, R. Molva, G. Tsudik and E. Van Herreweghen, "Robust and Secure Password/Key Change Method", 1994 European Symposium on Research in Computer Security, November 1994.

[17] ISO CD 9798-2, Information Technology: Security Techniques– Entity Authentication Mechanisms. Part 2: Entity Authentication Using Symmetric Techniques. July 1993.

[18] "Banking - Key management (wholesale)" ISO 8732, Geneva (1988).

[19] "OSI Directory - Part 8: Authentication Framework", ISO 9594-8, Geneva (1988).

[20] P. Janson and G. Tsudik, "Secure and Minimal Protocols for Authenticated Key Distribution", Computer Communications, September 1995.

[21] A. Kehne, J. Schoenwaelder, H. Langendoerfer, "A nonce-based protocol for multiple authentications", ACM OSR 26 4 (Oct.92) 84-89.

[22] R. Molva, G. Tsudik, E. Van Herreweghen, S. Zatti, "*KryptoKnight* authentication and key distribution system," Proc. ESORICS 92, Toulouse, France (23-25 Nov.92).

[23] R. Molva, D. Samfat and G. Tsudik, "Authentication of Mobile Users" IEEE Network, Special Issue on Mobile Communications, March/April 1994.

[24] M. Naor, M. Yung, "Universal One-Way Hash Functions and Their Cryptographic Applications," ACM Sym on Theo. of Computing, 1989.

[25] R. M. Needham, M. D. Schroeder, "Using encryption for authentication in large networks of computers," CACM 21 12 (1978) 993-998.

[26] R. M. Needham, M. D. Schroeder, "Authentication revisited", ACM OSR 21 1 (Jan.87) 7.

[27] B. C. Neuman, S. G. Stubblebine, "A note on the use of timestamps as nonces", ACM OSR 27 2 (Apr.93) 10-14.

[28] B. C. Neuman, T. Ts'O "Kerberos: An Authentication Service for Computer Networks", IEEE Communication Magazine, Sep. 1994.

[29] D. Otway, O. Rees, "Efficient and timely mutual authentication", ACM OSR 21 1 (Jan.87) 8-10.

[30] R. Rivest, "The MD5 Message Digest Algorithm", Internet draft, RSA Co. (Jul.91).

[31] J. Rompel. "One-Way Functions are Necessary and Sufficient for Digital Signature," ACM Sym. on Theo. of Computing, 1990.

[32] G. Steiner, C. Neuman, J. I. Schiller, "Kerberos: an authentication server for open network systems", Proc. Usenix Conf. (Winter 88).

[33] G. Tsudik, "Message authentication with one-way hash functions," Proc. IEEE Infocom 92, Florence, Italy (May 92).

[34] G. Tsudik, E. van Herreweghen, On Simple and Secure Key Distribution, 1-st ACM Conf. on Compu. and Comm. Security, 1993, 49-57.

# An Adaptable and Reliable Authentication Protocol for Communication Networks

Taekyoung Kwon Myeongho Kang Jooseok Song

Department of Computer Science
Yonsei University, Seoul 120-749, Korea

**Abstract**

*In this paper, we propose a new authentication and key distribution protocol which is adaptable and reliable for communication networks. The secrets for authentication, which are chosen from a relatively small space by common users, are easy to guess. Our protocol gives a solution to protect the weak secrets from guessing attacks. Compared with other related work, our protocol is more reliable because it is resistant to various kinds of attacks including guessing attacks, and more adaptable because it reduces several overheads which make the existing protocols more expensive. We show how to apply our protocol to the Q.931 calling sequences and to the World Wide Web model.*

## 1 Introduction

Secure transmission of information over insecure communication channels is a major issue in cryptography. To achieve the goal, cryptographic protocols for authentication and key exchange are needed[2]. Such protocols are typically the initial step on setting up a communication session. The purpose of them is to provide procedures for authentication of participants and for sharing of cryptographic keying material. Most of the important properties of the protocols do not depend on the underlying cryptographic algorithms, but rather on the structure of the messages exchanged. Bugs in and attacks to such protocols, therefore, usually do not come from the weak cryptographic algorithms, but from the mistakes in protocol design.

In recent years, a variety of protocols for authentication and key distribution have been proposed and applied to many communication systems. [1] describe procedures which allow the establishment of a common secret key by public messages. [2] proposes landmark protocols which use encryptions to achieve authenticated communications and is followed by a lot of protocols. In practice, they are applied to systems which require user-chosen secrets such as passwords for authentication. But it is well known that users choose easy-to-remember passwords that can be readily guessed[3]. The secrets chosen from a relatively small space are called weak secrets. Therefore, the existing protocols that utilize such weak secrets are susceptible to guessing attacks whereby an attacker iterates through a relatively small key space and verifies the correct guess[6]. Various protocols have been also proposed to be resistant to those attacks[6, 8, 7, 9]. However, they are more expensive in terms of the computation and communication costs than the protocols which do not strongly protect weak secrets[4]. The overheads, reduction of which can cause another vulnerability, make such protocols more expensive and impractical[5].

The aim of this paper is to propose a new authentication and key distribution protocol that is reliable and adaptable for various communication networks. Our protocol is resistant to various attacks and efficient in terms of overheads. We also attempt to show its adaptation to several communication networks. In the section 2, we clarify the problems and requirements with the summary of notations, and the section 3 outlines and verifies our protocol. The section 4 and 5 show adaptations of our protocol to the Q.931 call setup sequences for enhancing the Integrated Services Digital Network (ISDN) security and to the Hyper Text Transfer Protocol (HTTP) models for enhancing the World Wide Web (WWW) security.

## 2 Preliminary of Our Protocol Design

In this section, we clarify the problems and requirements for authentication and key exchange, and summarize notations to be used for protocol descriptions.

### 2.1 Problems and Requirements

Authentication protocols have potential attacks and overheads problems. First of all, we define several requirements to solve them.

**(1) Attacks**

There are various types of attacks on cryptographic protocols. Most of the attacks can be removed by



0-8186-7780-5/97 $10.00 © 1997 IEEE

careful corrections. But user-chosen keys make such protocols vulnerable to guessing attacks. These types of attacks explore the fact that user-chosen secrets are usually chosen from a relatively small space (eg. keyboard space, numerical keypad space or remindful word space). Such secrets are called poorly-chosen weak secrets or weakly-shared secrets. As a method to prevent the attacks, using strong secrets such as hard-coded or hard-wired random values for authentication is not flexible. In most cases, user-chosen passwords are utilized for authentication. Guessing attacks are performed by means of known-plaintext attacks or verifiable-text attacks [4]. Potential attacks in them can be divided into two classes.

- *Off-line guessing attacks* : An attacker eavesdrops messages and stores them locally. He or she guesses a password and tries iteratively to verify the guess in off-line manners. There is no need that a server should participate in verification, and so it cannot notice the attack[4].
- *On-line guessing attacks* : An attacker tries to use a guessed password iteratively in on-line manners. The attack is performed by replaying eavesdropped messages or impersonating other clients. Unless a protocol provides a server with sufficient information to detect the authentication failure, the server cannot notice the attack[5].

We should never forget that inside attackers(malicious participants) are able to obtain more information for attack than outside attackers(eavesdropper)[4, 5].

**(2) Overheads**

Protocols to prevent guessing attacks are more expensive in terms of the computation and communication costs than protocols not to protect weak secrets. Protocol overheads are defined as follows.

- *Computation costs* : They depend on the number of cryptographic values such as random numbers and the amount of calculations.
- *Communication costs* : They depend on the size of messages and the number of protocol steps.

**(3) Requirements**

To solve the above problems, we define several requirements for the protocol. For authentication and key distribution, various cryptographic messages are exchanged between communicating parties. On constructing them, following requirements should be satisfied to defeat known attacks and to reduce overheads.

- Confidentiality of sensitive information included in messages should be confirmed.
- Authenticity of sender and originator should be verified. While the originator is a real message builder, the sender is an intermediary of message.
- The sender should be able to confirm the delivery.
- Participants should share the same session key and confirm it.
- Unauthorized modification in messages should be detected.
- Freshness of message should be confirmed.
- Any participants should be able to detect a replay of message as soon as possible.
- Contents of messages should be understood and recognized by legitimate participants.
- Messages should contain redundant bits to defeat verification attacks and make the entropy for guessing some specific information in message very high.
- For efficiency, a small number of cryptographic values, cryptographic operations, and protocol steps should be assured. In addition, the size of each message should be minimized.

## 2.2 Summary of Notations

To describe our protocol clearly, we summarize notations to be used. $A$ and $B$ are system principals of communication participants, and $S$ is a principal of trusted center or a server. A weak secret and a public key of $A$ are denoted as $K_A$ and $P_A$, respectively. $K_S$ stands for a public key of $S$ and $CERT[S]$ for a certificate. $K$ means a session key. The $i$-th nonce value of $A$ is denoted as $na(i)$ and a bit length of $X$ as $|X|$. $\{M\}_K$ denotes a ciphertext of message $M$ under an encryption key $K$. $h()$ is a one-way hash function and $f()$ a simple predefined function. $H_A$ is a hash value owned by $A$ and $F_A$ a partial value of a message generated by $A$. The partial value means a bit stream extracted from the original message. $\oplus$ and , represent a bit-wise XOR and a concatenator, respectively. $A \rightarrow B : M$ denotes that $A$ sends $M$ to $B$.

# 3 K1 Protocol(K1P) Design

In this section, we describe our basic idea and our protocol which is called K1P. K1P is proved through the formal logic models such as BAN logic and GNY logic which are aimed for the analysis of knowledge and belief[13]. However, we use informal descriptions rather than the logics to represent verifications of our protocol, because the logics are not so much helpful in describing attacks and overheads.

### 3.1 Idea of Our Protocol

In most of other protocols, the weakly-shared secret has been used as a cryptographic key for authentication and key exchange. But it makes the necessary number of random values and cryptographic operations very large for countering guessing attacks[7, 9]. Another approach like EKE[8] requires a large number of protocol steps. Using a concept of one-time pad and a one-way hash function, we reduce those overheads.

**(1) Basic Authentication Statement**

We introduce a basic statement for authentication:

$$na1 \oplus na2, h(K_A \oplus na1, na2) \quad (1)$$

The statement is composed of two sufficiently large random values and a shared secret. We assume that the shared secret was chosen poorly from the relatively small space. Required operations are only a XOR and a hash operation. Only those who know $na1$, $na2$ and $K_A$ are able to construct the statement and to verify it. The weak secret, $K_A$, is masked by $na1$ and the result, $K_A \oplus na1$, is used to compute the hash value along with $na2$. The random values $na1$ and $na2$ endow randomness on the input image of hash function and serve as nonce values. If they are distributed securely, legitimate participants are able to confirm the authenticity of each other. Because $na1$ and $na2$ are sufficiently large random bits, it is computationally infeasible for intruders to obtain either $na1$ or $na2$ from $na1 \oplus na2$ without knowing any of them. Therefore, though attackers are able to guess the weak secret $K_A$, they cannot verify whether the guessed value is correct in the basic statement. It means that the additionally required entropy for guessing $K_A$ is $log2^{|na1|}$. This can defeat the guessing attacks. A method for sharing $na1$ and $na2$ is needed and this is fulfilled by public key encryptions. We explain this in the part (2).

**(2) Authentication and Key Distribution**

We add functions for sharing the random numbers and a new session key to the basic statement:

$$\begin{array}{lll} 1. & A \rightarrow S: & \{na1, na2, K_A \oplus na1\}_{K_S} \\ 2. & S \rightarrow A: & na1 \oplus na2 \oplus K, h(K_A \oplus na1, K, na2) \end{array} \quad (2)$$

For the purpose, a public key mechanism is needed. We call the statement base protocol. In step 1, $A$ generates two random numbers and encrypts them using $S$'s public key, $K_S$. A weakly-shared secret, $K_A$, is masked by $na1$ and the result, $K_A \oplus na1$, is also included in the message. After decryption, $S$ gets the random numbers and the masked value, and simply XORs them to authenticate $A$. In step 2, $S$ generates a new session key and encrypts it using $na1 \oplus na2$ as a one-time pad. That means, just a bitwise XORing operation is enough and the assumption, $|na1 \oplus na2| = |K|$, should be assured. Because $na1$ and $na2$ are nonce values, $na1 \oplus na2$ can be used as a one-time pad. Due to the one-time pad, $A$ derives the new session key in a simple and secure manner. By computing the hash value, $A$ can check the integrity and freshness of the new key, and confirm the result of authentication. $A$ can also authenticate $S$. While $A$ is authenticated by $S$ in step 1, the new session key is sent to $A$ and $S$ is authenticated by $A$ in step 2.

**(3) Discussion**

In our approach, there is no need to encrypt the key distribution message with a weak secret as in the existing protocols. Instead, the concept of one-time pad is used for the purpose. Therefore, the relatively fast operations such as XOR and hash computations are enough. The one-way hash function is used to make a small random value from large random inputs. The hash value is used for various purposes such as key integrity check, authentication confirmation, and counterpart authentication. Our usage of hash function is not originated from MAC, the Message Authentication Code, because ours has a unique format and is not intended for message authentication only.

In the message 2 of the base protocol (2), while $na1 \oplus na2 \oplus K$ makes the new key $K$ undetectable by outside attackers who do not know $K$ at all, $na1 \oplus na2$ defeats all attackers who try to guess $K_A$. That means, attacks on the new key, $K$, require the entropy of $log2^{2|K|}$ and guessing $K_A$ requires the entropy of $log2^{|na1|}$ at least. Under the condition of $|na1 \oplus na2| = |K|$, the additional entropy required to guess $K_A$ is $log2^{2|na1|}$ without knowledge of $K$ and it is same to the entropy to find $K$. If $K$ is known or compromised by some means later, the additional entropy to guess $K_A$ is $log2^{|na1|}$ and the minimum complexity to guess $K_A$ is still large. For an attack on integrity by finding collision pairs of hash value, the probability to find the same-sized pairs is extremely low. Even if they are found, it is infeasible to cheat participants without finding the correct random numbers. Thus such attacks do not work.

On actual implementation, the usage of public key algorithm might be burdensome. This problem is solved by using $K_S$ as a hard-wired or hard-coded conventional secret key rather than a publick key. This is not a poorly chosen secret but a well chosen secret at manufacturing time. However in this solution, security and flexibility is somewhat degraded. In addition, $S$ should maintain a $K_S$ table as different $K_S$ should be assigned to each machine.

Using the hash value $h(K_A \oplus na1, na2)$ as a Key Encryption Key(KEK), we can modify the base protocol as follows:

$$\begin{array}{lll} 1. & A \rightarrow S: & \{na1, na2, K_A \oplus na1\}_{K_S} \\ 2. & S \rightarrow A: & \{na1, K\}_{h(K_A \oplus na1, na2)} \end{array} \quad (3)$$

The entropy for guessing $K_A$ is as high as in the unmodified version but it is harder to find $K$ than in the base protocol (2). For an attacker, $2^{2|na1|+|K_A|}$ complexities are needed to find $K$. Only one disadvantage is that one more cipher operation is added. There are two purposes for the modification above. The first one is to distribute a session key of any size. In previous version, the size of random values, $na1$ and $na2$, was varied in proportion to that of $K$ under the condition of $|na1 \oplus na2| = |K|$. But we don't want the size of $na1$ to be abnormally large or small. The former is burdensome and the latter insecure. In the modified version, there is no need to preserve the condition. That means, the size of session key does not depend on that of $na1$. Therefore, regardless of the size, $K$ can be hidden securely in the message 2. We can maintain the size of nonce values as intended and apply various cryptosystems without worrying about the size of cryptographic key. Second is for reducing the number of blocks in the message 2. If the size of session key is smaller than that of the hash value, i.e. under 128 bits, the total length of the message 2 can be reduced in the modified base protocol (3). The hash value $h(K_A \oplus na1, na2)$ is used temporarily only for a key distribution during relatively short terms. In section 3.2 and 3.3, we describe K1P in detail.

## 3.2 Three Way K1P

On the basis of our idea, we propose a protocol for three way mutual authentication and key distribution. Three way K1P is as follows:

$$\begin{array}{lll} 1. & A \rightarrow B: & \{A, B, na1, na2, K_A \oplus na1\}_{K_S} \\ 2. & B \rightarrow S: & \{A, B, na1, na2, K_A \oplus na1\}_{K_S}, \\ & & \{B, A, nb1, nb2, K_B \oplus nb1\}_{K_S} \\ 3. & S \rightarrow B: & na1 \oplus na2 \oplus K, \\ & & h(K_A \oplus na1, K, na2, A \oplus B), \\ & & nb1 \oplus nb2 \oplus K, \\ & & h(K_B \oplus nb1, K, nb2, A \oplus B) \\ 4. & B \rightarrow A: & na1 \oplus na2 \oplus K, \\ & & h(K_A \oplus na1, K, na2, A \oplus B), \\ & & \{f(F_A), nb1 \oplus nb2\}_K \\ 5. & A \rightarrow B: & \{f(nb1 \oplus nb2)\}_K \end{array} \quad (4)$$

In step 1, $A$ generates the message as we introduced in the previous part and sends it to $S$ via $B$. $B$ is a legitimate counterpart of $A$. Identifiers of $A$ and $B$ are included in the message to inform that they are legitimate participants. In step 2, $B$ composes a similar message and sends it to $S$. The trusted center, $S$, can check the authenticity of both $A$ and $B$ as we mentioned earlier. In step 3, $S$ generates a session key, $K$, and replies with message 3 as we described. $A \oplus B$ is added to the hash inputs to make $A$ and $B$ confirm that $S$ authenticated them. $B$ gets the new session key, $K$, and confirms everything as we introduced in the section 3.1. In step 4, $B$ produces a challenge value using the partial bit stream of message 1 and $nb1 \oplus nb2$. The one-time pad, $nb1 \oplus nb2$, has a nonce property and can be used in the Challenge-Response operations. We define $f(x)$ as a simple function for $x+1$. In step 5, $A$ produces and sends a response value. As a result, $A$ and $B$ can authenticate each other and confirm that the session key is shared securely.

The entropy to find out a new session key, $K$, by brute force search is $log 2^{2|na1|}$ as we mentioned. That means, the attacks on $K$ require $2^{2|na1|}$ complexities and are computationally infeasible. To perform off-line guessing attacks on a weak secret, $K_A$ or $K_B$, at least $2^{|na1|}$ complexities are required. Assuming that $na1$ is sufficiently large, it is computationally infeasible. On-line guessing attacks are also defeated as they will be detected by $S$. Unless a guessed value is correct at first trial, $S$ can detect the failure and illegal trials finally. It is due to the fact that identifiers of participants are included in the first message. Therefore, it is also impossible to search the secret on line in a relatively small space. As a result, all attacks by replaying an eavesdropped message or by impersonating other clients are defeated in K1P.

While the GLNS protocol and the Gong's optimal protocol require too many random numbers and encryptions to defeat the guessing attacks[7, 9, 6], our K1P needs only two random numbers, one public key encryption, one hash operation, and two symmetric encryptions for each participant. Compared with other work strong to the guessing attacks, K1P is more efficient by reducing the overheads. It makes the protocol more practical and adaptable.

Three way K1P can be modified as we mentioned previously. A hard-wired or hard-coded symmetric key can be used as $K_S$. To distribute a session key of abnormal size or to reduce the message blocks, we can apply the modified base protocol (3) to K1P.

## 3.3 Two Party K1P

We also propose an adaptable and reliable protocol for two party's direct authentication and key distribution. Two party K1P is as follows:

$$\begin{array}{lll} 1. & A \rightarrow S: & \{A, na1, na2, K_A \oplus na1\}_{K_S} \\ 2. & S \rightarrow A: & na1 \oplus na2 \oplus K, \\ & & h(K_A \oplus na1, K, na2) \\ 3. & A \rightarrow S: & h(K_A \oplus na2, K, na1) \end{array} \quad (5)$$

In step 1, $A$ generates a message 1 in a similar way to the three way K1P and sends it to $S$. After decryption, $S$ authenticates $A$ and generates a one-time pad. In step 2, $S$ generates a new session key, $K$, and replies to $A$ as in the base protocol (2). In step 3, $A$ replies with a new hash value to inform an admission of $K$. Hash value of message 2 also serves as a Challenge-Response for $K$ with message 3. As a result, both participants authenticate each other and share the session key securely.

As we described previously, the guessing attacks on $K_A$ on line or off line are computationally infeasible. All methods to find $K$ are also countered. While our K1P requires only one public key encryption and two hash operations for each participant, two random numbers for the initiater $A$, and three protocol steps, other related work like GLNS, Gong's optimal and Strengthened EKE needs more of them for preventing the guessing attacks[7, 9, 8]. To reduce the overheads in them, the new weakness was made[5]. As in the three way K1P, the two party K1P is more efficient than other work strong to the guessing attacks.

Using $na2$ and $K$, a mutual key negotiation is possible in our protocol. For this purpose, a new session key $K'$ can be generated by several methods. For instance, a one-way hash function can be used as $K' = h(na2, K)$ or the Diffie-Hellman method as $K' = g^{xy} \bmod n$. In latter case, since its security is based on the difficulty of calculating discrete logarithms in a finite field[1], two random values should satisfy $na2 = g^x \bmod n$ and $K = g^y \bmod n$ where $n$ is a large prime and $g$ is a primitive mod $n$.

Our protocol can be modified to use $A$'s public key rather than $S$'s as follows:

$$\begin{array}{lll} 1. & A \rightarrow S: & \{P_A\}_{K_A} \\ 2. & S \rightarrow A: & \{ns, K, K_A \oplus ns\}_{P_A} \\ 3. & A \rightarrow S: & h(K_A \oplus ns, K, ns) \end{array} \quad (6)$$

In step 1, $A$'s public key $P_A$ is encrypted using $K_A$ and sent to $S$. Though $A$ is authenticated by $S$ in step 3, this modified version is as secure as the original one.

# 4 Adaptation to Q.931

We adapt our protocol to the Q.931 call setup sequences for enhancing the security of ISDN. Though the advent of Broadband ISDN (BISDN) makes the future of ISDN not bright, ISDN has the already confirmed standards and is operated in several countries[17]. Because of its speed and flexibility, ISDN is rapidly becoming the Internet access communication medium of choice for individuals and for business. Since ISDN is the integrated services network which provides users with a variety of digital services, it is vulnerable and sensitive to malicious attacks. Therefore, it is desirable that ISDN should provide security services for user information without decreasing the performance of network. To provide security services, a suitable cipher system and a confidential method for key sharing and authentication are required. We apply our protocol to Q.931 call setup signalling protocol for the purpose.

## 4.1 Construction of Q.931 Messages

ITU-T Q.931 recommends a standard signalling protocol for the user network interface (UNI) of ISDN. This protocol specifies procedures and messages for the end-to-end call control of ISDN. There are various messages in Q.931 and they are transmitted through D channel of ISDN. The maximum size of message is defined as 260 octets. Each message contains a header part and various information elements. Of the messages, SETUP, ALERTING, CONNECT, and DISCONNECT are related to over all networks, including the sending and the receiving reference points. The messages can include the user-user information (UUI) element as an option for the transmission of information between users, transparent to the network[14, 15, 16]. We make the messages of K1P included in this field. For the purpose, the caller $A$'s SETUP and USER INFORMATION messages, the callee $B$'s SETUP and CONNECT messages, and the trusted center $S$'s DISCONNECT message should include UUI element. The maximum size of UUI element is defined as 131 octets. The message 2 of the three way K1P has a maximum size in our protocols. When we accept the strong symmetric key which is embedded in each terminal equipment at the manufacturing time, there is no need to consider the size. But on using a public key, we should limit the size of key as 512 bits or use an additional USER INFORMATION message for the key of which size is larger than 512 bits.

## 4.2 K1P in Q.931

By applying the three way K1P to Q.931, it is possible to make ISDN provide a reliable authentication and key distribution. First of all, we describe the security model for the adaptation briefly. LE stands for a Local Exchange and is connected to other LEs or

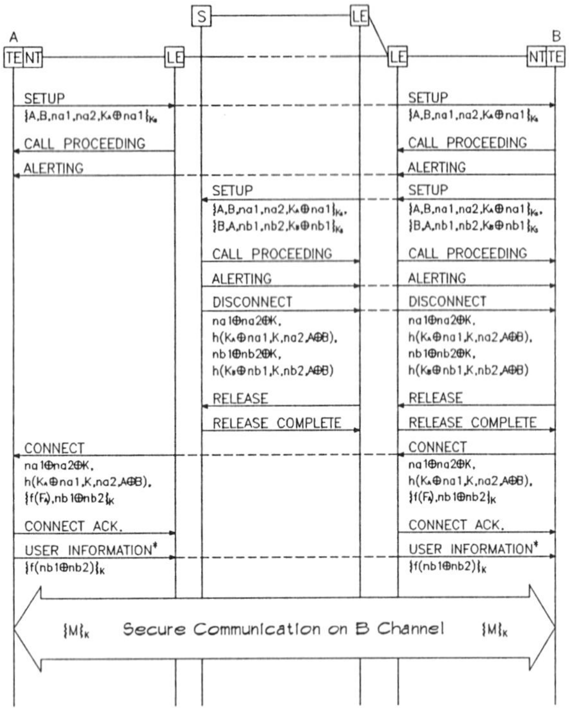


Figure 1: Three way K1P in Q.931

to Network Terminations (NTs). For secure services, each user should have registered to the trusted center and selected a password. The trusted center is a combination of TEs and NTs. User inputs the password using a small number of keys on Terminal Equipment (TE) anytime the services are needed.

As depicted in Figure 1, the Q.931 call setup procedure is preserved and the three way K1P is applied. By applying the two party K1P to Q.931, it is possible to provide two party's direct authentication in ISDN as shown in Figure 2.

## 5 Adaptation to WWW

The Internet is a vast cyberspace where we can gather, disseminate, and exchange all types of information. The WWW(web briefly) is accepted as the biggest service in the Internet and is also used for various commercial services and sensitive services. Therefore, the web has provided a simple authentication method. But it is a weak solution as passwords are transmitted over the Internet in a simple encoded text. We attempt to provide a clear authentication and key distribution mechanism for the web environment.

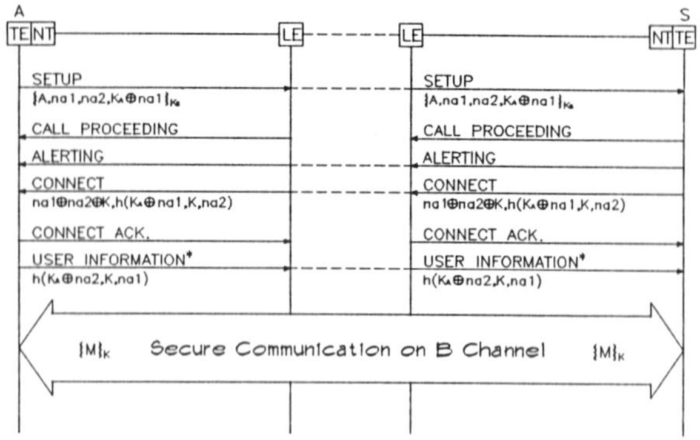


Figure 2: Two Party K1P in Q.931

### 5.1 Adaptation of K1P

The Hyper Text Transfer Protocol(HTTP) of the web runs as a stateless protocol that does not retain information about a connection from one request to the next. This is to achieve the goal to provide a simple algorithm with fast response time. Therefore, connection and disconnection are required for every request and response pair. However, the basic idea of our protocol is to require all participants to store states. A method to solve the stateless problem is discussed in the section 5.2. By making a little modification in the two party K1P, we can adapt it to the web. It is reasonable that $S$ sends its certificate $CERT[S]$ to $A$ while it is burdensome for $A$ to maintain a large number of public keys. Therefore, we start to modify our protocol as shown below.

1. $S \rightarrow A: \quad S, ns1, CERT[S]$ (7)
2. $A \rightarrow S: \quad \{A, na1, ns1, K_A \oplus na1\}_{K_S}$

The server $S$ generates a random number $ns1$ and sends it with its own certificate to the client $A$ who requested a sensitive data. $A$ confirms the server's certificate and obtains the server's public key. $A$ constructs the message 2 and sends it to $S$. This is similar to the message 1 of the base protocol. However, we should focus that $ns1$ is included instead of $na2$ for making confirm the freshness of message 2. This is an initial step. Because HTTP is a stateless protocol, authentication should be performed whenever the connection request is sent from a client. This makes the protocol design difficult. But our adapted K1P solves the problem easily.

1. $S \rightarrow A: na1 \oplus ns2, h(K_A \oplus na1, ns2, A \oplus S)$ (8)
2. $A \rightarrow S: na2 \oplus ns2, h(K_A \oplus na2, ns2, A \oplus S)$

$S$ generates a new random number $ns2$ and sends the message 1 to $A$. This is similar to the basic authentication statement. We assume that $S$ and $A$ know $na1$. $A$ confirm the freshness of message 1 by $na1$. $S$ sends the message 1 for requiring $A$ to send his password. $A$ confirms the message 1 and sends the message 2 as a response. By confirming the message 2, $S$ is able to authenticate $A$. While the protocol (7) performs an initialization, the protocol (8) is iterated whenever authentication is needed after the initialization. For iteration in (8), $na1$ and $na2$ is generalized as $na(i)$ and $na(i+1)$ where $i \geq 1$.

## 5.2 Secure Web Model for K1P

As we mentioned earlier, HTTP is a stateless protocol. To solve the problem, we use a Common Gateway Interface (CGI) and a HTTP cookie mechanism. The cookie is a general mechanism by which the server stores the state of each connection and retrieves later. CGI scripts are used to control the cookies. Cookies are stored on client side and included in the next message. Using those mechanisms, our protocol is implemented and adapted to the web completely. We describe a secure web model for adapting our protocol briefly. In the client side, a Client Security (CS) module is implemented and operated independently without communications with a web browser. In the server side, a Server Security (SS) module is implemented as a CGI application and operated when it is invoked through CGI by the web server. When the SS module is invoked, it communicates with the web server and the CS module. Different channels are established for web browser-web server and CS-SS. One is for HTTP and the other for the adapted K1P. Whenever the authentication is confirmed, the SS module obtains $na$ of a client $A$ and sends it to the web browser via the web server by constructing message in a cookie as follows.

$$COOKIE[\{A, na\}_{K_S}] \qquad (9)$$

The cookie is introduced to the client by including a Set-Cookie header as part of an HTTP response. After the web browser requests a sensitive document which needs authentication, it receives a set-cookie information in the response. When the web browser requests a similar sensitive document after initialization, it has to send the cookie in the request. Figure 3 shows the transactions in our secure web model. By HTTP, when the web browser requests a sensitive document, a corresponding GET URI message is sent to the web server. The URI stands for the Uniform Resource Identifier and means an Uniform Resource Locator (URL) or an Uniform Resource Name (URN). After that, the SS module is executed. By K1P, it sends AUTH_REQUEST to the corresponding CS module with the message 1 of the protocol

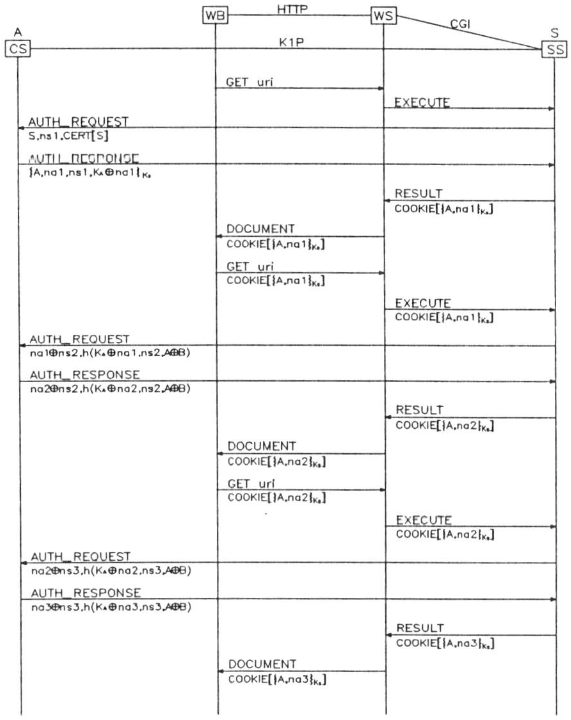


Figure 3: Adapted K1P in the web model

(7). The CS module replies with AUTH_RESPONSE and this command contains the message 2 of (7). In this step, the cookie is required because $na$ should be stored for the SS module. Therefore, the SS module sets the cookie as in (9) and is killed or dozed. It is due to the fact that the SS module is programmed as a CGI application. The web server sends a response including the corresponding document and the cookie to the web browser. These are all steps of initial authentication transaction. Next transactions are similar to the initial authentication transactions and performed iteratively but the messages of the protocol (8) are used instead of the messages of (7). On performing above transactions, two problems should be considered. One is the client's request to another sensitive document in another region and the other is the expiration of states. The first case does not matter in our secure web model. For example, in the mid step of Figure 3, when the client requests another sensitive document in another region, a cookie containing former data $COOKIE[\{A, na1\}_{K_S}]$ is sent to the new URL. But newly invoked SS module in another region ignores it and sends a new AUTH_REQUEST to the corresponding CS module. This new AUTH_REQUEST contains $S'$, $ns1'$, and $CERT[S']$ instead of $na1 \oplus ns2$

and $h(K_A \oplus na1, ns2, A \oplus S)$. Though the CS module contains the former data, it can reply to new AUTH_REQUEST as a usual initialization. The second case is solved by running and terminating the web browser and the CS client module together. The cookie expires when its expiration date comes. The CS module is executed as an independent application. All states are expired when the CS module is terminated or the cookies expire.

Our secure web model provides the functions of authentication securely. To provide an encryption of documents, an encryption key can be made as $K = h(na1) \oplus ns1$ and so on. For each document, a different encryption key is used and this makes the system secure.

## 6 Conclusions

We have designed the new reliable and adaptable protocol for authentication and key distribution. First we have clarified the problems and the requirements on authentication protocols, and represented our basic idea. We have verified our basic idea and proposed our protocol family, K1P. They are the three way mutual authentication protocol and the two party's direct authentication protocol. We have verified that our protocol is reliable and adaptable by informal description. Compared with other related work, ours has the superiority in terms of overheads and attacks. Adaptations of our protocol to ISDN and the web have been shown. We implemented the secure web model on a PC platform by applying K1P. Our protocol was applied to the models successfully. Our K1P is: (1) reliable because it is resistant to various attacks including guessing attacks; and (2) adaptable because it minimizes various kinds of overheads such as communication and computation costs.

## References


[1] W.Diffie, M.Hellman, "New Directions in Cryptography," *IEEE Transactions on Information Theory*, Vol. 17, pp. 1-100, 1987.

[2] R.Needham, M.Schroeder, "Using Encryption For Authentication in Large Networks of Computers," *Communications of the ACM*, Vol. 21, No. 12, pp. 993-999, 1978.

[3] R.Morris, K.Thompson, "Password Security: A Case Study," *Communications of the ACM*, Vol. 22, No. 11, pp. 594-597, 1979

[4] L.Gong, "Verifiable-text Attacks in Cryptographic Protocols," *Proceedings of IEEE INFOCOM'90*, pp. 686-693, 1990.

[5] Y.Ding, P.Horster, "Undetectable On-line Password Guessing Attacks," *ACM Operating Systems Review*, Vol. 29, No. 4, pp. 77-86, 1995.

[6] M.Lomas, L.Gong, J.Saltzer, R.Needham, "Reducing Risks from Poorly Chosen Keys," *ACM Operating Systems Review*, Vol. 23, No. 5, pp. 14-18, 1989.

[7] L.Gong, M.Lomas, R.Needham, J.Saltzer, "Protecting Poorly Chosen Secrets from Guessing Attacks," *IEEE Journal on Selected Areas in Communications*, Vol. 11, No. 5, pp. 648-656, 1993.

[8] S.Bellovin, M.Merritt, "Augmented Encrypted Key Exchange: A Password-based Protocols Secure Against Dictionary Attacks and Password File Compromise," *Proceedings of the 1st ACM Conference on Computer and Communications Security*, pp. 244-250, 1993.

[9] L.Gong, "Optimal Authentication Protocols Resistant to Password Guessing Attacks," *Proceedings of the 8th IEEE Computer Security Foundations Workshop*, pp. 24-29, 1995.

[10] D.Denning, G.Sacco, "Timestamps in Key Distribution Protocols," *Communications of ACM*, Vol. 24, No. 8, pp. 533-536, 1981.

[11] D.Otway, O.Rees, "Efficient and Timely Mutual Authentication," *ACM Operating Systems Review*, Vol. 21, No. 1, pp. 8-10, 1987.

[12] W.Fumy, M.Munzert, "A Modular Approach to Key Distribution," *Proceedings of Crypto'90*, pp. 274-283, 1991.

[13] L.Gong, R.Needham, R.Yahalom, "Reasoning about Belief in Cryptographic Protocols," *Proceedings of the IEEE Symposium on Research in Security and Privacy*, pp. 234-248, 1990.

[14] ITU-T Recommendation Q.931, Digital Subscriber Signalling System No.1 (DSS1), Network Layer, User-Network Management,

[15] W.Gifford, "ISDN User-Network Interfaces," *IEEE Journal on Selected Areas in Communications*, Vol. 4, No. 3, pp. 343-348, 1986

[16] S.Kano, "Layer 2 and 3 ISDN Recommendations," *IEEE Journal on Selected Areas in Communications*, Vol. 4, No. 3, pp. 355-359, 1986

[17] W.Burr, Security in ISDN, NIST Special Publication 500-189, 1991.

# An Algorithm to Compute Collusion Paths


Steven H. Low

Department of EEE
University of Melbourne
VIC 3052 Australia
slow@ee.mu.oz.au

Nicholas F. Maxemchuk

AT&T Research
Murray Hill
NJ 07974 USA
nfm@research.att.com



## Abstract

*In earlier work we have formulated a collusion problem that determines whether it is possible for a set of colluders to collectively discover a target set of information, starting from their initial knowledge, and have presented a complete solution for a special case of the problem. In this paper we present an algorithm that solves the general case. Given a collusion problem the algorithm determines whether it has a solution, and if it does, computes one. A solution to the collusion problem is a method with which the colluders can uncover the hidden information. Communications protocols that employ cryptographic techniques are increasingly used to protect privacy as well as to communicate. A cryptographic protocol defines a process by which information is transferred among some users while hidden from others. The algorithm presented here can be used to determine whether a subset of protocol users can discover, during or after the protocol's execution, the information that is designed to be hidden from them.*


## 1 Introduction

Complex communications protocols employing cryptographic building blocks are being developed not only to communicate, but also to protect privacy, e.g., in broadband networks [11, 10], in mobile networks [3], in electronic commerce [2, 5, 6], and in health insurance systems [9]. A cryptographic protocol defines a process by which some information is transferred among some users and hidden from others. The collusion problem determines whether it is possible for a subset of users to discover, through collusion, the information that is to be hidden from them after or during a protocol's execution. A solution to the problem is a specific way with which the colluders can uncover the hidden information.

It is not always possible for two users to collude. In order to collude they must share a common, unique piece of information pertaining to the protocol run. This may be necessary because, in practice, the sender and the receiver, such as banks in the anonymous credit card context [5, 6], may exchange a large number of messages corresponding to different protocol runs within a short time interval. It may not be sufficient, for example, for two banks to know that both have been involved in some transaction, because they may have been involved in a great many transactions within a short time interval. In order to combine their knowledge pertaining to a particular protocol run, they need to share a unique link pertaining to that run. There are two possible such links: 1) a unique message that is exchanged during that protocol run, or 2) a unique piece of data, e.g, two banks may have the unique social security number of a customer and hence can combine their knowledge about the customer. We stress however that our formulation includes as a special case in which two users can collude as long as one knows the other, even if they share no unique information.

The collusion problem is motivated by our earlier work [5] and [9] in which we designed multiparty communications protocols to protect privacy in credit card and health-care systems. In the credit card system, for instance, the protocol uses standard cryptographic techniques to hide different pieces of transaction information from different parties involved in the transaction so that at the end of a credit card transaction, no single party except the cardholder can associate the cardholder's identity with where or what she purchases. Moreover it takes many parties to collude in order to compromise the cardholder's privacy.




0-8186-7780-5/97 $10.00

In [8, 4] we first introduced a formal model for cryptographic protocols and their collusion analysis. The collusion problem is completely solved for the special case where two users can collude only if they have exchanged a message during the protocol's execution. An algorithm is presented in [8], and proved in [4], that determines whether a collusion problem has a solution and if so, computes one. In [7] we provide an algorithm that determines the existence of a solution for the general case where collusion can occur on unique data as well as on unique messages. In this paper we refine the algorithm of [7] so that it not only determines the existence of a solution, but also computes one when it exists.

We present our model and problem statement in §2. Roughly, the collusion problem determines whether it is possible for a subset of users to discover a target set of information, through a sequence of message exchanges among the colluders that satisfy the above collusion prerequisites. A solution to the problem, called a *collusion path*, is a specific sequence of message exchanges that uncovers the target set of information. The problem is formulated as a reachability analysis on a large transition system, exhaustive search on which is infeasible. It turns out, however, that the existence of a solution to the collusion problem, as well as the construction of a collusion path, can be determined by examining just the initial knowledge of all the colluders. This eliminates the need to explore the large transition system.

In §3 we review the special case where collusion is allowed only between two colluders sharing unique messages. We present a closed form expression specifying the condition under which a solution exists and clarify the simple structure of collusion paths.

The solution to the special case illustrates the structure of the problem and leads to the solution for the general case when collusion is allowed between colluders sharing unique data as well. This is explained in §4. We present an algorithm that determines whether a collusion problem has a solution and if it does, computes one. The algorithm includes the solution for the special case as its first step.

# 2 Model and Problem Formulation

In this section we present our model and formulate the collusion problem.

## 2.1 Notation

We use $(y_j, j \in J)$ to denote a vector with components $y_j$, $j$ spanning the index set $J$; the $j$th component $y_j$ is sometimes denoted $y.j$. For any set $A$, $|A|$ denotes the number of elements in $A$, $2^A$ denotes the collection of subsets of $A$, and $A^*$ denotes its Kleene closure.

If $d$ is a piece of data and $k$ is a cryptographic key, then $k(d)$ denotes the encryption of $d$ with $k$. A string $k_n \cdots k_1$ represents successive application of keys $k_1, \ldots, k_n$ in order. We use $\epsilon$ to denote the identity key: for any piece of data $d$, $\epsilon(d) = d$.

For any key $k$, $k^{-1}$ denotes its inverse with the cancellation rule $k^{-1}\, k = k\, k^{-1} = \epsilon$. For example, The keys $k$ and $k^{-1}$ are identical in secret-key cryptosystems, but not in public-key cryptosystems. When we refer to a string $\gamma$ of keys, we always assume that $\gamma$ is in reduced form that cannot be further simplified by application of the cancellation rule.

A *transition system* is a triple $\Theta = (Q, \Sigma, \delta)$, where $Q$ is a set of states, $\Sigma$ is a finite set of transition labels, and $\delta : Q \times \Sigma \to Q$ is a transition (partial) function. For example, a finite state machine is a special transition system in which $Q$ is finite. A *path* is a sequence of transitions. A concatenation of two paths $\rho_1$ and $\rho_2$ is denoted $\rho_1 \cdot \rho_2$.

## 2.2 Collusion Model

Consider a set of users we call colluders. Each colluder initially has a set of knowledge that includes a subset of messages that have been exchanged during a protocol run, the identity of some protocol users that have been involved in that protocol run, a set of data, possibly multiply encrypted, and a set of cryptographic keys. The colluders obtain this set of initial knowledge possibly by participating in the protocol run, or stealing messages over the communication channel; it is not important for our purpose how they obtain their initial knowledge.

The colluders' objective is to collectively discover a certain set of information, e.g., a cardholder's identity and what she purchases in the context of anonymous credit cards in [6]. A colluder first finds another colluder with which it can collude and then sends it its complete knowledge, including cryptographic keys in its possession. The recipient attempts to decrypt the combined knowledge with the keys it now has, and the process continues. We are interested in whether a given set of colluders can discover a target set of information. We now make these notions precise.

Collusion is carried out in an *environment* described by the 5-tuple $(U_p, D, K, U_c, L)$ where

1. $U_p$ is a finite set of protocol users;
2. $D$ is a finite set of data;
3. $K$ is a finite set of cryptographic keys, including the identity key $\epsilon$;
4. $U_c \subseteq U_p$ is a set of colluders;
5. $L \subseteq U_p \cup D \cup K$ is a set of information that determines whether two colluders can collude; see condition (2) below.

Define the *information set* as the set of every possible encryption and clear text combination of every piece of information in the system:

$$I \quad := \quad K^*(U_p \cup D \cup K)$$

For example, if $d \in U_p \cup D \cup K$ and $k_i \in K$, then $d$, $k_1(d)$, $k_2k_1(d)$, $k_1k_2k_1(d)$ are all in $I$.

Decryption is a function $\Delta : 2^I \rightarrow 2^I$ that is defined by the cancellation rule $k^{-1}\ k = k\ k^{-1} = \epsilon$, the identity key. For instance $\Delta(\{k(d)\} \cup \{k^{-1}\}) = \{d, k^{-1}\}$. $\Delta(A)$ represents the decryption of a set $A \subseteq I$ of information by the keys included in $A$ such that if $k_n \cdots k_1(d) \in \Delta(A)$ then $k_n^{-1} \notin \Delta(A)$. Whenever we refer to a subset of $I$ we always assume that it is in this reduced form.

The *knowledge set* is the combination of the messages and information:

$$W := 2^N \times 2^I$$

where $N$ is the set of unique message identifiers and $I$ is the information set. An element $w = (w.N, w.I)$ of $W$ represents a user's knowledge. It has two components: the first component $w.N \subseteq N$ represents all the messages the user has seen, and the second component $w.I \subseteq I$ represents all the information the user knows. As noted above $w.I$ is in reduced form. User $u$'s knowledge is denoted $w_u \in W$. We naturally assume that $u \in w_u.I$ for all $u \in U_p$.

As colluders in $U_c$ collude by exchanging messages, their knowledge is modified. This evolution is modeled by a transition system $\Theta = (W^{|U_c|}, \Sigma, \delta)$. Here, a state $w = (w_u, u \in U_c)$ in $W^{|U_c|}$ is the knowledge of all colluders. An event $\sigma = (s, r)$ in $\Sigma := U_c \times U_c$ describes the transfer of the sender's complete knowledge $w_s$ to the receiver $r$ to attempt to extract the hidden information at the receiver. The transition function $\delta$ describes the transformation of colluders' knowledge as a result of the message exchange.

For each state $w = (w_u, u \in U_c)$ and event $\sigma = (s, r)$, the next state $\delta(w, \sigma)$ is defined if and only if $r \in w_s.I$ and *at least* one of the following conditions is satisfied:

$$w_s.N \cap w_r.N \neq \phi \qquad (1)$$
$$w_s.I \cap w_r.I \cap L \neq \phi. \qquad (2)$$

The conditions, motivated in §1, says that for $s$ and $r$ to collude, $s$ must know $r$ and they must either share a unique message (condition (1)) or a unique piece of data in $L$ (condition 2)).

Note that if $L = U_c$ then since $u \in w_u$ for all $u$, $r \in w_s.I$ implies condition (2). Then the collusion prerequisites reduce to the special case in which collusion is allowed as long as the sender $s$ knows the receiver $r$.

We call an event $\sigma = (s, r)$ *enabled in state* $w$ if the next state $\delta(w, \sigma)$ is defined; we often say that $\sigma$ is *enabled* when the state from which the transition is made is understood. A path is *valid* if every transition on the path is enabled.

When the current state is $w = (w_u, u \in U_c)$ and an enabled transition $\sigma = (s, r)$ is made, the next state $w' := \delta(w, \sigma)$ is:

$$\begin{aligned} w'_y &= w_y \quad \text{if } y \neq r \\ w'_r.N &= w_r.N \cup w_s.N \\ w'_r.I &= \Delta(w_r.I \cup w_s.I) \end{aligned}$$

i.e., the receiver's knowledge is expanded to include that of the sender.

Note that the set of users that can collude can increase as users collude and information is combined. For instance, a sender can have encrypted information that includes the identity of a user and a unique piece of data that the sender and that user shares, and a receiver may have the key to decrypt that information. After the sender transfers its information to the receiver, the receiver can collude with the user that was hidden in the encrypted information.

We summarize our model in the following definition. The transition system $\Theta$ describes all the possible sequences of message exchanges among the colluders and how their knowledge evolves as collusion proceeds.

**Definition 1** *Given an environment* $(U_p, D, K, U_c, L)$*, a collusion system is the (unique) transition system* $\Theta = (W^{|U_c|}, \Sigma, \delta)$ *defined above.*

## 2.3 Problem formulation

The collusion problem is to determine if a subset of users can combine their information, by passing messages, and extract the hidden information after or during a protocol's execution. Suppose we have a collusion system $\Theta = (W^{|U_c|}, \Sigma, \delta)$.

**Collusion problem**

Given an initial state $w(0) \in W^{|U_c|}$ and a target set of unencrypted information $T \subseteq U_p \cup D \cup K$, does there exist a valid path $\rho$ in $\Theta$ that starts in $w(0)$ and terminates in a state $w(\rho)$ in which a colluder $c \in U_c$ knows $T$, i.e., $w_c(\rho).I \supseteq T$?

We call the valid path $\rho$ in the definition of the collusion problem a *collusion path*.

Though the collusion problem is simply a reachability analysis on the state machine $\Theta$, given $w(0)$, the reachable set contains up to $2^{|U_c|(|U_c|-1)}$ states. For example, for the simple protocol analysed in [6], $|U_c| = 8$ and the reachable set contains up to $10^{17}$ states. It is hence impractical to do an exhaustive search. In the next two sections we present a solution that avoids searching on $\Theta$.

For the rest of this paper, we make the following natural assumptions on the initial state $w(0)$ of the collusion problem. We assume that in state $w(0)$, if $(u, v)$ is enabled because $u$ and $v$ share a unique message (condition (1)), then they must know each other in $w(0)$ and hence $(v, u)$ must also be enabled, i.e., $w(0)$ satisfies the condition:

$$\begin{aligned} & w_u(0).N \cap w_v(0).N \neq \phi \\ \Rightarrow \quad & v \in w_u(0).I \text{ and } u \in w_v(0).I \end{aligned} \qquad (3)$$

# 3 Special case: $L = \phi$

In this section we consider the special case in which $L = \phi$, i.e., two users can collude only if they share a unique message that was exchanged during the protocol run (condition (1)). We present an algorithm that completely solves this special case. Given a collusion problem it determines whether it has a solution and if it does, computes one. The algorithm is a minor adaptation of the one derived in [8]. The adaptation makes it useful for solving the general case, presented in the next section. Results of this section are proved in [4].

For the rest of this paper, fix an environment $(U_p, D, K, U_c, L)$, an initial state $w(0)$ and a target information set $T$. In this section $L = \phi$ so that condition (2) is always violated. It is shown in [8, 4] that, to solve the collusion problem, it is necessary and sufficient to find a set of colluders who have exchanged messages among themselves during protocol execution and whose *initial* information in state $w(0)$, when combined, contains $T$.

Define $F = (U_c, E(w(0)))$ as a graph, depending on the initial state $w(0)$, that describes all the events that are initially enabled by condition (1). $F$ contains all colluders as its nodes. There is an edge $(u, v)$ in $E(w(0))$ if and only if $(u, v)$ is enabled in the initial state $w(0)$. According to assumption (3), $(u, v)$ is enabled in state $w(0)$ if and only if $(v, u)$ is also enabled. Hence we can take $F$ to be an undirected graph with each edge representing two directed edges in opposite directions.

Results of [8, 4] suggest Algorithm 1 below to solve the collusion problem. It first constructs the graph $F$. Then it finds each connected component $F' = (V, E)$ of $F$ using breadth-first search while, at the same time, constructing a candidate collusion path with the special structure described by [8, Theorem 3]. The candidate path has visited every node in the connected component when the search on the connected component is complete. Hence the last recipient on the path knows the combined knowledge $\Delta(\cup_{u \in V} w_u(0).I)$ of every colluder in the connected component. This combined knowledge is then checked to see if it contains the target information set $T$. A collusion path is found if it does; otherwise the search is repeated on a different connected component of $F$. When all connected components have been searched without producing a collusion path, it is proved in [4] that none exists.

The algorithm maintains several data structures. The adjacent lists *Adj*[$v$] represent the graph $F$. The variable *discovered*[$v$] stores the status of a node $v$ in $F$. It is initialized to be NO and becomes YES after node $v$ is discovered in the breadth-first search. $Q$ is a queue of nodes and HEAD[$Q$] is the node at the head of the queue. A node is appended to the end of $Q$ when it is first discovered and removed from the queue when all its neighbors have been discovered. The variable $\rho$ stores the path under construction and the variable *last* stores the last node visited by $\rho$. The algorithm extends $\rho$, whenever possible, by a directed edge from *last* to a newly discovered node.

The algorithm is adapted from [8] to also initialize a list *GROUP* of pairs $(\rho, i)$, where $\rho$ denotes a path or a set of colluders on the path, depending on context, and $i \in I$ is the combined information of colluders in $\rho$. *GROUP* is empty on entry of the algorithm; when returned it contains a pair $(\rho, i)$ for each connected component of $F$, with the interpretation that $\rho$ is a valid path that visits every colluder in the connected component and $i$ is the information of the last recipient if $\rho$ is followed. The list *GROUP* will be used to solve the general case in the next section.

**Algorithm 1**

**Input:** An initial state $w(0)$ and a target information set $T$.

**Output:** A collusion path $\rho$ if the collusion problem has a solution; *GROUP* otherwise.

1. Construct graph $F = (U_c, E)$ from $w(0).N$ and store it in *Adj*$[v]$
2. For each $v \in U_c$, *discovered*$[v] \leftarrow$ NO; *GROUP* $\leftarrow \phi$
3. For each $s \in U_c$
   If *discovered*$[s]$ = NO, then SEARCH$(s)$
4. Return (*GROUP*)

SEARCH$(s)$

1. *discovered*$[s] \leftarrow$ YES
2. $\rho \leftarrow$ NIL; *last* $\leftarrow s$; $Q \leftarrow \{s\}$
3. While $Q \neq \phi$
   $u \leftarrow$ HEAD$[Q]$
   For each $v \in$ *Adj*$[u]$
   If *discovered*$[v]$ = NO
   then $\rho \leftarrow \rho \cdot (last, v)$; *last* $\leftarrow v$
   *discovered*$[v]$ = YES;
   append $v$ to the end of $Q$
   Remove $u$ from $Q$
4. $i \leftarrow \Delta(\cup_{u \in \rho} w_u(0).I)$;
   append $(\rho, i)$ to *GROUP*
5. If $i \supseteq T$, then Return$(\rho)$

In the algorithm, the function SEARCH$(s)$ is an adaptation of a breadth-first search [1]. It finds a connected components of $F$ that contains the node $s$. It also constructs a path $\rho$ while it scans the connected component, by adding an edge from the last node of the current $\rho$ to a new node when the new node is first discovered. For a proof that the constructed path $\rho$ is valid, see [4]. It has visited every node in the connected component when the entire connected component has been scanned. The algorithm then adds the pair $(\rho, i)$ to the data structure *GROUP*, where $i$ is the combined initial information of all nodes on the path $\rho$. If $i$ contains $T$ then the candidate path $\rho$ is a collusion path and the algorithm returns. Otherwise, it repeats the search on a different connected component of $F$. If all connected components of $F$ have been searched without producing a collusion path then the algorithm returns *GROUP*. We summarize.

**Theorem 1** *The algorithm terminates. Moreover it returns a collusion path if the collusion problem has a solution and the linked list* GROUP *otherwise.*

## 4 General case: $L \supseteq \phi$

In the last section we show how to solve the collusion problem for the special case where collusion is allowed only on unique messages. In this section we solve the general case where collusion is allowed on unique data in $L \neq \phi$ as well.

For the special case the condition under which a solution exists can be described by a simple expression involving the initial knowledge of the colluders. This is no longer possible for the general case, but the solution can still be determined from just the initial state $w(0)$. We will provide an algorithm, Algorithm 2 below, that verifies if a collusion path exists and if so, computes one, without having to search the state machine $\Theta$ on which the collusion problem is defined.

Recall the graph $F$ that describes all events that are initially enabled in $w(0)$. The algorithm starts by calling Algorithm 1 of the last section. If there is a connected component of $F$ whose combined initial information contains the target information set $T$, then Algorithm 1 will identify it and returns a collusion path that involves only nodes in that connected component. Otherwise Algorithm 1 will have initialized the data structure *GROUP* to specify, for each connected component of $F$, a valid path through all nodes in the connected component and their combined initial information.

At any time, an element $(\rho, i)$ of *GROUP* identifies a group of colluders, a *valid* path $\rho$ that visits every

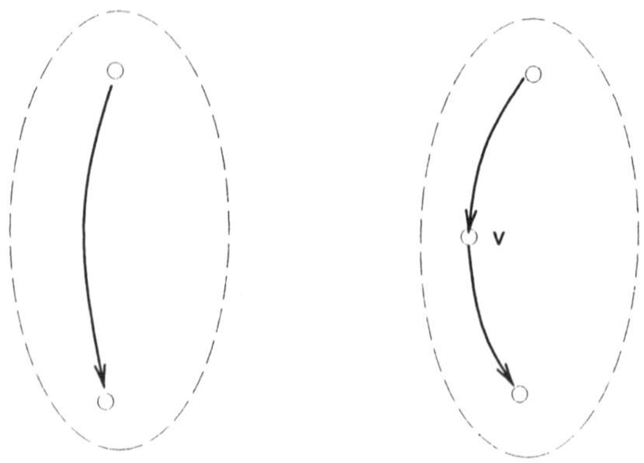


Figure 1: Elements $(\rho_1, i_1)$ and $(\rho_2, i_2)$ of *GROUP*

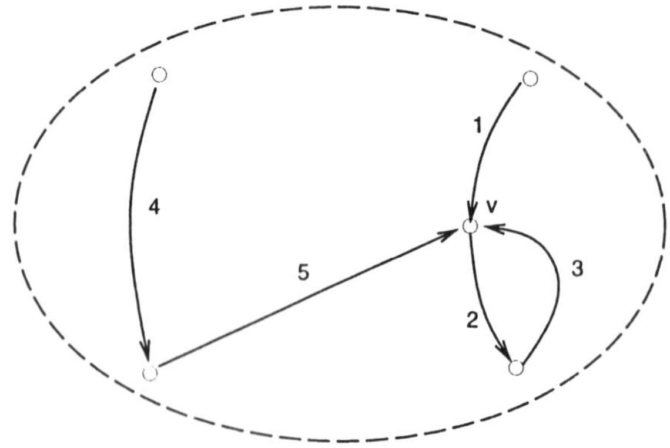


Figure 2: New element $(\rho_{12}, i_{12})$ of *GROUP*

colluder in the group and the combined initial information $i = \Delta\ (\cup_{u \in \rho}\ w_u(0).I)$ of the group. The last recipient of $\rho$, denoted TAIL$[\rho]$, knows the combined information $i$ when $\rho$ is followed. Immediately after Algorithm 1 returns without finding a collusion path, each element of *GROUP* corresponds to a connected component of $F$. As Algorithm 2 proceeds these elements are combined to form bigger and few groups, until either a collusion path is found or no further combination is possible. The collusion problem has no solution in the latter case.

Two colluders in different connected components of $F$ can collude only if they share a unique piece of information in $L$ (condition (2)). The algorithm searches for two elements in *GROUP*, identified by $(\rho_1, i_1)$ and $(\rho_2, i_2)$, such that TAIL$[\rho_1]$ knows a colluder $v$ in $\rho_2$ and shares a unique piece of information with TAIL$[\rho_2]$. Note that TAIL$[\rho_1]$ may not share a unique piece of information with $v$ to allow them to collude, nor may it know TAIL$[\rho_2]$ to collude with it. But TAIL$[\rho_2]$ certainly knows $v$ since $v \in \rho_2$ and hence can transfer all its knowledge to $v$. Then $v$ and TAIL$[\rho_1]$ indeed share a unique piece of information and can collude. In summary the path

$$\rho_{12} \quad := \quad \rho_2 \cdot (\text{TAIL}[\rho_2], v) \cdot \rho_1 \cdot (\text{TAIL}[\rho_1], v)$$

is valid. Moreover its last recipient $v$ knows the combined information $i_{12} := \Delta(i_1 \cup i_2)$. The construction of $\rho_{12}$ from $\rho_1$ and $\rho_2$ is illustrated in Figures 1 and 2.

If $i_{12}$ contains $T$, then the corresponding candidate path $\rho_{12}$ is a collusion path, and the algorithm returns. Otherwise, the two elements $(\rho_1, i_1)$ and $(\rho_2, i_2)$ are removed from *GROUP* and the new element $(\rho_{12}, i_{12})$ is added, and the search repeats. When no further elements in *GROUP* can combine their information the algorithm concludes that the collusion problem has no solution and returns NIL.

**Algorithm 2**

**Input:** An initial state $w(0)$ and a target information set $T$.

**Output:** A collusion path $\rho$ if the collusion problem has a solution; NIL otherwise.

1. Execute Algorithm 1
2. If collusion path $\rho$ is found, Return($\rho$)
3. While there are elements $(\rho_1, i_1)$, $(\rho_2, i_2)$ of *GROUP* satisfying $i_1 \cap \rho_2 \neq \phi$ and $i_1 \cap i_2 \cap L \neq \phi$
   Let $v \in i_1 \cap \rho_2$
   $\rho_{12} \leftarrow \rho_2 \cdot (\text{TAIL}[\rho_2], v) \cdot \rho_1 \cdot (\text{TAIL}[\rho_1], v)$
   $i_{12} \leftarrow \Delta(i_1 \cup i_2)$
   If $i_{12} \supseteq T$ then Return $(\rho_{12})$
   Remove $(\rho_1, i_1)$, $(\rho_2, i_2)$ from *GROUP*
   Add $(\rho_{12}, i_{12})$ to *GROUP*
4. Return (NIL).

The correctness of the algorithm is guaranteed by the following theorem.

**Theorem 2** *The algorithm terminates. Moreover it returns a collusion path if the collusion problem has a solution and* NIL *otherwise.*

We now briefly sketch why the theorem should hold. If there is a connected component of $F$ whose combined initial information contains $T$, then Algorithm 1 in the previous section will identify a collusion path, and the algorithm will terminate in step 2. Otherwise, Algorithm 1 will return the list *GROUP* that contains one element for each connected component of $F$. Each time the 'while' loop is entered the list *GROUP* is shortened by one. Hence Algorithm 2 must terminate, either inside the 'while' loop with a collusion path, or in step 4 without one. It is proved in [4] that it terminates inside the 'while' loop with a collusion path if and only if there exists one.

## 5 Conclusion

In earlier work [8] we have formulated a collusion problem which determines whether a set of colluders can, starting from their initial knowledge, collectively discover a target set of information, and have provided a complete solution for a special case. In this paper we have solved the general case with an algorithm that determines whether a collusion problem has a solution, and if it does, computes one. All results in [8] and this paper can be found in [4].

Communications protocols that employ cryptographic techniques are increasingly used to protect privacy as well as to communicate. A cryptographic protocol defines a process by which information is transferred among some users while hidden from others. The algorithm presented here can be applied to determine whether a subset of protocol users can collectively discover, during or after the protocol's execution, the information that is designed to be hidden from them; see [8, 6] for an example.

## References


[1] Thomas H. Cormen, Charles E. Leiserson, and Ronald L. Rivest. *Introduction to Algorithms.* The MIT Press, 1993.

[2] Semyon Dukach. SNPP: A Simple Network Payment Protocol. In *Proceedings of the Computer Security Applications Conference*, San Antonio, TX, November 1992.

[3] Hannes Federrath, Anja Jerichow, and Andreas Pfitzmann. Mixes in mobile communication systems: Location management with privacy. *Proc. Workshop on Information Hiding*, May 1996.

[4] S. H. Low and N. F. Maxemchuk. Collusion in cryptographic protocols. Technical report, University of Melbourne, Department of Electrical & Electronic Engineering, 1996.

[5] S. H. Low, N. F. Maxemchuk, and S. Paul. Anonymous credit cards. *Proceedings of the 2nd. ACM Conference on Computer and Communications Security*, November 2–4 1994.

[6] S. H. Low, N. F. Maxemchuk, and S. Paul. Anonymous credit cards and their collusion analysis. *IEEE/ACM Transactions on Networking*, 4(6):809–816, December 1996.

[7] Steven H. Low and Nicholas F. Maxemchuk. Collusion analysis of cryptographic protocols. In *Proc. of Globecom'96*, pages 1–5. London, UK, November 1996.

[8] Steven H. Low and Nicholas F. Maxemchuk. Modeling cryptographic protocols and their collusion analysis. In *Proc. of First International Workshop on Information Hiding*, Cambridge, U.K., May/June 1996. Ross Anderson, editor, Vol. 1174 of *Lecture Notes in Computer Science*, pages 169–186, Springer Verlag.

[9] N. F. Maxemchuk and S. H. Low. The use of communications networks to increase personal privacy. *Proceedings of Infocom'95*, pages 504–512, April 1995.

[10] A. Pfitzmann, B. Pfitzmann, and M. Waidner. ISDN-MIXes – Untraceable Communications with very Small Bandwidth Overhead. *Proc. IFIP/Sec'91*, pages 245–258, May 1991.

[11] A. Pfitzmann and M. Waidner. Networks without user observability. *Computers and Security*, 6(2):158–166, 1987.

# MetaRing Fairness Control Schemes in All-Optical WDM Rings*

M. Ajmone Marsan, A. Bianco, E. Leonardi, F. Neri, S. Toniolo
Dipartimento di Elettronica, Politecnico di Torino
E-mail: {ajmone,bianco,leonardi,neri}@polito.it

**Abstract**

*WDM rings are receiving significant attention in the field of all-optical networks because their implementation appears to be feasible with state-of-the-art components. Several MAC protocols were recently proposed in order to resolve contentions among nodes sharing the available wavelengths in WDM rings. These MAC protocols achieve high efficiency but unsatisfactory fairness, due to the asymmetric position of sources with respect to destinations. Thus, in order to improve fairness, it is necessary to adopt a fairness control scheme. In this paper we discuss the adaptation of the MetaRing fairness control scheme to the context of WDM multi-channel rings. Several alternatives are considered and compared via simulation.*

## 1 Introduction

We consider all-optical multi-channel networks with ring topology, the channel multiplicity being achieved by using WDM (wavelength division multiplexing) [1]. Space diversity can be further exploited to reduce the number of wavelengths that must be accommodated in one single fiber, but we do not consider this issue here. Each channel (i.e., each wavelength) is used to transfer packets to a subset of network destinations; different transmissions are time-multiplexed via a slotted MAC (medium access control) protocol. Since WDM channels are used as (group) destination addresses, nodes are equipped with one tunable transmitter and one fixed receiver.

We focus on networks with ring topology since they are considered an attractive solution for all-optical networks mainly thanks to the recent availability of optical amplifiers to compensate for insertion losses at intermediate nodes. An important feature of rings is to allow for an easier synchronization, thus permitting the adoption of slotted MAC protocols even at extremely high data rates. The main advantage of slotted MAC protocols is that they allow collision-free access to the available wavelengths with limited complexity; their main drawback is in the possible unfair sharing of the resources among users.

This paper considers fairness control techniques to be integrated within a slotted MAC protocol for all-optical WDM rings named SRR (Synchronous Round Robin), which was proposed and studied by the authors in previous papers [2, 3]. The proposed fairness control approaches are derived from those originally designed for the MetaRing MAN [4].

## 2 WDM Rings

We consider all-optical WDM rings with $M$ nodes and $W$ wavelengths (with $W \leq M$). Each node is equipped with one tunable transmitter and one fixed receiver; when a source node needs to transmit to a destination node, it must tune its transmitter to the wavelength on which the destination node is able to receive. Packets are always extracted from the ring at their destinations.

We assume slotted operations; thus $W$ slots (one for each wavelength) simultaneously reach each node at every slot time; we call *multi-slot* the set of $W$ parallel slots, and multi-ring the network topology.

Contentions among transmitters can arise due to the sharing of wavelengths; collisions are avoided with a wavelength inspection capability, which can be implemented by means of subcarrier multiplexing approaches [2]. The source node, prior to transmitting a packet to a given destination, inspects the next multi-slot at the appropriate wavelength; only if the slot at that wavelength is empty, the packet is inserted into the slot. If the slot is not empty, the transmission attempt is delayed.

The lack of receiver tunability simplifies the design of the MAC protocol: transmission attempts are scheduled according to the SRR MAC protocol, which will be described in Section 3.1.

In spite of the circular symmetry of the ring, the positions of sources are asymmetric with respect to transmissions to one specific destination; as a consequence, each node experiences easier access to wavelengths leading to some destinations, and worse access to other wavelengths leading to different destinations. When the number of wavelengths $W$ equals the number of nodes $M$, since each wavelength is dedicated to one destination, the slotted multi-ring can be mapped on a slotted staggered multi-bus, which is prone to unfairness when a simple empty slot access protocol is used. We will say that nodes are at high priority when they experience easy access on a wavelength, and at low priority when they must defer to transmissions of upstream nodes.

Considering the simple multi-ring depicted in Fig. 1, with $M = W = 4$, assuming that multi-slots propagate clockwise, it can be seen that node 0 has highest priority when transmitting to destination 3 on

*This work was supported in part by the Italian National Research Council, and the Italian Ministry for University and Scientific Research. S. Toniolo was supported by a grant from CSELT.



0-8186-7780-5/97 $10.00 © 1997 IEEE

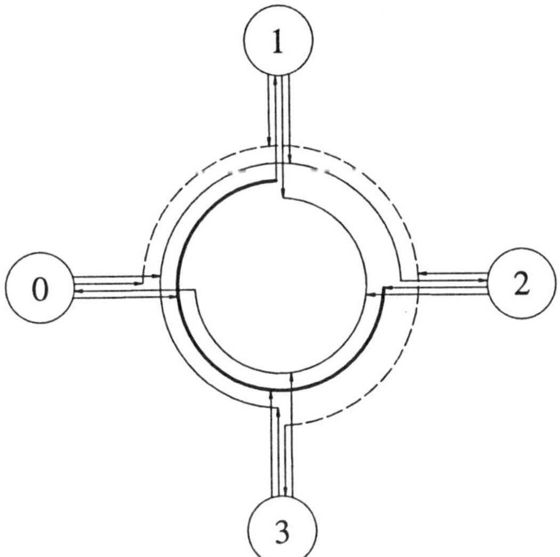

Figure 1: A WDM ring with $W = M = 4$

the dashed WDM channel, while it has to yield to all other nodes when transmitting to node 1 on the thick solid channel, on which node 2 has the highest priority.

When $W < M$, $W/M$ nodes receive at the same wavelength; still on each wavelength some nodes have a better access opportunity, and some worse, depending on their positions. Under the assumption that nodes are equipped with one fixed wavelength receiver and one wavelength tunable transmitter, different wavelengths are used to reach *disjoint subsets* of destinations. Since we always assume that the transmitted information is removed from the ring by the destination node, slots can be reused several times as they propagate along the network. The release of slots at their destinations partially compensates for the resource reduction due to the decreased number of wavelengths, since the equivalent bandwidth on each ring is larger than the raw data rate. The slot reuse capability somewhat helps in reducing unfairness, but more complex and still significantly biased behaviors can be observed. The additional capacity generated by slot reuse can be better exploited by nodes immediately following a node to which a large portion of traffic is directed, as well as by the node itself.

To alleviate unfairness and to maximize slot reuse in uniform traffic conditions, we assume in the paper that the destinations sharing one wavelength are equally spaced (in terms of number of nodes) along the multi-ring. This means that, if $W = M/D$, the $D$ destinations sharing the $i$-th wavelength are in positions $|i + dW|_M$, with $0 \leq d < D$, where $|\cdot|_M$ denotes the modulo $M$ operator.

# 3 The SRR Protocol and its Fairness Control

Several MAC protocols and fairness control schemes can be adopted to achieve good utilization of the transmission resources while alleviating unfairness. A description of some of the approaches investigated by the authors can be found in [3]; these MAC protocols are based only on local information, hence do not require any coordination among nodes. Moreover, they guarantee collision-free access to the available wavelengths, with an *a priori* (i.e., without any knowledge of the content of the incoming multi slot) choice of the packet to be transmitted. The packet is successfully transmitted if the slot at the appropriate wavelength is empty; otherwise a new packet is scheduled for transmission in the next multi-slot.

Among the proposed MAC protocols, SRR (Synchronous Round Robin) seems the most promising, due to its simplicity and very good utilization of the available wavelengths.

## 3.1 An overview of SRR

The aim of the SRR MAC protocol is to force the network behavior to approach TDMA (time division multiple access) under heavy load, avoiding the high delays of TDMA when the network is lightly loaded. In order to implement SRR, each node must keep one separate queue for every possible destination. Thus $M - 1$ queues are required at each node (nodes do not transmit to themselves); we denote by $Q_i$ the length of queue $i$ measured in packets. Packets are handled in FIFO order within each queue.

Let us first focus on multi-rings with $W = M$. The SRR scheduling algorithm works as follows. The $M-1$ queues are cyclically scanned by each node, looking for a packet to transmit. In an arbitrary time slot $s$, node $i$ deterministically schedules for transmission a packet selected from a specific queue. Introducing a variable $k = |s|_{M-1}$, that cycles over the range $0, 1, 2, \ldots, M-2$, the queue with packets directed to destination $|i + k + 1|_M$ is selected for transmission in the multi-slot labeled $s$. Only if such a scheduled queue is empty, the transmission of the first packet from the longest queue is attempted in multi-slot $s$. If a tie occurs for the longest queue, the longest queue associated with the most unfavorable destination is chosen for the transmission attempt. In any case, if transmission in multi-slot $s$ is not possible because it would generate a collision, in the following time slot (labeled $s + 1$) a *new* packet is selected for the transmission attempt according to the SRR scheduling algorithm.

Note that the selection of the next packet to be transmitted requires the information about the lengths of all queues, as well as a common knowledge by all nodes about the slot label $s$, i.e. a global (network-wide) synchronization on the slot sequence. This last requirement enforces also the equalization of the ring latency to a multiple of $M - 1$ slots.

The SRR scheduling algorithm becomes equivalent to TDMA when all nodes find a packet to be transmitted in the scheduled queue at each time slot; in other words, in overloaded uniform traffic, the SRR scheduling algorithm deterministically avoids contentions in the network. The possibility of transmitting a packet from the longest queue when the queue scheduled for transmission is empty avoids the high delays of TDMA under light traffic. Unfortunately, breaking the SRR schedule, which is mandatory to avoid a degeneration of the access protocol to TDMA, creates unfairness among nodes under unbalanced traffic conditions, as explained in the next section.

When $W < M$, i.e. when the number of wavelengths is smaller than the number of destinations, the SRR protocol behavior is somewhat more complex. Several variations of the protocol can be introduced (for a more complete description see [3]), since the simple extension of the SRR schedule would create deterministic conflicts among nodes due to the reduced network resources. The SRR-RND version, which we consider in this paper, requires nodes to keep a separate queue for each destination; the destination selected according to the SRR schedule identifies a wavelength, which is the wavelength on which the destination node receives. The packet whose transmission is attempted is randomly selected among all the destinations sharing the selected wavelength as receivers. Only if all queues referring to these destinations are empty, the SRR schedule is broken, and transmission is attempted of a packet taken from the longest queue.

### 3.2 Performance of SRR

In order to overview the behavior of the SRR protocol, we discuss simulation results for a 16-node network, with $W = 16$, considering throughput and average packet delay, referring to individual node-to-node traffic relations. The packet delay is the delay encountered by a packet prior to accessing the network, i.e., the time interval from the packet generation until the beginning of its successful transmission. We normalize delays to slot times, and express arrival rates and throughputs in packets per slot time.

Packets whose length equals the slot size are generated at node $i$ according to a Poisson process with fixed rate $\lambda_i$. The total traffic offered to the network is $\Lambda = \sum_{i=1}^{M} \lambda_i$.

We consider a simple client-server scenario : one "server" node (node 16) is present in the network; the remaining $M - 1$ "clients" direct half of their traffic to the server, while the other half of the traffic is uniformly distributed among clients. The server generates an amount of traffic equal to half the total traffic generated by clients, and evenly distributes it to clients.

We consider two load levels: $\Lambda = 2.7$ and $\Lambda = 6$. When $\Lambda = 2.7$, no wavelength is overloaded (a traffic equal to 0.9 is offered to the channel leading to the server); packet delays are examined in this case. When $\Lambda = 6$, the wavelength leading to the server is overloaded (offered traffic equal to 2), while the other wavelengths are lightly loaded (offered load equal to 0.26); we focus in this case on throughputs.

The SRR protocol provides very good performance when balanced traffic conditions are considered; performance indices under uniform traffic are not reported here due to lack of space, but the reader can refer to [2, 3] for details. Under unbalanced traffic, unfairness arises, both for delays over underloaded wavelengths, and for throughputs under overload, as reported in Fig. 2 when $W = M$ in the wavelength leading to the server. A similar but somewhat more complex behavior can be observed when $W = 4$ [3].

Unfairness is mainly induced by nodes transmitting packets selected from the longest queues because the scheduled queue is empty; if only one wavelength is overloaded, like in the client-server scenario, nodes try to transmit packets on the overloaded wavelength each time the scheduled queue is empty, since the longest queue is the one requiring the transmission on the overloaded wavelength. In this case, due to the priorities induced by the ring topology, some nodes have better access opportunity than others, and complete starvation of low priority nodes can occur when the traffic increases.

### 3.3 Fairness and the MetaRing Protocol

A possible solution to avoid starvation of sources at low priority on overloaded wavelengths is based on the adaptation of the MetaRing protocol presented in [4]. MetaRing is based on the circulation on the ring of a control message, named SAT. Nodes are assigned a transmission *quota* denoted by $K$, i.e. a maximum number of packets that can be transmitted between two SAT visits. On reception of the SAT, each node normally forwards it on the ring with no delay; nodes that are not satisfied, i.e. that were not able to transmit up to $K$ packets, delay the SAT transmission until either the node has sent its quota or the node packet buffer is empty. When nodes release the SAT, they renew their transmission quota.

Since we deal with multi-rings, we need to adapt the fairness control mechanism originally proposed for MetaRing to a multi-channel environment; we call MMR (Multi-MetaRing) the family of modified algorithms. We assume that one slot is devoted to the transmission of the SAT message; thus some bandwidth is wasted for the propagation of control information.

Since our rings provide $W$ wavelengths for transmission, we can use either one "global" SAT message, obtaining a global control over all wavelengths, or several SAT messages, one SAT for each wavelength, so as to control each wavelength separately. We identify the first option as MMR-SS (MMR Single SAT), the second as MMR-MS (MMR Multiple SAT).

When we focus on MMR-SS, we could associate the quota $K$ with all packets transmitted between two SAT visits, regardless of packet destinations, or keep a separate quota equal to $K_q = K/(M - 1)$ for each queue (i.e. wavelength). We consider only the latter option, since it can be easily shown that, under unbalanced traffic conditions, the former choice would significantly reduce the network throughput.

As regards MMR-MS, there is a correlation between the forwarding of the SAT on one wavelength and the transmission of packets on other wavelengths. While one node is delaying the SAT for one particular wavelength (because the quota $K_q$ was not reached for that wavelength and more packets are waiting in the transmission queues), the SRR access scheme may force the node to attempt transmissions on other wavelengths (where some quota is still available). Several variations of the basic algorithms can be introduced at this point (for example, packets to be transmitted on those wavelengths for which the SAT is being delayed could be given special attention), but we do not consider

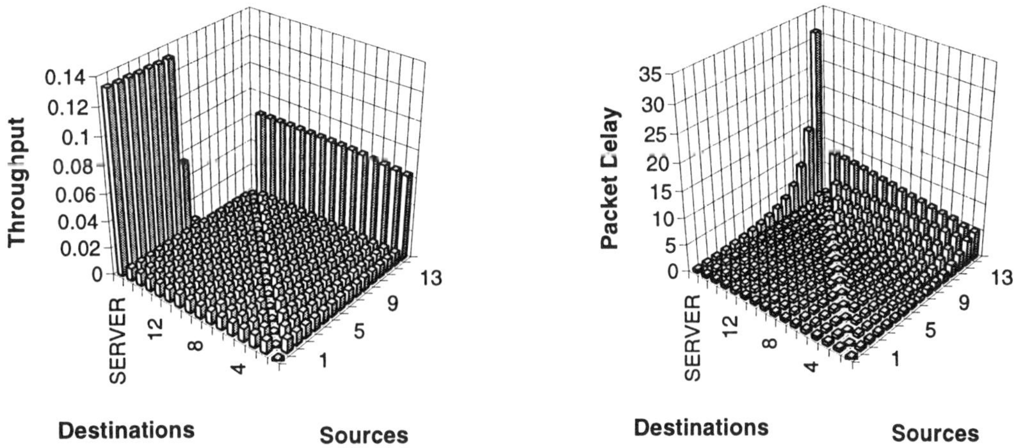


Figure 2: Throughputs ($\Lambda = 6.0$) and packet delays ($\Lambda = 2.7$) for the SRR access protocol when $W = M = 16$

them here.

For what concerns the node to which the SAT message must be forwarded, we can either choose to transmit the SAT to the upstream node or to the downstream node.

If we restrict our attention to network architectures only providing co-directional rings, the SAT message must propagate in the same direction of the regulated data. If the SAT is forwarded to the upstream node, the forwarding node is in a good shape as far as access opportunity, since it is at the highest priority on the wavelength leading to the intended destination (i.e., to the upstream node); unluckily, SAT propagation delays are very large, since the SAT message must traverse almost the entire network. We add the suffix U (Upstream) to MMR-SS and MMR-MS to identify the versions in which the SAT is forwarded to the upstream node with respect to the data stream; note that logically the SAT propagates counter-directionally with respect to data, even if physically the SAT message follows the same data direction.

Of course, it is possible to consider also the case where the SAT is forwarded to the downstream node; we label as D (Downstream) this option. In this case we can expect longer access delays due to the fact that the node acts as the lowest priority source when it has to forward the SAT, while the propagation delays are minimized.

We can also choose to devote one additional wavelength to SAT messages, in order to avoid or to reduce contention in SAT transmissions. This dedicated wavelength can be co-directional or counter-directional with respect to data propagation. We label as WDC (With Dedicated Channel) the options in which a dedicated wavelength is provided for SAT messages. It should be noted that dedicating one wavelength to SAT transmissions requires an increase in the available network resources, and results in a significant additional complexity in the node structure, since a receiving device must be devoted to SATs. When discussing the WDC option, we will consider a physically co-directional dedicated wavelength for the downstream SAT forwarding and a physically counter-directional dedicated wavelength for the upstream SAT forwarding; with the above choice nodes simply need to extract the incoming SAT, and no SAT addressing is required.

## 4 Simulation Results

In the presentation of a selection of the simulation results that we derived for the various configurations of all-optical WDM rings with SRR MAC protocol and MMR fairness control scheme, we first highlight the most important features common to all the network and protocol configurations; then we focus on a comparison among the various alternatives in different scenarios. Initially we consider the case $W = M$; later on we investigate the case of a smaller number of wavelengths.

Most of the analysis is based on the unbalanced traffic scenario resulting from the client-server environment that was previously described when overviewing the performance characteristics of the SRR protocol alone. We also briefly consider a different traffic pattern because it allows us to visualize some key differences between MMR-SS and MMR-MS.

All the results that will be presented refer to a network with $M = 16$ nodes, with inter-node distance $d_{ij}, \forall i, j$ equal to 15 slots. Recall that when we refer to the MetaRing quota $K_q$ we indicate the number of packets that each node is allowed to transmit to each destination node between two SAT visits.

A first important remark is that when nodes follow the SRR protocol and one of the different versions of the MMR fairness control mechanism, the throughput behavior of the network is perfectly fair, even when some wavelength is overloaded, as depicted in Fig. 3 for the particular case of MMR-SS-D, with $W = M$, and $\Lambda = 6$. In order to appreciate the impact of MMR, consider that Fig. 3 must be compared with the left hand side of Fig. 2. The starvation that was previously observed on the (overloaded) wavelength leading to the server has completely disappeared. Similar be-

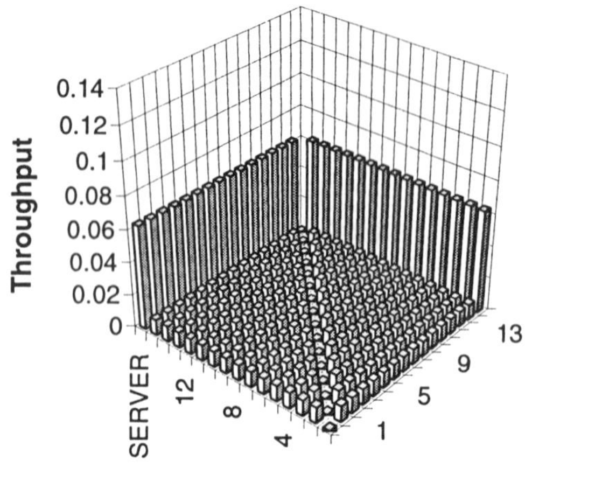


Figure 3: Effect of MetaRing (MMR-SS-D) on throughput; $W = M = 16$, $\Lambda = 6.0$, $K_q = 80$.

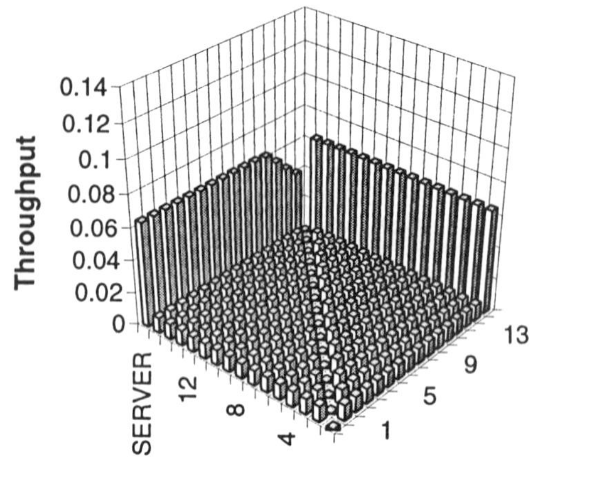


Figure 4: Effect of small queue size on the throughput of low priority nodes, when MMR-SS-D is considered; $W = M = 16$, $\Lambda = 6.0$, $K_q = 80$, $Q_i = 20$.

haviors will also be observed when $W = 4$ and $\Lambda = 6.0$ (Fig. 7). These results are achieved regardless of the chosen MMR version, provided that system parameters are appropriately dimensioned.

For a more compact presentation of results in the sequel, we note from Fig. 3 that, when MMR is used and $W = M$, the network performance can be captured with just three aggregate indices: the total throughput obtained on the wavelength leading to the server, the total throughput obtained any client-bound wavelength, and the total throughput obtained by the server as a transmitter. In Fig. 5 we will refer to these three indices for the comparison among different versions of MMR.

When no wavelength is overloaded, MMR does not influence the network behavior, and thus does not improve fairness in the packet delays observed by different sources. This is due to the fact that if wavelengths are not overloaded, it is very unlikely that sources delay SAT transmissions because they need more transmission resources. Consider moreover that MMR provides fairness control on a much longer timescale (of the order of magnitude of the ring latency) with respect to the packet delays achieved with SRR. This is true for all versions of MMR; for this reason we will not present delay results in the remainder of the paper.

### 4.1 Queue length effect

In order to obtain the fair behavior reported in Fig. 3, it is important to set the size of the $M - 1$ queues available in each node to a value not smaller than the transmission quota $K_q$. This is necessary because in a completely overloaded environment, higher priority nodes tend to exhaust their quota very quickly, whereas lower priority nodes are struggling to obtain their fair share of the bandwidth, because each time they try to transmit a packet following the SRR schedule they cannot find an empty slot. This behavior is mitigated by MMR, since higher priority nodes are forced to refrain from transmission (they exhaust their quota) due to the fact that lower priority nodes delay the SAT forwarding. When all the higher priority nodes are forced to stop transmitting, a lower priority node can start transmitting its quota of packets. However, since a node is forced to release the SAT when its transmission queue is empty, if the length of a queue $Q_i$ is significantly smaller that the quota $K_q$, the lower priority node is forced to release the SAT before completing the transmission of $K_q$ packets, and thus its throughput suffers.

This clipping effect, which limits the throughput obtained by lower priority nodes, can be observed on the wavelength leading to the server in Fig. 4, for the MMR-SS-D version with $K_q$ set to 80 and $Q_i = 20$, but it is a common features of all the considered versions of MMR.

### 4.2 Choosing the value of the quota $K_q$

We just observed that it is important to set the internal node queues to sizes larger than the quota $K_q$; however, we have not yet discussed the correct choice of the value for the quota so as to provide the best performance to networks with MMR fairness control; this point is discussed next, considering first just one wavelength for the sake of simplicity.

The performance of MetaRing in overload conditions is ruled by the fact that all nodes are able to transmit up to $K_q$ packets between two visits of the SAT. This means that the throughput is mainly regulated by the ratio between $K_q$ and the SAT circulation time; given $K_q$, the shorter the latter the higher the throughput. Thus, if the SAT circulation time increases, we are forced to use large values for $K_q$ if we want to obtain high utilization. More precisely, if we want to guarantee that the maximum achievable throughput (which is equal to 1 when $W = M$) can be obtained even when just one node is transmitting on a given wavelength, we must ensure that the quota $K_q$ is greater than the SAT propagation time in slots; if

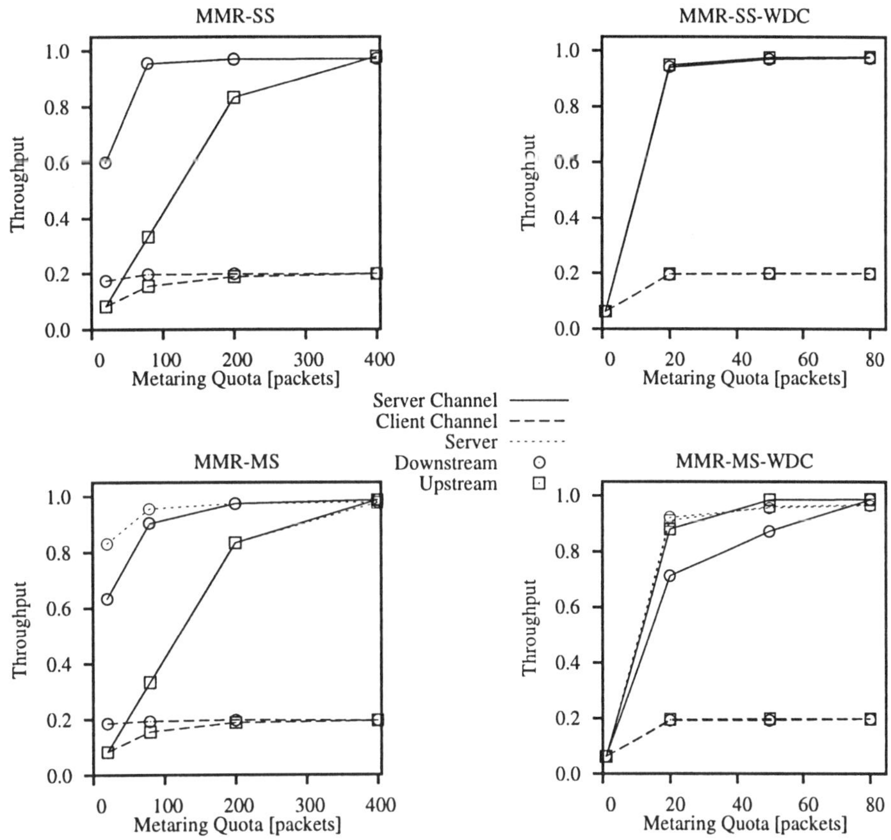


Figure 5: Throughput as a function of $K_q$ for MMR-SS and MMR-MS with and without dedicated channel; server bound wavelength as solid lines, one of the client bound wavelengths as a dashed line, total throughput out of the server as a dotted line; $W = M = 16$, $\Lambda = 6.0$.

a smaller $K_q$ is adopted, the transmitting node would refrain unnecessarily from transmission just to comply with the MMR rule. Since we assume that no other node needs to access the wavelength, the aggregate network throughput is reduced.

Large values of $K_q$ are thus necessary in order to achieve good efficiency, but it is important to remember that large values of $K_q$ not only mean that we are able to obtain a fair behavior only on a longer time scale: due to the clipping effect induced by short queue lengths, large values of $K_q$ also require large queues, of the order of magnitude of $M \times D$, where $D$ is the distance between the two nodes following upon in the reception of the SAT. This constraint can be critical, specially if we consider an upstream transmission of the SAT when no dedicated wavelength is available (MMR-SS-U or MMR-MS-U), since in this case the SAT propagation delays are equal to $M \times (d_{ij} \times (M - 1))$.

In order to visualize the effect of the quota $K_q$ on the network performance, we report in Fig. 5 the normalized throughput for several versions of the MMR protocol as a function of $K_q$ when W=16. In the picture, the solid line refers to the overloaded wavelength on which the server receives, the dashed line refers to one of the client-bound wavelengths, and the dotted line refers to the throughput achieved by server transmissions.

It can be immediately observed that a threshold value for $K_q$ exists. Above this threshold the maximum achievable throughput is obtained; smaller values of $K_q$ instead induce smaller aggregate throughputs on the overloaded wavelength leading to the server.

If the network provides a dedicated wavelength for SAT transmissions, as shown in the right hand side pictures, the limit throughput can be reached with a significantly smaller value of the quota $K_q$ with respect to the case of no dedicated wavelength shown in the left hand side pictures (about 80 against about 400 – consider that the total ring latency equals $16 \times 15 = 240$ slots).

Of course, providing a dedicated wavelength implies a significantly higher complexity in the system architecture, as discussed in the previous section. When no dedicated wavelength is provided for SAT transmissions, the MMR-U versions require higher values of $K_q$ in order to reach the maximum throughput, due to the longer propagation delays.

Downstream transmission (circular markers) without a dedicated channel provides another way of reducing the value of $K_q$ for which the limit throughput is obtained; note that nodes are at the lowest possible priority when accessing the channel to forward the SAT. This does not significantly influence the throughput results, while a noticeable increase in the access delays was observed for $\Lambda = 2.7$, i.e. in lightly loaded condition, especially for the MMR-MS (results not reported due to lack of space).

It is interesting to notice that, if we consider the limit throughputs that can be obtained in the different cases, i.e. we compare the different MMR versions for large $K_q$, no large performance advantage can be observed for any MMR version. This is in contrast with some of the previously published papers, where it was shown that the upstream forwarding of the SAT allows a higher throughput to be obtained [4] than the downstream SAT forwarding. Upstream forwarding is a more natural solution: upstream nodes have, more likely, exhausted their quota since they have been waiting for the SAT longer than other nodes. Moreover, in our setup, the node that delays the SAT because it was not able to transmit its quota can more easily access the wavelength due to the fact that upstream nodes, i.e. higher priority nodes on the considered wavelength, are likely to be the first nodes to refrain from transmission.

If no reuse is possible, as in the case $W = M = 16$ that we are considering, lower priority nodes can be made silent by the node delaying the SAT, which can be using all the available slots. However, when reuse is possible, as in the cases $W = 4$ or $W = 2$, lower priority nodes have an opportunity to exploit slot reuse to transmit to destinations on the considered wavelength. In this context, the upstream SAT forwarding can be quite beneficial and should be preferred to downstream SAT transmission. This is confirmed by the results for $W = 4$, and for $W = 2$, not shown for the sake of conciseness. Note that in our scenario the differences in the individual throughput figures cannot be expected to be very large: most of the traffic on the overloaded wavelength is still directed to the server, and nodes can only partially exploit slot reuse.

Finally, the MMR-MS options provide a somewhat higher throughput to the server transmissions, as it is shown by the dotted lines in Fig. 5. This phenomenon will be explained in Section 4.3.

In summary, we can state that the use of a dedicated wavelength for SAT transmissions can be considered beneficial not so much from the performance point of view, but surely in terms of the possibility of reducing the value of $K_q$ required to obtain the limit throughput. A similar reduction in the quota $K_q$ can also be obtained with a downstream forwarding of the SAT, but it must be remembered that when $W < M$, i.e. in the most interesting situation when a large network is to be implemented, the downstream forwarding impairs the performance of the network.

The most interesting solutions from a system perspective thus appear to be MMR-MS-U and MMR-SS-U, provided that it is acceptable to obtain fairness on a longer time scale; these solutions are feasible with simple node architectures [2], and do not require additional resources to propagate the SAT control messages. If we must choose one of the two alternatives, the fact that only one SAT message is required in the case of MMR-SS should lead to simpler algorithms, and appears thus to be preferable. However, some problems may be present if MMR-SS is used, as we shall see next.

### 4.3 Deficiency of MMR-SS

Consider a modified client-server traffic scenario, where the server transmits 1/4 of its traffic toward client 9, while the remaining 2/4 are uniformly distributed among other clients. The results for MMR-MS and MMR-SS in this case are presented in Fig. 6. We can immediately observe that the adoption of MMR-SS forces the server to drastically reduce its transmission rate towards client 9, with respect to MMR-MS.

Remember that on the wavelength leading to node 9, the server can transmit up to its quota $K_q$ towards destination node 9, then it must refrain from transmission until the SAT arrives. This holds for both MMR-SS and MMR-MS. However, when MMR-SS is considered, the SAT circulation time on the wavelength leading to node 9 is forced to be equal to the SAT circulation time on the wavelength leading to the server, since only one SAT exist in the network. On this overloaded wavelength, all nodes delay the SAT until they are able to transmit $K_q$ packets; as a consequence, the SAT circulation time grows, thus leading to starvation of the server on the wavelength leading to node 9.

In other words, the adoption of several SAT messages, one for each wavelength, allows nodes to balance their traffic wavelength by wavelength, not being forced to throttle transmissions on lightly loaded wavelengths because of congestion on other wavelengths which are overloaded.

This is an important reason to prefer MMR-MS to MMR-SS.

Note that the traffic pattern that we considered is not an artificial construction with little practical interest: whenever traffic is unbalanced on more than one wavelength, MMR-SS can dramatically limit the network throughput. Since throughput on overloaded wavelengths is determined by the ratio of the product $(M - 1) \times K_q$ to the SAT propagation delay, when MMR-SS is adopted, the SAT propagation delay is determined by the overloaded wavelength; if only few nodes try to transmit on a different underloaded wavelength, they are forced to block their transmissions when they reach their quota $K_q$, and this wavelength is underutilized. Conversely, when one SAT per wavelength is used, as in MMR-MS, nodes regulate transmissions on each wavelength separately, and no starvation on underloaded wavelengths can be induced by the circulation of the SAT messages providing fair access to the overloaded wavelengths. This phenomenon explains also the increase in the throughput obtained by the server when MMR-MS versions are considered as shown in Fig. 5.

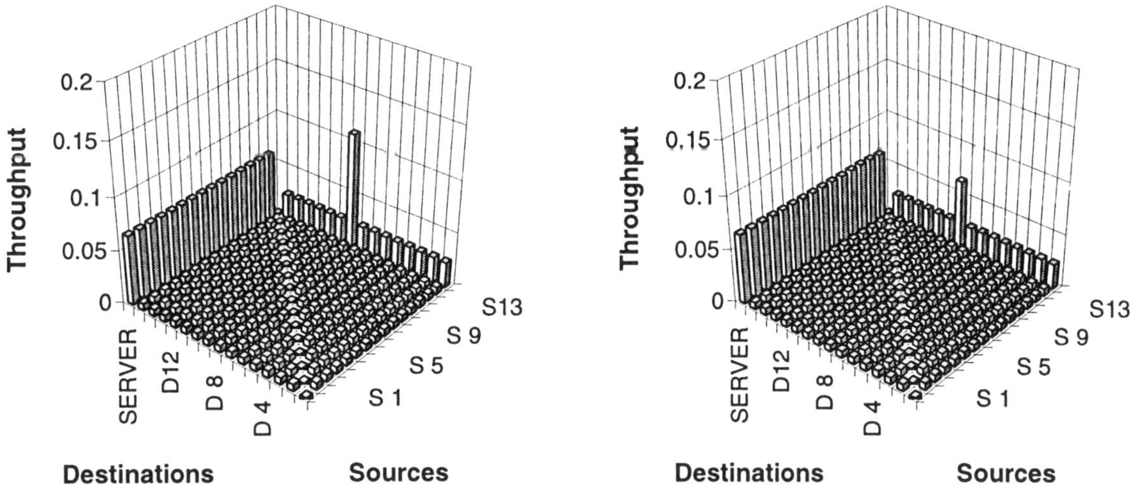


Figure 6: Throughputs for MMR-MS-U (right) and MMR-SS-D (left) in the modified server scenario; $W = 16$, $K_q = 400$, $\Lambda = 4$

### 4.4 MMR-MS when W < M

Let us now focus on the case in which the number of wavelengths is less than the number of nodes.

As shown in Fig. 7, a perfect fairness in the throughput figures is achieved by using a MMR-SS-D scheme also when $W < M$.

Remember that, when $W = M$, the number of SATs used to control the network behavior in the MMR-MS scheme was equal to the number of destinations, which is identical to the number of available wavelengths. When $W < M$ it could be possible to associate one SAT either to each of the $M$ destinations, or to each of the $W$ wavelengths. The results obtained with one SAT per destination are reported in Fig. 8.

Using one SAT per destination, besides requiring a higher number of control messages, gives poor performance as regards the server throughput towards clients. The reasons behind this performance loss are the following. The node upstream with respect to the server, i.e. node 15, experiences difficulty to obtain bandwidth on the wavelength leading to the server (node 16); since also nodes 4, 8 and 12 receive on that same wavelength, node 15 delays not only the SAT of the wavelength leading to the server, but also the SATs that control transmissions towards nodes 4, 8 and 12. Only when all the four SATs are in possession of node 15 this node can freely access the overloaded wavelength. In this situation the node should be able to transmit $K_q$ packets towards the server, and nodes 4, 8 and 12. This is only partly true: if node 15 exhausts its quota $K_q$ towards the server before the other quotas, it immediately forwards the corresponding SAT. The possession of the other SATs (call them SATs 4, 8 and 12) does not help the node in its transmission attempts towards such nodes, since other sources are allowed to transmit towards the server because the SAT relative to the server wavelength is rotating in the network. Only when node 15 receives again the SAT 16 that allows it to transmit to the server, node 15 is able to obtain enough bandwidth on the overloaded wavelength leading to the server. It can thus transmit to the server, as well as to nodes 4, 8 and 12. This implies that the propagation times of SATs referring to destination 4, 8 and 12 increase, thus reducing the source throughputs.

Numerical results indicate that node 15 has a probability higher than 1/4 of reaching the quota $K_q$ towards the server before reaching the quota on the wavelengths leading to nodes 4, 8 and 12. This is due to the fact that each time node 15 breaks the SRR scheduling algorithm while it is holding the four SATs it transmits packets taken from the longest queue, i.e. from the the queue of packets directed toward the server. This justifies the higher rotation times of the SATs associated to nodes 4, 8 and 12 when compared to the rotation delay of the SAT associated to the server; as a result the server throughput towards nodes 4, 8 and 12 is dramatically reduced, almost to zero.

For these phenomena, when considering a scenario in which the number of available wavelengths is less than the number of destinations, it seems wise to use one SAT to control the traffic on each wavelength; this avoids the problems that were just described, and also entails a reduction in the complexity of the system, since the SAT number is equal to $W$ which is less than $M$. By using one SAT per channel (MMR-MS-U case), performance similar to those observed in Fig. 7 can be achieved. The only (marginal) difference concerns the throughput obtained by server transmissions: while the same throughput is observed on those wavelengths where the server also receives, a slightly larger throughput is obtained on all other wavelengths. This is due to the ability of MMR-MS to separately control each wavelength as described in the previous section; even if it could seem that the behavior of the MMR-SS-D is more "fair" in the sense that the server obtains the same throughput towards all the client

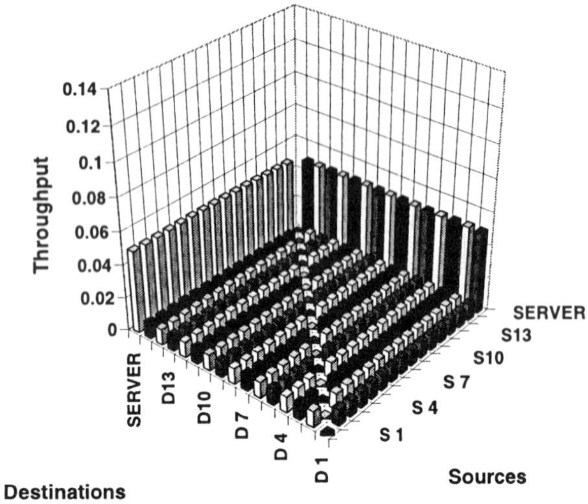


Figure 7: Throughputs for MMR-SS-D; $M = 16$, $W = 4$, $K_q = 400$, $\Lambda = 6.0$

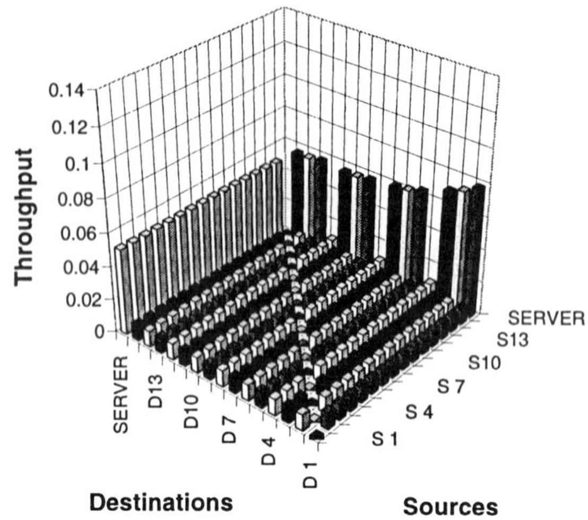


Figure 8: Throughputs for MMR-MS-U, one SAT per destination; $M = 16$, $W = 4$, $K_q = 400$, $\Lambda = 6.0$

nodes, the actual performance of MMR-MS is, on any wavelength, better of the one provided by MMR-SS; MMR-MS should still be preferred also in this context.

## 5 Conclusions

In this paper we considered algorithms for fairness control in all-optical WDM rings, assuming that the available wavelengths are associated with (groups of) destinations, and that transmissions are ruled by the SRR slotted MAC protocol.

The association of wavelengths with destinations allows their use as (group) destination addresses and the simplification of the MAC protocol, but leads to unsatisfactory fairness, due to the asymmetric positions of sources with respect to destinations. Thus, in order to improve fairness, it is necessary to adopt a fairness control scheme.

We defined and evaluated several variations of a fairness control scheme derived from the extension to a multi-channel context of the MetaRing proposal.

The simulation results on which the comparison was based provide many useful insights. First of all, it can be observed that all the proposed alternatives are capable of providing fairness on time scales much longer than packet delays. This means that it is possible to achieve throughput fairness (if we accept to average throughputs over relatively long time intervals), whereas little can be done as regards packet delay fairness. The downstream forwarding of SAT messages provides advantages due to the reduction of SAT propagation delays, as well as disadvantages due to the increase of SAT access delays and to throughput reductions in the case of a number of wavelengths smaller than the number of nodes. The availability of a dedicated wavelength for SATs appears not to be justified, since the performance improvements are marginal, whereas the possible system complexity increase may be quite significant.

The discovery of untoward behaviors in unbalanced traffic patterns, and the performance achievable when the number of wavelengths is smaller than the number of nodes suggests that using just one SAT to regulate fairness on all wavelengths is not a good choice, in spite of its potential simplicity. Moreover, the analysis of alternatives when the number of wavelengths is smaller than the number of nodes indicates that in this case the number of SATs should equal the number of wavelengths.

As a result, the best extension of the MetaRing fairness control scheme to a WDM ring seems to be the one using one SAT for each wavelength, which circulates together with data packets, and is always addressed to the node just upstream of the node that emits the SAT.

## References

[1] C.A.Brackett, "Dense Wavelength Division Multiplexing Networks: Principles and Applications", *IEEE Journal on Selected Areas in Communications,* vol. 8, n. 6, pp. 948-964, Aug. 1990

[2] M.Ajmone Marsan, A.Fumagalli, E.Leonardi, F.Neri, "R-Daisy: an All-Optical Packet Network," *EUROPTO European Symposium on Advanced Networks and Services,* Amsterdam, The Netherlands, Mar. 1995

[3] M.Ajmone Marsan, A.Bianco, E.Leonardi, M.Meo, F.Neri, "MAC Protocols and Fairness Control in WDM Multi-Rings with Tunable Transmitters and Fixed Receivers", *IEEE/OSA Journal on Lightwave Technology,* vol. 14, n. 6, pp. 1230-1244, June 1996

[4] J.Chen, I.Cidon, Y.Ofek, "A Local Fairness Algorithm for the MetaRing and its Performance Study," *IEEE Journal on Selected Areas in Communications,* vol. 11, n. 8, pp. 1183-1192, Aug. 1993

# $SR^3$: a Bandwidth-Reservation MAC Protocol for Multimedia Applications over All-Optical WDM Multi-Rings*

M. Ajmone Marsan, A. Bianco, E. Leonardi, A. Morabito, F. Neri
Dipartimento di Elettronica – Politecnico di Torino – Italy
E-mail: {ajmone,bianco,leonardi,neri}@polito.it

## Abstract

*The paper describes $SR^3$ (Synchronous Round Robin with Reservations), a collision-free medium access control protocol for all-optical slotted packet networks based on WDM multi-channel ring topologies where nodes are equipped with one fixed-wavelength receiver and one wavelength-tunable transmitter.*

*$SR^3$ is derived from the SRR and MMR protocols previously proposed by the same authors for the same class of all-optical networks. SRR and MMR already achieve an efficient exploitation of the available bandwidth, while guaranteeing a throughput-fair access to each node. $SR^3$, in addition, allows nodes to reserve slots, thereby achieving a stronger control on access delays; it is thus well suited to meet tight delay requirements, as it is the case for multimedia applications.*

*Simulation results show that $SR^3$ provides very good performance to guaranteed quality traffic, but also brings significant performance improvements for best-effort traffic.*

## 1 Introduction

In all-optical networks, data generated in the electronic domain by the source user are converted into the optical domain at the ingress UNI (User/Network Interface), and transported to the destination with no conversion into an electronic format before the egress UNI. Wavelength division multiplexing (WDM) [1] is normally used to partition the very large bandwidth available on the fiber into a number of channels whose rates match the speeds of electronic interfaces.

In this paper we consider all-optical networks where one logical channel is associated with each destination node. Logical channels are assumed to be obtained with a combination of WDM and space diversity, since in this case the feasibility of the proposed approach was verified [2, 3]. Since one channel for each destination exists, nodes are equipped with one tunable transmitter and one fixed receiver.

We focus on the particular case of ring topologies (more precisely on multi-channel rings), which have become an attractive solution for all-optical LANs and MANs, mainly thanks to the successful progress achieved in optical amplifiers to compensate for insertion losses at intermediate nodes. With respect to other topologies (e.g., stars) rings ease the synchronization at extremely high data rates, permitting a slotted access, hence an efficient and flexible use of the available optical bandwidth for packet communications.

Providing one channel for each destination means that all sources that need to transmit to the same destination must share the corresponding channel. Medium Access Control (MAC) protocols are thus needed to arbitrate the access to the shared channels. This paper proposes a collision-free access protocol, which, in spite of its simplicity, allows an almost optimal exploitation of the available resources while guaranteeing a fair access to all nodes. In addition, it permits a very efficient integration of guaranteed quality and best-effort services. For these reasons, it is well suited to support multimedia applications.

## 2 Network Topology

We consider ring networks providing one logical channel for transmissions to each destination. If we denote by $M$ the number of nodes in the network, a total of $M$ logical channels is available in the ring. All nodes that need to transmit to the same destination share the same logical channel.

Fig. 1 depicts the logical network architecture for the case $M = 4$. The $M$ logical channels run in parallel; they are slotted and synchronized, so that $M$ slots (one for each destination node) simultaneously arrive at a node every slot time. Full connectivity is achieved by tuning the transmitter at the source node on a packet-by-packet basis. Fixed-length data packets are transmitted, and the slot size is such that one packet exactly fits into one slot. Since each channel brings information to one destination, we assume that the transmitted information is removed from the channel by the destination node: each logical ring is interrupted at a (different) node, and the multi-channel ring can be viewed as a set of staggered logical busses folded in a physical ring layout.

In order to avoid collisions (i.e., simultaneous accesses to the same slot) among packets directed to the same destination, nodes exploit a channel inspection capability on each logical channel. Thus the source node, prior to transmitting a new packet with a given destination, inspects the activity on the channel associated with such destination. If an empty slot is observed, the packet can be transmitted, and it will reach its destination without collision; otherwise, contention

*This work was supported in part by the Italian National Research Council, and the Italian Ministry for University and Scientific Research.

6d.2.1

0-8186-7780-5/97 $10.00 © 1997 IEEE

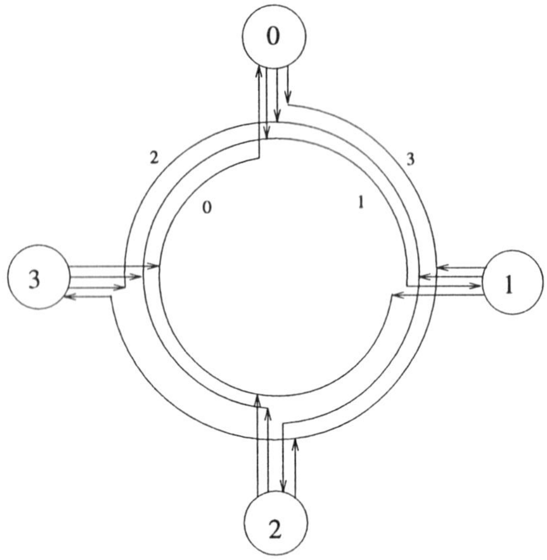


Figure 1: The logical network topology when $M = 4$

arises, and priority is given to in-transit packets: the transmission attempt is delayed. The channel inspection operation can be implemented with the subcarrier signalling technique (see [4]).

It can be observed that, due to ring symmetries, each node has a better-than-average access to the channels leading to some destinations, and a worse-than-average access to other channels, leading to other destinations. If we assume node numbers to be increasing in the transmission direction, the channel on which node $i$, $i = 0, 1, \cdots, M-1$, has the best access chance is the one leading to node[1] $|i-1|_M$, since to access this channel, node $i$ needs not defer to transmissions of any other node; the channel on which node $i$ has the worst access chance is the one leading to node $|i+1|_M$, since, to access this channel, node $i$ must defer to the possible transmissions of $M-2$ upstream nodes. We assume nodes not to transmit to themselves.

In Fig. 1, node 0 has the best access opportunity on channel 3 (leading to node 3), and the worst access opportunity on channel 1, where it must defer to transmissions of nodes 2 and 3.

We say that the traffic directed to node $j$ from node $i$ has lower access priority than traffic directed to $j$ from nodes $|j+1|_M, |j+2|_M, \cdots, |i-2|_M, |i-1|_M$. In particular, we say that node $i$ has access priority $|i-j|_M$ when transmitting to node $j$, 1 being the highest access priority, and $M-1$ the lowest. When a packet is ready for transmission from node $i$ to node $j$, the access must be delayed if the channel leading to $j$ is already occupied with a transmission by one of the nodes with higher access priority with respect to destination $j$.

## 3 Access Protocol

The access protocol that we propose, called Synchronous Round Robin with Reservations (SR$^3$), can be subdivided in three hierarchical layers: the access strategy, the fairness control scheme, and the reservation scheme.

### 3.1 Access strategy

The aim of the access strategy is to minimize the number of contentions among packets whose transmission is attempted in the same slot to the same receiver.

We consider access strategies with *a priori* packet selection: each transmitter selects the packet to be transmitted in a given slot without the knowledge of the channel status. This comes from the assumption that the selection of the packet whose transmission is attempted in a given slot is normally performed in the electronic domain, hence at low speed, during the previous slot interval, when the channel status is unknown. We further assume that only one packet can be transmitted per slot time, since only one transmitter is available at each node.

The access strategy called SRR (Synchronous Round Robin), presented in [5], avoids collisions and arbitrates contentions, permitting a good exploitation of the available bandwidth.

In order to implement the SRR protocol, nodes must keep one separate packet queue for every possible destination. Since we assume that a node does not transmit to itself, $M-1$ FIFO queues exist at each node. Each queue stores packets at a different priority in the channel access; such priority can be associated with the queue.

With SRR, in an arbitrary time slot identified by the label $s$, node $i$ schedules for transmission a packet with destination $|i+k+1|_M$, with $k = |s|_{M-1}$. If the corresponding queue is empty, the transmission of the first packet from the longest queue is attempted in slot $s$. If more then one longest queues exists (a tie for the longest queue occurs) the lowest priority among the longest queues is selected.

In any case, if transmission in slot $s$ is not possible because it would generate a collision, a *new* packet is selected in the following slot (labeled $s+1$).

We call *SRR frame* one SRR scheduling period, i.e., the time between two slots in which the same queue at one node has a preferential access. The duration of the SRR frame is $M-1$ slots.

The selection of the next packet to be transmitted requires the information about the lengths of all queues, as well as a common knowledge at all nodes about the slot label $s$, i.e., a global (network-wide) synchronization on the slot sequence. Moreover, the ring latency must be equalized in order to be a multiple of the SRR frame duration.

SRR tends to a Time Division Multiple Access (TDMA) scheme under high load, but allows a dynamic partitioning (i.e., statistical multiplexing) of the channel bandwidth among transmitting nodes under asymmetric traffic, and an unregulated access to the channel under light traffic.

SRR can cope, with minor modifications, also with several traffic classes at different user priorities (*U-priorities*[2]). In this case, nodes must be equipped with one queue for each traffic class for each destina-

[1] The notation $|\cdot|_M$ indicates the modulo $M$ operator.

[2] We use the term "U-priority" to make clear the differ-

tion. In an arbitrary time slot identified by the label $s$, node $i$ schedules for transmission a packet from the highest-U-priority non-empty queue with destination $d = |i + k + 1|_M$, where $k$ is defined as above. If all queues associated with destination $d$ are empty, the transmission of the first packet from the longest among non-empty highest-U-priority queues is attempted in slot $s$. If more than one non-empty highest-U-priority queue exists, the queue at lowest priority with respect to the access to the ring (i.e., packets directed to the closest destination) is selected.

### 3.2 Fairness scheme

SRR can lead to starvation of low access priority nodes in overloaded channels under unbalanced traffic patterns. We thus use on top of SRR a fairness control algorithm called MMR (Multi-MetaRing) [5, 6], derived from the Metaring fairness control algorithm proposal for high speed metropolitan area networks [7].

A complete description of the MMR scheme is reported in [6]. In this paper we only point out that fairness in MMR is granted by the circulation on the ring of $M$ control messages, named SAT's (standing for SATisfied). Each node has a transmission quota for each channel, which is restored when a SAT is received (i.e., only a given amount of packets can be transmitted between two SAT visits). Each SAT regulates the access on one channel: the $j$-SAT restores the quotas for channel $j$.

Each node forwards SAT messages to the upstream node, thus SAT messages logically rotate in the opposite direction with respect to data (although the physical propagation is obviously co-directional).

### 3.3 Reservation scheme

In the considered network packet access delays (i.e., the time elapsing from the instant when a packet reaches the head of its queue until transmission starts) experienced under non-uniform high-load conditions can be very large (see Fig. 2 in Sect. 5) when the SRR+MMR protocols are used. In order to obtain a stronger control on access delays, we rely on slot reservation. We propose a reservation scheme to be used in conjunction with SRR+MMR, which only requires a marginal algorithmic complexity increase, with no additional signaling messages.

A slot reserved by node $i$ on the channel leading to destination $j$ cannot be used by any higher access priority node (but can be effectively used by nodes at a lower priority, i.e., downstream on the logical bus leading to the intended destination). Nodes have therefore a guaranteed access to slots that were reserved. Only slots to which node $i$ has preferential access according to the SRR frame can be reserved on the channel leading to destination $j$, i.e., slots in position $|j - i|_M$ inside the SRR frame.

Time is subdivided into successive periods called *reservation frames*. Each reservation frame comprises $P$ SRR frames. Each node can reserve up to $P$ slots with a given destination per reservation frame, i.e., at most one slot per destination per SRR frame.

Reservations are effective if all network nodes are aware of other nodes' reservations. We use SAT messages to broadcast the reservation information: each SAT distributes information regarding current reservations on the channel it regulates.

We assume that each SAT contains a Reservation Field (SAT-RF), which is subdivided in $M - 1$ subfields; each sub-field is assigned to a particular node for reservations.

If node $i$ needs to reserve $h$ slots per reservation frame on channel $j$, it waits until it receives the $j$-SAT; it then forwards the reservation request by properly setting the $i$-th SAT-RF subfield to the value $h$.

The $j$-SAT visits all nodes during the next tour of the multi-ring. By the time node $i$ receives again the $j$-SAT, all nodes in the network are aware of the request of node $i$. Node $i$ can thus update its reservation request on channel $j$ every time it releases the $j$-SAT.

According to our reservation scheme, each SAT must carry channel reservation requests for every node in its SAT-RF. However, this does not limit the network scalability. Indeed, only the number of reserved slots, i.e., an integer $0 \leq h \leq P$, per reservation frame must be notified by a node to other nodes: the position of the $h$ reserved slots in the reservation frame is automatically established by running the SRR access strategy in every node (remember that a global synchronization on the slot sequence is assumed).

## 4 Reservation Strategies

The reservation scheme can be very effective in controlling queuing delays (i.e., the time from packet generation until packet transmission). We will see that this performance improvement is beneficial to best-effort datagram traffic transmitted on low priority channels in non-uniform traffic scenarios, and that it is even more effective when guaranteed-quality services are offered, or multiple traffic classes are to be handled.

In both cases, nodes must be able to evaluate whether they need to reserve slots: algorithms to determine the number of slots to be reserved must be provided. A very aggressive reservation policy, where nodes tend to reserve all reservable slots, would lead to performance limitations similar to those observed for the TDMA scheme. A very conservative reservation policy, instead, would leave us with delay and contention problems exhibited by SRR.

### 4.1 Reservation strategy for guaranteed-quality traffic

Applications with Quality of Service (QoS) requirements usually exploit connection-oriented protocols. At call set-up, the desired performance and the connection characteristics are specified. A Call Admission Control (CAC) algorithm can be introduced, using concepts similar to those developed in the ATM community (see, for example, [8, Sect. 4.3]); this would control the amount of statistical multiplexing in the network.

Since $SR^3$ allows nodes to reserve only preferential slots, no interference is observed among slots reserved

---

ence with the access priorities due to the considered network topology.

by different nodes on the same channel; each node can thus implement a call admission control policy based on local information, without any need for coordination with other nodes.

It is outside the aims of this paper to define an optimized bandwidth allocation strategy; we will show in Sect. 5 that by reserving slots it is possible to have a really strong control of access and queuing delays.

The nice characteristic of the proposed network is that the bandwidth allocation and connection establishment procedures can be naturally introduced in a system whose "native" mode of operation is connectionless. No hybrid solutions (i.e., different algorithms and access protocols) nor partitionings of the available resources between connection-oriented and datagram traffic are necessary. Packets belonging to guaranteed QoS streams do not necessarily have to be transmitted in reserved slots. Moreover, reserved slots not used by the node that made the reservation can be "reused" for transmission by downstream nodes. As a consequence, in multi-class traffic scenarios, network performances are not degraded because of too aggressive allocation policies.

Furthermore, connections with Variable Bit Rate (VBR) traffic, for which the average and peak bandwidth requirements are often not known, are more easily accommodated in our system. The amount of resources allocated to connections can be easily varied during the lifetime of each connection, thereby providing good flexibility.

### 4.2 Reservation strategy for datagram applications

In the case of datagram (best-effort) traffic, when a node observes a degraded access (i.e., large access delays) to a channel, it can improve the quality of its access on that channel by reserving slots. Nodes must however be able to evaluate the needed amount of reserved slots: if too many slots are reserved, they may go unused, leading to a degradation of the overall network performance.

We use packet queuing delays as a quality index of the channel access. When a node receives a SAT, the queuing delay experienced by the packet at the head of the corresponding transmission queue is used to compute the number of slots to be reserved.

We assume that nodes can increase, or decrease, *at most by one*[3] the number of reserved slots per reservation frame every time they update the reservation requests, i.e., every time they receive the SAT for that channel.

Nodes use two thresholds in order to decide whether the number of reserved slots must be increased, decreased, or left unchanged.

Let us define a High Threshold (HT) and a Low Threshold (LT), with (HT $\geq$ LT). Let $D$ be the queuing delay for the packet at the head of the queue; if $D < LT$, the number of reserved slots is decreased by one; if $LT \leq D < HT$, the number of reserved slots is left unchanged; finally, if $D \geq HT$, the number of reserved slots is increased by one.

Threshold values must be chosen so that nodes reserve only the number of slots necessary to improve their performance when experiencing problems in the access to the channel, without needlessly subtracting slots to other nodes.

As a first approximation, we can assume that a node has a degraded access to a given channel if, on the average, it has less than one transmission opportunity (i.e., it gets less than one free slot) per SRR frame on that channel. In this case, the queuing delay is expected to be greater than the one that the node would experience under a TDMA scheme. Each node could thus compare the experienced delay with the expected delay under TDMA, in order to decide whether a degraded access to the channel is being experienced, and the reservation of extra slots is necessary.

To compute the delay expected under TDMA, the amount of load offered at a node must be known. Nodes should therefore locally measure the traffic offered to each channel. Local load measures entail a non-negligible algorithmic complexity, and cannot be "cheaply" performed by nodes.

We therefore use the bandwidth allocation parameter $\rho_s = h/P$, equal to the ratio between the number $h$ of slots reserved per reservation frame and the maximum number $P$ of reservable slots, as an indicator of the local traffic offered to the network, and we define threshold values as a function of $\rho_s$. In particular we let LT $= 0$ when $h = 0$, LT $= C_1 \frac{M-1}{2(1-\rho_s)}$ when $0 < h < P$, and LT $=$ LT$_P$ when $h = P$; we let HT $= C_2 \frac{M-1}{2(1-\rho_s)}$ when $0 < h < P$, and HT $= \infty$ when $h = P$. $\frac{M-1}{2(1-\rho_s)}$ is the expression for the expected TDMA delay with node load $\rho_s$, and $C_1$, $C_2$, and LT$_P$ are constants, with $C_1 < C_2$. When $h = P$, hence $\rho_s = 1$, LT cannot be computed as a function of the expected TDMA delay, since the latter grows to infinity. Thus, the LT$_P$ constant was introduced, which can be computed similarly to LT for $0 < h < P$, with $\rho_s$ very close to 1 (e.g., $\rho_s = 0.98$).

By varying the values taken by constants $C_1$, $C_2$ and LT$_P$, it is possible to make the allocation strategy more or less aggressive.

It must be noted that an under-estimation of the locally offered load (i.e., of $\rho_s$) leads to an under-estimation of thresholds values; similarly, an over-estimation of the local load leads to an over-estimation of the thresholds values. As a consequence, the system tends to compensate differences between $\rho_s$ and the real offered load.

## 5 Simulation Results

This section presents simulation results for a 16-node multi-ring. The length of the multi-ring is 30 slots (i.e., 6 km at 1 Gb/s for slots of 1000 bits). Each node transmission queue can store up to 400 packets, and the MMR transmission quota $K$ (see [6]) is equal to 200. The reservation frame is set to 10 SRR frames.

We have already shown in [5] that SRR+MMR achieves an almost optimal exploitation of the avail-

[3] We could use only two bits to specify a unit reservation change in the SAT-RF subfields. We chose to load every time the current number $h$ of reserved slots for reliability considerations: differential systems are much more error prone.

| | $\rho_s = 0.0$ | $\rho_s = 0.2$ | $\rho_s = 0.3$ | $\rho_s = 0.5$ |
|---|---|---|---|---|
| $d_q$ | 1164.69 | 282.10 | 98.79 | 39.91 |
| $d_a$ | 60.87 | 54.93 | 41.36 | 26.13 |
| $\sigma_q$ | 744.81 | 224.59 | 85.59 | 31.98 |
| $\sigma_a$ | 344.01 | 55.96 | 42.91 | 25.99 |

Table 1: Queuing and access delays for different values of the bandwidth allocation parameter $\rho_s$ in overload conditions ($\Lambda = 3.3$)

| | $\rho_s = 0.0$ | $\rho_s = 0.2$ | $\rho_s = 0.3$ | $\rho_s = 0.5$ |
|---|---|---|---|---|
| $d_q$ | 152.07 | 70.93 | 58.68 | 36.72 |
| $d_a$ | 41.80 | 35.80 | 34.60 | 23.73 |
| $\sigma_q$ | 212.63 | 72.05 | 49.69 | 29.24 |
| $\sigma_a$ | 80.28 | 41.54 | 35.80 | 25.21 |

Table 2: Queuing and access delays for different values of the bandwidth allocation parameter $\rho_s$ ($\Lambda = 2.95$)

able bandwidth, while guaranteeing a throughput-fair access to every node. In this paper we focus on the benefits achievable by superposing the reservation scheme to SRR+MMR.

In the simulation model, packets are assumed to always fit into one slot, and to be generated according to a Poisson process with fixed rate $\lambda_i$ at node $i$. The total traffic in the network is $\Lambda = \sum_{i=0}^{M-1} \lambda_i$. We assume that nodes do not transmit to themselves.

We consider a simple client-server scenario: one 'server' (node 0) is present in the network; the remaining $M-1$ 'client' nodes direct half of their traffic to the server, while the other half of the traffic is uniformly distributed among clients. The server generates an amount of traffic equal to half the total traffic generated by clients, and evenly distributes it to clients.

### 5.1 Queuing delays for guaranteed quality traffic

This subsection presents simulation results to assess the performance of guaranteed quality traffic (which can be considered to belong to a traffic class at higher U-priority). We consider the following simple traffic pattern. All nodes generate datagram (best-effort) traffic according to the client-server scenario described above. In addition to this traffic, the client node $S_l$ at the lowest priority on the channel leading to the server also transmits to the server a traffic stream with a higher U-priority, which is meant to belong to a stream with QoS guarantee requirements. To study the effect of the reservation strategy on guaranteed traffic, we assume that reservations are issued *only* by node $S_l$.

The packets at higher U-priority are assumed to always fit into one slot, and to be generated according to a Poisson process with fixed rate $\lambda_{hp} = 0.2/(M-1)$. The Poisson assumption for the stream with QoS requirements was introduced for simplicity, and can be considered unrealistic, since the generation of packets with QoS requirements is usually strongly correlated.

We present simulation results for the average $d$ and standard deviation $\sigma$ of queueing (subscript $q$) and access delays (subscript $a$) experienced by node $S_l$.

The average and standard deviation of access delays provide meaningful information about the network behavior. In overload conditions the average access delay is equal to the reciprocal of the throughput, hence it tells whether the channel bandwidth is efficiently and fairly shared by nodes. The standard deviation of the access delay provides an even more important information. Large standard deviations mean that certain packets are facing much larger access delays than other packets; this also implies that queuing delays are large.

Table 1 refers to overload conditions. We can observe that, if no slot is reserved, node $S_l$ experiences large queuing delays on the channel leading to the server. $S_l$ does not experience losses of packets at the higher U-priority, because the MMR fairness scheme guarantees the bandwidth necessary for transmissions. However, the experienced standard deviation of the access delay is very large, since node $S_l$ gets free slots only when most of the nodes at higher priority on the server channel exhausted their quota.

By reserving slots, node $S_l$ can improve its access on the server channel. Table 1 shows that the average, and even more the standard deviation, of the access delay can be very effectively controlled by reserving slots. As mentioned above, the standard deviation of the access delay is the key parameter, and it can be reduced by more than an order of magnitude with slot reservations.

Table 2 shows results when the load on the server channel is slightly smaller than 1 (i.e., $\lambda_0 = 0.983$), i.e., just below channel saturation. Also in this case, node $S_l$ experiences large queuing delays on the channel leading to the server if it does not reserve any slot. The standard deviation of the access delay is still large, although appreciably smaller than in Table 1. By reserving slots, node $S_l$ can again significantly reduce the average and the standard deviation of its access delay, obtaining a large improvement of queuing delay performance.

The results presented in the tables show that, by reserving slots, nodes can quite effectively control their channel access, managing to almost completely decouple the performance of traffic streams with QoS guarantee requirements from the amount of best-effort traffic.

### 5.2 Queuing delays for best-effort traffic

In this subsection we show that slot reservation can improve the queuing delay performance of datagram (best-effort) applications as well.

All results presented in this subsection refer to a client-server traffic scenario in which the traffic from and to the server is very close to one ($\lambda_0 = 0.983$).

Figs. 2, 3, and 4 show, respectively, the average access delays, the standard deviations of the access delays, and the average queuing delays, when nodes do not reserve slots for any source/destination pair.

Focus first on the server performance. The server experiences an average access delay approximately equal to $M-1 = 15$ slots for the client-bound chan-

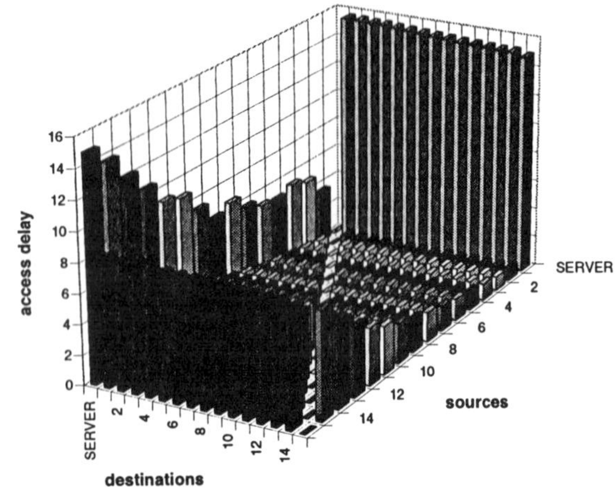


Figure 2: Average access delays for a client-server scenario with $\Lambda = 2.95$ when $\rho_s = 0.0$

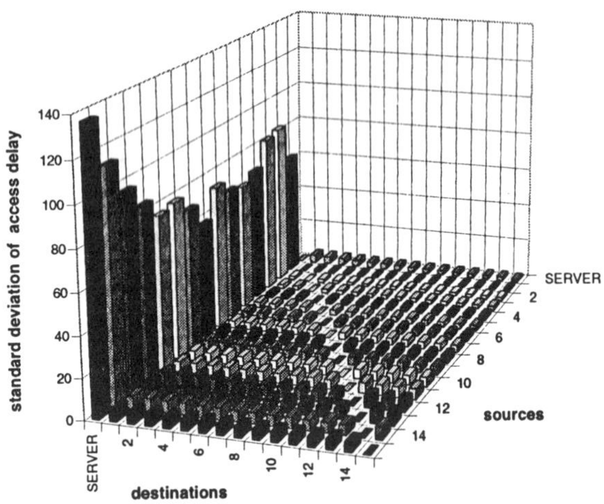


Figure 3: Standard deviations of the access delay for a client-server scenario with $\Lambda = 2.95$ when $\rho_s = 0.0$

nel at the highest priority, i.e., for the channel leading to node 15. Since the load is rather high (almost 1), the server executes an almost perfect round robin service of transmission queues. It may however happen that the server empties the queues at higher priorities, thus gaining some "extra slot" in which it can attempt transmissions of lower priority packets. However, these extra slots are not enough to compensate for slots "stolen" in a similar way by clients, so that the server still suffers a slight bandwidth loss on the lower priority channels (the experienced access delay is larger than $M - 1 = 15$).

The impact of this phenomenon on the queuing delays faced by the server (see Fig. 4) is very strong: very large queuing delays, and non-null loss probabilities, are experienced on client-bound channels where the server is at low priority.

For transmissions to the server, the client at the highest priority experiences a very small average and standard deviation of the access delay, and a very small average queuing delay, since it always observes a free channel, and can transmit packets to the server as soon as they are generated. Instead, clients at lower priorities towards the server experience larger average access delays (e.g., the average access delay of the lowest priority client is very close to 15), and access delay standard deviations, because they can transmit only if higher priority clients have not transmitted on the server channel. Also queuing delays are rather large. MMR does not influence the system behavior (i.e., the MMR blocking effect is negligible), as already shown in [5], in non-overload conditions.

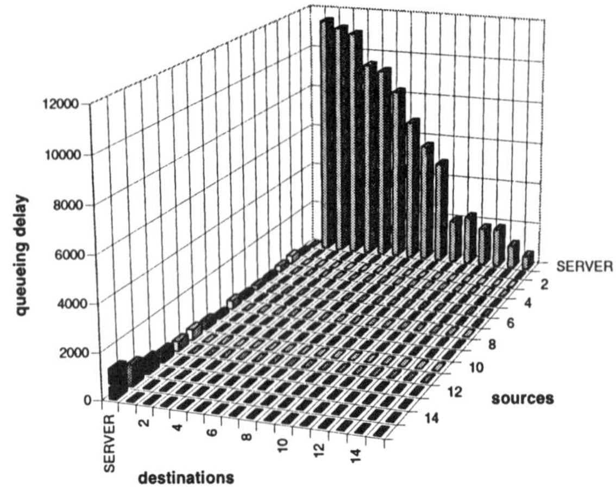


Figure 4: Average queuing delays for a client-server scenario with $\Lambda = 2.95$ when $\rho_s = 0.0$

A different behavior among client nodes is instead observed on client-bound channels. Clients with the higher priorities on the channel leading to the server exhibit a negligible access delay on client channels, while clients at lower priority when transmitting to the server face access delays slightly larger than $(M - 1)/2 = 7.5$ slots, i.e., slightly larger than half the SRR frame.

The transmission queues storing packets directed to the server at higher priority clients are empty most of the time, since these clients experience a small queuing delay on the server channel. As a consequence, higher priority clients very often attempt transmission of packets directed to other clients immediately after the packet is generated.

On the contrary, the transmission queues towards the server at lower priority clients are almost always non-empty and quite long, because lower priority clients experience large queuing delays on the server channel. Thus, client-to-client packets are transmitted only when the corresponding transmission queues are selected according to the SRR scheduling algorithm. The queuing delays of client-to-client packets are almost identical (this cannot be seen from Fig. 4 due to the very large vertical scale) to access delays, since the load is very small.

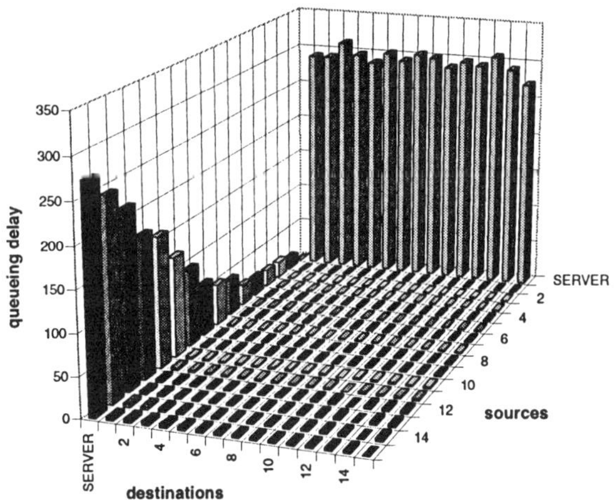


Figure 5: Average queuing delays for a datagram reservation strategy with $C_1 = 0.25$ and $C_2 = 0.4$

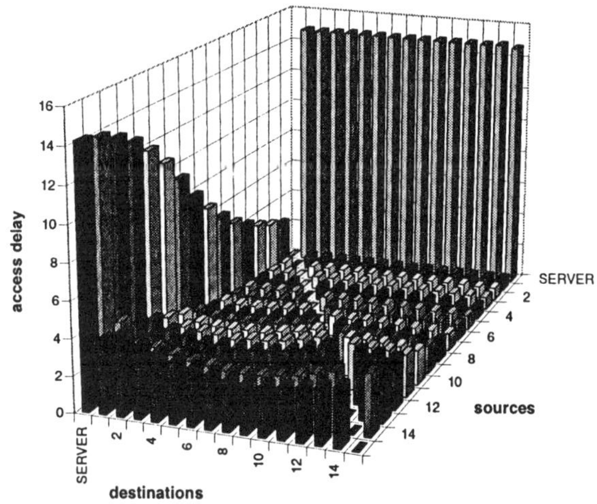


Figure 7: Average access delays for a datagram reservation strategy with $C_1 = 0.25$ and $C_2 = 0.4$

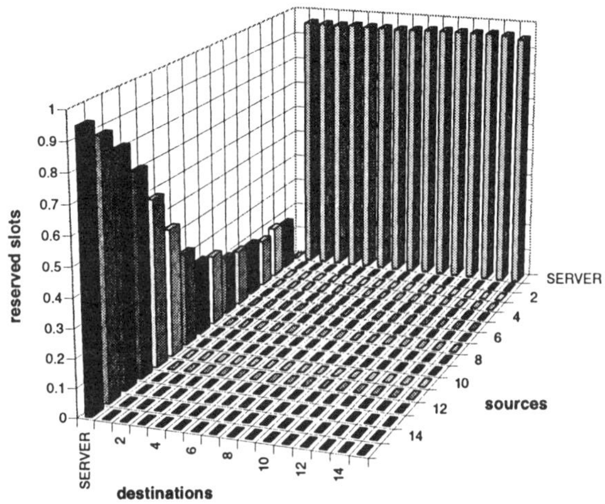


Figure 6: Normalized numbers of reserved slots for a datagram reservation strategy with $C_1 = 0.25$ and $C_2 = 0.4$

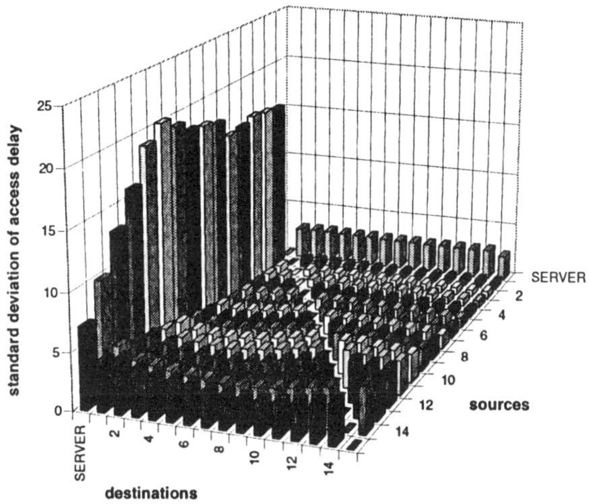


Figure 8: Standard deviations of the access delay for a datagram reservation strategy with $C_1 = 0.25$ and $C_2 = 0.4$

By reserving slots, it is possible to improve the performance of the server and of the clients at lower priority on the server channel. Figs. 5, 6, 7, and 8, show, respectively, the average queuing delays, the average normalized numbers of reserved slots (i.e., the average values of $\rho_s$), the average access delays and the standard deviations of the access delays, when nodes reserve slots according to the datagram reservation strategy described in Sect. 4.2. The values 0.25, 0.4, and 60 were respectively chosen for the constants $C_1$, $C_2$, and $LT_P$ of the reservation algorithm.

Similar queuing delays are experienced by the server on every client-bound channel; the values taken by these queuing delays are close to those experienced by the server on the highest priority channel when it does not reserve slots. No packet losses are observed on any client-bound channel. The server, indeed, reserves almost all reservable slots (see Fig. 6) on every client-bound channel, so that no client can "steal" slots from it. Average access delays are, in this case, below the $M - 1 = 15$ value, and standard deviations are very small.

Also clients at lower priorities on the server channel experience smaller queuing delays with respect to the case in which no reservations are allowed. Lower priority clients, indeed, by reserving slots can effectively control the standard deviation of the access delay on the server channel (see Fig. 8), thereby improving the queuing delay performance. It must be noted that, while lower priority clients are not successful in reducing their average access delay on the server channel by slot reservation, they achieve a beneficial reduction of the standard deviation of the access delay on the same channel.

Note that the average queuing delays experienced by lower priority clients on the server channel are smaller than those achievable in a pure TDMA system (which are approximately 450 slots). The average queuing delays, and the average and standard deviations of the access delays, instead, increase with respect to TDMA because of the unavailability of slots reserved by lower priority nodes.

Other simulation results not reported here, showed that the reservation strategy is not really sensitive to the values taken by its parameters $C_1$, $C_2$, and $LT_P$. As already mentioned, the behavior is self-adjusting, and the number of reserved slots rapidly adapts to the status of local queues.

## 6 Conclusions

The paper described $SR^3$, an access protocol designed for all-optical packet networks based on WDM multi-channel ring topologies devoting one logical channel for transmissions to each destination.

$SR^3$ is derived from the protocols already presented in [5, 6], which exhibit an efficient exploitation of the available bandwidth, and guarantee a throughput-fair access to each node. With respect to these protocols, $SR^3$ introduces a novel slot reservation scheme, which allows nodes to dynamically allocate a portion of the available bandwidth, and can thus provide quality of service guarantees for the support of multimedia applications.

The interesting feature of the proposed protocol is that, although its "native" mode of operation is the provision of connectionless best-effort services, connection-oriented guaranteed services are naturally supported without affecting the basic access mechanisms. The bandwidth left unused by guaranteed services can be very effectively shared by best-effort traffic, with a full exploitation of the advantages offered by statistical multiplexing.

Even for the basic best-effort service, that requires no service guarantee, the reservation scheme can be very beneficial: the averages and variances of access delays are greatly reduced when slots are reserved, leading to improved performance and fairness.

## References


[1] C.A. Brackett, "Dense Wavelength Division Multiplexing Networks: Principles and Applications", *IEEE Journal on Selected Areas in Communications,* vol. 8, n. 6, pp. 948-964, Aug. 1990.

[2] I. Chlamtac, A. Fumagalli, L.G. Kazovsky, P.T. Poggiolini, "A Multi-Gbit/s WDM Optical Packet Network with Physical Ring Topology and Multi-Subcarrier Header Encoding", *ECOC '93,* Montreux, Switzerland, Sept. 1993.

[3] M. Ajmone Marsan, A. Fumagalli, E. Leonardi, F. Neri, "R-Daisy: an All-Optical Packet Network," *EUROPTO European Symposium on Advanced Networks and Services,* Amsterdam, The Netherlands, March 1995.

[4] A. Budman *et al.,* "Multigigabit optical packet switch for self-routing networks with subcarrier addressing", *OFC'92,* paper Tu04, San José (CA), Febr. 1992.

[5] M. Ajmone Marsan, A. Bianco, E. Leonardi, M. Meo, F. Neri, "MAC Protocols and Fairness Control in WDM Multirings with Tunable Transmitters and Fixed Receivers", *IEEE/OSA Journal of Lightwave Technology,* vol. 14, n. 6, June 1996

[6] M. Ajmone Marsan, A. Bianco, E. Leonardi, F. Neri, S. Toniolo, "Metaring Fairness Control Schemes in All-Optical WDM Rings", *INFOCOM '97,* Kyoto, Japan, April 1997.

[7] I. Cidon, Y. Ofek, "MetaRing – a Full-Duplex Ring with Fairness and Spatial Reuse", *IEEE Transactions on Communications,* vol. 41, n. 1, pp. 110-120, Jan. 1993.

[8] R.O. Onvural, *Asynchronous Transfer Mode Networks - Performance Issues,* Artech House, 1994

# Scalable WDM Network Architecture Based on Photonic Slot Routing and Switched Delay Lines *

Imrich Chlamtac[a], Viktoria Elek[b], Andrea Fumagalli[c], Csaba Szabó[b]

[a] Boston University
Department of Electrical and Computer Engineering
E-mail: chlamtac@engc.bu.edu

[b] Technical University of Budapest
Department of Telecommunications
E-mail: {elekv,szabo}@hit.bme.hu

[c] Politecnico di Torino
Dipartimento di Elettronica
E-mail: andreaf@hp0tlc.polito.it

## Abstract

*Photonic Slot Routing (PSR) is a promising approach to solving the fundamental scalability problem of all-optical packet switched WDM networks. In this approach adjacent subnetworks can exchange wavelength sensitive traffic through bridges using wavelength non-selective devices which can be constructed using proven technologies. With photonic slot routing, packets sharing a common subnetwork destination are aggregated to form a photonic slot which is individually routed in order to reach the destination subnetwork. Photonic slots from different subnetworks can originate contentions at the bridge, leading to potential penalties of slot loss and retransmission.*

*This paper shows how slot contention penalties can be reduced through the use of Switched Delay Lines (SDL) at the bridges. The combination of these two innovative techniques, the photonic slot routing and the switched delay lines, leads to a unique solution that is shown to nearly achieve throughput and delay performance obtainable in absence of slot contentions.*

## 1 Introduction

Due to their many potential advantages the development of optical networks is attracting continued attention. With a practical realization of the well known all-optical network concept data, once sent into the network, does not need to be converted back to electronic form until it reaches the destination. Among optical multiplexing techniques, WDM (Wavelength Division Multiplexing) provides a promising solution for a practical utilization of this capacity as it allows the potential THz bandwidth to be multiplexed into multiple parallel channels, each operating at a speed compatible with the speed of electronics available today.

To support emerging, mixed traffic type applications, and growing system size, the successful deployment of optical networks requires packet switching capability and scalability to support a large number of nodes, and a large number of high capacity data streams resulting in large aggregate bandwidth.

So far, several solutions have been proposed to accommodate packet switching in all-optical WDM LANs, with a limited number of nodes [1, 3, 7, 11, 12]. These solutions achieved packet switching by using a "broadcast and select" approach (e.g., [1, 3]) or by addressing and (wavelength) routing the packet at the source node (e.g., [12]).

Attempts have recently been made to scale packet switched optical networks [7, 11] based on hierarchical architectures that provide wavelength channel reuse within each hierarchical level. Wavelength channels can be assigned dynamically to provide either intra- or inter-cluster communications, by means of slowly reconfigurable filters used at the gateways (hubs) interconnecting the clusters.[1] Due to their quasi-static

*This work is sponsored by ARPA under contract # MDA972-93-1-0028 and by NSF under contract # NCR-9406522.

[1] Extant technology does not include photonic switches which are both wavelength selective and sufficiently fast (reconfigurable) to support optical-rate packet switching. For example, in wavelength selective devices, such as Acousto Optic Tunable



0-8186-7780-5/97 $10.00 © 1997 IEEE

channel assignment these solutions encounter some drawbacks. i) The number of available wavelengths limits the number of levels in the hierarchy, and indirectly the size of the system. ii) Some of the wavelengths are not used at the higher levels of the hierarchy.

Another approach to achieve scalability in terms of coverage area, population and number of wavelengths is based on the more recent concept of *Photonic Slot Routing* (PSR) [10, 14, 15]. This approach is based on the combination of two ideas - the use of a backbone that connects (bridges) multiple LAN segments with limited number of nodes, and data bridging introducing the concept of Photonic Slot Routing. In this concept, packets transmitted simultaneously (in the same "photonic" slot) on all WDM channels are switched jointly in the bridges which connect the LAN segments with the backbone. Thus packets in a given slot remain transmitted on the same path, from the source LAN to the destination LAN. To make this possible, packets aggregated into the same slot share their destination LAN address using, what can be appropriately termed, a *sorting access protocol*.

Since in this case bridges do not have to separate packets belonging to the same slot in order to route them on different paths, wavelength *selective* inter-LAN data flows can be handled using wavelength *non-selective* devices [2]. This solution is thus unique in allowing to move the fundamental problem of switching limitations of wavelength selective devices at the bridges to a solvable problem of finding effective sorting access protocols to be used at the transmitting nodes.

PSR introduces several desirable properties. It reduces the complexity of the switching/routing operation by a factor of $w$ - the number of wavelengths, at the cost of additional processing required at the nodes (at the periphery of the network). Such solution is consistent with emerging high speed network paradigms, such as ATM. At the bridge, switching crosstalk in adjacent wavelength channels is avoided and the resulting solution is fully transparent to the data format. The proposed solution also eases power budget and loss constraints of optical systems, by keeping the number of nodes (hops) traversed by a signal at supportable level. In addition, the proposed architecture provides the well known general advantages of bridging operation: information does not have to be broadcast to the entire system (higher security and privacy), the network architecture is modular, it displays high fault tolerance and easy maintenance (if one segment is down, the rest of the communication network is unaffected), and leads to increased network capacity by using space diversity.

However, with PSR *slot contention* originating at the bridge due to un-coordinated transmissions in each LAN segment may limit the network capacity improvement obtainable through this approach. *Switched Delay Lines* (SDL) is a well know technique used in the past to optically resolve contentions arising among packets vying for common network resources [3, 6, 4, 5]. SDL consists of a combination of fiber delay lines and digital photonic switches that are controlled on a packet by packet basis, with the aim of delaying each packet until contentions are resolved. Due to the optical bandwidth transparency of SDL, this approach is well suited to also resolve contentions between photonic slots. In a PSR network this is accomplished by incorporating one SDL device at each bridge, so termed *SDL-bridge*. By so doing, slot contentions can be significantly reduced, leading to improved bandwidth efficiency, without compromising the above mentioned key features offered by the PSR architecture.

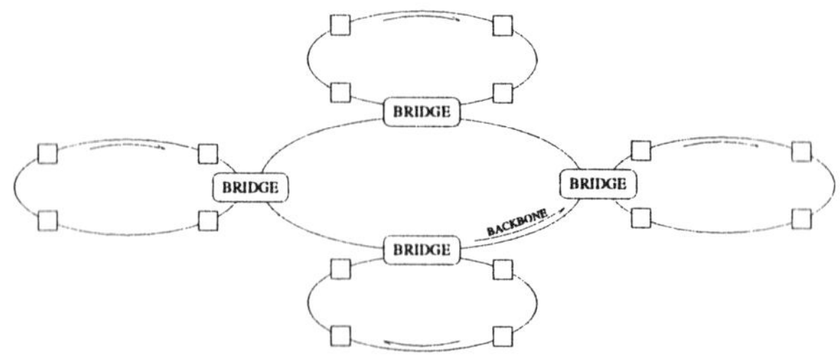


Figure 1: Architecture of segmented WDM network with ring backbone and ring segments.

## 2 Network architecture

Consider a segmented WDM network, where ($s$) WDM LANs are interconnected by means of a ring shaped backbone as shown in Fig. 1. Each LAN is connected to the backbone via an optical bridge. The bridge's function is to switch photonic slots between the LAN and the backbone towards their intended destination (LAN) segment. The WDM LAN's time is subdivided into time slots allowing only one fixed length packet to be transmitted in each slot per wavelength. Slots are synchronized across the wavelengths in order to form groups of aligned packets (the photonic slots) propagating within the fiber. Without loss of generality, in demonstrating the PSR solution we use here a WDM LAN ring topology to realize the individual LANs, as originally proposed in [12]. In this system each ring LAN connects $n$ nodes transmitting clockwise. Each node is assigned a reserved wavelength for reception, thus requiring $w = n$ wave-

Filters - AOTF [2], the current switching rate ($\sim \mu s$) and their crosstalk characteristics make packet switching on an individual wavelength basis impractical.

[2]Photonic digital switches, contrary to AOTF, are wavelength non-selective and can switch in the order of ns [9].

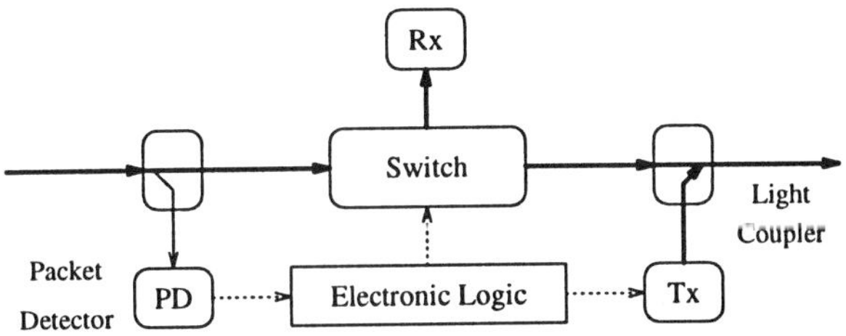


Figure 2: Schematic of the node in the ring segment.

length data channels in the LAN. [3] A data packet can be exchanged between any pair of nodes in the LAN by tuning the source's transmitter to the destination's receiver wavelength. The data packet is extracted from the network at the destination node.

To provide a seamless interconnection between nodes belonging to different LANs, identical channel and slot structures are used in all segments and in the backbone, thus ensuring that packets can be transferred from one segment to another via the backbone network without signal format (optical/electrical) or wavelength conversions. The network-wide slot synchronization required to achieve slot alignment at the bridge input fibers can be obtained across multiple segments by using the two level synchronization technique described in [15].

The node and bridge architectures required to realize a PSR system consist of basic optical devices that can be constructed using proven technologies as demonstrated next.

### 2.1 Node architecture

One possible node architecture is shown in Fig. 2. From right to left, following the data flow in the fiber, the optical signal reaches the *packet detector*, which informs the node of the wavelengths of the arriving packets and the LAN destination of the arriving slot (e.g., using the Multi-Subcarrier Signaling technique described in [12]). After that the *switch* extracts, from the LAN, the packets destined to the node and carried on the wavelength reserved to the node, e.g., $\lambda_i$. One possible implementation of such a filter is obtained by combining a wavelength demultiplexer with a fast photonic switch [9] followed by a wavelength multiplexer. If the arriving slot contains a packet for the node, the switch extracts the corresponding signal from the network, otherwise the signal remains in the network. Remaining packets propagating on the other wavelengths are let through the nodes unaffected. The *coupler* in Fig. 2 allows for the insertion of the newly transmitted packet, with carrier wavelength set by the tunable transmitter *Tx* (e.g., see [8]).

[3] In general, LANs with $n > w$ are also possible [13] using the same ring topology, with the addition of a fair channel sharing mechanism in the node access control that guarantees fair transmissions in the system.

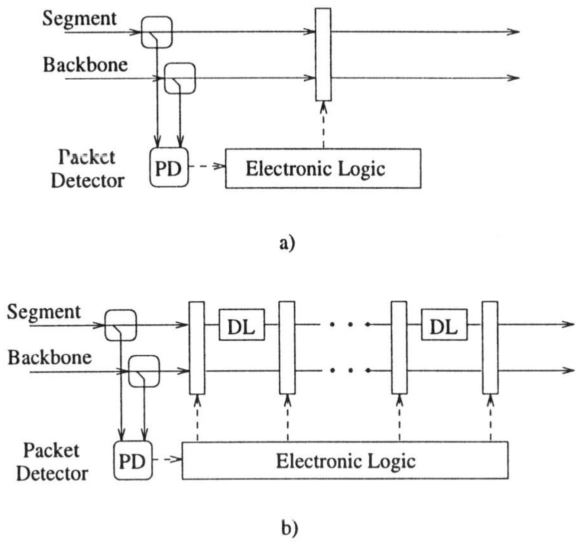


Figure 3: a) Original bridge architecture. b) SDL-bridge architecture.

### 2.2 Bridge architectures

The original bridge architecture consists of a single $2 \times 2$ space photonic switch controlled by an electronic logic (e.g., see [9]) and a packet detector connected to every input fiber (Fig. 3.a). The switch configuration (cross/bar) is determined on a slot basis. Arriving slots are detected and delayed before reaching the bridge in order to allow the electronic logic to process the information provided by the slot detectors and accordingly set the photonic switch prior to the slot arrivals.

SDL-bridge

The basic bridge architecture can be upgraded by adding the SDL device as shown in Fig. 3.b, creating the so called SDL-bridge. In general, the SDL consists of $dl$ delay lines (DL) and $dl + 1$ $2 \times 2$ space photonic switches [5].[4] The switching configuration is determined by the electronic logic on a slot basis, as for the basic bridge, based on information on the arriving slots, and on the slots already "stored" in the delay lines.

The optical hardware necessary to implement the node interface and the (SDL-)bridge reveals the attractive scalability and modularity properties of the proposed network architecture. Specifically, the number of segments and the bridge architecture do not affect the node interface. In particular, the same node architecture can be used in the single segment ring network as in the multi-segment network, thus providing for a modular growth of the network.

[4] Note that case $dl = 0$ degenerates into the original bridge architecture.

As the node interface is left unchanged, at any stage of the network evolution the node is always capable of transmitting to and receiving from any other node in the system at full speed.

The number of wavelength channels (i.e., the number of nodes in the segment) does not affect the bridge architecture as long as all the wavelengths fall into the passband of the optical components used at the bridge.

Due to its basic components, fiber and wavelength non-sensitive photonic switches, the inclusion of the SDL into the bridge architecture does not affect the key features of the PSR network. The optical bandwidth transparency and the proven feasibility of the SDL components guarantee compatibility and consistency between the original bridge and the SDL-bridge architectures, thus limiting the use of upgraded bridges only at those segments that require so.

Lastly, it is interesting to notice that the slots cross the same number of switches ($dl + 1$) at the bridge, independently of their actual route through the SDL unit. As switches are the principal cause for crosstalk and insertion loss in the proposed architecture, signal degradation grows therefore only linearly with $s$ and $dl$.

## 3 Transmission control

The following protocols are required to control the packet flow in the interconnected system.

- Packet transmission at the source node is coordinated by the *sorting access protocol* running independently at each node of the segment.
- Transmission of photonic slots between the segments and the backbone is controlled by the *bridge control* running independently at each bridge.
- By using SDL-bridge to connect segments to the backbone, slots arriving from the input links can be switched to the output links of the bridge or temporarily stored in the SDL unit. The *SDL control strategy* - running independently at the bridges - selects slots present at the bridge to be switched to the output links.
- As transmissions in each source LAN, destination LAN and at the bridges are not coordinated, slots may be dropped at the bridge due to unresolved contentions, thus *retransmission control* is required at both bridge and source node to ensure reliable packet delivery.

### Sorting access protocols

The sorting access protocol ensures collision-free channel access inside each segment (subnetwork), and organizes packets having the same destination into photonic slots. While crossing the subnetwork each photonic slot can be either assigned to a given destination segment, or (yet) un-assigned. The slot's destination is determined by the destination of the first packet placed into the slot which requires to cross the bridge in order to reach the destination node. (Packets destined to any node connected to the ring fiber between the source node and the bridge, are removed from the network prior to the arrival of the slot at the bridge, thus they do not determine the path of the slot throughout the bridge.)

At the source node, packets are stored in dedicated transmission queues according to their destination segment. The packet considered for transmission is the packet at the head of the queue associated with the destination segment of the arriving slot. Transmission will take place only if collision does not arise in the slot, i.e., the destination's channel is free. When the arriving slot is not assigned to a destination segment the oldest packet among the head of the line packets that do not generate collision is transmitted. The complexity of this destination-dependent queuing policy is proportional to the number of segments in the system, which can be considered relatively small when compared to the number of nodes in the system.

In order to prevent potential starvation at some nodes due to their relative position with respect to the bridge, fairness control must be included in the node's access protocol. Any of the available fairness control mechanisms proposed so far to regulate nodes' access to a WDM ring network (e.g., [13]) can be adjusted with minor changes to be used in the proposed network architecture.

### Bridge control

The bridge control handles the photonic slots arriving at the bridge and optically propagates them towards their intended destination segment. In the original PSR bridge architecture slots are forwarded to the output ports immediately upon arrival at the bridge. Thus when both of the slots reaching the bridge need to be forwarded through the same bridge output port (a contention), only one slot is successfully routed, whilst the other is dropped, thus requiring its retransmission. Intuitively, the control strategy that, under contention occurrence, chooses the successful slot must ensure that the overhead induced by the packet retransmission is minimized. This aspect requires some further elaboration.

Two types of slot contention may occur at the bridge. A *backbone contention*, which occurs when both arriving slots want to leave the bridge through the backbone, and a *segment contention*, which originates when both slots should be directed to the local segment.

To resolve contentions we propose a *backbone priority* strategy where priority is given to slots arriving on the backbone over slots arriving on the segment fiber. This ensures that only slots arriving from the segment might be dropped.

The backbone priority approach presents several advantages. 1) Once a slot (packets) reaches the backbone, its delivery to the destination is guaranteed. 2) Backbone bandwidth is not wasted by packet retransmissions. 3) A slot can be unsuccessful only at the bridge connected to the originating segment, thus the signaling necessary to inform the source nodes of an unsuccessful transmission attempt remains local to the segment. 4) As a consequence of point 3, a dropped packet is retransmitted within a round trip time in the segment, which can be relatively short when compared to the average end-to-end propagation time over the entire network.

SDL control strategy

When the SDL device is added to the bridge, contentions can be resolved without dropping slots as long as DLs are available to store arriving contending slots [5]. An SDL strategy determines, on a time slot basis, how photonic slots must be switched through the SDL in order to improve the bandwidth efficiency of the PSR, i.e., minimize the probability of slot loss. As shown in [5], the finite storing time and the particular architecture of the SDL make the optimal strategy not trivial to identify, however, good heuristics are available [5].

In the SDL-bridge the slots to transmit are selected based on the following rules:

1. Slots are transmitted using a *non-idling policy*: if there is at least one slot that can be transmitted in addition to the slot in the rightmost DL naturally leaving the bridge, this slot is transmitted. Intuitively, this policy minimizes the number of busy DLs, and maximizes the bridge throughput in terms of photonic slots.
2. If the rightmost DL is empty, both of the output links are available for transmission. In this case the slot selection is based on a *balancing policy*. The number of slots selecting each output port is compared, and a slot from the larger group is chosen for transmission. In this way the load of the two ports is balanced, decreasing the probability of future congestions that might lead to slot loss.

Following the above rules of operation a group of photonic slots *eligible for transmission* can be determined at each time slot. Which among the slots of the eligible group is chosen for actual transmission can be selected according to different metrics of interest, e.g.:

- control complexity is kept limited by choosing any photonic slot, e.g., the *rightmost* in the SDL,
- packet retransmission probability is reduced by choosing the slot carrying the *largest number of packets*.

Finally, observe that when contention cannot be resolved by the SDL, a slot will be dropped. It is easy to see that in such case it is advantageous to drop the photonic slot arriving at the bridge on the local segment. Other strategies are possible.

Retransmission control

When a slot is dropped the bridge requires packet retransmission by broadcasting a negative acknowledgment (NACK) message to the nodes of the local segment. The NACK message is piggy-backed in the first slot directed into the local segment leaving the bridge after contention. Note, that the ring topology of the segment allows for a simple retransmission control at the source node: the NACK signal reaches each source node exactly one round trip time after transmission of the unsuccessful packet. Since under contention occurrence the dropped slot is the one at the bridge input arriving on the segment fiber, the round trip time does not include any SDL delay, thus making the retransmission control independent from the number of delay lines.. In this way the node can determine whether packet retransmission is necessary based on the arrival time of the NACK signal as described next. Upon transmission of a packet *requiring to cross the bridge*, copy of it is stored in the outstanding buffer of the source node with a timeout equal to the round trip propagation time within the LAN segment. At timeout expiration the packet is removed from the outstanding buffer, and according to the ACK/NACK signaling carried by the arriving slot on the fiber it is dropped or re-inserted into the transmission queue in time order.

The advantage of this retransmission control is twofold. First, the signaling required to control retransmission is very simple: it is associated with the photonic slot rather than with each individual packet and it is localized within the source segment. Secondly, the size of the outstanding buffer is kept small and proportional to the round trip propagation time of the segment, thus it is not affected by the size of the global network.

Signaling and overall complexity

Since the proposed network is targeted toward very high speed interconnection systems, it is of fundamental importance that the signaling required by the network control has a contained complexity. The sorting access protocol requires a signaling complexity linear with $w$ and $s$, and is unaffected by the network geographical extension. The bridge control only requires the knowledge of the destination segment of the arriving slot, hence its signaling complexity is only a

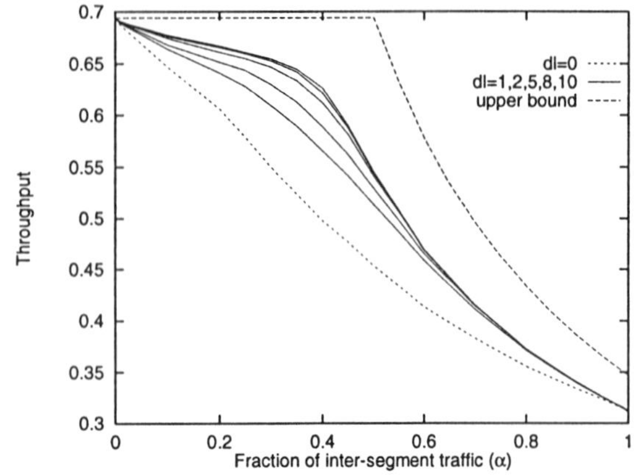


Figure 4: Per node throughput versus $\alpha$, the fraction of inter-segment traffic, under saturated load ($\lambda = 1$). A $s = 4$ segment network using bridge architectures with varying number of DLs ($dl = 0-10$) is simulated. The dotted curve shows the upper bound in Eqs. 1,2.

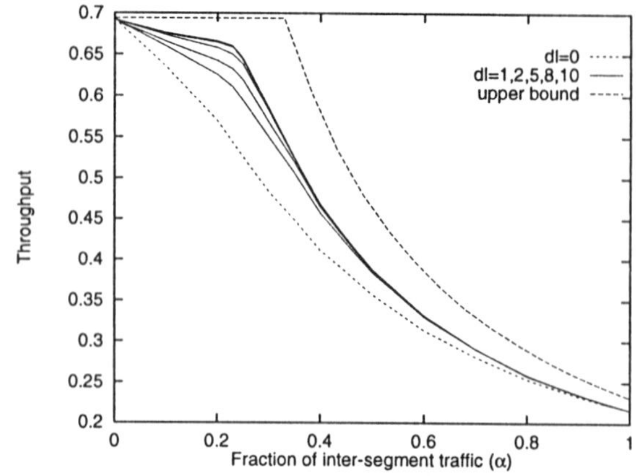


Figure 5: Per node throughput versus $\alpha$, the fraction of inter-segment traffic, under saturated load ($\lambda = 1$). A $s = 6$ segment network using bridge architectures with varying number of DLs ($dl = 0-10$) is simulated. The dotted curve shows the upper bound in Eqs. 1,2.

function of $s$. The complexity of the SDL control is linear with $dl$, and does not depend on $w$ and $s$. Last but not least, the signaling necessary to support the retransmission control does not depend on any of the above network parameters.

## 4 Performance analysis

This section evaluates the performance of the SDL based PSR system. The two considered metrics are conventional *per node throughput* ($th$), defined as the average number of packets per time slot successfully transmitted by every node, and the average number of *per packet transmissions* ($\bar{r}$) required to ensure data delivery through the network.

- $w$: number of wavelength channels (4)
- $n$: number of nodes per segment, $n = w$
- $s$: number of segments (4,6)
- $p$: total number of nodes, $p = n \times s$
- $dl$: number of delay lines in the SDL device
- $\lambda$: per node offered load
- $\alpha$: fraction of inter-segment traffic

Table 1: Parameters used in simulation.

Table 1 lists the assumptions made for this evaluation. Architecture and control of the segmented system are based on the description given in Sec. 2 and 3, respectively. The WDM system has $w$ wavelength channels, the ring backbone connects $s$ segments, each with $n = w$ nodes for a total of $p = w \times s$ nodes in the system. Nodes of the same segment do not share the same wavelength for reception. Transmitter's buffer is assumed to be infinite. SDL-bridges, making use of $dl$ DLs as described in section 2.2, connect the segments to the backbone, being case $dl = 0$ the original bridge architecture without SDL.

The traffic generated to test the systems is characterized by two parameters, $\lambda$ and $\alpha$. In each time slot every source node generates a packet with probability $\lambda$. The packet's destination is chosen uniformly with probability $\alpha$ among the nodes connected to a segment different from the source segment, thus also defining the *inter-segment* traffic. With probability $1-\alpha$ the destination is uniformally chosen among the nodes connected to the source segment (excluding the source node), defining the *intra-segment* traffic.

First, an upper bound on $th$ ($\tilde{th}$) and a lower bound on $\bar{r}$ ($\tilde{r}$) - assuming unlimited storage capacity at the bridges - are computed to determine the potential gain offered by the proposed approach. The behavior of the Head-Of-Line (HOL) blocking at the transmitter's buffer for $\alpha = 0$ can be analyzed using the model presented in [16] for a single ring network with $p = w$. For other values of $\alpha > 0$ the effect of the HOL blocking is more pronounced, thus further limiting the achievable per node throughput. Defining as $th(0)$ the per node throughput obtained in a single ring WDM network with $p = w$ nodes [16], an upper bound of the throughput, when the backbone bandwidth is not saturated, is thus

$$\tilde{th}(\alpha) = th(0) \qquad 0 \leq \alpha \leq \frac{s}{2} \tag{1}$$

Assuming fair transmission of inter- and intra-segment traffic, i.d., $\frac{th(\alpha)}{th_{inter}(\alpha)} = \frac{1}{\alpha}$ for $0 < \alpha \leq 1$ as demon-

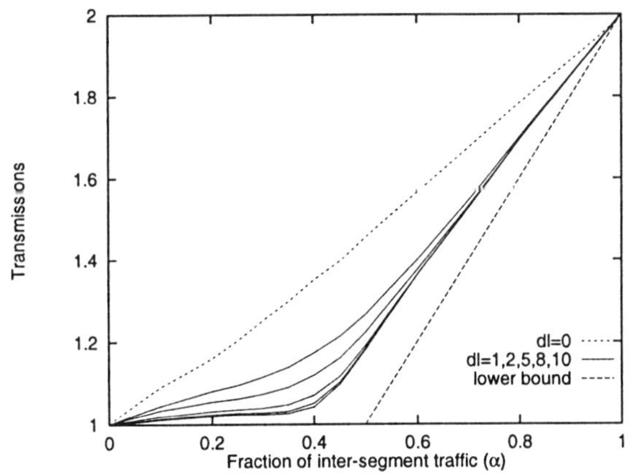


Figure 6: Average per packet transmissions versus $\alpha$, the fraction of inter-segment traffic, under saturated load ($\lambda = 1$). A $s = 4$ segment network using bridge architectures with varying number of DLs ($dl = 0-10$) is simulated. The dotted curve shows the upper bound in Eq. 3.

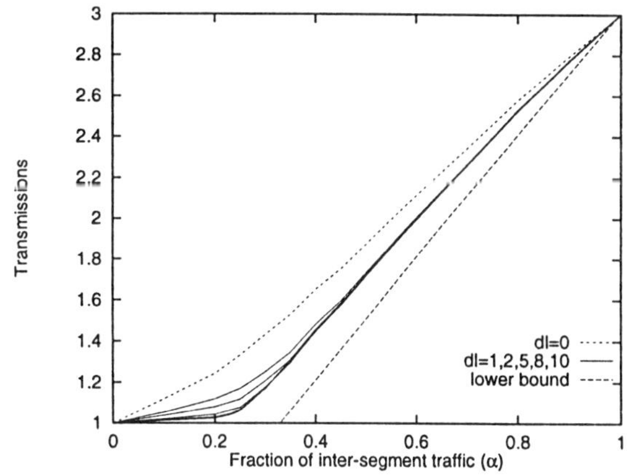


Figure 7: Average per packet transmissions versus $\alpha$, the fraction of inter-segment traffic, under saturated load ($\lambda = 1$). A $s = 6$ segment network using bridge architectures with varying number of DLs ($dl = 0-10$) is simulated. The dotted curve shows the upper bound in Eq. 3.

strated in [14], we have

$$\tilde{th}(\alpha) = \frac{2}{\alpha s} th(0) \qquad \frac{s}{2} < \alpha \leq 1 \qquad (2)$$

Similarly, a lower bound on the per packet average number of transmissions can be derived:

$$\tilde{r}(\alpha) = \begin{cases} 1 & 0 \leq \alpha \leq \frac{s}{2} \\ \frac{\alpha s}{2} & \frac{s}{2} < \alpha \leq 1 \end{cases} \qquad (3)$$

Figs. 4-7 show simulation results (solid curve) with confidence interval of 6% or less, at 99% confidence level, and the bound curves (dotted curve) obtained using Eqs. 1-3. Figs. 4 and 5 show $th$ versus $\alpha$ for a 4 and 6 segment network, respectively, under offered load $\lambda = 1$. In both systems, the use of SDL significantly improves the achievable throughput and consequently the bandwidth efficiency of the PSR approach. With as few as 5 DLs the gap between the upper bound and the actual performance of the system using the original bridge architecture is reduced by a factor up to 50%.

The positive effect of resolving slot contentions through the use of the SDL-bridge is also visible in Figs. 6 and 7, that plot $\bar{r}$ versus $\alpha$ under offered load $\lambda = 1$, using SDL devices with varying number of stages ($dl = 1, 2, 5$). With 5 DLs the SDL-bridge solution achieves a 50% (or higher) reduction of the gap between the actual $\bar{r}$ incurred in the PSR without SDL and its lower bound of Eq.3.

The graphs show that further increasing the number of DLs (e.g., $dl = 5$) does not improve the performance significantly. As optimal throughput is achieved with small number of DLs, the SDL bridging does not lead to significant additional transmission delay or signal attenuation.

Performance of the SDL-bridge based PSR network was evaluated using several SDL control strategies. The results showed that no essential improvement can be achieved by the strategies giving priority to the most loaded slot over the simple *rightmost* strategy. Based on this observation the latter strategy is preferred due to its lower complexity.

As shown in the plots the backbone capacity might become a limiting factor for the achievable inter-segment throughput. In those applications where this limitation is not acceptable, the backbone capacity can be increased using parallel multiple fibers, as described in [14].

## 5 Summary

This paper proposes the use of SDL in a PSR network to provide a *bandwidth efficient* solution to the *scalability* problem of all-optical packet switching WDM networks. Photonic Slot Routing (PSR) has been proposed in WDM systems to allow fast packet switching of wavelength sensitive traffic between subnetworks using wavelength non-selective devices based on proven technologies, thus making possible to scale an all-optical network comprising several LAN segments. By means of Switched Delay Lines (SDL) to optically resolve contention arising between photonic slots simultaneously reaching the bridge connecting adjacent subnetworks, the efficiency of a PSR network is significantly improved.

## References


[1] M. -S. Chen, N. R. Dono, R. Ramaswami, "A Media-Access Protocol for Packet-Switched Wavelength Division Multiaccess Metropolitan Area Networks," *IEEE Journal on Selected Areas in Communications*, vol. 8, no 6, pp. 1048-1057, August 1990.

[2] D. A. Smith and J. J. Johnson, "Switching speed of integrated acoustically-tunable optical filter," *Electronics Letters*, vol. 27, pp. 2102-2103, Nov. 1991.

[3] I. Chlamtac, A. Fumagalli, "QUADRO-Star: High Performance Optical WDM Star Networks," *IEEE Globecom'91*, Conf. Record, Phoenix, Arizona, December 1991, also in *IEEE Transactions on Communications*, vol. 42, no. 8, pp. 2582-2590, August 1994.

[4] A. Bononi, F. Forghieri, P. R. Prucnal, "Throughput Limitations in Ultra-Fast All-Optical Soliton Mesh Networks Using Deflection Routing," in *proc. OFC'93*, San Jose, CA, Feb. 1993.

[5] I. Chlamtac, A. Fumagalli, "An Optical Switch Architecture for Manhattan Networks," *Journal on Selected Areas in Communications.* vol. 11, no. 4, pp. 550-559, May 1993.

[6] Z. Haas, "The 'Staggering Switch': An Electronically Controlled Optical Packet Switch," *Journal of Lightwave Technology*, vol. 11, no. 5/6, pp. 925-936, May/June 1993.

[7] P. W. Dowd, et *al.*, "Hierarchical Scalable Photonic Architectures for High-Performance Processor Interconnection," *IEEE Transactions on Computers*, vol. 42, no. 9, pp. 1105-1120, Sept. 1993.

[8] N. K. Shankaranarayanan et *al.*, "Two-Section DBR Laser Transmitters with Accurate Channel Spacing and Fast Arbitrary-Sequence Tuning for Optical FDMA Networks," *OFC'94*, San Jose, Feb. 1994.

[9] W. H. Nelson, A. N. M. Masum Choudhury, M. Abdalla, R. Bryant, E. Meland, and W. Niland, "Wavelength and Polarization independent Large Angle InP/InGaAsP Digital Optical Switches with Extinction Ratio exceeding 20 dB," *IEEE Photon. Technol. Lett.*, vol. 6, pp. 1332-1334, 1994.

[10] A. Fumagalli, I. Chlamtac, "A Bridge for Packet Switched WDM Networks," *Ninth Annual Workshop on Computer Communications*, Hawk's Cay Resort and Marina, Duck Key, Marathon, Florida, October 1994.

[11] B. Kannan, S. Fotedar, M. Gerla, "A Two Level Optical Star WDM Metropolitan Area Network," in *proc. IEEE Globecom'94*, San Francisco, CA, Dec. 1994.

[12] I. Chlamtac, A. Fumagalli, L. G. Kazovsky, P. T. Poggiolini, "A Contention/Collision Free WDM Ring Network for Multi Gigabit Packet Switched Communication," *Journal of High Speed Networks* Vol. 4, No. 2, pp. 201-219, 1995.

[13] M. Ajmone Marsan, A. Bianco, E. Leonardi, M. Meo, F. Neri, "On the Capacity of MAC Protocols for All-Optical WDM Multi-Rings," in *proc. IEEE Infocom'96*, San Francisco, CA, March 1996.

[14] I. Chlamtac, V. Elek, A. Fumagalli, C. Szabó, "Scalable WDM Network Architecture Based on Photonic Slot Routing," *Boston University, ECE Dept. Technical Report #96-003*, Boston University, Boston, June 1996.

[15] I. Chlamtac, V. Elek, A. Fumagalli, C. Szabó, "A scalable optical network based on folded bus architecture," in *proc. SPIE-Europto'96*, Berlin, October 1996.

[16] M. Ajmone Marsan, A. Fumagalli, E. Leonardi, F. Neri, "Modeling Slotted Multi-Channel Ring All-Optical Networks," *MASCOTS Conference*, Israel, January 1997.

# STWnet: A High Bandwidth Space-Time-Wavelength Multiplexed Optical Switching Network

Rajgopal Kannan†, Radim Bartos‡, Kyungsook Y. Lee‡, Harry F. Jordan◇

† Dept. of CIS, University of Michigan-Dearborn, Dearborn, MI 48124

‡ Dept. of Mathematics and Computer Science, University of Denver, Denver, CO 80208

◇ Optoelectronics Computing Center*, University of Colorado-Boulder, Boulder, CO 80309

## Abstract

*We propose STWnet, a self-routing high bandwidth optical network architecture for interconnecting users, grouped together as g groups with w users per group. STWnet uses the three dimensions of space, time, and wavelength by combining the advantages of space and temporal switching with the benefits of wavelength parallel data transmissions. Technologically difficult switching of individual wavelengths is avoided by prearranging transmissions in a way that they can be switched in a wavelength insensitive manner. Wavelengths are reused within the network thus allowing for a larger switching fabric.*

*The proposed architecture can be internally expanded either in the spatial or temporal dimension to allow for multiple packets to be delivered to the same destination group. The expansion factor is determined based on the Group Knockout Principle and given typical traffic patterns is a small number. STWnet allows easy group to group multicasting and broadcasting while system-wide multicasts and broadcasts can be achieved through repetitive group-to-group transmissions. The network uses readily available components such as opto-electronic directional couplers, fixed wavelength transmitters, and diffraction based parallel receivers while avoiding the use of relatively slow and expensive tunable components.*

## 1 Introduction

Traditional communication networks utilize only one or two dimensions (such as space-division, space-time division, wavelength-division) for switching. For example, a $gw \times gw$ space-time switching system operating on $g$ parallel frames of $w$ time slots each can interconnect $N = gw$ end-users by switching or interchanging time slotted packets in different spatial and temporal positions. Optical space-time switching networks using simple $2 \times 2$ electro-optic directional couplers can be easy to control and exhibit superior performance as compared to the traditional Time Multiplexed (Space) Switching approach. $gw \times gw$ permuters and sorters with applications in circuit switched TDM systems and telecommunications have also been recently described [1].

An alternative approach for exploiting concurrency in optical media is Wavelength Division Multiplexing (WDM) in which a light beam is partitioned into combs of wavelengths, and packets are transmitted simultaneously on different wavelengths without interference. WDM systems are limited by several factors, primarily technological, such as the limited number of available wavelengths, power budget considerations, and speed of electro-optical components. Recently, a new category of optical network architectures broadly classified as switched optical networks [2, 3] have been proposed to overcome some of the limitations on pure WDM based systems. The basic idea is to perform a limited amount of optical switching and some form of wavelength selective routing so as to be able to reuse wavelengths in the network. While a number of tunable components (such as the Acousto-Optic Tunable Filter [4]) have been proposed recently, their operational parameters (especially the time to retune) are insufficient for most applications [5].

Multidimensional switching networks are networks that utilize more than one degree of freedom. It is hard to achieve a large number of distinct channels in one dimension due to limits set by physical factors (e.g., crosstalk, logic speed, finite spectrum). In [6] Sharony et. al. describe a generic approach to the design of high capacity, high connectivity communica-

*The Center is supported in part by the National Science Foundation Engineering Research Grant No. ECD 9015128 and by the Colorado Advanced Technology Institute (CATI).



0-8186-7780-5/97 $10.00 © 1997 IEEE

tion networks which meet the demands set by different applications such as multimedia and parallel processing by mixing and matching the three fundamental dimensions of space, time, and wavelength. This approach reduces network complexity while increasing connectivity to an extent not possible by using one or two dimensional networks. The authors give examples of both point-to-point and strictly nonblocking generalized switching networks using tunable transmitters, receivers and optical filters and photonic switching elements.

In [7], Aly and Dowd describe the design of a hierarchical time-space-wavelength network where nodes are clustered into groups. Space-division is used for local intra-group communication via passive metal buses, and wavelength-division at the global level (inter-group) through passive optical star-couplers. Time-division is used to provide conflict free access at both levels by means of an interleaved time-division multiple access scheme. Each group of nodes contains an asynchronous time-division multiplexer (ATDM) equipped with tunable transmitters and receivers which collects global packets from and receives to the local group. At the global level $g$ conflict free, wavelength multiplexed packets, one from each group are transmitted over the passive optical star coupler during a time slot, to be received by the ATDMs at each group and then retransmitted over local electronic buses to destination nodes within the group.

This paper considers an alternate approach to space-time-wavelength switching that increases the overall throughput by considering the introduction of wavelength-parallel channels into self-routing space-time networks. We propose a two-level hierarchical Space-Time-Wavelength network architecture (STWnet). The upper level interconnects groups of nodes using $2 \times 2$ wideband electro-optic directional couplers for switching and simultaneous routing over all input wavelengths. Groups at the lower level use self-routing space-time sorters, time slot routers, and passive diffraction based receivers [8] along with an address notification protocol for multiple wavelength reception at individual nodes. Since group-to-group switching at the higher level is wavelength insensitive, the function of the space-time network is to arrange data packets within a group into a form in which all wavelengths can be switched simultaneously.

The primary characteristics of STWnet are the ability to reuse wavelengths within different groups while avoiding the use of tunable (active) optical components for wavelength switching. STWnet allows easy group to group multicasting and broadcasting while system-wide multicasts and broadcasts can be achieved through repetitive group-to-group transmissions. The network can be internally expanded either in the spatial or temporal dimension to allow for multiple WDM packets to be delivered to the same destination group. The expansion factor is determined based on the Group Knockout Principle and given typical traffic patterns is a small number. STWnet uses readily available components such as opto-electronic directional couplers, fixed wavelength transmitters, and diffraction based parallel receivers. The control of the network is fully distributed.

The rest of this paper is organized as follows. Section 2 describes the STWnet architecture, with the group output and input interfaces, and the address notification protocol for wavelength multiplexed group-to-group transmissions. Section 3 contains a performance analysis of the network with respect to packet loss rates and network delay. Conclusions are presented in section 4.

## 2 STWnet Architecture

Figure 1 shows the overall schematic of STWnet. The network connects $g$ groups of users, with $w$ nodes/users per group, where a user typically refers to a LAN or high-bandwidth host. Each user in a group is connected to a group interface node, forming the lower level of the hierarchy. A group interface node is logically divided into two components: a Group Output Interface (GOI) and a Group Input Interface (GII). The function of a GOI is to receive packets from users in the group and group them by destination group address in a format suitable for WDM transmission. Transmitted information is in the form of WDM packets that are consistent in size with a cache line or ATM packet. At the upper level of the hierarchy, $g$ group interface nodes are connected to the central switch over high-speed WDM optical links as shown in the figure. The central switch non-blockingly routes WDM packets in a wavelength-insensitive manner to their destination group interface nodes. Diffraction based parallel receivers at the GIIs are then used to demultiplex packets over all wavelengths before transmission to individual end-users.

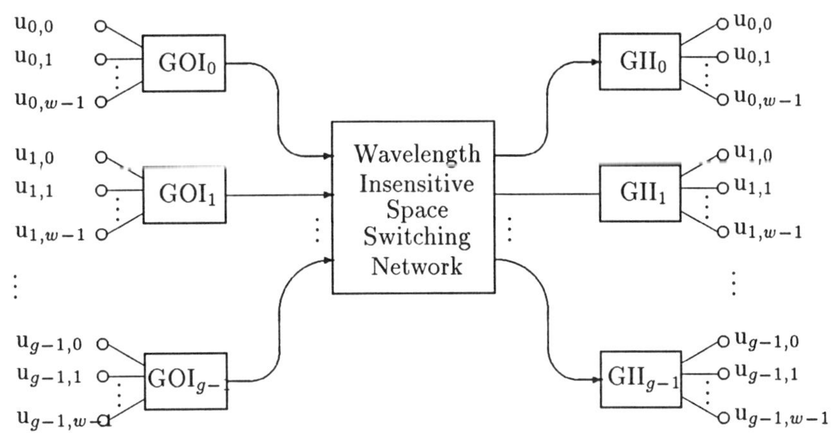


Figure 1: Space-Time-Wavelength Network architecture.

## 2.1 Wavelength Insensitive Central Switch

The wavelength insensitive central switch is a $g \times g$ reverse banyan network[1]. It consists of $\log g$ stages of $2 \times 2$ wideband switching elements (electro-optic directional couplers) [9] with $\frac{g}{2}$ switching elements per stage. A $2 \times 2$ switching element receives wavelength multiplexed signals on its input ports and is capable of routing a WDM signal from an input port to the destination output port in a wavelength insensitive manner.

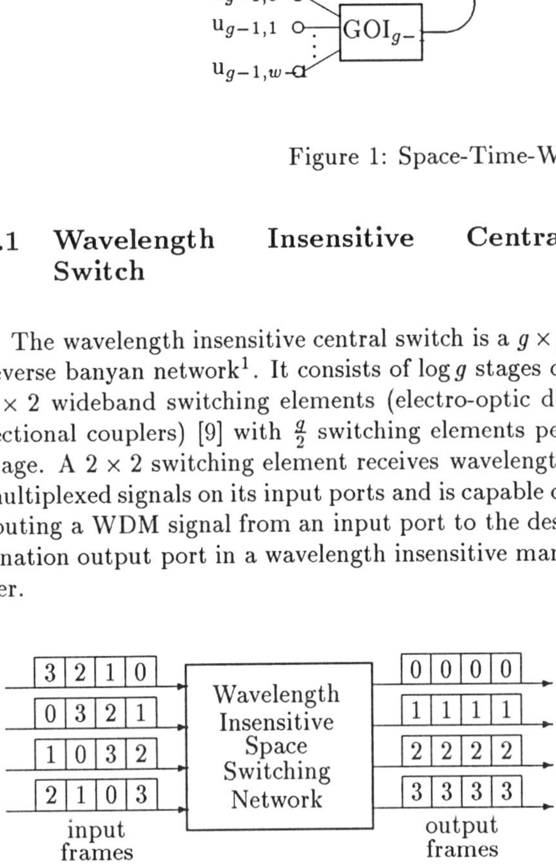


Figure 2: Example of wavelength insensitive routing within central switch.

The input to the $g \times g$ central switch consists of $g$ parallel frames of $g$ time slotted packets each, arriving from $g$ GOIs, as illustrated in Figure 2. Each packet in a time slot actually consists of $w$ wavelength multiplexed data packets and is referred to as a WDM packet. A WDM packet consists of two parts: intra-group addressing information followed by payload data as per the GOI transmitting protocol to be explained later.

A simple scheduling algorithm is used to transmit frames of time slotted WDM packets from the $g$ GOIs. Each GOI transmits to the central switch in such a way that WDM packets present in time slots at the same temporal position on different input frames form a cyclic permutation with respect to destination group address as shown in Figure 2. The same set of cyclic permutations is repeated every $g$ time slots. Since the reverse banyan network is non-blocking when the inputs form a cyclic permutation, WDM packets are routed without conflicts to their destination GIIs during each time slot. The repetitive nature of the routing schedule allows the switches of the reverse banyan to be set in a predetermined manner during each time slot. This eliminates the need to carry group destination address headers along with each WDM packet. Note that the above scheduling scheme requires time slot level synchronization among GOIs. This can be achieved by equalizing the delay between the group interfaces to the central switch and using a feedback self synchronization mechanism [10].

## 2.2 Group Interface Modules

The function of the GOI is to organize input packets from local users in such a manner that they can be wavelength multiplexed and transmitted to the central switch for wavelength insensitive routing in a non-blocking manner. The main purpose is to avoid the use of tunable wavelength filters and instead use a wide-bandwidth wavelength insensitive central switch

[1] A reverse banyan network can be obtained from the corresponding banyan by simply reversing inputs and outputs.

with simple control. Since the central switch cannot switch wavelengths, this implies that packets must be grouped by destination group address before being wavelength multiplexed and transmitted to the central switch for routing.

Figure 3 shows a block diagram of a GOI. Packets from local end-users arrive asynchronously at the GOI over $w$ spatial lines where they are stored in buffers before being output as $w$ synchronous parallel frames of $g$ time slots each. Routing within the GOI for each packet is carried out using a two part header consisting of group destination address and user address within the group.

A GOI consists of the following modules: First, a Space-Time Sorting Network (STSN) which sorts a $w \times g$ matrix of time slots in column major order by group destination address. This is followed by $w$ Time Slot Expander/Router (TSER) modules, one per output frame which expand each frame in either the space or time domain by a factor determined by the Group Knockout Principle [11], and route packets to appropriate time slots in a manner explained below. The TSER modules are followed by fixed wavelength transmitters, one per spatial output of a TSER module. Each transmitter transmits on a fixed wavelength unique within its GOI. The transmitters are connected to a passive coupler and the combined WDM signal is transmitted over optical fiber to the central switch during each time slot.

### 2.2.1 Space-Time Sorting Network

All packets received during a time slot by the fixed-wavelength transmitters at the outputs of the TSERs must be destined to the same group, so that they can be wavelength multiplexed and routed in a wavelength insensitive manner through the central switch. This can be achieved by a global control algorithm which looks at packets in the input buffers and delivers $w$ packets destined to the same group to the $w$ fixed wavelength transmitters. A self-routing Space-Time Sorting Network followed by Time Slot Expanders/Routers with simple local control provides an alternative solution to the problem.

A $w \times g$ STSN operates on $w$ synchronous parallel frames of $g$ time slots each [12]. The parallel frames may be considered as a $w \times g$ input matrix of packets which is processed as a whole by the STSN. The input matrix is sorted in column major order on the basis of monotonically increasing group destination address. The sorting network consists of $O(w \log_2^2 g)$ $2 \times 2$ electro-optic directional couplers with feedforward delay lines and is based on a space-time mapping of the Odd-Even merge algorithm. The sorter has a frame delay of $\frac{g}{2}\log_2(wg)$ time slots for the initial set of input frames. However it is fully pipelined and the frame delay does not affect the throughput of the switch.

### 2.2.2 Time Slot Expander/Router

The sorting network is followed by $w$ time slot expander/router modules, one per output frame. The goal of the TSER modules is to expand the sorted $w \times g$ output matrix of time slots into a $lw \times rg$ matrix satisfying the following format: The $j^{th}$ column of time slots in the matrix contains only those packets with group destination address $\lfloor \frac{j}{r} \rfloor$, where $0 \leq j \leq rg-1$, and $l$ and $r$ are constant expansion factors.

The need for expansion is based on the following observation: It is possible that there are more than $w$ packets within the $w \times g$ matrix destined to the same group. For a fixed number $w$ of transmitters, a fixed frame size of $g$ time slots, and the above matrix format, it would not be possible to wavelength multiplex and transmit all these excess packets. Under the Group Knockout Principle for uniform traffic [11], for a packet loss probability of $10^{-6}$ and a group size $w \geq 32$ it is sufficient to route at most $2w$ packets to a destination group in one output matrix. This can be achieved either by spatially expanding the $w \times g$ input matrix by a factor of 2, ($l = 2$, $r = 1$) using a space-domain TSER or through a temporal expansion of the same magnitude ($l = 1$, $r = 2$) using a time-domain TSER. A Space-domain (time-domain) TSER consists of an upfront space (time) expander/packet eliminator followed by a time slot packer and time slot router. Note that spatial expansion increases the internal network size and requires twice the number of transmitters whereas temporal expansion is achieved at the cost of a twofold internal speedup.

The purpose of the expander/eliminator is to distribute packets from a sorted input frame into $l$ spatial outputs and to drop excess packets when there are more than $l$ packets with the same group destination. The incoming frame of time slots is first copied onto $l+2$ output lines using a passive optical splitter. Inputs on the first two lines are fed to an address comparator which is linked to a packet eliminator that controls the activity bits of packets on the remaining $l$ lines. The input frame on the first line is delayed for a duration of $l$ time slots. The address comparator compares the group destination address of the packet in the current time slot $k$ with that of the packet appearing at the output of the delay loop, $0 \leq k \leq g-1$ and drops one of the packets in case of duplicates. The above scheme distributes packets among all $l$ parallel

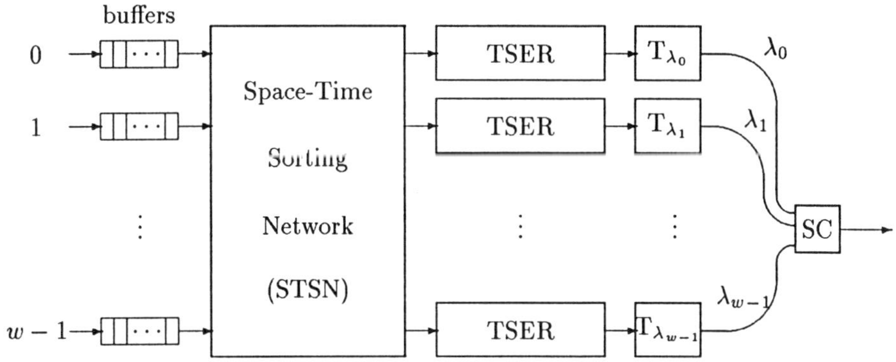


Figure 3: Group Output Interface (GOI).

frames while ensuring that none of the $l$ frames contains more than one packet with the same destination address [15].

The function of the time slot packer is to pack the active packets into the beginning of a frame while shifting inactive packets (empty time slots) to the end of the frame. A $1 \times N$ time slot packer packs an input frame of $N$ time slots containing up to $N$ active packets as illustrated in Figure 4. The packer consists of $\log_2 N$ stages of $K(\delta)$ switches [13], which are single-bit controlled $2 \times 2$ optical switching elements with feedback fiber delay loops of magnitude $\delta$ time slots. The $j^{th}$ stage of a packer consists of a $K(2^j)$ switch, $0 \leq j \leq \log_2 N - 1$. A $K(2^j)$ switch can be controlled by a single bit and is capable of interchanging packets which are $2^j$ time slots apart in the input frame. The $\log_2 N$ stage packing module in Figure 4 is thus the time-domain equivalent of a spatial $N \times N$ reverse banyan network and can pack up to $N$ active inputs in an $N$ time slot input frame in a stable manner [15].

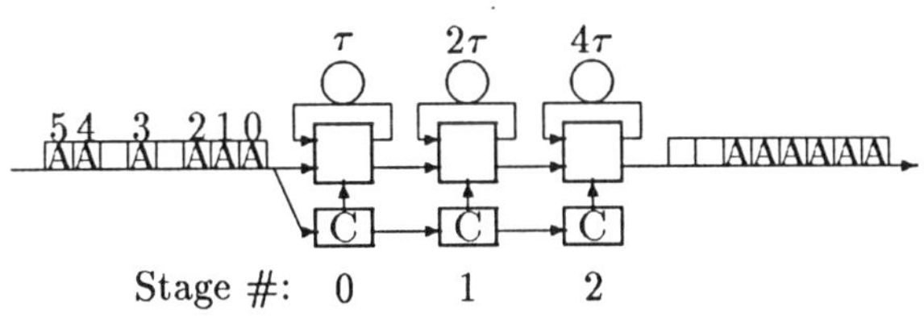


Figure 4: A $1 \times 8$ Time Slot Packer ($A$: Active Packet, C: Control Logic).

A $1 \times N$ time slot router is a time-domain implementation of the spatial $N \times N$ banyan network. It is well known that the banyan is non-blocking when the inputs are sorted and consecutive (without any inactive inputs between two active inputs). Since the input frame to each time slot router consists of consecutive active packets sorted by destination address (without duplicates), the time slot router can non-blockingly route packets to their destination time slots.

Figure 5 shows a complete example of routing in a GOI with $g = w = 4$.

### 2.2.3 GOI Transmitting Protocol

The last stage of a GOI consists of $w$ fixed wavelength transmitters $T_{\lambda_i}$ which are used to transmit WDM packets. The wavelength insensitive switching network routes each WDM packet to its destination GII. A GII consists of a splitter followed by $w$ diffraction based parallel receivers $R_{\lambda^*}$, one per destination user. A parallel receiver is capable of concurrent reception on all wavelengths. Figure 6 shows a block diagram of the interconnection between GOIs and GIIs through the wavelength insensitive space switching network.

As explained previously, a WDM packet consists of two components: intra-group addressing information, and payload data. The recently proposed MultiNet protocol [14] is used to facilitate intra-group notification during which $w$ destination nodes in a GII are informed about the wavelengths on which they are to receive source packets from $w$ transmitting nodes in the GOI.

The protocol provides for easy group-to-group multicasting and broadcasting as follows: The notification phase is divided into $w$ bit times for $w$ nodes. During bit time $i$, all nodes which have packets destined to node $i$ send a pulse on their respective wavelengths. The reception logic at each receiving node consists of $w$ shift registers, one per receiving wavelength, connected to buffers. The reception control

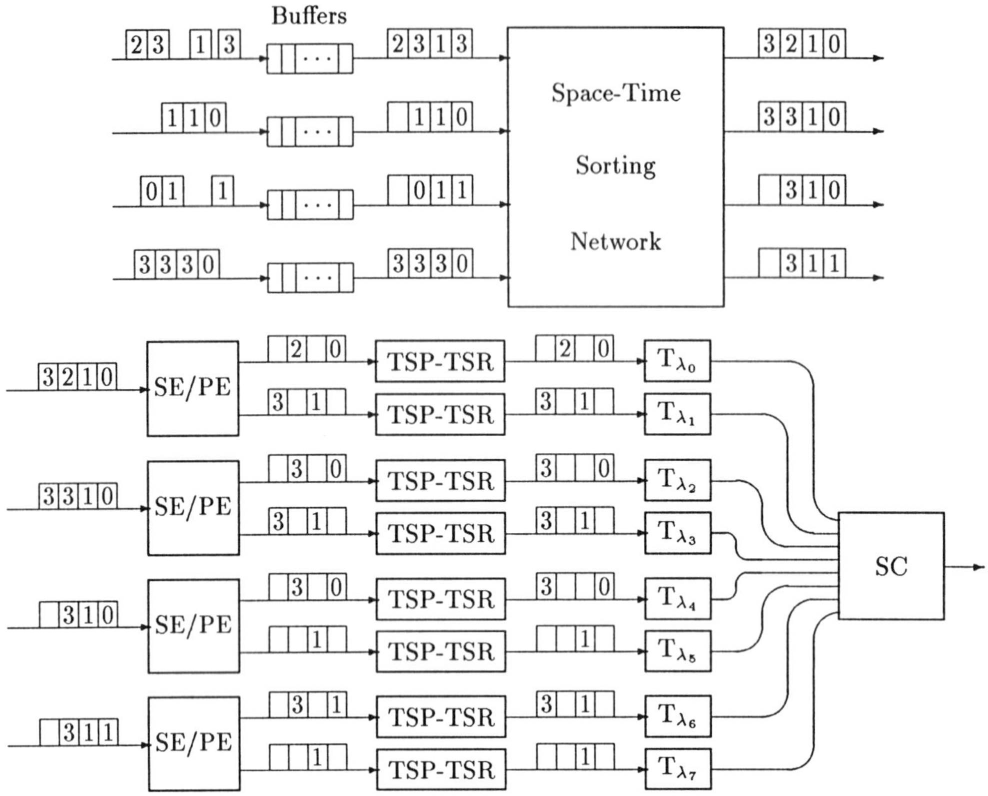


Figure 5: Routing with space expansion in a GOI with $g = w = 4$ ( SE/PE: Space Expander/Packet Eliminator, TSP-TSR: Time Slot Packer followed by Time Slot Router).

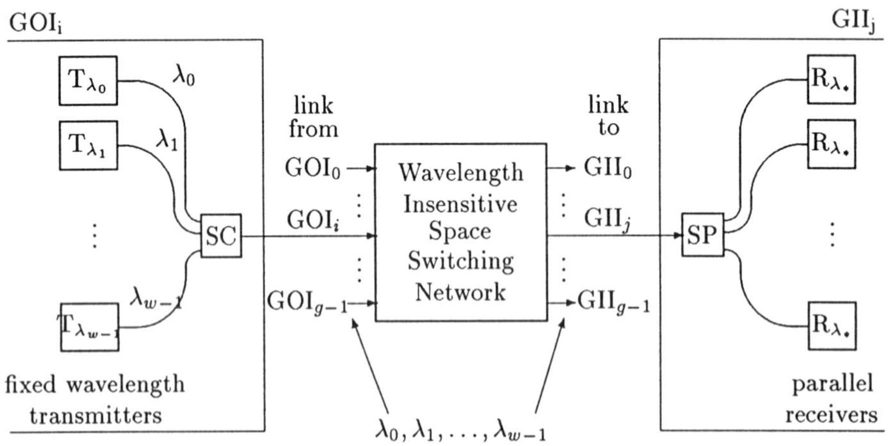


Figure 6: Wavelength-parallel transmission ($T_{\lambda_i}$: fixed-wavelength transmitter, $R_{\lambda *}$: parallel receiver, SC: star coupler, SP - splitter).

of node $i$, upon detecting a pulse during interval $i$ on wavelength $\lambda_j$ opens the gate to the associated shift register, $1 \leq j \leq w$. $w$ wavelengths and $w$ bit times thus provide an $w \times w$ matrix which allows the description of all possible permutations of group-to-group communication including multicasts and broadcasts. Network wide multicasts and broadcasts can be easily achieved through the central switch by repetitive group-to-group transmissions over $g$ time slots.

Figure 7 shows an example of signals exchanged during a notification phase in a system where $w = 4$. Potentially, four packets can be transmitted resulting in up to sixteen received packets, in a single cycle.

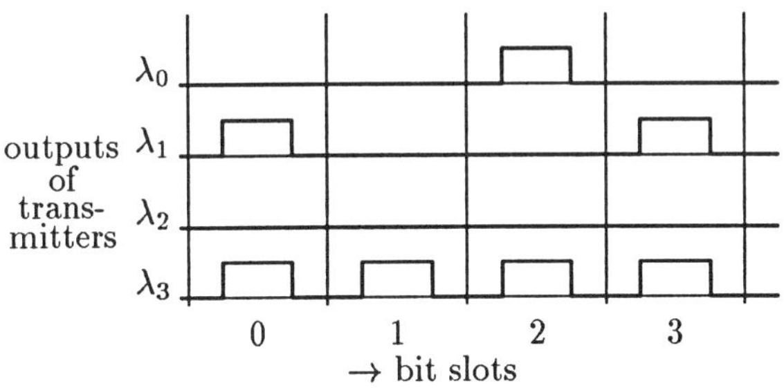


Figure 7: An example of a notification phase (node 0 transmits to 2, node 1 multicasts to 0 and 3, and node 3 broadcast to all nodes).

## 3 Performance Analysis

The maximum throughput of the network equals $lrgw$, the total number of available wavelength channels. Routing is conflict-free in the wavelength insensitive central switch and in the GIIs at the destination groups. The mean network latency of a packet is the time spent in its source GOI module. The space-time sorting network, the time slot packer and time slot router components in the GOIs contribute to the latency as they have a fixed frame delay for each $w \times g$ matrix of time slots. The frame delay of an STSN is $\frac{g\tau}{2}\log_2(gw)$ units. A $1 \times rg$ time slot packer and time slot router each has a frame delay of $rg\tau - 1$ units. Thus the total latency of a packet in a GOI is $g\tau(2r + \frac{\log_2(gw)}{2}) - 2$ units. Additionally, the GOI transmission protocol requires $w$ bit-times for the intra-group notification phase.

Consider the proposed switch with $gw$ users under a uniform traffic model where the packets have independent, uniform destination address distributions. Each GOI and GII serve a group of $w$ users and there are $g$ groups of users. Packet arrival processes to an input port of the space-time sorting network from the input buffers at a GOI during a time slot are independent Bernoulli processes with $\rho$ =Pr.[a packet arrives at input port]. The GOI processes the input in the form of a $g \times w$ matrix of time slots ($w$ parallel frames of $g$ time slots each) before transmission to the GIIs.

Consider a group $G$ of outputs served by a GII where $|G| = w$. Then the probability that there are exactly $k$ packets destined to $G$ over $g$ time slots in a GOI is the binomial distribution

$$P_{G=k} = \binom{gw}{k}\left(\frac{\rho}{g}\right)^k\left(1-\frac{\rho}{g}\right)^{gw-k}, \quad (1)$$

A GOI can deliver a maximum of $lrw$ packets to a destination GII during an expanded $lg \times rw$ matrix of time slots. Thus the expected number of packets destined to a GII and lost in a GOI due to the arrival of more than $lrw$ packets in the network is given as

$$E = \sum_{k=lrw+1}^{gw} (k - lrw)\binom{gw}{k}\left(\frac{\rho}{g}\right)^k\left(1-\frac{\rho}{g}\right)^{gw-k} \quad (2)$$

The packet loss probability (PLR) of a network is defined as [11]

$$\text{PLR} = \frac{\text{expected packet loss}}{\text{offered load}}. \quad (3)$$

The wavelength insensitive central switch is non-blocking and therefore no packets are lost in the switch. Furthermore we assume that there is no loss due to output buffer overflow at nodes in the GIIs and thus the only packet losses in the network are due to overflow at the GOIs. The offered load to a group of $g$ outputs served by a GII is $g\rho$ with an expected packet loss of $E$.

Figure 8 shows a graph of the packet loss rate of a fully loaded STWnet ($\rho = 100\%$) at different values of $g$, for varying space-time expansion factors $lr$ and a fixed number of wavelengths per group $w$. At a maximum offered load of 100% and $g = w = 32$, an expansion factor $lr = 2$ is sufficient to achieve a low packet loss rate of $6.66 \times 10^{-9}$. As the expansion factor is increased the packet loss rate rapidly decreases.

## 4 Conclusions

Traditional one or two dimensional communication networks have limited connectivity due to physical limitations such as number of available wavelengths,

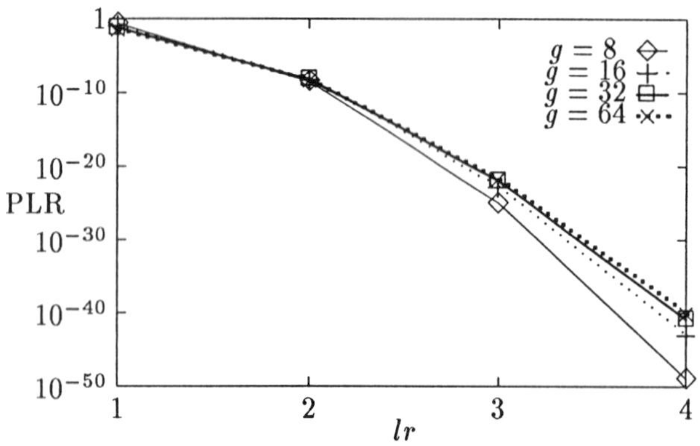


Figure 8: Packet loss rate in STWnet with $gw$ users where $w = 32$.

optical power budget, speed of electro-optic components etc. We propose an alternative solution by considering multidimensional space-time-wavelength networks that increase the overall throughput by introducing wavelength-parallel channels into self-routing space-time networks. STWnet is a two-level hierarchical high bandwidth optical network architecture for interconnecting groups of users. The network is self-routing with distributed control and uses readily available optical components such as opto-electronic directional couplers and fixed wavelength transmitters. Bandwidth limits in optical components mean that distinct wavelengths are a scarce resource. Thus re-use of wavelengths in different groups enhances scalability. The network avoids active switching of wavelengths requiring the use of wavelength sensitive switches.

## References

[1] D. K. Hunter, I. Andonovic, D. G. Smith, and B. Culshaw, "Architectures for optical TDM switching," *Electronics letters*, Vol. 28, No. 18, Aug. 1992.

[2] C. A. Brackett, "Dense wavelength division multiplexing networks: principles and applications," *IEEE JSAC*, Vol. 8, No. 6, pp. 948-964, Aug. 1990.

[3] K. Lee, V. O. K. Li, "A Wavelength convertible optical network," *IEEE/OSA J. of Light. Tech.*, Vol. 11, May/June 1993.

[4] D. A. Smith, J. E. Baran, J. J. Johnson, and K. W. Cheung, "Integrated-Optic acoustically-tunable filters for WDM networks," *IEEE JSAC*, Vol. 8, No. 6, Aug. 1990.

[5] R. Ramaswami, "Multiwavelength lightwave networks for computer communication," *IEEE Comm. Magazine,* pp. 78-88, Feb. 1993.

[6] J. Sharony, T. E. Stern, and Y. Li, "The universality of multidimensional switching networks," *IEEE/ACM Trans. on Networking*, Vol. 2, No. 6, pp. 602-612, Dec. 1994.

[7] P. W. Dowd and K. A. Aly, "Time-Space-Wavelength networks for low-complexity processor interconnection," *Proc. of Intnl. Conf. on Massively Parall. Proc. with Optical Interconnects*, pp. 281-292, Cancun, Apr. 1994.

[8] G. J. Cannell, A. Robertson, and R. Worthington, "Practical realization of a high density diode-coupled wavelength demultiplexer," *IEEE JSAC*, Vol. 8, No. 6, pp. 1141-1145, Aug. 1990.

[9] Theodor Tamir, Ed., *Guided Wave Optoelectronics*, Springer Series in Electronics and Photonics, Vol. 26, Springer-Verlag, New York 1988.

[10] R. Bartoš, R. Kannan, K. Y. Lee, and H. F. Jordan, "Distributed optical ATM switching architectures," *Proc. Globecom*, pp. 1751-1755, Nov. 1995.

[11] K. Y. Eng, M. Karol, and Y. S. Yeh, "A growable packet switch architecture: design principles and applications," *IEEE Trans. on Comm.*, Vol. 40, No. 2, pp. 423-430, Feb. 1992.

[12] R. Kannan, D. Lee, K. Y. Lee, and H. F. Jordan, "Optical TDM sorting networks for high-speed packet switching," *Proc. Globecom*, pp. 1948–1952, CA, Dec. 1994.

[13] H. F. Jordan, D. Lee, K. Y. Lee, and S. V. Ramanan, "Serial array time slot interchangers and optical implementations," *IEEE Trans. on Comp.*, Vol. 43, No. 11, pp. 1309-1318, Nov. 1994.

[14] R. Bartoš, R. Kannan, K. Y. Lee, and H. F. Jordan, "MultiNet: High-performance WDM interconnection architecture," *Proc. ICC'95*, pp. 277-281, June 1995.

[15] R. Kannan, R. Bartos, K. Y. Lee and H. F. Jordan, "Optical TDM switching architectures with distributed control," *Proc. of IEEE Milcom*, pp. 155–159, McLean, VA, Oct. 1996.

# PERFORMANCE AND CORRECTNESS OF THE ATM ABR RATE CONTROL SCHEME

*David Lee*
*Bell Laboratories*
*600 Mountain Ave.*
*Murray Hill, New Jersey*
*lee@research.bell-labs.com*

*K. K. Ramakrishnan*
*AT&T Research*
*600 Mountain Ave.*
*Murray Hill, New Jersey*
*kkrama@research.att.com*

*W. Melody Moh*
*San Jose State University*
*Dept. of Math.& Computer Sc.*
*San Jose, California*
*melody@jupiter.SJSU.EDU*

*A. Udaya Shankar*
*University of Maryland*
*Computer Sc. Dept.*
*College Park, Maryland*
*shankar@cs.umd.edu*

## ABSTRACT

We study both correctness and performance of the source/destination protocol of the Available Bit Rate (ABR) service in Asynchronous Transfer Mode (ATM) networks. Although the basic source/destination protocol for congestion management is relatively simple, the protocol specification has to cope with several "real-world" cases such as failures and delayed/lost feedback which may introduce complexity. Rigorous proofs of the correct functioning of the protocol based on a formal specification is necessary. We use a formal Extended Finite State Machine (EFSM) model to show that the ABR source/destination protocol is free of live-locks, so that under all conditions both Resource Management (RM) and data cells will be transmitted. We also show that the network options of Explicit Forward Congestion Indication (EFCI) and Explicit Rate (ER) interoperate correctly.

While ensuring the correct functioning of the protocol, it is essential that pathological situations do not result in abysmal performance, which is another form of incorrect operation. We use the understanding of the informal English description of the source/destination behavior and of our EFSM model to derive conditions that ensure that the source transmission rate is stable in the presence of delayed or lost feedback RM cells, especially under the operation of a source rule that requires the reduction of the source rate under these conditions. We arrive at bounds on the number of consecutive RM cell losses tolerated while the rate remains stable.

It is also of vital importance that the delay for feedback of network state is well understood. There are two components of this delay contributed by the source/destination protocol: the source delay for sending out the probe Forward RM cells and the destination delay to turn-around the Backward RM cell. We provide a worst-case analysis of the delay in turning around RM cells at the destination station and the worst-case inter-departure time of Forward RM cells from the source.

## 1. INTRODUCTION

The Available Bit Rate (ABR) service class for Asynchronous Transfer Mode (ATM) networks uses a rate control scheme to manage congestion. Sources adjust their rates such that the aggregate load on the network does not exceed the capacity of the network [ATM]. The protocol specification for the source and destination behavior to achieve overall congestion avoidance and control is specified using a relatively informal specification described in [ATM]. Many of the aspects of the protocol have been designed based on extensive performance analysis through simulation. Simulation has been used especially to determine correct parameter settings. There is little work in the literature that rigorously analyzes the performance and examines the correctness of the ABR protocol.

Some of the properties of the protocol, such as whether it is correct or not, are difficult to show using simulation. A formal specification is necessary for this purpose. Correctness relates to whether the specified protocol is free of any live-locks or other undesirable properties. We model the ABR protocol by an Extended Finite State Machine [LY] and show that the ABR protocol is live-lock free in terms of transmitting data cells and Resource Management (RM) cells, which act as source probes of the network conditions.

In addition, the ABR congestion management specification accommodates at least two different modes in which switches in the network may operate. The source/destination policies (the main focus of the specification) are designed to smoothly operate with any intermix of the two types of switches in the network - these are the Explicit Forward Congestion Indication (EFCI) and Explicit Rate (ER) switches. EFCI switches use a single bit to communicate congestion [RJ], when a queue threshold is exceeded. ER switches on the other hand compute a max-min fair rate [CCJ,CR] and communicate this rate to the sources. The source and destination use a common ABR protocol to interface to both types of switches. We examine whether the specification correctly interoperates with both types of switches, using the formal specification we have developed.

Rate based flow control mechanisms also need some form of protection against failures. For example, when the feedback from the network is not provided in a timely manner or is lost, it is desirable that the source reduces its rate so that the network is not overloaded by the source transmitting at an incorrectly high rate. ATM's ABR service also permits sources to start at a high initial rate so that higher layer protocols and applications such as Remote Procedure Calls (RPC) may transmit a short burst without a start-up delay of a full round-trip time for feedback from the network (Source Rule 6 in [ATM]). To avoid using this potentially high rate for too long, and thus exceeding the buffering in the network, the source rules specify a proportionate reduction in the rate in the absence of feedback from the network. This rate reduction may also be triggered in certain cases when the current transmission rate of RM cells by the source is mismatched with the rate at which RM cells return from the network, especially subsequent to a source rate increase. If the parameters are set inappropriately, this may



0-8186-7780-5/97 $10.00 

result in a net rate reduction in spite of feedback from the network to allow a rate increase. Some of this has been analyzed in the ATM Forum [JKFL] through simulation.

In this paper, we provide a quantitative analysis of the worst-case conditions under which a stable source transmission rate (ACR) is maintained in spite of source rule 6. It is particularly important to examine this in the presence of different types of RM cell loss, which is one of our main contributions. This is covered in the next section.

In conjunction with the problem of maintaining a stable rate, there is the need to ensure that the feedback from the network is timely. While some of the feedback delay contributed by the network is outside our framework, we quantify in this work, the contribution to the feedback delay due to the source/destination policies. Specifically, in Section 3, we estimate the turn-around time delay for Backward RM (BRM) cells and the inter-departure time intervals for Forward RM (FRM) cells from the source. The estimation provides useful information for appropriate parameter setting as well as for understanding the relationship between the rate and the network feedback delay.

In Section 4, we examine some correctness issues, in proving that there are no live-locks in the specified protocol, and in Section 5 we show that the interoperation of EFCI and ER mechanisms is correct.

The source/destination rules and various parameters and acronyms used in the paper are from [ATM]. For the formal specification that we used in this paper, see [LMRS, LRMS].

## 2. RATE ANALYSIS

The ABR source policy includes a mechanism that limits the use of a current transmission rate, called Allowed Cell Rate (ACR), in the absence of timely feedback from the network (source Rule 6). Under ''steady-state'' operation, where the rate is not changing, and there are no RM cells lost, the source end-system should be receiving a BRM cell for every FRM sent. When a rate change occurs, we may be sending FRM cells at a different rate (based on the new ACR) than the returning rate of BRM cells. When a source starts up and is transmitting at an Initial Cell Rate (ICR), the source runs the risk of overloading the network if this initial rate is too high. RM cells, however, return only one Round-trip Time (RTT) after start-up. Consequently, in the absence of feedback from the network, the source rules provide for a conservative correction of the rate until the feedback arrives. The Forum ABR policy has chosen to have sources start at an ICR that may be relatively high. On the other hand, one could choose to start at a relatively low rate, and then increase based on feedback [Kes]. The ATM Forum's ABR policy was chosen to allow for RPC-like flows to derive the benefit of a "fast-start", especially if the total amount of data transmitted in the "burst" is small enough not to exceed the buffering in the network.

Subsequent to start-up, when a significant increase in the rate occurs, once again, Rule 6 may be triggered. Consider the following (relatively general) scenario. Subsequent to a rate change at time $t=0$, the rate at which BRM cells return will correspond to the rate at which FRM cells were sent approximately one RTT earlier. Therefore, if the original rate is small, and the new rate at which the station is transmitting FRM cells is much higher, then potentially more than *Crm* (Missing RM-cell count) in-rate FRM cells may be transmitted prior to a BRM cell returning after the rate change at $t=0$. Rule 6 will be triggered upon sending *Crm* FRM cells. The reduction of source rate, *ACR*, is multiplicative and proportionate to the current ACR.

When a BRM cell is received, and the Explicit Rate, ER, (or the CI, NI bits for EFCI operation) allows the source rate to increase, then ACR is increased additively, by a fixed amount. Subsequent BRM cells received would continue to allow increasing the ACR, until it reaches the ER value or the Peak Cell Rate (PCR) for the connection. The ACR value from which we begin to increase is the rate achieved after any (zero or more) earlier reductions caused by Rule 6.

As a result, there are two counter-acting actions taking place at the source:

(1) A rate decrease as a result of Rule 6, when there are too many FRM cells transmitted before a BRM cell is received; and

(2) A rate increase, potentially, when a BRM cell returns indicating that the current source rate is below its target.

We examine below in Theorem 2.1 whether the rate increases that take place as a result of the BRM cells returning make up for the decreases caused while ''running blind'' awaiting the return of BRM cells. The analysis examines the case where there are $n$ decreases (as a result of (1)), before an increase takes place (as a result of (2)). We need to ensure that there is no ''net decrease'' in the rate at the source because of Rule 6.

### 2.1. Estimating ACR With No RM cell loss

In this subsection we examine the Allowed Cell Rate, *ACR*, in a single ''epoch'', where an epoch is the time interval between the arrival of two Backward RM (BRM) cells. Subsequent to the arrival of the first BRM cell of an epoch, we have possibly multiple decreases of the source rate, *ACR*, as a result of the repeated applications of Rule 6, if the next BRM cell arrives late.

Denote the current $ACR \equiv ACR_0$ and the $ACR$ after $k$ consecutive rate reductions from Rule 6 is:

$$ACR_k = ACR_0(1 - CDF)^k \quad , k = 1, 2, \cdots \tag{2.1}$$

**Lemma 2.1.** The time interval $t_k$ for the $k$th consecutive rate reduction from Rule 6 is:

$$t_1 = Crm \cdot \min \left\{ \max \left\{ \frac{Mrm}{ACR_0} , Trm \right\} + \frac{1}{ACR_0} , \frac{Nrm}{ACR_0} \right\} + t_0 , \tag{2.2a}$$

$$t_k = \min \left\{ \max \left\{ \frac{Mrm}{ACR_{k-1}} , Trm \right\} + \frac{1}{ACR_{k-1}} , \right. \tag{2.2b}$$

$$\left. \frac{Nrm}{ACR_{k-1}} \right\}, \; k = 2, \cdots$$

where

$$0 \le t_0 \le \min \left\{ \max \left\{ \frac{Mrm}{ACR_0}, Trm \right\}, \frac{Nrm - 1}{ACR_0} \right\}.$$

**Proof.** There are two cases when FRM cells are sent according to Source Rule (3)(a) [ATM].

Case 1: At a rate $ACR_j$, the source sends an FRM cell out after every $Nrm - 1$ cells, as long as there are data cells to be sent. This corresponds to the second factor in (2.2a).

Case 2: If instead, we have *Mrm* data cells sent out ($Mrm < Nrm - 1$) and the timer also expires after time *Trm* then an FRM cell is sent. This is the first factor in equation (2.2a).

Observe that a BRM cell may be received either right before the first FRM cell is to be transmitted or just after the transmission of the previous FRM cell. This gives us time interval $t_0$. The first rate reduction occurs after *Crm* FRM cells have been sent after receiving a BRM cell with $BN = 0$. The time interval of sending the *Crm* FRM cells is given in the first term of (2.2a). The sum of the two terms is the time interval $t_1$ in (2.2a). Afterwards, each FRM cell sent results in a rate reduction and that gives the time intervals $t_k$ in (2.2b) for the consecutive rate reductions. □

Consider the following scenario: we have a possible rate increase at time $T_0$ as a result of receiving a BRM cell. We examine what would be the maximum number of rate decreases occurring as a result of Rule 6, prior to the arrival of another BRM cell at time $(T_0 + \tau)$. Here $\tau$ is typically the inter-departure time of FRM cells from the source about one RTT time earlier (at $T_0 - RTT$) . For example, $\tau = (Nrm)/(ACR_{T_0 - RTT})$. The following lemma describes the rate decrease/increase in between two consecutive BRM cells with BN=0.

**Lemma 2.2.** Suppose that two consecutive BRM cells with BN=0 are received in time period $\tau$. Then after $n$ consecutive reductions, a rate increase occurs where:

$$n = \max \left\{ k : \sum_{i=1}^{k} t_i \le \tau \right\} \qquad (2.3)$$

where $t_i$ is given in (2.2).

Before the rate increase, the total rate reduction is:

$$ACR_0 - ACR_n = ACR_0 \left[ 1 - (1 - CDF)^n \right] . \qquad (2.4)$$

This net rate decrease occurs prior to the arrival of a BRM cell with BN=0, which allows a rate increase. □

After $n$ consecutive rate reductions, we have a BRM cell allowing a rate increase (by Source Rule 8) of:

$$r_{inc} = RIF \cdot PCR . \qquad (2.5)$$

Comparing the rate increase in (2.5) with the rate decrease in (2.4), we obtain:

**Theorem 2.1.** A necessary and sufficient condition that there is no net rate reduction after a BRM cell with BN=0 is received is:

$$\frac{RIF \cdot PCR}{ACR_0} + \left[ 1 - CDF \right]^n \ge 1 \qquad (2.6)$$

where $n$, given in (2.3), is the number of rate reductions due to Source Rule (6) since the previous BRM cell with BN=0 was received. □

Theorem 2.1 provides a relationship between the amount of decreases in the rate as a result of successive applications of Rule 6, prior to a rate increase that compensates for the decreases. The time between receiving two consecutive BRM cells (in the worst case, the first BRM cell was received just as the previous rate change occurred at $t=0$) may be $(1/ACR_0)$, if the rate was $ACR_0$ for at least one RTT prior to the rate change at time $t=0$. We assume that the time from the rate change, at $t=0$, to the present time is less than one RTT time. Condition (2.6) provides the value for *RIF* that should be large enough to compensate for the decreases in between the arrival of two consecutive BRM cells. This is the worst case behavior of Rule 6 when there is no loss of RM cells.

An important special case is when ACR is low: $ACR \le RIF \cdot PCR$. In this case there is no net rate reduction, since the first term in (2.6) is always greater than 1.

**Corollary 2.1.** Suppose that $ACR \le RIF \cdot PCR$. Then there is no net rate reduction after a BRM cell with BN=0 is received. □

We have also examined the asymptotic behavior of the rate when the network is consistently returning a fixed value of *ER* in the BRM cells, and examine if the reductions due to Rule 6 result in an overall decrease in the source rate, when observed over a long period of a number of BRM cell arrivals [LRMS2].

### 2.2. Rate Stability in the Presence of RM Cell Loss

Suppose that an end system is operating at "steady state", by transmitting at a rate $ACR = ER$. We want to assure that the cumulative reduction due to Rule 6 does not overcome the aggregate increase achieved by the returning BRM cells. In "steady state", the total number of FRM cells transmitted should correspond to the number of BRM cells received. In a sense, we are "integrating" the effect across multiple BRM cells returning to the source, without necessarily maintaining the constraint that there are reductions occurring between every arriving BRM cell. In some cases, a BRM cell may arrive prior to Rule 6 being triggered. We also compute the worst case when the maximal number of reductions occur.

The previous subsection looked at the case when there were no RM cells lost in the network. If there are RM cells lost, there is an increasing likelihood of rate reductions due to Rule 6. RM cell losses both in the forward (FRM cells) and backward (BRM cells) directions can result in the source experiencing a rate reduction. For the rest of this section, we will treat all RM cell losses as effectively being BRM cell losses (since when viewed from the source, a BRM cell does not arrive in time), for ease of exposition.

The first case we examine here is the effect of losing $\nu - 1$ *consecutive* BRM cells. Thus, the "epoch" between RM cell arrivals is now increased by $\nu - 1$ BRM cell inter-arrival times.

For clarity, we assume that with all possible reductions, $ACR \geq MCR$ and we know:

$$MCR \leq ACR \leq ER \leq PCR . \qquad (2.9)$$

In the following rate analysis, we consider the worst case scenario for rate reductions. Consequently, we assume $t_0 = 0$. Suppose that after initial start-up, the source rate, ACR, converges to *ER*. We assume as before that the network consistently returns a constant allocation of *ER* for the VC. We derive the conditions such that ACR remains stable at *ER* in the event of losing one or more BRM cells.

Suppose that $\nu - 1$ BRM cells were lost. Then the time interval between two consecutive BRM cells received with BN=0 is $\nu \cdot Nrm/ER$. The following proposition gives the condition that the rate ACR remains stable:

**Proposition 2.1.** Suppose that $\nu - 1$ BRM cells were lost consecutively. The rate ACR is stable if

$$n \leq \frac{\log\left(1 - \frac{RIF \cdot PCR}{ER}\right)}{\log(1 - CDF)} \qquad (2.10)$$

where

$$n = \max\left\{k : \sum_{i=1}^{k} t_i \leq \frac{Nrm}{ER} \cdot \nu\right\} \qquad (2.11)$$

where $t_i$ is the time interval for the *i*th consecutive rate reduction, given in (2.2).

**Proof.** The rate is stable if an increment of ACR from the arrival of a BRM cell with BN=0 offsets the decrements before its arrival. This can be derived directly from Theorem 2.1 with $ACR_0 = ER$, and $\tau = \nu \cdot Nrm/ER$. □

In the above proposition, the rate stability conditions depend on two intermediate parameters: $t_i$ and $n$. The condition and intuition derived from these are related to the number of reductions due to Rule 6 and the time for these. They are similar to the conditions on the system parameters that are specified in the ATM Forum [ATM]. We now go a significant further step, which is one of the main results of our paper: a quantification of how many BRM cells could be lost consecutively without affecting the rate stability, based on the system parameters only. A detailed proof is in Appendix.

**Theorem 2.2.** If $ER \leq RIF \cdot PCR$ then the rate remains stable. Otherwise, the rate ACR remains stable when no more than $\nu - 1$ consecutive BRM cells are lost, where:

$$\nu \leq \frac{1}{Nrm}\left\{(Mrm+1) \cdot \left[\frac{\log\left(1 - \frac{RIF \cdot PCR}{ER}\right)}{\log(1 - CDF)} - r\right] + Crm \cdot Nrm + (l - 1) \cdot Nrm + (r - l) \cdot (ER \cdot Trm + 1)\right\} \qquad (2.12)$$

where

$$l = \max\left\{0, \frac{\log \frac{Nrm}{Trm \cdot ER}}{\log(1 - CDF)}\right\} \qquad (2.13)$$

and

$$r = \max\left\{0, \frac{\log \frac{Mrm}{Trm \cdot ER}}{\log(1 - CDF)}\right\}. \qquad (2.14)$$

□

If the rate remains high, so that $Nrm/ACR \leq Trm$, the rate decreases are triggered after *Crm* FRM cells are sent. In this case, $t_1 = Crm \cdot Nrm/ACR_0$ and $t_i = Nrm/ACR_{i-1}$, $i = 2, \cdots, l$. Then, we have

$$n = \nu - Crm + 1 .$$

From Proposition 2.1, we have:

**Corollary 2.3.** If $ER \leq RIF \cdot PCR$ then the rate remains stable. Otherwise, suppose that the rate ACR satisfies $Nrm/ACR < Trm$. Then the number of allowed consecutive BRM cell losses is:

$$\nu \leq \frac{\log\left(1 - \frac{RIF \cdot PCR}{ER}\right)}{\log(1 - CDF)} + Crm - 1 . \qquad (2.15)$$

□

When the rate is low, i.e., $ER \leq RIF \cdot PCR$, then the rate remains stable because a single rate increase from a BRM cell overcomes the accumulated effect of rate decreases from Rule 6. The interesting region for the rate stability issue is when $ER > RIF \cdot PCR$. In this case, the number $\nu$ of consecutive losses tolerated depends on several parameters and the network feedback rate *ER*.

### 2.2.1. Numerical Results for Acceptable Number of Consecutive RM Cell Losses

We examine, numerically, the number of consecutive RM Cell Losses (called BRM cell loss for simplicity), for typical parameter values, as the source rate ACR varies. We restrict ourselves to the condition that $ER \geq RIF \cdot PCR$, and in particular when Corollary 2.3 applies. In Table 2.1, we examine the number of consecutive RM cell losses that may be tolerated, for different ratios of the "steady state" rate, ER, returned by the network to the peak rate, PCR.

| | ER/PCR=0.1 | ER/PCR=0.25 | ER/PCR=0.5 | ER/PCR=1.0 |
|---|---|---|---|---|
| CDF=1/2 | 31.245110 | 31.093110 | 31.048580 | 31.022720 |
| CDF=1/32 | 36.351370 | 33.032790 | 32.0 | 31.496030 |
| CDF=1/64 | 41.788370 | 35.098110 | 33.0160 | 32.0 |

**Table 2.1.** Bounds on Allowable Consecutive RM cell Loss for Varrying Values of CDF (RIF = 1/64)

The values of the parameters chosen for the table are as

follows:

The values chosen are $Crm = 32$, $Nrm = 32$, $Mrm = 2$ and $Trm =$ 100 milliseconds. We have chosen a somewhat conservative value of $RIF = 1/64$, based on our understanding of the need to minimize the burst load on the network when the source rate increases. We have chosen to vary the ratio of $ER/PCR$, so that it is applicable for a wide range of link speeds, and examine how many consecutive RM cell losses may be tolerated while keeping the source rate stable.

We examined equation (2.15) for different values of $CDF$, varying in powers of 2 from (1/2) to (1/128) [LRMS2]. Increasing ER reduces the tolerance for consecutive RM cell losses. When we consider realistic values of $CDF$ (we believe 1/64 or smaller), quite a large number of RM cell losses are tolerated. For $CDF = 1/64$, at a ratio of $ER/PCR$=0.1, the number of consecutive losses is almost 42, which is reasonable. With a larger $CDF$, there is less tolerance for loss, but still appears to be "safely" large. Hence, for low rates, $ER$, and for reasonable values of the parameters, RM cell losses are not such a substantial concern.

We now examine the tolerance to RM cell losses in the more realistic situation of having a higher ER rate. When the ratio $ER/PCR$ ranges from 0.1 to 1.0 the number of consecutive RM cell losses tolerated continues to reduce. For $CDF = 1/64$, when $ER/PCR$=1.0, the number of consecutive RM cell losses tolerated is 32. At intermediate rates of $0.1 < ER/PCR < 0.5$, smaller values of $CDF$ (not shown) allows for slightly greater loss tolerance.

### 2.3. Rate Analysis Under Probabilistic Assumptions of RM Cell Losses

We now examine the effect of RM cell losses in a probabilistic situation. We assume that our observation of the effect on the source rate, ACR, is over a sufficiently long period, covering multiple "epochs". As before, over this period, the total number of BRM cells (lost as well as those returned to source) is equal to the FRM cells transmitted. We derive for a given probability of loss $\rho$ of RM cells, the relationship between the parameters associated with Rule 6 ($CDF$, $Crm$) and the rate increase factor $RIF$ so that the expected rate is not below the starting value of $ACR$.

As before, we assume that the target rate $ER$ returned to the source in BRM cells is constant over the interval. Knowing a starting rate $ACR$ at time $t=0$ which is equal to the steady-state rate for the VC (i.e., $ACR = ER$ at $t = 0$), we examine the effect on $ACR$ when RM cells are lost.

Suppose that the cell loss probability of RM cells is $0 \le \rho \le 1$. If we observe the source events of interest, these are either sending FRM cells or receiving BRM cells. Given that, over a time period, we send $N$ FRM cells and receive $N \cdot (1 - \rho)$ BRM cells, the probability that the event is that of sending an FRM cell is $1/(2 - \rho)$, and the probability that the event is of receiving a BRM cell is $(1 - \rho)/(2 - \rho)$.

The expected amount of rate increases in the steady state over a fixed time interval is $RIF \cdot PCR[\,1 - 1/(2 - \rho)]$. Corresponding to the same time interval, a decrease is caused if more than $Crm$ consecutive FRM cells are sent. The probability of sending $Crm + i$ FRM cells consecutively (i.e., without an intervening event of a BRM cell returning) is $1/(2 - \rho)^{Crm+i}$, $i = 1, \cdots$, and each of these causes a rate decrease of $ACR[1 - (1 - CDF)^i]$. The expected rate reduction is then

$$\sum_{i=1}^{\infty} \frac{ACR[1 - (1 - CDF)^i]}{(2 - \rho)^{Crm+i}}$$

$$= \frac{ACR}{(2 - \rho)^{Crm-1}} \left[ \frac{1}{1 - \rho} - \frac{1}{2 - \rho - CDF} \right].$$

In summary, the expected rate change in the steady state with an initial rate of ACR is:

$$RIF \cdot PCR \left[ 1 - \frac{1}{2 - \rho} \right] -$$

$$\frac{ACR}{(2 - \rho)^{Crm-1}} \left[ \frac{1}{1 - \rho} - \frac{1}{2 - \rho - CDF} \right].$$

For the rate to be stable, statistically, the expected rate change should be non-negative. Thus, we have:

**Proposition 2.2.** With an RM cell loss probability $0 \le \rho \le 1$ and current transmission rate ACR, there is no expected rate decrease if:

$$RIF \cdot PCR \left[ 1 - \frac{1}{2 - \rho} \right] \ge \qquad (2.16)$$

$$\frac{ACR}{(2 - \rho)^{Crm-1}} \left[ \frac{1}{1 - \rho} - \frac{1}{2 - \rho - CDF} \right].$$

□

### 3. BRM CELL TURN-AROUND, FRM CELL TRANSMISSION INTERVALS, AND ACR

We first study the turn-around time for BRM cells at the receiving end-station. When an FRM cell arrives at an end-station with the current network information, it is converted into a turned-around BRM cell. Understanding the contribution of the destination in turning around the RM cell is critical to understand the time it takes to feedback information to the source to adjust the rate.

Informally, a source sends an FRM cell every $Nrm - 1$ data cells or based on an upper bound on the time, $Trm$. These FRM cells arrive in the data stream (sent on the same VC) at destination protocol machine of the remote station. After incurring queueing delays to have the hardware (adapter) process arriving cells (which we do not consider here), the FRM cell is handed to destination protocol machine. Our estimation of the turn-around delay starts from the point when the FRM cell is handed to the destination protocol machine.

The destination protocol machine follows its rules to take the information received in the FRM cell to create information to be sent in the turned-around BRM cell. Specifically, the DIR bit in the FRM cell is changed from "forward" to "backward" and BN, CI, NI, QL and SN fields are set if necessary. From this point onwards, the relevant turned-around BRM cells contain updated information to be handed to source. This process of updating the fields of an FRM cell can usually be done in hardware and the processing time is negligible.

There are rules in the destination which state that the information received in the FRM cell may be used to re-write any turned-around BRM cells already queued to the source protocol machine. For convenience, we call this *BRM re-writing*. Another alternative is to drop all queued turned-around BRM cells and queue this one to send to the source. We call it *BRM dropping*. It turns out that the turn-around time is invariant with respect to the two different rules.

The turned-around BRM cell is then processed through the protocol state machines at the receiver (source and scheduler machines) to eventually be transmitted back to the sending end-system. The significant turn-around delay is the time it takes for the BRM cell to receive its opportunity to be transmitted by the scheduler. The turn-around delay estimation ends at the point when the BRM cell is transmitted.

Our estimate of the turn-around time $\tau$, from the moment an FRM cell is received at the destination protocol machine to the time a corresponding BRM cell is sent to the network, is derived informally based on the original specification [ATM]. We chose to do so since it provides more insight. On the other hand, a formal derivation based on the EFSM may also be obtained.

We now estimate the delay of the BRM cell in the scheduler with the following assumptions:

**Assumption 3.1.** (1) $Mrm \geq 1$ and $Nrm \geq 2$; (2) $Mrm < Nrm$; and (3) $Trm > 1/MCR$. □

Note that the problem is only relevant under these assumptions. The first lemma is concerned with the ordering of the transmission of RM cells. It is crucial for the estimation of BRM cell turned-around time.

**Lemma 3.1.** Suppose that BRM cells are waiting for transmission and that an FRM cell has just been transmitted to the network by scheduler. Then, the next cell to be transmitted by the scheduler is a BRM cell. □

Implementations may be somewhat lax in interpreting the order in which BRM cells and queued data cells may be transmitted. However, the priority, according to the specification (source rule (3)(a)) is given to the waiting BRM cell.

**Theorem 3.1.** The turn-around delay $\tau$ of a BRM cell is bounded by:

$$\frac{1}{PCR} \leq \frac{1}{ACR} \leq \tau \tag{3.1}$$

$$\leq \min\left\{ \max\left\{ Trm, \frac{Mrm}{ACR} \right\} + \frac{1}{ACR}, \frac{Nrm}{ACR} \right\}$$

$$\leq \min\left\{ \max\left\{ Trm, \frac{Mrm}{MCR} \right\} + \frac{1}{MCR}, \frac{Nrm}{MCR} \right\}.$$

Furthermore, the bounds are tight.

**Proof.** We show that $\tau$ is primarily the time to transmit a BRM cell to the network by the scheduler. The lower bound in equation (3.1) is obvious; suppose that an FRM has been just sent to the network. Then by Lemma 3.1, a BRM cell is sent immediately in time $1/ACR$ according to the rate constraint. Since the rate PCR is attainable by ACR, the lower bound is tight.

For clarity, we denote the moment the BRM cell is queued to scheduler by $t_0$. Again from Lemma 3.1, the upper bound is determined by the time for a maximum number of data cells sent before sending an FRM cell and the time *Trm* that would have to elapse for an FRM to be sent. The bound can be achieved if and only if the last RM cell sent before $t_0$ is a BRM cell. There are two cases.

Case 1: We ignore the time constraint *Trm* then neither source rule (3)(a) nor (3)(b) hold until $Nrm - 1$ cells have been sent since the last FRM cell sent. To maximize the number of cells sent after $t_0$, we consider that the two cells sent before $t_0$ are an FRM cell followed by a BRM cell. Therefore, from $t_0$, $Nrm - 2$ data cells are sent followed by an FRM cell and then the BRM cell to be transmitted. The total number of cells sent after $t_0$ (including this BRM cell) is *Nrm*, in time $Nrm/ACR$.

Case 2: The timer may expire before $Nrm/ACR$ cells are sent. By Lemma 3.1, the longest possible time duration (after $t_0$ and before sending the BRM cell) occurs when the two cells sent right before $t_0$ are an FRM and then a BRM cell. The first FRM should have been sent at time $t_0 - 1/ACR$, and at time $(t_0 - 1/ACR) + Trm$ another FRM cell will be sent. By Lemma 3.1, it is followed by the BRM to be transmitted. Thus, it takes time $2/ACR$ to send these two RM cells, and, therefore, the total time duration from $t_0$ to the moment the BRM cell is sent is: $Trm + 1/ACR$.

On the other hand, in conjunction with the expiration of the timer, at lease *Mrm* in rate cells have to be sent before transmitting a BRM cell, which takes time $(Mrm + 1)/ACR$, including this BRM cell.

To summarize, the BRM cell is sent whenever one of the above two events happens first, and (3.1) is proved.

Since *ACR* is bounded below by *MCR* and the bound is tight, the upper bound on the right side of (3.1) is also tight. Since there are no other delays in the protocol state machines other than what is specified in equation (3.1), our estimation of BRM cell turn-around time is tight. □

### 3.1. FRM CELL INTER-DEPARTURE TIMES

RM cells act as the probes into the network to determine the capacity available for a VC. Frequent probes into the network introduce overhead, which may be excessive. However, sending probes too infrequently results in exposure of the network to congestion and delay in the source's reaction to network state. Here, we attempt to understand the bounds on the time between transmitting two consecutive FRM cells. We assume that there are sufficient data/BRM cells available for transmission. Otherwise, the inter-departure times for FRM cells is close to being constant, $Trm + 1/ACR$, until *ACR* increases above $Nrm/Trm$.

**Proposition 3.1.** Let $\tau$ be the time interval between two FRM cell transmissions. If there are data/BRM cells available for in-rate transmission, then

$$\max\left\{\frac{Mrm}{ACR}, Trm\right\} + \frac{1}{ACR} \leq \tau \qquad (3.2)$$

$$\leq \min\left\{\max\left\{\frac{Mrm}{ACR}, Trm\right\}, \frac{Nrm - 1}{ACR}\right\} + \frac{1}{ACR}.$$

**Proof.** The lower bound is ensured by source rule (3)(a)(i) and the upper bound is a corollary of Lemma 2.1. □

If there are no data/BRM waiting for in-rate transmission, by rule (3)(a)(i) the next in-rate cell shall be an FRM cell if and only if at least *Mrm* in-rate cells have been transmitted and at least *Trm* time has elapsed since the last FRM cell was sent. Consequently, the time interval $\tau$ is nondeterministic.

The source rate may change whenever FRM cells are sent. We now discuss the dependency of the rate ACR and FRM cell transmissions.

**Proposition 3.2.** Assume data/BRM cells are available for transmission. (1) If $ACR \geq Nrm/Trm$ then each FRM cell is transmitted after transmitting $(Nrm - 1)$ data/BRM cells. (2) If $Mrm/Trm \leq ACR < Nrm/Trm$ then FRM cells are transmitted every *Trm* time interval. (3) If $ACR < Mrm/Trm$ then each FRM cell is transmitted after transmitting *Mrm* data/BRM cells. □

From Proposition 3.2 and Lemma 2.1, we have the following relation between the rate ACR and BRM cell transmission.

**Corollary 3.1.** Assume that data and turned-around BRM cells are available for transmission. Then (1) If $ACR \geq Nrm/Trm$ then each turned-around BRM cell is transmitted after $(Nrm - 2)$ data cells and one FRM cell are sent. (2) If $Mrm/Trm \leq ACR < Nrm/Trm$ then turned-around BRM cells are transmitted every *Trm* time interval. (3) If $ACR < Mrm/Trm$ then each turned-around BRM cell is transmitted after $(Mrm - 1)$ data cells and one FRM cell being sent. □

We have also evaluated, numerically, the FRM cell inter-departure times [LRMS2]. The primary observation is that it is only in an "intermediate range" of source rates, the feedback delay to the source is impacted by the FRM inter-departure times (e.g., at a source rate of 1 cell/millisecond, or about 384 Kbits/second, the feedback occurs around once every 33 milliseconds). It is less of a concern at very low source rates or at much higher source rates. We have excluded this due to space constraints.

## 4. CORRECTNESS — SOURCE/DESTINATION PROTOCOL BEING LIVE-LOCK FREE

We now discuss whether there are worst case scenarios such that available data or RM cells are never sent out. When this occurs the protocol has a *live-lock* [Kur]. This concerns the correctness of the rate control scheme and is a necessary condition for the protocol to perform properly. We show that there are no such live-locks in ABR. We use the formal specification in [LRMS], and the reader is referred to that paper for details on the EFSM.

Note that sources queue data and RM cells instantly to scheduler whenever they are available. Therefore, delay of cells and ''livelocks'' can only occur in the scheduler. We now examine the scheduler behavior. We first show that the transitions from the active state $S_1$ are mutually exclusive and inclusive:

**Lemma 4.1.** In the scheduler machine at any moment one and exactly one of the transitions from the active state $S_1$ is executable.

**Sketch of Proof.** We ignore the condition $t \geq 1/ACR$, since it becomes TRUE as time elapses. Examine the predicates of the outgoing transitions from $S_1$. It is straightforward to check that the conjunction of any two predicates is FALSE. Therefore, at any moment, at most one of the transitions is executable. On the other hand, one checks that the disjunction of all the predicates is TRUE and this implies that at any moment at least one transition is executable. □

The above lemma shows that in the active state one and only one of the outgoing transitions is executable. It does not yet imply that the ABR protocol is live-lock free; we have to show that the transitions which transmit data cells and BRM cells will always be executed within a finite (bounded) amount of time.

**Theorem 4.1.** The ABR source/destination protocol is live-lock free; both data cells and RM cells waiting for transmission will be sent eventually. Specifically,

(1) So long as data cells are waiting for transmission, FRM cells are sent in a time interval no more than:

$$\tau_{FRM} = \min\left\{\max\left\{\frac{Mrm}{MCR}, Trm\right\}, \frac{Nrm - 1}{MCR}\right\}. \qquad (4.1)$$

(2) A turned-around BRM cell will be sent in time no more than

$$\tau_{BRM} = \min\left\{\max\left\{Trm, \frac{Mrm}{MCR}\right\} + \frac{1}{MCR}, \frac{Nrm}{MCR}\right\}. \qquad (4.2)$$

(3) Data cells waiting for transmission will be sent in time no more than:

$$\tau_{DATA} = \frac{4}{MCR}. \qquad (4.3)$$

**Proof.** Equation (4.1) can be derived from Proposition 3.1 where the time interval of sending FRM cells is derived. Equation (4.2) is a corollary of Theorem 4.1 where the turned-around delay of BRM cells is estimated.

We now analyze the waiting time for a data cell ready for transmission. Data cells are queued to scheduler immediately, and, therefore, the only delay occurs in the scheduler. There are three cases.

**Case 1:** The last cell sent was an FRM cell.

The corresponding transitions executed are either $T_2$; or $T_3$ followed by $T_4$; or $T_3$ followed by $T_5$. In all the cases, we are back in state $S_1$ with $X_1 + X_2 = 0$. There are two subcases.

(A) $X = 0$. In this case, among all the transitions from $S_1$, only $T_7$ is executable, since event $E$ is TRUE: there are data cells waiting for transmission, $X = 0$, and $X_1 + X_2 = 0 < Nrm - 1$. Therefore, $T_7$ is executed and the data cell waiting from transmission is sent. The delay is $1/ACR$.

(B) $X > 0$. In this case, only $T_6$ is executable, since $X > 0$ and $X_1 = 0$. Therefore, a BRM cell is sent and we are still in state $S_1$ with $X_1 = 1$. Now by a similar argument among all the transitions from $S_1$, only $T_7$ is executable. Note that $T_6$ is no longer executable since $(X_1 = 0) \,||\, !E = FALSE$. Therefore, $T_7$ is executed and the data cell is sent. The delay is $2/ACR$.

**Case 2:** The last cell sent was a BRM cell.

The corresponding transition for the transmission was $T_6$. After the execution of $T_6$, $X_1 > 0$ and $T_6$ is no longer executable since $(X_1 = 0) \,||\, !E = FALSE$. From Lemma 4.1, at least one of the transitions from $S_1$ is executable and, consequently, either an FRM cell or the data cell is sent upon execution. If an FRM cell is sent, then from Case 1 the data cell will be sent in time no more than $3/ACR$. Otherwise, the data cell is transmitted in time $1/ACR$.

**Case 3:** The last cell sent was a data cell.

The corresponding transition executed was $T_7$. By Lemma 4.1, among all the transitions from $S_1$ at least one of them is executable. Therefore, either $T_7$ is executed next and in this case the data cell is sent, or any one of the following transitions is executed: $T_2$; $T_3$ followed by either $T_4$ or $T_5$; or $T_6$. In any one of the cases, either an FRM cell or a BRM cell is sent. By the analysis in Case 1 and 2, the data cell is sent in time no more than $1/ACR + 3/ACR = 4/ACR \le 4/MCR$. □

## 5. INTEROPERATION OF EFCI AND ER SCHEMES

There are two rate control schemes in ABR: Explicit Forward Congestion Indication (EFCI) and Explicit Rate (ER). We now discuss their interoperation using the formal extended finite state machine specification in [LRMS].

Upon receiving BRM cells, the source adjusts ACR at state $S_2$ of the source machine. The four transitions involving rate changes are $T_4$, $T_5$, $T_6$, and $T_7$; they all go from state $S_2$ to $S_1$. We first show that these four rate-change transitions are mutually exclusive and inclusive:

**Lemma 5.1.** In the source machine, in the rate-change state $S_2$, upon arrival of a BRM cell, one and exactly one rate-change transition is executable from the rate-change state $S_2$.

**Sketch of Proof.** From the rate-change state $S_2$, we examine the predicates of the four rate-change transitions: $T_4$, $T_5$, $T_6$, and $T_7$. Upon arrival of a BRM cell, we only have to check that the conjunction of any two predicates is FALSE and that the disjunction of all these predicates is TRUE. □

We now discuss the interoperation of EFCI and ER in determining the rate ACR.

**Theorem 5.1.** EFCI and ER schemes inter-operate as follows:

(1) If both EFCI and ER indicate congestion, then the final resulting rate is the minimum of the two rates obtained by rate reductions determined by the two schemes, respectively.

(2) If both EFCI and ER indicate no congestion, then the final rate increase is the minimum of the two increases obtained by applying the two schemes, respectively, unless $NI = 1$ in which case there would be no rate increase.

(3) If there is a conflict, (one indicates congestion and the other indicates no congestion), then the final outcome is the rate reduction obtained by the option indicating congestion.

**Proof.** EFCI scheme indicates congestion by setting the $CI$ bit; ER scheme indicates congestion by setting $ER$ such that $ER \le ACR$. Obviously, there are three cases.

*Case 1: Both EFCI and ER indicate congestion.* In this case, $(CI = 1)\ \&\&\ (ER_{BRM} \le ACR)$. Source transition $T_4$ is enabled, and by Lemma 5.1 it is the one and only transition enabled; the result is the following rate change:

$$ACR := \max\{MCR, \min\{ACR \cdot (1 - RDF), ER_{BRM}\}\}.$$

Thus the final rate is the minimum of the two rates, determined by the two schemes, respectively.

*Case 2: Both EFCI and ER indicate no congestion.* In this case, $(CI = 0)\ \&\&\ (ACR < ER_{BRM})$, we consider two sub-cases:

(a) $NI = 0$: then, $(CI = 0)\ \&\&\ (NI = 0)\ \&\&\ (ACR < ER_{BRM})$, source $T_5$ is the one and only transition enabled; this results in the following rate change:

$$ACR := \min\{ER_{BRM}, PCR, ACR + (RIF \cdot PCR)\}.$$

Therefore the final rate increase is bounded by the minimum of the increases allowed by the two option.

(b) NI = 1: then, $(CI = 0)\ \&\&\ (NI = 1)\ \&\&\ (ACR < ER_{BRM})$, source $T_6$ is the one and only transition enabled; the result is no rate increase.

*Case 3: One indicates congestion and the other indicates no congestion.* Consider two sub-cases:

(a) EFCI indicates congestion but ER indicates no congestion. In this case, $(CI = 1)\ \&\&\ (ER_{BRM} > ACR)$, source $T_4$ is the one and only transition enabled, the result is the following rate change:

$$ACR := \max\{MCR, \min\{ACR \cdot (1 - RDF), ER_{BRM}\}\}.$$

Hence the final outcome is the rate reduction due to EFCI scheme since $ER_{BRM} > ACR$.

(b) EFCI indicates no congestion but ER indicates congestion In this case, $CI = 0\ \&\&\ ACR \ge ER_{BRM}$, source $T_7$ is the one and only transition enabled, this results in the following new rate:

$$ACR := \max\{MCR, ER_{BRM}\}.$$

Thus the final outcome is the rate reduction due to ER scheme. □

## 6. CONCLUSIONS

Protocol design has traditionally been an evolutionary process. First is the genesis of the algorithm and an informal specification of the algorithm using an English description. The protocol is subsequently refined as a result of additional scrutiny and performance analysis using simulations and other techniques. In the process, the protocol begins to accommodate complexity to address real-life situations where the initial design was inadequate. This has also been the evolution of the ATM Forum's ABR service description and congestion management protocol. Subsequent study based on formal methods is useful to understand the correctness and performance issues of the resulting protocol.

In this paper, we have examined the performance and correctness issues using a formal specification of the ABR service using an Extended Finite State Machine model. In the correctness domain, we have demonstrated using the EFSM that the protocol is live-lock free. This implies that if there are pending cells to be transmitted from a source, then they will eventually be transmitted. Furthermore, we computed the bounds on the time interval between successive transmissions of these cells. We have also demonstrated that the EFCI and ER options that have been accommodated in the ABR specification interoperate appropriately, with the source rate-change actions reflecting the minimum of the rates resulting from the two mechanisms when the network is congested. When a source is allowed to increase its rate, the rate is also allowed to increase to the minimum of the rate increases allowed by the two options. We believe these are needed to ensure that the protocol is robust without uncovered failure modes.

In the performance domain, there has been considerable work done in the past to understand various aspects of the mechanism in different network conditions. In this paper, we have examined, based on the understanding obtained from constructing the EFSM, several worst-case behaviors. One of the rules for the source is to have a " safety-valve" for the rate in the light of delayed or lost feedback from the network. We examine the stability of the source rate under various situations of RM cell loss and provide an understanding of the relationships between the different protocol parameters. In particular, the acceptable loss probability depends not only on parameters such as *RIF* and *CDF*, but also on the ratio (*ER* returned to source / *PCR*).

We also provided bounds on the worst-case delay for a destination to turn-around RM cells that carry the network feedback to the source. The predominant delay here is the "waiting" period for the Backward RM cell for its turn to be transmitted by the scheduler. Another important bound to understand is the time between transmissions of Forward RM cells from the source, which depends on the current value of the source rate as well as the other connection-level parameters. This has to be considered in the context of the connection's round trip time, to examine if the "RM-cell probes" are being transmitted adequately frequently.

## ACKNOWLEDGMENT

Melody Moh is supported in part by the CSU Research Grant and the SJSU Faculty Development Award.

## REFERENCES

[ATM]ATM Forum Traffic Management Specification Version 4.0, ATM Forum/95-0013R11, March 1996.

[CGS] Y. Chang, N. Golmie, and D. Su, "Study of Interoperability between EFCI and ER Switch Mechanisms for ABR Traffic in an ATM Network," *Proc. of the 4th International Conference on Computer Communications and Networks,* pp. 310-315, 1995.

[CCJ] A. Charny, D. D. Clark, and R. Jain, "Congestion Control with Explicit Rate Indication," *Proc. ICC,* June 1995.

[CR] Anna Charny and K. K. Ramakrishnan, "Time Scale Analysis of Explicit Rate Allocation in ATM Networks", *Proceedings of Infocom '96*, March 1996.

[JKFL]Raj Jain, Shiv Kalyanaraman, Sonia Fahmy and Fang Lu, "Parameter Values for Satellite Links", ATM Forum Contribution ATM Forum/95-972, August 1995.

[Kes] S. Keshav, "A Control-Theoretic Approach to Flow Control", *Proceedings of ACM Sigcomm '91*, September 1991.

[Kur] R. P. Kurshan, *Computer-aided Verification of Coordinating Processes,* Princeton University Press, Princeton, New Jersey, 1995.

[LY} D. Lee and M. Yannakakis, "Principle and Methods of Testing Finite State Machines - a Survey", *Proceedings of The IEEE*, Vol. 84, No. 8, August 1996.

[LMRS]D. Lee, W. M. Moh, K.K. Ramakrishnan, and U. Shankar, "An Extended Finite State Machine Representation of the Source/Destination Behavior", ATM Forum Contribution ATM_Forum/96-0231, Feb. 1996.

[LRMS]D. Lee, K.K. Ramakrishnan, W. M. Moh, and U. Shankar, "Protocol Specification Using Parameterized Communicating Extended Finite State Machines - A Case Study of the ATM ABR Rate Control Scheme", *Proc. ICNP*, pp. 208-217, October 1996.

[LRMS2]D. Lee, K.K. Ramakrishnan, W. M. Moh, and U. Shankar, "Performance and Correctness of the ATM ABR Rate Control Scheme", *Extended Version*, June 1996.

[RJ] K. K. Ramakrishnan and Raj Jain, "A Binary Feedback Scheme for Congestion Avoidance in Computer Networks", *ACM Transactions on Computer Systems*, May 1990.

#### APPENDIX: PROOF OF THEOREM 2.2

The first part of the theorem is a simple special case of Corollary 2.1.

Now suppose that $ER > RIF \cdot PCR$. During the stable period where the source's rate $ACR = ER$, each FRM cell is sent after $Nrm - 1$ data or BRM cells are sent. Including the transmission time of the FRM cell, the time interval each FRM sent is: $Nrm/ER$. The time interval between receipt of successive BRM cells with BN=0 is also $Nrm/ER$, if there is no loss.

Suppose that $\nu - 1$ consecutive FRM cells in a forward direction or BRM cells in a backward direction have been lost. The time interval between two BRM cells is

$$\tau = \frac{\nu \cdot Nrm}{ER}. \tag{A.1}$$

Before we analyze the rate stability, we observe that the problem is interesting when $ER - MCR > RIF \cdot PCR$ where $RIF \cdot PCR$ is the rate increase after receiving a BRM cell. Otherwise, a single rate increase will always take the source transmission rate, ACR, back to ER and the rate is always stable, independent of the amount of decrease due to Rule 6. We assume that $ER - MCR > RIF \cdot PCR$ and provide conditions such that consecutive rate decreases are no more than a rate increase from receiving a BRM cell.

We first estimate the time interval $t_k$ between consecutive rate decreases. We assume $Nrm - 1 \geq Mrm$, based on generally accepted ranges for these parameters.

We order the decreases in the rate in the following manner: for time instants $t_i = 0, \cdots, l$, when the rate is still high, FRM cells are sent after every $Nrm - 1$ data cells and BRM cell transmissions. Subsequently, the source rate $ACR$ is sufficiently lower that the FRM cells are sent by the timer, $Trm$, expiring. This occurs at time instants $t_i = l + 1, \cdots, r$. Finally, when the rate has reduced to small enough values, the FRM cells have to wait for $Mrm$ cells to be sent out, which occur after the timer $Trm$ has expired.

We define $l$ as the maximum number of time instants when the decrease is caused by $Crm$ FRM cells being transmitted when the rate is high. The time to transmit these FRM cells at the lowest rate in this phase is such that it is less than the timer value $Trm$. Also define $r$ as the maximum number of time instants when the FRM cell transmission is caused by the timer expiring, which implies that the time to send $Mrm$ cells at the smallest rate in this phase is less than the timer $Trm$.

$$\begin{aligned} l &= \max\left\{ i : \frac{Nrm}{ACR_{i-1}} \leq Trm \right\} \\ r &= \max\left\{ i : \frac{Mrm}{ACR_{i-1}} \leq Trm \right\} \end{aligned} \tag{A.2}$$

The condition $l = 0$ implies that it is always true that $Nrm/ACR_i > Trm$ and, similarly, the condition $r = 0$ implies that $Mrm/ACR_i > Trm$ is always true.

For large enough rates of $ACR$, Rule 6 is triggered based on sending $Crm$ FRM cells, each of which take $Nrm/ACR_{i-1}$ cell times. For lower (intermediate) rates of $ACR$, when the source has sent more than $Mrm$ cells but less than $Nrm$ cells in time $Trm$, then the decrease is triggered by $Crm$ FRM cells transmitted upon expiration of the timer $Trm$. For "very low rates", when $Trm$ has already expired, FRM cell transmission occurs only after the requisite minimum number of cells $Mrm$, classifying the connection as active, have been sent. From (2.2), we can derive:

$$t_i = \begin{cases} \dfrac{Crm \cdot Nrm}{ACR_0} & i = 1 \\ \dfrac{Nrm}{ACR_{i-1}} & i = 2, \cdots, l \\ Trm + \dfrac{1}{ACR_{i-1}}, & i = l+1, \cdots, r \\ \dfrac{Mrm + 1}{ACR_{i-1}} & i = r+1, \cdots, k \end{cases} \tag{A.3}$$

Therefore,

$$\sum_{i=1}^{k} t_i = Crm \cdot \frac{Nrm}{ACR_0} + \left[ \sum_{i=2}^{l} \frac{Nrm}{ACR_{i-1}} + (r - l) \cdot Trm + \sum_{i=l+1}^{r} \frac{1}{ACR_{i-1}} + \sum_{i=r+1}^{k} \frac{Mrm + 1}{ACR_{i-1}} \right]$$

From (2.1), $ACR_{i-1} = ER(1 - CDF)^{i-1}$, we have

$$\sum_{i=2}^{l} \frac{Nrm}{ACR_{i-1}} = \frac{Nrm}{ER \cdot CDF} \left[ \left( \frac{1}{1 - CDF} \right)^{l-1} - 1 \right]$$

$$\sum_{i=l+1}^{r} \frac{1}{ACR_{i-1}} = \frac{1}{ER \cdot CDF \cdot (1 - CDF)^{l}} \left[ \left( \frac{1}{1 - CDF} \right)^{r-l} - 1 \right]$$

and

$$\sum_{i=r+1}^{k} \frac{Mrm + 1}{ACR_{i-1}} = \frac{Mrm + 1}{ER \cdot CDF \cdot (1 - CDF)^{r}} \left[ \left( \frac{1}{1 - CDF} \right)^{k-r} - 1 \right].$$

We have

$$\sum_{i=1}^{k} t_i = Crm \cdot \frac{Nrm}{ER} + \frac{Nrm}{ER \cdot CDF} \left[ \left( \frac{1}{1 - CDF} \right)^{l-1} - 1 \right] + (r - l) \cdot Trm + \tag{A.4}$$

$$\frac{1}{ER \cdot CDF} \left[ \left( \frac{1}{1 - CDF} \right)^{r} - \left( \frac{1}{1 - CDF} \right)^{l} \right] + \frac{Mrm + 1}{ER \cdot CDF} \cdot \left[ \left( \frac{1}{1 - CDF} \right)^{k} - \left( \frac{1}{1 - CDF} \right)^{r} \right].$$

If we consider the boundary cases in (A.2), so that $(Nrm)/ACR_l = Trm$ and $Mrm/ACR_r = Trm$, then we obtain (2.13) and (2.14).

Since $CDF << 1$, we have

$$\left( \frac{1}{1 - CDF} \right)^{k} \approx 1 + \frac{k \cdot CDF}{1 - CDF}. \tag{A.5}$$

From (A.4) and (2.11), we have

$$\sum_{i=1}^{k} t_i \approx Crm \cdot \frac{Nrm}{ER} + \frac{(l - 1) \cdot Nrm \cdot CDF}{ER \cdot CDF \cdot (1 - CDF)} +$$

$$(r - l) \cdot Trm + \frac{r \cdot CDF - l \cdot CDF}{ER \cdot CDF \cdot (1 - CDF)} + \frac{(Mrm + 1) \cdot (k \cdot CDF - r \cdot CDF)}{ER \cdot CDF \cdot (1 - CDF)}$$

$$\approx Crm \cdot \frac{Nrm}{ER} + \frac{(l - 1) \cdot Nrm}{ER} + \frac{r - l}{ER} + \frac{(k - r) \cdot (Mrm + 1)}{ER} + (r - l) \cdot Trm \leq \frac{\nu \cdot Nrm}{ER}.$$

The number of decreases in the rate between receiving two consecutive BRM cells (with $\nu - 1$ RM cell losses in between) is:

$$n = \tag{A.6}$$

$$\max\left\{ k : k \leq \frac{\nu \cdot Nrm - \left[ Crm \cdot Nrm + (l - 1) \cdot Nrm + (r - l) + (r - l) \cdot ER \cdot Trm \right]}{Mrm + 1} + r \right\}.$$

On the other hand, from Proposition 2.1, we have

$$\frac{\nu \cdot Nrm - \left[ Crm \cdot Nrm + (l - 1) \cdot Nrm + (r - l) + (r - l) \cdot ER \cdot Trm \right]}{Mrm + 1} + r \tag{A.7}$$

$$\leq \frac{\log\left( 1 - \dfrac{RIF \cdot PCR}{ER} \right)}{\log (1 - CDF)}$$

A routine derivation from (A.7) yields (2.12).

# Performance Analysis of Rate Based Feedback Control for ATM Networks *

Lalita A. Kulkarni San-qi Li
Department of Electrical and Computer Engineering
University of Texas at Austin, Austin, TX 78712-1084

## Abstract

*Closed-loop input rate regulation schemes have come to play an important role in the transport of the Available Bit Rate (ABR) traffic service category for ATM. In this paper, we present a numerical approach to the performance study of a delayed feedback system with one congested node and multiple connections. This approach consists in modeling the feedback system as a finite Quasi-Birth-Death (QBD) process. Due to the peculiar block tri-diagonol nature of its generator, efficient techniques exist for its steady-state and transient solutions. Using these techniques, we examine a simple parsimonious feedback system for issues such as throughput/loss performance, fairness and stability. Our approach has the flexibility to study the effect of several additional factors such as asynchronous feedback, two-level control and explicit rate notification in the presence of underlying high-priority traffic. This study brings to light the trade-offs between system performance and the complexity of the feedback scheme. Our study shows that the time scales of correlation of the feedback system have a dominant effect on its performance. These time scales are associated with the feedback delay, the durations of active/idle periods of traffic sources and the time scales of the underlying high-priority traffic. We also examine the effect of the time scales on the convergence time for the transient queueing system.*

## 1 Introduction

The Asynchronous Transfer Mode (ATM) with its capability of supporting various Quality of Service (QoS) guarantees and bandwidth on demand has been recognized as the transport medium for the future B-ISDN networks. The diverse multimedia traffic can be supported with high bandwidth utilization only if effective traffic management is employed. This includes call admission control and congestion control within the network. While open-loop congestion control schemes are typically used for real-time communications such as Variable-Bit Rate (VBR) or Constant-Bit Rate (CBR) services, closed-loop control has proved to be a promising mechanism for the Available-Bit Rate (ABR) service category. Closed-loop rate control schemes have received a lot of attention in recent years. Researchers are constantly devising new and more effective schemes for dynamically allocating available capacity in the network. These schemes rely on feedback messages from congested switches in the network. Several schemes for feedback control have been proposed. These range from schemes involving a single bit (binary feedback) for congestion indication ([1],[2]) to explicit rate notification ([3],[4]) in which the network explicitly provides the source with its allowed rate. The authors in [5] present an excellent description of the evolution of the rate-based framework for the support of the ABR service.

Most feedback-based flow control strategies suffer from the large time constants associated with the adaptive processes ([6]). When the propogation delays are significantly large as compared to the durations of the bursts of the input traffic, feedback may prove to be ineffective in terms of limiting the cell loss behaviour or queueing delays. In contrast, the feedback control proves to be effective for applications which demand bandwidth for durations comparable to the propogation delays ([6]).Two important issues must be addressed by any feedback-based scheme viz. the fairness criteria and the time for the algorithm to converge. Most analysis of feedback-based congestion control schemes involve deterministic fluid traffic models and deterministic round-trip delays. Therefore the system behaviour is described by a set of deterministic delay-differential equations which may be solved to obtain the steady-state system behaviour. Most of the previous analysis assume lossless systems with the buffer overflow probabilities used to estimate the loss probabilities.

The related works along these lines may be found in [6],[7] and [8]. In reality, the traffic sources are stochastic and so too are the feedback delays. In [9], the authors model a simplified delayed feedback system with constant service rate and independent random arrivals with on/off source behaviour. In [10] and [11], the authors analyze a stochastic feedback system using Markov-modulated fluid models for the traffic sources, a fluid queue and exponentially distributed feedback delays. Thus, the model for the feedback system is a piecewise deterministic Markov process. In [12] and [13], the authors use a stochastic approach to analyze the feedback system but they ignore the effect of the feedback delays in their analysis.

Our approach is similar to [10], although we use a Quasi-Birth Death (QBD) model for the feedback system. Thus, the queue behaviour is not deterministic as in the fluid model assumed in [10]. The advantage of QBD-modeling lies in the efficient solution technique for systems of linear equations of the type $\vec{x}\mathbf{P} = \vec{a}$, for a matrix $\mathbf{P}$ with a block tri-diagonol structure. This solution technique is called the Generalized Folding Algorithm ([15]) which exploits the block tri-diagonol

*The research reported here was supported by NSF under grant NCR-9314387, Southwestern Bell, and Texas Advanced Research Program under grant TARP-33.



0-8186-7780-5/97 $10.00 © 1997 IEEE

structure of the matrix $\mathbf{P}$ to solve for $\vec{x}$. A special case would be the solution of $\vec{\pi}\mathbf{G} = \mathbf{0}$ which is the steady-state solution of a QBD system with generator $\mathbf{G}$.

Our main contributions are as follows. We study the interplay between the various parameters of a feedback system, along the lines of [10]. While their study involved only certain aspects of the steady-state behaviour, we endeavor to explore other steady-state issues such as two-level control, the effect of underlying high priority traffic and the performance of an explicit rate notification scheme. We also study the transient performance of the system. Specifically, we will address issues such as convergence time to steady-state, the fairness issue in short term behaviour and the transient queue lengths. In [16], we have already seen the dominant effect of the time scales of the arrival process relative to the service time on the transient queueing system. In that model the time scales of the arrival process were independent of the dynamics of the queue. In this case, the time scales of the arrival process are those imposed by the feedback delays and also by the threshold level chosen for congestion indication in the case of binary feedback, or the dynamics of the underlying traffic in the case of explicit rate notification. If the traffic sources have their own time scales associated with their active/idle periods, these will also come into play in the dynamics and will affect the effectiveness of the feedback scheme as suggested in [10]. The solution technique used in [10] is limited due to the inherent eigenvalue decomposition problem associated with the fluid-flow approach. Hence their numerical study is restricted to homogenous on-off sources, with constant service rate. Also, their model uses the overflow probability in an infinite buffer to approximate the cell loss in the case of a finite buffer. Our model uses an exact finite buffer analysis to find the cell loss probability. Further, the extension of their analysis to the transient case may be difficult if feasible.

The paper is organized as follows: In Section 2 we describe the system model. Section 3 briefly describes the solution technique for the QBD system which includes both the steady-state solutions and the transient solutions. Section 4 describes the numerical study for the feedback system. Finally, Section 5 concludes the study of the performance of the feedback system. The reader may refer to [15] and [16] for the detailed description of the GFA and its applications to the transient solutions of a QBD queueing system.

## 2 The System Model

The system consists of a single bottleneck node fed by multiple traffic sources located at different geographical distances from the bottleneck node. Traffic generated from the $k^{th}$-source has a forward propogation delay $d_{f,k}$ to reach the bottleneck node. In general, the forward propogation delay differs for each traffic source and is determined by the number of switches in the forward path from source to the congested node. In the case of the ABR traffic, the source periodically sends Resource Management (RM) cells along with the data cells. Upon receipt of the RM cells, the bottleneck node sends feedback information to the traffic sources to indicate its level of congestion. The feedback delay for the $k^{th}$-source is $d_{b,k}$. Thus, the round-trip delay for the $k^{th}$-source is $d_{r,k} = d_{f,k} + d_{b,k}$. The feedback information may be parsimonious (a single bit) which simply indicates congestion by 1 or non-congestion by 0. On the other hand, the feedback may explicitly indicate the instantaneous available link capacity. Both these schemes have trade-offs in terms of nodal processing versus effectiveness of the feedback scheme. The source behaviour on receipt of the feedback information may also vary. The most widely accepted scheme for binary feedback is that the source may linearly increase its sending rate on receipt of 0 and exponentially decrease its rate on receipt of 1. This slow rate of increase on non-congestion and fast rate of reduction on congestion is necessary to reduce the length of congestion period at the node and thus reduce the cell loss. When explicit rate notification is used based on the available link capacity, the source may adjust its rate to the value specified in the feedback message. The purpose of this study is to explore the effectiveness of each of the above mentioned schemes. We describe below in detail the system model including the traffic source behaviour, the nodal behaviour and the dynamics of the feedback information.

**The traffic sources:** The traffic source may be persistent, i.e., it is constantly transmitting at the allowable rate, or it may be alternating between periods of activity and inactivity. In the latter case, the periods of activity and inactivity are exponentially distributed with mean $\frac{1}{\alpha}$ and $\frac{1}{\beta}$ respectively. Thus, in the absence of the feedback process, the source behaves like an independent two-state Markov chain[1]. When the source is on and a feedback message is received, the traffic source changes its rate of transmission depending on the feedback information as well as its current rate. For instance, if the feedback bit is 0, the rate of transmission is increased by a small increment until it reaches its maximum allowable transmission rate; if the feedback is 1, the transmission rate is reduced to the minimum. In the language of the ABR service category, these would correspond to the peak cell rate (PCR) and minimum cell rate (MCR). The increase or decrease in the transmission rate is implemented by a flow control scheme such as the Leaky-Bucket which is not modeled here. If the source is inactive, it does not react on receipt of the feedback information. When the source becomes active again after some period of inactivity, it starts transmitting at the minimum possible rate. Thus, the source behaviour is governed by both the active/inactive periods as well as the feedback process.

**The Bottleneck Node:** It is represented by a finite buffer queueing system of size $K$. In general, the service capacity may not remain fixed throughout the connection duration. In addition to the traffic sources which are controlled by the closed-loop schemes, there may be real-time traffic arriving at the bottleneck which will have priority over the link bandwidth. The dynamics of this underlying traffic determine the available link bandwidth for the traffic sources being controlled by the closed-loop scheme. The service process may be described by a Markov chain with transition rate matrix $\mathbf{Q}_s$ and rate vector $\vec{\mu}_s$ i.e. the service times are exponentially distributed with mean $\frac{1}{\mu_k}$ when the service process is in state $k$, where $\mu_k \in \vec{\mu}_s$. It may be noted that the transitions of the service process are independent of the queue level

[1] The analysis may be extended to multiple-state Markov chains.

and also independent of the arrival process transitions. They are completely determined by the dynamics of the underlying high priority traffic. Since our purpose is to study the feedback system performance, we do not attempt to model the underlying traffic itself but only its effect on the available link capacity. The service discipline at the congested node for the closed loop traffic is considered to be FIFO.

**The Feedback Information:** The bottleneck node sends feedback information to each traffic source to inform the source of its status. For the time being, assume only one traffic source with round-trip delay $d_r = d_f + d_b$. In general, both $d_f$ and $d_b$ are random. The randomness in the forward paths arises due to the variable queueing delays at the intermediate nodes. Similarly, the randomness in the feedback path is caused by the variable delays suffered by the messages from the bottleneck node to the traffic source. Both these delays depend on the number of nodes that must be traversed between the source and the bottleneck node. In the interests of tractability, most analysis of feedback systems are deterministic which assume that both source behaviour and feedback delays are deterministic. In the case of ABR, the source injects RM cells every fixed number of data cells. They may suffer a random delay before they reach the congested node. Hence the instances at which the bottleneck node checks its congestion level and sends feedback messages are random rather than deterministic. The delay between these instances (i.e. between the arrival of RM cells) is assumed to be exponentially distributed with mean $\frac{1}{\lambda}$ for the purpose of Markovian modeling. Further, the feedback message receipt instant at the source coincides with a new message generation instant at the congested node. Most analysis assume that there is only one feedback message in the closed loop at any given instant. At this point, we make an approximation: during the average round-trip delay time $\bar{d}_r$, there is assumed to be a fixed number of messages $m$ on their way where $m\frac{1}{\lambda} \approx (\bar{d}_f + \bar{d}_b)$. In some sense, this assumption of a fixed number of messages with an exponentially distributed time spacing between them is analogous to using an Erlang distribution of $m$-phases to approximate the random round-trip delay of $d_r = d_f + d_b$. Let $\mathbf{S}(t) = [S(t-\tau_1)\ \ S(t-\tau_2)\ \ ...S(t-\tau_m)]$ represent the vector of $m$ feedback messages with the most recent message being $S(t-\tau_1)$ and the oldest message being $S(t-\tau_m)$. These feedback messages are instantaneous indicators of the congestion level. In the binary feedback based on queue threshold, $S(t-\tau_k) = 0$ if $Q(t-\tau_k) < K_T$ and $S(t-\tau_k) = 1$ if $Q(t-\tau_k) \geq K_T$ for all $1 \leq k \leq m$. In some sense, $\tau_1$ may be considered as the time that has elapsed since the most recent sample was sent and $\tau_m$ may be considered as the time since the oldest unreceived message has been sent. Thus, the next message to be received will be $S(t-\tau_m)$ after a time interval that is exponentially distributed with mean $\frac{1}{\lambda}$. The sequence of message generation instances (and message receipt instances) form a Poisson process with average rate $\lambda$.

In order to simplify the explanation, let us first consider only binary feedback based on the queue threshold $K_T$. Fig. 1 shows the source and feedback behaviour. The source shown in Fig. 1 is an on/off source whose response to a binary feedback message is as described earlier. The dynamics of the system are described below. An event may occur when any

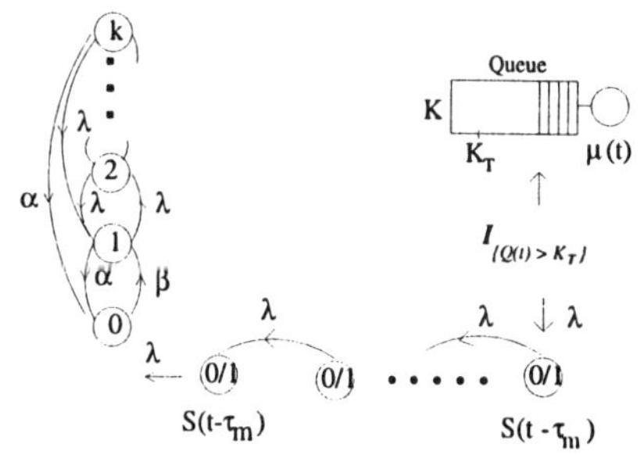


Figure 1: The feedback system behaviour for single traffic source.

of the following happen:

- The queue level $Q(t)$ may change: the queue level may decrease by 1 due to a service at rate $\mu(t)$, or increase by 1 due to an arrival at rate $\gamma(t-d_f)$.
- The available capacity $\mu(t)$ may change determined by $\mathbf{Q}_s$ and $\vec{\mu}_s$ for the service process.
- A new feedback message is received by the source and at the same time the queue level will be sampled to generate the latest feedback message. This occurs at rate $\lambda$. When the new message $S(t-\tau_m)$ is received, the vector $\mathbf{S}(t)$ makes a transition to $\mathbf{S}'(t)$ where $\mathbf{S}'(t) = [0\ \ S(t-\tau_1)\ \ S(t-\tau_2)...\ \ S(t-\tau_{m-1})]$ if $Q(t) < K_T$ or $\mathbf{S}'(t) = [1\ \ S(t-\tau_1)\ \ S(t-\tau_2)...\ \ S(t-\tau_{m-1})]$ if $Q(t) \geq K_T$. It is assumed that there is no delay between the message receipt at the source and the source response to that message. Thus, simultaneously with the above transition, the source also changes its transmission rate. In the above case if $S(t-\tau_m) = 0$ and the source is on, it changes its transmission state from $i$ to $min(i+1, k)$; if $S(t-\tau_m) = 1$, the source changes its transmission state to 1. In Fig. 1, state 1 represents the minimum transmission rate ($\gamma_{min}$) or MCR while state k represents the peak transmission rate ($\gamma_{max}$) or PCR when the source is on. If the feedback is not binary, then $S'(t-\tau_1)$ is the feedback message containing the explicit rate (depending on the available link capacity at the most recent time of feedback message generation). The source changes its transmission rate to that specified by the message. This may be modelled by discretizing the range of the link capacity to a certain finite number of values, each of which is represented by a state. Thus, if the avaliable link capacity varies over a range of $M$ discrete values, each feedback message $S(t-\tau_k)$ can take a value of $0, ..., M-1$.
- Independent of the feedback process, the traffic source may turn off (state 0) at rate $\alpha$ from any transmission state $1, .., k$. If the source is off, it may turn on at rate $\beta$ and start transmitting at $\gamma_{min}$ (state 1). The transition rate matrix of the Markov chain describing the source may be easily obtained from the above figure.

For $n$ traffic sources, each source may have its own vector $\mathbf{S}_k(t)$ associated with its feedback process. Thus, the sources are independent and their instances of message receipt are not synchronized. In other words, the instances of message generation at the node for different sources are also not synchronized. In this case, the $n$ Markov chains describing the state of the independent sources may be combined into a single Markov chain to represent the aggregate arrival process $\gamma(t)$. Let $\mathbf{Q}_k$ and $\mathbf{Q}$ be the transition rate matrices of the $k^{th}$ Markov chain and the aggregate Markov chain respectively. Then $\mathbf{Q} = \mathbf{Q}_1 \oplus \mathbf{Q}_2 \oplus ... \oplus \mathbf{Q}_n$, where $\oplus$ is the kronecker sum operator. If the dimension of the $k^{th}$ markov chain is $N_i$, the overall state space has dimension $N = N_1 \times N_2 \times ... \times N_n$ which grows rapidly with $n$. Similarly, the feedback vectors for all the traffic sources may be aggregated with $\mathbf{S}(t)$ representing the state of the aggregated feedback process. With the above description of the system, clearly $(Q(t), \gamma(t-d_f), \mu(t), \mathbf{S}(t))$ represents a continuous-time markov chain with generator $\mathbf{G}$. It may be noted that the arrival process $\gamma(t-d_f)$, server process $\mu(t)$ and the feedback process $\mathbf{S}(t)$ can also be described by an aggregate process $N(t)$ with generator $\mathbf{N}$. We thus have one composite process that describes the states of the traffic sources, the state of the server and the state of all the feedback information vectors. Given all the above assumptions, the system and its feedback dynamics can be described by the Markov process $(Q(t), N(t))$. The behaviour of the feedback information (the most recent feedback message $S(t-\tau_1)$) depends on whether the current queue level is above or below the given queue threshold $K_T$. Therefore the composite process $N(t)$ has a different generator $\mathbf{N}'$ when the current queue level is above the threshold $K_T$. Note that we may also use the same feedback vector with different positions to represent the oldest sample with respect to different sources (i.e the first to be received) as done in [11]. This causes a dramatic reduction in the size of the state space. However, it implies synchronism in message receipt among different connections. In this case, $\mathbf{Q}$ is not simply the kronecker sum as described above but can still be readily obtained. The synchronous assumption cannot model a situation where different feedback information is sent to different sources to satisfy some fairness or weighted fairness criteria. It also limits the maximum ratio of the delays suffered by two sources to $1 : m$. In our study, we compare the performances for synchronous and asynchronous feedback. If $N$ is the size of the state space of the aggregated traffic sources, $M$ the size of the state space of server and $m$ the length of the single feedback vector, then the aggregate process $N(t)$ has a state space of size $L = N \cdot M \cdot 2^m$ for binary feedback. For explicit rate notification $L = N \cdot M \cdot M^m$. To give some idea of the size of the state space for binary feedback with constant service rate ($M = 1$) and synchronous feedback, if $N = 16$, $m = 4$ and $K = 1024$, the total dimension of $\mathbf{G}$ is 262,144! Note that $N = 16$ may correspond to two heterogenous sources each of which has four adjustable transmission states. This large dimension of $\mathbf{G}$ motivates the use of efficient techniques for solving the steady-state and transient solutions of the system.

## 3 Analysis of the QBD System

Consider the Markov process $(Q(t), N(t))$ which describes the feedback system. The system can be considered as a finite Quasi-Birth-Death System (QBD) with finite generator $\mathbf{G}$ given by:

$$\mathbf{G} = \begin{bmatrix} (\mathbf{N}-\gamma_{dg}) & \gamma_{dg} & \mathbf{0}... & \\ \mu_{dg} & (\mathbf{N}-\gamma_{dg}-\mu_{dg}) & \gamma_{dg} & \mathbf{0}... \\ \ddots & \ddots & \ddots & \\ ...\mu_{dg} & (\mathbf{N}'-\gamma_{dg}-\mu_{dg}) & \gamma_{dg} & \mathbf{0}... \\ \ddots & \ddots & \ddots & \\ & ...\mathbf{0} & \mu_{dg} & (\mathbf{N}'-\mu_{dg}) \end{bmatrix}, \tag{1}$$

where $\gamma_{dg}$ and $\mu_{dg}$ are diagonol matrices containing the Poisson input rates and exponential service rates for each state of the composite process $N(t)$. The matrix $\mathbf{G}$ has dimension $L(K+1)$. It may be noted that in the above equation, the generator of the composite process is $\mathbf{N}'$ after level $K_T$. Our objective is to solve for the steady-state probability distribution of the queue and thus obtain the performance parameters of interest such as cell loss and throughput for each traffic type. As mentioned in the introduction, the block tri-diagonol structure of the matrix $\mathbf{G}$ lends itself easily to the solution for the steady-state distribution by the GFA. We can thus obtain all the above mentioned steady-state parameters of interest for the feedback system.

We apply the techniques developed in [16] to compute the transient queue distribution of the feedback system. This technique is now briefly described. The transient probability distribution is obtained as the solution of the matrix differential equation:

$$\frac{d}{dt}\vec{\pi}(t) = \vec{\pi}(0)\mathbf{G}, \qquad \vec{\pi}(0) = \vec{\pi}(t)|_{t=0} \tag{2}$$

where $\vec{\pi}(t) = [\pi_0(t)\ \pi_1(t)...]$ and $\vec{\pi}(0)$ is the initial probability distribution. Each $\pi_i(t) = [\pi_{i0}(t), ..., \pi_{i(L-1)}(t)]$ is the probability of being in level $i$ and phase $k$ for $k = 0$ to $L-1$ at time $t$. The solution for (2) is $\vec{\pi}(t) = \vec{\pi}(0)e^{\mathbf{G}t}$.

The large dimension of the matrix $\mathbf{G}$ precludes the use of any of the known methods for computing the matrix exponential ([17]). The Laplace Transform denoted by $\vec{\pi}^*(s)$ of the sequence $\vec{\pi}(t)$ exists for $Re\{s\} > 0$. The Laplace Transform of (2) may be expressed as:

$$\vec{\pi}^*(s)(s\mathbf{I} - \mathbf{G}) = \vec{\pi}(0). \tag{3}$$

The above equation represents a system of $L(K+1)$ linear equations with complex coefficients bearing the form: $\mathbf{xP} = \mathbf{a}$, where $(s\mathbf{I} - \mathbf{G})$ is a complex block tri-diagonol matrix. This expression lends itself easily to the form required by the GFA. The algorithm may be used to solve for $\vec{\pi}^*(s)$ for a series of values of $s$. Once $\vec{\pi}^*(s)$ has been computed at several discrete frequencies we may use any of the known techniques for the numerical inversion of Laplace Transforms. We chose the inversion method based on the Fourier Series expansion ([18]). Thus, $\vec{\pi}(t)$ may be obtained to any degree of accuracy.

This analysis can be extended to control based on multiple queue thresholds. We may wish to explore the possibility of two-level overload control for the feedback system. While this "hysteresial" scheme has been proposed by several researchers ([8],[9]), its performance has not been analyzed in the context of ABR traffic. In [9], the authors present some analysis on the two-level control scheme in a much simplified model of

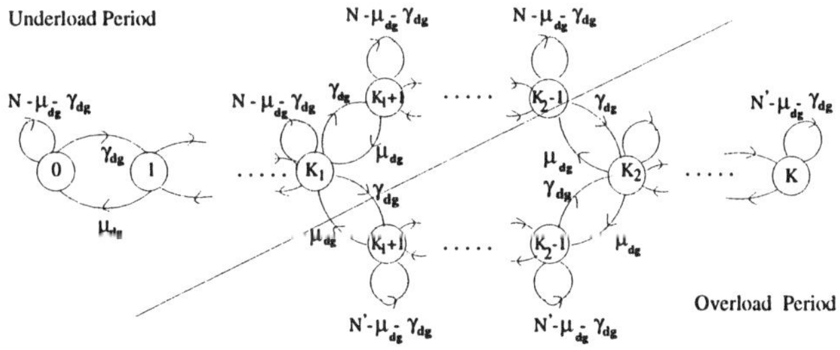

Figure 2: State Transition Diagram for the Overload Controlled System

a feedback system. They give some insight into the choice of the two thresholds for this model to optimize the system throughput. They compare the throughput of this two-level control policy with an open-loop policy subject to the same loss constraint. Our intent, however, is to compare the two-level control scheme with the single-level control in both the steady-state and transient regime.

Fig. 2 shows the state-transition diagram for a two-level overload control for the feedback system. The two thresholds are denoted by $K_1$ and $K_2$ as shown in the figure. The notion of congestion period is slightly different from the single threshold case described above. The congestion period starts from the instant the queue level exceeds $K_2$ and lasts until the level falls below $K_1$. As long as the system is in congestion, a feedback message of 1 is sent. This extends the congestion and non-congestion periods but it reduces their variance ([14]). This scheme is essential where the control-switching cost is not negligible. It may be observed that this system is not a QBD-system, hence the GFA cannot be directly applied without some modification. The analysis is carried out by partitioning the Markov chain describing the state of the system into overload (congestion) and underload (non-congestion) periods as shown in Fig. 2. Thus, the generator $\mathbf{G}$ may be partitioned as:

$$\mathbf{G} = \begin{bmatrix} \mathbf{G}_u & \mathbf{G}_{uo} \\ \mathbf{G}_{ou} & \mathbf{G}_o \end{bmatrix}, \qquad (4)$$

It may be noted that although the generator $\mathbf{G}$ no longer has the block tridiagonol structure as in a QBD process, the blocks $\mathbf{G}_u$ and $\mathbf{G}_o$ do have this special structure. The steady-state analysis of an overload controlled system based on this partitioning has already been done in [14]. The system is considered to be alternating between two transient processes and the steady-state probability distribution can be computed from the average sojourn times in each state of the two processes. Thus, the steady-state performance parameters for this overload controlled feedback system may be obtained. We now propose a new technique to compute the transient probability distribution for the system. Let $\vec{\pi}_u(t)$ and $\vec{\pi}_o(t)$ be the transient probabilities of being in the underload and overload states respectively. Thus, the overall transient probability distribution is represented by $\vec{\pi}(t) = [\vec{\pi}_u(t)\ \vec{\pi}_o(t)]$. The differential equation governing the evolution of the transient probabilities is:

$$\frac{d}{dt}[\vec{\pi}_u(t)\ \vec{\pi}_o(t)] = [\vec{\pi}_u(t)\ \vec{\pi}_o(t)]\mathbf{G}, \quad \vec{\pi}(0) = \vec{\pi}(t)|_{t=0}$$

$$\frac{d}{dt}\vec{\pi}_u(t) = \vec{\pi}_u(t)\mathbf{G}_u + \vec{\pi}_o(t)\mathbf{G}_{ou}$$

$$\frac{d}{dt}\vec{\pi}_o(t) = \vec{\pi}_o(t)\mathbf{G}_o + \vec{\pi}_u(t)\mathbf{G}_{uo}$$

Taking the Laplace Transform of the above equations:

$$\vec{\pi}_u^*(s)(s\mathbf{I} - \mathbf{G}_u) = \vec{\pi}_o^*(s)\mathbf{G}_{ou} + \vec{\pi}_u(0)$$

$$\vec{\pi}_o^*(s)(s\mathbf{I} - \mathbf{G}_o) = \vec{\pi}_u^*(s)\mathbf{G}_{uo} + \vec{\pi}_o(0).$$

We need to solve the above two equations iteratively for $\vec{\pi}_u^*(s)$ and $\vec{\pi}_o^*(s)$ at each $s$ employing the GFA in each iteration. The iterative procedure stops when the difference in values of $\vec{\pi}_o^*(s)$ and $\vec{\pi}_u^*(s)$ between successive iterations is less than a certain $\epsilon$. Thus, $\epsilon$ will determine the accuracy of the Laplace Transform computation. Once the Laplace Transform is computed for each $s$, it can be numerically inverted as before to obtain the time-dependent solutions. We will apply these techniques to solve for the steady-state and transient performance parameters of the feedback system.

## 4 Numerical Study

For our numerical study, we chose 2 sources with different round-trip delays at the same feedback rate $\lambda$. In most of the examples, unless otherwise stated, we use a single feedback message vector of length $m = 4$. Source 1 which is the nearer source uses the $S(t - \tau_1)$ as its next to be received sample whereas Source 2 which is the further source uses the $S(t-\tau_4)$ as its next to be received sample. In this synchronzed version of the feedback process, the length of the sample vector models the disparity in the round-trip delay for the two sources. Thus, the ratio between the round-trip delays is 1 : 4. On the other hand, the sources could have different feedback vectors to model an asynchronous version of their feedback process ([6]). We show some results for the asynchronous version as well. Our goal is to study the effect of the feedback delay on the loss and throughput performance of the two sources. Initially, we assume that the link capacity is fixed and the two sources are allowed to vary their transmission rates between $\gamma_{min}$ and $\gamma_{max}$. They do so in incremental steps of size $h$ on receipt of a 0 and jump to the minimum rate of $\gamma_{min}$ on receipt of a 1. All units for the time constants associated with the system are considered to be in terms of the average cell transmission time ($\Delta$) rather than absolute time. This is because of the scalability in the dynamics of the system with respect to the cell transmission time ([16]). Just to give a physical interpretation of the time constants associated with the system, let us assume that the output link is an OC-3 line of capacity 155 $Mbps$. The average transmission time for an ATM cell of 53 bytes is $\Delta = 2.8\mu s$. Thus, for $m = 4$ with the average delay between adjacent feedback messages $d = \frac{1}{\lambda} = 1000\Delta$, the average round-trip delay is $4000\Delta = 11.2ms$ for the further source and $1000\Delta = 2.8ms$ for the nearer source. Delays as large as this value may be seen in WAN network environments. Thus, we could adapt our parameters to suit various networking environments. We will frequently use the term time scales of the traffic sources and time scales of the underlying traffic. This describes the range of time over which these processes show significant correlation. The time scales of the traffic sources as well as those of the underlying traffic are also expressed in terms of

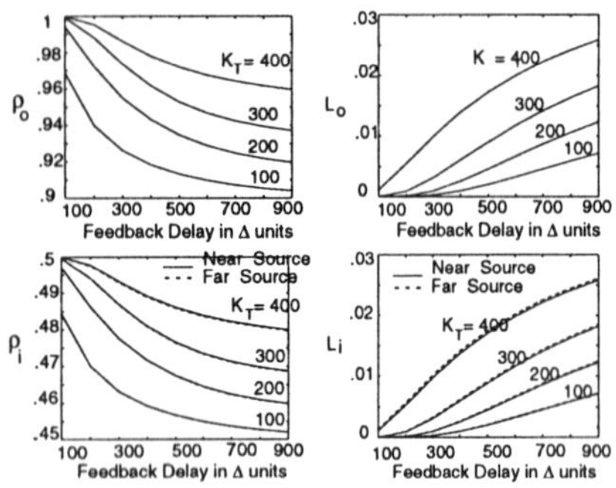


Figure 3: Effect of $d$ and $K_T$ on (a) $\rho_o$ (b) $L_o$ (c) $\rho_i$ and (d) $L_i$.

$\Delta$. The high priority underlying traffic may in general be VBR or CBR traffic which has very slow time-varying behaviour. Typically, if the CBR traffic are audio sources, their active/idle periods have time scales of the order $400ms$ and $600ms$ respectively. Similarly, the VBR traffic shows correlation over time scales as long as several hundred $ms$. These numbers correspond to time scales of the order of $10^5\Delta$ on an OC-3 link. Thus, all the time constants associated with the system may be conveniently expressed in terms of $\Delta$.

### 4.1 Stationary Behaviour

Initially, the sources are considered to be persistent, i.e., they are constantly transmitting data at the given rate with the cell interarrival times being exponentially distributed. The overall throughput of the system is interpreted as the probability of the system being non-empty. To calculate the individual throughputs, we compute the individual loss probabilities for each source from which we can compute the fraction of time spent transmitting cells of each source. Unless otherwise stated, the buffer size is fixed at $K = 512$. The threshold $K_T$ is varied between $100 - 400$, and the feedback is considered to be synchronous. We will use the following steady-state notations:

- $\rho_o$: Overall throughput of system, $\rho_i$: Individual throughput for each source
- $L_o$: Overall loss probability, $L_i$: Individual loss probability
- $d$: average delay between adjacent feedback messages
- $T_{sr}$: Time scales of the traffic sources $T_{sv}$: Time scales of the server process
- $K$: Buffer size, $K_T$: Queue threshold
- $\overline{\mu}_s$: average service rate, $\overline{q}$: Average queue level

**Effect of Round-trip Delay and Feedback Rate**

The round-trip delay may be changed by changing $d$ or $m$. In the study, $d$ is increased from $100\Delta$ to $900\Delta$ simultaneously for both sources, holding $m$ constant. The round-trip delay for the further source is 4 times that of the near source. The dynamic range for the transmission rates varies from $\gamma_{min} = 0.3\overline{\mu}_s$ to $\gamma_{max} = 0.6\overline{\mu}_s$ in increments of $h = 0.1\overline{\mu}_s$ for each source. Thus, the sources have a dynamic range of 4 transmission rates. The overall throughput $\rho_o$ is plotted in Fig. 3(a) for different $d$ and $K_T$. As may be expected, $\rho_o$ reduces as $d$ increases. Also, as $K_T$ increases, $\rho_o$ increases but at the cost of higher loss probabilities $L_o$ (Fig. 3(b)). Fig. 3(c) shows the individual throughputs $\rho_i$ and (d) shows the individual loss probabilities $L_i$. It is observed that in spite of the difference in the round-trip delays for the two sources, their $\rho_i$ are almost identical. Similarly, the difference in $L_i$ is also negligible with the closer source suffering a slightly better loss probability than the further source. Similar observations were made in the case of the two delay class sources in [11], where the sources alternate between two transmission rates. Thus, we see that fairness may not be an important consideration in the case of a single bottleneck node. In order to explore this further, we increase the dynamic range of transmission rates to $\gamma_{min} = 0.2\overline{\mu}_s$ and $\gamma_{max} = 0.8\overline{\mu}_s$ with $h = 0.2\overline{\mu}_s$. Fig. 4(a) and (b) shows the $\rho_o$ and $L_o$ for this increased dynamic range. A comparison of Fig. 3 and Fig. 4 shows the reduction in throughput and the increased loss rates achieved by the feedback. This shows that a better performance can be achieved if the sources vary their transmission rates over a smaller range with smaller increments. Also, some amount of unfairness is apparent with the nearer source achieving better throughput at a lower loss rate than the further source. Thus, in the interests of fairness as well as overall performance, the dynamic range of transmission rates should be kept small. So far, the sources were assumed to be synchronized in their receipt of feedback messages. In practice the feedback process to each source may not be synchronized. For ABR traffic, it would depend on the instances at which the RM cells of different connections arrive at the bottleneck node. In order to model this asynchronized version of the feedback process, we use different sample vectors for the two sources while keeping the ratio of the average round-trip delay the same as before viz. 1:4 and the same feedback rate $\lambda$ as that used in Figs. 3(a)-(d). The overall as well as in-

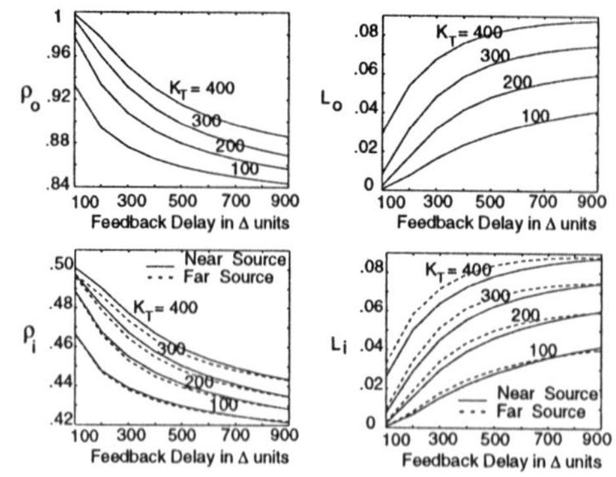


Figure 4: Effect of $(\gamma_{min}, \gamma_{max})$ on (a) $\rho_o$ (b) $L_o$ (c) $\rho_i$ and (d) $L_i$.

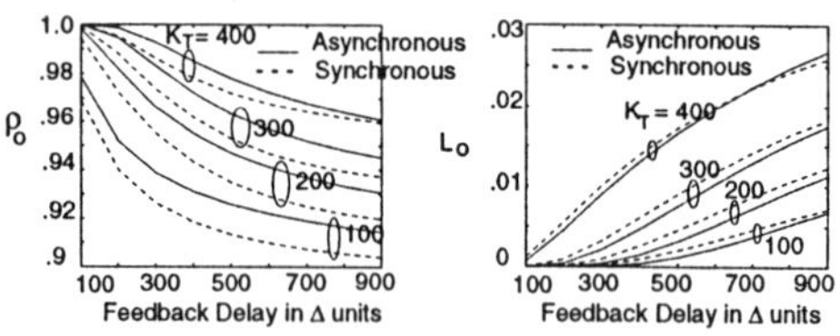


Figure 5: Effect of asynchronous feedback on (a) $\rho_o$ (b) $L_o$.

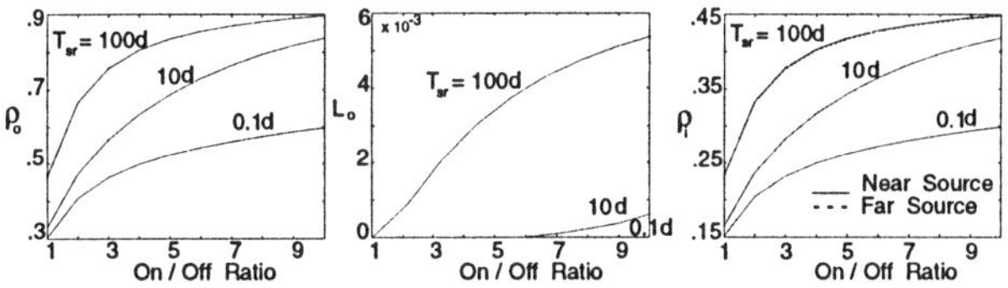


Figure 6: Effect of time scales of traffic sources on (a) $\rho_o$ (b) $L_o$ (c) $\rho_i$.

dividual statistics are plotted in Fig. 5. For the purpose of comparison, we have replotted the curves of Fig. 3(a) and (b) in Figs. 5(a)-(b). This shows that a slightly better $\rho_o$ can be achieved if the sources are not synchronized in their receipt of the feedback information. Asynchronism in feedback receipt also implies that the different sources may receive different feedback information depending on the instant at which the buffer level was observed for that source. This might mean some additional processing for the node which can be substantial if the number of active connections becomes large. The improvement in performance may be expected because by introducing the asynchronism in the sampling of the queue level, in effect the average time interval between the feedback samples for the overall system is reduced which results in better performance. Although asynchronous feedback does not significantly affect fairness in the two source case, its impact might be more apparent as the number of sources increases. Most analytical studies on feedback control with multiple delay classes assume that the feedback process is synchronous ([6],[11]). As the number of sources increases, we expect to see much better $\rho_o$ and $L_o$ with significant unfairness.

**Effect of Time Scales of Traffic Sources**

Next, we consider sources which have random active/idle periods. These periods are assumed to be exponentially distributed with mean $\frac{1}{\alpha}$ and $\frac{1}{\beta}$ respectively. In practice, these active/idle periods are associated with the window-flow control for the higher-layer protocol such as TCP. We vary the durations of the active period (time scales) from $0.1d$ to $100d$ where $d = 100\Delta$. The results are plotted for different ratios of on/off ranging from 1 to 10 in Fig. 6(a)-(c). The throughput for each source improves as the time scales of the active period relative to the round-trip delay increase, however at the cost of greater loss. It may be observed that the thoughput is substantially low when the time scales of the active period are small although it is at zero loss. This is because the source characteristics change several times between the receipt of feedback messages rendering them virtually useless. The time scales do not affect fairness (Fig. 6(c)).

Next, we explore the effect of different time scales ($T_{sr}$) for the two sources. These are three different cases:

**Case 1:** $T_{sr,1} = 0.1d$, $T_{sr,2} = d$, i.e. the nearer source has times scales smaller than the feedback delay but the further source has time scales which are comparable with the feedback delay.

**Case 2:** $T_{sr,1} = d$, $T_{sr,2} = 10d$, i.e. the nearer source has time scales which are comparable with the feedback delay but the further source has time scales which are 10 times that of feedback delay.

**Case 3:** $T_{sr,1} = d$, $T_{sr,2} = 0.1d$, i.e. the nearer source has time scales which are comparable with the feedback delay but the further source has time scales smaller than the feedback delay. We plot the individual $\rho_i$ with respect to different feedback delays for the above three cases in Fig. 7(a)-(c). All three cases are subject to a loss constraint of $10^{-5}$ in order to simplify the comparison. Obviously, the feedback process gives preferential treatment to the source whose time scales are comparable or larger than the feedback delay.

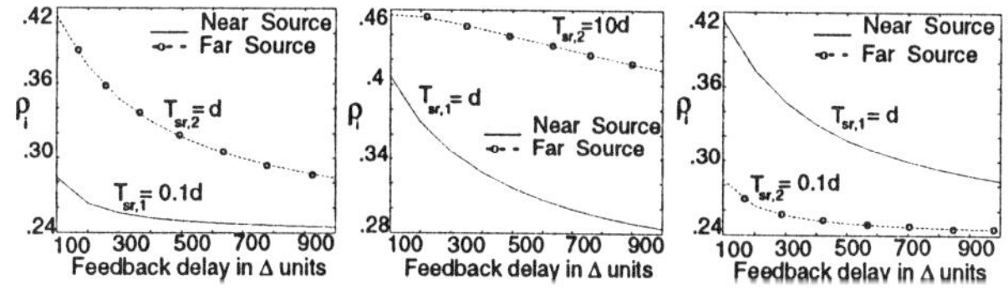


Figure 7: Effect of time scales of traffic sources on $\rho_i$ for (a) $T_{sr,1} = 0.1d$, $T_{sr,2} = d$ (b) $T_{sr,1} = d$, $T_{sr,2} = 10d$ and (c) $T_{sr,1} = d$, $T_{sr,2} = 0.1d$.

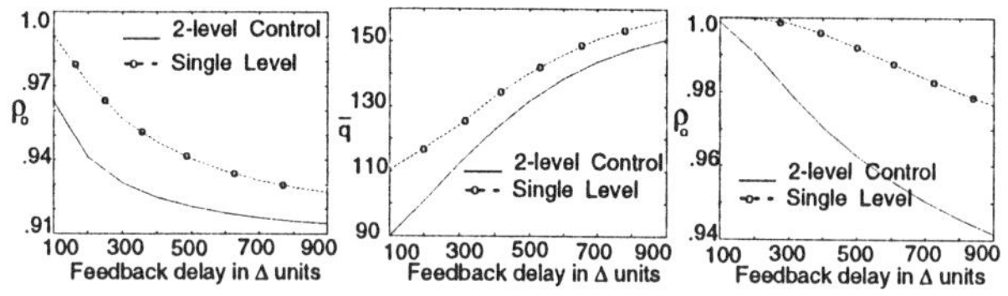


Figure 8: Comparision of 2-level control vs single level: (a)$\rho_o$ (b) $\overline{q}$ (c) $\rho_o$ ($K = 1024$).

**Two-level Congestion Control**

Next, we explore the effect of two-level control based on queue threholds. Our goal is to study this system for any performance improvement over the single-level control. The comparison is done subject to the same loss constraint of $10^{-5}$. We achieve this by the adjustment of the threshold level $K_T$ in the single level control. In Fig. 8(a), we plot the $\rho_o$ achieved by both two-level and single-level control given the same loss rate. The buffer size is taken to be $K = 512$ and the two control levels are set at $K_1 = 100$ and $K_2 = 250$. The feedback delay is varied from $100\Delta$ to $900\Delta$. For the above values of $K_1$ and $K_2$, $K_T$ is set in the range of $130 - 160$ depending on the feedback delay. We see that the two-level control does not have any advantage over the single-level in terms of the throughput. In fact, there is a negative effect due to the extended congestion and non-congestion periods which cause more cell loss. The two-level control does not however affect the fairness among the two sources. From Fig. 8(b), the average queue lengths $\overline{q}$ in the case of the single-level control scheme are seen to be somewhat higher than the two-level control scheme. The $\overline{q}$ affects the average queueing delay suffered by a cell. The ABR service is mainly used for delay-insensitive or delay-adpative traffic sources and hence the queueing delay is not an important issue in the comparison. In Fig. 8(c) we use a larger buffer $K = 1024$ with the two levels set to $K_1 = 200$ and $K_2 = 700$. Once again the performance of the system deteriorates in the two-level case given the same loss rates. Thus, the single level control scheme does consistently better than the two-level control.

**Effect of Underlying Traffic**

So far, we have assumed that the bandwidth available

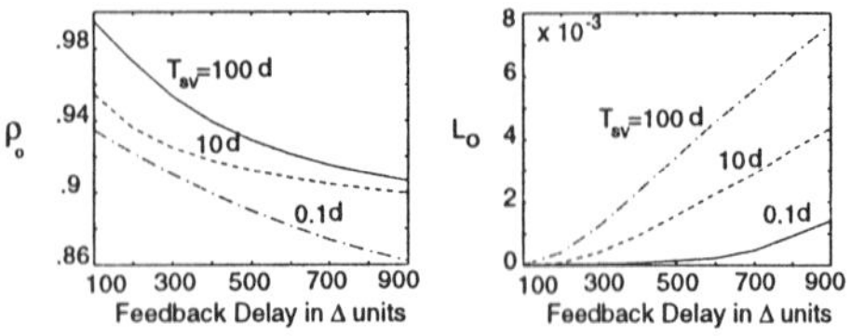


Figure 9: Effect of underlying traffic on (a)$\rho_o$ (b) $L_o$.

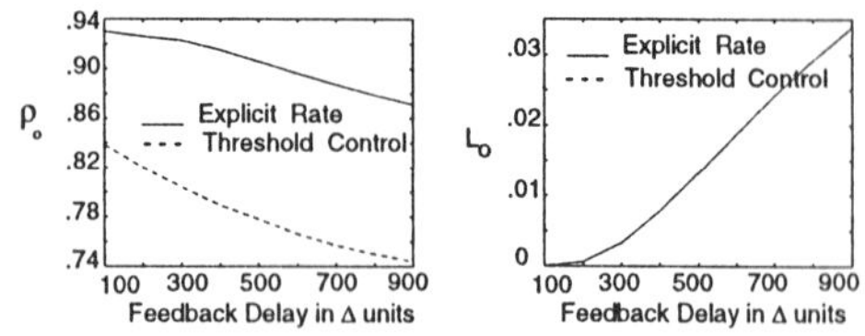


Figure 10: Comparision of binary feedback vs explicit rate notification for (a) $\rho_o$ (b) $L_o$.

for the ABR traffic is constant. This is not practical since the characteristics of the underlying high-priority traffic may be varying. For instance, this high-priority traffic could be real-time audio/video traffic. The variations in the available bandwidth may be very slow if the bandwidth is reserved on a connection level but may be faster if the bandwidth is reserved on the burst level. The burst level reservation is more interesting for bandwidth efficiency. This has not been studied before. We use a 5-state Markov Chain to represent the fluctuations in the available capacity. Its transition rate matrix has a single complex eigenvalue to characterize the time varying scales of the service process ([20])[2]. Our goal is to study the interplay between the time scales of the service process and those of the feedback process. As in the previous cases, we have two sources with different round-trip delays. The round-trip delays are in the ratio 1:4. The sources have the same behaviour as in the previous subsection, i.e. changing in the same dynamic range $(\gamma_{min}, \gamma_{max})$. The buffer size is taken to be $K = 1024$ with the threshold set to $K_T = 200$. The delay between messages is $d = 200\Delta$. The throughput and loss probabilities are computed with respect to $T_{sv} = 0.1d$, $10d$, $100d$, shown in Fig. 9(a) and (b). We observe that if the time scales are very small, a high throughput may be achieved at a small loss probability. The performance deteriorates as the time scales of the service process increase. When the time scales of the underlying traffic are very small, its fluctuations do not have much impact on the throughput. As the time scales of the service process increase, due to the long sojourn times in the overload states where the available link capacity can be consistently less than the arrival rate, the queue builds up quickly resulting in longer congestion periods and hence larger overall losses. Thus, the slow time scales of the service process have a detrimental effect on the queueing performance.

As mentioned earlier, there are several differences in the study of the time scales of the arrival process as compared to the study of the time scales of the service process. First of all, the time scales of the service process are independent of the buffer level and the feedback process. In the case of the arrival process, the time scales are those associated with the active/idle periods viz. $\alpha$, $\beta$ of the sources themselves as well as those induced by the feedback delay $d$ which is inherently tied to the buffer level. Therefore, the effectiveness of the feedback scheme depends on $\alpha$,$\beta$ relative to $d$. While we see an improvement in the throughput of the system as the source active/idle periods increase (at the cost of increased loss rates), we see a reduction in the throughput as the time scales of the service process increase. This may seem counter-intuitive as we would expect to see similar behaviour in both studies. This dissimilarity is due to the above mentioned independence property of the service process. The time scales of the service process have no significant effect on fairness.

**Explicit Rate Notification**

Another scheme that has been proposed for feedback-based control of ABR traffic is the explicit rate notification. In this scheme, the network explicitly provides the source with its allowed rate rather than with single-bit feedback ([3],[19]). Simulation studies have shown that this scheme results in improved throughput performance. We now investigate the performance of the explicit rate notification scheme using our stochastic model. The available capacity is modelled by a 5-state markov chain for which $T_{sv} = 10d$. We consider the effect of this scheme with only a single traffic source and the length of the feedback vector is $m = 2$. Each sample can take any of 5 possible values depending on the instantaneous available capacity. On receipt of the feedback message, the source modifies its rate to 90% of the available capacity. The throughput of this scheme is compared to the throughput obtained by the queue threshold based binary feedback, subject to the same loss probability. The values of $\gamma_{min}$ and $\gamma_{max}$ for the binary feedback have been chosen to obtain maximum achievable throughput for the same loss probability. The results are plotted in Fig. 10 for different values of feedback delay ranging from $100\Delta - 900\Delta$. In each case, we find that subject to the same loss constraint, the explicit rate notification scheme performs better than the single-bit feedback scheme. The explicit rate notification however means more computational complexity for the node. For highly correlated underlying traffic such as real-time video, the improved throughput may justify the additional complexity.

## 4.2 Transient Behaviour

Our transient analysis of the feedback scheme focuses on the transient average transmission rate $\overline{\gamma}(t)$ of each source and the transient average queue length $\overline{q}(t)$.

**Stochastic vs Deterministic System Behaviour**

Before the comprehensive study of the transient behaviour, we would like to compare the transient performance of a system having deterministic feedback delays to a system having exponential feedback delays. The results for deterministic delays are obtained through simulation while those for the stochastic case are obtained through the numerical procedure outlined in Section 3. The system under consider-

[2] The autocorrelation function for the markov chain with single complex eigenvalue is characterized by $R(\tau) = \psi e^{\lambda\tau}$, where $\lambda$ is complex. The normalized eigenvalue $\frac{\lambda}{2\pi\mu_s}$ which is directly associated with the average sojourn times in each state of the markov chain (relative to the cell transmission time $\Delta$) represents the time scales $T_{sv}$ of the process. We use this interpretation for time scales.

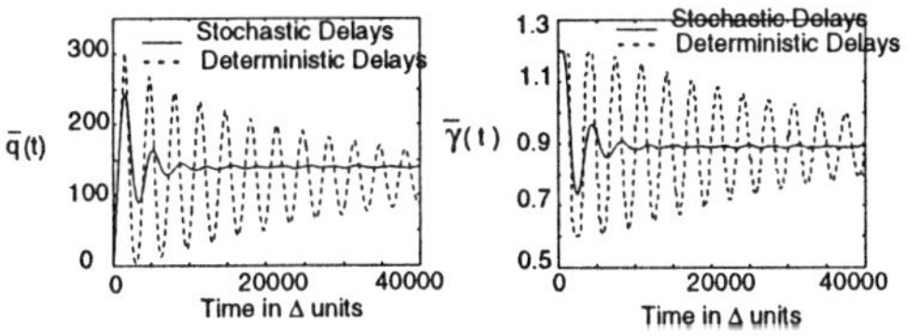


Figure 11: Comparision of deterministic vs stochastic delays for (a) $\overline{q}(t)$ (b) $\overline{\gamma}(t)$.

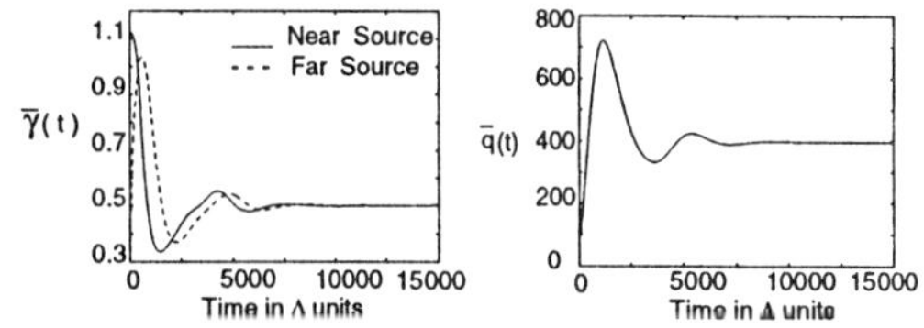


Figure 12: Effect of initial conditions for $d = 200\Delta$, $K_T = 200$ on (a) $\overline{\gamma}(t)$ (b) $\overline{q}(t)$.

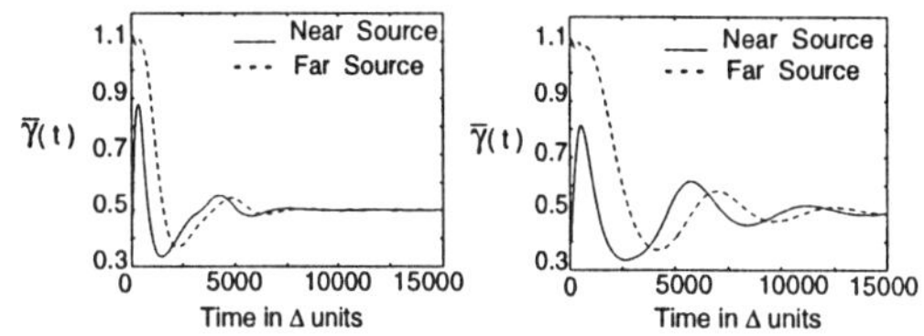


Figure 13: Effect of initial conditions for $K_T = 200$ on (a) $\overline{\gamma}(t)$ for $d = 200\Delta$ (b) $\overline{\gamma}(t)$ for $d = 400\Delta$.

ation is simple. We consider a single source with $d = 250\Delta$ and $m = 4$, which transmits at $\gamma_{max} = 1.2\overline{\mu}_s$ upon receipt of feedback 0 and transmits at $\gamma_{min} = 0.6\overline{\mu}_s$ upon receipt of feedback 1. Initially, the source is at $\gamma_{max}$ and the buffer is empty. We measure the $\overline{q}(t)$ and $\overline{\gamma}(t)$ for both the systems in Fig. 11(a) and (b) respectively. The deterministic system is highly unstable while the stochastic system converges much faster in the stochastic sense. Yet, the steady-state values of the two systems are almost identical. This observation tells us that randomness to some degree leads to stability of the feedback scheme. While the period of oscillations is almost the same, the peak overshoots for the stochastic system tend to reduce faster than the corresponding deterministic system. A similar observation was made by the authors of [6] where they found by simulations that adding a random exponential component to the deterministic delays led to a system with no oscillations. This is important because devising new schemes for feedback or evaluating old ones in a deterministic framework may be very different from the stochastic framework. Random feedback delays is also a more realistic scenario of the actual feedback process especially in congested networks since the message then experiences variable queueing delays at intermediate nodes.

### Effect of Initial Conditions

An interesting case study is when one source is at $\gamma_{max}$ while the other source is just activated (i.e. starting at $\gamma_{min}$). We are interested in knowing how long it takes for the two rates to converge to their steady-state. This will depend on several factors such as which source is at the higher transmission rate, the ratio of the round-trip delays, the dynamic range of the transmission rates and so on.

We consider a simple scenario in which the two sources transmit at one of two possible transmission rates $\gamma_{min} = 0.3\overline{\mu}_s$ and $\gamma_{max} = 1.1\overline{\mu}_s$. Assume that the buffer is initially empty, the near source is at $\gamma_{max}$ while the farther source is at $\gamma_{min}$. The ratio of the round-trip delays is 1:4 and $d = 200\Delta$. The buffer size is taken to be 1024 with the threshold set at $K_T = 200$. We used a larger buffer size in the transient study since we desired to study the fairness issue in the transient case subject to a loss constraint less than $10^{-5}$. The initial value of the sample vector $\mathbf{S}(t) = [0\ 0\ 0\ 0]$, i.e. it is assumed that the system has been uncongested at the past four sampling instants. Unless otherwise stated we keep the same initial conditions and values for $K$, $\gamma_{min}$, $\gamma_{max}$ and $m$ throughout the transient study. Fig. 12 shows the $\overline{\gamma}(t)$ of the two sources and $\overline{q}(t)$. The $\overline{\gamma}(t)$ and $\overline{q}(t)$ display an oscillatory behaviour which is related to the round-trip delays of the two sources. We observe that the scheme is still fair in that the $\overline{\gamma}(t)$ for one traffic source is just a delayed version of that for the second traffic source. The peak transmission rate for each source before they equalize is almost the same. Now we consider slightly different initial conditions: the farther source is transmitting at the $\gamma_{max}$ while the near source is just activated transmitting at $\gamma_{min}$. The $\overline{\gamma}(t)$ for the two sources are plotted in Fig. 13(a) for $K_T = 200$. As compared to Fig. 12(a), we find that although the time taken to converge is about the same, the farther source has a larger share of the available bandwidth until the two finally equalize at steady-state. The near source never achieves the same peak transmission rate as enjoyed by the farther source. Thus, in some sense this could be considered unfairness in the transient system. For a larger feedback delay $d = 400\Delta$, this unfairness is more evident (Fig. 13(b)). Thus, although it is often argued that in steady-state, the nearer sources tend to achieve better throughput, the farther sources may enjoy better thoughput in transience especially if the farther source has been active for a while with the near source just activated.

### Effect of Two-level Overload Control

In this final section, we would like to examine the transient behaviour of the two-level overload controlled system. We have two sources alternating between the same $\gamma_{max}$ and $\gamma_{min}$. We consider $K = 1024$, $K_1 = 175$ and $K_2 = 300$ and $d = 200\Delta$. The value of $K$, $K_1$ and $K_2$ were chosen so as to keep the loss constraint of $10^{-5}$. The $\overline{\gamma}(t)$ and $\overline{q}(t)$ for the system are plotted in Fig. 14(a) and (b) repectively. As compared to Fig. 12(a) and (b), we find that the two-level controlled feedback system converges much slower than the single-level controlled system. Also the peak value of $\overline{q}(t)$ is higher for the two-level controlled system since the congestion period gets extended. Thus, we see that even in the transient case, the single level of control does better than the two-level control. The scheme is fair in that the curve $\overline{\gamma}(t)$ for one source is simply a delayed version of the other.

Similar to the steady-state behaviour, the effects of the time scales of the traffic sources and the underlying traffic on the transient system have been studied. These results may be obtained from our web-site([21]).

One fact that is evident from this study is that the time

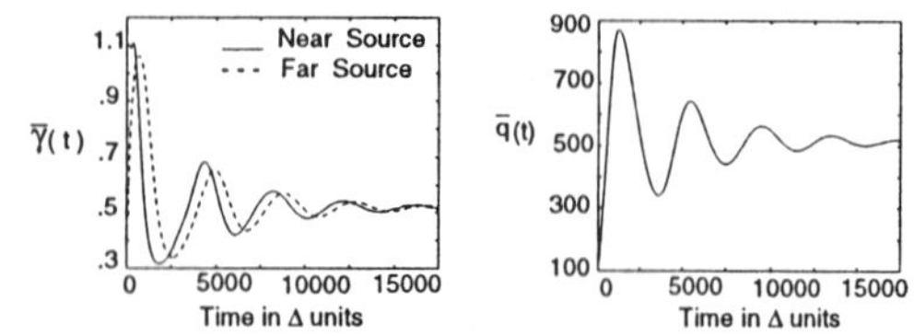


Figure 14: Effect of two-level control on (a) $\overline{\gamma}(t)$ (b) $\overline{q}(t)$.

scales of the overall feedback system have a dominant effect on its steady-state and transient performance.

## 5 Conclusion

In this paper we have presented a Quasi-Birth-Death model for the rate-based feedback system which can be numerically solved for various steady-state and transient solutions. We studied the effect of the different time constants associated with the system, viz. the feedback delay, the time scales of the source active/idle periods and the time scales of the underlying traffic. Our study shows that the longer time scales dominate both the steady-state and the transient performance of the system. We see that fairness is not an issue in steady-state for a single congested node. However, depending on the initial conditions it can be an issue in the transient regime. The study of a two-level controlled feedback system shows that due to the extension of the overload and underload periods, the throughput performance deteriorates. We have seen that asynchronism in feedback results in better system performance but may lead to some potential unfairness. In the presence of underlying high priority traffic, the comparison of the performance of a system using binary feedback based on the queue threshold vs a system using explicit rate notification shows that better throughput can be achieved in the latter. This is especially true when the underlying traffic has slow time varying scales. We would like to point out an important fact in the stochastic analysis of the feedback system viz. randomness in the feedback delays adds stability to an oscillating system. While the equivalent deterministic system may never converge (or converge very slowly), the stochastic system converges much faster.

## References

[1] K. Ramakrishnan and R. Jain, "A Binary Feedback Scheme for Congestion Avoidance in Computer Networks," *ACM Trans. Comput. Sys.*, 1990, vol. 8, no. 2, pp. 158-181.

[2] P. Newman, "Traffic Management for ATM Local Area Networks," *IEEE Comm. Mag.*, 1994, vol. 32, no. 8, pp. 44-50.

[3] A. Charny, D. Clark, R. Jain, "Congestion Control with Explicit Rate Indication," *Proc. ICC'95*, June 1995.

[4] R. Jain, S. Kalyanaraman, R. Vishwanathan, "The OSU Scheme for Congestion Avoidance using Explicit Rate Indication," OSU-CISRC-1/96-TR02, Jan. 1996.

[5] F. Bonomi and K. Fendick, "The rate-based flow control framework for the available bit rate ATM service," *IEEE Network Mag.*, Mar/Apr. 1995, pp. 25-39.

[6] F. Bonomi, D. Mitra and J. Seery, "Adaptive Algorithm for Feedback-Based Flow Control in High-Speed, Wide-Area ATM Networks," *IEEE J. Select. Areas on Commun.*, Sept. 1995, vol. 13, no. 7, pp. 1267-1283.

[7] M. Hluchyj and N. Yin, "On Closed-loop Rate Control for ATM Networks," *Proc. of IEEE INFOCOM'94*, 1994, pp. 99-108.

[8] H. Ohsaki, M. Murata, H. Suzuki, C. Ikeda and H. Miyahara, "Rate-Based Congestion control for ATM Networks," *Proc. ACM Sigcomm*, 1994.

[9] Y. T. Wang and B. Sengupta, "Performance Analysis of a feedback Congestion Control policy under nonnegligible propogation delay," *Proc. ACM Sigcomm,91*, 1991.

[10] R. Pazhyannur and R. Agarwal, "Feedback-Based Flow Control of B-ISDN/ATM Networks," *IEEE J. Select. Areas on Commun.*, Sept. 1995, vol. 13, no. 7, pp. 1252-1266.

[11] R. Pazhyannur and R. Agarwal, "Feedback-Based Flow Control in ATM Networks with Multiple Propogation Delays," *Proc. of IEEE INFOCOM'96*, 1996, vol. 2, pp. 585-593.

[12] J. Rubin and K. Lin, "A burst-level adaptive input-rate flow control scheme for ATM networks," *Proc. of IEEE INFOCOM'93*, 1993, pp. 386-394.

[13] T. Tedijanto and L. Gun, "Effectiveness of dynamic bandwidth management techniques in ATM networks," *Proc. of IEEE INFOCOM'93*, 1993, pp. 358-367.

[14] W. Lau and S. Q. Li, "Sojourn-time Analysis of Nodal Congestion in Broadband Networks and its Impact on QoS Specifications," *Proc. of IEEE INFOCOM'96*, 1996, pp. 1327-1337.

[15] S. Q. Li and H. Sheng, "A Generalized Folding Algorithm for Transient Analysis of Finite QBD Processes and its Queueing Applications," *Computations with Markov Chains, Proc. of the 2nd International Workshop on the Numerical Solution of Markov Chains*, 1995, edited by W. Stewart, pp. 463-482.

[16] L. Kulkarni and S.Q.Li "Transient Behaviour of Queueing Systems with Correlated Traffic," *Performance Evaluation*, vol. 27, 28, 1996, pp. 117-145.

[17] C. Moler, and C. Loan, "Nineteen Dubious ways to Compute the Exponential of a Matrix," *SIAM Rev.* Vol. 20, No. 4, Oct. 1978, pp. 801-836.

[18] F. Durbin, "Numerical Inversion of Laplace Transforms: An Efficient Improvement to Dubner and Abate's Method," *Comput. J*, vol. 17 (4) 1973, pp. 371-376.

[19] K. Y. Siu and H. Tzeng, "Adaptive Proportional Rate Control for ABR Service in ATM Networks," UC Irvine Technical Report No. 1102, Electrical and Computer Engineering, July 1994.

[20] S. Q. Li and C. L. Hwang, "Queue Response to Input Correlation Functions: Continuous Spectral Analysis," *IEEE/ACM Trans. Networking*, Vol. 1, No. 6, Dec. 1993, pp. 678-692.

[21] S.Q.Li, *http://mocha.ece.utexas.edu/ sanqi/papers.html.*

# An ABR Feedback Control Scheme with Tracking


*Cathy Fulton*
Austin Product Center-Research, Schlumberger
8311 N.FM 620, Austin, TX 78726

*San-qi Li*
Department of Electrical and Computer Engineering
The University of Texas at Austin, Austin, TX 78712

*Chang Soo Lim*
Communication Systems R&D Center
Samsung Electronics Co., Ltd



## Abstract

We propose an explicit-rate ABR feedback control scheme, UT (Uniform Tracking). The distinct feature of UT is that it achieves max-min fairness by tracking an effective number of sources; specific constraint information is not required. As a result, its implementation is much simpler than that of other fair control schemes; indeed, its complexity is similar to that of *unfair* explicit-rate controls. In the thorough simulation study, UT demonstrates its ability to scale with speed, distance, number of users (both persistent and bursty), and number of switches while remaining robust, efficient, and fair under stressing conditions with MPEG background traffic and multiple propagation delay loops.


## 1 Introduction

The ATM Forum Traffic Management Specification currently defines five different service classes to support the diverse requirements of multimedia traffic [1]: Constant Bit Rate (CBR), Real-Time Variable Bit Rate (RT-VBR), Non-Real-Time Variable Bit Rate (NRT-VBR), Available Bit Rate (ABR), and Unspecified Bit Rate (UBR). Both CBR and RT-VBR service classes provide stringent cell transmission delay (CTD), cell delay variation (CDV), and cell loss ratio (CLR) constraints. NRT-VBR service provides stringent CTD and CLR constraints but no CDV guarantees. These three classes rely on the network reservation of resources in order to provide the required quality of service (QoS).

ABR and UBR service classes are defined to increase network efficiency above that which can be achieved from reservation-based service alone. Separate logical buffers are provided to ensure that traffic belonging to these "reservationless" service classes does not interfere with the QoS of CBR and VBR traffic. UBR service is truly "best-effort" – the network provides no service guarantees. The problem with UBR service is that cell losses may result in retransmissions which further increase congestion resulting in more losses; the bulk of the UBR load may eventually be retransmissions.

To address the problem of inefficiency resulting from excessive loss, the ABR service class was defined. This service class guarantees a minimal (but unspecified) CLR through a feedback control mechanism and call admission; it is the only service class that uses feedback. The control scheme operates in the following manner. Each ABR source regularly generates Resource Management (RM) cells which are modified by the switches as they pass through the network. The modified RM cells are returned to the source which adjusts its transmission rate appropriately.

The specifics of this feedback control have not been determined; however, the ATM Forum has agreed on a set of criteria on which proposed control schemes will be judged. These criteria include the following: [1]

1. It must scale with speed, distance, number of users, and number of switches.
2. It must be fair to the different ABR sources.
3. It must be robust to minor perturbations and noncompliant sources.
4. It must converge to steady-state.
5. It must be easy to implement in a heterogeneous environment without requiring a specific switch architecture.
6. It must efficiently utilize resources with minimal buffer requirements.

The interested reader may refer to [2]–[4] for additional information on ABR traffic.

## 2 Contribution

This paper proposes an explicit-rate ABR feedback control scheme, Uniform Tracking (UT), which appears to satisfy the criteria established by the ATM Forum. The distinct feaure of UT is that it achieves max-min fairness automatically by tracking an effective number of sources, $N_{eff}$; the tracking allows each




0-8186-7780-5/97 $10.00 © 1997 IEEE

switch to deduce global information (number of active sources, bottlenecks and other constraints) in a distributed fashion. Since UT does not need to explicitly determine the number of sources or constraint information, its implementation is much simpler than that of other fair control schemes; indeed, its complexity is similar to that of *unfair* explicit-rate controls.

A discrete-event simulator is used to evaluate the performance of UT. To demonstrate that UT scales with speed, link capacities of 1.544 Mbps, 44.736 Mbps, 150 Mbps, and 622 Mbps are included. To indicate that UT scales with distance, the sources have different round-trip propagation delays ranging from 3–70 ms. To show that UT scales with number of users, 2–200 ABR sources compete for bandwidth. To illustrate that UT scales with number of switches, 1–10 switches are considered. The robustness of UT is tested by simultaneous activating all ABR sources with 1–30 MPEG sources as background traffic; in different cases the ABR sources may be persistent or bursty, constrained or unconstrained. The efficiency of UT is compared to the explicit-rate scheme OSU. Convergence and fairness of UT is evaluated both with and without background traffic.

This paper is organized in the following manner. Previously proposed control schemes are reviewed in Section 3. The new UT scheme is described in Section 4, a thorough single-switch simulation study is provided in Section 5, and a multiple-switch simulation study is contained in Section 6. This paper is then concluded in Section 7.

## 3 Background

The traffic descriptors for an ABR source are its Cell Delay Variation Tolerance (CDVT), Peak Cell Rate (PCR), and Minimum Cell Rate (MCR). We assume the network call admission policy will treat the MCR as a PCR for CBR service; feedback from the network will thus apply only to the rate above the MCR. We interpret fairness to mean that the sources which are using the least bandwidth above their MCR are receiving as much as they can use (max-min allocation above the MCR). Since the MCR is easily handled in this fashion, we will not mention it further. For scalability, we also assume each ABR source generates one RM cell after every $N_{RM}$ data cells rather than periodically with time; the RM cell traffic is thus $\frac{1}{N_{RM}}$ of the total ABR traffic irrespective of the number of sources.

A number of ABR control schemes have been proposed over the years simply because none have been entirely satisfactory. It is in general very difficult for a scheme to be efficient, fair, and practical to implement. In this section we review some common approaches to ABR feedback control. Since achieving fairness is an issue with all the schemes, we first begin with a discussion of max-min allocation in a multiple-switch network.

### 3.1 Max-Min Fairness

An active ABR source has data to transmit. A persistent source is always active; a bursty source alternates between periods of activity and inactivity. The Fair Share ($FS$) computed at a switch is the bandwidth allocated to each source in order to achieve max-min fairness. An unconstrained source can achieve the $FS$; a constrained source can not achieve $FS$ either because of physical (e.g., PCR) or network (e.g., bottleneck) limitation. An unconstrained environment is a network with only unconstrained sources from the reference point of a bottleneck switch; a constrained environment has at least one constrained source. A compliant source behaves within the guidelines specified by the control scheme.

Suppose there are $N_{tot}$ active ABR sources competing for $C_{avail}$, the current capacity available for ABR traffic. Let $N_{con}$ be the number of constrained sources and let $C_{con}$ be the capacity achievable by the constrained sources. The Fair Share rate is then defined by

$$FS = \frac{C_{avail} - C_{con}}{N_{tot} - N_{con}}. \tag{1}$$

For max-min fairness, the $N_{con}$ constrained sources should each send at their maximum permitted rates and the unconstrained sources should each transmit at $FS$. To determine how closely max-min fairness is achieved by a control scheme, we define the Fairness Metric ($\varepsilon_{FS}$) as

$$\varepsilon_{FS} = \sqrt{\frac{1}{N_{tot}} \sum_{i=1}^{N_{tot}} \left( \frac{\hat{r}_{A_i} - \bar{r}_{A_i}}{\hat{r}_{A_i}} \right)^2}, \tag{2}$$

where $\bar{r}_{A_i}$ and $\hat{r}_{A_i}$ are respectively the achieved and the max-min fair rate (time functions or averages) of the $i^{th}$ ABR source. To measure the efficiency of a control scheme, we define the Efficiency Metric ($\varepsilon_{\eta}$) as

$$\varepsilon_{\eta} = \frac{q_{max} - q_{B_{max}}}{\rho - \rho_B}, \tag{3}$$

where $q_{max}$ is the zero-loss buffer requirement, $q_{B_{max}}$ is the zero-loss buffer requirement for the background (CBR, VBR) traffic alone, $\rho$ is the total achieved load, and $\rho_B$ is the load achieved by the background traffic.

For a switch to determine $FS$, it must have a method of estimating $N_{tot}$, $C_{avail}$, $N_{con}$, and $C_{con}$. While $C_{avail}$ is readily measured, determination of $N_{tot}$ may not be easy in a realistic environment with bursty sources. It is not at all clear how $N_{con}$ and $C_{con}$ might be determined in practice. At best, the direct computation of $FS$ in a constrained environment adds a great deal of complexity.

### 3.2 Single-Bit Feedback

One class of proposed ABR control schemes uses single-bit feedback. While there are a number of variations, the basic procedure is as follows. The RM (or data) cells contain a Congestion Indicator (CI) bit which is initialized to 0 by each ABR source. If a switch along the route detects congestion, it sets CI=1. An ABR source decreases its rate by a multiplicative factor, the Rate Decrease Factor (RDF), until it receives a returned RM cell with CI=0. Upon receiving this positive feedback indicating no congestion along the route, the source increases its rate by an incremental amount, the Additive Increase to Rate (AIR). Both AIR and RDF are network default parameters. [2, 3, 5].

### 3.3 Explicit-Rate Feedback

To achieve more rapid convergence and offer greater flexibility in switch design, explicit-rate feedback schemes have been proposed [6]. Rather than simply indicating congestion existence with a single bit, the switches provide direct rate information to the ABR sources in the Explicit Rate (ER) field of the RM cell. The ABR sources can thus reach a near-optimal rate within a few round trips.

#### 3.3.1 OSU

The OSU [7] is a popular explicit-rate control scheme with the following behavior. A switch computes a load factor ($LF$) which is simply the ratio of the measured total ABR rate $r_A(n)$ divided by the difference between the threshold rate $\rho_T C$, where $\rho_T$ denotes a targeted utilization and $C$ denotes the link capacity, and the total background (CBR and VBR) rate $r_B(n)$:

$$LF = \frac{r_A(n)}{\rho_T C - r_B(n)}.$$

If $|LF - 1| > \Delta$, where $\Delta$ is a small fraction, then the switch writes the $LF$ in the ER field if it is larger than the presently stored value. If $|LF - 1| \leq \Delta$, the switch must compute the Fair Share where $C_{avail} = \rho_T C - r_B(n)$. As with the binary schemes, it is not clear how $C_{con}$, $N_{tot}$, and $N_{con}$ will be obtained.

For those ABR sources whose current rate is larger than the $FS$, the switch writes the value $\frac{LF}{1-\Delta}$ in the ER field if it is larger than the presently stored value. For those ABR sources whose current rate is smaller than the $FS$, the switch writes the value $\frac{LF}{1+\Delta}$ in the ER field if it is larger than the presently stored value. Upon receiving a returned RM cell, ABR sources adjust their rate by dividing their current rate by the ER value.

The advantage of the OSU scheme is that near-optimal bandwidth utilization can be achieved rapidly under certain conditions. The scheme is sensitive to high-frequency fluctuations, but this can be easily corrected by using the low-pass filtered rate $r_B(n)$ in the computation of $LF$ and $FS$. Fairness can only be achieved if the environment is relatively stable so that the $LF$ will be within $\Delta$ of 1 for a sufficiently long period of time. Fairness also relies on an accurate computation of $FS$; as we discussed in Section 3.1, this is a non-trivial task. Without fairness, the scheme is relatively simple to implement but does require that the sources be able to divide; with fairness, scheme complexity is certainly an issue. A major concern with the OSU scheme is stability, or more precisely lack thereof. As we see in the simulation study, the scheme may destabilize in the presence of background traffic and multiple round-trip delays.

#### 3.3.2 H2

The recently proposed H2 scheme [8] investigates ABR feedback in terms of traditional control theory for the case when there is a single congested switch and all ABR sources are persistent, unconstrained, and compliant. The H2 switch computes the $FS = \frac{\rho_T C - \tilde{r}_B(n)}{N_{tot}}$ and writes it to the RM cell ER field; the ABR sources simply set their rate equal to the ER value in the returned RM cells (no division). The $FS$ must be calculated using the low-pass filtered background rate $\tilde{r}_B(n)$ in order to provide stability. By explicitly assigning the Fair Share to each source, stability can be guaranteed under such conditions in the presence of multiple delay loops.

The contribution of this scheme is that it considers ABR feedback in a control-theory framework and demonstrates the conditions under which stability can be guaranteed in an unconstrained environment with persistent sources. How to handle a more realistic environment is not addressed. While OSU can operate (unfairly) without a $FS$ computation, H2 obviously can not.

## 4 UT

We propose a new scheme, UT, that addresses some of the difficulties observed with other feedback controls. The distinct feature of UT is that it achieves max-min fairness without requiring explicit knowledge of the number of active sources $N_{tot}$, the number of active constrained sources $N_{con}$, or the capacity achievable by the constrained sources $C_{con}$. Instead, UT tracks an effective number of active sources based on the current measured ABR rate and a moving average of previously assigned rates; max-min fairness is achieved automatically.

Each control interval the UT switch computes an effective Fair Share, $FS_{eff}$; this $FS_{eff}$ is written to the ER field of an RM cell if it is smaller than the presently stored value. Define $\tilde{FS}_{eff}$ to be a moving average of previously assigned $FS_{eff}$'s; this average should be taken over the maximum expected round-trip delay time of the ABR sources. The effective Fair Share is computed by

$$FS_{eff} = \frac{\rho_T C - \tilde{r}_B(n)}{N_{eff}} \tag{4}$$

where the effective number of sources $N_{eff}$ is tracked by

$$N_{eff} = \max\left\{\frac{r_A(n)}{\tilde{FS}_{eff}}, 1\right\}. \tag{5}$$

For faster tracking, the number of new sources admitted (terminated) during a control interval could conceivably be directly added (subtracted) to $N_{eff}$ if desired; this feature is *not* implemented in the following simulation study.

To minimize buffer requirements in the event that a large number of sources simultaneously go active, it may be desirable for each source to limit its rate of increase by an additive increment, AIR, negotiated during call admission. That is, an EFCI-type bound may be imposed on the rate of increase to give UT switches sufficient time to track the effective number of sources. Providing such ramping is optional but may improve performance. In either event, new sources should initially transmit at some small rate until they receive their first RM cell.

### 4.1 Discussion

To understand how UT achieves max-min fairness, let the system be in steady-state with $\tilde{r}_B(n)$ constant and $FS_{eff} = \tilde{FS}_{eff}$; for convenience, define $R \equiv \rho_T C - \tilde{r}_B(n)$. From (4) and (5), $r_A(n) = R$; the ABR sources use all available bandwidth. Assume there are $N_{tot}$ active ABR sources, $r_A(n) = \sum_{i=1}^{N_{tot}} r_{A_i}(n) \leq N_{tot} \times FS_{eff}$. If $r_A(n) = N_{tot} \times \tilde{FS}_{eff}$, each ABR source is transmitting at $FS_{eff}$ so max-min fairness is achieved; this is simply H2 control. If $r_A(n) < N_{tot} \times FS_{eff}$, there exists at least one constrained source $l$; this constraint could be of either source (PCR) or network (bottleneck) origin. Since $FS_{eff} > r_{A_l}(n)$, every constrained source will transmit at its maximum possible rate. Since $r_A(n) = \sum_{i=1}^{N_{tot}} r_{A_i}(n) = R$, the unconstrained sources transmitting at $FS_{eff}$ will use all extra bandwidth equally. Thus if steady-state is reached, max-min fairness is achieved without specific knowledge of $N_{tot}$, $N_{con}$, or $C_{con}$.

To understand how UT behaves in a transient, suppose steady-state has been achieved when $r_A(n)$ increases due to the activation of a source(s). From (5), the effective number of sources $N_{eff}$ increases due to the increase in the measured ABR rate $r_A(n)$. From (4), $FS_{eff}$ decreases; the ABR sources respond by reducing their rate. The effective number of sources reacts to environmental changes to return the system to steady-state.

### 4.2 Implementation

The sources are required to transmit one RM cell every $N_{RM}$ data cells or every 100 ms, whichever comes first. If no RM cells are received by an active source in a TMAX time interval, the network is presumed congested; the source must automatically decrease its rate by a factor RDF. Upon receipt of a returned RM cell, the sources set their rate to their current rate plus AIR or the value in the ER field, whichever is smaller. AIR, RDF, and TMAX are network default parameters. If ramping is not desired, AIR is set to the full link capacity.

The UT switch must perform control computations every control interval $t_c$. This interval must be chosen sufficiently large to obtain an accurate rate measurement and allow implementation; too large an interval, however, will lead to sluggish response. The measured ABR rate $r_A(n)$ will be a multiple of the rate resolution $\frac{1}{t_c}$; the control interval must be selected so that measurement of a solitary cell will not result in $r_A(n)$ being large compared to the link capacity. As a guideline, we require $t_c$ to be sufficiently large to produce a rate resolution of 0.5% of the target rate. To allow easy implementation at high link speeds, we further require that $t_c$ be no smaller than 10 ms; slower response times should be acceptable on high-speed links because of the smoothing effect of statistical multiplexing. Thus the control interval is selected from

$$t_c \approx \max\left\{\frac{1}{0.005\rho_T C}, 10 \text{ ms}\right\}, \tag{6}$$

where the link capacity $C$ has units of cells/ms.

Filtering of the background traffic eliminates the high-frequency fluctuations which are easily absorbed by buffering; the ABR rates should not be adjusted based on these short-duration background bursts. The number of points $L_B$ in the moving-average filter is selected to be 10. For slower link speeds, the filter delay is inversely proportional to the link capacity; at higher link speeds, statistical multiplexing lessens the impact of filtering and a constant 50 ms (one-half of 10 × 10 ms) filter delay is selected. This is a rough guideline that appears to work well. The number of points $L_{FS}$ in the moving-average filter for the effective Fair Shares is selected so that the filter delay is roughly one-half the maximum expected network delay experienced by ABR traffic,

$$L_{FS} \approx \max\left\{\frac{d_{max}}{t_c}, 1\right\}. \tag{7}$$

In the simulation study, $d_{max}$ is set equal to the maximum propagation delay plus 300 service times.

The UT switch must have a separate counter for background cells and for ABR cells ( if policing were performed, $r_A(n)$ could be determined from the ACR field of the RM cells rather than a counter). The sum of each of the two moving-average filter contents are stored for efficiency. Every control interval the switch must perform one integer subtraction, one integer addition, and one multiplication (by $\frac{1}{L_B} = 0.1$) to obtain $\tilde{r}_B(n)$. It then performs one subtraction, two multiplications (one to form $r_A(n)$), and one division to compute $FS_{eff}$. Finally it updates $\tilde{FS}_{eff}$ with one subtraction, one addition, and one multiplication (for $L_{FS} > 1$). To be thorough, we note the following. If $\rho_T C - \tilde{r}_B(n)$ is very small, $FS_{eff}$ is set equal to zero. If $\tilde{FS}_{eff}$ is smaller than some initial start-up rate, $FS_{eff}$ is set equal to this start-up rate. In the simulation study, this start-up rate is set equal to $(\rho_T C - \tilde{r}_B(n))/N_{max}$, where $N_{max}$ is the maximum number of connections expected on the network.

### 4.3 Advantages

The UT scheme achieves max-min fairness in a distributed fashion with relatively simple implementation. To achieve max-min fairness, other schemes must explicitly compute the Fair Share which requires knowledge of the active number of sources $N_{tot}$, the number of constrained sources $N_{con}$, and the capacity used by the constrained sources $C_{con}$. UT's tracking eliminates the need for these parameters. If a source suddenly increases its activity, the measured ABR traffic rate will rise resulting in a reduction in the next effective Fair Share; likewise if a source suddenly decreases its activity, the next effective Fair Share will be increased. Max-min fairness is achieved automatically without additional computation.

Among fair schemes, UT clearly has the simplest implementation. Indeed, its complexity is similar to that of the *unfair* OSU scheme. Both should obtain $r_A(n)$ and $\tilde{r}_B(n)$. The *unfair* OSU scheme additionally requires one division and one subtraction each control interval; also, the individual sources must divide their current rate by the $LF$ every returned RM cell. The UT scheme additionally requires one integer addition, one integer subtraction, and one multiplication to compute $\tilde{FS}_{eff}$ together with one division, one multiplication, and one subtraction each control interval.

The UT scheme can be viewed loosely as an adaptive H2 control; stability should not be a major concern. In the following simulation study, we investigate the stability, efficiency, fairness, and convergence properties of UT under diverse conditions. As the simulation study demonstrates, the UT scheme appears to satisfy the criteria set forth by the ATM Forum.

## 5 Single-Switch Simulation

A discrete-event simulator is employed to investigate the efficiency of the UT scheme in a more realistic environment. For this portion of the study, we consider a single congested switch; the switch calculates the background and ABR rates by counting cell arrivals, thus measurement errors are allowed. The round-trip propagation delays are quantized into ten loops with 7–70 ms delays; an ABR source on the $k^{th}$ loop experiences a $7k$ ms round-trip propagation delay, $3.5k$ ms in either direction. For most of the simulations, there are ten ABR sources competing for bandwidth; in one example, there are 200 sources. The sources transmit an RM cell every 35 data cells ($N_{RM} = 35$) and at least every 100 ms.

To determine $L_{FS}$ from (7), the maximum expected network delay is set at 70 ms plus 300 service times. The target utilization is 0.90 with control update performed according to (6). The initial transmission rate is set equal to $0.675/N_{max}$ of the link capacity where $N_{max}$ is the maximum number of ABR sources expected to simultaneously activate (the number of ABR calls admitted). UT is used without damping (AIR is set to the target rate $\rho_T C$), and TMAX is set to infinity so RDF is not needed. For the fair OSU scheme, $\Delta = 0.05$; for unfair OSU, $\Delta = 0$. Both the UT and OSU schemes perform filtering on the background traffic for stability.

The VBR background traffic consists of two-minute traces from the movie *Star Wars* coded in MPEG [9]. The original data is sampled at 24 Hz (frame-level) and recorded in bits. The bits are converted into cells which are assumed uniformly distributed over the frame to obtain slice-level (1.4 ms) information; the cells in each slice are assumed to arrive simultaneously at the switch (batch arrival). Two different backgrounds are considered: a single MPEG transmitted on a T1 line ($t_c = 61$ ms, $L_{FS} = 2$) and the aggregation of 30 MPEG transmitted on a T3 line ($t_c = 10$ ms, $L_{FS} = 7$).

Three different cases are considered for each background traffic. In each case, all ABR sources are turned on simultaneously at time 10 $t_c$ (allowing the background filter to properly initialize). In Case 1, the individual ABR sources are persistent (always have data to transmit) and unconstrained (can transmit at full link capacity). In Case 2, the individual ABR sources are persistent but constrained. For the first (closest) seven sources, the $k^{th}$ source has a PCR equal to $k$% of the link capacity. The eighth source has a PCR equal to 10% of the link capacity, the ninth source has a PCR equal to 14% of the link capacity, while the tenth source is unconstrained. The sources with the largest round-trip propagation delays have the largest PCR's. In Case 3, the individual ABR sources are bursty without constraint. At the time of every cell transmission, each source may turn off with fixed source-dependent probability; this probability is selected such that on average the source will turn off after ten round-trip delays. Silent sources resume transmission after waiting 1–141 cell transmission times (2 RM cells on average) also determined from a uniform distribution.

For the T3 line, an additional simulation is performed to show that UT scales with number of users. In Case 4, there are 200 persistent unconstrained ABR sources; each loop has 20 sources at the midpoint. As in the previous cases, all 200 sources activate simultaneously. Because of the difficulty in computing the Fair Share in a constrained environment, fair OSU is used for Case 1 and 4 while unfair OSU is used for Case 2 and 3.

### 5.1 BKG 1: 1 MPEG on T1

The background traffic consists of a single MPEG trace transmitted on a T1 line (1.544 Mbps); its original and filtered rate sample path are illustrated in Fig. 1. The mean arrival rate is 0.447 Mbps resulting in a utilization of 0.2895; the peak arrival rate is 4.58 Mbps. A 275 cell buffer is required to handle just the MPEG arrivals when no other traffic is present. The control time is set at 61.0 ms with $L_B = 10$ and $L_{FS} = 2$. The simulation duration is 120 seconds; all ten ABR sources simultaneously activate at time 610.0 ms ($L_B \times t_c$).

#### 5.1.1 Case 1: Unconstrained Persistent

The fair OSU scheme achieves a utilization of 0.902 with a maximum queue of 500 cells. The queue and aggregate ABR rate sample paths are shown in the top half of Fig. 3; the individual ABR sample paths are depicted in the bottom half. Each ABR source obtains a mean rate in the range 0.094–0.097 Mbps. The Fairness and Efficiency Metrics are respectively $\varepsilon_{FS} = 0.011$ and $\varepsilon_\eta = 367.3$.

The UT scheme achieves a utilization of 0.901 with a maximum queue of 465 cells. The queue and ABR rate sample paths are shown in Fig. 5. Each ABR source obtains the same mean rate of 0.094 Mbps. The Fairness and Efficiency Metrics are respectively $\varepsilon_{FS} = 0.000$ and $\varepsilon_\eta = 310.7$.

Although the metrics for UT are better than those for OSU, both schemes perform well in this case. For both, the queue closely follows the background traffic. From the figures one can see that there is somewhat more individual ABR rate variation with the OSU

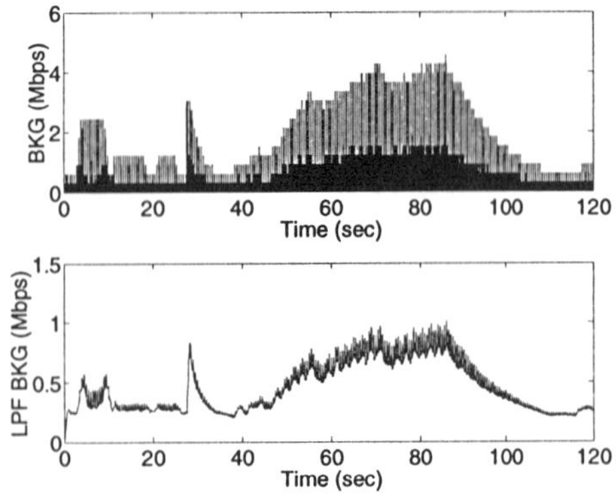


Figure 1: 1 MPEG at 1.544 Mbps

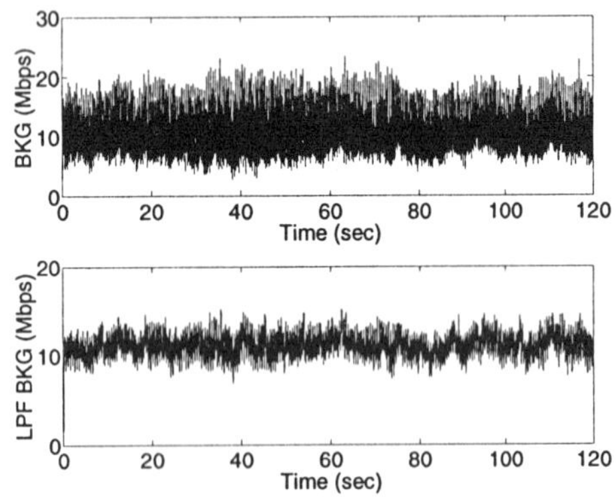


Figure 2: 30 MPEG at 44.736 Mbps

scheme than with the UT scheme; this observation is valid for all cases investigated.

#### 5.1.2 Case 2: Constrained Persistent

The *unfair* OSU scheme achieves a utilization of 0.902 with a maximum queue of 445 cells. The Efficiency Metric is $\varepsilon_\eta = 277.6$. The Fairness Metric is not defined for unfair OSU; fair OSU is not used due to the difficulty in computing the Fair Share with constrained sources.

The UT scheme achieves a utilization of 0.897 with a maximum queue of 515 cells. The UT scheme provides a fairly close approximation to max-min fairness with this highly variable MPEG background traffic. The Fairness and Efficiency Metrics are respectively $\varepsilon_{FS} = 0.084$ and $\varepsilon_\eta = 395.3$. The worst-case error in fairness occurs for the tenth ABR source which achieves an average bandwidth of 0.214 Mbps, 0.0366 Mbps larger than its fair-share bandwidth of 0.177 Mbps.

The Efficiency Metric for *unfair* OSU is better than that for UT in this case; fairness does have some cost in terms of the maximum queue. For both, the queue closely follows the background traffic. There is again more rate variation with the OSU scheme than with UT.

#### 5.1.3 Case 3: Unconstrained Bursty

The unfair OSU scheme achieves a utilization of 0.894 with a maximum queue of 546 cells. The queue and ABR rate sample paths are shown in Fig. 4. The individual ABR rates have severe rate oscillations, alternating between the full link capacity and zero. The aggregate ABR rate also varies greatly, in some instances achieving nearly four times the full link capacity. The queue no longer follows the background traffic. The Efficiency Metric is $\varepsilon_\eta = 448.3$.

The UT scheme achieves a utilization of 0.897 with a maximum queue of 435 cells. The queue and ABR rate sample paths are shown in Fig. 6. Each ABR source fairly receives a mean rate of 0.100–0.102 Mbps over the simulation time. The Fairness and Efficiency Metrics are respectively $\varepsilon_{FS} = 0.081$ and $\varepsilon_\eta = 263.5$.

The performance of UT is clearly superior to that of OSU in this case. While this is supported by the metrics, the figures provide the strongest evidence. The maximum individual ABR rates are almost an order of magnitude larger with the OSU scheme than with the UT scheme; stability with OSU is a definite concern. With UT, the queue still closely follows the background traffic; the same cannot be said with OSU.

### 5.2 BKG 2: 30 Random MPEG on T3

The background traffic consists of 30 MPEG traces with randomly assigned phases transmitted on a T3 line (44.736 Mbps); the original and filtered rate sample path are illustrated in 2. Because of the statistical multiplexing, the filtering has less of an impact than it had with the previous background. The mean arrival rate is 11.069 Mbps resulting in a utilization of 0.2474; the peak arrival rate is 23.51 Mbps. A buffer of 77 cells is required to handle the burst arrivals of the MPEG background when no other traffic is present.

The control time is set at 10.0 ms with $L_B = 10$ and $L_{FS} = 7$. The simulation duration is 120 seconds; all ten ABR sources simultaneously activate at time 100.0 ms ($L_B \times t_c$). The figures depict the first 10 seconds of the simulation.

#### 5.2.1 Case 1: Unconstrained Persistent

The fair OSU scheme achieves a utilization of only 0.253 with a maximum queue of 10588 cells. The queue and aggregate ABR rate sample paths for the first 10 seconds are shown in Fig. 7. The mean rates of the individual ABR sample paths range from 0.005–0.502 Mbps over the 120 second simulation time; fairness is certainly not achieved. In the presence of this background traffic with multiple delay loops, the OSU scheme is much worse than no feedback at all; adjusting rates by a multiplicative factor when delays are involved can be detrimental. The Fairness and Efficiency Metrics are respectively $\varepsilon_{FS} = 0.97$ and $\varepsilon_\eta = 1.75e6$.

The UT scheme achieves a utilization of 0.901 with a maximum queue of only 547 cells; the queue and aggregate ABR rate sample paths are depicted in Fig. 8. The individual ABR sources all obtain the same mean rate of 2.923 Mbps. UT has little difficulty with the simultaneous activation of unconstrained persistent sources with this background traffic. The Fairness

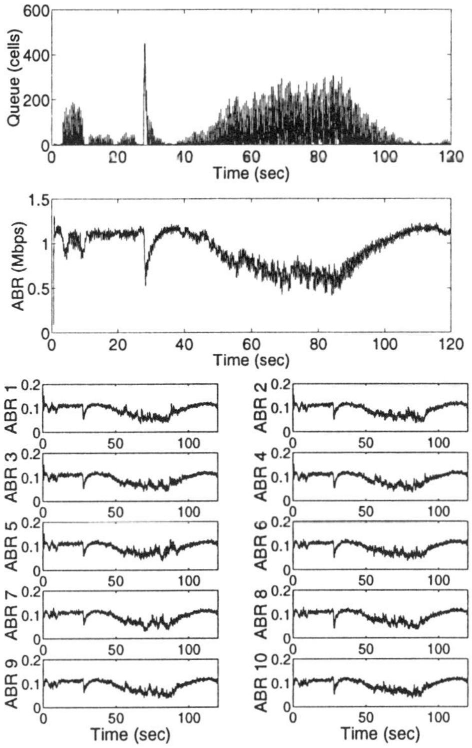


Figure 3: OSU: BKG 1, Case 1

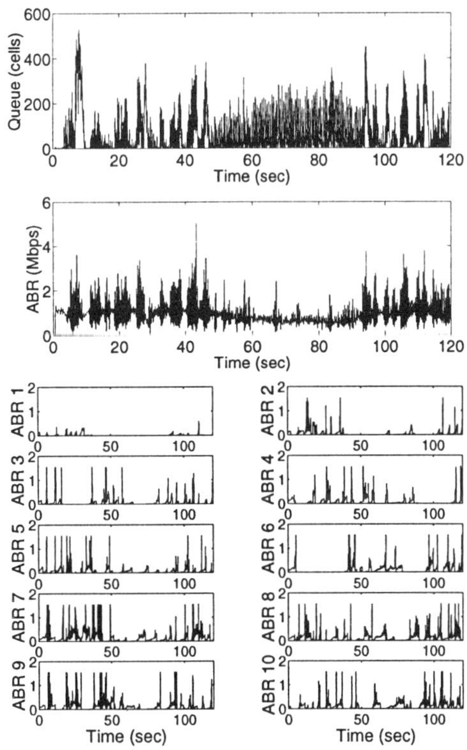


Figure 4: OSU: BKG 1, Case 3

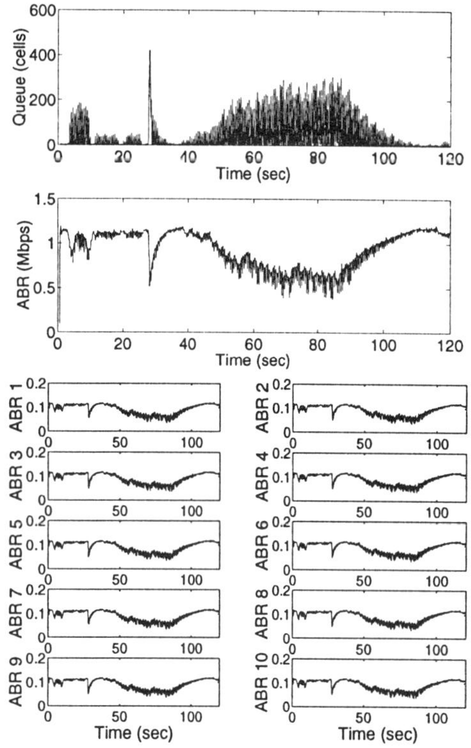


Figure 5: UT: BKG 1, Case 1

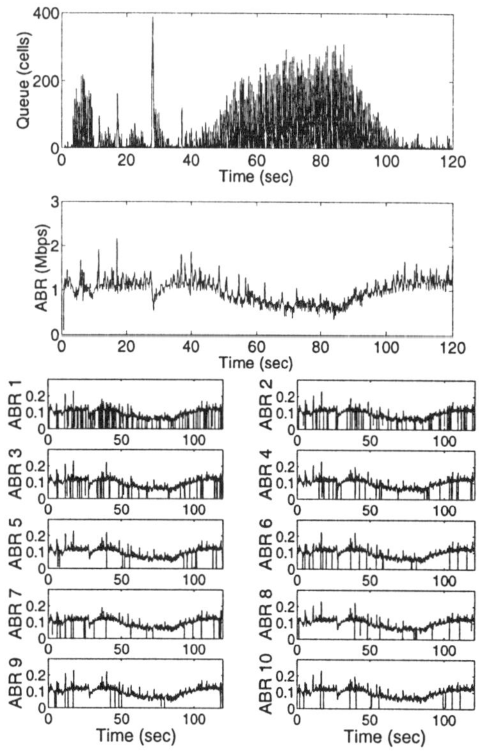


Figure 6: UT: BKG 1, Case 3

Table 1: Performance Metrics

| | | $\varepsilon_{FS}$ | | $\varepsilon_{\eta}$ | |
|---|---|---|---|---|---|
| | | OSU | UT | OSU | UT |
| BKG 1 | Case 1 | 0.011 | 0.000 | 367 | 311 |
| | Case 2 | N/A | 0.084 | 278 | 395 |
| | Case 3 | N/A | 0.081 | 448 | 264 |
| BKG 2 | Case 1 | 0.970 | 0.001 | 1.75e6 | 719 |
| | Case 2 | N/A | 0.007 | 4.51e3 | 672 |
| | Case 3 | N/A | 0.002 | 2.49e6 | 599 |
| | Case 4 | 0.005 | 0.002 | 1.74e4 | 644 |

and Efficiency Metrics are respectively $\varepsilon_{FS} = 0.001$ and $\varepsilon_{\eta} = 718.7$.

#### 5.2.2 Case 2: Constrained Persistent

The unfair OSU scheme achieves a utilization of 0.767 with a maximum queue of 2423 cells. The OSU performance improves with constrained sources, but it is still most unsatisfactory. The Efficiency Metric is $\varepsilon_{\eta} = 4.51e3$.

The UT scheme achieves a utilization of 0.899 with a maximum queue of 515 cells. Max-min fairness is achieved efficiently and automatically. The aggregate performance of UT is similar to that obtained in Case 1. The Fairness and Efficiency Metrics are respectively $\varepsilon_{FS} = 0.007$ and $\varepsilon_{\eta} = 671.8$.

#### 5.2.3 Case 3: Unconstrained Bursty

The unfair OSU scheme achieves a utilization of only 0.253 with a maximum queue of 15000 cells. As with the two previous cases, OSU simply does not perform well with this background traffic and multiple delay loops. The Efficiency Metric is $\varepsilon_{\eta} = 2.49e6$.

The UT scheme achieves a utilization of 0.900 with a maximum queue of 468 cells. The individual ABR sources all receive a mean rate of 2.921–2.928 Mbps. The aggregate performance is again very similar to Case 1. The Fairness and Efficiency Metrics are respectively $\varepsilon_{FS} = 0.002$ and $\varepsilon_{\eta} = 598.8$.

#### 5.2.4 Case 4: Multiple Unconstrained Persistent Sources Per Loop

The fair OSU scheme achieves a utilization of 0.900 with a maximum queue of 11427 cells. The individual ABR mean rates range from 0.145–0.148 Mbps over the simulation time. The Fairness and Efficiency Metrics are respectively $\varepsilon_{FS} = 0.005$ and $\varepsilon_{\eta} = 1.74e4$. Although the performance is not good, the additional sources have resulted in a marked improvement from Case 1.

The UT scheme achieves a utilization of 0.901 with a maximum queue of 498 cells. Of the 200 sources, 181 achieve their fair-share bandwidth of 0.146 Mbps; the remaining 19 sources average 0.147 Mbps over the simulation time. The Fairness and Efficiency Metrics are respectively $\varepsilon_{FS} = 0.002$ and $\varepsilon_{\eta} = 644.4$. The performance of UT is somewhat improved by the additional sources; it is clearly superior to that of OSU.

### 5.3 Single-Switch Summary

To demonstrate that UT scales with speed, two different backgrounds were investigated: 1 MPEG on a 1.544 Mbps line (BKG 1), and 30 MPEG on a 44.736 Mbps line (BKG 2). With each background, three different ABR source types were investigated: unconstrained persistent sources (Case 1 and 4), constrained persistent sources (Case 2), and unconstrained bursty sources (Case 3). To show the effect of number of users, ten sources were competing in Case 1–3 while 200 sources were competing in Case 4. To demonstrate that UT scales with distance, ten round-trip propagation delay loops of 7–70 ms were considered. The UT scheme was compared to the fair OSU scheme for Case 1 and 4; because it is not clear how OSU can compute $FS$ in a constrained environment, UT was compared to unfair OSU for the other two cases. In all cases the ABR sources were simultaneously activated.

The performance metrics for the simulations are summarized in Table 1; it is apparent from the Efficiency Metric that OSU was unstable with BKG 2. What is not evident from the metrics is that the OSU scheme consistently produced larger ABR rate variations than did the UT scheme, even for BKG 1. For BKG 1 Case 3, the individual rates controlled by OSU oscillated continually from full link capacity to zero; the peak individual rates controlled by UT were nearly an order of magnitude less than the link capacity. OSU behaved poorly because the sources multiplicatively adjusted their current rates based on delayed infor-

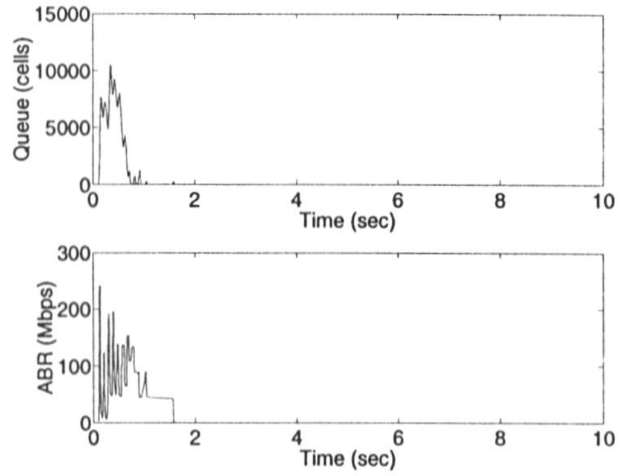


Figure 7: OSU: BKG 2, Case 1

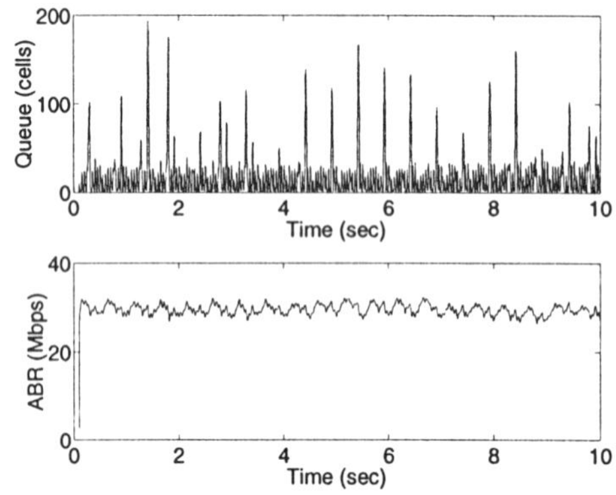


Figure 8: UT: BKG 2, Case 1

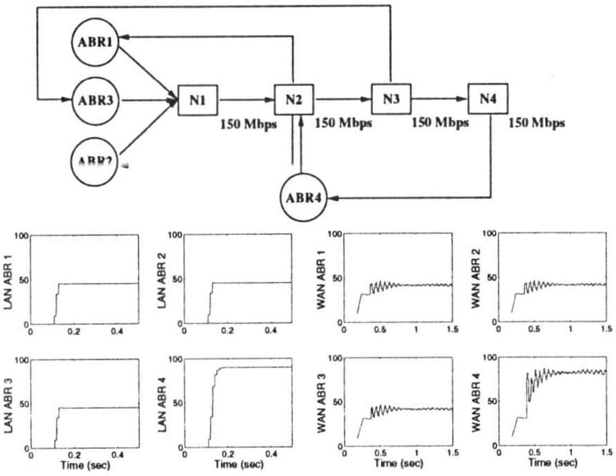


Figure 9: Four-Switch Example

mation. UT had no stability problems whatsoever.

# 6 Multiple-Switch Simulation

To some extent, the single-switch study with multiple delay loops and constrained sources captures the behavior of a multiple-switch environment; for completeness, however, we explicitly include the following multiple-switch examples. The sources transmit an RM cell every 35 data cells ($N_{RM} = 35$) and at least every 100 ms; the RM cell update is performed in the backwards direction. The RM cells are queued and treated as data cells in the forwards direction to accurately capture delay. Since traffic is not specified in the backwards direction, the backwards RM cell is delayed by the queue level in the forwards direction; introducing such extreme correlation stresses the system.

The target utilization is 0.90 and the initial transmission rate is set equal to $0.675/N_{max}$ where $N_{max} = 10$ for each of these examples. UT without damping is used (AIR is set to the link capacity). The sources are persistent, unconstrained, and simultaneously activate after the background filter has initialized. The background traffic when present consists of 30 MPEG sources entering the first switch, propagating through the series of switches, then exiting the final switch. As before, the switches calculate the background and ABR rates by counting cell arrivals, thus measurement errors are allowed.

## 6.1 Four-Switch Example

The fairness and convergence of UT in a four-switch, four-source network is evaluated using the discrete-event simulator. From Fig. 9 (top), ABR1 and ABR2 both see a round-trip propagation delay corresponding to 6 links (3 each way), while ABR3 and ABR4 both see a round-trip propagation delay corresponding to 8 links. The link speeds are all 150 Mbps.

For the LAN case, a 0.01 ms propagation delay is assigned to every link resulting in round-trip propagation delays of 0.06 ms and 0.08 ms; there is no background traffic. The individual ABR rates are depicted in Fig. 9 (bottom left). The first three sources converge to a rate of 45 Mbps while the fourth source converges to a rate of 90 Mbps; it is easy to show that these are the max-min fair-share bandwidths. The maximum queue at any output port is only 3 cells. To examine the effect of link speed, the bandwidth on each link is increased to 622 Mbps; again the sources converge rapidly to their max-min fair-share bandwidths (186.6 and 373.2 Mbps) with a maximum queue of 3 cells.

To examine a more stressing WAN environment, the propagation delays are all increased by three orders of magnitude so that the ABR sources see a minimum of 60 ms and 80 ms delays; in addition, 30 MPEG background sources enter the first switch and exit the fourth switch. The individual ABR rates are depicted in Fig. 9 (bottom right). The maximum queue at any output port in this WAN case with MPEG background is 66 cells.

## 6.2 Ten-Switch Parking Lot Example

This second example is a classic 10-switch parking lot. The ten switches are linked in series and numbered sequentially. There are ten ABR sources, and the $n^{th}$ source for $n > 1$ has entry switch $(n-1)$. The first ABR source shares entry switch 1 with the second ABR source. The tenth switch is the exit point for all ABR traffic. The round-trip propagation delay thus varies from 4 links for the tenth source to 22 links for the first and second source. The link speeds are all 25 Mbps.

The link propagation delays are first set at 0.01 ms to represent a LAN and then at 10 ms to represent a WAN; the round-trip propagation delay for the first source is thus 0.22 ms and 220 ms for the two cases. In both the LAN and WAN environments, all ten sources converge rapidly to their max-min fair-share bandwidths with a maximum queue at any output port of only 3 cells. For the LAN example, the link speeds are increased to 622 Mbps; again all sources rapidly achieve their max-min bandwidths with a maximum queue of 3 cells.

## 6.3 Generic Fairness Configuration GFC1

As a final example, we consider Generic Fairness Configuration 1 (GFC1) which consists of 5 switches with a series of 23 connections that are grouped into six classes A-F. The switches are serially connected with respective link capacities of 50 Mbps, 150 Mbps, 150 Mbps, and 100 Mbps between switches 1-2, 2-3, 3-4, and 4-5. This network is depicted in Fig. 10 (top).

For the LAN case, the links are 400m with propagation delays of 1 microsecond yielding a maximum round-trip propagation delay of 10 microseconds. The individual ABR rates are depicted in Fig. 10 (middle); in every case the max-min fair-share bandwidth is rapidly obtained using the desired utilization of 0.9. All connections in class A and D receive 5.0 Mbps, all connections in class B and E receive 10.0 Mbps, all connections in class C receive 30.0 Mbps, and the two connections in class F receive 45.0 Mbps. The maximum output queue is 535 cells.

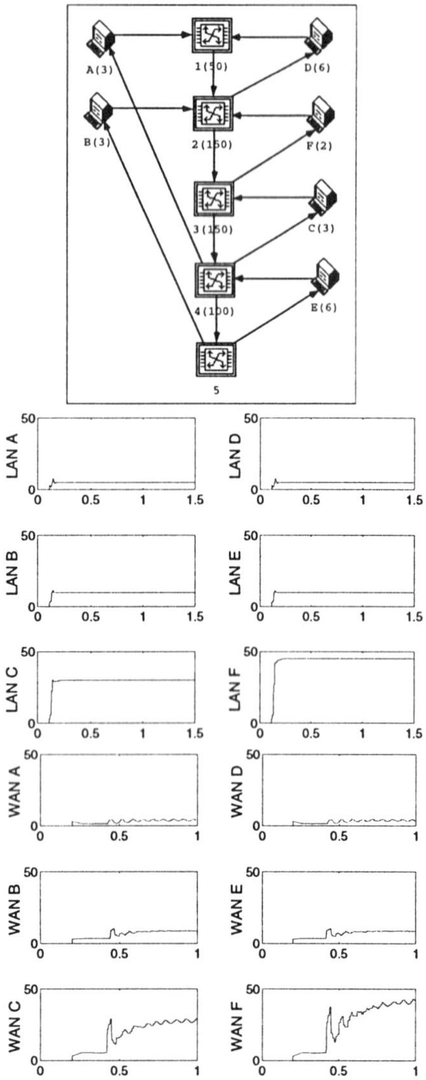


Figure 10: GFC1 Example

For the WAN case, the link propagation delays are all increased by four orders of magnitude yielding a maximum round-trip propagation delay of 100 ms. 30 MPEG background sources enter the first switch and exit the final switch. The individual ABR rates are depicted in Fig. 10 (bottom). They all approach their max-min fair-share bandwidth with the mean rate of the background traffic being 11.069 Mbps. The maximum queue at any output port is 272 cells.

## 7 Conclusion

Uniform Tracking (UT), a new explicit-rate ABR feedback control scheme, was proposed. UT differs from other schemes in that it achieves max-min fairness automatically without requiring constraint information; this is achieved by tracking an effective number of sources. Since UT does not need to explicitly determine the number of sources or constraint information, its implementation is much simpler than that of other fair control schemes; indeed, its complexity is similar to that of *unfair* OSU.

In the discrete-event simulations, UT demonstrated its ability to scale with speed (1.544–622 Mbps), distance (3–70 ms), number of users (3–200), and number of switches (1–10). It suffered no stability problems even with the simultaneous activation of all ABR sources multiplexed with 1–30 MPEG background sources; performance was consistent whether the ABR sources were persistent or bursty, constrained or unconstrained. UT achieves stability with scale through the use of low-frequency filtering in its computations; this filtering should also enable it to handle low-frequency windowing protocols (such as TCP) over ATM.

## References

[1] ATM Forum Traffic Management Specification, Version 4.0, 1995.

[2] R. Jain, "Congestion Control and Traffic Management in ATM Networks: Recent Advances and A Survey," invited submission to Computer Networks and ISDN Systems, 1995.

[3] F. Bonomi and K.W. Fendick, "The Rate-Based Flow Control Framework for the Available Bit Rate ATM Service," *IEEE Network Mag.*, Mar. 1995, pp. 25–39.

[4] K.K. Ramakrishnan and P. Newman, "Integration of Rate and Credit Schemes for ATM Flow Control," *IEEE Network Mag.*, Mar. 1995, pp. 49–56.

[5] Y. Zhao, S.Q. Li, S. Sigarto, "An Improved EFCI Scheme with Early Congestion Detection," AF-TM 96-1084, Feb. 1996.

[6] A. Charny, D. Clark, and R. Jain, "Congestion Control with Explicit Rate Indication," Proc. ICC'95, June 1995.

[7] R. Jain, S. Kalyanaraman, and R. Viswanathan, "The OSU Scheme for Congestion Avoidance Using Explicit Rate Indication," AF-TM 94-0883, Sept. 1994.

[8] Y. Zhao, S.Q. Li, and S. Sigarto, "A Linear Dynamic Model for Design of Stable Explicit-Rate ABR Control Schemes," AF-TM 96-0606, Apr. 1996.

[9] File MPEG.data obtained via anonymous ftp from thumper.bellcore.com in directory vbr.video.trace compliments of M.W. Garrett and A. Fernandez of Bellcore.

[10] R.O. Onvural, *Asynchronous Transfer Mode Networks: Performance Issues*, ARTECH HOUSE, Inc., Norwood, MA, 1995.

# The Effect of Bottleneck Service Rate Variations on the Performance of the ABR Flow Control

Michael Ritter
University of Würzburg, Institute of Computer Science
D-97074 Würzburg, GERMANY
email: ritter@informatik.uni-wuerzburg.de

## Abstract

*One of the main features of ABR services is the employment of a rate-based flow control mechanism. Feedback from the network switches to the end systems gives users the information necessary to adjust their transmission rates appropriately according to the current network load. This type of control has been investigated to some extent, assuming a constant transmission capacity on a bottleneck link.*

*In this paper we develop a discrete-time analysis to study the effect of bottleneck service rate variations on the performance of the ABR flow control mechanism. Looking at real systems, such variations occur on the one hand due to the establishment and release of ATM connections and on the other hand due to the varying bandwidth demand of VBR connections. To model the rate variations, the bottleneck service rate is assumed to follow a general probability density function.*

## 1 Introduction

Recent advances in the development of B-ISDNs led to the definition of a fourth ATM service category, the *Available Bit Rate* (ABR) service. Its primary goal is the economical support of applications with vague requirements for throughput and delay. With the ABR service category, the available bandwidth is allocated systematically and dynamically to the users by controlling the rate of offered traffic through feedback. To implement this framework, a closed-loop feedback control operating on a rate-oriented basis has been developed by the ATM Forum [2].

A distinguishing feature of ABR sources is their ability to submit cells into the network at a variable but controlled rate, the *Allowed Cell Rate* (ACR). This rate is always bounded between a *Minimum Cell Rate* (MCR) and a *Peak Cell Rate* (PCR) negotiated at connection setup. The ACR is controlled by the return of *Resource Management* (RM) cells, which are sent periodically by the source and are looped back by the destination.

As the RM cells travel through the network, the switches provide information about their current congestion status by modifying the content of these cells. When an RM cell arrives back at the source, the source resets its ACR based on the information carried by this cell. If congestion is indicated, the source must decrease its ACR, otherwise it may increase its ACR by a fixed amount. By implementing such a policy, network congestion is controlled or avoided and the available bandwidth is used economically.

In the recent past, feedback controls for communication networks have been investigated extensively [7, 9, 18]. A number of papers deals with the modeling of the dynamical system behavior during steady-state. The dynamics, which occur due to the feedback delay, are an undesirable characteristic of feedback controls [19, 20, 21]. Other authors analyze the dynamical behavior during initial and specific transient phases [6, 8]. Performance measures of interest are, e.g., the convergence of the mechanism [10, 14, 17], the size of the switch buffers required to avoid cell losses [12, 15, 22, 25, 26], fairness properties [5], and the speed of adapting the transmission rates to a changed system environment [4, 13].

Almost all analysis published on feedback controls are based on the assumption that the bottleneck service rate is constant or remains constant over long time periods. In real systems, however, the transmission capacity available for active ABR connections typically changes frequently. These fluctuations are caused on the one hand by the varying bandwidth demand of *Variable Bit Rate* (VBR) connections, whose cells are transmitted with a higher priority due to the real-time constraints. On the other hand, the establishment and release of ATM connections causes fluctuations of the bandwidth share available for a single ABR connection.

In this paper we present an analysis to study the effect of bottleneck service rate variations on the performance



0-8186-7780-5/97 $10.00 © 1997 IEEE

of the ABR flow control mechanism. Particularly, we are interested in the influence of the variations on the buffer size which must be provided in the switches in order to avoid cell losses. To model the rate variations described above, the transmission capacity available for a particular ABR connection is assumed to follow a general probability density function.

The paper is organized as follows. Section 2 describes the basic operation mode of the flow control mechanism and presents the network model used for our investigation. The analysis, which operates in the discrete-time domain, is outlined in Section 3. Numerical results to illustrate the accuracy of our algorithm and to discuss performance aspects with respect to the bottleneck service rate variations are presented in Section 4. The paper concludes with a brief summary in Section 5.

## 2 Basic operation and model

Once an ABR connection is set up and the ABR-specific parameters are identified, the source begins with cell transmission. It is allowed to schedule cells with a rate up to the ACR, which is dynamically adjusted to the network congestion status. To signal congestion, a switch modifies the content of the RM cells for those connections for which it constitutes a bottleneck.

The flow control mechanism developed by the ATM Forum supports two signaling modes. In the simple binary mode, the EFCI bit located in the header of data cells is set by the switches to indicate congestion for a particular connection. According to this information, the *Congestion Indication* (CI) bit in the backward RM cells is modified by the destination. At the return of an RM cell carrying positive feedback, i.e. no congestion was detected, the source may increase its ACR by a fixed increment *RIF·PCR*, but never exceeding the PCR. The *Rate Increase Factor* (RIF) is determined at connection setup. If the CI bit is set, i.e. congestion was detected, the ACR is decreased in a multiplicative manner by *RDF · ACR*, but never below the MCR. The speed of the reduction is determined by the *Rate Decrease Factor* (RDF).

In the more sophisticated explicit mode, a switch directly signals the rate it can support for a connection in the *Explicit Rate* (ER) field of the RM cells. This, however, requires the switch to be able to compute a fair bandwidth share for each connection. At the return of an RM cell, the ACR is reduced to the ER value if it is smaller than the current ACR and larger than the MCR. Otherwise it is increased in the same manner as described above, but never exceeding the ER. A more detailed description of the behavior of the *Source End System* (SES) and the *Destination End System* (DES) can be found in the ABR specification of the ATM Forum [3].

To investigate the feedback control we model a single ABR connection as shown in Figure 1. The SES and the DES communicate via a single switch, which constitutes a bottleneck in forward direction. In backward direction, no congestion occurs. As usual for the analysis of feedback controls, non-congested switches along the transmission path are omitted, since they do not influence the system in a major way. Congestion is detected by the switch when the buffer content exceeds an upper threshold $B_H$, and is regarded as terminated if the buffer content subsides to a lower threshold $B_L$.

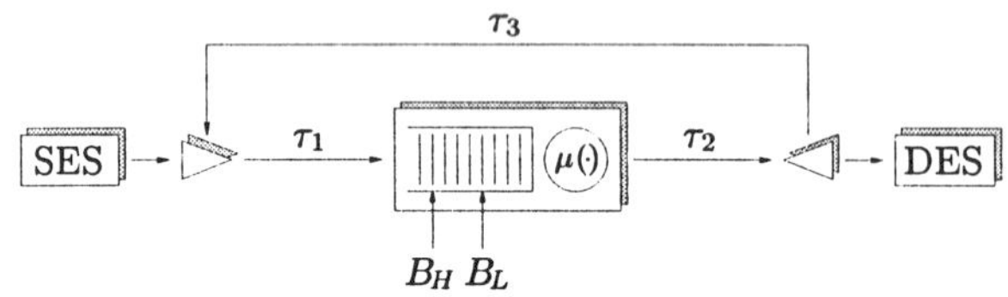


Figure 1: *Model of a single ABR connection*

The SES operates in a saturated condition, i.e. it always submits cells with the relevant ACR. The variables $\tau_1$ and $\tau_2$ denote the propagation delay between the SES and the switch, and between the switch and the DES, respectively. In backward direction, the propagation delay is given by $\tau_3 = \tau_1 + \tau_2$, which results in a *Round Trip Time* (RTT) of $\tau = 2(\tau_1 + \tau_2)$.

To model the variations of the bandwidth share available for the ABR connection, we assume, regarding the particular connection, that the cell inter-departure times at the switch follow a general probability density function $\mu(\cdot)$. This assumption is motivated by the fact that for a large number of connections the system noise introduced by other connections results in a frequent change of the bottleneck service rate with a low correlation structure [16].

A similar modeling was used in [1] and [16] where the authors considered autoregressive processes and random walks with a low variance respectively. The control mechanisms investigated are, however, not comparable to the one developed for the ABR service category. Furthermore, the papers do not address performance issues concerning the influence of the bottleneck service rate variations on the system behavior. They only focus on the stability of the control law and the derivation of system state estimators. The approach presented in [1] allows to estimate mean values for the transmission rate and the buffer content. Due to the oscillating system behavior, the usefulness of these values is only limited. In [11, 23] the transient behavior of a queueing system is investigated when the service rate is a non-linear function of the buffer occupancy. This, however, is not the case in the context of ABR services, where the bandwidth share is independent of the buffer occupancy.

The following section presents an algorithm to derive the probability density functions of the ACR and the buffer content at specific time instants within a control cycle. Using these density functions for an example scenario, the sensitivity of the ABR flow control mechanism to variations of the bandwidth share is discussed in Section 4.

# 3 Performance analysis

With the ABR flow control mechanism, network congestion can be signaled and controlled in different ways [3]. To give a short and understandable description of our analysis we focus on a scheme which uses the ER field to signal congestion. Of course, other control schemes, such as the binary mode, can be treated similarly.

As long as the switch does not detect congestion, the content of the RM cells remains unchanged. Thus, the ER field of returning RM cells contains the PCR, which is the initial value set by the SES. The ACR is therefore increased by a fixed amount at each return of a backward RM cell. During congestion periods, the switch signals an ER in each RM cell. We assume that this rate *ER* is constant and lower than the mean cell transmission rate $TR = \mathrm{E}[\mu(\cdot)]$ on the bottleneck link, which leads to a constant ACR during congestion periods.

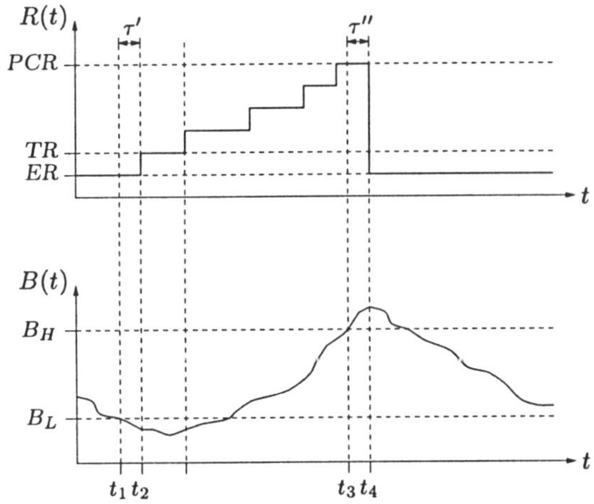


Figure 2: *Evolution of the ACR and the buffer content*

Considering this control law, the ACR $R(t)$ and the buffer content $B(t)$ evolve as depicted in Figure 2. After congestion release ($t_1$), it takes a feedback delay $\tau'$ until the SES receives positive feedback and starts to increase its ACR ($t_2$). As long as positive feedback is signaled ($t_3$), the ACR is increased at each return of a backward RM cell. If negative feedback is received ($t_4$), the ACR is set to the ER computed by the switch. It again takes a feedback delay $\tau''$ until the SES recognizes that the buffer content has exceeded $B_H$. After releasing congestion, the next cycle starts. The increase and the decrease of the buffer content varies with the bottleneck service rate and is therefore strongly non-linear. For the same reason, the ramp-up of the ACR during non-congestion periods is also non-linear.

Due to the slotted nature of the ATM environment, our analysis operates in the discrete-time domain. In the following we denote the discrete convolution of the probability density function of the cell inter-departure time $\mu(i)$ $k$ times with itself by

$$\mu_k(i) = \underbrace{\mu(i) \star \cdots \star \mu(i)}_{k} \quad , \tag{1}$$

and the corresponding complementary probability distributions by $\mu_k^c(i)$. Furthermore, the probability density function of the recurrence distribution of $\mu_k(i)$ and its corresponding complementary probability distribution are denoted by $\mu_k^r(i)$ and $\mu_k^{rc}(i)$ respectively.

Due to the stochastic process incorporated in our model, the system state is expressed by the probability density functions of the buffer content $B_t(i)$ and the ACR $R_t(i)$ at time $t$. Thus, the probability that the buffer contains $i$ cells at time $t$ is given by $B_t(i)$. Because of its non-integer nature, the ACR is mapped. In the following, $R_t(i)$ corresponds to the rate

$$r(i) = ER + i \cdot RIF \cdot PCR \quad . \tag{2}$$

The derivation of the probability density functions $B_t(i)$ and $R_t(i)$ at the time instants $t_1, \ldots, t_4$ within a control cycle (cf. Figure 2) is outlined in the next four subsections. To simplify the description, we consider the ACR that was relevant $\tau_1$ time units before $t$, i.e. we look at the cell arrival rate at the switch.

## 3.1 Density functions at the end of a congestion period

We start with the end of a congestion period ($t_1$), i.e. the time instant when the buffer content subsides to the lower threshold $B_L$.

### 3.1.1 Transmission rate density function

As long as the switch remains in the congestion state, an ER is signaled in the RM cells. Thus, recalling the mapping of Equation (2), we obtain

$$R_{t_1}(i) = \delta(i) \quad , \tag{3}$$

where $\delta(\cdot)$ is the Kronecker Delta defined by $\delta(k) = 1$ for $k = 0$, else $\delta(k) = 0$.

### 3.1.2 Buffer length density function

Since the buffer content at $t_1$ is equal to $B_L$, the corresponding density function is given by

$$B_{t_1}(i) = \delta(i - B_L) \quad . \tag{4}$$

Based on the density functions for the ACR and the buffer content, the system evolution is derived.

## 3.2 Density functions at the end of an ER signaling phase

The next time instant we look at is the moment just before the return of the first cell carrying positive feedback after congestion release ($t_2$). The time interval between $t_1$ and $t_2$ constitutes the feedback delay $\tau'$.

### 3.2.1 Transmission rate density function

Since at $t_2$ the positive feedback is not yet received, the SES still submits cells with the ER into the network, i.e.

$$R_{t_2}(i) = \delta(i) \quad . \tag{5}$$

### 3.2.2 Buffer length density function

During the feedback delay $\tau'$, the buffer content generally decreases, since the cell arrival rate *ER* is smaller than the mean departure rate *TR*. To compute the buffer length density function at $t_2$, we are first interested in the number of cells that depart from and arrive at the switch respectively, during a given time interval $t$.

The probability $D_t(i)$ that $i$ cells depart from the switch within $t$ time slots is given by

$$D_t(i) = \sum_{j=i}^{t} \mu_i(j) \cdot \mu_1^c(t-j) \qquad t = 1, \ldots, \infty \quad . \tag{6}$$

Due to the constant cell arrival rate *ER*, we derive the probability $A_t(i)$ that $i$ cells arrive at the switch within $t$ time slots by

$$A_t(i) = \delta(i - \lfloor ER \cdot t \rfloor) \qquad t = 1, \ldots, \infty \quad . \tag{7}$$

The computation of the number of departures and arrivals is only approximate, since the first inter-arrival and inter-departure time after congestion release follow different distributions. The error is, however, neglectable for practical purposes.

By adding the arrivals to and subtracting the departures from $Q_L$, we arrive at the buffer content $t$ time slots after $t_1$. This operation is expressed by the discrete-time convolution in case of the probability density functions. Consequently, the probability $H_t(i)$ that the buffer contains $i$ cells after $t$ time slots is

$$H_t(i) = \pi_0 \left[ B_{t_1}(i) \star A_t(i) \star D_t(-i) \right] \quad t = 1, \ldots, \infty, \tag{8}$$

where $\pi_0[\cdot]$ denotes the operator defined in [24]:

$$\pi_0[a(i)] = \begin{cases} 0 & : \; i < 0 \\ \sum_{j=-\infty}^{0} a(j) & : \; i = 0 \\ a(i) & : \; i > 0 \end{cases} \quad . \tag{9}$$

The total feedback delay $\tau'$ consists of the RTT $\tau$ and the time it takes until an RM cell is forwarded by the switch after congestion release. By weighting the density functions $H_t(i)$ with the probability that the total feedback delay is equal to $t$, we obtain the density function for the buffer length at $t_2$, i.e.

$$B_{t_2}(i) = \sum_{t=\tau}^{\infty} \mu^{\tau}_{N_{rm}}(t - \tau) \cdot H_t(i) \quad . \tag{10}$$

## 3.3 Density functions at the end of a non-congestion period

When the upper threshold $B_H$ is exceeded ($t_3$), the switch detects congestion and starts to signal negative feedback. Until this time instant, the ACR increases with every return of a backward RM cell as long as the PCR is not attained.

### 3.3.1 Transmission rate density function

Due to the non-deterministic bottleneck service rate, the lengths of the time intervals between two consecutive increase steps are in general different and thus, the ACR can have different values at congestion detection. To deal with this, we look at the buffer length density function at the end of a single increase step, which allows to determine the probability that the threshold $B_H$ is exceeded within this step. Using these probabilities, we compute the density function $R_{t_3}(i)$.

We proceed analogously to the last subsection. The probability $D_t(i)$ that $i$ cells depart from the switch within $t$ time slots is determined by Equation (6). Since the ACR is constant between two increase steps of the height *RIF·PCR* (cf. Section 2), we obtain the probability $A_t^k(i)$ that $i$ cells arrive at the switch within $t = 1, \ldots, \infty$ time slots by

$$A_t^k(i) = \delta(i - \lfloor (ER + k \cdot RIF \cdot PCR) \cdot t \rfloor) \quad , \tag{11}$$

if we are currently situated between the $k$-th and the $(k+1)$-th increase step. Performing a convolution operation, we arrive at the probability $H_t^k(i)$ that the buffer contains $i$ cells $t$ time slots after the $k$-th increase step, i.e.

$$H_t^k(i) = \pi_0\left[\sigma^{Q_H}\left[B_{t_2}^{k-1}(i)\right] \star A_t^k(i) \star D_t(-i)\right] \quad . \qquad (12)$$

The operator $\sigma^{Q_H}[\cdot]$ extracts the part lower than $Q_H$ from the density function and normalizes it. The initial condition is given by $B_{t_2}^0(i) = B_{t_2}(i)$.

Knowing that the inter-arrival time of backward RM cells follows $\mu_{N_{rm}}(i)$, we obtain for the density function of the buffer content $B_{t_2}^k(i)$ just before the ($k$+1)-th increase step

$$B_{t_2}^k(i) = \sum_{t=N_{rm}}^{\infty} \mu_{N_{rm}}(t) \cdot H_t^k(i) \quad . \qquad (13)$$

If we carry out the following summation, which includes a normalization factor, we arrive at the density function for the ACR at $t_3$:

$$R_{t_3}(i) = \sum_{j=B_H}^{\infty} B_{t_2}^i(j) \cdot \left(1 - \sum_{l=0}^{i-1} R_{t_3}(l)\right) \quad . \qquad (14)$$

Again, the computation involves a number of approximations to reduce the numerical complexity.

### 3.3.2 Buffer length density function

Since the buffer length at $t_3$ is equal to the threshold $B_H$, the corresponding density function is given by

$$B_{t_3}(i) = \delta(i - B_H) \quad . \qquad (15)$$

## 3.4 Density functions at the end of an increase phase

In this subsection we outline the computation of the system state density functions observed at the time instant when the first negative feedback is received by the source ($t_4$), i.e. when the buffer content reaches its maximum value within a control cycle.

### 3.4.1 Transmission rate density function

The density function of the ACR $R_{t_4}(i)$ can be computed similarly as outlined in the last subsection. Since this paper primarily focuses on the influence of the rate variations on the buffer occupancy, we omit the description.

### 3.4.2 Buffer length density function

As before, we first compute the density functions for the number of cells that depart from and arrive at the switch during a given time interval $t$. For the departures we refer to Equation (6). The derivation of the density function for the arrivals is more complex. Since the ACR is a non-deterministic value at $t_3$, we start with the conditional probabilities $A_t^j(i)$. They denote the probability that $i$ cells arrive at the switch within $t$ time slots for an initial ACR at $t_3$ which corresponds to $R_{t_3}(j)$ (cf. Equation (2)). If we take into account further increases of the ACR, which may occur during the feedback delay, the probabilities $A_t^j(i)$ are given by

$$\begin{aligned} A_t^j(i) \;=\; & \mu_{N_{rm}}^{rc}(t) \cdot \\ & \quad \delta(i - \lfloor r(j) \cdot t \rfloor) + \\ & \sum_{t_1=0}^{t} \mu_{N_{rm}}^{r}(t_1) \cdot \mu_{N_{rm}}^{c}(t - \sum_{k=1}^{1} t_k) \cdot \\ & \quad \delta(i - \lfloor r(j) \cdot t_1 + r(j+1) \cdot (t - t_1) \rfloor) + \\ & \vdots \end{aligned} \qquad (16)$$

The conditional density functions are weighted by the probabilities of the initial ACRs to arrive at the probability $A_t(i)$ that $i$ cells arrive at the switch within $t = 1, \ldots, \infty$ time slots:

$$A_t(i) = \sum_{j=0}^{\infty} R_{t_3}(j) \cdot A_t^j(i) \quad . \qquad (17)$$

By proceeding as in Subsection 3.2.2, we obtain the buffer length density function $H_t(i)$ observed after $t$ time slots by

$$H_t(i) = \pi_0\left[Q_{t_3}(i) \star A_t(i) \star D_t(-i)\right] \quad . \qquad (18)$$

Finally, the buffer length density function just before the decreases of the ACR to the ER is obtained by

$$Q_{t_4}(i) = \sum_{t=\tau}^{\infty} \mu_{N_{rm}}^{r}(t - \tau) \cdot H_t(i) \quad , \qquad (19)$$

taking into account all possible feedback delays $\tau''$.

The computation of the system performance at the time instants $t_2, \ldots, t_4$ depends on the initial density functions at $t_1$. In our case, the initial functions are well-defined and of a deterministic nature. Thus, the results obtained reflect the steady-state behavior of the explicit rate mechanism considered for the description of the analysis. In case of other mechanisms, e.g. the binary signaling mode, time instants with a well-defined system state do not exist. For the investigation of such mechanisms, the analysis has to be carried out iteratively starting with hypothetical density functions.

# 4 Numerical results

Since we made a number of simplifications to reduce the numerical complexity, ignored the time-out procedures defined in the end system behavior [3] and neglected synchronization effects occurring in real systems, our analysis is only of an approximate nature. Therefore, the numerical accuracy of our algorithm is studied first. To obtain simulation results, we implemented the complete source and destination behavior as defined in [3]. The following system configuration was used:

- the physical layer is based on a SONET STS-3c system, i.e. the links have a capacity of 155 *Mbps*,
- the propagation delays are $\tau_1 = 0.04$ *ms*, $\tau_2 = 0.04$ *ms* and $\tau_3 = 0.08$ *ms*,
- the thresholds are $B_L = 128$ and $B_H = 256$ cells,
- the mean bandwidth share available for the ABR connection is 25% of the link capacity and the cell inter-departure time process $\mu(i)$ is geometric,
- the RM cell frequency is $N_{rm} = 32$,
- the PCR is equal to the link capacity (155 *Mbps*),
- the ER equals 20% of the link capacity,
- and the RIF is set to 0.1%.

Figure 3 shows a good agreement for the buffer length density function $Q_{t_2}(i)$ measured at the end of an ER signaling phase. The main portion of the density function is located below the threshold $B_L$, since the cell arrival rate during the feedback delay is lower than the mean bottleneck service rate.

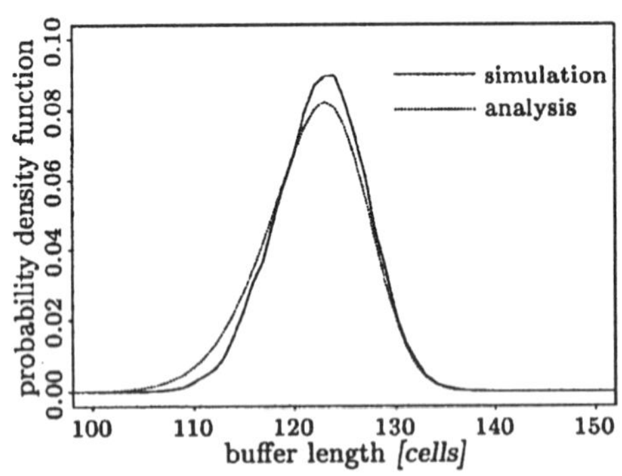


Figure 3: *Buffer length observed at* $t_2$

Theoretically, the mean buffer length at $t_2$ is equal to 122.2 cells. Comparing it with the results obtained from simulation and from our analysis, we observe a good agreement (cf. Table 1). Furthermore, Table 1 shows that both $10^{-3}$ quantiles are well approximated.

The next figure presents the buffer length density function noticed after an increase phase, i.e. at the time instant $t_4$. Again, a good agreement between simulation and analytical results is observed (cf. Figure 4).

| Measure | Simulation | Analysis |
|---|---|---|
| mean value | 122.6 | 121.9 |
| lower $10^{-3}$ quantile | 107 | 103 |
| higher $10^{-3}$ quantile | 136 | 135 |

Table 1: *Accuracy of the mean and the* $10^{-3}$ *quantiles*

The main portion of the probability density function is now located beyond $B_H$, since the cell arrival rate during the feedback delay is higher than the mean bottleneck service rate. A theoretical mean content of the buffer at this time instant can not be computed in such a way as before. The reason is the step-wise increase of the ACR during non-congestion periods, which may lead to different values of the ACR when congestion is detected.

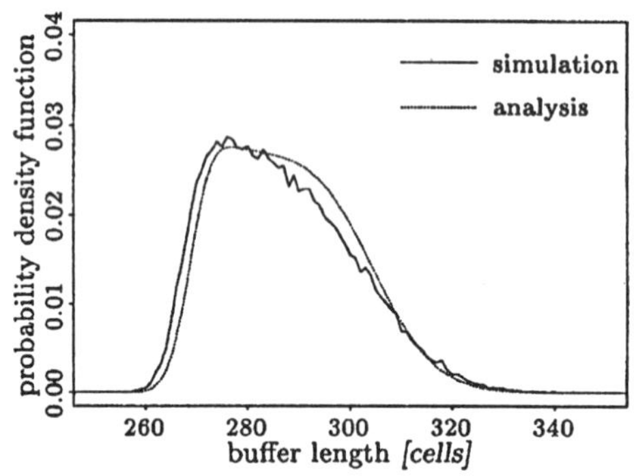


Figure 4: *Buffer length observed at* $t_4$

Table 2 compares the mean and the $10^{-3}$ quantiles obtained by simulation with those computed with our analysis. As already mentioned, the buffer content has its maximum at $t_4$ within a control cycle.

| Measure | Simulation | Analysis |
|---|---|---|
| mean value | 286.6 | 287.7 |
| lower $10^{-3}$ quantile | 259 | 261 |
| higher $10^{-3}$ quantile | 334 | 329 |

Table 2: *Accuracy of the mean and the* $10^{-3}$ *quantiles*

After checking the accuracy of our analysis, we study the influence of various system parameters on the density function of the buffer length. The first parameter we look at is the coefficient of variation of the cell inter-departure time process $\mu(i)$. Figure 5 shows the mean (solid lines) and the $10^{-3}$ quantiles (dotted lines) of the buffer length density functions at $t_2$ and $t_4$ as functions of the coefficient of variation. The cell inter-departure times are negative-binomially distributed with a mean equal to 4.0 and the other system parameters are set as described at the beginning of this section.

First, we observe that the mean variation of the queue length slightly increases with the coefficient of variation, in particular for the density function observed at $t_4$.

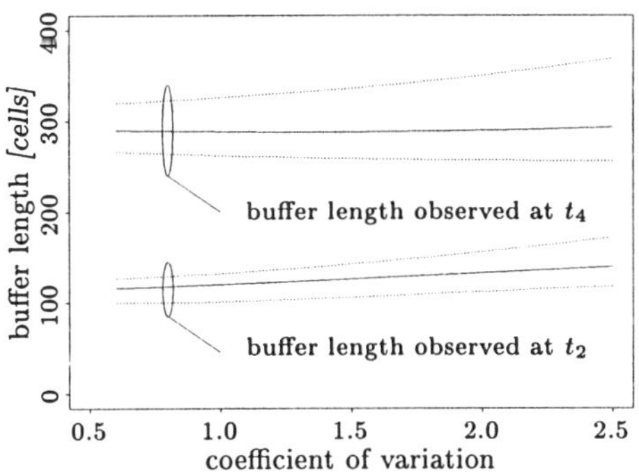


Figure 5: *Dependency on the coefficient of variation*

While the mean queue length at $t_4$ remains almost constant, it increases slowly and almost linearly if measured at $t_2$. For comparison, the queue lengths observed with a deterministic bandwidth share are 119 cells at $t_2$ and 303 cells at $t_4$, computed with the formulae presented in [22]. Thus, the degree of variation of the bottleneck service rate has only a minor influence on the mean queue length and the $10^{-3}$ quantiles at the observation instants $t_2$ and $t_4$.

The influence of the RTT on the system performance is studied in Figure 6. Using a negative-binomial distribution as before with a coefficient of variation equal to 1.0, we varied the round trip distance, i.e. twice the distance between the SES and the DES, from 10 to 100 *km*. Figure 6 indicates a linear dependency of the mean and the quantiles for both density functions. This observation was also made in [22] where the bandwidth share is assumed to be constant.

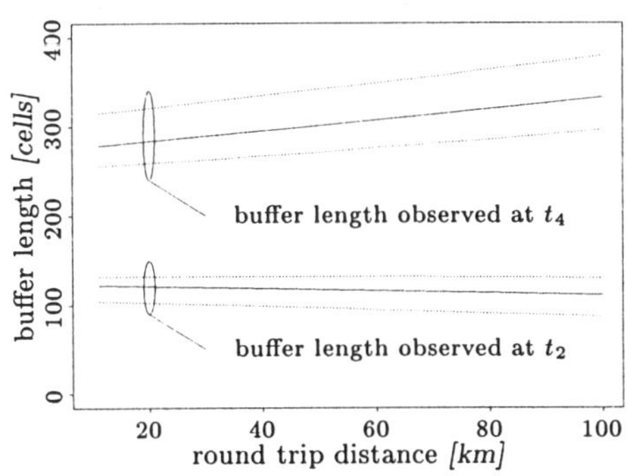


Figure 6: *Linear dependency on the RTT*

In the next two figures, the mean and the quantiles are plotted as functions of the ER and the RIF respectively. For the ER (cf. Figure 7) we again observe a linear dependency of the mean and the quantiles measured at $t_2$. The buffer length after an increase phase ($t_4$) is hardly influenced by this parameter.

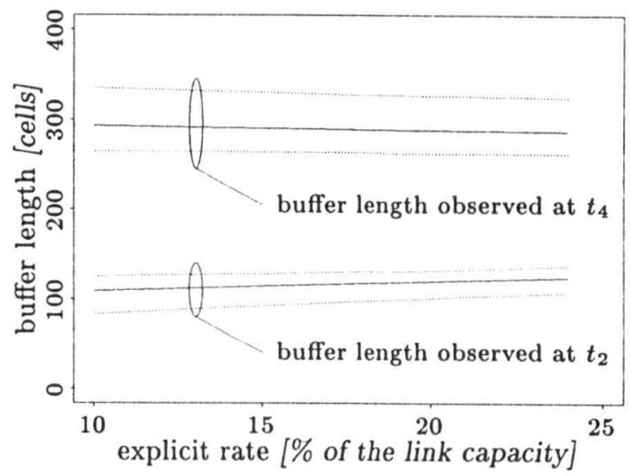


Figure 7: *Linear dependency on the ER*

In contrast, the buffer length density function observed at $t_2$ remains constant if we vary the RIF, as shown in Figure 8. In this case, the mean and the quantiles measured at $t_4$ increase fast with the RIF until the RIF is large enough so that the PCR is attained before congestion is signaled.

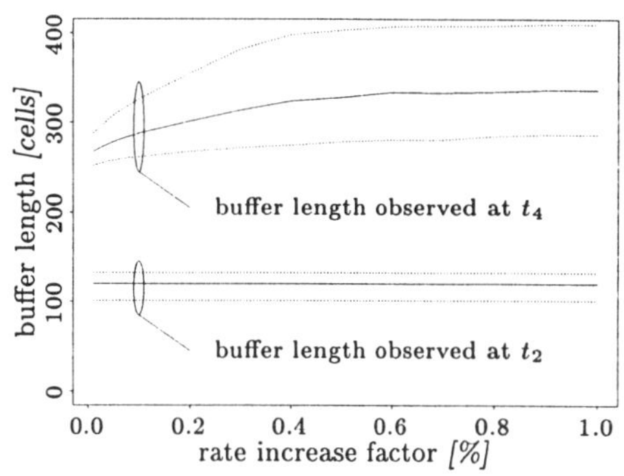


Figure 8: *Dependency on the RIF*

# 5 Conclusion

In this paper we presented an analysis to study the effect of bottleneck service rate variations on the performance of the ABR flow control. Such variations occur in real systems due to the establishment and release of ATM connections and due to the varying bandwidth demand of VBR connections. Our algorithm operates in the discrete-time domain and assumes a bottleneck service rate that varies according to a general probability density function. To investigate the influence of the variations on the system performance, we compute probability density functions for the buffer length observed at specific time instants within a control cycle.

The numerical results obtained with our algorithm show a high accuracy, in particular for the mean and for the quantiles of the density functions. We discovered a weak linear dependency of the mean and the quantiles on the degree of the rate variations. This behavior indicates that frequent variations of the bottleneck service rate have only a minor influence on the system performance, even if the degree of variation is large. An explanation for this observation are the different time scales on which the rate variations occur and the control process operates.

Our analysis can also be used to investigate other control schemes, such as the binary mode. Since the difference in time scales mentioned above is also given for other control schemes, we expect similar results.

# Acknowledgment

The author would like to thank Sven Wahler for the programming efforts during the course of this work. We also appreciate the support of the Deutsche Telekom AG.

# References

[1] E. Altman. F. Baccelli and J.-C. Bolot. *Discrete-Time Analysis of Adaptive Rate Control Mechanisms.* High Speed Networks and Their Performance (C-21), North-Holland 1994, pp. 121-140.

[2] The ATM Forum Technical Committee. *User-Network Interface Specification.* Version 3.1, September 1994.

[3] The ATM Forum Technical Committee – Traffic Management Working Group. *Traffic Management Specification.* Version 4.0, April 1996.

[4] J.-C. Bolot and A. U. Shankar. *Dynamical Behavior of Rate-Based Flow Control Mechanisms.* ACM SIGCOMM Comp. Comm. Review 20(2), 1990, pp. 35-49.

[5] F. Bonomi, D. Mitra and J. B. Seery. *Adaptive Algorithms for Feedback-Based Flow Control in High-Speed, Wide-Area ATM Networks.* IEEE JSAC 13(7), 1995, pp. 1267-1283.

[6] D. Cavendish, Y. Oie, M. Murata and H. Miyahara. *Proportional Rate-Based Congestion Control Under Long Propagation Delay.* Intern. Journal of Communication Systems 8, 1995, pp. 79-89.

[7] A. E. Eckberg, B. T. Doshi and R. Zoccolillo. *Controlling Congestion in B-ISDN / ATM: Issues and Strategies.* IEEE Comm. Magazine, September 1991, pp. 64-70.

[8] A. I. Elwalid. *Analysis of Rate-Based Congestion Control for High-Speed Wide-Area Networks.* IEEE ICC '95, Seattle, 1995, pp. 1948-1943.

[9] K. W. Fendick, D. Mitra, I. Mitrani, M. A. Rodrigues, J. B. Seery and A. Weiss. *An Approach to High-Performance, High-Speed Data Networks.* IEEE Comm. Magazine, October 1991, pp. 74-82.

[10] K. W. Fendick, M. A. Rodrigues and A. Weiss. *Analysis of a Rate-Based Control Strategy with Delayed Feedback.* IEEE Comm. Magazine, October 1991, pp. 74-82.

[11] J. Filipiak. *Modelling and Control of Dynamic Flows in Communication Networks.* Springer-Verlag, 1988.

[12] Y. Gong and I. F. Akyildiz. *Dynamic Traffic Control Using Feedback and Traffic Prediction in ATM Networks.* IEEE INFOCOM '94, Toronto, 1994, pp. 91-98.

[13] I. Iliadis. *A New Feedback Congestion Control Policy for Long Propagation Delays.* IEEE JSAC 13(7), 1995, pp. 1284-1295.

[14] R. Izmailov. *Adaptive Feedback Control Algorithms for Large Data Transfers in High-Speed Networks.* IEEE Trans. on Automatic Control 40(8), 1995, pp. 1469-1471.

[15] K. Kawahara, Y. Oie, M. Murata and H. Miyahara. *Performance Analysis of Reactive Congestion Control for ATM Networks.* IEEE JSAC 13(4), 1995, pp. 651-661.

[16] S. Keshav. *A Control-Theoretic Approach to Flow Control.* ACM SIGCOMM Comp. Comm. Review 21(4), 1991, pp. 3-15.

[17] A. Mukherjee and J. C. Strikwerda. *Analysis of Dynamic Congestion Control Protocols – A Fokker-Plank Approximation.* ACM SIGCOMM Comp. Comm. Review 21(4), 1991, pp. 159-169.

[18] P. Newman. *Traffic Management for ATM Local Area Networks.* IEEE Comm. Magazine, August 1994, pp. 44-50.

[19] H. Ohsaki, M. Murata, H. Suzuki, C. Ikeda and H. Miyahara. *Rate-Based Congestion Control for ATM Networks.* ACM SIGCOMM Comp. Comm. Review 25(2), 1995, pp. 60-72.

[20] R. S. Pazhyannur and R. Agrawal. *Feedback-Based Flow Control of B-ISDN/ATM Networks.* IEEE JSAC 13(7), 1995, pp. 1252-1266.

[21] G. Pecelli and G. Kim. *Dynamic Behavior of Feedback Congestion Control Schemes.* IEEE INFOCOM '95, Boston, 1995, pp. 253-260.

[22] M. Ritter. *Network Buffer Requirements of the Rate-Based Control Mechanism for ABR Services.* IEEE INFOCOM '96, San Francisco, 1996, pp. 1090-1097.

[23] D. Tipper and M. K. Sundareshan. *Numerical Methods for Modeling Computer Networks Under Nonstationary Conditions.* IEEE JSAC 8(9), 1990, pp. 1682-1695.

[24] P. Tran-Gia and H. Ahmadi. *Analysis of a Discrete-Time* $G^{[x]}/D/1-S$ *Queueing System with Applications in Packet-Switching Systems.* IEEE INFOCOM '88, New Orleans, 1988, pp. 861-870.

[25] N. Yin and M. G. Hluchyj. *On Closed-Loop Rate Control for ATM Cell Relay Networks.* IEEE INFOCOM '94, Toronto, 1994, pp. 99-108.

[26] N. Yin and M. G. Hluchyj. *A Dynamic Rate Control Mechanism for Source Coded Traffic in a Fast Packet Network.* IEEE JSAC 9(7), 1991, pp. 1003-1012.

# The APIC Approach to High Performance Network Interface Design: Protected DMA and Other Techniques†

Zubin D. Dittia
zubin@dworkin.wustl.edu

Guru M. Parulkar
guru@cs.wustl.edu

Jerome R. Cox, Jr.
jrc@cs.wustl.edu

Department of Computer Science, Washington University in St. Louis
St. Louis, MO 63130, USA.

## Abstract

*We are building a high performance 1.2 Gb/s ATM network interface chip called the APIC (ATM Port Interconnect Controller). In addition to borrowing useful ideas from a number of research and commercial prototypes, the APIC design embraces several innovative features, and integrates all of these pieces into a coherent whole. Some of the novel ideas incorporated in the APIC design include: Protected DMA and Protected I/O, which allow applications to queue data for transmission or reception directly from user-space, effectively bypassing the kernel. This argues for moving the entire protocol stack including the interface device driver into user-space, thereby yielding better latency and throughput performance than kernel-resident implementations. Pool DMA when used with Packet Splitting, is a technique that can be used to build true zero-copy kernel-resident protocol stack implementations, using a page-remapping technique. Finally, Orchestrated Interrupts and Interrupt Demultiplexing are mechanisms used to reduce the frequency of interrupts issued by the APIC.*

*Although many of these ideas have been developed in the context of an ATM network interface, we believe they are also applicable in other contexts. In particular, protected DMA and I/O are promising techniques for improving the performance of several different types of I/O devices.*

## 1 Introduction

Network interface design and the structuring of protocol implementations in operating systems are two areas of research that have received considerable attention in recent years [1,2,4,5,7,16,17]. The growing interest in these subjects can be attributed to the observed gross disparity between the raw bandwidth available from emerging gigabit networks, and the maximum effective throughput that can be delivered to end applications. The bottlenecks in end-systems that give rise to this disparity are far easier to identify than to rectify. Indeed, it is a well known fact that memory bandwidth limitations, coupled with the overhead of operations such as data copying, software checksumming, servicing of interrupts, and context switching are usually responsible for the observed poor performance. Several of the aforementioned research efforts have identified mechanisms that are at least partially effective in overcoming some of these handicaps. We have attempted to integrate a number of these "proven" good mechanisms, along with some new ones of our own creation, in our attempt to build a state-of-the-art high performance ATM network interface. Our research prototype of this network interface, which is called the APIC (ATM Port Interconnect Controller), is capable of supporting a full duplex link rate of 1.2 Gb/s. Since one of our overriding goals during the course of the project was to minimize cost (of a production version of the interface), the entire interface is being implemented on a single ASIC chip. In addition to being a network interface in the traditional sense, the APIC also has the capability to double as a building block for an I/O Desk-Area Network (DAN) [13,14]. This was achieved by building into the chip a small $2 \times 2$ ATM switch that would allow multiple APICs to be interconnected to create a small network; each APIC in this resulting network can directly interface either to an I/O device or to a computer system bus. An example of an APIC-based DAN is shown in Figure 1. An introduction to the APIC chip and APIC-based DANs, and a brief overview of the internal design of the APIC can be found in [5]. In this paper, we present several innovative mechanisms that have been incorporated in the APIC design with the objective of delivering very high performance (in terms of both throughput and latency) to end-applications running on the host computer.

### 1.1 A Brief Overview of APIC Features

The APIC has two ATM ports which can be connected either to an optical link interface, or to another APIC. Both ports implement ATM Forum's 16-bit wide UTOPIA (Universal Test and Operations PHY Interface for ATM) standard to connect to receive and transmit links. The prototype APIC interfaces to computer systems and devices over an external memory interface which supports three different bus standards: Sun's MBus, which is a 2.56 Gb/s (peak) 64-bit wide CPU-memory bus, and 32 and 64 bit wide versions of the PCI bus, which is a 1.056 Gb/s peak (for PCI-32, twice that for PCI-64) I/O bus. Thus, the APIC is capable of interfacing to a host system either over an I/O bus or over a CPU-memory bus. When interfacing to a CPU-memory bus, the APIC issues cache-coherent transactions to ensure cache consistency.

The capability of interfacing directly to a CPU-memory (main) bus is a noteworthy departure from most existing network interface designs, which typically interface to an I/O bus only. Main bus implementations of the network

† This work was supported in part by the Defense Advanced Research Projects Agency (DARPA), the National Science Foundation (NSF), Rome Laboratories, and an industrial consortium of Ascom Nexion, Bay Networks, Bell Northern Research, NEC America, NIH, NTT, Samsung, SBC, and Tektronix.



0-8186-7780-5/97 $10.00 © 1997 IEEE

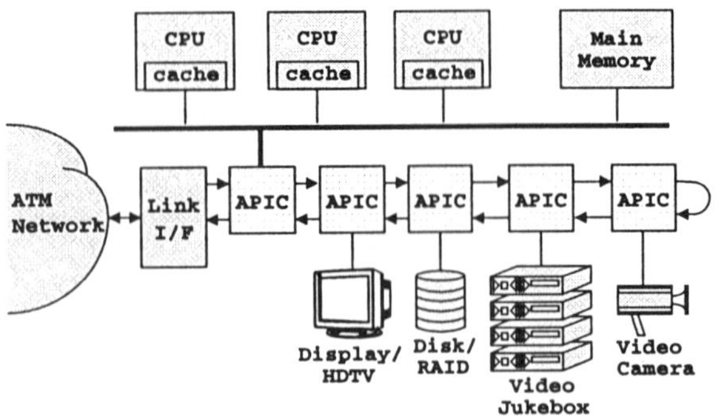


**Figure 1: An APIC based Desk-Area Network**

interface enjoy a number of benefits that I/O bus implementations cannot, not the least of which is improved performance. For example, an APIC that interfaces to a CPU-memory bus can physically address the entire range of physical memory in the machine, whereas an I/O bus implementation would, in most typical systems, be forced to use virtual mappings[1] to access physical memory that falls outside of the limits imposed by the I/O bus width. As networking becomes more an integral part of computer systems, we expect that network interfaces will migrate to the main bus on the motherboard in order to achieve maximum performance.

The APIC implements full **AAL-5 Segmentation and Reassembly** (SAR) functionality on-chip. The APIC does not store-and-forward entire AAL-5 frames; instead, it implements cut-through at cell granularity. For this reason, the APIC can make do with only 256 cells worth of buffering on-chip, and no off-chip buffers. This is in keeping with our objective of very low production costs, since APIC interface cards do not need any on-board memory and almost no glue logic. In addition to AAL-5 SAR, the APIC also supports transmission and reception of raw ATM cells (**AAL-0**).

Other features of the APIC chip include: multipoint and loopback connections, remote controllability, cell batching for larger bus transactions (and consequently higher throughput), cell pacing at rates that are individually specifiable on a per-connection basis, low delay priority for connections, best effort transmission of cells, and hardware assist for transport-level CRC generation and verification. Some of these features are described in detail elsewhere [5].

In addition to the above features, the APIC includes DMA mechanisms that are designed to support efficient implementations of zero-copy protocol stacks, and mechanisms designed to reduce the frequency of interrupts and interrupt service overhead. The focus of this paper is on these **DMA and interrupt related mechanisms**. For this reason, it will be sufficient for the rest of the paper to think of the APIC as a traditional network interface, and to ignore its desk-area networking capabilities.

The prototype APIC is being implemented in 0.5 micron CMOS, with a (conservatively) estimated die size of 1.8 square centimeters, and a package size of a little over 200 pins. The VHDL coding effort for the APIC is almost complete at the time of this writing. This version of the APIC will support a maximum of 256 transmit and 256 receive connections, which we felt was enough for prototype demonstration purposes.

### 1.2 Summary of Innovative Claims and Contributions

This paper introduces the following five techniques, in the context of the APIC interface design:

**Protected DMA:** This is a technique that is used to allow protocol libraries residing in user-space to queue buffers for transmission or reception directly to the APIC, without any kernel intervention, and without compromising the protection mechanisms of the operating system.

**Protected I/O:** Protected I/O is a technique that is used to allow protocol libraries residing in user space programmed I/O access to the memory-mapped registers on the APIC, with the specific access permissions to individual registers specifiable by the OS kernel.

**Pool DMA with Packet Splitting:** This technique enables true zero-copy[2] kernel-resident protocol stack implementations using page remapping.

**Orchestrated Interrupts:** When the CPU queues buffers for transmission or reception to the APIC, it can "mark" some of these buffers; the APIC will issue an interrupt whenever it encounters "marked" buffers. Such (pre-) *orchestrated interrupts* are useful for reducing the frequency of interrupts issued by the APIC.

**Interrupt Demultiplexing:** By allowing interrupts to be enabled/disabled on a per-connection basis, we can exploit the connection-oriented aspect of ATM networks to significantly reduce the frequency of interrupts raised by the APIC. We call this scheme "*interrupt demultiplexing*."

We would like to point out here that although the above techniques have been developed in the context of an ATM network interface, we believe that many of these ideas can be used to advantage in other scenarios too. In particular, we feel that it would be possible for other types of devices such as disks and video frame buffer cards to exploit protected DMA and protected I/O, and we intend to make this a subject for future study.

### 1.3 Organization of the Paper

The rest of this paper is organized as follows: Section 2 elaborates on the notion of protected I/O. Section 3 describes the three DMA mechanisms supported by the APIC. Section 4 outlines orchestrated interrupts and interrupt demultiplexing. Finally, Section 5 makes some concluding remarks. Throughout the paper, comparisons with related work are made where appropriate.

## 2 Protected I/O

The APIC device driver running on the host CPU communicates with the APIC by two mechanisms: through

[1] These would have to be setup in advance by the CPU in a special I/O MMU that is built into the bus adapter.

[2] The term "true zero-copy" is used to indicate that data moves directly between application data structures and the network interface without any intermediate copying. A definition of the term can be found in [9].

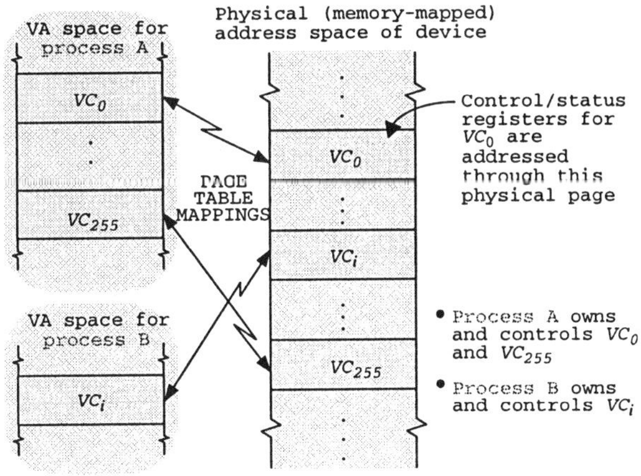


**Figure 2: Protection Mechanism Used for ADCs**

reading/writing memory-mapped on-chip registers, and through shared data structures in the host's main memory. The APIC's on-chip device registers fall into two categories: global registers, and per-connection registers. The set of global registers contain state that is of global relevance, such as the interrupt status registers, the software reset register, etc. There is one set of per-connection registers for each connection supported by the APIC; these hold state that varies from connection to connection, such as the connection identifier (VPI/VCI), the pacing bandwidth, etc. Protected I/O is designed to give untrusted user-space protocol implementations the ability to directly read or write per-connection registers, in a way that would not compromise the security or protection mechanisms of the operating system. Protected I/O should really have been called "protected programmed I/O," but we chose the former name in the interests of brevity. Protected I/O is really just an extension of the protection mechanism that was used by Druschel et al. to implement application device channels (ADCs) in the OSIRIS interface [7]. The U-Net interface from Cornell [9] also uses the same mechanism as ADCs. Both of these efforts attempt to give an application read/write access to only those memory-mapped I/O registers on the interface that correspond to connections that are "owned" by the application. An application is said to "own" a connection if it was responsible for initiating the connection setup. Figure 2 demonstrates how the ADC protection mechanism works. The per-connection registers on the interface are mapped into its memory-mapped I/O address space in such a way that all registers corresponding to a connection fall into the same physical page frame, and no page frame contains registers for more than one connection. Thus, all device registers for a particular connection can be accessed through physical addresses that fall within the same page frame (or set of page frames, if the machine's page size is not large enough to hold all the registers) in the physically addressed memory-mapped I/O space of the device. When a user process makes a connection setup request to the OS kernel, the kernel modifies the system page table entries such that the page corresponding to the connection is mapped into the process' virtual address space with read/write permissions. The process now becomes the owner of the connection, and it can control the connection by reading or writing the registers on

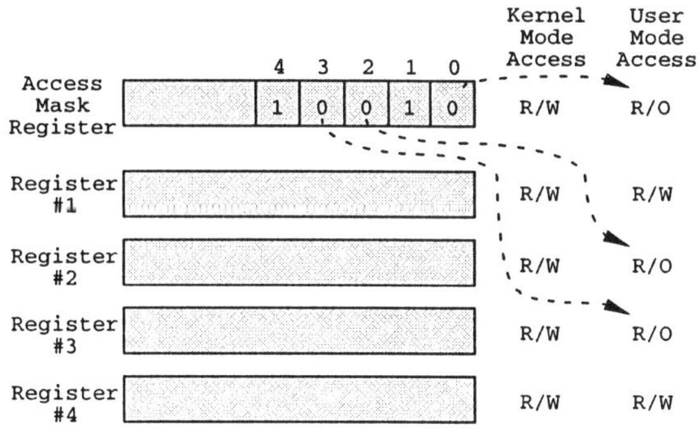


**Figure 3: Fine Grain Access Control using Protected I/O**

the interface directly, without having to make system calls or otherwise interact with any trusted code. This process cannot, however, control other connections that it does not also own, because the pages corresponding to those connections are not mapped into its virtual address space. To summarize, the system's virtual memory (VM) protection mechanisms are overloaded to provide protected access to per-connection device registers.

The ADC scheme does not allow the kernel fine grain control over which individual per-connection registers the application is given access to, or selectively control the type of access (no access, read-only, or read-write) to these registers. This is important because some administrators may be willing to grant more privileges to their users than others, and some processes may similarly be given more control by the operating system than others. For example: Should a user process be allowed to change the pacing rate for a connection that it owns? Should the operating system permit a user process to dictate under what conditions the interface will raise an interrupt, when a connection-specific event occurs? There is no way currently to use the ADC protection mechanism to provide this type of fine grain access control, short of mapping each device register into a separate page, and setting up page table entries and protections appropriately. This scheme is not acceptable because if there are many registers per connection, the number of page mappings in each process' context becomes large, resulting in inefficiencies from potentially slower page table lookups in the MMU, and thrashing in the TLB. Protected I/O provides the solution to this problem by extending the ADC protection idea to include the concept of an *access mask register*. The access mask register is a register that augments the set of per-connection device registers, so that each connection has an associated access mask register. In addition, all per-connection registers (including the access mask register) are mapped twice, and in different page frames, in the physically addressed memory-mapped I/O space of the device. Note that this means that each hardware per-connection register can be accessed (read or written) using two different physical addresses, each of which resides in a separate page frame. We term these two different methods of access as kernel-mode and user-mode accesses. The kernel ensures that the virtual memory page tables are setup in such a way that the kernel can use kernel mode accesses for all registers, but user processes are forced to use user-mode accesses. Furthermore, the ADC protection mechanism is used to ensure that only a process

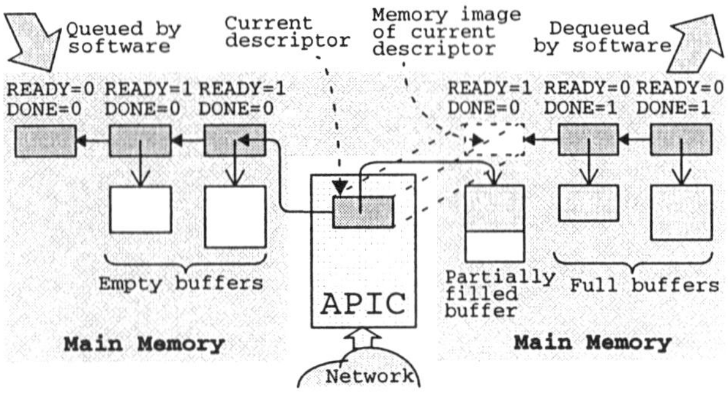


**Figure 4: Receiving Data using Buffer Descriptors**

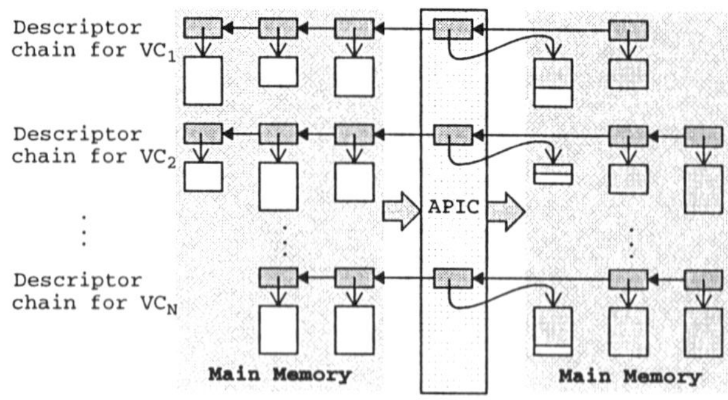


**Figure 5: Illustration of Simple DMA**

that owns a connection can access the corresponding per-connection registers (using user-mode accesses). The device (APIC) differentiates read or write accesses to a per-connection register based upon the access type. Only kernel-mode accesses are guaranteed to be successful. Thus, the kernel has full read/write access to all device registers, including the access mask registers for all connections. As shown in Figure 3, the access mask register contains one bit for every per-connection register that is associated with the corresponding connection; for each bit that is set, the device allows user-mode write access to the corresponding register. Otherwise, only read access is granted. The kernel is responsible for setting up the access mask register to grant appropriate permissions to the user process that owns the corresponding connection. Clearly, this scheme can be extended to allow the option of providing no access (in addition to R/W and R/O) to registers by having two bits per register instead of just one, in the access mask register.

# 3 APIC DMA Mechanisms

The APIC uses DMA for all movement of transmit/receive data from/to main memory. DMA is also used by the APIC to read/write control data structures stored in main memory called buffer descriptors, which are needed to support scatter/gather DMA. Buffer descriptors contain information about a data buffer in physical memory, such as the physical address of the buffer, its length, and the type of data in the buffer (AAL-0 or AAL-5). Buffer descriptors are used by the host CPU to queue buffers containing data to be transmitted, or to queue empty buffers that will be used to hold received data. Figure 4 demonstrates the use of buffer descriptors in receiving data. For transmission, the scenario is almost identical, except that the buffers on the right in the figure would contain data that has already been transmitted (or is in the process of being transmitted), while the buffers on the left hold data that has yet to be transmitted. To allow buffer descriptors to be queued, each descriptor contains the address of the next descriptor in a singly linked list (chain) of descriptors. One descriptor in a chain is always designated as the "current" descriptor; this is the descriptor that the APIC is currently using. When the APIC is done with the current descriptor (i.e., it has finished transmitting all the data in the corresponding buffer, or it has filled the buffer with received data), it writes the descriptor back to main memory, and fetches the next descriptor in the chain. The current descriptor (which is on-chip) is visible to software through APIC device registers. These registers are also used by the software to setup the first descriptor in the chain, at the time of connection initialization. Each descriptor contains two bits, called the `READY` and `DONE` bits, that are used to synchronize APIC and CPU accesses of the descriptors. The `READY` bit is set by the CPU to inform the APIC that the corresponding buffer is ready to be transmitted from, or received into. The `DONE` bit is set by the APIC when it has finished sending data from (or receiving data into) the corresponding buffer. The CPU can "catch up" with the APIC by chasing the next descriptor links until it comes to a descriptor that has its `DONE` flag set to zero (this is the current descriptor). In addition to the fields already mentioned, buffer descriptors contain several control and status flags. These include an `INTERRUPT` flag which can be set by the CPU to instruct the APIC to issue an interrupt when it first reads in the descriptor (see Section 4.1 for details on how this flag is used), an `END-OF-FRAME` flag, which is used to mark the last buffer of an AAL-5 frame, and a `CRC-OK` flag which is set by the APIC to inform the processor whether AAL-5 CRC verification was successful.

It should be noted that a single AAL-5 frame can span multiple data buffers. The APIC will always transmit all the data in a transmit buffer. However, the APIC does not allow data from more than one AAL-5 frame in a single receive buffer, so receive buffers may not be completely filled by the APIC (this happens if the portion of the received frame in the buffer is less than the size of the buffer).

The APIC supports three different types of scatter/gather DMA: Simple DMA, Pool DMA, and Protected DMA. We now go on to describe all three DMA mechanisms.

## 3.1 Simple DMA

With simple DMA, each connection supported by the APIC is associated with a separate and dedicated chain of descriptors, as shown in Figure 5. Simple DMA can be used by kernel-resident (or trusted user-level server) protocol stack implementations only. This is because if untrusted user-level programs were given write access to descriptors, they could queue arbitrary buffers from main memory for transmission or reception (including those not otherwise accessible to the process), thereby compromising the security and defeating the protection mechanisms of the operating system. Protected DMA, which is described in Section 3.3, is designed to be usable by untrusted user-level protocol stack implementations.

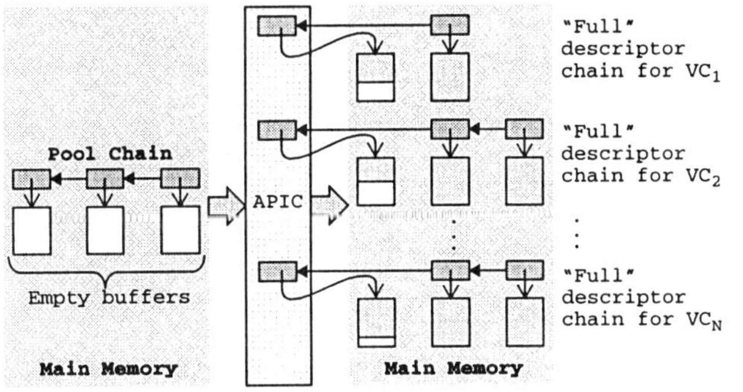


**Figure 6: Illustration of Pool DMA**

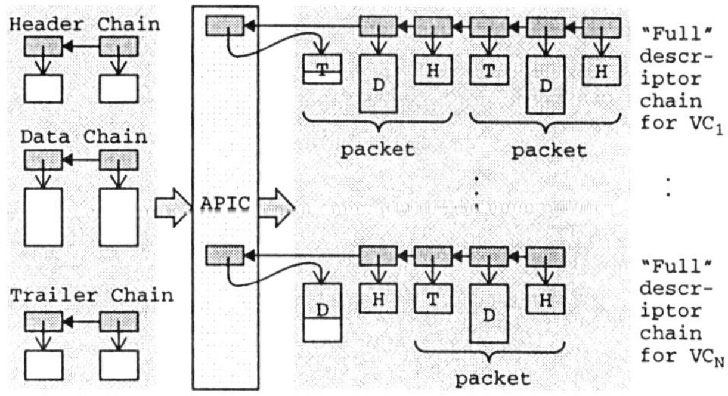


**Figure 7: Pool DMA with Packet Splitting**

Simple DMA can be used for both transmit and receive connections. However, simple DMA can be very inefficient in its use of memory resources if it is used for receiving data. This is because simple DMA requires free (or empty) buffers to be dedicated to each open receive connection. Because free buffers queued on one connection cannot be used by another, and because there is no way to anticipate when data will arrive on a connection, the amount of free buffer space required can be very large. Pool DMA is designed to overcome this limitation.

## 3.2 Pool DMA

Pool DMA allows a set of receive connections to all share the same pool of free buffers (see Figure 6). The APIC fetches a descriptor from a global "pool chain" whenever a connection needs a new empty buffer to place arriving data in. Before it writes the old "full" descriptor back, however, the APIC fills in the next descriptor pointer field in that descriptor with the address of the new descriptor. This results in the buffer descriptors (and buffers) getting demultiplexed into separate chains of "full" buffers, one per connection. Note that pool DMA is intended for use by receive connections only; transmit connections cannot use pool DMA. The prototype APIC supports four global pool chains, and it is possible to specify which of these chains to use for each connection. This can be useful, because we may know in advance that some connections always carry very small packets (DNS, for example), so we can use a pool of small buffers for all connections of that type. Other connections may draw from pools with larger sized buffers.

### 3.2.1 Pool DMA with Packet Splitting

The APIC allows a received packet (AAL-5 frame) to be split into a header portion, a data portion, and the AAL-5 trailer, with each of these portions written to buffers drawn from different pool chains. This is illustrated in Figure 7. The location of the header-data split is independently specifiable for each connection as an offset from the start of the packet; this "header length" is fixed for the lifetime of the connection. The location of the data-trailer split is determined by the APIC using the length field in the AAL-5 trailer.

The packet splitting feature of the APIC can be used to implement a true zero-copy protocol stack using page-remapping techniques, under the following assumptions: the network and transport protocol headers are of fixed size for each connection, and the amount of data in each packet is an exact multiple of the receiving host's page size[3]. The latter assumption required to get zero-copy behavior on the receiving end if we want to efficiently handle network errors and loss — to see this, note that if a packet is lost, there is a hole in the receive sequence space which must be filled by one or more received packets without a copy; this can be accomplished only if the retransmitted data fills the page frames in the "hole" completely. We are currently working on developing a high performance ATM transport protocol that satisfies both of the above assumptions.

The page-remapping strategy for implementing the receive side of a zero-copy protocol stack is illustrated by the example in Figure 8. The APIC splits received packets into headers and data (trailers, which are handled in the same way as headers, have intentionally been omitted to simplify the example). The header buffers are all drawn from a pool of buffers that are mapped into the kernel's address space. Buffers that will hold the data portion of packets are all drawn from a pool of free physical pages. Since each packet holds one or more pages worth of data, no page will be left partially filled. When packets are received, the operating system examines the header of the packet to determine where the corresponding data page(s) should reside in the application's address space; it then modifies the page table entries appropriately. The end-result is that data from consecutively sequenced packets appears contiguous in the application's address space. The (sometimes high) cost of modifying page table entries can be minimized by processing packets in batches, thereby avoiding the need to flush the TLB for every packet; this is known as lazy updating of page tables. The transmit side of the zero-copy protocol stack is considerably simpler: data can be transmitted directly from an application buffer using simple DMA; no page-remapping is needed.

Note that in a zero-copy protocol stack implementation, a BSD socket type of API cannot be presented to applications. A suitable API is provided by fbufs [8], container shipping [15], or UCMIO [3]. Also, note that using page-remapping to eliminate data copying is by no means a new idea. The Axon [16] network interface was among the first

[3] If there are multiple receiving hosts, and if we assume that pages are always a power of 2 in size, then the data portion of each packet would have to be a multiple of the largest of the page sizes of all receivers.

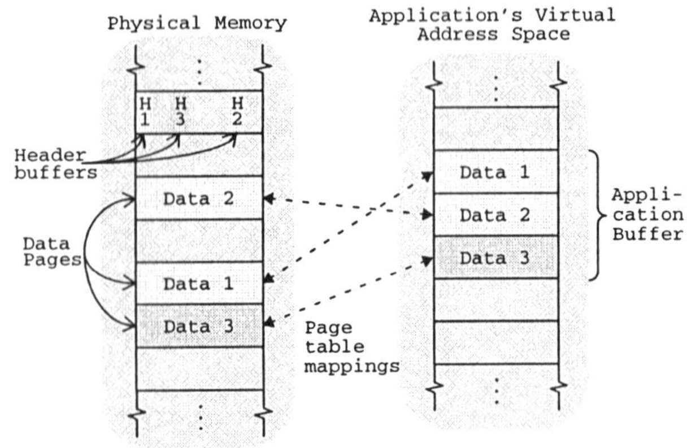


**Figure 8: Packet Splitting enables Zero-copy**

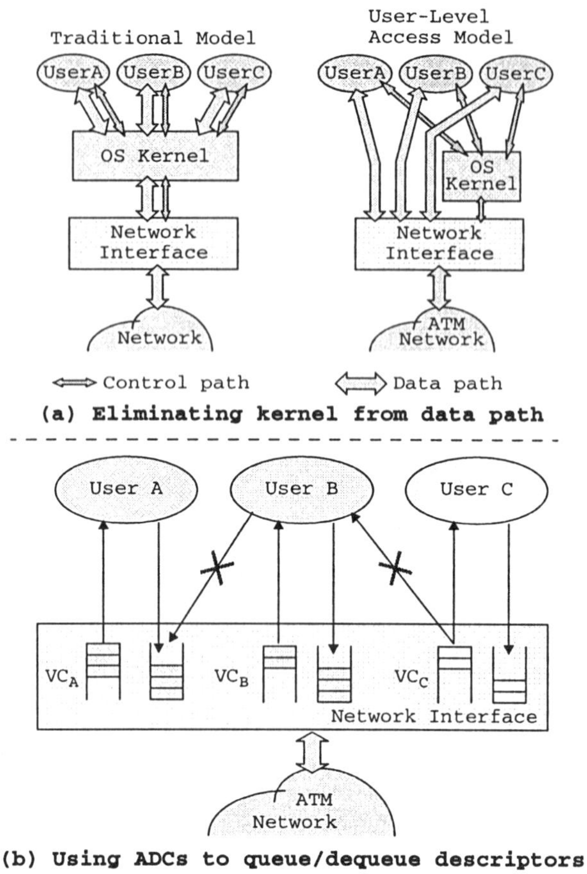


**Figure 9: User-Level Access to the Network Interface**

to introduce the use of page-remapping as a method for avoiding data copying.

## 3.3 Protected DMA

### 3.3.1 Motivation and Related Work

There have been several research efforts that have attempted to make user-level library implementations of protocol stacks. Most of these efforts have left the network interface device driver inside the kernel, thereby requiring the use of system calls for transmitting and receiving data. System calls are expensive; our experiments show that a null system call takes between 10 and 50 microseconds in state-of-the-art workstations running derivatives of the Unix operating system. This is bad from the viewpoint of minimizing end-to-end latency for latency-critical LAN applications (many distributed computing applications, RPC, and NFS fall in this category). But the high cost of system calls can also result in poor throughput if the protocols have not been implemented carefully. Most researchers exploring library implementations of protocols have given serious attention to amortizing the overhead of a system call over multiple operations by batching them into a single system call. We believe that this places an unnecessary burden on protocol coders, and makes the code less portable. Also, this technique does not solve the higher end-to-end latency problem discussed earlier.

To solve the afore-mentioned problems, system calls should be eliminated from the critical data path. As shown in Figure 9(a), the data path should be between the user-space and the network interface. The control path operations (for example, connection setup and teardown), can still pass through the kernel without incurring a significant performance penalty. With this objective in mind, Druschel et al. [7] proposed using ADCs (described earlier in Section 2) to queue buffer descriptors directly on the network interface. The ADC protection mechanism would ensure that one user could not queue/dequeue descriptors to/from another user's descriptor queue (see Figure 9(b)). The network interface was given the task of ensuring that buffer descriptors queued by an application pointed to valid buffers to which the application had appropriate read or write access. To make these checks feasible, the network interface relied on ownership and access information for buffers that was provided to it in advance (at connection setup time), by the operating system kernel. The checks themselves were performed by the two on-board *i*-960 processors that were part of the OSIRIS network interface. The U-Net interface from Cornell [9] also relied on these same ideas to achieve a direct data path between user-space and the network adapter, but this work was done by modifying the firmware for the on-board *i*-960 processor on Fore-System's SBA-200 ATM adapter.

There are two main problems with the OSIRIS/ADC and U-Net approaches that make them unsuitable for use with APIC-like network interfaces. First, information about valid communication buffers, as well as all buffer descriptors for queued buffers have to reside on the network interface board. For a gigabit network, the amount of memory needed on the board for these purposes can be substantial (a megabyte or more), which results in higher cost for the interfaces. The second problem is that both ADCs and U-Net approaches require fast on-board processor to perform buffer validity tests, since these tests are not easily amenable to hardware implementation.

Our approach to solving the problem of providing untrusted user-space protocols the ability to queue or dequeue data directly to/from the interface is called *Protected DMA*. This approach does not suffer from any of the three drawbacks mentioned above, and it is usable by both APIC and OSIRIS/U-Net types of interfaces.

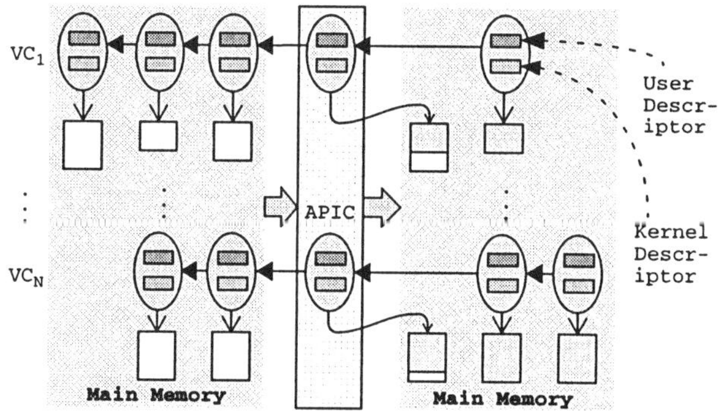


**Figure 10: Illustration of Protected DMA**

### 3.3.2 Description of Protected DMA

In protected DMA, all buffer descriptors reside in main memory. Protected DMA is in many ways similar to simple DMA; however, each buffer is associated with two descriptors instead of one (see Figure 10). We will call these *kernel descriptors* and *user descriptors*. Before the APIC uses a buffer, it always reads both descriptors for the buffer. The user descriptor contains values supplied by a user level program, so these values cannot be trusted. However, the kernel sets up descriptors in such a way that the kernel descriptor can be used to check the validity of the values supplied in the user descriptor. Thus, before the APIC begins using a buffer, it uses the contents of the kernel descriptor to validate, or *notarize*, the values supplied by the application in the user descriptor. The contents of the kernel descriptor are guaranteed by the operating system to be trustworthy; the kernel ensures this by using the VM protection mechanism of the system to disallow user-space access to kernel descriptors.

The association between communication buffers and their descriptors is done by the kernel at the behest of the user, through the use of system calls. When the user process makes such a request, the kernel first wires down the pages corresponding to the buffer in main memory, picks a pair of descriptors for the buffer, initializes the contents of the kernel descriptor, and returns the user descriptor to the user. If the buffer spans multiple non-contiguous physical pages, then multiple pairs of descriptors, one pair per page, will be associated with the buffer. Kernel descriptors always reside in a page that is not mapped into the user's virtual address space, and user descriptors always reside in a page to which the user has full read/write access. This ensures that user processes can only modify user descriptors, but not kernel descriptors.

**3.3.2.1 Buffer Notarization** Kernel descriptors are initialized by the kernel to contain the actual physical address of the buffer they reference, and its length (see Figure 11(a)). User descriptors are interpreted by the APIC to contain an offset into the buffer, and a length. Thus, the application is allowed to queue subsets of communication buffers. The APIC certifies the validity of a buffer by ensuring that the sum of the offset and length specified in the user descriptor is no greater than the length specified in the kernel descriptor. We call this checking process *buffer notarization*. If a buffer fails notarization, the corresponding connection is suspended and the APIC issues an exception interrupt to the processor; the kernel can then take whatever action it deems fit. If a buffer passes notarization, the APIC creates a new *resultant descriptor* which contains the length field from the user descriptor, and an address field which is computed as the sum of the address field from the kernel descriptor and the offset field from the user descriptor. This resultant descriptor is then used just like a normal (simple DMA) descriptor would. When the APIC is done transmitting or filling the buffer, it writes back the resultant descriptor to the location of the user descriptor. This allows the user process to be able to examine the status of the buffer/connection. The kernel descriptor is only read and never written, since the kernel is not responsible for keeping track of the state of the connection. Note also that the APIC needs on-chip storage for only one (resultant) descriptor per connection.

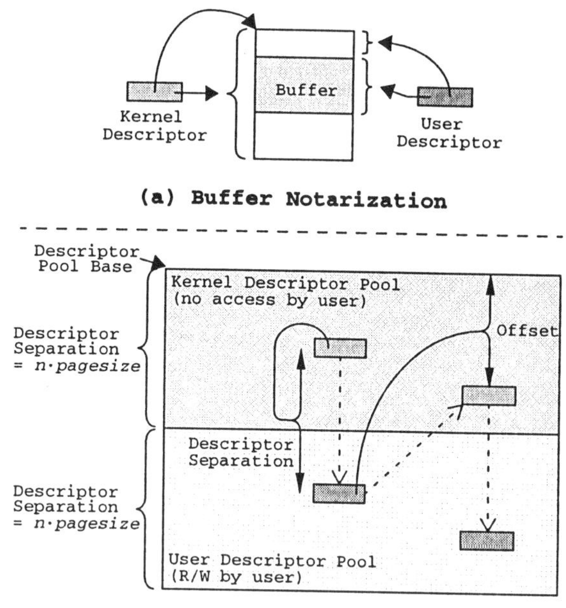


**Figure 11: Notarization for Protected DMA**

**3.3.2.2 Link Notarization** Although buffer notarization is sufficient to ensure that a user process never queues an illegal buffer, it cannot guarantee that the user will not queue an illegal descriptor. To get around this, the APIC has to subject the next descriptor link in user descriptors to another check which we call *link notarization*. Figure 11(b) shows how link notarization works. Every user process is allocated a dedicated set of $2{\cdot}n$ contiguous physical memory pages that will be used to hold user and kernel descriptors for that process — this can be likened to the file descriptor table for a process. The value of $n$ is fixed, and is configured into the operating system kernel at compile time. The first $n$ pages contain only kernel descriptors, and will be referred to as the kernel descriptor pool. Likewise, the last $n$ pages contain only user descriptors, and will be referred to as the user descriptor pool. Pairs of user and kernel descriptors are always allocated such that both descriptors are located at the same offset relative to the start of their respective descriptor pools. All the pages in the user descriptor pool are mapped with read/write permission into the process' virtual address space, while the pages in the kernel descriptor pool are accessible to the kernel only. The APIC per-connection state includes a pointer to the descriptor pool base of the process which owns the connection. This allows user processes to be able to use offsets within the descriptor pool to reference descriptors, rather than physical memory addresses. It also makes the job of link notarization easy for the APIC. As shown by the dotted arrows in the figure, the APIC always reads the kernel descriptor for a buffer before reading the corresponding user descriptor. Kernel descriptors always contain the relative offset of the corresponding user descriptor (this *descriptor separation* is always *n·pagesize*); the APIC uses this to determine the address of the user descriptor. User descriptors specify the link to the next descriptor as an offset into the descriptor page pool. In order to notarize this link, the APIC has to ensure that the next kernel (user) descriptor falls within the corresponding kernel (user) descriptor pool. It does this by making sure that the offset specified in the user descriptor is no larger than the descriptor separation specified in the corresponding kernel descriptor. If the link fails notarization, the APIC suspends the corresponding connection and issues an exception interrupt to the processor. If the link passes notarization, the APIC initializes the next descriptor link of the resultant descriptor to hold the address of the next kernel descriptor, which is computed as the sum of the descriptor pool base and the offset in the user descriptor.

Thus, with two simple inequality checks, the APIC ensures that no illegal buffers or buffer descriptors can be queued by a user process. Once a process has queued a buffer, it can inform the APIC that this has been done by issuing an *attention* command to the APIC (using protected I/O), thus completely removing the kernel and system calls from the critical data path. Protected DMA can therefore be used by untrusted user-space library protocol implementations, with the confidence that the security and protection mechanisms of the operating system will not be compromised.

We would like to point out here that although we have made all control path operations on the APIC pass through the kernel, there is no reason that they could not instead be made to pass through a trusted user-level server directly to the APIC. If this is done, then we have succeeded in moving almost the entire protocol stack including the APIC device driver, into user space (some kernel code would still be required to field interrupts from the APIC, but this code can be very small because all it needs to do is wake up relevant processes). This technique is particularly attractive for microkernel implementations, and has the potential to outperform monolithic kernel implementations that keep the entire device driver in the kernel.

# 4 APIC Interrupt Mechanisms

Interrupts are issued by the APIC to report the occurrence of asynchronous events, such as completion of transmission or reception of data, or an error condition. It is important that interrupts not be issued very frequently, because interrupt service overhead can be substantial. Furthermore, interrupts have a bad effect on cache performance. Our experiments with a prototype MBus test board have shown that the minimum interrupt service latency (the time from the instant when the interrupt was issued to the time when the first instruction of the device interrupt service routine is executed) for a Sun Sparcstation-10 running SunOS 4.*x* is 14 microseconds. This implies that the time to service even a null interrupt can be greater than the interarrival time between successive packets! Several researchers have recognized the importance of reducing the frequency of interrupts [7,12,17] to a host interface. All proposed solutions rely on batching multiple events so they can be handled with a single interrupt. Druschel et al. [7] suggest disabling transmit interrupts altogether, and checking for the completion of transmission as part of other driver activity. On receive, they interrupt only when new data arrives and there is no old data that has not already been dequeued by the OS; this has the desirable effect of the interrupt being asserted only once per burst of incoming packets. Traw et al. [17] suggest disallowing interface interrupts altogether, and instead polling the interface on periodic hardware clock interrupts. This scheme is shown to perform well for high bandwidth applications, but is unsuitable for latency-critical LAN applications because the time between successive clock interrupts is typically of the order of milliseconds. The APIC reduces interrupt frequency through two approaches: *orchestrated interrupts*, and *interrupt demultiplexing*.

## 4.1 Orchestrated Interrupts

As mentioned earlier, buffer descriptors used by the APIC contain an `INTERRUPT` bit flag. If this flag is set in a descriptor that has been queued on a transmit or receive chain, the APIC will interrupt the processor when it first reads that descriptor. This variety of interrupts are termed orchestrated, because they are issued in response to a fabricated and pre-orchestrated event (viz., the reading of the descriptor). This feature is very useful when transmitting data, because the processor can avoid getting interrupted for every packet, and only get interrupted when the last packet in a large burst has been transmitted. This is achieved by only setting the descriptor interrupt bit in the last descriptor corresponding to the last packet of the burst. Orchestrated interrupts are also used to notify the processor when a (transmit or receive) descriptor chain underflow is imminent. This is done by setting the interrupt bit in a descriptor that is located close to the end of a chain of descriptors; when the APIC reaches this descriptor, it will issue an interrupt and in response, the kernel can take steps to replenish buffers in the chain. Note that orchestrated interrupts can be used to advantage in both connection-oriented and traditional network interfaces.

## 4.2 Interrupt Demultiplexing

Interrupt demultiplexing is a strategy employed by the APIC to reduce the frequency of interrupts that are used to report packet arrivals. The connection-oriented aspect of ATM is exploited to differentiate (demultiplex) between applications with different traffic patterns and protocol and application processing requirements—hence the name *interrupt demultiplexing*.

In the APIC, interrupt demultiplexing is implemented by including a one-bit flag in the per-connection state which is used to tell whether interrupts are enabled for the connection. When an event (e.g., packet arrival) occurs on a particular connection, an interrupt is generated only if interrupts were enabled for that connection, and immediately following this the APIC automatically disables interrupts for that connection. Subsequent packet arrivals on that connection will not trigger an interrupt (although events on other connections might) until after the host CPU has specifically re-enabled interrupts by writing to an APIC per-connection command register. The CPU always re-enables interrupts for a connection after it has finished processing all outstanding packets that have arrived on that connection. Processing of packets belonging to latency-critical applications is always given higher priority than other types of packets. In fact, the higher the priority at which packets are processed, the lower the latency that such packets will experience. Clearly, a single interrupt would suffice for processing an entire burst of rapidly arriving packets. If a latency-critical packet arrives in the midst of a burst of packets belonging to a high bandwidth connection, the APIC would issue an interrupt which would result in the low latency packet getting immediate service, while service of the high bandwidth burst is postponed. More details on interrupt demultiplexing can be found in an expanded version of this work [6].

## 5 Conclusions

In this paper, we have presented several techniques for high performance network interface design. These techniques enable the APIC to efficiently support both high throughput and latency-critical applications. Note that this is achieved without imposing a specific structure on protocol implementations or the operating system. Instead, the programming interface presented by the APIC to the software includes several mutually exclusive mechanisms that can be mixed and matched in different ways by a systems programmer in order to extract the maximum performance from the interface. Furthermore, the connection-oriented nature of the underlying network allows different compositions of these mechanisms to be used for different applications, thereby allowing for customizing of protocol implementations. For instance, one application may choose to be interrupted by the interface on every packet arrival, while another may choose to be interrupted only once per burst of packets, and yet another may disable interrupts altogether and instead decide to poll the interface. Customization is further facilitated by the APIC's built-in support for user-space driver implementations.

In addition to interfacing to standard workstations, displays, and video cameras, the APIC is also going to be used to implement a high performance video storage server and a gigabit IP router. A future paper will report on the measured performance of prototype APIC-based systems in our gigabit local-ATM testbed.

While all the mechanisms described in this paper were presented in the context of the APIC network interface, we are convinced that some of these mechanisms can be used to advantage in other types of I/O devices too. This conviction is based on the fact that I/O typically involves multiple sequential streams of data, with individual streams associated with different applications. This property is reminiscent of ATM connections. It should therefore be possible to use techniques like protected DMA, protected I/O, and interrupt demultiplexing for other types of I/O devices. In particular, protected DMA and protected I/O can be used to off-load the task of controlling hardware in the system to applications running in user space. This facilitates the construction of new kernel architectures such as the MIT Exokernel [11]. By exposing the hardware to applications (as opposed to hiding it under an abstraction), significant performance gains are possible. Our research plans include exploring the feasibility of using protected DMA and protected I/O mechanisms for other types of devices, and in particular for mass storage devices like disks and RAIDs.

## References


[1] Banks, D., and Prudence, M., "A High Performance Network Architecture for a PA-RISC Workstation," *IEEE JSAC*, Vol. 11 No. 2, Feb. 1993.

[2] Clark, D.D., and Tennenhouse, D.L., "Architectural Considerations for a New Generation of Protocols," *Proc. ACM SIGCOMM 90*, Aug. 1990.

[3] Cranor, C.D., and Parulkar, G.M., "Design of Universal Continuous Media I/O," *Proc. 5th Intl. Workshop on Network and Operating System Support for Digital Audio and Video*, Apr. 1995.

[4] Davie, B.S., "The Architecture and Implementation of a High-Speed Host Interface," *IEEE JSAC*, Vol. 11, No. 2, Feb. 1993.

[5] Dittia, Z.D., Cox, J.R., and Parulkar, G.M., "Design of the APIC: A High Performance ATM Host-Network Interface Chip," *Proc. IEEE INFOCOM 95*, April 1995.

[6] Dittia, Z.D., Parulkar, G.M., Cox, J.R., "The APIC Approach to High Performance Network Interface Design: Protected DMA and Other Techniques," Washington University Technical Report WUCS-96-12, 1996.

[7] Druschel, P., Peterson, L., and Davie, B.S. "Experiences with a High-Speed Network Adaptor: A Software Perspective," *Proc. ACM SIGCOMM 94*, Sep. 1994.

[8] Druschel, P., and Peterson, L., "Fbufs: A High-Bandwidth Cross-Domain Transfer Facility," *Proc. 14th Symposium on Operating System Principles (SOSP)*, Dec. 1993.

[9] Eicken, T. von, Basu, A., Buch, V., Vogels, W., "U-Net: A User-Level Network Interface for Parallel and Distributed Computing," *Proc. 15th ACM Symposium on Operating System Principles*, Dec. 1995.

[10] Eicken, T. von, Culler, D.E., Goldstein, S.C., and Schauser, K.E., "Active Messages: A Mechanism for Integrated Communication and Computation," *Proc. 19th ISCA*, May 1992.

[11] Engler, D.R., Kaashoek, M.F., and O'Toole, J., "Exokernel: An Operating System Architecture for Application-Level Resource Management," *Proc. 15th ACM Symposium on Operating System Principles*, Dec. 1995.

[12] Forin, A., Golub, D., and Bershad, B., "An I/O System for Mach 3.0," *Proc. USENIX Mach Symposium*, Nov. 1991.

[13] Hayter, M.D., and McAuley, D.R., "The Desk Area Network," *Operating Systems Review*, Vol. 25, No. 4, Oct. 1991.

[14] Houh, H.H., Adam, J.F., Ismert, M., Lindblad, C.J., and Tennenhouse, D.L., "The VuNet Desk Area Network: Architecture, Implementation, and Experience," *IEEE JSAC* Vol. 13, No. 4, May 1995.

[15] Pasquale, J., Anderson, E., and Muller, P.K., "Container Shipping: Operating System Support for I/O-Intensive Applications," *IEEE Computer*, Vol. 27, No. 3, Mar. 1994.

[16] Sterbenz, J., and Parulkar, G.M., "Axon: Host-Network Interface Architecture for Gigabit Communication," *Protocols for High Speed Networking*, Elsevier, 1991.

[17] Traw, C.B.S., and Smith, J.M., "Hardware/Software Organization of a High Performance ATM Host Interface," *IEEE JSAC* Vol. 11, No. 2, Feb. 1993.

# Implementation and Analysis of PCC (Parallel Connection Control)

Malathi Veeraraghavan
Bell Laboratories
Room 4F-509
101 Crawfords Corner Road
Holmdel, NJ 07733
Email: mv@bell-labs.com

Gagan L. Choudhury
AT&T Laboratories
Room 1L-238
101 Crawfords Corner Road
Holmdel, NJ 07733
gagan@buckaroo.att.com

Madhu Kshirsagar
Bell Laboratories
Room 4F-513
101 Crawfords Corner Road
Holmdel, NJ 07733
mmk@dnrc.bell-labs.com

## Abstract

*In earlier papers, we proposed the PCC (Parallel Connection Control) algorithm for the setup and release of on-demand ATM (Asynchronous Transfer Mode) connections. This paper describes an implementation and analysis of PCC. The PCC algorithm is implemented on a testbed of three types of ATM switches from which service time measurements (software execution times) are obtained. These measured service times are used as input data for an analytical queueing network model to characterize the PCC end-to-end setup delay and maximum throughputs. Assuming all connections pass through ten switches, for this measured data, PCC has a theoretical maximum throughput of 343 calls/sec/switch, and at about 90% of this maximum limit (i.e., at 310 calls/sec/switch), the mean end-to-end connection setup delay is only 43ms. We also compare PCC performance against an equivalent sequential connection setup/release approach. We observe that PCC end-to-end setup delay is much smaller than the sequential setup delay (34% at low load and even smaller at higher load). Also, the per-switch maximum throughput of the PCC approach is 80% more compared to the sequential approach.*

## 1 Introduction

ATM (Asynchronous Transfer Mode) networks are based on connection-oriented communication in that a connection is set up prior to data exchange and released after data exchange. The commonly accepted solution for ATM connection management is the ATM Forum PNNI (Private Network-Network Interface) standard [1]. This standard consists of two protocols: the PNNI routing protocol and the PNNI signaling protocol. During connection setup, switches consult the data updated by the PNNI routing protocol to determine the "shortest-path" route for the connection. The first switch in each PNNI peer group on the path of the connection determines the "shortest-path" route of the connection through that peer group. Following this route computation, connection setup is performed at each switch within the peer group sequentially.

We observe that since the first switch in a peer group identifies the switches in that peer group through which the connection will be routed, connection setup at these switches can be accomplished in parallel. This will improve end-to-end connection setup delay. However, the first switch will have the added burden of sending messages to the switches on the selected route within its peer group, and coordinating responses. This will negatively impact the call handling capacity of switches which are already expected to be short on computing resources. To address this drawback, we propose separating the route computation function from other connection management functions performed in switches (such as switch resource management), and locating the route computation function in new servers called *connection servers* distinct from switches. This improves per-switch call handling capacity by reducing the number of functions performed by the switch processors. These two concepts of parallelizing connection setup operations at switches, and performing route computation in separate servers, constitute the PCC (Parallel Connection Control) algorithm, proposed in [2, 3]. Using this scheme, connection setup actions at the switches on the computed route *within each peer group* are executed *in parallel*. Connection setup proceeds *sequentially from one peer group to the next* on the route of the connection.

Section 2 gives a brief overview of the PCC approach. The PCC implementation is described in Section 3, and service time measurements obtained from this implementation are listed in Section 4. Using the measured data, a comparative analysis of the PNNI signaling solution and the PCC solution is carried out as described in Section 5. Conclusions drawn from this analysis are provided in Section 6.

## 2 Parallel Connection Control (PCC)

In the PCC solution, connection control functionality is distributed between two entities, *connection servers* and *switch resource servers*, as shown in Fig. 1. A switch resource server is associated with each switch. Multiple connection servers are present in each peer group of a PNNI-standards-based network. The PNNI routing proto-



0-8186-7780-5/97 $10.00 © 1997 IEEE

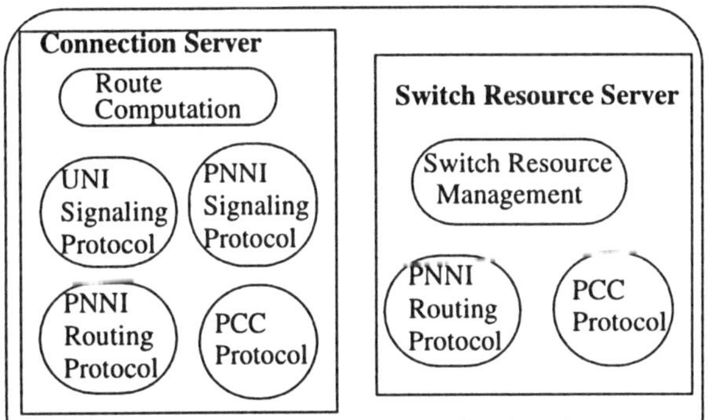


**Fig. 1 PCC functionality distribution**

col software at switches send topology state packets to connection servers rather than to each other. This removes the software needed to receive and parse PNNI routing protocol topology state packets from the switch processors. In addition, UNI (User-Network Interface) [4] and PNNI signaling, and route computation modules are also moved out of the switch processors to connection servers.

The bidirectional two-party PCC connection setup procedure is summarized here. Readers are referred to [2, 3] for details. Upon receiving a *Setup-connections* message, the route computation module of the connection server (Fig. 1) determines the route of the connection using the topology data collected by the PNNI routing protocol. This computation is similar to the DTL (Designated Transit List) computation in PNNI networks. The connection server then establishes the first segment of the connection through switches in its peer group by executing switch setup actions *in parallel* using a *two-phase* message exchange. In the *first phase*, it requests the switch resource servers of the switches on the route within its peer group to reserve resources for the connection using the *Reserve-resources* messages (one message per switch). This phase is executed *in parallel* at these switches.

The switch resource management module of each switch resource server (Fig. 1) receives this message and performs two steps:

- Step 1: CAC (Connection Admission Control) procedures to determine if the new connection can be admitted without disrupting any QoS (Quality-of-Service) guarantees given to pre-existing connections.
- Step 2: Selection of VPI/VCIs (Virtual Path Identifiers/Virtual Channel Identifiers) on the ports to the neighbor switches. The selected channel identifiers are included as parameters in the *responses*.

If this first phase is successful, the connection server initiates the *second phase* in which the switch resource servers configure the switches by sending *Configure-switch* messages (one message per switch). This phase is also executed in parallel at the switches on the route in the peer group. Each switch resource server performs the next two steps of connection setup:

- Step 3: Port/VPI/VCI translation table entries are made for user plane ATM data cell routing; and
- Step 4: Parameters for runtime algorithms such as scheduling, priority control, and usage parameter control, are set based on the QoS requirements.

Upon successful completion of this phase, the segment through the first peer group is fully established. The reason we use a two-phase approach is that channels selected by each switch in the first phase (Step 2) are needed to configure switches in the second phase (Step 3).

If the connection spans multiple peer groups, the connection server sends a PNNI signaling message [1] to a connection server in the next peer group to request the setup of the next segment of the connection. Upon completion of setup through the last peer group, the connection server in this peer group sends an *Offer-connections* message to the far end host. If accepted, data transmission is initiated by the connection server sending a *Start-traffic* message. Response to the segment setup PNNI signaling messages traverse backwards through connection servers until the first connection server is reached. This entity then sends a *Start-traffic* message to its end host to initiate data transmission from the first end host.

UNI (User Network Interface) [4] signaling messages, can be used for communication between end hosts and connection servers. For example, the UNI SETUP message can be used instead of the *Setup-connections* message.

## 3 Implementation

In this section, we describe an implementation of the PCC algorithm. The ATM testbed network available in our research laboratory is shown in Fig. 2. It consists of two

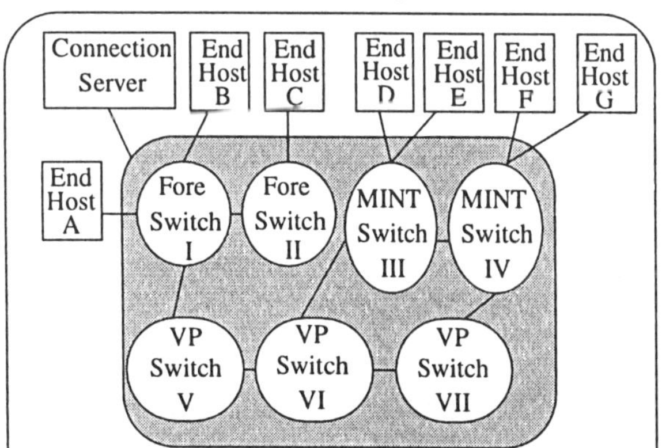


**Fig. 2 Prototype test bed configuration**

*MINT*[1] *switches* [5] and two *Fore Systems switches*, and three *VP switches*. There are two types of *multimedia end hosts*, those connected to Fore switches and those connected to MINT switches. The end hosts connected to the Fore switches are SUN workstations with a Fore ATM interface adapter card, and a JPEG video card. The audio capability is built-in with the workstation. The end hosts connected to the MINT switches are SUN workstations connected via ethernet to terminal adapters. Each terminal adapter has a control processor, executing the VxWorks operating system, an ATM network interface card, an audio card, and an NTSC video card. Details about the MINT terminal adapter can be obtained from [6].

The PCC software consists of three distinct types of UNIX™ processes: *connection server, switch resource server,* and *end host signaling process*. The *connection server* is shown as an explicit "box" in Fig. 2 to illustrate that it is run on a separate SUN workstation. The switch resource servers are collocated with ATM switches. Three types of *switch resource servers* are implemented, one for each type of ATM switch. One end host signaling process is executed per end host.

The different processes communicate with each other using IP over ATM or IP over ethernet. The PCC messages shown in Fig. 2 are transported in TCAP (Transaction Capabilities Application Part) transactions, where TCAP is part of the SS7 (Signaling System No. 7) protocol for invoking remote operations [7]. We transport TCAP messages as UDP/IP (User Datagram Protocol/Internet Protocol) [8] packets instead of using the lower layers of the SS7 stack.

For experimentation purposes, we only execute one instance of the connection server for this group of ATM switches (all assumed to be in one peer group), though, in general, multiple instances of the connection server can be executed in the same peer group.

## 4 Measurements

Having implemented a proof-of-concept prototype of the PCC algorithm, the next phase is to characterize the performance of this approach. We created scripts to set up and release bidirectional two-party connections, and measured processing times for different functions (subroutines) in the PCC software. Processing time measurements are taken using the *Quantify* software tool from Pure Software Inc. The connection server and switch resource servers are executed on SPARCstation 10 hosts running SUNOS 4.1.3. A processing model for an intra-peer group (involving only one connection server) PCC connection setup procedure is shown in Fig. 3. The model for the release procedure is shown in Fig. 4. We use the notation $CS^i$ to represent the $i^{th}$ processing session in the connection server and $SRS_k^j$ to represent the $j^{th}$ processing session in the $k^{th}$ switch resource server. EA and EB represent the ends of the connection, i.e., end hosts A and B, respectively.

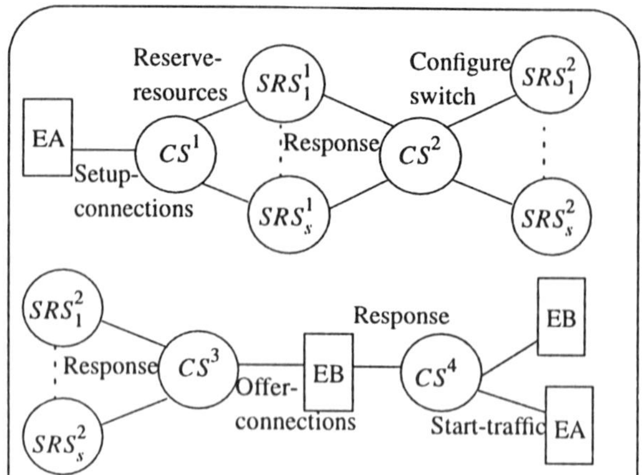


**Fig. 3 Model for PCC connection setup**

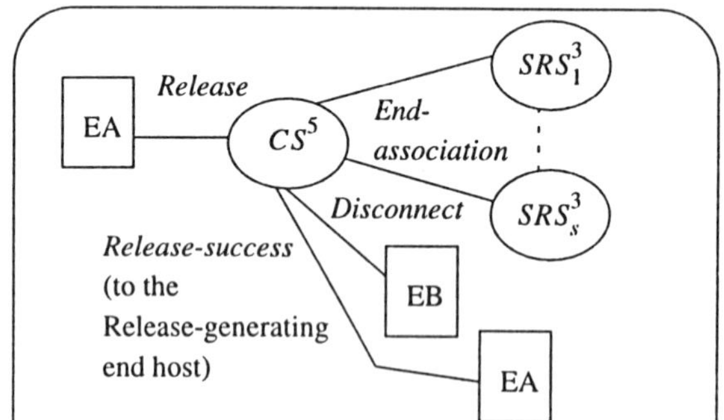


**Fig. 4 Model for PCC connection release**

The measured times for each processing session in the connection server are listed in Table 1. Parts of the processing are dependent on the number of switches on the connection, $s$. The measured service times for the processing sessions in the switch resource servers are listed in Table 2. Some of the data in these two tables are listed as symbols since they represent environment-dependent service times. The values measured for these environment-

**Table 1: Connection server processing times**

| Time | Processing Time (in µsec) |
|---|---|
| $CS^1$ | $107.4 + t_R + 112.4\ s + t_{rcv} + st_{snd}$ |
| $CS^2$ | $252.2\ s + s(t_{snd} + t_{rcv})$ |
| $CS^3$ | $101.2\ s + 178.4 + st_{rcv} + t_{snd}$ |
| $CS^4$ | $365.36 + t_{rcv} + 2t_{snd}$ |
| $CS^5$ | $281.23 + 89.19\ s + t_{rcv} + (s+2)t_{snd}$ |

1. MINT (Multimedia Integrated Network for Telecommunications) was an ATM research project in AT&T Bell Labs.

**Table 2: Switch resource server processing times**

| Time | Processing Time (in μsec) |
|---|---|
| $SRS_1^1, \ldots, SRS_K^1$ | $268.8 + t_{rcv} + t_{snd}$ |
| $SRS_1^2, \ldots, SRS_K^2$ | $203 + t_{rcv} + t_{snd} + t_{prog}$ |
| $SRS_1^3, \ldots, SRS_K^3$ | $143.7 + t_{rcv}$ |

dependent processing times are listed in Table 3. Processing times $t_{snd}$ and $t_{rcv}$, the times to send and receive a UDP/IP message respectively, are dependent on the operating system. The time for route computation $t_R$ is dependent on the size of the network, and the time to program a switch (i.e., perform Steps 3 and 4 described in Section 2), defined as $t_{prog}$, is dependent on the switch hardware. We measured these four quantities separately and listed them in Table 3.

To measure $t_{snd}$ and $t_{rcv}$ accurately, we used the UNIX™ function call *getrusage* to measure the time for system calls, *sendmsg* and *recvmsg*, used to send and receive UDP messages. While measuring the processing time data in the connection server and switch resource servers using the *Quantify* tool, we excluded system calls

**Table 3: Environment-dependent processing times**

| Parameter | Value |
|---|---|
| $t_{snd}$ | 240μs |
| $t_{rcv}$ | 220μs |
| $t_R$ | 33.94μs to 15ms |
| $t_{prog}$ | 1.16ms to 15ms |

due to accuracy problems. The parameters $t_{snd}$ and $t_{rcv}$ are environment dependent since in other implementations, TCAP transactions may be transported over S-AAL (Signaling ATM Adaptation Layer) and ATM layers rather than on UDP/IP. This will impact the times to send and receive a message.

The route computation time $t_R$ was measured to be 33.94 μs in our prototype network consisting of seven switches. For larger networks, if Dijkstra's algorithm is used to perform on-the-fly route computation, this time could be as large as 15ms as reported in [9] for a 200-node network. We thus carry out a sensitivity analysis based on this variation of $t_R$.

Finally, $t_{prog}$ is switch hardware-dependent. In our implementation, we measured this time for two types of switches. For the MINT switch, the switch resource server is executed as a VxWorks (a realtime operating system) task running on a i960 processor. This task directly sends control ATM cells to program the switch fabric. The measurement indicates that a bidirectional fabric configuration can be done in 1.16ms. On the other hand, to program the switch fabric of the VP switch shown in Fig. 2 for a bidirectional connection, we require 15ms, since it uses a message-based interface (on an RS-232 serial link) between the processor executing the switch resource server and the shelf controller that, in turn, programs the fabric.

# 5 Analysis

In order to characterize the benefits of the parallel connection control (PCC) approach over the switch-by-switch sequential setup approach (referred to as the "PNNI approach") for use within a peer group, we construct models for the latter. Estimates of processing times for the PNNI approach are obtained from the PCC measured service times presented in Section 4. Given the service times and call flows for the two models, we can carry out a queueing analysis for the end-to-end connection setup delay for different call arrival rates. In addition to the queueing delay and service times at the control processors, link emission delays are also included. Message length details are not provided in this paper due to space considerations, but can be obtained from the authors. A signaling link rate of 1.5Mbps is assumed.

Using this combination of measured service times for PCC, estimated service times for PNNI, and estimated link emission delays, we carry out a *comparative delay-throughput analysis*, and also compare the *theoretical maximum throughputs* in the two approaches. This section is organized as follows: Section 5.1 describes the models of the PNNI signaling setup and release procedures and lists estimates of the processing times for the PNNI approach; Section 5.2 describes the analysis methodology; and Section 5.3 presents the results of the analysis.

## 5.1 Model of the switch-by-switch sequential approach (the PNNI approach)

The PNNI signaling procedure [1], illustrated in Fig. 5, is an example of a switch-by-switch sequential approach. In Fig. 5, $SW_1$ represents a typical originating switch; $SW_3$ a typical terminating switch; and $SW_2$ a typical transit switch. If there are more than 3 switches in a connection, all the transit switches between the originating switch and the terminating switch will behave like $SW_2$. EA and EB represent the ends of the connection, i.e., end hosts A and B, respectively.

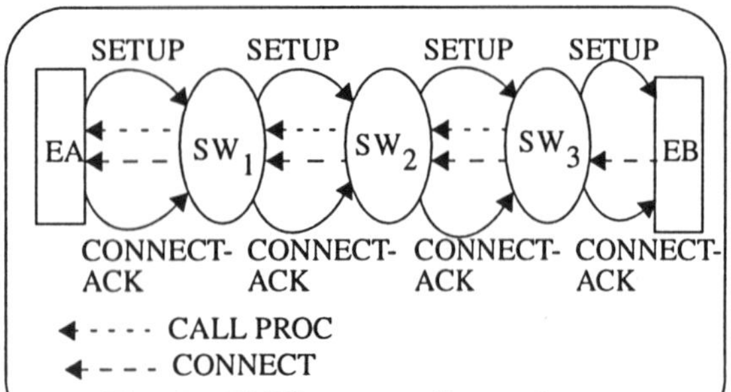


**Fig. 5 PNNI connection setup**

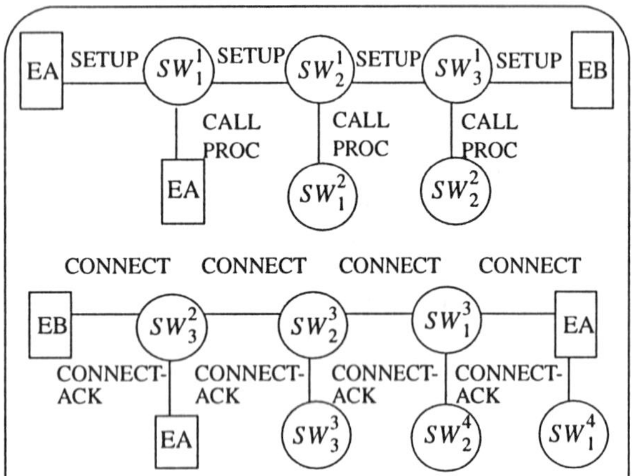


**Fig. 6 Model for PNNI connection setup**

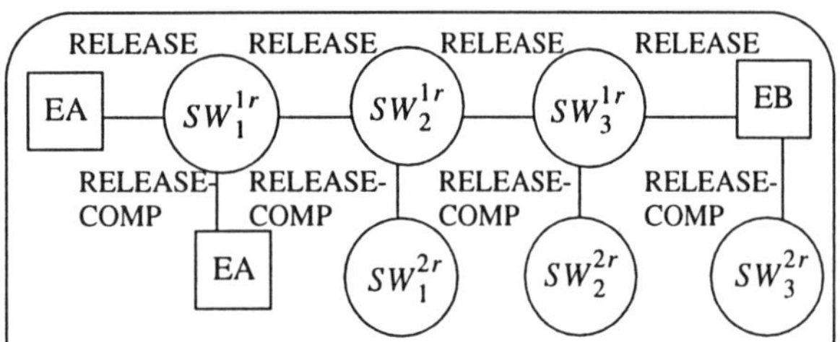


**Fig. 7 Model for PNNI connection release**

Models for the setup and release of a connection using the PNNI approach are shown in Figs. 6 and 7, respectively. We use the notations $SW_j^i$ and $SW_j^{ir}$ to represent the $i^{th}$ processing session at switch $j$ during the connection setup and release phase, respectively. The service times for different processing sessions (shown in Figs. 6 and 7) in the three types of switch resource servers are shown in tables 4 and 5 for setup and release, respectively. We did not implement PNNI signaling. Instead, we estimated the times for these processing sessions using the data obtained from the PCC implementation measurements. Effectively, since many of the actions that need to be performed are the same in both models, this estimation should be accurate.

**Table 4: PNNI connection setup processing times**

| Time | Value (μs) |
|---|---|
| $SW_1^1$ | $398.8+t_R+2t_{snd}+t_{rcv}$ |
| $SW_2^1$ | $374.3 + 2t_{snd}+t_{rcv}$ |
| $SW_1^2$ | $101.7+t_{rcv}$ |
| $SW_3^1$ | $447.2 + 2t_{snd}+t_{rcv}$ |
| $SW_2^2$ | $101.7+t_{rcv}$ |
| $SW_3^2$ | $426.56 +t_{prog}\ 2t_{snd}+t_{rcv}$ |
| $SW_3^3$ | $101.2+t_{rcv}$ |
| $SW_2^3$ | $355.6+t_{prog}+2t_{snd}+t_{rcv}$ |
| $SW_1^3$ | $351 +t_{prog} + 2t_{snd}+t_{rcv}$ |
| $SW_2^4$ | $101.2+t_{rcv}$ |
| $SW_1^4$ | $101.2+t_{rcv}$ |

**Table 5: PNNI connection release processing times**

| Time | Value (μs) |
|---|---|
| $SW_1^{1r}$ | $340.92+t_{rcv}+2t_{snd}$ |
| $SW_2^{1r}$ | $308+t_{rcv}+2t_{snd}$ |
| $SW_3^{1r}$ | $302.3+t_{rcv}+2t_{snd}$ |
| $SW_1^{2r}$ | $94.7+t_{rcv}$ |
| $SW_2^{2r}$ | $94.6+t_{rcv}$ |
| $SW_3^{2r}$ | $94.7+t_{rcv}$ |

## 5.2 Analysis methodology

The queueing analysis for both the PCC and PNNI approaches are done by representing the system as a queueing network. The processing elements, Connection Servers (CSs), Switch Resource Servers (SRSs) in the PCC approach, Switches (SWs) in the PNNI approach, and the transmission elements (the links interconnecting the processing elements) are represented as nodes of the queueing network. The delay analysis at each individual node is done through a decomposition assumption which essentially treats each node as an M/G/1 queue, i.e., each processing/transmission session at a node is represented as an independent Poisson arrival. The critical path of the connection setup delay is treated as an activity graph. The end-to-end delay distribution is obtained by inverting the Laplace transform of the distribution which in turn is obtained as the product of the Laplace transforms of individual distributions assuming independence among them. See [10] for details of the procedure.

It is assumed that there are a large number of switches in the system, and, on the average, a call involves $N$ switches. However, the particular call for which we do delay analysis involves $N_p$ switches. In general, $N$ and $N_p$ need not be the same. Also, we assume that each switch of the system is equally likely to be chosen in a particular call so that the load is evenly balanced across the switches.

All processing on the critical path of the connection setup delay is done serially in the PNNI architecture. However, as shown in Fig. 3, there is a lot of parallelism in the PCC architecture which we take into account in the models. As an example, consider the processing phase that starts at $CS^1$ and ends at $CS^3$ in Fig. 3, which represents the network portion of the connection setup delay (i.e., excluding the end host portions). In $CS^1$, $s$ messages are sent to the $SRSs$, which perform the processing session $SRS^1$ in parallel. As part of this session, each SRS sends one message, which is received in $CS^2$. After $CS^2$ receives all of these messages, it sends $s$ messages to the $SRSs$, which perform their processing sessions $SRS^2$ in parallel, and send messages, which are received in $CS^3$. In addition to the parallelism among the SRSs, there is *a second source of parallelism* in $CS^2$ and $CS^3$ since we assume that by the time the last message arrives at $CS^2$ or $CS^3$, they have already processed the earlier ones. Therefore, referring back to Table 1, the critical path of the connection setup delay includes all of the processing work in $CS^1$, all of the transmission piece of the processing work in $CS^2$ and $CS^3$, and only a fraction (corresponding to just 1 and not $s$ $SRSs$) of the receiving piece of the processing work in $CS^2$ and $CS^3$. Specifically, the total receiving piece of work in $CS^2$ and $CS^3$ are $s(101.7 + t_{rcv})$ μs (this is not separated out in Table 1 for the sake of simplicity) and $s(101.2 + t_{rcv})$ μs, respectively. Of these, the pieces appearing on the critical path of connection setup delay are only $(101.7 + t_{rcv})$ μs and $(101.2 + t_{rcv})$ μs, respectively. In addition to processing delay, there are, of course, queueing delays which are appropriately taken into account.

In the PCC approach, it is assumed that there are as many Connection Servers (CS) in the system as there are Switch Resource Servers (SRSs), and the load is evenly balanced among the CSs and among the SRSs. Also, the processing power (MIPS, Millions of Instructions Per Second, for the same set of applications) of a CS is the same as that of a SRS.

## 5.3 Analysis results

We present the variation of the mean and 95th percentile of the end-to-end connection setup delay with the:

- throughput (call arrival rate),
- number of switches in the connections, and
- the environment-dependent parameters, $t_R$, the route computation time, and $t_{prog}$, the switch programming time.

*Cases 1-4* represent four sets of values for the parameters $t_R$, $t_{prog}$, and $N$ (in all cases, we assume $N$, the average number of switches on a connection, to equal the number of switches on a particular connection, $N_p$):

- Case 1: ($t_R = 33.94\mu s$), ($t_{prog} = 1.16ms$), and $N = N_p = 2$ switches,
- Case 2: ($t_R = 33.94\mu s$), ($t_{prog} = 1.16ms$), and $N = N_p = 10$ switches,
- Case 3: ($t_R = 15ms$), ($t_{prog} = 15ms$), and $N = N_p = 10$ switches, and
- Case 4: ($t_R = 15ms$), ($t_{prog} = 15ms$), and $N = N_p = 5$ switches.

*Fig. 8 shows the delay-throughput results* for cases 2 and 3, while *Table 6 shows the theoretical maximum throughput* achievable in each of the four cases at 100% utilizations of the various servers (CS and SRS in the PCC approach, and SW in the PNNI approach). It is to be noted that the theoretical maximum throughputs shown in Table 6 are not achievable in practice since queueing delays approach infinity at those throughput values. However, they show which of the two approaches can sustain higher traffic load.

Finally, *Fig. 9 shows the variation of the mean and 95th percentiles of the end-to-end setup delay with varying* $N_p$, the number of switches in a particular connection, while keeping throughput (call arrival rate), $\lambda$, and the mean number of switches per connection, $N$, fixed for the following two cases:

- Case 5: ($t_R = 33.94\mu s$), ($t_{prog} = 1.16ms$), $\lambda = 150$calls/sec/switch, and ($N = 5$),
- Case 6: ($t_R = 15ms$), ($t_{prog} = 15ms$), $\lambda = 35$calls/sec/switch, and ($N = 5$).

**Description of Fig. 8:**

*Fig. 8* represents the cases when all connections are routed through 10 switches. Even at a low load of 10 calls/sec/switch, the mean setup delay for PCC (14.29ms) is about 34% of the PNNI approach (41.45ms) for 10-switch connections. At higher load, the difference increases. The end-to-end setup delay (mean and 95th percentile) for Case 3 is greater than for Case 2 for both the PNNI and PCC approaches, as seen in Fig. 8. This is because the larger values of $t_R$ and $t_{prog}$, shown in Table 3, are used for Case 3. As mentioned earlier, the route computation time, $t_R$, is sensitive to the size of the network and the

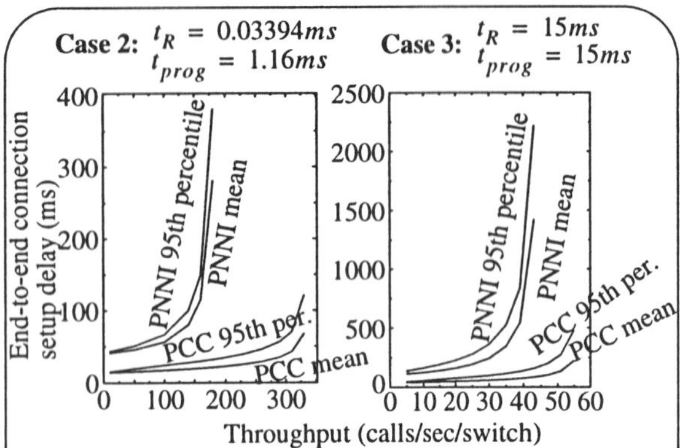


**Fig. 8 Cases 2 and 3:** $N = N_p = 10$

switch resource management time, $t_{prog}$, is sensitive to the type of ATM switch hardware and device driver used. Compare Cases 2 and 3, both of which use 10-switch connections, at a loading of 10 calls/sec/switch. As stated earlier for Case 2, the PCC setup delay is 34% of the PNNI setup delay at this load. In Case 3, at this load, the PCC mean end-to-end setup delay is 46.72ms, which is only 20% of the PNNI mean end-to-end setup delay (230.08ms). Thus, the reductions in setup delay using the PCC approach is more significant the greater the switch programming time.

**Description of Table 6:**

We now consider the issue of *throughput*. Table 6 shows the theoretical maximum throughput that can be achieved in Cases 1 to 4. We discuss *four* observations noted from the results of Table 6:

- The difference in total throughput between the two approaches;
- The difference in per-switch throughput between the two approaches;
- The variation of the theoretical maximum throughputs with the number of switches on connections; and
- The effect of the environment-dependent variable $t_{prog}$ (switch programming time) on the theoretical maximum throughputs.

First consider the difference in the *total throughput* of the two approaches (PCC and PNNI). As mentioned in Section 5.2, the PCC approach has as many CSs as there are SRSs, and the processing power of a CS is the same as that of an SRS. This implies that the total processing capacity (measured, for example, in MIPS) assumed for the PCC approach is two times compared to the total processing capacity assumed for the PNNI approach. The corresponding increase in throughput should be two-fold if exactly the same amount of work is done in both approaches. However, this is not true. Both approaches

**Table 6: Theoretical maximum throughput at 100% server utilizations**

| Case | Throughput at 100% server utilization (calls/sec/switch) | | |
|---|---|---|---|
| | PCC | | PNNI |
| | Connection Server | Switch Resource Server | Switch |
| Case 1 | 319.68 | 342.99 | 192.05 |
| Case 2 | 500.60 | 342.99 | 190.63 |
| Case 3 | 286.19 | 59.68 | 48.59 |
| Case 4 | 189.63 | 59.68 | 45.31 |

accomplish the same overall task of setting up and releasing connections. However, for *connection setup* of $n$-switch connections, the total work in the PNNI approach consists of performing route computation once, performing switch resource management functions (consisting of the four steps listed in Section 2) $n$ times, and handling $4n$ incoming[2] and $4n$ outgoing signaling messages. In the PCC approach, besides all this work (distributed between the connection server and switch resource servers), the connection server receives an additional 2 messages and sends an additional 3 messages. However, for *connection release*, the PCC procedure is simpler than the PNNI procedure (see Figs. 4 and 7). In PCC, we simply use unidirectional messages for release assuming that the lower layer of the protocol stack ensures reliable delivery of messages.

These two effects, the larger setup processing and the smaller release processing, work at cross-purposes, causing the total throughput numbers to be dependent on the number of switches traversed by connections. In the PCC approach, given that the CSs and SRSs reach saturation at different loads, the relative numbers of these servers have to be varied to make them both equally loaded. For example, in Case 2 (see results in Table 6), by reducing the number of connection servers by a factor of $(342.99/500.60)$, both connection servers and switch resource servers will achieve the same theoretical maximum throughput at 342.99 calls/sec. This implies that one unit of processing power in the PCC approach will yield a theoretical maximum throughput of $342.99/(1 + (342.99/500.60))$, which is equal to 203.5 calls/sec. On the other hand, one unit of processing power

2. The terminating switch receives 1 less incoming message, as seen in Fig. 5. Presumably, this effect is small.

in the PNNI approach yields a theoretical maximum throughput of 190.63 calls/sec. Thus, the PCC approach yields a higher total throughput for Case 2. This is true for Case 3 (49.38 calls/sec for PCC vs. 48.59 calls/sec for PNNI), and Case 4 (45.39 calls/sec for PCC vs. 45.31 calls/sec for PNNI) also.

However, in Case 1 (two-switch connections), using a similar computation, one unit of processing power in the PCC approach yields the theoretical maximum throughput of 165.46 calls/sec/switch, while in the PNNI approach, the corresponding figure is 192.05 calls/sec/switch. For connections with a small number of switches, the reduced release processing in PCC is dominated by the processing of the extra five signaling messages needed for connection setup. If we remove the effect of the reduced processing for connection release (under the assumption that the PNNI release procedure can be changed to only use unidirectional messages), then we note that the processing per connection setup in PCC is more than that for PNNI by a fixed amount, which is independent of the number of switches in the connection. Thus, in the limit, as the number of switches per connection approaches infinity, the total theoretical maximum throughput of both approaches will be the same.

*Next, consider the second throughput measure: the per-switch theoretical maximum throughput.* As seen in Fig. 8, the PCC approach achieves higher throughput, i.e., the processors can sustain a higher load (calls/sec/switch) before reaching saturation than in the PNNI approach (also seen in Table 6). The reason for this behavior is that, in the PNNI approach, a switch performs many more functions than a switch resource server in the PCC approach. Thus, the theoretical maximum throughput is higher for an SRS in the PCC approach than for an SW in the PNNI approach.

In the PCC approach, there are two types of servers, CSs and SRSs. The connection servers also do not reach saturation as fast as the PNNI switch processors. In the case of connection servers, each server does perform more work per connection than a switch in the PNNI approach. Based on the data shown in Tables 1 and 4, the total work done at a connection server per connection setup is greater than at a PNNI switch. However, the call arrival rate experienced by a connection server is less than that experienced by a PNNI switch. Since each connection requires $s$ switches, and just one CS, and we assume the same number of CSs and SRSs in the system (with the load evenly distributed among all CSs and SRSs), the call arrival rate witnessed by a CS is only $1/s$ of the per-switch call arrival rate. Thus, in the PCC approach, even though a connection server has more work per connection setup than a PNNI switch, it still reaches 100% utilization at much higher per-switch call arrival rate than a switch in the PNNI approach, as shown in *Table 6*.

*The third observation from the results presented in Table 6 is about the variation of the theoretical maximum throughput with the number of switches in connections.* As $s = N = N_p$ increases from 2 to 10, the theoretical maximum throughput of the SRS remains unchanged while that of the CS goes up as seen in Table 6. As a result, the system bottleneck in the PCC approach shifts from the CS to the SRS as we move from Case 1 ($S = 2$) to Case 2 ($S = 10$). We explain the reason behind this phenomenon as follows.

Let $\lambda_{CS}$, $T_{CS}$ and $\rho_{CS}$ represent the call arrival rate, the processing time per call and the load per call, respectively at the CS. Let $\lambda_{SRS}$, $T_{SRS}$ and $\rho_{SRS}$, represent the corresponding quantities at the SRS. Clearly,

$$\rho_{CS} = \lambda_{CS}T_{CS} \text{ and } \rho_{SRS} = \lambda_{SRS}T_{SRS}. \quad \text{EQ 1}$$

By definition, for a fixed calls/sec/switch, the quantity $\lambda_{SRS}$ is independent of $s$. From Table 2, we see that $T_{SRS}$ is also independent of $s$. Therefore, the load $\rho_{SRS}$ is independent of $s$ as well. Now, since each call requires $s$ SRSs, and just one CS, and we assume the same number of CSs and SRSs in the system (with the load evenly distributed among all CSs and SRSs), we see

$$\lambda_{CS} \propto \frac{1}{s} \quad \text{EQ 2}$$

From Table 1, we see that,

$$T_{CS} \propto a + bs \quad \text{EQ 3}$$

where $a$ and $b$ are positive constants. Combining (EQ 2) and (EQ 3), we get,

$$\rho_{CS} = \lambda_{CS}T_{CS} \propto b + \frac{a}{s}. \quad \text{EQ 4}$$

Therefore, the load at a CS decreases with increasing $s$ for a fixed calls/sec/switch. This explains why at lower values of $s$, the CS is more loaded than the SRSs, but at higher values of $s$, CS becomes less loaded than the SRSs, causing the bottleneck to shift with increasing $s$.

As for the switch in the PNNI approach, the theoretical maximum throughput may increase or decrease with the number of switches on connections, based on the values of $t_R$ and $t_{prog}$. For the first two cases, there is a slight reduction in the number of calls that can be handled before the switch processor is 100% utilized in Case 2 relative to Case 1. The reason for this difference is that the end switch processes one less segment (see Fig. 6: $SW_3$ has only three processing segments, while $SW_1$ and $SW_2$ have four each) compared to other switches. If the number of switches per connection increases, then, on average, fewer switches would act as terminating switches, and hence the average processing load per switch would go down slightly. On the other hand, for the last two cases, there is a slight increase in the number of calls that can be handled before the switch processor is 100% utilized in Case 3 relative to Case 4. The reason for this behavior is that route computation time ($t_R$) is only needed in the originating switch. This is significant (15ms) compared to the reduced terminating switch processing time (321.7μ s). Thus, in Case 3, since there are more switches, fewer switches act as originating switches, and hence the average processing load per switch would increase. In Case 1 and Case 2, $t_R$ is only 33.94μ s, and hence the dominant effect is that of reduced load of terminating switches.

The *final observation made from the results presented in Table 6 is the effect of the environment-dependent variable $t_{prog}$ (switch programming time) on the theoretical maximum throughputs.* The servers reach 100% utilization at much lower call arrival rates for Cases 3 and 4, relative to Cases 1 and 2, due to the increased service times required for route computation and switch programming tasks. For higher values of the switch programming time $t_{prog}$, the switch resource server becomes the bottleneck. Hence, the difference between the per-switch theoretical maximum throughput that can be achieved using PCC and PNNI becomes smaller at higher values of $t_{prog}$. However, as already explained, the gain in setup delay increases at these higher values of $t_{prog}$. Thus, at lower values of $t_{prog}$, a much higher per-switch theoretical maximum throughput can be achieved with PCC, while the end-to-end setup delay reduction for PCC (relative to PNNI) is not as high, while the opposite is true at higher values of $t_{prog}$.

**Description of Fig. 9:**

Fig. 9 shows the variation of the mean and 95th percentile of the end-to-end connection setup delay with the number of switches on the route of a connection, for different values of $t_R$ and $t_{prog}$ (Cases 5 and 6, as defined at the start of this section). In Cases 1-4, we assumed that all connections are routed through the same number of switches. Thus, in Case 1, all connections are routed through 2 switches, in Case 2, through ten switches, etc. However, in a typical situation, different connections will be routed through a varying numbers of switches. To handle this, as stated earlier (Section 5.2), we create two variables $N$ and $N_p$, to represent the average number of switches in a connection, and the number of switches in a particular connection, respectively. From a throughput perspective, if a switch experiences an arrival rate of $\lambda$ calls/sec, each connection server will experience $\lambda/N$ calls/sec (EQ 2, where $s = N$). For Cases 5 and 6, we keep $\lambda$ and $N$ fixed, and therefore, the load at all servers fixed as well, but just study how the end-to-end connection setup delay varies with $N_p$, the number of switches in a particular connection.

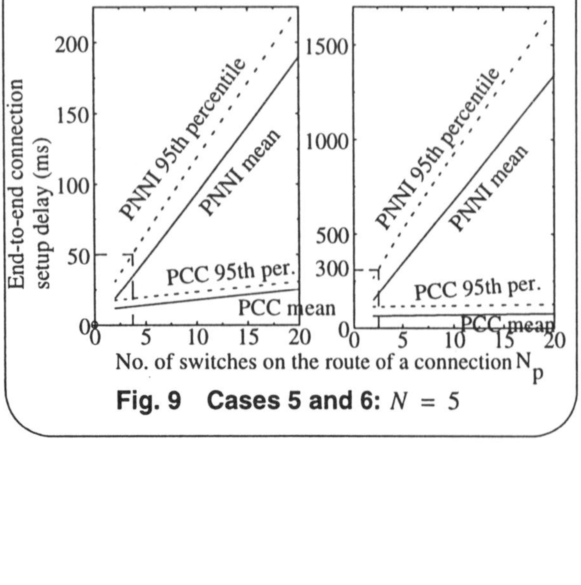

**Fig. 9 Cases 5 and 6:** $N = 5$

Case 5 of Fig. 9 assumes the smaller values of $t_R$ and $t_{prog}$, and sets the switch throughput at 150 calls/sec. The mean number of switches per connection is assumed to be 5. Thus, a connection server experiences 150/5 or 30 calls/sec. At this load, the connection server utilization is 34.2% and switch resource server utilization is 43.7% in the PCC solution. The switch in the PNNI solution is 78.5% loaded at this throughput.

Case 6 of Fig. 9 shows the variation of setup delay with $N_p$ for the higher values of $t_R$ and $t_{prog}$. Since we assume $N = 5$, the results for Case 4 can be consulted to select an appropriate call arrival rate. At a loading of 35 calls/sec/switch, servers in neither approach are as yet saturated. Hence, we use this call arrival rate to study the variation of the end-to-end setup delay with $N_p$, for Case 6. At this load, the connection server utilization is 18.5% and switch resource server utilization is 58.6% in the PCC solution. The switch in the PNNI solution is 77.2% loaded at this throughput.

The major observation from Fig. 9 is that in the PNNI approach the end-to-end setup delay increases fast with $N_p$, whereas the rate of increase is much slower in the PCC approach. The reason for this difference lies in the increased service time caused by sequential processing rather than parallel processing. With both approaches, the load is fixed since calls/sec/switch and $N$ are fixed. This implies that the queueing delay during each visit at a server does not change. Given the sequential nature of the PNNI approach, and the fact that $N_p$ switches are visited, each time with fixed processing and queueing delays, the mean connection setup delay is roughly of the form $aN_p$, where $a$ is a positive constant. By contrast, in the PCC approach, due to the inherent parallelism of work among the SRSs (Section 5.2), and also due to further parallelism of work at the CSs, the mean connection setup delay is roughly of the form $aN_p + b$, where $a$ and $b$ are positive constants with $a \ll b$.

Case 5 of Fig. 9 shows that for a given 95th percentile end-to-end setup delay requirement of 50 ms, a connection can be routed through a maximum of 3 switches in the PNNI approach, while in the PCC approach, the limit is several hundreds. In Case 6 of Fig. 9, for a given 95th percentile end-to-end setup delay of 300 ms, no more than 2 switches must be located on the route of the connection in the PNNI approach, while there is practically no upper limit in the PCC approach even if the delay requirement is only two-thirds as much (i.e., 200 ms). The implication of these results is that a reduced number of provisioned virtual path connections (used to decrease the number of switches that need setup for on-demand connections) is required in the PCC approach relative to the PNNI approach in order to meet the specified end-to-end delay requirement. The use of fewer provisioned VPCs leads to better network utilization for the PCC approach relative to the PNNI approach as was demonstrated in [2].

## 6 Conclusions

This paper described an implementation of PCC (Parallel Connection Control), reported measured service times (software execution times) obtained from this implementation, and used the measured data in a queueing analysis to quantify the benefits of PCC over PNNI (the standards approach) signaling. At low loads (removing the effect of queueing delays), the PCC *end-to-end setup delay* is only 20% of the PNNI setup delay for the larger values of the route computation and switch programming times, and it is only 34% of the PNNI setup delay for the smaller values of these times, assuming ten-switch connections. The difference between the two types of delays is much more at higher loads. Thus, significant gains in end-to-end setup delay are obtained by exploiting two forms of parallelism (across switch resource servers on a connection, and between connection servers and switch resource servers). The PCC end-to-end setup delay grows much slower with the number of switches on connections than the PNNI setup delay. This allows far fewer VPCs (Virtual Path Connections) to be provisioned in the PCC approach, leading to better network utilization. To achieve a 300-ms 95th percentile end-to-end setup delay, in the PNNI approach, connections can only pass through 2 switches (assuming the higher values of the route computation and switch programming times). On the other hand, there is no discernible limit for PCC.

The *per-switch throughput* of the PCC approach is 80% more than that of the PNNI approach for smaller values of the route computation and switch programming times, and 23% more than that of the PNNI approach for larger values of these times, assuming ten-switch connections (assuming equal processing capacities for the PNNI switch and PCC switch). As for the *total throughput*, PCC and PNNI are about the same in all cases, given that the same overall "work" of setting up and releasing connections is performed.

## 7 Acknowledgment

We thank Clark Woodworth, W. H (Tony) Lau, and Kai Eng for providing us the hardware ATM platform on which we implemented the PCC software. We also thank Sunil Malhotra, Sizheng Wei, Tom La Porta, Ram Ramjee, and Maribel Lopez, for helping with the software implementation.

## References

[1] The ATM Forum Technical Committee, "Private Network-Network Specification Interface v1.0 (PNNI 1.0)," af-pnni-0055.000, March 1996.

[2] M. Veeraraghavan, M. Kshirsagar, G. L. Choudhury, "Concurrent ATM Connection Setup Reducing Need for VP Provisioning," *Proc. of Infocom '96*, pp. 303-311.

[3] M. Veeraraghavan and M. Kshirsagar, "Parallel Connection Control (PCC) Algorithm for ATM Networks," *Proc. of ICC '96*, pp. 1635-1641.

[4] The ATM Forum Technical Committee, "ATM User-Network Interface (UNI) Signalling Specification, Version 4.0," ATM Forum 95-1434R9, January 1996.

[5] C. B. Woodworth, M. J. Karol and R. D. Gitlin, "A Flexible Broadband Packet Switch for a Multimedia Integrated Network," *Proc. of ICC '91, pg. 3.2.*

[6] C. B. Woodworth, G. D. Golden, R. D. Gitlin, "An Integrated Multimedia Terminal for Teleconferencing," *Proc. of Globecom '93, pp. 399-405.*

[7] CCITT, "Signaling System No. 7, Transactions Capabilities Application Part," Q.771-Q.775, 1988.

[8] D. E. Comer, "Internetworking with TCP/IP," Prentice-Hall, 1991.

[9] M. Steenstrup, Editor, "Routing in Communications Networks," Prentice Hall 1995, pg. 144.

[10] G. L. Choudhury and D. Houck, "Combined Queueing And Activity Network Based Modeling Of Sojourn Time Distributions In Distributed Telecommunication Systems," Proc. of the 14th *International Teletraffic Congress*, Antibes Juan-les-Pins, France, 6-10 June, 1994, pp. 525-534.

# Performance Analysis of Generalized Multihop Shuffle Networks

Chiang-Ling Ng
NEC Logistics, Ltd.
13-16 Mita 3-Chome, Minato-ku
Tokyo 108, Japan

Seung-Woo Seo
School of Electrical Engr.
Seoul National University
Seoul, Korea 151-742

Hisashi Kobayashi
Department of Electrical Engr.
Princeton University
Princeton, NJ 08544, U.S.A

## Abstract

*This paper describes the performance analysis of a class of two-connected multihop shufflenets, known as generalized shuffle networks. The topology of such networks is described mathematically by the equation $N = kn$, where $N$ is the total number of nodes in the network, $k$ the number of stages in the network and $n$ the number of nodes in each stage. Compared to classical shufflenets, the definition of generalized shuffle networks allows a larger number of feasible network structures that are realizable for a given network size $N$. In attempting to find an optimum network structure, network characteristics are discussed and system performance is evaluated. Important relationships and interdependencies among the various network parameters are developed to facilitate cross-structural comparison.*

## 1 Introduction

In multihop packet-switching networks, packets traverse a number of intermediate nodes until they arrive at their destinations. At each node, switching decisions should be made so that packets can take appropriate output links. The switching algorithm at each node decides on the best possible channel allocation to the packets in its incoming links without regard for the packet dispatch decisions at the rest of the nodes in the network. As much as this improves the network reliability and throughput by allowing autonomy at each node, packets may contend for the limited resources in the node. One possible way to allev iate this contention problem is to use deflection routing. In this environment, packets that neither get routed through their shortest path nor stored in the local buffer will be sent out through the unoccupied output [1, 2, 3].

The shufflenets have been extensively studied for a possible multihop network topology [4]. These networks have one and only one network topology to speak of. For any *possible* $N$, the total number of nodes, the network topology is uniquely determined by finding $p$ and $k$ that satisfy $N = kp^k$, where $p$ represents the number of links into or out of each node and $k$ represents the number of physical node stages in the network. Consequently, the number of nodes at each stage is $p^k$ nodes.

Performance analysis of the classical shufflenets has been thoroughly treated in previous studies [5, 6, 7, 8, 9]. The tight relationship between the number of stages in the network and the number of nodes per stage effectuates a regular node-hopping behavior that yields a relatively straight-forward mathematical model. However, this regular connectivity severely limits the number of realizable structures.

This paper explores a class of shufflenets known as shuffle-ring networks [5], generalized shuffle networks (GSNs) [10], and generalized shuffle-exchange-based multihop networks (GEMNETs) [11], where the tight constraint relating the number of nodes per stage and the number of stages is relaxed. For any *possible* $N$, the total number of nodes in the network, these networks are mathematically given by $N = kn$. The parameter $k$ represents the number of physical node stages, while $n$ represents the number of nodes per stage. The only binding condition in these shuffle networks is that which restricts $n$ to be a base-$p$ integer (we assume $p$=2 for the rest of this paper). This maintains a certain level of regularity in network connectivity and keeps the mathematical analysis of these network structures tractable.

This less restrictive constraint on node arrangement presents us with a few choices of network topology for any given $N$ that satisfies the condition as prescribed above. This paper attempts to find a simple rule that will get us the best network layout for all instances of realizable $N$. Network performance will be analyzed and compared. To relate this paper to existing works pertaining to the study of shufflenets, the analysis will be based on the same performance measures, i.e., the effect of network traffic on the expected number of hops taken by a packet to reach its destination and the normalized throughput of the networks.



0-8186-7780-5/97 $10.00 

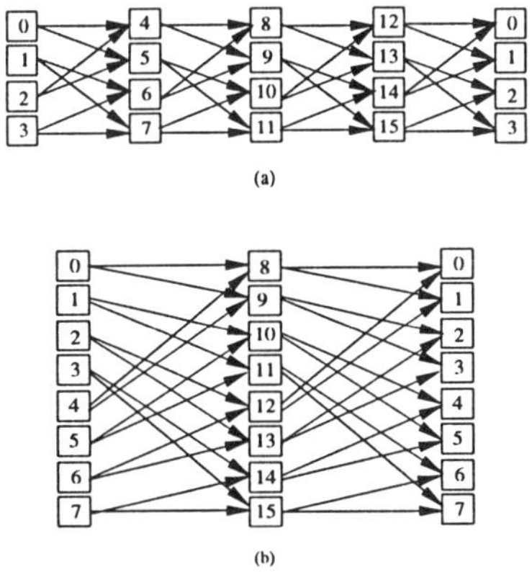


Figure 1: For $N = 16$, (a) XSN with $k = 4, k' = 2$ and (b) RSN with $k = 2, k' = 3$

The rest of this paper is organized as follows. In Section 2, two sub-classes of the GSNs are described, i.e., the extra-stage and reduced-stage shuffle networks. The performance modeling and analysis of extra-stage networks are given in Sections 3. Interpretation of the probability of deflection is discussed in detail in Section 4. Section 5 show the performance of reduced-shuffle networks. Results of this paper are summarized in Section 6 with some remarks.

## 2 A Benchmark in Analyzing Generalized Shuffle Networks

In analyzing the GSNs, it is helpful to further define two sub-classes of networks that fall into the category of GSNs [10]. These two sub-classes are defined based on their relationship with a parameter $k'$, termed the *virtual number of stages*, where $k' = log_2 n$. The parameter $k'$ represents the minimum number of hops to reach a node-stage where all nodes at that particular node-stage will be reachable by the packet at its present stage-location. A GSN characterized by $k \geq k'$ is called an extra-stage shuffle network (XSN), while one characterized by $k < k'$, is called a reduced-stage shuffle network (RSN). Figure 1 illustrates the distinction between the two sub-classes of GSNs with a 16-node network.

In XSNs, there are generally one or more node-stages where a packet can reach all nodes in its first visit to that stage. Under perfect routing conditions, a packet whose destination node is located $h$ stages away from its present stage-location, with $h \geq k'$, will reach its destination in exactly $h$ hops. This exactly equals its physical stage distance. Stages that are less than $k'$ hops away have nodes that are unreachable by the packet during its first traverse through the stage and thus will have to allow the packet to recirculate through the whole network before these nodes may be reached. RSNs, however, have comparatively less node-stages and packets will have to revisit all stages at least once more so as to be able to reach all nodes at all stages.

As a node structure in the networks, we assume in this paper that each node has two input/output links, one transmitter (TX) and one receiver (RX), and a buffer of one-packet size. This simple node structure is crucial in high-speed optical networks, where each node structure should have minimal processing requirement. With the two sub-classes of GSN structures clearly defined, we proceed to discuss the performance of simpler XSNs.

## 3 Extra-Stage Shuffle Networks

When observing the connectivity of any node with the rest of the nodes in any XSN, a regular spanning tree structure is evident. A packet from any source node has $2^h$ possible destinations at its $h$th hop. However, when and after it reaches the point where $h = k$, some nodes are revisited. Furthermore, the number of new nodes reachable is also limited by the physical number of nodes per stage. As such, for $h \geq k$, the number of new nodes met decreases as $h$ increases. The algorithm that may be used to calculate the number of reachable nodes at each hop from its source node is presented in [10].

The furthest hopping distance any packet would need to take to reach any destination without deflection is found to be $k + k' - 1$, where $k$ is derived from the number of physical stages in the network and $k' - 1$ accounts for the number of previously traversed stages during which certain nodes were unreachable, due to the inherent structural constraints. Then average number of hops a packet will take to reach its destination without deflection, denoted $E[D_0]$, is given as follows:

$$E[D_0] = \frac{1}{N-1} \sum_{i=1}^{k+k'-1} i \cdot n_i, \qquad (1)$$

where $i$ is the number of hops required to reach the destination node and $n_i$ is the number of nodes at distance $i$ hops away. This average value corresponds to the shortest path routing without any deflection in the routing process.

Given the structural setup in multihop networks, only one packet may be received or sent out through each of the two outputs at each time-slot. However,

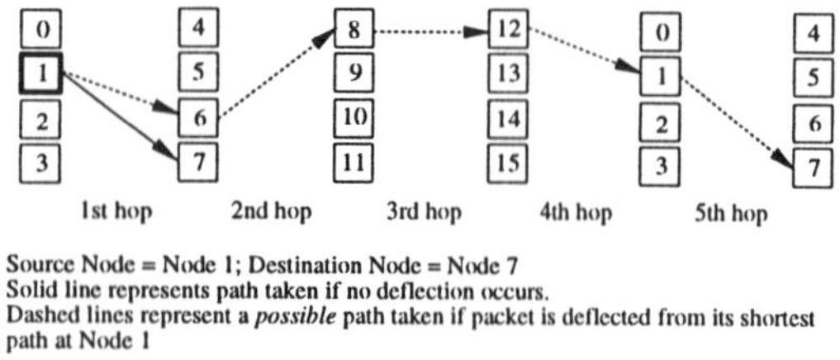


Figure 2: An illustration of deflection routing for network with $N = 16$, $k = 4$, $k' = 2$

if multiple packets desire to use the same output, it is inevitable that output contention within a node will ensue. Thus we need to consider network performance under packet contention. In this paper, we adopt deflection routing as a means of alleviating contention problems. Some possible contention resolution schemes under deflection routing are discussed in [3, 9]. Regardless of the chosen scheme, the packet that is sent out through the less preferred output channel and has to take more than the minimum required number of node hops to reach its destination is said to be deflected from its shortest path. It consequently takes a *detour* as it tries to reach its desired destination. Figure 2 compares a possible route of a packet that experiences deflection against that of an undeflected one. For this purpose, we define a parameter $P_{def}$ as the probability that a packet will be deflected from its shortest path. This number represents the probability that both input packets at a node will contend for the same output channel for shortest path routing *and* the monitored packet has to give way to the other packet.

The performance of XSNs can be analyzed using a Markov chain model. We construct a Markov chain where the states represent the distance between the packet and its destination node. As previously mentioned, the furthest possible distance in such networks is $k + k' - 1$. We include in this Markov chain the zero-distance state to represent the absorbing state, when the packet arrives at its desired destination. Then the state space of such a Markov chain will be completely defined with $k + k'$ states. A diagrammatic illustration is depicted in Figure 3 for $N$=64 case.

In modeling the behavior of packet movement in the presence of possible deflection, note that deflection is only possible if the packet resides in a *care node* [2]. Due to the regular connectivity of the network, a deflected packet has to recirculate through all the other stages, return to its current stage, which imply a total of $k - 1$ extra hops, before it can proceed to cover its

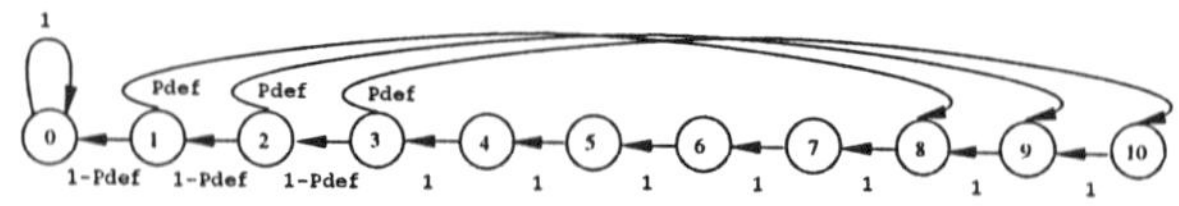


Figure 3: Node-distance-state Markov chain for $N = 64$, $k = 8$, $k' = 3$

original remaining distance. In other words, for any probability of deflection given by $P_{def}$, a packet at distance $i$ from its destination will be $i + k - 1$ hops away from its destination upon a deflection. And with probability $(1 - P_{def})$, the packet is not deflected and proceeds to the state where it will be at distance $i - 1$ away from its destination. Let

$$D_i = \text{E[number of hops when the tagged packet is at distance } i \text{ from its destination} \mid \text{probability of deflection} = P_{def}], \quad i < k + k'. \tag{2}$$

From the Markov chain of Figure 3, we can derive the following one-hop state transition equations:

$$D_i = \begin{cases} P_{def} D_{i-1+k} + (1 - P_{def}) D_{i-1} + 1, & 1 \le i \le k', \\ D_{k'} + (i - k'), & k' + 1 \le i \le k + k' - 1. \end{cases} \tag{3}$$

Using the above state-transition equations, we can obtain

$$D_i = \begin{cases} i + \frac{k}{(1-P_{def})^{k'}}[1 - (1 - P_{def})^i], & 1 \le i \le k', \\ D_{k'} + (i - k'), & k' + 1 \le i \le k + k' - 1, \end{cases} \tag{4}$$

where

$$D_{k'} = \frac{k}{(1 - P_{def})^{k'}} + k' - k. \tag{5}$$

Thus, $E[D]$ in terms of $P_{def}$ is given as

$$E[D] = \frac{1}{N-1} \sum_{i=1}^{k+k'-1} D_i n_i. \tag{6}$$

Note that the above expression reduces to $E[D_0]$ of Equation (1) when $P_{def} = 0$.

In a similar manner, we can find $E[N]$, the expected number of Don't Care nodes traversed by a packet during its lifetime on the network. Let

$$N_i = \text{E[number of Don't Care nodes that a tagged packet at distance } i \text{ visits in its lifetime]}, \quad i < k + k'. \tag{7}$$

Then, we find

$$N_i = \begin{cases} P_{def} N_{i-1+k} + (1 - P_{def}) N_{i-1}, & 1 \le i \le k', \\ N_{k'} + (i - k'), & k' + 1 \le i \le k + k' - 1, \end{cases} \tag{8}$$

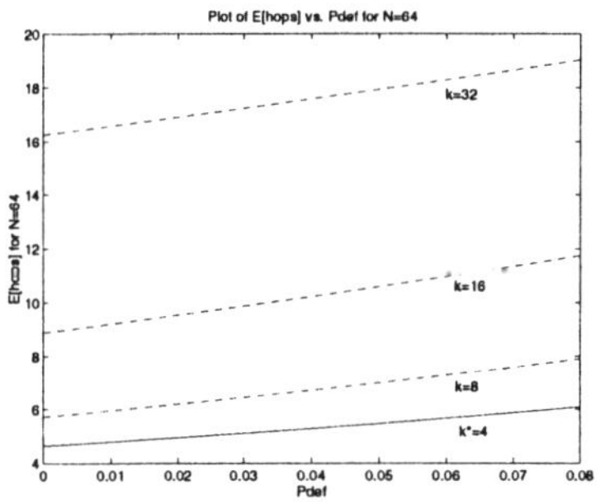


Figure 4: Plot of expected number of hops vs. $P_{def}$ for $N = 64$

$$= \begin{cases} D_i - \frac{1-(1-P_{def})^i}{P_{def}(1-P_{def})^{k'}}, & 1 \le i \le k', \\ N_{k'} + (i - k'), & k'+1 \le i \le k+k'-1. \end{cases} \quad (9)$$

Consequently, we get $E[N]$ as

$$E[N] = \frac{1}{N-1} \sum_{i=1}^{k+k'-1} N_i n_i, \quad (10)$$

and $P_{dc}$, the probability of visiting Don't Care nodes, may be derived using the following relation:

$$P_{dc} = \frac{E[N]}{E[D]}. \quad (11)$$

If we substitute $k' = k$ into Equations (4) and (9), i.e., the case where the physical number of node-stages equals the virtual number of node-stages, we get the results in [9] for classical shufflenets. This not only verifies the validity of the newly formulated equations, but also suggests that the classical shufflenet is a special case of XSNs.

Using Equation (6) derived in the previous section, we obtain a plot of $E[D]$ against $P_{def}$, shown in Figure 4. This graphical result suggests that network topology commands a significant influence on the performance of the network. The somewhat constant offset in $E[D]$ between any two network topologies is a consequence of the regular connectivity of the networks. Thus, the *comparative performance* of the different topologies will not vary with statistical significance for any value of $P_{def}$. This suggests that comparison of network performance can be fully accounted for by using the $E[D]$ values at $P_{def} = 0$.

Also from Figure 4, we learn that for any given $N$, the optimal XSN network topology will be the one which has the largest number of nodes per stage, hence the smallest number of physical stages. Thus, if a classical shufflenet structure for that given value of $N$ exists, then that structure is the optimal one. It is also noted that the larger the number of stages, the greater the probability of meeting a Don't Care node. This is true since the wider the network diameter, the greater the number of shortest paths a packet has. This indefinitely increases the packet's probability of visiting Don't Care nodes.

Network performance improves as the probability of encountering Don't Care nodes decreases. Don't Care nodes allow for some flexibility in packet switching that alleviates packet contention problems. However, the graphs suggest that the tighter the routing constraints, the better the performance in terms of expected number of hops, regardless of network load.

## 4 Validity of $P_{def}$

In the analysis so far, the relationship between network performance measures and $P_{def}$ has been carefully studied. However, this does not get us to the bottom of the network model – in the physical system, $P_{def}$ is internal to the network. Thus, relating the performance measures to $P_{def}$ does not describe as yet the response of the network to any exogenous factor, of which the most fundamental is the response of the network to the offered load, $g$. Figure 5 pictorially illustrates this point.

Thus, we need to find the relationship between $P_{def}$ and $g$. To do this, we use the definition of offered load $g$ as described in [1, 3, 8]. This defines $g$ as the load seen by the network. Note that this does not necessarily equate the load offered by the user. Under high network traffic conditions, packets that the user would have liked to transmit may not be successfully transmitted. This occurs in situations when the output channels are taken up by the packets in the input channels or the memory buffer – thus, none of the output channels are available for the transmission of new packets. This being the case, we will have to consider issues like re-transmission or temporary storage of packets, double-counting of re-transmitted packets in the queue, rules for discarding packets upon packet contention, and so forth. To fully model this behavior will be phenomenally difficult.

However, if we are looking at network performance in terms of the *throughput of the system*, we can claim that using $g$ as our reference parameter suffices our analysis. This is because whatever the actual load offered by the user, call it $p$, the network will only be able to optimize on $g$, regardless of $p$. The buffer temporarily mediates between the network capacity and the node-user's transmission demand, and the node-user may continue to request for data transmission.

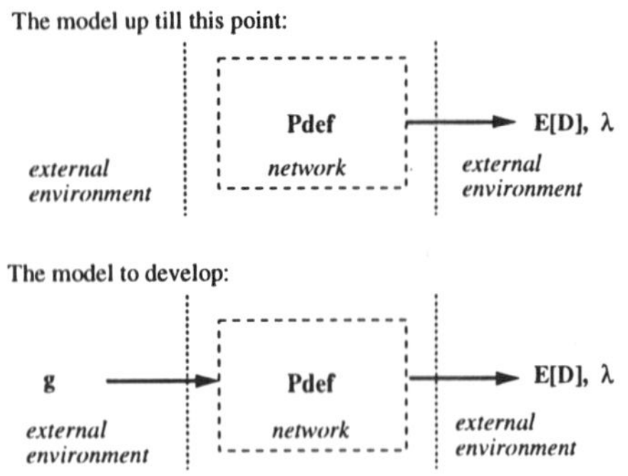


Figure 5: The relationship between $P_{def}$ and g

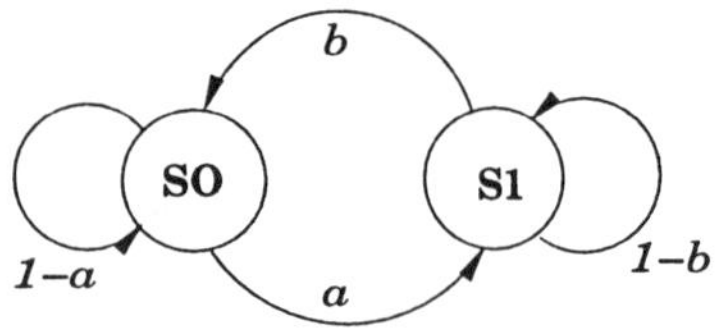


Figure 6: Node-state state-transition diagram

Thus, we can assume $p = g$, the dynamic equilibrium of which adheres to Little's Law and will allow the network to operate properly. As such, we can confidently pursue our model development with $g$ as the exogenous offered load parameter.

The crucial factor that determines the relationship between $P_{def}$ and $g$ is the structure of each node in the network. If we assume that the packet in memory is serviced with the highest priority as in the case of optical networks (otherwise optical signals may be degraded to undetectable level), the only situation where deflection could possibly occur is when the memory buffer is occupied. In all other circumstances, at least one packet will always be properly routed; if there are two incoming packets and they contend for the same output channel for shortest path routing, the packet that does not get assigned to the appropriate output channel will unquestionably be sent to the memory buffer. Although this constitutes a delay in the time sense, it is by definition not a deflection. Recirculating via the memory buffer does not de-track the packet from its shortest path. Thus it suffices our requirements to model the system using a two-state Markov chain, where the states are determined by the state of the memory. Define State 0 (S0) as the state when the memory buffer is empty and State 1 (S1) as that when the memory buffer holds a packet. Figure 6 illustrates such a Markov chain.

It is also appropriate to mention at this point that the two-state Markov chain does not over-simplify the state space that models the relationship between $P_{def}$ and $g$. Elaborate consideration of all possible combinations of inputs into the node is not necessary due to the fact that within every time-slot, all other states are transient. This is because whether a deflection occurs depends crucially on the vacancy or non-vacancy of the memory buffer. This is, in effect, a consequence of the adopted priority routing rule that confers the packet residing in the memory buffer with the highest routing priority. To formulate the one-state transition matrix of the above Markov chain, let $a$ represent the probability of changing from S0 to S1, and $b$ the probability of changing from S1 to S0 at any time-slot.

For a state-change from S0 to S1 at any time-slot, there must have been two Care packets entering the node via the input channels. If both incoming packets contend for the same output channel for shortest path routing, then one of the packets will be routed to the memory buffer, thus causing a state-change to S1. The probability of this occurrence $a$ is given by $\frac{1}{2}P_u^2$, where $P_u$ is the probability that an input channel brings in a Care packet into the node [3] and is given by $u(1-P_{dc})$.

The parameter $P_{dc}$ is given in Equation (11) and $u$, the probability of slot occupancy in a single-buffer node, is given by

$$u = \frac{\sqrt{\alpha^2 + g^2\{(1-\alpha)^2 + \frac{1}{4}(1-P_{dc})^2\}} - \alpha}{g\{(1-\alpha)^2 + \frac{1}{4}(1-P_{dc})^2\}}, \quad (12)$$

where $\alpha = 1/E[D]$.

Likewise, in deriving the probability of a state-change from S1 to S0, we find that this can only occur in the following situations:

1. when there are no packets coming in from the input channels;
2. when there is only one input packet and the input packet is either a Don't Care packet or does not require the same output channel as that taken up by the packet in the memory buffer.

The probability of this occurrence, represented by $b$ in Figure 6, can therefore be given by

$$\begin{aligned} b &= (1-u)^2 + u(1-u)[P_{dc} + \frac{1}{2}(1-P_{dc})] \\ &= (1-u)[1 - \frac{u}{2}(1-P_{dc})]. \end{aligned} \quad (13)$$

As mentioned before, the only time when packet deflection is possible is when the memory buffer is occupied at the beginning of that particular time-slot, i.e., when the starting state of that clock-cycle is S1.

Hence, to derive the steady-state $P_{def}$, we first need to know the steady-state probability of S1. Define $\pi_i$ as the steady-state probability that the node is in State $i$ ($i$=0,1). We can find $\pi_1$ by solving the following limiting probability matrix:

$$[\pi_0 \quad \pi_1] \begin{bmatrix} a & 1-a \\ 1-b & b \end{bmatrix} = [\pi_0 \quad \pi_1], \tag{14}$$

which readily yields

$$\pi_1 = \frac{1-a}{2-a-b}. \tag{15}$$

We find that $P_{def}$ is given by

$$P_{def} = \frac{1}{8}\pi_1 u(1-P_{dc})^2. \tag{16}$$

Described in words, $P_{def}$ is the probability that *all* of the following occur:

1. the node initially has a packet in the memory buffer $\Rightarrow$ probability $\pi_1$;
2. the packet in question is at a Care node $\Rightarrow$ probability $1-P_{dc}$;
3. the other input channel also brings in a Care packet $\Rightarrow$ probability $u(1-P_{dc})$;
4. the packet is deflected under contention $\Rightarrow$ probability $\frac{1}{2}$; and
5. all three packets contend for the same output channel $\Rightarrow$ probability $(\frac{1}{2})^3 + (\frac{1}{2})^3$.

Although these relations allow us to numerically solve for $P_{def}$ for any given offered load $g$, complexities pervade as the equation we need to solve is not only a polynomial in the variable $P_{def}$, the degree of which depends on the size and structure of the network we wish to analyze, but also embedded with summation terms, whose expanded form is absolutely unilluminating.

A simpler method of working this out is to specify a value for $P_{def}$ and algorithmically work the equations backward to solve for $g$. For any given $P_{def}$, we can easily obtain $P_{dc}$ and $\alpha$ using Equations (6), (10) and (11). Therefore, expansion of Equation (16) will yield a fixed-degree polynomial in terms of the variable $u$ regardless of network size and network structure. Finding the roots to this equation yields only one root within the logical range of [0,1]. This suggests that this reverse method is probably a viable solution. Following this, we may use Equation (12) to find the corresponding $g$.

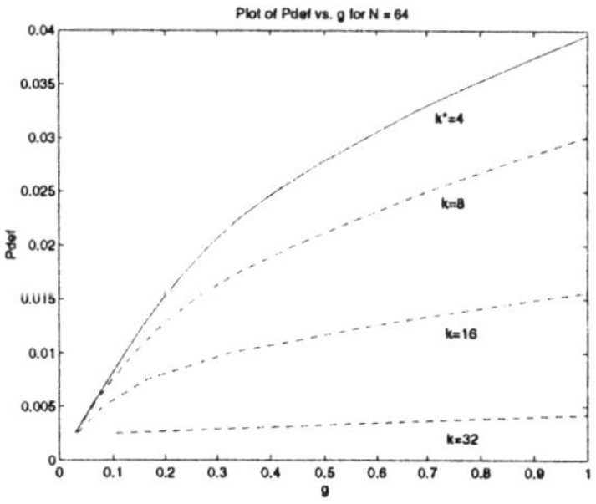


Figure 7: Plot of $P_{def}$ vs g for $N = 64$

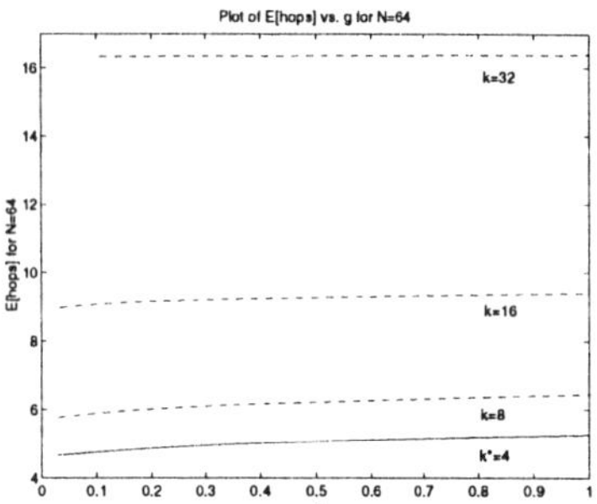


Figure 8: Plot of E[hops] vs g for $N = 64$

With $g$ in hand, we will be able to find $\lambda$, the normalized throughput of the network:

$$\lambda = 2\alpha \frac{\sqrt{\alpha^2 + g^2\{(1-\alpha)^2 + \frac{1}{4}(1-P_{dc})^2\}} - \alpha}{g\{(1-\alpha)^2 + \frac{1}{4}(1-P_{dc})^2\}}. \tag{17}$$

Figure 7 shows the plots of $P_{def}$ against $g$ for $N = 64$ with different network topologies. We observe that $P_{def}$ increases with the offered load and the slope of increase appears to reach a constant after $g$ reaches approximately 0.5. For $k = 32$, the probability of deflection, $P_{def}$, is almost negligible. For the optimum case where $k = 4$, $P_{def}$ terminates at a maximum value of $P_{def} = 0.04$, and increases monotonically with $g$.

Similarly, we derive plots of the relationship between $E[D]$ and $\lambda$, the normalized throughput against $g$ in Figure 8 and Figure 9, respectively. Both plots reiterate the point made in the previous section that the optimum structure among XSNs is that with the smallest number of node-stages and that the network topology has a dominating impact on network performance.

The analysis of RSNs has to be treated with a different approach due to the irregularity of the network structure. By irregularity, we mean that the network connectivity of every single node is not same, but different nodes meet a different number of new nodes for

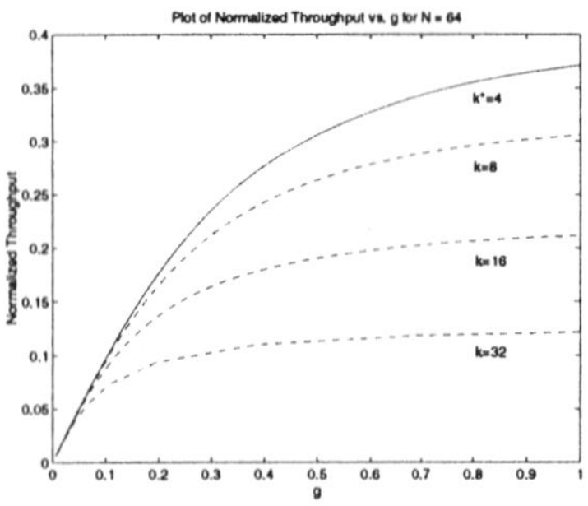


Figure 9: Plot of normalized throughput vs g for $N = 64$

any given number of hops taken. This is due to the fact that node-stages have to be repeatedly revisited as the packet tries to reach some nodes that had been inaccessible for the number of hops already taken. We find that the hop-distance distribution of each node in the network varies, depending on the size of the network and the position of the reference (source) node in relation to the rest of the nodes in the network. This evokes a very complex model.

Furthermore, the number of stages in a network also determines the node-hopping behavior of a packet upon deflection from its shortest path route. It is observed that the smaller the number of stages, the greater the node-hoping variation. For example, if there is only one stage in the network, a deflection that takes place when the packet is one hop away from its desired destination will bring the packet to any distance away from its destination in the hop-distance state space, including its current state, but none closer than its current distance, depending on the reference position of the node it currently resides.

Given the fact that the $E[D_0]$ in Equation (1) gives a good indication of comparative system performance under ideal conditions, i.e., the environment where no packet deflection occurs, we may calculate the lower bound on $E[D]$ for all RSN network topologies simply by finding the proportion of new nodes met at every hop.

Table 1 shows the tabulated results of the $E[D]$ values for the various RSN topologies for $P_{def} = 0$. The results show that two-stage networks give the lowest $E[D]$ values across the investigated network sizes.

To see the effects of offered load on $E[D]$ and $\lambda$, the normalized throughput, an approximate Markov chain model is obtained by taking the weighted-average probability of the different resultant distance from destination that a deflection will cause. Figure 10 depicts the Markov chain model for the two-stage 64-node network.

Table 1: $E[D]$ values for various values of $N$ and $n$.

| | $n$=16 | $n$=32 | $n$=64 | $n$=128 | $n$=256 |
|---|---|---|---|---|---|
| $N$=32 | 3.565 | 3.649 | | | |
| $N$=64 | 4.635 | 4.448 | 4.532 | | |
| $N$=128 | 6.614 | 5.559 | 5.379 | 5.460 | |
| $N$=256 | | 7.561 | 6.514 | 6.336 | 6.417 |

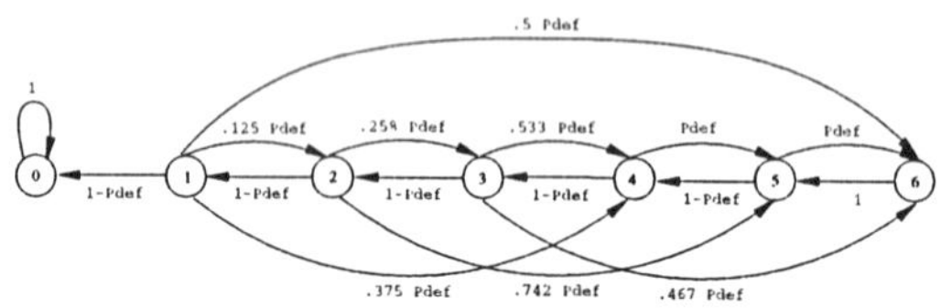

Figure 10: Node-distance-state Markov chain for $N$=64, $k$=2

Following the analytical steps as before, we obtain plots of $E[D]$ and $\lambda$ with respect to $g$ for various 64-node RSNs as shown in Figure 11 and Figure 12 respectively. The solid line in the graphs represents the performance of the optimal XSN topology, included as a point of reference. As we can see from the graphs, the two-stage network yields the best network performance in terms of both expected number of hops and normalized throughput. Our result agrees with the observation made by Iness, *et al.* in [11], where they found a two-stage network gives the minimum average hop distance when the number of nodes is even.

## 5 Conclusion

This paper compares the performance of all generalized shuffle networks for a given $N$. We find that the

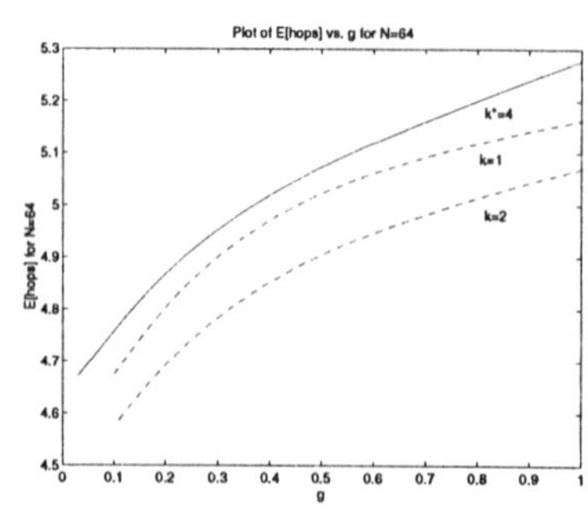


Figure 11: Plot of E[hops] vs g for $N = 64$ (RSN)

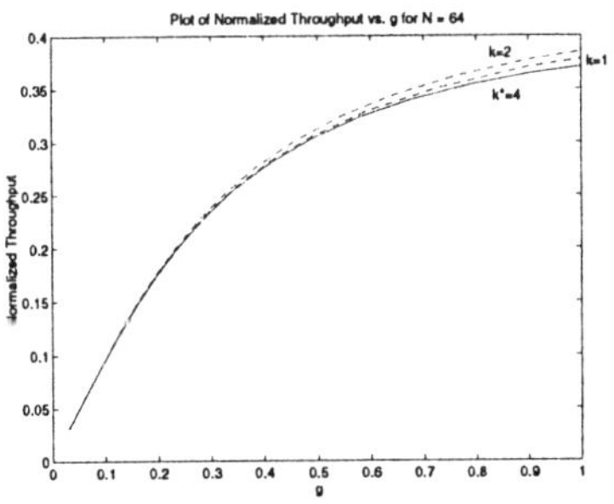


Figure 12: Plot of normalized throughput vs g for $N = 64$ (RSN)

larger the network diameter, the more the node-stages and thus the higher the probability of a node visiting a Don't Care node. This yields a certain extent of flexibility in the choice of routing a packet through a shortest path. Consequently, the probability of packet deflection also decreases. On the other hand, we find that as the number of node-stages increases, the system throughput falls.

We also find that the structure that yields the best performance in terms of system throughput and expected number of hops a packet takes on the network is the two-stage network for $N$=64. In such a network, the shortest path to the desired destination is mostly unique. Even with high offered loads, networks with high node-access efficiencies still perform better in terms of hop instances. In other words, routing flexibility does not improve the performance of multihop networks.

## Acknowledgements

This work has been supported, in part, by ARPA/Hanscom, NSF Postdoctoral Fellowship, NSF Research Grant (#NCR-9404947), and the Ogasawara Foundation for the Promotion of Science and Engineering.

## References

[1] A. Bononi and P. R. Prucnal, "New structures of the optical node in transparent optical multihop networks using deflection routing," *Proc. of IEEE INFOCOM*, pp. 415 - 422, 1994.

[2] A. Bononi, "Novel Schemes and Performance Analysis of Ultrafast Packet-Switching Transparent Optical Networks," *Ph.D Dissertation, Department of Electrical Engineering, Princeton University*, June 1994.

[3] F. Forghieri, A. Bononi and P. R. Prucnal, "Analysis and Comparison of Hot-Potato and Single-Buffer Deflection Routing," *IEEE Transactions on Communications*, Vol. 43, No. 1, pp. 88-98, Jan. 1995.

[4] M.G. Hluchyj and M.J. Karol, "ShuffleNet: An application of generalized perfect shuffles to multihop lightwave networks," *Proc. of IEEE INFOCOM*, pp. 4B.4.1-4B.4.5, 1988.

[5] A. Krishna and B. Hajek, "Performance of Shuffle-Like Switching Networks with Deflection," *IEEE INFOCOM*, Vol. 2, pp.473-480, 1990.

[6] N.F. Maxemchuk, "Comparison of deflection and store-and-forward techniques in the Manhattan street and shuffle-exchange networks," *Proc. of IEEE INFOCOM*, pp. 800-809, 1989.

[7] A. Acampora and S. Shah, "Multihop Lightwave Networks: A Comparison of Store-and-Forward and Hot-Potato Routing," *IEEE Transactions on Communications*, Vol. 40, No.6, pp. 1082-1090, June 1992.

[8] S. G. Chan and H. Kobayashi, "Analysis of the Shufflenet with Different Contention Resolution Schemes," *Proc. of 94' CISS*, pp. 261-270, March, 1994.

[9] S. G. Chan and H. Kobayashi, "Performance Analysis of Shufflenet with Deflection Routing," *IEEE GLOBECOM*, pp. 854-859, 1993.

[10] S. Seo, P. R. Prucnal, H. Kobayashi and J. B. Lim, " On the Performance of a Class of Multihop Shuffle Networks," *Proc. of '95 International Conference on Communications*, Vol. 2, pp. 1211-1215, Seattle, June 1995.

[11] J. Iness, S. Banerjee, and B. Mukherjee, "GEMNET: A Generalized, Shuffle-Exchange-Based Regular, Scalable, Modular, Multihop, WDM Lightwave Network," *IEEE/ACM Transactions on Networking*, Vol. 3, No. 4, pp. 470-476, Aug. 1995.

# An Analysis of Internet Inter-Domain Topology and Route Stability

*Ramesh Govindan* *Anoop Reddy*

USC/Information Sciences Institute
Marina Del Rey, CA 90292
{govindan,areddy}@isi.edu

## Abstract

*The Internet routing fabric is partitioned into several* domains. *Each domain represents a region of the fabric administered by a single commercial entity. Over the past two years, the routing fabric has experienced significant growth. From more than a year's worth of inter-domain routing traces, we analyze the Internet inter-domain topology, its route stability behavior, and the effect of growth on these characteristics. Our analysis reveals several interesting results. Despite growth, the degree distribution and the diameter of the inter-domain topology have remained relatively unchanged. Furthermore, there exists a four-level hierarchy of Internet domains classified by degree. However, connectivity between domains is significantly non-hierarchical. Despite increased connectivity at higher levels in the topology, the distribution of paths to prefixes from the backbone remained relatively unchanged. There is evidence that both route availability and the mean reachability duration have degraded with Internet growth.*

## 1 Introduction

In the past two years, we have witnessed the emergence of a commercial Internet infrastructure. Today, the Internet routing fabric is partitioned into different administrative *domains*. A campus or internal corporate network is an example of a domain. Data exchange between campus or corporate domains is facilitated by one or more *provider* domains; these domains offer, as a service, transmission and switching facilities for data exchange between their customers. Providers usually interconnect at Internet *exchange points*, and can vary in the geographical scope of their operations from regional, to national and international.

Domains may need to exercize traffic access restrictions and express transit preferences. Currently, domains realize these *policies* by selectively disseminating routing information. The Border Gateway Protocol (BGP) version 4 [15], an *inter-domain* hop-by-hop routing protocol, is used for this purpose. In BGP, a domain may originate one or more *routes*. Routes advertise reachability to IP *address prefixes* within a domain. A domain realizes its traffic policies by independently selecting, and selectively propagating routes heard from its neighbors or *peers*. Associated with each route is a list of identifiers for domains traversed by the route. This list is the route's AS_PATH.

The collection of domains, their policies and peering relationships, and the address prefixes they advertise defines the Internet *inter-domain routing system*. The inter-domain routing system is large. In December 1995, there were more than 900 domains, and nearly 31,000 address prefixes. Paralleling the growth of the Internet, the routing system has also rapidly increased in size. Between mid 1994 and late 1995, domains and address prefixes have each nearly doubled.

The inter-domain routing system provides the foundation for Internet wide-area communication. Two characteristics of the routing system can impact the performance of such communication:

*Inter-domain topology:* This is the graph of domains and the inter-domain peering relationships. A link in this graph signifies route exchange—and presumably IP traffic exchange—between the corresponding domains.

*Route stability:* The routing system experiences transient changes in routes, caused by router and link failures or router misconfiguration.

With the growth of the routing system, it is reasonable to expect significant changes in these characteristics.

With the emergence of the World-Wide Web and Mbone-based applications, wide-area communication is becoming more prevalent [13]. Understanding the topology and route stability behavior of the routing system is important for end-to-end protocol design and evaluation. However, the geographic extent of the routing system precludes an accurate analysis of these characteristics.

From traces of routing updates seen at a large Internet service provider and at a popular Internet exchange point, this paper *approximately* characterizes the routing system and its growth. This approximation is possible because most large service providers carry routes to almost all IP-connected destinations and BGP's AS_PATHs contain some inter-domain topology information.

Our analysis reveals several interesting results about the inter-domain topology. Despite the growth of the routing system, the diameter and degree distribution in the inter-domain topology have remained relatively constant. The path "redundancy"—the number of distinct paths to

[0] This work was supported by the National Science Foundation under Cooperative Agreement NCR-9321043. Any opinions, findings, and conclusions or recommendations expressed in this material are those of the author(s) and do not necessarily reflect the views of the National Science Foundation.



0-8186-7780-5/97 $10.00 © 1997 IEEE

a prefix—has also not changed significantly, despite increased connectivity. A closer analysis of the degree distribution reveals the existence of a four-level hierarchy of domains. Connectivity between domains, however, appears to be significantly non-hierarchical.

While routes to prefixes were highly available (more than 90% of the address prefixes were available for more than 95% of the time), there was some evidence of degradation of availability with growth. Not surprisingly, more than 80% of the prefixes were reachable for more than 95% of the time by a single *primary* path. The mean reachability duration for a prefix shows wide variation, but a noticeable degradation with growth. This reachability duration, however, appears to be correlated with the length of the primary path.

Section 2 motivates the need for a study of routing system growth. Section 3 studies the inter-domain topology, and the effect of growth on the topology. Section 4 analyzes route stability and its variation with growth. Finally, Section 5 describes related work and Section 6 presents our conclusions.

## 2 Background and Motivation

In this section, we briefly describe Internet inter-domain routing. We also motivate the need for an analysis of the inter-domain routing system.

### The Internet Inter-Domain Topology

A domain is an autonomously administered portion of the Internet's routing fabric. Domains vary in size, geographic extent, and function. *Backbones* provide national or inter-continental transit, *regionals* serve a metropolitan area or a collection of such areas, and *stubs* provide campus level IP connectivity. Domains interconnect in several ways. The larger providers usually exchange traffic at neutral *exchange points*, such as MAE-East in Washington DC and the NSF-sponsored NAPs [9]. Stubs usually connect to their providers using direct leased lines.

By abstracting out the internal topology of domains, we can describe the Internet as an undirected graph whose nodes are the domains and whose links are the inter-domain interconnects. In the early Internet, this *inter-domain topology* was approximately tree-structured. A single national *backbone* provided cross-country transit to several regional providers. Campus networks obtained global IP connectivity by attaching to their respective regionals. With the advent of commercial IP service, the structure of this graph has become more complex. Several backbones now interconnect in a partial mesh. A regional provider may interconnect with other regionals serving the same or adjacent geographical area, as well as with one or more backbones. Finally, a stub may connect to one or more regionals or backbones.

### The Border Gateway Protocol

The Border Gateway Protocol (BGP) is used to achieve inter-domain routing information exchange. The unit of information exchanged by BGP-speakers is an *update*. An update contains a collection of address prefixes. Address prefix *X* represents the topological region of the Internet in which hosts and routers' network-layer addresses have *X* as a prefix; a route from a peer containing prefix *X* advertises that peer's reachability to some entity within that topological region. Address prefixes are usually represented by an IP address and a prefix length.

For each address prefix it contains, an update defines a *routing transition*. We distinguish between two kinds of transitions: *unreachables*, and routes. An unreachable for prefix *X* advertises the sender's inability to reach destinations in *X*. Conversely, a route for prefix *X* advertises the sender's reachability to destinations in *X*. Associated with each route is an `AS_PATH`. The `AS_PATH` for prefix *X* lists the domain-level path to destinations in *X*.

In today's Internet, each domain originates routes to all address prefixes within its borders. Usually, the domain's border routers learn of these address prefixes through a separate *intra-domain* routing protocol. BGP allows domains to realize access restrictions and transit preferences—domain traffic *policy*—by selectively propagating routing information. A domain that receives two or more routes to an address prefix can independently select one of the routes, thereby exercising its transit preference. A domain can also independently restrict the advertisement of a selected route to a neighbor, thereby realizing its access restrictions.

### Characterizing the Inter-Domain Routing System

The inter-domain routing system determines the perceived quality of wide-area communication in the Internet. Such wide-area communication is becoming increasingly prevalent; studies at one campus indicate that wide-area TCP connections originating at that campus domain grew exponentially [13]. Several factors, including the rapid growth of the World-Wide Web, and the increasing use of the Mbone, account for this increase. Another measure of the growth in wide-area communication is the growth in aggregated backbone traffic; the utilization of the MAE-East Gigaswitch nearly doubled in the five months between May and September 1995 [8].

To understand the impact of the routing system on wide-area communication, we focus on two characteristics of the routing system: the inter-domain topology and route stability. What factors influence inter-domain topology and route stability? In today's Internet, the inter-domain topology is determined by bilateral transit agreements between providers. The presence of several exchange points enables increased domain connectivity. Router failure or temporary router overload is one reason for route instability. Loss of link connectivity either within a domain or between domain border routers is another. Routing misconfiguration is a third—currently, most inter-domain route exchange is effected by manual policy configuration.

When analyzing topology and route stability, it is important to understand how these characteristics change with *growth*. A unique feature of the Internet is the relatively rapid growth in the topology and the number of routed address prefixes, caused by the rapid increase in the number of connected hosts [12] and the deployment of a commercial Internet infrastructure. In June 1994, the routing system consisted of about 400 domains and 18,000 prefixes. By November 1995, it had grown to 900 domains and 31,000 prefixes.

Why might an analysis of routing system topology and route stability be useful? First, such an analysis enables a better understanding of how these characteristics impact end-to-end communication performance. Second, this analysis can impact the design of routing protocols and route distribution mechanisms, as well as the implementation and provisioning of routers. Finally, a better understanding of the routing system can improve modeling of internetwork topologies [16], and of end-to-end delay and loss characteristics [5].

Accurately analyzing the routing system and its growth is extremely difficult. Because the Internet is geographically distributed, no *complete* map of the inter-domain topology exists today. Efforts are underway to establish Internet policy registries containing such information [2, 4]. Because the Internet is administratively decentralized, it is difficult to obtain a composite picture of the inter-domain topology and route stability.

### Overview of Approach

In this paper, we characterize routing system topology and route stability, and the impact of growth on the routing system, using two chronological traces of routing transitions:

- $\mathcal{D}_A$ contains nearly 6.6 million BGP updates heard from a backbone router of a major IP service provider between June 7 1994 and June 26 1995[1].
- $\mathcal{D}_M$ contains nearly 5.1 million BGP updates heard from more than twenty large and small IP service providers attached to a large Internet exchange point (MAE-East in Washington DC) between August 1995 to November 1995. $\mathcal{D}_M$ was collected at an experimental facility, the MAE-East Route Server.

These traces are incomplete in parts, caused by failures at the trace collection points. In our analysis, we have been careful to eliminate the effect of these trace flaws.

A macroscopic examination of the trace data reveals nearly linear growth in the number of prefixes, links, and domains [10]. On average, a new prefix appears in the routing system every 25 minutes, a new domain every 12 hours, and a new inter-domain link every 8 hours.

Of interest to us, however, are more detailed measures of growth in topology and changes in route stability. For this, we focused on three different *snapshots* (Section 3) of these traces, separated by nearly six months. Each snapshot contains some inter-domain connectivity information, namely the AS_PATHs associated with updates. Using this, we derive an approximate characterization of the inter-domain topology. This enables us to quantitatively analyze the growth of several characteristics of this topology: the number and size of domains, the extent of inter-domain connectivity, the number of different domain-level paths to address prefixes, and so on. From the snapshots, we also obtain distributions for two measures of route stability: availability of a path to a prefix, and the mean reachability duration for a prefix.

[1] Advanced Networks and Services, who operated the now defunct NSFNET backbone service

| | Domains | Links | Address Prefixes |
|---|---|---|---|
| $\mathcal{S}_a$ | 531 | 709 | 21524 |
| $\mathcal{S}_b$ | 746 | 1000 | 26945 |
| $\mathcal{S}_c$ | 909 | 1369 | 31470 |

Table 1: *Snapshots:* We obtain an approximate representation of the routing system topology from 21-day segments of our traces. This table shows the number of domains, links, and address prefixes in the topologies obtained from our three snapshots.

The results presented in this paper are approximate, because they are based on routing data collected at a single point in the Internet. While we expect backbone routers to see routes to all prefixes, our snapshots may not contain all the domains or inter-domain links in the Internet. This is because routes containing these domains and links in their AS_PATHs may not have propagated to our observation points, having been restricted by domain policy.

## 3 Topology

In this section, we obtain approximate characterizations, called *snapshots* of the inter-domain topology from three different segments of our traces. Using these snapshots, we study the following properties of the topology, and their variation over time: domain degree distribution, diameter, and connectivity.

### Snapshots

Two artifacts of the traces preclude our using the entire traces for analyzing routing system topology, reliability and availability. First, the traces contain several gaps, primarily caused by outages at the trace collection routers. Second, $\mathcal{D}_M$ was collected at an experimental facility (the Mae-East Route Server) and is incomplete in parts.

Nevertheless, there exist segments of these traces that are devoid of these artifacts. From these segments, we can derive an approximate "instantaneous" characterizations (*snapshots*) of the routing system. By comparing widely separated snapshots, we can observe the variation of routing system characteristics with growth. This is the methodology we use in this and the next section. For our analysis, we chose three snapshots: $\mathcal{S}_a$, corresponding to the routing system in November 1994; $\mathcal{S}_b$, corresponding to the routing system in May 1995; and, $\mathcal{S}_c$, corresponding to the routing system in November 1995. Table 1 gives the sizes of the topology and address prefixes obtained from these snapshots.

From the AS_PATHs in a snapshot, we can derive the inter-domain topology. Each element of an update's AS_PATH defines a node in the topology and each successive pair of domains in the AS_PATH represents the endpoints of a link. Furthermore, the collection of unique address prefixes seen in the snapshot approximately represents the routed destinations at that instant.

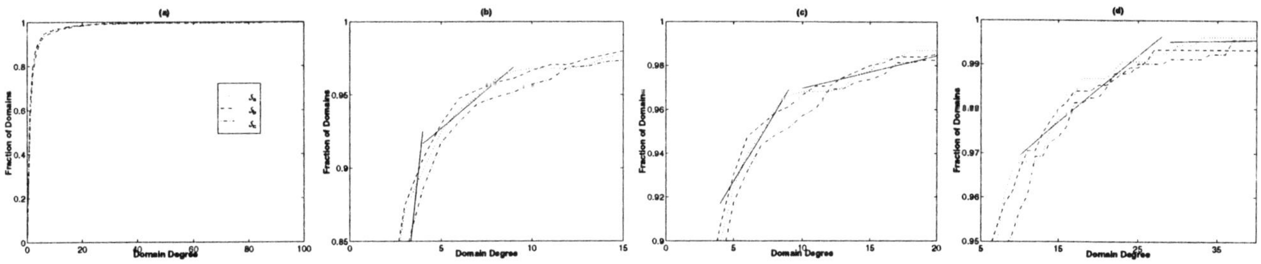


Figure 1: *Degree Distribution:* The cumulative fraction of domains plotted against degree. (a) The distributions are nearly identical for the three snapshots. A closer look at the distribution ((b), (c), and (d)) shows that domains can be divided into different classes based on frequency of occurrence. The solid line segments in each of (b), (c) and (d) demarcate different classes of domains (see text).

The longer the segment of the trace chosen, the more complete our snapshot is likely to be. However, a longer duration trace segment may represent significant growth and thereby skew our snapshot. We empirically chose 21-day segments of our traces. In each 21-day segment, the number of domains, links, and prefixes grows by no more than 10%. Further, the routing activity in the Internet is such that in each segment, at least two transitions are seen for more than 99% of all prefixes seen in the window. For this reason, we believe that our choice of segment length is likely to capture most of the routed address prefixes in the routing system at the time. We validated this by comparing the address prefix count in our snapshots with an independently collected history of the size of backbone routing tables [6]. In each case, our approximation was within 5% of the size of the routing table at the corresponding instant.

This technique provides a richer view of the topology than an instantaneous dump of the routing table. This is because we may see more than one AS_PATH to an address prefix over the 21-day trace segment. However, there is still a likelihood of "missing" some of the inter-domain links, and a smaller likelihood of "missing" some domains as well. In general, we expect that this technique gives a fairly good picture of the topology closer to the trace collection locations (i.e. in the North American portion of the Internet). The "fuzziness" of our snapshots is likely to increase with with increasing topological distance from the trace collection locations.

We now describe the diameter, degree distribution, and connectivity characteristics of the inter-domain topology.

## Degree Distribution

A link in the inter-domain topology represents BGP peering between the end-points of the link. Usually, such peering is based on bilateral data traffic exchange agreements between domains. The number of such peerings, the domain's degree, is therefore an approximate measure of its size. The distribution of domain degree illustrates the range of domain sizes in the Internet.

An analysis of our snapshots reveals that the average degree of domains is 2.67, 2.68, and 2.99 respectively. This indicates that the inter-domain topology is, by and large, sparse. This observation is illustrated better by plotting the cumulative fraction of domains against node degree (Figure 1(a)). Nearly 75% of the domains have a degree of 1 or 2.

| Class | Degree Range | Approximate Fraction of Domains in Class |
|---|---|---|
| $\mathcal{C}_1$ | >= 28 | 0.9% |
| $\mathcal{C}_2$ | 10-27 | 3.1% |
| $\mathcal{C}_3$ | 4-9 | 9% |
| $\mathcal{C}_4$ | 1-3 | 87% |

Table 2: *Degree Classification:* The degree distribution can be well approximated by a piecewise linear function with four components. This suggests a classification of domains by degree range. Within a degree range, the frequency of occurrence of domains of a certain degree is similar.

The average degree has also increased only slightly across the different snapshots, even though the number of domains and links has doubled between $\mathcal{S}_a$ and $\mathcal{S}_c$. This may indicate that the rate of growth has been approximately *uniform* across all sizes of domains. The degree distribution confirms this—the distributions for the three snapshots appear *identical* (Figure 1(a)). This suggests that as the Internet has grown, the fraction of domains having a given degree has remained approximately constant.

The degree distribution is well approximated by a piecewise linear function with four components (Figure 1(b), (c), and (d)). Each component defines a degree range. Within a degree range, the fraction of nodes with a given degree is similar. We believe that these four degree ranges represent a "natural" hierarchy of domains classified by function. Table 2 describes this hierarchy. We think that the $\mathcal{C}_1$ domains correspond to national or international backbones, the $\mathcal{C}_2$ domains correspond to large North American regional providers or European national networks, the $\mathcal{C}_3$

domains correspond to smaller regional providers and large metropolitan area providers, and the $C_4$ domains correspond to smaller metropolitan area providers and multi-campus corporate or academic networks. In some instances, particularly for classes $C_1$ and $C_2$, we have been able to validate this correspondence. The constancy of the degree distribution implies that the Internet has been growing "laterally", adding domains to the different levels of the hierarchy in proportion to growth.

## Diameter

The diameter of the three inter-domain topologies is 9, 10, and 10 respectively. The path taken by packets between two domains is a function of domain policies, and can exceed this figure. This figure is consistent with our domain classification above. Between two stub domains, there are at most 3 or 4 domain-level hops each to $C_1$ providers. As we show below, connectivity within $C_1$ is rather high, so the shortest path between $C_1$ providers should be between 2 and 4.

More importantly, despite the near doubling in the number of domains and links between $S_a$ and $S_c$, the domain-level *diameter of the Internet has remained relatively constant.* Despite this, however, it is likely that the *router-level* diameter has increased with growth; our traces do not contain the information necessary to confirm this.

## Connectivity Between Domain Classes

The degree distribution revealed a hierarchy of domains by size and function. Are inter-domain links also largely hierarchical? That is, is a domain primarily connected to domains in classes immediately above and below its own? In this section, we investigate domain connectivity within and between classes.

Figure 2 depicts the sub-graph of the inter-domain topology containing domains in $C_1$ and $C_2$, for the three snapshots. This figure reinforces the uniform growth in the number of domains in $C_1$ and $C_2$. In addition, this visual representation of the topology reveals several important features of domain-level connectivity in $C_1$ and $C_2$. Between $S_a$ and $S_c$, the connectivity within $C_1$ has increased significantly. A similar observation may be made about the connectivity within $C_2$. Between $S_a$ and $S_c$, the connectivity between $C_1$ and $C_2$ has also increased. Each $C_2$ node appears to peer directly with more $C_1$ nodes on average. We attribute these trends to the establishment of several tens of Internet exchange points which facilitate inter-provider connectivity. Quantitatively, the fraction of links within $C_1$ has nearly quadrupled, the fraction of links between $C_1$ and $C_2$ has nearly doubled, and the fraction of links within $C_2$ has increased by nearly a half.

The fraction of links within and between other classes remain approximately constant. However, it is interesting to note that connectivity between domains is significantly non-hierarchical. Table 3 shows the fraction of links between different classes in $S_c$. Nearly a quarter of the total number of links is between $C_4$ domains and $C_1$ domains. There appear to also be some evidence of "backdoor" links between domains in the same class; about 3% of all links are each within $C_2$ and $C_3$.

| | $C_1$ | $C_2$ | $C_3$ | $C_4$ |
|---|---|---|---|---|
| $C_1$ | 0.012 | 0.053 | 0.064 | 0.250 |
| $C_2$ | | 0.030 | 0.059 | 0.236 |
| $C_3$ | | | 0.034 | 0.164 |
| $C_4$ | | | | 0.098 |

Table 3: *Connectivity between classes:* An element of this matrix indicates the fraction of the total number of links in $S_c$ that exist between the corresponding classes. Links are significantly non-hierarchical; noticeable, nearly half of all the links are between domains in $C_4$, and domains in $C_1$ and $C_2$.

## Redundancy in Domain-Level Paths

If the inter-domain connectivity has become increasingly meshed, the number of domain-level paths between any two domains must also have increased.

Recall that the route—and implicitly, the path—actually traversed by packets to a destination is a function of domain policy. For policy reasons, many of these redundant paths may not be available at backbone provider. What is the level of redundancy in the number of paths to destinations? The `AS_PATH` associated with a route update indicates the domain-level path to the address prefixes in the update. We use the number of distinct `AS_PATH`s seen for an address prefix as a measure of the redundancy to destinations within that address prefix.

Figure 3 plots the fraction of address prefixes in each of the snapshots for which $n$ different `AS_PATH`s are seen, for different values of $n$. To more than half the destinations, we see exactly one domain-level path. To about a fourth, we see exactly two domain-level paths. This is not surprising. Route distribution, and hence, a route's `AS_PATH`, is governed by routing policy. Routing policy is usually set by bilateral transit agreements. In most cases, a domain negotiates a primary and, possibly, one backup transit to a collection of destinations.

Surprisingly, this distribution has *not changed significantly* from $S_a$ to $S_c$. This indicates that the routing policies expressed in the Internet have remained relatively simple, despite the growth of the topology. It is conceivable that the lack of tools to configure and analyze inter-domain routing has prevented providers from realizing more complicated policies [1].

## Discussion

In this section, we described several characteristics of the Internet inter-domain topology and its growth. However, our snapshot technique is likely to underestimate the topology. This is particularly true of portions of the topology distant from our observation points on the North American provider mesh. However, it is likely that each snapshot equally underestimates the "instantaneous" topology. We believe, therefore, that these results—obtained by *comparing* snapshots—are reliable estimators for the variation of the inter-domain topology with growth.

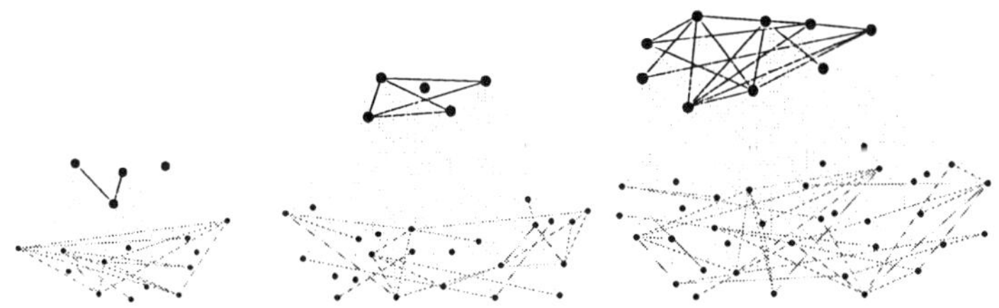

Figure 2: $\mathcal{C}_1$ *and* $\mathcal{C}_2$ *Topology:* The three graphs describe the subgraph of the inter-domain topology containing $\mathcal{C}_1$ and $\mathcal{C}_2$ nodes, for $\mathcal{S}_a$, $\mathcal{S}_b$, and $\mathcal{S}_c$ respectively, from left to right. The larger circles represent $\mathcal{C}_1$ nodes and the smaller circles $\mathcal{C}_2$ nodes. The solid black lines indicate links between $\mathcal{C}_1$ nodes, the faint lines indicate links between $\mathcal{C}_1$ and $\mathcal{C}_2$ nodes, and the gray lines links between $\mathcal{C}_2$ nodes.

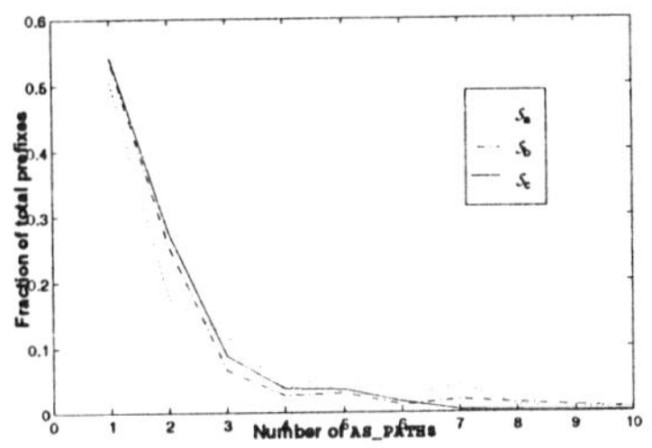


Figure 3: *Path redundancy:* The fraction of all address prefixes in a snapshot for which a given number of paths are seen has not changed significantly over the three snapshots.

## 4 Route Stability

In this section, we describe inter-domain route stability behavior. Route stability affects reachability to prefixes. From the perspective of routes to a single prefix, two stability measures are of interest: 1) prefix *availability*, the fraction of time that a prefix is reachable, and 2) prefix *steadiness*, the average time that a prefix is continuously reachable. We study the distribution of these measures.

Route stability can vary with the size of the topology. It is important, therefore, to factor out the rapid growth of the Internet when analyzing our traces. For this reason, we use the same trace *snapshot* methodology described in the previous section. We assume that the inter-domain topology has remained static within a snapshot. Recall that a snapshot is long enough to capture at least two transitions for more than 99% of the prefixes seen. On average, however, each snapshot contains more than a hundred transitions per prefix.

To study the effect of growth on route stability, we compare the distributions of these stability measures across snapshots. For this purpose, we consider only snapshots $\mathcal{S}_a$ and $\mathcal{S}_b$, and not $\mathcal{S}_c$. $\mathcal{S}_c$ is extracted from $\mathcal{D}_M$, and this trace was obtained at an experimental facility, the MAE-East Route Server. In these traces, we observe frequent downtimes for peering sessions with clients of the Route Server. These trace flaws prevent a reliable estimation of route stability behavior from $\mathcal{D}_M$ in general. On average, however, route server clients remained highly available, and we have no reason to suspect the collection of AS_PATHs seen in $\mathcal{S}_c$, or our conclusions about the growth of topology (Section 3).

### Prefix Availability

We define the *availability* of a prefix as the fraction of time for which it was reachable in the interval between when the prefix was first seen and the end of the snapshot. Figure 4 plots the cumulative fraction of prefixes in a snapshot against prefix availability. In general, prefix availability is high; about 10% of the prefixes were available for less than 95% of the time.

However, between $\mathcal{S}_a$ and $\mathcal{S}_b$, there is some evidence of degradation in availability. In $\mathcal{S}_a$, 90% of the prefixes are available for more than 99.6% of the time. In $\mathcal{S}_b$, only 83% of the prefixes are available for that time. There are two possible explanations for this degradation. First, the number of routers and links in paths to prefixes could have increased between the two snapshots. This increases the likelihood of router or link failure in these paths. Second, the errors due to routing misconfiguration could have increased, owing to an increase in the complexity of the inter-domain topology.

To nearly half the prefixes in each snapshot, we saw more than one AS_PATH (Section 3). Given that routing on the Internet is based on relatively static metrics, we might hypothesize that one of these paths is used for a significant fraction of the time that a prefix is reachable. Call this most frequently used path to a prefix its *primary* path. We can then define the *primary availability* of a prefix as that fraction of its reachable time for which the prefix was reachable by its primary path. Figure 4 also shows the cumulative distribution of the fraction of prefixes against primary availability. For more than 80% of the prefixes, the primary availability is greater than 95%. For most prefixes, then, the primary path is unavailable for a very small fraction of time. The figure also shows improved primary availability in $\mathcal{S}_b$, despite decreased overall availability.

### Prefix Steadiness

We define the *steadiness* of a prefix as the mean duration of all intervals in a snapshot over which the prefix was con-

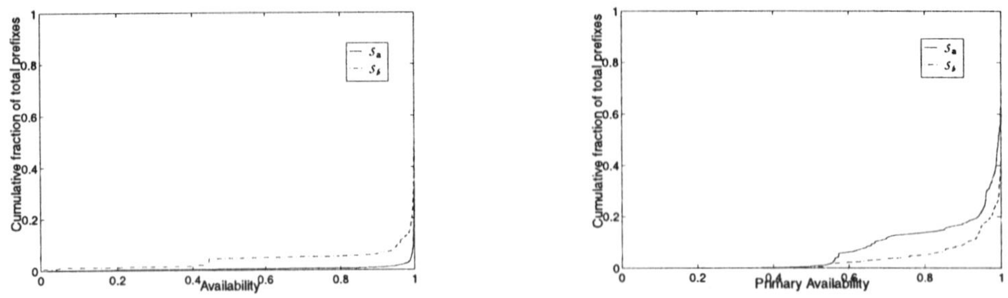


Figure 4: *Prefix Availability:* More than 90% of the prefixes are available for more than 95% of the time. More than 80% of the prefixes are reachable through a primary path for more than 95% of the time.

tinuously reachable. Figure 5 plots the cumulative distribution of the fraction of prefixes seen in each snapshot against steadiness. There is a wide variation in prefix steadiness. Remarkable, however, is the fact that almost 80% of the prefixes have steadiness values of more than 1 day! There is some evidence that prefix steadiness decreases with growth in the Internet; $\mathcal{S}_b$ 's distribution of prefix steadiness is almost completely to the "left" of that of $\mathcal{S}_a$. Furthermore, the steadiness distribution shows several "steps", indicating that there exist clusters of prefixes with similar steadiness behavior. A closer examination of our traces reveals that prefixes in a cluster appear to share a common primary path.

We have already shown that, to most prefixes, there exists a highly available primary path. We might hypothesize that a prefix's steadiness is determined by the number of routers and links in its primary path. To a first approximation, we study a prefix's steadiness as a function of the number of domains in its primary path. Figure 5 also plots the cumulative distribution of the fraction of prefixes seen in each snapshot against steadiness, for different path lengths. In a distribution sense, the steadiness of prefixes appears to generally decrease with path length. There is one exception. In $\mathcal{S}_b$, prefixes whose primary path length is three appear steadier than prefixes whose primary path length is two. A possible explanation for this is the existence of other factors, such as routing misconfiguration, that affect steadiness.

### Discussion

Our prefix stability behavior is as observed from a single point on the backbone mesh. The behavior of individual prefixes is likely to differ when observed at different points on this mesh. However, we believe that the *distribution* of prefix availability and steadiness is likely to be similar at other backbone providers.

## 5 Related Work

To our knowledge, no prior work has attempted to characterize the Internet inter-domain topology and its growth. Several researchers have proposed inter-domain topology models [3, 11, 16]. These models posit a three- or four-level provider hierarchy. Some of these models also assume that domains in a class primarily connect to domains in classes above or below their own. Our analysis confirms the existence of a four-level hierarchy. However, our classification exposes a significant level of connectivity within classes, as well as connectivity between non-adjacent classes.

Two other studies have attempted to characterize Internet route stability. One analyzes a 12-hour trace of routing traffic on the now defunct NSFNET backbone network [7]. The Internet topology has changed significantly since then. This study analyzes routing protocol behavior: the frequency and size of updates, routing protocol convergence times and so on. It does not analyze prefix availability and steadiness characteristics.

A second, more recent, study [14] uses the `traceroute` tool to sample availability and steadiness characteristics of paths between a small set of host pairs. Their end-to-end path availability estimates of 97% or higher appear to match our estimated host availability distribution; they too observe a degradation in host availability with Internet growth. Their distribution of the path with the highest availability, observed at "AS granularity" between host pairs, closely matches our primary prefix availability distribution.

## 6 Conclusions

There are two major conclusions about Internet inter-domain routing that emerge from our findings. First, the Internet has grown "laterally". Second, route stability behavior has degraded with growth. At a high level, these conclusions are not very surprising. The ubiquity of provider connectivity afforded by Internet exchange points encourages "lateral" growth (many providers at different levels, and constant number of levels) rather than "vertical" growth. The widespread use of manual routing configuration on the Internet today, and the lack of sophisticated routing analysis and debugging tools probably accounts for the decreased route stability.

We see no reason to believe that the pattern of growth in the inter-domain topology will change significantly in the near future. However, an increasingly commercial and competitive infrastructure is likely to spur the development of automated routing analysis and engineering tools, resulting in better route stability.

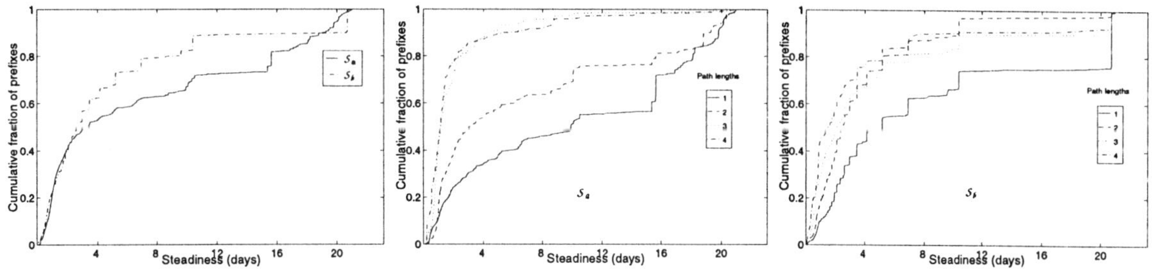


Figure 5: *Prefix Steadiness:* There is a wide variation in prefix steadiness, but nearly 80% of the prefixes have a steadiness greater than 1 day. Longer paths have worse steadiness characteristics, with one exception (in $\mathcal{S}_b$, for path lengths 2 and 3).

## Acknowledgements

Several members of the Routing Arbiter team have contributed to this work: Cengiz Alaettinoğlu, Rusty Eddy, Deborah Estrin, Bill Manning, Satish Kumar, Jon Postel, Yakov Rekhter, and Kannan Varadhan. Many thanks to Curtis Villamizar for providing the ANS traces, and the anonymous referees for their suggestions regarding the content and presentation of the material.

## References

[1] C. Alaettinoğlu. Scalable Router Configuration for the Internet. *Proceedings of the 1996 International Conference on Networking Protocols*, October 1996.

[2] C. Alaettinoğlu, T. Bates, E. Gerich, D. Karrenberg, M. Terpstra, and C. Villamizar. Routing Policy Specification Language (RPSL). Internet Draft draft-ietf-rps-rpsl-00.txt, Network Information Center, March 1996. Revised, June 1996.

[3] C. Alaettinoğlu and A. U. Shankar. The Viewserver Hierarchy for Interdomain Routing: Protocols and Evaluation. *Journal on Selected Areas in Communications*, 13(8):1396–1410, October 1995.

[4] T. Bates, E. Gerich, L. Joncheray, J-M. Jouanigot, D. Karrenberg, M. Terpstra, and J. Yu. Representation of ip routing policies in a routing registry. Technical Report ripe-181, RIPE, RIPE NCC, Amsterdam, Netherlands, October 1994.

[5] J. C. Bolot. End-to-end Packet Delay and Loss Behavior in the Internet. In *Proceedings of the ACM SIGCOMM Symposium on Communication Architectures and Protocols*, pages 289–298, San Francisco, CA, Sep 1993.

[6] E. J. Bos. Routing Table Growth. http://nic.surfnet.nl/netmanagement/ip/cidr, 1995.

[7] B. Chinoy. Dynamics of Internet Routing Information. In *Proceedings of the ACM SIGCOMM '93*, pages 45–52, San Francisco, CA, Sep 1993.

[8] MFS Datanet. Mae-East Traffic Statistics. http://www.mfsdatanet.com/MAE/east.stats.html/.

[9] National Science Foundation. Network Access Point Manager, Routing Arbiter, Regional Network Providers and Very High-Speed Services Provider for NSFNET and NREN(SM) Programs. Program Solicitation 93-52, May 1993.

[10] R. Govindan and A. Reddy. An Analysis of Internet Inter-Domain Topology and Route Stability. Technical Report 96-642, Computer Science Dept., University of Southern California, Nov 1996.

[11] S. M. Hotz. *Routing Information Organization To Support Scalable Interdomain Routing With Heterogeneous Path Requirements*. PhD thesis, University of Southern California, 1996.

[12] M. Lottor. Internet Domain Survey. Technical report, Network Information Systems Center, SRI International, October 1993.

[13] V. Paxson. Growth Trends in Wide-Area TCP Connections. *IEEE Network*, pages 8–17, July/August 1994.

[14] V. Paxson. End-to-end Routing Behavior in the Internet. In *Proceedings of the ACM SIGCOMM Symposium on Communication Architectures and Protocols*, San Francisco, CA, September 1996.

[15] Y. Rekhter and T. Li. A Border Gateway Protocol 4 (BGP-4). Request for Comments 1771, Internic Directory Services, March 1995.

[16] E. W. Zegura, K. L. Calvert, and Samrat Bhattacharjee. How to Model an Internetwork. In *Proceedings of IEEE INFOCOMM*, pages 40–52, San Francisco, CA, September 1996.

# Implementation and Analysis of IP Multicast over ATM

Maryann P. Maher, Suresh K. Bhogavilli *
USC/Information Sciences Institute
4350 N. Fairfax Drive, Ste 620, Arlington, VA 22203
{maher, suresh}@isi.edu

**Abstract**

*Today it is evident that ATM technology will have its role in the future of Internetworking. Two major Internet backbone service providers, Sprint and MCI, have marketed their investments in ATM as a way to push more bandwidth into their Internet infrastructures. Regardless of whether ATM technology will thrive in the WAN or LAN, it is also evident that the Internet Protocol (IP), which has been the glue of the Internet allowing it to endure exponential growth, must be well supported over ATM. IP multicast (protocol extensions to IP that allow IP packets from one source to be distributed to multiple destinations) is an essential part of IP which has allowed multimedia applications, for example, to more efficiently use Internet resources. In this paper we describe an implementation of one model of supporting IP multicast over ATM, the Multicast over ATM model [1] developed by the IETF. We discuss empirical measurements gathered in a testbed with both a WAN and a LAN component that give insights into the behavior of this model. We detail some of the shortcomings of this model and discuss potential modifications to improve it. Ideas for other approaches to IP multicast over ATM are also described.*

## 1 Introduction

The Multicast over ATM model described in "Support for Multicast over UNI 3.0/3.1 based ATM Networks" [1] (MC_over_ATM) is one model for supporting connectionless IP multicast over connection-oriented ATM networks. This model defines support for network layer multicasting over ATM using two different modes of operations. In one mode, senders of IP multicast traffic create ATM virtual channel connections (VCC) to the other members of the particular multicast group. In the other mode, the senders send their traffic to an intermediary server, the multicast server, which in turn relays the data to the members of the multicast group. In this paper we discuss the implementation of MC_over_ATM that includes both these modes of operation and the behavior of each in a testbed where the ATM hosts were connected in a LAN and WAN. A WAN topology was to gain insight into the effects of larger propagation delays on the MC_over_ATM model.

Throughout this paper the word "group" or words "multicast group" are used to mean network layer multicast group. In addition, the words "group address" or "multicast address" are used to mean network layer multicast group address.

## 2 Overview of MC_over_ATM

There are three main entities in the MC_over_ATM model:

- the Multicast Address Resolution Server (MARS),
- the MARS client (a Classical IP over ATM entity [2] running MARS client code), and
- the Multicast Server (MCS).

These entities communicate using a query-response style protocol. The MARS keeps a database that maps network layer multicast addresses to ATM layer addresses. A host wishing to receive data from a particular network layer multicast group registers its ATM address with the MARS for that group address. A host wishing to send data to a particular group address queries the MARS for the list of ATM addresses that are registered for that group. The sending host can then set up a point-to-multipoint (p2mpt) VCC that includes as leaves all the hosts specified by the list of ATM addresses. If the list of ATM addresses contains the addresses of the actual group members, then the group is said to be operating in a VCC-mesh mode, or simply mesh mode. This corresponds to the first mode of operation described in the previous section. If however, the MARS returns a list containing

*This research is supported by Sprint Corporation, Research & Development, Overland Park, KS 66212-6333, under the IPARS '95 contract.

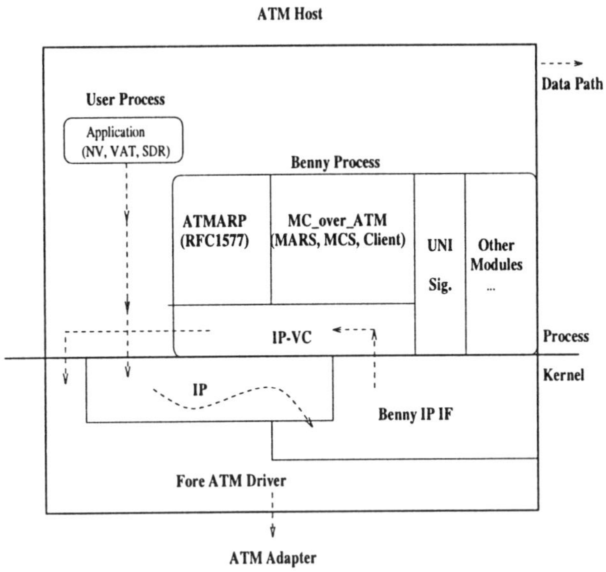


Figure 1: Benny IP over ATM Host Architecture

the ATM address of a single MCS, the sender will simply establish a p2mpt VCC with the MCS as the only leaf. This will be the case if an MCS has previously registered with the MARS to support that particular multicast group. This mode of operation is termed MCS mode.

The ingenious feature of the MC_over_ATM model is that group senders need not be aware of what mode of multicast support is taking place. From the point of view of the group sender, MCS mode appears to be the same as mesh mode but with a single group member.

## 3 Overview of Host Architecture

The implementation described in this paper was done in the framework of "Benny". Benny is a derivative of VINCE, a freely available ATM software package developed at the US Naval Research Laboratory [3]. Benny includes many enhancements to VINCE and new code modules such as the MC_over_ATM implementation. Benny has been developed at USC/ISI and is freely available [4].

IP multicasting as defined in RFC 1112 [5] was designed as an extension to the normal IP layer found in a system kernel. In order to support basic IP over ATM, there needs to be some added "glue" in the kernel between IP and the ATM layer, specifically there must be a layer that maps IP packet flows to ATM VCCs. We call this layer the IP-VC layer in Benny. In order to support IP multicast over ATM, the IP-VC layer must also distinguish between unicast and multicast packets and create the appropriate type of VCCs, namely point-to-point (pt2pt) or p2mpt.

Figure 1 shows a diagram of the software and hardware components making up our IP over ATM host platform. In our testbed we use Fore Systems' SBA-200 ATM host adapters and Fore Systems' ASX-200 and ASX-200BX ATM switches.

### 3.1 Benny Host Kernel Support

Benny implements a "lightweight" ATM driver that attaches an IP multicast capable interface to the system kernel. (The only operating systems supported at this time are SunOS 4.1.3 and 4.1.4.) We describe the Benny driver as "lightweight" because although it implements an IP interface, it does not go as far as controlling the hardware of the ATM adapter. Through this interface, Benny receives IP packets routed to it and does the needed interfacing with the MARS client entity if the packets are destined for a multicast address. Furthermore, IGMP JoinLocalGroup and LeaveLocalGroup are processed by triggering the MARS client to issue the corresponding MARS_JOINs and MARS_LEAVEs.

Clearly an ATM driver is an essential part of doing any host side IP over ATM development. The Benny driver therefore has been a key component of our prototype even though there exist drawbacks in using it. The main disadvantage is that because this driver does not control the hardware, the data that comes down to the Benny driver must be sent to the hardware via the vendor supplied API. In the case of the FORE SBA platform, the FORE API is used. This means that data takes an extra 'hop' from kernel space to user space. When the Benny driver receives an IP packet, the packet is sent to the Benny process running in user space. In figure 1 the arrows show the data path in our test host. Packets generated by an application are routed by IP to the Benny interface which in turn sends the packet up to the IP-VC layer of the Benny process. The IP-VC layer determines if there is a VCC for this packet, if so, it hands it to the FORE driver via the FORE API. If there is not a VCC, Benny triggers the necessary MARS client and ATM signalling behavior, then sends the packet to the FORE driver for transmission. The extra kernel-process-kernel hop undoubtedly affects performance. Therefore, when we take performance measurements in our experiments we must factor in this delay.

The remarkable advantage of using the Benny driver is that it is highly portable. It can easily be used along side any ATM vendor's adapter and driver software by merely swapping the API calls in Benny and including the corresponding API libraries.

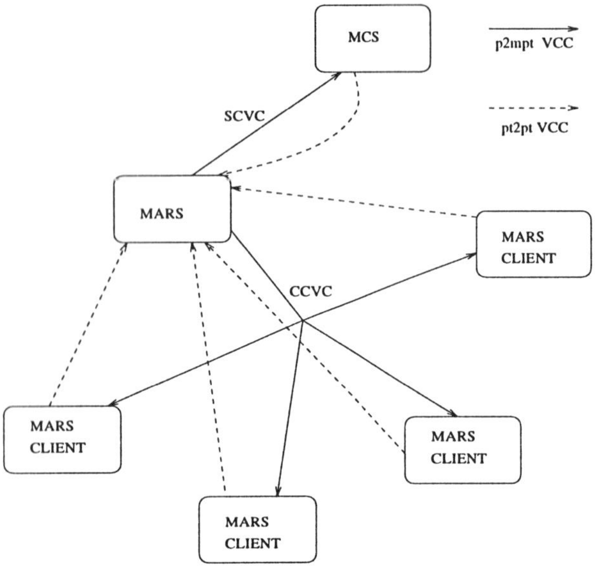


Figure 2: MARS Cluster and its control VCCs

# 4 Protocol Implementation

This section describes the MC_over_ATM protocol in more detail. All the procedures described here are implemented in the Benny MC_over_ATM code. Those familiar with MC_over_ATM may choose to skip this section. Throughout this paper the terms "host" or "client" refer to an ATM endsystem running MARS client code.

Figure 2 shows a MARS cluster and its control VCCs. A host that wishes to be supported by the MARS creates a pt2pt VCC to the MARS and registers with it. All future messages to the MARS are transmitted on this VCC. The MARS maintains a list of registered MARS clients and maintains a p2mpt control VCC, called Cluster Control VC (CCVC), to those clients.

When a host issues an IGMP JoinLocalGroup for a multicast group, the MARS client entity generates a MARS_JOIN for that network layer group. MARS maintains a database of network layer group address to ATM layer address, called the host map. MARS updates the host map to reflect the latest membership information for the multicast group. In response to an IGMP LeaveLocalGroup, the MARS client entity generates a MARS_LEAVE, and the MARS removes its ATM address from the host map for that group.

When the MARS client wishes to send data to a multicast group to which it has no existing VCC and has no translation for that group address, it generates a MARS_REQUEST for that group. The MARS responds with a MARS_MULTI containing a list of ATM addresses of the clients who have MARS_JOINed that group. The client opens a p2mpt VCC with those ATM addresses as leaf nodes. Further packets to the multicast group are forwarded on that VCC by the Benny IP-VC layer and are transparent to the MARS client entity. MARS retransmits the join and leave messages on the CCVC, so that clients with open VCCs to the multicast group can add or drop the corresponding MARS client on their VCC to the group.

As a way to conserve the number of VCCs required by the mesh mode to support the multicast group described above, a system administrator could configure a host to serve as an MCS. An MCS is a multicast server which relays data sent to it to all the members of a multicast group. The MCS registers with the MARS through a registration MARS_MSERV message. The MARS adds the MCS to a p2mpt Server Control VC (SCVC), which is used to distribute group membership updates.

The hosts registered with a MARS constitute a MARS cluster and can open direct VCCs to one another. Two such MARS clusters could be connected together through a multicast IP router (mrouter). An mrouter forwards multicast packets between different clusters. Refer to [1] for further details on MARS protocol entities.

# 5 Testing MC_over_ATM

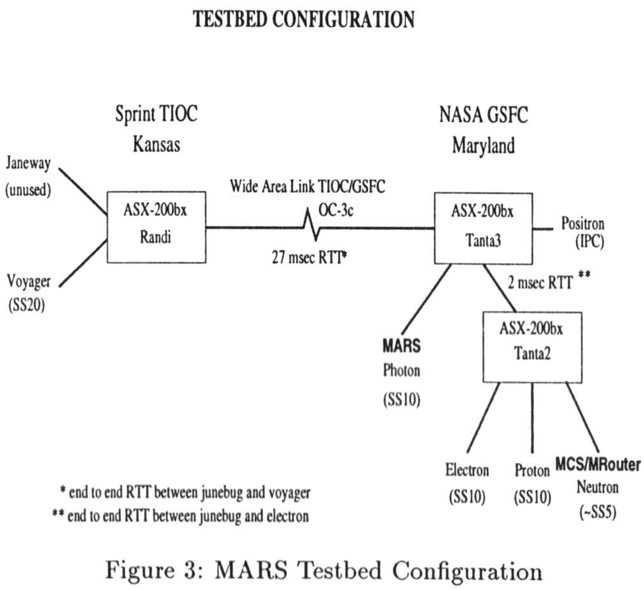


Figure 3: MARS Testbed Configuration

A configuration of the experimental testbed is shown in Figure 3. A requisite for testing IP multicast over ATM is to have a multicast capable host. In our testbed, SunOS 4.1.3 and SunOS 4.1.4 hosts were augmented with Xerox PARC's public domain "IP Multicast Extensions" package version 3.5 [6]. The common MBone [7] applications such as SD, VAT, and NV, were run on the test hosts in order to generate multicast traffic.

In our experimental MARS cluster, which equated to an IP subnet, a group of ATM endsystems at the NASA Goddard Space Flight Center (GSFC) in Maryland were connected in a LAN. The maximum propagation delay over ATM between any two of these endsystems was two milliseconds. In addition, there were two other endsystems located in the Sprint Technical Integration Operation Center (TIOC) in Kansas connected to the rest of the cluster via a wide area OC-3c link. The maximum propagation delay between endsystems at GSFC and the TIOC was 27 milliseconds. For the endsystem at Sprint TIOC, Voyager, connectivity to any other MARS client was burdened with the WAN propagation delays. Endsystems in the LAN-sized group at GSFC incurred the WAN link delays whenever they added Voyager as a leaf onto a p2mpt VCC. The MARS, MCS, and MRouter where all located at the GSFC site for these experiments. It would be interesting to place the MARS at Sprint in future experiments.

An initial goal of this prototyping was to gauge the general performance of the MC_over_ATM model. The Benny code is instrumented with code that time stamps MARS and UNI signalling [8] messages in order to gather various latency measurements. The measurements taken were the following:

- Latency in joining a group: time transpired between the sending of a MARS_JOIN and receiving a confirmation copy on the CCVC
- Address translation latency: time transpired between the sending of a MARS_REQUEST until receiving a MARS_MULTI.
- Related to the measurement above, the latency between the initiation of an address translation request (triggered by the arrival of an IP packet at Benny driver for transmission) until a multipoint VCC is setup.

## 6 MC_over_ATM Protocol Measurements

In our experiments, we view the testbed topology from the perspective of the location of the MARS. This implies that all the hosts that are in a close proximity to the MARS are considered "LAN" clients. Since the MARS is located at GSFC for all the experiments, we refer to the hosts at GSFC as LAN clients. Following the same reasoning, the hosts at TIOC are referred to as "WAN" clients.

Table 1: Test Results Involving One WAN Client and Two LAN Clients (all times in *msec*).

| WAN Client Latencies: 1st Client (Voyager) | | | |
|---|---|---|---|
| Group | Join | Addr Res | Mpt VCC Setup |
| 1 | 61.2840 | 31.0740 | 708.9580 |
| 2 | 38.0000 | 31.3360 | 628.3360 |
| 3 | 33.5500 | 30.9640 | 627.7230 |
| 4 | 43.7500 | 32.0090 | 825.1230 |
| 5 | 37.7960 | 32.6110 | 878.3570 |
| Avg | 42.8760 | 31.5988 | 733.6994 |

| LAN Latencies: 2nd Client (Electron) | | | |
|---|---|---|---|
| Group | Join | Addr Res | Mpt VCC Setup |
| 1 | 7.3290 | 9.1520 | 179.0010 |
| 2 | 12.8440 | 9.2410 | 165.9940 |
| 3 | 11.3330 | 5.9310 | 156.3960 |
| 4 | 8.7710 | 7.0770 | 162.3030 |
| 5 | 10.3440 | 6.5290 | 189.8350 |
| Avg | 10.3242 | 7.5860 | 170.7058 |

| LAN Latencies: 3rd Client (Proton) | | | |
|---|---|---|---|
| Group | Join | Addr Res | Mpt VCC Setup |
| 1 | 12.2740 | 6.3530 | 328.5450 |
| 2 | 10.3560 | 9.0390 | 345.4440 |
| 3 | 11.8330 | 8.5520 | 317.1330 |
| 4 | 11.2080 | 6.4000 | 335.4350 |
| 5 | 11.0860 | 8.2900 | 289.9820 |
| Avg | 11.3514 | 7.7268 | 323.3078 |

In this section, we present various latencies of interest, measured over several MARS experiments. Note that the results only emphasize trends of the scalability of various MC_over_ATM entities. Since MARS entities are implemented in the process space, the measured latencies, to some extent, depend on the system load and are therefore coarse measurements. Nevertheless, every effort is made to minimize these effects.

Table 1 lists the latency measurements in an experiment involving one WAN client and two LAN clients. The first client to join a multicast group, with no prior registered group members, is referred to as the "first" client. For each experiment, five different multicast groups were used to measure the latencies of the three targeted metrics. Each row of the tables corresponds to a group and the column lists the respective metric.

### 6.1 Multicast Group Join

The first column in table 1 depicts the MARS join latencies for all the three clients joining a group. All the hosts in the MARS cluster open a pt2pt VCC to

Table 2: Test Results Involving Three LAN Clients (all times in *msec*).

| First Client Latencies (Electron) | | | |
|---|---|---|---|
| Group | Join | Addr Res | Mpt VCC Setup |
| 1 | 21.4150 | 6.4170 | 170.1400 |
| 2 | 19.3080 | 6.1890 | 180.5140 |
| 3 | 28.5000 | 5.9570 | 168.2510 |
| 4 | 15.9040 | 7.8140 | 178.5100 |
| 5 | 8.4560 | 7.3040 | 175.4270 |
| Avg | 18.7166 | 6.7362 | 174.5684 |

| Second Client Latencies (Proton) | | | |
|---|---|---|---|
| Group | Join | Addr Res | Mpt VCC Setup |
| 1 | 7.5660 | 19.2520* | 206.6350 |
| 2 | 10.3460 | 5.5190 | 183.2080 |
| 3 | 8.0030 | 6.6300 | 169.9050 |
| 4 | 10.7730 | 6.0200 | 184.5700 |
| 5 | 33.1980* | 7.4210 | 215.6560 |
| Avg | 9.1720 | 6.3975 | 191.9948 |

| Third Client Latencies (Positron) | | | |
|---|---|---|---|
| Group | Join | Addr Res | Mpt VCC Setup |
| 1 | 21.4750 | 10.7520 | 1460.3730 |
| 2 | 19.2390 | 9.3480 | 1013.3480 |
| 3 | 19.5760 | 9.6500 | 1047.0550 |
| 4 | 26.1060 | 10.3830 | 1309.9020 |
| 5 | 18.4440 | 10.2470 | 2144.9950* |
| Avg | 20.9680 | 10.076 | 1207.6695 |

* excluded from average computations

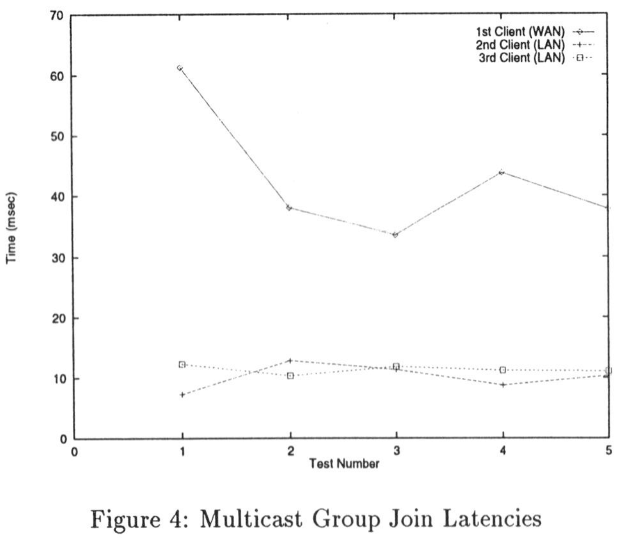


Figure 4: Multicast Group Join Latencies

the MARS to be used for all communication with the MARS. When the MARS receives a multicast group join message from a host, it first checks the host map for the group to determine if the host already joined that group. The host map for the group is updated only if it does not already include the ATM address of the host. The host's group join message is then acknowledged on the existing pt2pt VCC between the MARS and the host.

The multicast group join latency is measured as the difference between the time a host sends a MARS_JOIN message to the MARS to the time the MARS acknowledges this message to the host. As the number of hosts joined in a group increases, the time taken by the MARS to check an existing group membership increases. This results in increased MARS join latencies. Notice in table 1 that the average delay of 10.32 msec for the third client is longer than the 11.35 msec delay of the second client. The first client being a WAN client took longer than the other two because of its remoteness.

These measurements are also plotted in fig. 4, which shows a slight increase in latencies from the second to the third client. These differences are so minute that they are occasionally overridden by the extraneous effects of system load on Benny process scheduling, as is evident from the data points for the second group in this figure. These effects are also visible in the address resolution measurements presented in the next section.

Table 2 shows the equivalent data for a cluster where all the members are connected over a LAN sized network. The MARS implementation dependencies are more visible in the MARS join data of the first client. In this case, the server has to insert a new MARS table entry for the new group the client is joining. This seems to take longer than the insertion of a new ATM address into an existing group translation entry, when a client joins an already known multicast group.

### 6.2 Address Resolution

As the number of hosts that have joined a multicast group increases, the number of addresses copied into the MARS_MULTI message by the MARS increases. This results in increased latency of address resolution from host to host, as shown in table 1, where on the average, the second client's requests were resolved in 7.5 msec, whereas the third client's requests were resolved in 7.7 msec. The first client's resolution time of 31.6 msec includes the 27 msec RTT, since this is a WAN client. These values are plotted in fig. 5. Table 2 shows similar results for the case where all the

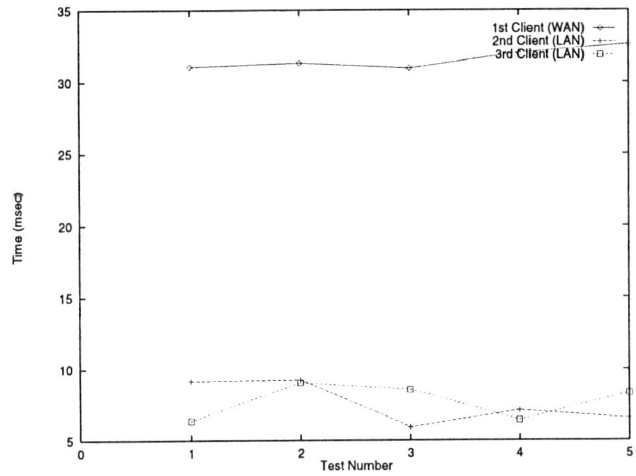


Figure 5: Address Resolution Latencies

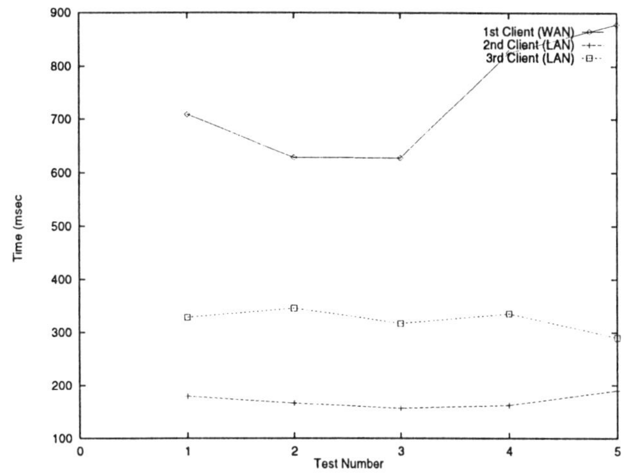


Figure 6: Multipoint VCC Setup Latencies

clients are connected over a LAN sized network.

Also, on average, address resolutions are faster than multicast group joins. This is purely an implementation issue. Joining a group requires the operation of inserting a new entry into a table. In addition, before inserting the ATM address (NSAP) of the new member, the current list of NSAPs has to be checked in order to avoid duplicate entries. In the case of the first client, even though the table is empty, the process of checking has to be done. In our implementation we have an efficient hash table lookup and message generation and so the processing of a MARS_REQUEST is more efficient than processing a JOIN. This behavior appears to hold well for the number of hosts in the testbed. However, as the size of the cluster increases, the address resolution latencies are expected to exceed the group join latencies.

It is worth noting that it is advantageous for senders to have address resolution and VCC setup occur as quickly as possible, since delay in this process could result in packets being dropped before transmission.

### 6.3 Point-to-Multipoint VCC Setup

In table 1, the third column shows the time period from the point where a multicast IP packet arrives at the Benny interface for transmission, to the point when a p2mpt VCC for the group is established. A p2mpt VCC is considered to be established when a first leaf is successfully added.

As shown in fig. 6, the multipoint VCC setup times for the first client are considerably larger than those of the other two, since this client has to do address resolution and VCC setup across a WAN. WAN setup delays include both multipoint signalling and NNI routing delays at each switch hop. Since Benny is only a host ATM stack implementation, these network delays cannot be independently quantified through Benny.

Table 3: Test Results Involving an MCS (all times in *msec*)

| Grp | Regist | Mserv | Addr Res | MptVC Setup |
|---|---|---|---|---|
| 1 | 137.1980 | 5.6680 | 6.3320 | 171.7180 |
| 2 | 133.8020 | 7.3100 | 6.6110 | 163.4350 |
| 3 | 132.8110 | 6.7510 | 6.7660 | 875.2850 |
| 4 | 165.4450 | 6.0690 | 5.4720 | 141.3490 |
| 5 | 165.2640 | 5.8460 | 5.5640 | 185.8750 |
| Avg | 146.9040 | 6.3288 | 6.1490 | 307.5324 |

The second and third clients reflect multipoint VCC setups that occurred in the LAN portion of the testbed. For this reason, these delay measurements are less than those of the first client. In this particular experiment, these two clients were actually connecting to a multicast router, also located in the LAN part of the testbed, as their first leaf.

In table 2, the measurements for the third client are those for Positron, a Sparc IPC, which is considerably slow compared to a SparcStation 10. It appears that the capabilities of the host significantly affect the latencies of VCC setup. Therefore, it seems wise to choose high performance machines for the critical entities such as the MARS and the MCS.

### 6.4 Multicast Server Latencies

The latencies associated with various MCS control messages are tabulated in table 3. Any entity that wishes to act as an MCS should first register with the MARS. This registration latency, measured at an MCS, is the elapsed time between the transmission of registration request to the MARS and the reception of an acknowledgement from the MARS. In our implementation, when the MARS receives an MCS registration request, it adds the MCS as a leaf to the server control VCC (SCVC) before acknowledging the request. If an MCS could not be added to the SCVC within a certain number of retries, the registration request is not acknowledged and the MCS retries its request to the MARS. The registration latencies shown in 3, therefore include a leaf setup, MARS' MCS table update, and a round trip propagation delay.

The Mserv latency is the time taken by an MCS to "join" the multicast group that it wishes to serve. The MCS acts as a relay for packets destined to this multicast group. The latency measured is the time taken by MARS to update its MARS table and a round trip latency. The address resolution times are the time taken by an MCS to get the ATM addresses of the endstations that joined the multicast group from the MARS.

An MCS sets up a p2mpt VCC for data transmission to the group in response to a MARS_SJOIN message relayed on the SCVC by the MARS. Hence the VCC setup latencies listed are measured from the time the first MARS_SJOIN message is received by the MCS to the time the VCC is created.

Trial three in table 3 was performed with an MCS in the LAN portion of the cluster and the first client to join the MCS supported group on the WAN part. Furthermore, the machine used as an MCS was a Sparc IPC, which took almost an order of magnitude longer than the LAN counterparts with a more efficient SparcStation 10 acting as an MCS. This signifies the importance of having a high performance machine for the MCS.

The metrics for comparing a mesh supported group against an MCS supported group are data latency and completion of full connectivity between all the participants in the group. In case of a mesh supported group, the latencies purely depend on the distance between the data sender and the receiver. However, in case of an MCS supported group, they largely depend on the location of the MCS itself, relative to the location of the multicast group members. When the group members are geographically distributed, the members close to the MCS experience lower data latencies compared to distant members. Ideally, there should be multiple MCSs, supporting a given multicast group. Each MCS supporting the senders / receivers in its physical proximity. A protocol specification to this effect is currently being developed by the IETF.

An MCS supported group is also limited by the quality of service of the p2mpt VCC between the MCS and the other multicast group members. In case of a mesh supported group, every sender has a dedicated p2mpt VCC to all the receivers in the group. The QoS of this VCC could be better tailored to the requirements of the receiving entities than that of an MCS, which is effectively shared by all senders.

However, an MCS could result in significant savings in the number of VCCs needed to support a large multicast group. A mesh supported group with $m$ senders and $n$ receivers requires $m*n$ VCCs. An MCS supported group, on the other hand, would only need $m+n$ VCCs.

# 7 Observations and Conclusions

## 7.1 Behavior of MBone Conferencing Tools

In our research of IP multicast over ATM, it was our goal to gather empirical data in a testbed running common Internet multicast applications. That is the reason for choosing the popular MBone audio (*VAT*), video (*NV*), and session management (*SDR*) tools. These applications are freely available, well maintained by researchers, and enjoy a large user base. The use of these tools is growing rapidly and so is the amount of traffic that they generate on the Internet. We were therefore interested in studying how these applications performed in an ATM network with MC_over_ATM.

An early observation we made was that a model like MC_over_ATM, whose scaling properties, particularly in mesh mode, depend on the number of multicast senders, may not be the best suited for the current MBone environment. The mismatch is mainly a product of the way the MBone tools work. A feature of all the current MBone tools is that they cannot be run purely in *receive-only* mode, even when the intent is to only receive data destined to the multicast group. These applications transmit status reports periodically, though at a low frequency, to the multicast group joined. For example, VAT sends a session message every 6 seconds containing information about each participant's identity and participation status. This information is transmitted whether or not audio data is ever transmitted by the participant.

This trickle of session messages results in the creation of a VCC, either pt2pt or p2mpt, wasting valuable VCC resources. It seems that it would be beneficial to enhance such conferencing tools with options that give users the capability of adjusting the frequency with which the advertisements are sent to the group when the host is in the receive-only mode. If advertisements were transmitted in order of minutes, it would allow VCCs to be released between advertisements, therefore not tying up network resources during the life of the session. Another modification which would conserve network resources would be to send advertisements for multiple groups to a single reserved group.

One could argue that a fix to this problem would be to use MCSs for all MBone multicast sessions. While this is a possibility, the transmission latencies that can be introduced by an MCS are least desired when running real-time conferencing applications like VAT and NV.

### 7.2 Interactions with UNI Signalling

In the experiments involving both LAN and WAN clients, the general data latencies clients experience depended on the order in which clients joined the group. As mentioned earlier, when the p2mpt VCC setup is initiated with the WAN client as the first member, the average startup latency experienced by the other members in the groups increases. For example, in case of a group supporting audio transmission, the audio starts off with greater latencies and or loss of data.

There is a potential to decrease the initial VCC setup delay by adding a bit of "smarts" to the MARS client. When the MARS_MULTI message received by a MARS client includes a set of destination ATM addresses, VCC setup latencies could be minimized if the client could identify any destination that is "local", for example, with the same prefix (HO-DSP part) in the NSAP address, and use it as the first leaf.

While the MARS model addresses the problem of achieving multicasting within a cluster, several other issues, such as efficient VCC allocation, bandwidth conservation, and support for applications' QoS need to be addressed for multicast deployment across cluster boundaries.

### 7.3 Scalability Issues

Several issues need to be addressed to work towards provisioning a scalable and manageable IP multicast service over ATM. The foremost issue is that of VCC scalability. The number of VCCs used for a particular multicast group is determined, to some extent, by the multicast routing protocols running between IP routers connecting different MARS clusters. DVMRP, the most widely deployed multicast routing protocol, uses source based trees, in which a distinct multicast tree is calculated for every source network for the same group. Also, packets destined to a multicast group are periodically flooded across the down stream interfaces to guarantee the delivery of multicast datagrams to all the receivers whose group membership could be varying dynamically.

The MC_over_ATM specification suggests that the multicast routers connected to a cluster join a block of multicast group addresses. When a router has to flood/forward IP multicast packets to a particular group, it gets a translation for the group from the MARS. This translation includes all the routers which promiscuously joined that group, in addition to any end stations that are also members in that group. A p2mpt VCC is setup from the router to the group members to carry the multicast packets destined to that group. In a cluster with $n$ senders and $m$ groups, this results in a total of $n * m$ VCCs created between the same set of routers. For example, 20 routers sending traffic to 50 groups in a block would result in 1000 VCCs between the same set of routers, which is about the maximum number of VCCs supported per ATM physical interface on majority of current IP routers. Also, in the absence of any downstream routers or hosts, the routers will receive IP multicast traffic only to be dropped by the IP layer, resulting in the wastage of valuable link bandwidth.

The VCC consumption could be reduced by: using a mesh of pt2pt VCCs between all the routers in the clusters, or setting up a p2mpt VCC from every router to every other router.

In case of pt2pt VCCs, each VCC could be used as a dedicated link between two routers. IP multicast traffic for a group would be forwarded across a VCC, only if a prune message is not received on that VCC for that group. This could be achieved completely independent of the existence of a MARS. The main advantage of this model is that the costs of utilization of the physical link can be accurately determined for any customer. However, this results in multiple copies of the same packet transmitted on the physical interface resulting in wasted buffer space in the router and bandwidth on the physical link.

Alternatively, routers could use the p2mpt VCC set to the *all routers* group for forwarding multicast packets on the downstream interfaces for a group. This results in the delivery of multicast traffic to the IP-VC interface of every router, regardless of the prune status of that interface.

As yet another possibility, VCC resources could be conserved by reusing an existing p2mpt VCC with leaves that is a superset of the new targeted receivers. However, this complicates the algorithms used for VCC management, since dynamic joins and leaves by the clients to different multicast groups could change the domain of the end systems served by a VCC map to one or more multicast groups.

In order to conserve VCC resources and also to prune unwanted traffic at the ATM level to the extent possible, the IP multicast group address space could be divided into pre-defined number of blocks. Each block in turn maps to a single VCC. Multicast routers that need to forward data of a particular group within a block will have to be added as a leaf to the VCC serving that block. A particular IP multicast group could be hashed into one of the blocks to uniformly distribute VCC load across multiple blocks. This technique would reduce the amount of unpruned traffic delivered to an IP-VC interface of the router, but does not totally eliminate it, emulating the behavior of a multicast extended ethernet interface.

Unlike DVMRP, which created a source based tree for every sender, the Protocol Independent Multicasting protocol in Sparse Mode (PIM-SM) creates just one multicast tree per multicast group, independent of the number of senders to the group. This indirectly saves a number of VCCs that need to be created when DVMRP like protocols are used at the IP level. Therefore PIM-SM is highly recommended for deployment over a wide area network, compared to DVMRP.

## 8 Alternative Models

The MC_over_ATM model is a server based model and as such suffers from the disadvantages associated with such models. They include availability, scalability, and reliability. Attempts to add counter measures frequently result in increased protocol complexity, as evident from the efforts of the IETF to produce separate specifications [9][10], each addressing some of these issues.

Distributed models, on the other hand, have a potential to offer a cleaner and more reliable solution at the expense of some extra complexity. One such model is the support for group addressing at the ATM layer. By using the ATM group addressing support defined in [11], an ATM end system could do the IP to ATM group address translation by algorithmically mapping one from the other independent of any server. With this capability, a sender to a multicast group could specify an ATM group address as the destination of the data VCC. It would be the job of PNNI [12] routing to create a VCC that reached all members of the multicast group. The PNNI routing protocol would need to be extended to do group address based routing. Furthermore, the "leaf initiated join" capability in UNI 4.0 signalling could be incorporated in PNNI to allow p2mpt VCCs from senders to be dynamically modified to add new group members.

The final component of this distributed model would be a mechanism for hosts to advertise themselves as members of a multicast group. Hosts could use an IGMP-style protocol to inform the ATM switch to which they are connected what multicast groups they wish to be members of. PNNI should ensure that this information gets distributed across the ATM network.


## Acknowledgements

This research has greatly benefited from discussions had with Allison Mankin. The authors would also like to thank Bill Edwards, Frank DeNap, and Ann Demirtjis of Sprint Corporation for guiding and funding this research. We gratefully acknowledge the support of Pat Gary, Javad Boroumand, and Paul Diggins of NASA GSFC for providing testbed resources and their valuable time.


## References


[1] Armitage, G., "Support for Multicast over UNI 3.0/3.1 based ATM Networks", RFC 2022, Bellcore, November 1996.

[2] Laubach, M., "Classical IP and ARP over ATM", RFC 1577, Hewlett-Packard Laboratories, January 1994.

[3] ftp://ftp.cmf.nrl.navy.mil/pub/vince

[4] ftp://ftp.isi.edu/pub/isi-east/benny.tar.gz

[5] Deering, S., "Host Extensions for IP Multicasting", RFC 1112, Stanford University, August 1989.

[6] ftp://ftp.parc.xerox.com/pub/net_research/ipmulti/ipmulti3.5-sunos41x.tar.Z

[7] ftp://ftp.isi.edu/pub/mbone.faq.txt

[8] The ATM Forum, "ATM User-Network Interface Specification", Prentice-Hall, 1994.

[9] Luciani, J., Armitage, G., Halpern, J., "Server Cache Synchronization Protocol (SCSP) - NBMA", Internet-Draft, April 1996.

[10] Talpade, R., Ammar, M., "Multicast Server Architectures for MARS-based ATM multicasting", Internet-Draft, June 1996.

[11] The ATM Forum, "ATM User-Network Interface (UNI) Signalling Specification v4.0", June 1996.

[12] The ATM Forum, "Private Network-Network Interface (PNNI) v1.0", June 1996.

# SEAM: Scalable and Efficient ATM Multicast

Matthias Grossglauser*

INRIA
Sophia Antipolis, France
Matthias.Grossglauser@inria.fr

K.K. Ramakrishnan

AT&T Labs-Research
Murray Hill, NJ
kkrama@research.att.com

**Abstract**

This paper proposes a multipoint-to-multipoint multicast architecture for ATM networks. The necessity for such an architecture stems from the scalability requirements, both in terms of state to be maintained in the network and in terms of the group population dynamics, of a wide range of networking applications.

We argue that approaches of using multicast servers or meshes of point-to-multipoint Virtual Circuits (VCs) may be inadequate solutions to this problem. We propose a true multipoint-to-multipoint architecture called SEAM, which uses a single VC for a multicast group consisting of multiple senders and receivers. We achieve this without changes to ATM's AAL5. SEAM relies on an additional switching feature we call cut-through forwarding, which enables the mapping of several incoming VCs into outgoing VCs.

We believe that SEAM is both an important and necessary step in the evolution of ATM. It will enable applications relying on group multicast to benefit directly from ATM's quality of service support and scalable bandwidth and the resulting performance advantages. Also, it considerably simplifies the problem of supporting IP multicast over large ATM networks.

## 1 Introduction

Support for multi-party communications is viewed as a critical building block for enabling transparent, scalable communication. In most of the existing work on IP and ATM multicasting, human collaborative applications such as audio/video-conferencing and shared interactive workspaces are cited as one of the primary applications to benefit from a multicast service. Since bandwidth has been and continues to be a scarce resource in the Internet, one of the main goals of these studies has been the gain in bandwidth efficiency that multicast offers over unicast. The obvious goal of minimization of resource usage to a single transmission of a message over a given link has been paramount. We believe that another fundamental attractiveness for multicasting is its ability to abstract the identity of individual members of the group to a single common group identity. This enables scaling of the communication mechanism to arbitrarily large numbers of participants and network sizes.

The emphasis on human collaborative applications and bandwidth efficiency has led to design decisions that can impede scalability for other more general uses of multicast. Multicast sessions for human collaboration, based on the nature of human behavior, can be expected to be relatively static. Also, the set of senders to the group is small: a person is often unable to look and listen to even a few speakers at the same time. Thus, scalability has been addressed only in terms of the size of the receiver population. This has led to designs based on per-source distribution trees, such as DVMRP [1], MOSPF [2], and ATM UNI 4.0 [3].

Multicast serves as a communication *abstraction* between a set of group members. In many circumstances, the group members are all potential senders; furthermore, the group population can be large and highly dynamic. The main motivation for using a multicast service then lies in the decoupling of the application and the group membership management. In other words, the application is relieved of the burden of tracking group membership; it can address the group as a single entity. This proves important in many distributed systems, where requiring the application to track membership and manage member arrivals and departures results in complexity and is an additional computational burden. Such applications include distributed interactive simulation (DIS), distributed databases and caches [4], and distributed games.

In DIS, a multicast group represents a cell of simulated terrain, and group members are processes representing objects moving in the corresponding cell of the terrain. Objects "inform" other interested objects

*This author was supported in part by a grant from France Telecom/CNET.



0-8186-7780-5/97 $10.00 © 1997 IEEE

(i.e., objects in the same cell) of their actions (movement, state changes etc.) Thus, all objects are potential senders. Also, the objects' movements between cells can translate into frequent membership changes.

In summary, in order for a multicast service to efficiently support a wide range of applications, we believe it has to offer the following:

1. Membership management symmetry for senders and receivers.

2. Scalability in the total network size, the group size, and the frequency of membership changes.

These requirements impose certain design choices. First, the multicast group should be represented by a single tree shared by all group members (senders and receivers) [5]. We will elaborate on this in Section 2. Second, only network nodes (switches or routers) on the tree for a group should have to maintain state concerning that corresponding group. Otherwise, the cost of setting up and maintaining a large number of sparse groups will become excessive, as has been observed with DVMRP. Third, it must be possible to support member-initiated group membership changes. If all membership changes have to be processed centrally, the burden of communication and processing overhead, latency, and unreliability can become excessive.

It is important to note that these issues are fundamentally tied to the scalability requirements of multiparty communication, and do not depend on the particular network protocol, such as IP or ATM. Note that the clear distinction of the connection-less nature of IP and the connection-oriented nature of ATM vanishes for multicast: both protocols have to maintain per-connection state in network nodes. The only difference lies in how this state is set up and maintained. IP has traditionally preferred soft-state approaches based on periodic refreshes, while ATM has preferred hard-state approaches based on explicit state creation and deletion.

The only protocols proposed so far recognizing the need for a shared tree are CBT [5] and the sparse mode of PIM [6]. In ATM, member-initiated join and leave has been incorporated into ATM Forum UNI version 4.0 for point-to-multipoint communication. However, there has been no proposal for a "convenient" multipoint-to-multipoint communication mechanism. While MARS [7] uses a single tree spanning all receivers, rooted at a multicast server, senders have to create point-to-point (unicast) connections to the server, violating the network state scalability requirement above. Also, the server may be both a bottleneck (due to the necessity to perform reassembly-segmentation in the server) and a single point of failure. The number of Virtual Circuits (VCs) used on the link to the server may be a scarce resource as well.

In this paper, we propose a true multipoint-to-multipoint architecture for ATM, called SEAM. It is compatible with the requirements elaborated earlier, and is therefore based on a single, shared tree. A single VC per link is used to send cells from all the senders of the multicast group to the receivers in the group. Conceptually, SEAM is closest to CBT, while it maintains the cell-switched nature of ATM. Cell switching, i.e., forwarding small, fixed-sized cells, has been introduced in ATM to simplify the switch's hardware architecture, and providing for higher performance. However, manipulating sub-packet units means that we need to be careful when forwarding from more than one incoming VC into one (or several) outgoing VC, because cells belonging to one packet need to remain in sequence. We solve this problem through a small modification to cell forwarding, called *cut-through forwarding*. *Short-cutting* is a proposed signalling mechanism that sets up the cell forwarding tables so that packets span the shared tree, reducing delay and increasing bandwidth efficiency. Short-cutting is an emulation of reverse path forwarding on the shared tree through an appropriate mapping of the incoming VCs onto the outgoing VCs belonging to the same SEAM tree. SEAM achieves the multipoint-to-multipoint communication over AAL5, with no changes to the cell headers, and does not require switches to examine the cell-payload.

One of the ancillary goals in our proposing SEAM is a desire to support IP multicasting in ATM networks. An ATM backbone may have many IP routers at the periphery. A straightforward mapping of a large number of IP multicast addresses among these routers using point-to-point VCs results in excessive state to be maintained and managed in the ATM backbone. SEAM overcomes this by having a single virtual channel associated with each IP multicast address.

The remainder of this paper is structured as follows. Section 2 explores the necessity of having a single shared tree in more detail. Section 3 discusses signalling, and Section 4 discusses data forwarding. Section 5 concludes the paper.

## 2 Necessity of a Single Shared Tree

In this section, we show that the necessity of a single shared tree derives directly from our assumptions of sender/receiver symmetry and scalability. More specifically, we focus on three aspects of scalability: network state, dynamic membership management, and membership coherence.

## 2.1 Network State

Even when the group membership is static, group connectivity based on per-source trees or on a multicast server results in a number of VCs equal to the number of potential sources on the links towards the receivers or the multicast server. This may be reasonable in an environment of a few senders and a large number of receivers. However, a large number of applications rely on a model where all group members are receivers and potential senders.

## 2.2 Membership Management

We use simulation to illustrate the difference in join performance for multicast groups based on a shared tree (such as CBT and SEAM) and groups based on source-based trees (such as DVMRP or ATM UNI 4.0). We first generate random network topologies, using the algorithm proposed by Waxman [8]. The topologies we generate have 1000 nodes and an average outdegree of approximately 7[1]. We then randomly select nodes of this graph as group members. There are three types of possible group members: pure senders, pure receivers, or members that are both senders and receivers. We then create a multicast group connecting the members. There are two types of group connectivity: shared-tree groups (SEAM) and source-based tree groups. For shared-tree groups, we use the following heuristic to determine the core node. We select as the core the node of the random topology closest to the center of mass of the set of receivers. For source-based tree groups, we set up a shortest path tree for each sender (including members that are senders and receivers) to all of the receivers. We then randomly select a node among the non-member nodes to issue a join request. This new node can request to join as a receiver, as a sender, or as both.

We consider two metrics to evaluate the performance of the join request, namely latency and resource consumption. "Latency" measures the time it takes to create the state in the network to include the new member in the group. For shared-tree groups (SEAM groups), *join latency* is the time to reach the existing tree on the shortest path towards the core.[2] For source-based tree groups (meshes of point-to-multipoint VCs), join latency is the maximum of the join latencies to all of the source-based trees. In other words, we assume that the multiple joins can progress in parallel. Each hop traversed by the join contributes a unit of time to the latency. *Resource consumption* measures the total amount of processing a join requires in the network. We simply count how many hops are traversed by signalling messages related to this join. As in a SEAM group, there is only one signalling message, this is of course equal to the distance in hops between the new node and the tree.

For each random topology, we generate fifty multicast groups and one join of each type to this group (receiver join, sender join, sender-receiver join). As a stop criterion, we require that the 90 % confidence interval of both metrics for the three types of joins be within ±10% of the estimated mean.

We consider two types of group members. For the first type of group members, we assume only sending *and* receiving members. Fig. 1 and 2 depict the latency and resource consumption as a function of the group size. The join latency for the shared tree is considerably lower than for the collection of source-based trees. This is because it is very likely that at least one of the joins to the source-based trees has to travel quite far to reach the existing tree. Of course, the exact extent of the performance advantage of the shared tree over the collection of source-based trees depends on the network and the group topologies as well as on the core placement. The difference in terms of resource consumption is extremely large, and continues to grow with group size (cf. Fig. 2). This is because a new group member in the source-based tree case has to build up a new tree rooted at itself to all the existing receivers, and it has to join all of the existing source-based trees. Thus, the join cost grows approximately proportional to the group size, whereas for the shared tree, the cost actually gets lower as the group size increases, as on the average, the join hits the tree of a large group earlier.

For the second type of group members, we assume there are only pure senders and pure receivers in the group. The size of the receiver population is fixed at 100. We vary the number of senders. Fig. 3 and 4 depict the join latency and resource consumption for both new senders and new receivers. We see the excellent join performance, both in terms of join latency and of resource consumption, of the shared tree. For the group based on source-based trees, the join latency for senders is worst. This is because a new tree has to be built up, and therefore the latency is determined by the longest path between the new sender and any of the existing receivers. In terms of resource consumption, we again observe more than two orders of magnitude in difference between the shared-tree group and the source-based tree group. Only for small numbers of potential senders are receiver joins comparably cheap to the shared tree. Again, the join cost for receivers scales up approximately linearly with the number of sources.

[1] This outdegree is relatively large, but for random topologies of this size, it is computationally hard to get smaller outdegrees, as graphs tend to be disconnected with high probability.

[2] For senders, it is sufficient to reach any part of the shared tree, while receivers have to connect to a node on the receiver-spanning tree.

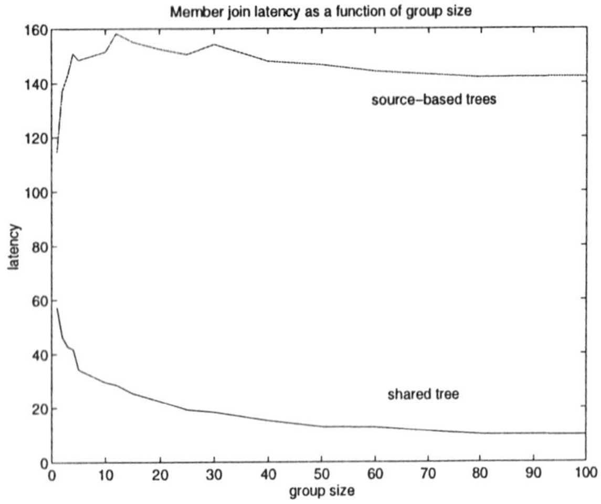


Figure 1: The join latency for members as a function of the number of members. A member is both a sender and a receiver.

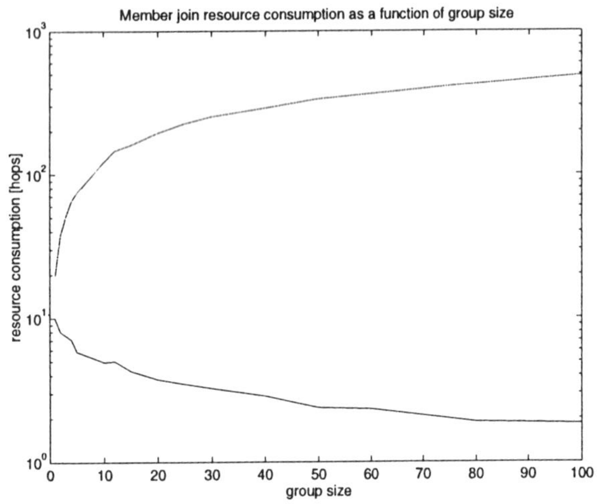


Figure 2: The join resource consumption for members as a function of the number of members. A member is both a sender and a receiver.

Our simulation results suggest that a single shared tree is a good solution for large scale multicast groups, where the number of senders is not negligible.

## 2.3 Membership Coherence

In a per-source tree environment, providing the current membership information to a new sender/receiver is problematic as well. One way to provide information on the existing sources and receivers is to have a *repository* of such information somewhere in the network. The problems of keeping the repository up-to-date, ensuring that access to the repository is not a bottleneck in the presence of constant membership change and

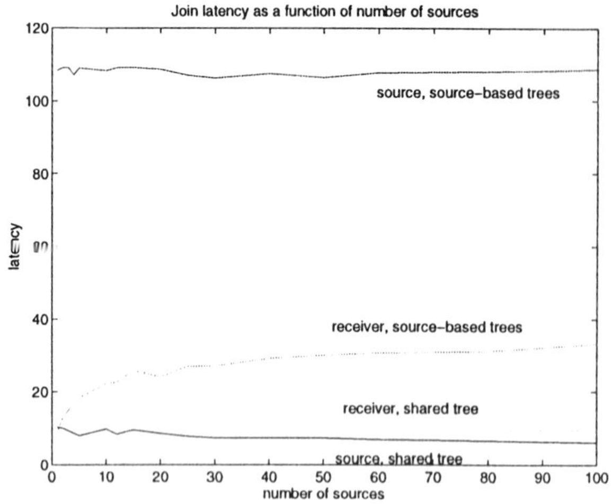


Figure 3: The join latency for senders and receivers as a function of the number of senders. The number of receivers is 100.

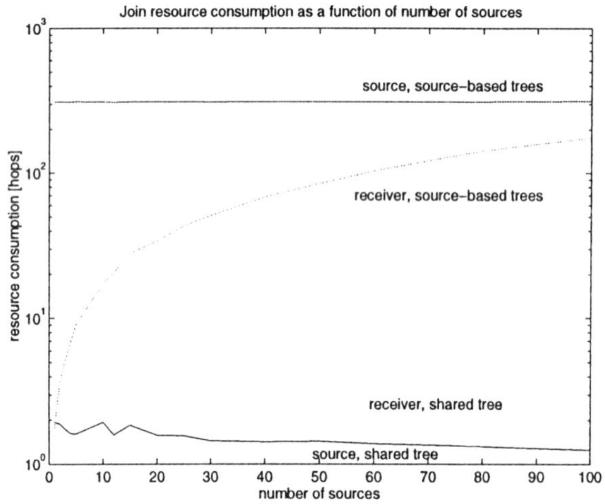


Figure 4: The join resource consumption for senders and receivers as a function of the number of senders. The number of receivers is 100.

providing a coherent view to new participants have to be addressed. For example, it is difficult to deal with the situation of providing coherent information to new receivers while we are setting up a new source. If we fail to provide the appropriate information, a receiver would have no way of knowing that it is not connected to all the current sources. A similar situation applies to a new source, as it may not be able to ensure all currently interested receivers have been "joined" into the group. The obvious dependence on a highly reliable repository exists, and recovery from the failure of a repository is not trivial.

With SEAM, the group abstraction provided by the

shared tree avoids the need for such a repository. The core serves as a "beacon" towards which senders and receivers issue joins to the single shared tree. The join terminates at the point where a new branch has to be added to the existing tree. There is no danger of a receiver not "seeing" all the sources, and vice versa. Furthermore, failure of a switch (including the core) does not result in any failure of continued operation of the multicast group (other than the natural partitioning of the network). Recovery from a failure also is simple, since the failed switch does not have to maintain/recover any state of the current group membership.

### 2.4 Delay Issues

The major disadvantage of shared trees are delays to receive data that are potentially higher than in the case of shortest-path sender-based trees [9]. However, it should be kept in mind that most networks exhibit a certain degree of hierarchy. Even in a local area network, where the network may be physically connected in an arbitrary mesh, the routing layer typically organizes the network in a hierarchical fashion. For example, routing protocols such as OSPF or IS-IS use hierarchy to control the amount of routing information that is being distributed all over the network. Given this hierarchy, it can be expected that sender-based trees will not offer significantly different delays than shared trees, because the hierarchical structure reduces the number of alternative paths from a sender to a receiver. For example, a campus network is usually connected to the Internet over a single leased line. This may be the most likely bottleneck in a wide-area multicast session. Both shared trees and sender-based trees would have to choose this link to reach all members on the campus. We recognize the need to substantiate this claim further through simulations, which is the subject of our future work.

## 3 Signalling Support for SEAM

We first address the requirements on signalling and group management.

### 3.1 Group Creation

When senders or receivers want to join a multicast group, they send a join message towards the core. In other words, the choice of a core needs to be made prior to setting up any part of the multicast tree. The question is: who is responsible for setting up the core?

We propose to have an "initiator", who may or may not be a future member of the group, responsible for defining the core and disseminating the existence of the core to the potential members. This can happen, for example, through a name service, as proposed in [5], or through directly contacting the members, depending on the semantics of the group.

Note that it does not need to be the initiator's responsibility to choose what switch in the network is elected as core. In our view, the network would offer core selection as a service. The initiator could convey some information about the expected group membership (e.g., geographical information) in order for the network to optimize the choice of a core. The network answers a core selection request with a handle that the initiator may use to advertise the group. Since any switch may potentially act as a core, one may envisage some form of load distribution among several of them in the network to act as cores for different multicast groups.

### 3.2 Member Initiated Joins

It is obvious from the discussions in [5, 6] that member-initiated joins are a necessity for a scalable multicast service. The advantages of a member initiated join approach over a root initiated approach are twofold. First, the root of a multicast tree (in our case the core) does not need to know about or keep track of the membership of the group. This means saving processing resources and state space. Second, a join to a group that already has a tree set up can be terminated at the point where a new branch will be added to the existing tree. This means saving bandwidth (due to signalling messages traveling smaller distances, or hops), processing resources in the switches and reduced latency.

New members who wish to join the multicast group either as senders or receivers issue a join request. This join request travels towards the core on the shortest path, until it hits a switch that is already on the requested group's tree. A new branch is then created from that switch to the joining member. Basically, the procedure is similar to that of receivers joining a point-to-multipoint VC in UNI 4.0 [3], but we generalize it to both sending and receiving members. Similar options as proposed originally for UNI 4.0 (without sender participation, with sender notification, with sender permission) may be used.

### 3.3 The Receivers-Downstream (RD) Bit

The use of a single shared tree among all receivers and senders requires us to introduce a small amount of per-link state to avoid wasting resources by transmitting to sender-only end-systems. In order to avoid forwarding packets to members who are only senders, we associate a flag with the group at each "on-tree" switch. The flag, called the "Receivers Downstream" bit, indicates if there are any receivers downstream from this port. Consider situation (a) in Fig. 5: RD=0 at switches S1-S3 means that the respective

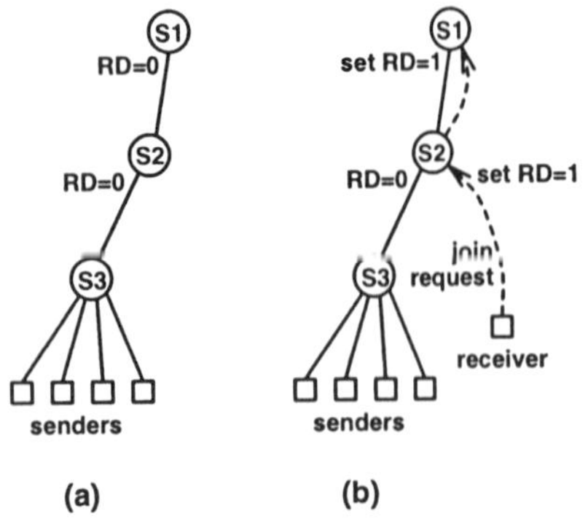


Figure 5: Updating of the RD bit upon receiver join.

ports only have senders downstream, and therefore no packets need to be forwarded on these ports.

If a new receiver connects to the existing tree at a port that has the RD bit cleared, then the forwarding table in some upstream switches have to be updated, so that packets will be forwarded down to the new receiver. The join request therefore has to travel towards the core on the tree and update the forwarding table in each switch. The join request stops when it hits the core or a switch with the RD bit set on at least one other port, which means that packets sent to the group already reach this switch. At each switch traversed on the tree, forwarding tables have to be updated such that packets will be forwarded towards the new receiver.

The core acts as any other SEAM switch. The only exception is that all data gets forwarded to the core, even if it does not have receivers on its other ports. This is because the RD bit is not helpful since receiver joins only go as far as the core. There is no clean way to have the signalling progress beyond the core to the set of switches downstream, until the point where we reach switches that all have their RD bit set. Therefore, by requiring the data to be forwarded to the core, irrespective of the RD bit, switches in the tree are led to believe that there are always receivers on the other side of the core.

### 3.4 Core Initiated Joins

Using a single tree means that several group members can be added in one step, initiated by the core. In a scheme using per-sender trees, this is not possible: either each sender has to set up a tree to all the receivers, which means that the set of receivers has to be communicated to the senders, or the receivers join the sender tree of each of the senders, which means that, in turn, the receivers need to know the set of senders. This can be an important performance consideration for applications that depend on rapid setup of centrally controlled groups. An example would be the setting up of a group teleconferencing session with the help of a centralized server. The function of the centralized server may be to provide security screening, the appropriate translation functions needed for the different participants and other coordinating functions prior to the start of the session. Unlike "simple teleconferencing" with member-initiated joins, we also envisage a need for a small set of multicasting applications that are centrally coordinated and managed. Here a core-initiated join is advantageous.

### 3.5 Short-Cutting

This is the second building block of SEAM, wherein we avoid having all the transmissions go to the core (which may be an end-system, or a switch with cut-through capability) before being forwarded to the receivers. Anytime a cell is received at a switch S on a VC H, and if the context for VC H has been established (i.e., the switch knows it is in the spanning tree for conversation H), then the switch forwards the arriving cell on all the links of the spanning tree other than the one it was received on. This is the concept of Reverse Path Forwarding (RPF) that protocols such as DVMRP exploit as well. The only constraint is that the forwarding is only on the links where the "Receivers Downstream" (RD) bit is set. We leave the issue of how the spanning tree is built to the routing protocol.

Short-cutting is enabled by modifications in the signalling path of the switch implementation, and does not require any changes in the data path. Figure 6 illustrates how forwarding tables have to be set to achieve short-cutting.

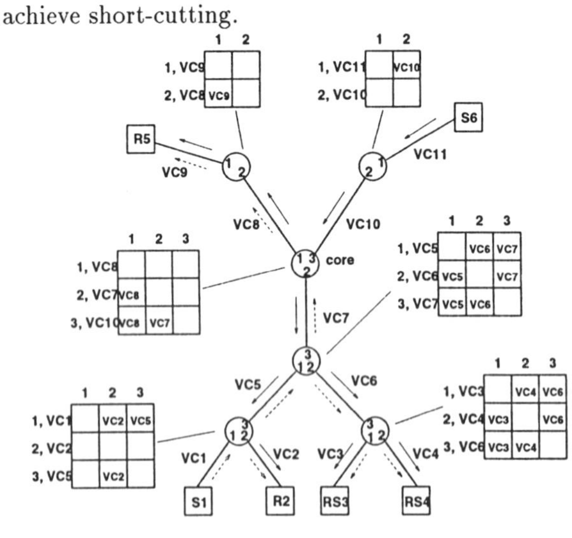


Figure 6: Forwarding tables for short-cutting. The paths followed by a packet from S1 and from S6 are shown.

In principle, SEAM also allows reconfiguration of

"segments" of the shared tree upon link failure, rather than reconfiguration of the entire shared tree. This may require appropriate signalling support to not 'clear' the entire multicast call upon a link failure: only those receivers/senders downstream of the failed link need to be notified and requested to re-issue joins towards the core (with an alternate path provided by the routing infrastructure). This enhances reliability and scalability.

## 4 Data Forwarding Issues

For our multicast scheme to work, we need to be able to map multiple incoming VCs into one or several outgoing VCs at switches. If this is done simply on a cell-by-cell basis, then cells belonging to different packets will interfere with each other (they will be interleaved, resulting in packet corruption).

One way to circumvent this problem is by reassembling the packets, perform packet-level scheduling, and re-segment one packet after the other onto an outbound point-to-multipoint VC (or mesh of point-to-point VCs). A multicast server typically used to do this function of reassembly and forwarding [7] makes for an obvious performance bottleneck and means that switches have to process packets. We show in this section that it is possible to achieve the same without reassembly and segmentation, by taking advantage of the fact that the AAL5 end-of-packet identifier is part of the ATM cell header.

A handle H for the group is used at the time of signalling to set up the SEAM VC. There is a one-to-one correspondence between the handle H and the VC on each individual link. Although the VC id may be different on each link, we will use the same term "H" for the SEAM VC, whenever this does not lead to confusion.

When multiple senders transmit to the same multicast group, identified by the handle, then their packets arrive on the same VC. The constraint imposed by ATM is that the data on a particular VC is ordered, and therefore, there is no need to identify cells as belonging to a particular packet. With AAL5, when a end-of-packet cell is received, all the previous cells received on that VC belong to that packet. When multiple senders send packets on the same VC, these need to be unambiguously ordered and forwarded so that there is no corruption of the data transmissions. We do this by having switches perform a function we call *cut-through forwarding*. Switches performing cut-through forwarding complete whole packets at a time, while buffering incoming packets from other input ports until an End-of-Packet (EOP) cell has been forwarded. Then, another port with an incoming VC for this group is selected for forwarding.

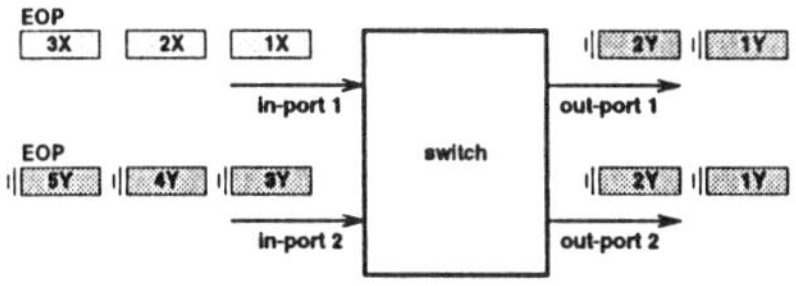


Figure 7: Cut through for VC H: Packet Y gets forwarded, while Packet X is buffered until cell 5Y with EOP for packet Y goes through switch.

With cut-through, the receivers do not have to distinguish cells of different packets arriving on the same VC (an impossible task). The specific actions for cut-through at a switch S are: the first cell of a packet arriving from any input port on VC H determines that this packet arriving on that input port gets unconditional priority to be forwarded on the outgoing VC H. Let this packet be Y from source B. Then, all of the cells of packet Y are forwarded first (e.g., Figure 7). Any other packet arriving on any other input port is queued at switch S for forwarding subsequent to the transmission of packet Y. When the last cell of packet Y (signified by the end-of-packet cell) is transmitted, then the cells queued for packet X are transmitted from switch S on the spanning tree. From that point onwards, packet X gets priority for being transmitted on VC H. A switch that is not a "merge point" would perform pure cell-switching for the multicast VC, even when following the above actions. Unicast VCs are unaffected by cut-through.

Thus, our requirement on switch S performing cut-through is to identify the first cell of an incoming packet on a given multicast VC H, and to transmit cells received on that input port only, until the last cell of that packet has been transmitted. The cells from other input ports that arrive in the meanwhile on VC H are queued for forwarding subsequent to sending the last cell of the packet currently being forwarded. Once the EOP cell is forwarded, another input port with cells awaiting transmission for the multicast VC is selected on a round-robin basis for transmission. Every switch (at least every *merge point* for multicast communication) on the tree is expected to be able to perform cut-through. We assume the support of per-VC queueing in the switches at least for multicast VCs.

Thus, a requirement we impose on switches is the need to recognize the EOP bit (for an AAL5 packet) to enable cut-through. AAL5 support of this nature is becoming more and more prevalent in ATM switches. This is because the notion of packet-discard is becoming a necessary aid to manage congestion, requiring switches to recognize the EOP flag. It is precisely this feature we exploit to achieve the ability to cut-through, in addition to the storage of cells of a packet, while a previous packet is being forwarded for that VC. A similar mechanism is briefly described in [10] in the context of multicast servers (called "hardware resequencers"). However, implementation issues have not been studied in detail.

The *fundamental* advantage of SEAM achieved with cut-through is that we do *not* have to look at the payload of the cell to do efficient multipoint-to-multipoint communication, and no changes are required for the cell header or AAL5 trailer.

Another observation we make is that LAN Emulation and IP Multicast over ATM (wherein a framework of point-to-multipoint VCs is used in conjunction with a multicast server to achieve the multipoint-to-multipoint service) use multicast servers. It is anticipated that switch vendors will begin to incorporate the server in the switch itself, so as to make ATM more attractive for deployment in traditional LAN environments. These switches will therefore incorporate the ability to switch frames. SEAM can exploit this functionality, and take advantage of switching frames only when essential (when there are multiple packets for the same SEAM VC contending for an output port of the switch), and allowing the switch to take full advantage of cell-switching whenever possible. Furthermore, we avoid reassembly and segmentation.

### 4.1 Recovery from Lost EOP Cells

Loss of an end-of-packet (EOP) cell causes cut-through to have somewhat more serious consequences than the unicast case. Just as in the unicast case, the loss of an EOP cell results in that packet not being successfully reassembled at the destination. That packet is lost. However, in multicast with SEAM, the loss of an EOP cell for a packet on a given input port also results in the continued queueing of the cells for that multicast VC on other input ports. Only the transmission of a subsequent packet on that same input port (and the forwarding of its EOP cell) would result in the queued cells on other ports being released. An approach for recovering from the loss of an EOP cell is to use a timer. If no cell (including an EOP cell) has been received for that multicast VC on an input port which is currently forwarding a packet for a period of time, then we may time-out that input port. The actions taken upon timeout would be:

1) To generate an EOP cell for that VC with a "null payload" so as to complete the packet loss event. This allows other switches to avoid the overhead associated with identifying the packet loss and having a timeout.

2) Once the EOP cell is forwarded, then allow the normal process of cut-through to continue. Another input port with cells awaiting transmission for the multicast VC is selected on a round-robin basis for transmission.

The setting of the timer for the multicast VC would have to be appropriate so that the loss of an EOP cell does not result in excessive delays. This is a function of the link speeds, and certainly based on the minimum rate that the VC may transmit at. One timer would be required per multicast VC at each independent forwarding point (one per SEAM VC for the switch, if it is an input buffered switch; or one timer per SEAM VC for each output port, if it is an output buffered switch).

### 4.2 When to Perform Cut-Through

When there is a slow input port on a switch with heterogeneous ports (of different speeds), a pure cut-through design may lead to unnecessary delay for cells arriving on the higher speed input ports for the same SEAM VC. Consider a switch with a fast output link and two input links, one that is fast (comparable to the output link) and another that is a slow input link. A packet arriving from the fast input link is able to saturate the output link. We can cut-through such a packet without potentially wasting downstream bandwidth by blocking packets for the same group arriving on other ports. On the other hand, a packet arriving on the slow incoming link cannot saturate the output port. During the time this packet uses the output port, link bandwidth proportional to the bandwidth difference between the fast output port and the slow input port is lost. Ideally, we would like this lost bandwidth to be exploited by packets concurrently arriving on the fast link. Therefore, we propose to store-and-forward packets arriving on incoming links that cannot saturate the output links. In other words, these input links would receive an entire packet before contending for access. More specifically, we suggest to perform cut-through on input port $i$ if

$$C_i \geq \min_{o \in O}\{C_o\} \quad (1)$$

and store-and-forward otherwise, where $C_j$ is the link bandwidth of port $j$, and $O$ is the set of output ports for this multicast group.

When there are multiple "active" input ports, then the switch follows a round-robin policy (motivated by fairness issues) to determine which input port's cells should be forwarded. A "cut-through port" is active if it has at least one cell queued. A "store-and-forward port" is active if it has at least one packet queued.

## 5 Conclusions

SEAM is an efficient scheme for multipoint-to-multipoint communication in ATM networks, with the potential to scale up to large, dynamic groups. SEAM uses a single shared spanning tree for all senders and receivers.

We proposed the use of a unique handle (translates to a single VC on a link) to identify all packets associated with a given multicast group. Each multicast group has an associated "core", which is used as the focal point for routing signalling messages for the group. The handle is a tuple (core address, unique-id at core) that is unique across the network. We allow for member-initiated joins to the single core-based tree by senders and receivers as well as core-initiated joins. We exploit the proposed capabilities of leaf-initiated joins in ATM networks specified in UNI 4.0.

We compared through simulation the performance differences for member joins in a shared tree versus source-based trees. We observed that the SEAM join latency for a new member is significantly smaller than with source-based trees because the join travels far fewer hops. The consumption of resources by joins reduces (especially for senders) with a shared tree as the group size increases (for a given network topology). This is in contrast to a dramatic increase in resource consumption by joins (especially for receivers) in a source-based tree.

We introduced two new features in SEAM: "cut-through" forwarding and "short-cutting" to achieve efficient multicasting with low-latency for communication between senders and receivers. Cut-through forwarding in a switch enables the mapping of several incoming VCs into outgoing VCs at a switch. A switch capable of cut-through forwards a multicast packet from one input port at a time, taking advantage of the AAL5 end-of-packet cell to identify when to "switch" to forwarding a new packet. Incoming packets from other input ports are buffered until it is their turn, thus ensuring packets are transmitted on an outgoing VC atomically. Our preliminary simulation results indicate that the buffer requirements imposed by cut-through are modest. Short-cutting is the signalling mechanism allowing packets to follow the shortest path along the shared tree by emulating reverse-path forwarding. We avoid the packet having to go all the way to the core and then be forwarded back to the receivers, and therefore avoid it traversing links twice. No changes are needed to the cell header.

We believe no scheme is complete without addressing issues of migration. We have worked out the details of a SEAM-based environment working quite efficiently along with islands of non-SEAMable switches. The interoperability is such that only "boundary" SEAM switches need to be concerned with non-SEAMable islands, and within those islands, we fully exploit the point-to-multipoint capabilities of current ATM signalling.

Thus, we believe we have proposed a truly scalable and efficient ATM multicasting architecture. Issues of traffic management and reliable multicasting, both important topics, are the subject of our future work.

## References


[1] S. E. Deering, "Multicast Routing in Internetworks and Extended LANs," in *Proc. ACM SIGCOMM '88*, (Stanford, Calif.), August 1988.

[2] J. Moy, "Multicast Extensions to OSPF," in *Request For Comments 1584*, (Network Working Group, IETF), March 1994.

[3] P. Samudra, "UNI Signalling 4.0 (draft), ATM Forum/95-1434R9," Dec 1995.

[4] K. P. Birman, "The Process Group approach to reliable distributed computing," *Communications of the ACM*, December 1993.

[5] T. Ballardie, P. Francis, and J. Crowcroft, "Core Based Trees (CBT)," in *Proc. ACM SIGCOMM '93*, (San Francisco, Calif.), September 1993.

[6] S. Deering *et al.*, "An Architecture for Wide-Area Multicast Routing," in *Proc. ACM SIGCOMM '94*, (London), August 1994.

[7] G. J. Armitage, "Multicast and Multiprotocol support for ATM based Internets," *ACM Sigcomm Computer Communication Review*, vol. 25, April 1995.

[8] B. M. Waxman, "Routing of multipoint connections," *IEEE JSAC*, vol. 6, no. 9, 1988.

[9] L. Wei and D. Estrin, "The Trade-Offs of Multicast Trees and Algorithms," in *Proc. Int'l Conference on Computer Communications and Networks*, (San Francisco), September 1994.

[10] L. Wei, F. Liaw, D. Estrin, A. Romanow, and T. Lyon, "Analysis of a Resequencer Model for Multicast over ATM Networks," in *Proc. 3rd Intl. Workshop on Network and Operating System Support for Digital Audio and Video (NOSSDAV '92)*, (San Diego, Calif.), Nov 1992.

# Restricted Dynamic Steiner Trees for Scalable Multicast in Datagram Networks

Ehud Aharoni Reuven Cohen
Dept. of Computer Science
Technion, Haifa 32000
Israel

## abstract

*The paper addresses the issue of minimizing the number of nodes involved in the routing over a multicast tree and in the maintenance of such a tree in a datagram network. It presents a scheme where the tree routing and maintenance burden is laid only upon the source node and the destination nodes associated with the multicast tree. The main concepts behind this scheme is to view each multicast tree as a collection of unicast paths, and to locate only the multicast source and destination nodes on the junctions of their multicast tree. The paper shows that despite of this restriction, the cost of the created multicast trees is not necessarily higher than the cost of the trees created by other algorithms that do not impose the restriction and therefore require all the nodes along the data path of a tree to participate in the routing over the tree and in the maintenance of the tree.*

## 1 Introduction

In a point-to-point communication network multicast is treated as the problem of creating, maintaining and updating efficient multicast trees, rooted at the multicast source nodes and spanning the groups of destination nodes. A multicast tree is dynamically created, as network nodes join and leave the destination group. It is maintained by some of the network nodes, mainly those sitting on its data path. It needs to be updated following changes in the connectivity or in the load of the underlying network topology.

Internet employs the distance vector multicast routing protocol (DVMRP) [9] in order to construct a shortest path tree for every multicast {source, group} pair. This protocol, which is a "pruning" variant of the reverse path forwarding (RPF) algorithm [7], suffers from two main scaling problems as follows [2, 8]. First, each network node has to maintain routing information per every multicast tree[1]. Second, prune messages should be periodically exchanged between the network nodes in order to maintain an updated version of each multicast tree.

The protocols presented in [2, 8, 4] address these problems. A tree spanning the members of the group is established in the network, and only the nodes sitting on the data path of the tree are required to maintain routing information associated with the tree. When a new node joins the multicast group, all the nodes on the shortest path between the new node and some node on the tree (the pre-determined core in [2], the rendezvous point(s) in [8] or the closest node in [4]) join the tree and update their multicast routing tables accordingly.

However, when multicast becomes pervasive more techniques must be employed in order to avoid scaling problems. If thousands of trees are created, deleted and updated every minute, the processing burden on the network nodes will be excessive, even if the burden associated with every multicast tree is laid only upon the nodes sitting on the data path of that tree. This is because these nodes will have to respond very often to join or delete requests, and to changes in the load or connectivity of the underlying network. This burden can be significantly reduced using the concept of tunneling [17] as follows. The multicast packets are routed over a tree formed by a collection of *multicast links* (tunnels), where each multicast link is a simple unicast route. The intermediate nodes of each multicast link do not have to maintain routing information for the multicast tree, because they are involved only in regular unicast routing. Only the end points of each multicast link have to maintain routing information for every tree established over the link. For instance, consider a multicast source $s$, a multicast group $Z = \{z_1, z_2, z_3, z_4, z_5\}$, and the multicast tree depicted in Figure 1. This tree can be viewed as a collection of the following 6 multicast links: $s \leadsto b$, $b \leadsto z_2$, $b \leadsto z_1$, $z_1 \leadsto d$, $d \leadsto z_5$, $d \leadsto z_3$ and $d \leadsto z_4$. The end points of these multicast links are $Z \cup \{s\} \cup U$, where $U$ is the set of nodes not in $Z \cup \{s\}$ that have at least three links in the tree ($b$ and $d$ in Figure 1). Packets sent by the source $s$ have two pairs of source/destination addresses. One pair is of the multicast source $s$ and multicast group $Z$. This pair remains fixed for the entire routing. The other pair is the addresses of the source and destination of the multicast link over which the packet is routed. This pair is replaced when the packet reaches the end of the multicast link. In terms of Figure 1, a multicast packet

[1]Except in section 6, it is assumed that all network nodes have multicast routing capability.



0-8186-7780-5/97 $10.00 

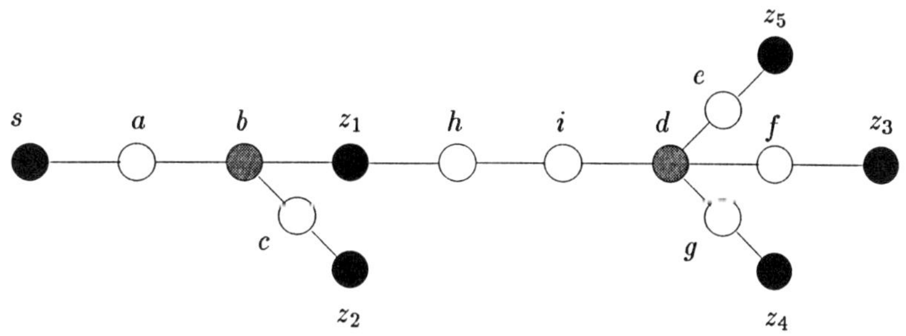


Figure 1: A Multicast Tree

created by the source has a multicast address pair[2] $(s,G)$ and a unicast address pair $(s,b)$. The packet is routed through $a$ based on the unicast address pair. Node $a$ does not need to know anything about the multicast destination $G$. When the packet is received by the unicast destination $b$, it is processed by the multicast routing procedure. In the multicast table of $b$ it is indicated that a multicast packet from $s$ to $G$ should be forwarded to $z_2$ and to $z_1$. The copy destined for $z_2$ has the unicast address pair $(b,z_2)$. It is sent to $c$ and routed as a regular unicast packet whose destination is $z_2$. At $z_2$, the packet is processed by the multicast routing procedure. The latter uses its multicast routing table, and deduces that the packet is destined for the local node and that it should not be forwarded elsewhere[3]. Node $z_1$, in contrast, deduces from its multicast routing table that it needs to keep a copy of the packet for itself, and to send another copy on the multicast link $z_1 \rightsquigarrow d$.

The concept of tunneling is already used for multicast routing in the Internet MBONE [10]. However, its purpose is not to reduce the maintenance and routing burden at the multicast nodes, but to connect multicast-capable nodes through the general IP network. If all the Internet routers had multicast capability, as in the model considered in this paper, tunneling would not have been used.

It can be easily shown by induction that in a multicast tree rooted at source $s$ and spanning the group $Z$, the number $l$ of multicast links (tunnels) is $|Z| \leq l \leq 2|Z| - 1$. In addition, only less than half of the nodes that are actively involved in the maintenance of the tree and in the routing of multicast packets from $s$ to $Z$ (i.e. the nodes whose multicast procedure is invoked when a multicast packet from $s$ to $G$ is received) do not belong to $Z \cup \{s\}$. It turns out, however, that in a datagram network it is practically impossible to keep the details of a multicast tree transparent to the intermediate nodes of the multicast links. When a new member $v$ joins an existing multicast group, it might need to connect to some intermediate node, $v'$ say, of a multicast link $v'' \rightsquigarrow v'''$, in which case $v'' \rightsquigarrow v'''$ is removed from the tree and three multicast links: $v'' \rightsquigarrow v'$, $v' \rightsquigarrow v'''$, $v' \rightsquigarrow v$, are added. For this process to take place, node $v'$ needs to know that it participates in the multicast tree and to maintain some parameters describing its position in the tree, like the identities of the end nodes of the multicast link for which it acts as an intermediate node. This information needs to be refreshed not only when multicast links are added or removed due to changes in the destination group, but also when the unicast routing tables change. For instance, if in Figure 1 the unicast routing tables are updated such that the shortest path from $d$ to $z_4$ goes through nodes $j$ and $k$ rather than through $g$, nodes $g$, $j$ and $k$ must be updated. The conclusion is that the *concept of tunneling does not remove the tree maintenance burden from the intermediate nodes of the multicast links.* It just removes from these nodes the memory and processing burden associated with multicast routing decisions.

In this paper we suggest an approach to solve the scalability problem of establishing, updating, maintaining and routing over a great number of multicast trees in a datagram network. According to this approach, for every multicast tree rooted at a source node $s$ and spanning a set $Z$ of destination nodes, only the nodes in $\{s\} \cup Z$ need to keep and update information related to the tree routing and maintaining. This is achieved by *viewing a multicast tree as a collection of multicast paths (tunnels)* and ensuring that *only nodes in $\{s\} \cup Z$ are selected as end points of the multicast links* (namely the set $U$ mentioned above is empty). In terms of Figure 1, this means that nodes $b$ and $d$, that do not belong to $\{s\} \cup Z$, cannot function as end nodes of multicast links but only as intermediate nodes.

The main advantage of the proposed scheme is that for every multicast tree only the nodes in $\{s\} \cup Z$, which *in any case must keep routing and maintenance information regarding the tree,* are required to do so.

[2]Throughout the paper, $G$ represents a multicast address whereas $Z$ represents a dynamic set of nodes that want to receive the multicast packets sent by $s$ to $G$.

[3]In terms of the Internet, $z_2$ as well as any other node in the multicast group $Z$ can be viewed as a border router connecting an autonomous network of some destination host(s) to the Internet backbone. Thus, the packet will be forwarded by $z_2$ into the autonomous network and multicast to the destination hosts by means of an internal multicast protocol [16].

The existence of the tree is absolutely transparent to any other network node, even to those nodes that sit on the tree data path and route packets of the tree as intermediate nodes of multicast links. Neither changes in the unicast routing tables that affect the routes between the end points of multicast links, nor changes in the multicast destination group can put any maintenance burden on nodes not in $\{s\} \cup Z$.

The constraint imposed by the proposed scheme, where only nodes in $\{s\} \cup Z$ can be located in the tree junctions and serve as end nodes of the multicast links, may lead to the creation of inefficient multicast trees. This issue is extensively studied in the paper. As will be shown, the differences between the cost of the trees generated without this constraint and the trees generated under this constraint are minor, and may therefore justify the significant reduction in the maintenance overhead.

The problem of establishing a low cost tree spanning a partial set of the network nodes is known as the Steiner tree problem. When the set of nodes dynamically changes, a different problem – referred to as the dynamic Steiner tree (DST) – is defined [13]. Section 2 discusses these problems and presents the dynamic greedy algorithm (DGA) [13] for establishing and updating a low cost multicast tree when the destination group dynamically changes and when there is no restriction to locate only nodes from $\{s\} \cup Z$ in the junctions of the multicast trees. In Section 3 we present a new algorithm, referred to as R-DGA (restricted DGA), that locates only nodes from $\{s\} \cup Z$ in the junctions of the multicast trees. Based on R-DGA, we then present a possible protocol for creating, updating and maintaining low cost multicast trees.

In Section 4 the performance of R-DGA is studied. We first prove that despite of the restriction, the worst case performance ratio of R-DGA is the same as of DGA. Then we present simulation results that show that the differences in the actual cost of the trees established by R-DGA and the trees established by DGA are not significant. We also calculate the average number of nodes not in $\{s\} \cup Z$ that are included in the trees generated by DGA and by shortest path algorithm (as suggested in [2, 8]). We use the result in order to compare the burden laid on an average network node by R-DGA and by the other protocols. In Section 5 we discuss the problem of creating, maintaining and updating low cost multicast trees that guarantee some upper bound on the distance between the source node and every destination node. Such a requirement might be of importance for many multicast applications. A new algorithm, referred to as C-R-DGA (constrained R-DGA) is presented and its performance is studied. In section 6 we describe and study the performance of a method to adapt R-DGA and other multicast protocols to the case where only some of the network nodes have multicast capability. Section 7 concludes the paper.

A full version of this paper appears in [1].

## 2 The Dynamic Steiner Tree Problem

The Steiner tree problem can be formulated as follows:

> Given a graph $G(V, E)$, a non-negative weight for each $e \in E$ and a subset $Z \subseteq V$, find a subnetwork $T$ of $G$ such that there is a path between every pair of vertices in $Z$ and the total cost of $T$ is a minimum.

The Steiner tree problem is NP-complete [11]. It remains NP-complete even if all edge weights are equal. Several heuristics are known for this problem [20]. One of them, suggested in [12, 18], is the minimum spanning tree heuristic (MST). This heuristic has a worst case performance of two times the optimum cost solution [5]. No heuristic with a better worst case performance is known [20]. The MST heuristic works as follows [20]:

**Step 1:** Choose an arbitrary vertex $z$ from $Z$. Let $Z' = \{z\}$ and $T = \{z\}$.

**Step 2:** Find in $Z - Z'$ the vertex $z$ closest to $T$. Add $z$ to $Z'$, and add to $T$ the minimum cost path joining $z$ to $T$.

**Step 3:** If $Z' \neq Z$ return to Step 2. Otherwise, $T$ is the solution.

When the set $Z$ represents a multicast group, it cannot be assumed to be known in advance since nodes can dynamically join and leave the multicast group. This is known as the dynamic Steiner tree (DST) problem, formally stated as follows [13]. Let $R = \{r_0, r_1 \cdots r_K\}$ be a sequence of requests, where each $r_i$ is a pair $(v_i, \rho_i)$, $v_i \in V$, $\rho_i \in$ {add,remove}. Let $Z_i$ be the set of nodes in the multicast group after step $i$, consisting of every node $v$ for which there exists $j \leq i$ such that $r_j = (v, \text{add})$ and $r_l \neq (v, \text{remove})$ for all $j < l \leq i$. Then,

> Given a graph $G(V, E)$, a non-negative weight for each $e \in E$ and a sequence $R$ of requests, find a sequence of multicast trees $\{T_1, T_2 \cdots T_K\}$ where $T_i$ spans $Z_i$ and has a minimum cost.

DST can be solved using any heuristic for the static Steiner tree problem, like the MST heuristic mentioned above, if we allow the multicast tree to be completely rebuilt after each change. This is however an unrealistic approach since it requires a lot of coordination among the network nodes [3], and it is very likely that a new request $r_i$ will come up before $T_{i-1}$ is ready. The non-rearrangeable version of DST, referred to as DST-N [13], requires that if $r_i$ is an add request, $T_i$ must include $T_{i-1}$ as a subgraph (namely, no link can be removed from the old tree), whereas if $r_i$ is a remove request, $T_{i-1}$ must include $T_i$ as a subgraph (namely, no link can be added to the new tree).

Imase and Waxman have shown [13] that when the request sequence consists of only add requests, for any algorithm $A$ that solves DST-N there exists an instance such that for every $i$ $0 < i \leq K$

$$\frac{A(Z_i)}{OPT(Z_i)} \geq 1 + \frac{1}{2}\lfloor log(|Z_i| - 1)\rfloor$$

where $K$ is the length of the request sequence, $OPT(Z_i)$ is the optimum solution for a tree spanning $Z_i$, and $A(Z_i)$ is the cost of a tree spanning $Z_i$ created by $A$. They have also presented the dynamic greedy algorithm (DGA), where a new node appended to the multicast group is connected to the existing multicast tree through the cheapest path leading to any node in the tree, and shown that DGA has a worst-case performance ratio (competitiveness) of $\lceil log(|Z_i|) \rceil$ — that is within two of the optimal algorithm.

If both add and remove requests are allowed and if the tree cannot be re-arranged, no upper bound on the worst-case performance ratio exists [13]. Several algorithms [4, 13, 14] have been proposed in order to accommodate both add and remove requests while restricting the number of rearrangements required in order to derive a new efficient tree $T_i$ from the old one $T_{i-1}$.

## 3 R-DGA Heuristic for Scalable Multicast

In this section we describe a new algorithm, referred to as the restricted dynamic greedy algorithm (R-DGA), and then present an R-DGA based protocol for creating and maintaining dynamic multicast trees. Throughout the paper we assume that unicast routing from $v$ to $v'$ is performed over the shortest path $v \rightsquigarrow v'$. We also assume that every node $v'$ knows the cost of the shortest path $v \rightsquigarrow v'$ from every other network node $v$. This kind of information can be provided by the protocol that updates the unicast routing tables, even in the general case where the cost function and the delay function are different, or the costs of $v' \rightsquigarrow v$ and $v \rightsquigarrow v'$ are different.

R-DGA responds differently to add requests and to remove requests. When a request $r_i$ to add a node $v$ to the existing multicast group $Z_{i-1}$ is received, R-DGA uses DGA with a small but significant change: the new node $v$ can be connected *only to a node in the former multicast group* $Z_{i-1}$. The cost of the path $v' \rightsquigarrow v$ is checked for every $v' \in Z_{i-1}$. The node $v' \in Z_{i-1}$ for which the cost of $v' \rightsquigarrow v$ is minimum is selected as the parent of $v$, and a new multicast tree $T_i$ is created by appending the multicast link $v' \rightsquigarrow v$ to the previous multicast tree $T_{i-1}$. When a request $r_i$ to remove $v$ from a multicast group $Z_{i-1}$ is received, $v$ is removed from $T_{i-1}$ along with all the multicast links connecting $v$ to its parent and to its children. Then, every child $v'$ of $v$ in $T_{i-1}$ is connected to a new parent $v'' \in Z_i(v')$ from which the shortest path is of minimum cost. The set $Z_i(v')$ is a subset of $Z_i = Z_{i-1} - \{v\}$ consisting of all the nodes in $Z_i$ that have joined the tree (in the last time) before $v'$. The selected node $v''$ becomes the new parent of $v$ in $T_i$ by appending the multicast link $v'' \rightsquigarrow v$ to $T_{i-1}$.

This algorithm is demonstrated in Figure 2. The original graph is shown in Figure 2(a), and the multicast source is node $s$. The number near every link indicates the cost and the delay on the link for both directions. When node $g$ is added to the multicast group, it joins the tree through the unicast path multicast link $s \rightsquigarrow g$ whose cost is 6. When node $c$ is added, it can join the existing tree by a multicast link from $s$ or from $g$. Since the latter is cheaper (3 versus 7), $c$ joins the tree through the multicast link $g \rightsquigarrow c$. Packets from the source $s$ to $c$ will be routed through $s \rightsquigarrow g$ and then through $g \rightsquigarrow c$, namely over the path $s - f - g - f - c$. Other multicast algorithms, like those based on DGA or on the shortest path algorithm [2, 8, 13] would avoid this unnecessary loop between $f$ and $g$ by creating three multicast links: $s \rightsquigarrow f$, $f \rightsquigarrow g$ and $f \rightsquigarrow c$. However, this is the price we pay by requiring that only the source node and destination nodes will be located in the forks of the tree. The next node added to the multicast group is $d$. It can join the existing tree by a multicast link from $s$, from $g$ or from $c$. The cost of $s \rightsquigarrow d$ is 8, of $g \rightsquigarrow d$ is 2 and of $c \rightsquigarrow d$ is 3. Thus, $g \rightsquigarrow d$ is added to the tree, and the resulting tree is shown in Figure 2(b). Next, suppose that $g$ is removed from the multicast group. The multicast links $s \rightsquigarrow g$, $g \rightsquigarrow c$ and $g \rightsquigarrow d$ are removed, and new parents should be selected for $c$ and $d$. For node $c$, only node $s$ can serve as the new parent of $c$, because no node in the updated destination group has joined the group in the last time before $c$. Thus, the multicast link $s \rightsquigarrow c$ is added to the tree. Regardless of the new parent selected for $c$, both $s$ and $c$ can become the new parent of $d$. Since $c \rightsquigarrow d$ is cheaper than $s \rightsquigarrow d$ (3 versus 8), $c \rightsquigarrow d$ is added to the tree. The resulting tree is shown in Figure 2(c).

A possible protocol based on R-DGA for creating and maintaining a multicast tree is as follows. A node $v$ wishing to join a multicast group $G$ sends a request message to the source $s$ over a reliable unicast (TCP) connection. The source $s$ responds with a list $Z_{i-1}$ of the identities of the nodes currently in $G$. Then it generates an updated list $Z_i \leftarrow Z_{i-1} \cup \{v\}$. When node $v$ receives the response from $s$, it selects as a parent the node $u$ from $Z_{i-1} \cup \{s\}$ for which $u \rightsquigarrow v$ is of minimum cost. It then sends a message asking $u$ to be its parent. Node $u$ updates its multicast routing table, by adding the multicast link $u \rightsquigarrow v$. Consequently, when $u$ receives later a message for $G$, it will send one copy to $v$ over the unicast route $u \rightsquigarrow v$. When a node $v$ wants to leave $G$, it sends a remove request to $s$. It attaches to this request a list of identities of its children in the current tree. Node $s$ generates an updated list $Z_i$ of the multicast group, by removing $v$ from $Z_{i-1}$. Then, for every child $u$ of $v$ in the existing tree, $s$ determines the list $Z_i(u)$ of nodes that had joined $G$ before $u$ and have not left it yet. A response message is then sent back to $v$, containing a different list for every child of $v$. Node $v$ then sends a message to every child $u$, asking $u$ to find a new parent from the list $Z_i(u)$provided by $s$. The multicast link from $v$ to $u$ can be removed either when $v$ asks $u$ to find a new parent, or after $u$ notifies $v$ that it has a connection to the tree through a new parent. In either case some of the packets sent by $s$ might not be received by $u$ due to the change.

In the following we discuss some of the properties of this protocol. The most important property is that the protocol can handle many multicast trees that dynamically change, because it requires that a minimum number of nodes will participate in the multicast rout-

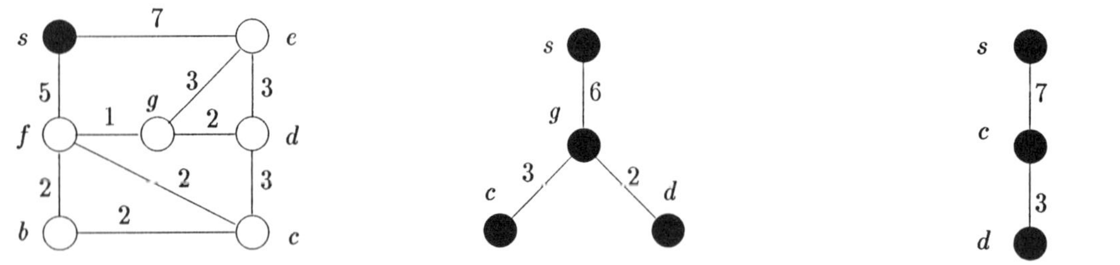


(a) the network graph (b)$g$, $c$ and $d$ are added (c) $g$ is deleted

Figure 2: R-DGA Execution Example

ing over each tree and in maintaining and updating each tree. This is achieved in three steps. Firstly, in order to avoid keeping at every network node routing and maintenance information associated with every active group (as in MBONE), the multicast trees are set up and updated dynamically, according to the exact structure of the destination group. This removes from the picture those network nodes that do not sit on the tree data path. Secondly, the concept of multicast over unicast paths (tunneling) is employed in order to avoid routing burden from nodes sitting on the data path a tree. Finally, only the nodes directly related to the multicast tree, namely the source and the destinations, are located in the end points of the multicast links. This eliminates the routing and maintenance burden from all the other nodes in the tree. The result of these three steps is that only those nodes directly related to each multicast tree will have to encounter the burden associated with routing over the tree, maintaining the tree, and updating the tree following changes in the destination group or in the underlying unicast routing.

Another important property of the protocol is that the established trees are efficient. In a first glance it seems that due to the restriction to have only nodes from $\{s\} \cup Z$ in the junctions of the tree, the trees would be of a high cost. This hypothesis can be supported by the example in Figure 2 as discussed before. However, the next section shows that despite of the restriction, the worst case performance ratio of R-DGA is the same as of DGA. It also shows that the differences in the actual cost of the trees established by R-DGA and the trees established by DGA are minor, and in many cases do not exist at all.

A third property of the protocol is its *fast* response to changes in the destination group. When a new node is added, a new multicast link is created without affecting the rest of the tree. When a node is removed, then unlike other algorithms that try to minimize the *number* of re-arrangements [4, 13, 14], R-DGA minimizes the rearrangement *time*. All the affected nodes, whose parent has left the group, join the new tree independently of each other. Consequently, the time needed to re-arrange the tree following a remove request is roughly equal to the time needed to address a single add request. As for the *number* of rearrangements, while it may be as high as $|Z| - 1$ for extreme cases, it is less than 1 on the average case. This is because the average degree of a node in a tree is less than 2, and therefore the average number of children of a node in the multicast tree is less than 1.

Finally, the protocol is not affected by unicast routing changes, except in those rare cases where the connectivity between end points of a multicast link is broken. If the unicast route between the end points of a multicast link changes, the tree might be less or more efficient, and the changes will be taken into consideration when subsequent add/remove requests are accommodated. However, since the protocol does not consider the intermediate nodes of a multicast link as part of the tree, the unicast routing changes will be transparent to the tree. If a multicast link $u \rightsquigarrow v$ is broken due to loss of connectivity, node $v$ will access the source $s$ and will be treated as a node whose parent has left the tree.

## 4 The Performance of R-DGA

In this section the performance of R-DGA is compared to the performance of DGA. We first compare the worst case performance of both algorithms, and then present simulation results for the average case. As stated in Section 2, when the request sequence consists of only add requests, DGA has a worst-case performance ratio (competitiveness) of $\lceil log(|Z_i|) \rceil$, where $i$ is the number of add requests and $|Z_i|$ is the number of nodes in the destination group after these requests are handled. If both add and remove requests are allowed, no upper bound on the worst-case performance ratio exists. Both claims are proven in [13].

In [1] we prove that any bound that applies to the performance of DGA on every sequence of only add requests applies to R-DGA as well. Moreover, such a bound applies to R-DGA even if the sequence also contains remove requests. Recall that since we employ the unicast routing as the underlying layer of the multicast routing, R-DGA can use only the shortest path between two nodes, regardless of its cost. In order to compare the performance of these algorithms we shall assume throughout this section that the cost function is proportional to the delay function. This implies that the shortest path between two nodes is also the cheapest path. A private case of this assumption would be to consider equal delay and cost functions. We show in [1] that under these assumptions the following theorem holds:

**Theorem 1** *Consider an execution of R-DGA on a sequence $\alpha$ of $i$ add/remove requests. Let $Z_i$ be the set of nodes in the multicast group following this sequence. Let R-DGA($\alpha$) the cost of the tree created by R-DGA and let OPT be the optimal tree spanning $Z_i$. Then,*

$$\frac{\text{R-DGA}(\alpha)}{\text{OPT}} \leq \lceil \log(|Z_i|) \rceil$$

The proof of this theorem appears in the full paper [1]. It is interesting to note that though R-DGA can be viewed as a restricted version of DGA, applying to DGA the R-DGA approach for handling remove requests would not retain the logarithmic bound. An example is given in [1].

So far we have shown that the worst case performance of R-DGA is at least as good as of DGA. In order to compare the average performance we have tested DGA, R-DGA, and a third algorithm referred to as improved-R-DGA on 100 randomly generated networks. Improved-R-DGA allows a wider selection for a node $v$ whose parent is deleted from the tree. Instead of sending $v$ a list of the nodes that have joined the group in the last time before $v$ and have not left since then, the source sends $v$ (via $v$'s old parent) the entire list of nodes in the tree except those in the subtree of $v$. Recall that the average number of sons of a deleted node is less than 1, but if a deleted node has several sons, $N$ say, then in order to avoid the creation of cycles, the root arranges the sons in some arbitrary order $v_1, v_2, \cdots v_N$ and allows $v_i$ to connect to any node in the tree except those in the subtree of $v_j$ for every $i < j \leq N$. Note that implementing the improved-R-DGA would require the source to know the exact structure of its tree; namely the identity of the parent of every destination node. R-DGA, in contrast, needs to know only the order according which the destination nodes have joined the tree. This new requirement of the improved-R-DGA leads to a small modification of the multicast protocol presented in Section 3 as follows. A node $v$ that selects a parent, either because $v$ has just joined the multicast group or because its previous parent has left the tree, needs to inform $s$ about its new parent.

The simulated networks were created as in [6]. One hundred nodes were randomly distributed on a $[0 \cdots 400][0 \cdots 400]$ grid. An edge was then added between every pair of nodes $u$ and $v$ with probability $\beta \cdot \exp(-\frac{d_{u,v}}{576\alpha})$, where $d_{u,v}$ is the Euclidean distance between $u$ and $v$. The values selected for $\alpha$ and $\beta$ are 0.1 and 0.4 respectively. The network was then made connected by randomly selecting nodes from distinct components of the graph and connecting them with an edge. The cost and length of each edge are set to the Euclidean distance between the edge nodes.

The add/remove sequence of requests was created by adding a non-member node with probability $P_{in}$ and removing a member node with probability $P_{out}$. These values determine the average density of the multicast group. We tried densities ranging from 5% to 95% (a density of p% means an average of p% of the network nodes were members of the multicast group at any given time). The created trees were tested after sequences of 500 requests.

The metrics used for comparison is the competitiveness of each heuristic. Since calculating the optimal tree is NP-complete, we considered the cost of the tree generated by the static MST heuristic (see Section 2) as the optimal tree. Thus for all the following simulations we define competitiveness of an algorithm $A$ as the ratio between the cost of the tree constructed by $A$ and the tree constructed by the MST heuristic[4].

The simulation results are depicted in Figure 3. The graph reflects 2400 executions on different networks and different group sizes. For each group size, the average performance of 25 executions is presented. The results show the extra cost R-DGA pays due to the restriction of connecting new nodes only to nodes in the group or to the source is more than desirable. For instance, when the density of the multicast group is larger than 30%, the competitiveness of R-DGA gets larger than 1.3, while DGA's competitiveness drops below 1.2. This is because the penalty for putting only group members in the junctions of the multicast trees becomes heavier as the group gets more dense. The improved-R-DGA yields much better results, which are similar to those gained by DGA. When the density of the multicast group is smaller than 20%, the results of the improved-R-DGA become distinctly better than those of DGA, whereas for larger groups it retains a reasonable competitiveness.

In order to view the advantage of R-DGA, we've considered the number of nodes in the multicast tree that are *not* members of the multicast group, under DGA and SPATH. The simulation results were that for almost all sizes of multicast groups, the multicast tree created by SPATH or DGA contains 10 to 25 network nodes which are not members of the group. All these nodes have to maintain and update state information in any case, and routing information in the case where the concept of tunneling is not employed, regarding multicast trees for which they serve as intermediate nodes only. Of course when the network size increases these numbers increase as well. For instance, for a 500-node network an average tree with 40-60 destination nodes has about 60-70 non-destination nodes. Graphs depicting the full results can be found in [1].

It follows from these results that R-DGA is most effective when the destination group consists of no more than 10-30% of the total network nodes. In such a case the cost of the improved-R-DGA algorithm is *smaller* than the cost of DGA, and the number of nodes that need to encounter routing and maintenance burden is reduced by 50%.

[4] Recall that the MST heuristic has a worst case performance of two times the optimum [5]. However, simulations show [19] that its actual performance is only 5% worst than the optimum.

burden from all the nodes in the tree that are not in $\{s\} \cup Z$, while imposing a tight upper bound on the delays, without increasing the cost of the tree at all. Relaxing the delay constraint makes C-R-DGA's performance become closer to that of R-DGA. This shows that C-R-DGA can tradeoff the cost of the tree and the maximum delay.

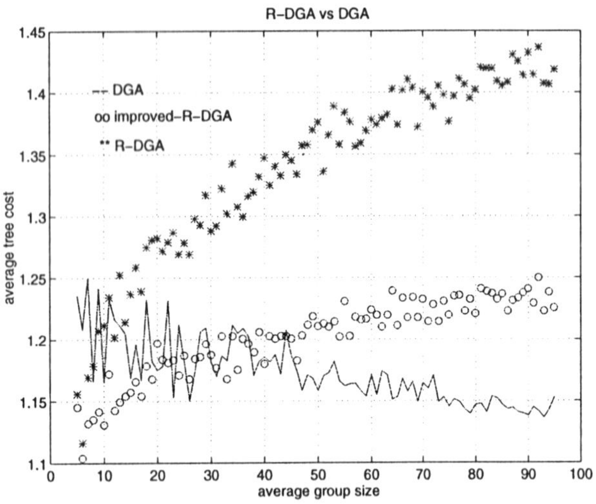


Figure 3: Average Cost of R-DGA vs. DGA

# 5 Delay Constrained Multicast Trees

In the previous section we considered only the cost of the multicast tree, and ignored the distance between the source and each destination node. However, for many future multicast applications it will be desirable to bound the latency between the source and each member of the destination group [15].

To address this problem we have created a version of R-DGA, referred to as C-R-DGA (constraint R-DGA). Like R-DGA, C-R-DGA aims at finding a low cost tree rooted at $s$ and spanning the destination group $Z$ such that only nodes from $\{s\} \cup Z$ are located in the tree forks. In addition, C-R-DGA ensures that the the path from $s$ to any member of the multicast group is not longer than some threshold $\Delta$. C-R-DGA is similar to R-DGA, except that whenever a node selects a parent node, it is careful not to select a parent too distant from the source.

The full description of C-R-DGA, proofs for the claims presented in this section and the simulation results can be found in [1].

The worst case performance of C-R-DGA is $|Z|$ which is optimal for a non-rearrangeable algorithm that guarantees a bound on the latency between the source and each member of the destination group. The average performance depends upon the delay constraint. When it is tight, the performance of C-R-DGA is almost identical to the shortest path algorithm. This result means that we can apply the restriction that removes the routing and maintenance

# 6 Restricted Multicast Capability

In this section we consider a different model of the network, where only part of the nodes have multicast capability and may therefore participate in the creation and maintenance of the multicast tree. These nodes will be referred to as *multicast capable* nodes. A non-multicast capable node $v$ wishing to join the multicast group must connect to a multicast capable node via a multicast link, and the selected multicast capable node must connect to the source. The multicast capable node through which node $v$ is connected to the source will be referred to as $v$'s multicast hub. A multicast tree in this model consists of two parts. The first part is the *core tree* connecting the multicast capable nodes by means of multicast links. The second part consists of the multicast links from each group member and the source node to their multicast hubs. Note that such a multicast link can be an empty path if a group member is a multicast capable node. The cost of the multicast tree is the sum of the costs of the two parts.

Let $G(V, E)$ be the network graph, $M \subseteq V$ the group of multicast capable nodes, $s$ the multicast source and $Z = \{v_1, ..., v_n\} \subseteq V$ the destination group. Also, let $Z'$ denote the set of multicast hubs chosen by the nodes of $Z \bigcup \{s\}$. Note that if $Z'$ is given, the problem of finding the core tree is identical to finding the steiner tree spanning $Z'$ in $G'(M, E')$ where $E'$ connects every two nodes of $M$ and the cost of an edge $(u, v) \in E'$ is the distance between $u$ and $v$ in $G$.

This suggests a method to adapt a multicast protocol to this model as follows. Each node $v$ will choose the closest multicast capable node $v'$ as its multicast hub and will establish the multicast link $v' \rightsquigarrow v$. The multicast hubs will use the original multicast protocol to establish the core tree. The original protocol will run on the virtual network $G'(M, E')$, where each edge is a unicast path in the real network.

In [1] we analyze the worst case performance of protocols adapted this way, and prove the following theorem:

**Theorem 2** *Assume a multicast protocol MP has a worst case performance ratio bounded by $\mathcal{F}(|Z|)$. Then the adapted version for networks with restricted multicast capability has a worst case performance bounded by $2\mathcal{F}(|Z|) + 1$.*

For example, adapting the minimum spanning tree heuristic [5], whose worst case performance ratio is 2, would yield a static algorithm whose worst case performance ratio is 5. Adapting R-DGA would yield a fast dynamic protocol whose worst case performance ratio is $2 \log |Z| + 1$, since from Theorem 1 follows that R-DGA has a worst case performance ratio of $\log |Z|$.

# 7 Conclusions

The paper has presented an approach for solving the scalability problem of routing over, updating, and maintaining a great number of multicast trees in a datagram network. According to the presented approach only the nodes directly related to a multicast tree, namely the source node and destination group nodes, need to keep information related to the tree routing and maintenance. This is achieved by viewing a multicast tree as a collection of multicast paths, and imposing a restriction where only the source node and destination nodes can be located in the tree junctions, as end points of multicast links. Based on this restriction two algorithms were presented: R-DGA and C-R-DGA. R-DGA aims at establishing a low cost tree, whereas C-R-DGA aims at establishing such a tree while imposing a constraint on the distance from $s$ to every node in the destination group. The paper has shown that both algorithms can be efficiently implemented by a multicast protocol that can guarantee fast response to changes in the destination group. The paper has also shown that despite of the restriction imposed by the proposed approach, both R-DGA and C-R-DGA yield a good performance. The worst case performance of C-R-DGA is the best any non-rearrangeable algorithm may yield, whereas the worst case performance of R-DGA is within two times the best any non-rearrangeable algorithm may yield. In terms of their average performance, both algorithms perform as well as (and in many cases even better than) other known and applicable algorithms that do not impose the restriction and therefore require all the nodes along the data path of a tree to participate in the routing over the tree or in the maintenance of the tree. Finally, the paper has shown a general method to adapt any multicast protocol to a network where only some of the nodes have multicast capability. This method roughly doubles the worst case performance of the original protocol while maintaining its other properties.

# References


[1] E. Aharoni and R. Cohen. "Restricted Dynamic Steiner Trees for Scalable Multicast in Datagram Networks," Technical Report LPCR 9606, Technion, Dept. of Computer Science.

[2] T. Ballardie, P. Francis, and J. Crowcroft. Core based trees (CBT). In *SIGCOMM*, 1993.

[3] F. Bauer and A. Varma. Distributed algorithms for multicast path setup in data networks. In *GLOBECOM*, November 1995.

[4] F. Bauer and A. Varma. ARIES: a rearrangeable inexpensive edge-based on-line steiner algorithm. In *INFOCOM*, March 1996.

[5] K. Bharath-Kumar and J. Jaffe. Routing to multiple destinations in computer networks. *IEEE Transactions on Communications*, 31:343–351, March 1983.

[6] R. Bryant. Graph-based algorithms for boolean function manipulation. *IEEE Transactions on Communications*, 34(8):677–691, May 1986.

[7] Y. Dalal and R. Metcalfe. Reverse path forwarding of broadcast packets. *Communications of the ACM*, 21(12):1040–1048, 1978.

[8] S. Deering, D. Estrin, D. Farinacci, V. Jacobson, C. Liu, and L. Wei. Protocol independent multicast (PIM): Motivation and architecture. Internet draft, January 1995.

[9] S. Deering, C. Partridge, and D. Waitzman. Distance vector multicast routing protocol. RFC-1075, November 1988.

[10] H. Eriksson. MBone: The Multicast Backbone. *Communications of the ACM*, Vol. 37, No. 8, Aug. 1994.

[11] M. Garey and D. Johnson. *Computers and Intractability.* W.H. Freeman and Company, 1979.

[12] E. Gilbert and H. Pollak. Steiner minimal tree. *SIAM J. Appl. Math.*, 16, 1968.

[13] M. Imase and B. Waxman. Dynamic Steiner tree algorithm. *SIAM J. Disc. Math.*, 4(3), August 1991.

[14] J. Kadirire. Comparison of dynamic multicast routing algorithms for wide-area packet switched networks. In *INFOCOM*, April 1995.

[15] V. Kompella, J. Pasquale, and G. Polyzos. Multicast routing for multimedia communication. *IEEE Transactions on Networking*, 1(3), June 1993.

[16] J. Moy. Multicast routing extensions for OSPF. *Communications of the ACM*, Vol. 37, No. 8, Aug. 1994.

[17] W. Simpson. IP in IP tunneling. RFC-1853, October 1995.

[18] H. Takahashi and A. Matsuyama. An approximate solution for the Steiner problem in graphs. *Math. Japonica*, 24:573–577, 1980.

[19] B. Waxman. Routing of multipoint connections. *IEEE Journal on Selected Areas in Communications*, 6(9):1617–1622, 1988.

[20] P. Winter. Steiner problem in networks: A survey. *NETWORKS*, 17:129–167, 1987.

# The Ordered Core Based Tree Protocol

Clay Shields J. J. Garcia-Luna-Aceves
{clay, jj}@cse.ucsc.edu
Department of Computer Engineering
University of California—Santa Cruz
Santa Cruz, CA 95064

## Abstract

*This paper presents a new protocol, the Ordered Core Based Tree (OCBT) protocol, which remedies several shortcomings of the Core Based Tree (CBT) multicast protocol. We show that the CBT protocol can form loops during periods of routing instability, and that it can consistently fail to build a connected multicast tree, even when the underlying routing is stable. The OCBT protocol provably eliminates these deficiencies and reduces the latency of tree repair following a link or core failure. OCBT also improves scalability by allowing flexible placement of the cores that serve as points of connection to a multicast tree. Simulation results show that the amount of control traffic in OCBT is comparable to that in CBT.*

## 1 Introduction

Multicast routing protocols build routing trees for the dissemination of messages to a select group of other stations. In some protocols, such as the Distance Vector Multicast Routing Protocol (DVMRP) [1] and the Protocol Independent Multicast-Dense Mode (PIM-DM) protocol [2] the receiving group is assumed to be fairly dense and the sender initiates the multicast assuming all routers in the network are interested in receiving the multicast. If any receiver does not wish to receive the multicast, it must take explicit action and send a message called a *prune* to remove itself from the tree. These types of protocols are termed *sender initiated* as the receivers are not required to take any action to receive the multicast. In each of these protocols the routing tree is formed along the shortest path between each sender and receiver. The overhead at a router $O(n \cdot s)$, where $n$ is the number of multicast groups and $s$ is the number of sources in the group.

In both the Core Based Tree (CBT) multicast protocol [3] and in the Protocol Independent Multicast-Sparse Mode (PIM-SM) protocol [4] [5], a single *shared tree* is created for all sender and receivers in the group, and receivers initiate their own connection to the tree. In each of these *receiver initiated* protocols a well known router exists that accepts connection requests from other routers. This router is known as the *rendezvous point* in PIM; in CBT it is called a *core*. The returning acknowledgment builds a branch of the tree back to the initiator along the reverse path of the connection request. Instead of forwarding each packet on a per-group per-source basis, each data packet is instead forwarded over every on-tree link for that group except the one on which it was received. Accordingly, the router does not have to maintain information about each source for each group and has instead a single entry for each group. The router overhead is therefore $O(n)$, giving the shared tree approach superior scalability. However, because each packet no longer travels over its shortest path to each receiver, shared trees incur longer average delay in the delivery of a data packet.

This work was supported in part by the Office of Naval Research (ONR) under Grant No. N00014-94-1-0688 and by the Defense Advanced Research Projects Agency (DARPA) under Grant No. F19628-96-C-0038.

During times of underlying unicast instability CBT can form loops. Loops in a shared multicast tree are disastrous. When a data packet enters a loop, it circulates the loop endlessly until its time-to-live expires; as a circulating data packet passes through a router that has an off-loop branch, the packet gets forwarded down that branch. This leads to multiple transmissions of each packet in the loop to the rest of the tree. As more traffic finds its way into the loop this situation gets worse, as more and more off-loop transmissions occur. Eventually, the loop can start forwarding so many packets to the rest of the tree that all links on the tree become saturated. We present a new protocol for the construction of shared multicast trees that eliminates this looping problem and other problems that can keep a multicast tree from forming in CBT. We call this protocol the Ordered Core Based Tree protocol.

The next section describes the ways in which CBT can fail. Section 3 describes and specifies the OCBT protocol. Section 4 provides an example of how OCBT handles link failures and is followed in Section 5 with simulation results showing the performance of OCBT and CBT, based on the CBT specifications of April 1996 [6]. We discuss some aspects of core placement in Section 6 before presenting our conclusions.

## 2 Looping in CBT

CBT [3] [7] [8] [6] forms a *backbone* within a connected group of nodes called cores. The backbone is formed by selecting one router, called the *primary core*, to serve as a connection point for the other cores, called *secondary cores*. Secondary cores remain disconnected from the primary core until they are required to join the multicast group. A router wishing to participate in the multicast session sends a *join-request* towards the closest core. This request travels hop-by-hop on the shortest path to the core, forcing other off-tree nodes to join the branch that the router is forming. When the join-request reaches a core or an on-tree node, a *join-acknowledgment* is sent back along the reverse path, forming a new branch from the tree to the requesting router. If the core that is reached is a secondary core and is off-tree, it connects to a primary core using the same process. Once the tree is constructed, data packets flow from any source to its parent and children. Each parent node forwards the packet to all children other than the sender and to its parent until the data packet reaches the backbone. Each packet is then sent along the backbone and down all other branches, ensuring that all group members receive it.

In the event of a link or node failure, the child node that detects the failure follows a particular strategy in order to reconnect to the tree. If that node's next hop to the nearest core is through one of its immediate children, it sends a message, called a *flush message*, to its children. The flush message travels down the tree, forwarded from parent to child, removing the connection between the parent and child. This message tears down the tree to the individual receivers, which then attempt to reconnect along their best path to a core. If


0-8186-7780-5/97 $10.00 © 1997 IEEE

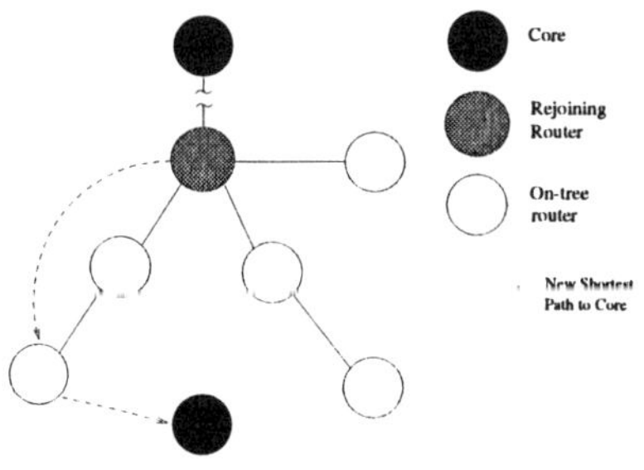


Figure 1: Looping in a disconnected subtree

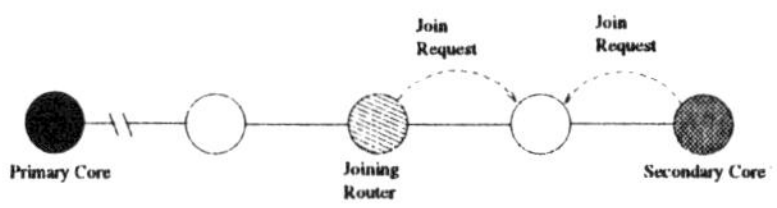


Figure 2: Deadlock or loop formation in tree formation

the next hop to the core is not through a child, the detecting node attempts to reconnect itself by sending a rejoin-request towards the nearest core and does not send the flush message to its children. When the request reaches an on-tree node, that node returns a join acknowledgment that rebuilds the branch down to the sending node. It also sends the rejoin-request to its parent for forwarding to the primary core. The forwarding of the rejoin-request back up the constructed tree is a mechanism used to detect loops that may have formed. If a node receives a rejoin-request that it originated, then a loop has formed. The node detecting the loop removes the link to its parent by sending a message called a *quit-request* and again attempts to rejoin. Otherwise, if the rejoin-request is received at the primary core, that core sends a unicast acknowledgment to the originator of the rejoin request to verify the absence of a loop. This unicast message is needed because if a loop had formed and the rejoin-request was lost before it was returned to the originator, then the loop would not have been detected. However, if the originator never receives the ack, it can assume that a loop has formed, quit from its parent by sending a quit message, and attempt to rejoin again.

Surprisingly, there have been no prior attempts to show that CBT is correct, that is, that CBT creates multicast trees in finite time and that it does not form loops. In fact, CBT does not always form a tree. Part of the tree can remain disconnected when a router seeks to rejoin the multicast tree in response to a failure in the link to its parent. The router detecting the link failure attempts to maintain the sub-tree below it while rejoining the rest of the tree by sending a rejoin-request towards the core. If the path to the core is through an immediate child, the sub-tree is destroyed by transmission of a flush message. Otherwise, the rejoining router sends a rejoin-request towards the core. If this request reaches a descendent in the sub-tree, it is acknowledged and a link forms between the descendent and the rejoining router, completing a loop. Figure 2 shows the topography of a CBT sub-tree subject to this transient looping. The grey node is attempting to rejoin along a newly formed shortest path to the next reachable core. Because its path passes through a descendent child, a loop is formed. This type of loop can occur even when the underlying routing algorithm, which a CBT node uses to determine the path to the core, does not contain loops and is said to be *stable*.

As a loop detection mechanism, the descendent node forwards the rejoin request to its parent, and this message is passed up tree until it reaches the originating router, at which point the loop is detected and action taken to correct it. According to the CBT protocol specification of April 1996 [6], the rejoining router simply sends a quit request to its parent to remove the loop. This correction mechanism can fail, however, as the rejoining router takes no action to destroy its sub-tree and instead attempts to rejoin again, possibly along the same path forming the same loop. Each time the router reconnects along the same path, the same loop forms. This continual looping denies multicast service to the disconnected sub-tree, but it can be stopped if upon detecting a loop, the rejoining router is allowed to flush the tree by forwarding a flush message to all of its children, after which each receiver or sender on the sub-tree connects directly to the core along the shortest path.

If the rejoining router is a secondary core that must reconnect to the primary core, then flushing the tree does not always solve the looping problem. In this case, flushing the tree can initiate a race condition in which local routers attempt to join the secondary core as it attempts to join the primary core. Upon receiving a flush message, routers with members of their subnets desiring the multicast immediately send a join-request on a hop-by-hop basis towards the closest core. That could be a secondary core which is trying to connect to the primary core. If a router that lies on the path to the primary core has attempted to join the secondary core, then it is possible that by the time the join request from the secondary core, which is destined for the primary core, reaches the router, the router will be awaiting an acknowledgment to its own join-request. In this join-pending state the router will accept the local core's request, as illustrated in Figure 2. This will lead to a temporary deadlock, until the appropriate timeouts occur. If these timeouts occur close together and there is no mechanism for selecting an alternate primary core, or if the receiver group near the disconnected secondary core is dense so that each path to the primary core is blocked, this race condition can occur many times, leading to a long latency in reconnecting the sub-tree, if the sub-tree is able to connect at all. A solution to this would be to force routers receiving a flush message to back off for some period of time before attempting to rejoin. While this would prevent the routers from winning the race, it would also lead to long latency times for routers attempting to rejoin the multicast tree.

The same situation that prevents proper reconstruction of the tree following a link failure can also prevent initial construction of the tree, and it can form a loop in a disconnected sub-tree. If a secondary core receives a join-request from a router that lies on the path from the secondary core to the primary core, the secondary core will be unable to form a link to the primary core as all join-requests the secondary core sends will be stopped at the first hop towards the joining router. In Figure 2, this occurs at the white colored router between the joining router and secondary core. In this case the race is always won by the joining router, as it has a head start in sending its join request. As the secondary core sends a join-acknowledgment to the router before attempting to connect to the primary core, the nodes on the path back to the joining router will consider themselves to be on-tree and will acknowledge the secondary core's join-request if the acknowledgment arrives before the secondary core's join-request. A loop, which is undetected by CBT, will then be formed between the router which is the first hop to the joining router and the secondary core. Notice that this loop does not form when secondary core is attempting to reconnect; in the case in which reconnection is occurring the forwarding of the rejoin-request back to the secondary router removes the loop, though the

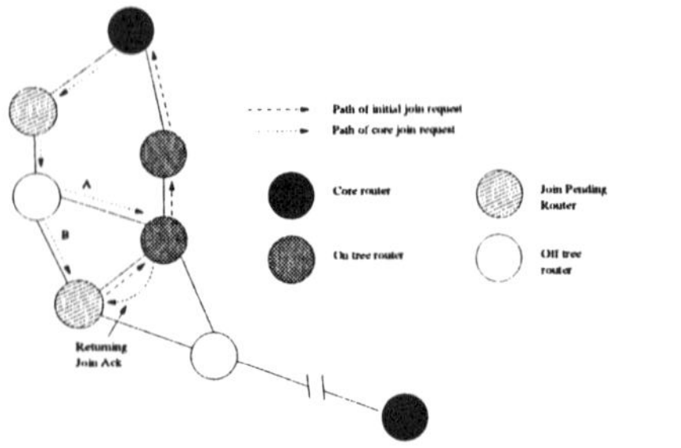


Figure 3: Undetected loop during tree construction

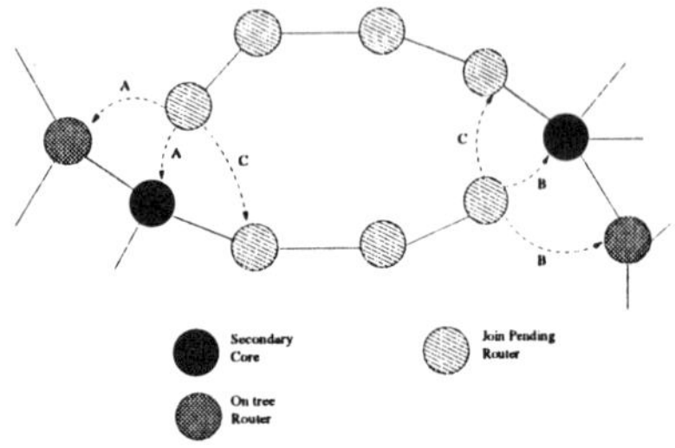


Figure 4: Permanent loops in the core backbone

secondary core will still be unable to connect to the primary core. If the secondary cores do not send a join acknowledgment before sending a join-request, then deadlock can occur as described above.

If the network is unstable during construction, the secondary core's attempt to join the multicast tree can again lead to undetected loops in the disconnected sub-tree. Assume that a router sends a join-request to a secondary core, which is currently off-tree. When the join-request reaches the core, the core acknowledges it and attempts to join the primary core by sending a join-request of its own. If this request travels a different path due to unicast routing instability and traverses a branch of its sub-tree, the join-request will be accepted and acked as shown in Figure 3. The transmission of the ack will occur immediately if the receiving node is on the branch, indicated by path A, or as soon as the ack traveling from the core reaches that point on the branch, indicated by path B. This ack will travel back to the core and form a loop that will not be detected; traffic will circulate within the loop endlessly, dumping repeat copies of data packets down each other off-loop branch as it goes by. Again, this type of loop can only be formed during the initial build of the tree; if the core is attempting to reconnect and uses a rejoin-request instead of a join-request, the loop detection mechanism will detect the loop when the rejoin is forwarded to the core.

There is one similar undetected loop that can form when the tree is constructed during times of network instability or when secondary cores are attempting to contact different primary cores. In this situation it is possible that the primary core is thought to be unreachable by part of the secondary core group without that information having been disseminated through the rest of the group. This inconsistency can occur, due to the mechanism causing deadlock described above, if some secondary core has been unable to reach the primary core because its children blocked the connection and it is now attempting to reach an alternate primary core. If the branches being formed by two secondary cores cross, either due to differences in the destination of the join-request or because of looping in the unicast routing, a loop can be formed. If the loop is formed during the initial construction of the tree, it will be undetected and will not be removed.

If two secondary cores are attempting to form the backbone and their branches meet in a way that forms a loop, one of two things will happen. In the best case, join-pending nodes on each branch receive the request of the other. This is illustrated in Figure 4, where each join-pending node chooses the hop labeled C. No loop will be formed as no acks will be sent; instead, each branch will wait for an ack until they time out.

In the second case, one or both of the forming branches will meet the other at a core or an on-tree node that is a descendent of the core. The core or on-tree router that receives the request will acknowledge it. The ack will travel back along the reverse path forming the branch, possibly getting forwarded back down the other branch that was forming as well. In this case, a loop has been formed in the backbone that will not be detected. Any traffic entering the loop will circle it endlessly, and each time it reaches a router with an interface leading out of the loop, and additional copy will travel down the tree to all receivers. Additional traffic flowing into the loop only serves to exacerbate the situation, resulting in a denial of service as the tree is flooded with the same packets repeatedly. Figure 4 shows how the loop will form if either of any of the next hop choices labeled A or B are taken.

## 3 The OCBT Protocol

CBT builds a multicast tree from a single level of secondary cores which join at a single primary core. Looping and disconnected sub-trees occur in CBT because the protocol does not enforce any ordering in the way in which nodes and cores attempt to join the tree. In contrast, OCBT maintains a *logical level* for each node and core. The logical level is a label indicating the cores place in the hierarchy of cores. The cores' logical levels are fixed when the core is selected; the nodes levels are not fixed but are assigned when the node joins the tree. Any node or cores level is always less than or equal to the level of its parent; OCBT uses this property to guarantee that no transient or permanent loops ever form in the structure of the tree and that the protocol is safe and live even when routing-table loops occur in the underlying routing protocols. OCBT has been shown to be free of loops at every instant and to be safe and live [9]. OCBT also reduces control traffic following a link failure, allows for flexible core placement, and does this without increasing the complexity of the protocol.

When a router has a member wishing to receive the multicast session, it locates the nearest core and sends a join-request towards that core. Join-requests force any off-tree routers they reach on their path to the core to forward the request and attempt to join the tree. In OCBT, join-requests also carry a field which contains the level a node must have to safely acknowledge the request. Join-requests from an off-tree router carry a level of zero to indicate that any on-tree node or core can safely acknowledge the request. If a node receives a join-request carrying a level higher than its level, it quits from its parent and joins the branch that the join-request is forming. In this way, OCBT forces lower-level branches to break to allow the construction of higher-level branches. This prevents the cases in CBT in which a node or core attempting to rejoin following a link failure is unable to connect to a core because it is blocked by its sub-tree, preventing that sub-tree from joining the main multicast tree.

OCBT limits control messages to within a particular logical level and distributes the processing of control messages over a larger number of cores. When a link fails, flush messages travel down-tree only as far as the next lower level of cores; join-requests need only travel as far as the next higher level of cores. This results in less traffic following a link failure than in CBT, in which flush messages from near a core or rejoin messages originating far from the core have to travel relatively long distances. More recent specifications for CBT [6] have a single primary core that forms a point of connection for secondary cores that stay off-tree until required to join. This single primary core is a limiting factor to the scalability of CBT, as it must receive and respond to all passive join-requests from the entire multicast tree. OCBT has no similar single point of traffic concentration, as cores need only respond to traffic within its logical level.

Other differences between CBT and OCBT include changes in the mechanism by which nodes destroy the connection formed with their parent. OCBT replaces the *quit request* of CBT with a *quit notice*, and in OCBT nodes sending the quit request do not wait for an acknowledgment before leaving the tree. In contrast, under CBT, nodes must wait for an acknowledgment from the parent before leaving the tree. OCBT uses a keep-alive mechanism to detect lost quit-notices and flush messages instead of using explicit acknowledgments. A *parent-assert* message is included in OCBT to insure that consistent state information is maintained between nodes. A parent keeps track of reception of keep-alive packets from its children. In the event that the parent does not receive a keep-alive from a child in a set period of time, it sends a parent assert message to ascertain if the child still is its child; if no reply or a negative reply to a parent assert is received, the child is assumed to have quit. This guarantees eventual consistent information about the state of the link between child and parent, even if messages are lost. Because no node accepts or forwards an on-tree data packet from an off-tree link, no data packets are received twice, even if a quit-notice or flush message is lost.

OCBT is quite similar in complexity to the original CBT. OCBT takes $O(n)$ to create a spanning tree, where $n$ is the number of links in the spanning tree and is dependent on the network, core placement and multicast group members. The load on the routers is only marginally increased. In addition to the state variable required for CBT, each on-tree router in OCBT is additionally required to track its level and to maintain level information for each of its children, as well as a marker as to whether that child has transmitted a keep-alive packet recently.

OCBT's specification is shown in Figure 5. Function names are in **bold**. A call to another function or the name of a particular type of message is capitalized. Parameters that are part of a received message are in *italics*. Names of the variables maintained within the node are plain, lower case.

Each of the cores and routers maintains variables representing the state of the node in regard to OCBT's operation. Each node has an entry for its OCBT state (on-tree or off-tree or join-pending, and core or non-core), level, parent, the core it last attempted to reach, and a list maintaining the list of the node's children and their level. Core nodes also have one additional state variable, which is the logical level of their parent. This entry is used to track the core state in case it is coerced to a higher level; if for some reason it receives a flush message from its parent, it can flush all children of level greater than the original core level and return to that level.

Examination of OCBT's specifications reveals that descriptions of some called functions are missing. In particular, **Next Hop**, **Find Core**, **Subnet Member** and **Send Message** were omitted for brevity, but are explained below.

**Subnet Member** determines whether the router has some member on its local network wishing to receive the multicast; if it does, this function returns true.

**Send Message** transmits a message to the designated recipient that includes the information specified; if the message being sent is a join-request, **Send Message** also starts the timeout timer. Receipt of an appropriate acknowledgment cancels the timer.

**Next Hop** examines the unicast routing table and returns the neighbor node on the next hop to take towards a given destination.

**Find Core** returns the nearest core of a specified level; if level 0 is specified, it returns the closest core of any level. **Find Core** was omitted as the actual OCBT code depends on the means used to distribute core information. If some means of scoping is desired, **Find Core** may not return the closest core, but instead one that lies within the scoped area. **Find Core** changes the node variable `core`; each time **Find Core** is called, `core` is updated to whatever it returns. In addition to locating cores, **Find Core** also detects partitions in the network when higher-level cores are unreachable and instigates a partition-recovery mechanism. In order to do this, it maintains a list of cores that have been contacted but failed to respond; this list is cleared when the node is joining and receives an ack.

## 4 Tree Maintenance in OCBT

OCBT builds a distribution tree in which each member has a logical level equal to or less than its parent. The logical level changes only at a core or a *graft*. Grafts occur where a lower-level branch is broken to make way for a higher level branch to form, and the lower level branch is maintained below the break. Figure 6 shows the structure of an OCBT tree. The large nodes are cores and show their levels. The smaller black nodes are on-tree nodes and have the link to their parent labeled with their level. The striped node is a graft node which formed when the $(n+1)$-level branch broke to allow the $(n+2)$-level branch to connect to the $(n+2)$ core.

When a link failure requires recovery of the tree, cores and grafts respond in different manners. A core attempts to reconnect for its children; a graft flushes the tree below it and expects a core or receiver below it to attempt reconnection. Figure 7 illustrates this by showing the state of the tree after a link failure. Following the link failure, the $(n+1)$-level core and the leftmost level-$n$ core would each attempt to reconnect to their higher-level core. If the network remained partitioned and the $(n+2)$-level core was unreachable, the multicast tree would form up to the $(n+1)$-level core, which would then wait until the partition was corrected to rejoin the multicast tree.

## 5 Simulation Results

To examine the performance of CBT and OCBT in a realistic manner, we created a simulation of each protocol using a simulation package* that supports protocol layering. These simulations ran on top of a unicast routing layer that implemented the distributed

*The protocols presented in this paper were simulated using the C++ Protocol Toolkit (CPT) by Rooftop Communications Corp. of Los Altos, CA.

```
Add Child (child,level)
  Add Child to List (child, level)
  Send Message (Join Ack, child, level)

Break Branch (source, message level,
                    core, originator)
  Send Message (Quit-Notice, parent)
  if (state = On-Tree Core) or
  (state = Join-Pending Core)
    parent level = message level
  parent = Next Hop (core)
  if (On Child List (parent))
    Remove Child from List (parent)
  Add Child (source, message level)
  send message (Join-Request, parent,
          message level, core, originator)
  if (state = On-Tree Core)
    state = Join-Pending Core
  else
    state = Join-Pending

Forward Message (type, source)
  for each child
    if (child ! = source)
      Send Message (type, child)
  if (parent ! = source)
    Send Message (type, parent)

Join Tree (level)
  if state = Join-Pending Core
    parent = Next Hop (Find Core(level + 1))
    Send Message (Join-Request, parent,
                    level + 1, core)
  else /* level = 0 */
    parent = Next Hop (Find Core(level))
    Send Message (Join-Request, parent,
                    level, core)
    state = Join-Pending

Multicast Message (type, level)
  for each child on list
    if (level = 0) or (level < child level )
      Send Message (type, child, level)

Quit Tree ()
  parent = null
  if (state = On-Tree Core)
    or (state = Join-Pending Core)
    parent level = core level
    state = off-tree core
  else
    state = off-tree
    level = 0
  halt /* do not return */

Remove Children (level)
  for each child on list
    if (level = 0) or (level < child level )
      Remove Child from List (child)
  if (child list = null)
    and not (Subnet Receiver)
    Quit Tree
  else
    return to calling function

Remove Child (child)
  Remove Child from List (child)
  if (child list = null) and
    not (Subnet Receiver)
    Send Message (Quit-Notice, parent)
    Quit Tree
  else
    return to calling function

Send Data (source, data)
  if (source = parent) or
    (On Child List (source))
      Forward Message (data, source)
    else
      drop the packet and
      do not forward to subnet

Join-Pending or
On-Tree Router (message type, message level,
                    source, core, originator)
  case (message type)
    Join-Request
      if (on child list (source))
        Remove Child from List (source)
        if (message level > level)
          Break Branch (message level,
                        core, originator)
        else
          if (state = On-Tree Router)
            Add Child (level)
          else
            Add Child to List (source)
    Quit-Notice
      if (on child list (source))
        Remove Child (source)
    Flush Message
      if (source = parent)
        Forward Message (Flush Message, source)
        Remove Children (0)
        /* only reached if above function returns */
        level = 0
        Join Tree (level)
    Join Ack
      if (state = Join-Pending Router)
        if (source = parent)
        and (message level >= level)
          level =message level
          Forward Message (Join Ack, level,source)
    Data
      Send Data (data, source)

Off-Tree Router (message type, message level,
                    source, core, originator)
  case (message type)
    Join-Request
      parent = Next Hop (core)
      level = message level
      Send Message (Join-Request, parent,
                    level,core)
      state = Join-Pending

Join-Pending Core or
On-Tree Core (message type, message level,
                    source,core,originator)
  case (message type)
    Join-Request
      if (on child list (source))
      /* previous quit-notice was lost */
        Remove Child from List(source)
      if (message level <= level)
        Add Child (source, level)
      else
        if (message level > parent level)
          Break Branch (message level,
                        core, originator)
        else
          if (On-Tree Core)
            Add Child (source, parent level)
          else
            if (originator = self)
              /*message looped - unicast instability */
              Send Message (Quit-Notice, parent)
              Send Message (Flush Message,source)
              parent level = level + 1
              parent = Next Hop (Find Core(level + 1))
              Send Message (Join-Request, parent,
                            level + 1, core)
            else
              Add Child to List (source, message level)
    Quit-Notice
      if (on child list (source))
        Remove Child (source)
    Flush Message
      if (source = parent)
        Multicast Message (flush message, level)
        Remove Children (level)
        /* only reached if above function returns */
        state = Join-Pending Core
        Join Tree (level)
    Join Ack
      if (Join-Pending Core)
        if (source = parent)
        and (message level > level)
          parent level = message level
          foreach child on list
            if (child level > core level) and
            (child level <= parent level)
              send message (Join Ack, child, parent level)
          state = On-Tree Core
    Data
      if (On Tree Core)
        Send Data (data, source)

Off-Tree Core (message type, message level,
                    source, core, originator)
                    case (message type)
    Join-Request
      if (message level <= level)
        Add Child (source,level)
        parent = Next Hop (Find Core(level + 1))
        parent level = level +1
        Send Message (Join-Request, parent,
                        level + 1, core)
      else
        Add Child to List (source, message level)
        parent = Next Hop (core)
        parent level = message level
        Send Message (Join-Request, parent,
                        message level, core)
      state = Join-Pending Core

On Time Out
  case (state)
    Join-Pending Core
      if (parent level > core level + 1)
        for each child on list
          if (child level > level)
            Remove Child from List (child)
      if (child list ! = null) or (Subnet Member)
        parent = Next Hop (Find Core(level + 1))
        parent level = level + 1
        Send Message (Join-Request, parent,
                        level, core)
      else
        parent = null
        parent level = level
        state = Off-Tree Core

    Join-Pending Router
      for each child on list
        Remove Child from List (child)
      parent = null
      level = 0
      if (Subnet Member)
        Join Tree (0)
      else
        state = Off-Tree Router

On Parent Link Failure
  case (state)
    On-Tree Core or
    Join-Pending Core
      Multicast Message (Flush Message, level)
      for each child
        if (child level > level)
          Remove Child from List (child)
      if (Subnet Member) or (child list ! = null)
        state = Join-Pending Core
        Join Tree (level)
      else
        parent = null
        parent level = level
        state = Off-Tree Core

    On-Tree Router or
    Join-Pending Router
      Forward Message (Flush Message, parent)
      for each child
        Remove Child from List (child)
      level = 0
      if (Subnet Member)
        Join Tree (level)
      else
        parent = null
        state = Off-Tree Router
```

Figure 5: OCBT Protocol Specification

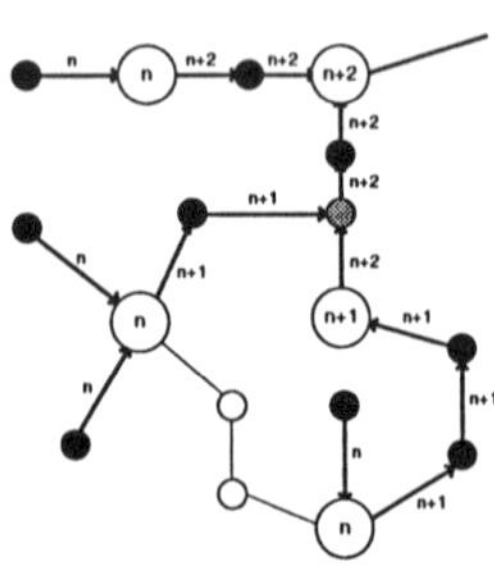


Figure 6: HCBT Tree

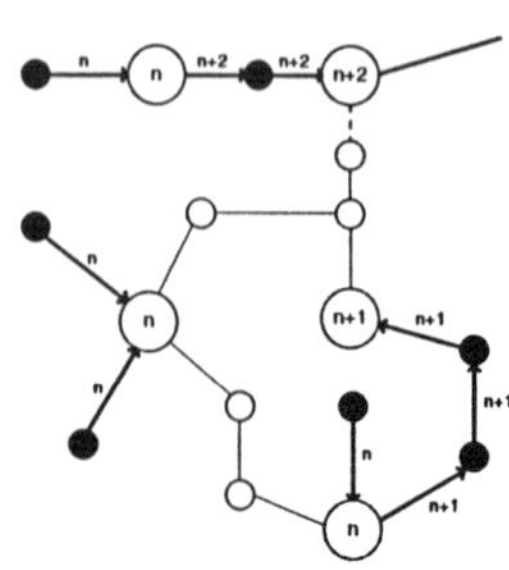


Figure 7: Link Failures

Bellman-Ford algorithm and used routing information from the unicast layer. Using this simulation we measured the end-to-end delay of data packets traversing the tree, the number of messages of each type sent before and after a link failure, and the number of times CBT formed of transient loops requiring explicit action from CBT to remove. In addition, each case in which a CBT sub-tree was un-

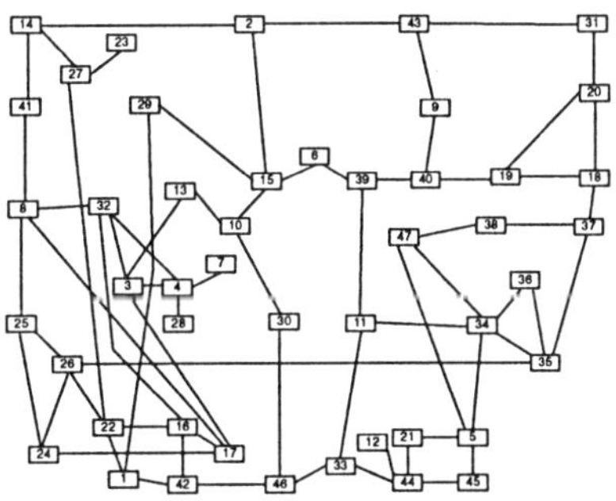

Figure 8: Arpanet Simulation Topography

able to reconnect to the tree, as shown in Figure 2, was recorded. We also recorded the number of times OCBT did not form transient loops when CBT would have.

For our simulations we used the Arpanet topology shown in Figure 8, which contains 47 nodes and 69 edges. We examined the performance of OCBT and CBT under realistic conditions: the links on the network were configured to run at 200 kilobits per second, with a 1 millisecond delay between hops; the unicast routing updates occurred four times as frequently as the CBT and OCBT keep-alive messages. We chose this update period to allow the unicast routing time to disseminate routing information; this was important because one indication of a link failure was a change in the unicast routing table. We selected two receiver groups for the simulation - a dense group consisting of all nodes and a sparse group consisting of 11 widely distributed nodes. The same single source was used with each receiver group.

For each run of the simulation, we chose a particular set of cores using what is probably the same "trivial heuristic" used by Ballardie [3], that is, looking at a picture of the network we picked distributed nodes of relatively high degree to serve as cores. For OCBT, the cores were divided into two logical levels. We constructed the CBT backbone before allowing receivers to connect even though the current protocol specification does not; we did this because of the difficulty CBT has in connecting secondary cores to the primary cores. Building each of the trees for each receiver group, we measured the construction costs in terms of the traffic required. We then sent a stream of data packets from the source to all receivers and recorded the delay each data packet encountered. Finally, we made each link in the network fail individually and measured the number of messages required to reconnect the tree and any loops that were formed.

In our simulation, link failures were detected in two ways. First, failure of a parent or child to respond to a set number of keep-alive messages created the link-down condition. Second, every time a message was sent, the unicast routing was checked to see if the next hop to the destination had changed. Changes in the next hop information reflect a change in the underlying unicast routing that came about as result of a link failure. This allowed the protocol to detect link failures before the set number of keep-alive messages were lost.

The simulations used the 12 different core sets shown in Figure 1, with the results summarized in Table 2. Each run shows the average performance of OCBT and CBT for a sparse and dense receiver group for the selected core set. The delay and the variance of the delay are normalized to the delay and variance of a source based

| Run Number | Level 1 Cores | Level 2 Cores |
|---|---|---|
| 1 | 3 40 34 | 15 33 26 |
| 2 | 32 33 | 40 26 |
| 3 | 40 26 32 33 | 3 40 |
| 4 | 2 10 46 | 8 37 |
| 5 | 33 | 15 |
| 6 | 26 33 | 40 |
| 7 | 40 26 32 33 | 15 |
| 8 | 26 44 18 | 30 |
| 9 | 40 26 32 33 | 2 10 46 |
| 10 | 37 | 2 46 |
| 11 | 14 24 31 45 | 15 30 |
| 12 | 17 44 31 | 34 32 |

Table 1: Cores used in simulation

| Run # | Build Messages | Repair Messages | Average Delay | Delay Variance | Trans. Loops | Disconn. Subtrees | Loops Prevented |
|---|---|---|---|---|---|---|---|
| 1 | | | | | | | |
| OCBT | 71 | 4.4 | 1.5 | 2.5 | - | - | 0 |
| CBT | 70 | 14.2 | 1.5 | 2.7 | 0 | 9 | - |
| 2 | | | | | | | |
| OCBT | 72.5 | 4.2 | 1.4 | 2.0 | - | - | 0 |
| CBT | 68 | 4.4 | 1.4 | 1.9 | 0 | 17 | - |
| 3 | | | | | | | |
| OCBT | 71 | 4.3 | 1.3 | 1.6 | - | - | 0 |
| CBT | 73 | 4.4 | 1.9 | 3.5 | 0 | 19 | - |
| 4 | | | | | | | |
| OCBT | 80 | 5.5 | 1.2 | 1.5 | - | - | 0 |
| CBT | 72 | 4.5 | 1.7 | 3.0 | 0 | 18 | - |
| 5 | | | | | | | |
| OCBT | 72 | 5.2 | 1.3 | 1.6 | - | - | 0 |
| CBT | 70 | 15.3 | 1.2 | 1.6 | 0 | 17 | - |
| 6 | | | | | | | |
| OCBT | 70 | 4.5 | 1.5 | 2.1 | - | - | 0 |
| CBT | 66 | 10.9 | 1.5 | 2.1 | 1 | 18 | - |
| 7 | | | | | | | |
| OCBT | 79.5 | 4.3 | 1.6 | 2.8 | - | - | 0 |
| CBT | 69 | 12 | 1.6 | 2.4 | 1 | 13 | - |
| 8 | | | | | | | |
| OCBT | 80 | 7.4 | 1.4 | 1.8 | - | - | 0 |
| CBT | 69 | 4.1 | 1.4 | 1.8 | 0 | 10 | - |
| 9 | | | | | | | |
| OCBT | 78.5 | 4.5 | 1.6 | 3.0 | - | - | 4 |
| CBT | 73 | 21.4 | 1.2 | 0.5 | 1 | 11 | - |
| 10 | | | | | | | |
| OCBT | 75 | 6.0 | 1.7 | 3.1 | - | - | 2 |
| CBT | 72 | 4.9 | 1.2 | 0.5 | 0 | 23 | - |
| 11 | | | | | | | |
| OCBT | 87.5 | 5.9 | 1.2 | 1.5 | - | - | 2 |
| CBT | 71 | 4.1 | 1.5 | 2.1 | 0 | 20 | - |
| 12 | | | | | | | |
| OCBT | 75 | 4.8 | 1.4 | 1.8 | - | - | 0 |
| CBT | 68 | 3.6 | 1.4 | 1.8 | 0 | 12 | - |
| **Average** | | | | | | | |
| OCBT | 76 | 5.1 | 1.43 | 2.1 | - | - | .67 |
| CBT | 70 | 8.7 | 1.46 | 2.0 | .25 | 15.6 | - |
| Source | 72 | | 1.00 | 1.00 | | | |
| **.95 C.I.** | | | | | | | |
| OCBT | 72.7-79.3 | 4.5-5.7 | 1.3-1.5 | 1.7-2.5 | - | - | 0.0-1.5 |
| CBT | 68.7-71.5 | 4.9-12.4 | 1.3-1.6 | 1.4-2.6 | 0.0-0.5 | 12.8-18.4 | - |

Table 2: OCBT vs. CBT

tree. The source based tree was created using CBT with a single core located at the sender for the same two receiver groups. The delay results were then averaged. The Transient Loops entry for CBT shows the number of transient loops that were able to be corrected. The Disconnected Subtree column shows the number of times a CBT sub-tree was unable to reconnect to the main tree following a link failure. The Loops Prevented entry shows the number of loops caused by instability in the unicast routing that OCBT detected and which would have formed transient loops in CBT.

The results demonstrate that the major advantage of OCBT is its loop freedom and its ability to correctly reconstruct a multicast tree following a link failure. In our simulations, a CBT sub-tree was frequently unable to reconnect to the multicast tree following a link failure as described in section 2. As each set of simulation runs included 138 runs of the CBT protocol, and an average of 15.6 disconnected sub-trees were formed during those runs, we found a disconnection rate of 11.3% under the current protocol specifications [6]. Clearly, a routing protocol that is unable to find a correct path when one exists one time out of nine is hardly suitable for use in a large Internet.

The message count for the CBT protocol was kept artificially low in situations when a sub-tree was unable to reconnect, as our simulation enforced a timeout period for any rejoining node that detected a loop. Had those routers been allowed to attempt to connect as quickly as possible, the total number of messages would have been much higher. In addition, we formed the CBT backbone before the receivers were allowed to join; this also lowered the total message count as it prevented situations in which a secondary core could not connect to the primary core.

On average, OCBT requires some additional work to build the tree, but once it is constructed the traffic required to maintain the tree is reduced. Intuitively, one might expect the OCBT tree to require less traffic to build, as lower-level cores remain in an off-tree state until they receive a join-request. If a particular core never receives a request for the multicast session, it can remain off-tree and no traffic is required to build the tree out to it. However, we found that the OCBT takes slightly more messages to form the multicast tree than that of the version of CBT we tested. This is because many children tried to connect in close succession to lower-level cores that were off-tree. As these lower-level cores sent join acks to the joining nodes before attempting to reach a higher-level core, many links were formed between the core and its new children. The lower-level core was then forced to break some of these existing links to reach the higher-level core. Links formed this way required five messages to form - two for the initial node to core join, two for the link to form from between the lower-level core and the higher-level core, and one quit-notice sent from the child to its former parent as it was coerced to join the higher-level branch that was forming.

OCBT did reliably reform the tree after a link failure with fewer messages than CBT. The branches of the CBT tree can grow fairly long, and messages can be required to traverse the entire length of the branch in the event of a link failure. If the failure is near the bottom of the branch and a rejoin occurs, CBT requires that a passive rejoin be forwarded the length of the branch to the primary core, which then sends a unicast message to the originator acknowledging the passive rejoin-request to ensure that there is no loop formed. As the unicast message does not necessarily traverse the multicast tree on its return to the originator, we did not include it in our message count as it may not contribute to on-tree congestion.

Similarly, if the failure is near the backbone and the branch is flushed, then the flush must travel the length of the branch to the receivers which then send a join-request back to a core, resulting in messages traversing the branch twice. OCBT reduces the traffic requirements in both cases. OCBT does not require that a rejoin-request be forwarded to the highest-level core; instead it only travels as far as the next higher core as required to rejoin the tree. The flush message cannot destroy a branch all the way from the highest-level core down to the receivers as control traffic is limited to a single logical level.

As expected, the multicast trees produced by CBT and OCBT produce more delay in delivering packets than do source-based trees. This can be seen intuitively as the path a packet would take in a core based tree might not be the shortest to each receiver since it must detour to pass through a core. The actual delay from a source to a receiver is dependent on core placement, as no additional delay will be incurred if the core lies on the shortest path. With poor core placement in an OCBT tree, this could be exacerbated as the packet may be routed further off the shortest path to pass through several cores. In our simulation, the delays experienced by data packets in OCBT were on average about 43% greater than the delay experienced by a packet from a source-based tree. Data packets sent over the tree formed by CBT experienced an average delay about 46% greater than the source based tree. Using OCBT, it is possible that this could be reduced by making each source a lower level core. Nearby nodes would then connect directly to the source, while nodes further away would receive the multicast over the shared backbone.

Both CBT and OCBT construct and operate a fixed tree. This has the clear drawback of requiring all data packet transmissions to traverse specific links in the network, regardless of congestion. This can create *hot spots* at cores that must handle an excessive amount of traffic. CBT is more susceptible to hot spots, particularly at the primary core which must receive and reply to each passive rejoin request. Using more cores can alleviate hot spots somewhat, as this spreads the traffic over more cores, though this does not reduce the traffic at CBT's primary core. OCBT is more amenable to use of additional cores, and does not require any single core to answer messages from the entire multicast group. Another partial solution to congestion over fixed links is to allow children to quit from their parents and connect on a shorter path to the core if one becomes available. This in fact was first suggested by Ballardie for CBT [7], but has not yet been included in our simulation. Another improvement to be investigated will be to make each source a local core so that near by nodes can join directly to it, reducing the delay to those nodes.

The slightly increased number of messages required in the construction of the tree is a very small price to pay for OCBT compared to its major advantage: it works correctly. CBT, in contrast, is incorrect and does not always form a complete multicast tree during construction or following a link failure. Permanent, undetected loops can form in CBT that can cause complete saturation of every link on the tree containing the loop. This is clearly an undesirable characteristic of CBT; OCBT suffers from no similar detrimental traits and can be used safely. In addition, in a tree with many link failures, OCBT's reduced repair costs actually makes the amortized cost of construction lower than CBT.

## 6 Core Placement

There are a number of issues concerning the placement of cores in the network and the distribution of information about the core location. Currently, we assume that some mechanism for distributing core information is universally available and that each router can find the address and level of any core. In reality, this is neither desirable nor possible. A leaf router within the United States has little use for information about local cores in other countries, nor does it have the space to maintain what could be large core lists. Instead, some mechanism for leaf nodes to discover local cores and for lower-level cores to become aware of nearby higher-level cores is needed. This could take the form of a multicast group server able to respond with the identities of local cores, similar to the DNS service.

Alternatively, cores could follow a distributed scheme for disseminating their location and level, broadcasting or flooding their identity and location with an increasing time-to-live over each of their interfaces, or they could join a multicast group that existed solely for the purpose of core location dissemination. Cores need only know the addresses of the same level and next higher-level cores, so some method of limiting the core information that gets distributed is desirable. Multicast distribution schemes could also work well in a situation in which the multicast was being limited to a particular *scope*, that is, limiting the area of the network in which the multicast tree forms. Each level of cores in the scoped area could have its own local multicast address. A scheme similar to this was proposed in HPIM [10]. The issue of core information distribution is an area of future work for OCBT and other protocols based on shared trees.

After the cores are identified and a means of determining the location of nearby cores is established, the issue arises of whether or not to build a backbone of cores prior to allowing any leaf nodes or lower level to connect. In OCBT this is not strictly necessary, although it can help prevent some worst case behavior, in which the highest-level cores are forced to break many existing links if other connections are made before the backbone forms. In CBT it is not necessary unless one wants to be certain that secondary cores can join the tree. In OCBT the backbone is formed by choosing one core of the highest-level to be a connection point for all of the other highest-level cores. This core undergoes a temporary promotion to one level higher then the rest of the highest level cores. The other highest-level cores then join the promoted core.

The core placement in OCBT has an important effect on the performance of the protocol in terms of the amount of control traffic generated and the delay imposed on data packet delivery. This is true in CBT and PIM-SM as well. While determining optimal core placement remains an open problem, there have been suggestions made as to methods of migrating cores to provide better service [11] [10]. We believe that core placement can be made a matter of policy rather than optimality if the scope of the multicast is limited at each level. The flexibility of adding additional cores in OCBT supports this approach. Core placement and migration are important issues for our future work.

## 7 Conclusions

We have described an ordered extension to CBT, called OCBT, that increases scalability, reduces repair latency, completely eliminates loops, and is provably correct in forming a multicast tree. By distributing cores throughout the network and by maintaining logical level information, OCBT allows for a flexible multicast group in which the core structure does not have to be fixed in advance. The distribution of cores reduces the amount of repair traffic by limiting the distance over which repair messages have to travel to within the logical level.

OCBT eliminates the loops and disconnected sub-trees that occur in the CBT protocol [9]; our simulation results corroborate our verification work. The cost of OCBT is a slight increase in the initial number of messages required to construct the multicast tree. This is somewhat balanced by a reduction in the amount of traffic required to repair the tree following a link failure, and a guarantee that the tree will reform correctly. The increase in tree construction traffic is a result of the mechanism that breaks lower-level tree branches to allow formation of a higher-level branch; in some cases, this mechanism also adversely affects the number of messages it takes to repair a failure in the tree. On average, however, OCBT reconstructs the tree with less traffic than CBT and does so correctly; in all cases the multicast tree will be formed correctly and will reform correctly following a link or node failure.

The delay induced in end-to-end packet delivery by OCBT is comparable to that of CBT: both increase the average delay by about 50% over the delay of a source-based tree. The actual delay incurred is dependent on the location of the cores. It may be possible to reduce the delay in OCBT trees by making each source a local core. Nearby nodes would then be able to connect directly to the source, minimizing their perceived delay, while more remote receivers would connect via the shared tree.

The relative number of messages and delay induced by CBT and OCBT are hardly indicative of the overall performance of each protocol. The Core Based Tree protocol is incorrect; it does not prevent or detect looping nor does it consistently build a correct multicast tree. The correct construction of the multicast tree in all instances and the guarantee of loop freedom in the Ordered Core Based tree protocol make it superior in operation to CBT; it is only an added bonus that it does so with a reduced amount of control traffic. The changes that make OCBT perform correctly and more efficiently than CBT are simple and extensible; work done on the placement of cores and security mechanisms for CBT are applicable to OCBT with little or no modification. The need for a scalable multicast routing protocol in the Internet of the future highlights the importance of a shared tree protocol; OCBT meets that need with correct and efficient performance.

## REFERENCES


1. S. E. Deering, *Multicast routing in a datagram internetwork.* PhD thesis, Stanford University, Palo Alto, California, Dec. 1991.
2. D. Estrin, D. Farinacci, V. Jacobson, C. Liu, L. Wei, P. Sharma, and A. Helmy, "Protocol independent multicast-dense mode (PIM-DM): Protocol specification," Internet Draft draft-ietf-idmr-pim-dm-spec-01.txt, U.S.C, L.Bl., CISCO, January 1996.
3. A. Ballardie, P. Francis, and J. Crowcroft, "Core based trees (CBT)," in *Proc.of the ACM SIGCOMM93*, (San Francisco, California), pp. 85–95, ACM, Sept. 1993.
4. S. Deering, D. Estrin, D. Farinacci, M. Handley, A. Helmy, V. Jacobson, C. Liu, P. Sharma, D. Thaler, and L. Wei, "Protocol independent multicast-sparse mode (PIM-SM):protocol specification," Internet Draft draft-ietf-idmr-pim-sm-spec-02.txt, XEROX, USC, CISCO, UCL, LBL, UMICH, May 1996.
5. S. Deering, D. Estrin, D. Farinacci, V. Jacobson, C. Liu, and L. Wei, "An architecture for wide-area multicast routing," in *Proc.of the ACM SIGCOMM94*, (London, UK), pp. 126–135, Sept. 1994.
6. A. Ballardie, S. Reeve, and N. Jain, "Core based trees (CBT) multicast protocol specification," Internet Draft I-D, University College London, April 1996. Work in progress.
7. A. Ballardie, *A New Approach to Multicast Communications in a Datagram Internetwork.* PhD thesis, University College London, University of London, London, U.K., 1995.
8. A. Ballardie, "Core based trees (CBT) multicast architecture," Internet Draft I-D, University College London, February 1996. Work in progress.
9. C. Shields, "Ordered core based trees," Master's thesis, University of California, Santa Cruz, Santa Cruz, California, June 1996.
10. M. Handley, J. Crowcroft, and I. Wakeman, "Hierarchical protocol indepenent multicast (HPIM)." University College London, November 1995.
11. K. Calvert, R. Madhavanand, and E. Zegura, "A comparison of two practical multicast routing schemes," Tech. Rep. GIT-CC-94/25, College of Computing, Georgia Institute of Technology, Atlanta, Georgia 30332-0280, February 1994.

# An Efficient Priority-Based Dynamic Channel Allocation Strategy for Mobile Cellular Networks*

Xuefeng Dong and Ten H. Lai
Department of Computer and Information Science
The Ohio State University
{dong, lai}@cis.ohio-state.edu

## Abstract

*Priority-based dynamic carrier allocation strategies can be classified into three categories: static-priority, dynamic-priority, and hybrid-priority strategies. Strategies based on static priorities do not consider the local carrier reuse conditions, while dynamic-priority strategies do take these conditions into consideration. Intuitively, one would expect dynamic-priority strategies to perform better than static- and hybrid-priority strategies, but in the literature it is the other way around — existing dynamic-priority strategies are outperformed by some static- and hybrid-priority strategies.*

*In this paper, we propose a dynamic-priority strategy that significantly improves over all existing strategies. Under various traffic conditions, our simulation results indicated that the proposed strategy could reduce call blocking/failure rate by a margin ranging from 15% to 95%.*

## 1. Introduction

This paper considers the problem of carrier allocation in a mobile cellular network [5] that employs both TDMA and FDMA multiplexing techniques such as the GSM pan-European mobile radio network [6]. The area covered by the cellular network is divided into a set of hexagonal *cells*. The bandwidth available for the network is divided into a set of *carriers* by frequency division. Each carrier is further divided into a number of *channels* by time division. Each channel can support a call. If a carrier is assigned to a cell, then all channels in that carrier are available for use in that cell. A carrier can be used by two different cells if their geographic distance is greater than a certain threshold called *minimum reuse distance*. The *problem of carrier allocation* is concerned with the assignment of carriers to cells. (The reader is referred to [8] for an introduction to this topic.)

Various dynamic carrier allocation (DCA) strategies (e.g., [1, 7, 9]) have been proposed for better carrier reuse. In a DCA strategy, a carrier is assigned an *acquisition-priority* and a *release-priority* in each cell. The priorities of the carriers determine the order by which the carriers will be acquired or released. In fact, among all the available carriers, the one that has the highest acquisition-priority will be acquired first; among all the carriers in use, the one that has the highest release-priority will be released first.

DCA strategies differ from each other in the way priorities are calculated. Depending on whether carrier reuse conditions in the neighborhood are taken into consideration in the calculation, DCA strategies can be classified into three classes: static-priority, hybrid-priority, and dynamic-priority strategies. In a *static-priority* strategy such as the Geometric strategy [1], each carrier in each cell is assigned a fixed priority that does not change over time. In a *dynamic-priority* strategy such as the Nanda-Goodman [7] and Locally-Optimized strategies [9], a carrier's priority is dynamically computed. A *hybrid-priority* scheme is something in between: a carrier's priority is calculated as a static base-priority plus a dynamic adaptive-priority. The borrow with channel ordering strategies [4, 9] belong to this class.

Intuitively, one would expect dynamic-priority strategies to outperform static/hybrid-priority strategies. But in the literature, it is not the case. The *Locally-Optimized* dynamic-priority strategy is known to be outperformed by the *Borrowing with Directional Channel-Locking* (BDCL) hybrid-priority strategy [9]; and the *Nanda-Goodman* dynamic-priority strategy, by the *Geometric* static-priority strategy [1].

In this paper, we derive a new dynamic-priority strategy, called *Two-Step dynamic-priority* (TSDP) strategy, from the Nanda-Goodman strategy. The new strategy adopts the *optimal carrier reuse pattern* concept, and significantly improves over all existing static/hybrid/dynamic-priority strategies: the TSDP strategy could reduce the call blocking/failure rate by a margin of 15% to 95% under both uniform and non-uniform traffic distributions.

The paper is organized as follows. Section 2 presents the cellular model and illustrates the basic resource operations and the consistency requirement of priority assignment schemes. Section 3 reviews the Geometric, BDCL,

*This work is supported in part by the National Science Foundation under grant CDA-9413962.



0-8186-7780-5/97 $10.00 © 1997 IEEE

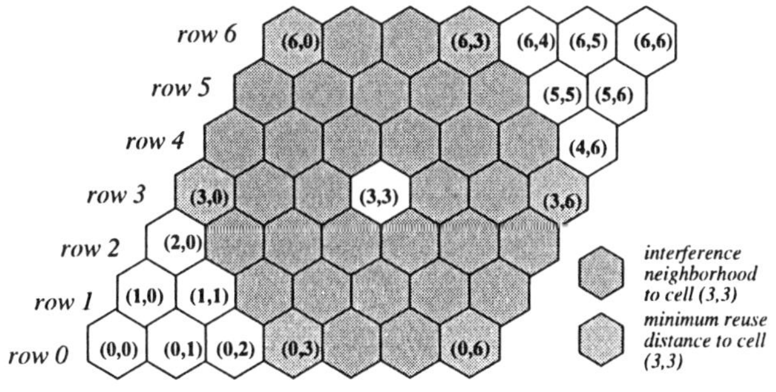


**Figure 1. Hexagonal Cellular Model**

and Nanda-Goodman strategies. The optimal carrier reuse pattern is discussed in section 4. Section 5 describes Two-Step dynamic-priority strategy, which is compared with other strategies in section 6. Section 7 concludes the paper.

## 2. Preliminary

### 2.1. Cellular Network Model

The cellular network is regarded as a regular grid of hexagonal cells of radius $R$. An $n \times m$ cellular network has $n$ rows and $m$ columns of cells. (Fig. 1 shows a $7 \times 7$ cellular network.) The cell at row $\tilde{r}$ and column $\tilde{c}$ is denoted by $(\tilde{r}, \tilde{c})$.

Each cell has a geometric center. In the rectangular Cartesian coordinates system with the $x$-axis pointing to the direction of row 0, the coordinates $(x, y)$ of the center of cell $(\tilde{r}, \tilde{c})$ can be calculated as:

$$(x, y) = (\tilde{c}, \tilde{r}) \begin{pmatrix} \sqrt{3}R & 0 \\ \frac{\sqrt{3}}{2}R & \frac{3}{2}R \end{pmatrix} \quad (1)$$

The *distance* between two cells $c_1$ and $c_2$, denoted by $\text{dist}(c_1, c_2)$, is defined to be the Euclidean distance between their centers. Thus, given their Cartesian coordinates $c_1 = (x_1, y_1)$ and $c_2 = (x_2, y_2)$, the distance between $c_1$ and $c_2$ is $\text{dist}((x_1, y_1), (x_2, y_2)) = \sqrt{(x_1 - x_2)^2 + (y_1 - y_2)^2}$.

A conservative way to guarantee interference-free carrier reuse is to choose a *minimum reuse distance*, $D_{\min}$, such that two cells with a distance at least $D_{\min}$ between them can use the same carrier without interfering each other. The value of $D_{\min}$ is chosen to meet the prescribed requirement even in the worst case interference scenario. Since each cell has six nearest interfering cells, the worst case $C/I$ ratio is given by $[C/I]_{\min} = [(D_{\min}/R) - 1]^4/6$, if a fourth-power law attenuation is assumed [1, 5]. Although the DCA strategies under study in this paper do not depend on any specific value of $D_{\min}$, we will assume $D_{\min} = 3\sqrt{3}R$ for ease of presentation. With $D_{\min} = 3\sqrt{3}R$, $[C/I]_{\min} \approx 17dB$, which is a reasonable value in practice.

**Definition 1** Given a cell $c$, the *interference neighborhood* of $c$, denoted by $IN(c)$, is the set of all cells whose distance to $c$ is smaller than the minimum reuse distance:

$$IN(c) = \{c' \mid \text{dist}(c, c') < D_{\min}\}$$

Fig. 1 shows that an interference neighborhood may contain as many as 30 cells if $D_{\min} = 3\sqrt{3}R$. Two cells in each other's interference neighborhood cannot use the same carrier simultaneously due to the interference-free constraint.

### 2.2. Wireless Resources

**Definition 2** The status of a carrier $r$ in a cell $c$, denoted by $status(r, c)$, is defined as follows:

- $r$ is a *used carrier* for $c$, written as $\text{status}(r, c) = UC$, if at least one channel of $r$ is currently used by some user in $c$ (in supporting a call).
- $r$ is an *interfered carrier* for $c$, written as $\text{status}(r, c) = IC$, if there is a cell $c' \in IN(c)$ such that $\text{status}(r, c') = UC$.
- otherwise, $r$ is an *available carrier* for $c$, i.e., $\text{status}(r, c) = AC$.

For convenience, we write $U(c)$, $I(c)$, and $A(c)$ to denote the set of *used*, *interfered*, and *available* carriers for $c$, respectively. Also, we say that a channel in a used carrier is either a *busy* or a *free* channel depending on whether it is currently supporting a call.

There are four basic operations for resource allocations:

- *Channel Acquisition:* when a call arrives, an available channel, if any, is allocated to it.
- *Channel Release:* when a call terminates, the channel assigned to it is released.
- *Carrier Acquisition:* an available carrier is assigned to a cell. (A cell needs a new carrier when a new call arrives at it and finds that all channels in the used carriers are busy.)
- *Carrier Release:* a used carrier is released to the system when all channels on the carrier become free. A release operation is usually aided by channel switch operations.

### 2.3. Intra-cell Handoff

There are two basic channel/carrier reallocation operations:

- *Channel Switch:* a free channel is assigned to a call to replace the channel currently used by that call; the former channel becomes busy and latter becomes free.

- *Carrier Switch:* all busy channels of a used carrier are released and their users are assigned the channels of another available carrier.

Channel switch operations are extremely important for efficient carrier use. If a cell has many free channels, it should pack its busy channels into as few carriers as possible and release the newly freed carriers. Such packing is done by switching the calls on the highest release-priority (used) carrier to the free channels in lower release-priorities carriers.

Carrier switch operations rearrange the carrier reuse pattern to achieve a better carrier reuse efficiency. A carrier switch operation is carried out only when a newly available carrier has a higher acquisition-priority than some used carriers. It consists of one or more channel switch operations, i.e., all calls on the highest release-priority (used) carrier are switched to the newly available carrier.

Channel switch and carrier switch operations, which are also called *intra-cell handoffs*, are important for DCA strategies to meet the rapidly changing demand and to achieve better resource utilization [2].

### 2.4. Consistent Priority Assignment Scheme

**Definition 3** (priority consistency) A priority assignment scheme is *consistent* if the following is true for any two carriers $r_1$ and $r_2$ in any cell $c$: acquisition-priority$(r_1, c) >$ acquisition-priority$(r_2, c) \iff$ release-priority$(r_1, c) <$ release-priority$(r_2, c)$.

It is important that acquisition-priorities and release-priorities are consistent, or the system may be unstable as illustrated in the following example.

**Example 1** Assume that three carriers $r_1, r_2, r_3$ are in $U(c)$ and their priorities are inconsistent: acquisition-priority$(r_1, c) >$ acquisition-priority$(r_2, c) >$ acquisition-priority$(r_3, c)$ and release-priority$(r_1, c) >$ release-priority$(r_2, c) >$ release-priority$(r_3, c)$.

Because $r_1$ has the highest release-priority, it will be released first. Once $r_1$ is released and becomes available, a carrier switch will take place between $r_1$ and $r_2$. Once $r_2$ becomes available, a new carrier switch will again take place between $r_2$ and $r_1$. This leads to endless switches between $r_1$ and $r_2$.

## 3. Previous Work

### 3.1. Geometric Strategy

In the *Geometric* strategy [1], the set of all cells is divided into $k$ subsets $G_0, G_1, \ldots, G_{k-1}$ such that no two cells in the same subset have a distance less than $D_{\min}$, i.e., no two cells interfere with each other. The set of all carriers is split into $k$ subsets $P_0, P_1, \ldots, P_{k-1}$, and the carriers in $P_i$ are called the *first-choice* carriers for the cells in $G_i$ $(i = 0, 1, \ldots, k-1)$. The carriers in each subset form an *ordered* list. Let $\tilde{P}_i$ denote the ordered list of the carriers in $P_i$. When a cell $c \in G_i$ needs a carrier, it checks the lists $\tilde{P}_i, \tilde{P}_{i+1}, \ldots, \tilde{P}_{k-1}, \tilde{P}_0, \ldots, \tilde{P}_{i-1}$, in that order, and acquires the first available carrier encountered.

### 3.2. Borrowing with Directional Channel-Locking (BDCL) Strategy

In the BDCL strategy [9], the set of all cells is divided into $k$ subsets $G_0, G_1, \ldots, G_{k-1}$. The carriers are split into $k$ subsets $P_0, P_1, \ldots, P_{k-1}$, and the carriers in $P_i$ are called the *nominal* carriers for the cells in $G_i$ $(i = 0, 1, \ldots, k-1)$. The nominal carriers for each cell are prioritized. During carrier acquisition, a cell acquires the available nominal carrier that has the highest priority. If none of the nominal carriers is available, it borrows the carrier that has the lowest priority from the "richest" *IN* cell, i.e., the cell with the most unassigned nominal carriers. Hence, the priority of a borrowed (non-nominal) carrier is the original fixed priority of the carrier plus the "richness" factor of the neighboring cells in which it is a nominal carrier.

### 3.3. Nanda-Goodman Strategy

In the *Nanda-Goodman* strategy [7], the acquisition-priorities and release-priorities of the carriers are calculated dynamically as follows. Given a cell $c$, the acquisition-priority of an available carrier $r$ in $c$ is defined as the number of cells in $IN(c)$ in which $r$ is an *interfered* carrier, i.e.,

$$\text{acquisition-priority}(r, c) = |\{c' \in IN(c) \mid \text{status}(r, c') = IC\}| \quad (2)$$

Thus, a carrier has a higher acquisition-priority in $c$ if its use in $c$ will cause a smaller number of new cells in $IN(c)$ to become interfered.

The release-priority of a used carrier $r$ is defined as the number of cells in $IN(c)$ in which $r$ will become available should $r$ be released by $c$, i.e.,

$$\text{release-priority}(r, c) = |\{c' \in IN(c) \mid \zeta(r, c') = 1\}| \quad (3)$$

where $\zeta(r, c')$ is the number of cells in $IN(c')$ in which the carrier $r$ is currently used. Thus, a carrier has a higher release-priority in $c$ if its release from $c$ will make itself available in more $IN(c)$ cells. It is easy to verify that Eq. 2 and Eq. 3 are consistent.

## 4. Foundation

We have reviewed three representative DCA strategies; their performances have been studied in [1, 7, 9] by simulation. Without looking at such simulation results, it is not obvious which of these strategies might outperform the others. In this section, we propose the concept of the *optimal carrier reuse pattern* which will help us see previous strategies' relative strengths and weaknesses and will, thereby, lead us to a more efficient new strategy.

### 4.1. Optimal Reuse Pattern

**Definition 4** The *reuse pattern* of a carrier $r$, denoted by $S(r)$, is the set of cells in which $r$ is in use, i.e.,

$$S(r) = \{c \mid \text{status}(r, c) = UC\}.$$

The *reuse frequency* of a carrier $r$, denoted by $f(r)$, is the number of cells in $S(r)$, i.e.,

$$f(r) = |S(r)|.$$

The co-channel interference constraint requires that a carrier can be reused in two cells if and only if the distance between the two cells is at least $D_{\min}$. Hence, there is an upper bound on $f(r)$. A carrier's possible largest reuse pattern is referred to as the *optimal reuse pattern*, and its corresponding reuse frequency the *optimal reuse frequency*.

In the following, we define an equivalent relation $\Gamma$ on the set of all cells $C$ which partitions $C$ into equivalent classes. We will establish a one-to-one correspondence between equivalent classes and optimal reuse patterns. Although the existence of such a correspondence do not depend on any specific $D_{\min}$, we will assume $D_{\min} = 3\sqrt{3}R$ for the sake of simplicity and clarity.

**Definition 5** Let $C$ be the set of all cells in a cellular network and assume $D_{\min} = 3\sqrt{3}R$. For any two cells $c_1, c_2 \in C$, define $(c_1, c_2) \in \Gamma$ if and only if one of the following holds true.

- $c_1 = c_2$;
- $\text{dist}(c_1, c_2) = D_{\min}$;
- there exists a cell $c$ such that $(c_1, c) \in \Gamma$ and $(c, c_2) \in \Gamma$.

**Theorem 1** *$\Gamma$ is an equivalence relation on $C$.*

It is easy to verify that $\Gamma$ is an equivalence relation, which partitions $C$ into 9 equivalence classes: $G_0, G_1, \cdots, G_8$ (Fig. 2).

For the notion of optimal reuse patterns to be meaningful, the cellular network under study must be large enough so that the boundary of the network will not significantly affect the results. Since a carrier can be reused every three cells in the same row or column (Fig. 2), we assume that the layout of the cellular network is $(3k_1) \times (3k_2)$. Hence, the set of cells are partitioned by $\Gamma$ into 9 classes, each containing

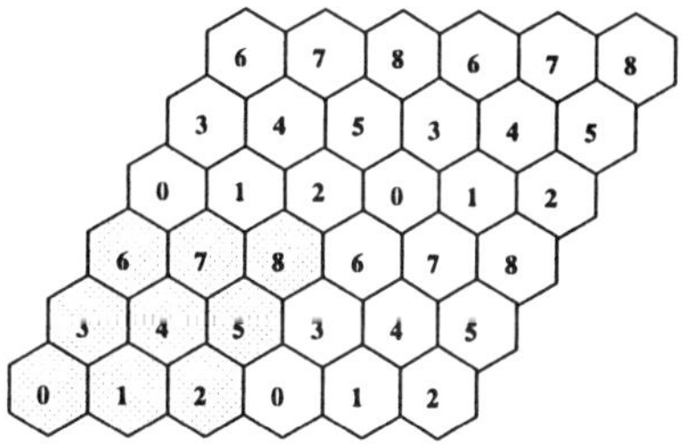


**Figure 2. Cells are partitioned into nine equivalence classes with $D_{\min} = 3\sqrt{3}R$.**

$k_1 * k_2$ cells. Furthermore, in order not to be distracted by the boundary's insignificant effect, we employ a "wrapped-around" cellular network model, in which the left-most column of cells is regarded as adjacent to the right-most column of cells and the top-row of cells is adjacent to the bottom-row. Thus, the cell at row $i$ and column $j$ has six closest neighbors: $((i-1)_{3k_1}, j)$, $((i-1)_{3k_1}, (j+1)_{3k_2})$, $(i, (j+1)_{3k_2})$, $((i+1)_{3k_1}, j)$, $((i+1)_{3k_1}, (j-1)_{3k_2})$, and $(i, (j-1)_{3k_2})$, where $(X)_y$ denotes $((X) \bmod y)$. A mobile host may roam from one cell to any of its six closest neighbors.

**Theorem 2** *In a $(3k_1) \times (3k_2)$ wrapped-around cellular network with $D_{\min} = 3\sqrt{3}R$, the optimal reuse frequency of any carrier is $k_1 * k_2$, which is achieved if and only if the carrier's reuse pattern is identical to an equivalence class.*

A formal proof of the theorem can be found in [3]. The theorem can be explained as follows. If a carrier $r$ is not used by any cell outside $G_i$, then its optimal reuse frequency will be achieved when every cell in $G_i$ uses $r$. However, if $r$ is used by cells from different equivalent classes, it will not achieve the optimal reuse pattern.

The assumption that $D_{\min} = 3\sqrt{3}R$ in the above theorem is not crucial. Similar results hold for other $D_{\min}$ values. For instance, if $D_{\min} = \sqrt{21}R$, the cells are partitioned into 7 equivalent classes; and in a $(k_1) \times (7k_2)$ wrapped-around cellular network, the optimal reuse frequency of a carrier is $k_1 * k_2$ and it can be achieved if and only if the carrier's reuse pattern is identical to some equivalence class.

Obviously, a static/hybrid-priority strategy such as the Geometric or BDCL strategy will not fulfill its potential unless the cells are partitioned following the optimal reuse patterns (see section 3.1 and 3.2). Hence, we assume that, given $D_{min}$, the cells are partitioned in $k$ subsets $G_i$ $(i = 0, 1, \ldots, k-1)$ in a static/hybrid-priority strategy, and each subset is an optimal reuse pattern.

### 4.2. Analysis of Previous Work

In the Geometric strategy, when a cell in $G_i$ needs a carrier, it acquires the first available carrier encountered in the lists $P_i, P_{i+1}, \ldots, P_{k-1}, P_0, \ldots, P_{i-1}$. The main strength of this strategy is that when traffic is uniform, most carriers in $P_i$ are used by the cells in $G_i$ and thus most carriers in $P_i$ can achieve the optimal reuse pattern. Its weakness, on the other hand, is that when traffic is non-uniform, "hot" cells (i.e., cells with heavy traffic) will acquire a lot of non-first-choice carriers. Since the non-first-choice carriers are acquired according to a fixed order regardless of the reuse patterns of the candidate carriers, this results in less compact reuse patterns and thus low reuse efficiency of the non-first-choice carriers.

The BDCL strategy is basically the same as the Geometric method except that when a cell has to borrow a carrier from other classes, it does not follow a pre-specified order but borrows the carrier from the "richest" neighboring cell. Borrowing from "richest" neighboring cell will reduce the number of acquisitions of the borrowed carriers (see example 2). Thus, it should not be a surprise that the BDCL strategy outperforms the Geometric strategy, although not by much.

**Example 2** Assume $c_1, c_2$, and $c_3$ are three neighboring cells, and $P_i$ ($i = 1, 2, 3$) is the nominal carriers in $c_i$. Assume that $P_1$, $P_2$ and $P_3$ have 0, 1, and 2 available carriers in $c_1$, respectively. When $c_1$ needs a carrier, it will acquire a carrier in $P_3$ in the BDCL strategy because it has more available carriers than $P_2$. Later, when both $c_2$ and $c_3$ need a new carriers, they both can acquire a nominal carrier. There is only one acquisition of a borrowed carrier. However, if $c_1$ borrows the available carrier in $P_2$, then $c_2$ will have to borrow a carrier when it needs a new carrier. In this case, there are two acquisitions of the borrowed carriers.

Both the Geometric and BDCL strategies are based on the notion of optimal reuse patterns. The *Nanda-Goodman* strategy [7], on the other hand, ignores such a notion. It is a simple greedy method in which a cell $c$ tries to acquire carriers that seem to have been used by many cells in $c$'s neighborhood such that the reuse pattern of the acquired carrier is more compact than others. The value defined in Eq. 2 is used as an indicator of the reuse frequency of a carrier in $c$'s neighborhood.

As such, one would expect the Geometric and BDCL strategies to outperform the Nanda-Goodman strategy in a uniform traffic condition, in which Geometric and BDCL strategies have better chances to achieve optimal or near optimal reuse patterns.

On the other hand, the Nanda-Goodman strategy can perform as well as, maybe better than, the Geometric and BDCL strategies under non-uniform traffic distribution. Because the "hot" cells may require much more carriers than the "normal" cells, many carriers acquired in the "hot" cells are non-first-choice (non-nominal) carriers in the Geometric and BDCL strategies. Thus, the reuse efficiency of these non-first-choice (non-nominal) carriers will be relatively low. However, the carrier allocations in the Nanda-Goodman strategy is fully adaptive to local carrier reuse conditions. The reuse pattern of any carrier, though may not be optimal, is always as compact as possible. This guarantees relatively high reuse efficiency even under non-uniform traffic distribution.

## 5. Two-Step Dynamic-Priority DCA Strategy

The main ideas of our dynamic-priority strategy are: (1) dynamically assign primary/secondary status to carriers, and (2) compute priorities in a way so that primary carriers' reuse patterns are brought toward the optimal reuse patterns and secondary carriers' reuse patterns are kept compact.

### 5.1. Primary and Secondary Carriers

Recall that the set of all cells is partitioned into optimal reuse patterns $G_0, G_1, \ldots, G_{k-1}$ by the equivalence relation $\Gamma$. Due to the hexagonal shape of cells, for each cell $c \in G_i$, there are exactly six cells in $G_i$ with distance $D_{\min}$ to $c$. These cells are referred to as $c$'s *locally-optimal reuse pattern*, denoted by $LOP(c)$.

**Definition 6** For any cell $c \in G_i$, $LOP(c) = \{c' \in G_i : \text{dist}(c, c') = D_{\min}\}$.

For instance, in Fig 1, the locally-optimal reuse pattern of cell $(3,3)$ is $\{(0,3), (0,6), (3,6), (6,3), (6,0), (3,0)\}$.

**Definition 7** Let $\lambda$ be a fixed integer between 0 and 7 inclusively. A carrier $r$ is said to be a *primary carrier* for cell $c$ if $r$ is currently used by at least $\lambda$ cells in $LOP(c)$. Otherwise, $r$ is a *secondary carrier* for $c$.

In the definition, the value of $\lambda$ is left unspecified. It could be any value between 0 and 7. If $\lambda = 0$, then every carrier is primary; if $\lambda = 7$, then every carrier is secondary. (Since $|LOP(c)| = 6$, it is meaningless to have a $\lambda$ greater than 7.) Choosing an appropriate value for $\lambda$ is an important design issue, which we will address in Section 5.5.

### 5.2. Priorities of Primary Carriers

The acquisition-priority of a primary carrier in a cell $c$ is:

$$\text{acquisition-priority}(r, c) = \sum_{c' \in LOP(c)} \text{weight}(r, c') \quad (4)$$

where the *weight* function is defined as:

$$\text{weight}(r, c') = \begin{cases} N & \text{if status}(r, c') = UC \\ 1 & \text{if status}(r, c') = AC \\ 0 & \text{if status}(r, c') = IC \end{cases} \quad (5)$$

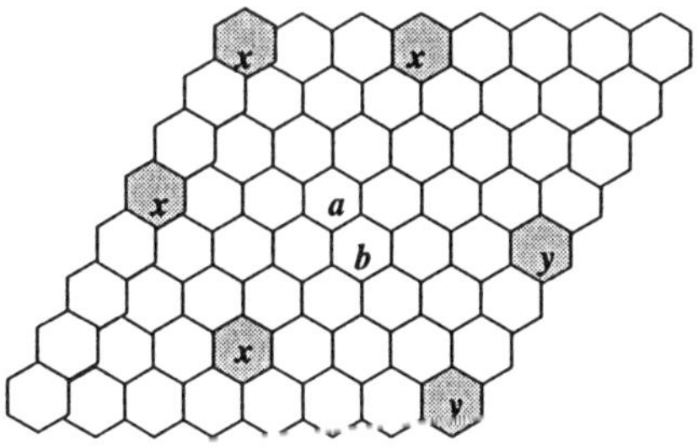


**Figure 3. Upgrade property: a primary carrier has a higher acquisition-priority than a secondary carrier.**

where $N$ is a positive number greater than the number of cells in $IN(c)$. In other words, if $r$ is used by exactly $p$ cells in $LOP(c)$ and is available in exactly $q$ cells in $LOP(c)$ (where $p+q \leq 6$), then acquisition-priority$(r, c) = p*N+q$. Suppose $x$ and $y$ are both primary carriers for cell $c$. If $x$ is used by more cells in $LOP(c)$ than is $y$, then $x$ has a higher acquisition-priority than $y$. If $x$ and $y$ are used by the same number of cells in $LOP(c)$, then the one that is available in more cells in $LOP(c)$ is assigned a higher acquisition-priority.

To be *consistent* with the acquisition-priority, the release-priority of a primary carrier is defined as

$$\text{release-priority}(r, c) = -\text{acquisition-priority}(r, c) \quad (6)$$

### 5.3. Priorities of Secondary Carriers

For secondary carriers, we wish to reuse them as compactly as possible. A priority function that assigns a higher acquisition-priority to those carriers which are reused in more neighboring cells will serve our purpose. Here, we borrow the Nanda-Goodman priority functions as defined in section 3.3. Thus, for a secondary carrier $r$ in a cell $c$,

$$\text{acquisition-priority}(r, c) = |\{c' \in IN(c) : \text{status}(r, c') = IC\}|$$

$$\text{release-priority}(r, c) = |\{c' \in IN(c) : \zeta(c', r) = 1\}|$$

### 5.4. Analysis of the TSDP Strategy

In the very beginning, before any carrier has been acquired by any cell, every carrier is a secondary carrier. In this stage, our strategy is no difference from Nanda-Goodman's dynamic-priority strategy since we use their priority functions for secondary carriers. Once a secondary carrier is used by $\lambda$ cells in $LOP(c)$, it is *upgraded* to a primary carrier and its priority is computed according to a different formula. The effect of such upgrading is illustrated in the following example.

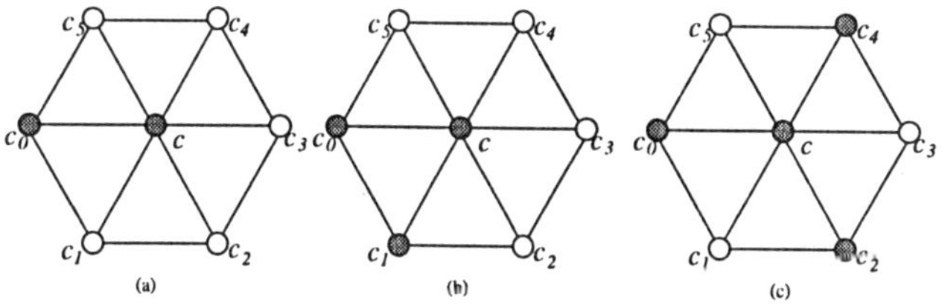

**Figure 4. Wave property: a carrier becomes primary in at least (a) 6 ($\lambda = 1$), (b) 4 ($\lambda = 2$), (c) 3 ($\lambda = 3$) LOP(c) cells.**

**Example 3** Suppose there are only two carriers, $x$ and $y$; $x$ is used by four cells in $LOP(a)$ and $y$ is used by two cells in $LOP(b)$ (Fig. 3). Using Nanda-Goodman's strategy, when $b$ needs a new carrier, it will acquire $x$ because more cells in $IN(b)$ are interfered by $x$ than by $y$. Later, when $a$ needs a carrier, it will acquire $y$. Hence, neither $x$ nor $y$ is reused following the locally-optimal pattern. Using our TSDP strategy, $b$ will acquire $y$ and $a$ will acquire $x$ because $y$ and $x$ are a primary carrier for $b$ and $a$, respectively (assume$\lambda \leq 2$). Both $x$ and $y$ are reused following the locally-optimal patterns.

The TSDP strategy has an interesting and useful *wave* property: if a cell $c$ acquires a primary carrier $r$, $r$ becomes primary in some $LOP(c)$ cells. Fig. 4 shows the best case for $\lambda = 1, 2, 3$, respectively. In Fig. 4(a) where $\lambda = 1$, $r$ becomes primary in all cells in $LOP(c)$ after $c$ acquires the primary carrier $r$. In Fig. 4(b) where $\lambda = 2$, $r$ becomes primary in four cells in $LOP(c)$ (e.g. $c_0, c_1, c_2, c_5$). In Fig. 4(c) where $\lambda = 3$, $r$ becomes primary in three cells in $LOP(c)$ (e.g. $c_1, c_3, c_5$).

The upgrade and wave properties of the TSDP strategy help bring the reuse pattern of a primary carrier closer to the optimal reuse patterns. As such, both primary carriers and secondary carriers are reused efficiently: primary carriers' reuse patterns follow the optimal reuse patterns, and the secondary carriers' reuse patterns are compact. It should not come as a surprise that the TSDP strategy outperforms all previous static/hybrid/dynamic-priority strategies in our simulation under both uniform and non-uniform traffic distributions.

### 5.5. The value of $\lambda$

If $\lambda$ is too large, then not many carriers will become primary and TSDP's strength will hardly be seen. (If $\lambda = 7$, TSDP will become the Nanda-Goodman strategy.) On the other hand, if $\lambda$ is too small, a carrier will easily become primary in many cells belonging to different optimal reuse classes, in which case the carrier cannot reach the optimal reuse frequency (Theorem 2).

| | |
|---|---|
| mean inter-arrival rate in a cell | $\Upsilon$ |
| mean inter-handoff rate in a cell | *1/60s* |
| mean service time | *180s* |

**Table 1. Assumed values for the simulation of the uniform traffic distribution.**

Question is, what values are too large and what values are too small? According to our simulation results, TSDP has best performance when $\lambda = 2$, followed by $\lambda = 1$ and $\lambda = 3$, in that order.

## 6. Comparisons

We compare the proposed strategy with the Geometric, BDCL and Nanda-Goodman strategies in terms of *cost*, and *performance*. The cost of a DCA strategy is measured by communication/computation overhead for updating the carriers' priorities. The performance of a DCA strategy is measured by the *failure rate* $R_f = R_b + (1 - R_b) * R_d$, where $R_b$ is the blocking rate and $R_d$ the dropping rate. The blocking rate is the percentage of new calls that are blocked due to insufficient resources, and the dropping rate is the percentage of on-going calls that are dropped during inter-cell handoffs due to insufficient resources.

### 6.1. Cost

The cost of the Geometric strategy is zero because the priorities of the carriers are static. There is a little cost in the BDCL strategy in determining which neighboring cell is the "richest". The cost of the Nanda-Goodman strategy and proposed strategy are much higher than the BDCL strategy because the priorities of the carriers will be changed whenever an operation such as a carrier acquisition or a carrier release occurs in a neighboring cell. Also, in the proposed strategy, extra cost is incurred to distinguish the primary carriers from secondary carriers.

### 6.2. Performance

The performance of each DCA strategy is simulated under both uniform and non-uniform traffic distributions. The cellular network is a wrapped-around layout with $15 * 15$ cells. The total number of available carriers in the system is 72, with four channels per carrier.

Under uniform traffic distribution, traffic in each cell is characterized by the mean inter-arrival time, mean service time, and mean inter-handoff time, all assumed to be negative exponentially distributed. The assumed values of the simulation parameters of the uniform traffic model are shown in Table 1.

| | |
|---|---|
| mean rate of change from normal state to hot state | *1/1800s* |
| mean rate of change from hot state to normal state | *1/180s* |
| mean inter-arrival rate in a normal state cell | $\Upsilon$ |
| mean inter-arrival rate in a hot state cell | $3\Upsilon$ |
| mean inter-handoff rate in normal state cell | *1/60s* |
| mean inter-handoff rate in a hot state cell | *1/180s* |
| mean service time | *180s* |

**Table 2. Assumed values for the simulation of the non-uniform traffic distribution.**

Under non-uniform traffic distribution, a cell can be in one of two states: *hot state* or *normal state*. A cell in the hot state is characterized by high inter-arrival rate and low inter-handoff rate to picture more arriving new users and/or prevailing stationary users. On the contrary, a cell in the *normal* state is characterized by low inter-arrival rate and high inter-handoff rate. Each cell can dwell in either state for an exponentially distributed time, independent of each other. We also assume that the inter-arrival rate, the service time, and the inter-handoff time are all negative exponentially distributed in each state. The assumed values of the simulation parameters are shown in Table 2.

For each inter-arrival rate, the mean blocking/failure rate is obtained via collecting a large number of samples such that the confidence interval is reasonably small. In most cases, the 95% confidence interval for the mean blocking/failure rate is less than 10% of the sample mean. The results of the simulations are shown in Fig. 5 to Fig. 6 and can be summarized as follows:

- The proposed strategy has the best performance. Compared with the Geometric, BDCL and Nanda-Goodman strategies, the new strategy could reduce the call blocking/failure rate by a margin of 15% to 95% under both uniform and non-uniform traffic distributions.
- The BDCL strategy is slightly better than the Geometric strategy.
- The Nanda-Goodman strategy has the worst performance under uniform traffic condition. It has slightly better performance than the Geometric and BDCL strategies under non-uniform traffic condition.

## 7. Conclusion

We classified the DCA strategies into three classes: static/hybrid/dynamic-priority strategies, and developed the

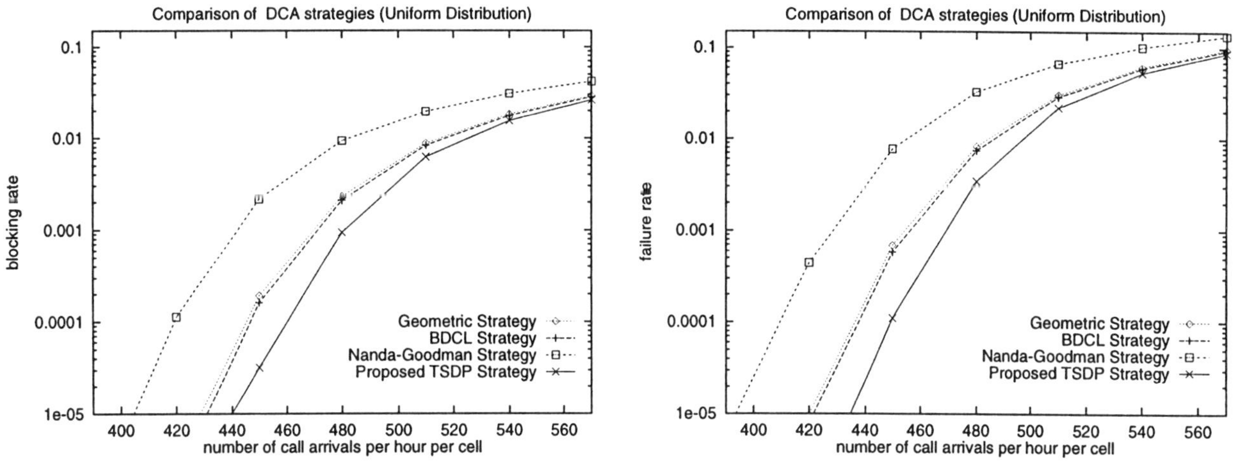


**Figure 5. DCA strategies under uniform traffic conditions: blocking rate and failure rate.**

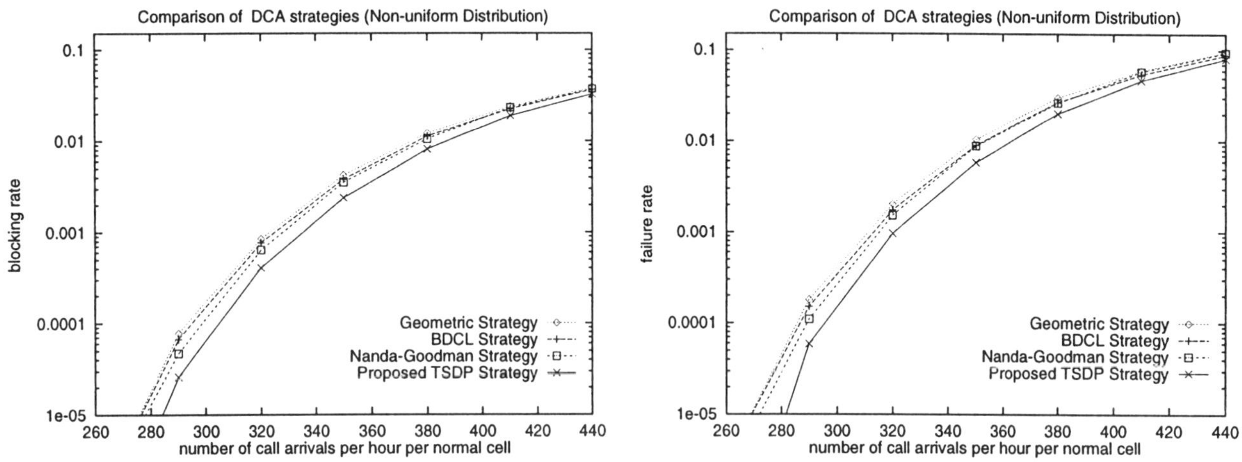


**Figure 6. DCA strategies under non-uniform traffic conditions: blocking rate and failure rate.**

concept of optimal carrier reuse pattern as a foundation for designing efficient DCA strategies. We proposed the Two-Step dynamic-priority DCA strategy which has better performance than all other static/hybrid/dynamic-priority DCA strategies under both uniform and non-uniform traffic distributions.

## References

[1] A. Baiocchi, F. D. Priscoli, F. Grilli, and F. Sestini. The geometric dynamic channel allocation as a practical strategy in mobile networks with bursty user mobility. *IEEE Trans. Vehicular Tech.*, 44(1):14–23, Feb. 1995.

[2] R. Beck and H. Panzer. Strategies for handover and dynamic channel allocation in micro-cellular mobile radio systems. In *Vehicular Tech. Conf.* IEEE, May 1989.

[3] X. Dong and T. H. Lai. Dynamic carrier allocation strategies for mobile cellular networks. Technical Report OSU-CISRC-10/96-TR48, Dept. of Comp. and Info. Sci., Ohio State University, 1996.

[4] S. M. Elnoubi, R. Singh, and S. C. Gupta. A new frequency channel assignment algorithm in high capacity mobile communication systems. *IEEE Trans. Vehicular Tech.*, 31(3), 1982.

[5] W. C. Y. Lee. *Mobile Cellular Telecommunications: Analog and Digital Systems*. New York: McGraw-Hill, 1995.

[6] M. Mouly and M. B. Pautet. *The GSM System for Mobile Communications*. the authors, 1992.

[7] S. Nanda and D. Goodman. Dynamic resource acquisition: Distributed carrier allocation for TDMA cellular systems. In *Globecom*, pages 883–889. IEEE, 1991.

[8] S. Tekinay and B. Jabbari. Handover and channel assignment in mobile cellular networks. *IEEE Comm. Magazine*, pages 42–46, Nov. 1991.

[9] M. Zhang and T.-S. Yum. Comparisons of channel-assignment strategies in cellular mobile telephone systems. *IEEE Trans. Vehicular Tech.*, 38(4):211–215, Nov. 1989.

# A Unified Framework and Algorithm for (T/F/C)DMA Channel Assignment in Wireless Networks

S. Ramanathan
BBN Systems and Technologies
Cambridge, MA 02138
email: ramanath@bbn.com

## Abstract

*Channel assignment problems in the time, frequency and code domains have thus far been studied separately. Exploiting the similarity of "constraints" that characterize assignments within and across these domains, we introduce the first unified framework for the study of assignment problems. Our framework identifies eleven atomic constraints underlying most current and potential assignment problems, and characterizes a problem as a combination of these constraints. Based on this framework, we present a unified algorithm for efficient (T/F/C)DMA channel assignments to nodes or to inter-nodal links in a (multihop) wireless network. The algorithm is parametrized to allow for tradeoff-selectable use as three different variants called RAND, MNF, and PMNF. Using theoretical analysis, we show that the worst-case performance guarantee of PMNF is an order of magnitude better than that of the traditional RAND and MNF for most networks. We also experimentally study the relative performance for one node and one link assignment problem. We observe that PMNF performs the best, and that a larger fraction of unidirectional links degrades the performance in general.*

## 1 Introduction

While the rapidly growing area of wireless networking promises to bring ubiquitous mobile services into the everyday realm, it is also likely to place an extremely high premium on the communications spectrum. The scarcity of spectrum necessitates efficient channel assignment mechanisms. Whether the channel sharing is based upon Time Division Multiple Access (TDMA), Frequency Division Multiple access (FDMA), Code Division Multiple Access (CDMA), or a combination thereof, there exists a fundamental limit on the number of users sharing the same channel simultaneously. This has motivated the need for *spatial reuse* of the channel, that is, having users sufficiently far apart use the same frequency band, time slot, or code. Attesting to the importance of the issue, the literature is replete with considerations of several *specific* assignment problems (references [3]-[16]).

In this paper, we postulate the *generalized* problem of channel assignment in the context of achieving efficient spatial reuse. The generalization stems primarily from two observations: that whatever the access technology, the solution depends largely on the nature of the *constraints*[1] to which an assignment must adhere; and that most (Time/Frequency/Code) Division Multiple Access assignments are characterized by a combination of a handful of underlying constraints. In this generalized formulation, the channel in question could be time, frequency, or code, and the assignment of channels may be to *nodes* or to *links* between nodes in the network. We develop a unified framework that identifies a set of eleven constraints as *atomic*, that is, as building blocks for the generation of *constraint sets* that characterize an assignment problem. Based on this framework, we present a unified algorithm and analysis for channel assignment that is applicable to 144 well-known or potential assignment problems in both cell-based and *multihop* wireless networks. A multihop wireless network is one in which a packet may have to traverse multiple wireless links in order to reach its destination. Examples include *Packet Radio networks* [1], and *ad hoc networks* [2].

### 1.1 Previous work

Much of the prior work in the spatial reuse of channel assignment in multihop wireless networks may be classified based on the technology – FDMA, TDMA or CDMA – that they cater to. Frequency assignment has been well studied, mostly in the context of cellular networks [3]. In [4, 5], the TDMA scheduling of broadcasts is considered, while in [6, 7], TDMA link scheduling is considered. Distributed scheduling algorithms are the subject of [8, 4, 15], and the work of [4, 9] addresses re-scheduling when the network topology is dynamic. With regard to CDMA, [11] studies the complexity of the problem, and [10, 11, 12] propose code assignment algorithms. Distributed algorithms are given in [12, 11].

Many assignment problems in this area have been shown to be NP-complete, including TDMA broadcast scheduling [5, 18], link scheduling [18] (even when the graphs are planar [16]), FDMA frequency assignment [3], and CDMA code assignment [11]. Indeed, for some of these problems, even constant times optimum polynomial algorithms appear highly unlikely (i.e., unless P=NP) [16].

The work presented in this paper differs significantly from the previous works mentioned above. We use a unified framework and a generalization based on the constraints, which in turn results in the first algorithmic and analytical unification within and across (T/F/C)DMA domains. In particular, our algorithm allows for the constraints as well as the topology to be part of the input parameters, and each of our performance analysis results are valid for not just one but a *class*

[1] An example of a constraint is: Two nodes that are adjacent to a common node must not use the same code. We shall discuss this in detail in section 2.2.



0-8186-7780-5/97 $10.00 © 1997 IEEE

of problems. Also, most of the prior work assumed links to be bidirectional, whereas we do not.

### 1.2 Our Contributions: An Overview

We use the traditional graph coloring problem as a convenient equivalent for channel assignment. However, our graphs are *directed*, and can thus model networks containing unidirectional links. Communicating equipment forming a wireless link may differ in terms of transmission power levels, multipath interference experienced, and noise or jamming experienced. Thus, the assumption that links are bidirectional, made in several previous works (e.g. [4, 5, 6, 9, 11, 12]) is unrealistic. The generalization to directed graphs, however, is non-trivial as far as problem complexity is concerned, as will be evident from the analysis in section 4.

Using this graph-theoretic model, we develop in section 2 a unified framework for the postulation of 16 node and 128 link assignment problems in time, frequency, and code based networks. From among these, we pick as examples eight problems that have a "real-life" counterpart in TDMA, FDMA and CDMA based networks, and map them into their corresponding constraint sets. In the context of this unified framework, we present a unified algorithm for coloring a graph, which translates into a channel assignment for the corresponding network. The algorithm is parametrized to accept as input the set of constraints characterizing the problem and for the choice of the assignment heuristic. We study three greedy heuristics, each using a different ordering in the way the vertices are considered for coloring.

We present, in section 4, analysis characterizing the worst-case performance of our algorithm on a wide variety of assignment problems. We show that, for most problem classes, a novel "progressive minimum neighbors first" (PMNF) ordering on the vertices produces significantly better worst-case and in-practice performance than the traditional random (RAND) ordering.

In section 5, we present experimental results characterizing the in-practice performance of our algorithm on a large number of randomly generated multihop network topologies. The performance (number of slots/frequencies/codes used) is studied as a function of the number of nodes, the range of each node, and the fraction of unidirectional links (introduced by having unequal transmission ranges, see section 5 for details). We observe that, for the problems studied, PMNF improves upon RAND by about 8 % to 13 %, and provides an in-practice guarantee of 1.1 times optimum.

## 2 A Unified Framework for Assignment Problems

In this section, we describe our network model, terminology, and concepts, and develop a unified framework within which our channel assignment algorithm can be conveniently described and analyzed.

### 2.1 Graphical Respresentation

Our presentation is based on a standard representation of a (multihop) wireless network as a directed graph G = (V,A). Here, V is a set of *vertices* denoting the nodes comprising the wireless network and A is a set of *directed edges* between vertices representing inter-node wireless links. For any two distinct vertices $u, v \in$ V, the edge from $u$ to $v$, denoted by $(u \rightarrow v)$, is in A if and only if $v$ can receive $u$'s transmission. Note that we do not assume that the edges of the graph are bidirectional. That is, $(u \rightarrow v) \in$ A does not necessarily imply that $(v \rightarrow u) \in$ A.

Assignment of channels to nodes corresponds in a natural fashion to *coloring* the corresponding graph. Depending on the nature of the assignment problem, it is either the vertices or the edges of the graph that receive colors. The mapping is one-to-one, that is, two nodes/links are assigned different channels if and only if the corresponding vertices/edges have different colors.

Formal definitions of terms we use throughout this paper are as follows. Two vertices are *adjacent* if there is an edge from one to the other, and two edges are adjacent if they have a common vertex. If $(v \rightarrow w)$ is an edge, then $v$ is an *in-neighbor* of $w$ and $w$ is an *out-neighbor* of $v$. A *neighbor* is a vertex that is an in-neighbor or an out-neighbor. The *in-degree* of a vertex $v$ is the number of in- neighbors of $v$ and the *out-degree* of $v$ is the number of out-neighbors of v. The *total degree* (or simply *degree*) of a vertex is the sum of its in- and out-degrees. The *maximum in/out/total-degree* of a graph is the maximum of the (in/out/total) degrees taken over all vertices of the graph and will be denoted by $\rho_{in}$ / $\rho_{out}$ / $\rho$. The *maximum degree ratio* is a measure of the asymmetry of the graph and is defined as $\delta_r = max(\frac{\rho_{out}}{\rho_{in}}, \frac{\rho_{in}}{\rho_{out}})$. A *planar* graph is one that can be embedded in the plane such that no two edges intersect. The *thickness* of a graph G is the minimum number of planar subgraphs of G whose union is G, and will be denoted by $\theta$. With respect to algorithmic concepts, we use terminology from [17]. Notably, the *performance guarantee* $R_A$ of an approximation algorithm $A$ is the maximum, taken over all problem instances $I$, of $A(I)/OPT(I)$, where $A(I)$ and $OPT(I)$ are, respectively, the "sizes" (colors or slots for the purposes of this paper) of the solution given by an algorithm $A$ and an optimum algorithm.

### 2.2 Constraints

We define a *constraint* as a symmetric relation between two vertices or two edges in a graph. If two vertices/edges are mutually related by some constraint $c$, we say that the vertices/edges are *constrained.* A constraint imposes a restriction on coloring: two vertices/edges that are mutually constrained must receive different colors for an assignment to be legal. Different constraints and combinations thereof give rise to different coloring problems, as discussed below.

We classify constraints according to whether they are between vertices or edges, the "separation" between them, and whether it is a transmitter and/or a receiver based constraint. Specifically, a constraint $c$ is denoted using the syntax $c =< \varepsilon >^{<s>}_{<d>}$, where $\varepsilon \in \{N, E\}, s \in \{0,1\}, d \in \{tr, tt, rr, rt\}$. Here, $\varepsilon$ is the entity (Node or Edge) being constrained, $s$ is the forbidden separation between two vertices or edges, and $d$ qualifies the separation by specifying its direction with respect to the transmitter and receiver. A separation of 0 between two vertices (edges) means that the vertices (edges) are adjacent, and a separation of 1 between two vertices (edges) means that there is one vertex (edge) between them. For example, if $c = V^1_{tt}$, then two vertices $u$ and $v$ that are separated by another vertex $w$ ( i.e., $s = 1$) with an edge from the transmitters (i.e., $d = tt$) of $u, v$ to $w$ are constrained. Figure 1 illustrates the various atomic constraints in our framework.

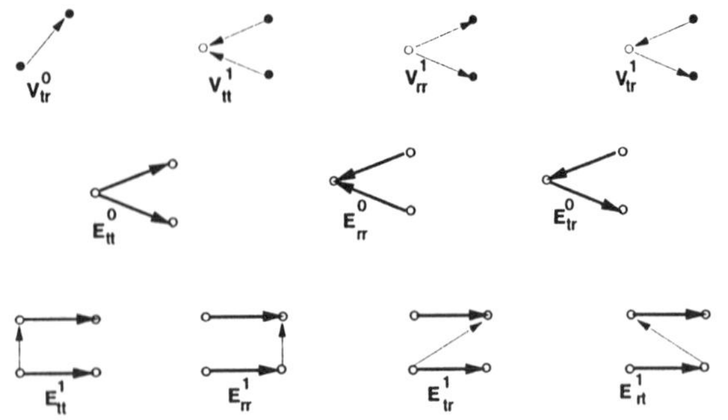


Figure 1: The eleven atomic constraints constituting the unified framework. The first row are vertex constraints, and the next two rows are edge constraints. The darkened vertices/edges are the ones that are mutually constrained, with the other vertices/edges causing the constraint.

Two constraints subsumed by this framework, namely $V^0_{tt}$ and $V^0_{rr}$ are invalid, since if two vertices are adjacent, then one of them must be the transmitter and the other the receiver. Note that $V^0_{tr}$ and $V^0_{rt}$ are equivalent constraints, as are $E^0_{tr}$ and $E^0_{rt}$. Henceforth, we shall treat $V^0_{tt}$ and $V^0_{rr}$ as "null" constraints and treat $V^0_{tr}$ ($E^0_{tr}$) as a "null" constraint when $V^0_{rt}$ ($E^0_{rt}$) is already present, and vice-versa.

Assignment problems are characterized by one or a combination of constraints, that is, a *constraint set*. For instance, $C$ = { $V^0_{tr}$, $V^1_{tt}$, $V^1_{rr}$ } is a constraint set. A problem characterized by a constraint set requires an assignment that satisfies *each* of the constraints in the constraint set. For instance, in an assignment problem characterized by $C$ = { $V^0_{tr}$, $V^1_{tt}$, $V^1_{rr}$ } two vertices cannot receive the same color if they are either adjacent (the $V^0_{tr}$ constraint), or have a common out-neighbor (the $V^1_{tt}$ constraint), or have a common in-neighbor (the $V^1_{rr}$ constraint). Formally,

**Definition 2.1** *An assignment characterized by a constraint set $C$, or a* **C-assignment** *of a graph $G$, is a coloring of $G$ such that for any two vertices/edges, if these vertices/edges are constrained by $c \in C$, then they are colored different.*

Although our framework allows for a constraint set to contain a mixture of vertex and edge constraints, we are not aware of any practical application that demands this flexibility, and therefore, restrict our attention in this paper to constraint sets in which all constraints are either vertex based, or edge based.

The objective of this paper is to study the *optimization* version of the $C$-assignment problem for various $C$, that is, to minimize the number of colors used in the assignment.

Given an assignment problem $P$, we shall denote the set of constraints characterizing it by $\Gamma$(P). We shall describe a constraint set by enumerating its contents explicitly, or express it using standard set theoretic notation, using the variables $s$, $x$, and $y$. For instance, { $V^s_{ty}$, $s \in \{0,1\}, y \in \{t,r\}$ } is equivalent to { $V^0_{tt}$, $V^0_{tr}$, $V^1_{tt}$, $V^1_{tr}$ } and { $E^1_{xx}$, $x \in \{t,r\}$ } is equivalent to { $E^1_{tt}$, $E^1_{rr}$ }.

Using the 4 *vertex* constraints illustrated in Figure 1, 16 different constraint sets are possible, and correspondingly 16 assignment problems. Similarly, using the 7 *edge* constraints illustrated in Figure 1, 128 different constraint sets are possible, and correspondingly 128 assignment problems. As a study of each problem individually is clearly impractical, we use the notion of a *class of problems*, as defined below.

**Definition 2.2** *A class of assignment problems* **covered** *by a constraint set $C$, or a* **C-covered class** *is the set $P$ of problems such that, for every $C_i \subseteq C$, the $C_i$-constrained assignment problem is an element of $P$.*

For instance, the class of problems covered by $\{E^0_{tt}, E^1_{tr}\}$ is the set {P1,P2,P3,P4} of problems where P1 is characterized by $\{E^0_{tt}\}$, P2 is characterized by $\{E^1_{tr}\}$, P3 is characterized by $\{E^0_{tt}, E^1_{tr}\}$, and P4 is characterized by {} (no constraints on coloring). Such groupings are very useful since performance bounds, a subject of section 4, can often be established for a class as a whole.

### 2.3 Common Assignment Problems

Several of the assignment problems arising in practice can be mapped into corresponding constraint sets in the context of our framework. We identify 8 real-life problems, identified P1 through P8 for easy reference, along with the constraint set characterizing each problem and a brief explanation of each. Unless otherwise specified, half duplex communications is assumed.

**P1:** Cellular network frequency assignment, is characterized by constraint set $\{V^0_{tr}\}$. Two adjacent vertices (denoting cells) must receive different colors (frequencies), and thus are $V^0_{tr}$ constrained.

**P2:** TOCA/ROCA CDMA code assignment, is characterized by constraint set $\{V^1_{tt}\}$. In both Transmitted Oriented (TOCA) and Receiver Oriented (ROCA) code assignments, it is required that if there is a node that can hear two nodes A, B (the $V^1_{tt}$ constraint), then A, B use different codes [10, 11, 12].

**P3:** (T/F)DMA Broadcast Schedule/Assignment, is characterized by constraint set $\{V^0_{tr}, V^1_{tt}\}$ and arises in multihop networks when a node's transmission is intended for all of its neighbors. Thus, if a node X is assigned a time-slot/frequency $q$, then every out-neighbor Y of X should not be assigned $q$ ($V^0_{tr}$ constraint), and every in-neighbor Z of Y should also not be assigned $q$ ($V^1_{tt}$ constraint) [4, 18, 14].

**P4:** POCA CDMA code assignment, has constraint set $\{E^0_{rr}, E^0_{tr}, E^0_{tt}\}$. In Pairwise Code (POCA) assignment, no two links sharing the same node are assigned the same code ($E^0_{tt}$,$E^0_{rr}$,$E^0_{tr}$) [12].

**P5:** (T/F)DMA link schedule/assignment, has constraint set $\{E^0_{rr}, E^0_{tt}, E^0_{tr}, E^1_{tr}\}$. Here, links between nodes are to be assigned time slots/frequency bands such that interference is completely avoided. This requires that if two links are assigned the same slot/frequency, then there be no link from the transmitter of one link to the receiver of the other link ($E^1_{tr}$). Moreover, half duplex implies that no two adjacent links are assigned the same slot/frequency ($E^0_{tt}$,$E^0_{rr}$,$E^0_{tr}$). This problem has been considered in [18, 14, 6].

**P6:** Full Duplex (T/F)DMA link schedule/assignment, has constraint set $\{E^0_{rr}, E^0_{tt}, E^1_{tr}\}$. This is the version of P5 when the nodes are capable of full duplex communications, that is, can transmit and receive simultaneously. The $E^0_{tr}$ constraint can then be removed.

**P7:** (T/F)DMA link schedule/assignment when there are multiple directional antennas, has constraint set $\{E^0_{rr}, E^0_{tr}\}$. In this case, multiple transmissions on the same time/frequency channel are possible without interference. Further, the transmission being directional, it does not cause interference with transmissions from other nodes. Thus, the $E^0_{tt}$ and $E^1_{tr}$ constraints can be removed from P5.

**P8:** with constraint set $\{ E^0_{rr}, E^0_{tt}, E^0_{tr}, E^1_{tt}\}$ arises in RTS-CTS protocols. In wireless LAN protocols such as IEEE 802.11, a control handshake (request-to-send (RTS), clear-to-send (CTS)) is required before data packets can be exchanged. Suppose a node A sends an RTS packet to a node B and is waiting for a response. Then, no node C that A can hear is allowed to transmit to any node, since the transmission will collide with the CTS packet from B to A. This manifests itself as an $E^1_{tt}$ constraint, along with the usual $E^0_{xy}$ constraints.

While the above list is by no means exhaustive, the development of this paper will be guided by problems in this set, as they seem to have a relatively important relevance for today's applications.

# 3 A Unified Algorithm

We now describe a unified algorithm for (T/F/C) DMA channel assignment (henceforth referred to as Algorithm UxDMA). Given a graphical representation of a (multihop) wireless network, algorithm UxDMA produces an assignment of positive integers ("colors") to vertices or edges of G, subject to a set of constraints on the assignment.

The algorithm consists of two phases - a *labelling* phase and a *coloring* phase. In the labelling phase, each vertex in the graph is assigned a *unique* label between 1 and $n$, where $n$ is the total number of vertices. The coloring phase follows the labelling phase. Here, vertices are considered in decreasing order of labels, and if it is edge coloring, then the edges incident to the considered vertex are colored, or if it is vertex coloring, the considered vertex itself is colored. The color is chosen in a *greedy* fashion. That is, the least color (integer) that can be assigned without violating any of the constraints is chosen. After the vertex labelled 1 one is colored, the algorithm terminates.

The crux of the algorithm lies in *how the labelling is done.* Several *ordering* heuristics are possible, but in this paper we have studied only three, as follows.

**Random** (RAND). This is the simplest ordering, and as the name indicates, the vertices are labelled in random order.

**Minimum Neighbors First** (MNF). Here, vertices that have a smaller number of neighbors are assigned a smaller label. Consequently, the coloring is done by first picking high neighborhood vertices first.

**Progressive Minimum Neighbors First** (PMNF). This is similar to MNF with a subtle but crucial difference - after labelling a vertex, this vertex and the edges incident on this vertex are ignored while processing the rest of the vertices (one could think of it as "deleting" the vertex and the edges or just the edges). The result is that unlike MNF, the neighborhood of a vertex changes as other vertices are processed. The ordering could be significantly different from MNF, as could the performance.

Many of the heuristics mentioned in packet-radio channel assignment literature (e.g. [5, 4, 6, 12]) are equivalent to our algorithm with a RAND ordering. Its appeal lies in its simplicity and relative ease with which a distributed version can be implemented. However, as we mentioned in section 1, and as we shall see in sections 4, the RAND ordering is significantly inferior to PMNF in terms of worst-case guarantees and somewhat inferior to both MNF and PMNF in terms of expected performance.

A notable feature of our algorithm is that a single implementation can be made to function, by a runtime choice of parameters, either as a simple RAND assigner, or a sophisticated PMNF/MNF assigner. This should be clear from the specification below.

## 3.1 Formal Specification

The main algorithm is given first, followed by the procedures it uses. Indentation is used to delineate block structure.

**Algorithm UxDMA** **Input:** (1) Directed graph G = (V, A), (2) element type $\Psi \in$ {V(ertex), E(dge)} to be colored (assigned), (3) constraint set $C$ which is either $C \subseteq \{ V^0_{tr}, V^1_{tt}, V^1_{tr}, V^1_{rr} \}$, or $C \subseteq \{ E^0_{tt}, E^0_{tr}, E^0_{rr}, E^1_{tt}, E^1_{tr}, E^1_{rt}, E^1_{rr} \}$ (4) ordering $\omega \in$ {RAND, MNF, PMNF}
**Output:** A C-constrained assignment of $q$ colors 1 through $q$ to vertices (if $\Psi$ = V) or edges (if $\Psi$ = E) of G

```
begin
1. for all elements e of type Ψ do
2.    color(e) ←0
3. Assign-Label(G, ω)
4. for j from largest down to smallest label do
5.    let u ←vertex with label j
6.    for each elem e in Surround(G, Ψ, u) do
7.       color(e) ←First-Available-Color(G, e, C)
end
```

**Procedure** Assign-Label( G = (V,A), $\omega$ )

```
1. for labels l from 1 through |V| do
2.    if ω is RAND then
3.       u ←unlabelled random vertex
4.    if ω is MNF then
5.       u ←unlabelled min. neighbor vertex in G
6.    if ω is PMNF then
7.       u ←unlabelled min. neighbor vertex in G
8.       delete all edges incident on u from G
9.    label(u) ←l
```

**Procedure** Surround(G, $\Psi$, $u$)

```
1. if Ψ is VERTEX then S ←u
2. else S ←set of edges incident on u
3. return(uncolored subset of S)
```

**Procedure** First-Available-Color(G, $e$, $C$)
*Return the least color that e can be assigned*

```
1. Taken ←{ }
2. for each constraint c ∈ C do
3.    for each colored elem f of type same as e
      such that e, f, are related by c do
4.       Taken ←Taken ∪ color(f)
5. return(smallest color ∉ Taken)
```

## 4 Theoretical Analysis

The correctness of Algorithm UxDMA follows from the fact that the color chosen for an element (line 7 of UxDMA) is never in the set of constraining elements' colors (line 3,4 of First-Avail-Color). In this section, we analyze the worst-case performance and running time of UxDMA.

We present results on the worst-case performance for Algorithm UxDMA as a function of the input parameters, in particular the constraint set and the ordering. These results generalize those given in [16] to directed graphs. Due to space constraints, we have only presented the proof for Theorem 4.2. The proofs of all of the other theorems are contained in an expanded version of the paper, obtainable from [20].

The results are presented in the order of decreasing cardinality of the constraint set covering the problem class. That is, we first describe loose upper bounds on the performance for a large class of problems, then describe tighter bounds for a subclass, still tighter bounds for a sub-sub-class and so on. A similar attitude is taken toward the ordering - first results that are applicable to all three orderings are presented, and then results applicable only to PMNF. Note that each of the theorems below is applicable to not just *one* assignment problem, but a *class* of assignment problems, namely those covered by indicated constraint set.

**Theorem 4.1** *For the class of assignment problems covered by $C = \{\Psi^s_{xy}, \Psi \in \{V,E\}, x,y \in \{t,r\}, s \in \{0,1\}\}$, algorithm UxDMA with any ordering $\in$ {RAND,MNF,PMNF} has a performance guarantee of $O(\rho^2)$.*

**Theorem 4.2** *For the class of assignment problems covered by $C = \{V^0_{xy}, V^1_{xx}, x,y \in (t,r)\}$, algorithm UxDMA with any ordering $\in$ {RAND,MNF,PMNF} has a performance guarantee of $O(\rho)$*

**Proof.** Let $P$ be an assignment problem. We consider two cases (recall that $\Gamma(P)$ denotes the constraint set characterizing $P$):

(1) $\underline{V^1_{xx} \notin \Gamma(P)}$. That is, the problem is characterized by zero-separation constraints only. Consider a vertex $u$ picked in line 5 of Algorithm UxDMA. Since only $V^0_{xy}$ constraints are present, exactly the vertices adjacent to $u$ are picked for $f$ in line 3 of Procedure First-Available-Color. Since there are at most $\rho$ such adjacent vertices, no more than $\rho$ different colors can be used up for them, leaving the $(\rho+1)^{th}$ color for $u$. Therefore, the graph can be colored using $\rho + 1$ colors, and since the optimum is trivially at least 1, the performance guarantee is $O(\rho)$.

(2) $\underline{V^1_{xx} \in \Gamma(P)}$. That is, both zero and one separation constraints are present. In this case, in line 3 of First-Available-Color, vertices adjacent to the vertex $u$ picked in line 5 of UxDMA as well as vertices adjacent to these vertices are candidates for $f$ (refer Figure 2). Suppose that vertices $v_i$, $1 \leq i \leq n$ adjacent to $u$ and and vertices $w_{ij}$, $1 \leq j \leq m_i$ adjacent to $v_i$ are picked for $f$. Clearly, $u$ can be colored with a color at most

$$color(u) = 1 + n + \sum_{i=1}^{n} m_i \qquad (1)$$

Consider a vertex $v_b$ adjacent to $u$ and the vertices $w_{bj}$ adjacent to $v_b$ that were picked for $f$ in line 3 of Procedure

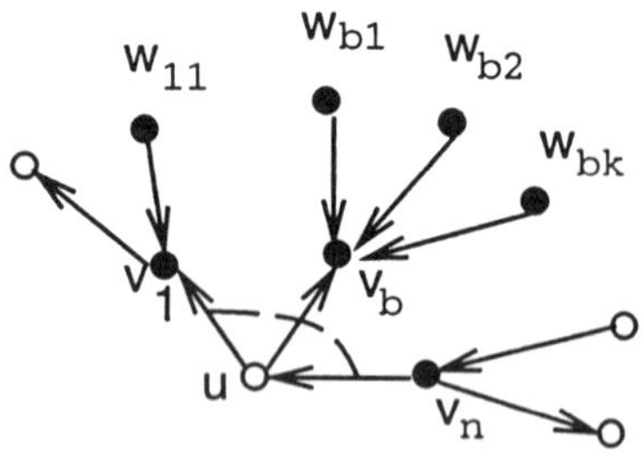


Figure 2: Example showing color restricting vertices (darkened) for vertex $u$, when the constraint set is $\{V^0_{tr}, V^1_{tt}\}$.

First-Available-Color. Suppose that a vertex $w_{bq}$ constrains $u$ by $c \in C$. Then, by definition, $c \in \{V^1_{tt}, V^1_{rr}\}$. However, for either of these two constraints, every vertex $w_{bl}$, $l \neq q$, is related by the same constraint $c$ to $w_{bq}$. In other words, the $w_{ij}$ vertices, $1 \leq j \leq m_i$, constrain each other. Figure 2 illustrates a scenario when the separation-1 constraint is $V^1_{tt}$ (the $V^1_{rr}$ case is similar). Notice that the $w_{bi}$ vertices are mutually $V^1_{tt}$ constrained. Therefore, these vertices must receive different colors in any coloring, including the optimum coloring. Clearly then, if OPT denotes optimum number of colors,

$$OPT \geq MAX(m_1, m_2, ... m_n) \qquad (2)$$

From (1),

$$\begin{aligned} color(u) &\leq 1 + n + n \cdot MAX(m_1, m_2, ..., m_n) \\ &\leq 1 + n \cdot OPT + n \quad (from\ 2) \\ &\leq 1 + \rho \cdot (OPT + 1) \quad (since\ n \leq \rho) \end{aligned}$$

Thus, at most $1 + \rho \cdot (OPT+1)$ colors are used by UxDMA to color the input graph. It follows that the performance guarantee is $O(\rho)$. □

If there are no unidirectional edges, then $V^1_{tt}$ would imply $V^1_{rr}$, and hence the above theorem would be valid for $C = \{V^s_{xy}, s \in \{0,1\}, x,y \in \{t,r\}\}$.

**Theorem 4.3** *For the class of assignment problems covered by $C = \{E^s_{xy}, s \in \{0,1\}, x,y \in \{t,r\}\}$ such that for each problem $P$ in the class, $\{E^0_{xy}, x,y \in \{t,r\}\} \subseteq \Gamma(P)$, algorithm UxDMA with any ordering has performance guarantee $O(\rho)$.*

**Theorem 4.4** *For the class of assignment problems covered by $C = \{E^0_{xy}, x,y \in \{t,r\}\}$ algorithm UxDMA with any ordering has performance guarantee O(1).*

The above theorems are applicable no matter what ordering was used. The theorems below show that improved performance guarantees can be obtained if the PMNF ordering is used.

**Theorem 4.5** *For the class of assignment problems covered by $C = \{V^s_{xy}, x \in \{t,r\}, s \in \{0,1\}\}$, and ordering PMNF (Progressive Minimum Neighbors First), Algorithm UxDMA has a performance guarantee of $O(\delta_r \theta)$.*

| Pi | Cnstrnt Set | RAND,MNF | PMNF |
|---|---|---|---|
| P1 | $V^0_{tr}$ | $O(\rho)$ (4.2) | $O(\theta \cdot \delta_r)$ (4.5) |
| P2 | $V^1_{tt}$ | $O(\rho)$ (4.2) | $O(\theta \cdot \delta_r)$ (4.5) |
| P3 | $V^0_{tr}$, $V^1_{tt}$ | $O(\rho)$ (4.2) | $O(\theta \cdot \delta_r)$ (4.5) |
| P4 | $E^0_{rr}$, $E^0_{tr}$, $E^0_{tt}$ | O(1) (4.4) | O(1) (4.4) |
| P5 | $E^0_{rr}$, $E^0_{tt}$, $E^0_{tr}$, $E^1_{tr}$ | $O(\rho)$ (4.3) | $O(\theta)$ (4.7) |
| P6 | $E^0_{rr}$, $E^0_{tt}$, $E^1_{tr}$ | $O(\rho^2)$ (4.1) | $O(\rho \cdot \theta)$ (4.6) |
| P7 | $E^0_{rr}$, $E^0_{tr}$ | O(1) (4.4) | O(1) (4.4) |
| P8 | $E^0_{rr}$, $E^0_{tt}$, $E^0_{tr}$, $E^1_{tt}$ | $O(\rho)$ (4.3) | $O(\theta)$ (4.7) |

Table 1: Best performance guarantees for eight real-life problems identified in section 2.3. The first column denotes the problem label (refer section 2.3). The second and third column give the performance guarantee and the theorem number (in paranthesis) that covers this constraint set - second column for RAND and MNF, third column for PMNF.

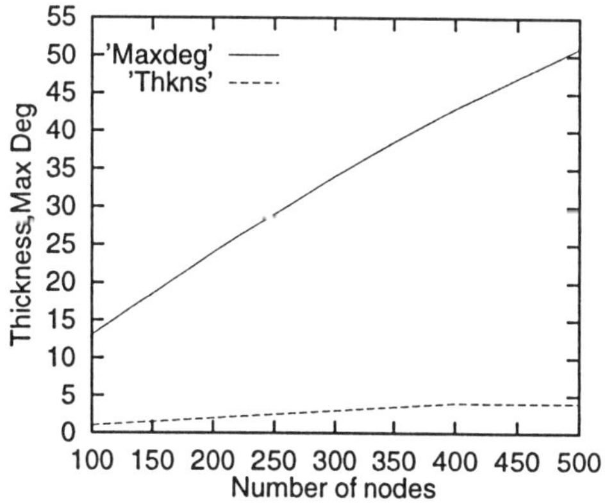


Figure 3: Max. degree and thickness versus number of nodes, with each node having a range of 40 units.

**Theorem 4.6** *For the class of assignment problems covered by* $C = \{E^s_{xy},\ s \in \{0,1\},\ x,y \in \{t,r\}\}$ *algorithm UxDMA with PMNF ordering has a performance guarantee of* $O(\rho \cdot \theta)$.

**Theorem 4.7** *For the class of assignment problems covered by* $C = \{\ E^s_{xy},\ s \in \{0,1\},\ x,y \in \{t,r\}\ \}$ *such that each problem P in the class,* $\{\ E^0_{xy},\ x,y \in \{t,r\}\ \} \subseteq \Gamma(P)$, *algorithm UxDMA with PMNF ordering has a performance guarantee of* $O(\theta)$.

The applicability of the foregoing theorems to the eight real-life problems P1-P8 mentioned in section 2.3 is given in Table 4.

We note that the PMNF ordering results in colorings that are guaranteed to be within $O(\theta)$ of the optimum colorings for many problems, where $\theta$ is the *thickness* of the topology graph. Algorithms in most previous works were only able to guarantee performance bounds of $O(\rho)$ where $\rho$ is the maximum graph degree (see for example [5, 4, 6, 12]). Our study shows that in typical multihop wireless networks, the thickness is several orders of magnitude less than $\rho$. Figure 4 shows[2] the growth in thickness[3] compared to growth in maximum degree for increasing network size and transmission range, respectively. Clearly, solutions with guarantees proportional to network thickness are more scalable than those based on maximum degree. Our algorithm does not require the calculation of thickness itself in its operation and hence is of polynomial time complexity.

**Running Time.** Let $v$ and $e$ denote the number of vertices and edges in the graph. Then, lines 1,2 of UxDMA takes $O(e)$. Line 3 (Assign- Label) takes $O(v)$ for RAND, $O(v^2)$ for MNF and $O(v \cdot (v+\rho))$ for PMNF using simple (linear search) structures[4]. Lines 6,7 take $O(\rho^2)$, and hence lines 4 through 7 take $O(e \cdot \rho^2)$. Thus, the worst-case running time is $O(v \cdot (v+\rho) + e \cdot \rho^2)$ for PMNF,MNF (simple structures) and is $O(e \cdot \rho^2)$ for RAND.

## 5 Experimental Results

For our experimental study, we have taken as representatives one node assignment problem, namely P3 (T/F DMA broadcast schedule/assignment), and one link assignment problem, namely P5 (T/F DMA link schedule/assignment).

Our experiments have been conducted under the assumption of a noiseless, immobile radio network, where the nodes are distributed in a given area and may each have a different transmission range. In this context, the network may be represented by the 3-tuple (N, $R_i$, P), where N is the number of nodes, $R_i$ is the transmission range of node $i$ and P = { ($x_i$, $y_i$, $1 \leq i \leq N$ } is the set of locations for each of the nodes. The location of a node is generated randomly, using a uniform distribution for its X and Y coordinates, in a given area. We convert this network into a graph G = (V,A), so that |V| = N, and (u,v) $\in$ A if and only if the Euclidean distance between ($x_u$, $y_u$) and ($x_v$, $y_v$) is less than or equal to $R_u$. Note that this might result an in unidirectional edge, but only if $R_u \neq R_v$.

We have studied the experimental performance of our algorithms by generating a large number of random graphs in an area of 400x400 units for values for N from 100 to 500 nodes and $R_i$ from 20 to 60 units. For each of the broadcast and link assignments, we study the performance (number of slots (colors) used) by Algorithm UxDMA for each ordering (RAND,MNF,PMNF), along with a lower bound for the optimum [5]. Figures 4 and 5 show, respectively, the number of slots for broadcast scheduling (number 3) and link scheduling (number 5) as a function of N, with $R_i$ = R = 40 units. Figures 6 and 7 show, respectively, the number of slots for broadcast and link scheduling as a function of $R_i$ = R, with N = 500 nodes. To study the effect of unidirectional links, we experimented with unequal transmission ranges, by giving

[2]Experiments conducted by placing nodes randomly on a 400x400 unit grid. Details in section 5.

[3]Since determining the exact thickness of a graph is itself NP-Complete [13], we have used an upper bound based on tree decompositions [19].

[4]The use of Fibonacci Heaps will reduce the time for PMNF to $O(e + v \cdot log(v))$.

[5]The problem being NP-complete, it is prohibitively time-consuming to compute the optimum number of slots. The lower bound for broadcast scheduling is $\rho_{in}$ and is fairly tight, and for link scheduling is the maximal number of mutually constrained edges in the vicinity of the maximum degree vertex and is quite loose.

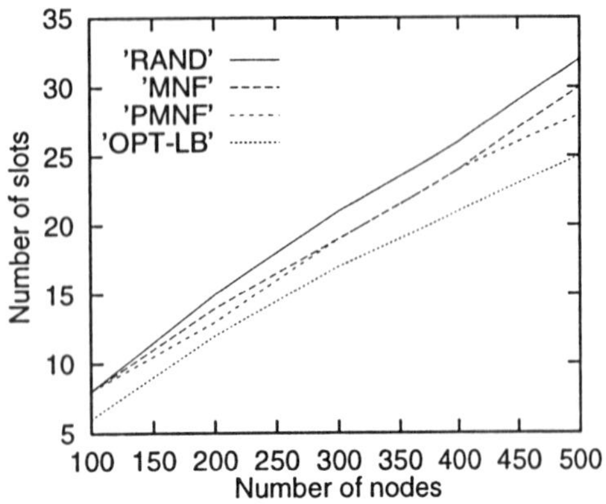


Figure 4: Size dependence, Node Assignment

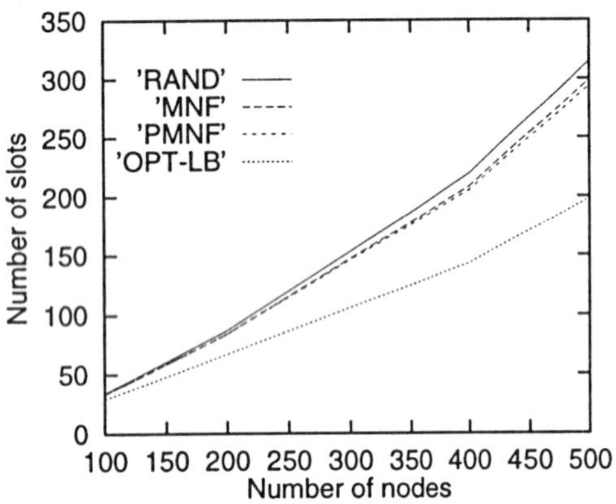


Figure 5: Size dependence, Link Assignment

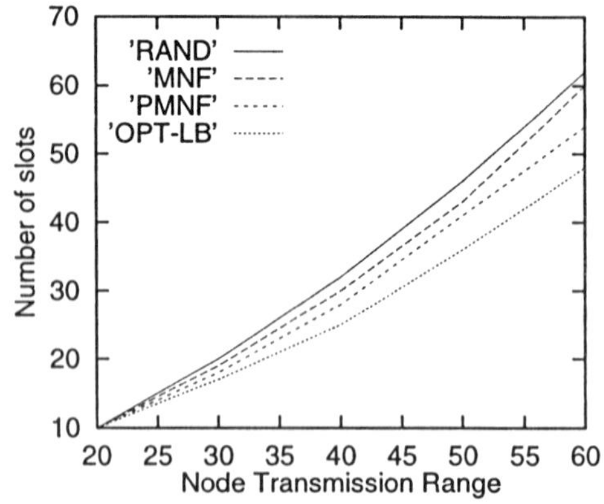


Figure 6: Range dependence, Node Assignment

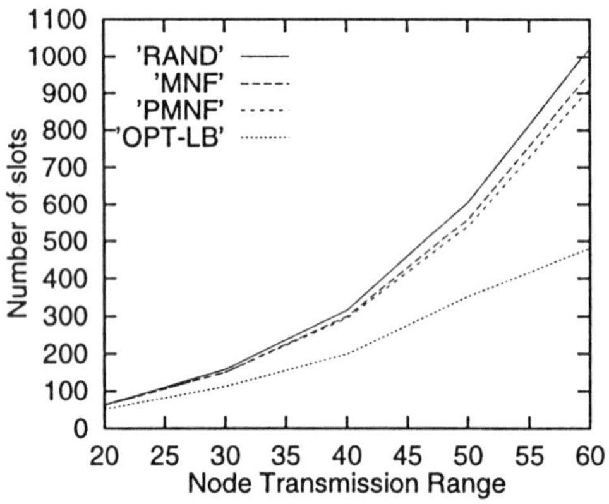


Figure 7: Range dependence, Link Assignment

each node a random range uniformly distributed between R + $r$ and R - $r$. Figures 8 and 9 show the number of slots as a function of $\frac{r}{R} \cdot 100$ (percent variability) for 2 values of R, for broadcast and link scheduling respectively.

As expected, the number of slots used by each of RAND, MNF, and PMNF, as well as the slots needed (i.e., the optimum) increases with both network size and node range. This is true for both broadcast and link scheduling. The increase appears to be more rapid with increasing range, especially for link scheduling. This is probably because adding more nodes results in a linear increase in a neighborhood (nodes per unit area) of a given node, whereas increasing the range results in a quadratic increase ($\pi R^2$ nodes per unit area).

PMNF performs best in practice, followed by MNF, and then RAND. On average, PMNF uses 9.6 % fewer slots than RAND for broadcast schedules, and 8.2 % fewer slots for link schedules. The difference tends to be larger for higher sizes and ranges. For N = 500, and R = 60, the performance improvement is as much as 12.9 % and 10.7 % for broadcast and link scheduling, respectively. MNF is somewhere in the middle for broadcast schedules, but performs nearly as well as PMNF for link schedules.

PMNF performs quite close to optimum. For the broadcast schedule case, even for the extreme case N=500,R=60, it is within 1.113 of the optimum, and in most typical cases, much less. The corresponding figure for link scheduling is 1.898 using the extremely loose lower bound on optimum. We expect the in- practice performance to be much better than this.

For both broadcast and link scheduling, the number of slots used by UxDMA for PMNF as well as RAND increases gradually with increasing variability of transmission range (Figure 8,9). Note that increasing the variability in transmission range typically increases the fraction of unidirectional links. The increase in number of slots used seems to be more pronounced at higher ranges, especially for link scheduling. Although not shown in order to avoid cluttering the plot, the MNF and the optimum lower bounds show similar behavior. Thus, everything else being same, unidirectional links seem to consume more spectrum compared to bidirectional links.

## 6 Concluding Remarks

We have developed a unified framework which captures a number of current and potential channel assignment problems. Such an unification is not only of pedagogical interest, but has useful practical implications as well. For instance, it obviates the need to come up with a new algorithm for each new assignment problem that the ever-changing wireless hardware and environment might present. Solution to an assignment problem can be obtained simply by identifying the set of atomic constraints characterizing the problem, and using algorithm UxDMA with the constraint set as a

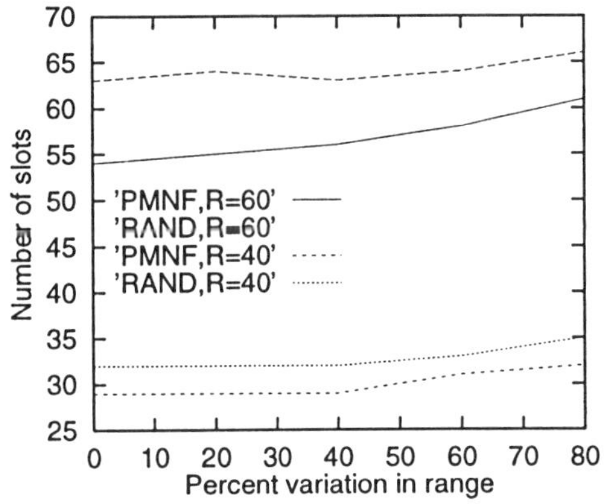


Figure 8: Range Variability dependence, Node Assgnmt

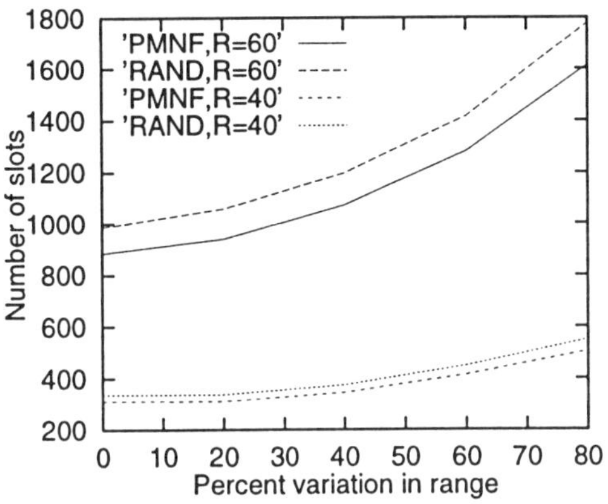


Figure 9: Range Variability dependence, Link Assgnmt

parameter. The user has a runtime choice, within the same algorithm/implementation, of three variants RAND, MNF, and PMNF, each offering a different tradeoff between simplicity (running time), and performance. Our theoretical and experimental analyses are useful in predicting how the algorithm will perform for each problem and variant. Our analysis shows that PMNF, although a little more complicated, and slightly more expensive in terms of running time, not only has a significantly improved worst-case bound in comparison to RAND, but also does 8-12 % better in practice. Since assignments are often made once and used repeatedly, the investment appears worthwhile, especially under scarce-bandwidth conditions.

Due to space constraints, we have not been able to describe distributed algorithms, which facilitate node mobility. We note, however, that the unification itself is completely orthogonal to obtaining a distributed version of UxDMA, which can be done by generalizing the specific-problem distributed algorithms of [15, 16] for PMNF, and the schemes of [5, 6] for RAND and [11] for MNF.

## Acknowledgments

We are grateful to Sudha Kapali, Northeastern University, and Martha Steenstrup, BBN Corp., for their valuable comments and suggestions on improving this paper. We also acknowledge the contribution of Prof. Errol Lloyd, University of Delaware, who supervised the dissertation upon which some of the results are based.

## References

[1] J. Jubin, J.D. Tornow, "The DARPA packet radio network protocols," *Proc. of the IEEE*, Vol. 75, 1987.

[2] W. Diepstraten, G. Ennis, P. Berlanger, "DFWMAC: Distributed Foundation Wireless Medium Access Control," *IEEE Document P802.11-93/190, Nov 1993*

[3] W.K. Hale, "Frequency Assignment: Theory and Applications," *Proceedings of the IEEE*, Vol. 68, No. 12, Dec. 1980.

[4] I. Chlamtac and S. Kutten, "A spatial reuse TDMA/FDMA for mobile multi-hop radio networks", *Proc. INFOCOM*, 1985.

[5] A. Ephremedis and T. Truong, "Scheduling Broadcasts in Multihop Radio Networks," *IEEE Transactions on communications*, vol COM-38, Apr. 1990, pp. 456-460.

[6] I. Chlamtac and A. Lerner, "Fair Algorithms for Maximal Link Activation in Multihop Radio Networks," *IEEE Transactions on Communications, vol COM-35*, Jul. 1987, pp. 739-746.

[7] A. Ephremedis and J.E. Wieselthier and D.J. Baker, "A design concept for reliable mobile radio networks with frequency hopping signalling," *Proceedings of the IEEE*, vol 75, No. 1, Jan. 1987, pp. 56-73.

[8] I. Cidon and M. Sidi, "Distributed assignment algorithms for multihop radio networks," *IEEE Transactions on Computers*, vol. 38, no. 10, Oct. 1989, pp. 1353-1361.

[9] I. Chlamtac and A. Farago, "Making Transmission Schedules Immune to Topology Changes in Multi-Hop Packet Radio Networks," *IEEE/ACM Transactions on Networking*, Vol. 2, No. 1, Feb. 1994, pp. 23-29.

[10] T. Makansi, "Transmitter Oriented Code Assignment for Multihop Packet Radio", *IEEE Transactions on Information Theory*, Vol. 34, No. 5, Sep. 1988.

[11] A. A. Bertossi, M. A. Bonuccelli, "Code Assignment for Hidden Terminal Interference Avoidance in Multihop Packet Radio Networks", In *Proceedings of the INFOCOM*, 1992.

[12] L. Hu, "Distributed Code Assignments for CDMA Packet Radio Networks", *Proceedings of the INFOCOM*, 1991.

[13] A. Mansfield, "Determining the thickness of graphs is NP-Hard," *Math. Proc. Cambridge Philos. Soc.*, Vol. 93, pp. 9-23, 1983.

[14] S. Ramanathan, E. L. LLoyd, "Scheduling Algorithms for Multihop Radio Networks," *IEEE/ACM Transactions on Networking*, Vol. 1., No. 2, April 1993.

[15] E.L. Lloyd and S. Ramanathan, "Efficient Distributed Algorithms for Channel Assignment in Multihop Radio Networks," Journal of High Speed Networks, Vol. 2, No. 4, 1993.

[16] S. Ramanathan, "Scheduling Algorithms for Multihop Radio Networks," *Ph.d Thesis*, University of Delaware, 1992.

[17] M.R. Garey and D.S. Johnson, *Computers and Intractability: A Guide to the Theory of NP-completeness*, New York, NY:Freeman, 1979.

[18] S. Even, O. Goldreich, S. Moran, P. Tong, "On the NP-completeness of certain network testing problems," *Networks*, Vol. 14, 1984.

[19] T. Nishizeki and N. Chiba, ""Planar Graphs : Theory and Algorithms (Annals of Disc. Math. 32)," North-Holland Publishers, 1988.

[20] Anonymous FTP: ftp.bbn.com:/pub/ramanath/infocom97.ps

# Channel Carrying: A Novel Handoff Scheme for Mobile Cellular Networks *

Junyi Li  Ness B. Shroff†  Edwin K.P. Chong

School of Electrical and Computer Engineering
Purdue University, West Lafayette, IN 47907, U.S.A.
E-mail: {junyi, shroff, echong}@ecn.purdue.edu

## Abstract

We present a new scheme that addresses the call handoff problem in mobile cellular networks. Efficiently solving the handoff problem is important for guaranteeing Quality of Service (QoS) to already admitted calls in the network. Our scheme is based on a new concept called *channel carrying*: when a mobile user moves from one cell to another, *under certain mobility conditions*, the user is allowed to *carry* its current channel. We propose a new channel assignment scheme to ensure that this movement of channels will not lead to any extra co-channel interference or channel locking. *In our scheme, the mobility of channels relies entirely on localized information, and no global coordination is required.* Therefore, the scheme is simple and easy to implement. We further develop a hybrid channel carrying scheme that allows us to maximize performance under various constraints.

We provide numerical results comparing our scheme with the traditional channel reservation types of techniques. We find that our scheme outperforms the reservation scheme over a broad range of traffic parameters.

## 1 Introduction

The use of cellular systems is a popular means for enhancing the capacity of wireless communication networks. In such a system, the service area is divided into cells, and *channels* are reused among those cells. A channel can be thought of as a generic network resource; for example, a frequency band in FDMA, a time-slot in TDMA, or a specific spread spectrum code in CDMA. This definition is consistent with that in [4]. Channels that are used in one cell cannot be used in other cells that are closer than the *minimum reuse distance*. Handoff occurs when a mobile subscriber moves from one cell to another. A handoff call may be blocked if there is no free channel in the new cell. However, studies have shown that blocking a handoff call is less desirable than blocking a new call. Therefore, specific schemes have been developed to prioritize handoff calls. Two prioritization schemes have been commonly studied in the literature [1]. They are:

(i) *Channel reservation schemes*: In this type of schemes, a number of channels are reserved solely for the use of handoff, allowing both handoff and new calls to compete for the remaining channels [5]. Specifically, in each cell a threshold is set, and if the number of channels currently used in the cell is below that threshold, both new and handoff calls are accepted. However, if the number of channels used exceeds this threshold, an incoming new call is blocked and only handoff calls are admitted.

(ii) *Queueing schemes*: In this type of schemes handoff requests are queued, and may be later admitted into the network in case channels free up [2].

The above two schemes can also be integrated together to improve the handoff blocking probability and the overall channel utilization. The scheme we propose in this paper is also readily integrated with the queueing schemes. Therefore, we compare our scheme only with the reservation scheme.

Our method for treating the handoff problem stems from the following simple idea. A user requesting a handoff always occupies a channel in its current cell. *Therefore, if that channel could be carried into the new cell, the handoff request would not be blocked.* From a practical point of view this is not difficult to achieve. For example, in an FDMA based system, suppose a user requesting handoff to some cell $A$ communicates over a frequency band $x$ that cell $A$ is not allowed to use. Now, if normal handoff is not possible the user (or its current base-station) could signal cell $A$ giving it permission to communicate over channel $x$ with it. In a similar way, channels can be carried in CDMA and TDMA systems.

However, when a channel is allowed to move into another cell, it shortens the reuse distance and may violate the minimum reuse distance requirement [1, 3]. To solve this problem, we propose a new channel assignment method that allows channels to be "carried" into a neighboring cell. Furthermore, with an *a priori* agreement on channel movement, channel coordination can be achieved locally. This helps to significantly

*This research was supported in part by AT&T special purpose grant 670-1285-2569, by NSF through grants NCR-9624525, ECS-9410313, and ECS-9501652, and by the U.S. Army Research Office through grant 33980-EL-FRI.

†Please address all correspondence to this author, Tel. (317) 494-3471, FAX. (317) 494-3358.



0-8186-7780-5/97 $10.00 © 1997 IEEE

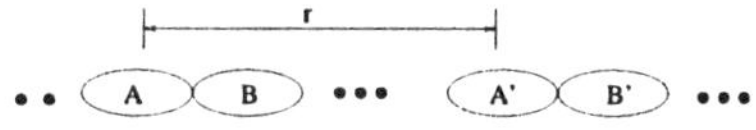


Figure 1: Linear Cellular System

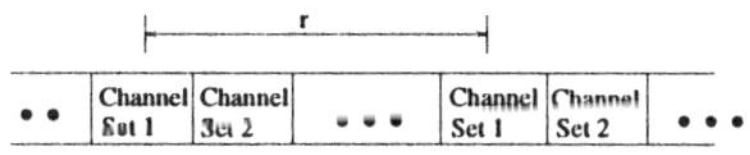


Figure 2: $r-$Channel Assignment

simplify the implementation. The new handoff scheme proposed in this paper is called *channel carrying.*

We next describe how the channels are assigned for the channel carrying scheme, and then present our basic handoff algorithm.

## 2 Channel Assignment

For simplicity, we describe our channel carrying scheme using a *linear cellular system* model. In this system, cells (or base stations) are arranged in a linear configuration, as shown in Figure 1. Let $N$ denote the total number of distinct channels that are available in the cellular system. Two cells can use the same set of channels as long as they are at least $r$ cells apart. This distance $r$ is called the *minimum reuse distance* or *reuse factor.* In the conventional fixed channel assignment scheme, the channels are assigned such that the same channels are reused exactly $r$ cells apart, as shown in Figure 2. Therefore, the total number of distinct channels available to each cell is $N/r$. We refer to this channel assignment as *r-channel assignment.*

In our channel carrying scheme, we alleviate blocking due to handoff by allowing calls to "carry" channels from one cell to another. However, using $r$-channel assignment, a call that carries a channel to an adjacent cell may violate the minimum reuse distance requirement. For example, in Figure 1, cells $A$ and $A'$ use the same set of channels. Suppose a call in cell $A$ uses a channel $y$, and carries it to cell $B$. Now, if a user arrives in cell $A'$ and uses channel $y$, then the two $y$ channels are only a distance of $r-1$ cells apart, thus violating the minimum reuse distance requirement. One way to overcome this problem is to have global coordination algorithms that use *channel locking* [3] to ensure that such situations do not occur. However, such schemes are computationally expensive and therefore difficult to implement [3]. Moreover, channel locking also degrades efficiency.

To ensure that the minimum reuse distance requirement is not violated, we use an $(r+1)$*-channel assignment* scheme. In other words, the same channels are reused exactly $r+1$ cells apart, as shown in Figure 3. In this case, the total number of distinct channels available to each cell is $N/(r+1)$. To ensure that the same channels do not get closer than $r$ cells apart (due to channel carrying), we restrict channel movement in the following way. Each channel is allowed to be carried in only one direction, left or right. This restriction thus divides the channels assigned to each

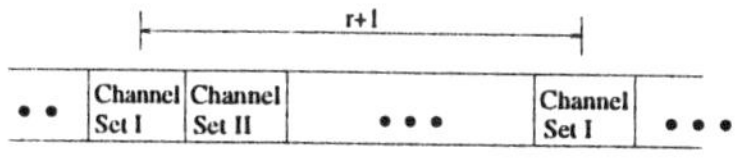


Figure 3: $(r+1)$-Channel Assignment

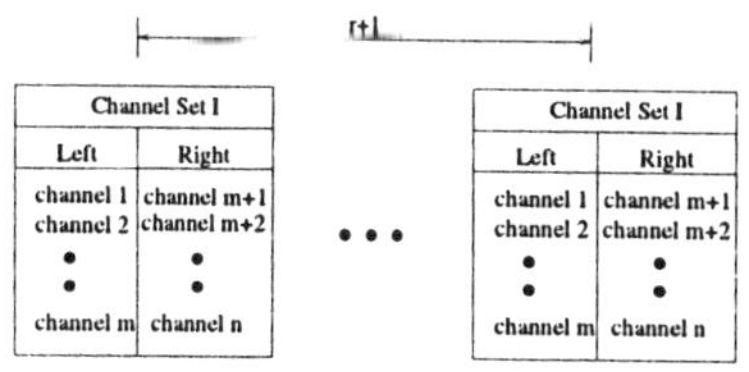


Figure 4: Channel Division in the $(r+1)$-Channel Assignment Scheme

cell into two types. Further, as shown in Figure 4, exactly the same division is used in cells that are a distance $r+1$ apart. Using this $(r+1)$-channel assignment scheme, and the channel carrying algorithm described in the next section, we ensure that there is no co-channel interference due to channel movement, while avoiding the need for global coordination.

## 3 Handoff Algorithm

### 3.1 Algorithm Description

To describe our handoff algorithm, we first focus our attention on a particular (arbitrary) cell, which we call the *local cell.* The adjacent cells to the left and right of the local cell are called *foreign cells.* The channels that have been assigned to the local cell are called *local channels,* and are divided into two types: *local-left* (LL) and *local-right* (LR) channels as shown in Figure 4. An LL (LR) channel is one that can be carried to the left (right) cell during handoff. In other words, an LL (LR) channel can be used by a call in the local cell as well as in the foreign cell to the left (right). A channel from a foreign cell that is being used in the local cell is called a *foreign channel.* Foreign channels from the left cell are called *foreign-left* (FL) channels and foreign channels from the right cell are called *foreign-right* (FR) channels.

Our algorithm can be described in five main parts, corresponding to five different possible scenarios: *arrival of a new call, handoff from a foreign cell, handoff to a foreign cell, termination of a call,* and when *a local channel becomes idle.*

#### 3.1.1 Arrival of a new call

When a new call arrives, we check if there are any idle (unused) local channels. If there are, the new call is accepted and assigned the idle channel; otherwise, the call is rejected (blocked).

#### 3.1.2 Handoff request from a foreign cell

When a handoff call request is received from a foreign (left or right) cell, we check if there are any idle local channels available. If there are, the handoff call is accepted and assigned the idle channel; otherwise, the foreign cell is notified that there are no idle local channels.

### 3.1.3 Handoff to a foreign cell

For simplicity, suppose a user $U$ in the local cell wants to move to the *left* foreign cell. The handoff operation is attempted according to the following order:

1. If user $U$ is currently using a foreign-left (FL) channel, then it simply carries it back to the left cell; otherwise, step 2 is initiated.

2. We check if there is an FL channel being used by some other user $V$ in the local cell. If so, user $U$ exchanges its channel with user $V$ and then executes step 1 above; if not, we perform step 3.

3. We send a handoff request to the left foreign cell. The foreign cell then executes the procedure in Section 3.1.2. If the handoff is accepted, user $U$ moves to the left cell and releases its own channel; if not, step 4 is initiated.

4. If user $U$ is currently using a local-left (LL) channel, then it carries it to the left cell; otherwise, step 5 is initiated.

5. We check if there is an idle LL channel currently in the local cell. If so, $U$ releases its own channel, grabs the idle LL channel, and carries it to the left cell; otherwise step 6 is initiated.

6. We check if there is an LL channel being used by some other user $W$ in the local cell. If so, user $U$ exchanges its channel with user $W$, and executes step 4 above.

7. If all the above conditions do not hold, then the handoff cannot be accomplished. Normally, this would result in the handoff call being blocked.

A similar procedure would be applied if a user in the local cell wanted to move to the right foreign cell.

### 3.1.4 Termination of a call

When a call $U$ is terminated (either due to the normal end of the call, or due to handoff blocking), we first check if the channel being used by $U$ is a foreign channel. If so, we release the foreign channel and return it to its originally assigned cell. Otherwise, $U$ is using a local channel—the call is then terminated and the channel becomes idle.

### 3.1.5 Local channel becomes idle

This scenario arises in the following situations:

1. Termination of a call in the local cell.

2. Handoff from the local cell to a foreign cell without carrying.

3. Return of an idle local channel from a foreign cell (when a local channel is released in the foreign cell and returned to the local cell).

When a local channel becomes newly idle, we check if there is a user $V$ using a foreign channel in the local cell. If so, user $V$ is assigned the newly idle local channel, and the foreign channel is released and returned to its originally assigned cell.

## 3.2 Salient Features of the Algorithm

The following are some of the significant features of our algorithm. Again, for simplicity, we focus only on handoff from the local cell to the *left* foreign cell.

(i) An important feature of our algorithm is that no global coordination is necessary, thus facilitating implementation. At the same time, the algorithm ensures that there is no co-channel interference due to channel movement.

(ii) In our algorithm, handoff calls have access to a larger portion of the system capacity than new incoming calls. To see this, note that a new call is blocked if and only if there is no idle (local) channel in the local cell. On the other hand, a handoff request to the (left) foreign cell is *blocked if and only if all the left-local (LL) channels are being used in the foreign cell.* This occurrence is relatively rare because it requires that all three of the following conditions are simultaneously true:

(a) All the FL channels are being used by users in the left foreign cell.

(b) All the channels in the left foreign cell are being used.

(c) All the LL channels have been previously carried to the left foreign cell.

It is therefore apparent that in our channel carrying scheme, handoff call requests are favored over new call requests. Meanwhile, we do not require channels to be reserved *a priori* for handoff calls. This helps increase the efficiency of our scheme compared to reservation schemes, as demonstrated in Sections 4.3 and 5.2.

(iii) In our algorithm, we prefer to use local channels whenever possible. We refer to this policy as a *return-as-soon-as-possible* policy. For example, whenever a channel becomes idle, we always return the foreign channel (if any) instead of keeping that idle channel waiting for a potential call in the local cell. The policy serves to protect potential handoff calls, because the accumulation of foreign channels may block further handoff requests from the foreign cell.

# 4 Performance Analysis

## 4.1 Channel Carrying Scheme

In this section we develop a Markov chain model to analyze the performance of our handoff algorithm. The QoS measures that we are interested in are:

- $P_{bN}$, the steady state probability of blocking a new call; and

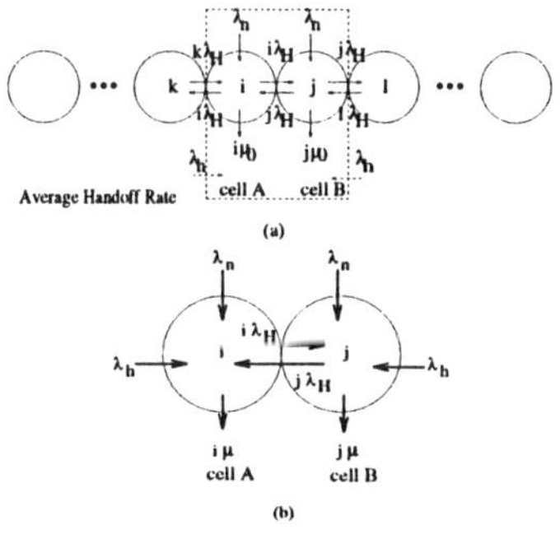


Figure 5: (a) Linear Cellular system with various traffic parameters. (b) Two-Cell model with the corresponding traffic parameters.

- $P_{bH}$, the steady state probability of blocking a handoff call.

The system that we are interested in modeling is the linear cellular system shown in Figure 5(a). The traffic is assumed to be symmetrically distributed over all the cells, for example, the new call arrival rate at every cell is $\lambda_n$. The handoff rates between cells is assumed to be directly proportional to the number of users in that cell, so if a cell has $i$ users the handoff rate to its neighboring cell is $i\lambda_H$, as shown in Figure 5(a). Analysis of this entire system is computationally infeasible. Therefore, the performance analysis of call handoff schemes in wireless systems is typically done by focusing on a single cell which results in a one dimensional Markov chain. However, the one-cell model does not accurately capture the essence of our algorithm. For example, suppose that a user in the local cell wants to move to the left foreign cell. Whether or not it carries a channel during handoff depends not only on the availability of FL and LL channels in the local cell but also on whether there is an idle channel in the left foreign cell. Hence, the availability of channels in adjacent cells is coupled.

To alleviate difficulties with a one-cell model we consider a two-cell model, as shown in Figure 5(b). We assume that in each cell $A$ and $B$, new call requests arrive according to Poisson processes with rate $\lambda_n$. The time it takes for each call in a cell to request a handoff to the other cell is assumed to be exponentially distributed with mean $1/\lambda_H$. Call handoffs arrive from outside the two-cell subsystem according to a Poisson process with rate $\lambda_h$. The time until a call terminates is assumed to be exponentially distributed with mean $1/\mu_0$. Therefore the time until a call leaves the two-cell system (either due to handoff or call termination) is exponentially distributed with mean $1/\mu = 1/(\mu_0 + \lambda_H)$. Now, assuming that all of the above mentioned processes (new arrival, call handoff request, and call termination) are mutually independent, we can analyze our two-cell system using a Markov Chain.

Recall that the total number of local channels in each cell is $M = N/(r+1)$. To further simplify the model, we assume that the total number of local channels, $M$, is divided into an equal number, $m = M/2$, of local left (LL) and local right (LR) channels.

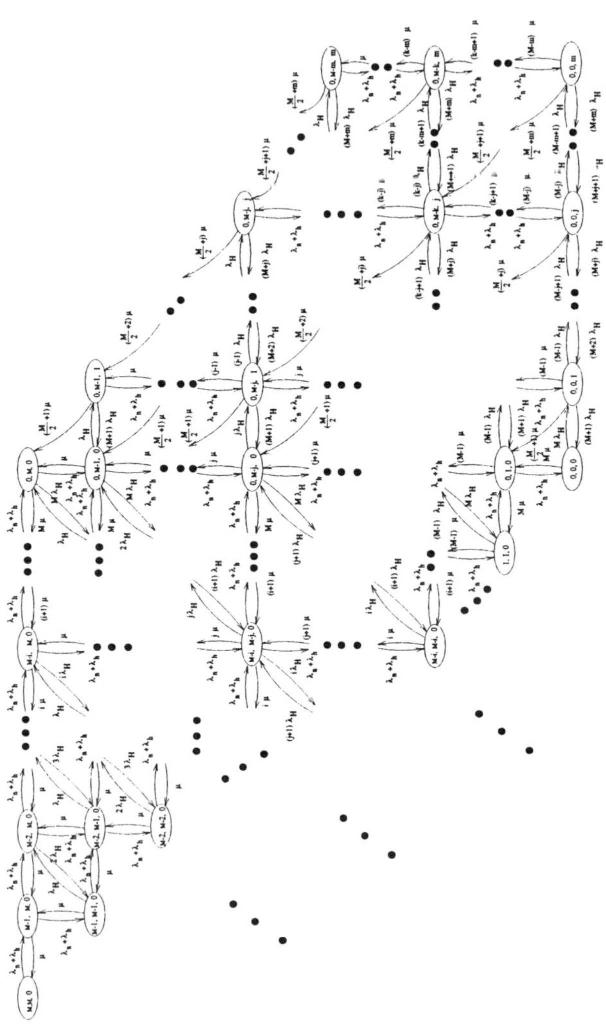

Figure 6: Markov Chain for the Channel Carrying Scheme using the Two-Cell model. Note that $m = M/2$, and $M = N/(r+1)$.

Our Markov chain model is shown in Figure 6. To describe the model, let $N_A \in \{0, \ldots, M\}$ and $N_B \in \{0, \ldots, M\}$ represent the number of idle local channels in cell $A$ and cell $B$, respectively. Next, let $N_{B\to A} \in \{-\frac{M}{2}, \ldots, 0, \ldots, \frac{M}{2}\}$ represent the following. If $N_{B\to A} \geq 0$, it denotes the number of foreign channels from cell $B$ that are being used in cell $A$. On the other hand, if $N_{B\to A} \leq 0$, it denotes the number of foreign channels from cell $A$ that are being used in cell $B$. Hence, $N_{B\to A}(t)$ can take values from $-\frac{M}{2}$ to $\frac{M}{2}$. The triple $(N_A, N_B, N_{B\to A})$ represents the state of the Markov chain. Although there are three components in each state, the state transition diagram of the Markov chain can be represented in a planar fashion. To see this, recall that a foreign channel will move into a cell only when there is no idle local channel in that cell. Also, whenever service is terminated, the foreign channel within the local cell will be returned immediately. Thus, if we neglect the additional time it would take to return or carry a channel, it follows that $N_{B\to A} > 0 \Rightarrow N_A = 0$, and $N_{B\to A} < 0 \Rightarrow N_B = 0$. These equations help restrict one degree of freedom thereby resulting in the planar or two-dimensional Markov chain shown in Figure 6.

Note that, because of the symmetric nature of the Markov chain, i.e., $P\{N_A = i, N_B = j, N_{B\to A} = k\} = P\{N_A = j, N_B = i, N_{B\to A} = -k\}$, only half of the Markov chain is shown in the figure. Let $P_{i,j,k} = P\{N_A = i, N_B = j, N_{B\to A} = k\}$ denote the steady state probability of the state $\{N_A = i, N_B = j, N_{B\to A} = k\}$. We obtain these probabilities by exploiting the above mentioned symmetry and by applying standard numerical Markov chain techniques.

Now observe Figures 5(a) and 5(b) again. In Figure 5(b) we have focussed only on cells $A$ and $B$ of Figure 5(a). Let the cells to the right of cell $B$ and to the left of cell $A$ be called *external cells*. The handoff rate $\lambda_h$ in the two-cell model of Figure 5(a) is actually the average of the state dependent handoff rate from their neighboring external cells. Averaging over all the states, $\lambda_h$ is given by

$$\lambda_h = \sum_{i=0}^{M}(M-i)\lambda_H \sum_{j=0}^{M}\sum_{k=-m}^{m} P_{i,j,k}, \qquad (1)$$

where $m = M/2$. Since $\lambda_h$ depends on $P_{i,j,k}$, we iteratively solve the Markov chain. Having determined $P_{i,j,k}$, we calculate $P_{bN}$, and $P_{bH}$ as follows:

$$P_{bN} = \sum_{k=0}^{m}\sum_{j=0}^{M-k} P_{0,j,k}; \quad P_{bH} = \sum_{j=0}^{M-m-1} P_{0,j,m}, \qquad (2)$$

### 4.2 Channel Reservation Scheme

In this section we develop a Markov chain model, shown in Figure 7, to analyze the system performance using the traditional channel reservation scheme. As in the channel carrying scheme, we focus on the two-cell model shown in Figure 5. The parameters $\lambda_h$, $\lambda_n$, $\lambda_H$, and $\mu$ are defined as before. Since no channel movement is allowed, the pair $(N_A, N_B)$, $N_A \in \{0,\ldots,M'\}$, $N_B \in \{0,\ldots,M'\}$, suffices to characterize the state of the two-cell system. Here, $M' = N/r$ is the total number of distinct channels available to each cell, and $N_A$ ($N_B$) is the total number of idle channels in cell $A$ (cell $B$). The resulting Markov chain is shown in Figure 7. Again, because of the symmetric nature of the Markov chain, i.e., $P\{N_A = i, N_B = j\} = P\{N_A = j, N_B = i\}$, only half of the Markov chain is shown in Figure 7. Let $P_{ij} \triangleq P\{N_A = i, N_B = j\}$ denote the steady state probability of the state $\{N_A = i, N_B = j\}$. Then, as in the channel carrying scheme, $\lambda_h$, the average external handoff arrival rate, is given by:

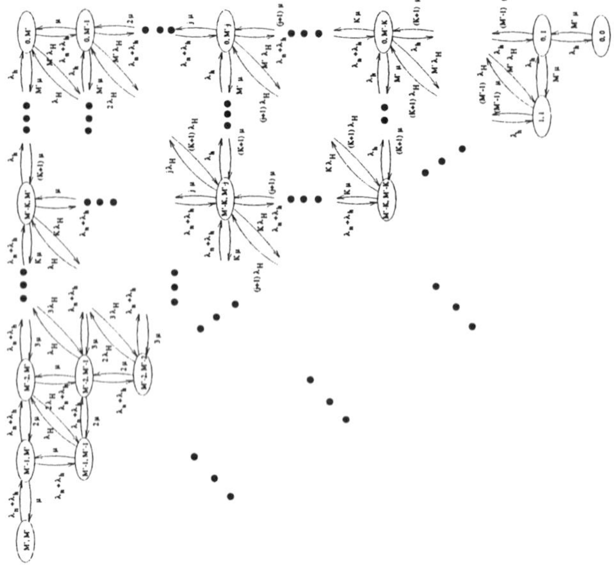

Figure 7: Markov Chain for the Channel Reservation Scheme using the Two-Cell model. Note: $M' = N/r$.

$$\lambda_h = \sum_{i=0}^{M'}(M'-i)\lambda_H \sum_{j=0}^{M'} P_{i,j}. \qquad (3)$$

Since $\lambda_h$ depends on $P_{i,j}$, we iteratively solve the Markov chain in Figure 7. Now $P_{bN}$ and $P_{bH}$ are given by

$$P_{bN} = \sum_{i=0}^{M'-K}\sum_{j=0}^{M'} P_{i,j}; \quad P_{bH} = \sum_{j=0}^{M'} P_{0,j} \qquad (4)$$

It is instructive to compare the state transition diagrams in Figures 6 and 7. The number of local channels in each cell is $M' = N/r$ in the reservation scheme (Figure 6) instead of $M = N/(r+1)$ in the carrying scheme (Figure 7). The difference is $d = M' - M = \frac{N}{r(r+1)}$, which is the cost we pay for channel mobility. Clearly, when the reuse factor $r$ is large, this difference is marginal. Also, because of channel reservation, new calls have to be blocked when the number of occupied local channels exceeds a threshold $K$ in Figure 7. Then, the arrival rate is reduced from $\lambda_n + \lambda_h$ to $\lambda_h$, which is a disadvantage of the reservation scheme compared to the channel carrying scheme.

### 4.3 Numerical Results

In this section, we provide numerical results to compare the performance of the channel carrying scheme and the reservation scheme.

We use our Markov chain model for computing the performance measures $P_{bN}$ and $P_{bH}$ and also simulate the system under the carrying and reservation schemes. Our simulation consists of a 120 cell linear

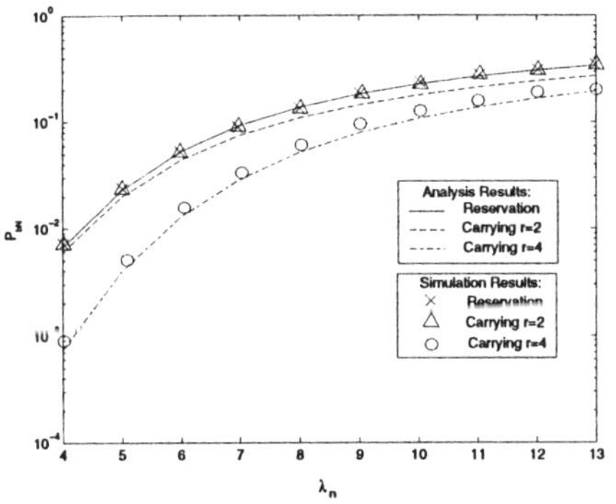


Figure 8: Plot of $P_{bN}$ versus $\lambda_n$.

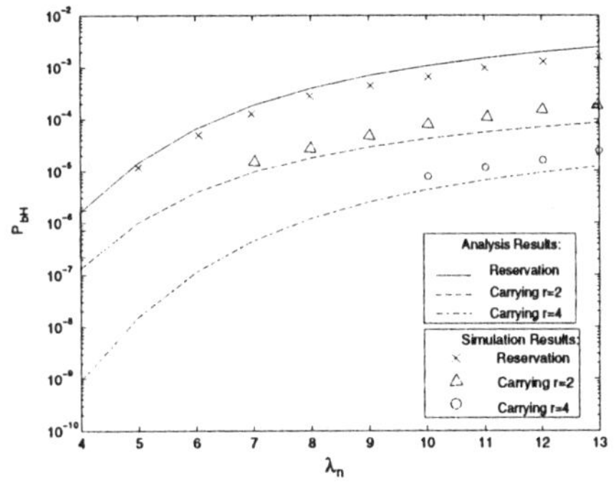


Figure 9: Plot of $P_{bH}$ versus $\lambda_n$.

cellular system, such as the one shown in Figure 5(a). Since we are interested in the performance of a typical cell, the statistics are averaged over all cells. Throughout the paper, we find that the simulation and analytical results match quite well, which indicates that the two-cell model works well in characterizing the behavior of the algorithm in a linear cellular system.

In Figure 8 we plot $P_{bN}$, and in Figure 9, we plot $P_{bH}$ for both the channel carrying and the reservation scheme under different traffic loads $\lambda_n$, ranging from 4 calls to 13 calls per unit time. The call handoff rate is $\lambda_H = 1$ call per unit time, and the call termination rate is $\mu_0 = 1$ call per unit time.

For the channel carrying case, two values for the reuse distance are considered: $r = 2$, the minimum possible reuse distance, and $r = 4$, a more typical value for the reuse distance. Further, in both figures, $M' = N/r = 15$; hence, $N = 30$ when $r = 2$, and $N = 60$ when $r = 4$.

Note, that in the channel reservation scheme, for a given arrival rate, we can vary the threshold $K$ to give us different values of $P_{bN}$ and $P_{bH}$. We find that if we choose $K = M = N/(r+1)$, then the values of $P_{bN}$ for the reservation scheme are close to those for the carrying scheme. The reason for this is that if the number of occupied local channels in a cell reaches $K$ (or $M$), any new call in the reservation (or carrying, respectively) scheme is now blocked. For $r = 2$, we choose $K = M = 10$, and we can observe in Figure 8 that the new call blocking probability ($P_{bN}$) curves for the reservation and carrying schemes are in fact very close. However, for the same parameters, the call handoff blocking probability ($P_{bH}$) as shown in Figure 9 is at least about one order of magnitude lower in the carrying scheme than in the reservation scheme. When the value of the reuse distance is increased to $r = 4$, and we set $K = 10$, the carrying scheme significantly outperforms the reservation scheme in terms of both $P_{bN}$ and $P_{bH}$. This result can be observed in Figure 8, where the $P_{bN}$ curve in the carrying case is up to one order of magnitude lower than in the reservation scheme, and in Figure 9, where the $P_{bH}$ curve in the carrying scheme is up to three orders of magnitude lower than in the reservation scheme.

We next develop a hybrid channel carrying scheme which attempts to maximize performance, under various constraints, by allowing us to vary the number of channels that can be carried.

# 5 Hybrid Channel Carrying Scheme

## 5.1 Description

In the numerical examples of the previous section, we observe that the channel carrying scheme results in a large difference between the values of $P_{bH}$ and $P_{bN}$. In particular, when the load is high, the value of $P_{bN}$ is much higher than that of $P_{bH}$. For example, for $\lambda_n = 13$ and $r = 4$, the value of $P_{bH}$ is only about $10^{-5}$ while that of $P_{bN}$ is greater than $10^{-1}$. This observation suggests that our channel carrying scheme excessively favors handoff requests over new calls. We next present a hybrid scheme that allows trading off potential handoff blocking for availability of idle channels for new calls.

Recall that in the $(r+1)$-channel assignment scheme, the number of channels assigned to each cell is $M = N/(r+1)$, and every channel can be carried either to the left or to the right. On the other hand, in the $r$-channel assignment scheme, the number of channels assigned to each cell is $N/r$, but none of the channels can be carried to foreign cells. In our hybrid scheme, we divide the total number of channels $N$ into two distinct groups of size $N_1$ and $N_2$, such that $N = N_1 + N_2$. The $N_1$ channels are assigned according to the $r$-channel assignment scheme, and cannot be carried to foreign channels. The $N_2$ channels, however, are assigned according to the $(r+1)$-channel assignment scheme, and can be carried either to the left or to the right, just as in the previous channel carrying scheme. Therefore, in the hybrid scheme, each cell is assigned

$$M_{hybrid} = \frac{N_1}{r} + \frac{N_2}{r+1} \qquad (5)$$

channels, where the two terms in the sum corresponds to the two groups of channels. As before, the $N_2/(r+1)$ channels of the second type are themselves divided into two types: left and right.

The hybrid scheme above defines a family of channel assignments that encompasses both the pure $r$-

and $(r+1)$-channel assignment schemes. Specifically, $N_1 = 0$ corresponds to the $(r+1)$-channel assignment scheme, while $N_2 = 0$ leads to the $r$-channel assignment scheme. The $N_2$ channels allow us to trade off the ability to carry (and hence avoid handoff blocking) with a reduced number of channels available to each cell. In particular, the number of channels that we sacrifice in using $(r+1)$-channel assignment instead of $r$-channels assignment is

$$d_{hybrid} = \frac{N_2}{r} - \frac{N_2}{r+1} = \frac{1}{r}\left(\frac{N_2}{r+1}\right). \qquad (6)$$

Thus, $d_{hybrid}$ serves as a design parameter that we can adjust to balance the requirements of the performance measures $P_{bN}$ and $P_{bH}$, analogous to the threshold parameter $K$ in the channel reservation scheme. The larger the value of $d_{hybrid}$ in the hybrid scheme, the more we favor handoff calls because there are more movable channels. Hence, as $d_{hybrid}$ increases, we expect $P_{bH}$ to decrease and $P_{bN}$ to increase. A similar observation holds for the design parameter $K$ in the reservation scheme. Also note that, as in the original channel carrying case, for a fixed number of channels $N_2$ that are allowed to move, the price we pay for the $(r+1)$-channel assignment scheme (in terms of $d_{hybrid}$) decreases with increasing $r$.

## 5.2 Numerical Results

For the purpose of performance evaluation, we adopt the two-cell model and make the same assumptions here as we did in Section 4.3. The resulting Markov chain has exactly the same structure as in Figure 6, the only difference being that we substitute $m_{hybrid} = \frac{N_2}{2(r+1)}$ in place of $m$. We can then solve for the steady state probabilities in the Markov chains for the hybrid and reservation schemes, and compute $P_{bH}$ and $P_{bN}$ as before. Also, as in Section 4.3, for our simulations we use a 120-cell linear cellular system.

We now provide plots of $P_{bN}$ under varying load conditions for the hybrid and reservation schemes. The performance measures depend on the parameters $d_{hybrid}$ and $K$ in the hybrid and reservation schemes, respectively. To meaningfully compare our hybrid scheme with the reservation scheme, we determine the optimal values of $P_{bN}$ for the two schemes, given a constraint on $P_{bH}$. Therefore, in the hybrid scheme, to appropriately choose $d_{hybrid}$, we consider the following optimization problem:

$$\underset{d_{hybrid}}{\text{minimize}} \quad P_{bN}, \qquad \text{subject to } P_{bH} \leq H_{max}, \qquad (7)$$

where $H_{max}$ denotes a prespecified maximum level for $P_{bH}$. A similar optimization problem can be defined for the reservation scheme, where the decision variable $d_{hybrid}$ above is replaced with the threshold parameter $K$. For a fair comparison of our hybrid scheme with the reservation scheme, we calculate the optimal values of $P_{bN}$ for the two schemes, given the same $H_{max}$. The optimal values can be computed numerically using the Markov chains in Figures 6 and 7. Figure 10

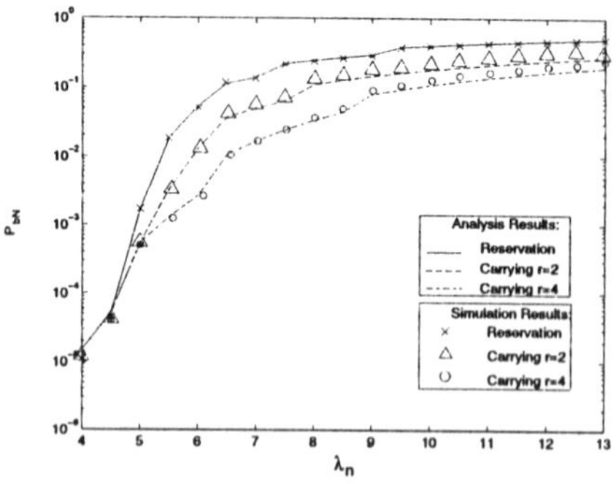


Figure 10: Plot of optimal $P_{bN}$ versus $\lambda_n$ for the problem defined in Equation (7).

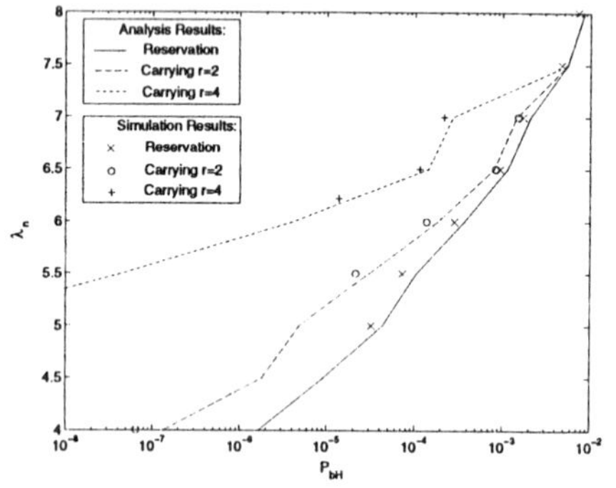


Figure 11: Plot of optimal $\lambda_n$ versus $P_{bH}$ for the problem defined in Equation (8).

shows plots of the optimal values of $P_{bN}$ for the reservation and hybrid schemes under varying $\lambda_n$. For this figure we have used the following parameters: $\lambda_H = 1$, $\mu_0 = 1$, $M' = 15$. Therefore, $N = 30$ for $r = 2$, and $N = 60$ for $r = 4$. For the constraint on $P_{bH}$, we used $H_{max} = 10^{-4}$, a typically desirable constraint for the handoff blocking probability. We can see that the hybrid scheme achieves uniformly lower values of $P_{bN}$ than the reservation scheme. As expected, increasing the value of $r$ further decreases $P_{bN}$ in the channel carrying case.

Next, in Figure 11, we plot a graph in which we compare the maximum new call arrival rate $\lambda_n$ that can be admitted by the carrying scheme and the reservation scheme for various handoff blocking probabilities $P_{bH}$. More precisely we define the following optimization problem for the channel carrying scheme:

$$\underset{d_{hybrid}}{\text{maximize}} \quad \lambda_n,$$
$$\text{subject to} \quad P_{bN} \leq N_{max}, \; P_{bH} = H. \qquad (8)$$

Here the constraint $H$ for $P_{bH}$ is varied between $10^{-8}$ and $10^{-2}$ and the corresponding maximum value of $\lambda_n$ is obtained. A similar optimization problem is defined for the reservation scheme by replacing $d_{hybrid}$ by $K$. In Figure 11 we plot the optimal values of $\lambda_n$ versus

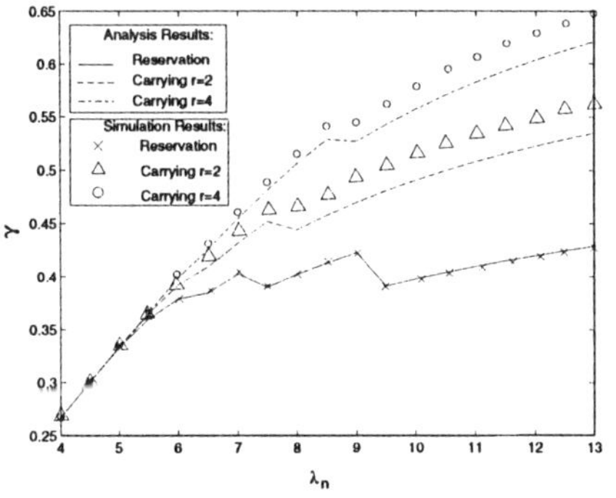


Figure 12: Plot of optimal $\gamma$ versus $\lambda_n$ for the problem defined in Equation (9).

$P_{bH}$ for the reservation scheme and the channel carrying scheme with $r = 2$ and $r = 4$. For this figure we use the following parameters: $\lambda_H = 1$, $\mu_0 = 1$, $M' = 15$, $N_{max} = 10^{-2}$. From Figure 11 one can observe that the hybrid carrying scheme allows a higher new call rate than the reservation scheme over all values of $P_{bH}$. For large values of $P_{bH}$ all the schemes perform essentially the same since it corresponds to the case when no carrying is necessary in the hybrid case ($N_2 = 0$) and no reservation is necessary ($K = N/r$) in the reservation scheme. However, for a typical value of $P_{bH} = 10^{-4}$, the hybrid scheme with $r = 4$ can admit approximately 20% more calls into the network than the reservation scheme. As is shown in the figure, for lower handoff probability constraints, this difference is even larger.

From a network provider's point of view, a more useful parameter of interest is the *normalized channel utilization*, $\gamma$ , defined as

$$\gamma \triangleq \frac{\text{average number of users in one cell}}{\text{total number of available channels in one cell}},$$

where the total number of available channels in one cell is $M' = N/r$. The parameter $\gamma$ is directly related to the revenue of a cellular network because it incorporates both new and handoff calls.

To plot the values of $\gamma$ under varying loads for the hybrid scheme, we define the optimization problem

$$\max_{d_{hybrid}} \gamma, \quad \text{subject to } P_{bH} \leq H_{max}. \quad (9)$$

Once again, we define a similar optimization problem for the reservation scheme by replacing the decision variable $d_{hybrid}$ by $K$. In Figure 12 we plot values of $\gamma$ under varying $\lambda_n$. The parameters used for this figure are: $\lambda_H = 1$, $\mu_0 = 1$, $M' = 15$, $H_{max} = 10^{-4}$. The hybrid scheme achieves uniformly higher values of $\gamma$ under various loads. The difference between the hybrid and reservation schemes is most apparent at high loads. At such loads, a low value of $K$ is required in the reservation scheme to maintain the QoS constraint on $P_{bH}$, thus resulting in a low value of $\gamma$. On the other hand, due to the mobility of channels in the hybrid scheme, the sacrifice in the number of local channels to maintain the QoS constraint on $P_{bH}$ is not as great. When $r = 4$, the channel utilization for the channel carrying scheme at high loads is over 50% more than the reservation scheme. Further, this advantage will be even more significant as $r$ increases

## 6 Conclusion

We have presented a novel channel carrying scheme to address the problem of handoffs in mobile cellular systems. Our basic idea is to allow mobile users to carry their current channels into new cells under certain conditions. We use the $(r+1)$-channel assignment scheme to avoid co-channel interference due to channel movement. This affords us channel mobility at the expense of some capacity. An attractive feature of the channel carrying scheme is that it does not require complex power control techniques or global channel coordination, which simplifies its implementation.

We develop a two-cell model to analyze our channel carrying scheme and the traditional channel reservation technique. We find through numerical results that even in the case of the minimum possible reuse distance, $r = 2$, the channel carrying scheme outperforms the reservation technique.

We further consider a refinement to the channel carrying scheme, which provides a useful design parameter that allows us to optimize various parameters of interest. We again find that our scheme scheme uniformly and significantly improves the system performance, in some cases resulting in over 50% better network utilization than the channel reservation scheme.

## References


[1] S. Tekinay and B. Jabbari, "Handover and channel assignment in mobile cellular networks," *IEEE Communications Magazine*, vol.29, pp.42–46, Nov. 1991.

[2] G.N. Senarath and D.H. Everitt, "Performance of handover priority and queueing systems under different handover request strategies for microcellular mobile communications systems," *Proc. IEEE Veh. Technol. Conf.*, pp.897–901, 1995.

[3] H. Jiang and S.S. Rappaport, "CBWL: a new channel assignment and sharing method for cellular communication systems," *IEEE Trans. Veh. Technol.*, vol.VT-43, pp.313–322, May 1994.

[4] E.D. Re, R. Fantacci and G. Giambene, "Handover and dynamic channel allocation techniques in mobile cellular networks," *IEEE Trans. Veh. Technol.*, vol.VT-44, pp.229-237, May 1995.

[5] R. Ramjee, R. Nagarajan and D. Towsley, "On optimal call admission control in cellular networks," *Proc. INFOCOM.*, pp43–50, March 1996.

# Effects of Erlang Call Holding Times on PCS Call Completion

Yi-Bing Lin
Dept. Comp. Sci. & Info. Engr.
National Chaio Tung University
Hsinchu, Taiwan, R.O.C.
Fax:+886-35-724-176
Email: liny@csie.nctu.edu.tw

Imrich Chlamtac
Dept. of Elect., Comp., & Sys. Engr.
Boston University
44 Cummington Str.
Boston, MA 02215
Email:chlamtac@bu.edu

## Abstract

Previous performance studies of PCS channel allocation assumed that call holding times have an exponential distribution. The exponential call holding time assumption is justified for existing cellular systems, where wireless calls are charged based on the length of the call holding time. Future PCS systems may exercise flat rate billing, and consequently a more general distribution is desirable to model the call holding times. This paper models the call holding times by the Erlang distribution (a generalization of the exponential distribution) to investigate the effect of the variance of the call holding times on the call completion probability. Our analysis indicates that the call completion probability decreases as the variance of the call holding times decreases. This effect becomes more pronounced as the variance of the cell residence times decreases.

## 1 Introduction

A *personal communications services* (PCS) network [2, 12] allows users to communicate with the network while on the move. During a communication session, a radio link is established between the portable (the *mobile phone* or *mobile computer*) and a *base station* of the PCS network, if the portable is in the *cell* or the coverage area of the base station. If, during the conversation, the portable moves from one cell to another, the radio link between the old base station and portable is removed and in order to continue the call the portable must obtain a new radio link in the new cell. If no radio link is available the call is *forced terminated* [7].

Performance modeling of a PCS system can be conducted at two levels. The first level modeling uses the number of radio channels in cells as an input parameter to determine the new call blocking probability and the forced termination probability. Second level modeling uses the new call blocking and the forced termination probabilities to study the call completion probability (or the probability that a call is successfully completed).

This paper focuses on the second level modeling. Since existing cellular systems are typically engineered at 1-2% new call blocking and forced termination, these default values may be used as the reference input parameters for the second level modeling. However, the call completion probability cannot be derived directly from these two probabilities. Both the cell residence times and the call holding times of portables are required to investigate the call completion probability. To provide an accurate analysis, the cell residence time and the call holding time distributions must be carefully chosen to reflect the real system. In our model, a general cell residence time distribution is considered, which can be used to accommodate any real PCS system. The selection of the call holding time distribution is subtle. In the early wireline telephone network modeling, the call holding times were typically assumed to be exponentially distributed. Such an assumption seems to be reasonable when the calls are charged based on the lengths of the call holding times. The assumption is no longer valid for modern telephone services with flat rate billing programs. Flat rate billing encourages people to make long calls (for example, people may log on from their PCs at home to main computers at their workplace through the local telephone links and keep the connections for hours or even days). Thus, long tails are observed for the call holding time distributions. In recent telephone network engineering, lognormal distributions [4] have been used to approximate the wireline call holding times.

For most existing cellular systems the wireless calls



0-8186-7780-5/97 $10.00 © 1997 IEEE

are charged based on the call holding times, and these systems can be appropriately modeled using exponential call holding time distributions [9, 10]. However, for future PCS systems (especially low power PCS systems such as CT-2 [13], DECT [3], or PACS [11]), flat rate billing programs have been proposed [1]. Thus, it is important to follow the wireline telephone network engineering approaches, i.e. use a lognormal-like distribution to represent the call holding time distribution.

In this paper, we consider the Erlang call holding time distribution. The Erlang distribution is a special case of the gamma distribution. Statistically, both the lognormal and gamma distributions have the same capability to approximate measured data [5]. An important advantage of the Erlang/gamma distribution over the lognormal distribution is that the Erlang/gamma distribution has a simple Laplace transform format, a desirable property in our modeling.

## 2 Assumptions

In this paper, we derive the call completion probability with the following three assumptions. The first two assumptions follow those given in our previous work [8]. The third assumption, generalizes the results presented in [8].

- The call arrivals form a Poisson process with arrival rate $\lambda$.

- The *cell residence times* (the intervals that a portable stays in the cells) have identical but arbitrary non-lattice distribution with mean $1/\eta$. The call completion probability $p_c$ will be derived under the general residence time distribution. Then gamma residence time distribution is used in the numerical examples. For a gamma residence time distribution with the shape parameter $\gamma$ and the scale parameter $\beta = \gamma\eta$ (and the variance of the distribution is $V = \dfrac{(\gamma+1)}{\gamma\eta^2}$), the density function $f(t)$ is expressed as

$$f(t) = \frac{\beta^\gamma t^{\gamma-1} e^{-\beta t}}{\Gamma(\gamma)} \quad \text{where} \quad \gamma > 0 \qquad (1)$$

Note that the $\gamma$ value is a positive real number. As pointed out in [8], the gamma distribution is selected because the distribution is a good second approximation for the data measured from the PCS field trials.

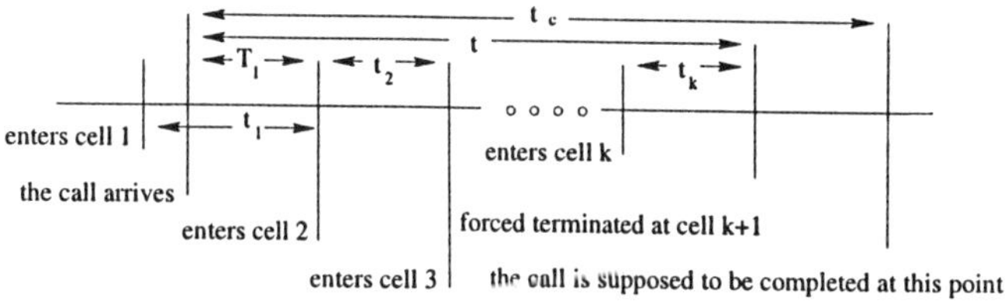


Figure 1: The timing diagram for a forced terminated call

- The call holding times have an Erlang distribution with the shape parameter $m$ and the scale parameter $\alpha = m\mu$ where $\frac{1}{\mu}$ is the expected call holding time, and the variance is $V = (m+1)/(m\mu^2)$. The density function $f_c$ for the call holding time $t_c$ is expressed as

$$f_c(t_c) = \frac{(\alpha t_c)^{m-1}}{(m-1)!}\alpha e^{-\alpha t_c} \quad \text{where} \quad m = 1, 2, 3, \ldots \qquad (2)$$

Note that an Erlang distribution is a special case of the gamma distribution where the shape parameter $m$ is a positive integer. When $m = 1$, the call holding time has an exponential distribution. Similar to the gamma distribution, the Erlang distribution can be used to approximate the measured data for some special cases. It can also be used to illustrate the effects of the variance and the skewness of the call holding time distribution on the call completion probability.

## 3 The Derivation for the Call Completion Probability

This section derives the call completion probability $p_c$. We note that the derivation of Equation (6) is exactly the same as that in [8]. The only difference is that in this paper the exponential call holding time distribution in [8] is replaced by the Erlang distribution. We note that this distinction is non-trivial. First of all, the derivation of $p_c$ based on the Erlang call holding time distribution is much more difficult than that based on the exponential distribution. Secondly, with the Erlang distribution, we are able to observe the effects of the variance of the call holding time distribution on the call completion probability.

To this end we first consider the effective call holding time $t$ for an incomplete call. Figure 1 illustrates the timing diagram for deriving $t$. In this figure, $t_1$ is the time that the portable resides at cell 1, and $t_i$ (where $i \geq 2$) is the residence time at cell $i$. We assume that $t_1, t_2, t_3, \ldots, t_k$ are independent and identically distributed random variables with an arbitrary non-lattice density function $f(\cdot)$ with the mean $\frac{1}{\eta}$. Let $f^*(s)$ be the Laplace Transform of the cell residence time distribution. Then

$$f^*(s) = \int_{\tau=0}^{\infty} f(\tau)e^{-s\tau}\,d\tau$$

Suppose that a call for the portable occurs when the portable is in cell 1. In Figure 1 (a), $T_1$ is the interval between when the call arrives and when the portable moves out of cell 1. Let $r(T_1)$ and $r^*(s)$ be the density function and the Laplace Transform of the $T_1$ distribution, respectively. Since the call arrivals are a Poisson process, from the *residual life theorem* [6] we have

$$r(T_1) = \eta \int_{\tau=T_1}^{\infty} f(\tau)d\tau \qquad (3)$$

From (3) and the Laplace Transform Rule P.1.1.6 in [14], we have

$$r^*(s) = \frac{\eta}{s}\Big[1 - f^*(s)\Big] \qquad (4)$$

Let $t = T_1 + t_2 + ... + t_k$. Then its density function $f_k(t)$ is expressed as the convolution of the density functions for $T_1, t_2, ..., t_k$. That is,

$$\begin{aligned} f_k(t) &= \int_{T_1=0}^{t}\int_{t_2=0}^{t-T_1}\cdots\int_{t_{k-1}=0}^{t-T_1-...-t_{k-2}} r(T_1)f(t_2)\cdots \\ &\times\ f(t_{k-1})f(t - T_1 - ... - t_{k-1})dT_1dt_2...dt_{k-1} \qquad (5)\end{aligned}$$

Next we define the probabilities used in this paper.

- $p_o$: the probability that a new call attempt is blocked (i.e., the call is never connected)
- $p_f$: the probability that a handover call is forced terminated.
- $p_c$: the probability that a call is completed (i.e., the call is connected and completed).

¿From the definitions of $p_o$ and $p_c$, the probability of an incomplete call (i.e., the call is connected but is eventually forced terminated) is $1 - p_o - p_c$, and is expressed as

$$\begin{aligned} & 1 - p_o - p_c = (1 - p_o)p_f \\ \times & \sum_{k=1}^{\infty}\left\{\int_{t=0}^{\infty}\int_{t_c=t}^{\infty} f_k(t)(1-p_f)^{k-1}f_c(t_c)dt_cdt\right\} \\ = & (1-p_o)p_f \\ \times & \sum_{k=1}^{\infty}\left\{\int_{t=0}^{\infty} f_k(t)(1-p_f)^{k-1}\left[\int_{t_c=t}^{\infty} f_c(t_c)dt_c\right]dt\right\} \end{aligned} \qquad (6)$$

In (6), the term in $\{\cdot\}$ is the probability that a call is forced terminated at the $k$th handover (note that the call is connected with the probability $1-p_o$, and then makes $k-1$ successful handovers with the probability $(1-p_f)^{k-1}$, and is forced terminated at the $k$th handover with the probability $p_f$). The call incompletion probability is the summation of the probabilities for $1 \le k < \infty$. From (2), we have

$$\begin{aligned} \int_{t_c=t}^{\infty} f_c(t_c)dt_c &= \int_{t_c=t}^{\infty}\frac{(\alpha t_c)^{m-1}}{(m-1)!}\alpha e^{-\alpha t_c}dt_c \\ &= \sum_{i=0}^{m-1}\frac{(\alpha t)^i}{i!}e^{-\alpha t} \end{aligned}$$

and (6) is rewritten as

$$\begin{aligned} & 1 - p_o - p_c = (1-p_o)p_f \\ \times & \sum_{k=1}^{\infty}\left\{\int_{t=0}^{\infty} f_k(t)(1-p_f)^{k-1}\left[\sum_{i=0}^{m-1}\frac{(\alpha t)^i}{i!}e^{-\alpha t}\right]dt\right\} \\ = & (1-p_o)p_f \\ \times & \sum_{k=1}^{\infty}\left[\sum_{i=0}^{m-1}(1-p_f)^{k-1}\left(\frac{\alpha^i}{i!}\right)\int_{t=0}^{\infty} t^i f_k(t)e^{-\alpha t}dt\right] \end{aligned} \qquad (7)$$

$$\begin{aligned} = & (1-p_o)p_f \\ \times & \sum_{i=0}^{m-1}\left\{\sum_{k=1}^{\infty}(1-p_f)^{k-1}\left(\frac{\alpha^i}{i!}\right)\left[\left.\frac{(-1)^i d^i f_k^*(s)}{d^i s}\right|_{s=\alpha}\right]\right\} \end{aligned} \qquad (8)$$

where $f_k^*(s)$ is the Laplace Transform of $f_k(t)$, and is derived from (5) as follows. The Convolution property of the Laplace Transform (Rule P.1.2.2 [14]) states that

$$h(t) = \int_{\tau=0}^{t} g(\tau)f(t-\tau)d\tau \Rightarrow h^*(s) = g^*(s)f^*(s)$$

Thus, the Laplace Transform $f_k^*(s)$ for $f_k(t)$ is expressed as

$$f_k^*(s) = r^*(s)\Big[f^*(s)\Big]^{k-1} \qquad (9)$$

From (9) and (4)

$$f_k^*(s) = \frac{\eta}{s}\Big[1 - f^*(s)\Big]\Big[f^*(s)\Big]^{k-1} \qquad (10)$$

Also note that (8) is derived from (7) by using the fact (Rule P.3.1.1 in [14]) that

$$g(t) = tf(t) \Rightarrow g^*(s) = -\frac{df^*(s)}{ds}$$

From (8) we have

$$p_c = 1 - p_o - X(m) \tag{11}$$

where

$$\begin{aligned} X(m) &= \sum_{j=0}^{m-1} \left\{ \sum_{k=1}^{\infty} (1-p_o)(1-p_f)^{k-1} p_f \left( \frac{\alpha^j}{j!} \right) \right. \\ &\times \left. \left[ \frac{(-1)^j d^j f_k^*(s)}{d^j s} \bigg|_{s=\alpha} \right] \right\} \end{aligned} \tag{12}$$

Denote $p_c(m)$ as the $p_c$ value when the Erlang call holding time distribution has the shape parameter $m$. For $m = 1$, $p_c(1)$ can be derived as follows. From (10) we have [8]

$$\begin{aligned} X(1) &= \sum_{k=1}^{\infty} (1-p_o)(1-p_f)^{k-1} p_f \left( \frac{\eta}{s} \right) \\ &\times [1 - f^*(s)][f^*(s)]^{k-1} \\ &= \frac{\eta(1-p_o)[1-f^*(\alpha)]p_f}{\alpha[1-(1-p_f)f^*(s)]} \end{aligned} \tag{13}$$

From (11), and (13) we have

$$p_c(1) = (1-p_o)\left\{ 1 - \frac{\eta\,[1-f^*(\alpha)]\,p_f}{\alpha[1-(1-p_f)f^*(\alpha)]} \right\} \tag{14}$$

For $m1$, in order to derive $X(i)$, we need to compute the derivatives of $f_k^*(s)$ and $f^*(s)$. Let

$$f_k^{(i)}(s) = \frac{d^i f_k^*(s)}{ds^i} \quad \text{and} \quad f^{(i)}(s) = \frac{d^i f^*(s)}{ds^i}$$

Then from (10)

$$\begin{aligned} f_k^{(1)}(s) &= -\frac{\eta}{s^2}[1-f^*(s)][f^*(s)]^{k-1} \\ &- \frac{\eta}{s}\left[ \frac{df^*(s)}{ds} \right][f^*(s)]^{k-1} \\ &+ \frac{\eta}{s}[1-f^*(s)](k-1)[f^*(s)]^{k-2}\left[ \frac{df^*(s)}{ds} \right] \\ &= -f_k^*(s)\left[ \frac{1}{s} + \frac{f^{(1)}(s)}{1-f^*(s)} \right. \\ &+ \left. \frac{f^{(1)}(s)}{f^*(s)} - \frac{kf^{(1)}(s)}{f^*(s)} \right] \qquad (15) \\ &= -A(s)[f^*(s)]^{k-1} + B(s)k[f^*(s)]^{k-1} \qquad (16) \end{aligned}$$

where

$$\begin{aligned} A(s) &= \frac{\eta[1-f^*(s)]}{s}\left[ \frac{1}{s} + \frac{f^{(1)}(s)}{1-f^*(s)} + \frac{f^{(1)}(s)}{f^*(s)} \right] \\ B(s) &= \frac{\eta f^{(1)}(s)[1-f^*(s)]}{sf^*(s)} \end{aligned} \tag{17}$$

Consider $m = 2$. From (12) and (16), we have

$$\begin{aligned} X(2) &= X(1) \\ &+ \sum_{k=1}^{\infty}(1-p_o)(1-p_f)^{k-1}p_f \left[ -\alpha \frac{df_k^*(s)}{ds} \right] \bigg|_{s=\alpha} \\ &= X(1) + \left[ \frac{\alpha(1-p_o)p_f}{f^*(\alpha)(1-p_f)} \right] \\ &\times \left\{ A(\alpha)\left\{ \sum_{k=1}^{\infty}[(1-p_f)f^*(\alpha)]^k \right\} \right. \\ &- \left. B(\alpha)\left\{ \sum_{k=1}^{\infty} k[(1-p_f)f^*(\alpha)]^k \right\} \right\} \\ &= X(1) + \alpha(1-p_o)p_f \\ &\times \left\{ \frac{A(\alpha)}{1-(1-p_f)f^*(\alpha)} - \frac{B(\alpha)}{[1-(1-p_f)f^*(\alpha)]^2} \right\} \end{aligned}$$

Consider $m = 3$. From (15), we have

$$\begin{aligned} f_k^{(2)}(s) &= -f_k^{(1)}(s)\left[ \frac{1}{s} \right. \\ &+ \left. \frac{f^{(1)}(s)}{1-f^*(s)} - \frac{(k-1)f^{(1)}(s)}{f^*(s)} \right] - f_k^*(s) \\ &\times \left\{ -\frac{1}{s^2} + f^{(2)}(s)\left[ \frac{1}{1-f^*(s)} - \frac{(k-1)}{f^*(s)} \right] \right. \\ &+ \left. \left\{ \frac{f^{(1)}(s)}{[1-f^*(s)]^2} + \frac{(k-1)f^{(1)}(s)}{[f^*(s)]^2} \right\} f^{(1)}(s) \right\} \\ &= A(s)\left[ \frac{1}{s} + \frac{f^{(1)}(s)}{1-f^*(s)} + \frac{f^{(1)}(s)}{f^*(s)} \right][f^*(s)]^{k-1} \\ &- A(s)\left[ \frac{f^{(1)}(s)}{f^*(s)} \right] k[f^*(s)]^{k-1} \\ &- B(s)\left[ \frac{1}{s} + \frac{f^{(1)}(s)}{1-f^*(s)} + \frac{f^{(1)}(s)}{f^*(s)} \right] k[f^*(s)]^{k-1} \\ &+ B(s)\left[ \frac{f^{(1)}(s)}{f^*(s)} \right] k^2[f^*(s)]^{k-1} \\ &+ \frac{\eta[1-f^*(s)]}{s}\left\{ \frac{1}{s^2} - \frac{f^{(2)}(s)}{1-f^*(s)} + \frac{f^{(2)}(s)}{f^*(s)} \right. \\ &- \left. \left[ \frac{f^{(1)}(s)}{1-f^*(s)} \right]^2 - \left[ \frac{f^{(1)}(s)}{f^*(s)} \right]^2 \right\}[f^*(s)]^{k-1} \\ &+ \frac{\eta[1-f^*(s)]}{s}\left\{ \frac{f^{(2)}(s)}{f^*(s)} - \left[ \frac{f^{(1)}(s)}{f^*(s)} \right]^2 \right\} k[f^*(s)]^{k-1} \\ &= C(s)[f^*(s)]^{k-1} + D(s)k[f^*(s)]^{k-1} \\ &+ E(s)k^2[f^*(s)]^{k-1} \end{aligned} \tag{18}$$

where

$$C(s) = A(s)\left[ \frac{1}{s} + \frac{f^{(1)}(s)}{1-f^*(s)} + \frac{f^{(1)}(s)}{f^*(s)} \right]$$

$$
\begin{aligned}
& + \frac{\eta[1-f^*(s)]}{s}\left\{\frac{1}{s^2}-\frac{f^{(2)}(s)}{1-f^*(s)}+\frac{f^{(2)}(s)}{f^*(s)}\right. \\
& - \left.\left[\frac{f^{(1)}(s)}{1-f^*(s)}\right]^2-\left[\frac{f^{(1)}(s)}{f^*(s)}\right]^2\right\} \\
D(s) &= \frac{\eta[1-f^*(s)]}{s}\left\{\frac{f^{(2)}(s)}{f^*(s)}-\left[\frac{f^{(1)}(s)}{f^*(s)}\right]^2\right\} \\
& - A(s)\left[\frac{f^{(1)}(s)}{f^*(s)}\right] \\
& - B(s)\left[\frac{1}{s}+\frac{f^{(1)}(s)}{1-f^*(s)}+\frac{f^{(1)}(s)}{f^*(s)}\right] \\
E(s) &= B(s)\left[\frac{f^{(1)}(s)}{f^*(s)}\right] \qquad (19)
\end{aligned}
$$

From (12) and (18), we have

$$
\begin{aligned}
X(3) &= X(2) \\
&+ \sum_{k=1}^{\infty}(1-p_o)(1-p_f)^{k-1}p_f\left[\left(\frac{\alpha^2}{2}\right)\frac{d^2f_k^*(\alpha)}{ds^2}\right]\Bigg|_{s=\alpha} \\
&= X(2)+\left[\frac{\alpha^2(1-p_o)p_f}{2f^*(\alpha)(1-p_f)}\right] \\
&\times \left\{C(\alpha)\sum_{k=1}^{\infty}[(1-p_f)f^*(\alpha)]^k\right. \\
&+ D(\alpha)\sum_{k=1}^{\infty}k[(1-p_f)f^*(\alpha)]^k \\
&+ \left.E(\alpha)\sum_{k=1}^{\infty}k^2[(1-p_f)f^*(\alpha)]^k\right\} \\
&= X(2)+\left[\frac{\alpha^2(1-p_o)p_f}{2}\right]\left\{\frac{C(\alpha)+E(\alpha)}{1-(1-p_f)f^*(\alpha)}\right. \\
&+ \frac{D(\alpha)-E(\alpha)}{[1-(1-p_f)f^*(\alpha)]^2} \\
&+ \left.\frac{2E(\alpha)}{[1-(1-p_f)f^*(\alpha)]^3}\right\}
\end{aligned}
$$

## 4 Discussion

In this paper, we assume a PCS system such as AMPS, GSM, or PACS, where the channel assignments for handover calls and the new calls are identical. That is $p_f = p_o$. Based on Equation (11), we plot $p_c$ as the function of $p_o(= p_f)$, $\eta$, $\gamma$, $\mu$, and $m$. Note that the variance of the Erlang call holding times is $(m+1)/(m\mu^2)$, and a large $m$ implies a small variance. Similarly, the variance of the gamma cell residence times is $(\gamma+1)/(\gamma\eta^2)$, and a large $\gamma$ implies a small variance. In a PCS system, a typical value for $1/\mu$ is 3 minutes.

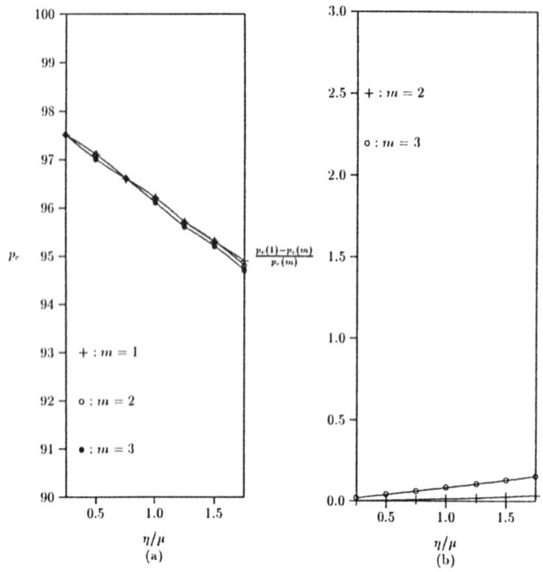


Figure 2: The effect of $\eta$ ($\gamma = 0.1$)

Figures 2-4 indicate that for the Erlang call hold time distributions, $p_c$ decreases as $m$ increases for different $\eta$ values. This effect is insignificant when $m$ is small (e.g., $m \leq 2$) or when the $\gamma$ value of the gamma cell residence time distribution is small (e.g., $\gamma \leq 1$). On the other hand, the effect becomes significant when $m$ is large (e.g., $m = 3$ in our example) and when $\gamma$ is large (e.g., $\gamma \geq 10$). Figures 2 (b) and 3 (b) (when $\gamma$ is small) indicate that when $m$ increases, the decrease of $p_c$ is more significant when $\eta$ is large than when $\eta$ is small. However, reverse result is observed in Figure 4 (b) (when $\gamma$ is large).

Figures 5-7 show that for the Erlang call hold time distributions, $p_c$ decreases as $m$ increases for different $p_o(= p_f)$ values. Similarly to the effect observed in Figure 2-4, this effect is insignificant when $m$ is small (e.g., $m \leq 2$), or when the $\gamma$ value of the gamma cell residence time distribution is small (e.g., $\gamma \leq 1$). On the other hand, the effect becomes significant when $m$ is large (e.g., $m = 3$ in our example) and when $\gamma$ is large (e.g., $\gamma \geq 10$). In Figure 5-7 (b), we observe that when $m$ increases, the decrease of $p_c$ is more significant when $p_o$ is large than when $p_o$ is small. The above discussion leads to an important observation: The call completion probability decreases as the variance of the call holding times decreases. This effect becomes more significant as the variance of the cell residence times

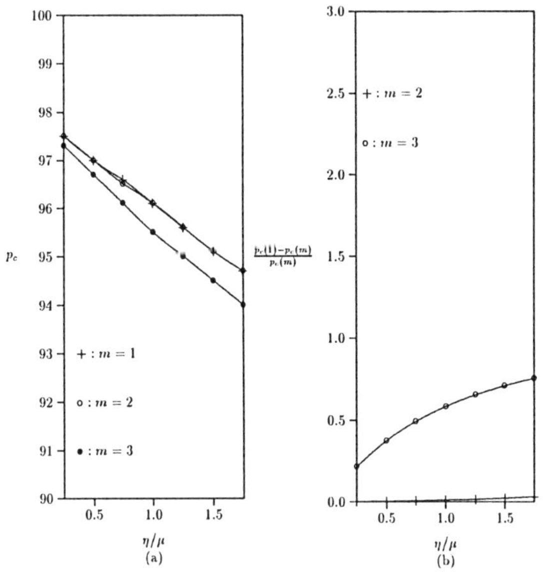


Figure 3: The effect of $\eta$ ($\gamma = 1$)

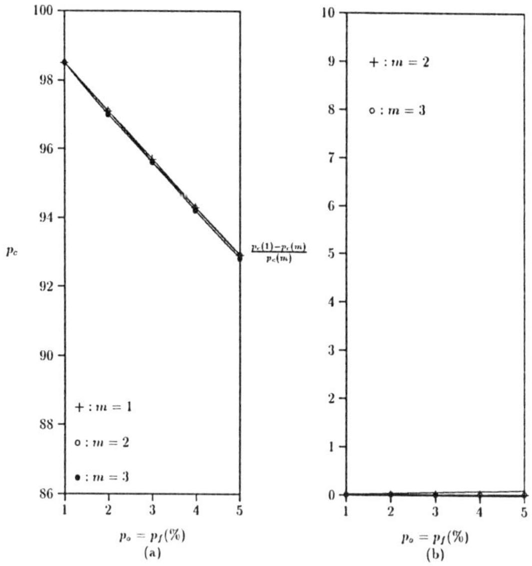


Figure 5: The effect of $p_o(= p_f)$ ($\gamma = 0.1$)

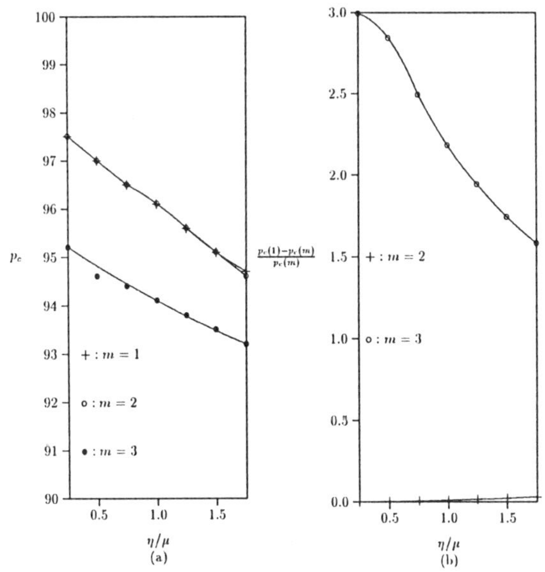


Figure 4: The effect of $\eta$ ($\gamma = 10$)

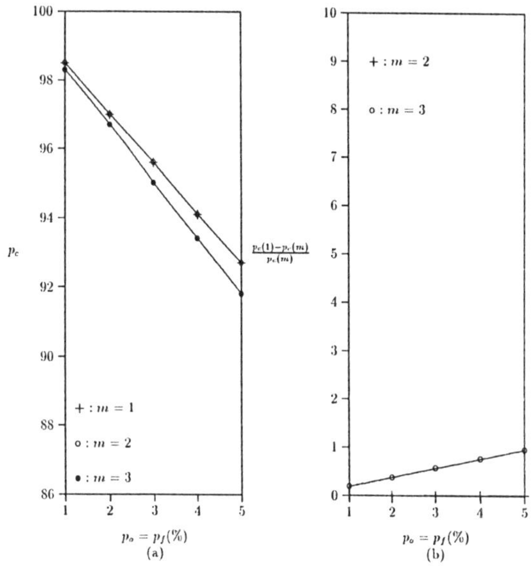


Figure 6: The effect of $p_o(= p_f)$ ($\gamma = 1$)

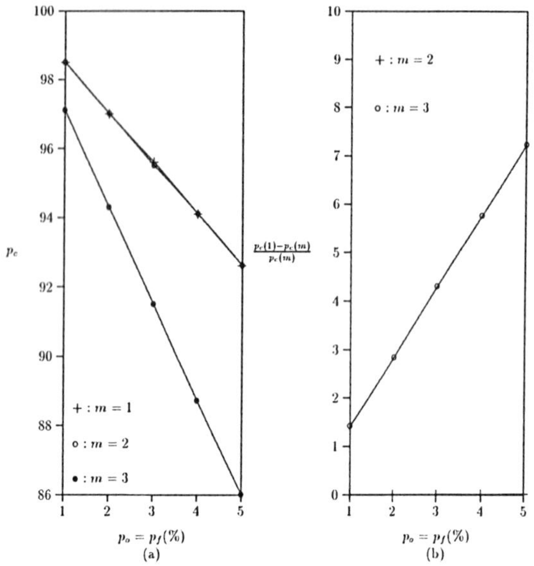


Figure 7: The effect of $p_o(= p_f)$ $(\gamma = 10)$

decreases.

## 5 Conclusions

This paper introduced a model for studying emerging PCS cellular systems which are expected to exercise flat rate billing programs. In this case a more general distribution for modeling the call holding times is necessary. By characterizing the call holding times via the Erlang distribution (a generalization of the exponential distribution) we were able to investigate the effect of the variance of the call holding times on the call completion probability. Using this model it was possible to make the significant observation that in these systems the call completion probability decreases as the variance of the call holding times decreases. This effect becomes more significant as the variance of the cell residence times decreases.

## References


[1] Bellcore. Private Communications, 1995.

[2] Cox, D.C. Wireless Personal Communications: What Is It? *IEEE Personal Commun. Mag.*, pages 20–35, April 1995.

[3] ETSI. Digital European Cordless Telecommunications Services and Facilities Requirements Specification. Technical Report ETSI DI/RES 3002, European Telecommunications Standards Institute, 1991.

[4] Hastings, N.A.J., and Peacock, J.B. *Statistical Distributions.* John Wiley & Sons, 1975.

[5] Johnson, N.L. *Continuous Univariate Distributions-1.* John Wiley& Sons, 1970.

[6] King, P.J.B. *Computer and Communication Systems Performance Modeling.* Prentice Hall, 1990.

[7] Lee, W.C.Y. *Mobile Cellular Telecommunications Systems.* McGraw-Hill, 1995.

[8] Lin, Y.-B. and Chlamtac, I. . Effective Call Holding Times for a PCS Network. 1996.

[9] Lin, Y.-B., Mohan, S., and Noerpel, A. Queueing Priority Channel Assignment Strategies for Handoff and Initial Access for a PCS Network. *IEEE Trans. Veh. Technol.*, 43(3):704–712, 1994.

[10] Lin, Y.-B., Noerpel, A., and Harasty, D. The Sub-rating Channel Assignment Strategy for PCS Hand-offs. *IEEE Trans. Veh. Technol.*, 45(1), February 1996.

[11] Noerpel, A.R., Lin, Y.-B., and Sherry, H. PACS: Personal Access Communications System – A Tutorial. *IEEE Personal Communications Magazine*, June 1996.

[12] Padgett, J.E., Gunther, C.G., and Hattori, T. Overview of Wireless Personal Communications. *IEEE Communications Magazine*, pages 28–41, January 1995.

[13] Steedman, R. The Common Air Interface MPT 1375. *Cordless Telecommunications in Europe*, 1990. Tuttlebee, W.H.W. ed., (Springer Verlag).

[14] Watson, E.J. *Laplace Transforms and Applications.* Birkhauserk, 1981.

# Author Index


Acharya, A. .......... 1046
Aharoni, E. .......... 876
Ajmone Marsan, M. .......... 752, 761
Akar, N. .......... 1105
Akyildiz, I.F. .......... 1422
Almeroth, K.C. .......... 1333
Ammar, M.H. .......... 1388
Andersen, A.T. .......... 196
Armitage, J. .......... 244
Azizoglu, M. .......... 499, 1278, 1286
Badrinath, B.R. .......... 1046
Baldi, M. .......... 683
Bambos, N. .......... 634
Banerjee, D. .......... 269
Barry, R.A. .......... 499
Bartos, R. .......... 777
Baruah, S. .......... 584
Berry, R.A. .......... 277
Bestavros, A. .......... 1210
Bhattacharjee, S. .......... 1388
Bhogavilli, S.K. .......... 858
Bianchi, G. .......... 711
Bianco, A. .......... 752, 761
Biersack, E.W. .......... 471
Biswas, S.K. .......... 649
Böcking, S. .......... 1245
Bonomi, F. .......... 1054
Breiter, F. .......... 611
Brustoloni, J.C. .......... 1122
Carter, R.L. .......... 1014
Chan, A.K.M. .......... 1373
Chan, C.W. .......... 525
Chandra, P. .......... 1324
Chandranmenon, G. .......... 557
Chaney, T. .......... 2
Chang, C.-J. .......... 955
Chang, C.-S. .......... 436
Chang, K. .......... 619
Chanson, S.T. .......... 667
Che, H. .......... 177
Chen, K.-C. .......... 236
Chen, K.-J. .......... 336
Chen, P.-N. .......... 1157
Chen, X.H. .......... 642
Cheng, M.-H. .......... 932
Cheng, R.-G. .......... 955
Chiussi, F.M. .......... 406
Chlamtac, I. .......... 769, 916
Choe, J. .......... 549
Choi, H. .......... 1286
Choi, H.-A. .......... 1286
Choi, S. .......... 1030
Chong, E.K.P. .......... 908
Choudhury, G.L. .......... 832
Chung, J.-K. .......... 626
Cidon, I. .......... 92, 541
Cohen, R. .......... 876
Corson, M.S. .......... 1405
Cox Jr, J.R. .......... 823
Crochat, O. .......... 244
Crovella, M.E. .......... 1014
Crow, B.P. .......... 126
Dan, A. .......... 1333
Danzig, P.B. .......... 973
DeHart, J. .......... 213
DeLucia, D. .......... 463
Dittia, Z.D. .......... 823
Dong, X. .......... 892
Duan, H. .......... 20
Elek, V. .......... 769
Elwalid, A. .......... 444
Estrin, D. .......... 222
Fei, Z. .......... 1388
Feldmann, A. .......... 1096
Feng, W.-C. .......... 58
Figueira, N.R. .......... 1063
Fingerhut, J.A. .......... 2
Firoiu, V. .......... 310
Fisher, A. .......... 1324
Floyd, S. .......... 222
Flucke, M. .......... 2
Fulton, C. .......... 805
Fumagalli, A. .......... 769
Garcés, R. .......... 134

Garcia-Luna-Aceves, J.J. ...............101, 134,
Garcia-Luna-Aceves, J.J. ..............884, 1182
Ge, Y. ......................................................380
Gerla, M.......................................118, 1365
Gerstel, O. ..............................................507
Ghani, N. ..............................................1315
Giordano, S.............................................168
Gorinsky, S.............................................584
Govindan, R. ..........................................850
Graf, M. ....................................................48
Greenberg, A. ........................................1054
Grossglauser, M. ............................867, 981
Guérin, R. ..................................................75
Han, C.-C. .............................................1261
Hao, R. ....................................................230
Harai, H. .................................................516
Hasegawa, T. ........................................1114
Hashemi, M.R. .................................29, 533
Hegde, M.V. ..............................................12
Higaki, H. ...............................................998
Hjálmtýsson, G. ......................................601
Hood, C.S. .............................................1147
Hou, C.-J. ...................................361, 1261
Hua, K.A. ....................................990, 1357
Huang, G. ...............................................380
Huang, N.-F. ..........................................1397
Huang, Y. ..............................................1080
Ikeda, H. .................................................480
Iness, J. ...................................................261
Ishibashi, Y. ...........................................692
Ishizaki, F. ............................................1088
Jacob, L. .................................................939
Jacobson, V. ............................................222
Jagerman, D.L. .......................................427
Jamin, S. .................................................973
Janson, P. ...............................................725
Jelenkovic, P.R. ......................................187
Ji, C. ......................................................1147
Jiau, J.-C. ...............................................336
Jordan, H.F. ............................................777
Kahale, N. .............................................1414
Kakuda, Y. ............................................1253
Kalampoukas, L. ...................................1227
Kang, M. .................................................737
Kang, S.M. ................................................20
Kannan, R. ....................................253, 777
Kantawala, A. ..........................................213
Keshav, S. .............................................1131
Khamisy, A. .............................................541
Kikuno, T. .............................................1253
Kim, G. .................................................1210
Kim, H.S. ................................................345
Kim, J.G. .................................................126
Kim, K.S. ..................................................12
Kim, Y.Y. ..............................................1022
Kobayashi, H. ..........................................842
Kolarov, A. ..............................................293
Konheim, A.G. .........................................601
Kosak, C. ...............................................1324
Krunz, M. ..................................................67
Kshemkalyani, A.D. ................................143
Kshirsagar, M. .........................................832
Kühn, S. ...................................................611
Kulkarni, L.A. .........................................795
Kumar, V.P. .............................................406
Kung, H.T. ...................................619, 1218
Kung, L.-Y. ............................................1174
Kurose, J. ......................................310, 675
Kurose, J.F. .............................................480
Kwon, T. ..................................................737
Lai, T.H. ..................................................892
Lakshman, T.V. ..............................38, 1199
Lam, C.H. ................................................947
Lam, S.S. .................................................388
Lang, T. ...................................................642
Lapid, Y. ................................................1191
Lazar, A.A. ..............................................187
Le Boudec, J.-Y. .............................168, 244
Lee, D. .....................................................785
Lee, D.-S. .................................................318
Lee, K.Y. ..................................................777
Lee, T.T. ..................................................947
Lee, W.-T. ..............................................1174
Leonardi, E. ........................752, 761, 1365
Leon-Garcia, A. ................................29, 533
Li, B. .....................................................1397
Li, C. .......................................................160
Li, J. ........................................................908
Li, S.-Q. ..................177, 283, 795, 805, 1022
Li, V.O.K. ..................................1341, 1349

Liao, J.-W. ....1174
Liao, W. ....1349
Libman, L. ....1006
Liebeherr, J. ....576
Liew, S.C. ....525
Lim, C.S. ....805
Lin, C.R. ....118
Lin, D. ....398
Lin, M. ....1237
Lin, R.H. ....947
Lin, S.-Y. ....955
Lin, Y.-B. ....916
Lin, Y.-D. ....1165
Liu, T.-L. ....1397
Lo Presti, F. ....675
Lockwood, J.W. ....20
Low, S.H. ....745
Ma, G.-K. ....1157
Madhow, U. ....1199
Mah, B.A. ....592
Maher, M.P. ....858
Makowski, A.M. ....419
Mark, B.L. ....427
Mark, J.W. ....1315
Marlowe, T.J. ....584
Marz, T. ....213
Mason, L. ....353, 924
Maxemchuk, N.F. ....745
Mayor, G. ....205
McKinley, P.K. ....1080
Melen, R. ....711
Min, P.S. ....12
Mishra, P.P. ....38
Misic, J. ....667
Mitra, D. ....444
Miyahara, H. ....516
Miyoshi, N. ....1114
Moh, W.M. ....785
Morabito, A. ....761
Morgan, S.P. ....1131
Morris, R. ....455, 619
Mouftah, H. ....302
Muir, A. ....1182
Mukherjee, B. ....261, 269
Murakami, K. ....345
Murata, M. ....516
Murthy, S. ....101
Nakamura, M. ....1253
Neri, F. ....752, 761, 1365
Ng, C.-L. ....842
Nielsen, B.F. ....196
Nikolopoulos, S.D. ....370
Nonnenmacher, J. ....471
Obraczka, K. ....463
Oechslin, P. ....168
Ofek, Y. ....683
Ohba, Y. ....566
Oksman, J. ....642
Orda, A. ....75, 659, 1006
Palnati, P. ....1365
Park, J. ....939
Park, V.D. ....1405
Parulekar, M. ....419
Parulkar, G. ....213
Parulkar, G.M. ....823
Pasquale, J. ....1063
Periyannan, A. ....1237
Peyravian, M. ....143
Pitsillides, A. ....370
Plotkin, N.T. ....1304
Polyzos, G.C. ....1380
Raha, A. ....160
Ramakrishnan, K.K. ....38, 785, 867, 1227
Ramamurthy, B. ....261
Ramamurthy, G. ....293, 427, 963
Ramanathan, R. ....900
Ramaswami, R. ....489, 507
Reddy, A. ....850
Reeves, D.S. ....84
Ren, Q. ....963
Rexford, J. ....58, 1054
Ritter, M. ....815
Robert, S. ....168
Roche, C. ....1365
Rohrs, C.E. ....277
Rom, R. ....92, 1191
Rouskas, G.N. ....1270
Rulnick, J.M. ....634
Saito, H. ....1072
Sakai, P. ....126

Salama, H.F. ....84
Sasaki, G.H. ....489, 507
Schill, A. ....611
Schuba, M. ....152
Schwartz, M. ....1038
Sengodan, S. ....1341
Sengupta, B. ....649
Seo, S.-W. ....842
Shacham, N. ....701
Shah, V. ....1388
Shankar, A.U. ....785
Sharma, P. ....222
Shavitt, Y. ....92
Shenker, S.J. ....973
Sheu, S. ....990, 1357
Shieh, S.-P. ....718
Shields, C. ....884
Shima, K. ....998
Shimkin, N. ....659
Shin, K.G. ....1030, 1295
Shioda, S. ....1072
Shiue, Y.-R. ....955
Shroff, N.B. ....549, 908
Sidi, M. ....541, 1191
Sigarto, S. ....283
Silvester, J. ....205
Singer, D. ....1237
Sitaram, D. ....1333
Sivaraman, V. ....1270
Sohraby, K. ....1105
Somani, A.K. ....499, 1278
Song, J. ....737
Steenkiste, P. ....1122, 1324
Stiliadis, D. ....326
Stoyenko, A.D. ....584
Su, C.-J. ....109
Subramaniam, S. ....499
Sudan, M. ....701
Sun, H.-M. ....718
Suri, S. ....557
Suter, B. ....1199
Sydir, J.J. ....1304
Szabó, C. ....769
Sze, M.-T. ....626
Tachikawa, T. ....998
Takagi, H. ....1139
Takine, T. ....1088
Takizawa, M. ....998
Talukdar, A.K. ....1046
Tasaka, S. ....692
Tassiulas, L. ....109
Tetzlaff, W.H. ....1333
Tipper, D. ....370
Toniolo, S. ....752
Towsley, D.F. ....310, 480, 675
Tripathi, S.K. ....67
Tsai, W.K. ....380
Tse, D. ....981
Tsudik, G. ....725
Tsuji, A. ....692
Turner, J.S. ....2
Twu, D.-C. ....236
Varghese, G. ....557
Varma, A. ....326, 1227
Veeraraghavan, M. ....832
Viniotis, Y. ....84
Wang, A.H. ....1038
Wang, B. ....1261
Wang, J.-Y. ....1174
Wang, J.Z. ....990, 1357
Wang, K. ....932
Wang, S.Y. ....1218
Wang, Y.-T. ....1397
Whitt, W. ....1096
Widjaja, I. ....126
Will, J.D. ....20
Wong, A. ....1054
Wong, E.W.M. ....1373
Wrege, D.E. ....576
Wright, P.E. ....1414
Wu, C.-J. ....1165
Wu, C.-S. ....336, 1157
Wu, J. ....230
Wu, J.-S. ....626
Xia, Y. ....406
Xie, G.G. ....388
Xiong, Y. ....353, 924
Xylomenos, G. ....1380
Yagyu, S. ....1139
Yamada, Y. ....1114

Yamamoto, M. ....................................480
Yan, P.Y. ....................................12
Yang, O.W. ....................................302
Yen, W. ....................................1422
Yener, B. ....................................683, 1422
Yin, W.-M. ....................................1165
Yoon, H. ....................................939
Yum, T.-S.P. ....................................1373
Yung, M. ....................................725
Zegura, E.W. ....................................1388
Zhang, H. ....................................302
Zhang, X. ....................................1295
Zhang, Z.-L. ....................................675
Zhao, W. ....................................160
Zhao, Y. ....................................283
Zheng, Q. ....................................1295